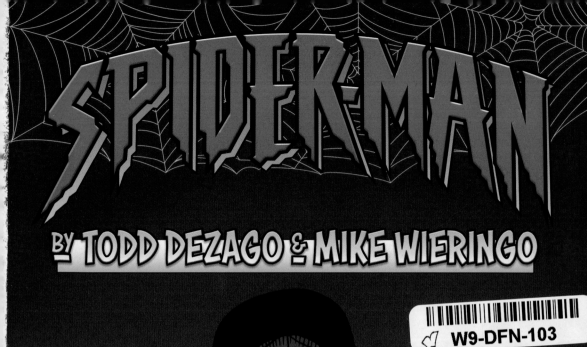

SPIDER-MAN

BY TODD DEZAGO & MIKE WIERINGO

SPIDER-MAN

BY TODD DEZAGO & MIKE WIERINGO

WRITERS
TODD DEZAGO & RICH CASE WITH MIKE WIERINGO
PENCILERS
MIKE WIERINGO, LUKE ROSS, JOSH HOOD, RICH CASE, JASON ARMSTRONG & TODD NAUCK WITH POP MHAN
INKERS
AL WILLIAMSON, RICH CASE, JOHN LOWE, RON BOYD, ROB STULL & ANDREW HENNESSY WITH MIKE WIERINGO & SCOTT HANNA
COLORISTS
GREGORY WRIGHT, JOE ANDREANI, MALIBU & GRAPHIC COLORWORKS WITH MARK BERNARDO
LETTERERS
RICHARD STARKINGS & COMICRAFT'S LIZ AGRAPHIOTIS, KIFF SCHOLL, KOLJA FUCHS & CO.

ASSISTANT EDITORS
MARK BERNARDO, JOE ANDREANI & MATT HICKS
EDITOR
RALPH MACCHIO

FRONT COVER ARTISTS
MIKE WIERINGO, RICH CASE & VERONICA GANDINI
BACK COVER ARTISTS
MIKE WIERINGO & RICH CASE

SPIDER-MAN CREATED BY **STAN LEE** AND **STEVE DITKO**

COLLECTION EDITOR **MARK D. BEAZLEY** • ASSISTANT EDITOR **CAITLIN O'CONNELL**
ASSOCIATE MANAGING EDITOR **KATERI WOODY** • ASSOCIATE MANAGER, DIGITAL ASSETS **JOE HOCHSTEIN**
SENIOR EDITOR, SPECIAL PROJECTS **JENNIFER GRÜNWALD** • VP PRODUCTION & SPECIAL PROJECTS **JEFF YOUNGQUIST**
RESEARCH **DARON JENSEN** • LAYOUT **JEPH YORK** • PRODUCTION **RYAN DEVALL, COLORTEK & ROMIE JEFFERS**
BOOK DESIGNER **JAY BOWEN** • SVP PRINT, SALES & MARKETING **DAVID GABRIEL**

EDITOR IN CHIEF **AXEL ALONSO** • CHIEF CREATIVE OFFICER **JOE QUESADA**
PRESIDENT **DAN BUCKLEY** • EXECUTIVE PRODUCER **ALAN FINE**

SPECIAL THANKS TO **MIKE HANSEN** & **DOUG SHARK** OF *MYCOMICSHOP.COM*

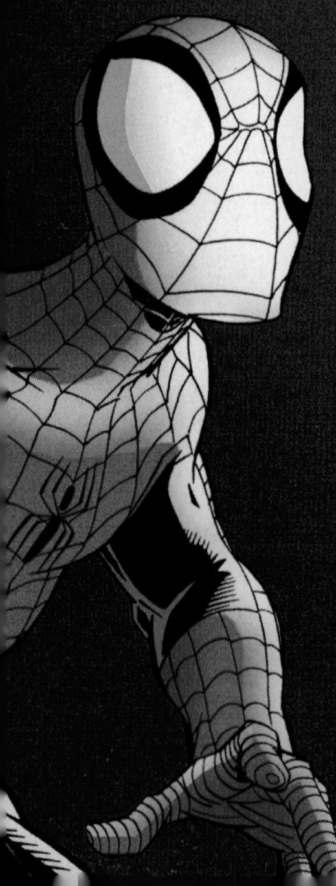

SPIDER-MAN BY TODD DEZAGO & MIKE WIERINGO VOL. 1. Contains material originally published in magazine form as SENSATIONAL SPIDER-MAN (1996) #7-24 and #-1. First printing 2017. ISBN# 978-1-302-90699-3. Published by MARVEL WORLDWIDE, INC., a subsidiary of MARVEL ENTERTAINMENT, LLC. OFFICE OF PUBLICATION: 135 West 50th Street, New York, NY 10020. **Printed in the U.S.A.** DAN BUCKLEY, President, Marvel Entertainment; JOE QUESADA, Chief Creative Officer; TOM BREVOORT, SVP of Publishing; DAVID BOGART, SVP of Business Affairs & Operations, Publishing & Partnership; C.B. CEBULSKI, VP of Brand Management & Development, Asia; DAVID GABRIEL, SVP of Sales & Marketing, Publishing; JEFF YOUNGQUIST, VP of Production & Special Projects; DAN CARR, Executive Director of Publishing Technology; ALEX MORALES, Director of Publishing Operations; SUSAN CRESPI, Production Manager; STAN LEE, Chairman Emeritus. For information regarding advertising in Marvel Comics or on Marvel.com, please contact Vit DeBellis, Integrated Sales Manager, at vdebellis@marvel.com. For Marvel subscription inquiries, please call 888-511-5480. **Manufactured between 3/31/2017 and 5/2/2017 by LSC COMMUNICATIONS INC., SALEM, VA, USA.**

10 9 8 7 6 5 4 3 2 1

TODD DEZAGO AND MIKE WIERINGO'S RUN BEGAN DURING AN EVENTFUL TIME IN SPIDER-MAN'S LIFE. PETER PARKER'S CLONE, NOW CALLING HIMSELF BEN REILLY, RETURNED FROM FIVE YEARS ON THE ROAD. THE TWO PERFORMED A TEST THAT, SHOCKINGLY, INDICATED THAT BEN HAD BEEN THE ORIGINAL SPIDER-MAN ALL ALONG, AND PETER THE CLONE. PETER SOON LOST HIS POWERS, AND RETIRED AS SPIDER-MAN TO FOCUS ON HIS WIFE MARY JANE AND THEIR UNBORN BABY. BEN DYED HIS HAIR BLOND AND TOOK ON THE MANTLE OF SPIDER-MAN, WITH AN UPDATED COSTUME AND WEAPONRY.

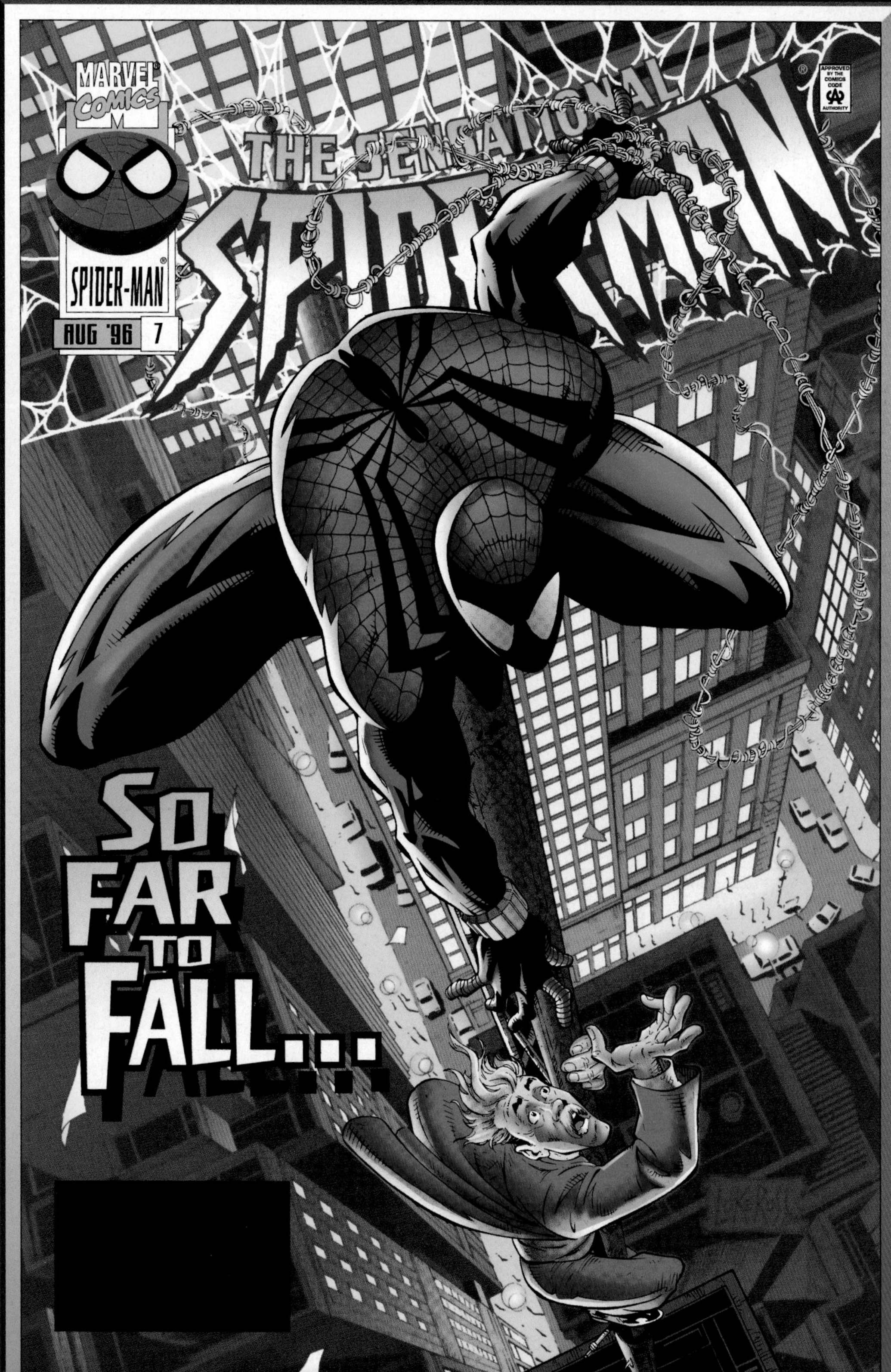
MARVEL COMICS
SPIDER-MAN
AUG '96
7
APPROVED BY THE COMICS CODE AUTHORITY
SO FAR TO FALL...

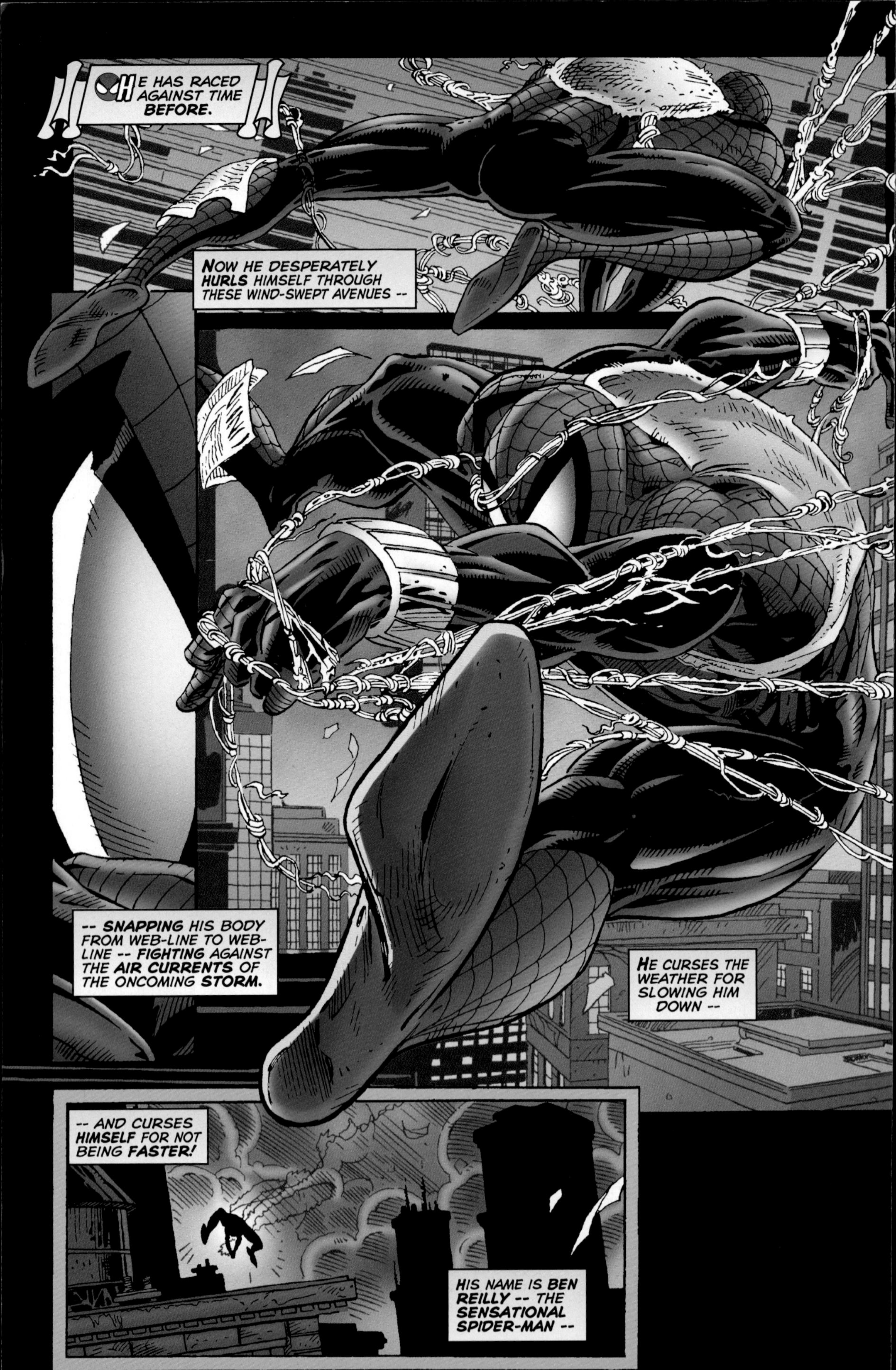
HE HAS RACED AGAINST TIME BEFORE.
NOW HE DESPERATELY HURLS HIMSELF THROUGH THESE WIND-SWEPT AVENUES --
-- SNAPPING HIS BODY FROM WEB-LINE TO WEB-LINE -- FIGHTING AGAINST THE AIR CURRENTS OF THE ONCOMING STORM.
HE CURSES THE WEATHER FOR SLOWING HIM DOWN --
-- AND CURSES HIMSELF FOR NOT BEING FASTER!
HIS NAME IS BEN REILLY -- THE SENSATIONAL SPIDER-MAN --

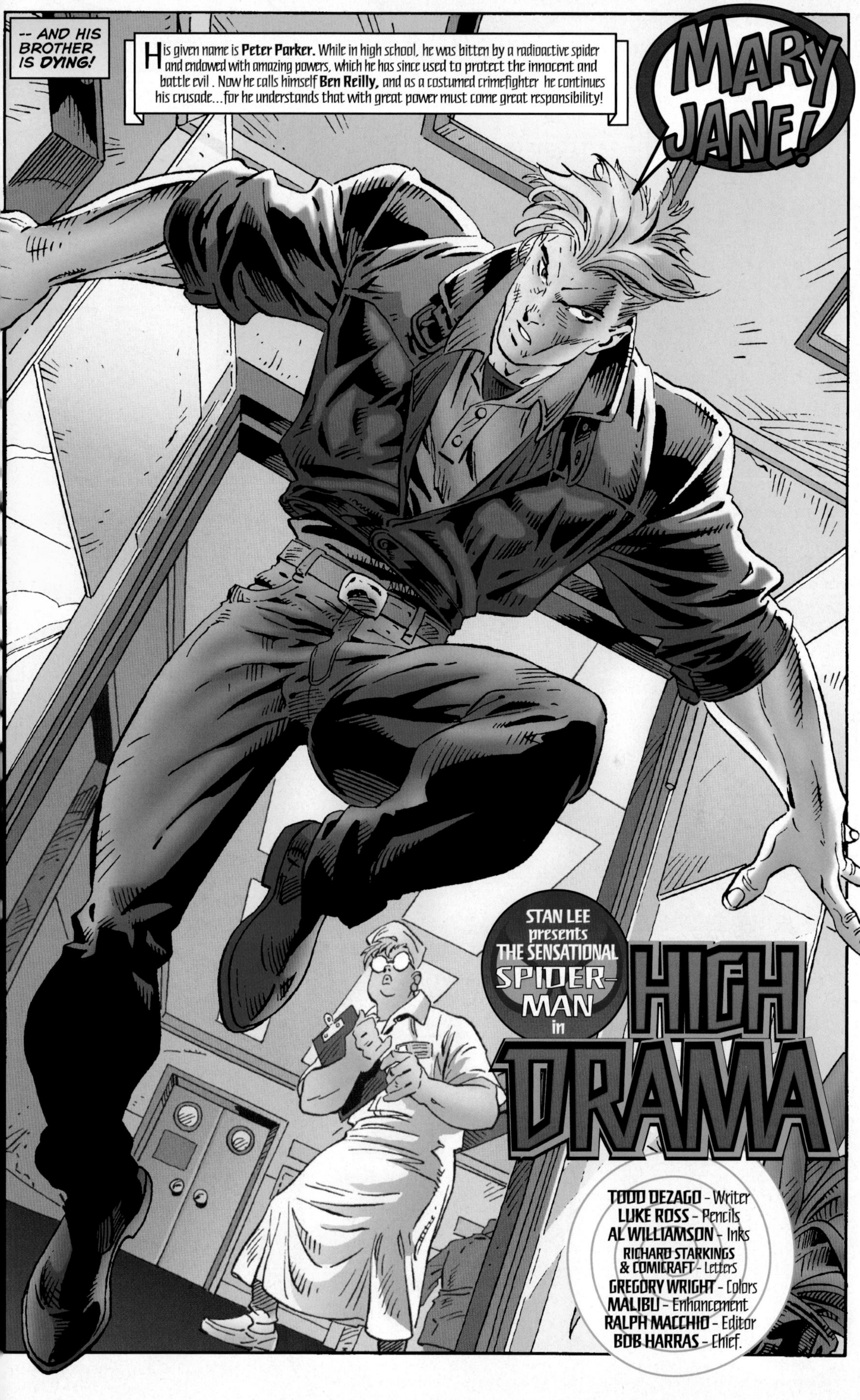
-- AND HIS BROTHER IS DYING!
His given name is Peter Parker. While in high school, he was bitten by a radioactive spider and endowed with amazing powers, which he has since used to protect the innocent and battle evil . Now he calls himself Ben Reilly, and as a costumed crimefighter he continues his crusade...for he understands that with great power must come great responsibility!
MARY JANE!
STAN LEE presents THE SENSATIONAL SPIDER-MAN in
HIGH DRAMA
TODD DEZAGO - Writer
LUKE ROSS - Pencils
AL WILLIAMSON - Inks
RICHARD STARKINGS & COMICRAFT - Letters
GREGORY WRIGHT - Colors
MALIBU - Enhancement
RALPH MACCHIO - Editor
BOB HARRAS - Chief.

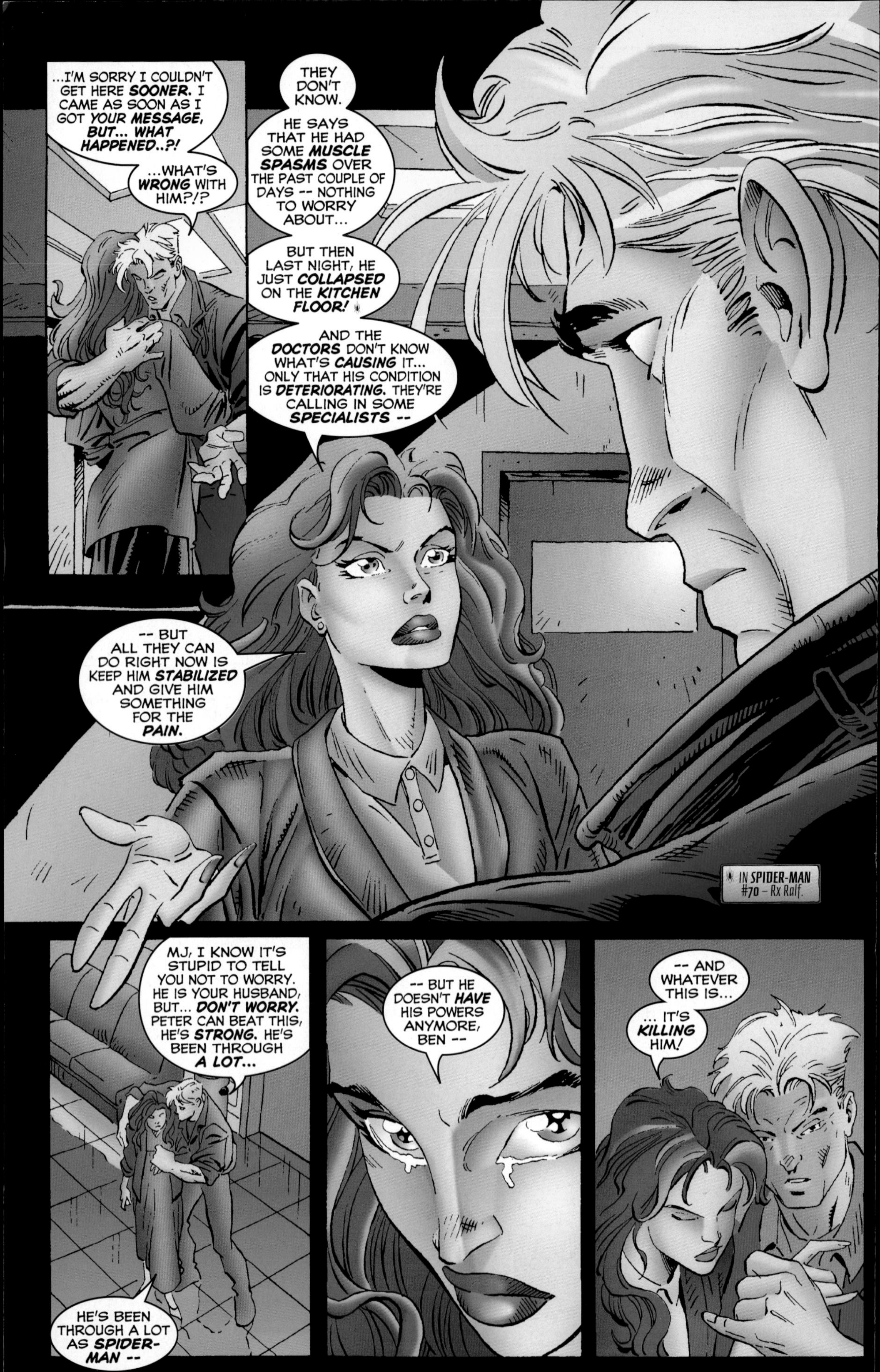

...I'M SORRY I COULDN'T GET HERE SOONER. I CAME AS SOON AS I GOT YOUR MESSAGE, BUT... WHAT HAPPENED..?!
...WHAT'S WRONG WITH HIM?!?
THEY DON'T KNOW.
HE SAYS THAT HE HAD SOME MUSCLE SPASMS OVER THE PAST COUPLE OF DAYS -- NOTHING TO WORRY ABOUT...
BUT THEN LAST NIGHT, HE JUST COLLAPSED ON THE KITCHEN FLOOR!
AND THE DOCTORS DON'T KNOW WHAT'S CAUSING IT... ONLY THAT HIS CONDITION IS DETERIORATING. THEY'RE CALLING IN SOME SPECIALISTS --
-- BUT ALL THEY CAN DO RIGHT NOW IS KEEP HIM STABILIZED AND GIVE HIM SOMETHING FOR THE PAIN.
IN SPIDER-MAN #70 – Rx Ralf.
MJ, I KNOW IT'S STUPID TO TELL YOU NOT TO WORRY. HE IS YOUR HUSBAND, BUT... DON'T WORRY. PETER CAN BEAT THIS, HE'S STRONG. HE'S BEEN THROUGH A LOT...
HE'S BEEN THROUGH A LOT AS SPIDER-MAN --
-- BUT HE DOESN'T HAVE HIS POWERS ANYMORE, BEN --
-- AND WHATEVER THIS IS...
... IT'S KILLING HIM!

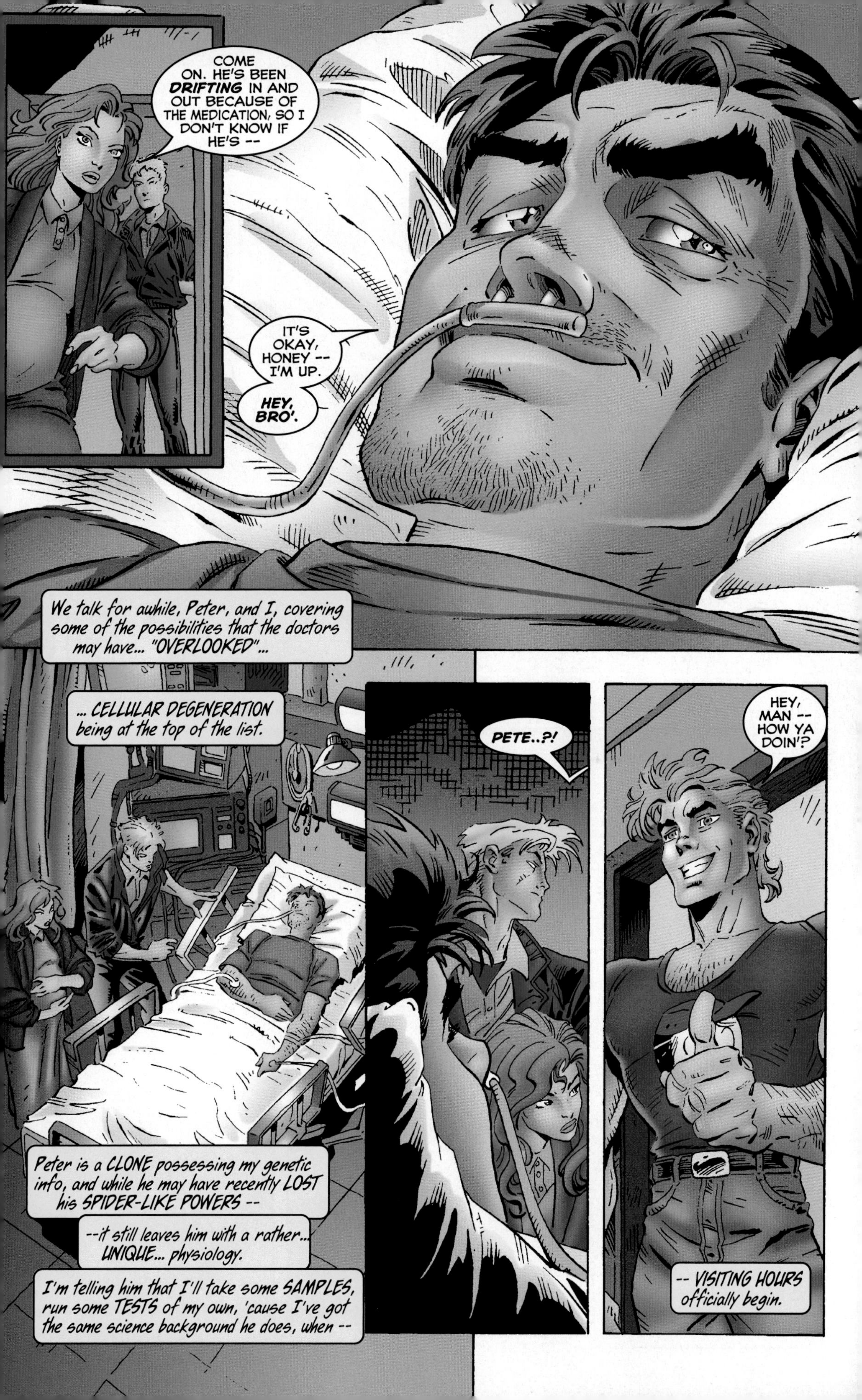
COME ON. HE'S BEEN DRIFTING IN AND OUT BECAUSE OF THE MEDICATION, SO I DON'T KNOW IF HE'S --
IT'S OKAY, HONEY -- I'M UP.
HEY, BRO'.
We talk for awhile, Peter, and I, covering some of the possibilities that the doctors may have... "OVERLOOKED"...
... CELLULAR DEGENERATION being at the top of the list.
Peter is a CLONE possessing my genetic info, and while he may have recently LOST his SPIDER-LIKE POWERS --
--it still leaves him with a rather... UNIQUE... physiology.
I'm telling him that I'll take some SAMPLES, run some TESTS of my own, 'cause I've got the same science background he does, when --
PETE..?!
HEY, MAN -- HOW YA DOIN'?
-- VISITING HOURS officially begin.

THAT **BED** LOOKS COMFY.

I'D BE HAPPY TO **TRADE PLACES** WITH YOU.

I step to one side as Peter and Flash cut on each other.

FLASH THOMPSON. Who'da thunk after all those years of him **BULLYING** and **TORMENTING** me... US... back in high school... that we could actually be **FRIENDS?**

We might be the same **PERSON,** Peter Parker, but I think you're much more **FORGIVING** than I.

It isn't very long before more people start to arrive --

--LIZ OSBORN, the widow of one of Pete's closest friends, and little NORMIE --

-- and I notice something... well...

... COOL ...

... is happening.

...Peter drifts IN and OUT...

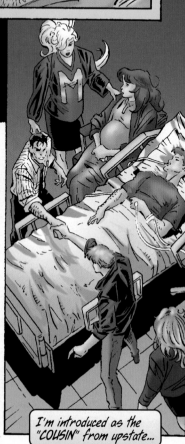

OLD FRIENDS and new continue to show up, offering SMILES and words of COMFORT and SUPPORT...

I'm introduced as the "COUSIN" from upstate...

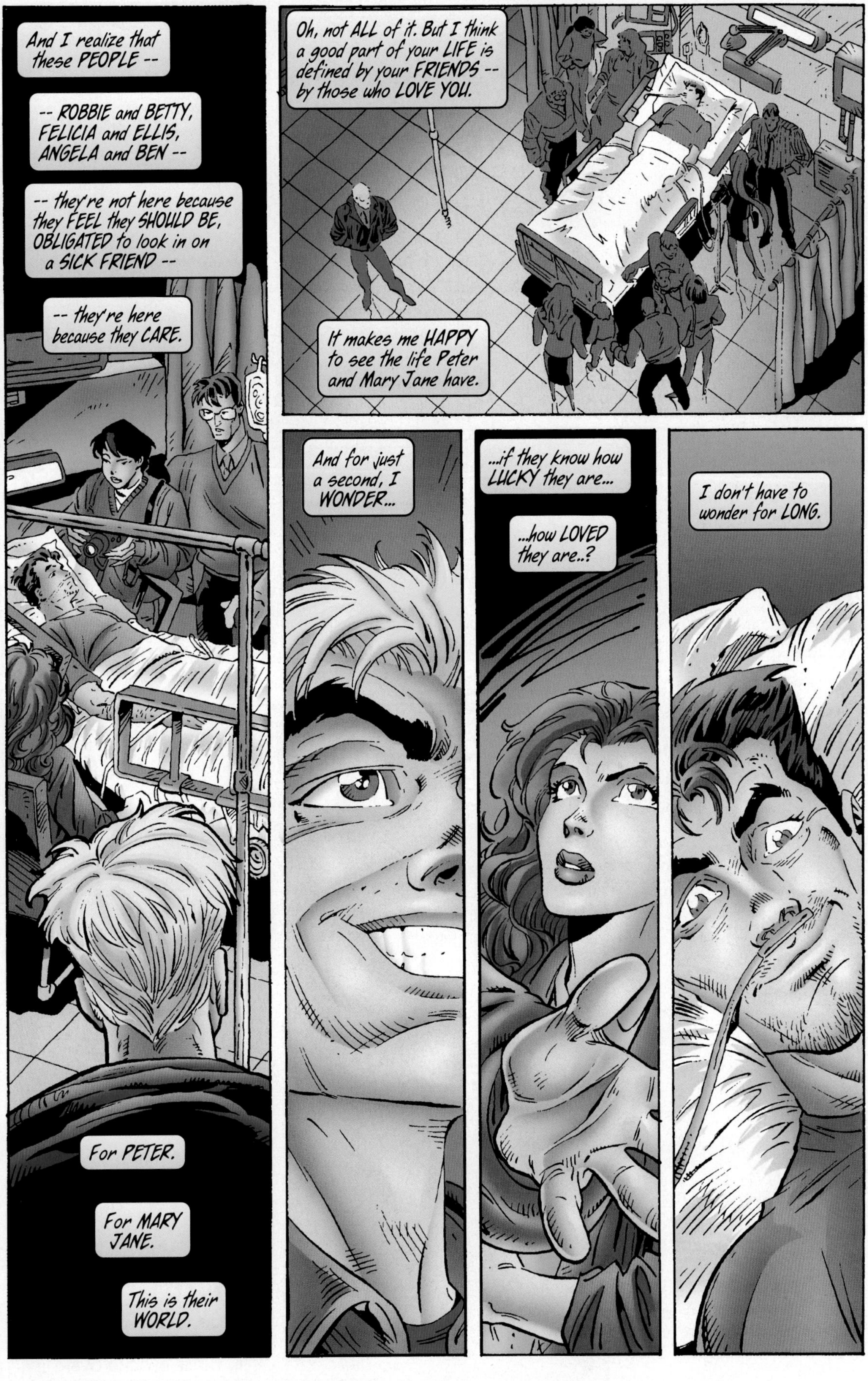

And I realize that these PEOPLE --
-- ROBBIE and BETTY, FELICIA and ELLIS, ANGELA and BEN --
-- they're not here because they FEEL they SHOULD BE, OBLIGATED to look in on a SICK FRIEND --
-- they're here because they CARE.
For PETER.
For MARY JANE.
This is their WORLD.
Oh, not ALL of it. But I think a good part of your LIFE is defined by your FRIENDS -- by those who LOVE YOU.
It makes me HAPPY to see the life Peter and Mary Jane have.
And for just a second, I WONDER...
...if they know how LUCKY they are...
...how LOVED they are..?
I don't have to wonder for LONG.

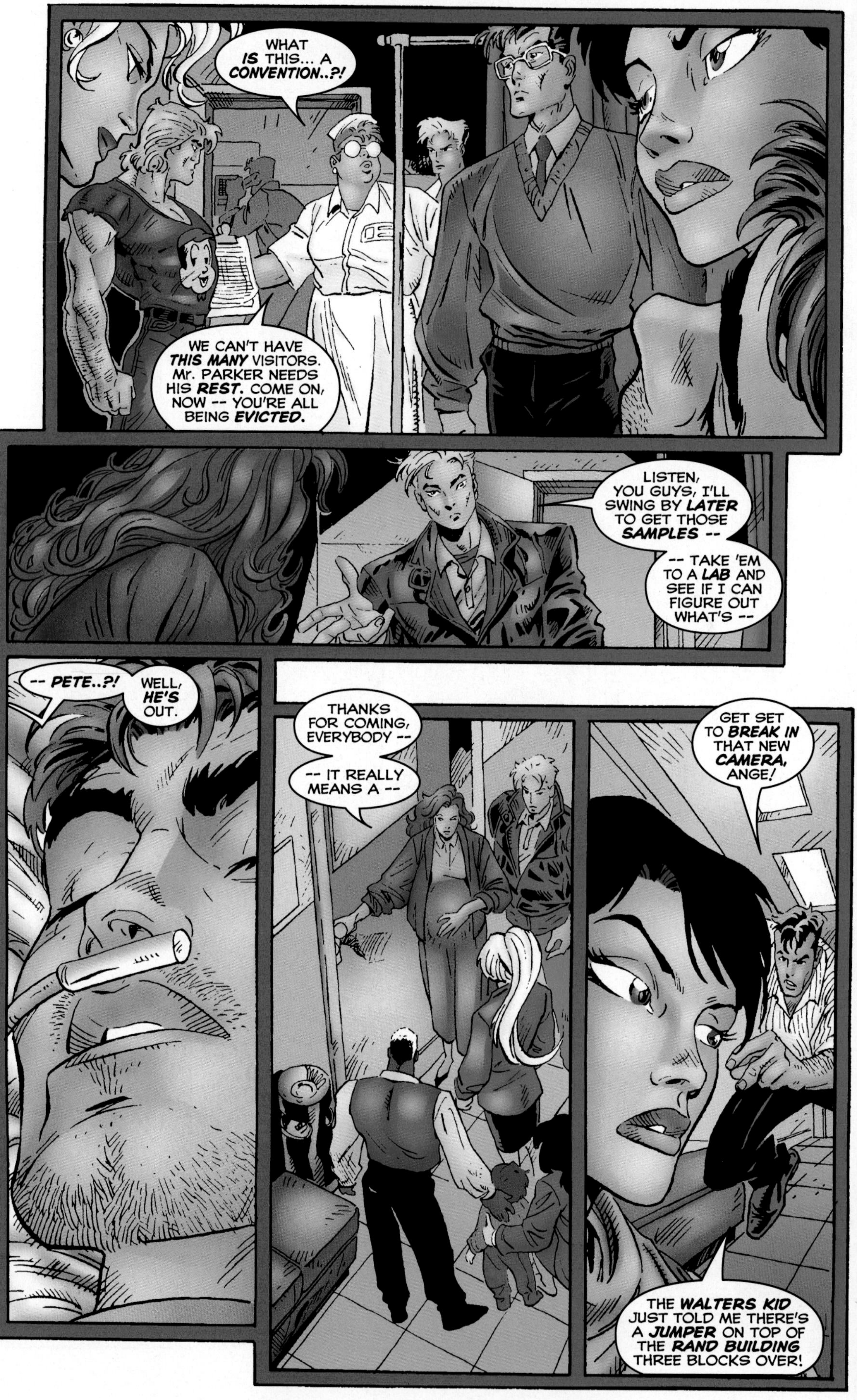
WHAT IS THIS... A CONVENTION..?!
WE CAN'T HAVE THIS MANY VISITORS. Mr. PARKER NEEDS HIS REST. COME ON, NOW -- YOU'RE ALL BEING EVICTED.
LISTEN, YOU GUYS, I'LL SWING BY LATER TO GET THOSE SAMPLES --
-- TAKE 'EM TO A LAB AND SEE IF I CAN FIGURE OUT WHAT'S --
-- PETE..?!
WELL, HE'S OUT.
THANKS FOR COMING, EVERYBODY --
-- IT REALLY MEANS A --
GET SET TO BREAK IN THAT NEW CAMERA, ANGE!
THE WALTERS KID JUST TOLD ME THERE'S A JUMPER ON TOP OF THE RAND BUILDING THREE BLOCKS OVER!

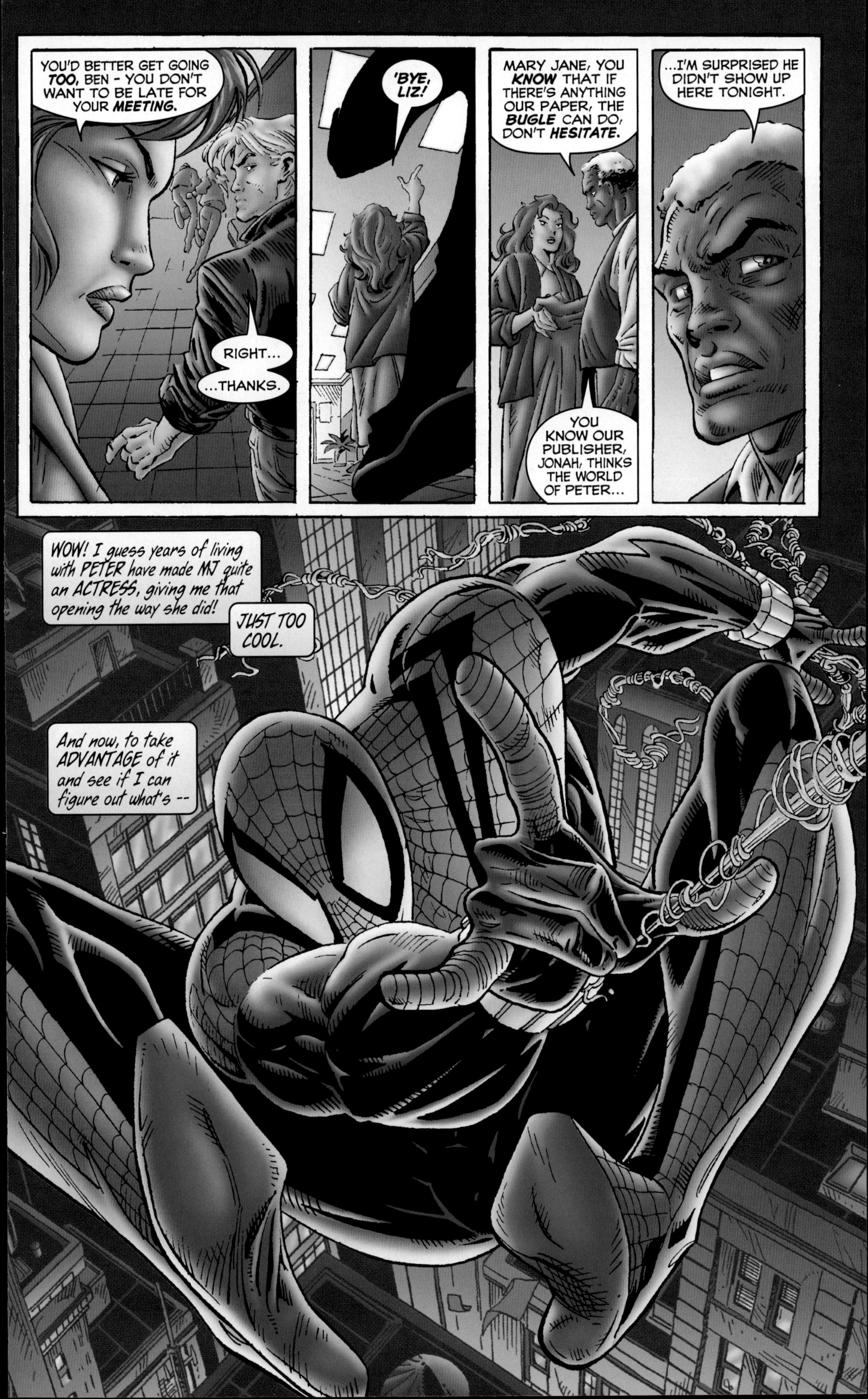

YOU'D BETTER GET GOING TOO, BEN - YOU DON'T WANT TO BE LATE FOR YOUR MEETING.
RIGHT...
...THANKS.
'BYE, LIZ!
MARY JANE, YOU KNOW THAT IF THERE'S ANYTHING OUR PAPER, THE BUGLE CAN DO, DON'T HESITATE.
YOU KNOW OUR PUBLISHER, JONAH, THINKS THE WORLD OF PETER...
...I'M SURPRISED HE DIDN'T SHOW UP HERE TONIGHT.
WOW! I guess years of living with PETER have made MJ quite an ACTRESS, giving me that opening the way she did!
JUST TOO COOL.
And now, to take ADVANTAGE of it and see if I can figure out what's --

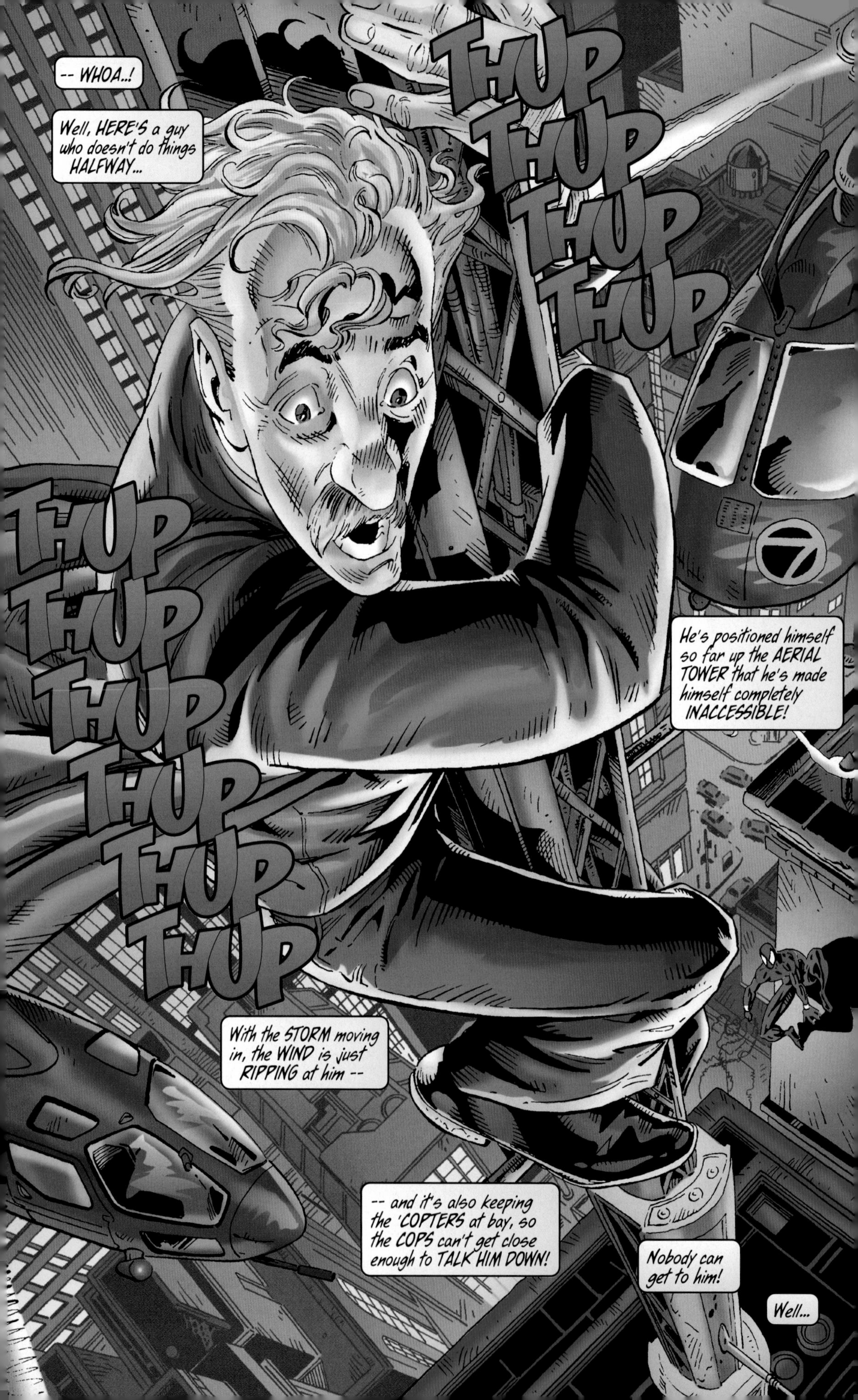
-- WHOA..!
Well, HERE'S a guy who doesn't do things HALFWAY...
THUP THUP THUP THUP
THUP THUP THUP THUP THUP THUP
He's positioned himself so far up the AERIAL TOWER that he's made himself completely INACCESSIBLE!
With the STORM moving in, the WIND is just RIPPING at him --
-- and it's also keeping the 'COPTERS at bay, so the COPS can't get close enough to TALK HIM DOWN!
Nobody can get to him!
Well...

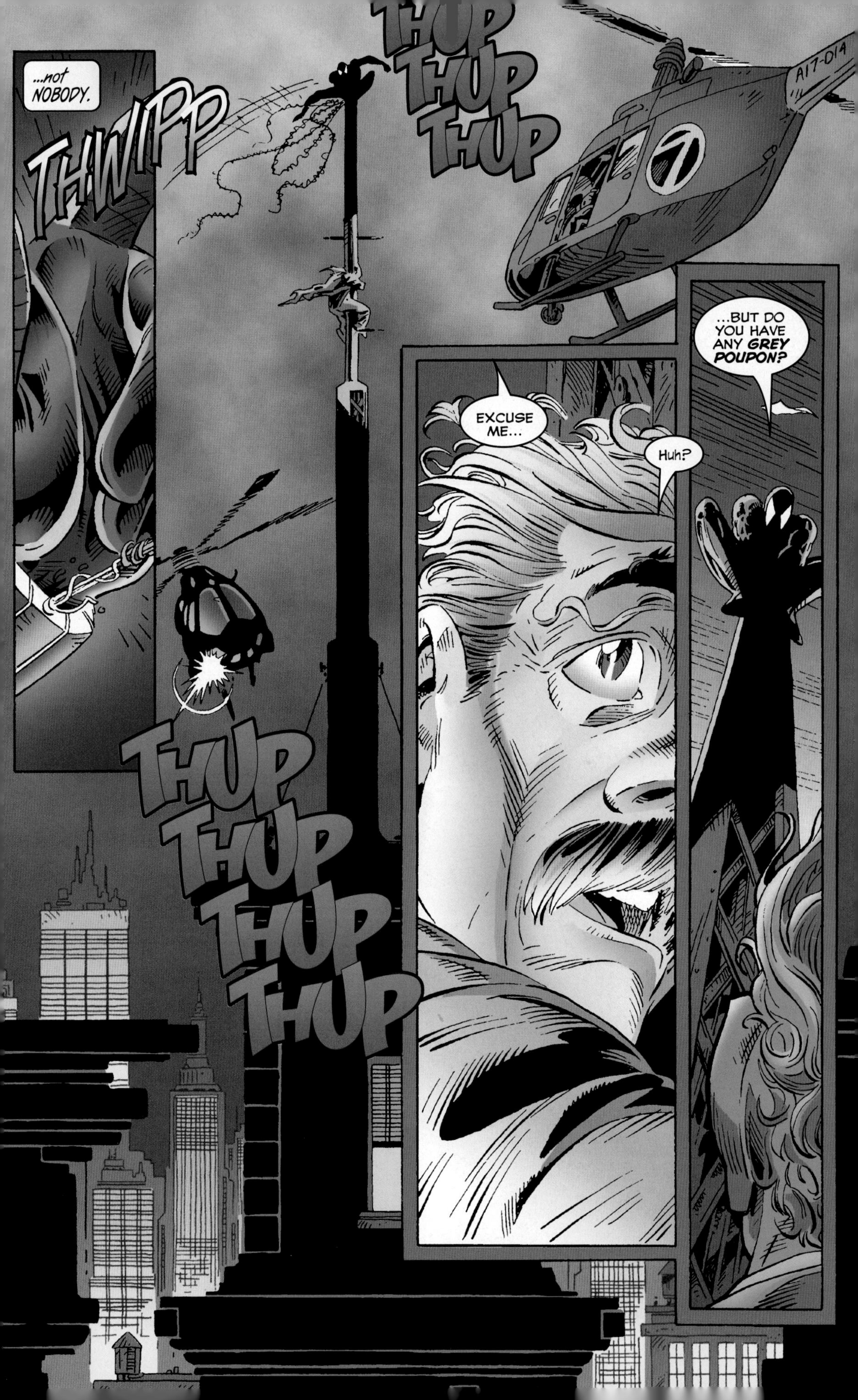

...not NOBODY.
THWIPP
THUP THUP THUP
A17-D1A
7
THUP THUP THUP THUP
EXCUSE ME...
Huh?
...BUT DO YOU HAVE ANY GREY POUPON?

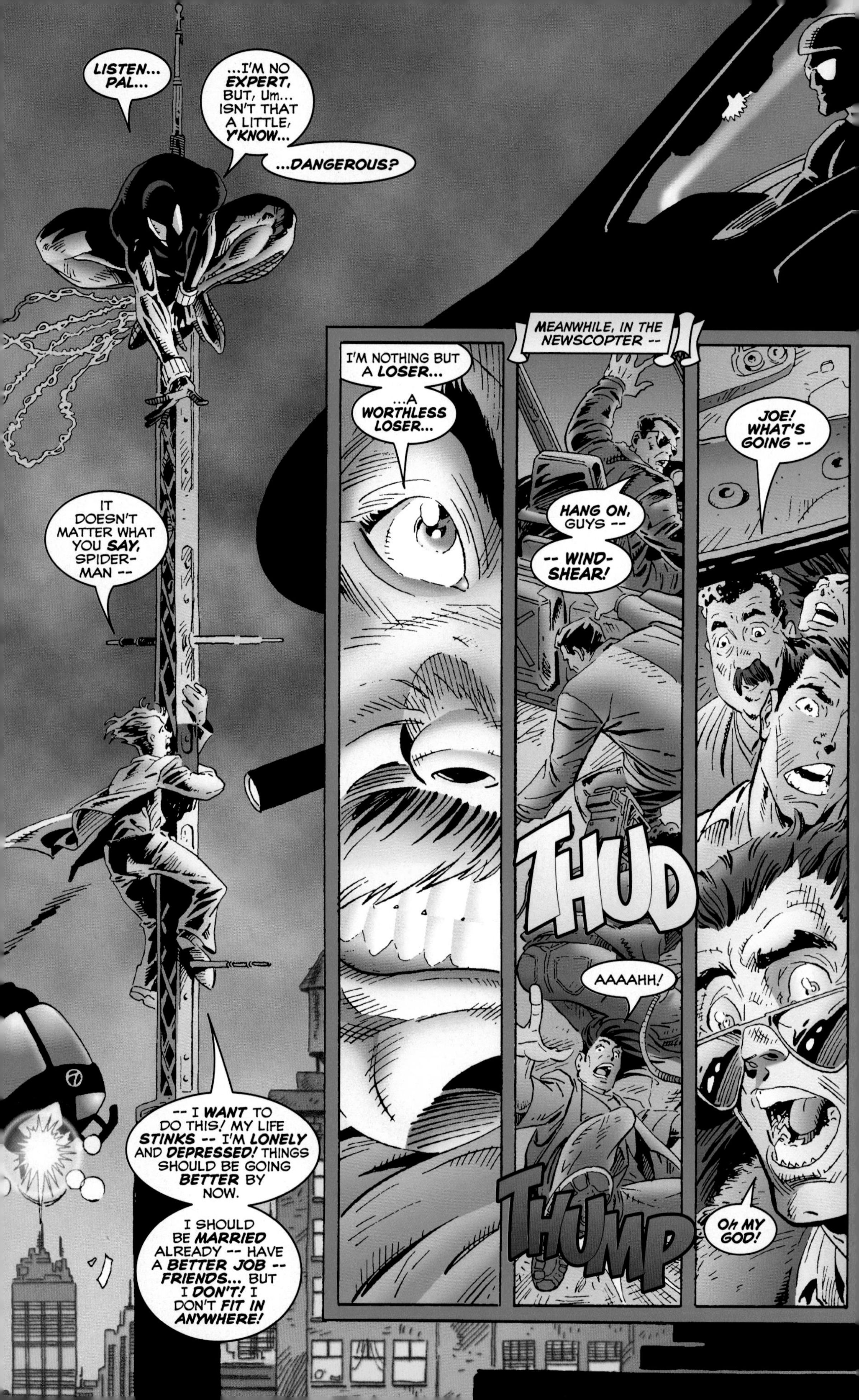

LISTEN... PAL...
...I'M NO EXPERT, BUT, Um... ISN'T THAT A LITTLE, Y'KNOW...
...DANGEROUS?
IT DOESN'T MATTER WHAT YOU SAY, SPIDER-MAN --
-- I WANT TO DO THIS! MY LIFE STINKS -- I'M LONELY AND DEPRESSED! THINGS SHOULD BE GOING BETTER BY NOW.
I SHOULD BE MARRIED ALREADY -- HAVE A BETTER JOB -- FRIENDS... BUT I DON'T! I DON'T FIT IN ANYWHERE!
MEANWHILE, IN THE NEWSCOPTER --
I'M NOTHING BUT A LOSER...
...A WORTHLESS LOSER...
HANG ON, GUYS --
-- WIND-SHEAR!
THUD
AAAAHH!
THUMP
JOE! WHAT'S GOING --
Oh MY GOD!

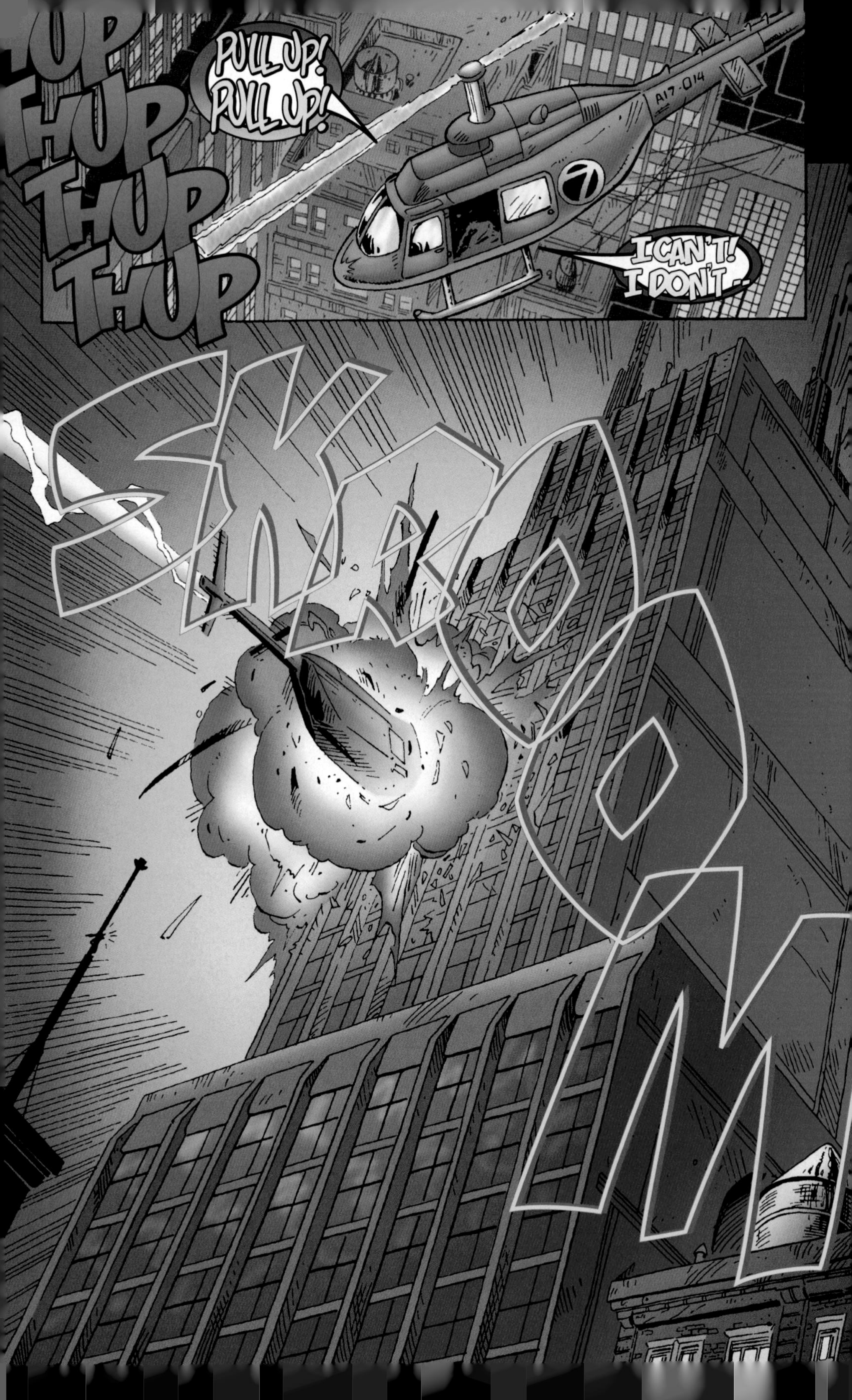
THUP THUP THUP THUP
PULL UP! PULL UP!
A17-014
I CAN'T! I DON'T...
SKROOOM

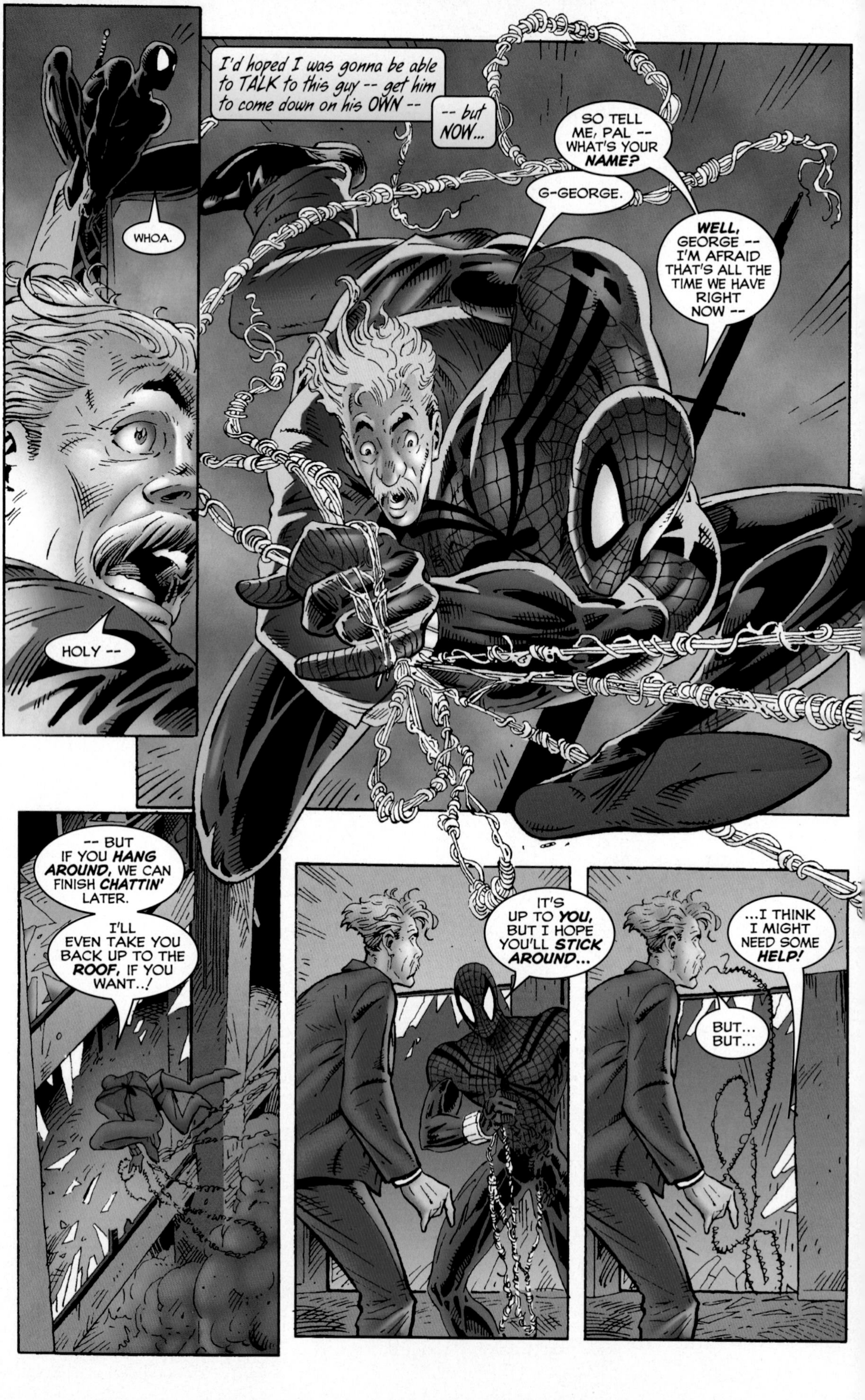
WHOA.
HOLY --
I'd hoped I was gonna be able to TALK to this guy -- get him to come down on his OWN --
-- but NOW...
SO TELL ME, PAL -- WHAT'S YOUR NAME?
G-GEORGE.
WELL, GEORGE -- I'M AFRAID THAT'S ALL THE TIME WE HAVE RIGHT NOW --
-- BUT IF YOU HANG AROUND, WE CAN FINISH CHATTIN' LATER.
I'LL EVEN TAKE YOU BACK UP TO THE ROOF, IF YOU WANT..!
IT'S UP TO YOU, BUT I HOPE YOU'LL STICK AROUND...
...I THINK I MIGHT NEED SOME HELP!
BUT... BUT...

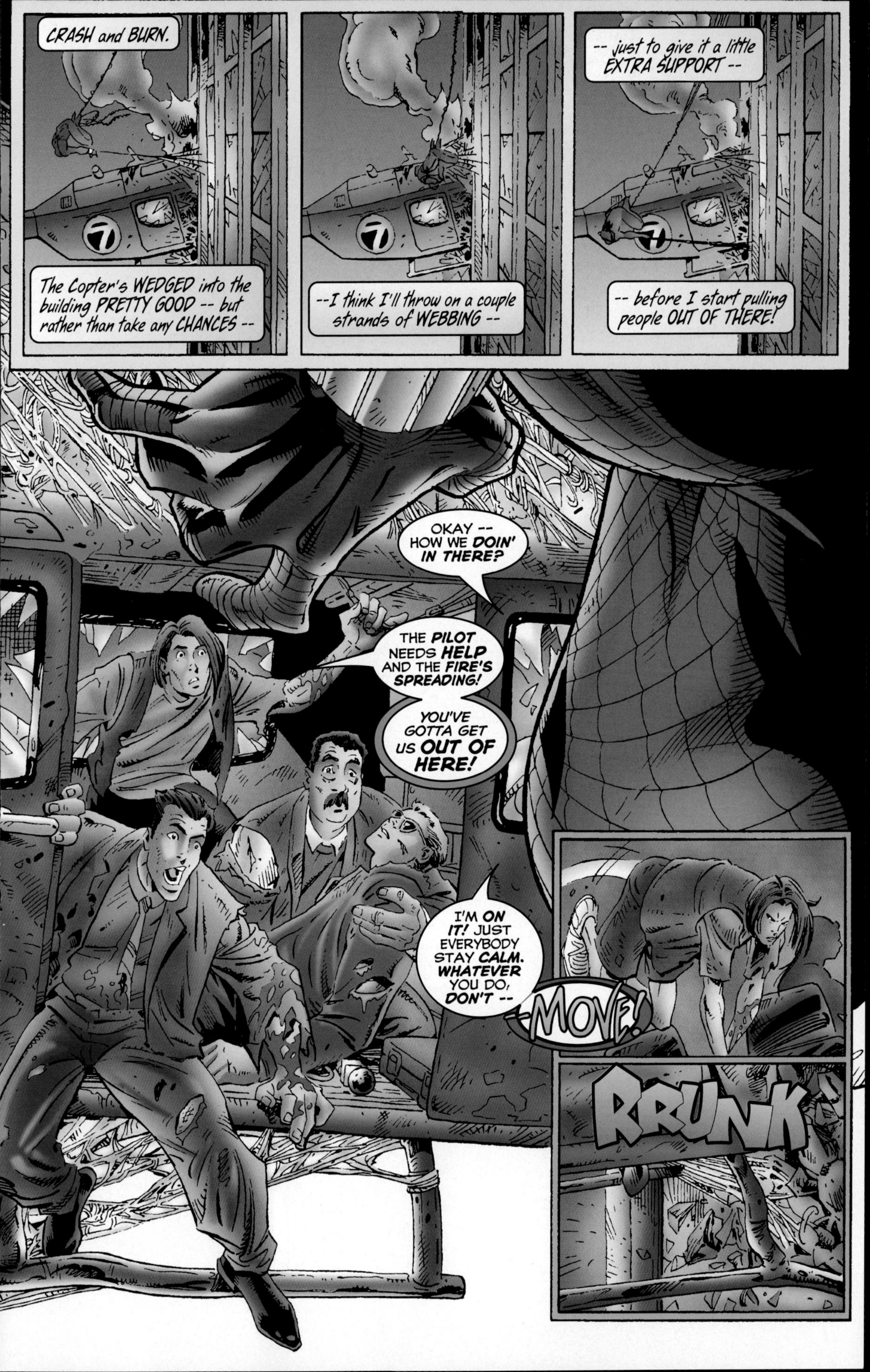
CRASH and BURN.
The Copter's WEDGED into the building PRETTY GOOD -- but rather than take any CHANCES --
--I think I'll throw on a couple strands of WEBBING --
-- just to give it a little EXTRA SUPPORT --
-- before I start pulling people OUT OF THERE!
OKAY -- HOW WE DOIN' IN THERE?
THE PILOT NEEDS HELP AND THE FIRE'S SPREADING!
YOU'VE GOTTA GET US OUT OF HERE!
I'M ON IT! JUST EVERYBODY STAY CALM. WHATEVER YOU DO, DON'T --
MOVE!
RRUNK

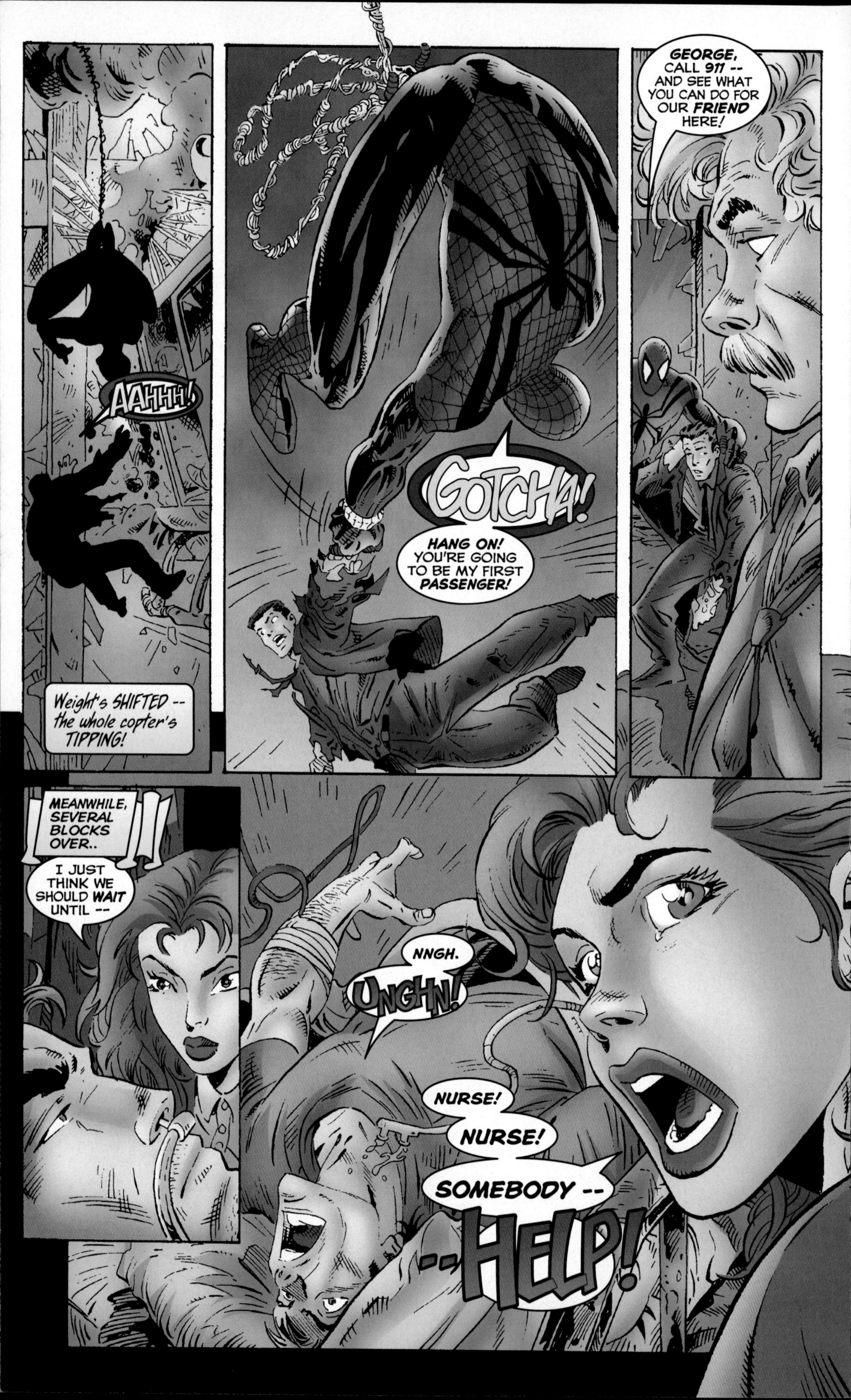
AAHHH!
Weight's SHIFTED -- the whole copter's TIPPING!
GOTCHA!
HANG ON! YOU'RE GOING TO BE MY FIRST PASSENGER!
GEORGE, CALL 911 -- AND SEE WHAT YOU CAN DO FOR OUR FRIEND HERE!
MEANWHILE, SEVERAL BLOCKS OVER..
I JUST THINK WE SHOULD WAIT UNTIL --
NNGH.
UNGHN!
NURSE!
NURSE!
SOMEBODY --
--HELP!

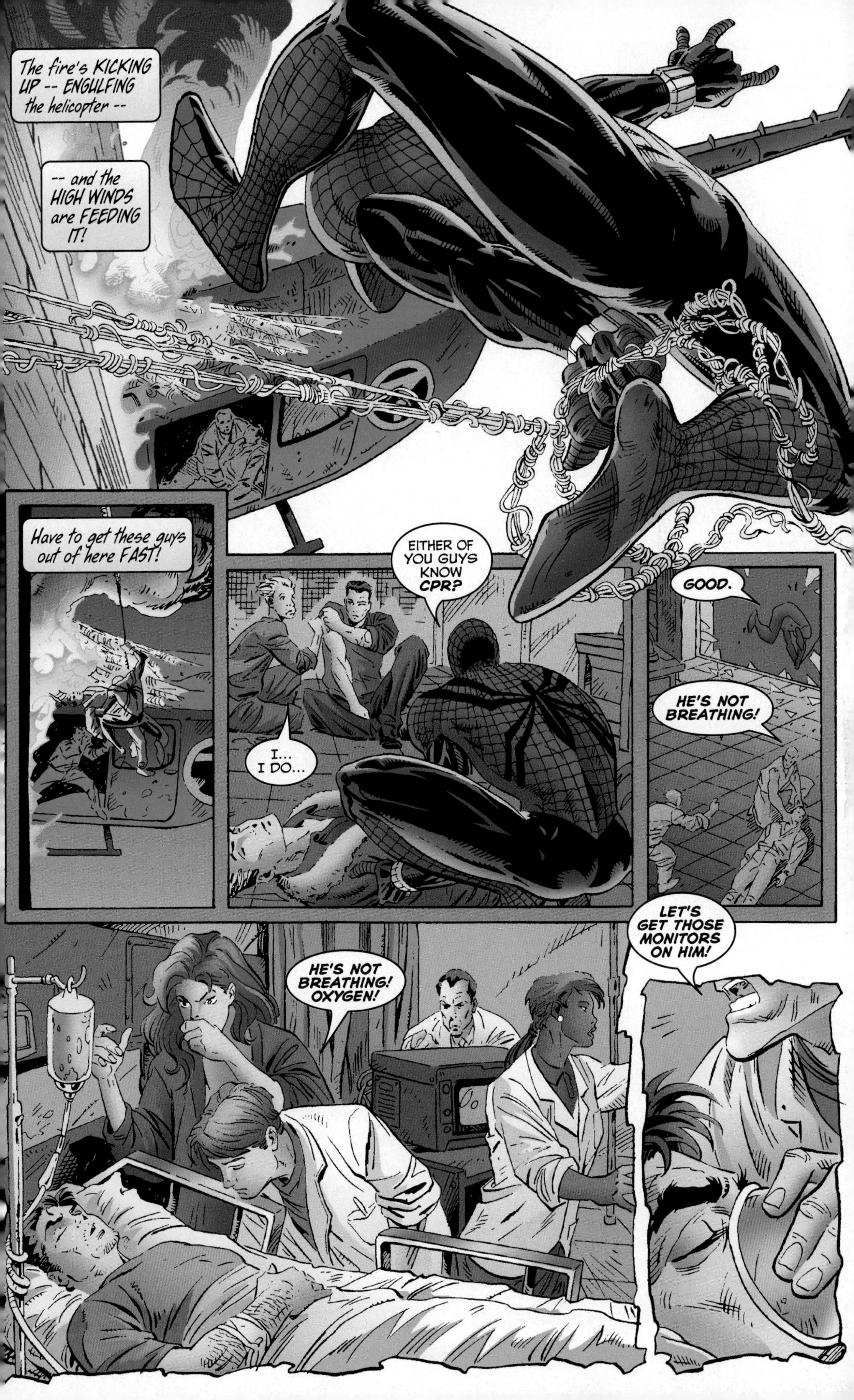
The fire's KICKING UP -- ENGULFING the helicopter --
-- and the HIGH WINDS are FEEDING IT!
Have to get these guys out of here FAST!
EITHER OF YOU GUYS KNOW CPR?
I... I DO...
GOOD.
HE'S NOT BREATHING!
HE'S NOT BREATHING! OXYGEN!
LET'S GET THOSE MONITORS ON HIM!

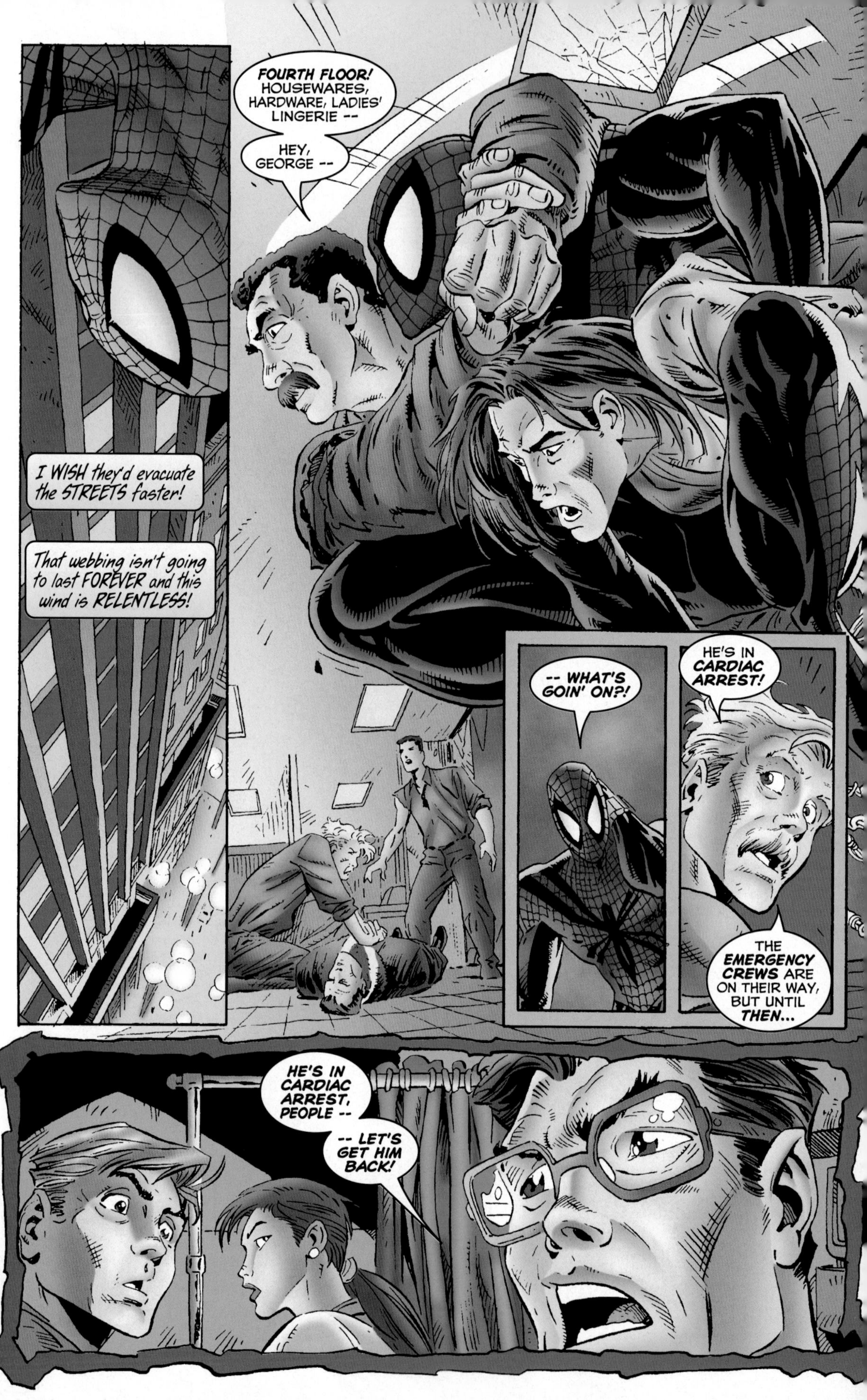
FOURTH FLOOR! HOUSEWARES, HARDWARE, LADIES' LINGERIE --
HEY, GEORGE --
I WISH they'd evacuate the STREETS faster!
That webbing isn't going to last FOREVER and this wind is RELENTLESS!
-- WHAT'S GOIN' ON?!
HE'S IN CARDIAC ARREST!
THE EMERGENCY CREWS ARE ON THEIR WAY, BUT UNTIL THEN...
HE'S IN CARDIAC ARREST, PEOPLE --
-- LET'S GET HIM BACK!

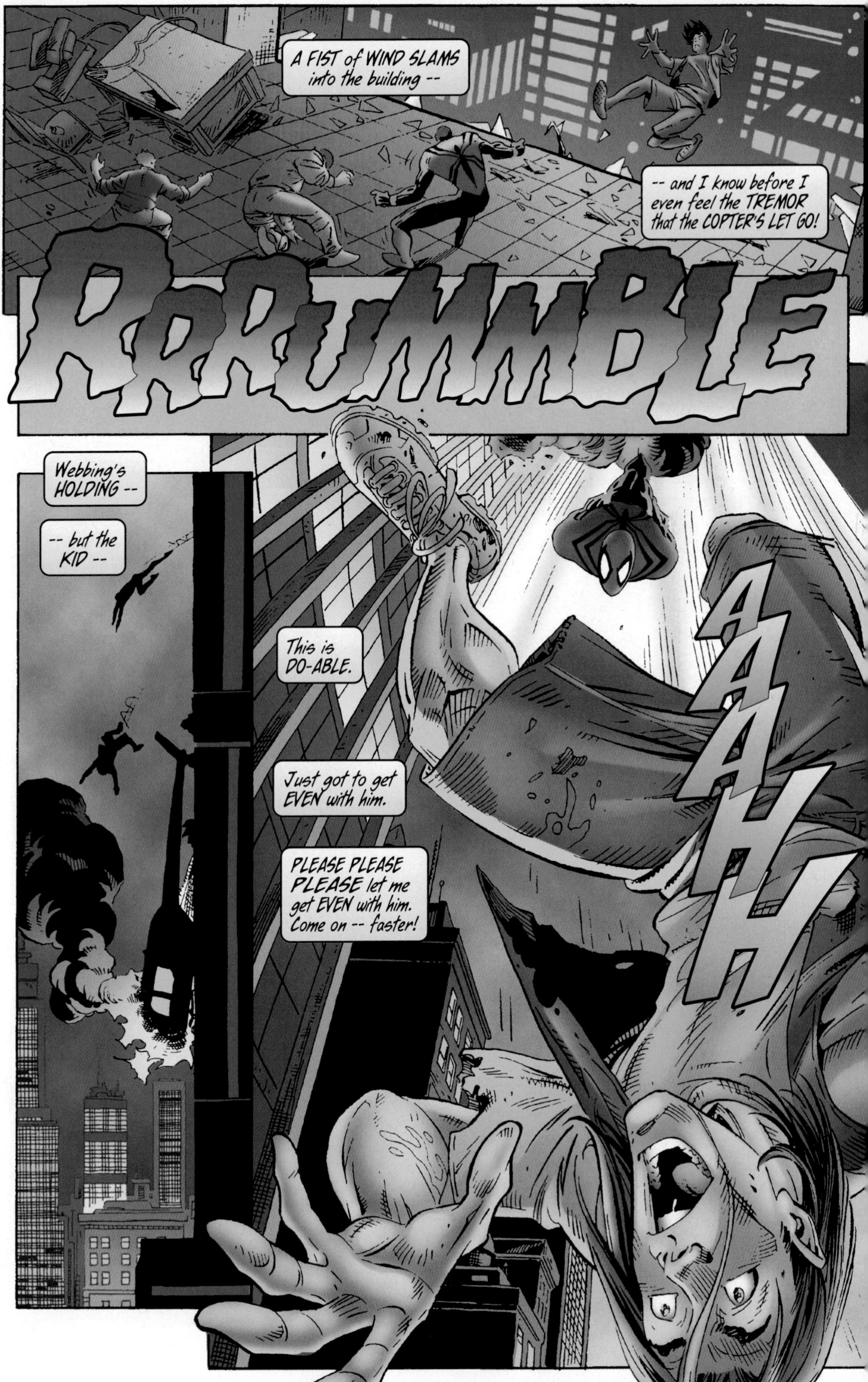
A FIST of WIND SLAMS into the building --
-- and I know before I even feel the TREMOR that the COPTER'S LET GO!
RRRUMMBLE
Webbing's HOLDING --
-- but the KID --
This is DO-ABLE.
Just got to get EVEN with him.
PLEASE PLEASE PLEASE let me get EVEN with him. Come on -- faster!
AAAAH

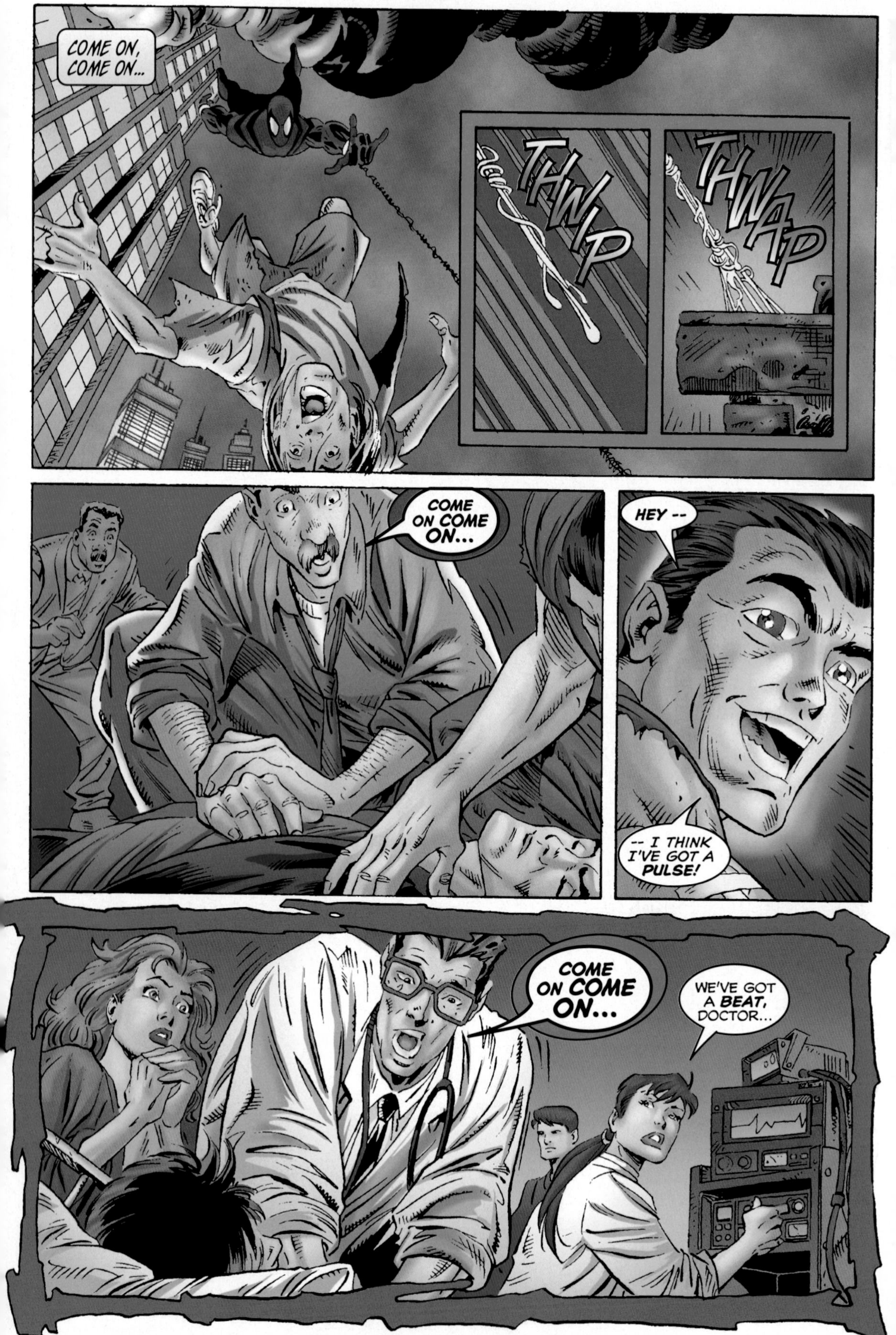
COME ON, COME ON...
THWIP
THWAP
COME ON COME ON...
HEY --
-- I THINK I'VE GOT A PULSE!
COME ON COME ON...
WE'VE GOT A BEAT, DOCTOR...

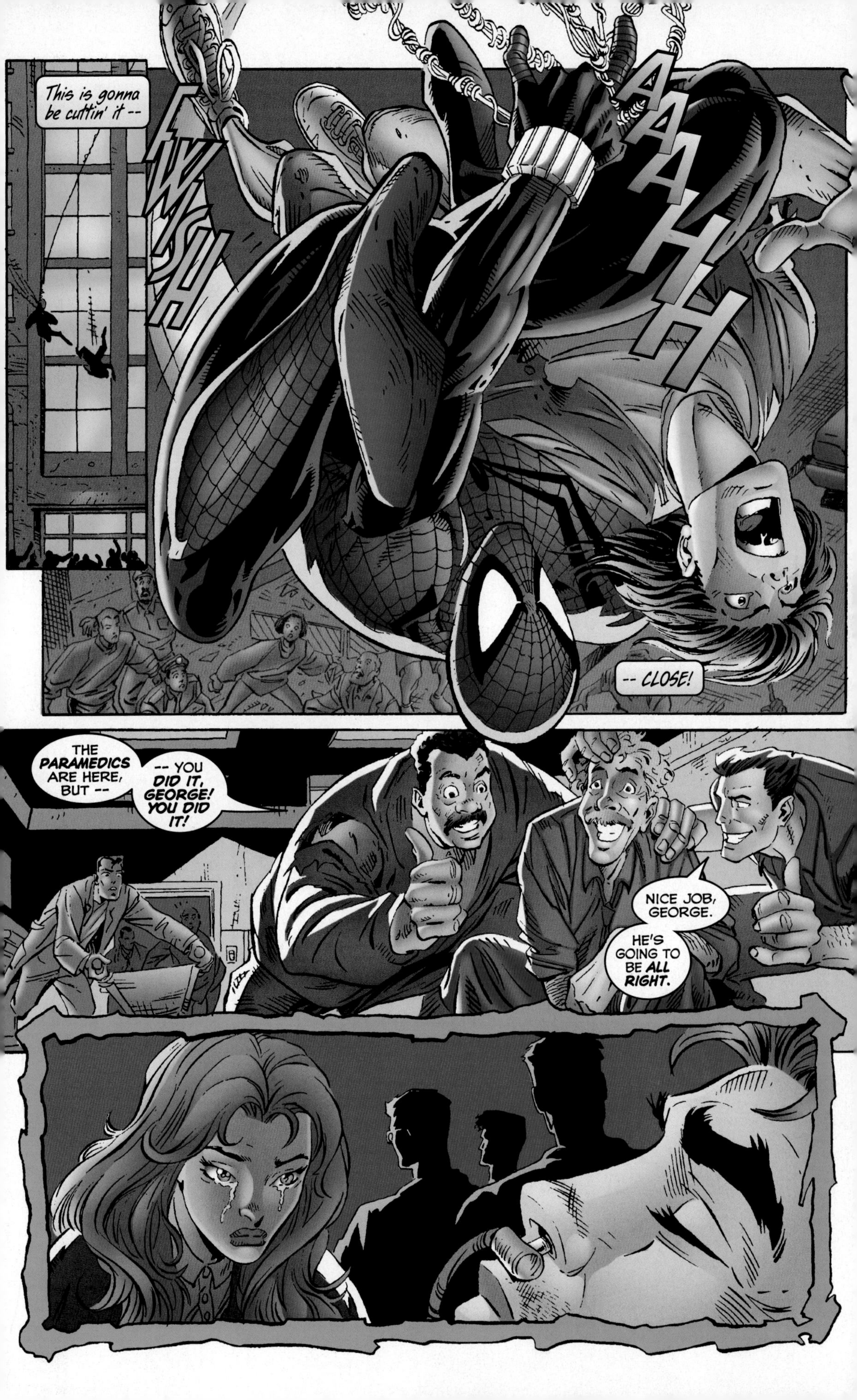

This is gonna be cuttin' it --
FWSHH
AAAHHH
-- CLOSE!
THE PARAMEDICS ARE HERE, BUT --
-- YOU DID IT, GEORGE! YOU DID IT!
NICE JOB, GEORGE.
HE'S GOING TO BE ALL RIGHT.

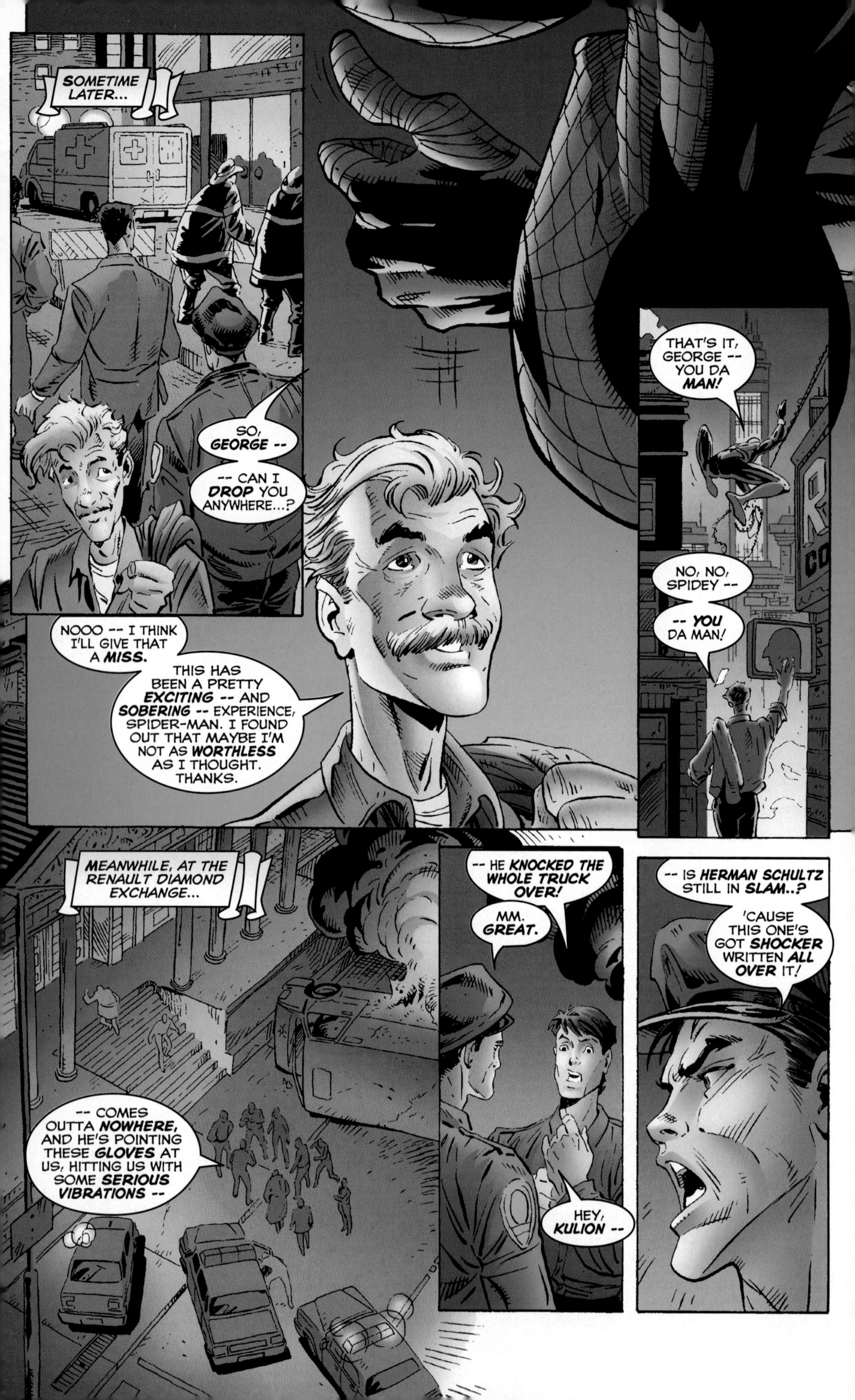
SOMETIME LATER...
SO, GEORGE --
-- CAN I DROP YOU ANYWHERE...?
NOOO -- I THINK I'LL GIVE THAT A MISS.
THIS HAS BEEN A PRETTY EXCITING -- AND SOBERING -- EXPERIENCE, SPIDER-MAN. I FOUND OUT THAT MAYBE I'M NOT AS WORTHLESS AS I THOUGHT. THANKS.
THAT'S IT, GEORGE -- YOU DA MAN!
NO, NO, SPIDEY --
-- YOU DA MAN!
MEANWHILE, AT THE RENAULT DIAMOND EXCHANGE...
-- COMES OUTTA NOWHERE, AND HE'S POINTING THESE GLOVES AT US, HITTING US WITH SOME SERIOUS VIBRATIONS --
-- HE KNOCKED THE WHOLE TRUCK OVER!
MM. GREAT.
HEY, KULION --
-- IS HERMAN SCHULTZ STILL IN SLAM..?
'CAUSE THIS ONE'S GOT SHOCKER WRITTEN ALL OVER IT!

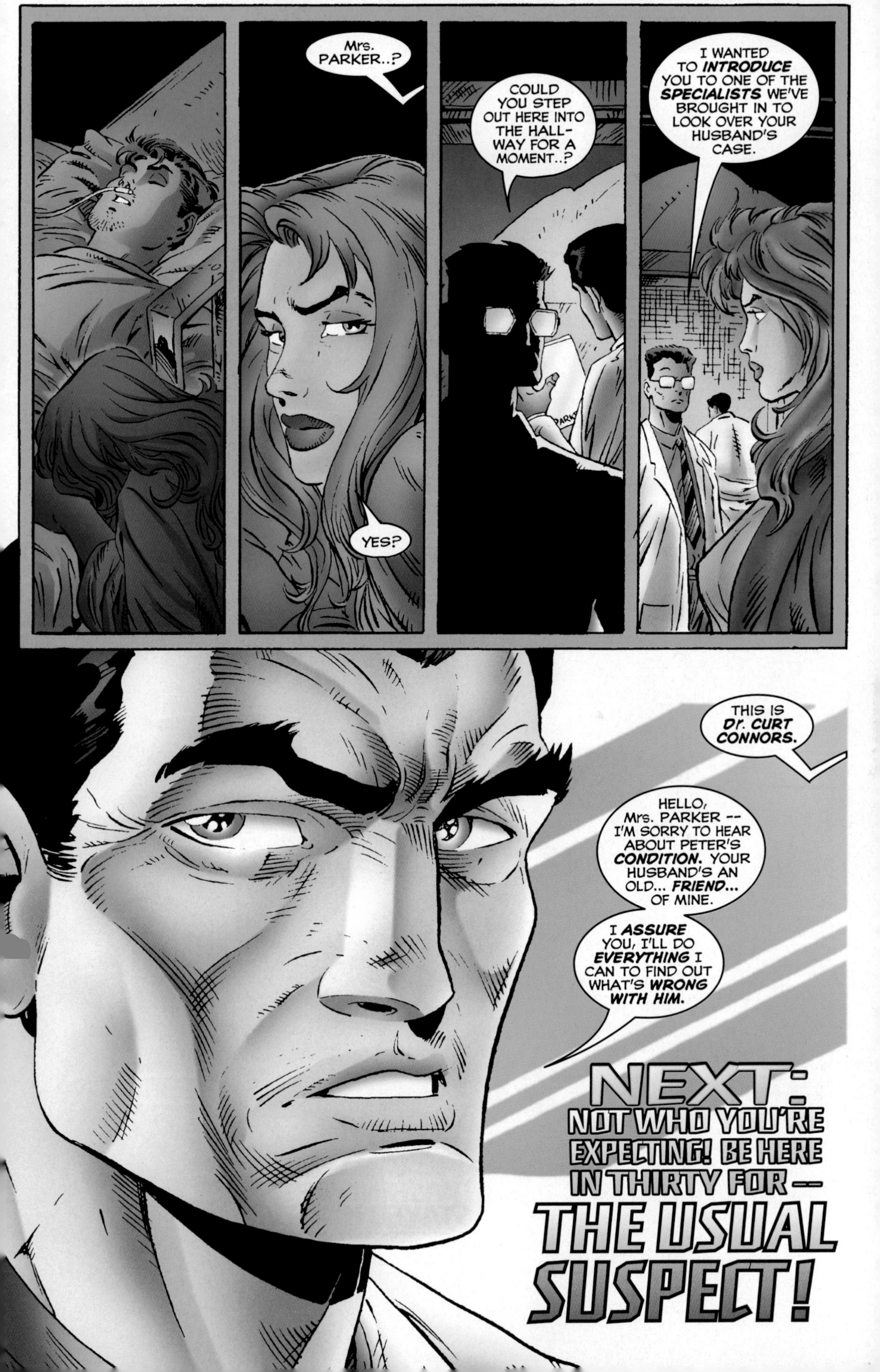
Mrs. PARKER..?
YES?
COULD YOU STEP OUT HERE INTO THE HALL-WAY FOR A MOMENT..?
I WANTED TO INTRODUCE YOU TO ONE OF THE SPECIALISTS WE'VE BROUGHT IN TO LOOK OVER YOUR HUSBAND'S CASE.
THIS IS Dr. CURT CONNORS.
HELLO, Mrs. PARKER -- I'M SORRY TO HEAR ABOUT PETER'S CONDITION. YOUR HUSBAND'S AN OLD... FRIEND... OF MINE.
I ASSURE YOU, I'LL DO EVERYTHING I CAN TO FIND OUT WHAT'S WRONG WITH HIM.
NEXT: NOT WHO YOU'RE EXPECTING! BE HERE IN THIRTY FOR --
THE USUAL SUSPECT!

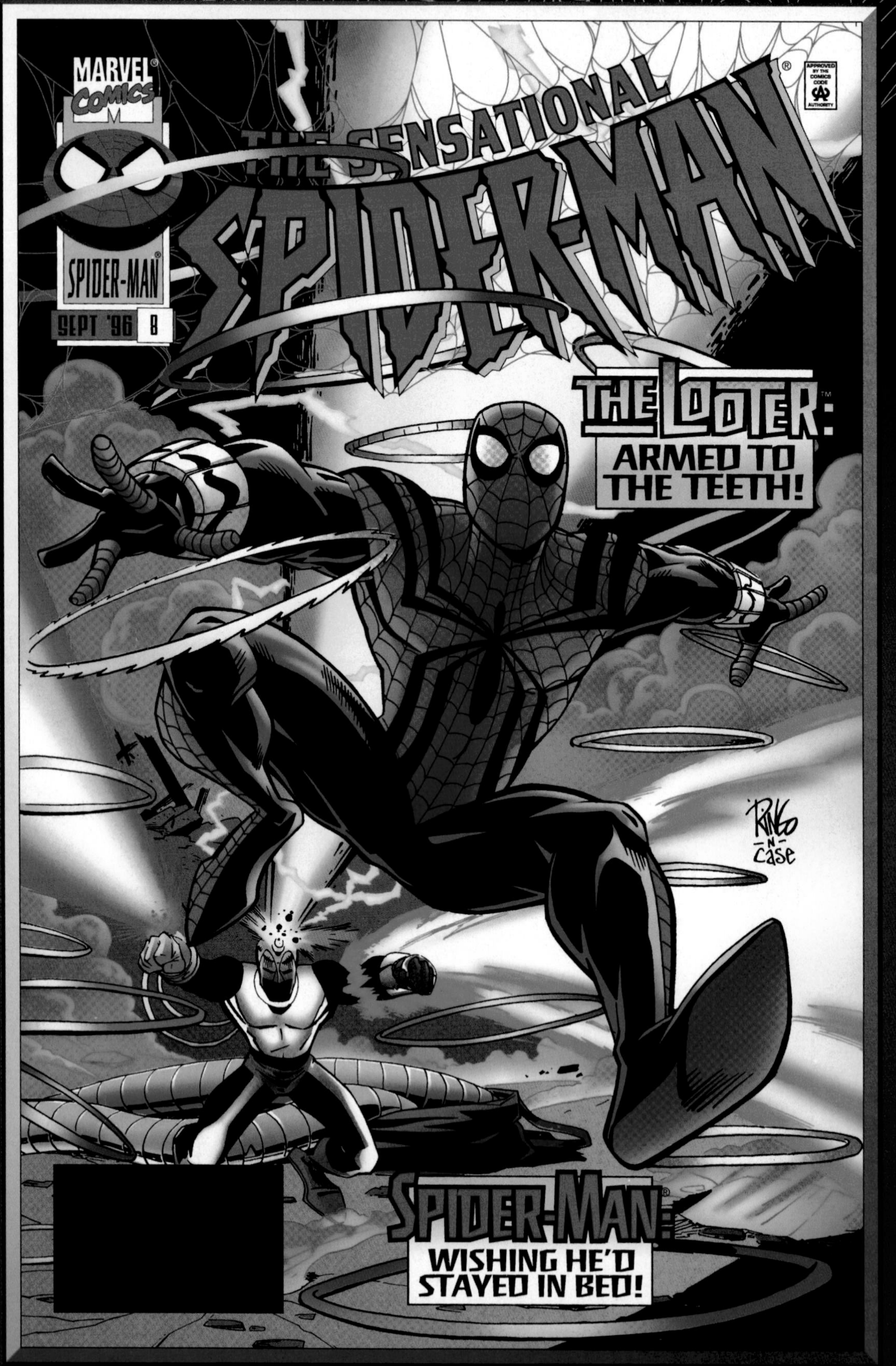
MARVEL COMICS
SPIDER-MAN
SEPT '96 8
APPROVED BY THE COMICS CODE AUTHORITY
THE SENSATIONAL SPIDER-MAN
THE LOOTER:
ARMED TO THE TEETH!
Ringo -n- Case
SPIDER-MAN:
WISHING HE'D STAYED IN BED!

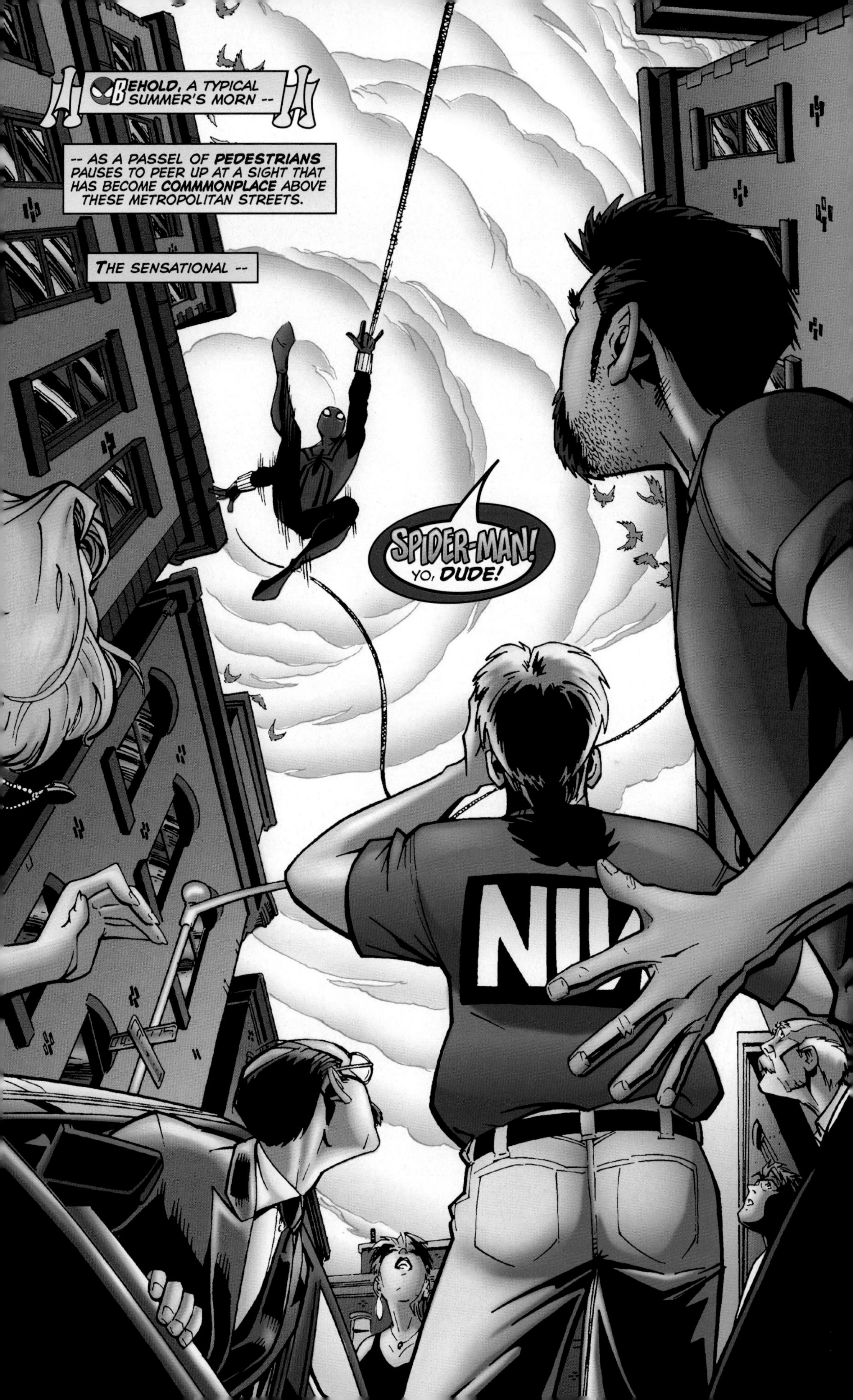

BEHOLD, A TYPICAL SUMMER'S MORN --
-- AS A PASSEL OF PEDESTRIANS PAUSES TO PEER UP AT A SIGHT THAT HAS BECOME COMMMONPLACE ABOVE THESE METROPOLITAN STREETS.
THE SENSATIONAL --
SPIDER-MAN! YO, DUDE!

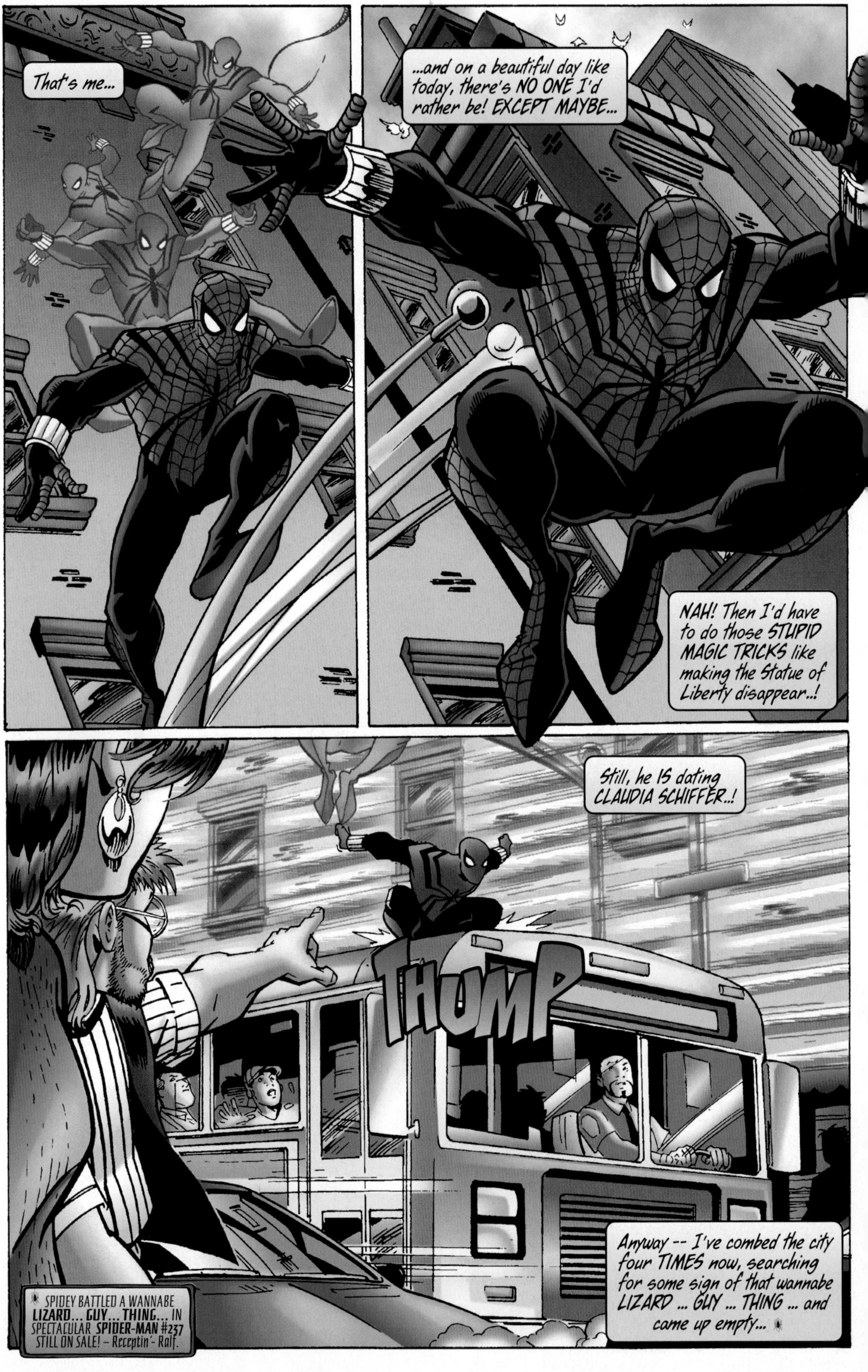
That's me...
...and on a beautiful day like today, there's NO ONE I'd rather be! EXCEPT MAYBE...
NAH! Then I'd have to do those STUPID MAGIC TRICKS like making the Statue of Liberty disappear..!
Still, he IS dating CLAUDIA SCHIFFER..!
THUMP
SPIDEY BATTLED A WANNABE LIZARD... GUY... THING... IN SPECTACULAR SPIDER-MAN #237 STILL ON SALE! – Receptin'- Ralf.
Anyway -- I've combed the city four TIMES now, searching for some sign of that wannabe LIZARD ... GUY ... THING ... and came up empty...

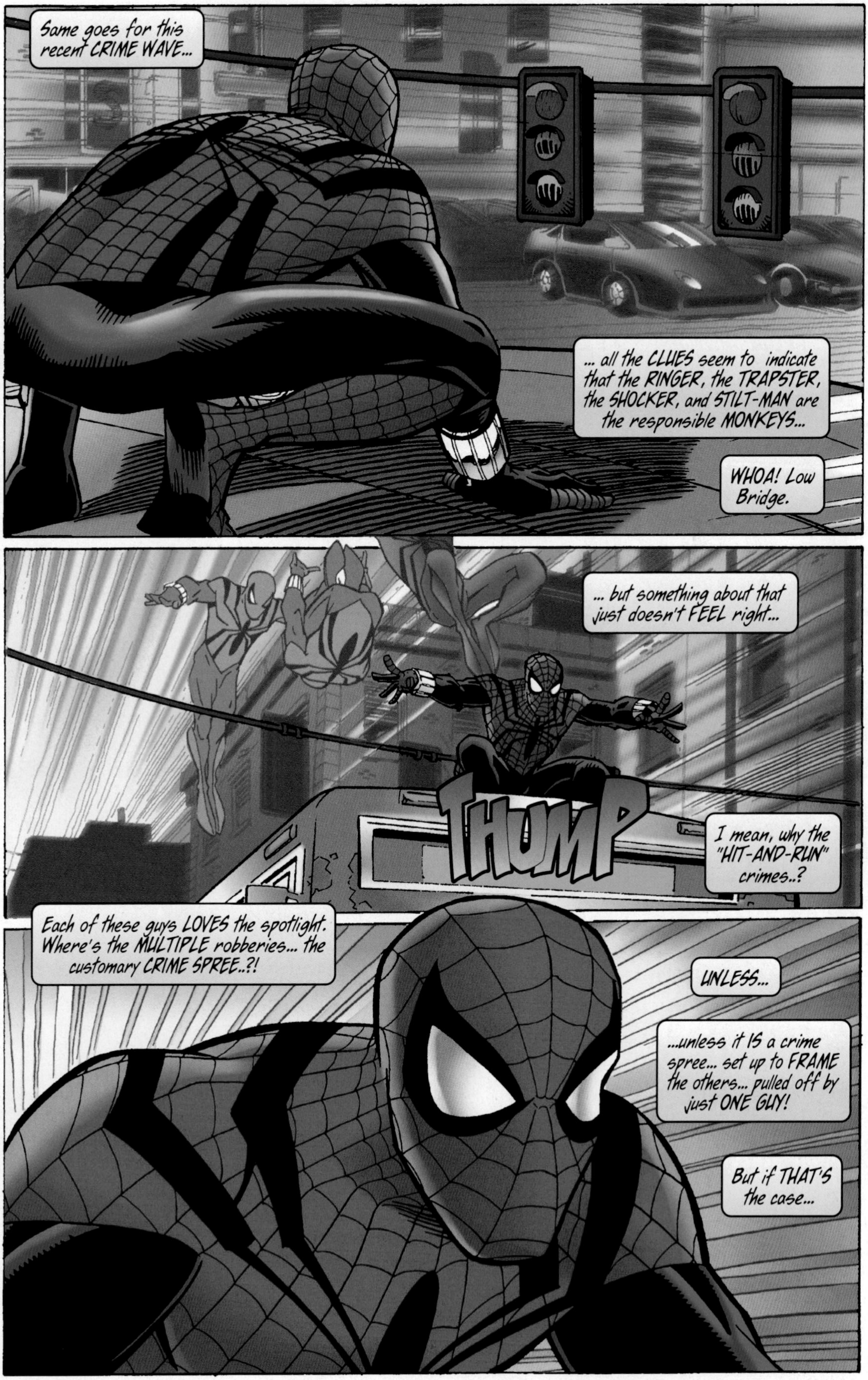
Same goes for this recent CRIME WAVE...
... all the CLUES seem to indicate that the RINGER, the TRAPSTER, the SHOCKER, and STILT-MAN are the responsible MONKEYS...
WHOA! Low Bridge.
... but something about that just doesn't FEEL right...
THUMP
I mean, why the "HIT-AND-RUN" crimes..?
Each of these guys LOVES the spotlight. Where's the MULTIPLE robberies... the customary CRIME SPREE..?!
UNLESS...
...unless it IS a crime spree... set up to FRAME the others... pulled off by just ONE GUY!
But if THAT'S the case...

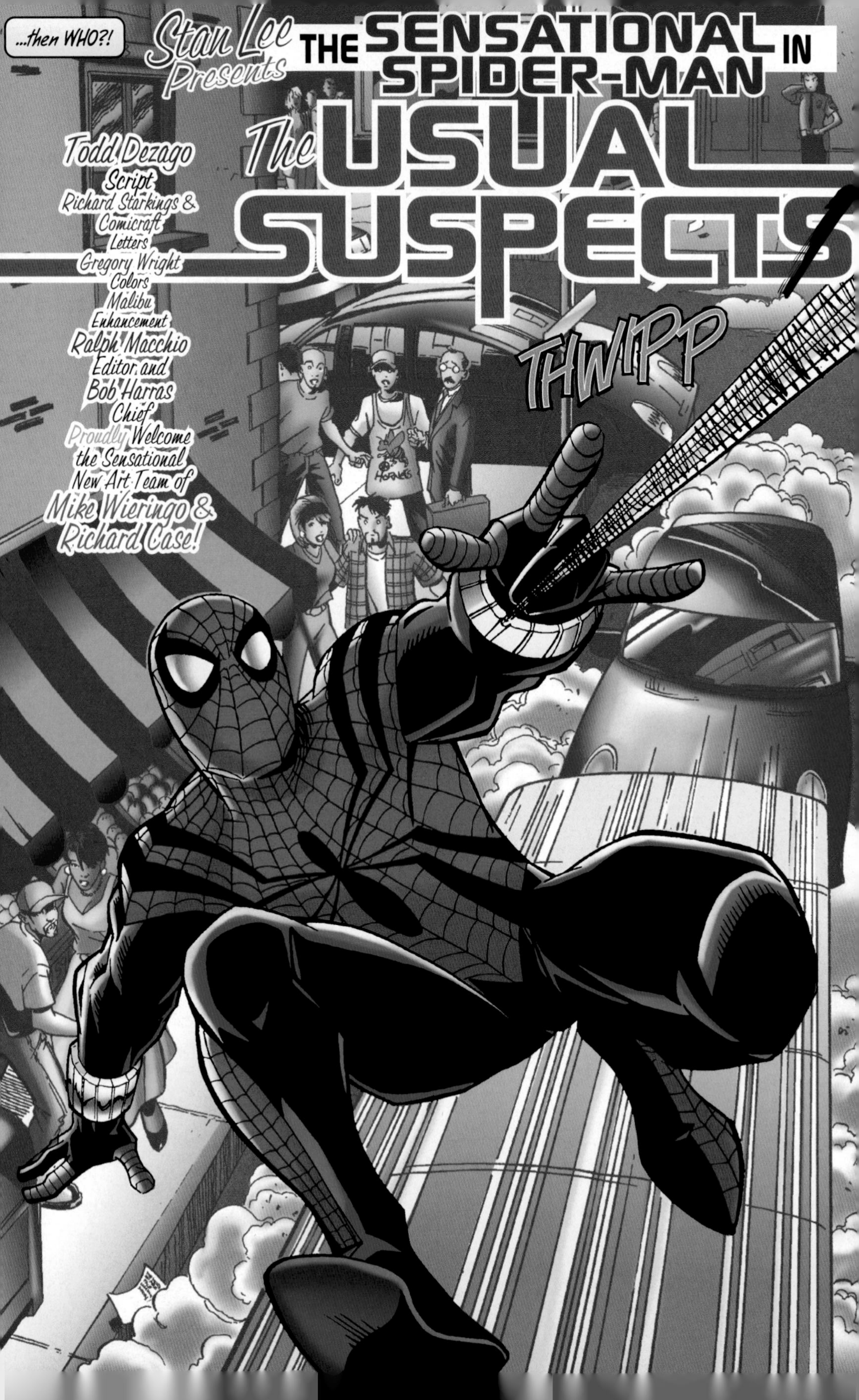
...then WHO?!
Stan Lee Presents
THE SENSATIONAL SPIDER-MAN IN
The USUAL SUSPECTS
Todd Dezago Script
Richard Starkings & Comicraft Letters
Gregory Wright Colors
Malibu Enhancement
Ralph Macchio Editor and
Bob Harras Chief
Proudly Welcome the Sensational New Art Team of
Mike Wieringo & Richard Case!
THWIPP

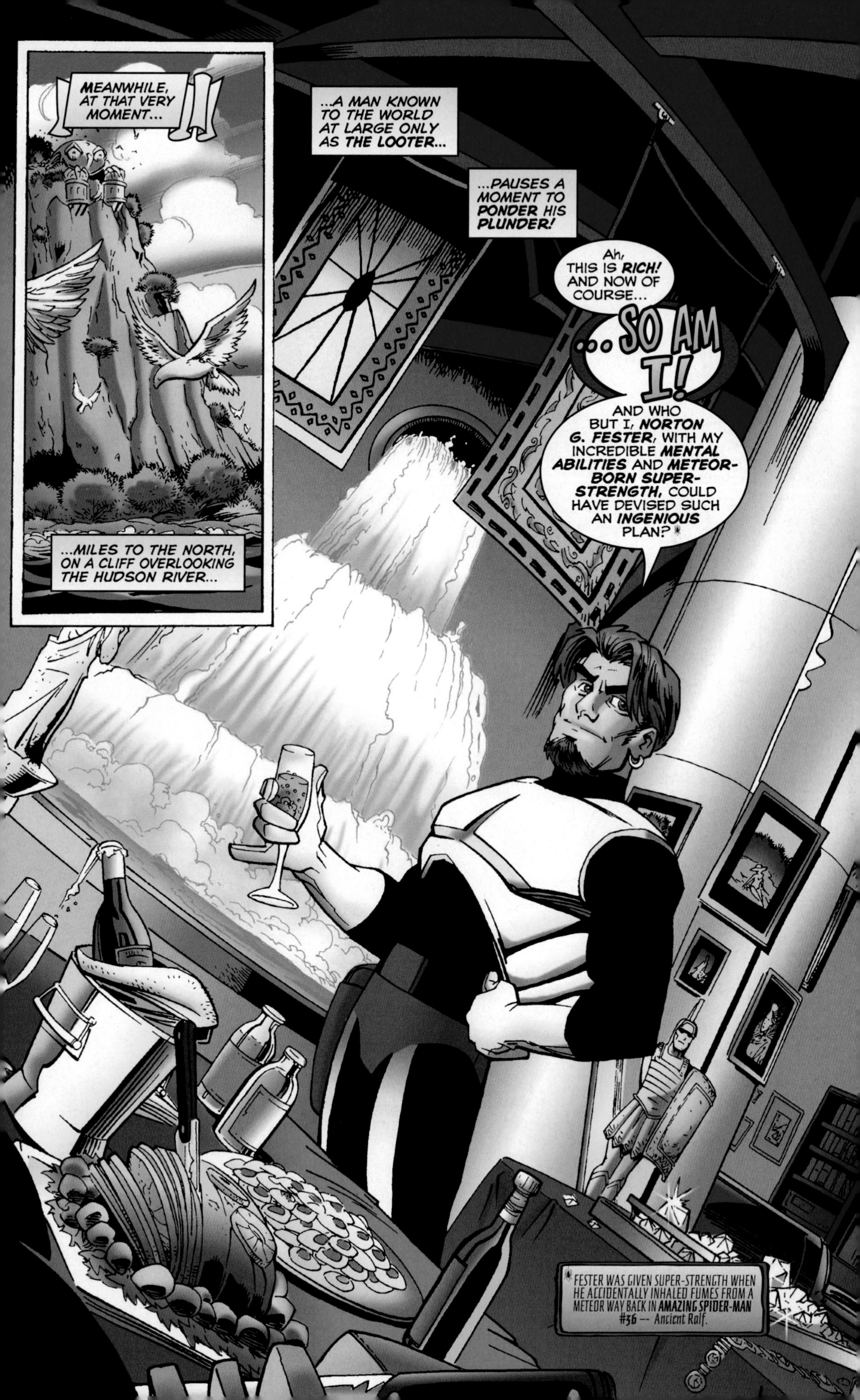
MEANWHILE, AT THAT VERY MOMENT...
...MILES TO THE NORTH, ON A CLIFF OVERLOOKING THE HUDSON RIVER...
...A MAN KNOWN TO THE WORLD AT LARGE ONLY AS THE LOOTER...
...PAUSES A MOMENT TO PONDER HIS PLUNDER!
Ah, THIS IS RICH! AND NOW OF COURSE...
...SO AM I!
AND WHO BUT I, NORTON G. FESTER, WITH MY INCREDIBLE MENTAL ABILITIES AND METEOR-BORN SUPER-STRENGTH, COULD HAVE DEVISED SUCH AN INGENIOUS PLAN?*
*FESTER WAS GIVEN SUPER-STRENGTH WHEN HE ACCIDENTALLY INHALED FUMES FROM A METEOR WAY BACK IN AMAZING SPIDER-MAN #36 -- Ancient Ralf.

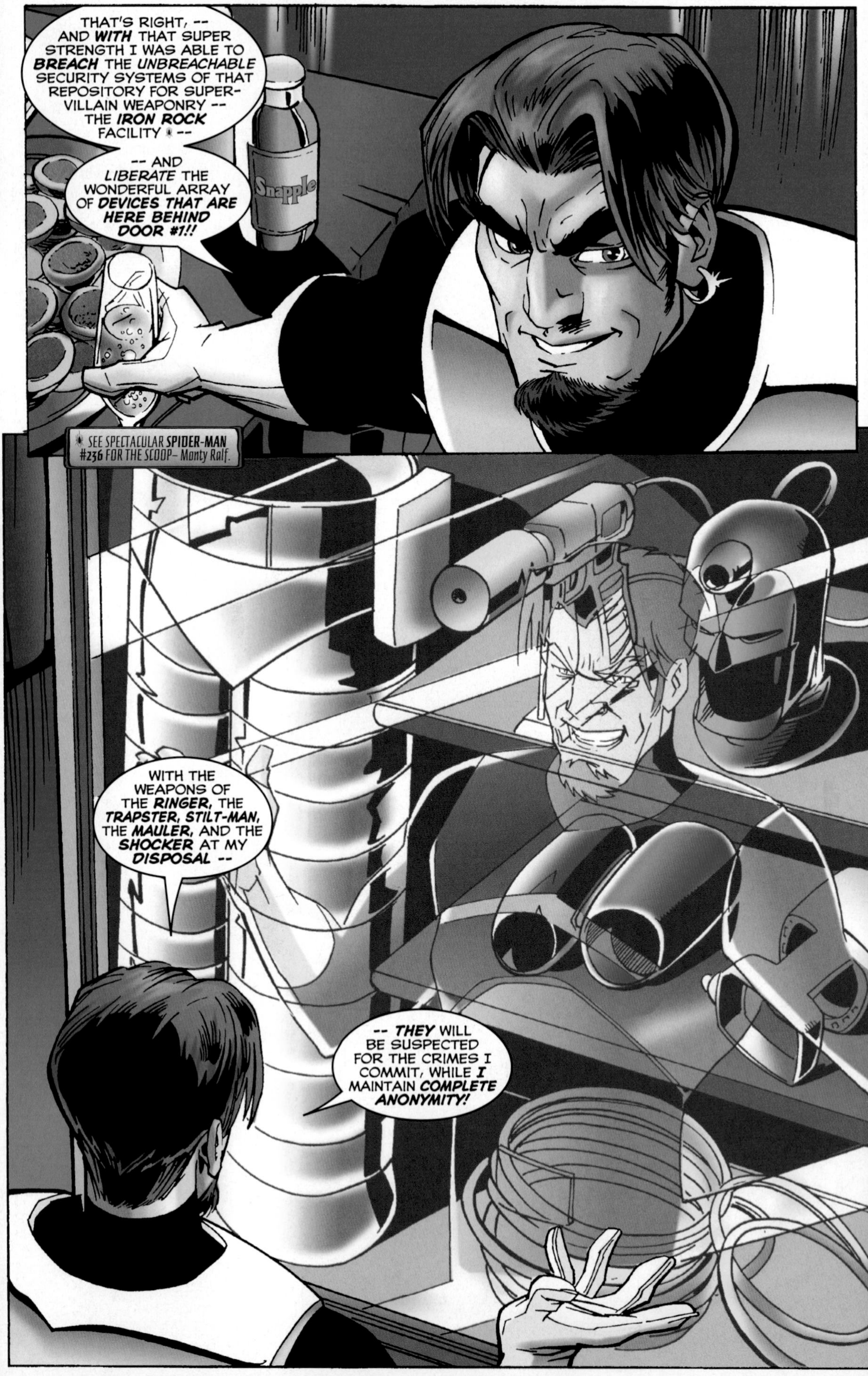
THAT'S RIGHT, -- AND WITH THAT SUPER STRENGTH I WAS ABLE TO BREACH THE UNBREACHABLE SECURITY SYSTEMS OF THAT REPOSITORY FOR SUPER-VILLAIN WEAPONRY -- THE IRON ROCK FACILITY --
-- AND LIBERATE THE WONDERFUL ARRAY OF DEVICES THAT ARE HERE BEHIND DOOR #1!!
Snapple
SEE SPECTACULAR SPIDER-MAN #236 FOR THE SCOOP– Monty Ralf.
WITH THE WEAPONS OF THE RINGER, THE TRAPSTER, STILT-MAN, THE MAULER, AND THE SHOCKER AT MY DISPOSAL --
-- THEY WILL BE SUSPECTED FOR THE CRIMES I COMMIT, WHILE I MAINTAIN COMPLETE ANONYMITY!

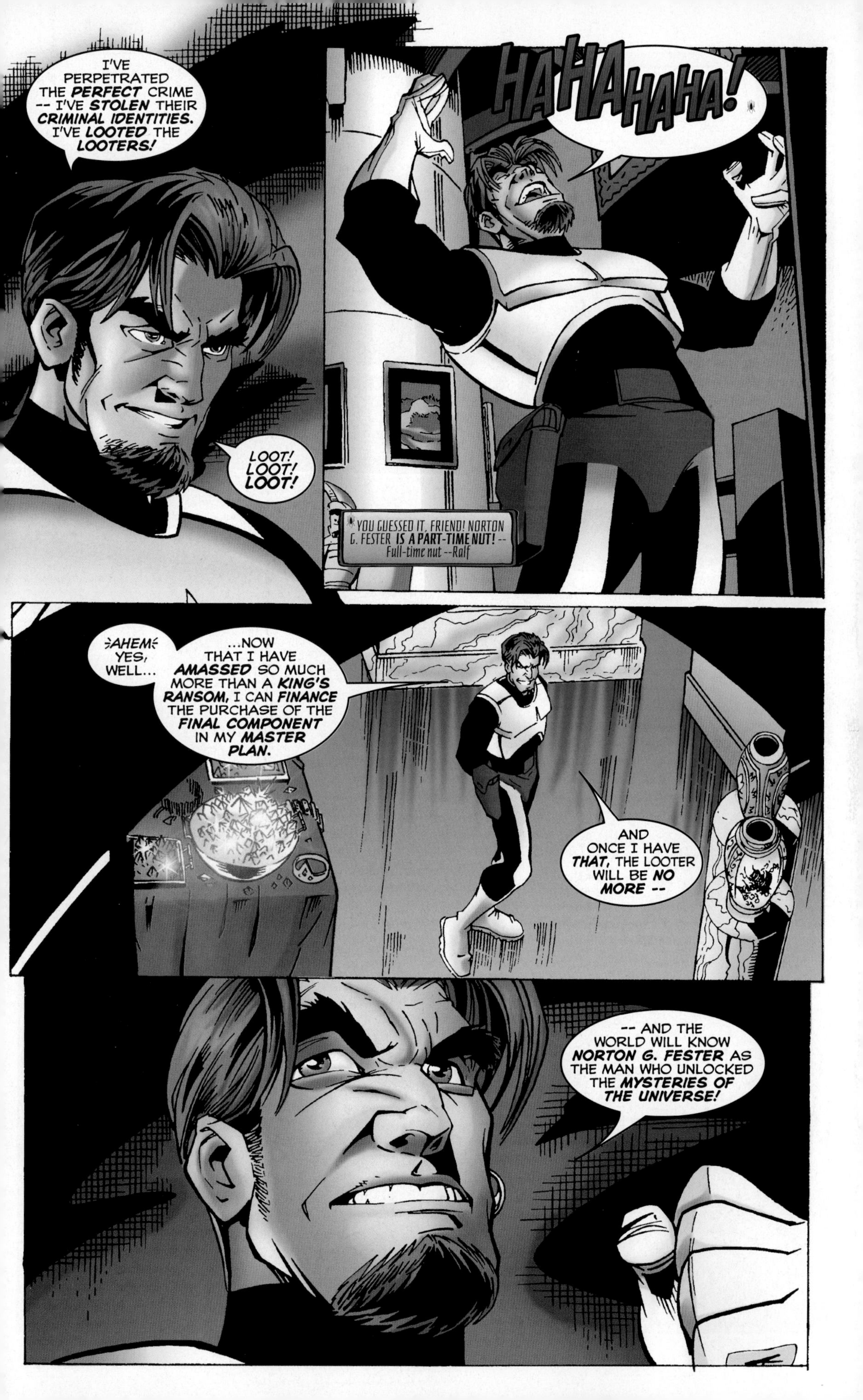
I'VE PERPETRATED THE PERFECT CRIME -- I'VE STOLEN THEIR CRIMINAL IDENTITIES. I'VE LOOTED THE LOOTERS!
LOOT! LOOT! LOOT!
HAHAHAHAHA!
YOU GUESSED IT, FRIEND! NORTON G. FESTER IS A PART-TIME NUT! -- Full-time nut --Ralf
AHEM YES, WELL...
...NOW THAT I HAVE AMASSED SO MUCH MORE THAN A KING'S RANSOM, I CAN FINANCE THE PURCHASE OF THE FINAL COMPONENT IN MY MASTER PLAN.
AND ONCE I HAVE THAT, THE LOOTER WILL BE NO MORE --
-- AND THE WORLD WILL KNOW NORTON G. FESTER AS THE MAN WHO UNLOCKED THE MYSTERIES OF THE UNIVERSE!

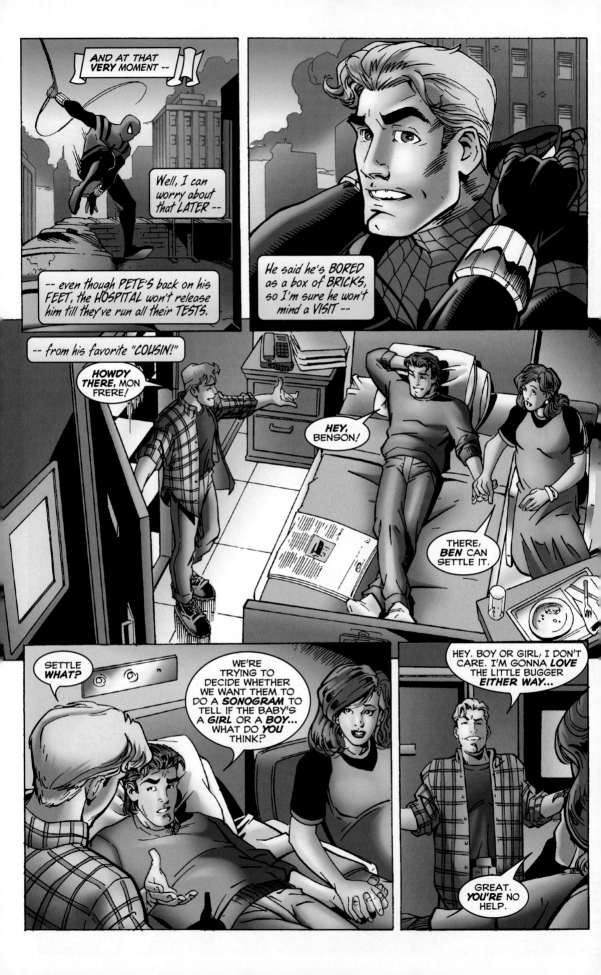

AND AT THAT VERY MOMENT --

Well, I can worry about that LATER --

-- even though PETE'S back on his FEET, the HOSPITAL won't release him till they've run all their TESTS.

He said he's BORED as a box of BRICKS, so I'm sure he won't mind a VISIT --

-- from his favorite "COUSIN!"

HOWDY THERE, MON FRERE!

HEY, BENSON!

THERE, BEN CAN SETTLE IT.

SETTLE WHAT?

WE'RE TRYING TO DECIDE WHETHER WE WANT THEM TO DO A SONOGRAM TO TELL IF THE BABY'S A GIRL OR A BOY... WHAT DO YOU THINK?

HEY. BOY OR GIRL, I DON'T CARE. I'M GONNA LOVE THE LITTLE BUGGER EITHER WAY...

GREAT. YOU'RE NO HELP.

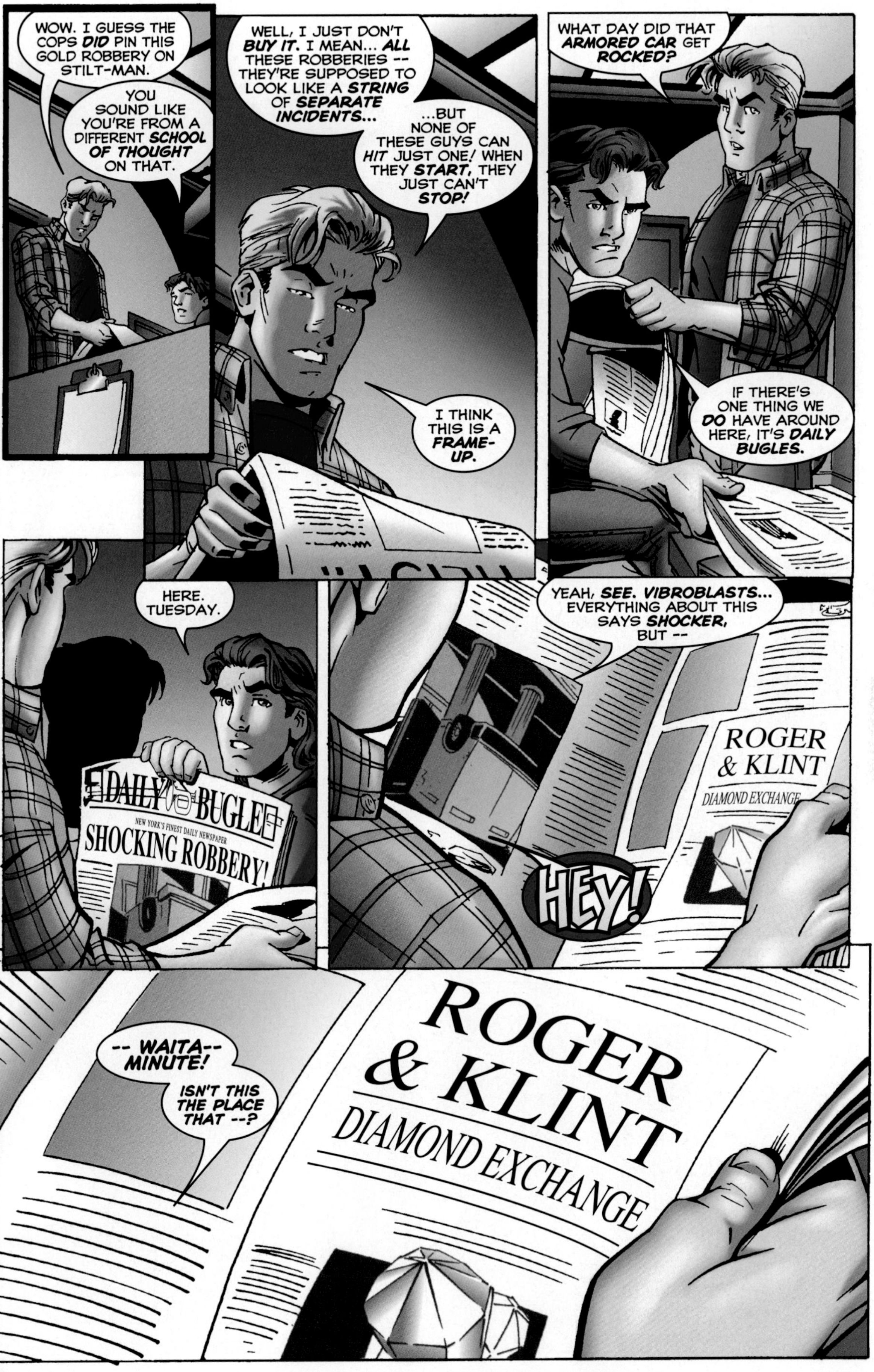
WOW. I GUESS THE COPS DID PIN THIS GOLD ROBBERY ON STILT-MAN.
YOU SOUND LIKE YOU'RE FROM A DIFFERENT SCHOOL OF THOUGHT ON THAT.
WELL, I JUST DON'T BUY IT. I MEAN... ALL THESE ROBBERIES -- THEY'RE SUPPOSED TO LOOK LIKE A STRING OF SEPARATE INCIDENTS...
...BUT NONE OF THESE GUYS CAN HIT JUST ONE! WHEN THEY START, THEY JUST CAN'T STOP!
I THINK THIS IS A FRAME-UP.
WHAT DAY DID THAT ARMORED CAR GET ROCKED?
IF THERE'S ONE THING WE DO HAVE AROUND HERE, IT'S DAILY BUGLES.
HERE. TUESDAY.
DAILY BUGLE
NEW YORK'S FINEST DAILY NEWSPAPER
SHOCKING ROBBERY!
YEAH, SEE. VIBROBLASTS... EVERYTHING ABOUT THIS SAYS SHOCKER, BUT --
ROGER & KLINT
DIAMOND EXCHANGE
HEY!
-- WAITA-- MINUTE!
ISN'T THIS THE PLACE THAT --?
ROGER & KLINT
DIAMOND EXCHANGE

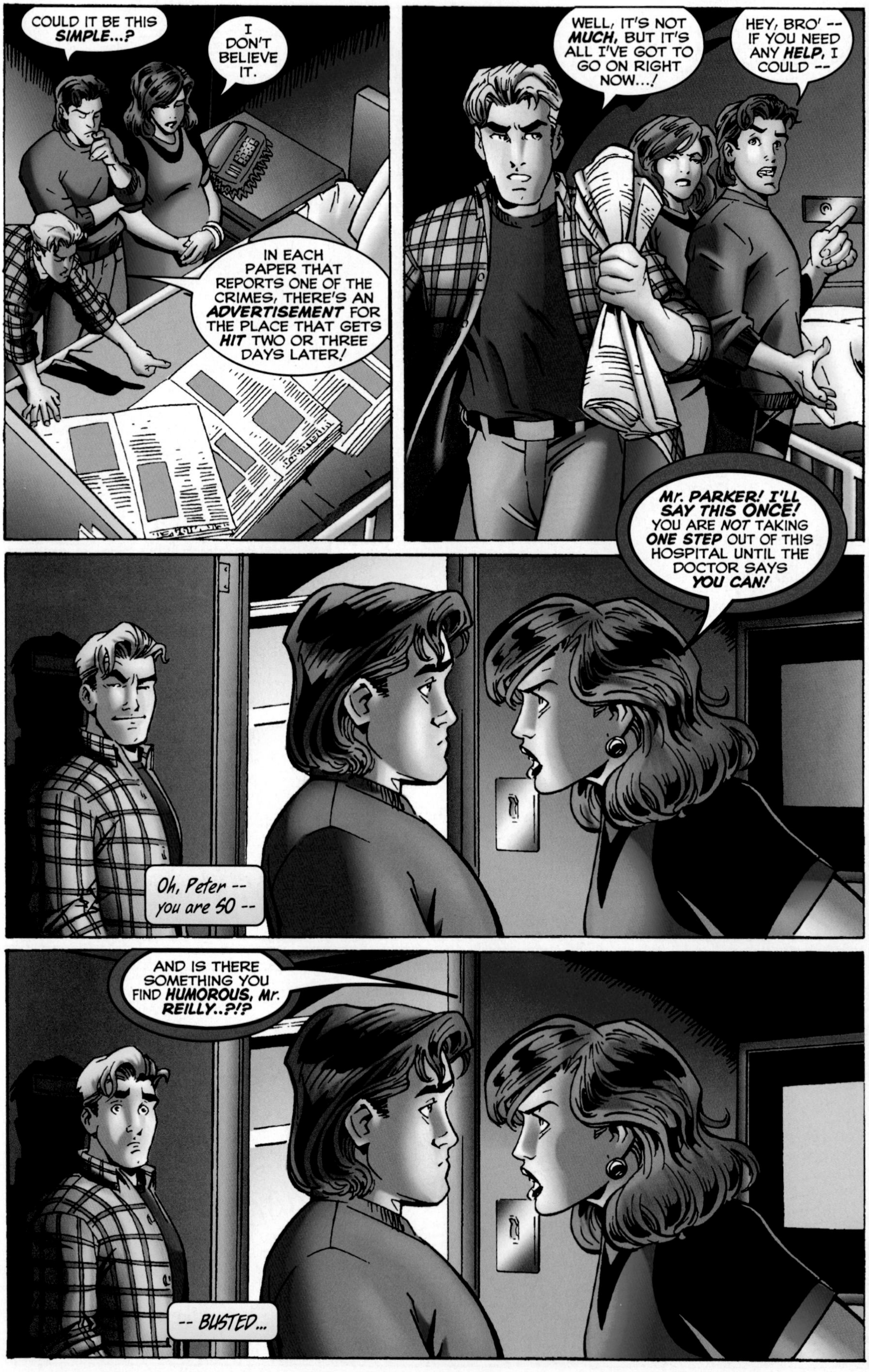
COULD IT BE THIS SIMPLE...?
I DON'T BELIEVE IT.
IN EACH PAPER THAT REPORTS ONE OF THE CRIMES, THERE'S AN ADVERTISEMENT FOR THE PLACE THAT GETS HIT TWO OR THREE DAYS LATER!
WELL, IT'S NOT MUCH, BUT IT'S ALL I'VE GOT TO GO ON RIGHT NOW...!
HEY, BRO' -- IF YOU NEED ANY HELP, I COULD --
Mr. PARKER! I'LL SAY THIS ONCE! YOU ARE NOT TAKING ONE STEP OUT OF THIS HOSPITAL UNTIL THE DOCTOR SAYS YOU CAN!
Oh, Peter -- you are SO --
AND IS THERE SOMETHING YOU FIND HUMOROUS, Mr. REILLY..?!?
-- BUSTED...

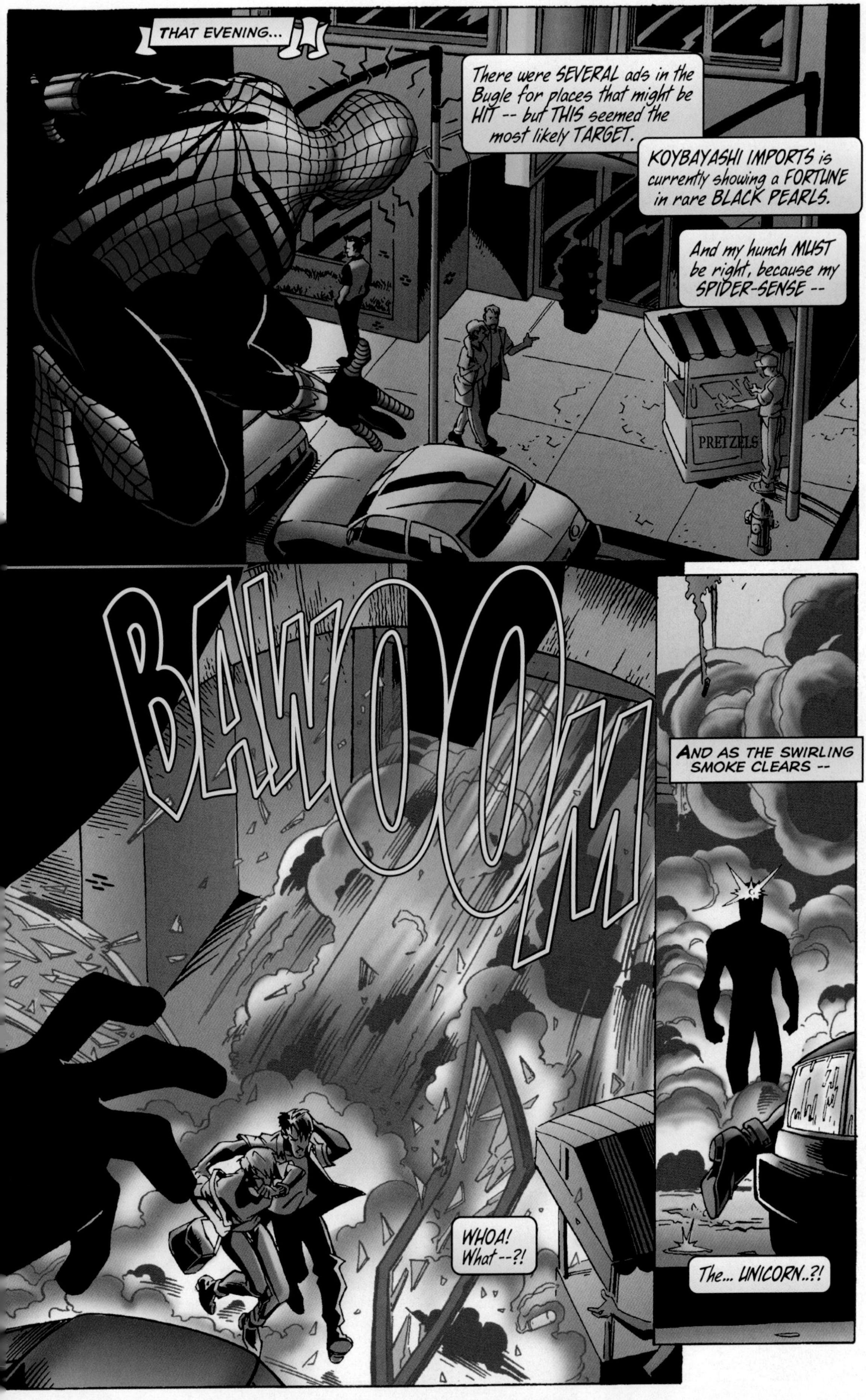
THAT EVENING...
There were SEVERAL ads in the Bugle for places that might be HIT -- but THIS seemed the most likely TARGET.
KOYBAYASHI IMPORTS is currently showing a FORTUNE in rare BLACK PEARLS.
And my hunch MUST be right, because my SPIDER-SENSE --
PRETZELS
BAWOOOM
WHOA! What --?!
AND AS THE SWIRLING SMOKE CLEARS --
The... UNICORN..?!

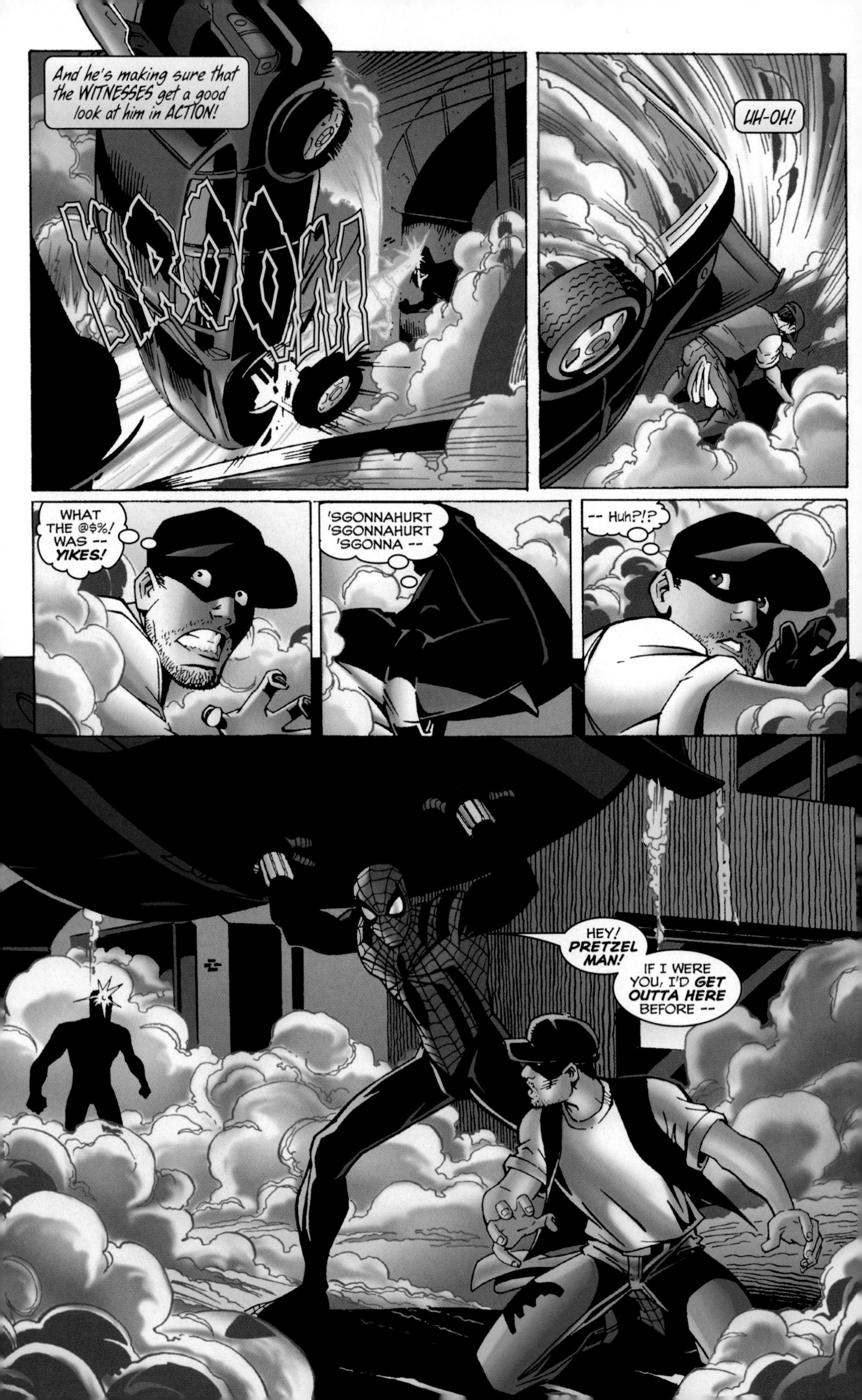
And he's making sure that the WITNESSES get a good look at him in ACTION!
VROOM
UH-OH!
WHAT THE @$%! WAS -- YIKES!
'SGONNAHURT 'SGONNAHURT 'SGONNA --
-- Huh?!?
HEY! PRETZEL MAN!
IF I WERE YOU, I'D GET OUTTA HERE BEFORE --

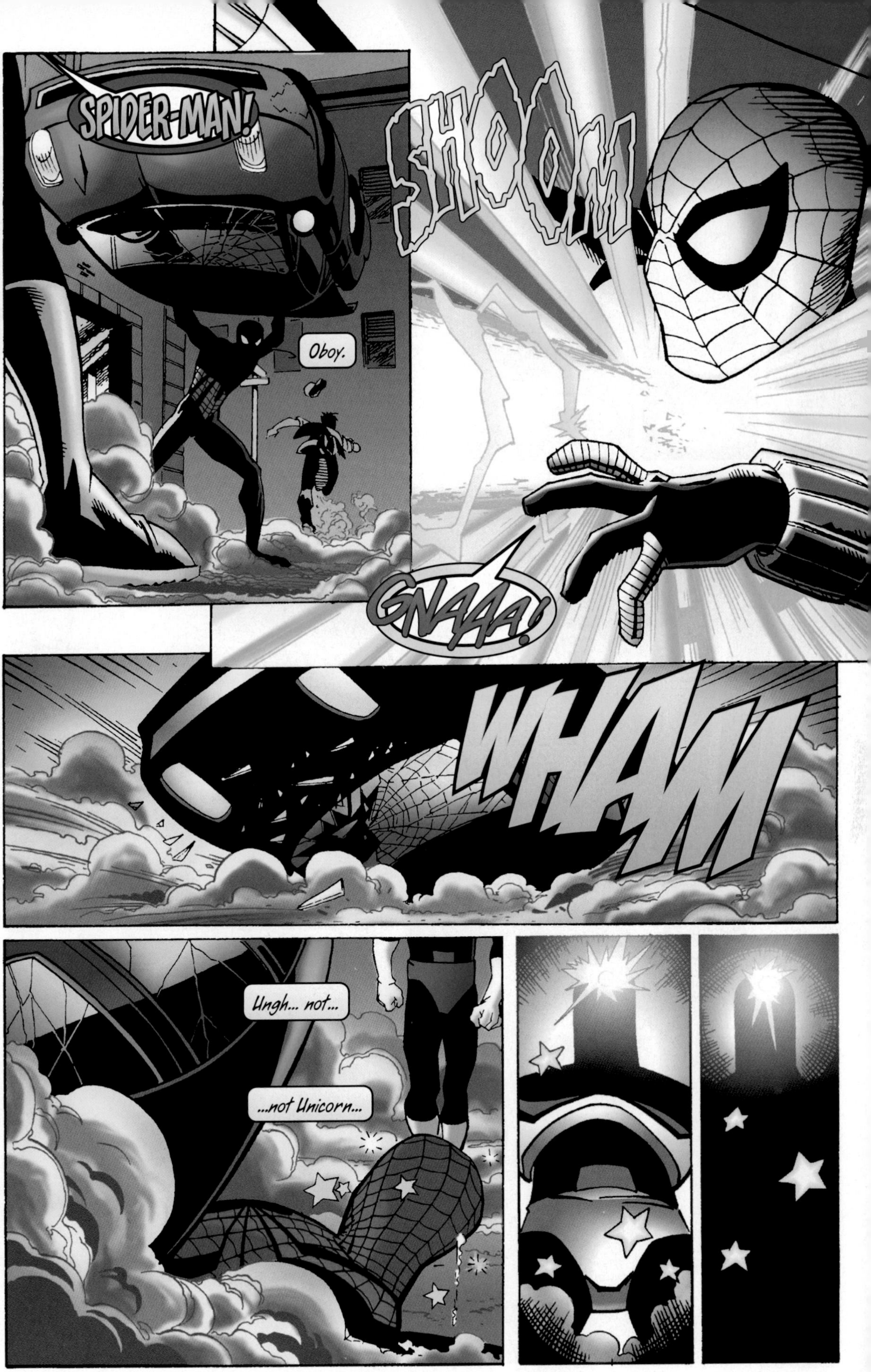
SPIDER-MAN!
Oboy.
SHOOM
GNAAA!
WHAM
Ungh... not...
...not Unicorn...

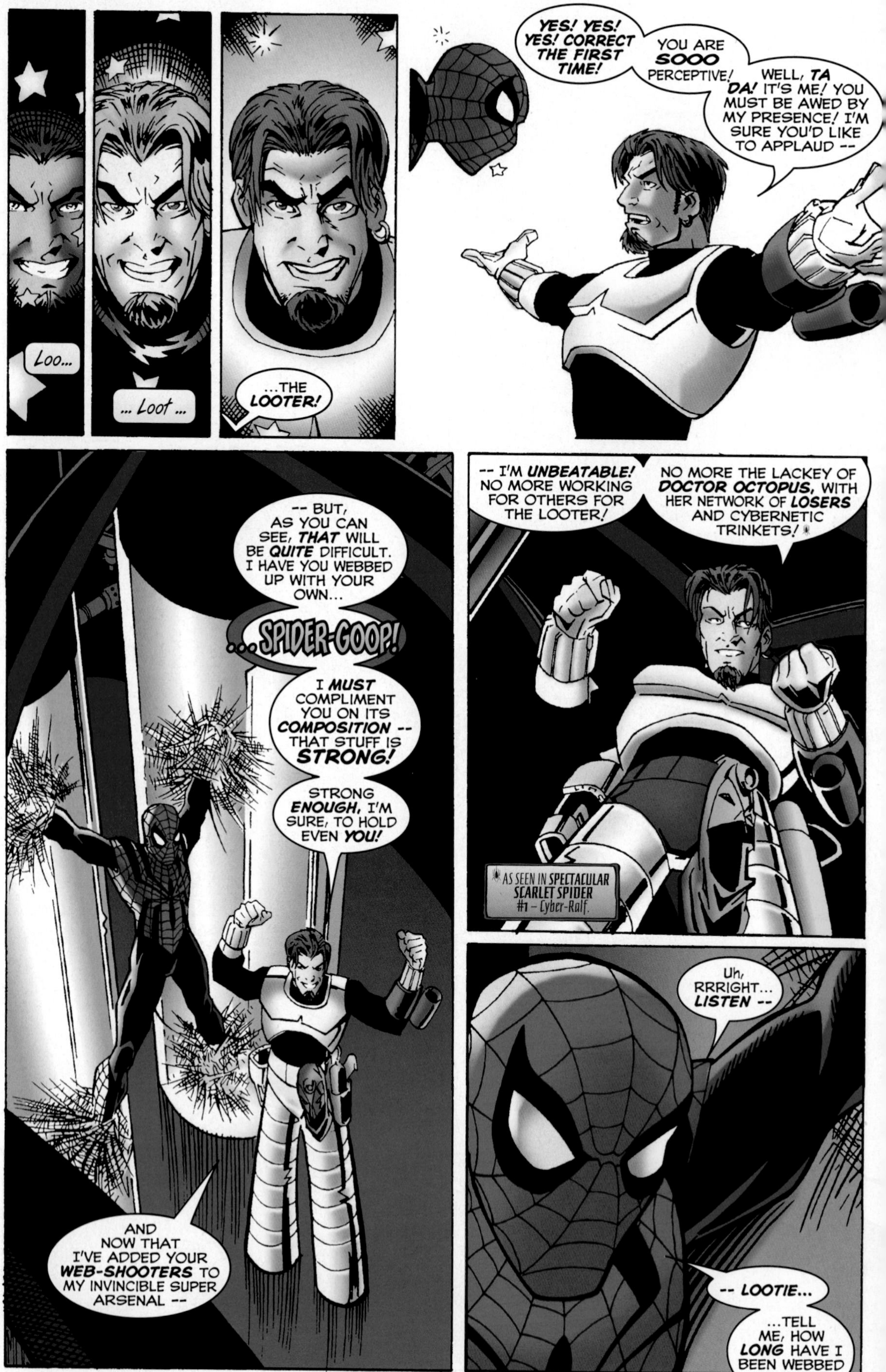

Loo...
... Loot ...
...THE LOOTER!
YES! YES! YES! CORRECT THE FIRST TIME!
YOU ARE SOOO PERCEPTIVE!
WELL, TA DA! IT'S ME! YOU MUST BE AWED BY MY PRESENCE! I'M SURE YOU'D LIKE TO APPLAUD --
-- BUT, AS YOU CAN SEE, THAT WILL BE QUITE DIFFICULT. I HAVE YOU WEBBED UP WITH YOUR OWN...
...SPIDER-GOOP!
I MUST COMPLIMENT YOU ON ITS COMPOSITION -- THAT STUFF IS STRONG!
STRONG ENOUGH, I'M SURE, TO HOLD EVEN YOU!
AND NOW THAT I'VE ADDED YOUR WEB-SHOOTERS TO MY INVINCIBLE SUPER ARSENAL --
-- I'M UNBEATABLE! NO MORE WORKING FOR OTHERS FOR THE LOOTER!
NO MORE THE LACKEY OF DOCTOR OCTOPUS, WITH HER NETWORK OF LOSERS AND CYBERNETIC TRINKETS!
AS SEEN IN SPECTACULAR SCARLET SPIDER #1 – Cyber-Ralf.
Uh, RRRIGHT... LISTEN --
-- LOOTIE...
...TELL ME, HOW LONG HAVE I BEEN WEBBED UP HERE?

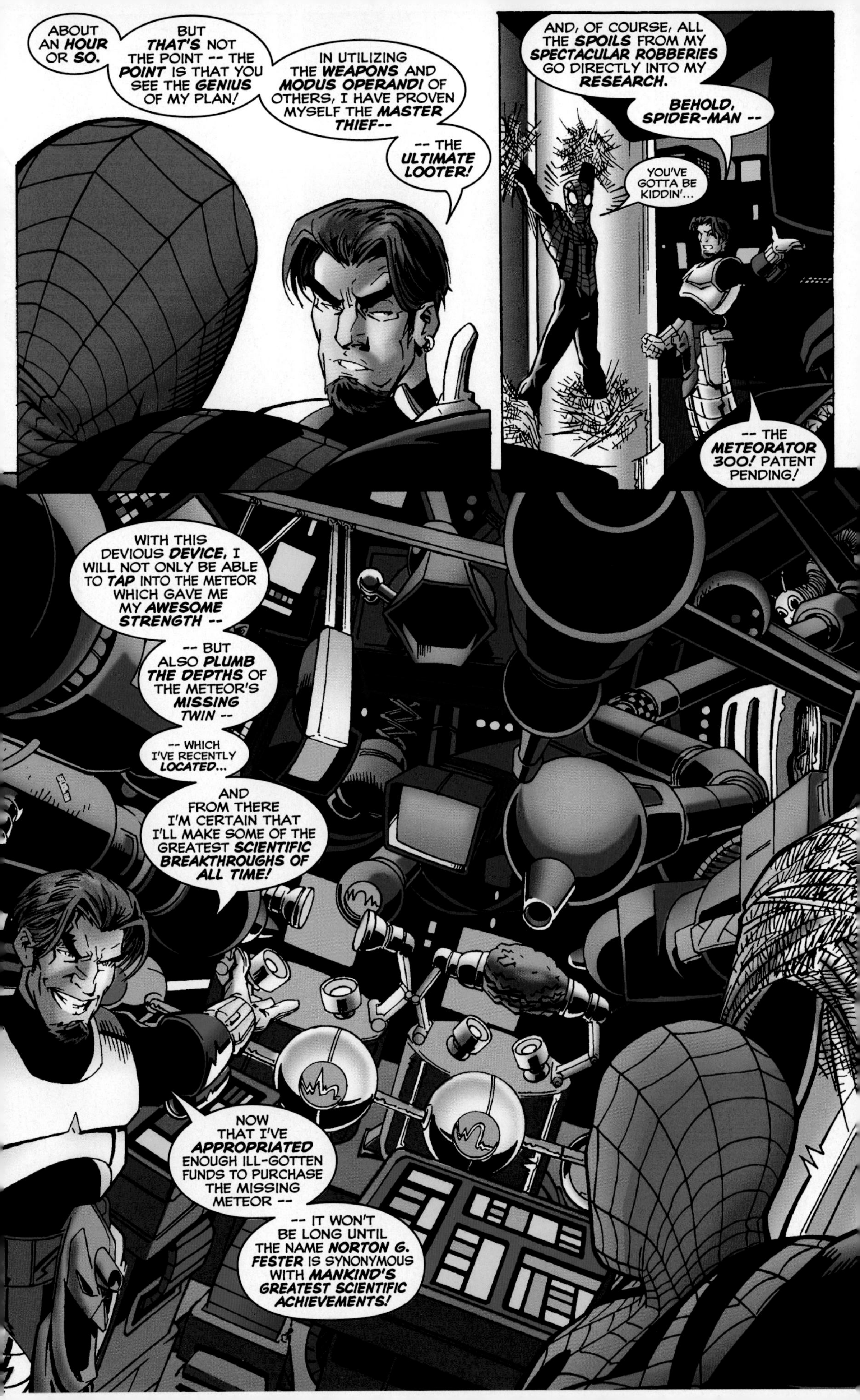
ABOUT AN HOUR OR SO.
BUT THAT'S NOT THE POINT -- THE POINT IS THAT YOU SEE THE GENIUS OF MY PLAN!
IN UTILIZING THE WEAPONS AND MODUS OPERANDI OF OTHERS, I HAVE PROVEN MYSELF THE MASTER THIEF--
-- THE ULTIMATE LOOTER!
AND, OF COURSE, ALL THE SPOILS FROM MY SPECTACULAR ROBBERIES GO DIRECTLY INTO MY RESEARCH.
BEHOLD, SPIDER-MAN --
YOU'VE GOTTA BE KIDDIN'...
-- THE METEORATOR 300! PATENT PENDING!
WITH THIS DEVIOUS DEVICE, I WILL NOT ONLY BE ABLE TO TAP INTO THE METEOR WHICH GAVE ME MY AWESOME STRENGTH --
-- BUT ALSO PLUMB THE DEPTHS OF THE METEOR'S MISSING TWIN --
-- WHICH I'VE RECENTLY LOCATED...
AND FROM THERE I'M CERTAIN THAT I'LL MAKE SOME OF THE GREATEST SCIENTIFIC BREAKTHROUGHS OF ALL TIME!
NOW THAT I'VE APPROPRIATED ENOUGH ILL-GOTTEN FUNDS TO PURCHASE THE MISSING METEOR --
-- IT WON'T BE LONG UNTIL THE NAME NORTON G. FESTER IS SYNONYMOUS WITH MANKIND'S GREATEST SCIENTIFIC ACHIEVEMENTS!

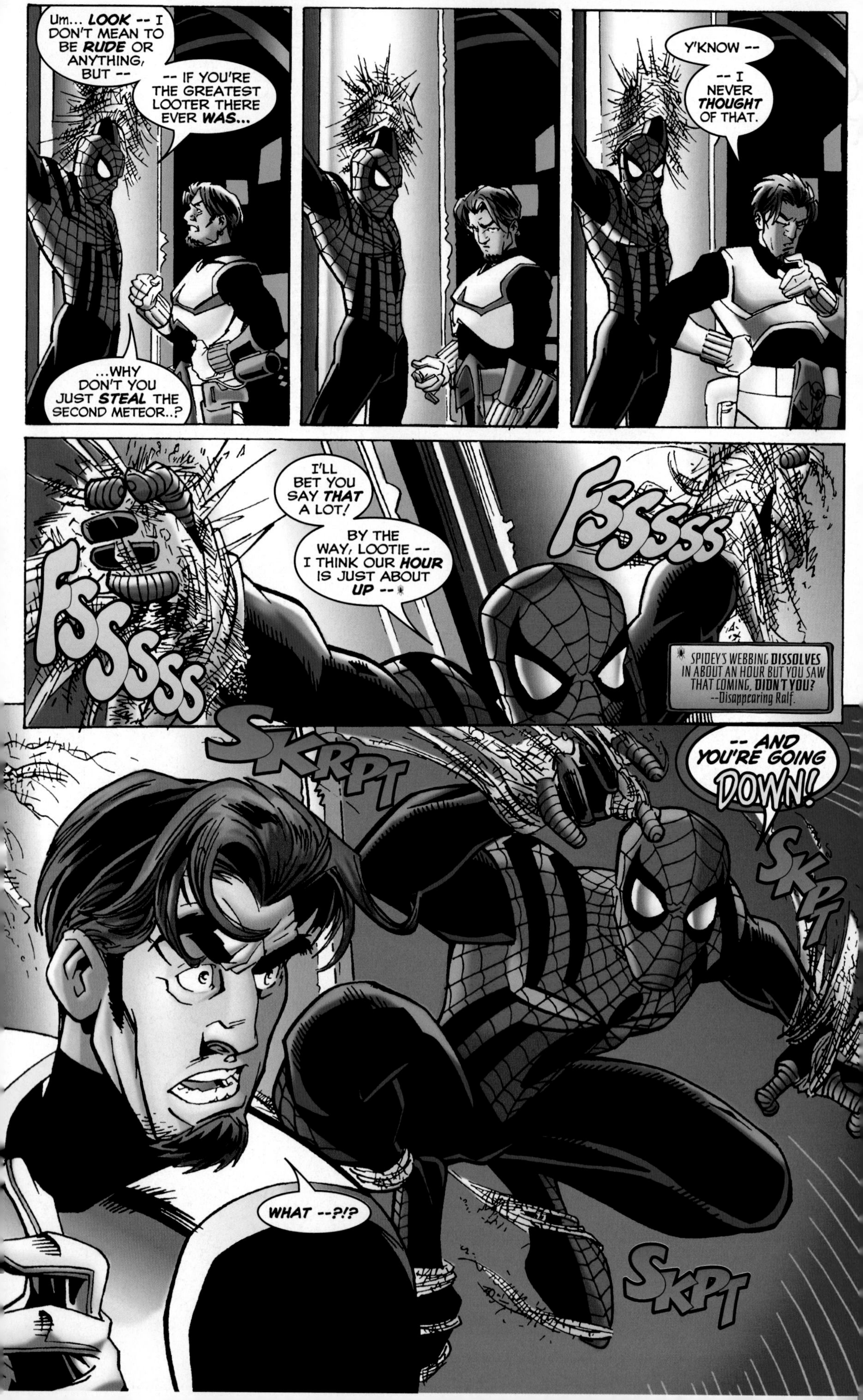

Um... LOOK -- I DON'T MEAN TO BE RUDE OR ANYTHING, BUT --
-- IF YOU'RE THE GREATEST LOOTER THERE EVER WAS...
...WHY DON'T YOU JUST STEAL THE SECOND METEOR..?
Y'KNOW --
-- I NEVER THOUGHT OF THAT.
I'LL BET YOU SAY THAT A LOT!
BY THE WAY, LOOTIE -- I THINK OUR HOUR IS JUST ABOUT UP --
FSSSSS
FSSSSS
SPIDEY'S WEBBING DISSOLVES IN ABOUT AN HOUR BUT YOU SAW THAT COMING, DIDN'T YOU? --Disappearing Ralf.
SKRPT
-- AND YOU'RE GOING DOWN!
SKPT
WHAT --?!?
SKPT

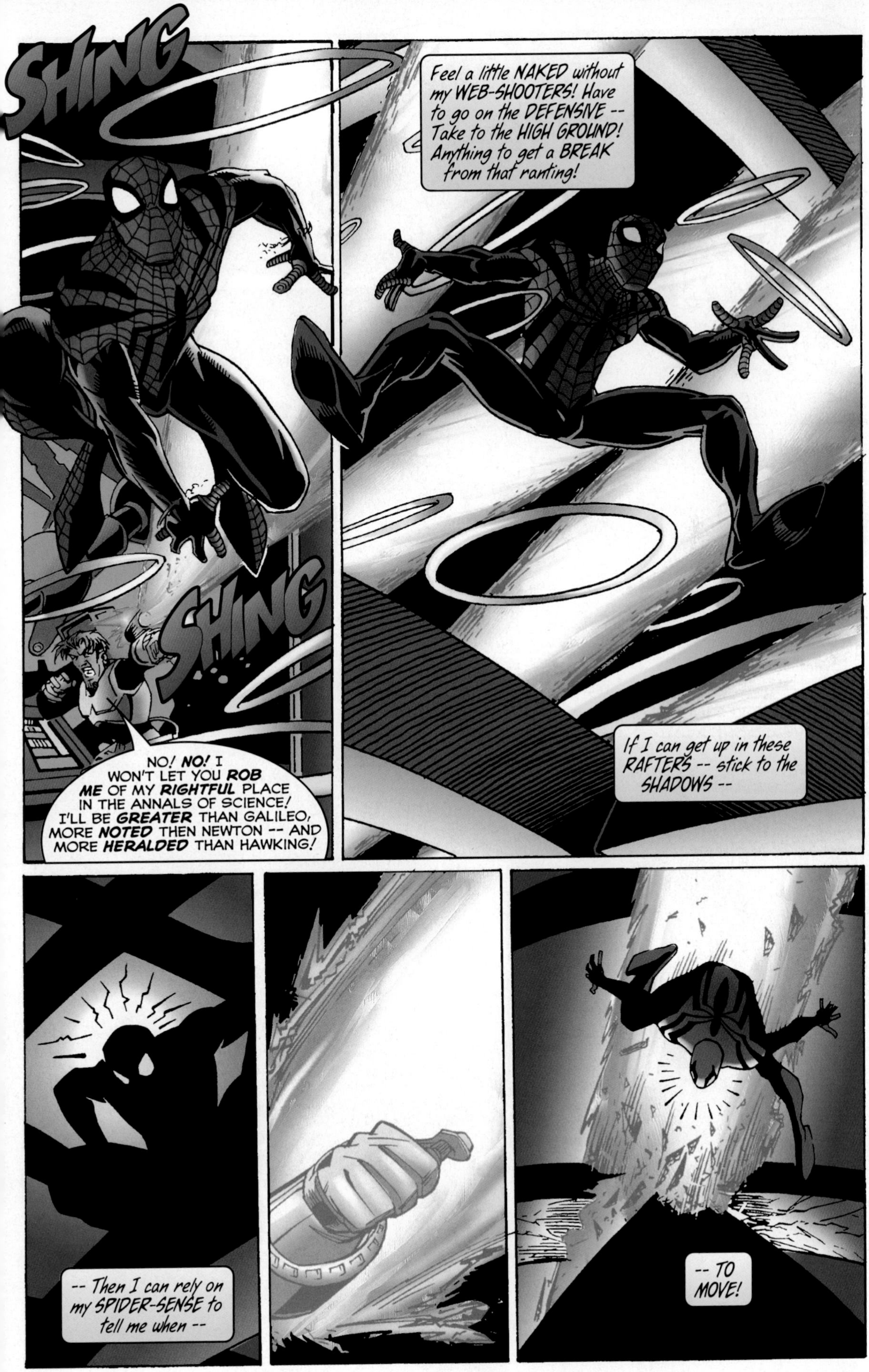
SHING
Feel a little NAKED without my WEB-SHOOTERS! Have to go on the DEFENSIVE -- Take to the HIGH GROUND! Anything to get a BREAK from that ranting!
SHING
NO! NO! I WON'T LET YOU ROB ME OF MY RIGHTFUL PLACE IN THE ANNALS OF SCIENCE! I'LL BE GREATER THAN GALILEO, MORE NOTED THEN NEWTON -- AND MORE HERALDED THAN HAWKING!
If I can get up in these RAFTERS -- stick to the SHADOWS --
-- Then I can rely on my SPIDER-SENSE to tell me when --
-- TO MOVE!

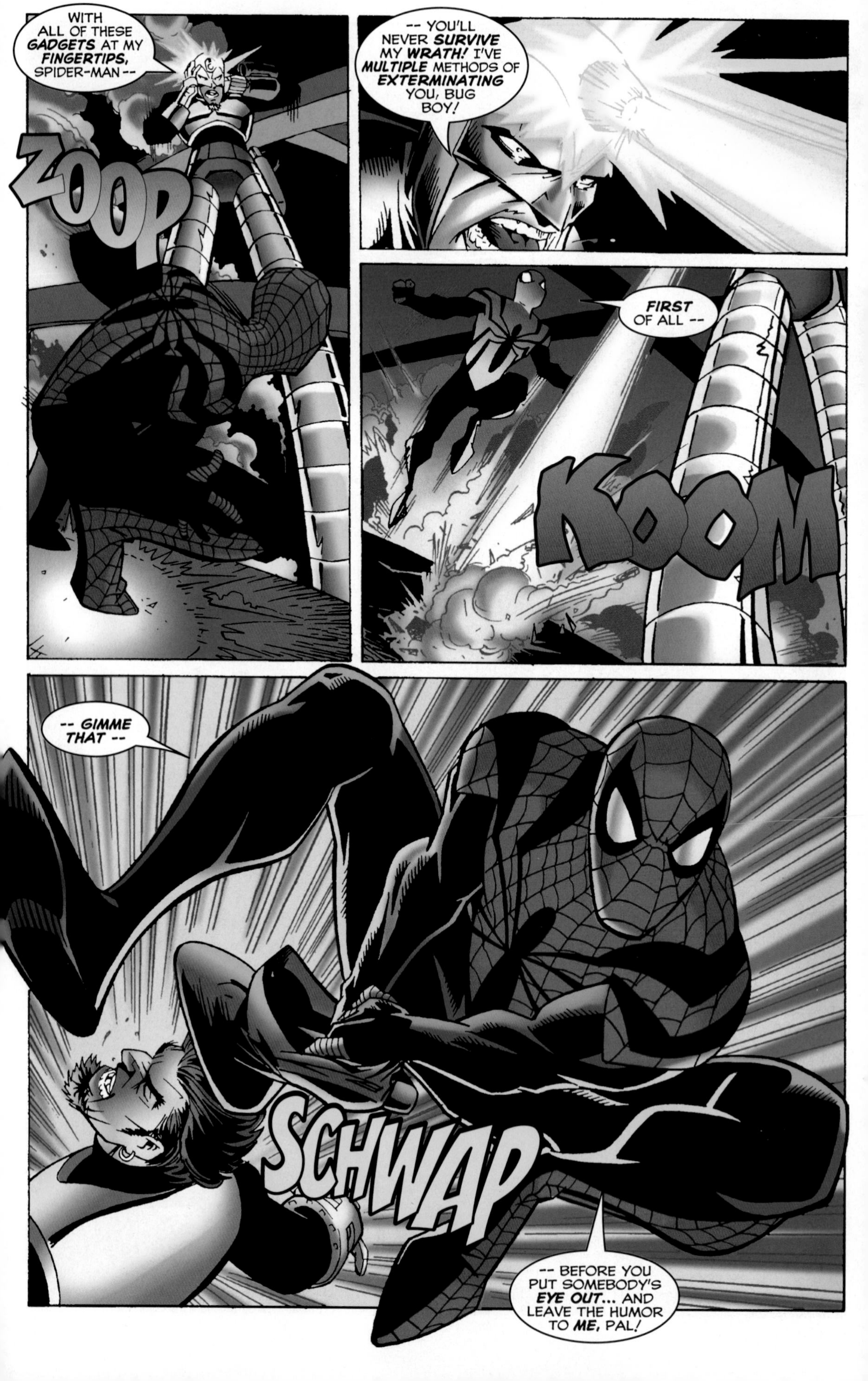
WITH ALL OF THESE GADGETS AT MY FINGERTIPS, SPIDER-MAN --
ZOOP
-- YOU'LL NEVER SURVIVE MY WRATH! I'VE MULTIPLE METHODS OF EXTERMINATING YOU, BUG BOY!
FIRST OF ALL --
KOOM
-- GIMME THAT --
SCHWAP
-- BEFORE YOU PUT SOMEBODY'S EYE OUT... AND LEAVE THE HUMOR TO ME, PAL!

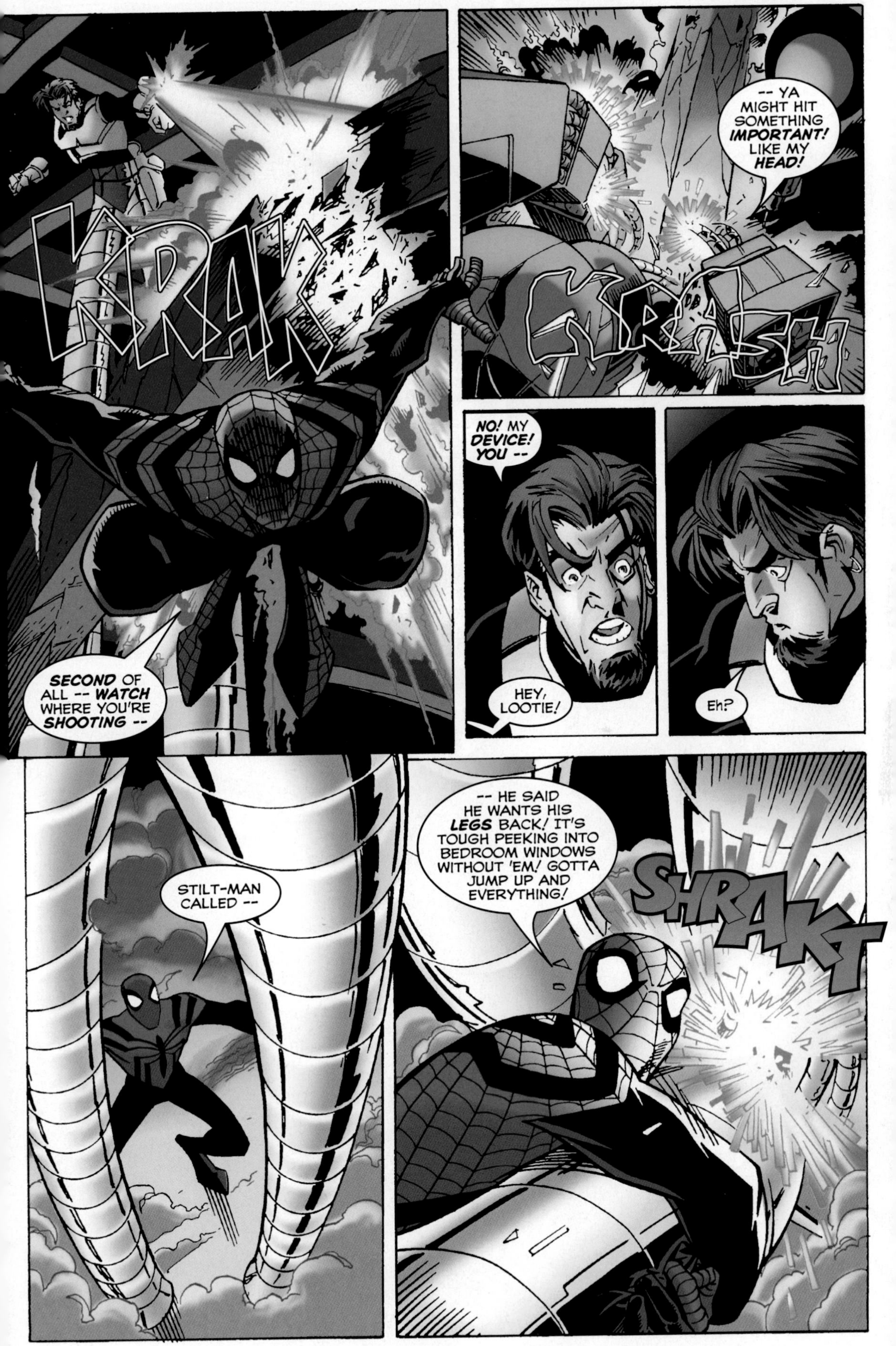
KRAK
SECOND OF ALL -- WATCH WHERE YOU'RE SHOOTING --
-- YA MIGHT HIT SOMETHING IMPORTANT! LIKE MY HEAD!
KRASH
NO! MY DEVICE! YOU --
HEY, LOOTIE!
Eh?
STILT-MAN CALLED --
-- HE SAID HE WANTS HIS LEGS BACK! IT'S TOUGH PEEKING INTO BEDROOM WINDOWS WITHOUT 'EM! GOTTA JUMP UP AND EVERYTHING!
SHRAKT

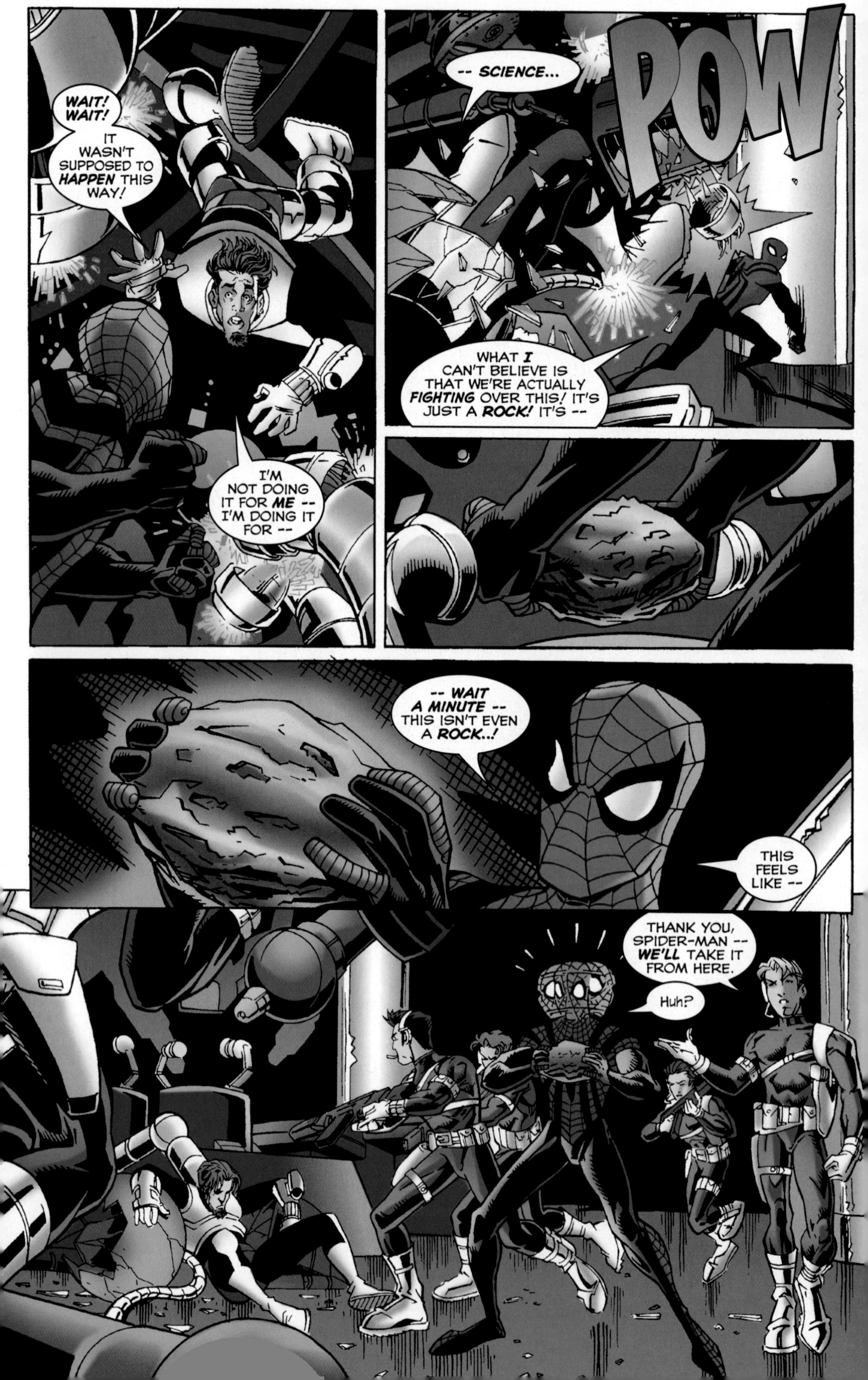

WAIT! WAIT!
IT WASN'T SUPPOSED TO HAPPEN THIS WAY!
I'M NOT DOING IT FOR ME -- I'M DOING IT FOR --
-- SCIENCE...
POW
WHAT I CAN'T BELIEVE IS THAT WE'RE ACTUALLY FIGHTING OVER THIS! IT'S JUST A ROCK! IT'S --
-- WAIT A MINUTE -- THIS ISN'T EVEN A ROCK..!
THIS FEELS LIKE --
THANK YOU, SPIDER-MAN -- WE'LL TAKE IT FROM HERE.
Huh?

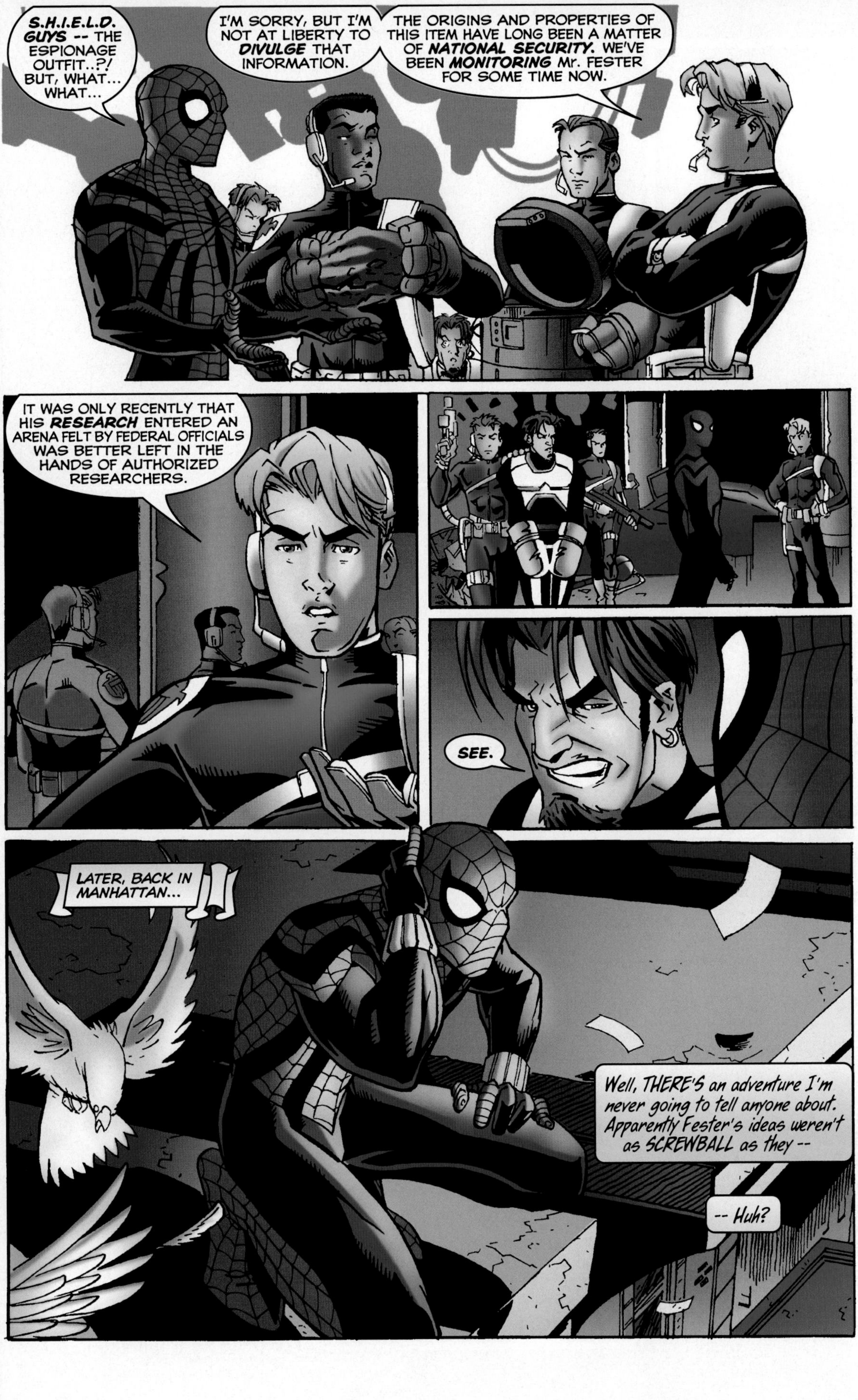
S.H.I.E.L.D. GUYS -- THE ESPIONAGE OUTFIT..?! BUT, WHAT... WHAT...
I'M SORRY, BUT I'M NOT AT LIBERTY TO DIVULGE THAT INFORMATION.
THE ORIGINS AND PROPERTIES OF THIS ITEM HAVE LONG BEEN A MATTER OF NATIONAL SECURITY. WE'VE BEEN MONITORING Mr. FESTER FOR SOME TIME NOW.
IT WAS ONLY RECENTLY THAT HIS RESEARCH ENTERED AN ARENA FELT BY FEDERAL OFFICIALS WAS BETTER LEFT IN THE HANDS OF AUTHORIZED RESEARCHERS.
SEE.
LATER, BACK IN MANHATTAN...
Well, THERE'S an adventure I'm never going to tell anyone about. Apparently Fester's ideas weren't as SCREWBALL as they --
-- Huh?

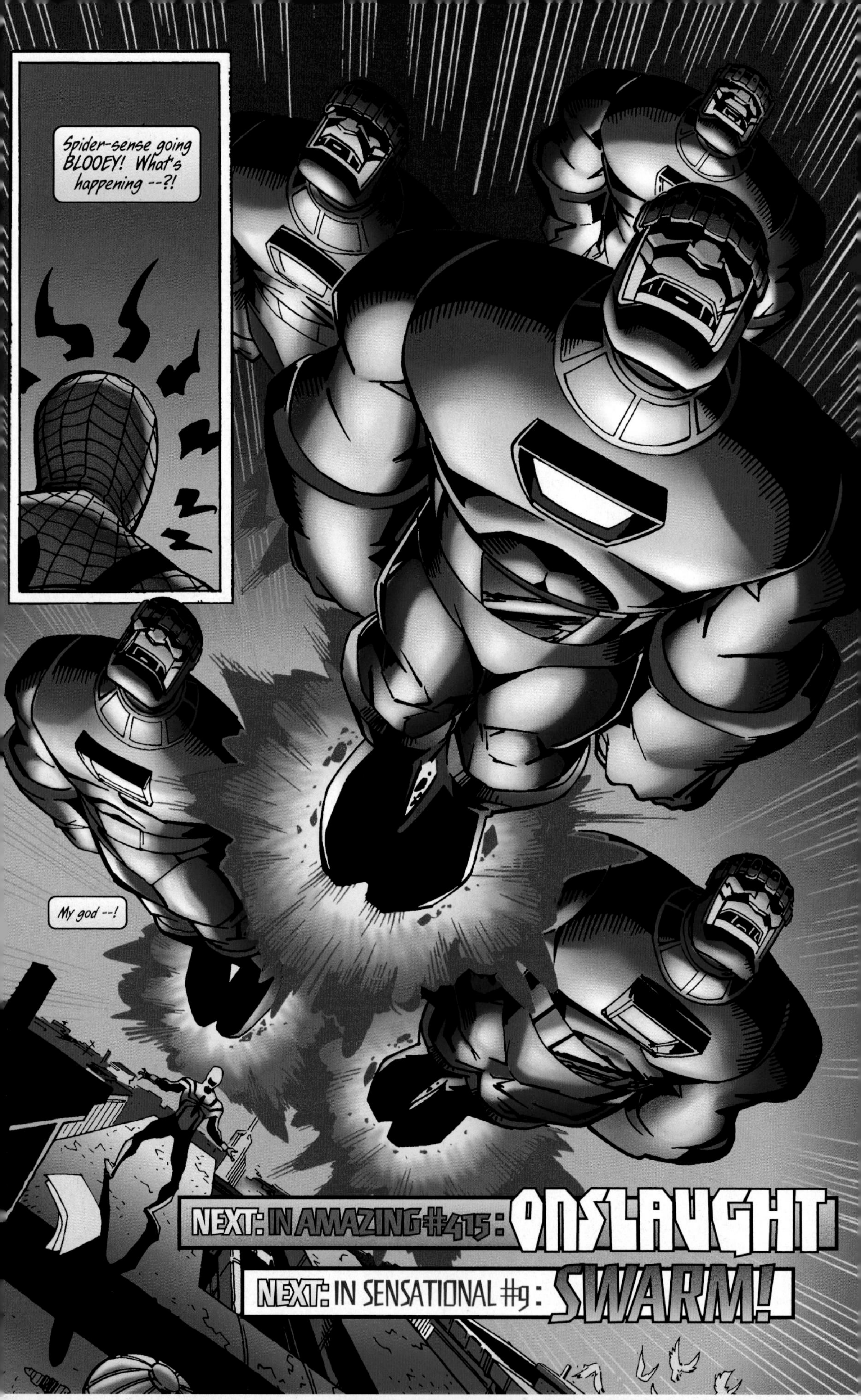
Spider-sense going BLOOEY! What's happening --?!
My god --!
NEXT: IN AMAZING #415 : ONSLAUGHT
NEXT: IN SENSATIONAL #9 : SWARM!

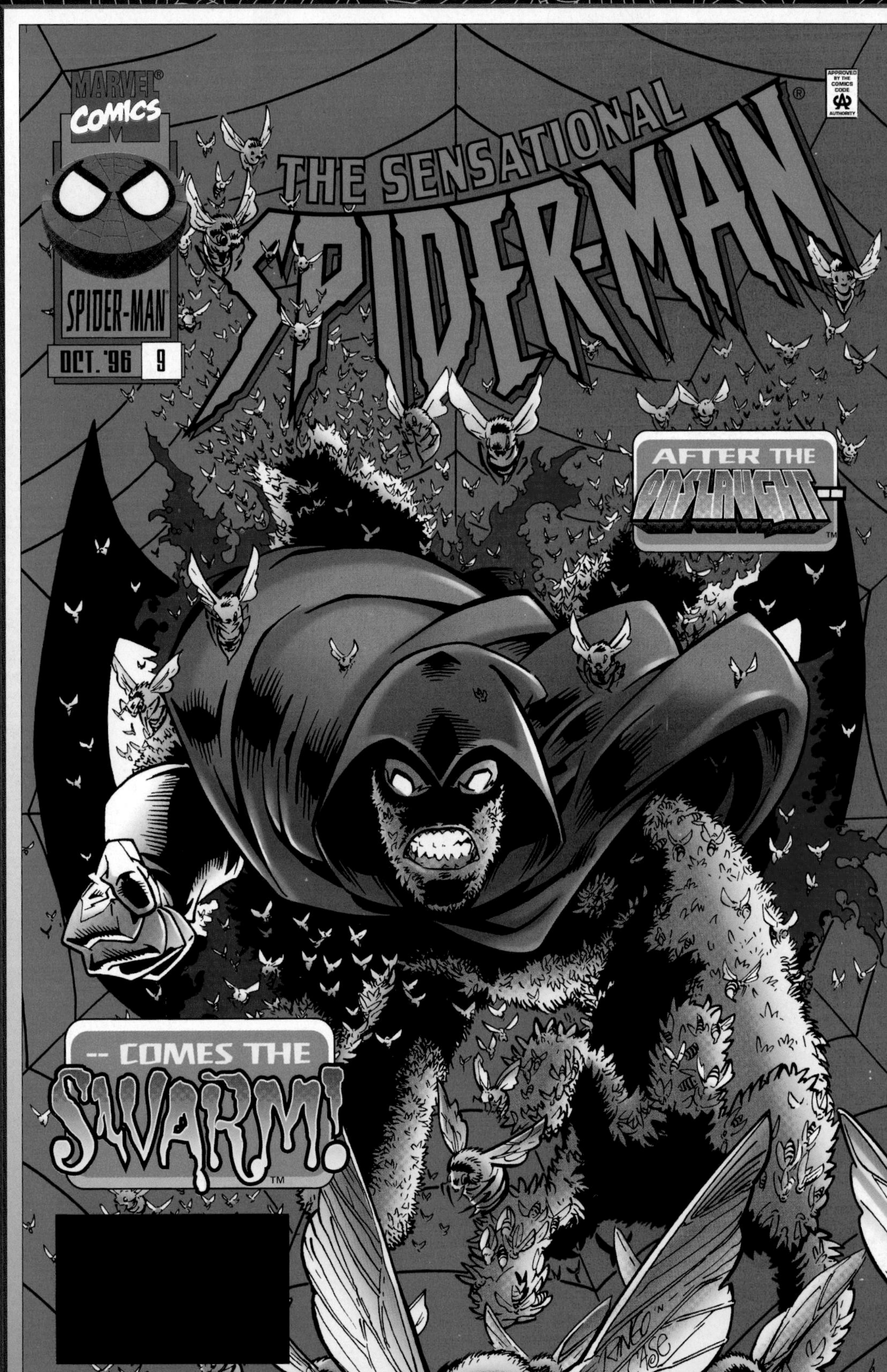
MARVEL COMICS
SPIDER-MAN
OCT. '96 9
APPROVED BY THE COMICS CODE AUTHORITY
THE SENSATIONAL
SPIDER-MAN
AFTER THE
ONSLAUGHT--
-- COMES THE
SWARM!

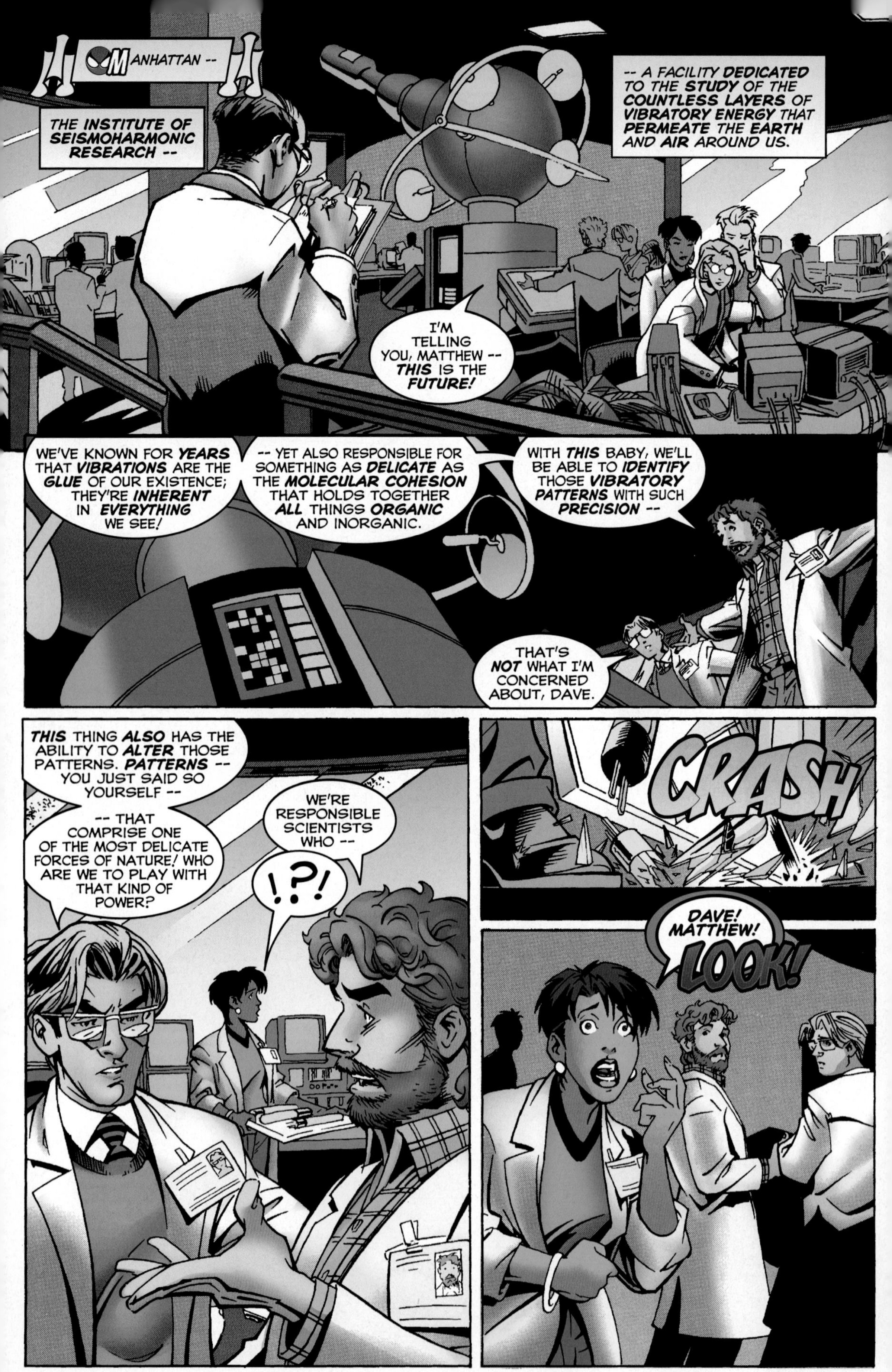
MANHATTAN --
THE INSTITUTE OF SEISMOHARMONIC RESEARCH --
-- A FACILITY DEDICATED TO THE STUDY OF THE COUNTLESS LAYERS OF VIBRATORY ENERGY THAT PERMEATE THE EARTH AND AIR AROUND US.
I'M TELLING YOU, MATTHEW -- THIS IS THE FUTURE!
WE'VE KNOWN FOR YEARS THAT VIBRATIONS ARE THE GLUE OF OUR EXISTENCE; THEY'RE INHERENT IN EVERYTHING WE SEE!
-- YET ALSO RESPONSIBLE FOR SOMETHING AS DELICATE AS THE MOLECULAR COHESION THAT HOLDS TOGETHER ALL THINGS ORGANIC AND INORGANIC.
WITH THIS BABY, WE'LL BE ABLE TO IDENTIFY THOSE VIBRATORY PATTERNS WITH SUCH PRECISION --
THAT'S NOT WHAT I'M CONCERNED ABOUT, DAVE.
THIS THING ALSO HAS THE ABILITY TO ALTER THOSE PATTERNS. PATTERNS -- YOU JUST SAID SO YOURSELF --
-- THAT COMPRISE ONE OF THE MOST DELICATE FORCES OF NATURE! WHO ARE WE TO PLAY WITH THAT KIND OF POWER?
WE'RE RESPONSIBLE SCIENTISTS WHO --
!?!
CRASH
DAVE! MATTHEW! LOOK!

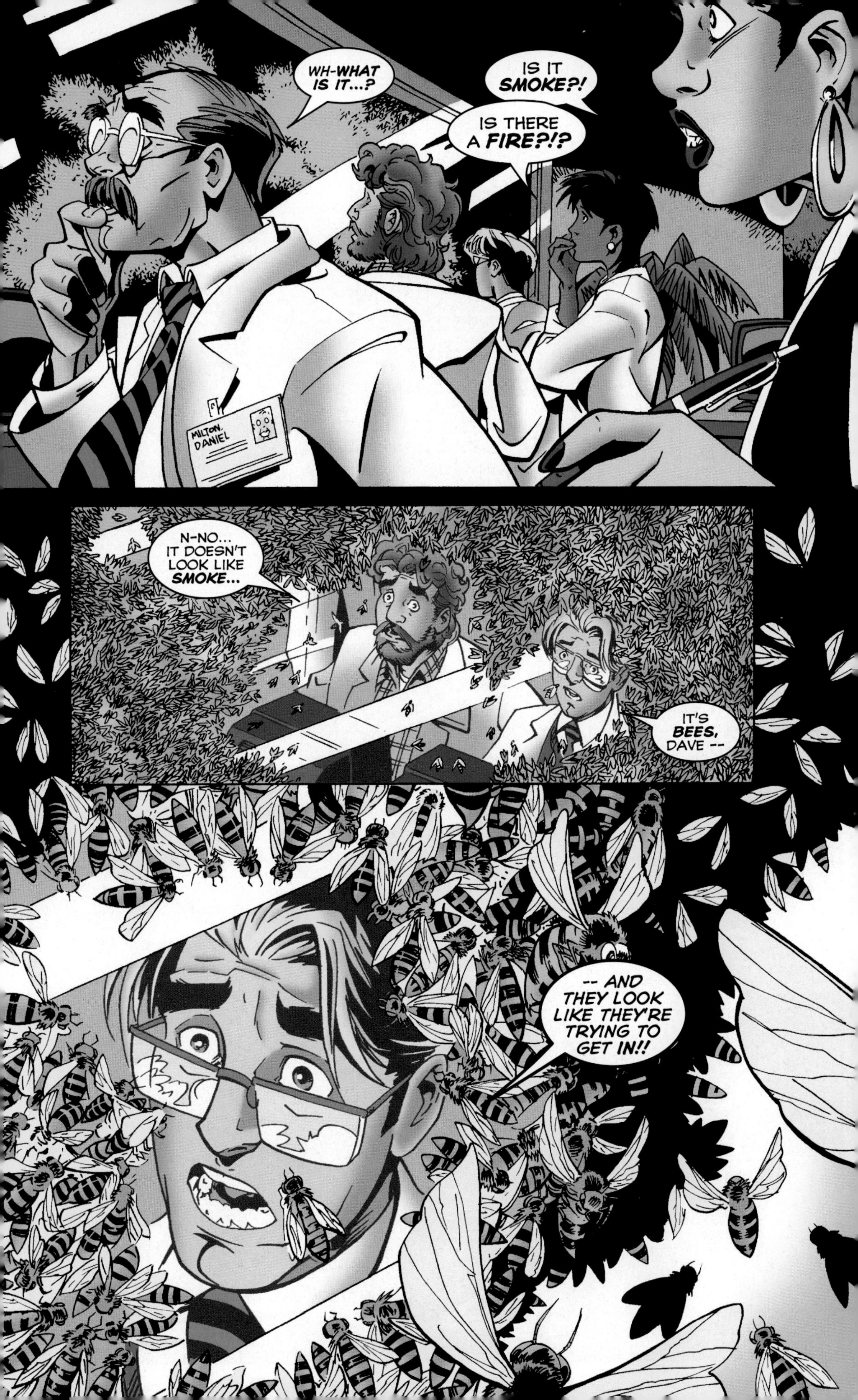
WH-WHAT IS IT...?
IS IT SMOKE?!
IS THERE A FIRE?!?
MILTON, DANIEL
N-NO... IT DOESN'T LOOK LIKE SMOKE...
IT'S BEES, DAVE --
-- AND THEY LOOK LIKE THEY'RE TRYING TO GET IN!!

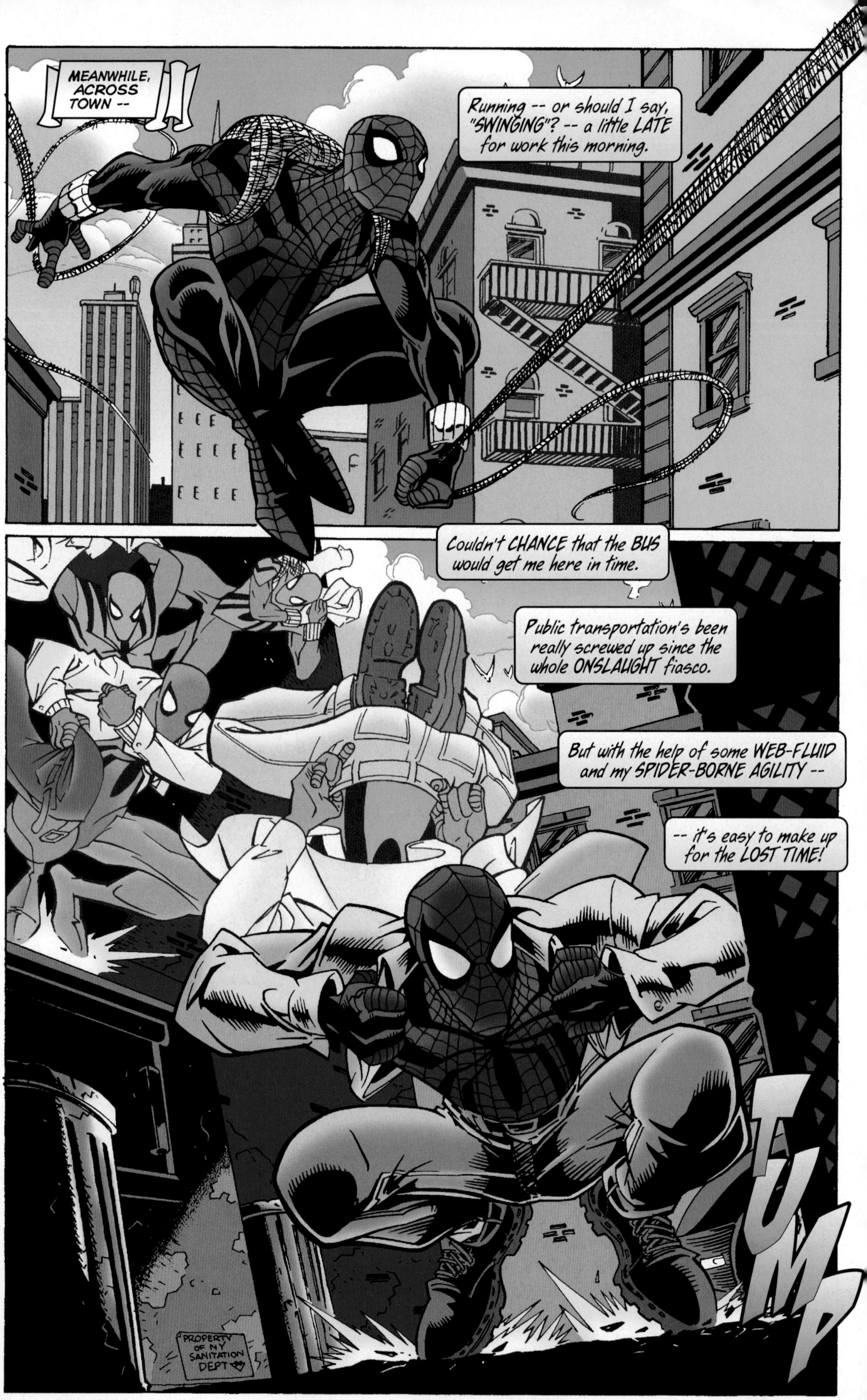
MEANWHILE, ACROSS TOWN --
Running -- or should I say, "SWINGING"? -- a little LATE for work this morning.
Couldn't CHANCE that the BUS would get me here in time.
Public transportation's been really screwed up since the whole ONSLAUGHT fiasco.
But with the help of some WEB-FLUID and my SPIDER-BORNE AGILITY --
-- it's easy to make up for the LOST TIME!
TUMP
PROPERTY OF NY SANITATION DEPT

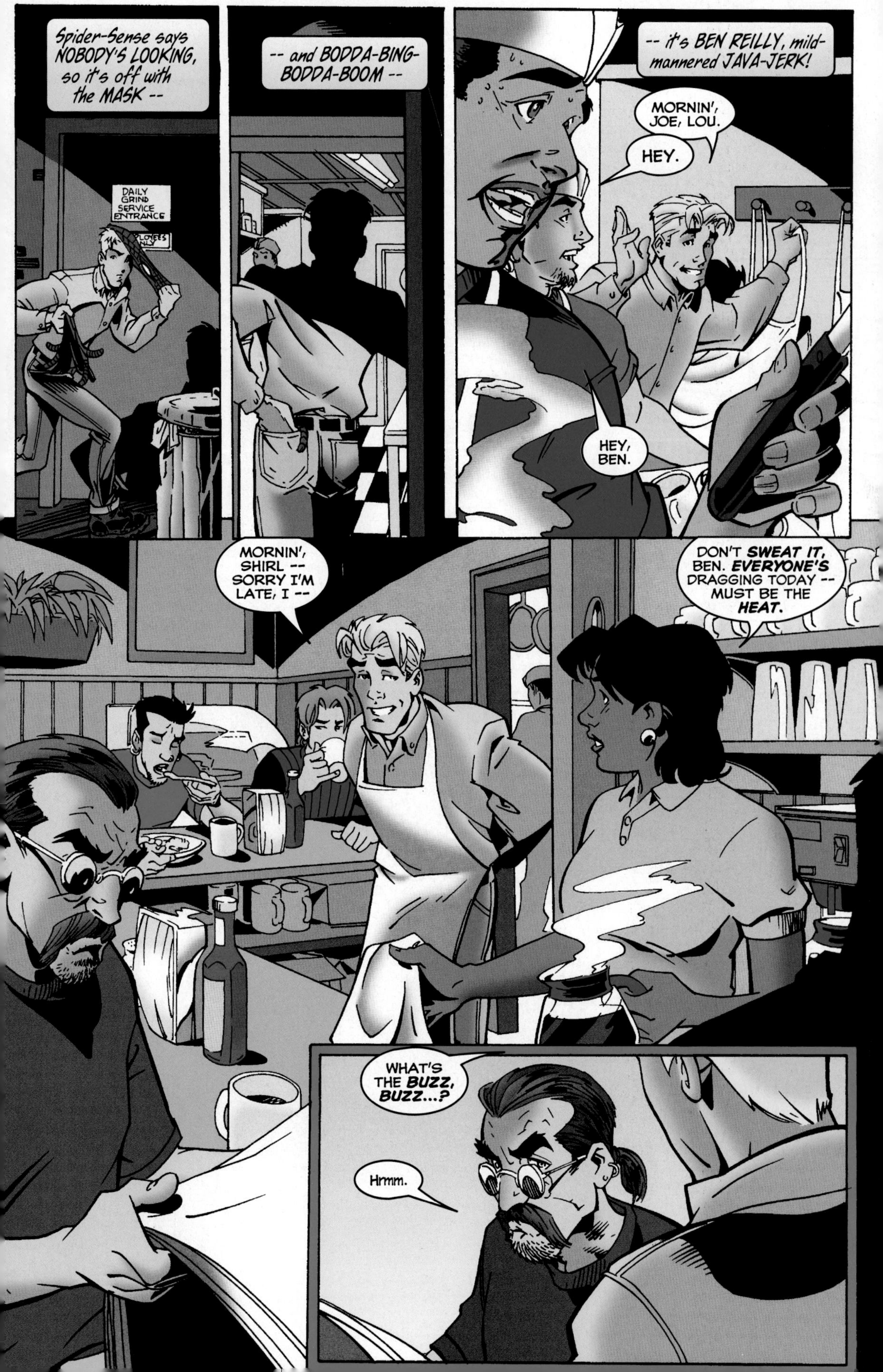
Spider-Sense says NOBODY'S LOOKING, so it's off with the MASK --
DAILY GRIND SERVICE ENTRANCE
-- and BODDA-BING-BODDA-BOOM --
-- it's BEN REILLY, mild-mannered JAVA-JERK!
MORNIN', JOE, LOU.
HEY.
HEY, BEN.
MORNIN', SHIRL -- SORRY I'M LATE, I --
DON'T SWEAT IT, BEN. EVERYONE'S DRAGGING TODAY -- MUST BE THE HEAT.
WHAT'S THE BUZZ, BUZZ...?
Hrmm.

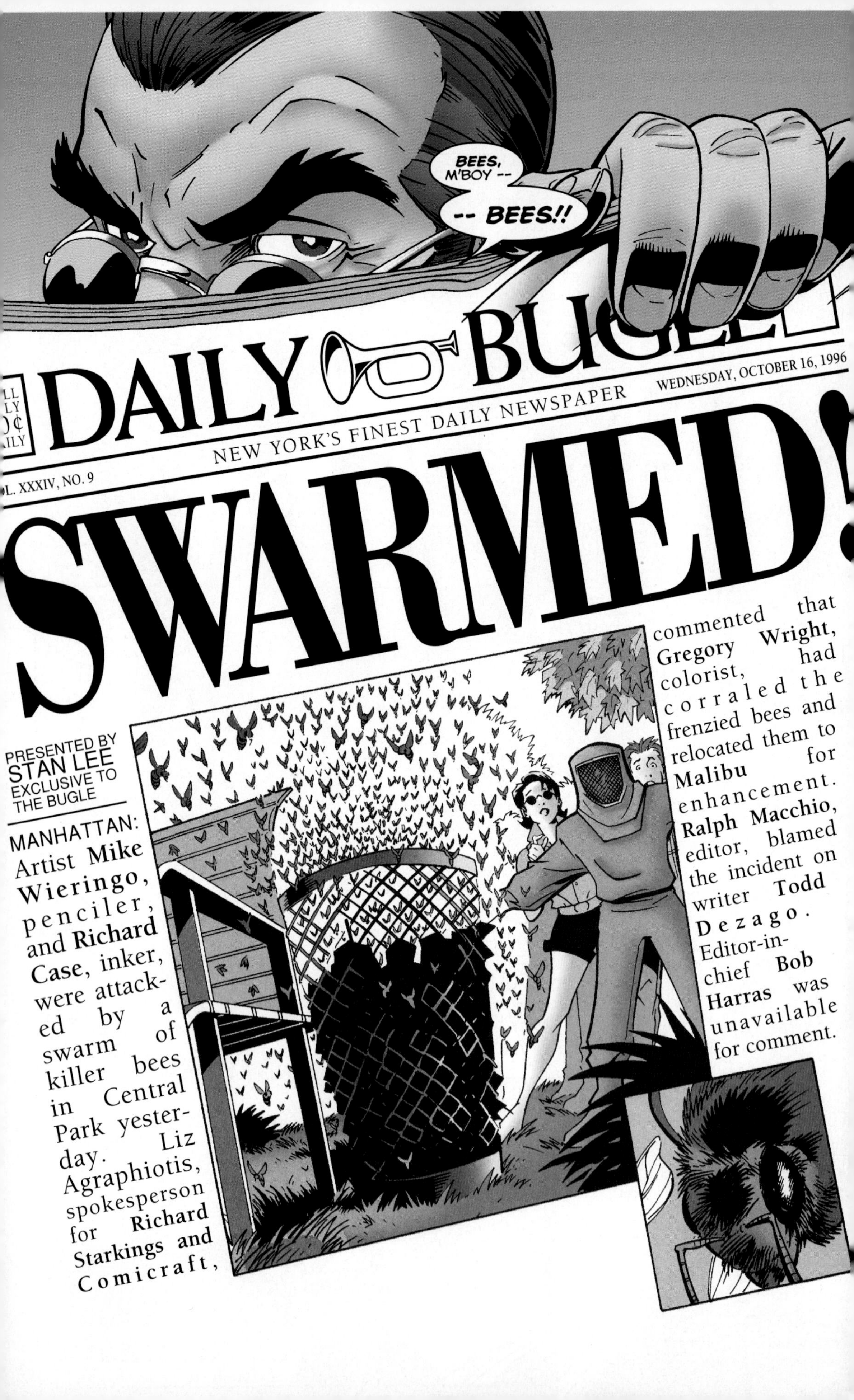

BEES, M'BOY --
-- BEES!!
DAILY BUGLE
WEDNESDAY, OCTOBER 16, 1996
NEW YORK'S FINEST DAILY NEWSPAPER
L. XXXIV, NO. 9
SWARMED!
PRESENTED BY STAN LEE EXCLUSIVE TO THE BUGLE
MANHATTAN: Artist Mike Wieringo, penciler, and Richard Case, inker, were attacked by a swarm of killer bees in Central Park yesterday. Liz Agraphiotis, spokesperson for Richard Starkings and Comicraft, commented that Gregory Wright, colorist, had corraled the frenzied bees and relocated them to Malibu for enhancement. Ralph Macchio, editor, blamed the incident on writer Todd Dezago. Editor-in-chief Bob Harras was unavailable for comment.

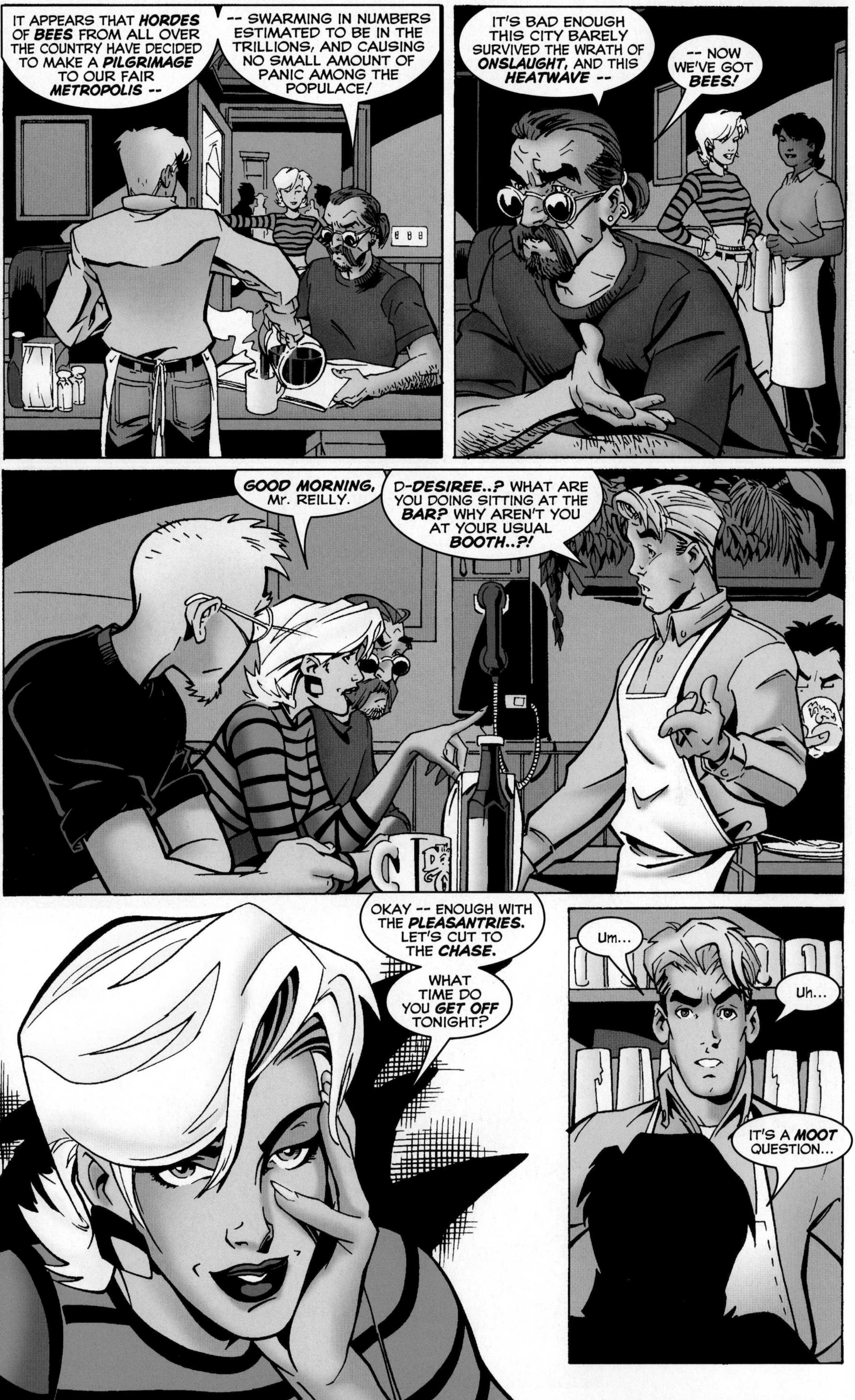
IT APPEARS THAT HORDES OF BEES FROM ALL OVER THE COUNTRY HAVE DECIDED TO MAKE A PILGRIMAGE TO OUR FAIR METROPOLIS --
-- SWARMING IN NUMBERS ESTIMATED TO BE IN THE TRILLIONS, AND CAUSING NO SMALL AMOUNT OF PANIC AMONG THE POPULACE!
IT'S BAD ENOUGH THIS CITY BARELY SURVIVED THE WRATH OF ONSLAUGHT, AND THIS HEATWAVE --
-- NOW WE'VE GOT BEES!
GOOD MORNING, Mr. REILLY.
D-DESIREE..? WHAT ARE YOU DOING SITTING AT THE BAR? WHY AREN'T YOU AT YOUR USUAL BOOTH..?!
OKAY -- ENOUGH WITH THE PLEASANTRIES. LET'S CUT TO THE CHASE.
WHAT TIME DO YOU GET OFF TONIGHT?
Um...
Uh...
IT'S A MOOT QUESTION...

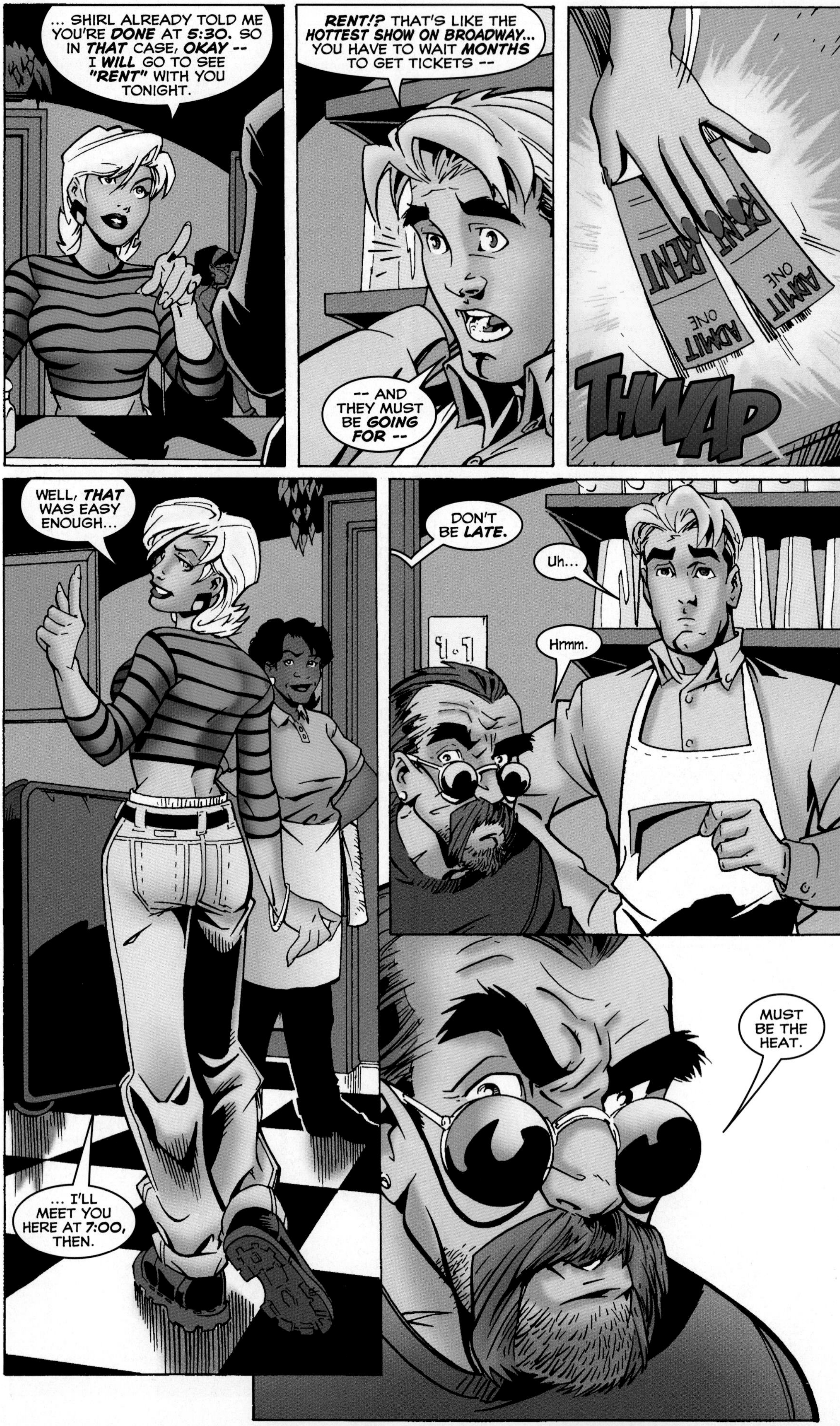

... SHIRL ALREADY TOLD ME YOU'RE DONE AT 5:30. SO IN THAT CASE, OKAY -- I WILL GO TO SEE "RENT" WITH YOU TONIGHT.
RENT!? THAT'S LIKE THE HOTTEST SHOW ON BROADWAY... YOU HAVE TO WAIT MONTHS TO GET TICKETS --
-- AND THEY MUST BE GOING FOR --
RENT
ADMIT ONE
RENT
ADMIT ONE
THWAP
WELL, THAT WAS EASY ENOUGH...
... I'LL MEET YOU HERE AT 7:00, THEN.
DON'T BE LATE.
Uh...
Hrmm.
MUST BE THE HEAT.

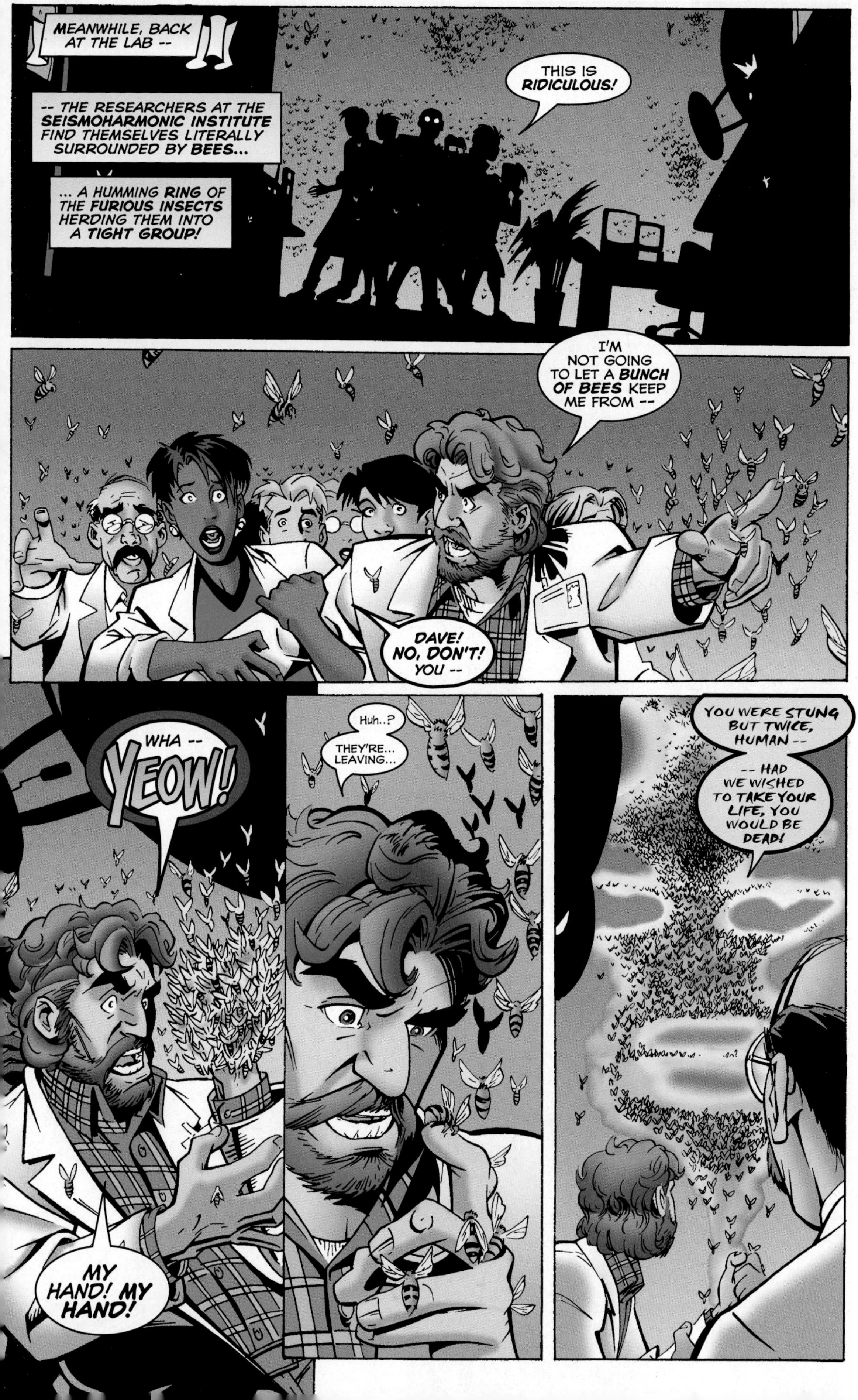

MEANWHILE, BACK AT THE LAB --
-- THE RESEARCHERS AT THE SEISMOHARMONIC INSTITUTE FIND THEMSELVES LITERALLY SURROUNDED BY BEES...
... A HUMMING RING OF THE FURIOUS INSECTS HERDING THEM INTO A TIGHT GROUP!
THIS IS RIDICULOUS!
I'M NOT GOING TO LET A BUNCH OF BEES KEEP ME FROM --
DAVE! NO, DON'T! YOU --
WHA -- YEOW!
MY HAND! MY HAND!
Huh..?
THEY'RE... LEAVING...
YOU WERE STUNG BUT TWICE, HUMAN --
-- HAD WE WISHED TO TAKE YOUR LIFE, YOU WOULD BE DEAD!

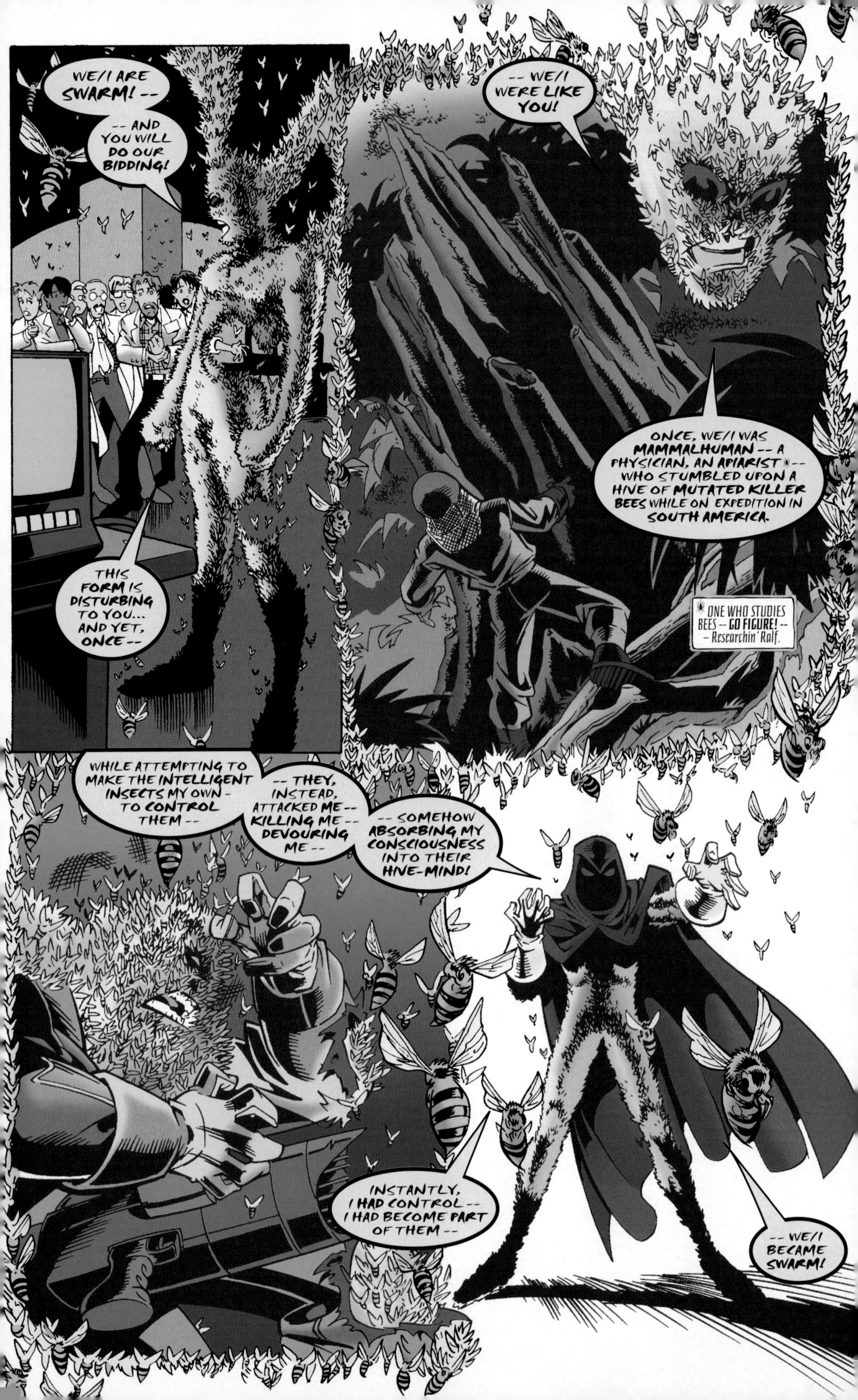
WE/I ARE SWARM! --
-- AND YOU WILL DO OUR BIDDING!
THIS FORM IS DISTURBING TO YOU... AND YET, ONCE --
-- WE/I WERE LIKE YOU!
ONCE, WE/I WAS MAMMALHUMAN -- A PHYSICIAN, AN APIARIST* -- WHO STUMBLED UPON A HIVE OF MUTATED KILLER BEES WHILE ON EXPEDITION IN SOUTH AMERICA.
*ONE WHO STUDIES BEES -- GO FIGURE! -- – Researchin' Ralf.
WHILE ATTEMPTING TO MAKE THE INTELLIGENT INSECTS MY OWN - TO CONTROL THEM --
-- THEY, INSTEAD, ATTACKED ME -- KILLING ME -- DEVOURING ME --
-- SOMEHOW ABSORBING MY CONSCIOUSNESS INTO THEIR HIVE-MIND!
INSTANTLY, I HAD CONTROL -- I HAD BECOME PART OF THEM --
-- WE/I BECAME SWARM!

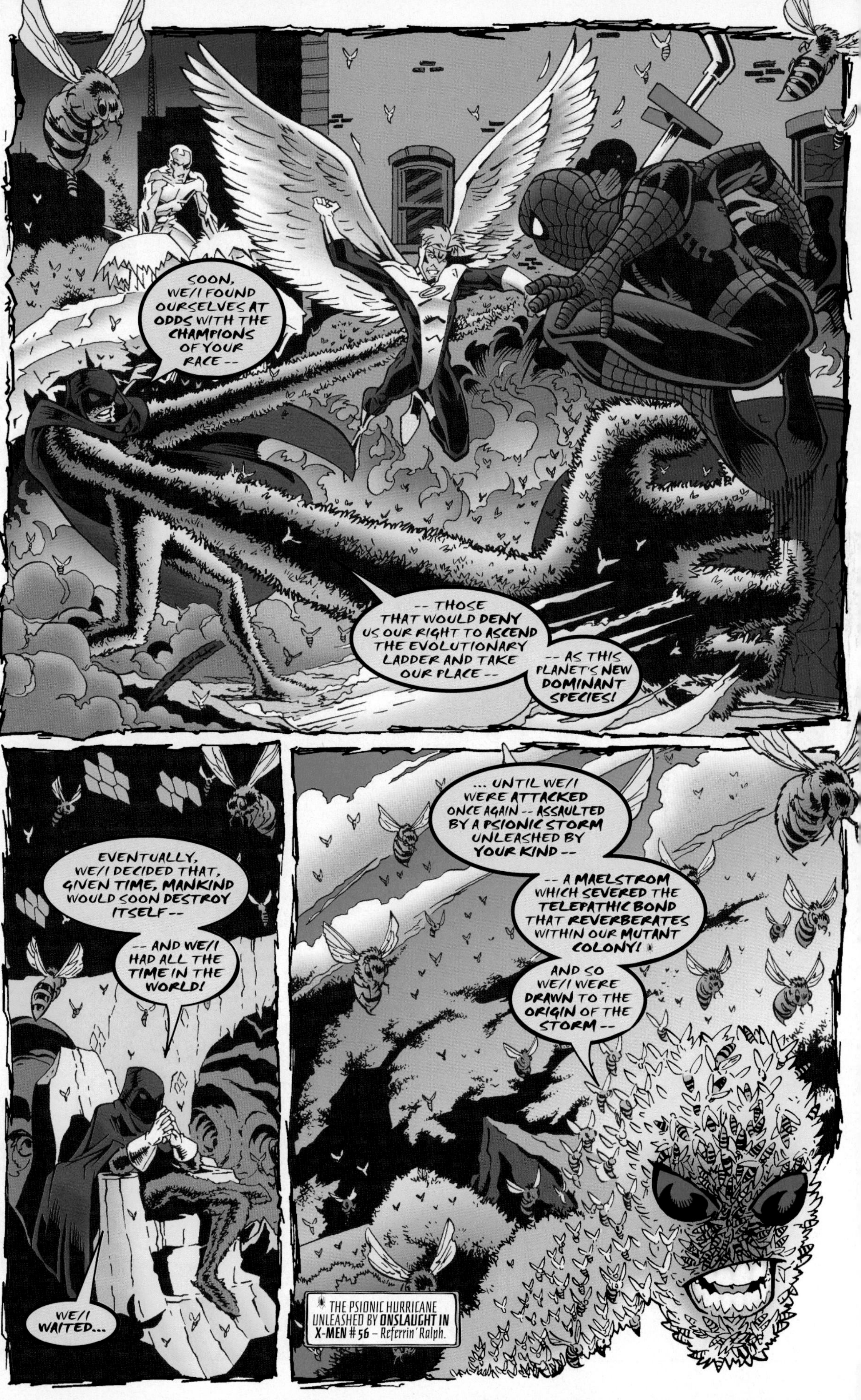
SOON, WE/I FOUND OURSELVES AT ODDS WITH THE CHAMPIONS OF YOUR RACE --
-- THOSE THAT WOULD DENY US OUR RIGHT TO ASCEND THE EVOLUTIONARY LADDER AND TAKE OUR PLACE --
-- AS THIS PLANET'S NEW DOMINANT SPECIES!
EVENTUALLY, WE/I DECIDED THAT, GIVEN TIME, MANKIND WOULD SOON DESTROY ITSELF --
-- AND WE/I HAD ALL THE TIME IN THE WORLD!
WE/I WAITED...
... UNTIL WE/I WERE ATTACKED ONCE AGAIN -- ASSAULTED BY A PSIONIC STORM UNLEASHED BY YOUR KIND --
-- A MAELSTROM WHICH SEVERED THE TELEPATHIC BOND THAT REVERBERATES WITHIN OUR MUTANT COLONY!
AND SO WE/I WERE DRAWN TO THE ORIGIN OF THE STORM --
THE PSIONIC HURRICANE UNLEASHED BY ONSLAUGHT IN X-MEN #56 – Referrin' Ralph.

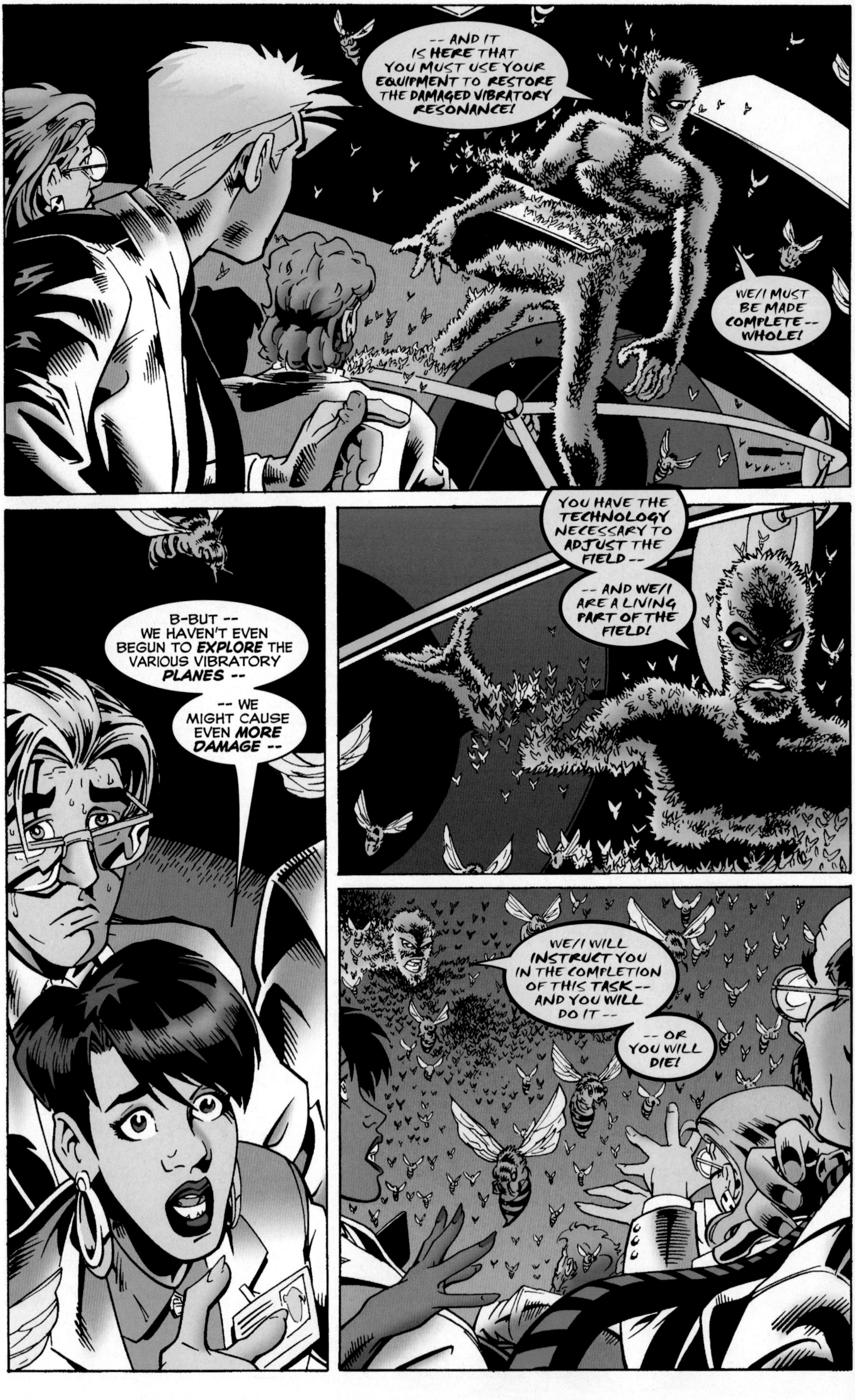
-- AND IT IS HERE THAT YOU MUST USE YOUR EQUIPMENT TO RESTORE THE DAMAGED VIBRATORY RESONANCE!
WE/I MUST BE MADE COMPLETE -- WHOLE!
B-BUT -- WE HAVEN'T EVEN BEGUN TO EXPLORE THE VARIOUS VIBRATORY PLANES --
-- WE MIGHT CAUSE EVEN MORE DAMAGE --
YOU HAVE THE TECHNOLOGY NECESSARY TO ADJUST THE FIELD --
-- AND WE/I ARE A LIVING PART OF THE FIELD!
WE/I WILL INSTRUCT YOU IN THE COMPLETION OF THIS TASK -- AND YOU WILL DO IT --
-- OR YOU WILL DIE!

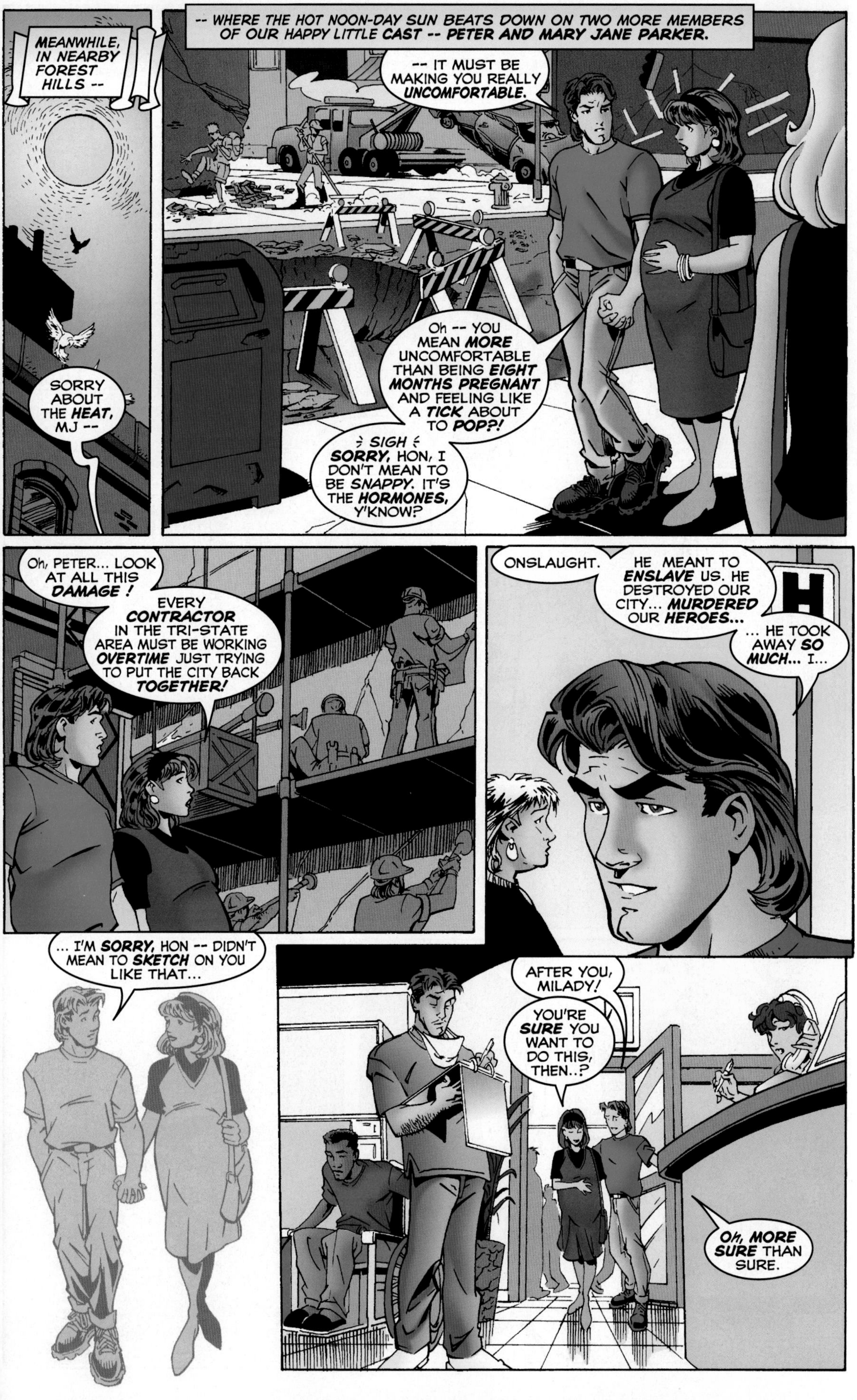

MEANWHILE, IN NEARBY FOREST HILLS --
-- WHERE THE HOT NOON-DAY SUN BEATS DOWN ON TWO MORE MEMBERS OF OUR HAPPY LITTLE CAST -- PETER AND MARY JANE PARKER.
SORRY ABOUT THE HEAT, MJ --
-- IT MUST BE MAKING YOU REALLY UNCOMFORTABLE.
Oh -- YOU MEAN MORE UNCOMFORTABLE THAN BEING EIGHT MONTHS PREGNANT AND FEELING LIKE A TICK ABOUT TO POP?!
SIGH
SORRY, HON, I DON'T MEAN TO BE SNAPPY. IT'S THE HORMONES, Y'KNOW?
Oh, PETER... LOOK AT ALL THIS DAMAGE!
EVERY CONTRACTOR IN THE TRI-STATE AREA MUST BE WORKING OVERTIME JUST TRYING TO PUT THE CITY BACK TOGETHER!
ONSLAUGHT.
HE MEANT TO ENSLAVE US. HE DESTROYED OUR CITY... MURDERED OUR HEROES...
... HE TOOK AWAY SO MUCH... I...
... I'M SORRY, HON -- DIDN'T MEAN TO SKETCH ON YOU LIKE THAT...
AFTER YOU, MILADY!
YOU'RE SURE YOU WANT TO DO THIS, THEN..?
Oh, MORE SURE THAN SURE.

Mr. AND Mrs. PARKER! HELLO! WE ARE READY TO TAKE SOME *PICTURES*, NO?

MORE THAN READY, Dr. HAJETI!

I'M SO *EXCITED* I COULDN'T EVEN *SLEEP* LAST NIGHT...

TO BE EXPECTED.

MY *APOLOGIES*. THE *BELLY JELLY* IS COLD -- BUT NECESSARY TO GET A GOOD *PICTURE*.

I ALWAYS TELL THE BABY, "SAY *CHEESE!*"

AND THERE IT *IS*, THE FIRST PHOTOGRAPH OF YOUR LITTLE BABY --

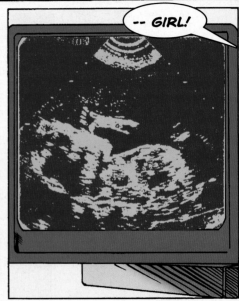

-- GIRL!

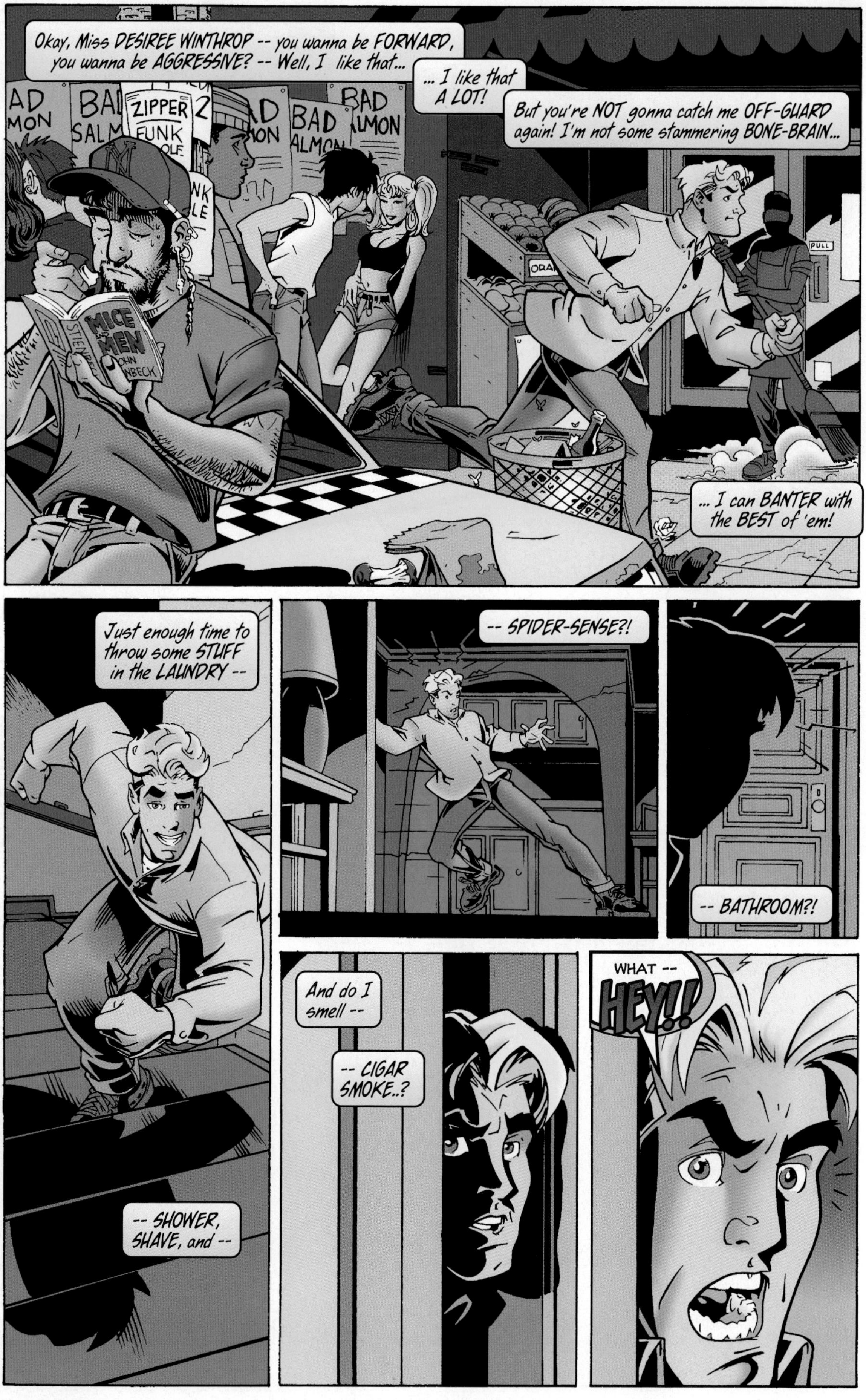
Okay, Miss DESIREE WINTHROP -- you wanna be FORWARD, you wanna be AGGRESSIVE? -- Well, I like that...
... I like that A LOT!
But you're NOT gonna catch me OFF-GUARD again! I'm not some stammering BONE-BRAIN...
BAD SALMON
ZIPPER FUNK
MICE AND MEN
STEINBECK
PULL
... I can BANTER with the BEST of 'em!
Just enough time to throw some STUFF in the LAUNDRY --
-- SHOWER, SHAVE, and --
-- SPIDER-SENSE?!
-- BATHROOM?!
And do I smell --
-- CIGAR SMOKE..?
WHAT --
HEY!!

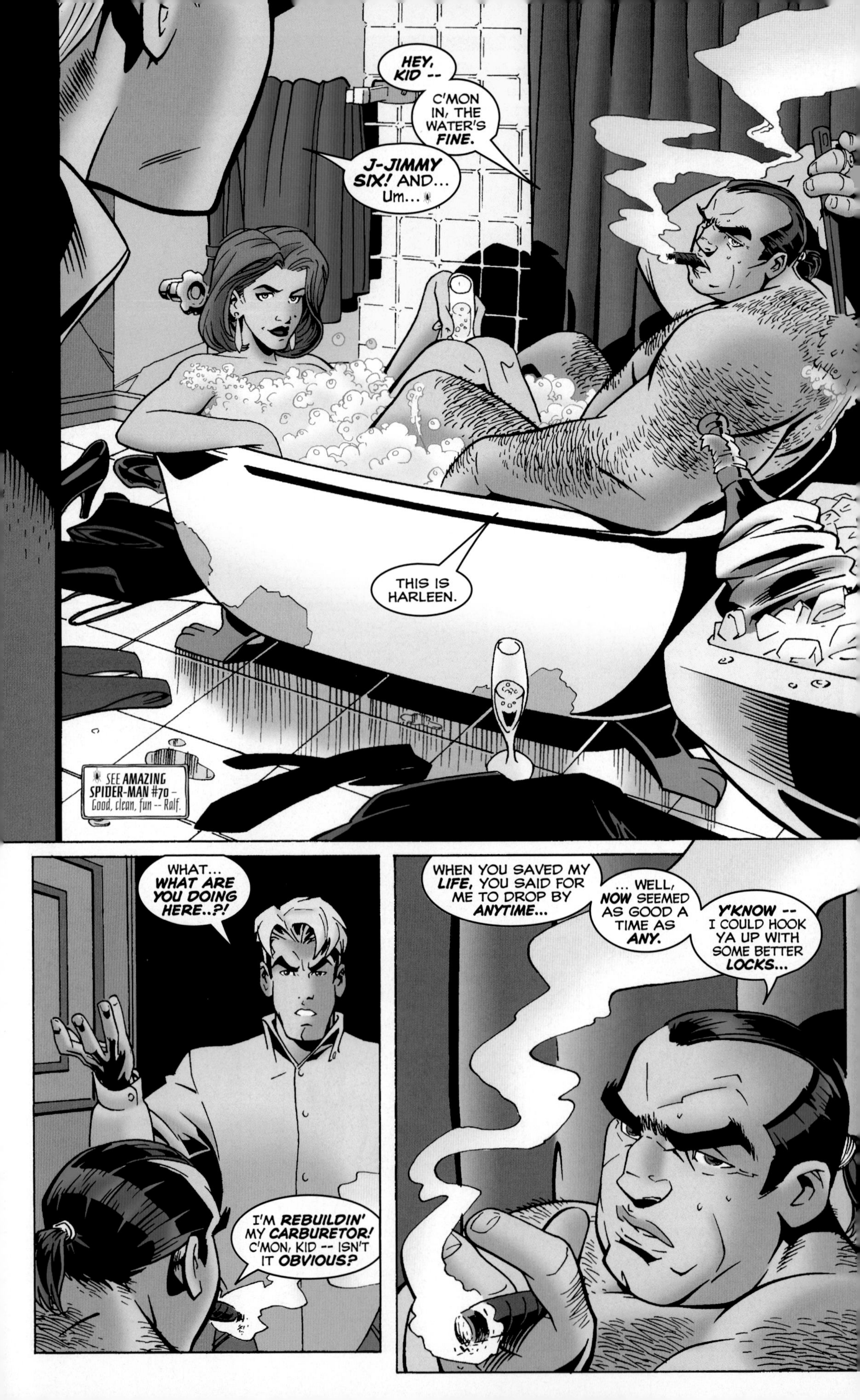
HEY, KID --
C'MON IN, THE WATER'S FINE.
J-JIMMY SIX! AND... UM...
THIS IS HARLEEN.
SEE AMAZING SPIDER-MAN #70 -- Good, clean, fun -- Ralf.
WHAT... WHAT ARE YOU DOING HERE..?!
I'M REBUILDIN' MY CARBURETOR! C'MON, KID -- ISN'T IT OBVIOUS?
WHEN YOU SAVED MY LIFE, YOU SAID FOR ME TO DROP BY ANYTIME...
... WELL, NOW SEEMED AS GOOD A TIME AS ANY.
Y'KNOW -- I COULD HOOK YA UP WITH SOME BETTER LOCKS...

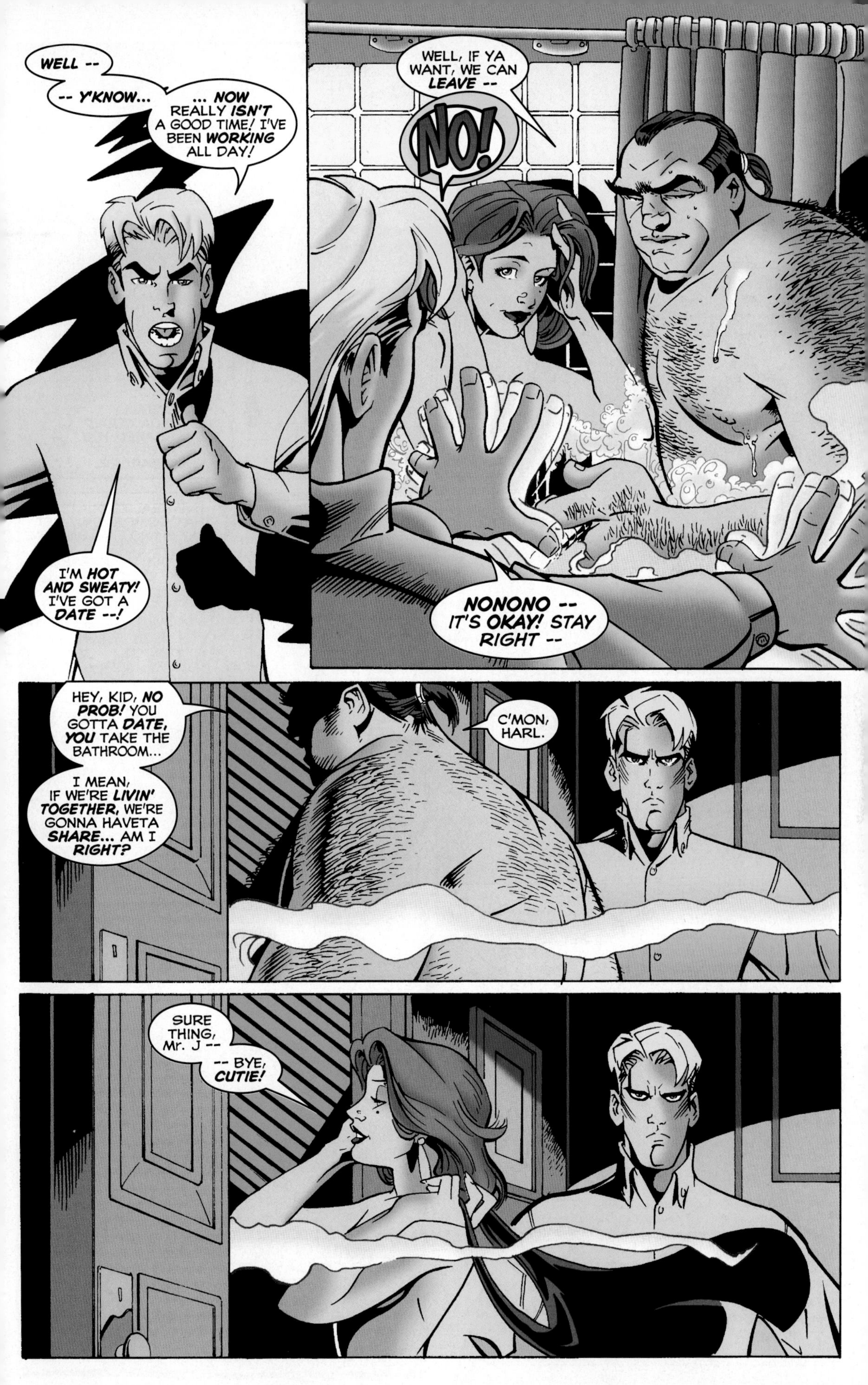
WELL --
-- Y'KNOW...
... NOW REALLY ISN'T A GOOD TIME! I'VE BEEN WORKING ALL DAY!
I'M HOT AND SWEATY! I'VE GOT A DATE --!
WELL, IF YA WANT, WE CAN LEAVE --
NO!
NONONO -- IT'S OKAY! STAY RIGHT --
HEY, KID, NO PROB! YOU GOTTA DATE, YOU TAKE THE BATHROOM...
I MEAN, IF WE'RE LIVIN' TOGETHER, WE'RE GONNA HAVETA SHARE... AM I RIGHT?
C'MON, HARL.
SURE THING, Mr. J --
-- BYE, CUTIE!

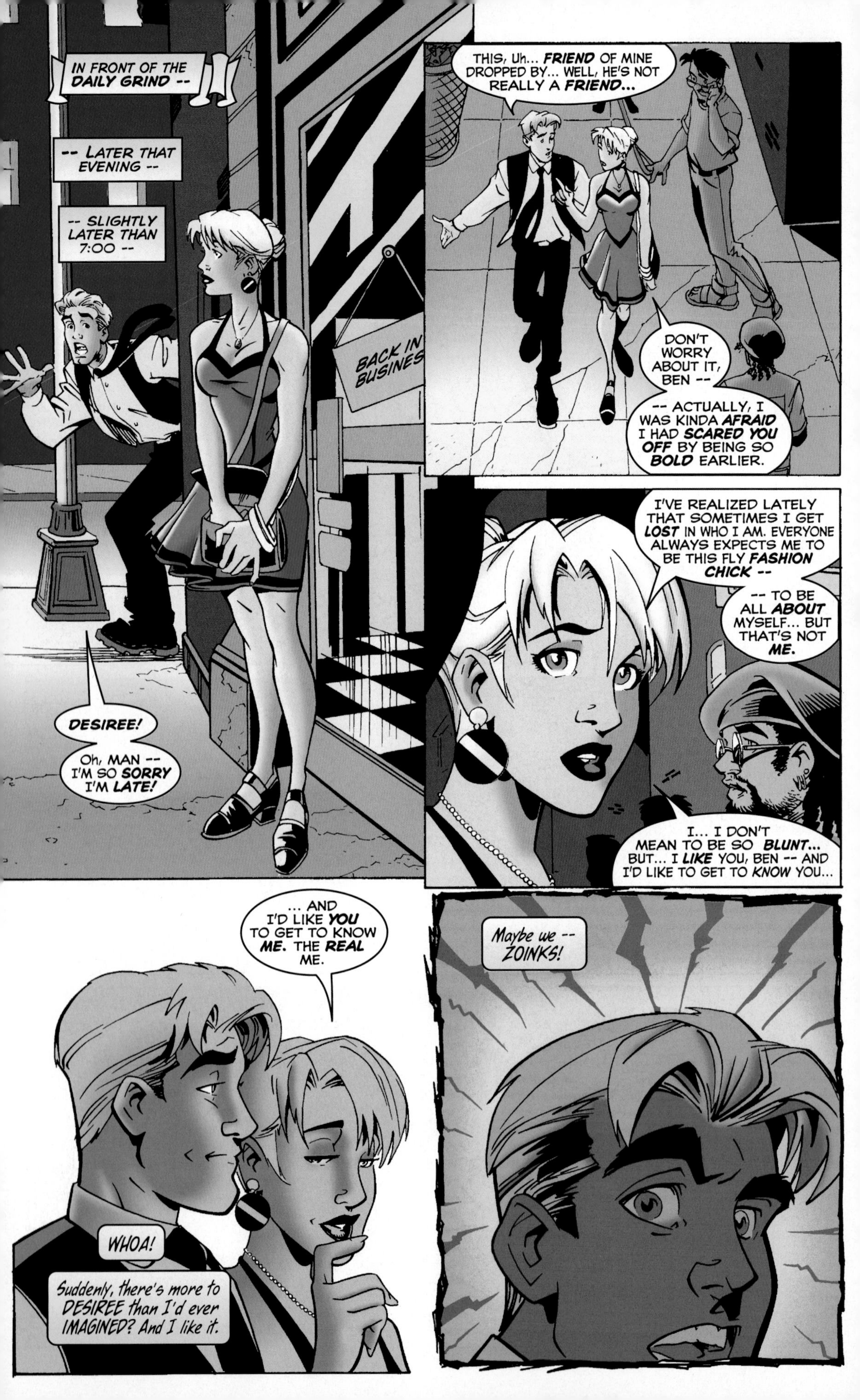
IN FRONT OF THE DAILY GRIND --
-- LATER THAT EVENING --
-- SLIGHTLY LATER THAN 7:00 --
BACK IN BUSINES
DESIREE!
Oh, MAN -- I'M SO SORRY I'M LATE!
THIS, Uh... FRIEND OF MINE DROPPED BY... WELL, HE'S NOT REALLY A FRIEND...
DON'T WORRY ABOUT IT, BEN --
-- ACTUALLY, I WAS KINDA AFRAID I HAD SCARED YOU OFF BY BEING SO BOLD EARLIER.
I'VE REALIZED LATELY THAT SOMETIMES I GET LOST IN WHO I AM. EVERYONE ALWAYS EXPECTS ME TO BE THIS FLY FASHION CHICK --
-- TO BE ALL ABOUT MYSELF... BUT THAT'S NOT ME.
I... I DON'T MEAN TO BE SO BLUNT... BUT... I LIKE YOU, BEN -- AND I'D LIKE TO GET TO KNOW YOU...
... AND I'D LIKE YOU TO GET TO KNOW ME. THE REAL ME.
WHOA!
Suddenly, there's more to DESIREE than I'd ever IMAGINED? And I like it.
Maybe we -- ZOINKS!

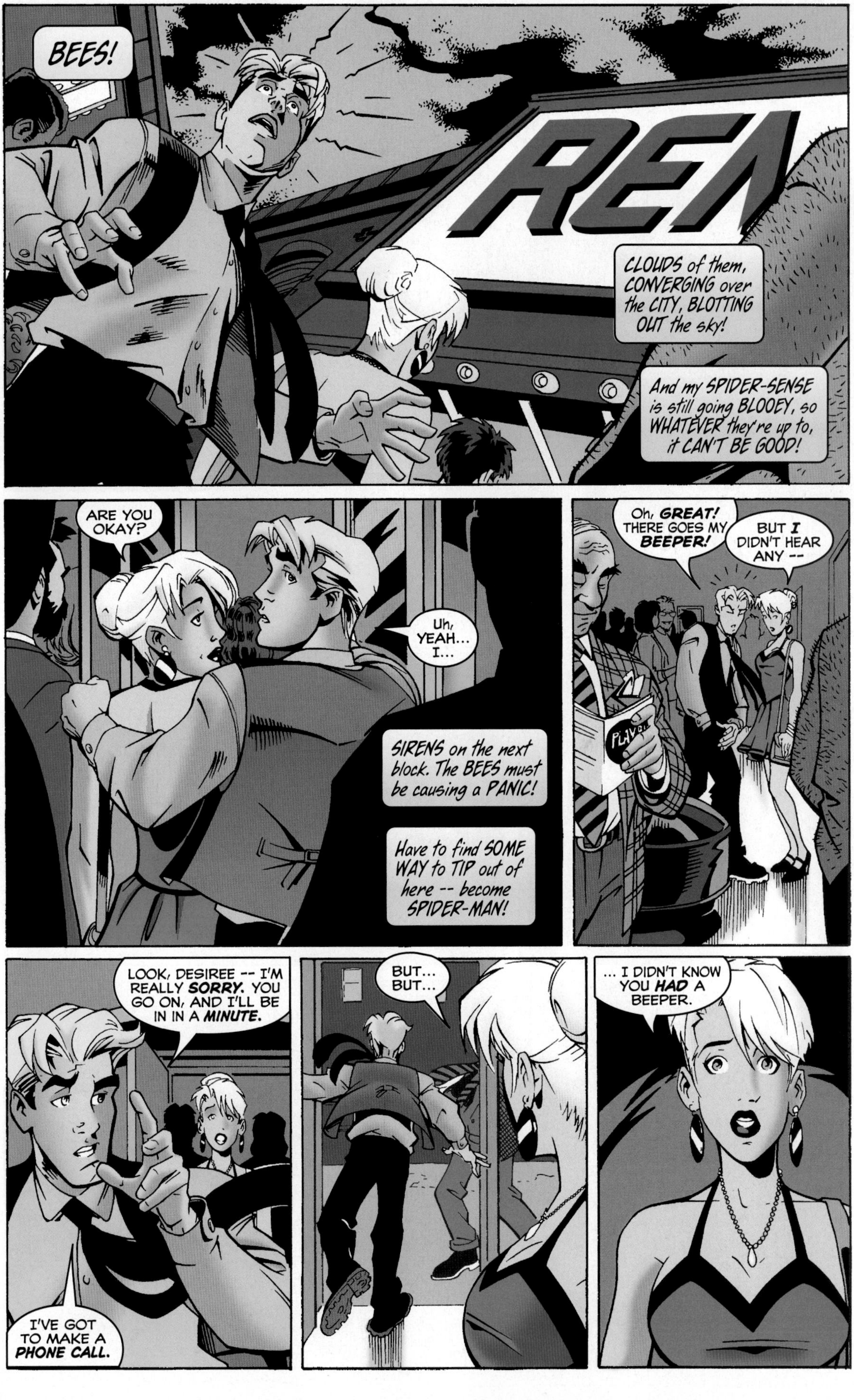
BEES!
REA
CLOUDS of them, CONVERGING over the CITY, BLOTTING OUT the sky!
And my SPIDER-SENSE is still going BLOOEY, so WHATEVER they're up to, it CAN'T BE GOOD!
ARE YOU OKAY?
Uh, YEAH... I...
SIRENS on the next block. The BEES must be causing a PANIC!
Have to find SOME WAY to TIP out of here -- become SPIDER-MAN!
Oh, GREAT! THERE GOES MY BEEPER!
BUT I DIDN'T HEAR ANY --
LOOK, DESIREE -- I'M REALLY SORRY. YOU GO ON, AND I'LL BE IN IN A MINUTE.
I'VE GOT TO MAKE A PHONE CALL.
BUT... BUT...
... I DIDN'T KNOW YOU HAD A BEEPER.

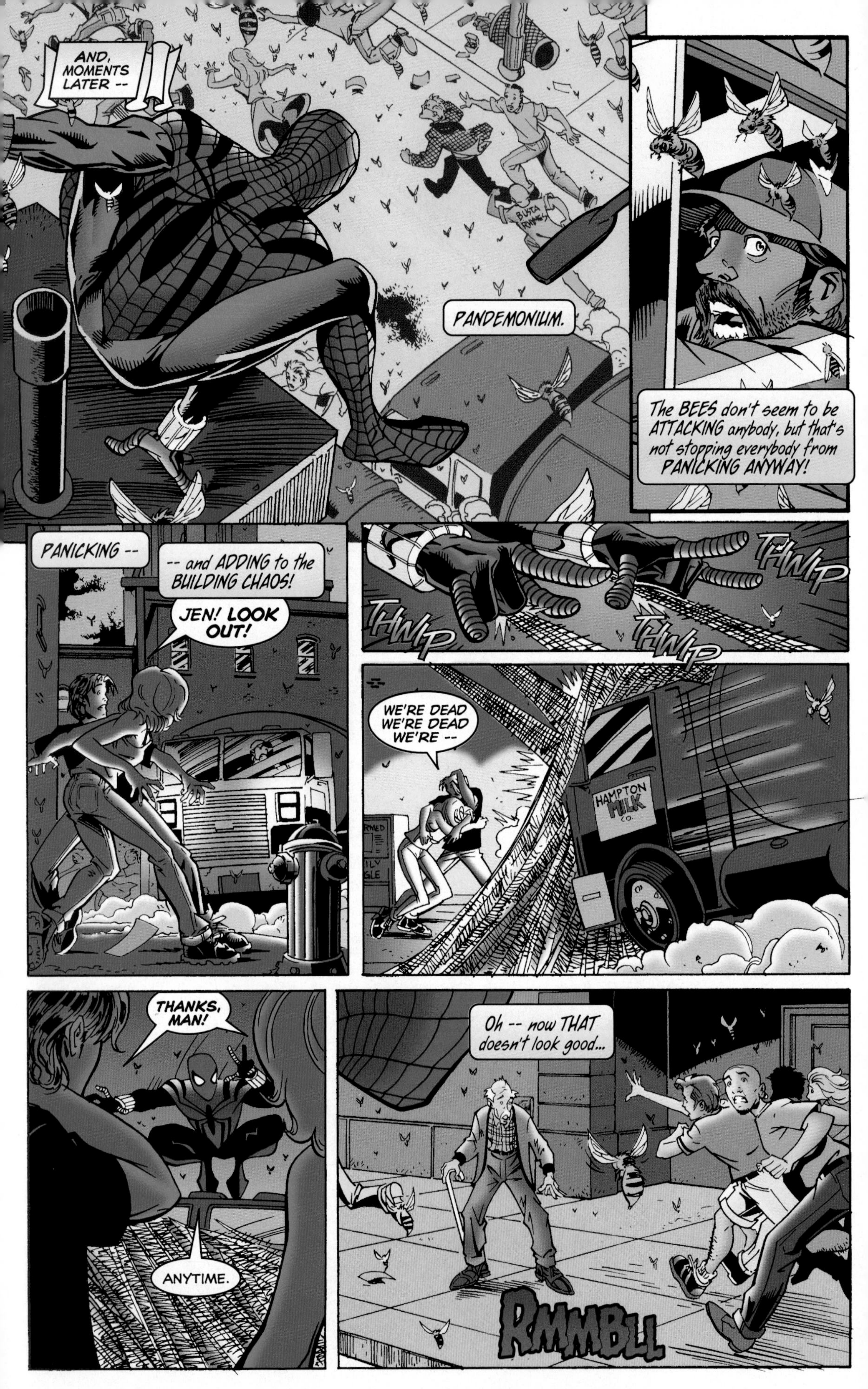
AND, MOMENTS LATER --
PANDEMONIUM.
BUSTA RHYMES
The BEES don't seem to be ATTACKING anybody, but that's not stopping everybody from PANICKING ANYWAY!
PANICKING --
-- and ADDING to the BUILDING CHAOS!
JEN! LOOK OUT!
THWIP
THWIP
THWIP
WE'RE DEAD WE'RE DEAD WE'RE --
HAMPTON MILK CO.
THANKS, MAN!
ANYTIME.
Oh -- now THAT doesn't look good...
RMMBLL

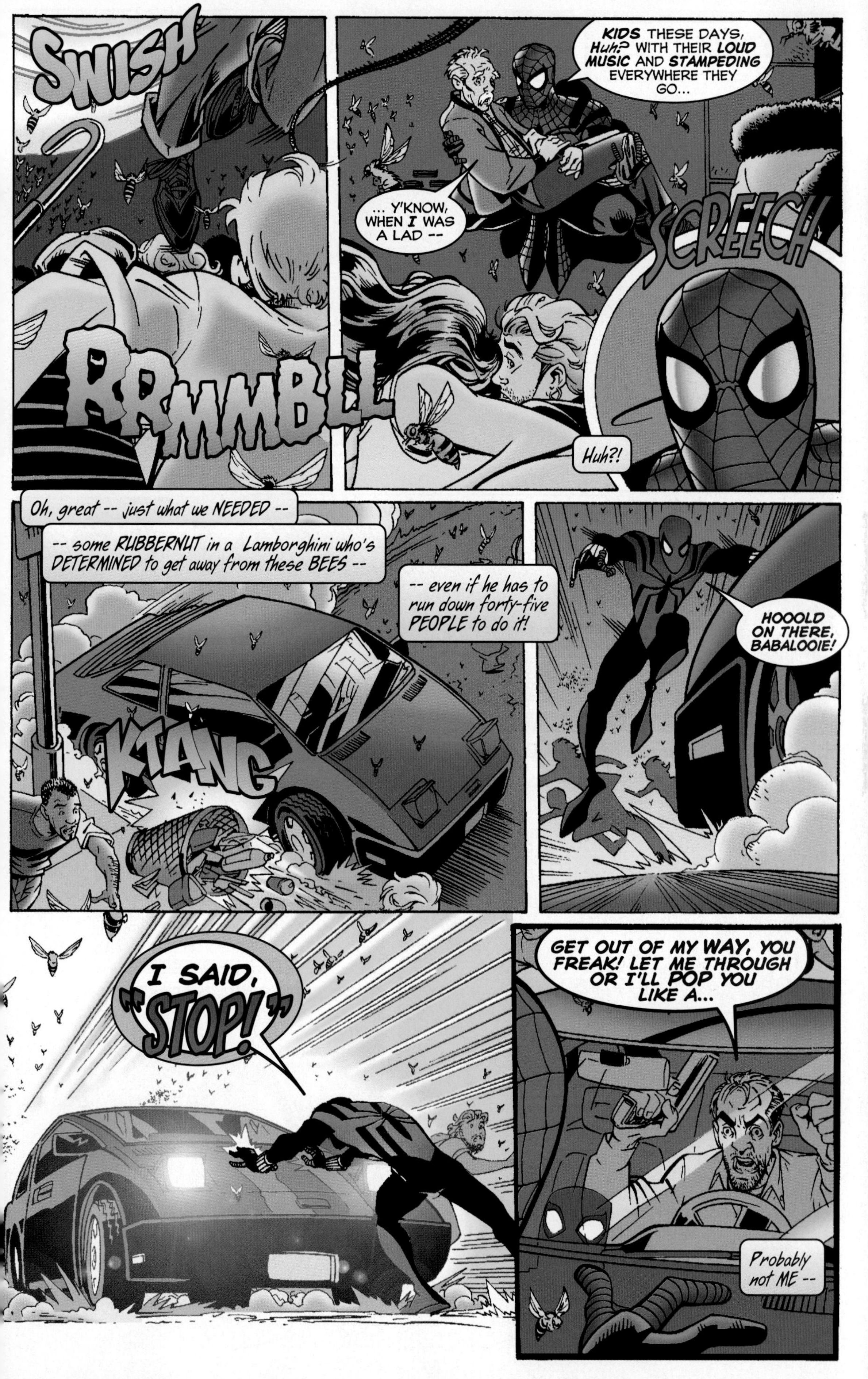
SWISH
RRMMBLL
KIDS THESE DAYS, HUH? WITH THEIR LOUD MUSIC AND STAMPEDING EVERYWHERE THEY GO...
... Y'KNOW, WHEN I WAS A LAD --
SCREECH
Huh?!
Oh, great -- just what we NEEDED --
-- some RUBBERNUT in a Lamborghini who's DETERMINED to get away from these BEES --
-- even if he has to run down forty-five PEOPLE to do it!
KTANG
HOOOLD ON THERE, BABALOOIE!
I SAID, "STOP!"
GET OUT OF MY WAY, YOU FREAK! LET ME THROUGH OR I'LL POP YOU LIKE A...
Probably not ME --

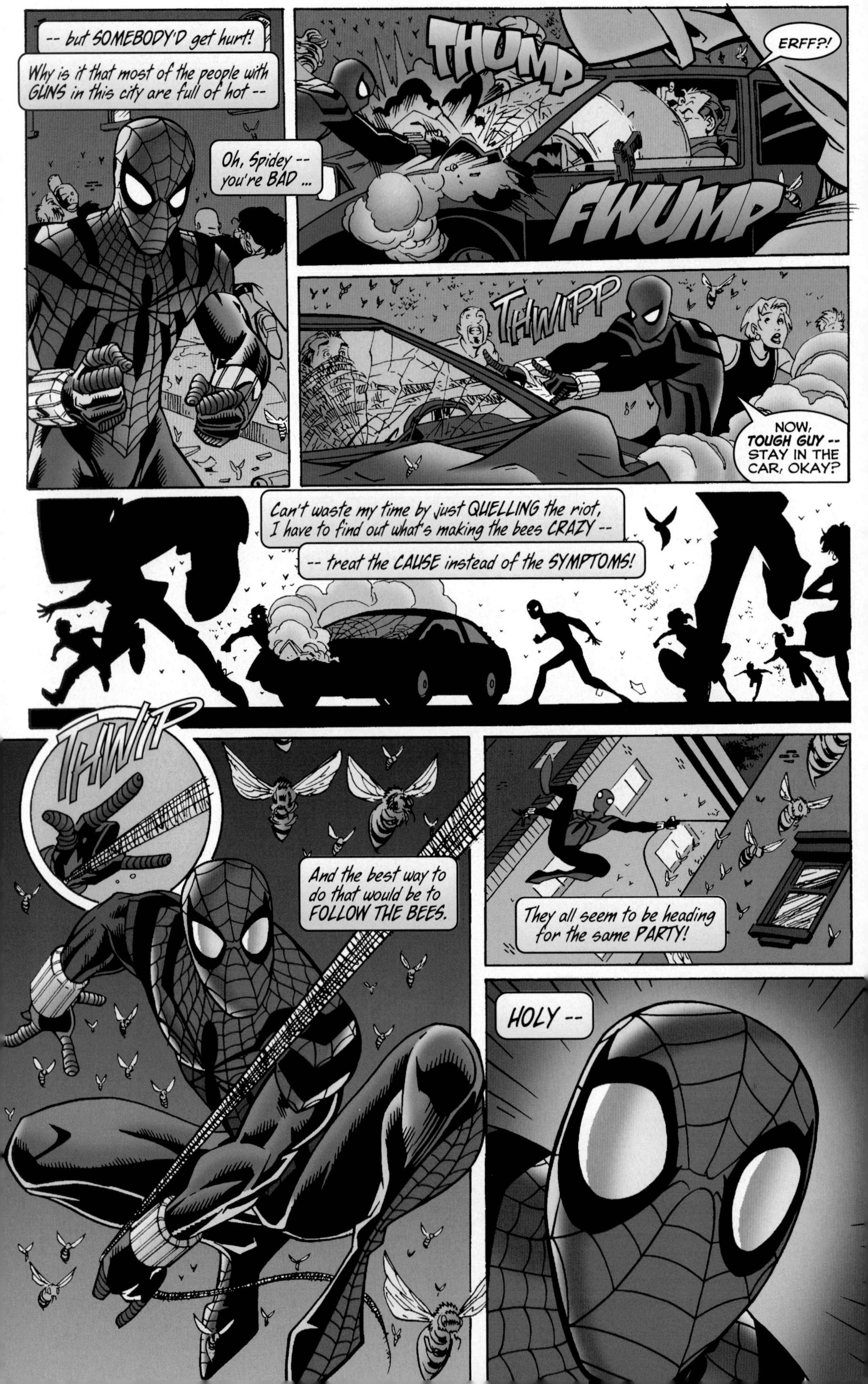

-- but SOMEBODY'D get hurt!
Why is it that most of the people with GUNS in this city are full of hot --
Oh, Spidey -- you're BAD ...
THUMP
ERFF?!
FWUMP
THWIPP
NOW, TOUGH GUY -- STAY IN THE CAR, OKAY?
Can't waste my time by just QUELLING the riot, I have to find out what's making the bees CRAZY --
-- treat the CAUSE instead of the SYMPTOMS!
THWIP
And the best way to do that would be to FOLLOW THE BEES.
They all seem to be heading for the same PARTY!
HOLY --

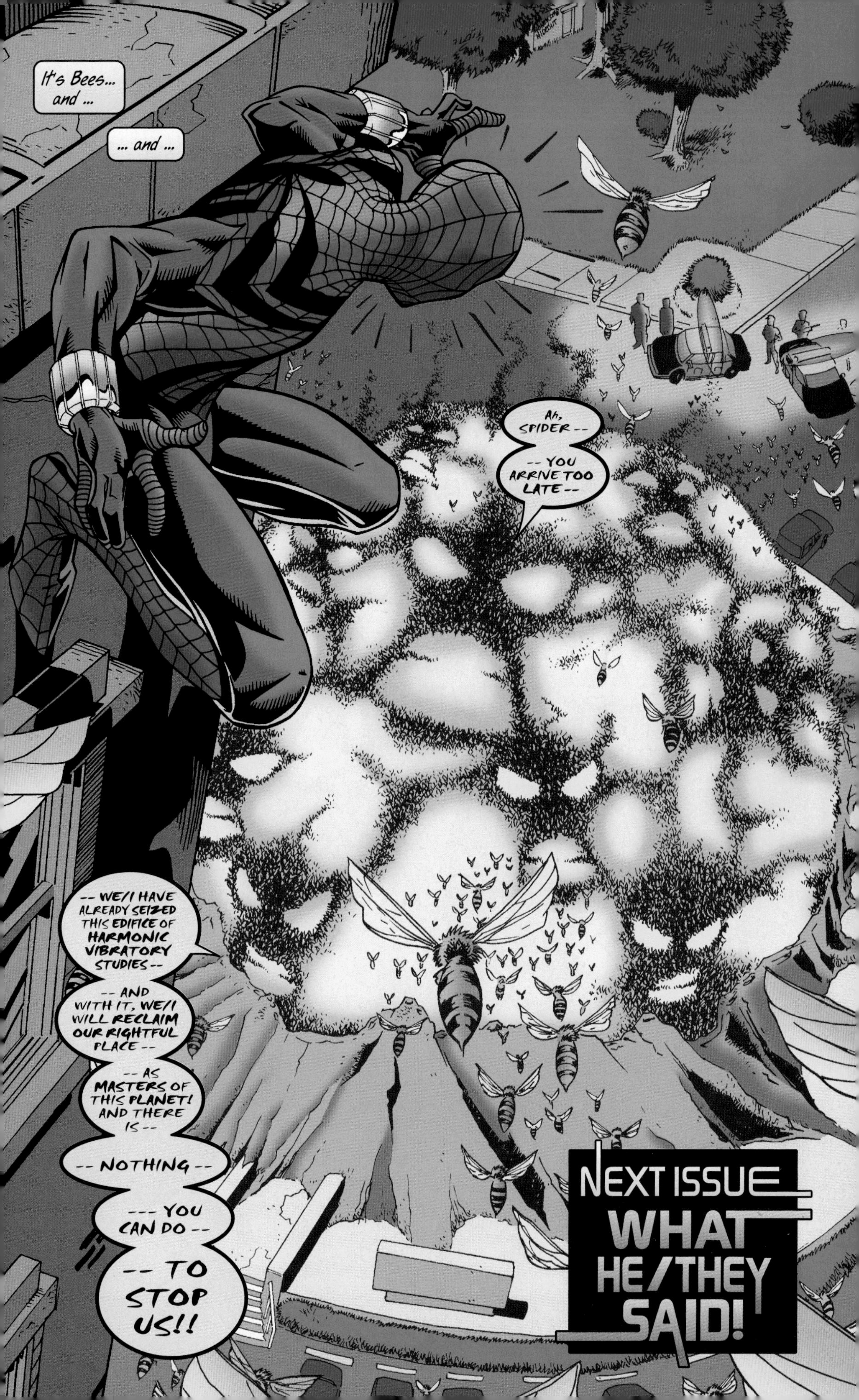
It's Bees... and ...
... and ...
Ah, SPIDER --
-- YOU ARRIVE TOO LATE --
-- WE/I HAVE ALREADY SEIZED THIS EDIFICE OF HARMONIC VIBRATORY STUDIES --
-- AND WITH IT, WE/I WILL RECLAIM OUR RIGHTFUL PLACE --
-- AS MASTERS OF THIS PLANET! AND THERE IS --
-- NOTHING --
--- YOU CAN DO --
-- TO STOP US!!
NEXT ISSUE
WHAT HE/THEY SAID!

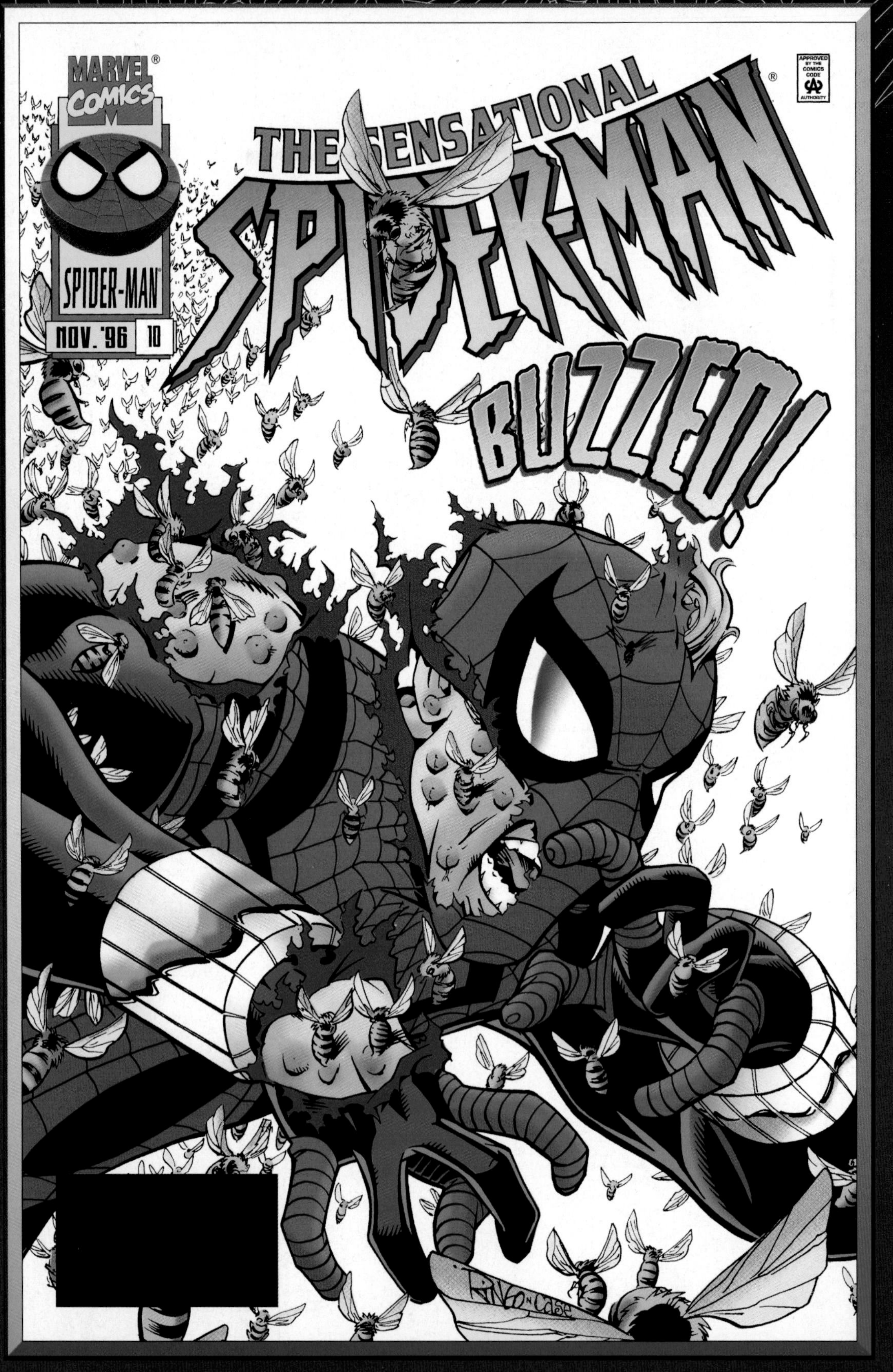
MARVEL COMICS
SPIDER-MAN
NOV. '96
10
APPROVED BY THE COMICS CODE AUTHORITY
THE SENSATIONAL SPIDER-MAN
BUZZED!
RINGO 'N CASE

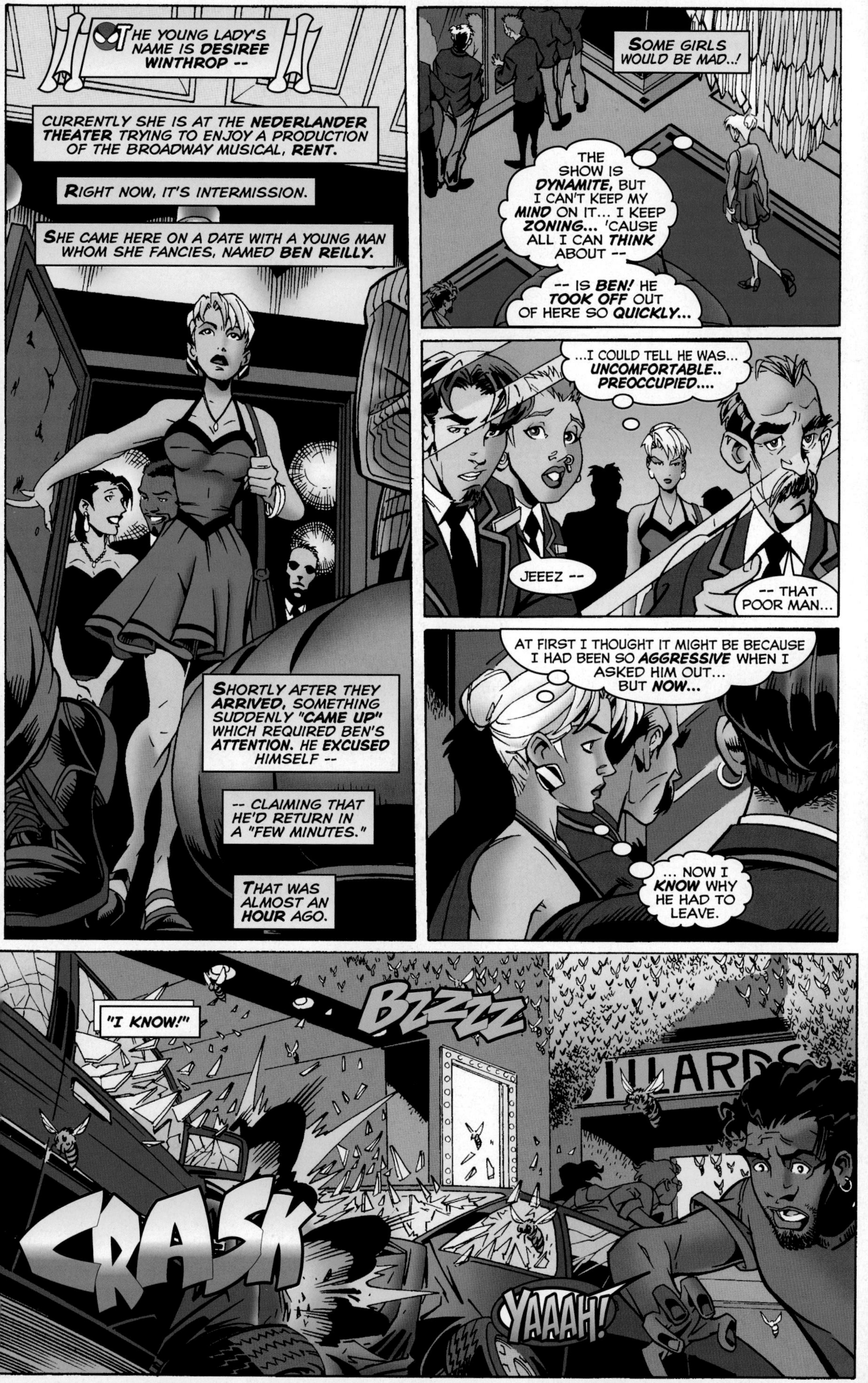
THE YOUNG LADY'S NAME IS DESIREE WINTHROP --
CURRENTLY SHE IS AT THE NEDERLANDER THEATER TRYING TO ENJOY A PRODUCTION OF THE BROADWAY MUSICAL, RENT.
RIGHT NOW, IT'S INTERMISSION.
SHE CAME HERE ON A DATE WITH A YOUNG MAN WHOM SHE FANCIES, NAMED BEN REILLY.
SHORTLY AFTER THEY ARRIVED, SOMETHING SUDDENLY "CAME UP" WHICH REQUIRED BEN'S ATTENTION. HE EXCUSED HIMSELF --
-- CLAIMING THAT HE'D RETURN IN A "FEW MINUTES."
THAT WAS ALMOST AN HOUR AGO.
SOME GIRLS WOULD BE MAD..!
THE SHOW IS DYNAMITE, BUT I CAN'T KEEP MY MIND ON IT... I KEEP ZONING... 'CAUSE ALL I CAN THINK ABOUT --
-- IS BEN! HE TOOK OFF OUT OF HERE SO QUICKLY...
...I COULD TELL HE WAS... UNCOMFORTABLE.. PREOCCUPIED....
JEEEZ --
-- THAT POOR MAN...
AT FIRST I THOUGHT IT MIGHT BE BECAUSE I HAD BEEN SO AGGRESSIVE WHEN I ASKED HIM OUT... BUT NOW...
... NOW I KNOW WHY HE HAD TO LEAVE.
"I KNOW!"
BZZZZ
CRASH
YAAAH!

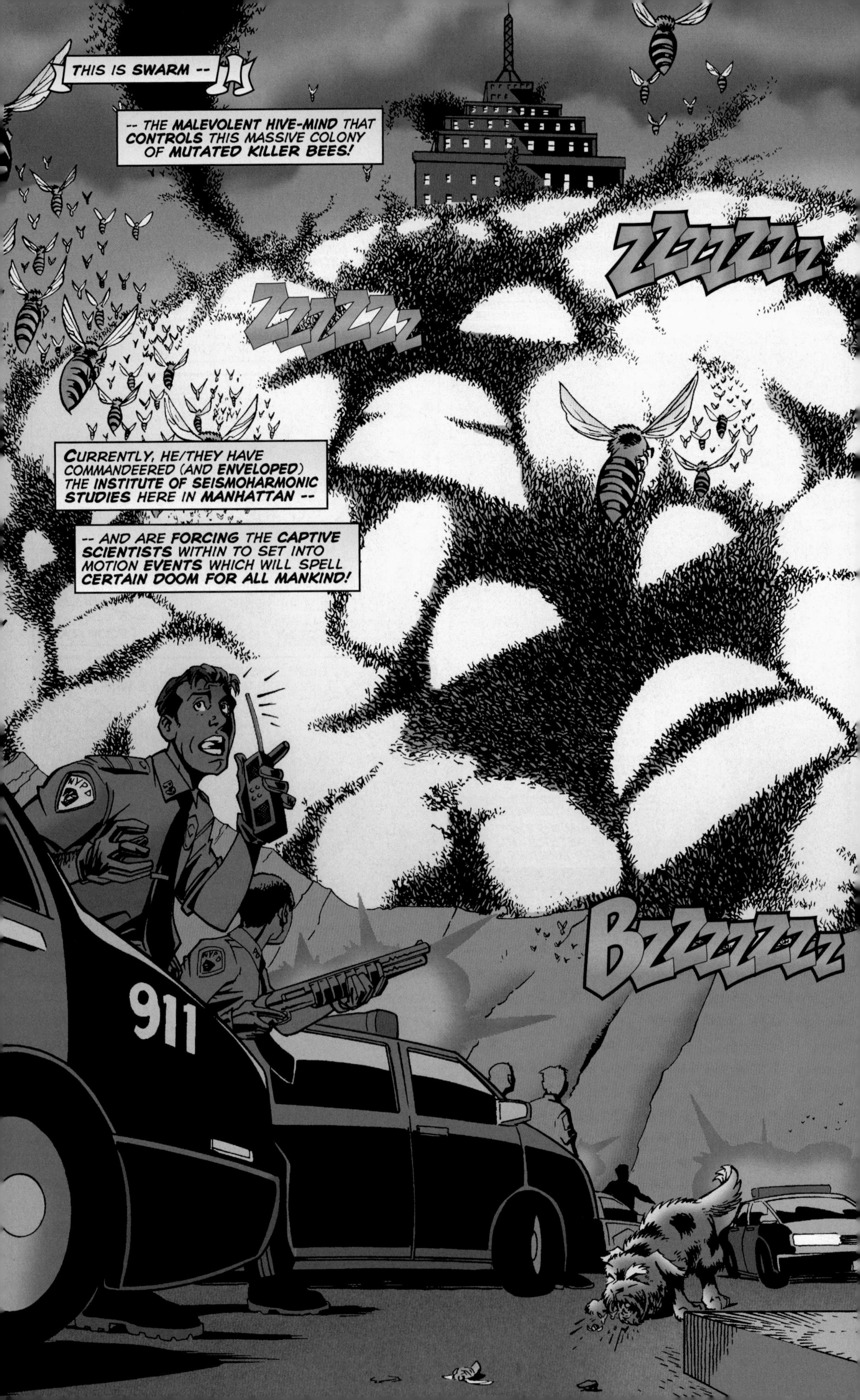
THIS IS SWARM --
-- THE MALEVOLENT HIVE-MIND THAT CONTROLS THIS MASSIVE COLONY OF MUTATED KILLER BEES!
ZZZZZZZz
ZZZZZZz
CURRENTLY, HE/THEY HAVE COMMANDEERED (AND ENVELOPED) THE INSTITUTE OF SEISMOHARMONIC STUDIES HERE IN MANHATTAN --
-- AND ARE FORCING THE CAPTIVE SCIENTISTS WITHIN TO SET INTO MOTION EVENTS WHICH WILL SPELL CERTAIN DOOM FOR ALL MANKIND!
Bzzzzzzz
911

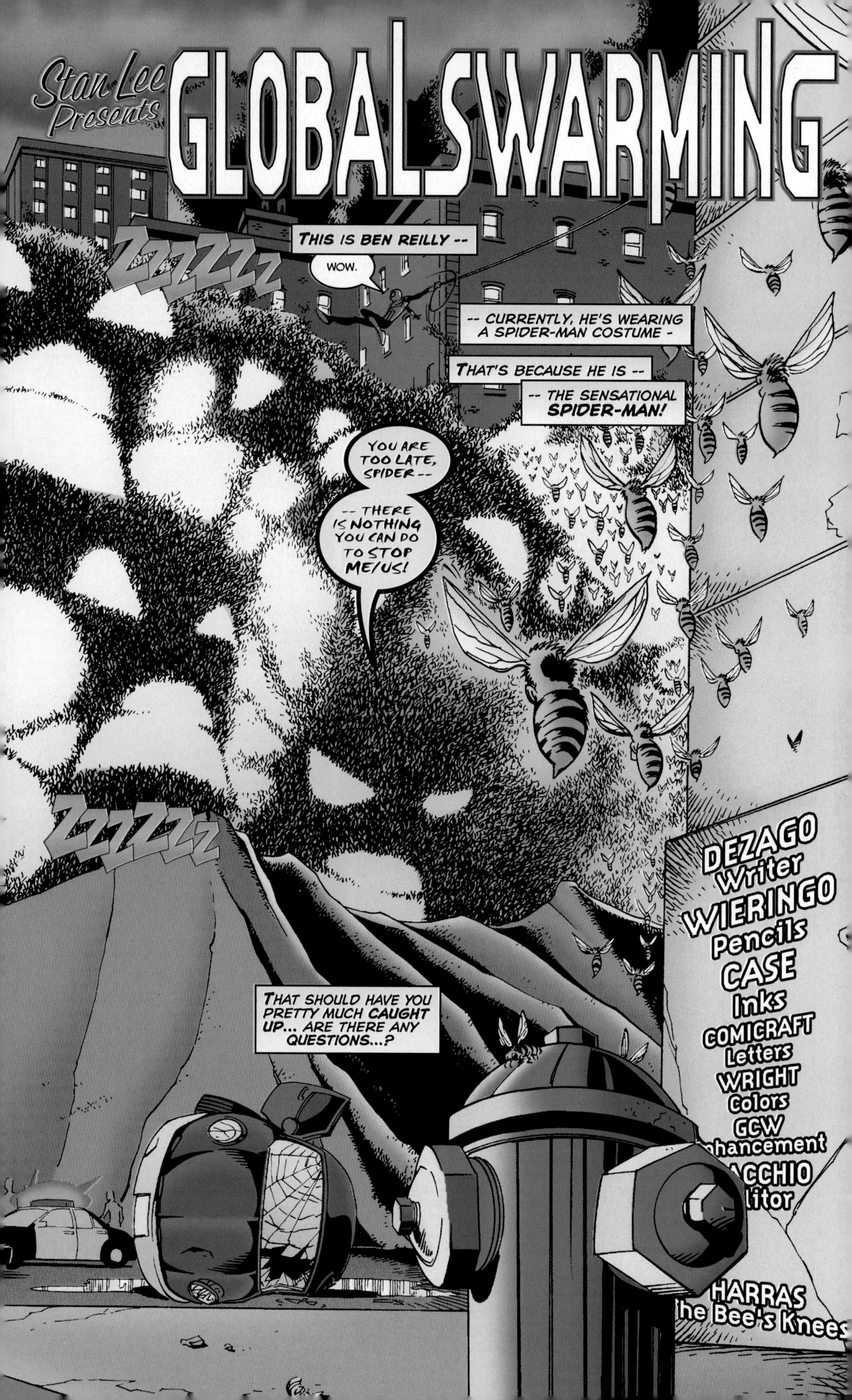

Stan Lee Presents
GLOBAL SWARMING
ZZZZZZ
THIS IS BEN REILLY --
WOW.
-- CURRENTLY, HE'S WEARING A SPIDER-MAN COSTUME -
THAT'S BECAUSE HE IS --
-- THE SENSATIONAL SPIDER-MAN!
YOU ARE TOO LATE, SPIDER --
-- THERE IS NOTHING YOU CAN DO TO STOP ME/US!
ZZZZZZ
THAT SHOULD HAVE YOU PRETTY MUCH CAUGHT UP... ARE THERE ANY QUESTIONS...?
DEZAGO Writer
WIERINGO Pencils
CASE Inks
COMICRAFT Letters
WRIGHT Colors
GCW
HARRAS

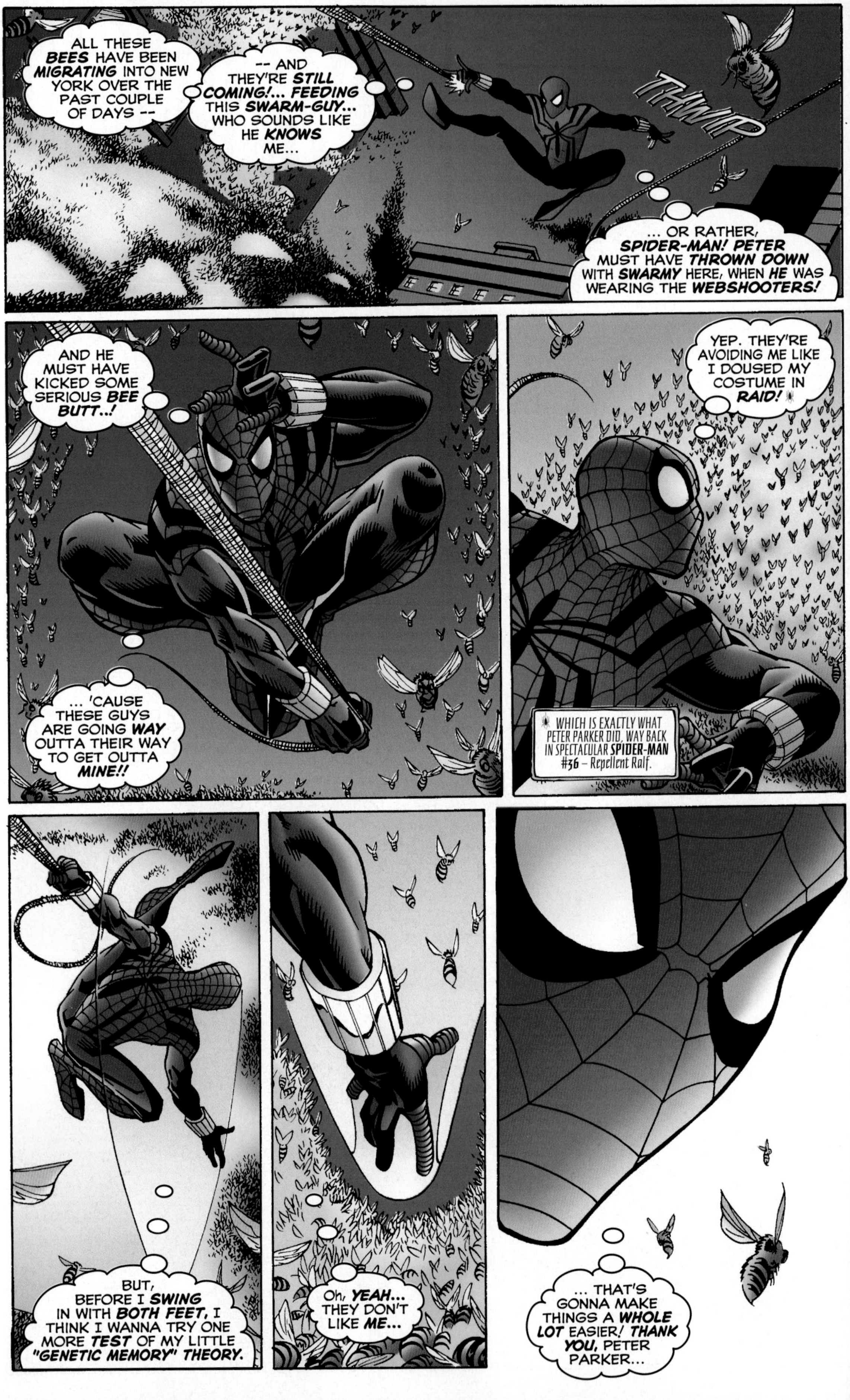
ALL THESE BEES HAVE BEEN MIGRATING INTO NEW YORK OVER THE PAST COUPLE OF DAYS --
-- AND THEY'RE STILL COMING!... FEEDING THIS SWARM-GUY... WHO SOUNDS LIKE HE KNOWS ME...
THWIP
... OR RATHER, SPIDER-MAN! PETER MUST HAVE THROWN DOWN WITH SWARMY HERE, WHEN HE WAS WEARING THE WEBSHOOTERS!
AND HE MUST HAVE KICKED SOME SERIOUS BEE BUTT..!
... 'CAUSE THESE GUYS ARE GOING WAY OUTTA THEIR WAY TO GET OUTTA MINE!!
YEP. THEY'RE AVOIDING ME LIKE I DOUSED MY COSTUME IN RAID!
WHICH IS EXACTLY WHAT PETER PARKER DID, WAY BACK IN SPECTACULAR SPIDER-MAN #36 – Repellent Ralf.
BUT, BEFORE I SWING IN WITH BOTH FEET, I THINK I WANNA TRY ONE MORE TEST OF MY LITTLE "GENETIC MEMORY" THEORY.
Oh, YEAH... THEY DON'T LIKE ME...
... THAT'S GONNA MAKE THINGS A WHOLE LOT EASIER! THANK YOU, PETER PARKER...

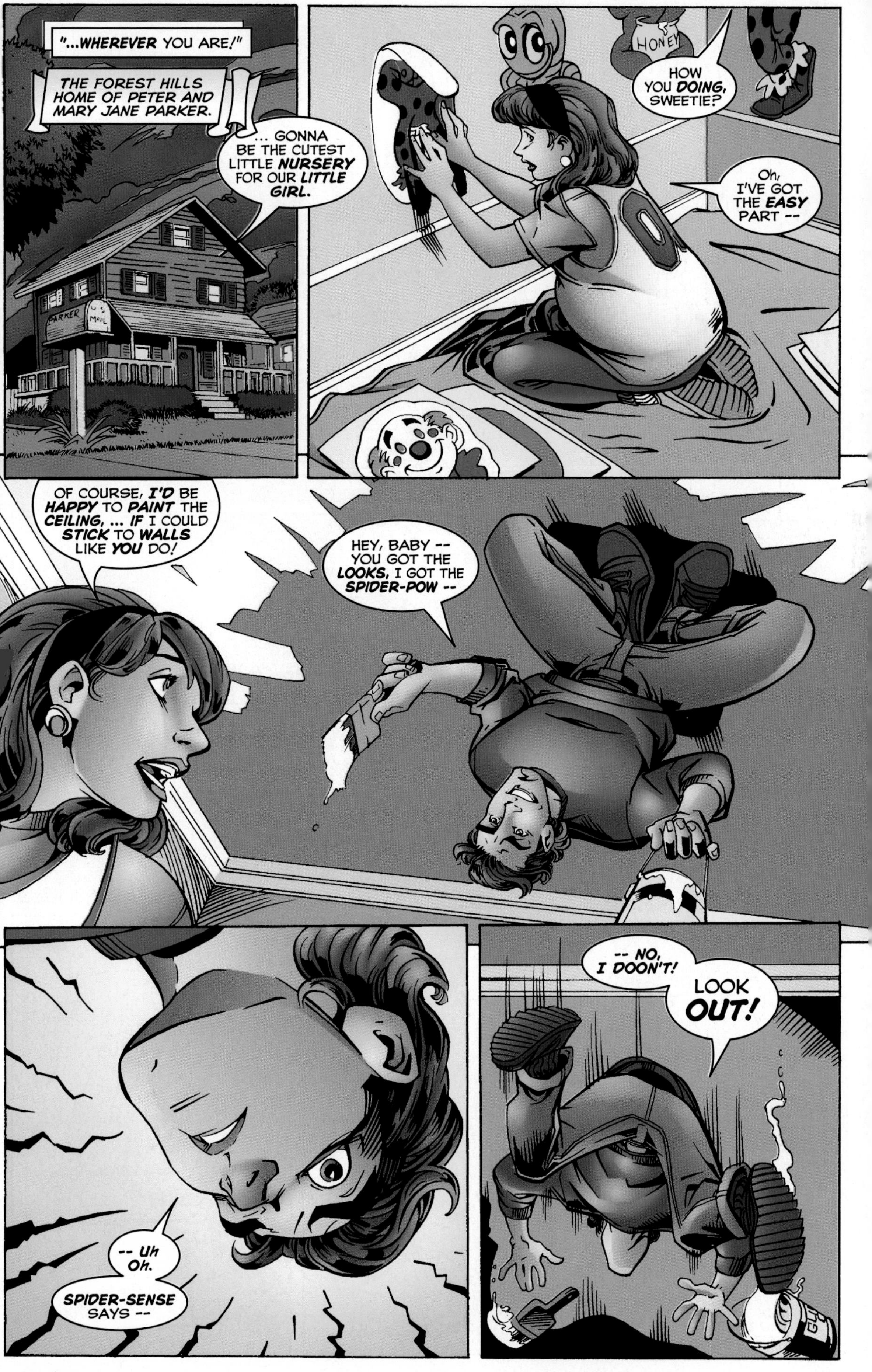
"...WHEREVER YOU ARE!"
THE FOREST HILLS HOME OF PETER AND MARY JANE PARKER.
... GONNA BE THE CUTEST LITTLE NURSERY FOR OUR LITTLE GIRL.
HONEY
HOW YOU DOING, SWEETIE?
Oh, I'VE GOT THE EASY PART --
OF COURSE, I'D BE HAPPY TO PAINT THE CEILING, ... IF I COULD STICK TO WALLS LIKE YOU DO!
HEY, BABY -- YOU GOT THE LOOKS, I GOT THE SPIDER-POW --
-- Uh Oh.
SPIDER-SENSE SAYS --
-- NO, I DOON'T!
LOOK OUT!

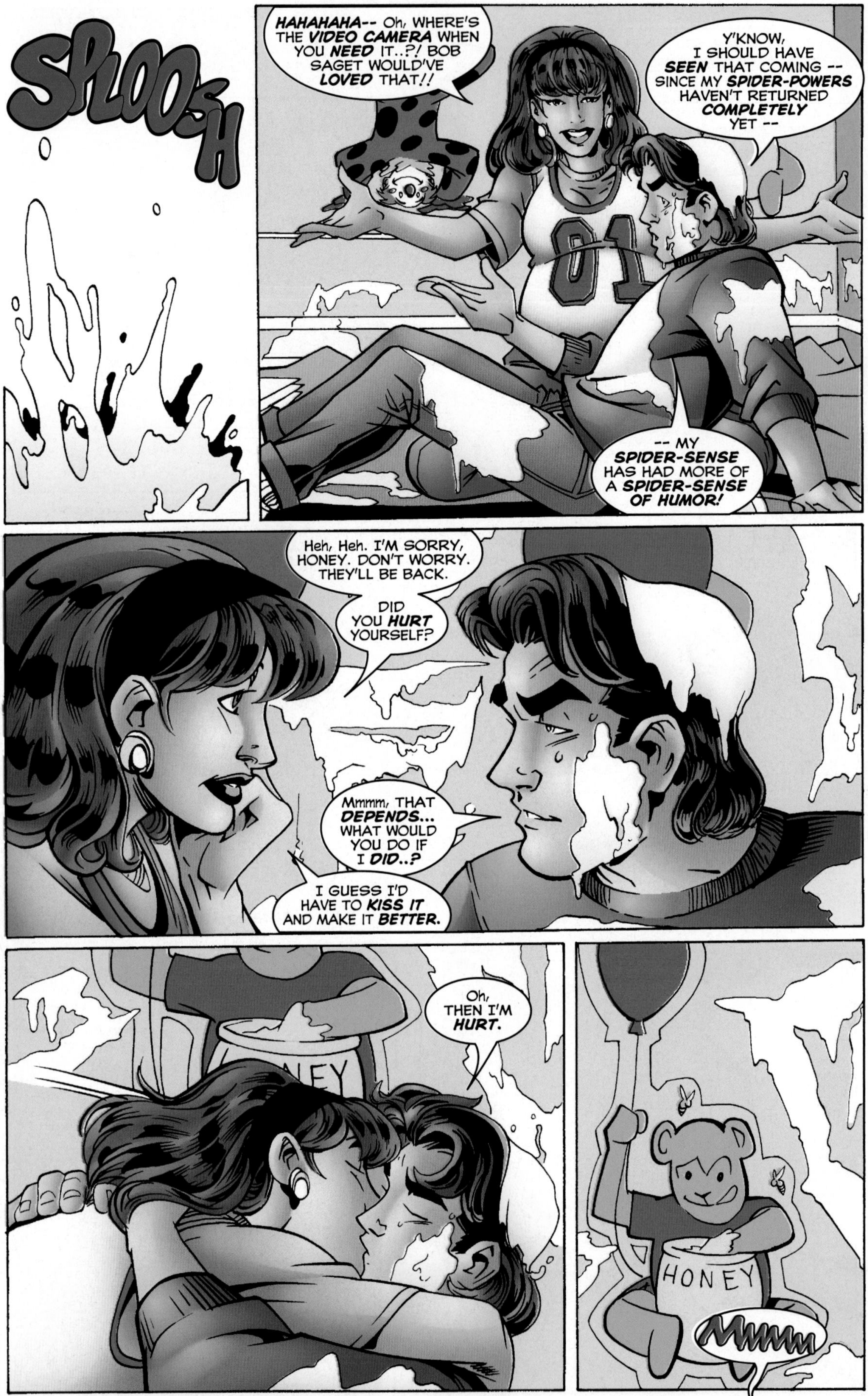

SPLOOSH
HAHAHAHA-- Oh, WHERE'S THE VIDEO CAMERA WHEN YOU NEED IT..?! BOB SAGET WOULD'VE LOVED THAT!!
Y'KNOW, I SHOULD HAVE SEEN THAT COMING -- SINCE MY SPIDER-POWERS HAVEN'T RETURNED COMPLETELY YET --
-- MY SPIDER-SENSE HAS HAD MORE OF A SPIDER-SENSE OF HUMOR!
Heh, Heh. I'M SORRY, HONEY. DON'T WORRY. THEY'LL BE BACK.
DID YOU HURT YOURSELF?
Mmmm, THAT DEPENDS... WHAT WOULD YOU DO IF I DID..?
I GUESS I'D HAVE TO KISS IT AND MAKE IT BETTER.
Oh, THEN I'M HURT.
HONEY
Mmmm

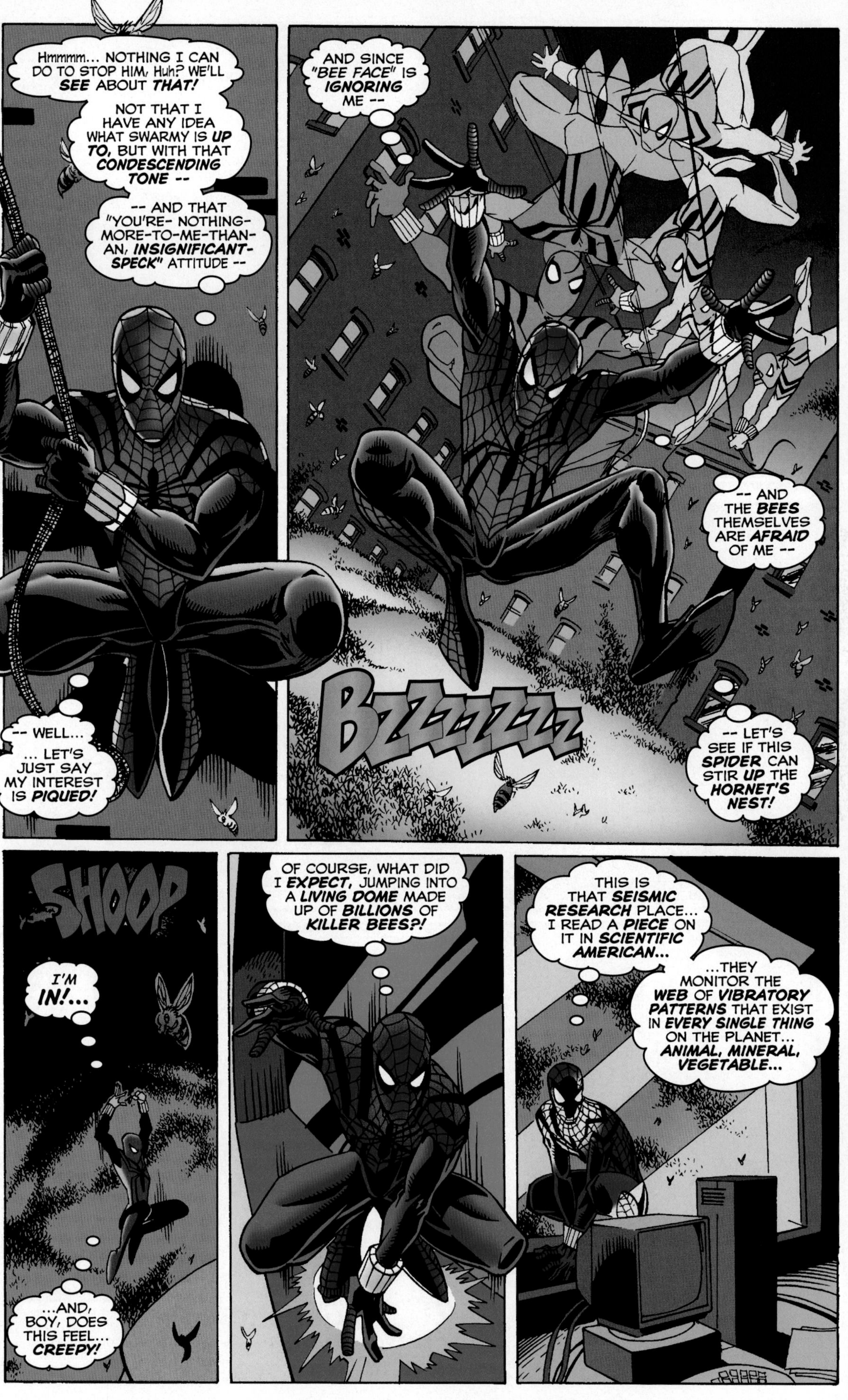
Hmmmm... NOTHING I CAN DO TO STOP HIM, Huh? WE'LL SEE ABOUT THAT!
NOT THAT I HAVE ANY IDEA WHAT SWARMY IS UP TO, BUT WITH THAT CONDESCENDING TONE --
-- AND THAT "YOU'RE- NOTHING- MORE-TO-ME-THAN- AN, INSIGNIFICANT- SPECK" ATTITUDE --
-- WELL...
... LET'S JUST SAY MY INTEREST IS PIQUED!
AND SINCE "BEE FACE" IS IGNORING ME --
-- AND THE BEES THEMSELVES ARE AFRAID OF ME --
BZZZZZZZ
-- LET'S SEE IF THIS SPIDER CAN STIR UP THE HORNET'S NEST!
SHOOP
I'M IN!...
...AND, BOY, DOES THIS FEEL... CREEPY!
OF COURSE, WHAT DID I EXPECT, JUMPING INTO A LIVING DOME MADE UP OF BILLIONS OF KILLER BEES?!
THIS IS THAT SEISMIC RESEARCH PLACE... I READ A PIECE ON IT IN SCIENTIFIC AMERICAN...
...THEY MONITOR THE WEB OF VIBRATORY PATTERNS THAT EXIST IN EVERY SINGLE THING ON THE PLANET... ANIMAL, MINERAL, VEGETABLE...

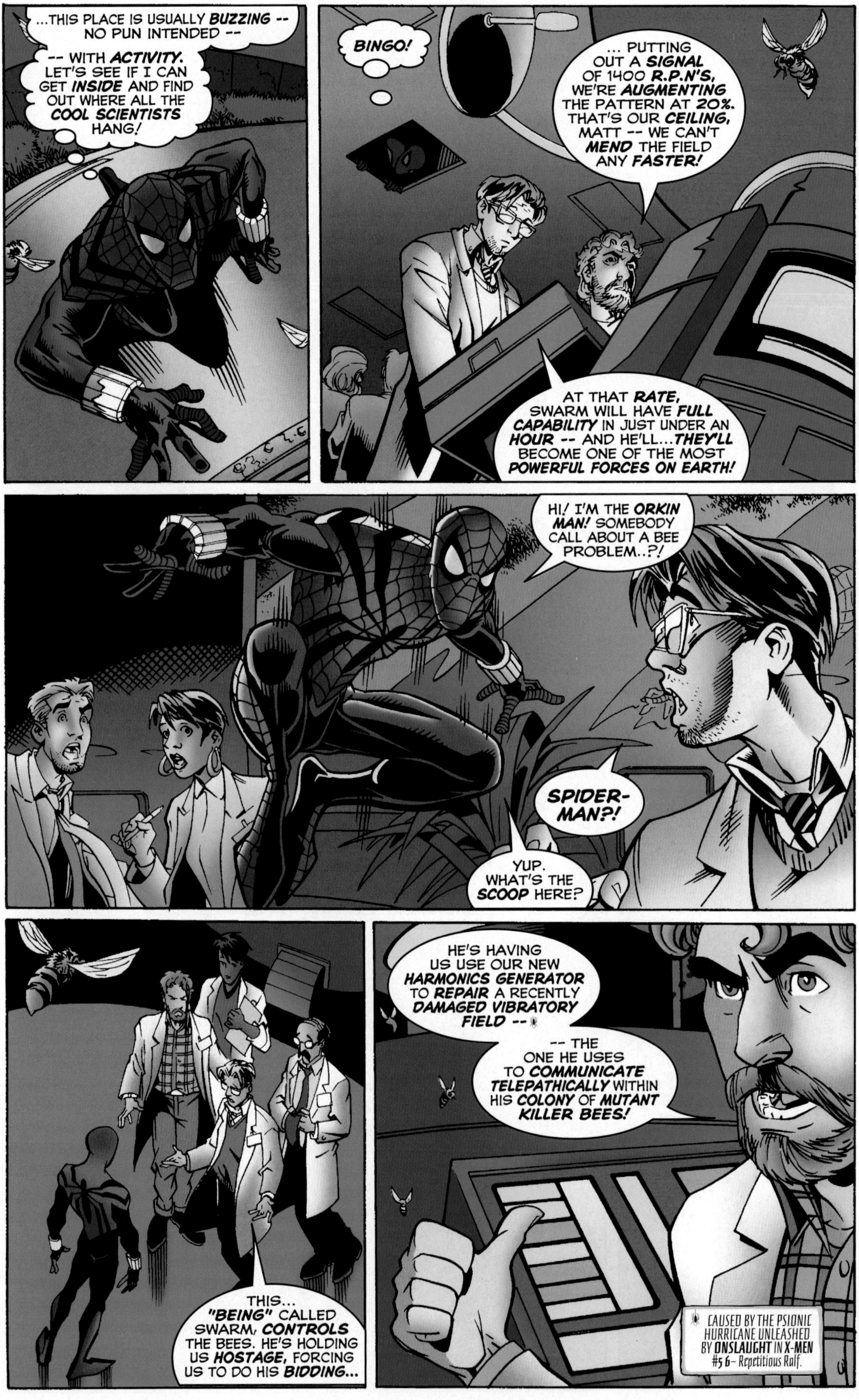
...THIS PLACE IS USUALLY BUZZING -- NO PUN INTENDED --
-- WITH ACTIVITY. LET'S SEE IF I CAN GET INSIDE AND FIND OUT WHERE ALL THE COOL SCIENTISTS HANG!
BINGO!
... PUTTING OUT A SIGNAL OF 1400 R.P.N'S, WE'RE AUGMENTING THE PATTERN AT 20%. THAT'S OUR CEILING, MATT -- WE CAN'T MEND THE FIELD ANY FASTER!
AT THAT RATE, SWARM WILL HAVE FULL CAPABILITY IN JUST UNDER AN HOUR -- AND HE'LL...THEY'LL BECOME ONE OF THE MOST POWERFUL FORCES ON EARTH!
HI! I'M THE ORKIN MAN! SOMEBODY CALL ABOUT A BEE PROBLEM..?!
SPIDER-MAN?!
YUP. WHAT'S THE SCOOP HERE?
THIS... "BEING" CALLED SWARM, CONTROLS THE BEES. HE'S HOLDING US HOSTAGE, FORCING US TO DO HIS BIDDING...
HE'S HAVING US USE OUR NEW HARMONICS GENERATOR TO REPAIR A RECENTLY DAMAGED VIBRATORY FIELD --
-- THE ONE HE USES TO COMMUNICATE TELEPATHICALLY WITHIN HIS COLONY OF MUTANT KILLER BEES!
CAUSED BY THE PSIONIC HURRICANE UNLEASHED BY ONSLAUGHT IN X-MEN #56 – Repetitious Ralf.

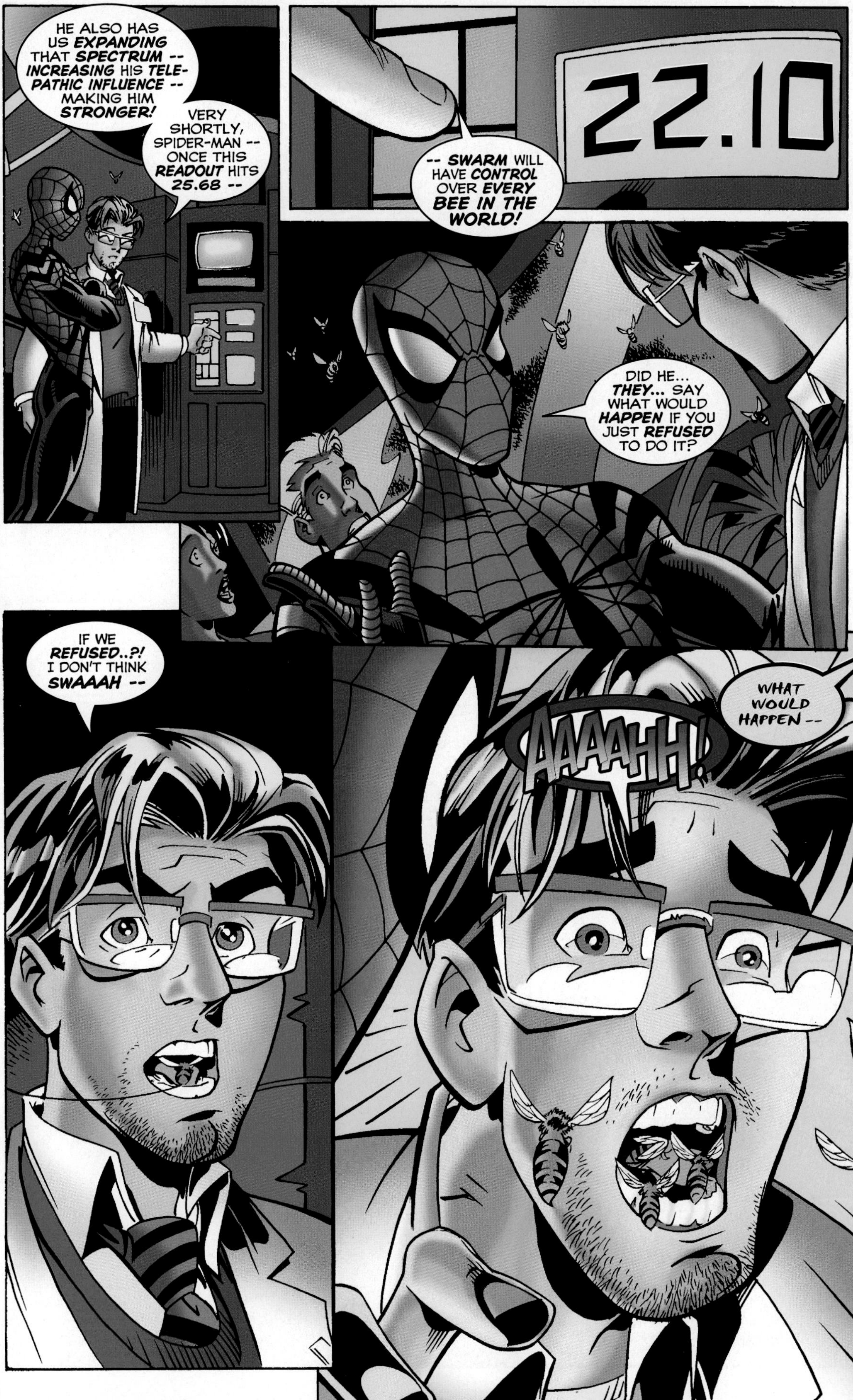
HE ALSO HAS US EXPANDING THAT SPECTRUM -- INCREASING HIS TELEPATHIC INFLUENCE -- MAKING HIM STRONGER!
VERY SHORTLY, SPIDER-MAN -- ONCE THIS READOUT HITS 25.68 --
22.10
-- SWARM WILL HAVE CONTROL OVER EVERY BEE IN THE WORLD!
DID HE... THEY... SAY WHAT WOULD HAPPEN IF YOU JUST REFUSED TO DO IT?
IF WE REFUSED..?! I DON'T THINK SWAAAH --
WHAT WOULD HAPPEN --
AAAAHH!

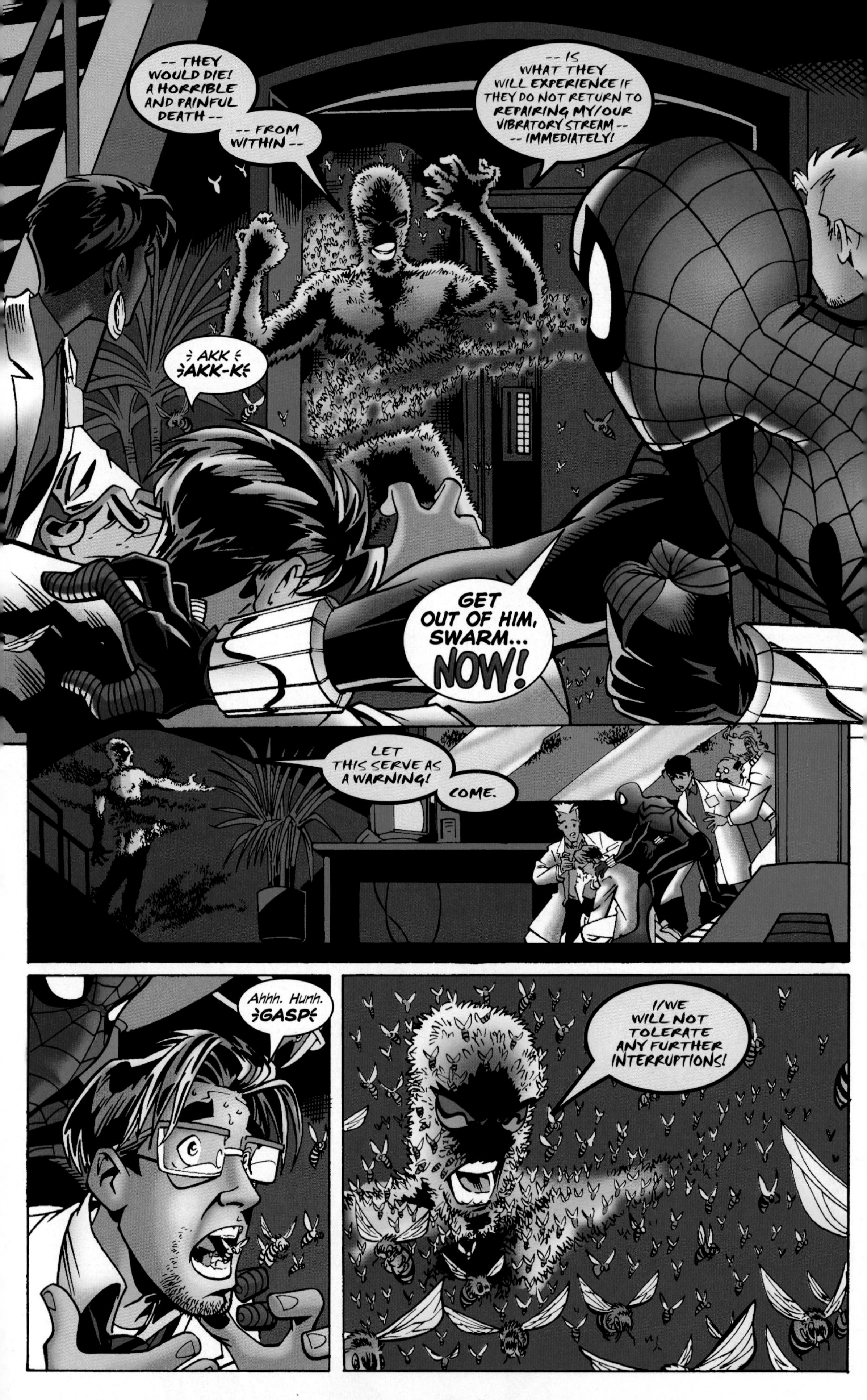
-- THEY WOULD DIE! A HORRIBLE AND PAINFUL DEATH --
-- FROM WITHIN --
-- IS WHAT THEY WILL EXPERIENCE IF THEY DO NOT RETURN TO REPAIRING MY/OUR VIBRATORY STREAM --
-- IMMEDIATELY!
AKK AKK-K
GET OUT OF HIM, SWARM... NOW!
LET THIS SERVE AS A WARNING!
COME.
Ahhh. Hunh. GASP
I/WE WILL NOT TOLERATE ANY FURTHER INTERRUPTIONS!

LISTEN, YOU GUYS -- I CAN'T TELL YOU WHAT TO DO BUT I'VE GOT AN *IDEA*..!

IF I REMEMBER MY *BIOLOGY* -- AND I THINK I *DO* -- BEES DON'T FLY LIKE *BIRDS* DO -- THEY DON'T *RIDE* THE AIR CURRENTS --

-- THEY *CUT THROUGH THEM* BY MOVING THEIR WINGS SO *FAST* THEY CREATE A *VIBRATORY PATTERN* THAT THEY *RIDE ON!*

SAME GOES FOR *HUMMINGBIRDS.*

SO... WITH THAT IN MIND --

-- DO YOU THINK ANY OF THIS *FANCY EQUIPMENT* COULD ...

...I DON'T KNOW... *DISRUPT* THAT?

YYYEAH, WE COULD DO THAT... BUT...

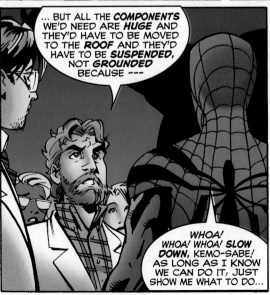

... BUT ALL THE *COMPONENTS* WE'D NEED ARE *HUGE* AND THEY'D HAVE TO BE MOVED TO THE *ROOF* AND THEY'D HAVE TO BE *SUSPENDED,* NOT *GROUNDED* BECAUSE ---

WHOA! WHOA! WHOA! SLOW DOWN, KEMO-SABE! AS LONG AS I KNOW WE CAN DO IT, JUST SHOW ME WHAT TO DO...

...'CAUSE *TIME* IS *RUNNING OUT!*

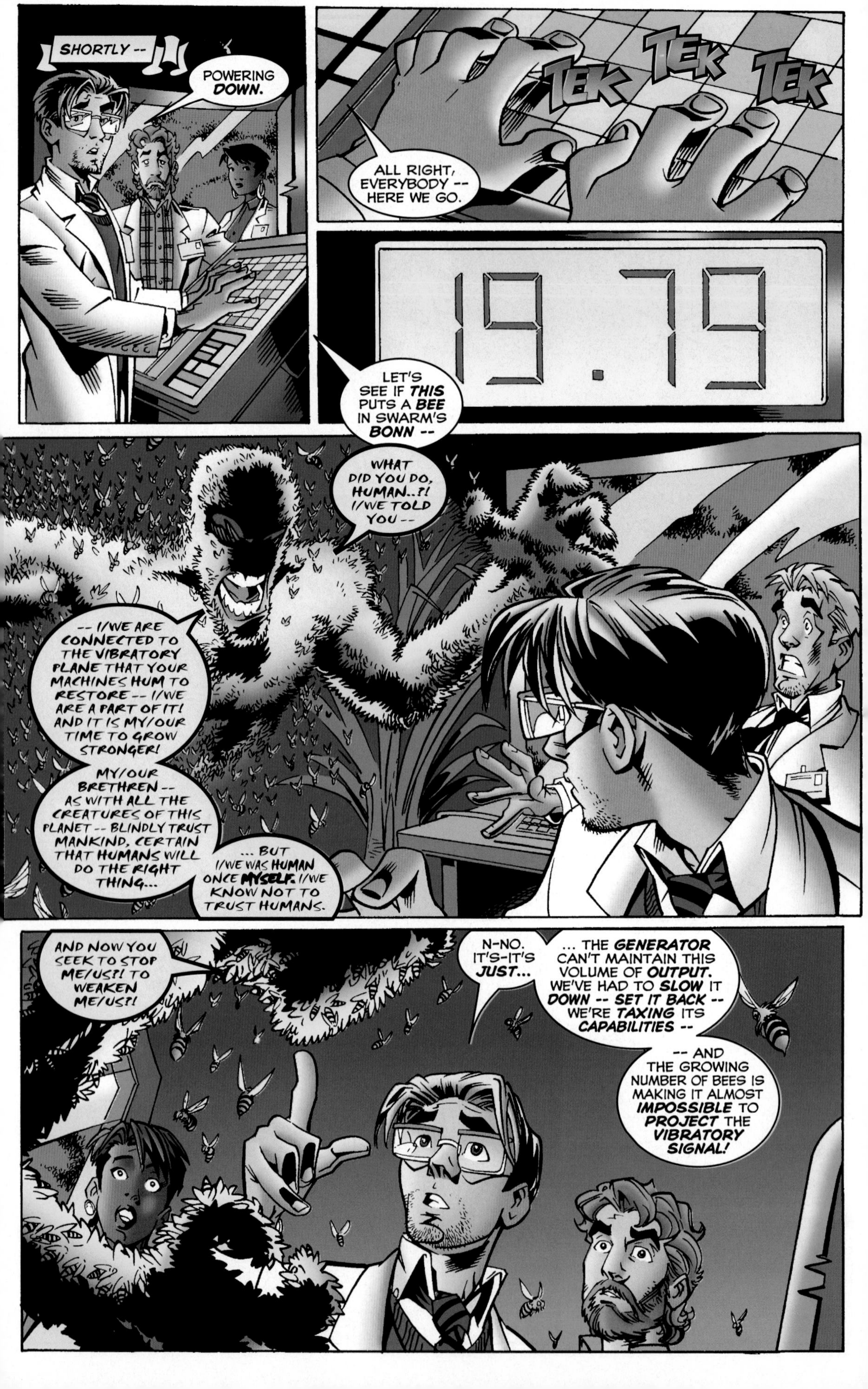
SHORTLY --
POWERING DOWN.
TEK TEK TEK
ALL RIGHT, EVERYBODY -- HERE WE GO.
19.79
LET'S SEE IF THIS PUTS A BEE IN SWARM'S BONN --
WHAT DID YOU DO, HUMAN..?! I/WE TOLD YOU --
-- I/WE ARE CONNECTED TO THE VIBRATORY PLANE THAT YOUR MACHINES HUM TO RESTORE -- I/WE ARE A PART OF IT! AND IT IS MY/OUR TIME TO GROW STRONGER!
MY/OUR BRETHREN -- AS WITH ALL THE CREATURES OF THIS PLANET -- BLINDLY TRUST MANKIND, CERTAIN THAT HUMANS WILL DO THE RIGHT THING...
... BUT I/WE WAS HUMAN ONCE MYSELF. I/WE KNOW NOT TO TRUST HUMANS.
AND NOW YOU SEEK TO STOP ME/US?! TO WEAKEN ME/US?!
N-NO. IT'S-IT'S JUST...
... THE GENERATOR CAN'T MAINTAIN THIS VOLUME OF OUTPUT. WE'VE HAD TO SLOW IT DOWN -- SET IT BACK -- WE'RE TAXING ITS CAPABILITIES --
-- AND THE GROWING NUMBER OF BEES IS MAKING IT ALMOST IMPOSSIBLE TO PROJECT THE VIBRATORY SIGNAL!

WE CAN DO IT! WE HAVE THE *TECHNOLOGY!* BUT MUCH OF THAT *EQUIPMENT* IS *TOO HEAVY!* NO WAY COULD *ANY OF US* GET THAT STUFF UP TO THE --

NO! THE PSIONIC FIELD MUST BE RESTORED! I/WE NEED... NEED...

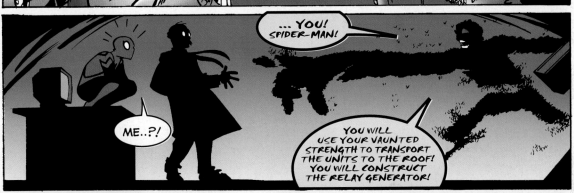

... YOU! SPIDER-MAN!

ME..?!

YOU WILL USE YOUR VAUNTED STRENGTH TO TRANSPORT THE UNITS TO THE ROOF! YOU WILL CONSTRUCT THE RELAY GENERATOR!

AND YOU WILL DO IT, OR --

WHA -- HEY!

BUZZZ

NO! WAIT! -- I'LL DO IT.

LET HIM GO.

HE BOUGHT IT.

REELED HIM IN.

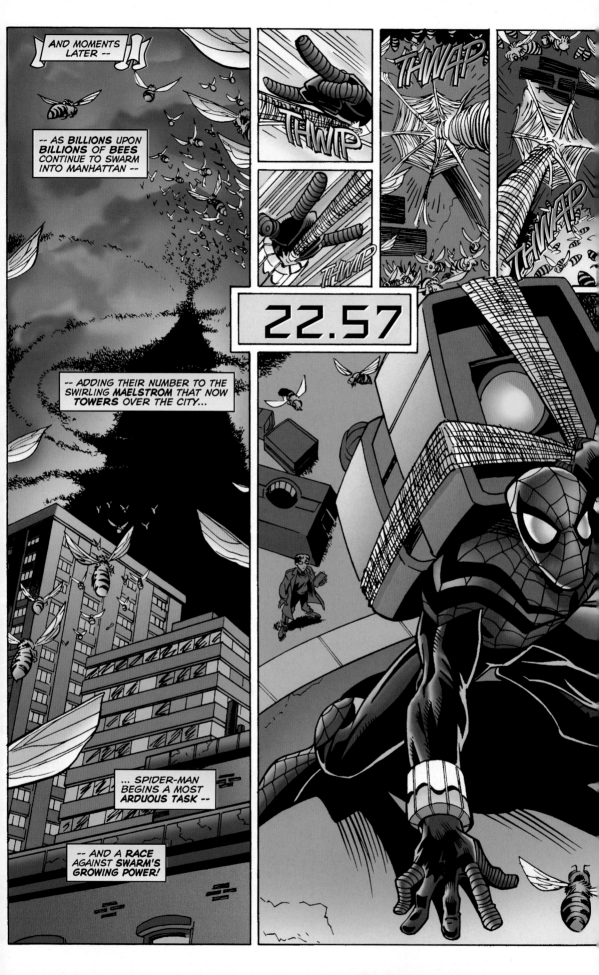

AND MOMENTS LATER --

-- AS BILLIONS UPON **BILLIONS** OF BEES CONTINUE TO SWARM INTO MANHATTAN --

-- ADDING THEIR NUMBER TO THE SWIRLING **MAELSTROM** THAT NOW **TOWERS** OVER THE CITY...

THWIP

THWIP

THWAP

THWAP

THWAP

22.57

... SPIDER-MAN BEGINS A MOST **ARDUOUS TASK** --

-- AND A **RACE** AGAINST **SWARM'S** GROWING POWER!

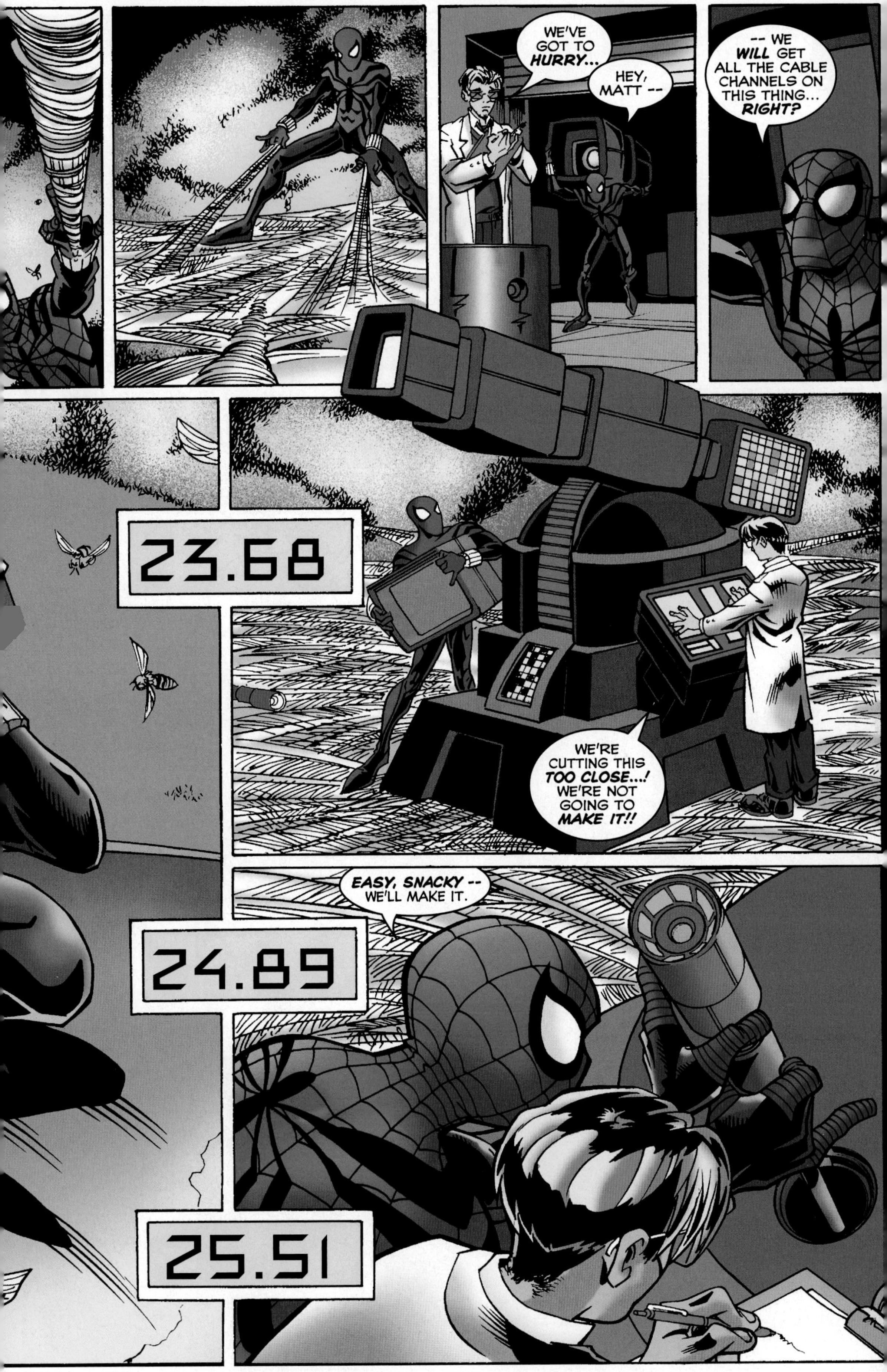
WE'VE GOT TO HURRY...
HEY, MATT --
-- WE WILL GET ALL THE CABLE CHANNELS ON THIS THING... RIGHT?
23.68
WE'RE CUTTING THIS TOO CLOSE...! WE'RE NOT GOING TO MAKE IT!!
EASY, SNACKY -- WE'LL MAKE IT.
24.89
25.51

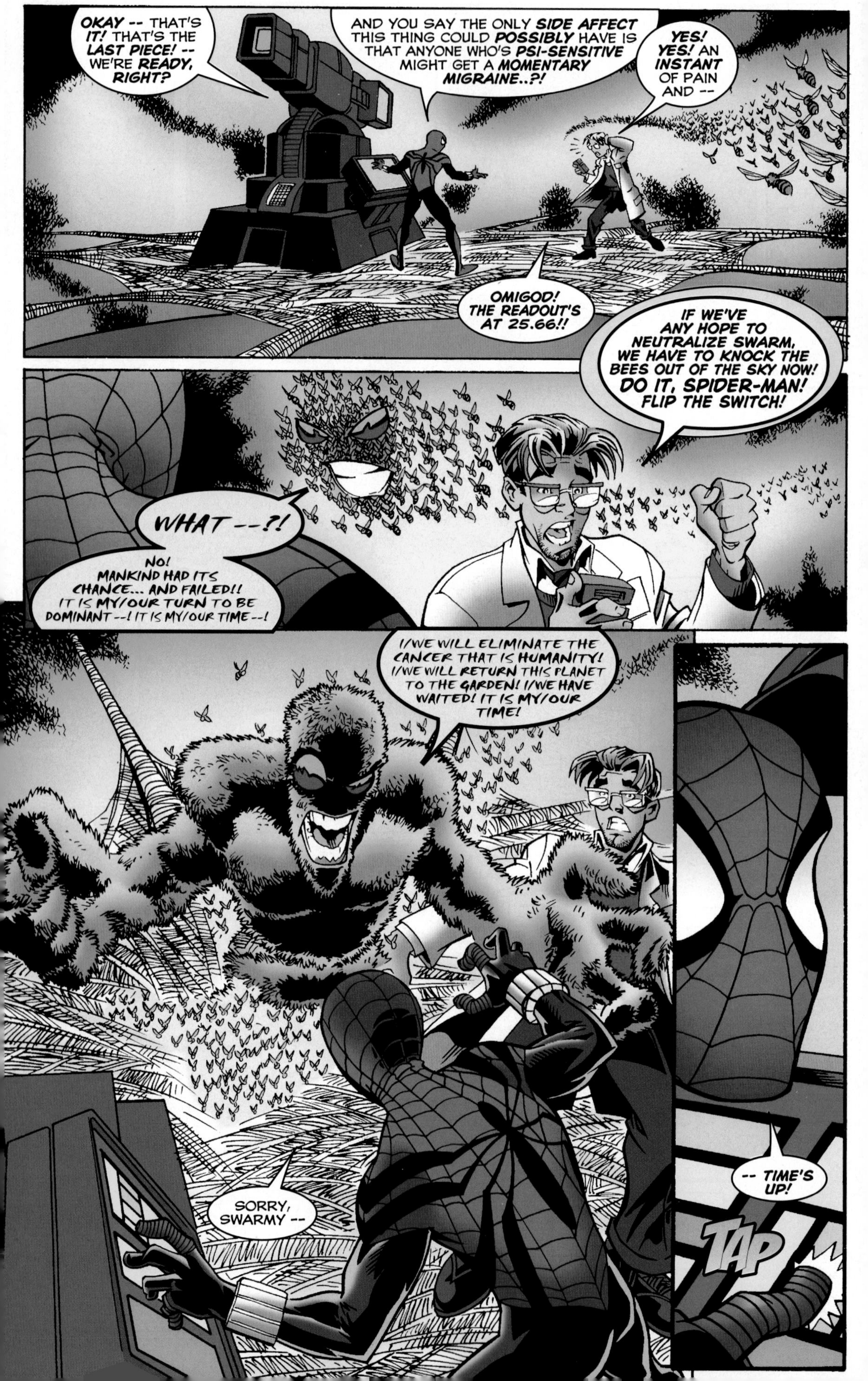
OKAY -- THAT'S IT! THAT'S THE LAST PIECE! -- WE'RE READY, RIGHT?
AND YOU SAY THE ONLY SIDE AFFECT THIS THING COULD POSSIBLY HAVE IS THAT ANYONE WHO'S PSI-SENSITIVE MIGHT GET A MOMENTARY MIGRAINE..?!
YES! YES! AN INSTANT OF PAIN AND --
OMIGOD! THE READOUT'S AT 25.66!!
IF WE'VE ANY HOPE TO NEUTRALIZE SWARM, WE HAVE TO KNOCK THE BEES OUT OF THE SKY NOW! DO IT, SPIDER-MAN! FLIP THE SWITCH!
WHAT --?!
NO! MANKIND HAD ITS CHANCE... AND FAILED!! IT IS MY/OUR TURN TO BE DOMINANT --! IT IS MY/OUR TIME --!
I/WE WILL ELIMINATE THE CANCER THAT IS HUMANITY! I/WE WILL RETURN THIS PLANET TO THE GARDEN! I/WE HAVE WAITED! IT IS MY/OUR TIME!
SORRY, SWARMY --
-- TIME'S UP!
TAP

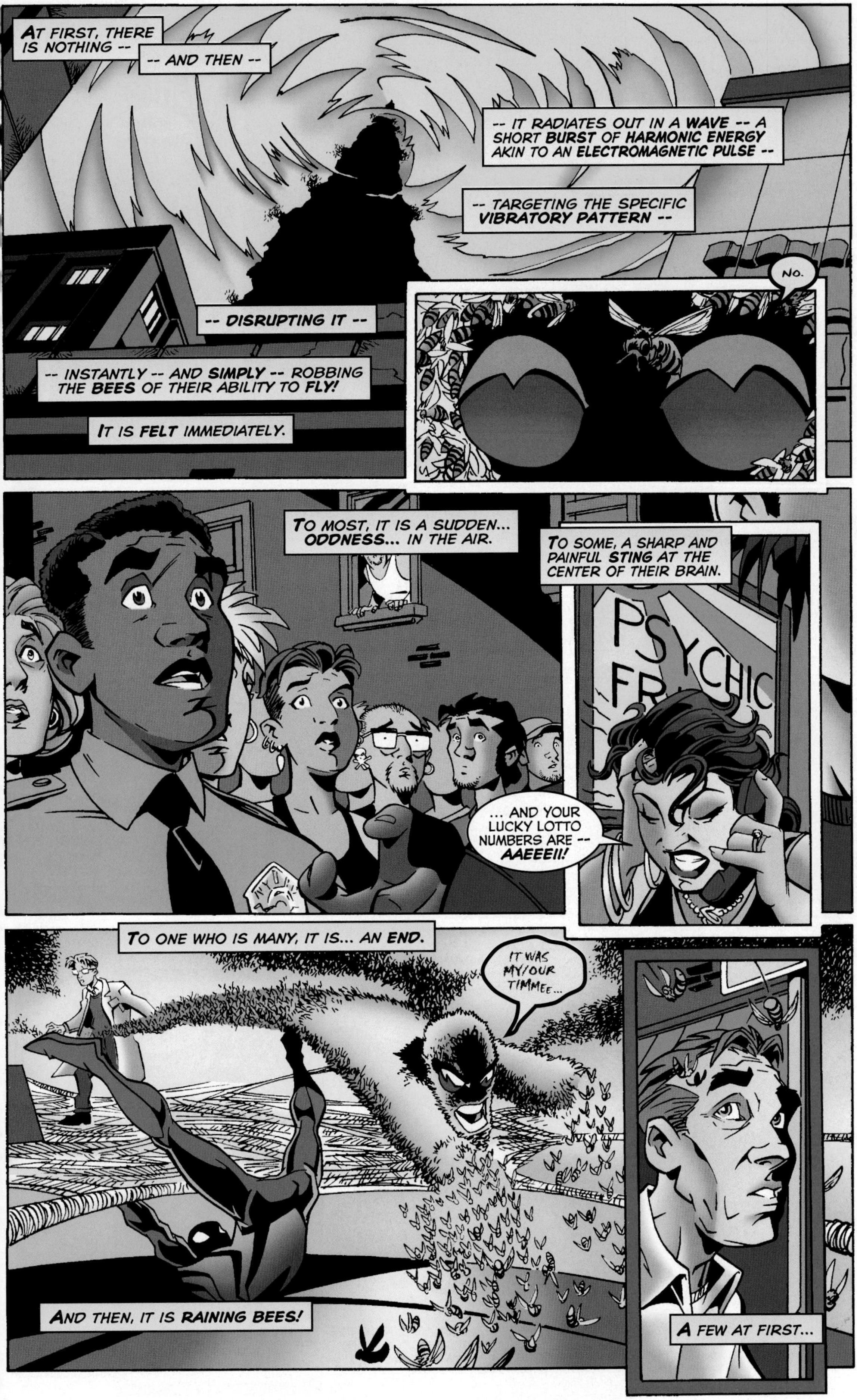
AT FIRST, THERE IS NOTHING --
-- AND THEN --
-- IT RADIATES OUT IN A WAVE -- A SHORT BURST OF HARMONIC ENERGY AKIN TO AN ELECTROMAGNETIC PULSE --
-- TARGETING THE SPECIFIC VIBRATORY PATTERN --
-- DISRUPTING IT --
-- INSTANTLY -- AND SIMPLY -- ROBBING THE BEES OF THEIR ABILITY TO FLY!
IT IS FELT IMMEDIATELY.
NO.
TO MOST, IT IS A SUDDEN... ODDNESS... IN THE AIR.
TO SOME, A SHARP AND PAINFUL STING AT THE CENTER OF THEIR BRAIN.
PSYCHIC
... AND YOUR LUCKY LOTTO NUMBERS ARE -- AAEEEII!
TO ONE WHO IS MANY, IT IS... AN END.
IT WAS MY/OUR TIMMEE...
AND THEN, IT IS RAINING BEES!
A FEW AT FIRST...

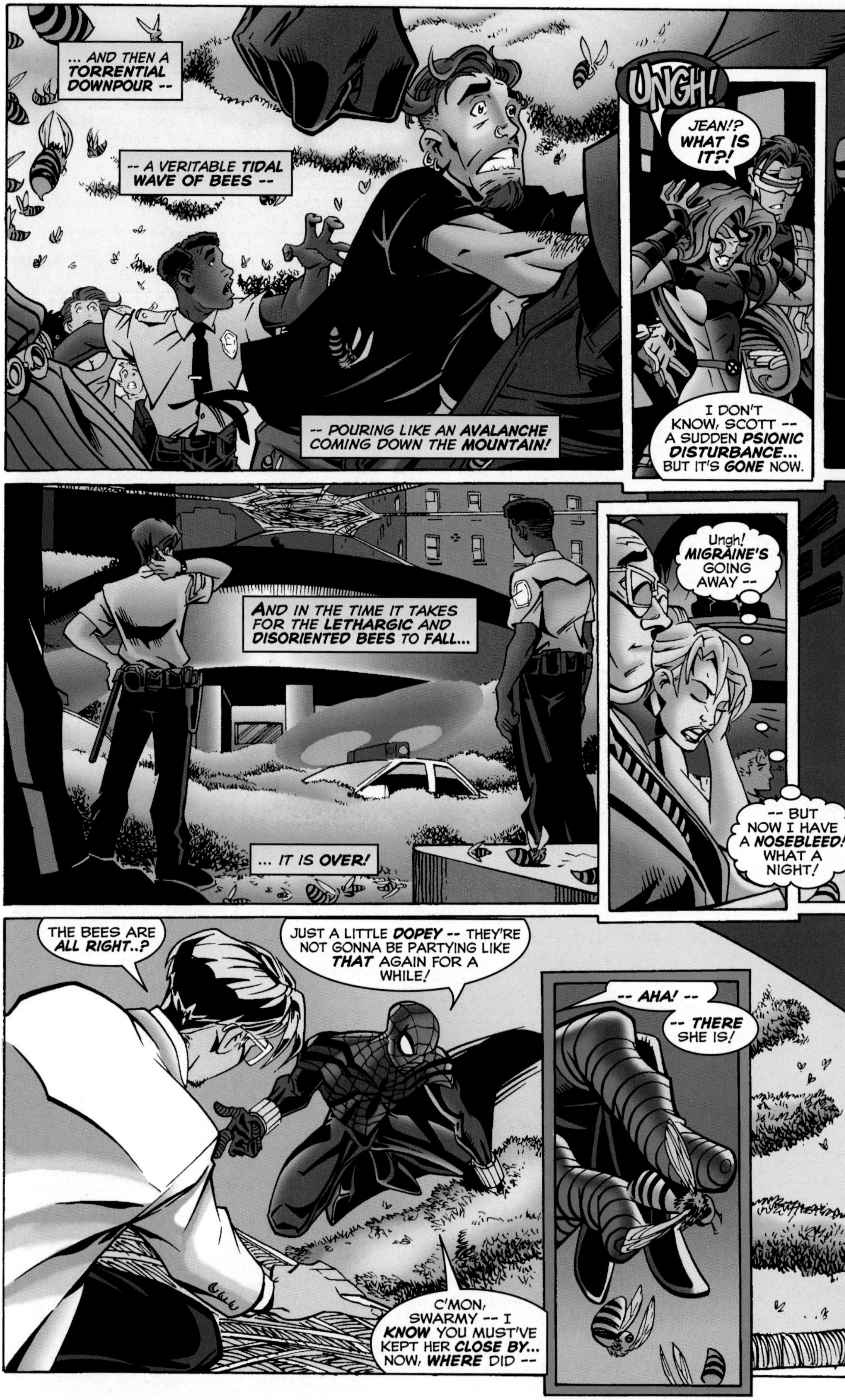
... AND THEN A TORRENTIAL DOWNPOUR --
-- A VERITABLE TIDAL WAVE OF BEES --
-- POURING LIKE AN AVALANCHE COMING DOWN THE MOUNTAIN!
UNGH!
JEAN!? WHAT IS IT?!
I DON'T KNOW, SCOTT -- A SUDDEN PSIONIC DISTURBANCE... BUT IT'S GONE NOW.
AND IN THE TIME IT TAKES FOR THE LETHARGIC AND DISORIENTED BEES TO FALL...
... IT IS OVER!
Ungh! MIGRAINE'S GOING AWAY --
-- BUT NOW I HAVE A NOSEBLEED! WHAT A NIGHT!
THE BEES ARE ALL RIGHT..?
JUST A LITTLE DOPEY -- THEY'RE NOT GONNA BE PARTYING LIKE THAT AGAIN FOR A WHILE!
C'MON, SWARMY -- I KNOW YOU MUST'VE KEPT HER CLOSE BY... NOW, WHERE DID --
-- AHA! --
-- THERE SHE IS!

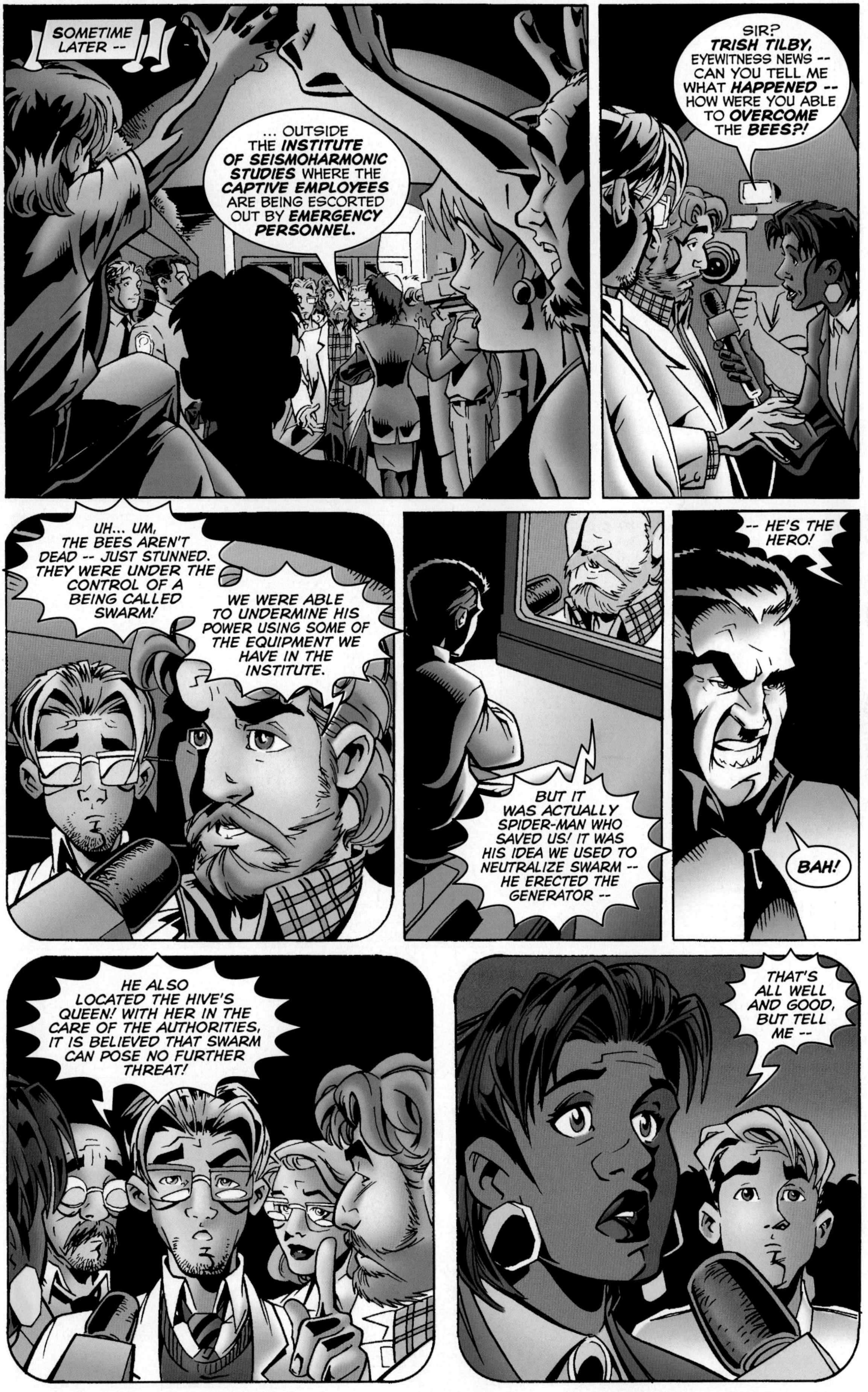
SOMETIME LATER --
... OUTSIDE THE INSTITUTE OF SEISMOHARMONIC STUDIES WHERE THE CAPTIVE EMPLOYEES ARE BEING ESCORTED OUT BY EMERGENCY PERSONNEL.
SIR? TRISH TILBY, EYEWITNESS NEWS -- CAN YOU TELL ME WHAT HAPPENED -- HOW WERE YOU ABLE TO OVERCOME THE BEES?!
UH... UM, THE BEES AREN'T DEAD -- JUST STUNNED. THEY WERE UNDER THE CONTROL OF A BEING CALLED SWARM!
WE WERE ABLE TO UNDERMINE HIS POWER USING SOME OF THE EQUIPMENT WE HAVE IN THE INSTITUTE.
BUT IT WAS ACTUALLY SPIDER-MAN WHO SAVED US! IT WAS HIS IDEA WE USED TO NEUTRALIZE SWARM -- HE ERECTED THE GENERATOR --
-- HE'S THE HERO!
BAH!
HE ALSO LOCATED THE HIVE'S QUEEN! WITH HER IN THE CARE OF THE AUTHORITIES, IT IS BELIEVED THAT SWARM CAN POSE NO FURTHER THREAT!
THAT'S ALL WELL AND GOOD, BUT TELL ME --

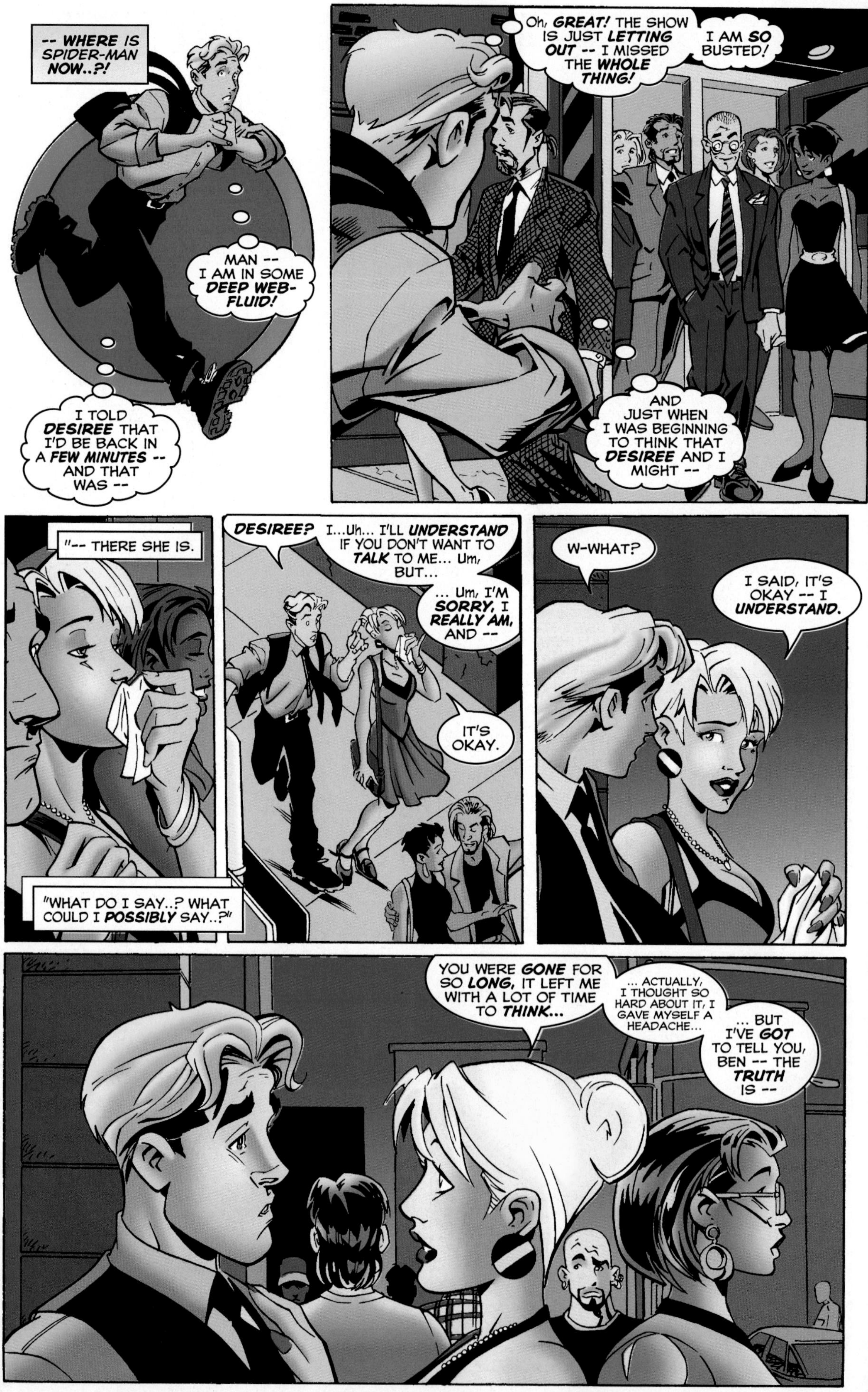
-- WHERE IS SPIDER-MAN NOW..?!
MAN -- I AM IN SOME DEEP WEB-FLUID!
I TOLD DESIREE THAT I'D BE BACK IN A FEW MINUTES -- AND THAT WAS --
Oh, GREAT! THE SHOW IS JUST LETTING OUT -- I MISSED THE WHOLE THING!
I AM SO BUSTED!
AND JUST WHEN I WAS BEGINNING TO THINK THAT DESIREE AND I MIGHT --
"-- THERE SHE IS.
"WHAT DO I SAY..? WHAT COULD I POSSIBLY SAY..?"
DESIREE?
I...Uh... I'LL UNDERSTAND IF YOU DON'T WANT TO TALK TO ME... Um, BUT...
... Um, I'M SORRY, I REALLY AM, AND --
IT'S OKAY.
W-WHAT?
I SAID, IT'S OKAY -- I UNDERSTAND.
YOU WERE GONE FOR SO LONG, IT LEFT ME WITH A LOT OF TIME TO THINK...
... ACTUALLY, I THOUGHT SO HARD ABOUT IT, I GAVE MYSELF A HEADACHE...
... BUT I'VE GOT TO TELL YOU, BEN -- THE TRUTH IS --

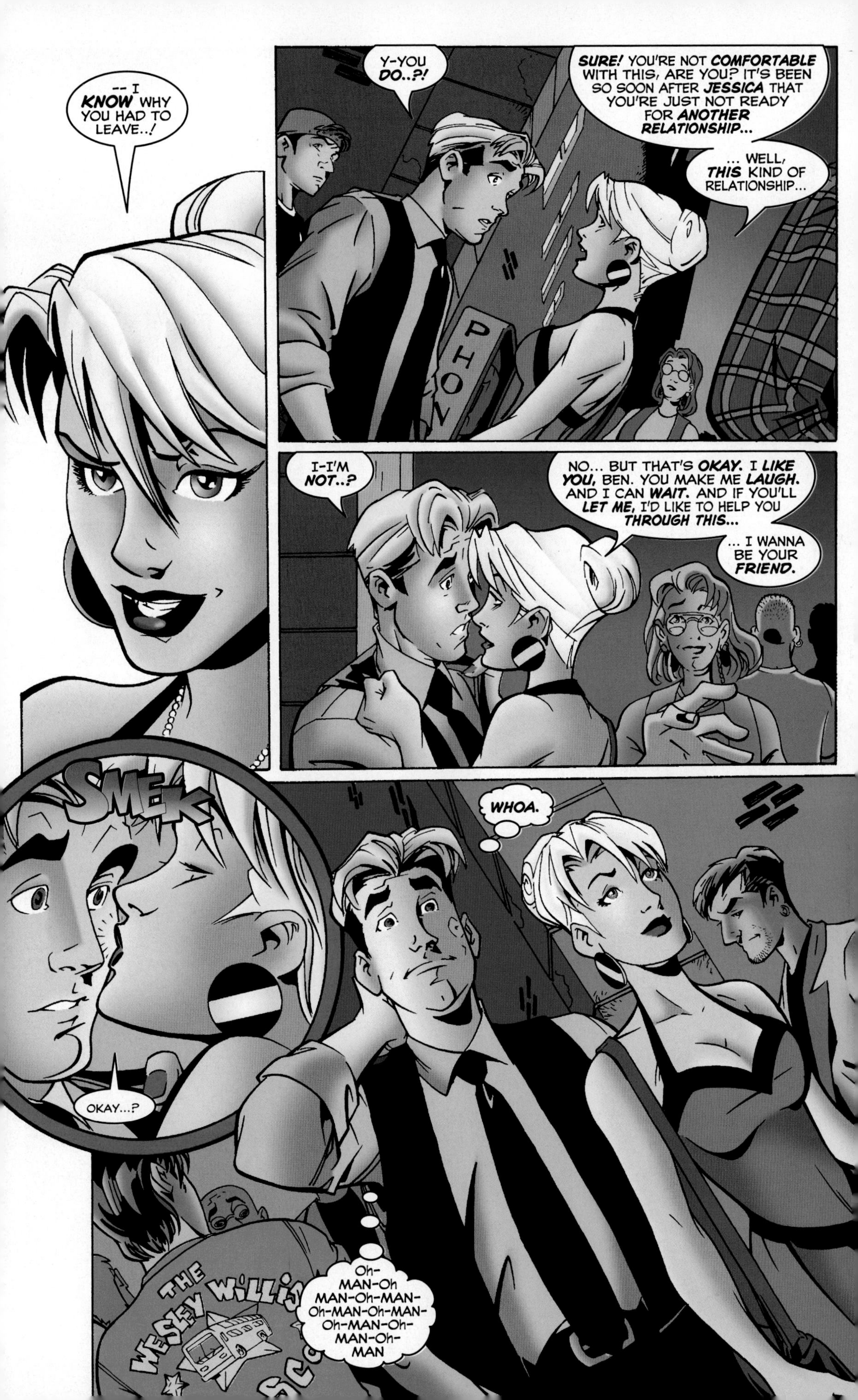
-- I KNOW WHY YOU HAD TO LEAVE..!
Y-YOU DO..?!
SURE! YOU'RE NOT COMFORTABLE WITH THIS, ARE YOU? IT'S BEEN SO SOON AFTER JESSICA THAT YOU'RE JUST NOT READY FOR ANOTHER RELATIONSHIP...
... WELL, THIS KIND OF RELATIONSHIP...
PHON
I-I'M NOT..?
NO... BUT THAT'S OKAY. I LIKE YOU, BEN. YOU MAKE ME LAUGH. AND I CAN WAIT. AND IF YOU'LL LET ME, I'D LIKE TO HELP YOU THROUGH THIS...
... I WANNA BE YOUR FRIEND.
SMEK
OKAY...?
WHOA.
Oh-MAN-Oh MAN-Oh-MAN-Oh-MAN-Oh-MAN-Oh-MAN-Oh-MAN-Oh MAN
THE WESLEY WILLIS

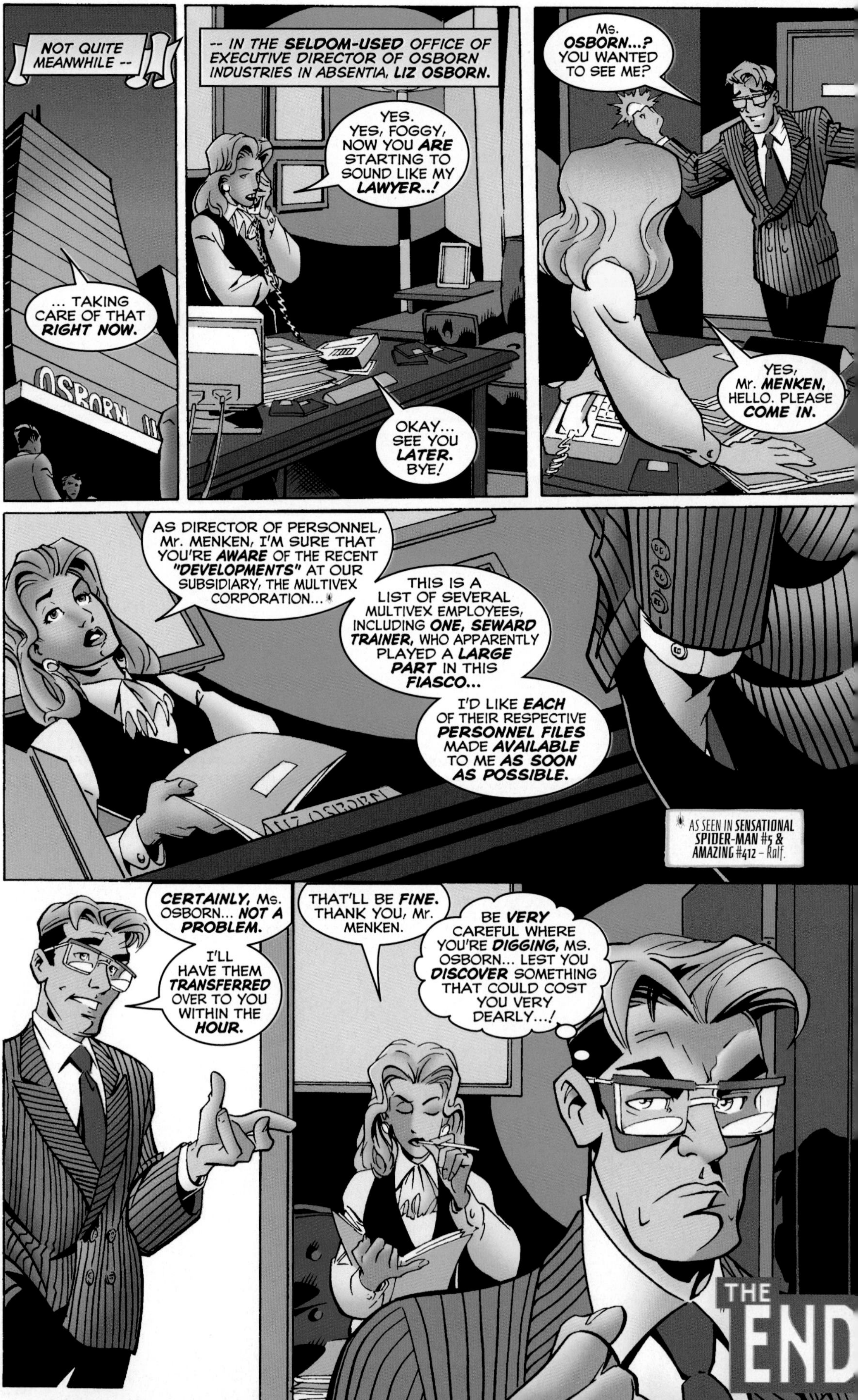
NOT QUITE MEANWHILE --
... TAKING CARE OF THAT RIGHT NOW.
OSBORN
-- IN THE SELDOM-USED OFFICE OF EXECUTIVE DIRECTOR OF OSBORN INDUSTRIES IN ABSENTIA, LIZ OSBORN.
YES. YES, FOGGY, NOW YOU ARE STARTING TO SOUND LIKE MY LAWYER..!
OKAY... SEE YOU LATER. BYE!
Ms. OSBORN...? YOU WANTED TO SEE ME?
YES, Mr. MENKEN, HELLO. PLEASE COME IN.
AS DIRECTOR OF PERSONNEL, Mr. MENKEN, I'M SURE THAT YOU'RE AWARE OF THE RECENT "DEVELOPMENTS" AT OUR SUBSIDIARY, THE MULTIVEX CORPORATION...
THIS IS A LIST OF SEVERAL MULTIVEX EMPLOYEES, INCLUDING ONE, SEWARD TRAINER, WHO APPARENTLY PLAYED A LARGE PART IN THIS FIASCO...
I'D LIKE EACH OF THEIR RESPECTIVE PERSONNEL FILES MADE AVAILABLE TO ME AS SOON AS POSSIBLE.
AS SEEN IN SENSATIONAL SPIDER-MAN #5 & AMAZING #412 – Ralf.
CERTAINLY, Ms. OSBORN... NOT A PROBLEM.
I'LL HAVE THEM TRANSFERRED OVER TO YOU WITHIN THE HOUR.
THAT'LL BE FINE. THANK YOU, Mr. MENKEN.
BE VERY CAREFUL WHERE YOU'RE DIGGING, MS. OSBORN... LEST YOU DISCOVER SOMETHING THAT COULD COST YOU VERY DEARLY...!
THE END

IN SPECTACULAR SPIDER-MAN #240, "REVELATIONS" PART 1, BEN'S FRIEND DR. SEWARD TRAINER WAS FORCED TO REVIVE A VILLAIN CALLED GAUNT FOR A MYSTERIOUS MASTERMIND WHO HAD BEEN TARGETING BEN AND PETER FOR SOME TIME. SEWARD IMPLIED THAT HE WAS ALSO MADE TO INTERFERE IN THE TEST THAT DETERMINED WHICH OF THEM WAS THE CLONE. WHEN SEWARD DISCOVERED THE MASTERMIND'S IDENTITY HE TRIED TO WARN BEN, BUT GAUNT AND THE MASTERMIND KILLED HIM. MEANWHILE, A MENACING WOMAN NAMED ALISON MONGRAIN TOOK A JOB AT THE DAILY GRIND…

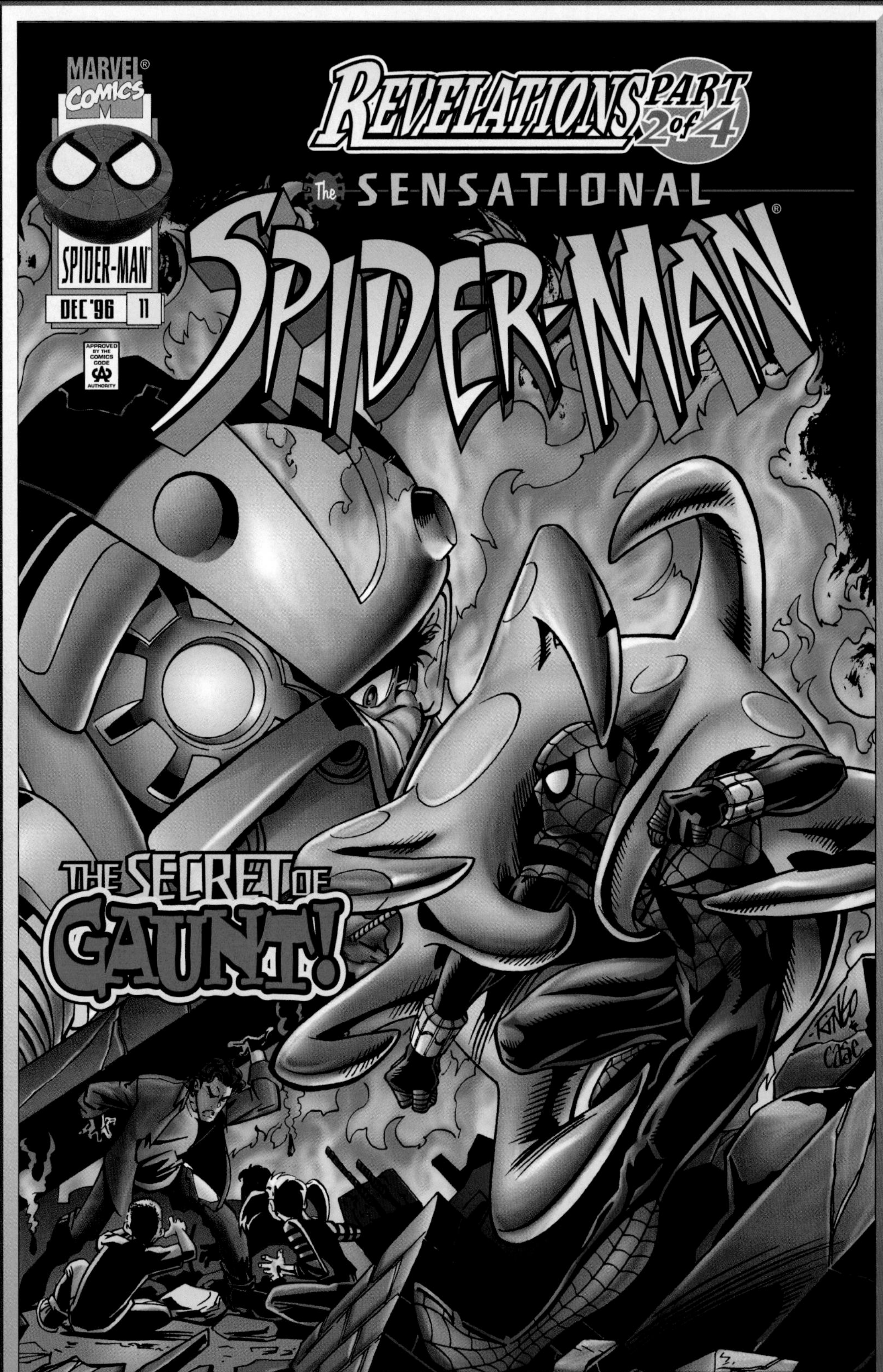

MARVEL COMICS
REVELATIONS PART 2 of 4
The SENSATIONAL SPIDER-MAN
SPIDER-MAN
DEC '96 11
APPROVED BY THE COMICS CODE AUTHORITY
THE SECRET OF GAUNT!

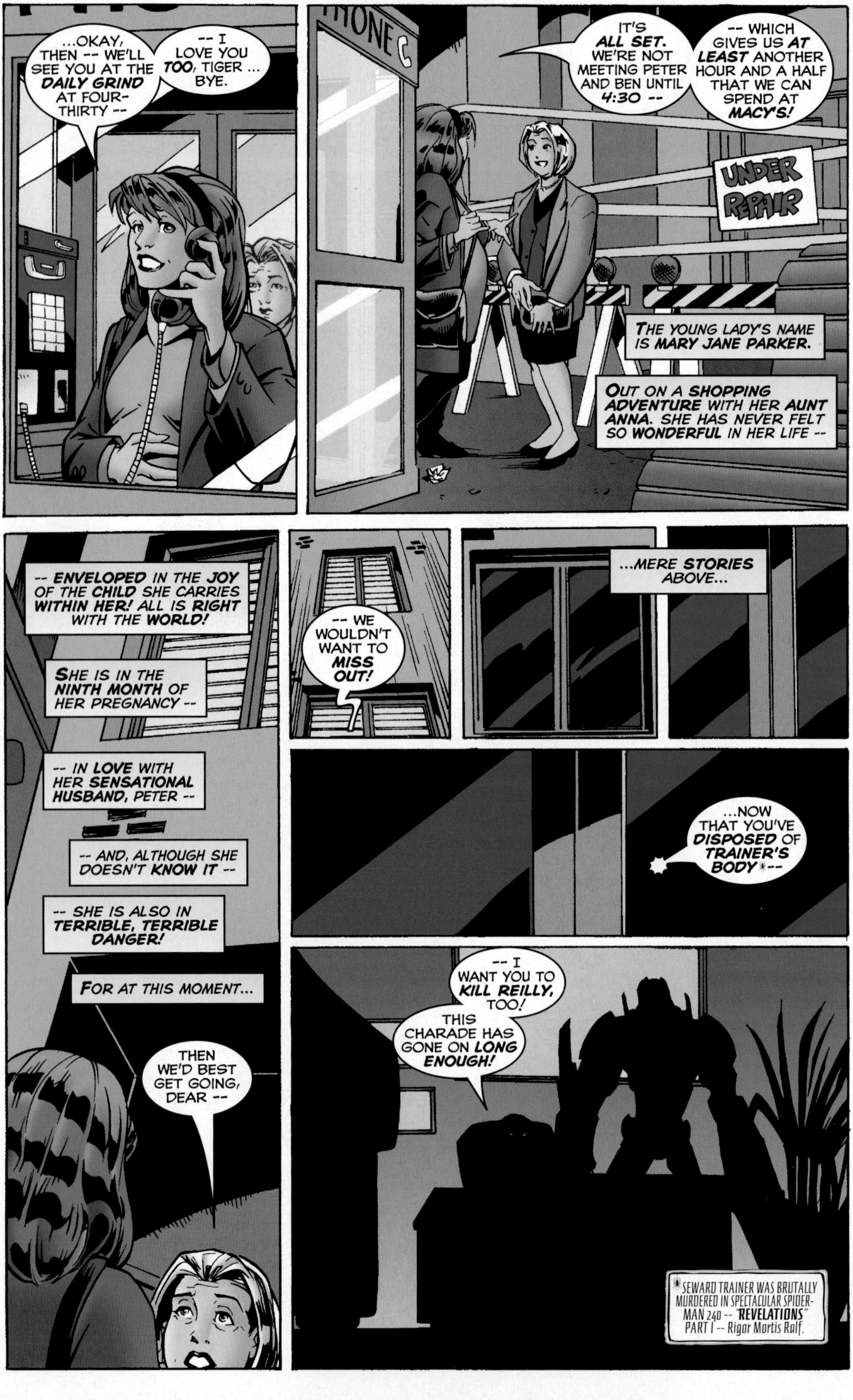

...OKAY, THEN -- WE'LL SEE YOU AT THE DAILY GRIND AT FOUR-THIRTY --
-- I LOVE YOU TOO, TIGER ... BYE.
PHONE
IT'S ALL SET. WE'RE NOT MEETING PETER AND BEN UNTIL 4:30 --
-- WHICH GIVES US AT LEAST ANOTHER HOUR AND A HALF THAT WE CAN SPEND AT MACY'S!
UNDER REPAIR
THE YOUNG LADY'S NAME IS MARY JANE PARKER.
OUT ON A SHOPPING ADVENTURE WITH HER AUNT ANNA. SHE HAS NEVER FELT SO WONDERFUL IN HER LIFE --
-- ENVELOPED IN THE JOY OF THE CHILD SHE CARRIES WITHIN HER! ALL IS RIGHT WITH THE WORLD!
SHE IS IN THE NINTH MONTH OF HER PREGNANCY --
-- IN LOVE WITH HER SENSATIONAL HUSBAND, PETER --
-- AND, ALTHOUGH SHE DOESN'T KNOW IT --
-- SHE IS ALSO IN TERRIBLE, TERRIBLE DANGER!
FOR AT THIS MOMENT...
THEN WE'D BEST GET GOING, DEAR --
-- WE WOULDN'T WANT TO MISS OUT!
...MERE STORIES ABOVE...
...NOW THAT YOU'VE DISPOSED OF TRAINER'S BODY --
-- I WANT YOU TO KILL REILLY, TOO!
THIS CHARADE HAS GONE ON LONG ENOUGH!
SEWARD TRAINER WAS BRUTALLY MURDERED IN SPECTACULAR SPIDER-MAN 240 -- "REVELATIONS" PART I -- Rigor Mortis Ralf.

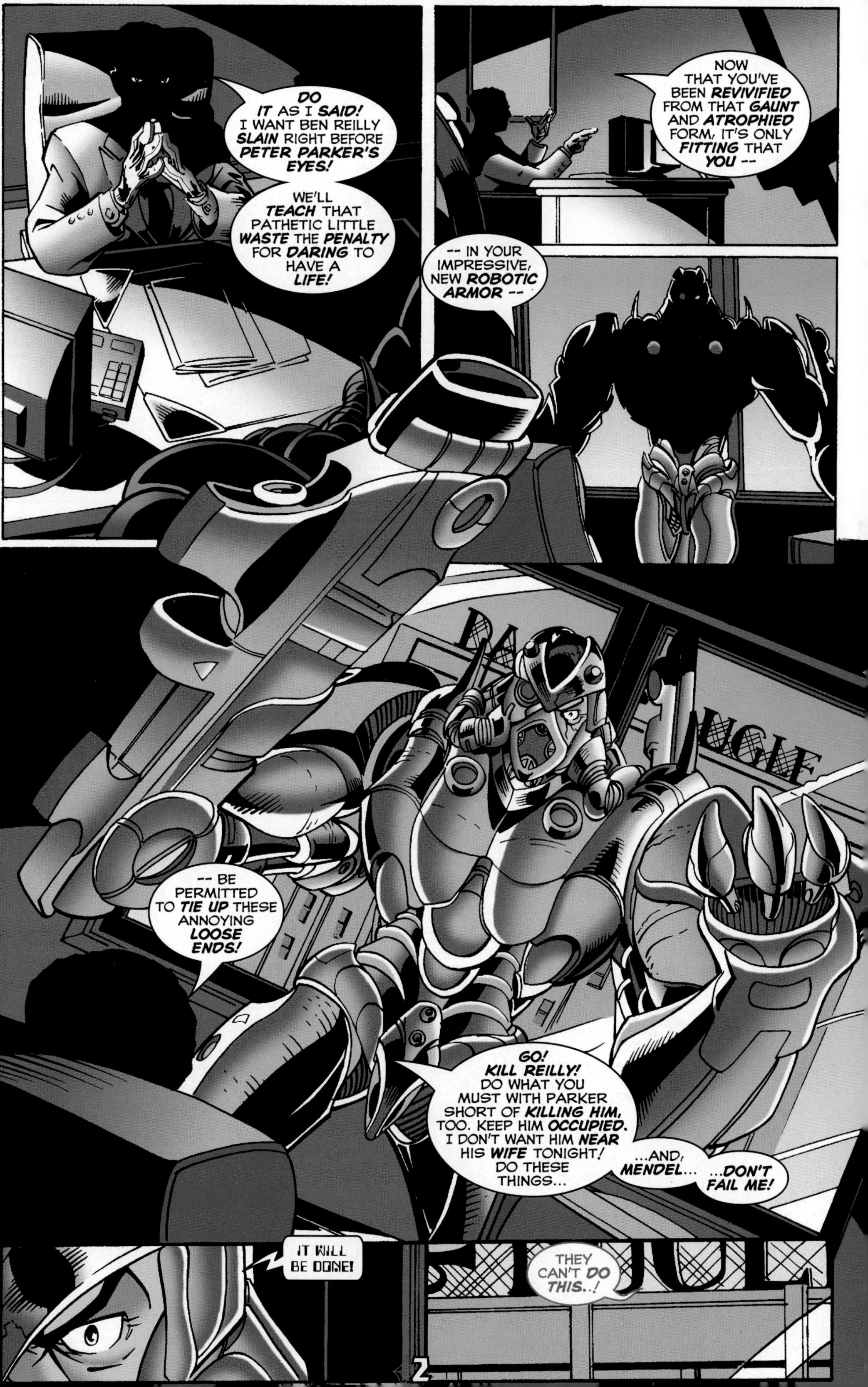
DO IT AS I SAID! I WANT BEN REILLY SLAIN RIGHT BEFORE PETER PARKER'S EYES!
WE'LL TEACH THAT PATHETIC LITTLE WASTE THE PENALTY FOR DARING TO HAVE A LIFE!
NOW THAT YOU'VE BEEN REVIVIFIED FROM THAT GAUNT AND ATROPHIED FORM, IT'S ONLY FITTING THAT YOU --
-- IN YOUR IMPRESSIVE, NEW ROBOTIC ARMOR --
-- BE PERMITTED TO TIE UP THESE ANNOYING LOOSE ENDS!
GO! KILL REILLY! DO WHAT YOU MUST WITH PARKER SHORT OF KILLING HIM, TOO. KEEP HIM OCCUPIED. I DON'T WANT HIM NEAR HIS WIFE TONIGHT! DO THESE THINGS...
...AND, MENDEL...
...DON'T FAIL ME!
IT WILL BE DONE!
THEY CAN'T DO THIS..!

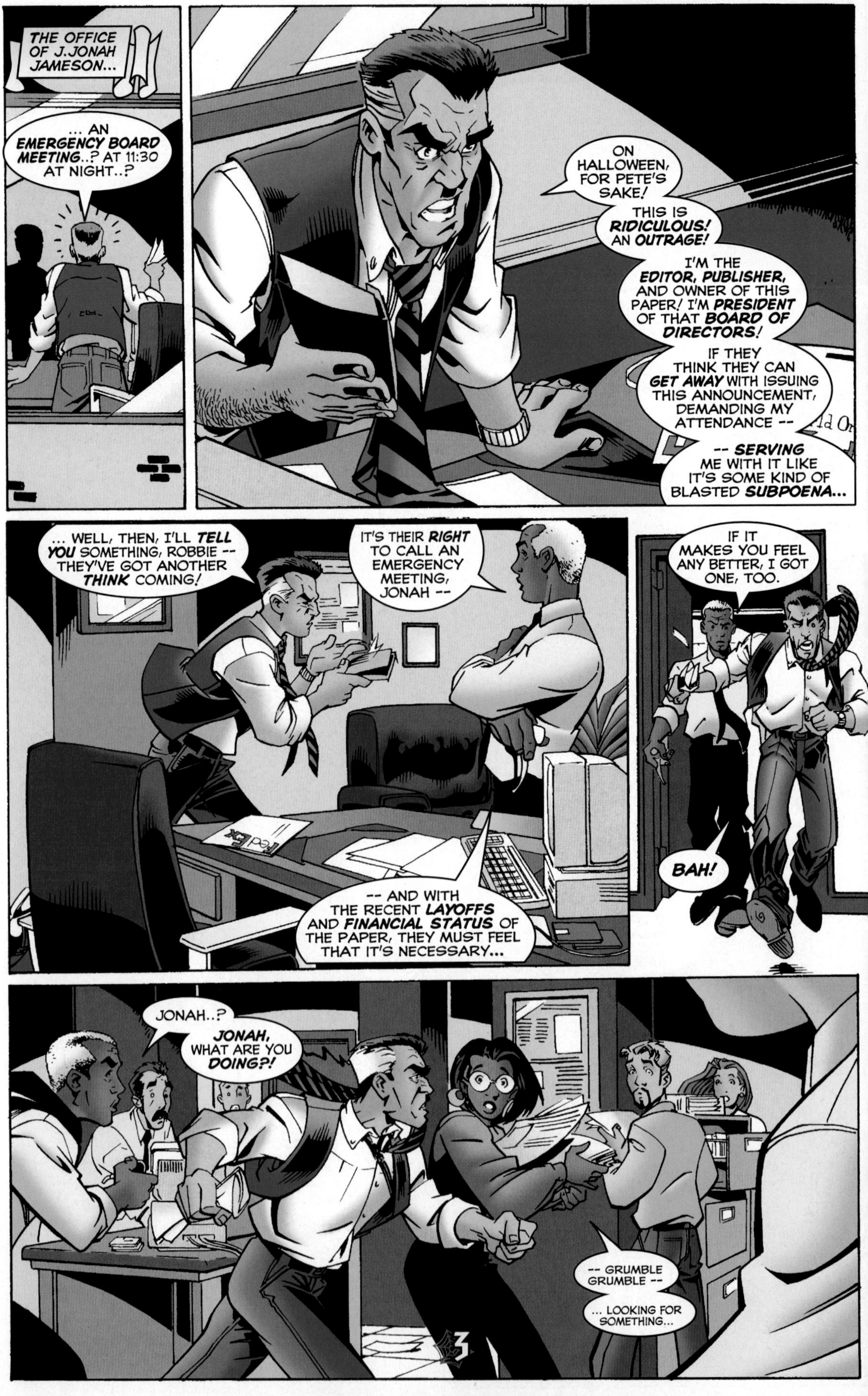
THE OFFICE OF J. JONAH JAMESON...
... AN EMERGENCY BOARD MEETING..? AT 11:30 AT NIGHT..?
ON HALLOWEEN, FOR PETE'S SAKE!
THIS IS RIDICULOUS! AN OUTRAGE!
I'M THE EDITOR, PUBLISHER, AND OWNER OF THIS PAPER! I'M PRESIDENT OF THAT BOARD OF DIRECTORS!
IF THEY THINK THEY CAN GET AWAY WITH ISSUING THIS ANNOUNCEMENT, DEMANDING MY ATTENDANCE --
-- SERVING ME WITH IT LIKE IT'S SOME KIND OF BLASTED SUBPOENA...
... WELL, THEN, I'LL TELL YOU SOMETHING, ROBBIE -- THEY'VE GOT ANOTHER THINK COMING!
IT'S THEIR RIGHT TO CALL AN EMERGENCY MEETING, JONAH --
-- AND WITH THE RECENT LAYOFFS AND FINANCIAL STATUS OF THE PAPER, THEY MUST FEEL THAT IT'S NECESSARY...
IF IT MAKES YOU FEEL ANY BETTER, I GOT ONE, TOO.
BAH!
JONAH..?
JONAH, WHAT ARE YOU DOING?!
-- GRUMBLE GRUMBLE --
... LOOKING FOR SOMETHING...

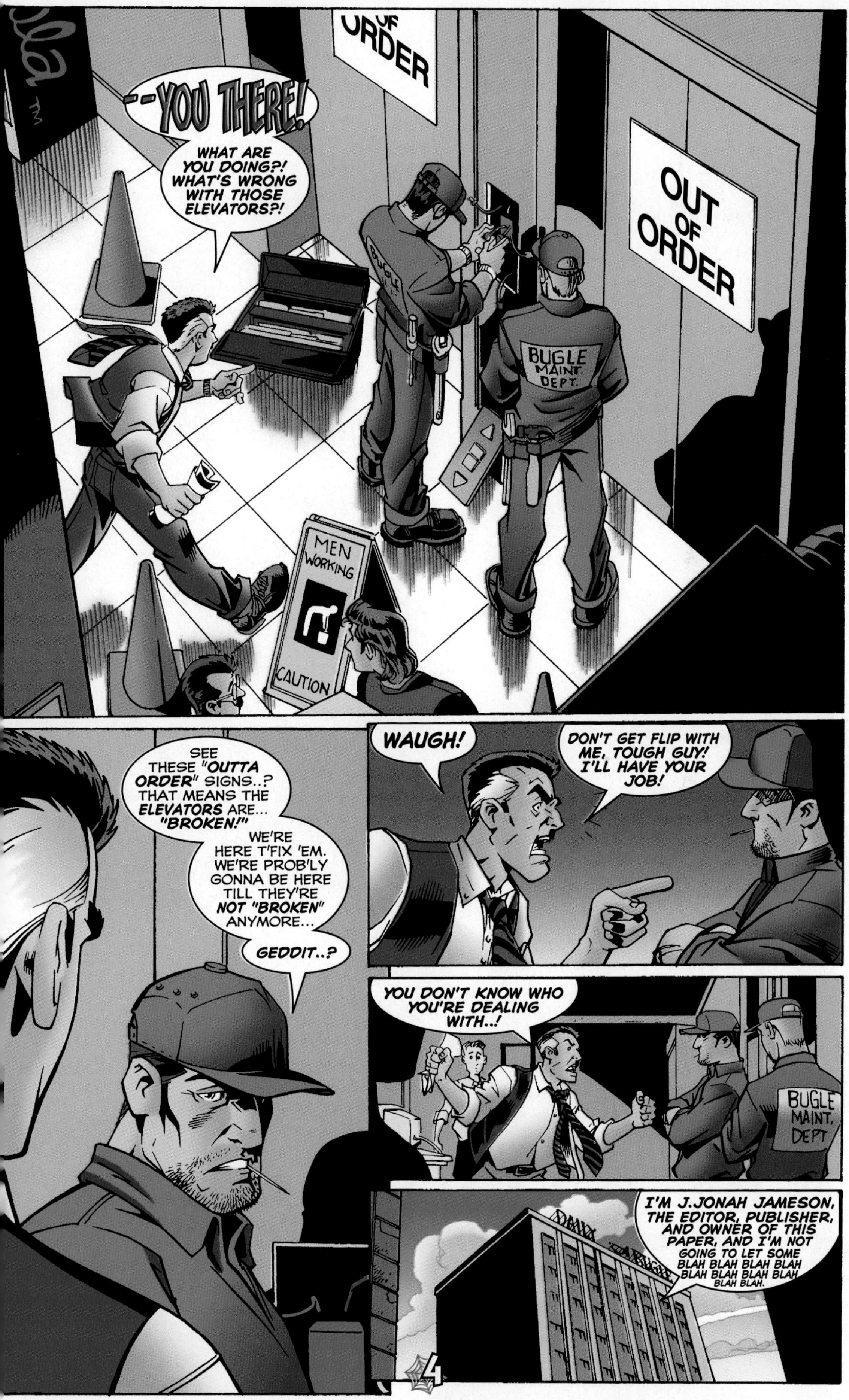
OF ORDER
--YOU THERE!
WHAT ARE YOU DOING?! WHAT'S WRONG WITH THOSE ELEVATORS?!
OUT OF ORDER
BUGLE MAINT. DEPT.
MEN WORKING
CAUTION
SEE THESE "OUTTA ORDER" SIGNS..? THAT MEANS THE ELEVATORS ARE... "BROKEN!"
WE'RE HERE T'FIX 'EM. WE'RE PROB'LY GONNA BE HERE TILL THEY'RE NOT "BROKEN" ANYMORE...
GEDDIT..?
WAUGH!
DON'T GET FLIP WITH ME, TOUGH GUY! I'LL HAVE YOUR JOB!
YOU DON'T KNOW WHO YOU'RE DEALING WITH..!
BUGLE MAINT. DEPT
I'M J.JONAH JAMESON, THE EDITOR, PUBLISHER, AND OWNER OF THIS PAPER, AND I'M NOT GOING TO LET SOME BLAH BLAH BLAH BLAH BLAH BLAH BLAH BLAH BLAH BLAH.

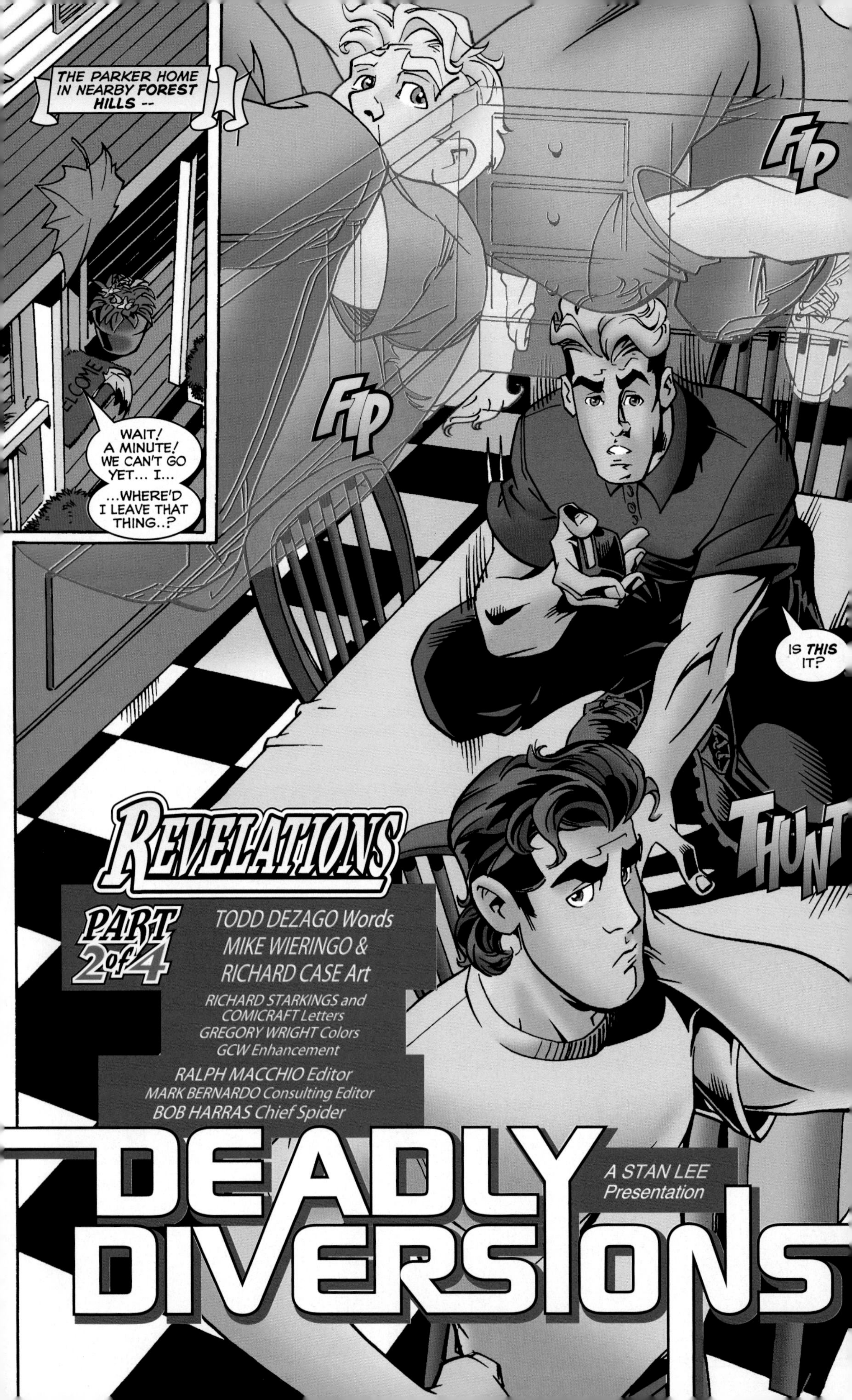
THE PARKER HOME IN NEARBY FOREST HILLS --
WAIT! A MINUTE! WE CAN'T GO YET... I...
...WHERE'D I LEAVE THAT THING..?
FTP
FTP
IS THIS IT?
THUNT
REVELATIONS
PART 2 of 4
TODD DEZAGO Words
MIKE WIERINGO & RICHARD CASE Art
RICHARD STARKINGS and COMICRAFT Letters
GREGORY WRIGHT Colors
GCW Enhancement
RALPH MACCHIO Editor
MARK BERNARDO Consulting Editor
BOB HARRAS Chief Spider
DEADLY DIVERSIONS
A STAN LEE Presentation

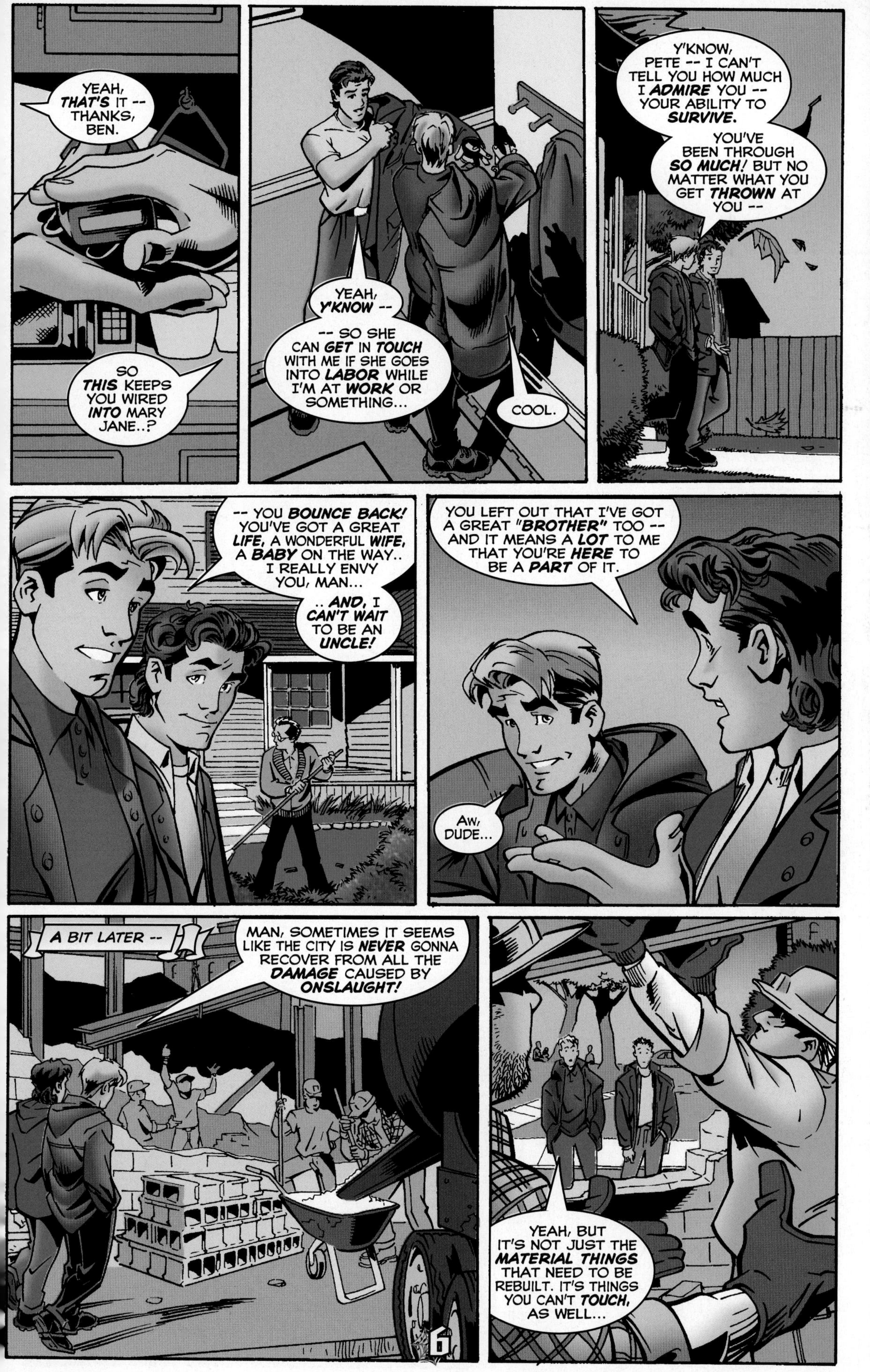

YEAH, THAT'S IT -- THANKS, BEN.
SO THIS KEEPS YOU WIRED INTO MARY JANE..?
YEAH, Y'KNOW --
-- SO SHE CAN GET IN TOUCH WITH ME IF SHE GOES INTO LABOR WHILE I'M AT WORK OR SOMETHING...
COOL.
Y'KNOW, PETE -- I CAN'T TELL YOU HOW MUCH I ADMIRE YOU -- YOUR ABILITY TO SURVIVE.
YOU'VE BEEN THROUGH SO MUCH! BUT NO MATTER WHAT YOU GET THROWN AT YOU --
-- YOU BOUNCE BACK! YOU'VE GOT A GREAT LIFE, A WONDERFUL WIFE, A BABY ON THE WAY.. I REALLY ENVY YOU, MAN...
.. AND, I CAN'T WAIT TO BE AN UNCLE!
YOU LEFT OUT THAT I'VE GOT A GREAT "BROTHER" TOO -- AND IT MEANS A LOT TO ME THAT YOU'RE HERE TO BE A PART OF IT.
AW, DUDE...
A BIT LATER --
MAN, SOMETIMES IT SEEMS LIKE THE CITY IS NEVER GONNA RECOVER FROM ALL THE DAMAGE CAUSED BY ONSLAUGHT!
YEAH, BUT IT'S NOT JUST THE MATERIAL THINGS THAT NEED TO BE REBUILT. IT'S THINGS YOU CAN'T TOUCH, AS WELL...
6

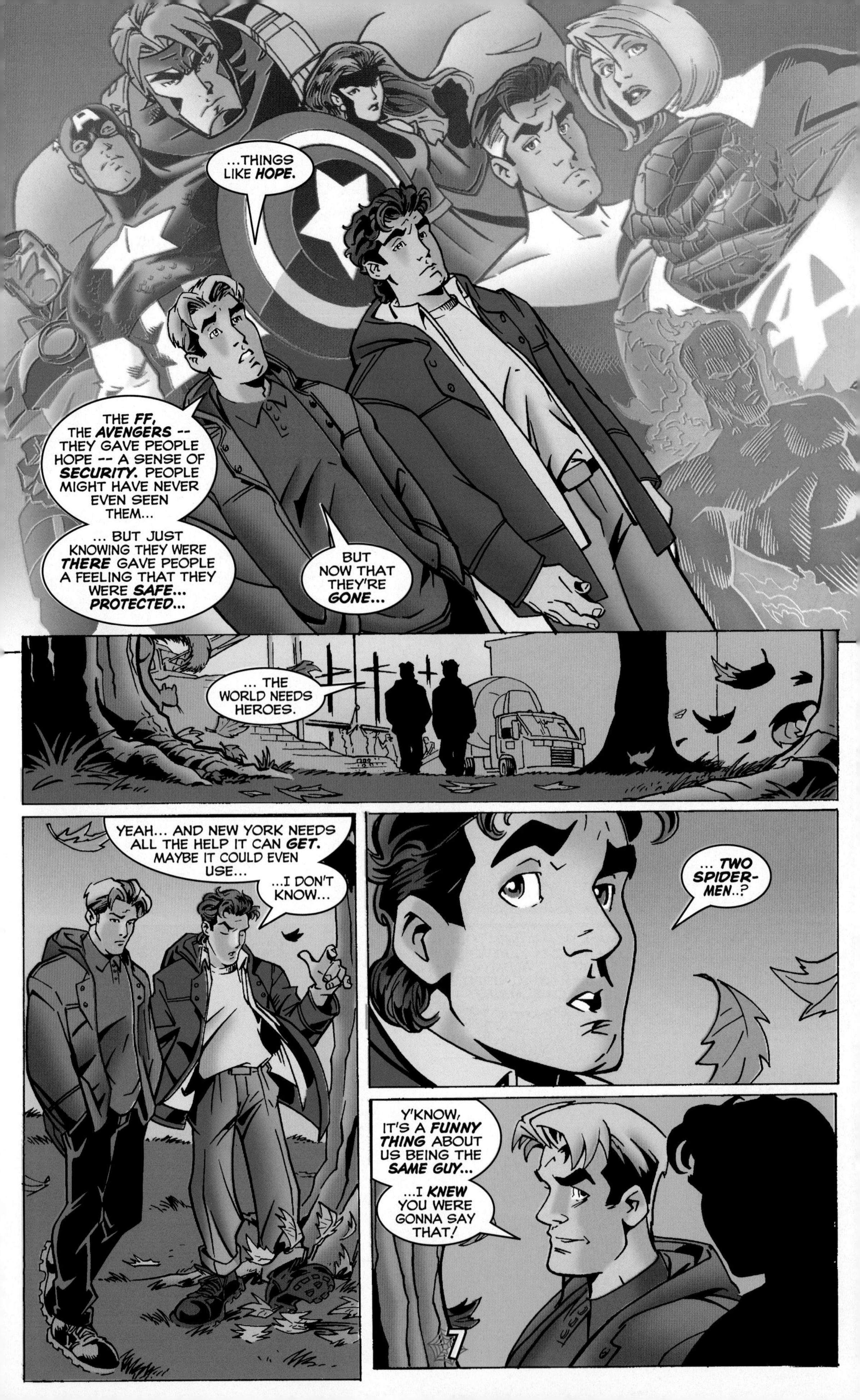
...THINGS LIKE HOPE.
THE FF, THE AVENGERS -- THEY GAVE PEOPLE HOPE -- A SENSE OF SECURITY. PEOPLE MIGHT HAVE NEVER EVEN SEEN THEM...
... BUT JUST KNOWING THEY WERE THERE GAVE PEOPLE A FEELING THAT THEY WERE SAFE... PROTECTED...
BUT NOW THAT THEY'RE GONE...
... THE WORLD NEEDS HEROES.
YEAH... AND NEW YORK NEEDS ALL THE HELP IT CAN GET. MAYBE IT COULD EVEN USE...
...I DON'T KNOW...
... TWO SPIDER-MEN..?
Y'KNOW, IT'S A FUNNY THING ABOUT US BEING THE SAME GUY...
...I KNEW YOU WERE GONNA SAY THAT!
7

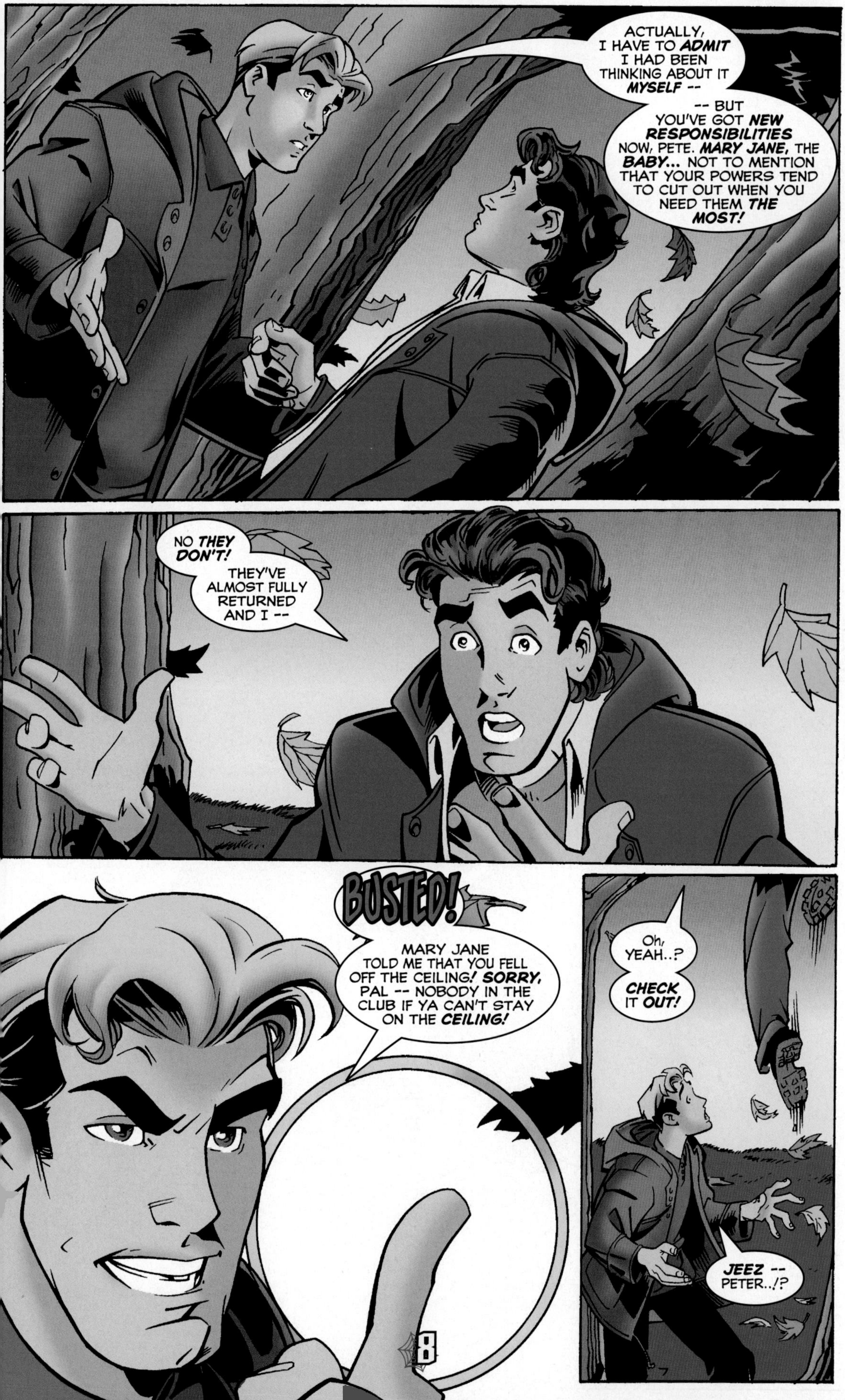
ACTUALLY, I HAVE TO ADMIT I HAD BEEN THINKING ABOUT IT MYSELF --
-- BUT YOU'VE GOT NEW RESPONSIBILITIES NOW, PETE. MARY JANE, THE BABY... NOT TO MENTION THAT YOUR POWERS TEND TO CUT OUT WHEN YOU NEED THEM THE MOST!
NO THEY DON'T!
THEY'VE ALMOST FULLY RETURNED AND I --
BUSTED!
MARY JANE TOLD ME THAT YOU FELL OFF THE CEILING! SORRY, PAL -- NOBODY IN THE CLUB IF YA CAN'T STAY ON THE CEILING!
Oh, YEAH..?
CHECK IT OUT!
JEEZ -- PETER..!?

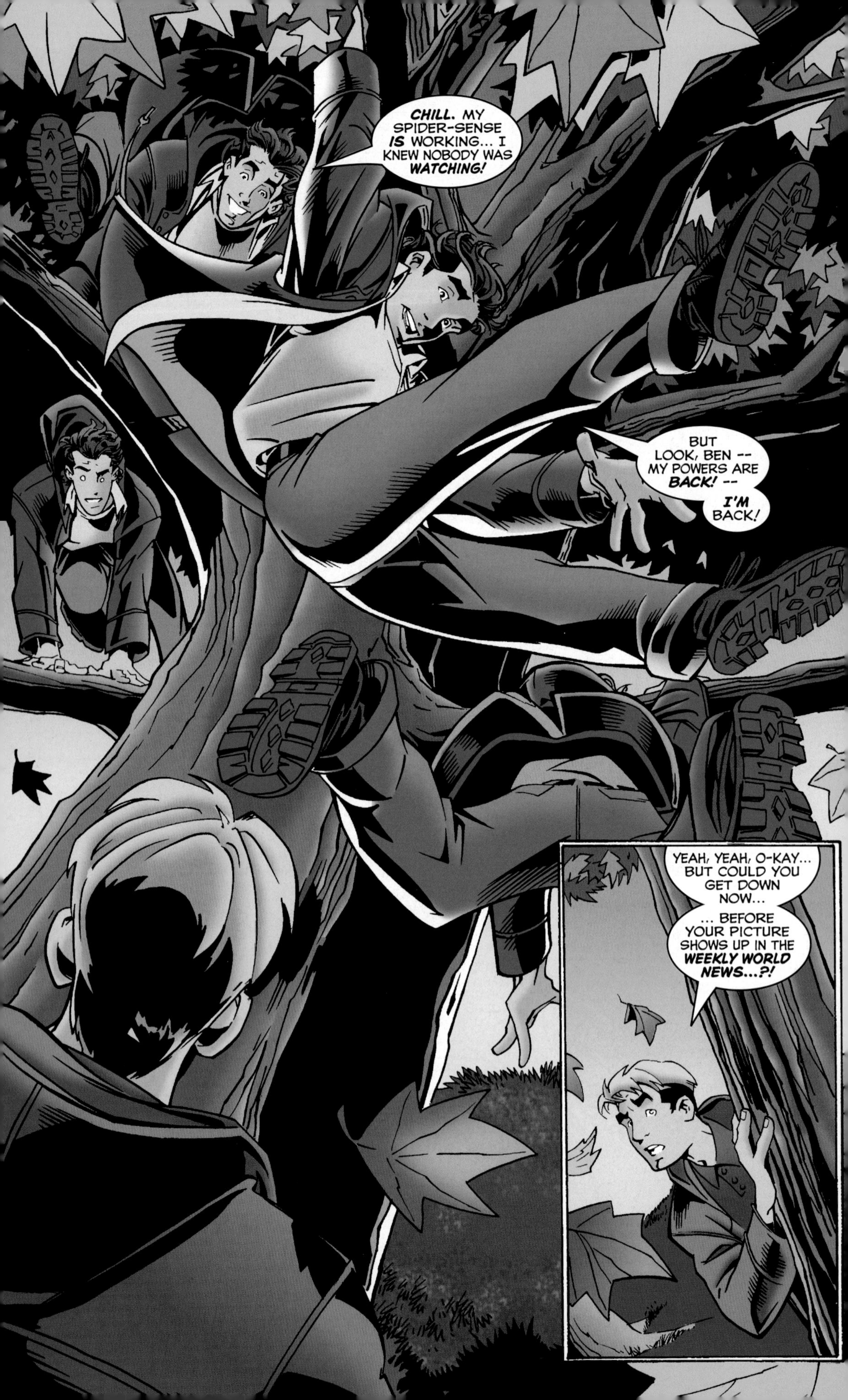
CHILL. MY SPIDER-SENSE IS WORKING... I KNEW NOBODY WAS WATCHING!
BUT LOOK, BEN -- MY POWERS ARE BACK! --
I'M BACK!
YEAH, YEAH, O-KAY... BUT COULD YOU GET DOWN NOW...
... BEFORE YOUR PICTURE SHOWS UP IN THE WEEKLY WORLD NEWS...?!

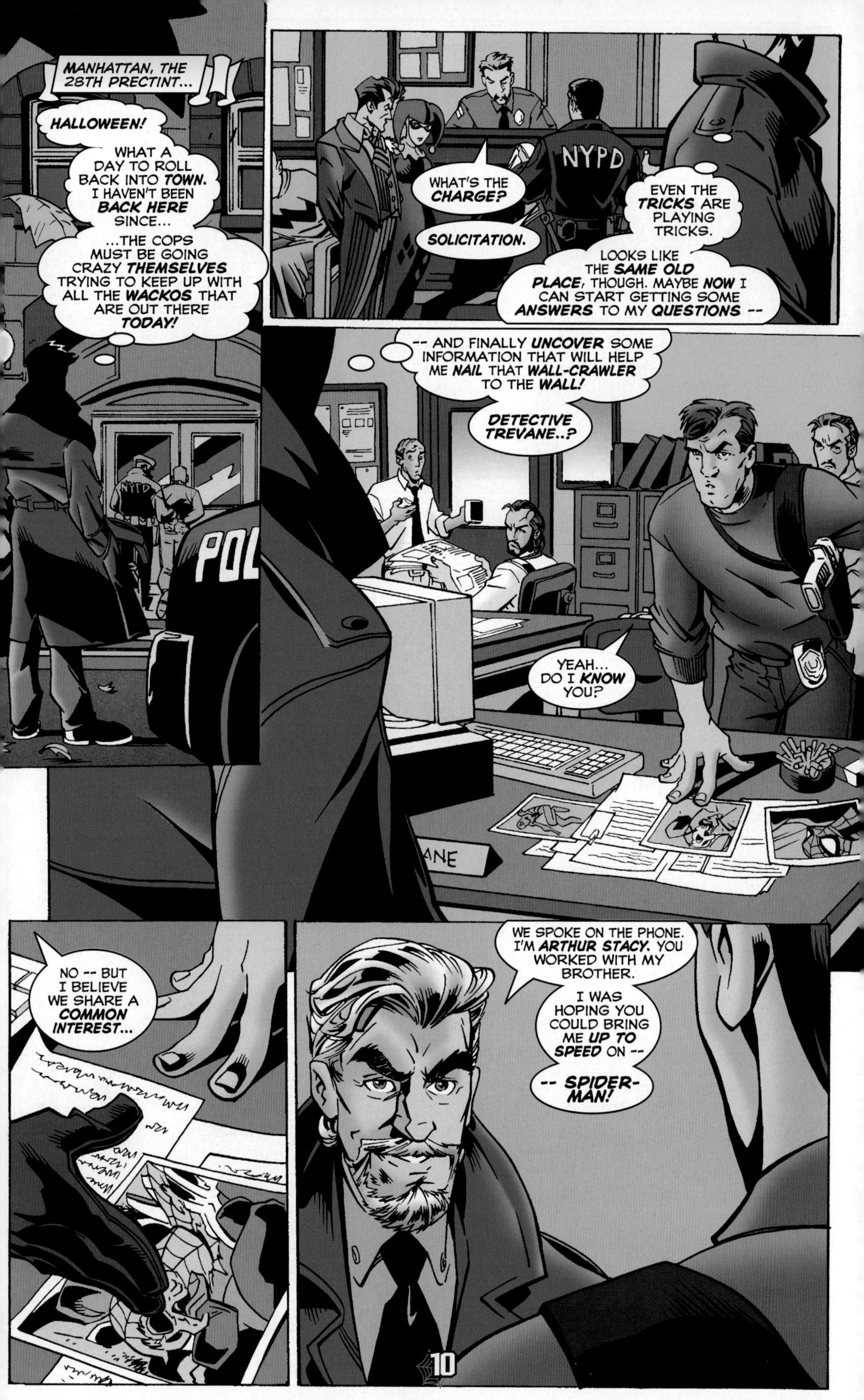

MANHATTAN, THE 28TH PRECTINT...
HALLOWEEN!
WHAT A DAY TO ROLL BACK INTO TOWN. I HAVEN'T BEEN BACK HERE SINCE...
...THE COPS MUST BE GOING CRAZY THEMSELVES TRYING TO KEEP UP WITH ALL THE WACKOS THAT ARE OUT THERE TODAY!
NYPD
WHAT'S THE CHARGE?
SOLICITATION.
EVEN THE TRICKS ARE PLAYING TRICKS.
LOOKS LIKE THE SAME OLD PLACE, THOUGH. MAYBE NOW I CAN START GETTING SOME ANSWERS TO MY QUESTIONS --
-- AND FINALLY UNCOVER SOME INFORMATION THAT WILL HELP ME NAIL THAT WALL-CRAWLER TO THE WALL!
DETECTIVE TREVANE..?
NYPD
POL
YEAH... DO I KNOW YOU?
ANE
NO -- BUT I BELIEVE WE SHARE A COMMON INTEREST...
WE SPOKE ON THE PHONE. I'M ARTHUR STACY. YOU WORKED WITH MY BROTHER.
I WAS HOPING YOU COULD BRING ME UP TO SPEED ON --
-- SPIDER-MAN!

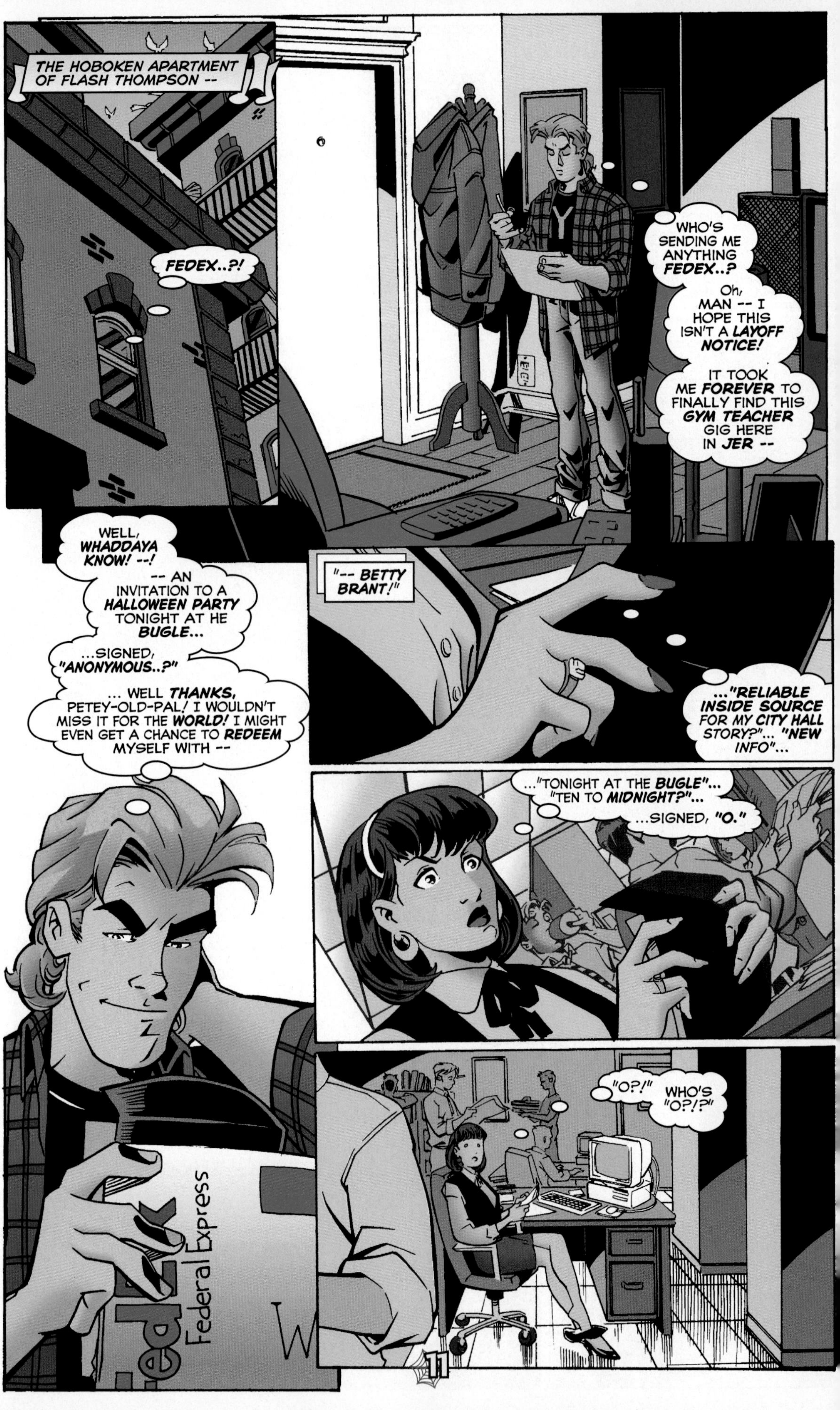
THE HOBOKEN APARTMENT OF FLASH THOMPSON --
FEDEX..?!
WHO'S SENDING ME ANYTHING FEDEX..?
Oh, MAN -- I HOPE THIS ISN'T A LAYOFF NOTICE!
IT TOOK ME FOREVER TO FINALLY FIND THIS GYM TEACHER GIG HERE IN JER --
WELL, WHADDAYA KNOW! --!
-- AN INVITATION TO A HALLOWEEN PARTY TONIGHT AT HE BUGLE...
...SIGNED, "ANONYMOUS..?"
... WELL THANKS, PETEY-OLD-PAL! I WOULDN'T MISS IT FOR THE WORLD! I MIGHT EVEN GET A CHANCE TO REDEEM MYSELF WITH --
Federal Express
"-- BETTY BRANT!"
..."RELIABLE INSIDE SOURCE FOR MY CITY HALL STORY?"... "NEW INFO"...
..."TONIGHT AT THE BUGLE"... "TEN TO MIDNIGHT?"...
...SIGNED, "O."
"O?!" WHO'S "O?!?"

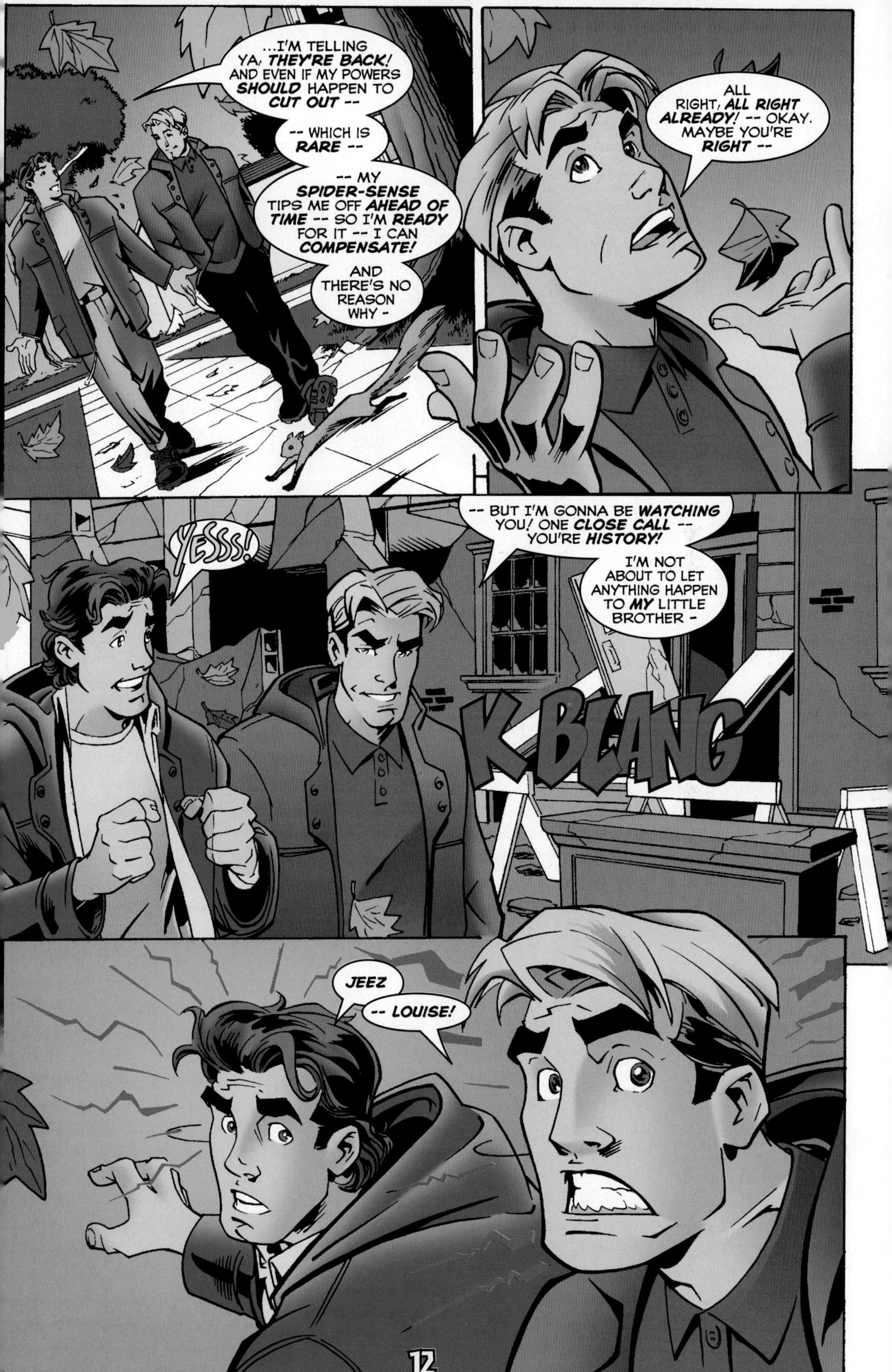
...I'M TELLING YA, THEY'RE BACK! AND EVEN IF MY POWERS SHOULD HAPPEN TO CUT OUT --
-- WHICH IS RARE --
-- MY SPIDER-SENSE TIPS ME OFF AHEAD OF TIME -- SO I'M READY FOR IT -- I CAN COMPENSATE!
AND THERE'S NO REASON WHY -
ALL RIGHT, ALL RIGHT ALREADY! -- OKAY. MAYBE YOU'RE RIGHT --
YESSS!
-- BUT I'M GONNA BE WATCHING YOU! ONE CLOSE CALL -- YOU'RE HISTORY!
I'M NOT ABOUT TO LET ANYTHING HAPPEN TO MY LITTLE BROTHER -
K-BLANG
JEEZ
-- LOUISE!

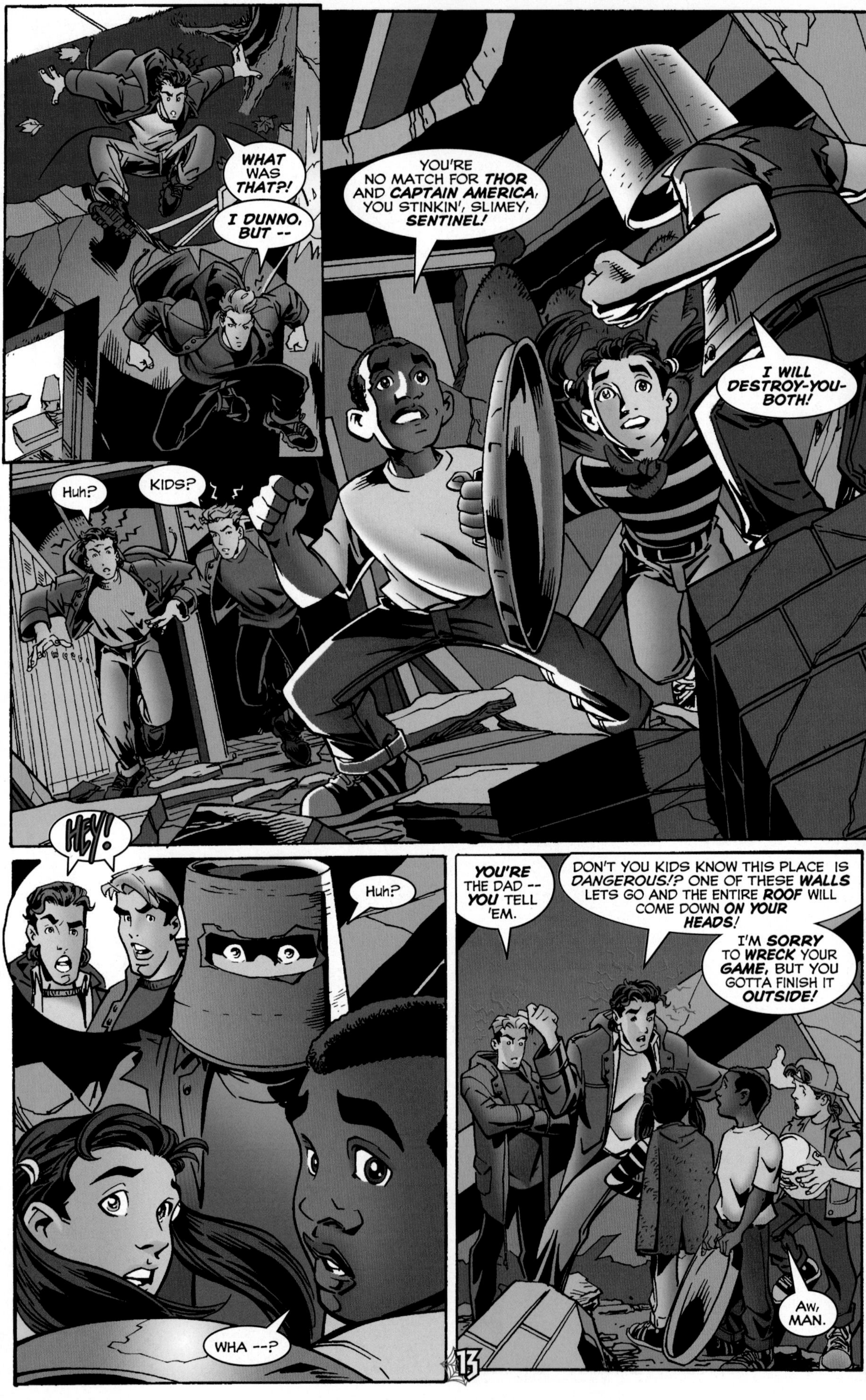
WHAT WAS THAT?!
I DUNNO, BUT --
YOU'RE NO MATCH FOR THOR AND CAPTAIN AMERICA, YOU STINKIN', SLIMEY, SENTINEL!
I WILL DESTROY-YOU-BOTH!
Huh?
KIDS?
HEY!
Huh?
WHA --?
YOU'RE THE DAD -- YOU TELL 'EM.
DON'T YOU KIDS KNOW THIS PLACE IS DANGEROUS!? ONE OF THESE WALLS LETS GO AND THE ENTIRE ROOF WILL COME DOWN ON YOUR HEADS!
I'M SORRY TO WRECK YOUR GAME, BUT YOU GOTTA FINISH IT OUTSIDE!
AW, MAN.

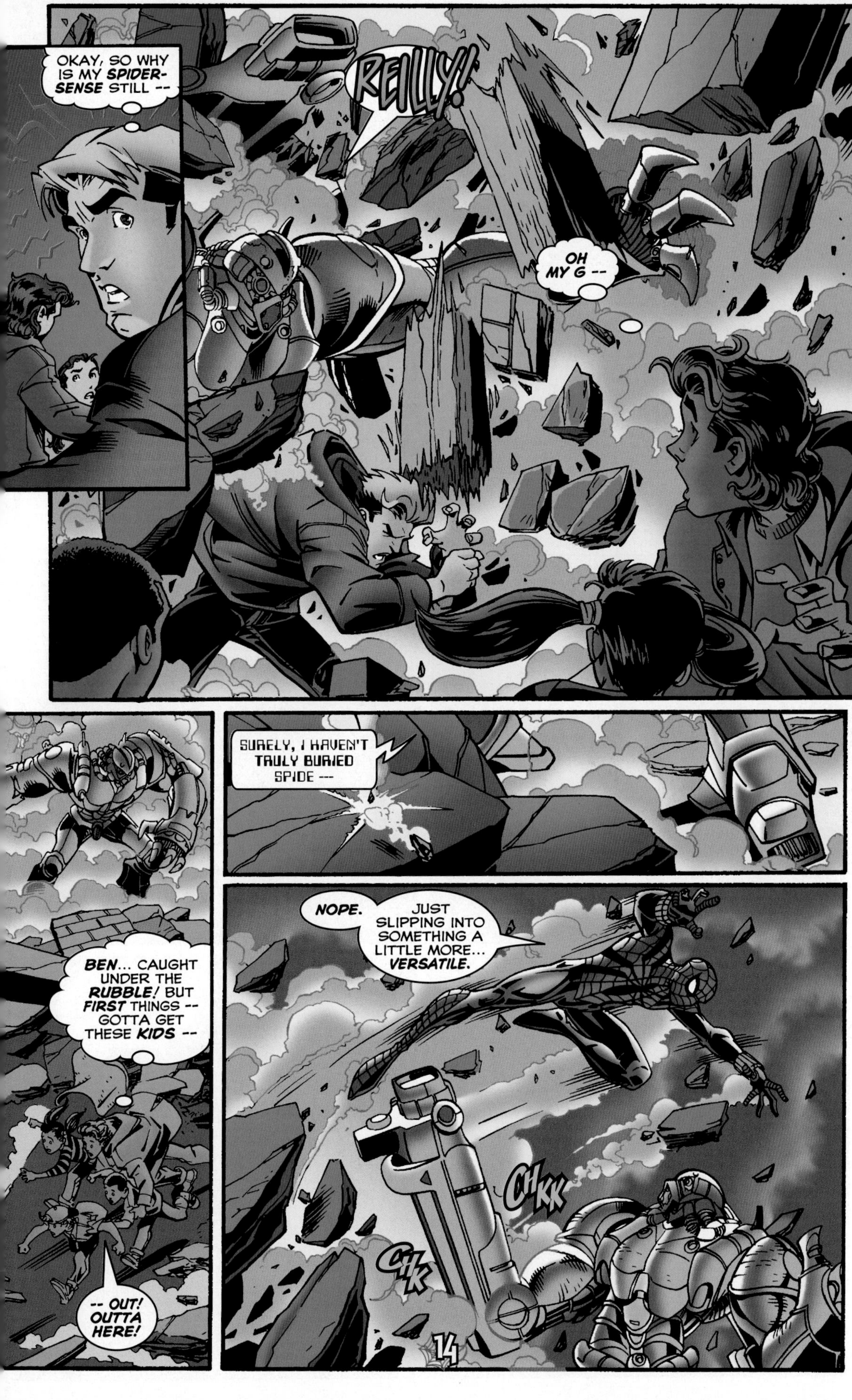
OKAY, SO WHY IS MY SPIDER-SENSE STILL --
REILLY!
OH MY G --
SURELY, I HAVEN'T TRULY BURIED SPIDE ---
BEN... CAUGHT UNDER THE RUBBLE! BUT FIRST THINGS -- GOTTA GET THESE KIDS --
-- OUT! OUTTA HERE!
NOPE.
JUST SLIPPING INTO SOMETHING A LITTLE MORE... VERSATILE.
CHKK
CHK

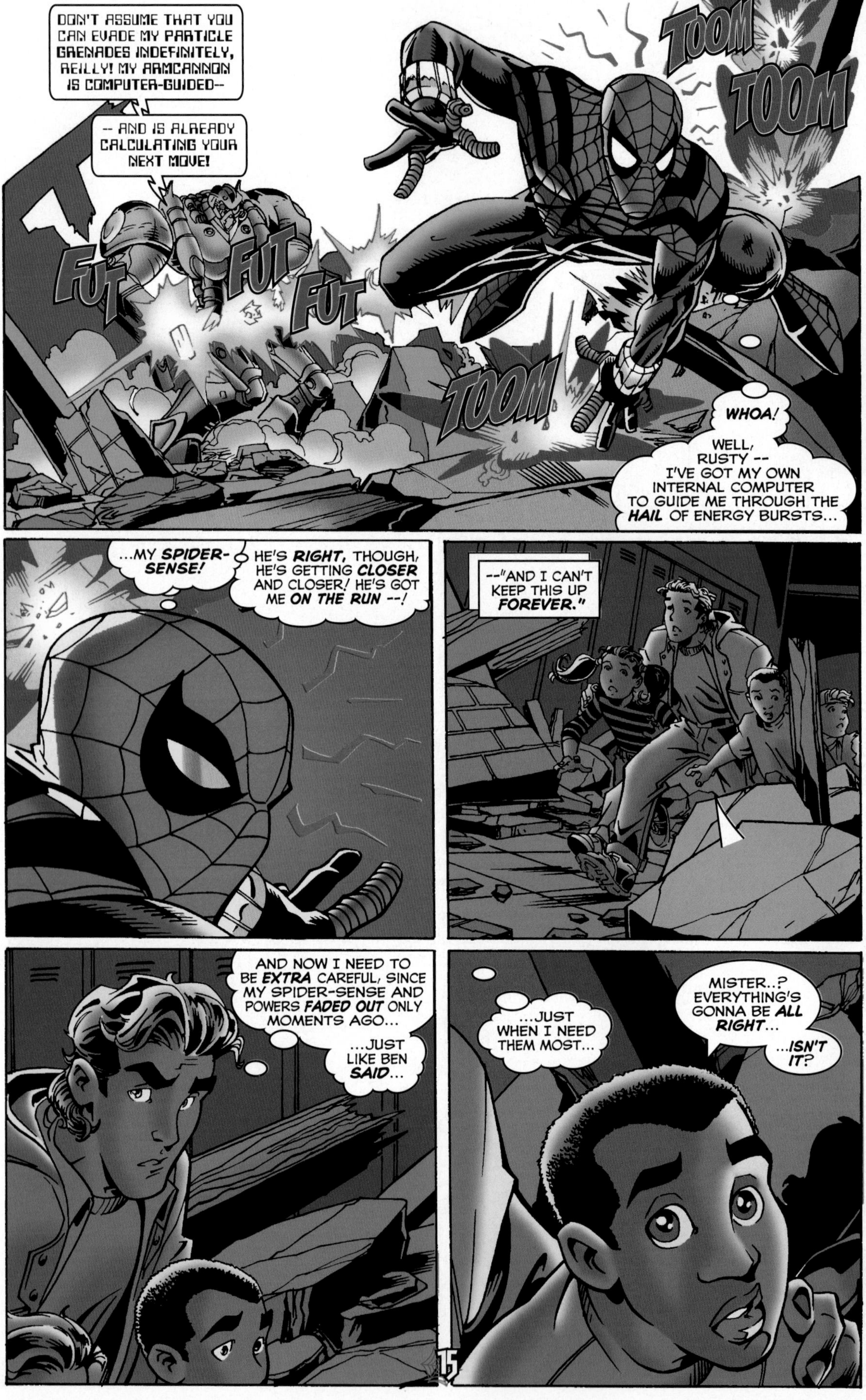
DON'T ASSUME THAT YOU CAN EVADE MY PARTICLE GRENADES INDEFINITELY, REILLY! MY ARMCANNON IS COMPUTER-GUIDED--
-- AND IS ALREADY CALCULATING YOUR NEXT MOVE!
TOOM
TOOM
FUT
FUT
FUT
TOOM
WHOA!
WELL, RUSTY -- I'VE GOT MY OWN INTERNAL COMPUTER TO GUIDE ME THROUGH THE HAIL OF ENERGY BURSTS...
...MY SPIDER-SENSE!
HE'S RIGHT, THOUGH, HE'S GETTING CLOSER AND CLOSER! HE'S GOT ME ON THE RUN --!
--"AND I CAN'T KEEP THIS UP FOREVER."
AND NOW I NEED TO BE EXTRA CAREFUL, SINCE MY SPIDER-SENSE AND POWERS FADED OUT ONLY MOMENTS AGO...
...JUST LIKE BEN SAID...
...JUST WHEN I NEED THEM MOST...
MISTER..? EVERYTHING'S GONNA BE ALL RIGHT...
...ISN'T IT?

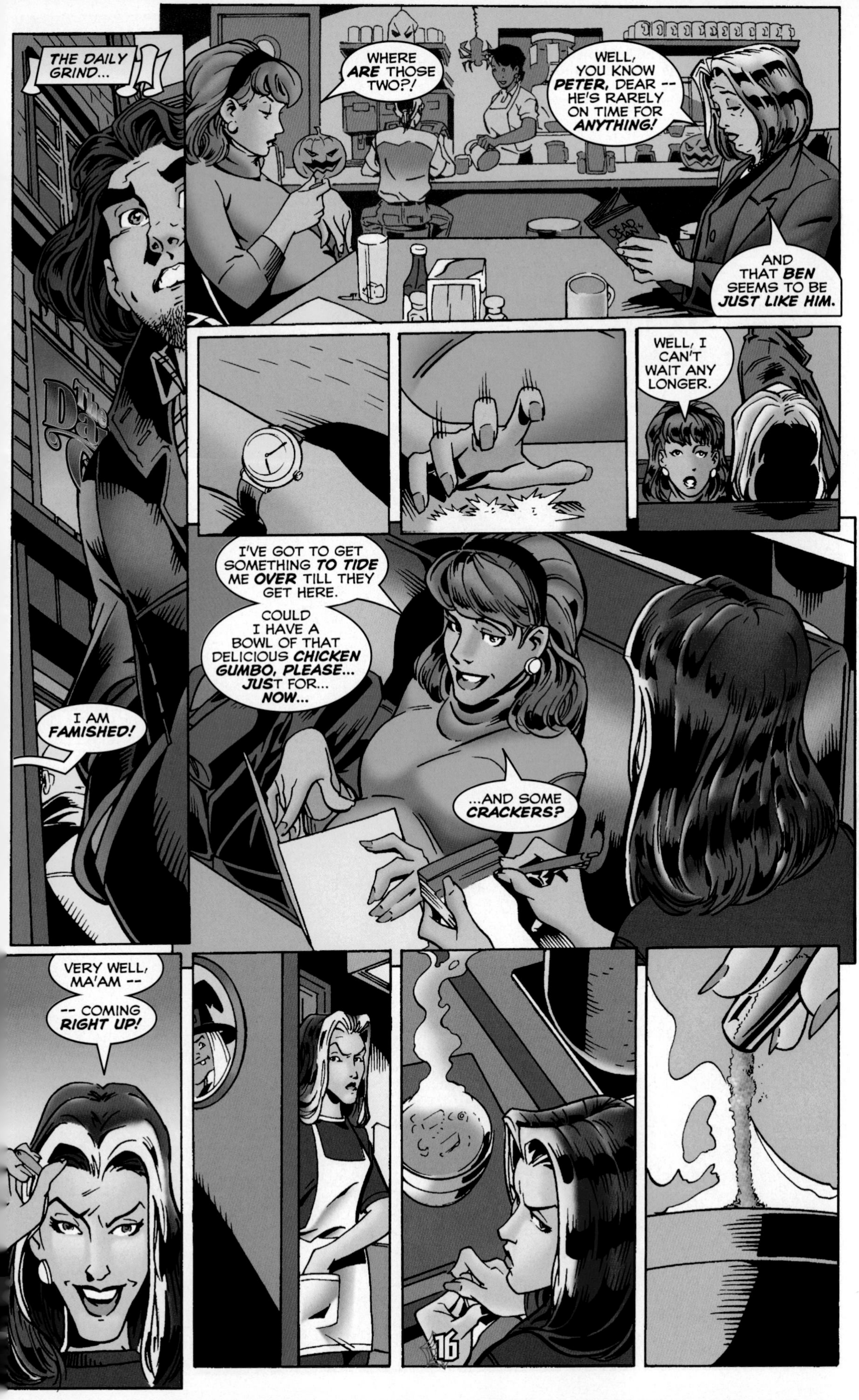
THE DAILY GRIND...
WHERE ARE THOSE TWO?!
WELL, YOU KNOW PETER, DEAR -- HE'S RARELY ON TIME FOR ANYTHING!
AND THAT BEN SEEMS TO BE JUST LIKE HIM.
WELL, I CAN'T WAIT ANY LONGER.
I'VE GOT TO GET SOMETHING TO TIDE ME OVER TILL THEY GET HERE.
COULD I HAVE A BOWL OF THAT DELICIOUS CHICKEN GUMBO, PLEASE... JUST FOR... NOW...
...AND SOME CRACKERS?
I AM FAMISHED!
VERY WELL, MA'AM --
-- COMING RIGHT UP!

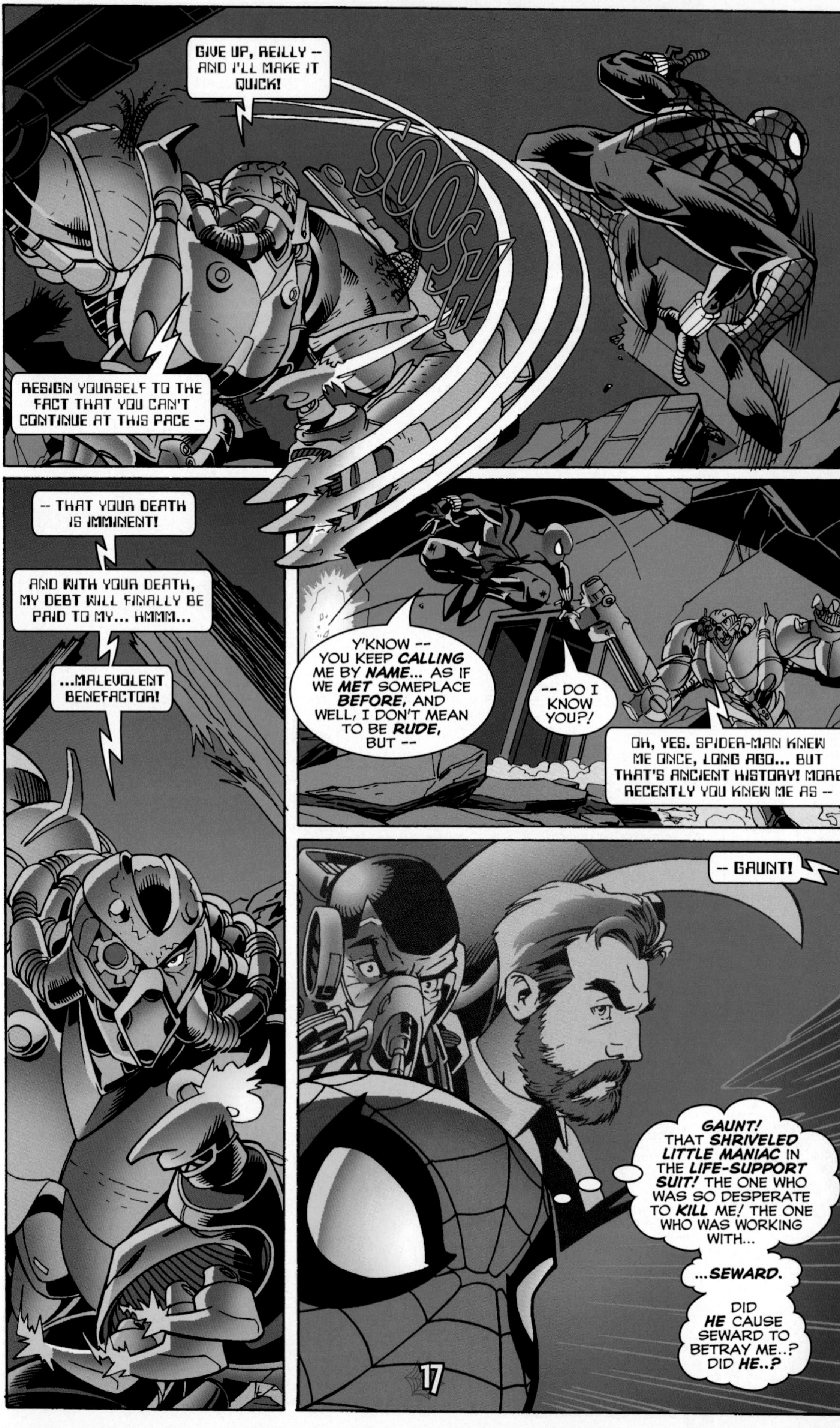
GIVE UP, REILLY -- AND I'LL MAKE IT QUICK!
SOOSH!
RESIGN YOURSELF TO THE FACT THAT YOU CAN'T CONTINUE AT THIS PACE --
-- THAT YOUR DEATH IS IMMINENT!
AND WITH YOUR DEATH, MY DEBT WILL FINALLY BE PAID TO MY... HMMM...
...MALEVOLENT BENEFACTOR!
Y'KNOW -- YOU KEEP CALLING ME BY NAME... AS IF WE MET SOMEPLACE BEFORE, AND WELL, I DON'T MEAN TO BE RUDE, BUT --
-- DO I KNOW YOU?!
OH, YES. SPIDER-MAN KNEW ME ONCE, LONG AGO... BUT THAT'S ANCIENT HISTORY! MORE RECENTLY YOU KNEW ME AS --
-- GAUNT!
GAUNT! THAT SHRIVELED LITTLE MANIAC IN THE LIFE-SUPPORT SUIT! THE ONE WHO WAS SO DESPERATE TO KILL ME! THE ONE WHO WAS WORKING WITH...
...SEWARD.
DID HE CAUSE SEWARD TO BETRAY ME..? DID HE..?

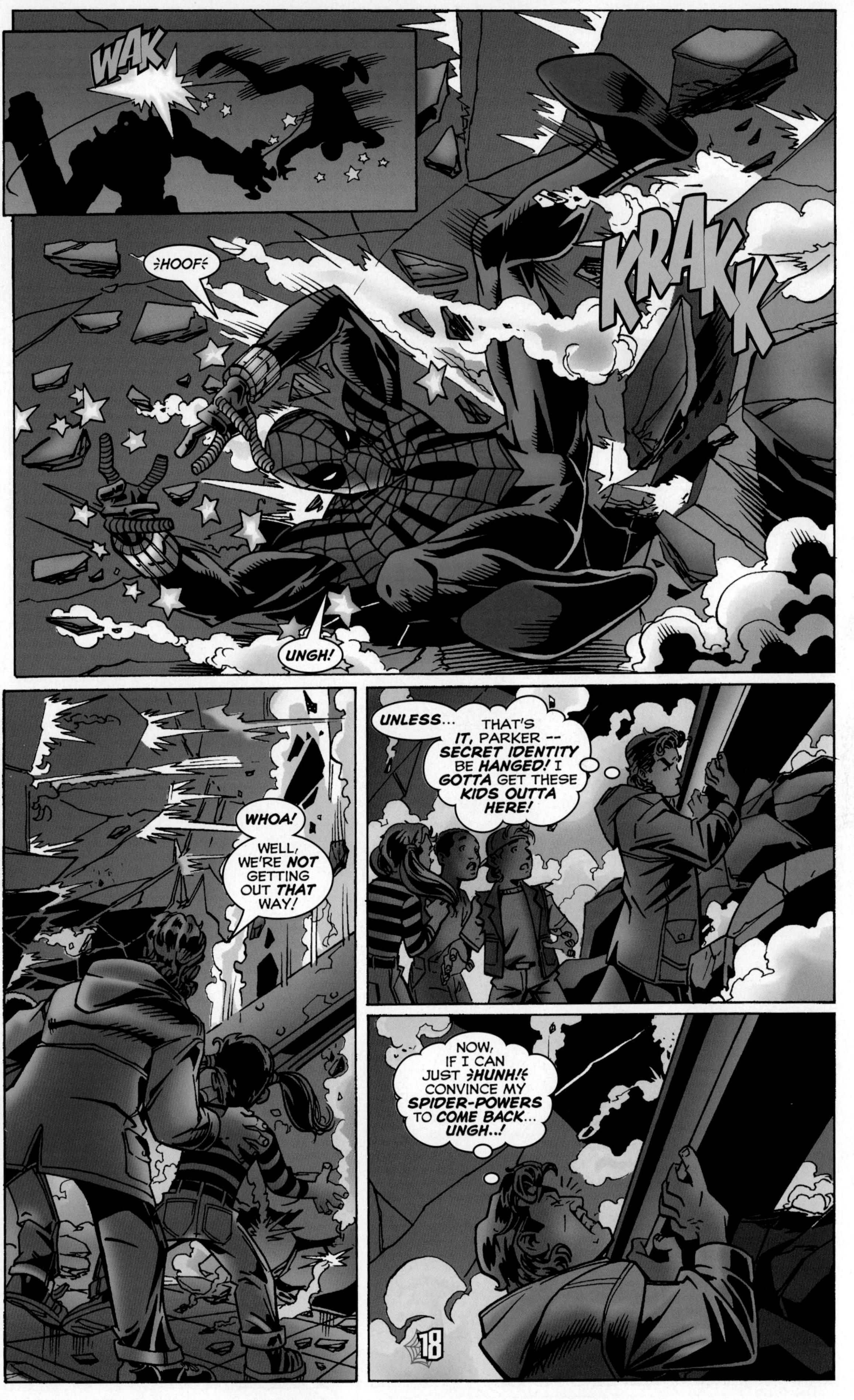
WAK
KRAKK
HOOF
UNGH!
WHOA!
WELL, WE'RE NOT GETTING OUT THAT WAY!
UNLESS... THAT'S IT, PARKER -- SECRET IDENTITY BE HANGED! I GOTTA GET THESE KIDS OUTTA HERE!
NOW, IF I CAN JUST HUNH! CONVINCE MY SPIDER-POWERS TO COME BACK... UNGH..!

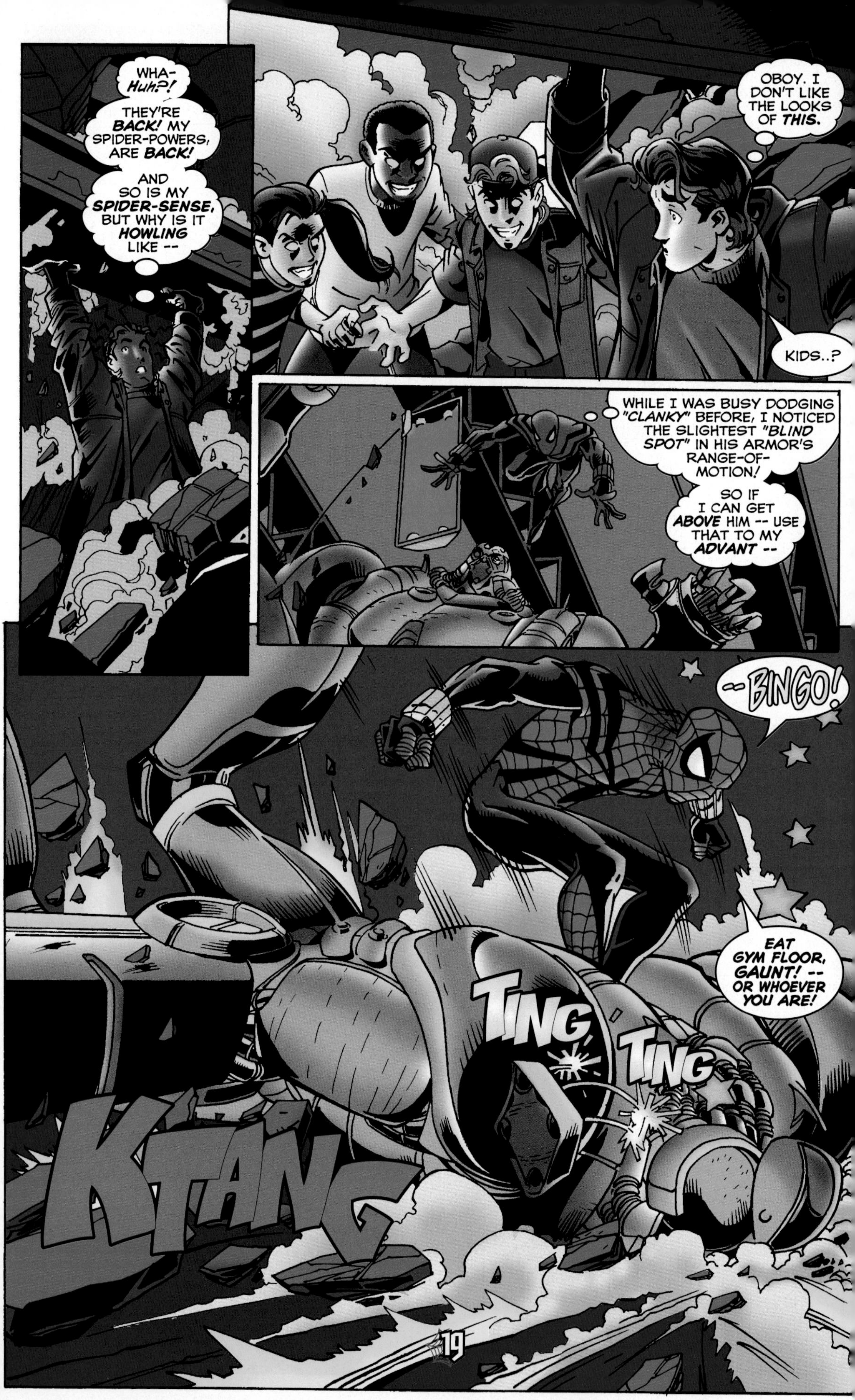
WHA- Huh?!
THEY'RE BACK! MY SPIDER-POWERS, ARE BACK!
AND SO IS MY SPIDER-SENSE, BUT WHY IS IT HOWLING LIKE --
OBOY. I DON'T LIKE THE LOOKS OF THIS.
KIDS..?
WHILE I WAS BUSY DODGING "CLANKY" BEFORE, I NOTICED THE SLIGHTEST "BLIND SPOT" IN HIS ARMOR'S RANGE-OF-MOTION!
SO IF I CAN GET ABOVE HIM -- USE THAT TO MY ADVANT --
--BINGO!
EAT GYM FLOOR, GAUNT! -- OR WHOEVER YOU ARE!
TING TING
KTANG

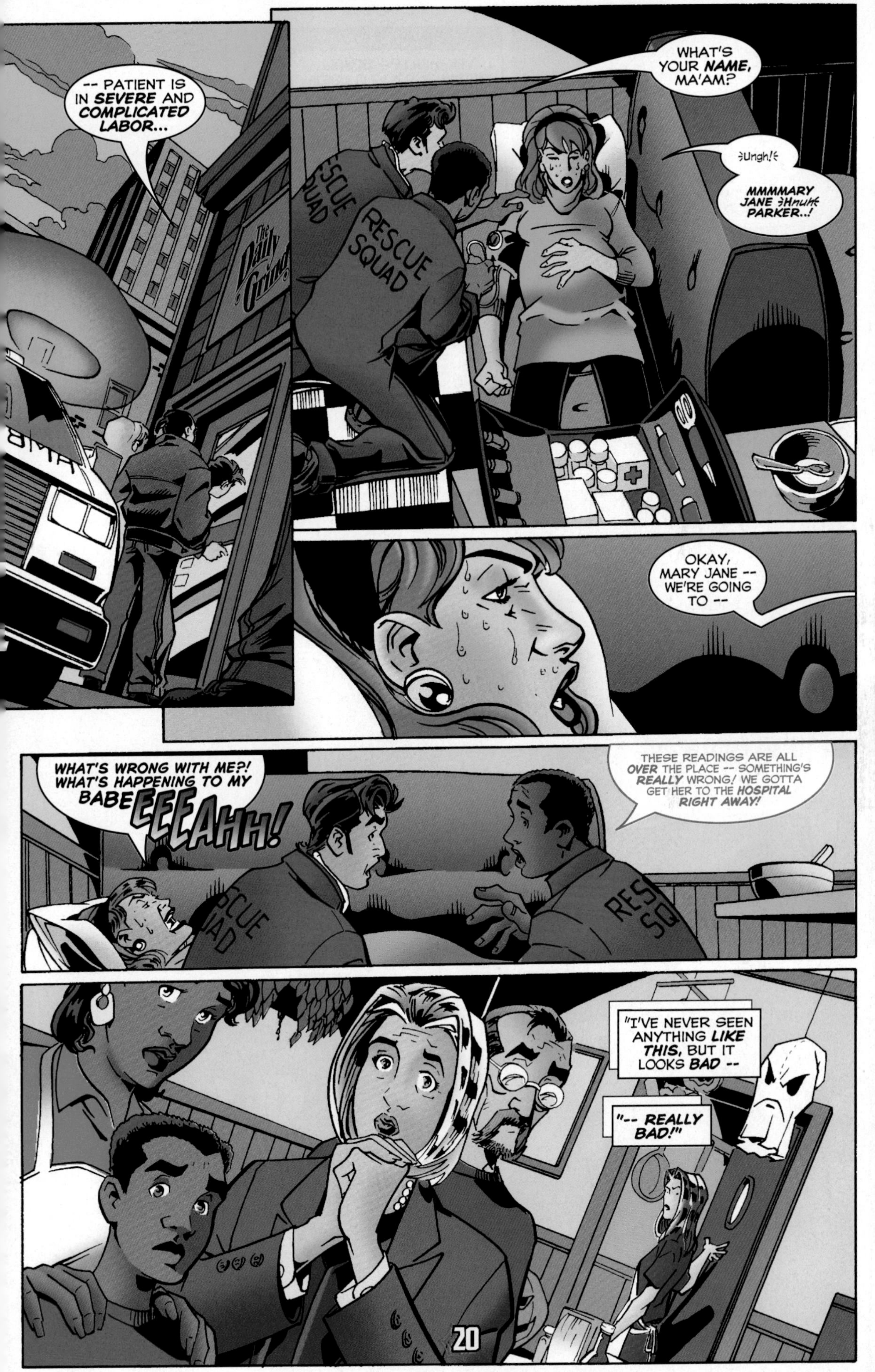
-- PATIENT IS IN SEVERE AND COMPLICATED LABOR...
AMB
The Daily Grind
WHAT'S YOUR NAME, MA'AM?
RESCUE SQUAD
RESCUE SQUAD
Ungh!
MMMMARY JANE Hnuh PARKER...!
OKAY, MARY JANE -- WE'RE GOING TO --
WHAT'S WRONG WITH ME?! WHAT'S HAPPENING TO MY BABEEEEAHH!
THESE READINGS ARE ALL OVER THE PLACE -- SOMETHING'S REALLY WRONG! WE GOTTA GET HER TO THE HOSPITAL RIGHT AWAY!
"I'VE NEVER SEEN ANYTHING LIKE THIS, BUT IT LOOKS BAD --
"-- REALLY BAD!"

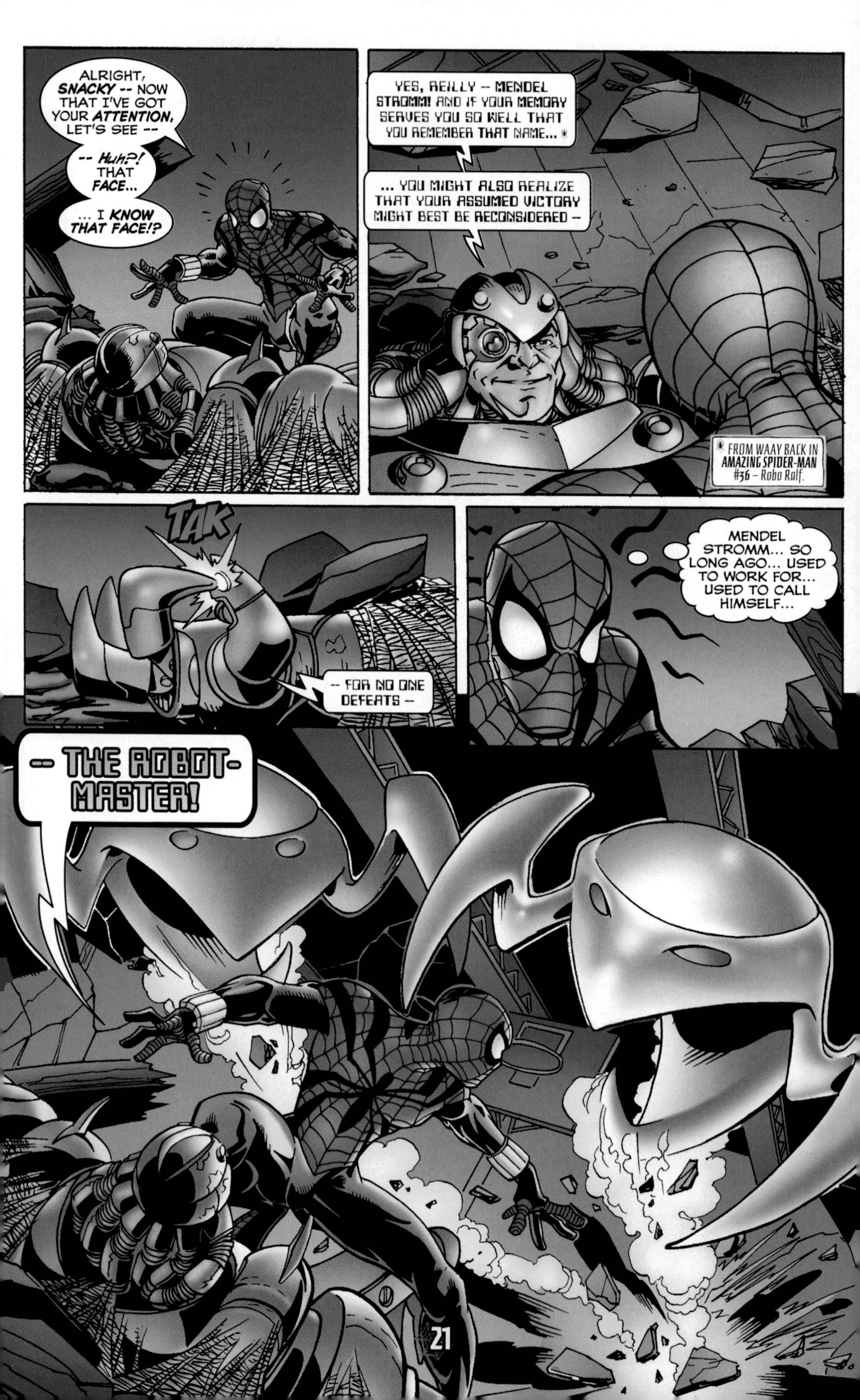
ALRIGHT, SNACKY -- NOW THAT I'VE GOT YOUR ATTENTION, LET'S SEE --
-- Huh?! THAT FACE...
... I KNOW THAT FACE!?
YES, REILLY -- MENDEL STROMM! AND IF YOUR MEMORY SERVES YOU SO WELL THAT YOU REMEMBER THAT NAME...
... YOU MIGHT ALSO REALIZE THAT YOUR ASSUMED VICTORY MIGHT BEST BE RECONSIDERED --
FROM WAAY BACK IN AMAZING SPIDER-MAN #36 – Robo Ralf.
TAK
-- FOR NO ONE DEFEATS --
MENDEL STROMM... SO LONG AGO... USED TO WORK FOR... USED TO CALL HIMSELF...
-- THE ROBOT-MASTER!

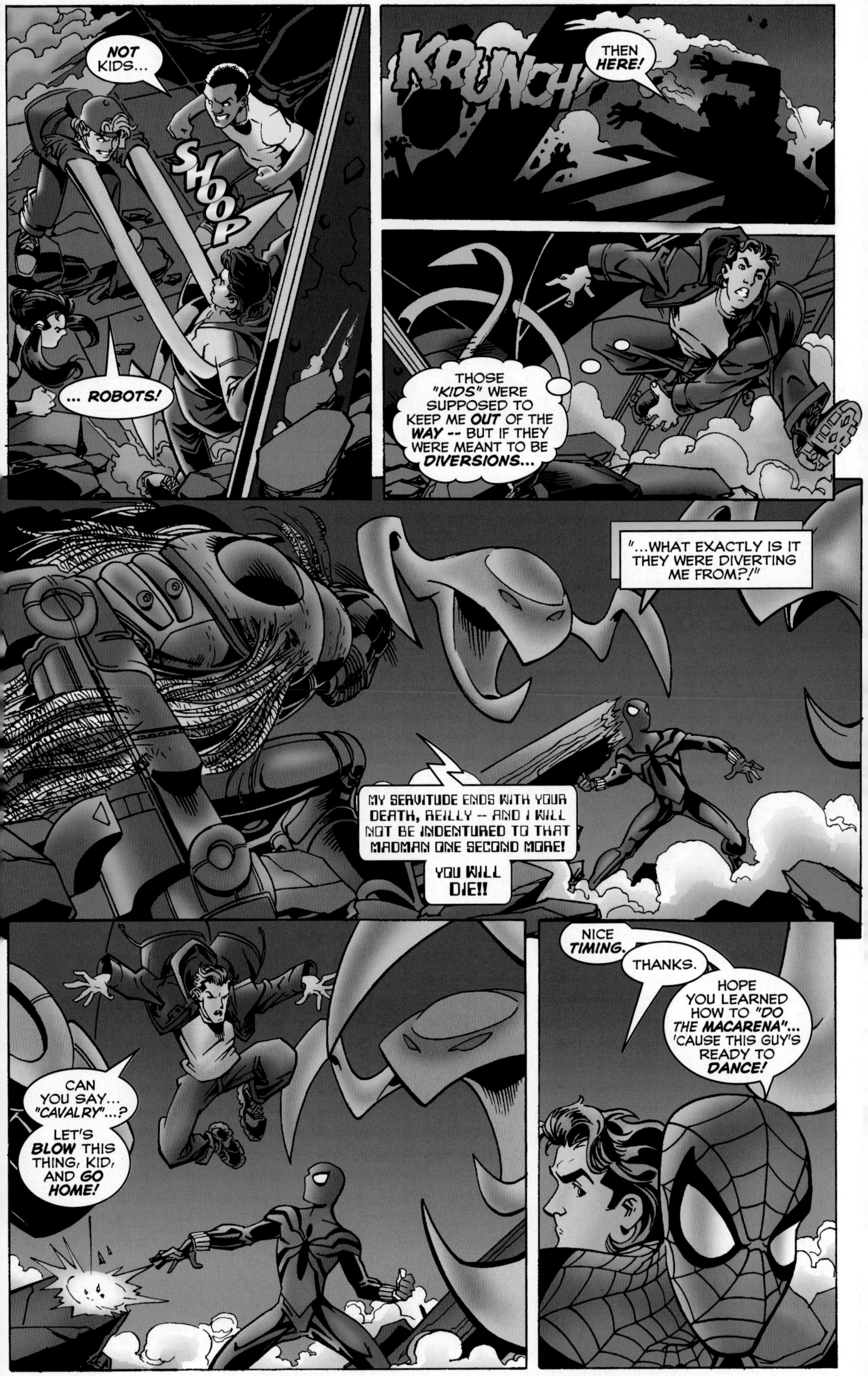
NOT KIDS...
SHOOP
... ROBOTS!
KRUNCH
THEN HERE!
THOSE "KIDS" WERE SUPPOSED TO KEEP ME OUT OF THE WAY -- BUT IF THEY WERE MEANT TO BE DIVERSIONS...
"...WHAT EXACTLY IS IT THEY WERE DIVERTING ME FROM?!"
MY SERVITUDE ENDS WITH YOUR DEATH, REILLY -- AND I WILL NOT BE INDENTURED TO THAT MADMAN ONE SECOND MORE!
YOU WILL DIE!!
CAN YOU SAY... "CAVALRY"...?
LET'S BLOW THIS THING, KID, AND GO HOME!
NICE TIMING.
THANKS.
HOPE YOU LEARNED HOW TO "DO THE MACARENA"... 'CAUSE THIS GUY'S READY TO DANCE!

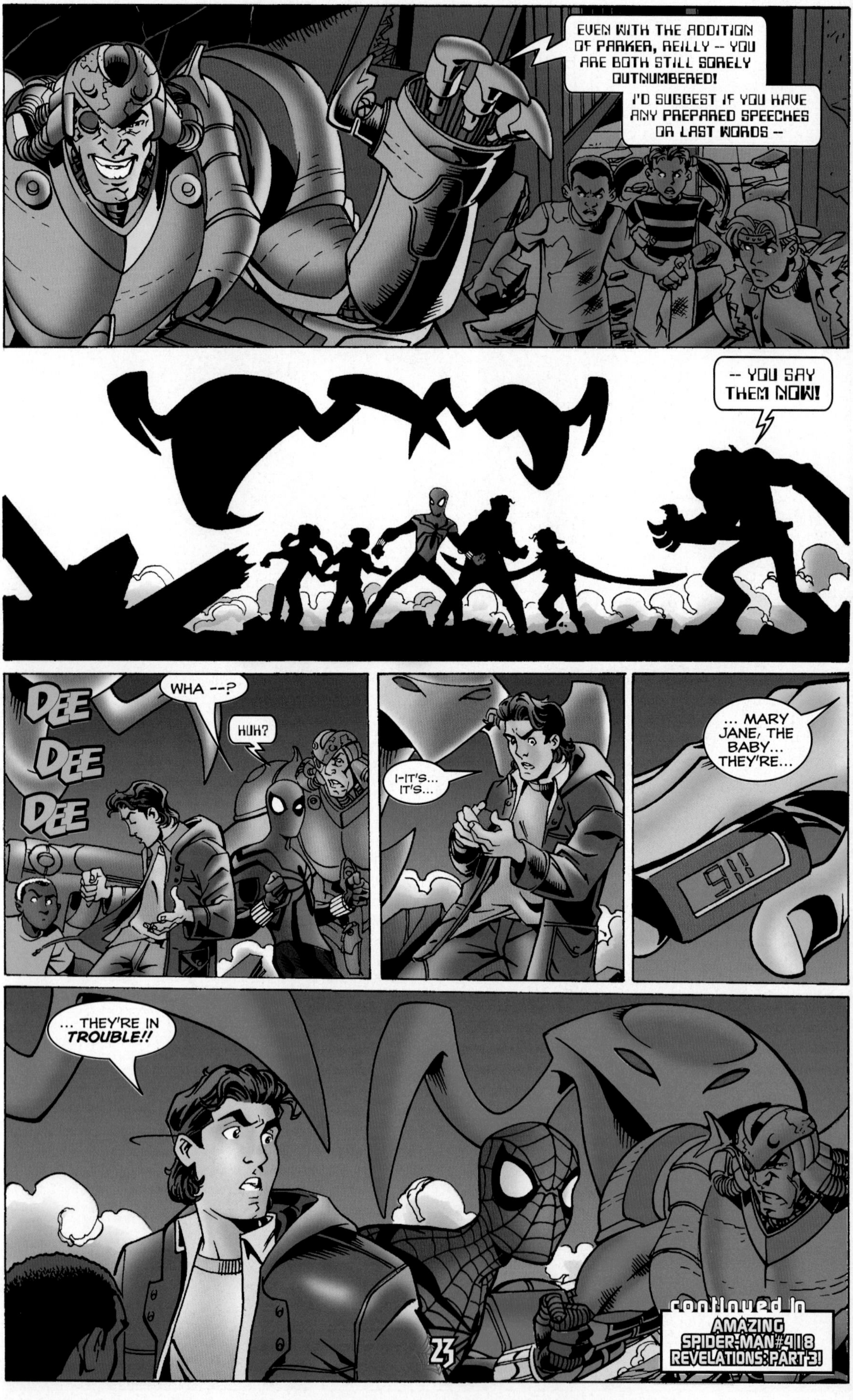

EVEN WITH THE ADDITION OF PARKER, REILLY -- YOU ARE BOTH STILL SORELY OUTNUMBERED!
I'D SUGGEST IF YOU HAVE ANY PREPARED SPEECHES OR LAST WORDS --
-- YOU SAY THEM NOW!
DEE DEE DEE
WHA --?
HUH?
I-IT'S... IT'S...
... MARY JANE, THE BABY... THEY'RE...
911
... THEY'RE IN TROUBLE!!
continued in AMAZING SPIDER-MAN #418 REVELATIONS: PART 3!

IN *AMAZING SPIDER-MAN* #418 AND *SPIDER-MAN* #75, "REVELATIONS" PARTS 3-4, TRAGEDY STRUCK. BEN AND PETER DEFEATED GAUNT, BUT ALISON'S POISON CAUSED MARY JANE TO MISCARRY. ALISON AND GAUNT'S MASTER REVEALED HIMSELF AS NORMAN OSBORN, THE LONG-THOUGHT-DEAD GREEN GOBLIN. WITH THE BUGLE STAFF AS HOSTAGES, NORMAN BATTLED BEN AND PETER. BEN ULTIMATELY SACRIFICED HIS LIFE TO SAVE PETER'S — AND DISSOLVED INTO DUST, REVEALING THAT HE HAD BEEN THE CLONE ALL ALONG. TO HONOR BEN AND HIS LOST CHILD, A GRIEVING PETER BECAME SPIDER-MAN ONCE AGAIN.

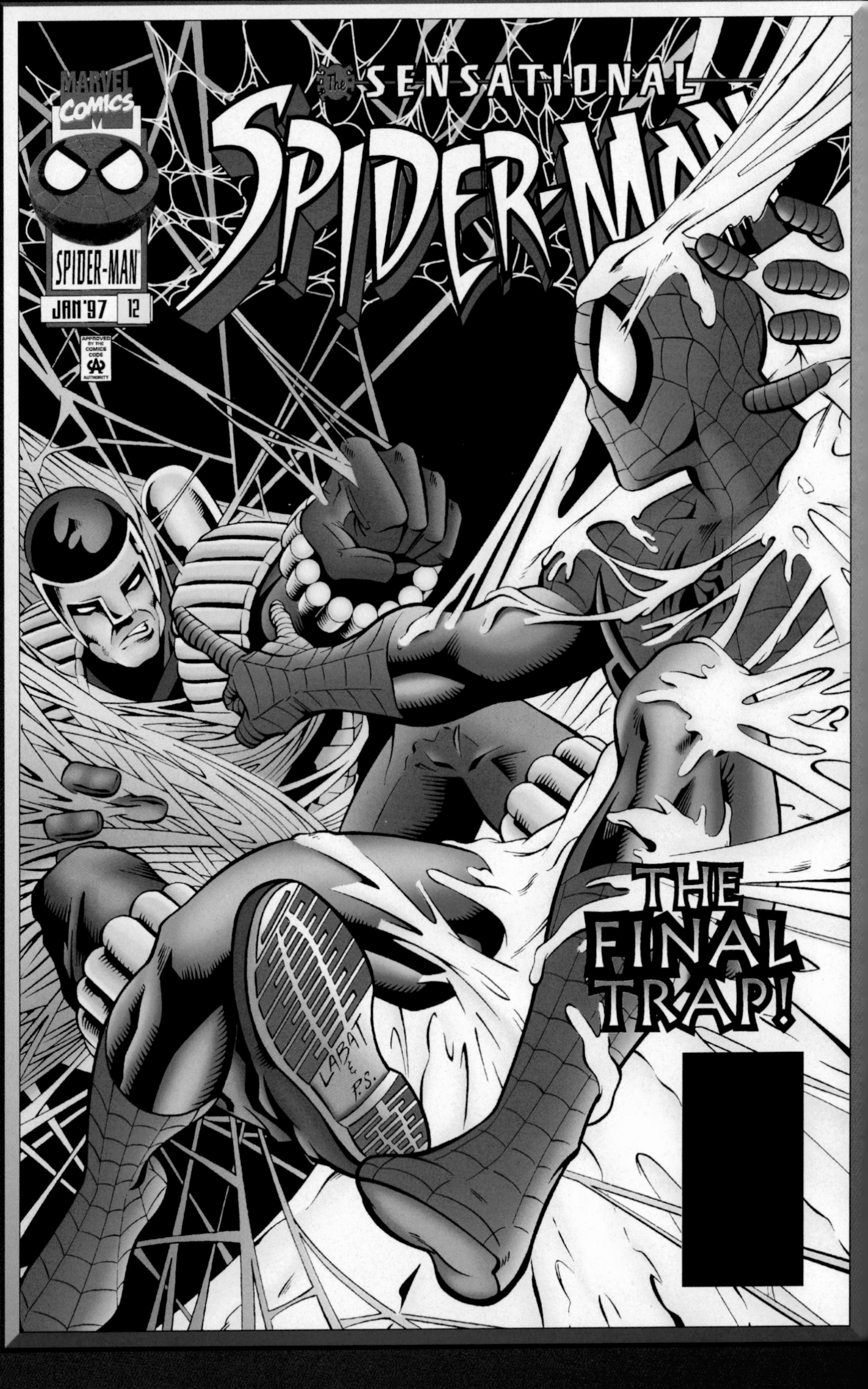
MARVEL COMICS
SPIDER-MAN
JAN '97 12
APPROVED BY THE COMICS CODE AUTHORITY
The SENSATIONAL SPIDER-MAN
THE FINAL TRAP!
LABAT & P.S.

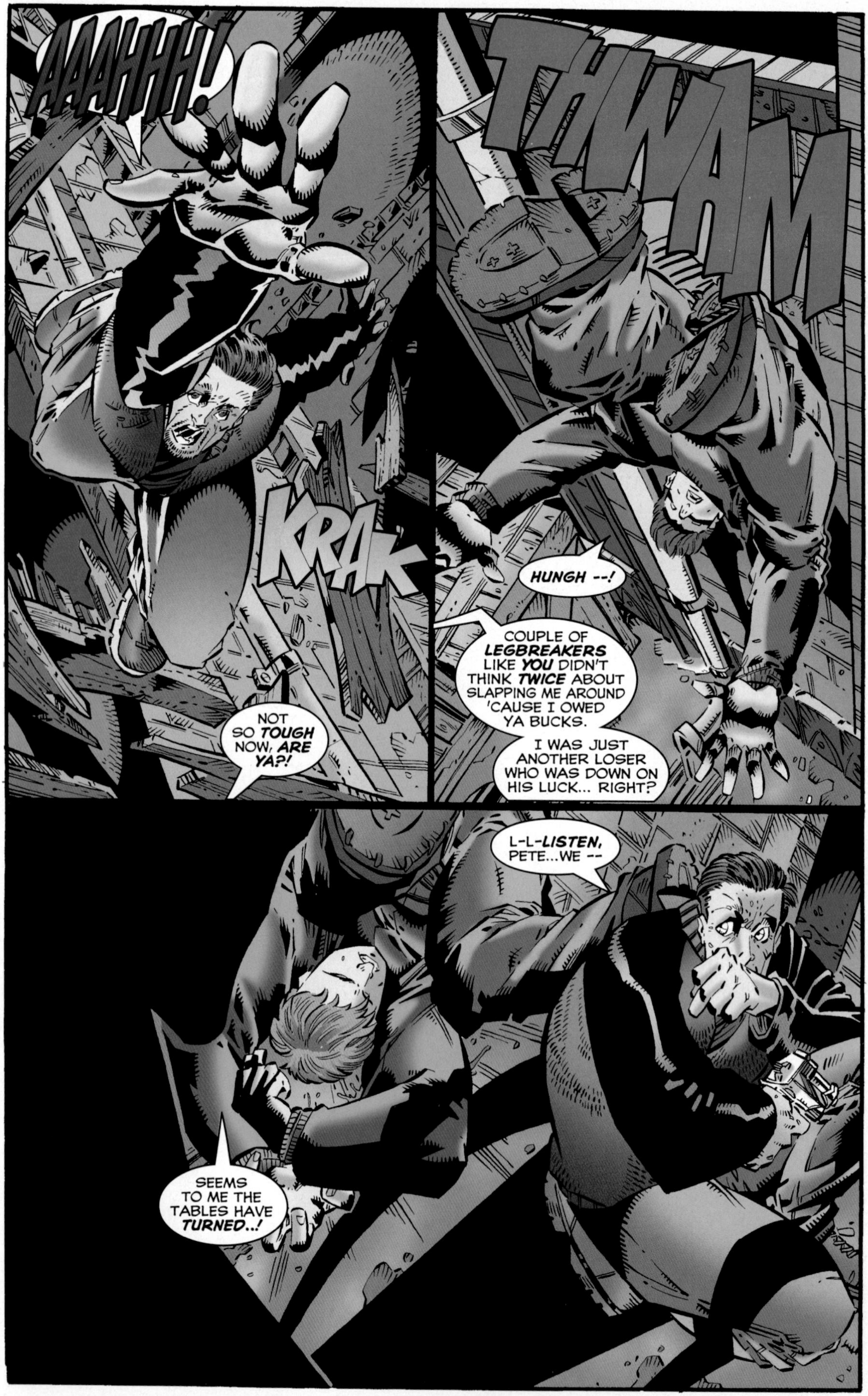
AAAHHH!
KRAK
NOT SO TOUGH NOW, ARE YA?!
THWAM
HUNGH --!
COUPLE OF LEGBREAKERS LIKE YOU DIDN'T THINK TWICE ABOUT SLAPPING ME AROUND 'CAUSE I OWED YA BUCKS.
I WAS JUST ANOTHER LOSER WHO WAS DOWN ON HIS LUCK... RIGHT?
L-L-LISTEN, PETE...WE --
SEEMS TO ME THE TABLES HAVE TURNED..!

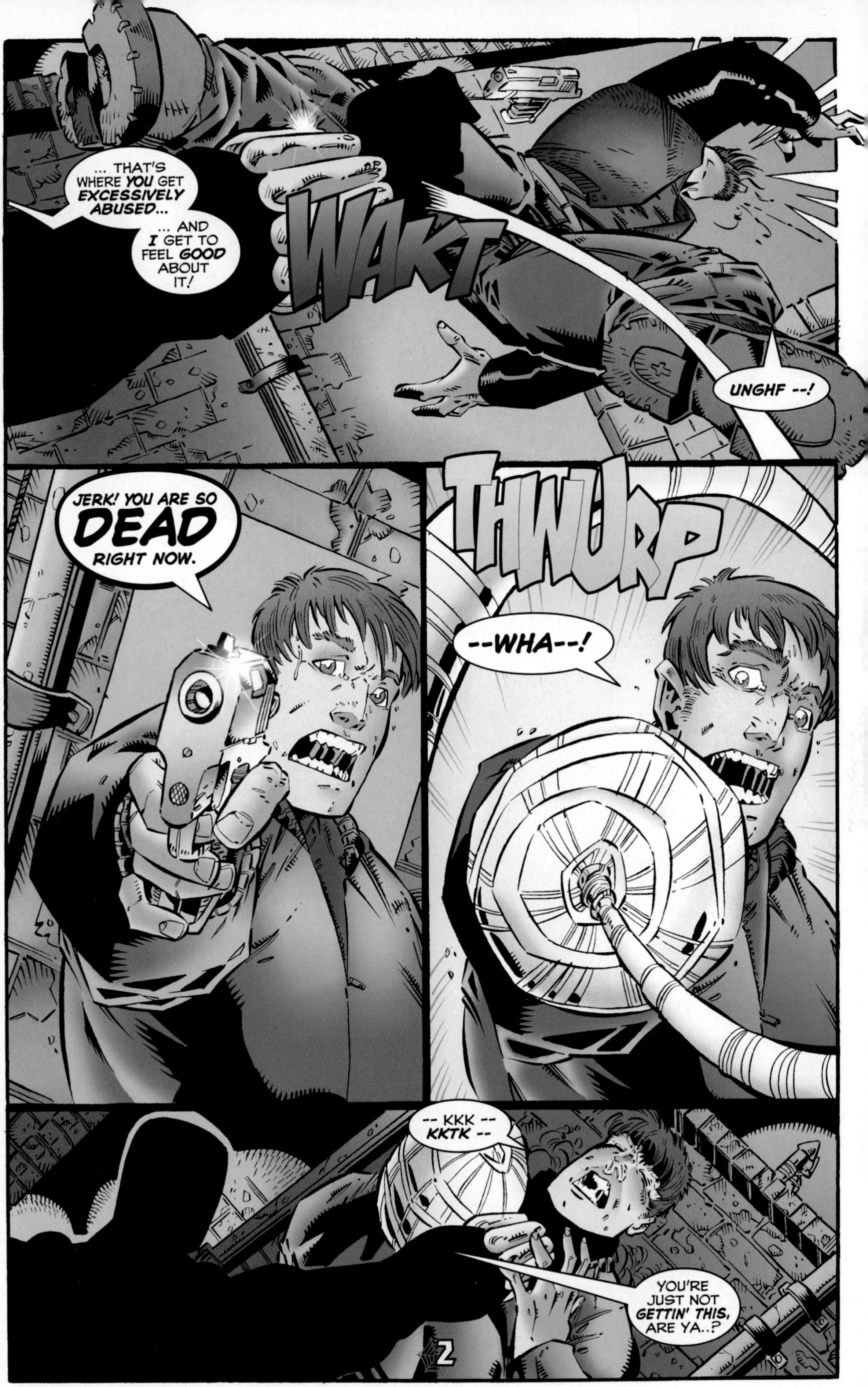

... THAT'S WHERE YOU GET EXCESSIVELY ABUSED...
... AND I GET TO FEEL GOOD ABOUT IT!
WAKT
UNGHF --!
JERK! YOU ARE SO DEAD RIGHT NOW.
THWURP
--WHA--!
-- KKK -- KKTK --
YOU'RE JUST NOT GETTIN' THIS, ARE YA..?

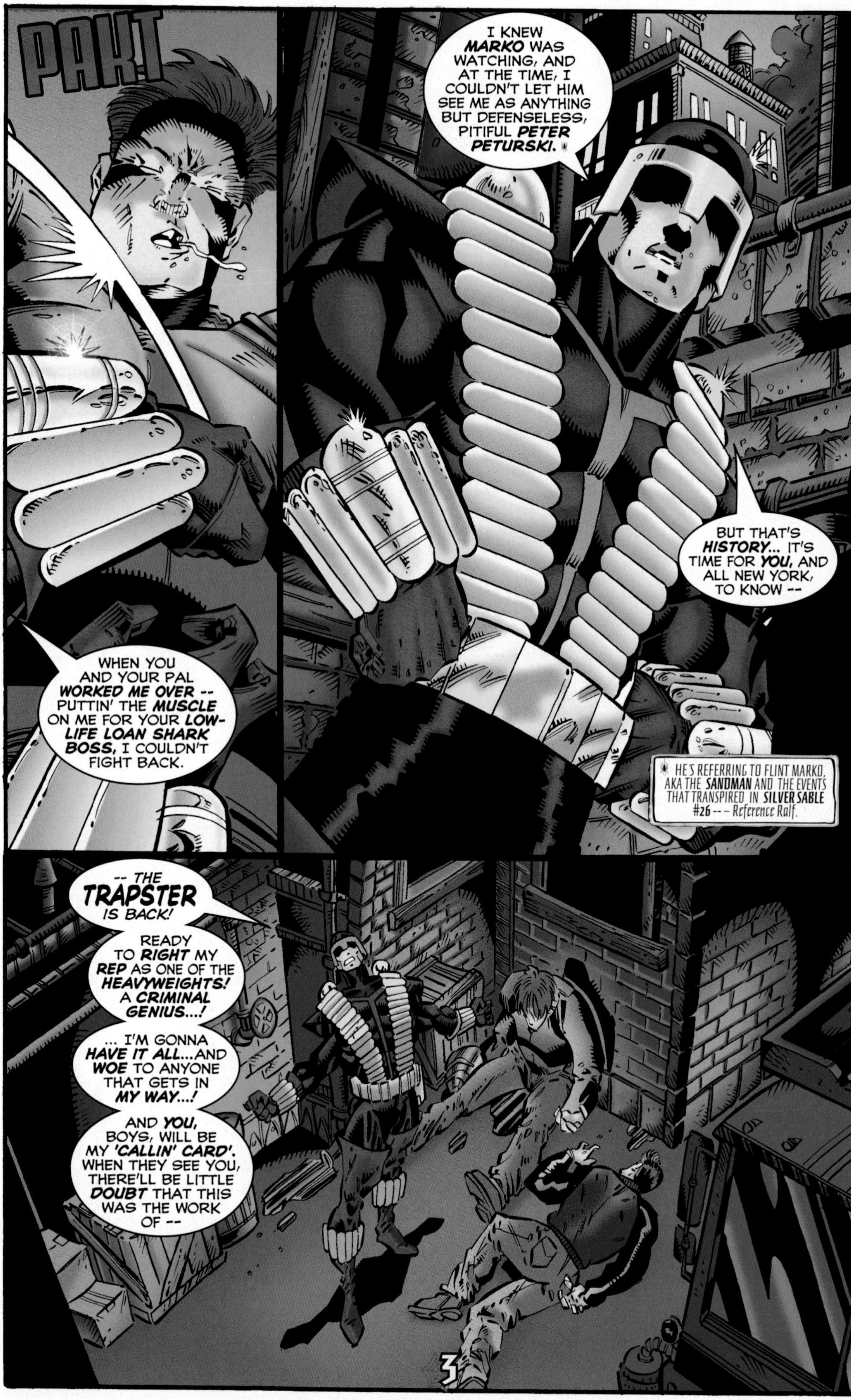
PAKT
WHEN YOU AND YOUR PAL WORKED ME OVER -- PUTTIN' THE MUSCLE ON ME FOR YOUR LOW-LIFE LOAN SHARK BOSS, I COULDN'T FIGHT BACK.
I KNEW MARKO WAS WATCHING, AND AT THE TIME, I COULDN'T LET HIM SEE ME AS ANYTHING BUT DEFENSELESS, PITIFUL PETER PETURSKI.
BUT THAT'S HISTORY... IT'S TIME FOR YOU, AND ALL NEW YORK, TO KNOW --
HE'S REFERRING TO FLINT MARKO, AKA THE SANDMAN AND THE EVENTS THAT TRANSPIRED IN SILVER SABLE #26 -- – Reference Ralf.
-- THE TRAPSTER IS BACK!
READY TO RIGHT MY REP AS ONE OF THE HEAVYWEIGHTS! A CRIMINAL GENIUS...!
... I'M GONNA HAVE IT ALL...AND WOE TO ANYONE THAT GETS IN MY WAY...!
AND YOU, BOYS, WILL BE MY 'CALLIN' CARD'. WHEN THEY SEE YOU, THERE'LL BE LITTLE DOUBT THAT THIS WAS THE WORK OF --
3

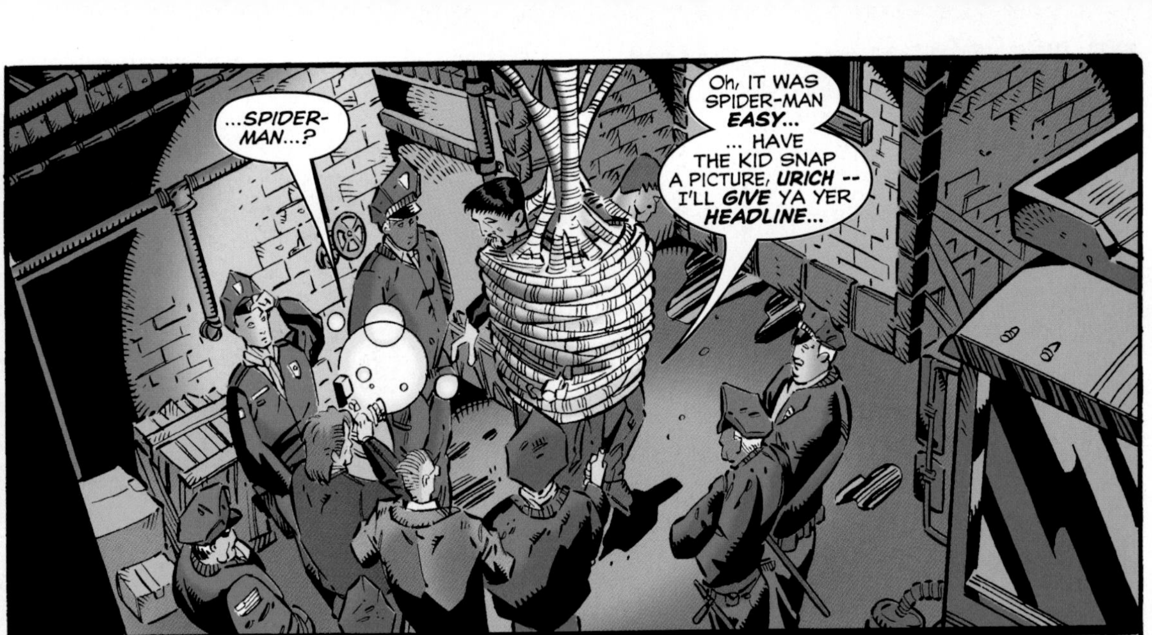
...SPIDER-MAN...?
Oh, IT WAS SPIDER-MAN EASY...
... HAVE THE KID SNAP A PICTURE, URICH -- I'LL GIVE YA YER HEADLINE...

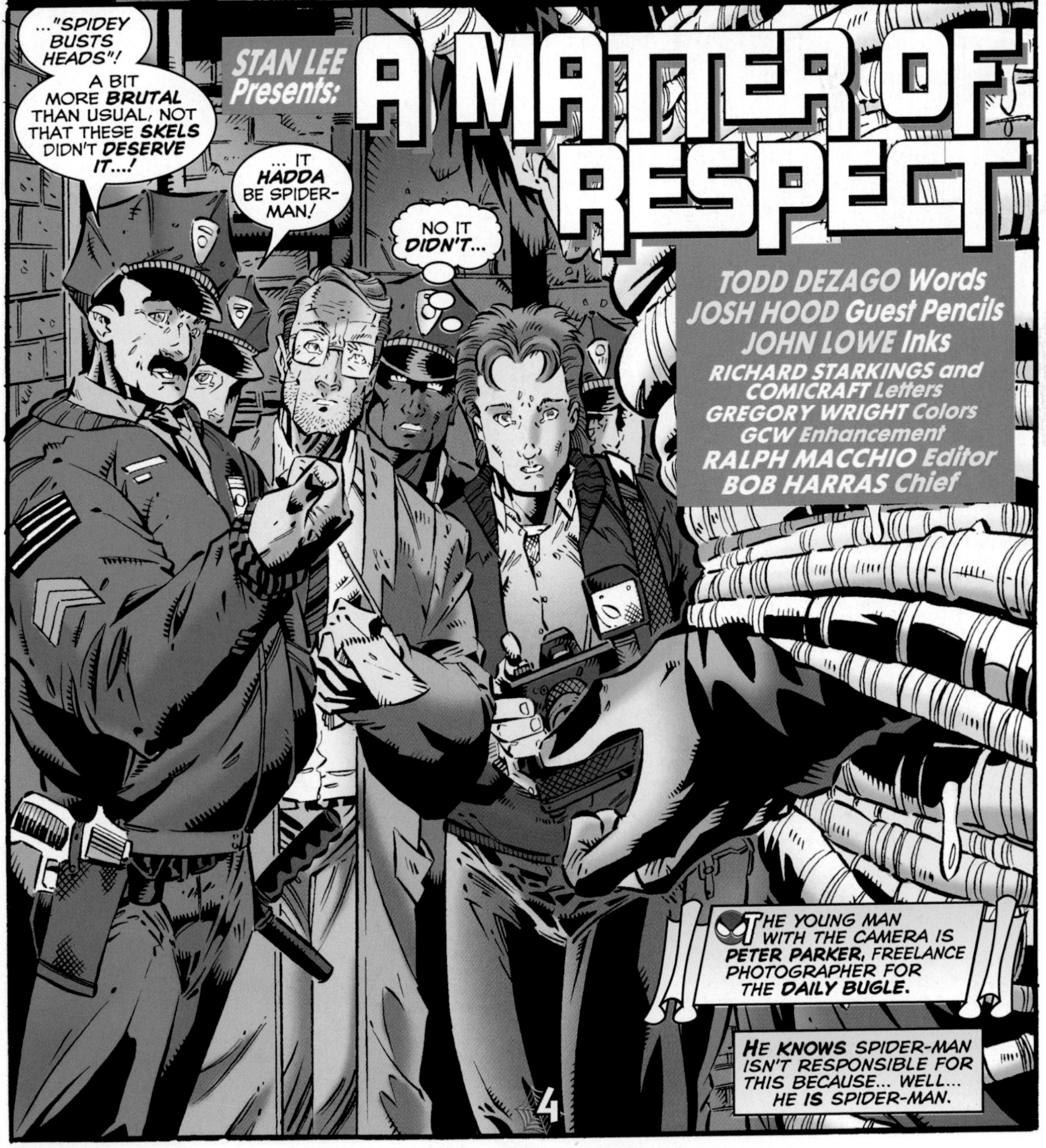
..."SPIDEY BUSTS HEADS"!
A BIT MORE BRUTAL THAN USUAL, NOT THAT THESE SKELS DIDN'T DESERVE IT...!
STAN LEE Presents:
A MATTER OF RESPECT
... IT HADDA BE SPIDER-MAN!
NO IT DIDN'T...
TODD DEZAGO Words
JOSH HOOD Guest Pencils
JOHN LOWE Inks
RICHARD STARKINGS and COMICRAFT Letters
GREGORY WRIGHT Colors
GCW Enhancement
RALPH MACCHIO Editor
BOB HARRAS Chief
THE YOUNG MAN WITH THE CAMERA IS PETER PARKER, FREELANCE PHOTOGRAPHER FOR THE DAILY BUGLE.
HE KNOWS SPIDER-MAN ISN'T RESPONSIBLE FOR THIS BECAUSE... WELL... HE IS SPIDER-MAN.

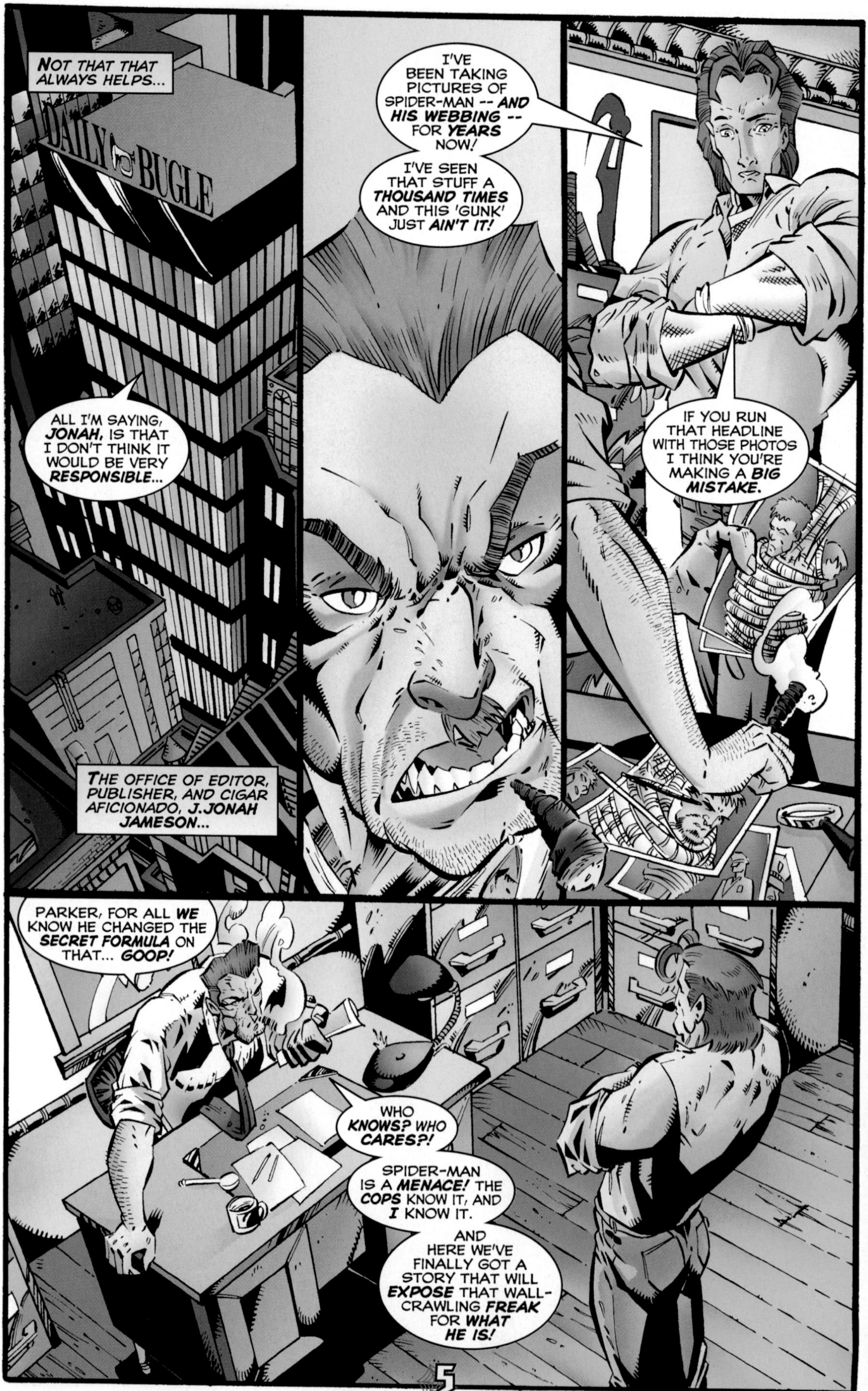
NOT THAT THAT ALWAYS HELPS...
DAILY BUGLE
ALL I'M SAYING, JONAH, IS THAT I DON'T THINK IT WOULD BE VERY RESPONSIBLE...
THE OFFICE OF EDITOR, PUBLISHER, AND CIGAR AFICIONADO, J.JONAH JAMESON...
I'VE BEEN TAKING PICTURES OF SPIDER-MAN -- AND HIS WEBBING -- FOR YEARS NOW!
I'VE SEEN THAT STUFF A THOUSAND TIMES AND THIS 'GUNK' JUST AIN'T IT!
IF YOU RUN THAT HEADLINE WITH THOSE PHOTOS I THINK YOU'RE MAKING A BIG MISTAKE.
PARKER, FOR ALL WE KNOW HE CHANGED THE SECRET FORMULA ON THAT... GOOP!
WHO KNOWS? WHO CARES?!
SPIDER-MAN IS A MENACE! THE COPS KNOW IT, AND I KNOW IT.
AND HERE WE'VE FINALLY GOT A STORY THAT WILL EXPOSE THAT WALL-CRAWLING FREAK FOR WHAT HE IS!

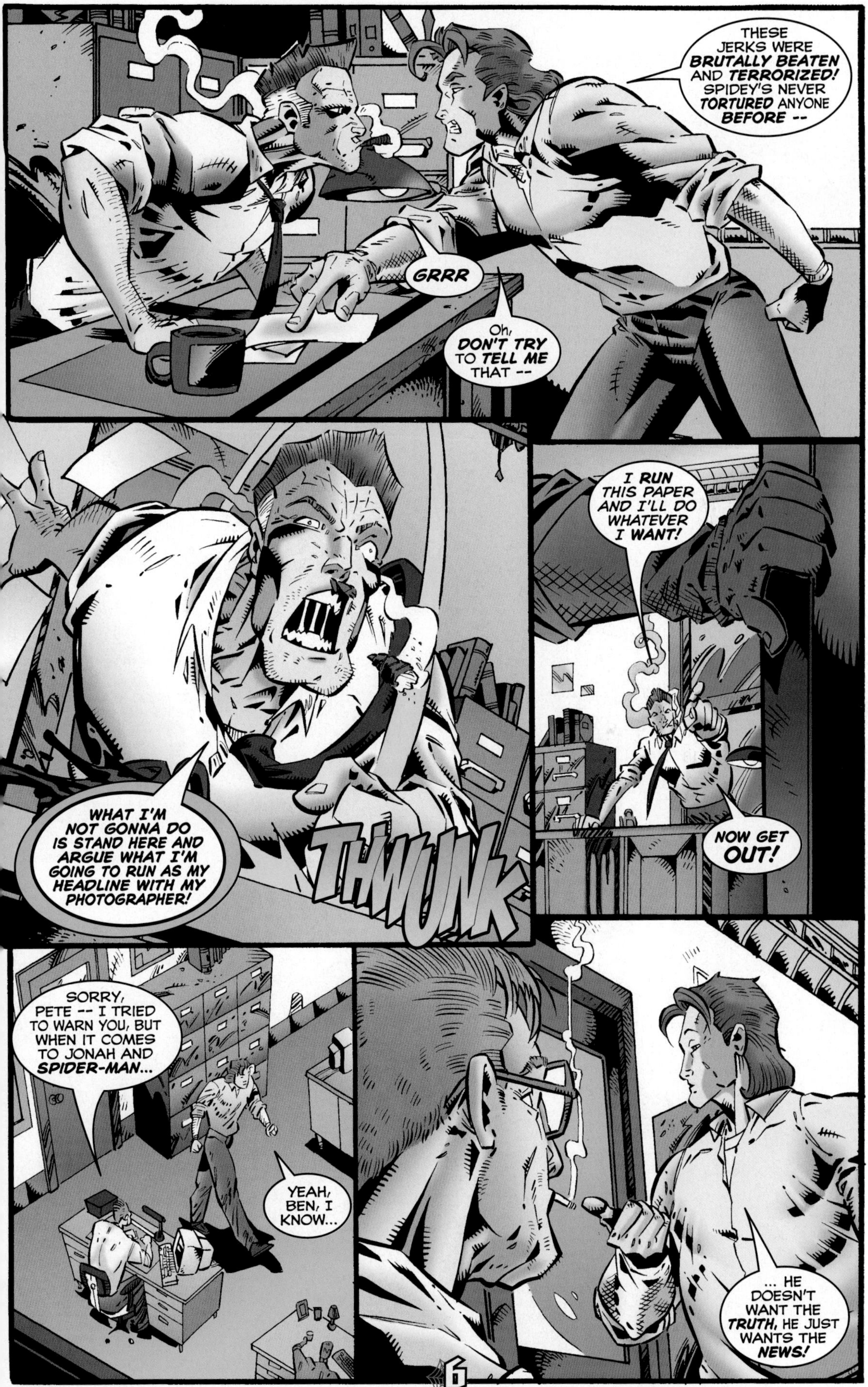
THESE JERKS WERE BRUTALLY BEATEN AND TERRORIZED! SPIDEY'S NEVER TORTURED ANYONE BEFORE --
GRRR
Oh, DON'T TRY TO TELL ME THAT --
WHAT I'M NOT GONNA DO IS STAND HERE AND ARGUE WHAT I'M GOING TO RUN AS MY HEADLINE WITH MY PHOTOGRAPHER!
THWUNK
I RUN THIS PAPER AND I'LL DO WHATEVER I WANT!
NOW GET OUT!
SORRY, PETE -- I TRIED TO WARN YOU, BUT WHEN IT COMES TO JONAH AND SPIDER-MAN...
YEAH, BEN, I KNOW...
... HE DOESN'T WANT THE TRUTH, HE JUST WANTS THE NEWS!

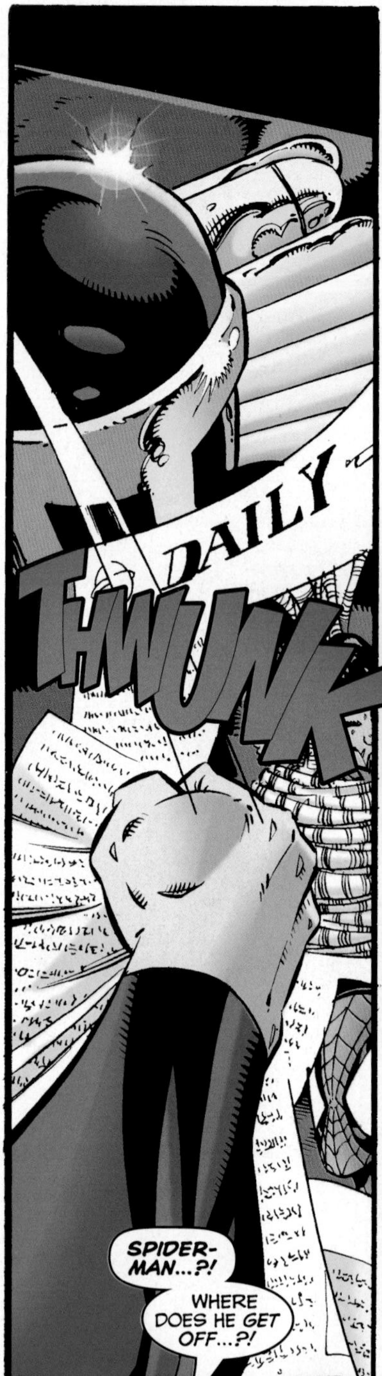
DAILY
THWUNK
SPIDER-MAN...?!
WHERE DOES HE GET OFF...?!

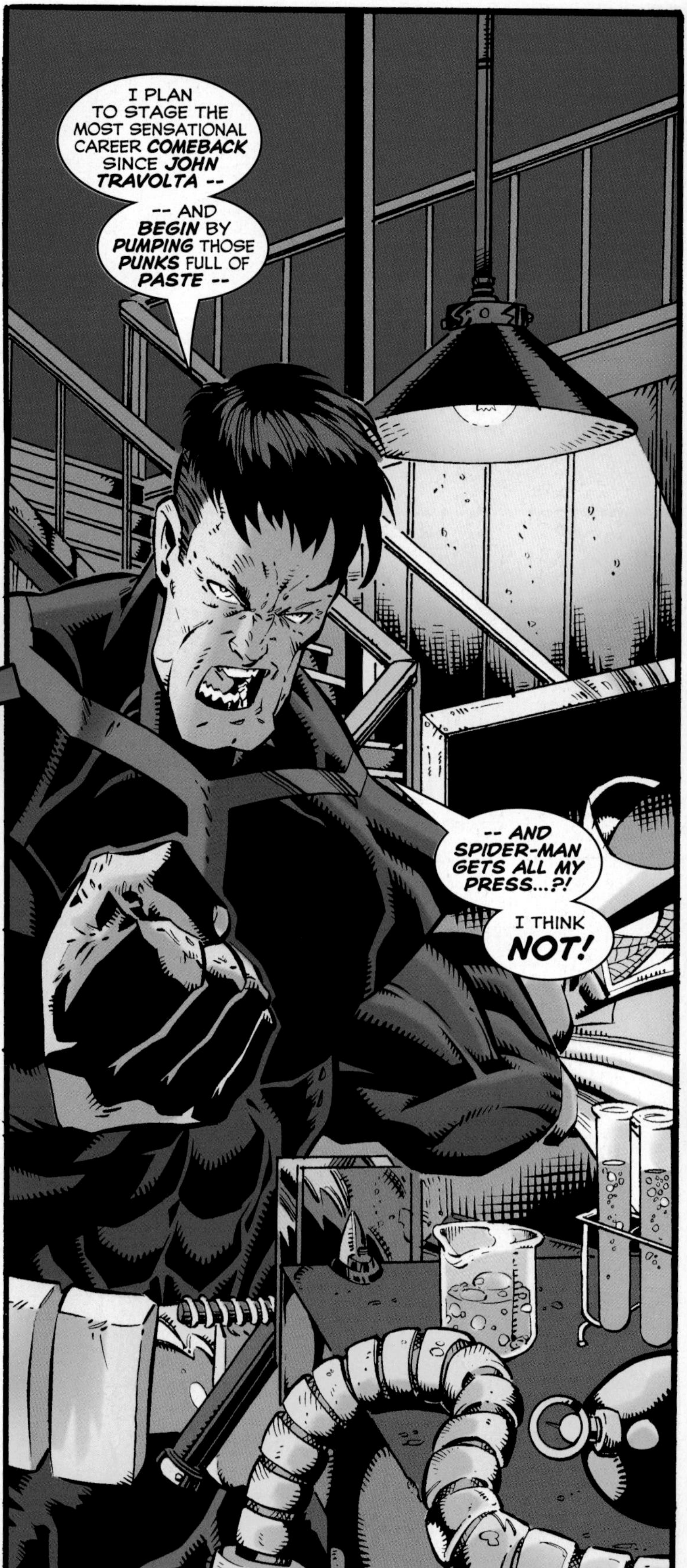
I PLAN TO STAGE THE MOST SENSATIONAL CAREER COMEBACK SINCE JOHN TRAVOLTA --
-- AND BEGIN BY PUMPING THOSE PUNKS FULL OF PASTE --
-- AND SPIDER-MAN GETS ALL MY PRESS...?!
I THINK NOT!

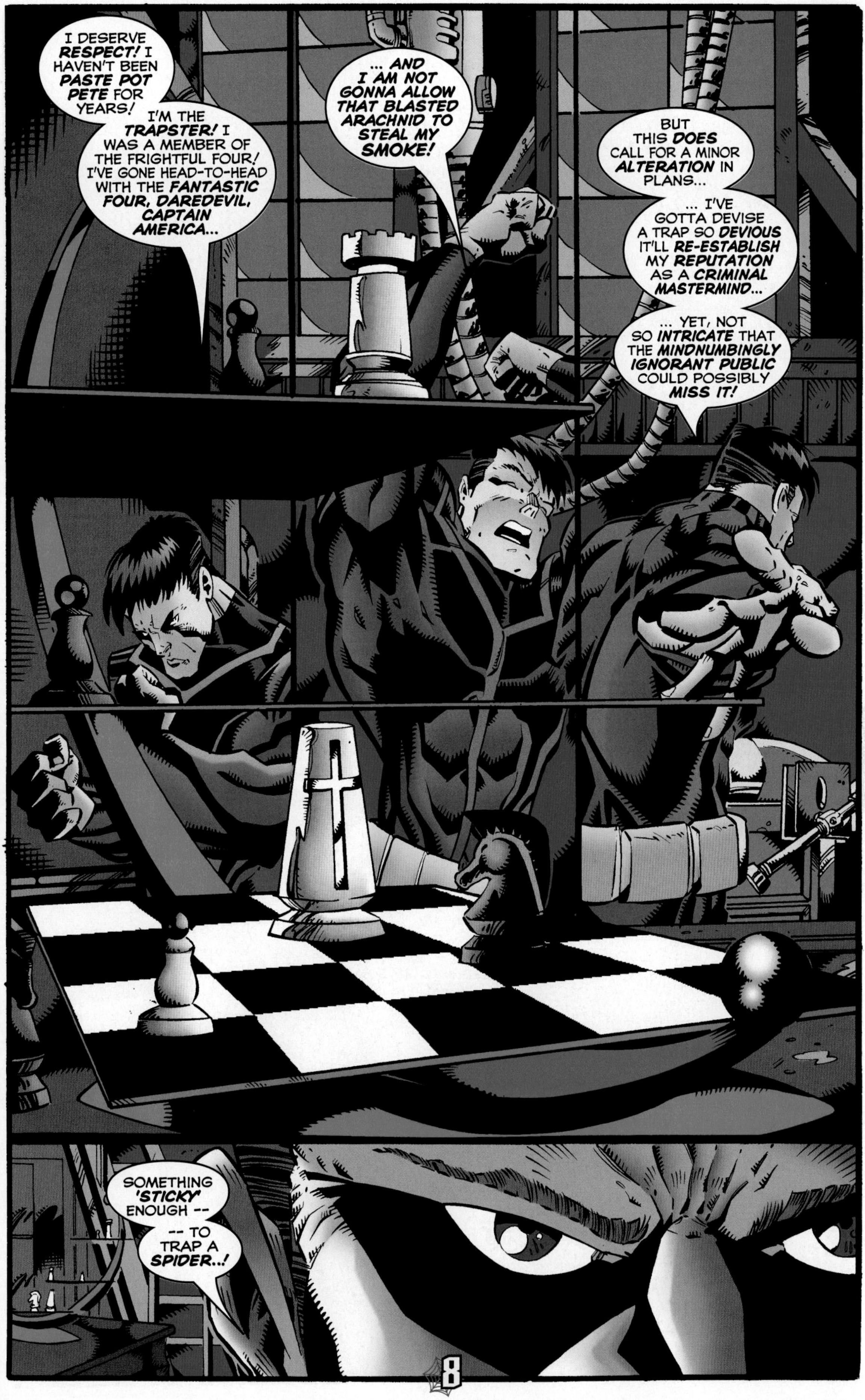
I DESERVE RESPECT! I HAVEN'T BEEN PASTE POT PETE FOR YEARS!
I'M THE TRAPSTER! I WAS A MEMBER OF THE FRIGHTFUL FOUR! I'VE GONE HEAD-TO-HEAD WITH THE FANTASTIC FOUR, DAREDEVIL, CAPTAIN AMERICA...
... AND I AM NOT GONNA ALLOW THAT BLASTED ARACHNID TO STEAL MY SMOKE!
BUT THIS DOES CALL FOR A MINOR ALTERATION IN PLANS...
... I'VE GOTTA DEVISE A TRAP SO DEVIOUS IT'LL RE-ESTABLISH MY REPUTATION AS A CRIMINAL MASTERMIND...
... YET, NOT SO INTRICATE THAT THE MINDNUMBINGLY IGNORANT PUBLIC COULD POSSIBLY MISS IT!
SOMETHING 'STICKY' ENOUGH --
-- TO TRAP A SPIDER...!

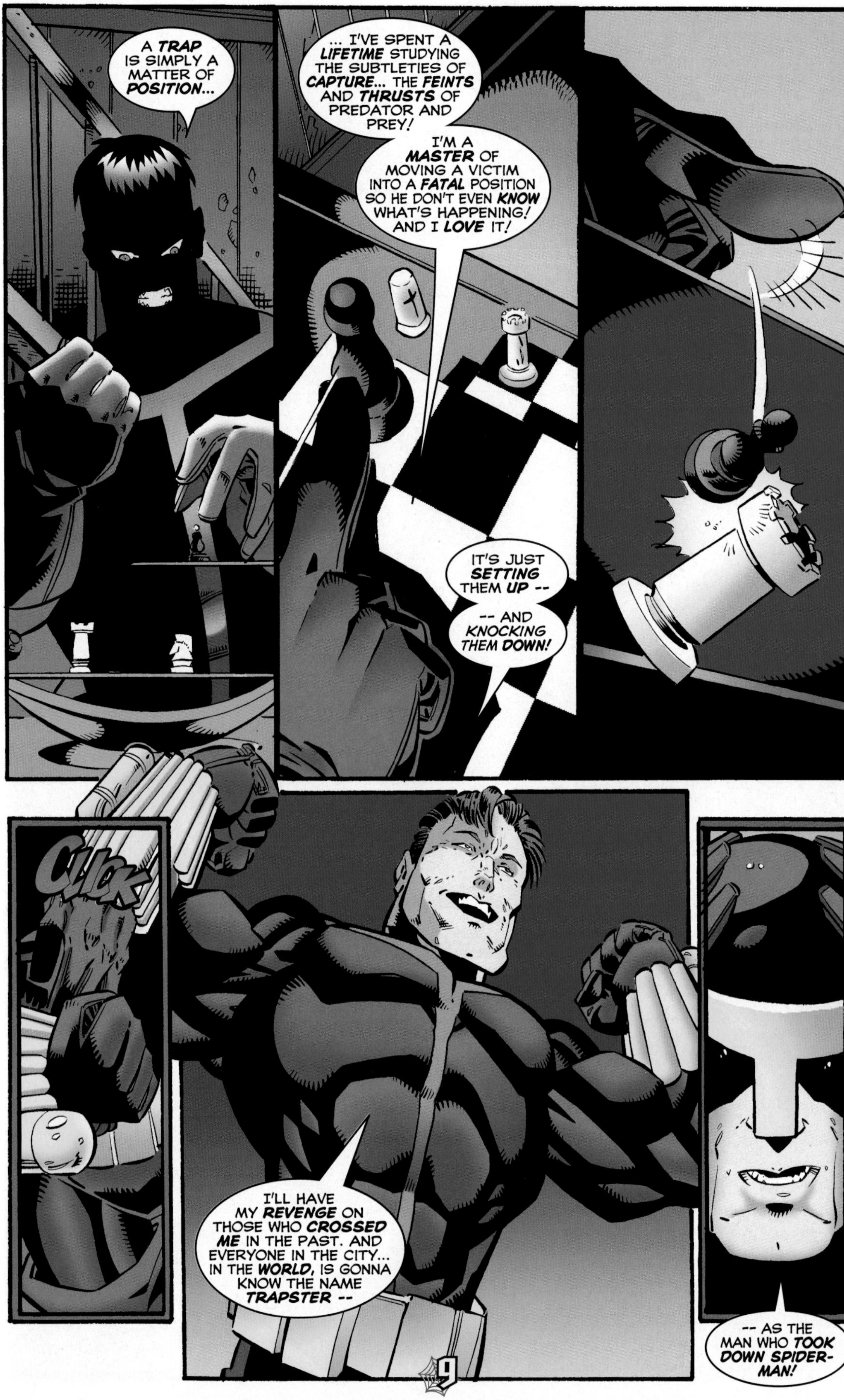
A TRAP IS SIMPLY A MATTER OF POSITION...
... I'VE SPENT A LIFETIME STUDYING THE SUBTLETIES OF CAPTURE... THE FEINTS AND THRUSTS OF PREDATOR AND PREY!
I'M A MASTER OF MOVING A VICTIM INTO A FATAL POSITION SO HE DON'T EVEN KNOW WHAT'S HAPPENING! AND I LOVE IT!
IT'S JUST SETTING THEM UP --
-- AND KNOCKING THEM DOWN!
CLICK
I'LL HAVE MY REVENGE ON THOSE WHO CROSSED ME IN THE PAST. AND EVERYONE IN THE CITY... IN THE WORLD, IS GONNA KNOW THE NAME TRAPSTER --
-- AS THE MAN WHO TOOK DOWN SPIDER-MAN!

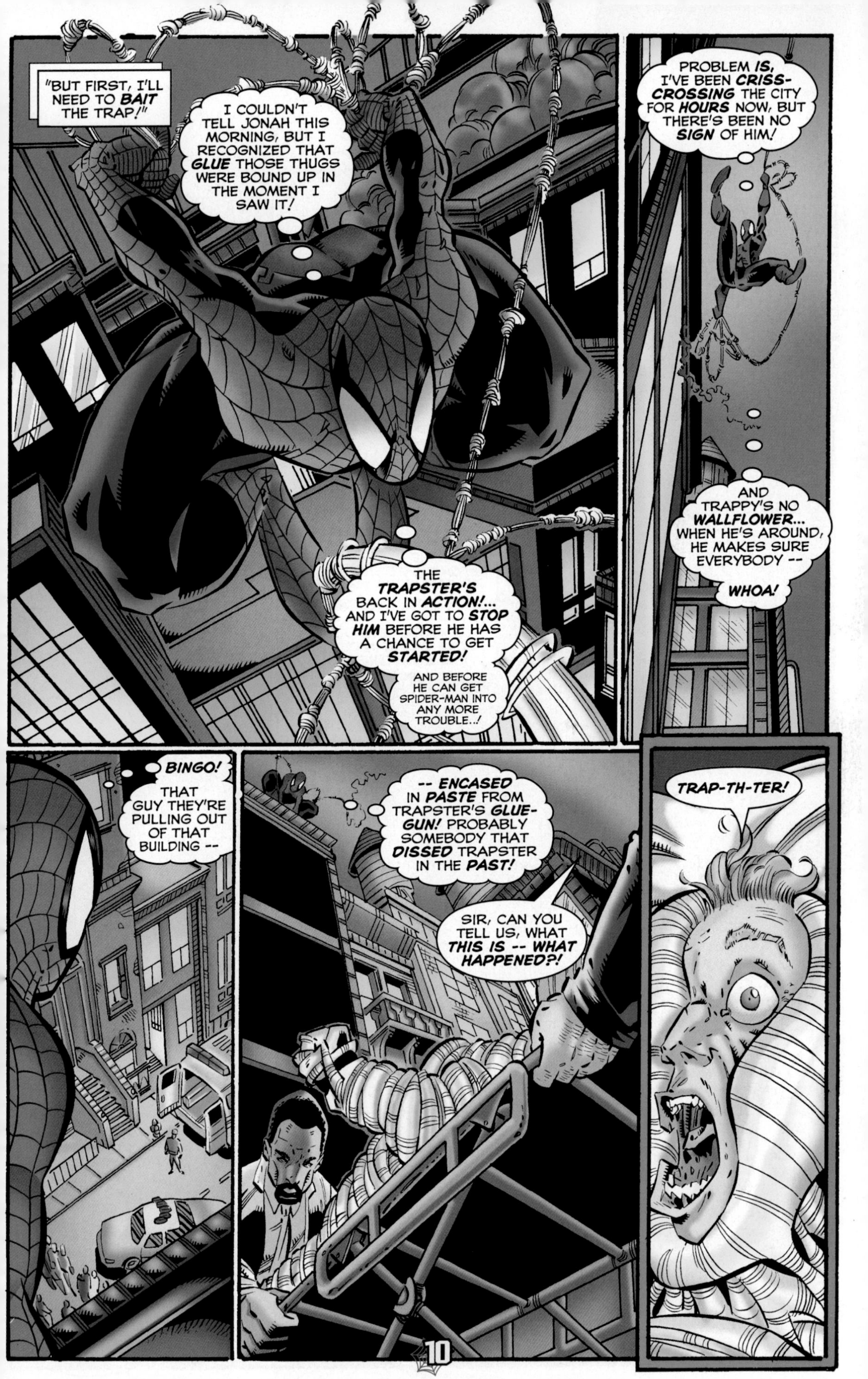
"BUT FIRST, I'LL NEED TO BAIT THE TRAP!"
I COULDN'T TELL JONAH THIS MORNING, BUT I RECOGNIZED THAT GLUE THOSE THUGS WERE BOUND UP IN THE MOMENT I SAW IT!
THE TRAPSTER'S BACK IN ACTION!... AND I'VE GOT TO STOP HIM BEFORE HE HAS A CHANCE TO GET STARTED!
AND BEFORE HE CAN GET SPIDER-MAN INTO ANY MORE TROUBLE..!
PROBLEM IS, I'VE BEEN CRISS-CROSSING THE CITY FOR HOURS NOW, BUT THERE'S BEEN NO SIGN OF HIM!
AND TRAPPY'S NO WALLFLOWER... WHEN HE'S AROUND, HE MAKES SURE EVERYBODY --
WHOA!
BINGO!
THAT GUY THEY'RE PULLING OUT OF THAT BUILDING --
-- ENCASED IN PASTE FROM TRAPSTER'S GLUE-GUN! PROBABLY SOMEBODY THAT DISSED TRAPSTER IN THE PAST!
SIR, CAN YOU TELL US, WHAT THIS IS -- WHAT HAPPENED?!
TRAP-TH-TER!

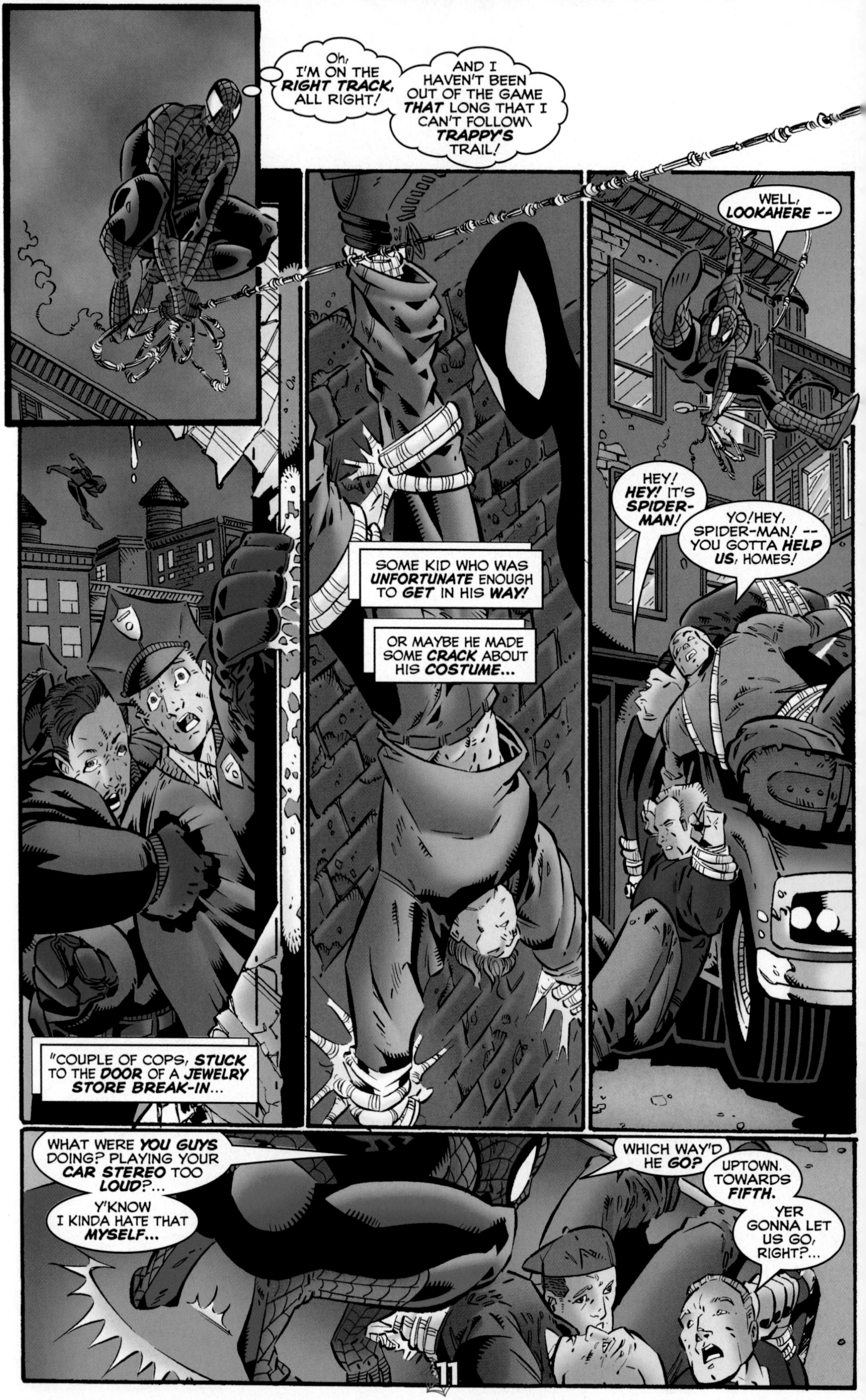

Oh, I'M ON THE RIGHT TRACK, ALL RIGHT!
AND I HAVEN'T BEEN OUT OF THE GAME THAT LONG THAT I CAN'T FOLLOW TRAPPY'S TRAIL!
"COUPLE OF COPS, STUCK TO THE DOOR OF A JEWELRY STORE BREAK-IN...
SOME KID WHO WAS UNFORTUNATE ENOUGH TO GET IN HIS WAY!
OR MAYBE HE MADE SOME CRACK ABOUT HIS COSTUME...
WELL, LOOKAHERE --
HEY! HEY! IT'S SPIDER-MAN!
YO! HEY, SPIDER-MAN! -- YOU GOTTA HELP US, HOMES!
WHAT WERE YOU GUYS DOING? PLAYING YOUR CAR STEREO TOO LOUD?...
Y'KNOW I KINDA HATE THAT MYSELF...
WHICH WAY'D HE GO?
UPTOWN. TOWARDS FIFTH.
YER GONNA LET US GO, RIGHT?...

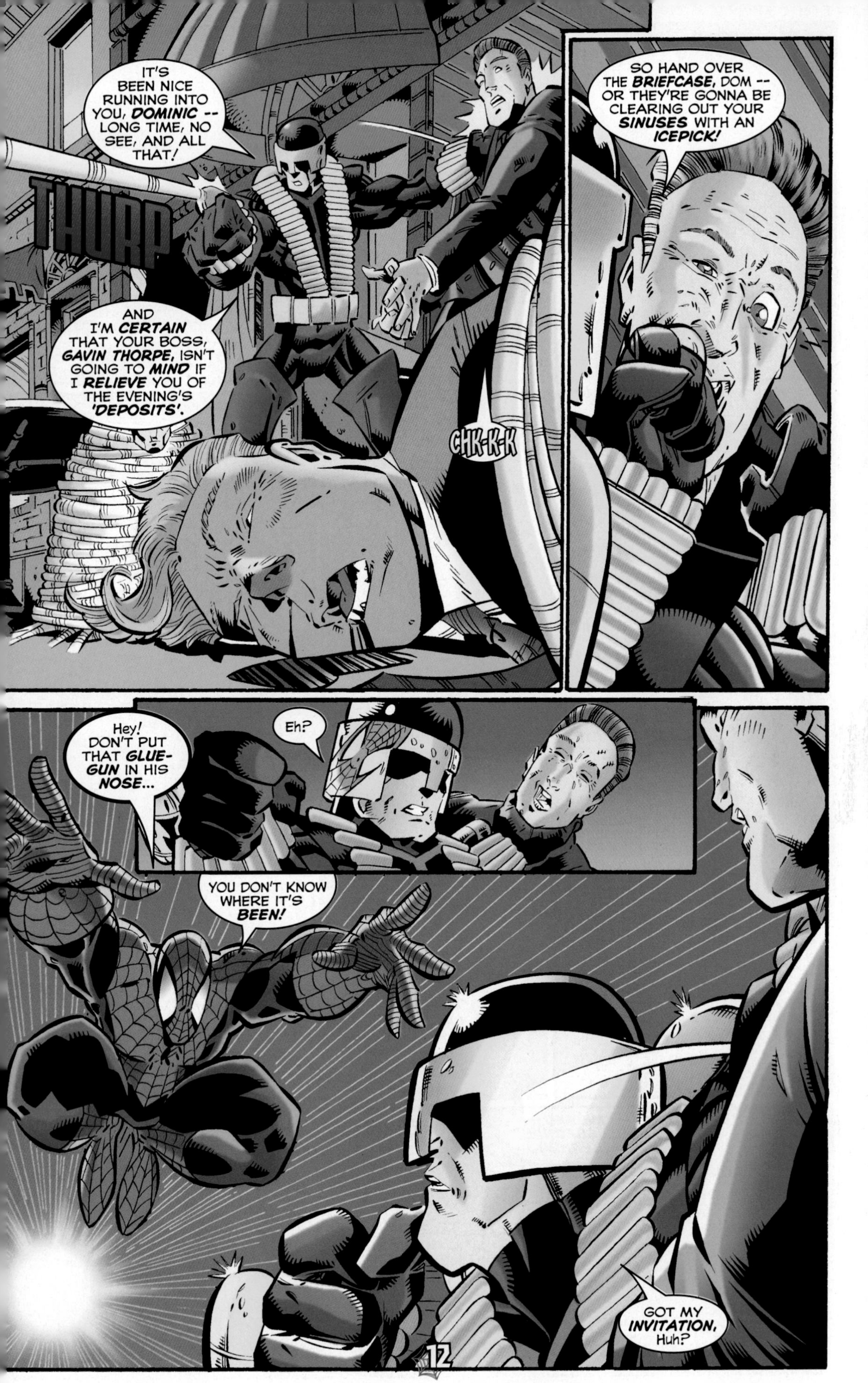
IT'S BEEN NICE RUNNING INTO YOU, DOMINIC -- LONG TIME, NO SEE, AND ALL THAT!
THURP
AND I'M CERTAIN THAT YOUR BOSS, GAVIN THORPE, ISN'T GOING TO MIND IF I RELIEVE YOU OF THE EVENING'S 'DEPOSITS'.
CHK-K-K
SO HAND OVER THE BRIEFCASE, DOM -- OR THEY'RE GONNA BE CLEARING OUT YOUR SINUSES WITH AN ICEPICK!
Hey! DON'T PUT THAT GLUE-GUN IN HIS NOSE...
Eh?
YOU DON'T KNOW WHERE IT'S BEEN!
GOT MY INVITATION, Huh?

YOU ONLY LEFT THEM **ALL OVER TOWN.**

I WASN'T SURE YOU'D **COME.** BELIEVE THAT, WEBS?

LET GO OF THE **'INNOCENT BYSTANDER'**, TRAPPY.

YOU **WANT** HIM, **TAKE HIM!**

UNGH!

ME?... I'M GONNA TAKE A **CAB!**

IGOT HIMIGOT HIMIGOT HIM --

THURP

WAKT

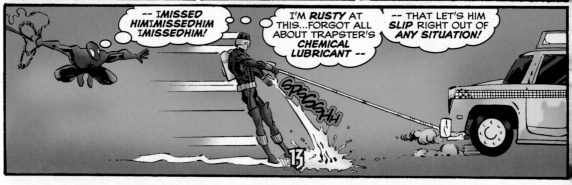

-- IMISSED HIMIMISSEDHIM IMISSEDHIM!

I'M **RUSTY** AT THIS...FORGOT ALL ABOUT TRAPSTER'S **CHEMICAL LUBRICANT** --

-- THAT LET'S HIM **SLIP** RIGHT OUT OF **ANY SITUATION!**

GPSPLSSHHH

13

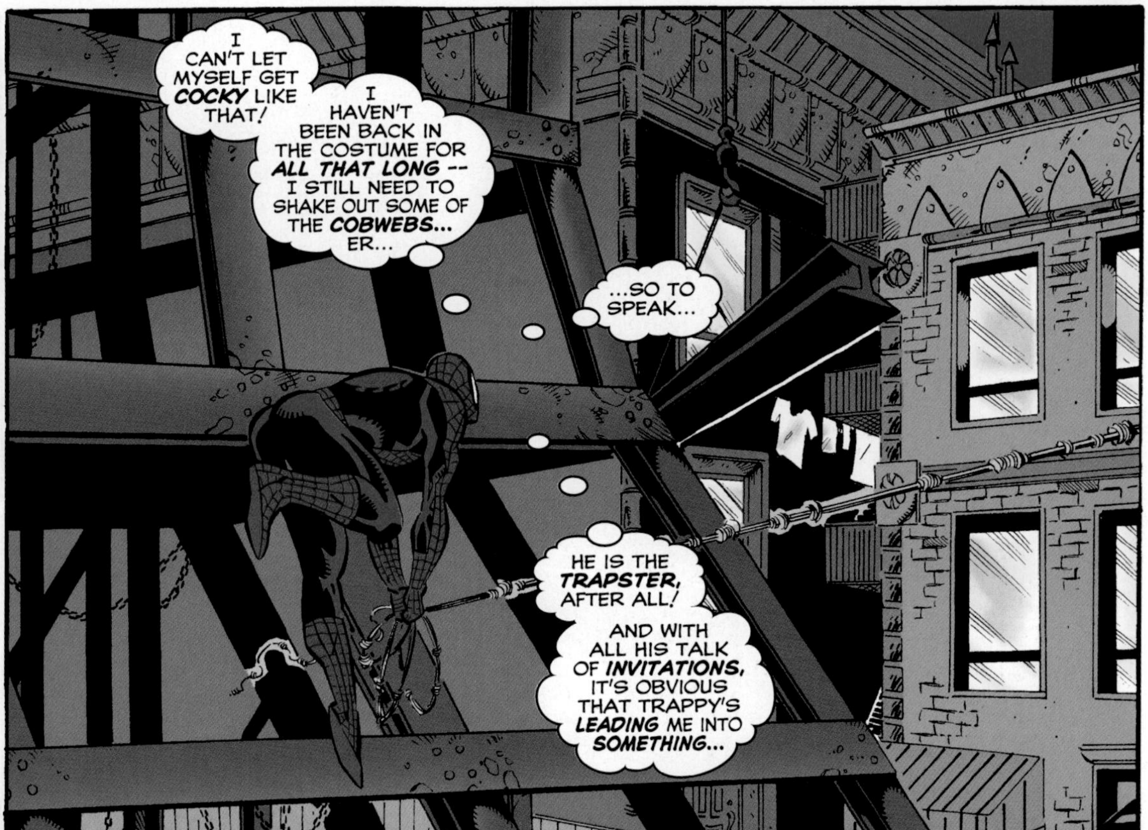
I CAN'T LET MYSELF GET COCKY LIKE THAT!
I HAVEN'T BEEN BACK IN THE COSTUME FOR ALL THAT LONG -- I STILL NEED TO SHAKE OUT SOME OF THE COBWEBS... ER...
...SO TO SPEAK...
HE IS THE TRAPSTER, AFTER ALL!
AND WITH ALL HIS TALK OF INVITATIONS, IT'S OBVIOUS THAT TRAPPY'S LEADING ME INTO SOMETHING...

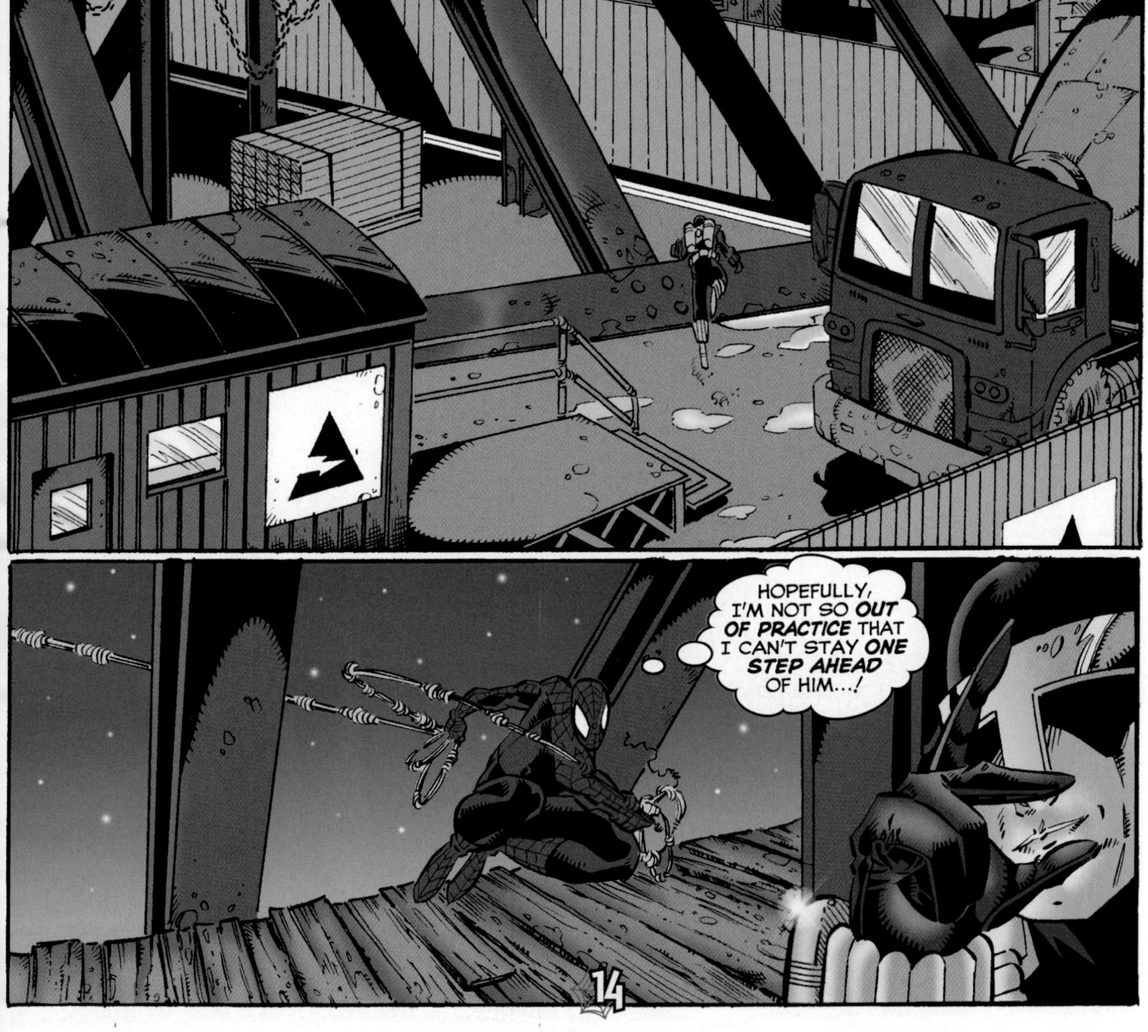
HOPEFULLY, I'M NOT SO OUT OF PRACTICE THAT I CAN'T STAY ONE STEP AHEAD OF HIM...!

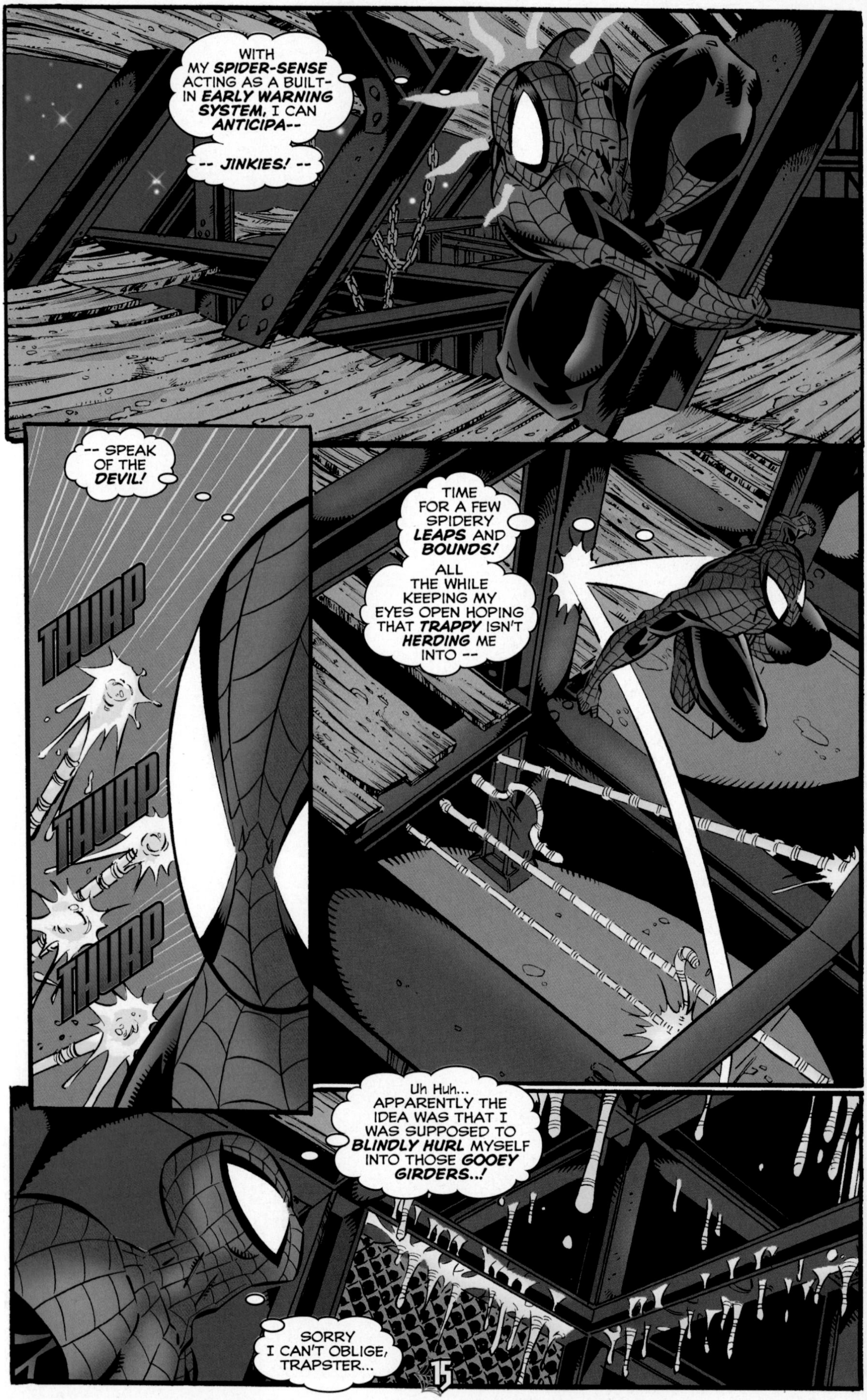
WITH MY SPIDER-SENSE ACTING AS A BUILT-IN EARLY WARNING SYSTEM, I CAN ANTICIPA--
-- JINKIES! --
-- SPEAK OF THE DEVIL!
THUMP
THUMP
THUMP
TIME FOR A FEW SPIDERY LEAPS AND BOUNDS!
ALL THE WHILE KEEPING MY EYES OPEN HOPING THAT TRAPPY ISN'T HERDING ME INTO --
Uh Huh... APPARENTLY THE IDEA WAS THAT I WAS SUPPOSED TO BLINDLY HURL MYSELF INTO THOSE GOOEY GIRDERS..!
SORRY I CAN'T OBLIGE, TRAPSTER...

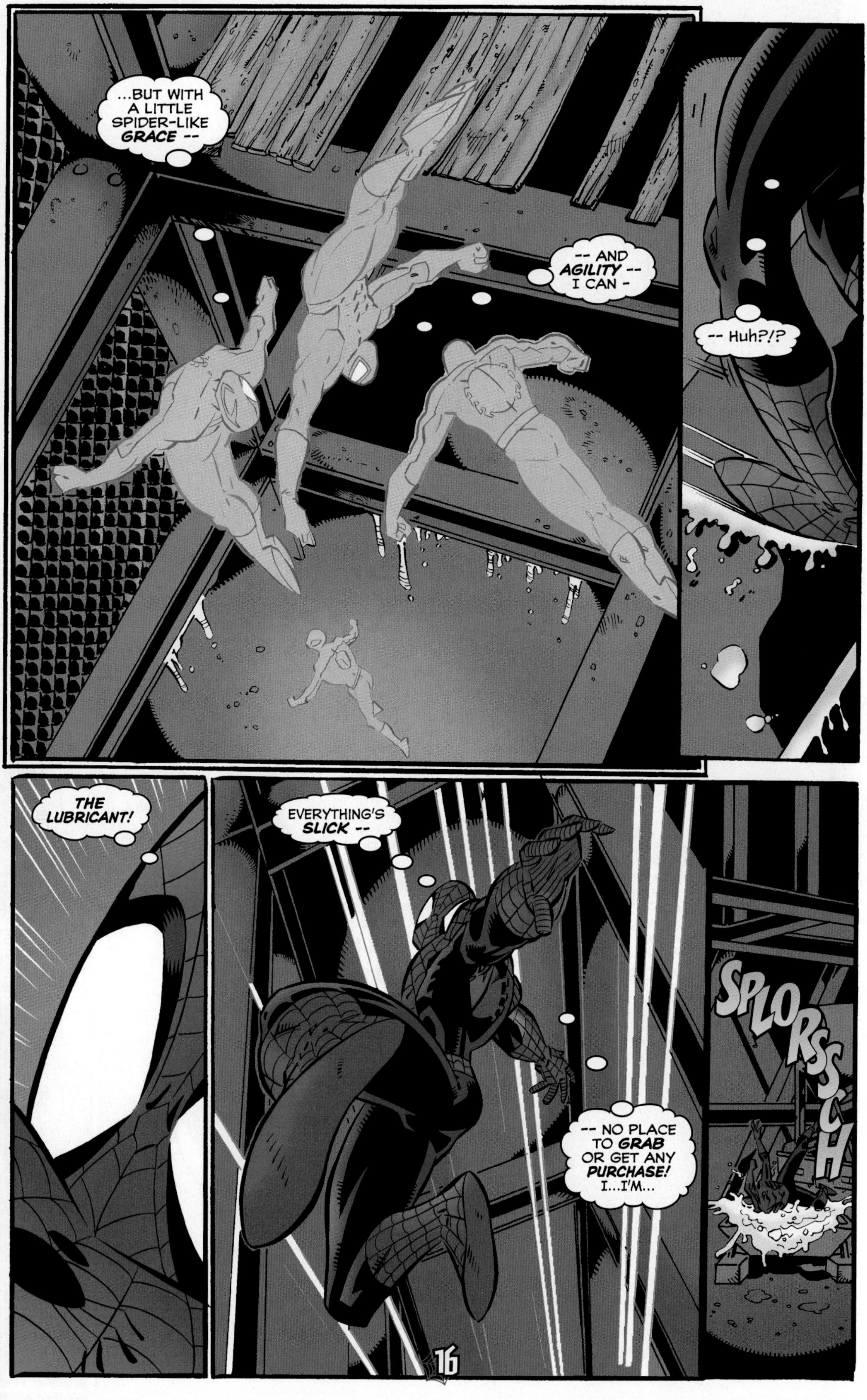
...BUT WITH A LITTLE SPIDER-LIKE GRACE --
-- AND AGILITY -- I CAN -
-- Huh?!?
THE LUBRICANT!
EVERYTHING'S SLICK --
-- NO PLACE TO GRAB OR GET ANY PURCHASE! I...I'M...
SPLORSSCH

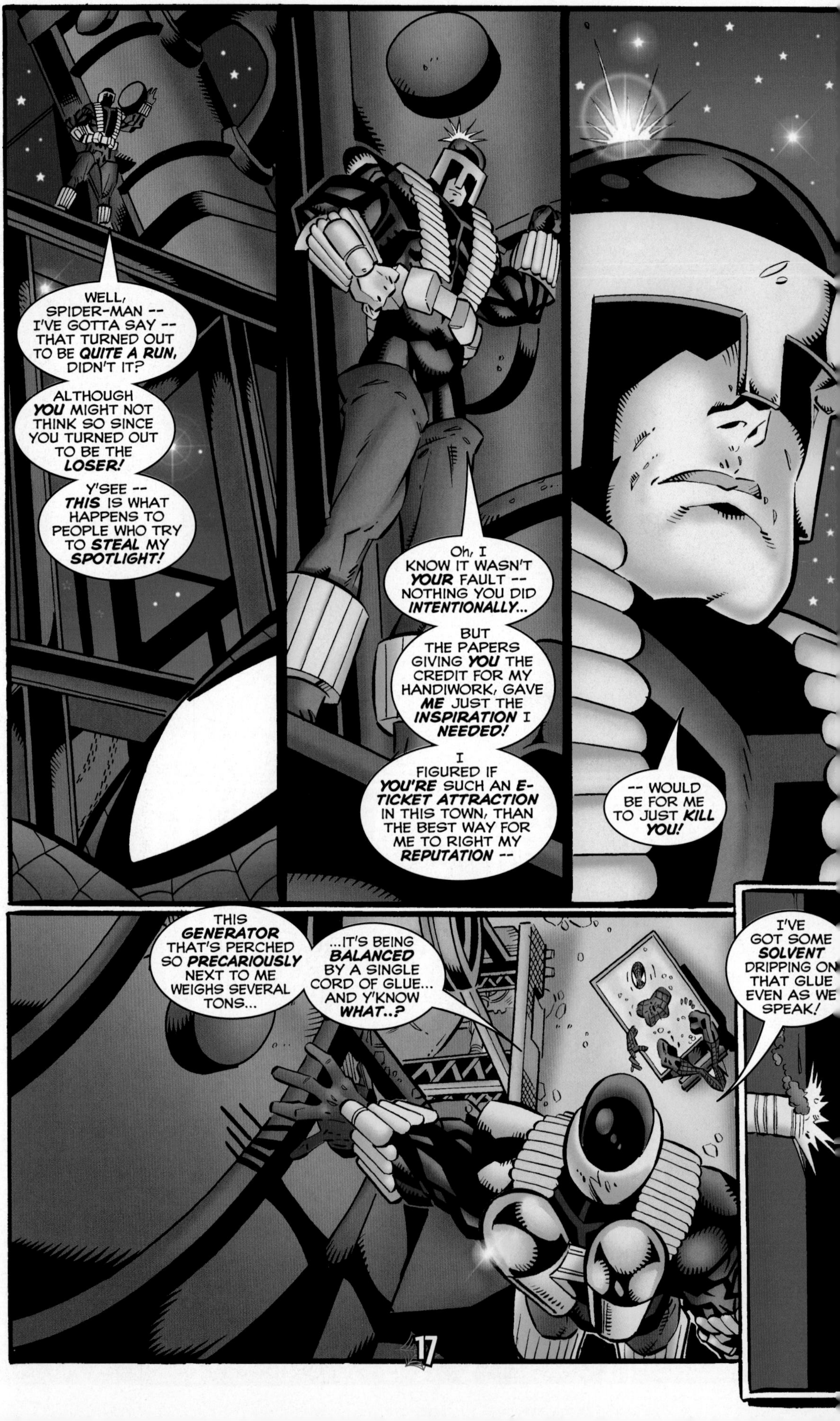
WELL, SPIDER-MAN -- I'VE GOTTA SAY -- THAT TURNED OUT TO BE QUITE A RUN, DIDN'T IT?
ALTHOUGH YOU MIGHT NOT THINK SO SINCE YOU TURNED OUT TO BE THE LOSER!
Y'SEE -- THIS IS WHAT HAPPENS TO PEOPLE WHO TRY TO STEAL MY SPOTLIGHT!
Oh, I KNOW IT WASN'T YOUR FAULT -- NOTHING YOU DID INTENTIONALLY...
BUT THE PAPERS GIVING YOU THE CREDIT FOR MY HANDIWORK, GAVE ME JUST THE INSPIRATION I NEEDED!
I FIGURED IF YOU'RE SUCH AN E-TICKET ATTRACTION IN THIS TOWN, THAN THE BEST WAY FOR ME TO RIGHT MY REPUTATION --
-- WOULD BE FOR ME TO JUST KILL YOU!
THIS GENERATOR THAT'S PERCHED SO PRECARIOUSLY NEXT TO ME WEIGHS SEVERAL TONS...
...IT'S BEING BALANCED BY A SINGLE CORD OF GLUE... AND Y'KNOW WHAT..?
I'VE GOT SOME SOLVENT DRIPPING ON THAT GLUE EVEN AS WE SPEAK!

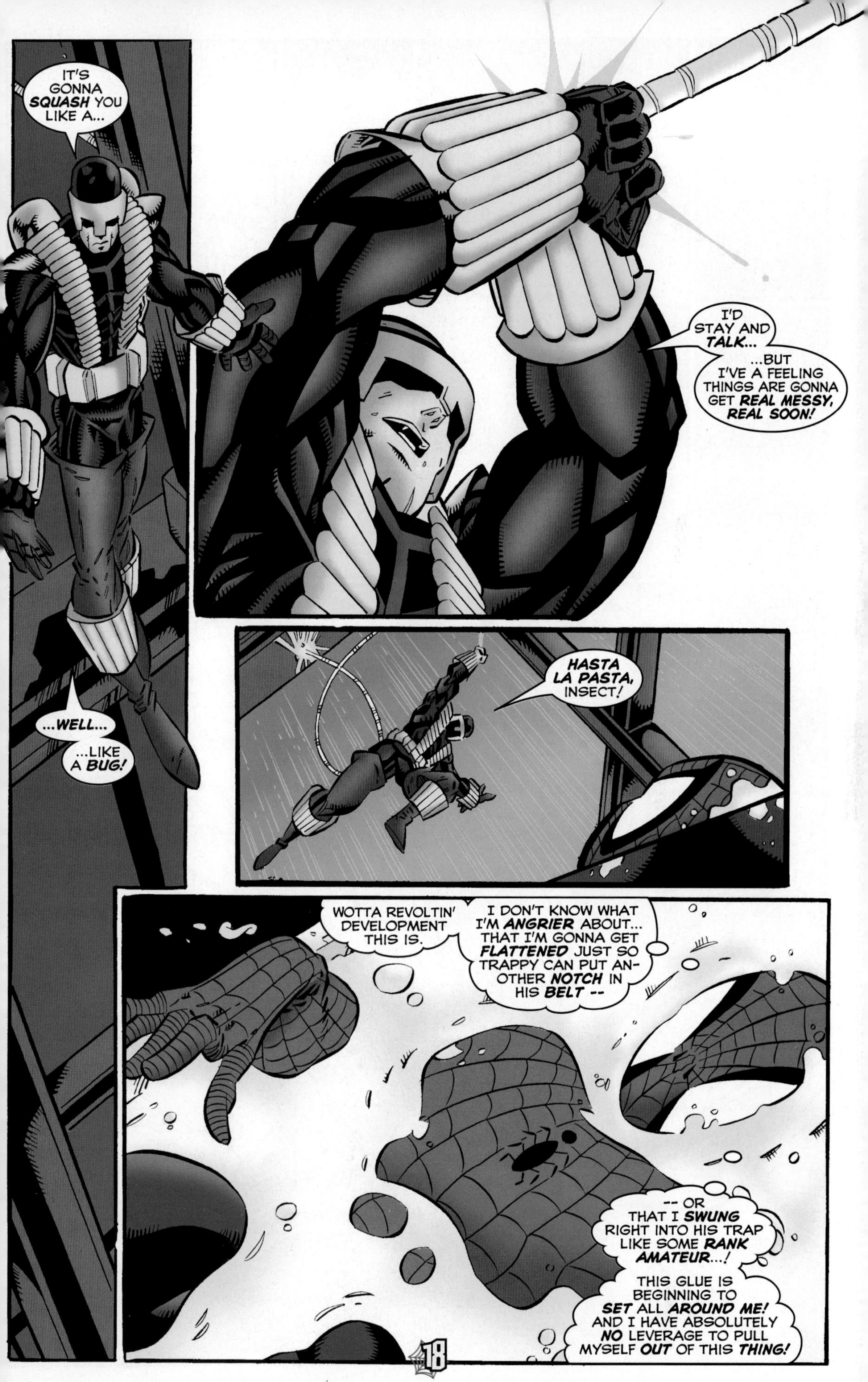
IT'S GONNA SQUASH YOU LIKE A...
I'D STAY AND TALK...
...BUT I'VE A FEELING THINGS ARE GONNA GET REAL MESSY, REAL SOON!
...WELL...
...LIKE A BUG!
HASTA LA PASTA, INSECT!
WOTTA REVOLTIN' DEVELOPMENT THIS IS.
I DON'T KNOW WHAT I'M ANGRIER ABOUT... THAT I'M GONNA GET FLATTENED JUST SO TRAPPY CAN PUT AN-OTHER NOTCH IN HIS BELT --
-- OR THAT I SWUNG RIGHT INTO HIS TRAP LIKE SOME RANK AMATEUR...!
THIS GLUE IS BEGINNING TO SET ALL AROUND ME! AND I HAVE ABSOLUTELY NO LEVERAGE TO PULL MYSELF OUT OF THIS THING!

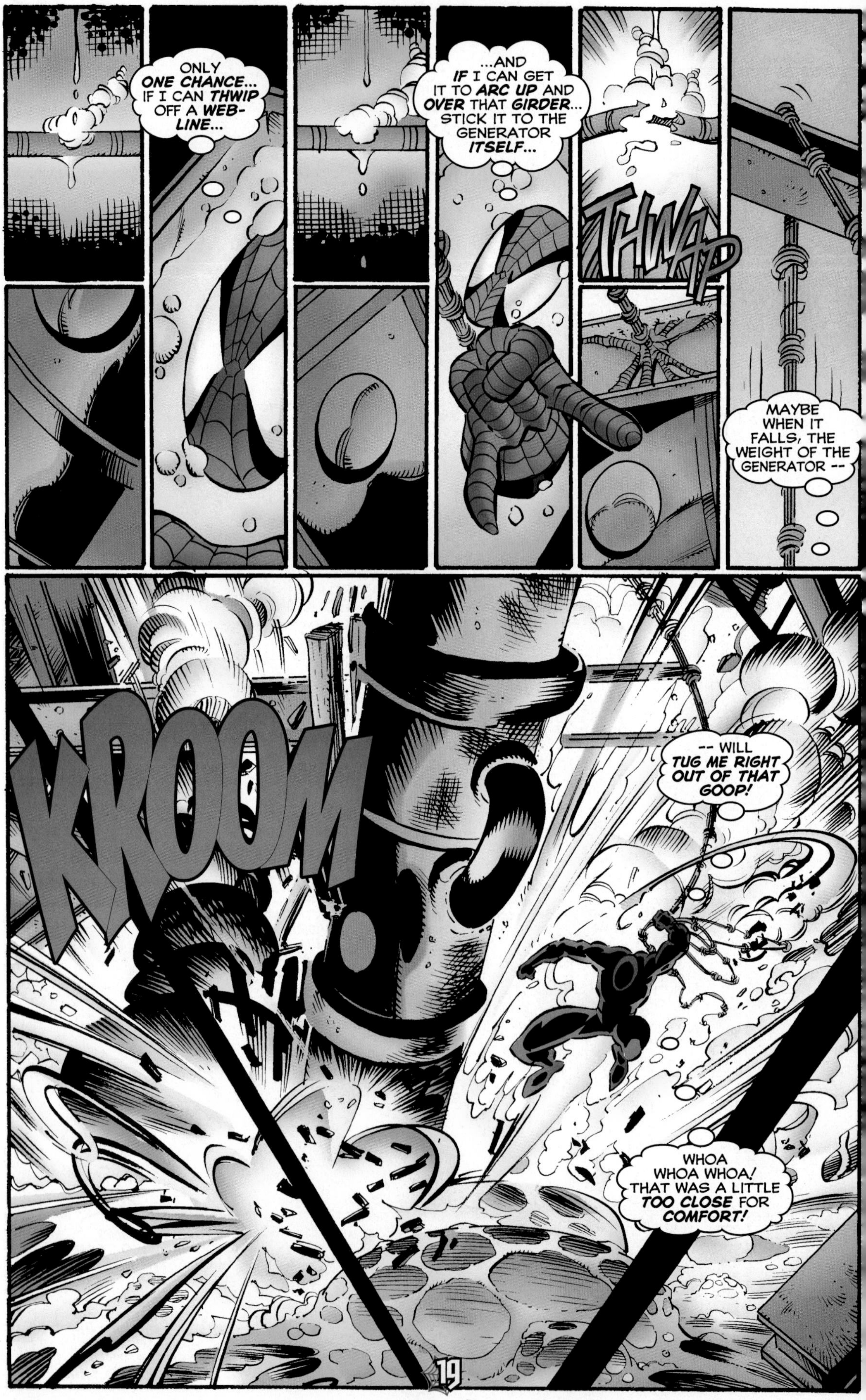
ONLY ONE CHANCE... IF I CAN THWIP OFF A WEB-LINE...
...AND IF I CAN GET IT TO ARC UP AND OVER THAT GIRDER... STICK IT TO THE GENERATOR ITSELF...
THWAP
MAYBE WHEN IT FALLS, THE WEIGHT OF THE GENERATOR --
KROOM
-- WILL TUG ME RIGHT OUT OF THAT GOOP!
WHOA WHOA WHOA! THAT WAS A LITTLE TOO CLOSE FOR COMFORT!

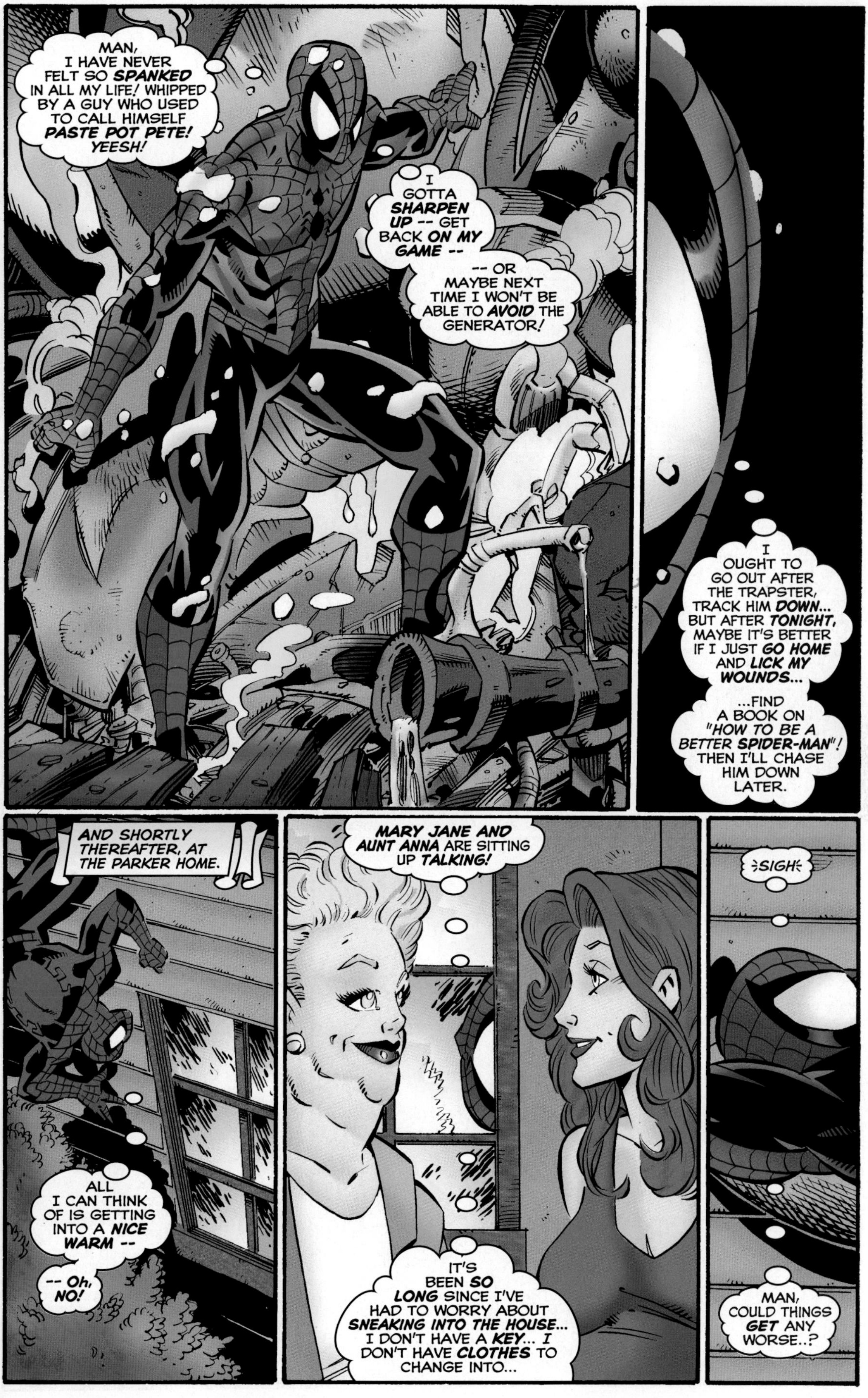
MAN, I HAVE NEVER FELT SO SPANKED IN ALL MY LIFE! WHIPPED BY A GUY WHO USED TO CALL HIMSELF PASTE POT PETE! YEESH!
I GOTTA SHARPEN UP -- GET BACK ON MY GAME --
-- OR MAYBE NEXT TIME I WON'T BE ABLE TO AVOID THE GENERATOR!
I OUGHT TO GO OUT AFTER THE TRAPSTER, TRACK HIM DOWN... BUT AFTER TONIGHT, MAYBE IT'S BETTER IF I JUST GO HOME AND LICK MY WOUNDS...
...FIND A BOOK ON "HOW TO BE A BETTER SPIDER-MAN"! THEN I'LL CHASE HIM DOWN LATER.
AND SHORTLY THEREAFTER, AT THE PARKER HOME.
ALL I CAN THINK OF IS GETTING INTO A NICE WARM --
-- Oh, NO!
MARY JANE AND AUNT ANNA ARE SITTING UP TALKING!
IT'S BEEN SO LONG SINCE I'VE HAD TO WORRY ABOUT SNEAKING INTO THE HOUSE... I DON'T HAVE A KEY... I DON'T HAVE CLOTHES TO CHANGE INTO...
SIGH
MAN, COULD THINGS GET ANY WORSE..?

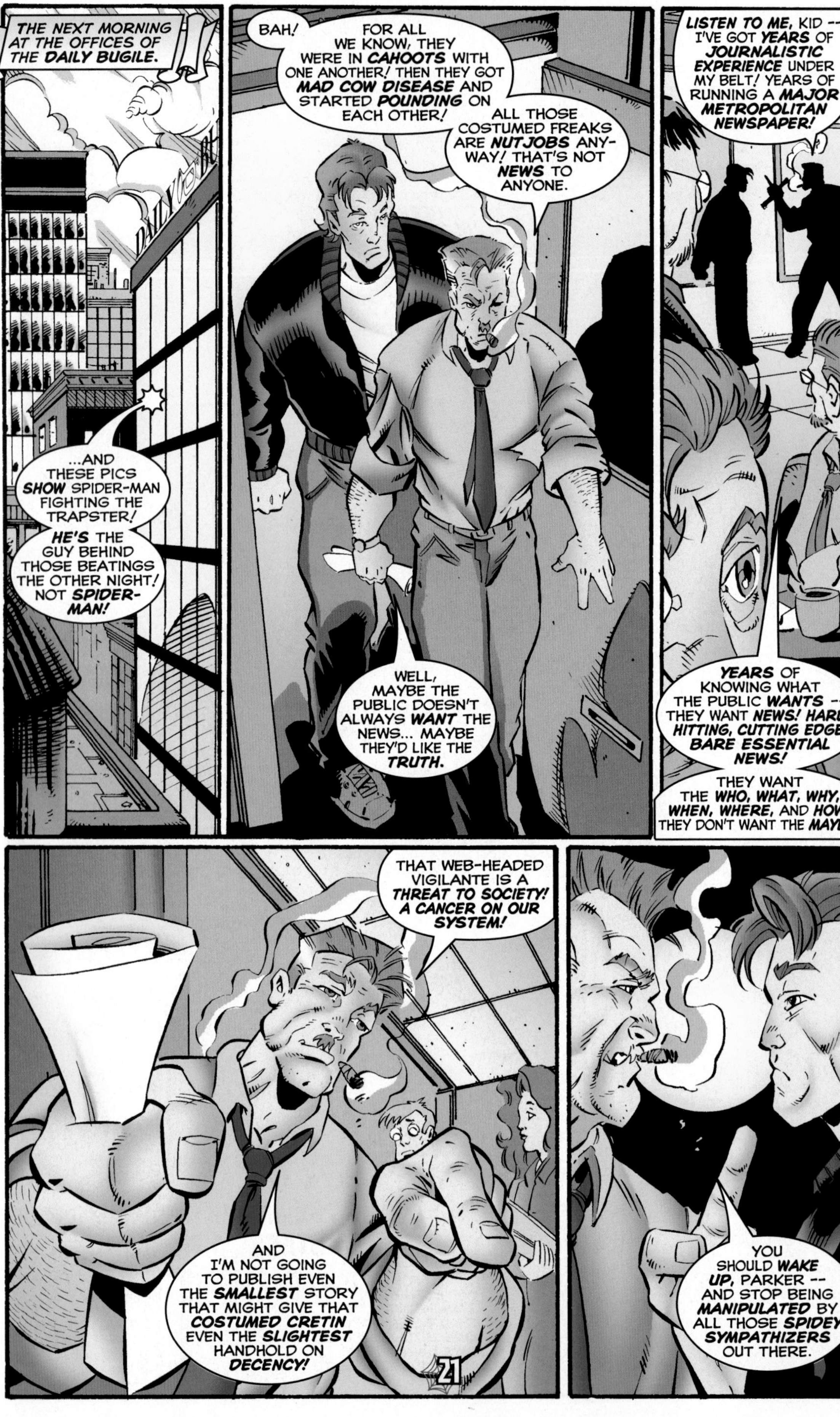

THE NEXT MORNING AT THE OFFICES OF THE DAILY BUGILE.
...AND THESE PICS SHOW SPIDER-MAN FIGHTING THE TRAPSTER!
HE'S THE GUY BEHIND THOSE BEATINGS THE OTHER NIGHT! NOT SPIDER-MAN!
BAH!
FOR ALL WE KNOW, THEY WERE IN CAHOOTS WITH ONE ANOTHER! THEN THEY GOT MAD COW DISEASE AND STARTED POUNDING ON EACH OTHER!
ALL THOSE COSTUMED FREAKS ARE NUTJOBS ANYWAY! THAT'S NOT NEWS TO ANYONE.
WELL, MAYBE THE PUBLIC DOESN'T ALWAYS WANT THE NEWS... MAYBE THEY'D LIKE THE TRUTH.
LISTEN TO ME, KID -- I'VE GOT YEARS OF JOURNALISTIC EXPERIENCE UNDER MY BELT! YEARS OF RUNNING A MAJOR METROPOLITAN NEWSPAPER!
YEARS OF KNOWING WHAT THE PUBLIC WANTS -- THEY WANT NEWS! HARD-HITTING, CUTTING EDGE, BARE ESSENTIAL NEWS!
THEY WANT THE WHO, WHAT, WHY, WHEN, WHERE, AND HOW! THEY DON'T WANT THE MAYBE!
THAT WEB-HEADED VIGILANTE IS A THREAT TO SOCIETY! A CANCER ON OUR SYSTEM!
AND I'M NOT GOING TO PUBLISH EVEN THE SMALLEST STORY THAT MIGHT GIVE THAT COSTUMED CRETIN EVEN THE SLIGHTEST HANDHOLD ON DECENCY!
YOU SHOULD WAKE UP, PARKER -- AND STOP BEING MANIPULATED BY ALL THOSE SPIDEY SYMPATHIZERS OUT THERE.

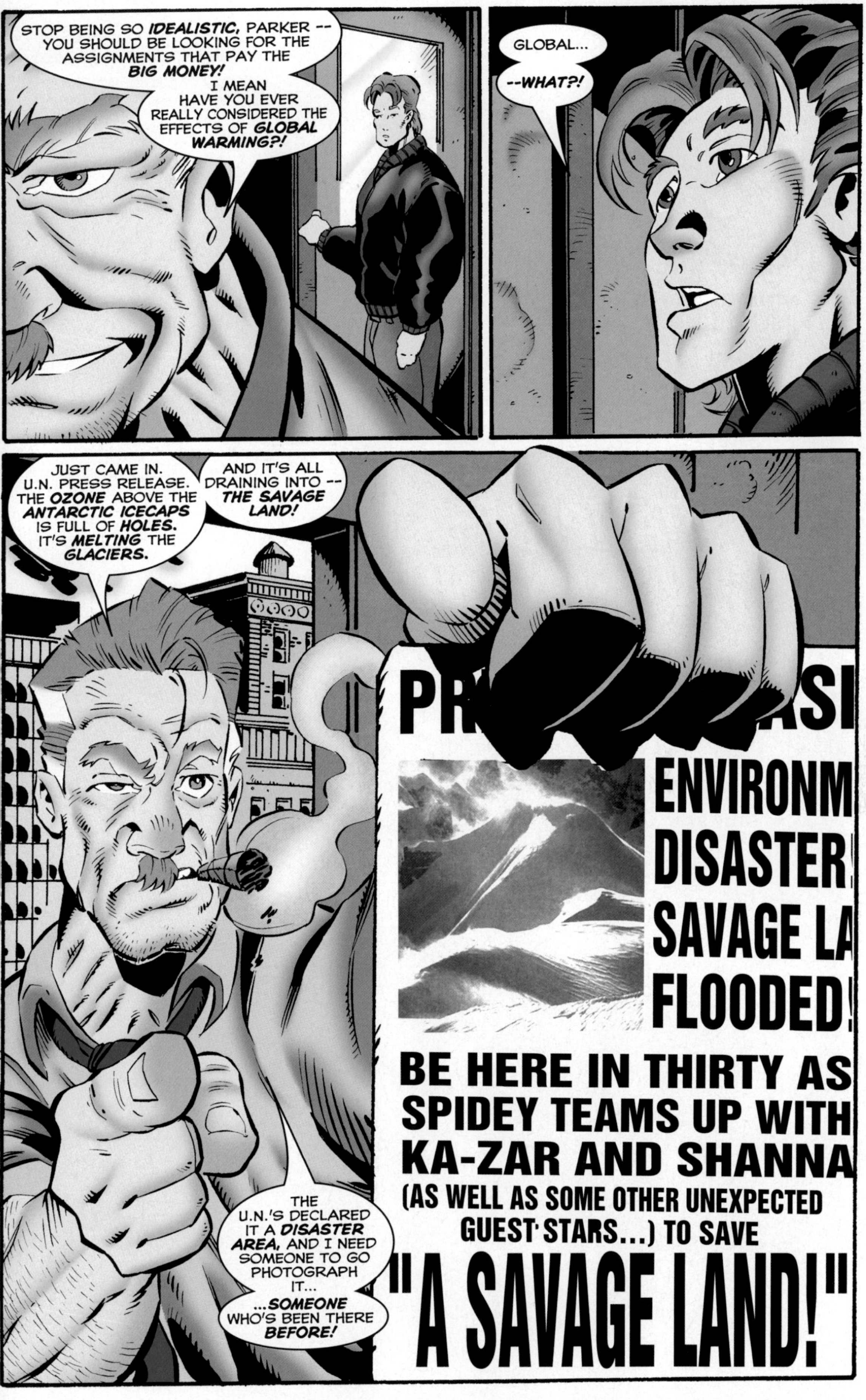
STOP BEING SO IDEALISTIC, PARKER -- YOU SHOULD BE LOOKING FOR THE ASSIGNMENTS THAT PAY THE BIG MONEY!
I MEAN HAVE YOU EVER REALLY CONSIDERED THE EFFECTS OF GLOBAL WARMING?!
GLOBAL...
--WHAT?!
JUST CAME IN. U.N. PRESS RELEASE. THE OZONE ABOVE THE ANTARCTIC ICECAPS IS FULL OF HOLES. IT'S MELTING THE GLACIERS.
AND IT'S ALL DRAINING INTO -- THE SAVAGE LAND!
THE U.N.'S DECLARED IT A DISASTER AREA, AND I NEED SOMEONE TO GO PHOTOGRAPH IT...
...SOMEONE WHO'S BEEN THERE BEFORE!
PR ASI
ENVIRONM
DISASTER
SAVAGE LA
FLOODED!
BE HERE IN THIRTY AS
SPIDEY TEAMS UP WITH
KA-ZAR AND SHANNA
(AS WELL AS SOME OTHER UNEXPECTED
GUEST STARS...) TO SAVE
"A SAVAGE LAND!"

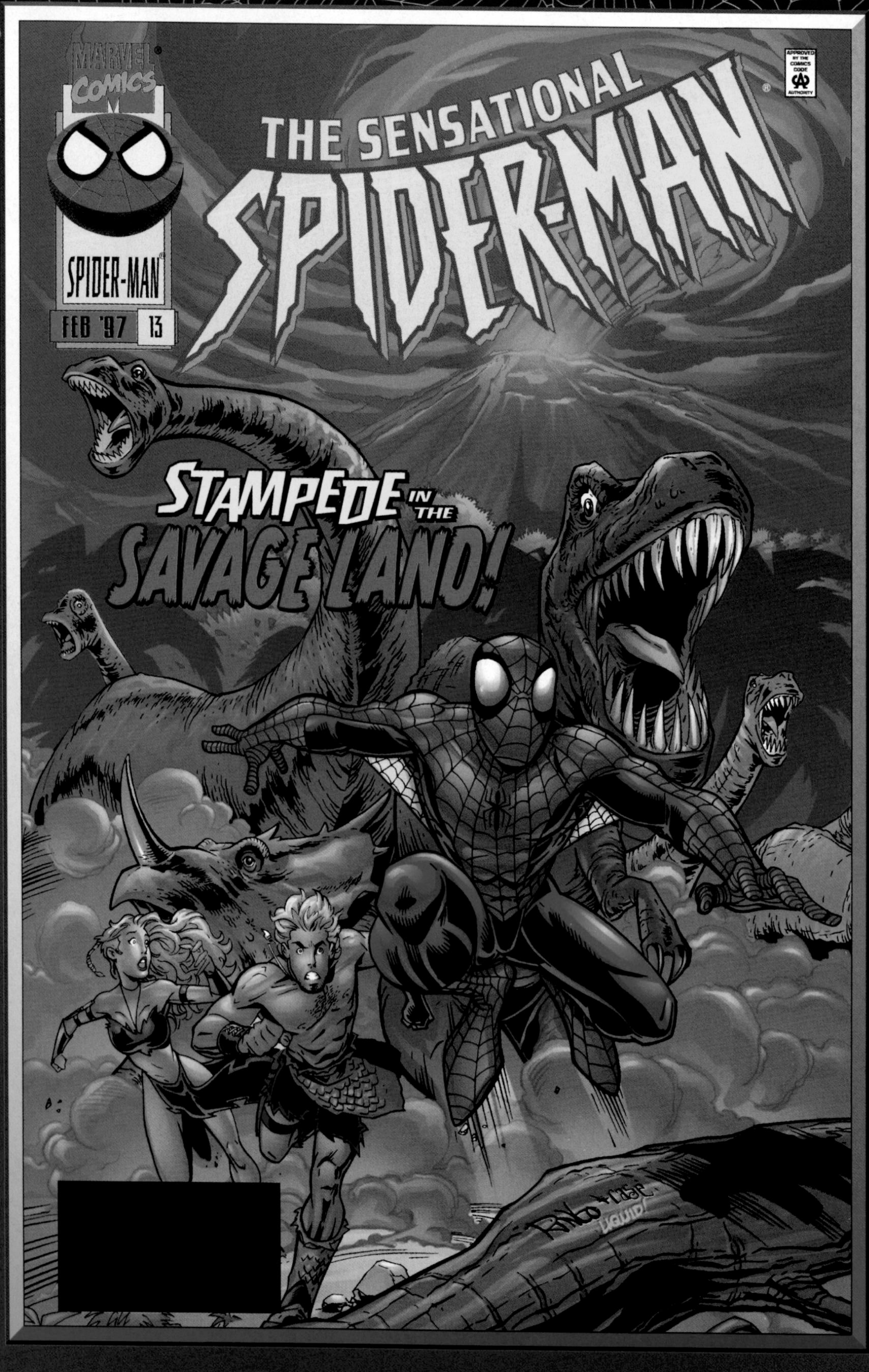
MARVEL COMICS
APPROVED BY THE COMICS CODE AUTHORITY
THE SENSATIONAL
SPIDER-MAN
SPIDER-MAN
FEB '97 13
STAMPEDE IN THE
SAVAGE LAND!

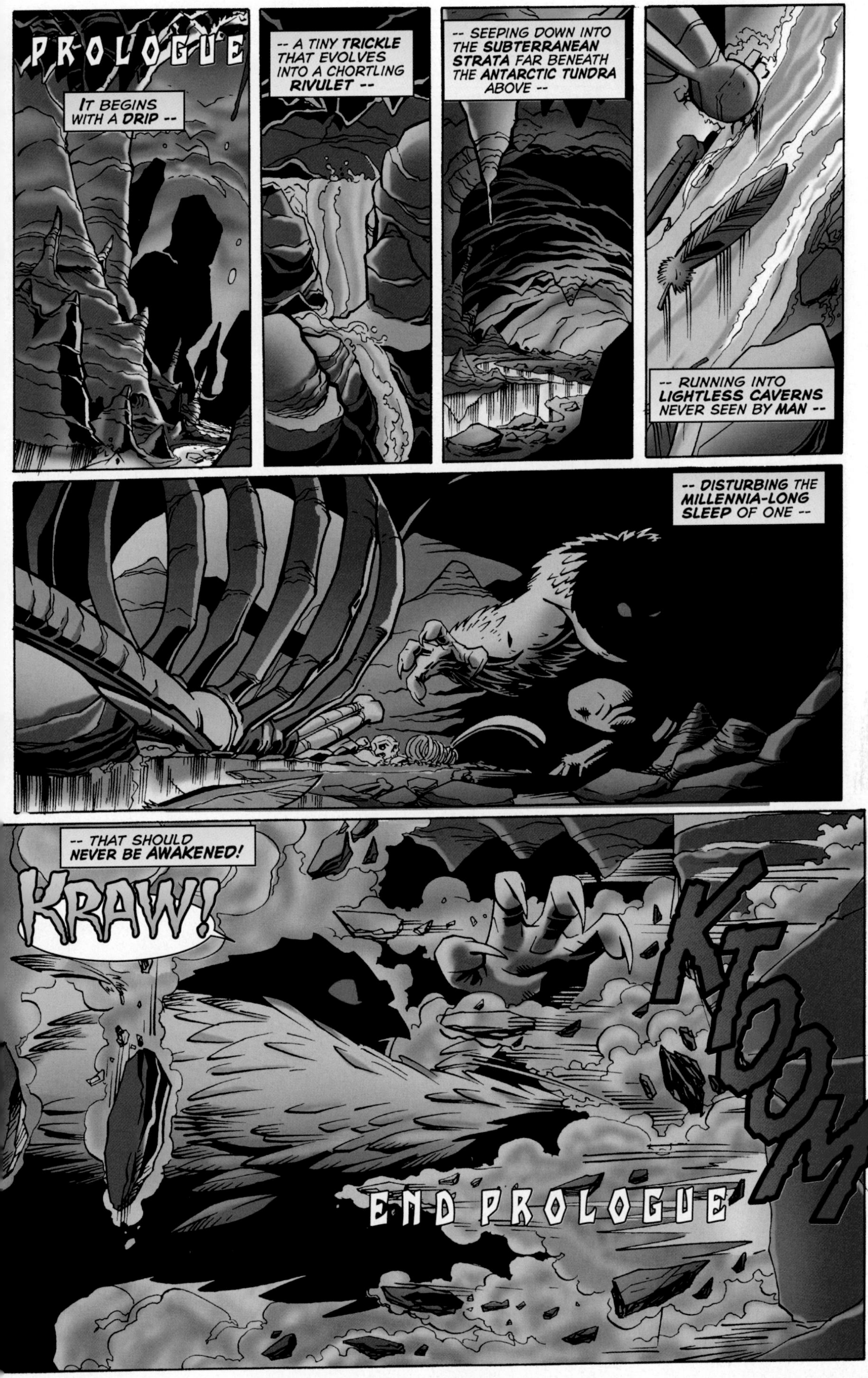
PROLOGUE
IT BEGINS WITH A DRIP --
-- A TINY TRICKLE THAT EVOLVES INTO A CHORTLING RIVULET --
-- SEEPING DOWN INTO THE SUBTERRANEAN STRATA FAR BENEATH THE ANTARCTIC TUNDRA ABOVE --
-- RUNNING INTO LIGHTLESS CAVERNS NEVER SEEN BY MAN --
-- DISTURBING THE MILLENNIA-LONG SLEEP OF ONE --
-- THAT SHOULD NEVER BE AWAKENED!
KRAW!
KTOOOM
END PROLOGUE

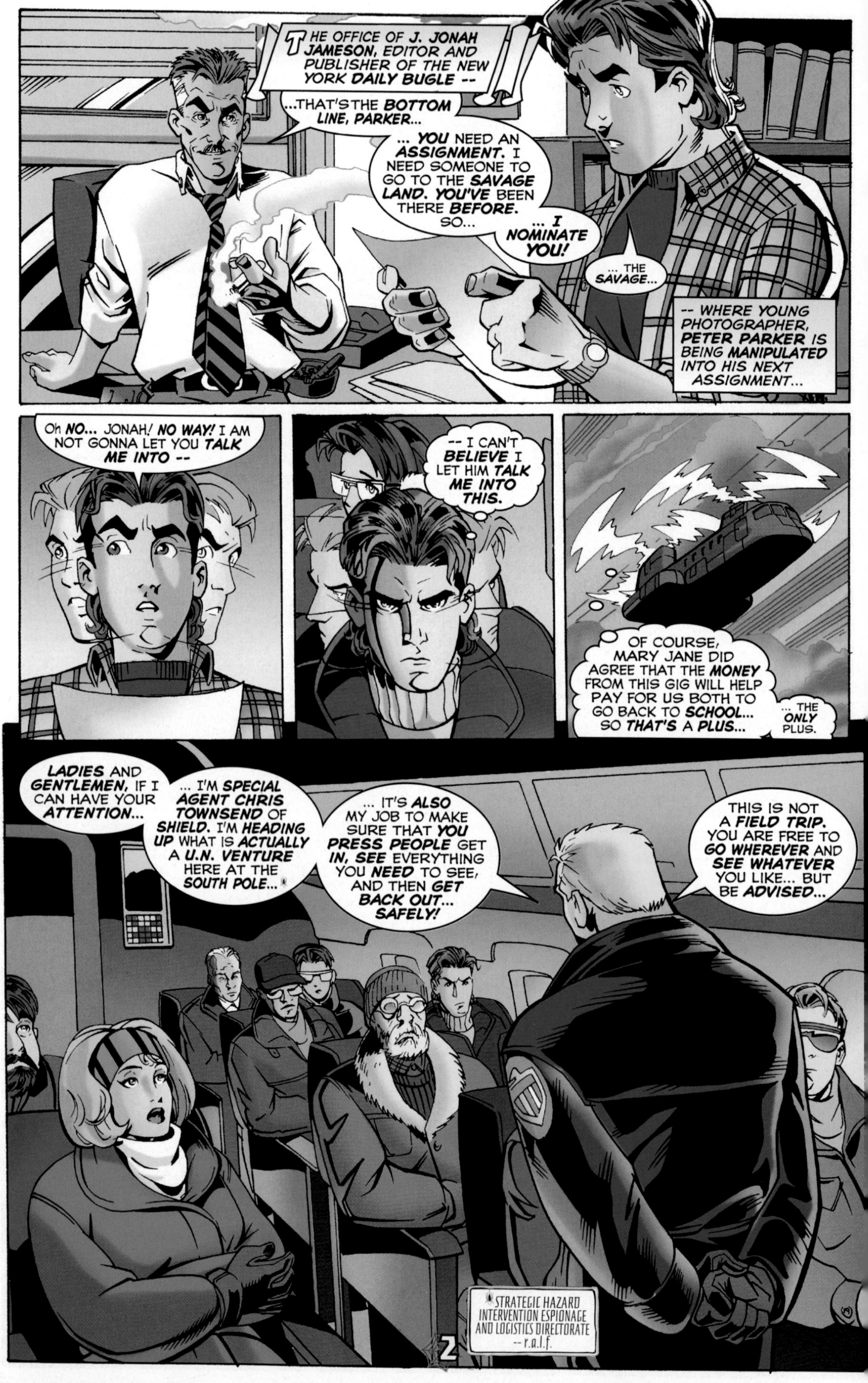
THE OFFICE OF J. JONAH JAMESON, EDITOR AND PUBLISHER OF THE NEW YORK DAILY BUGLE --
...THAT'S THE BOTTOM LINE, PARKER...
... YOU NEED AN ASSIGNMENT. I NEED SOMEONE TO GO TO THE SAVAGE LAND. YOU'VE BEEN THERE BEFORE. SO...
... I NOMINATE YOU!
... THE SAVAGE...
-- WHERE YOUNG PHOTOGRAPHER, PETER PARKER IS BEING MANIPULATED INTO HIS NEXT ASSIGNMENT...
Oh NO... JONAH! NO WAY! I AM NOT GONNA LET YOU TALK ME INTO --
-- I CAN'T BELIEVE I LET HIM TALK ME INTO THIS.
OF COURSE, MARY JANE DID AGREE THAT THE MONEY FROM THIS GIG WILL HELP PAY FOR US BOTH TO GO BACK TO SCHOOL... SO THAT'S A PLUS...
... THE ONLY PLUS.
LADIES AND GENTLEMEN, IF I CAN HAVE YOUR ATTENTION...
... I'M SPECIAL AGENT CHRIS TOWNSEND OF SHIELD. I'M HEADING UP WHAT IS ACTUALLY A U.N. VENTURE HERE AT THE SOUTH POLE...
... IT'S ALSO MY JOB TO MAKE SURE THAT YOU PRESS PEOPLE GET IN, SEE EVERYTHING YOU NEED TO SEE, AND THEN GET BACK OUT... SAFELY!
THIS IS NOT A FIELD TRIP. YOU ARE FREE TO GO WHEREVER AND SEE WHATEVER YOU LIKE... BUT BE ADVISED...
STRATEGIC HAZARD INTERVENTION ESPIONAGE AND LOGISTICS DIRECTORATE -- r.a.l.f.

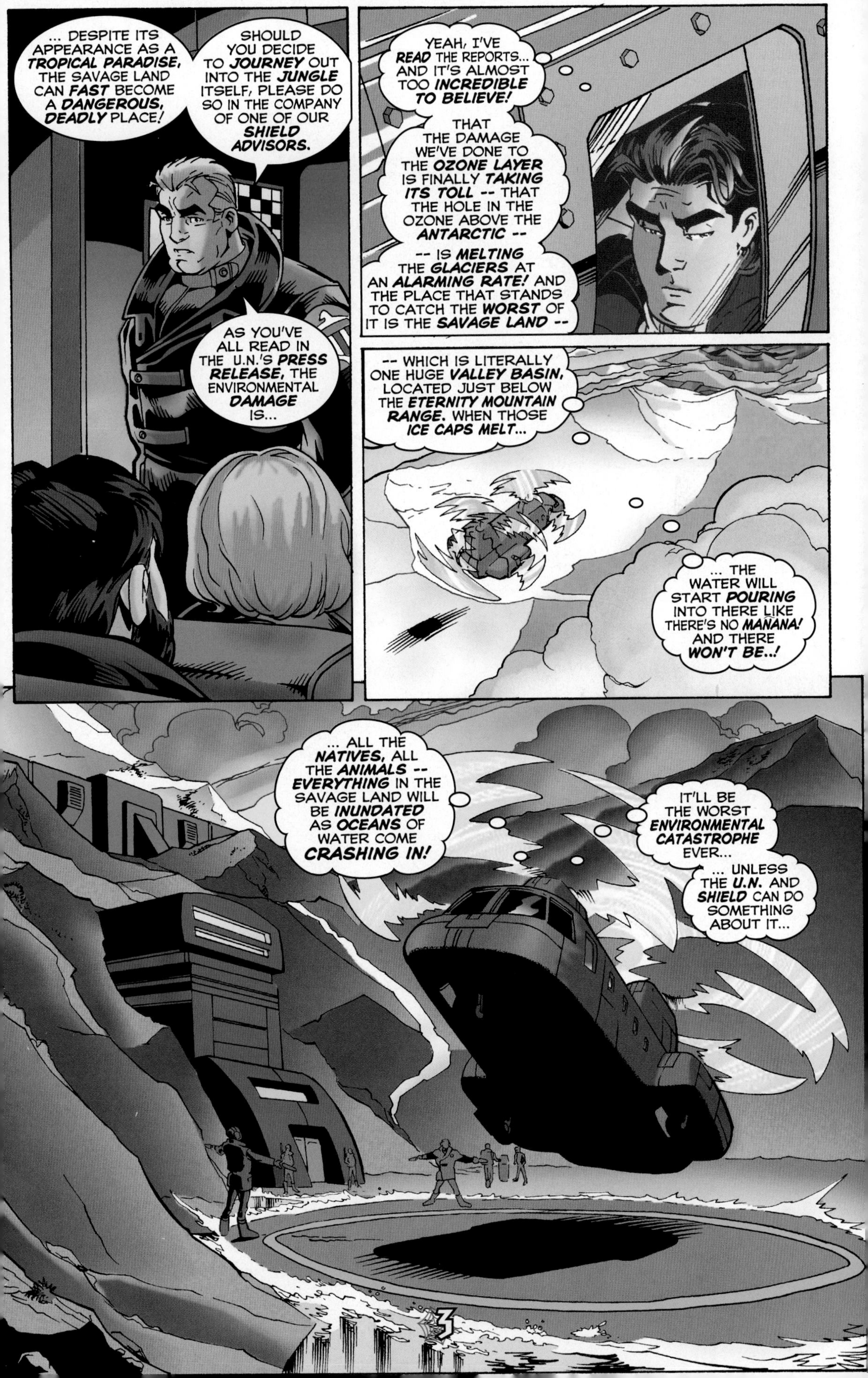
... DESPITE ITS APPEARANCE AS A TROPICAL PARADISE, THE SAVAGE LAND CAN FAST BECOME A DANGEROUS, DEADLY PLACE!
SHOULD YOU DECIDE TO JOURNEY OUT INTO THE JUNGLE ITSELF, PLEASE DO SO IN THE COMPANY OF ONE OF OUR SHIELD ADVISORS.
AS YOU'VE ALL READ IN THE U.N.'S PRESS RELEASE, THE ENVIRONMENTAL DAMAGE IS...
YEAH, I'VE READ THE REPORTS... AND IT'S ALMOST TOO INCREDIBLE TO BELIEVE!
THAT THE DAMAGE WE'VE DONE TO THE OZONE LAYER IS FINALLY TAKING ITS TOLL -- THAT THE HOLE IN THE OZONE ABOVE THE ANTARCTIC --
-- IS MELTING THE GLACIERS AT AN ALARMING RATE! AND THE PLACE THAT STANDS TO CATCH THE WORST OF IT IS THE SAVAGE LAND --
-- WHICH IS LITERALLY ONE HUGE VALLEY BASIN, LOCATED JUST BELOW THE ETERNITY MOUNTAIN RANGE. WHEN THOSE ICE CAPS MELT...
... THE WATER WILL START POURING INTO THERE LIKE THERE'S NO MAÑANA! AND THERE WON'T BE..!
... ALL THE NATIVES, ALL THE ANIMALS -- EVERYTHING IN THE SAVAGE LAND WILL BE INUNDATED AS OCEANS OF WATER COME CRASHING IN!
IT'LL BE THE WORST ENVIRONMENTAL CATASTROPHE EVER...
... UNLESS THE U.N. AND SHIELD CAN DO SOMETHING ABOUT IT...
3

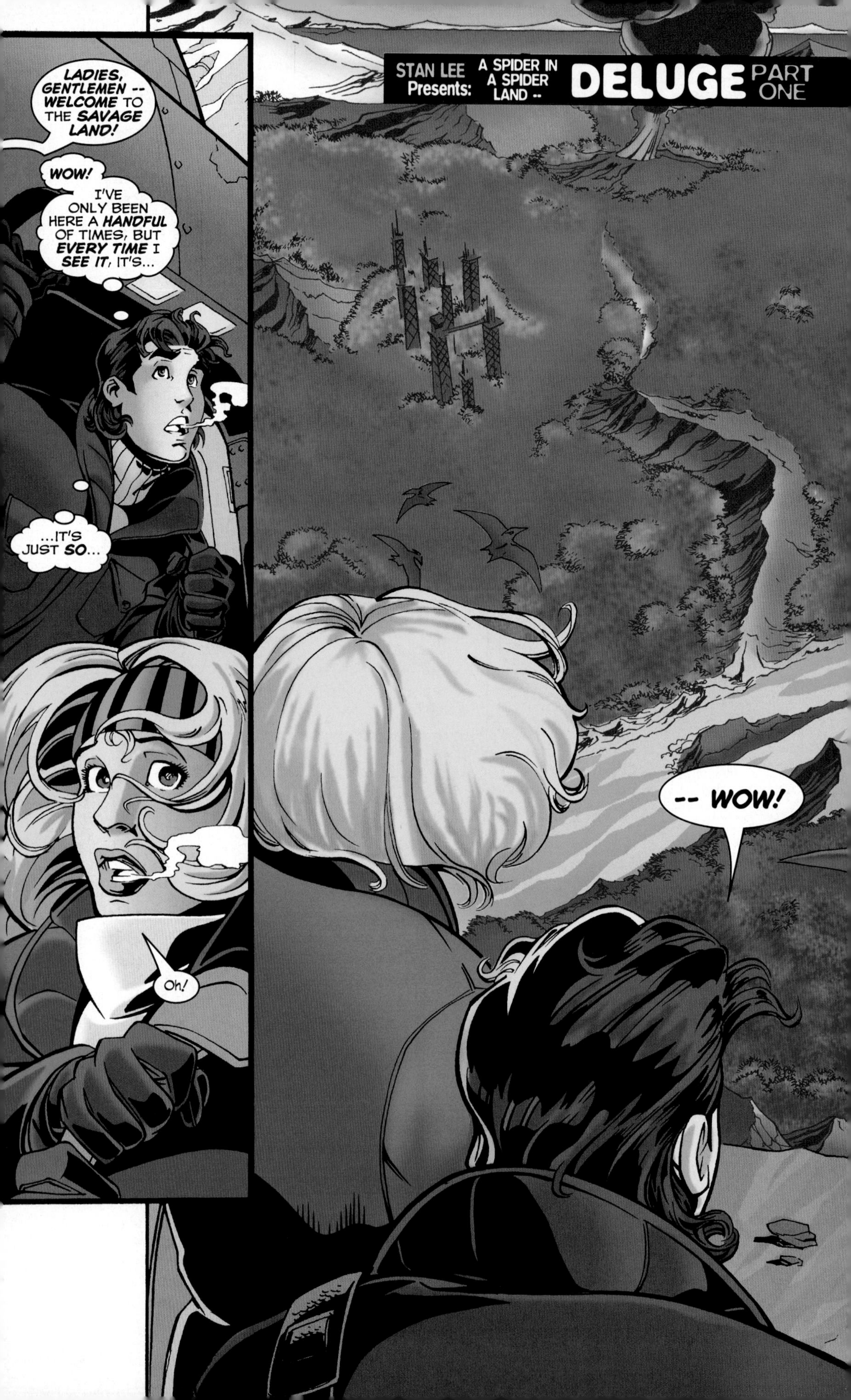
STAN LEE Presents:
A SPIDER IN A SPIDER LAND --
DELUGE PART ONE
LADIES, GENTLEMEN -- WELCOME TO THE SAVAGE LAND!
WOW!
I'VE ONLY BEEN HERE A HANDFUL OF TIMES, BUT EVERY TIME I SEE IT, IT'S...
...IT'S JUST SO...
-- WOW!
Oh!

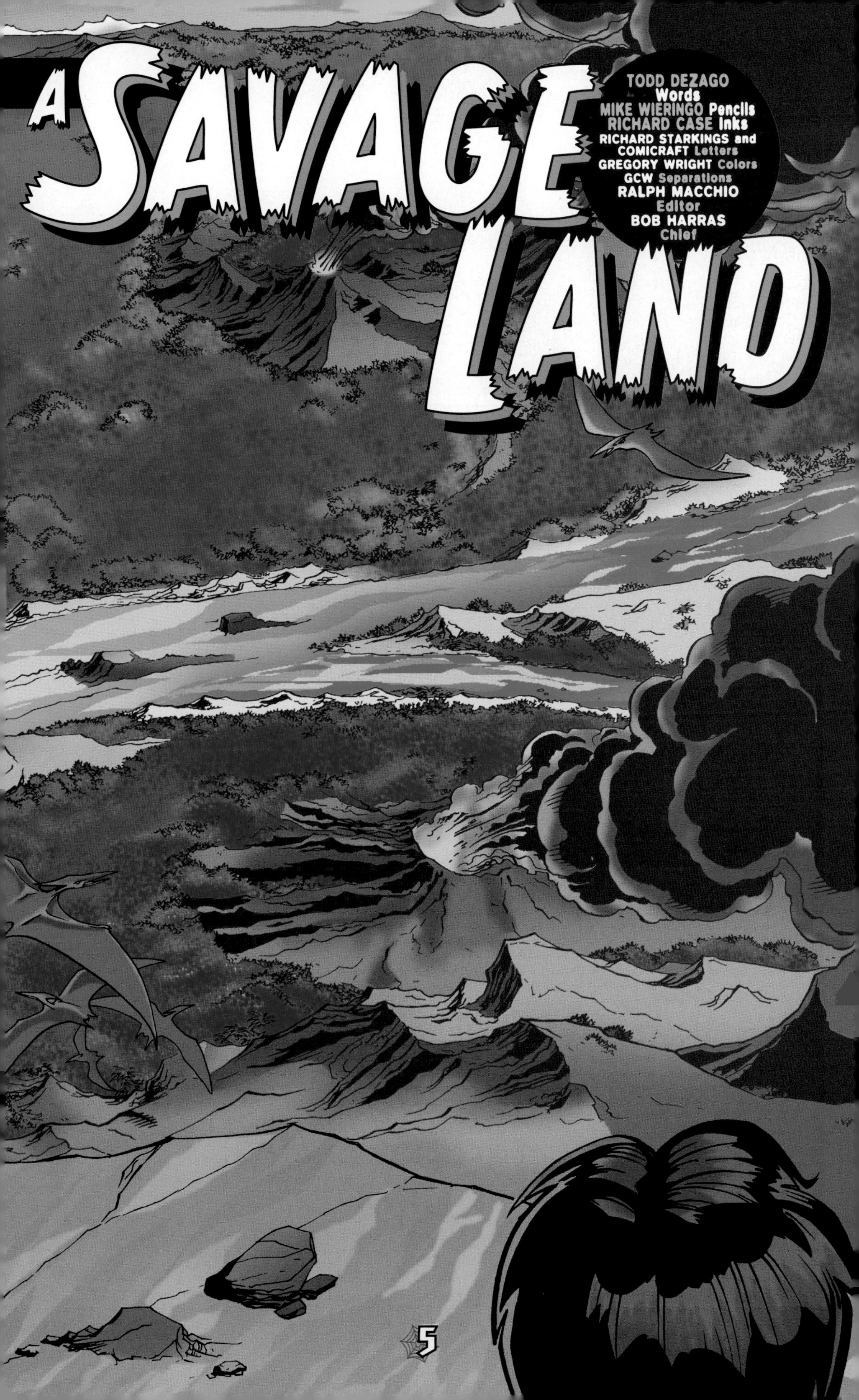
A SAVAGE LAND
TODD DEZAGO Words
MIKE WIERINGO Pencils
RICHARD CASE Inks
RICHARD STARKINGS and COMICRAFT Letters
GREGORY WRIGHT Colors
GCW Separations
RALPH MACCHIO Editor
BOB HARRAS Chief

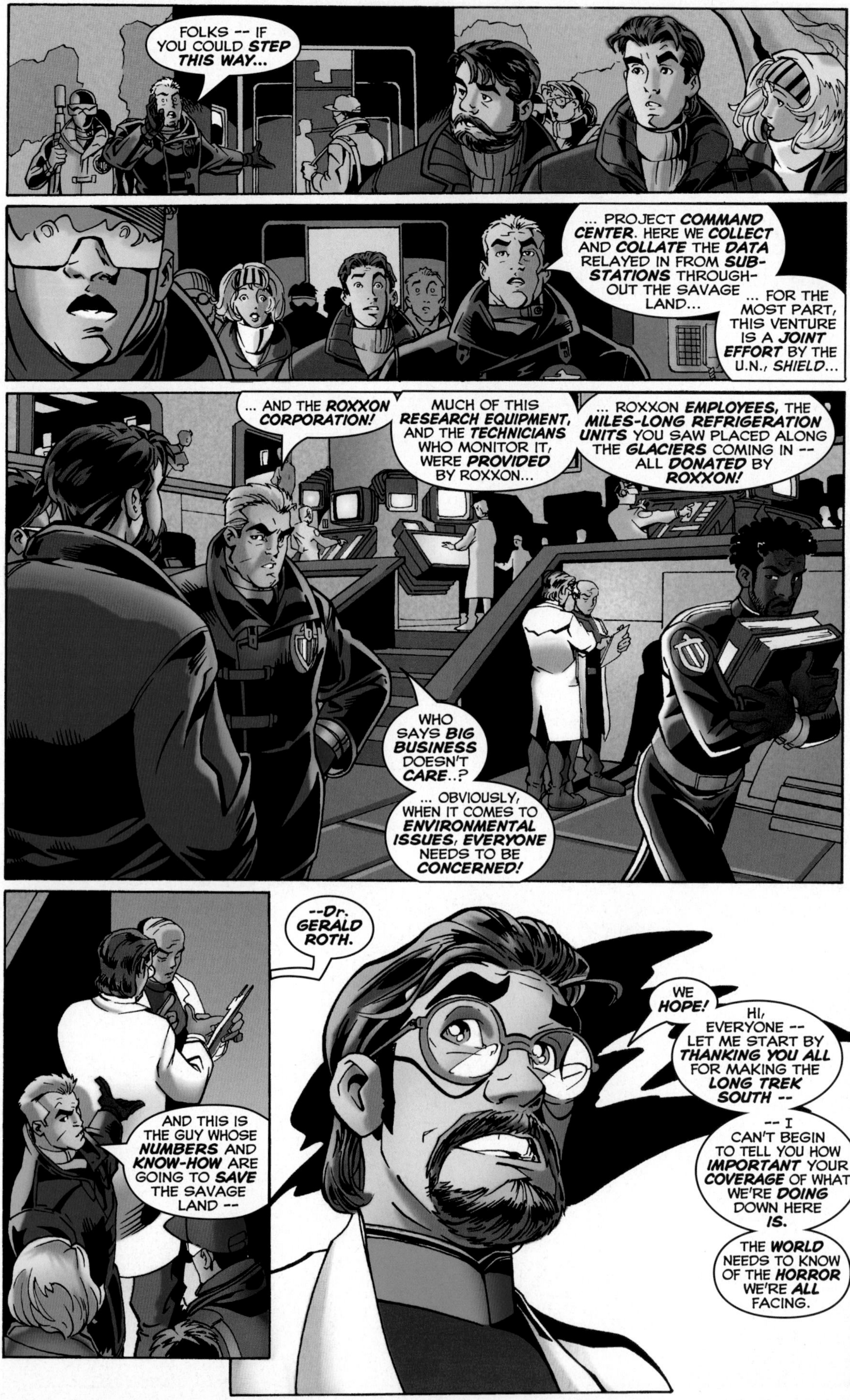
FOLKS -- IF YOU COULD STEP THIS WAY...
... PROJECT COMMAND CENTER. HERE WE COLLECT AND COLLATE THE DATA RELAYED IN FROM SUB-STATIONS THROUGH-OUT THE SAVAGE LAND...
... FOR THE MOST PART, THIS VENTURE IS A JOINT EFFORT BY THE U.N., SHIELD...
... AND THE ROXXON CORPORATION!
MUCH OF THIS RESEARCH EQUIPMENT, AND THE TECHNICIANS WHO MONITOR IT, WERE PROVIDED BY ROXXON...
... ROXXON EMPLOYEES, THE MILES-LONG REFRIGERATION UNITS YOU SAW PLACED ALONG THE GLACIERS COMING IN -- ALL DONATED BY ROXXON!
WHO SAYS BIG BUSINESS DOESN'T CARE..?
... OBVIOUSLY, WHEN IT COMES TO ENVIRONMENTAL ISSUES, EVERYONE NEEDS TO BE CONCERNED!
AND THIS IS THE GUY WHOSE NUMBERS AND KNOW-HOW ARE GOING TO SAVE THE SAVAGE LAND --
--Dr. GERALD ROTH.
WE HOPE!
HI, EVERYONE -- LET ME START BY THANKING YOU ALL FOR MAKING THE LONG TREK SOUTH --
-- I CAN'T BEGIN TO TELL YOU HOW IMPORTANT YOUR COVERAGE OF WHAT WE'RE DOING DOWN HERE IS.
THE WORLD NEEDS TO KNOW OF THE HORROR WE'RE ALL FACING.

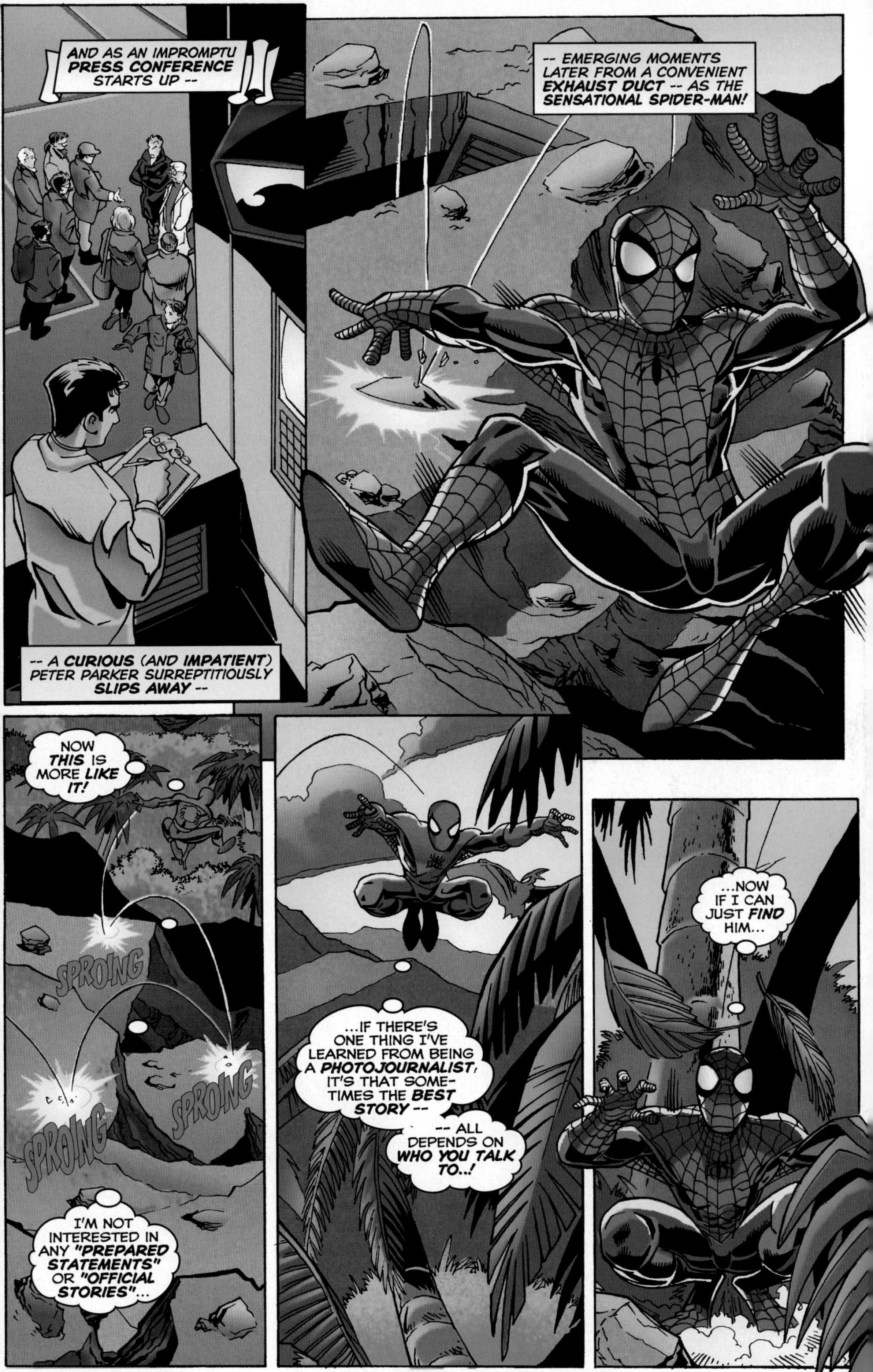
AND AS AN IMPROMPTU PRESS CONFERENCE STARTS UP --
-- A CURIOUS (AND IMPATIENT) PETER PARKER SURREPTITIOUSLY SLIPS AWAY --
-- EMERGING MOMENTS LATER FROM A CONVENIENT EXHAUST DUCT -- AS THE SENSATIONAL SPIDER-MAN!
NOW THIS IS MORE LIKE IT!
SPROING
SPROING
SPROING
I'M NOT INTERESTED IN ANY "PREPARED STATEMENTS" OR "OFFICIAL STORIES"...
...IF THERE'S ONE THING I'VE LEARNED FROM BEING A PHOTOJOURNALIST, IT'S THAT SOMETIMES THE BEST STORY --
-- ALL DEPENDS ON WHO YOU TALK TO..!
...NOW IF I CAN JUST FIND HIM...

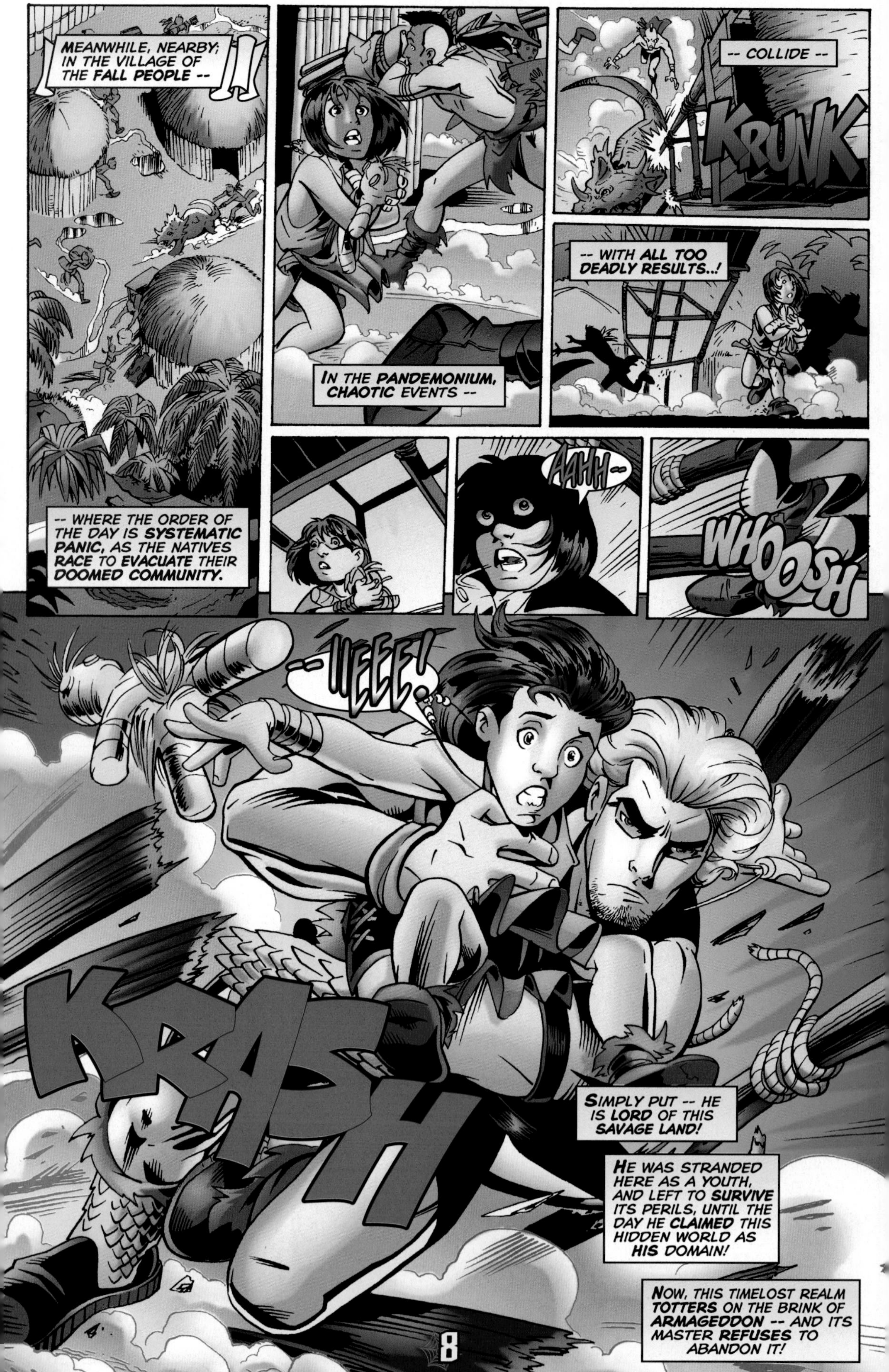

MEANWHILE, NEARBY; IN THE VILLAGE OF THE FALL PEOPLE --
-- WHERE THE ORDER OF THE DAY IS SYSTEMATIC PANIC, AS THE NATIVES RACE TO EVACUATE THEIR DOOMED COMMUNITY.
IN THE PANDEMONIUM, CHAOTIC EVENTS --
-- COLLIDE --
KRUNK
-- WITH ALL TOO DEADLY RESULTS..!
AAHH--
WHOOSH
--IIEEE!
KRASH
SIMPLY PUT -- HE IS LORD OF THIS SAVAGE LAND!
HE WAS STRANDED HERE AS A YOUTH, AND LEFT TO SURVIVE ITS PERILS, UNTIL THE DAY HE CLAIMED THIS HIDDEN WORLD AS HIS DOMAIN!
NOW, THIS TIMELOST REALM TOTTERS ON THE BRINK OF ARMAGEDDON -- AND ITS MASTER REFUSES TO ABANDON IT!

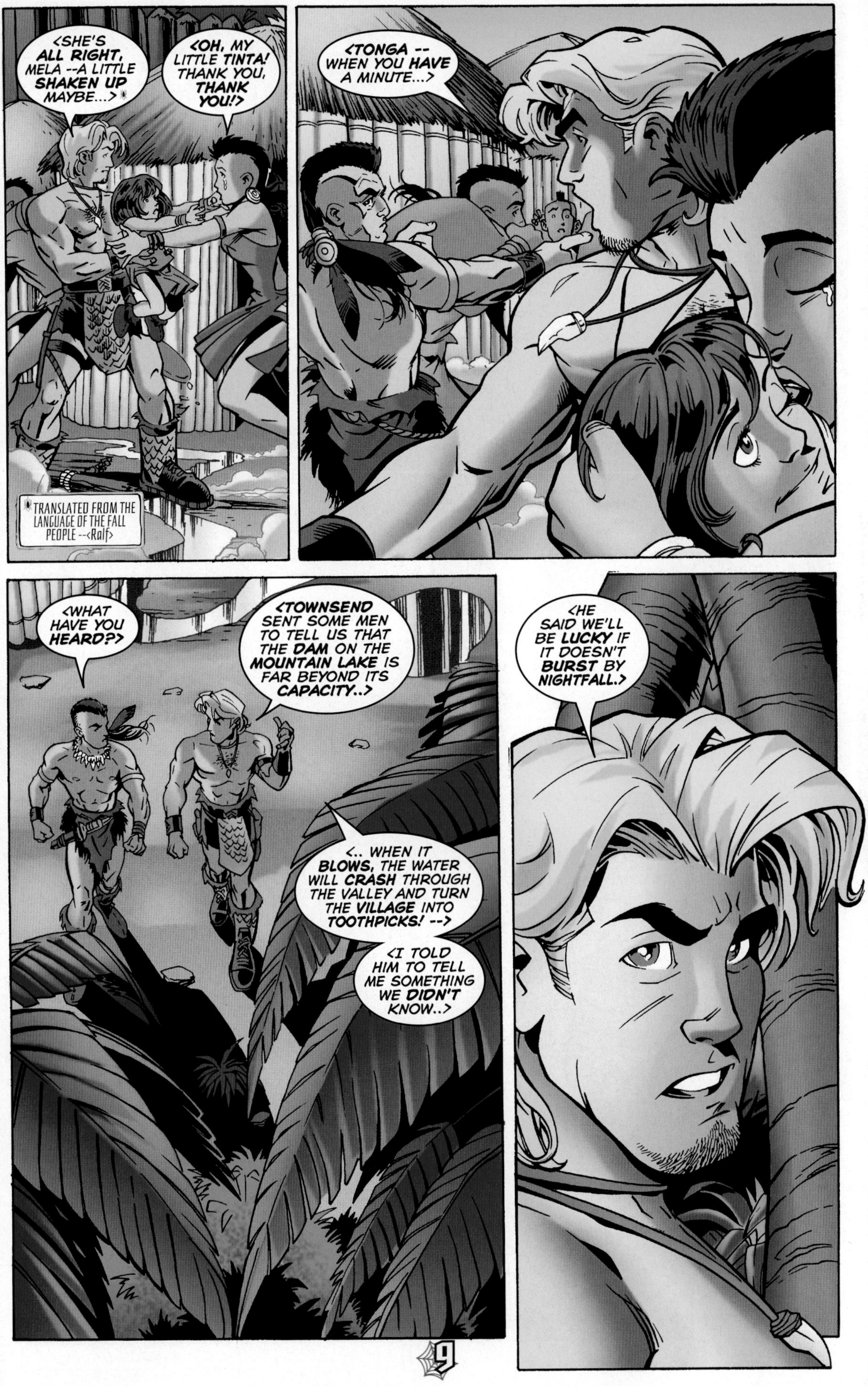
<SHE'S ALL RIGHT, MELA --A LITTLE SHAKEN UP MAYBE...>
<OH, MY LITTLE TINTA! THANK YOU, THANK YOU!>
TRANSLATED FROM THE LANGUAGE OF THE FALL PEOPLE --<Ralf>
<TONGA -- WHEN YOU HAVE A MINUTE...>
<WHAT HAVE YOU HEARD?>
<TOWNSEND SENT SOME MEN TO TELL US THAT THE DAM ON THE MOUNTAIN LAKE IS FAR BEYOND ITS CAPACITY..>
<.. WHEN IT BLOWS, THE WATER WILL CRASH THROUGH THE VALLEY AND TURN THE VILLAGE INTO TOOTHPICKS! -->
<I TOLD HIM TO TELL ME SOMETHING WE DIDN'T KNOW..>
<HE SAID WE'LL BE LUCKY IF IT DOESN'T BURST BY NIGHTFALL.>

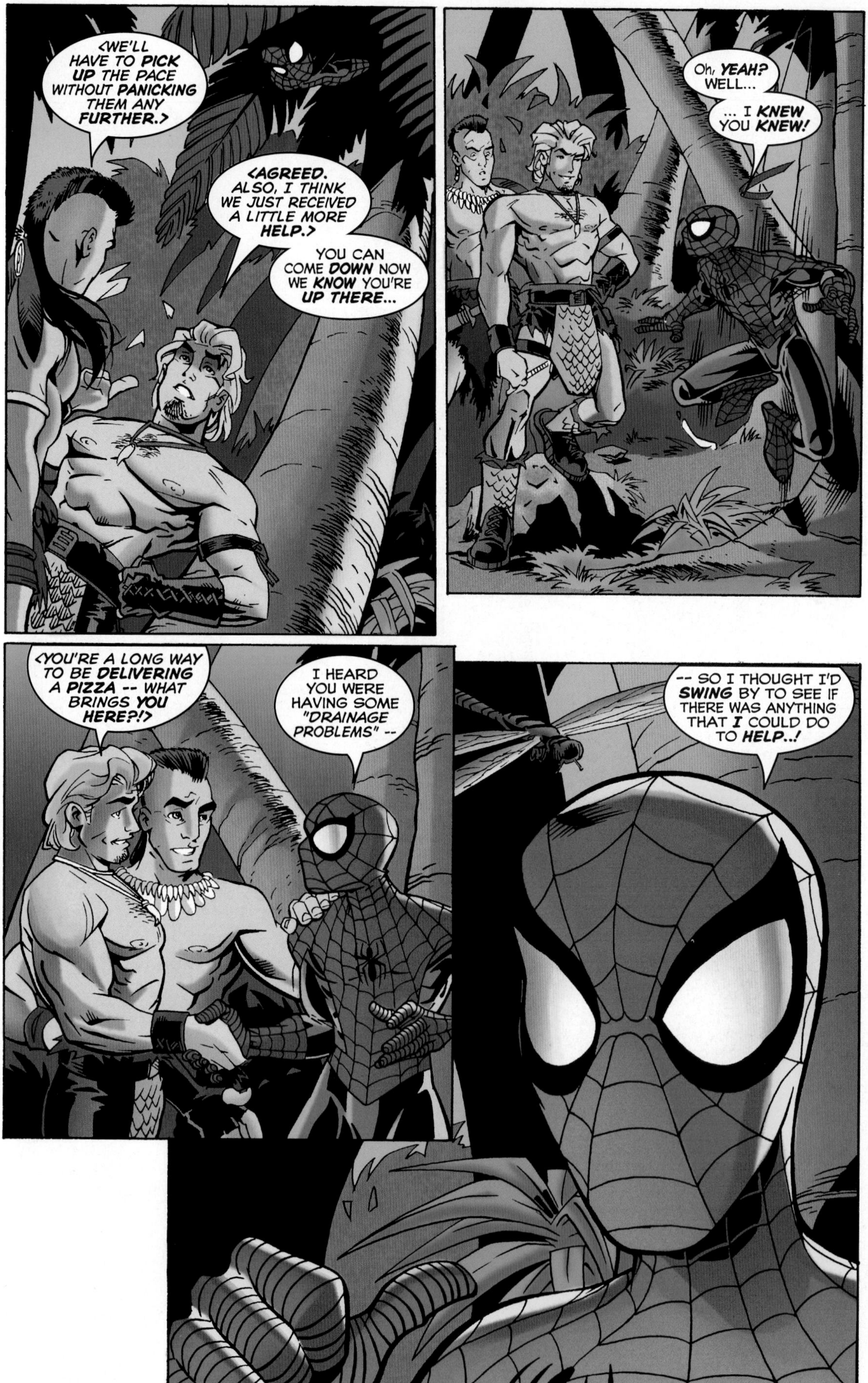

<WE'LL HAVE TO PICK UP THE PACE WITHOUT PANICKING THEM ANY FURTHER.>
<AGREED. ALSO, I THINK WE JUST RECEIVED A LITTLE MORE HELP.>
YOU CAN COME DOWN NOW WE KNOW YOU'RE UP THERE...
Oh, YEAH? WELL...
... I KNEW YOU KNEW!
<YOU'RE A LONG WAY TO BE DELIVERING A PIZZA -- WHAT BRINGS YOU HERE?!>
I HEARD YOU WERE HAVING SOME "DRAINAGE PROBLEMS" --
-- SO I THOUGHT I'D SWING BY TO SEE IF THERE WAS ANYTHING THAT I COULD DO TO HELP..!

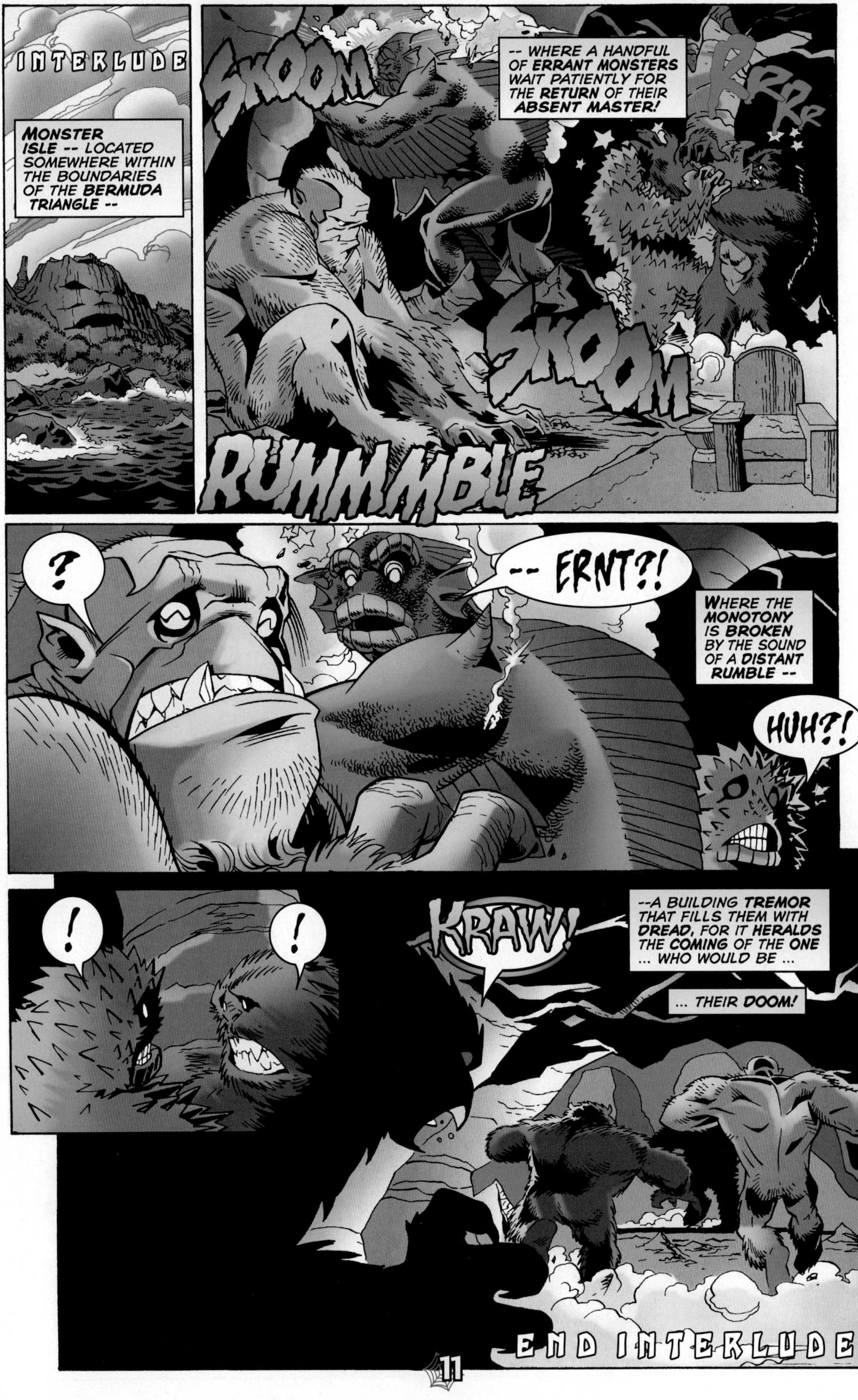

INTERLUDE
MONSTER ISLE -- LOCATED SOMEWHERE WITHIN THE BOUNDARIES OF THE BERMUDA TRIANGLE --
SKOOM
-- WHERE A HANDFUL OF ERRANT MONSTERS WAIT PATIENTLY FOR THE RETURN OF THEIR ABSENT MASTER!
RRRRR
SKOOM
RUMMMBLE
?
-- ERNT?!
WHERE THE MONOTONY IS BROKEN BY THE SOUND OF A DISTANT RUMBLE --
HUH?!
!
!
KRAW!
--A BUILDING TREMOR THAT FILLS THEM WITH DREAD, FOR IT HERALDS THE COMING OF THE ONE ... WHO WOULD BE ...
... THEIR DOOM!
END INTERLUDE

MEANWHILE --

... THE **REFRIGERATION UNITS** CONTINUE TO OPERATE AT **PEAK EFFICIENCY**...

... BUT EVEN WITH THAT, THEY CANNOT POSSIBLY **KEEP UP** WITH THE **RATE** AT WHICH THE **GLACIERS** ARE **MELTING!**

WE'RE FIGHTING AGAINST **NATURE** AND IT'S A **LOSING BATTLE**...

... BY Dr. ROTH'S CALCULATIONS, EVEN WITH THE **FREEZER UNITS** CONTINUING AT **MAXIMUM OUTPUT** --

-- THE **SAVAGE LAND** WILL BE COMPLETELY **UNDERWATER** IN A **MONTH'S TIME!**

THAT'S **IT**, THEN...

... WE'RE **FINISHED**...

-- MEANWHILE -- MANY METERS ABOVE --

-- THE MELTING GLACIER YIELDS UP ITS OWN **BAD NEWS** --

-- AS THE FLOWING WATERS GRADUALLY **REVEAL** THE SLOWLY THAWING FORM OF THE ONE WHO IS CALLED --

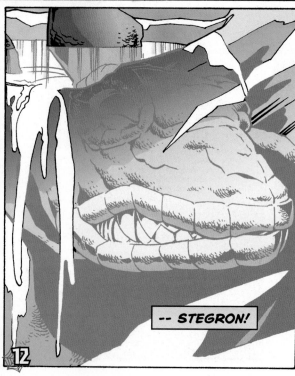

-- STEGRON!

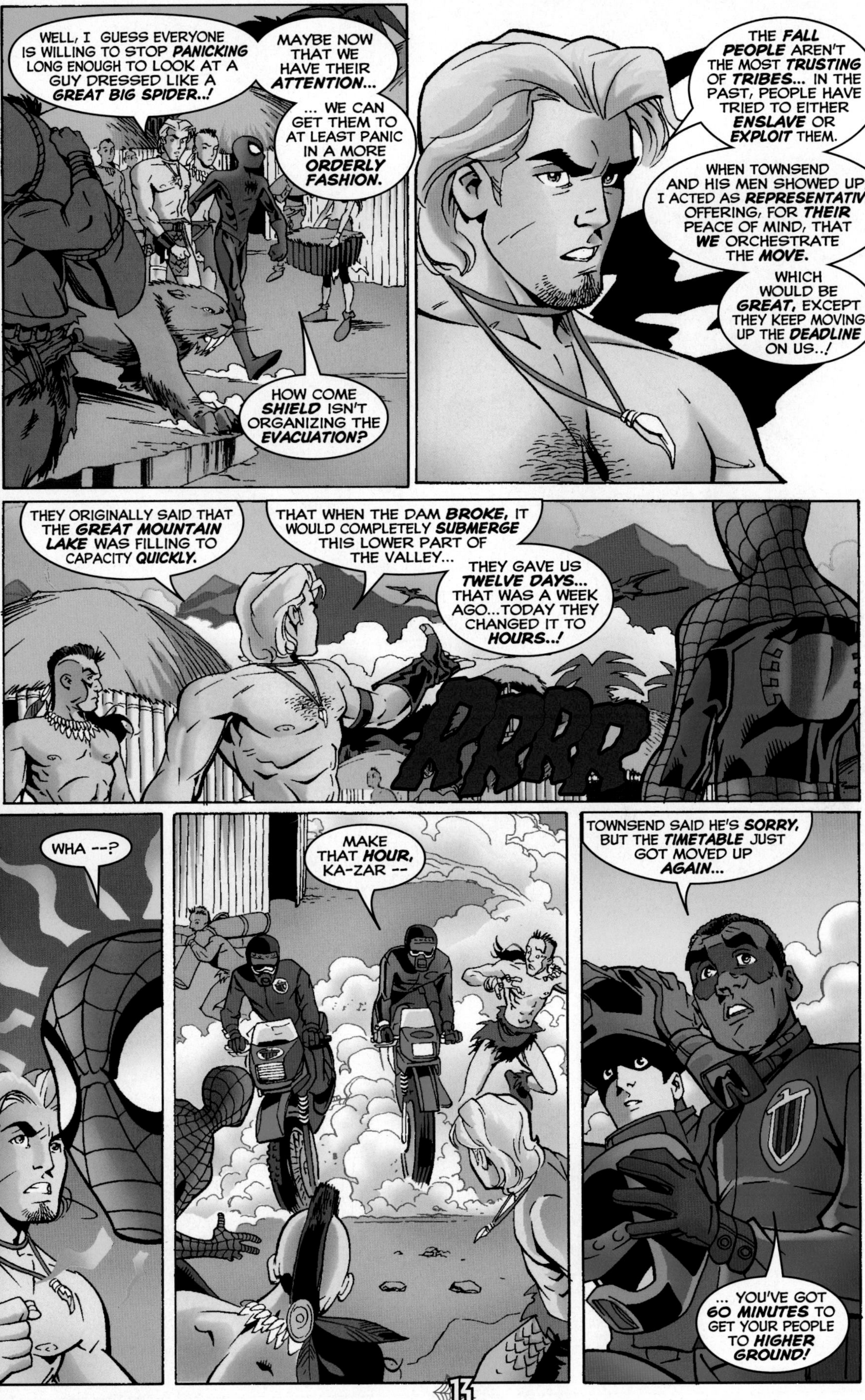
WELL, I GUESS EVERYONE IS WILLING TO STOP PANICKING LONG ENOUGH TO LOOK AT A GUY DRESSED LIKE A GREAT BIG SPIDER..!
MAYBE NOW THAT WE HAVE THEIR ATTENTION...
... WE CAN GET THEM TO AT LEAST PANIC IN A MORE ORDERLY FASHION.
HOW COME SHIELD ISN'T ORGANIZING THE EVACUATION?
THE FALL PEOPLE AREN'T THE MOST TRUSTING OF TRIBES... IN THE PAST, PEOPLE HAVE TRIED TO EITHER ENSLAVE OR EXPLOIT THEM.
WHEN TOWNSEND AND HIS MEN SHOWED UP, I ACTED AS REPRESENTATIVE, OFFERING, FOR THEIR PEACE OF MIND, THAT WE ORCHESTRATE THE MOVE.
WHICH WOULD BE GREAT, EXCEPT THEY KEEP MOVING UP THE DEADLINE ON US..!
THEY ORIGINALLY SAID THAT THE GREAT MOUNTAIN LAKE WAS FILLING TO CAPACITY QUICKLY.
THAT WHEN THE DAM BROKE, IT WOULD COMPLETELY SUBMERGE THIS LOWER PART OF THE VALLEY...
THEY GAVE US TWELVE DAYS... THAT WAS A WEEK AGO...TODAY THEY CHANGED IT TO HOURS..!
RRRRR
WHA --?
MAKE THAT HOUR, KA-ZAR --
TOWNSEND SAID HE'S SORRY, BUT THE TIMETABLE JUST GOT MOVED UP AGAIN...
... YOU'VE GOT 60 MINUTES TO GET YOUR PEOPLE TO HIGHER GROUND!

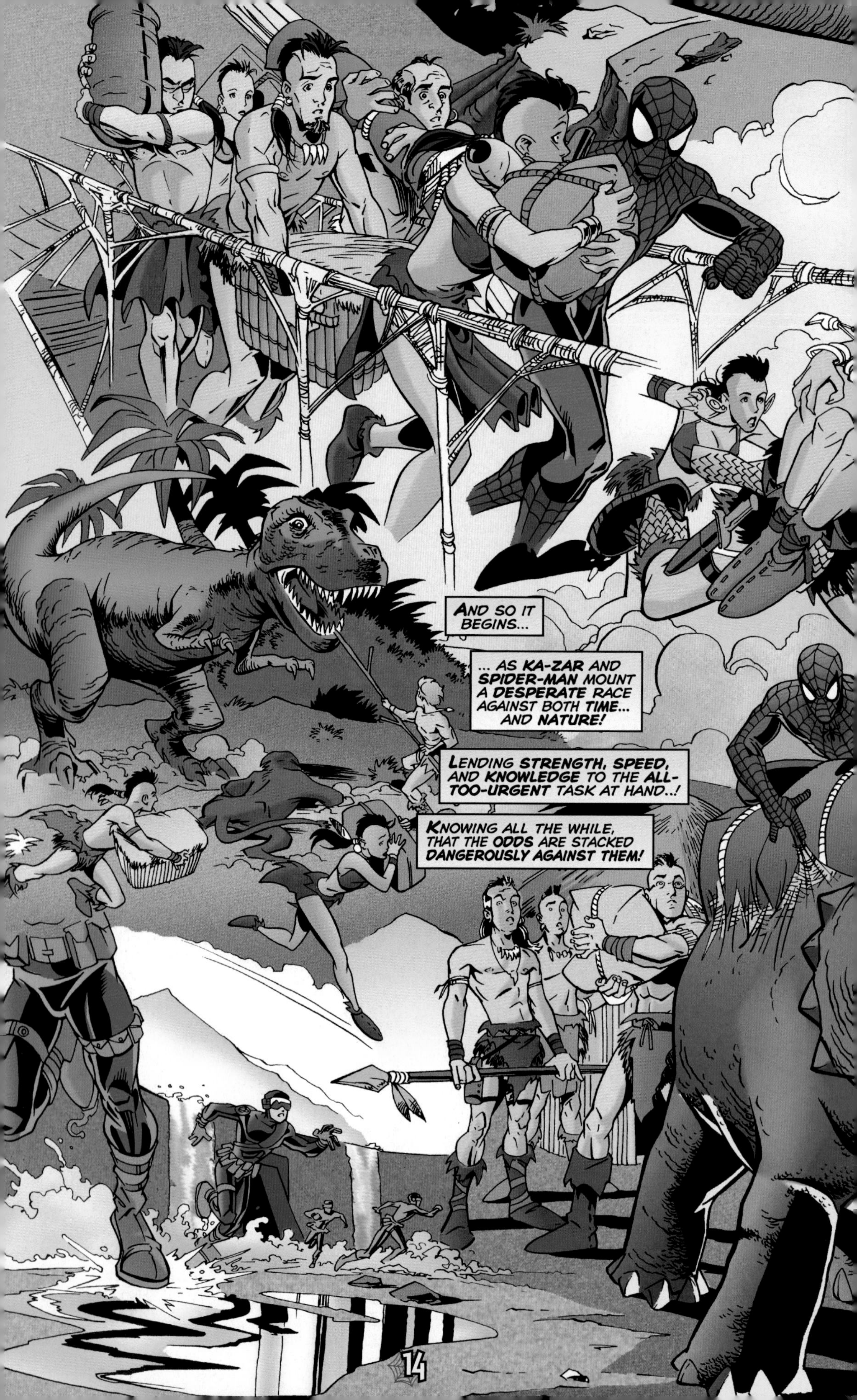
AND SO IT BEGINS...
... AS KA-ZAR AND SPIDER-MAN MOUNT A DESPERATE RACE AGAINST BOTH TIME... AND NATURE!
LENDING STRENGTH, SPEED, AND KNOWLEDGE TO THE ALL-TOO-URGENT TASK AT HAND..!
KNOWING ALL THE WHILE, THAT THE ODDS ARE STACKED DANGEROUSLY AGAINST THEM!
14

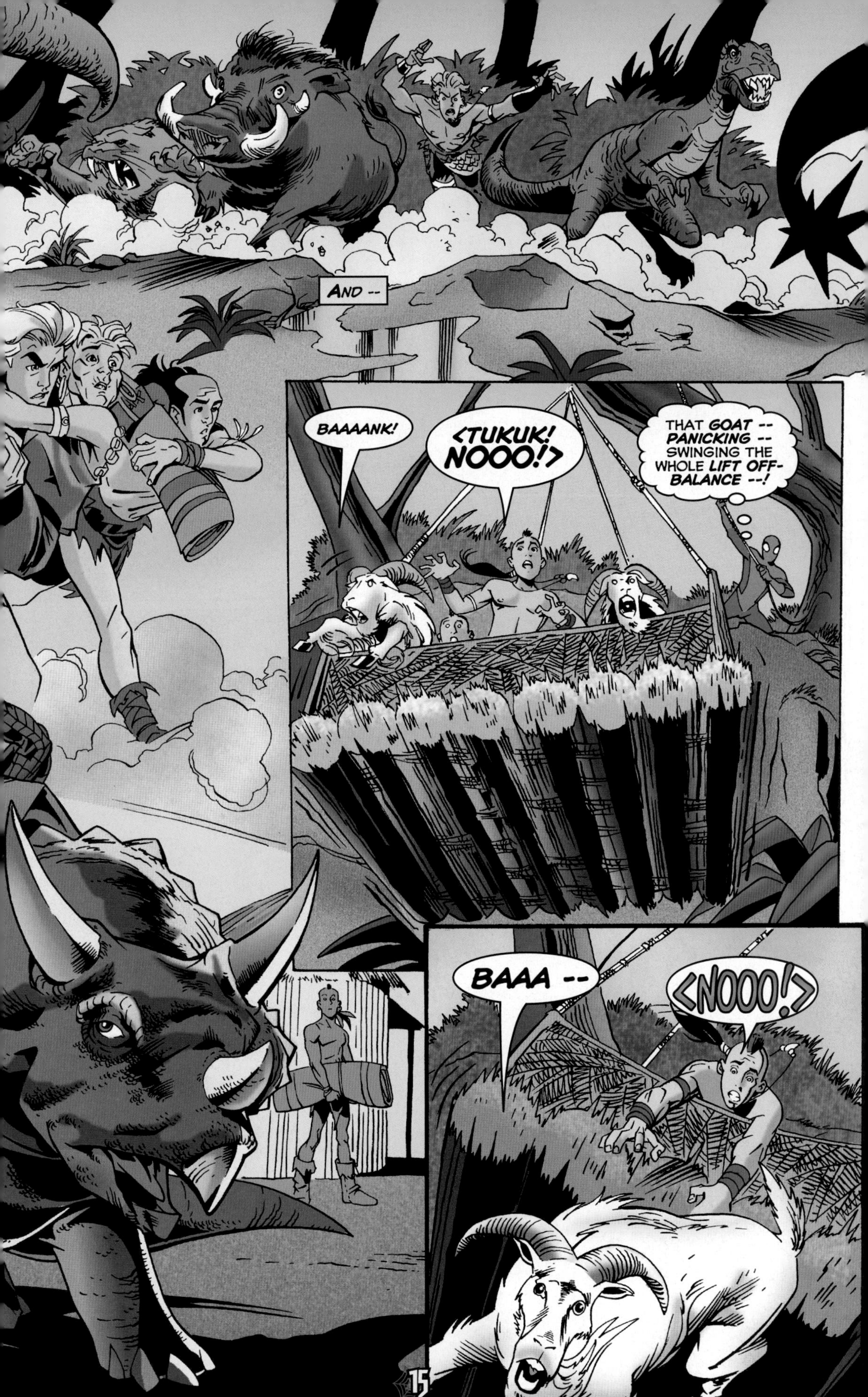

AND --
BAAAANK!
<TUKUK! NOOO!>
THAT GOAT -- PANICKING -- SWINGING THE WHOLE LIFT OFF-BALANCE --!
BAAA --
<NOOO!>

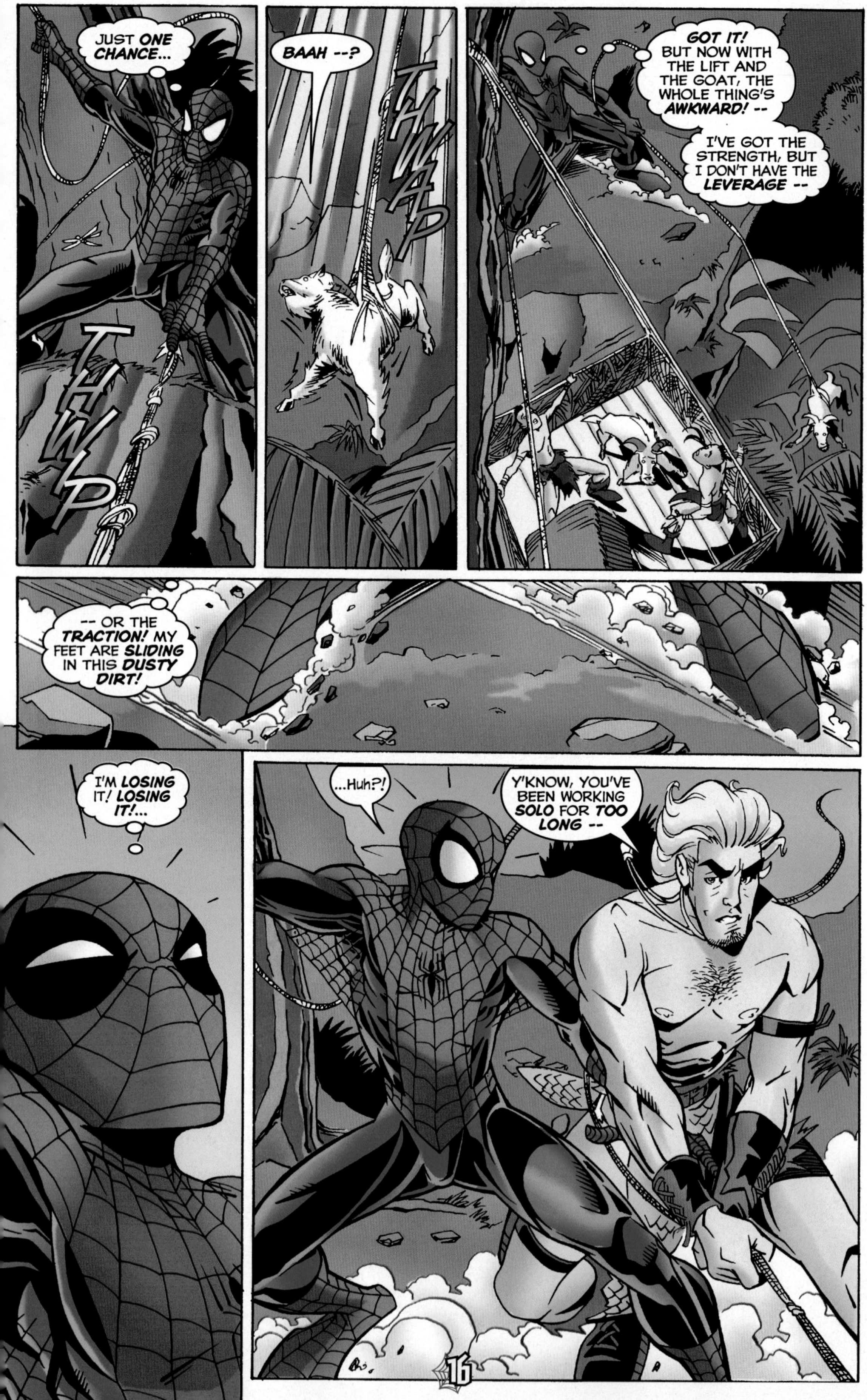

JUST ONE CHANCE...
THWAP
BAAH --?
THWAP
GOT IT! BUT NOW WITH THE LIFT AND THE GOAT, THE WHOLE THING'S AWKWARD! --
I'VE GOT THE STRENGTH, BUT I DON'T HAVE THE LEVERAGE --
-- OR THE TRACTION! MY FEET ARE SLIDING IN THIS DUSTY DIRT!
I'M LOSING IT! LOSING IT!...
...Huh?!
Y'KNOW, YOU'VE BEEN WORKING SOLO FOR TOO LONG --

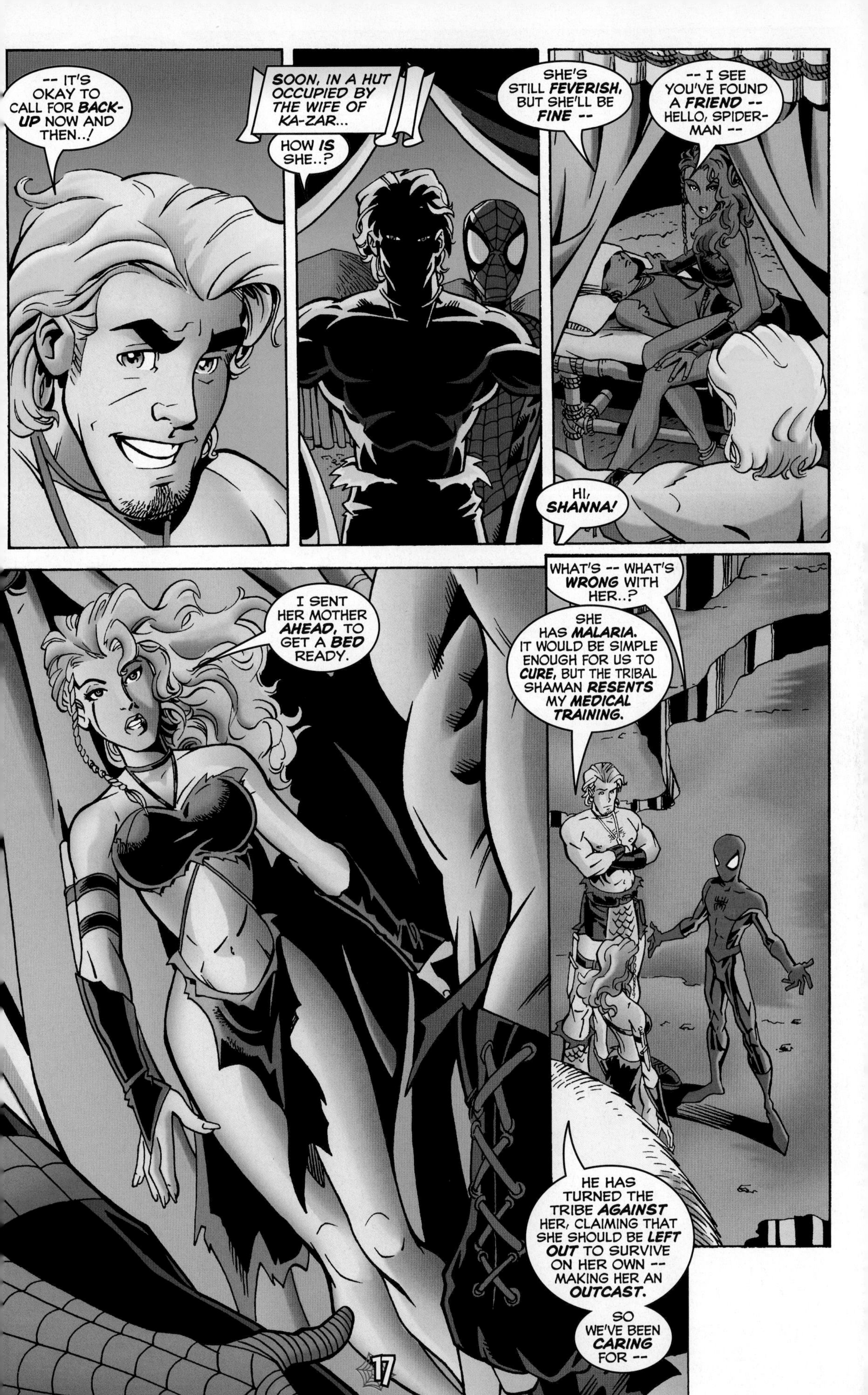
-- IT'S OKAY TO CALL FOR BACK-UP NOW AND THEN..!
SOON, IN A HUT OCCUPIED BY THE WIFE OF KA-ZAR...
HOW IS SHE..?
SHE'S STILL FEVERISH, BUT SHE'LL BE FINE --
-- I SEE YOU'VE FOUND A FRIEND -- HELLO, SPIDER-MAN --
HI, SHANNA!
I SENT HER MOTHER AHEAD, TO GET A BED READY.
WHAT'S -- WHAT'S WRONG WITH HER..?
SHE HAS MALARIA. IT WOULD BE SIMPLE ENOUGH FOR US TO CURE, BUT THE TRIBAL SHAMAN RESENTS MY MEDICAL TRAINING.
HE HAS TURNED THE TRIBE AGAINST HER, CLAIMING THAT SHE SHOULD BE LEFT OUT TO SURVIVE ON HER OWN -- MAKING HER AN OUTCAST.
SO WE'VE BEEN CARING FOR --

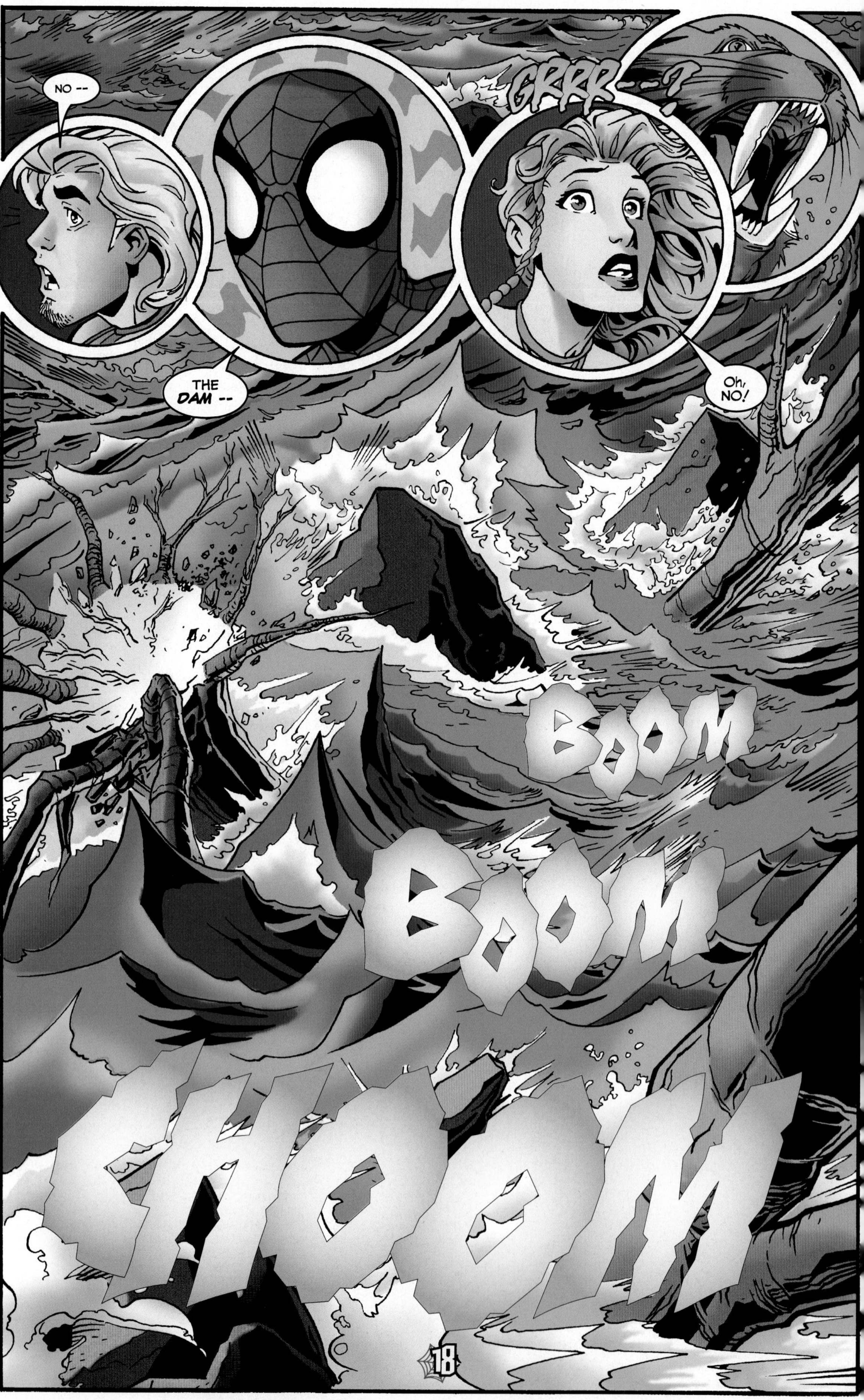
NO --
THE DAM --
GRRR--?
Oh, NO!
BOOM
BOOM
SHOOM

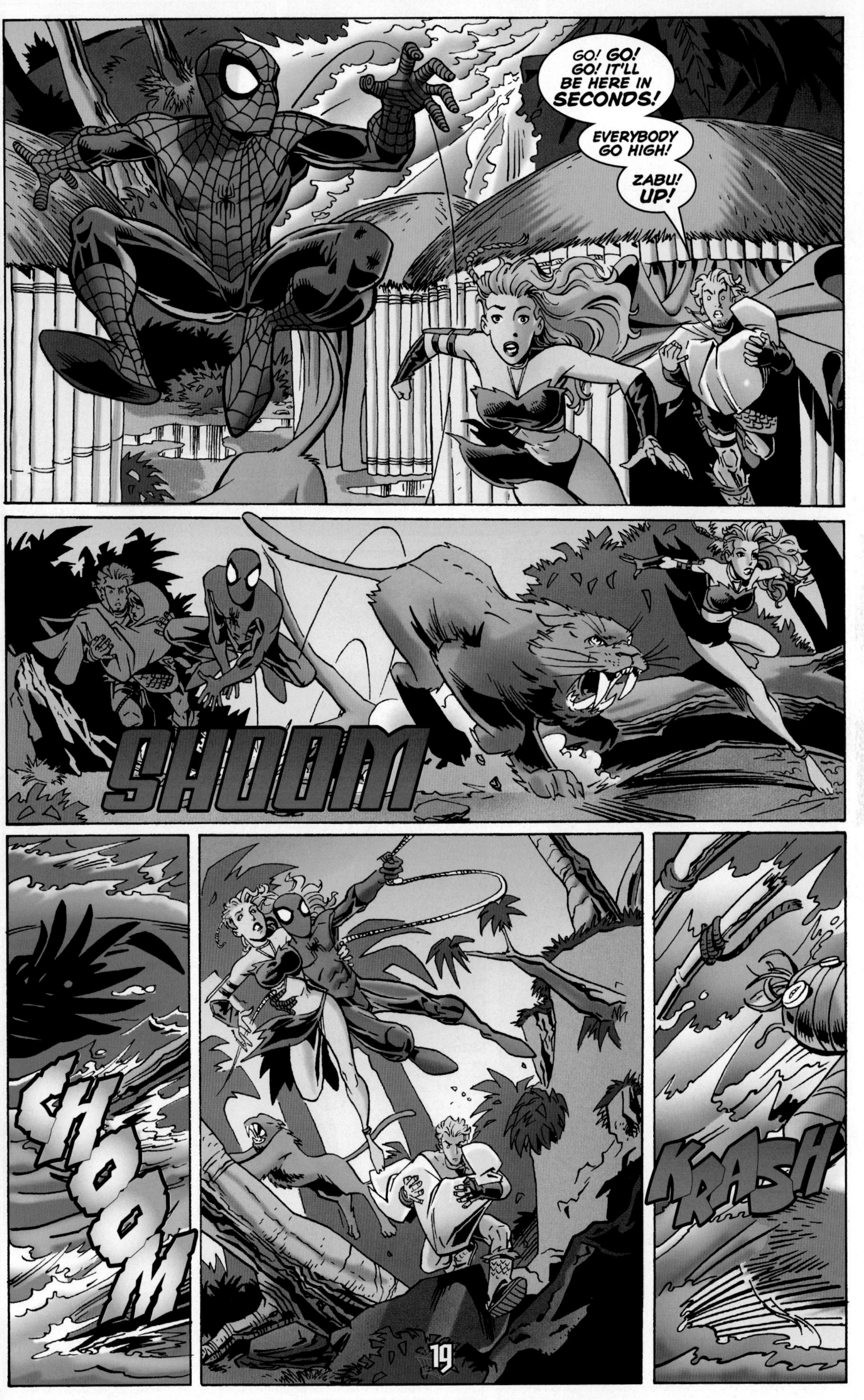

GO! GO! GO! IT'LL BE HERE IN SECONDS!
EVERYBODY GO HIGH!
ZABU! UP!
SHOOM
CHOOM
KRASH

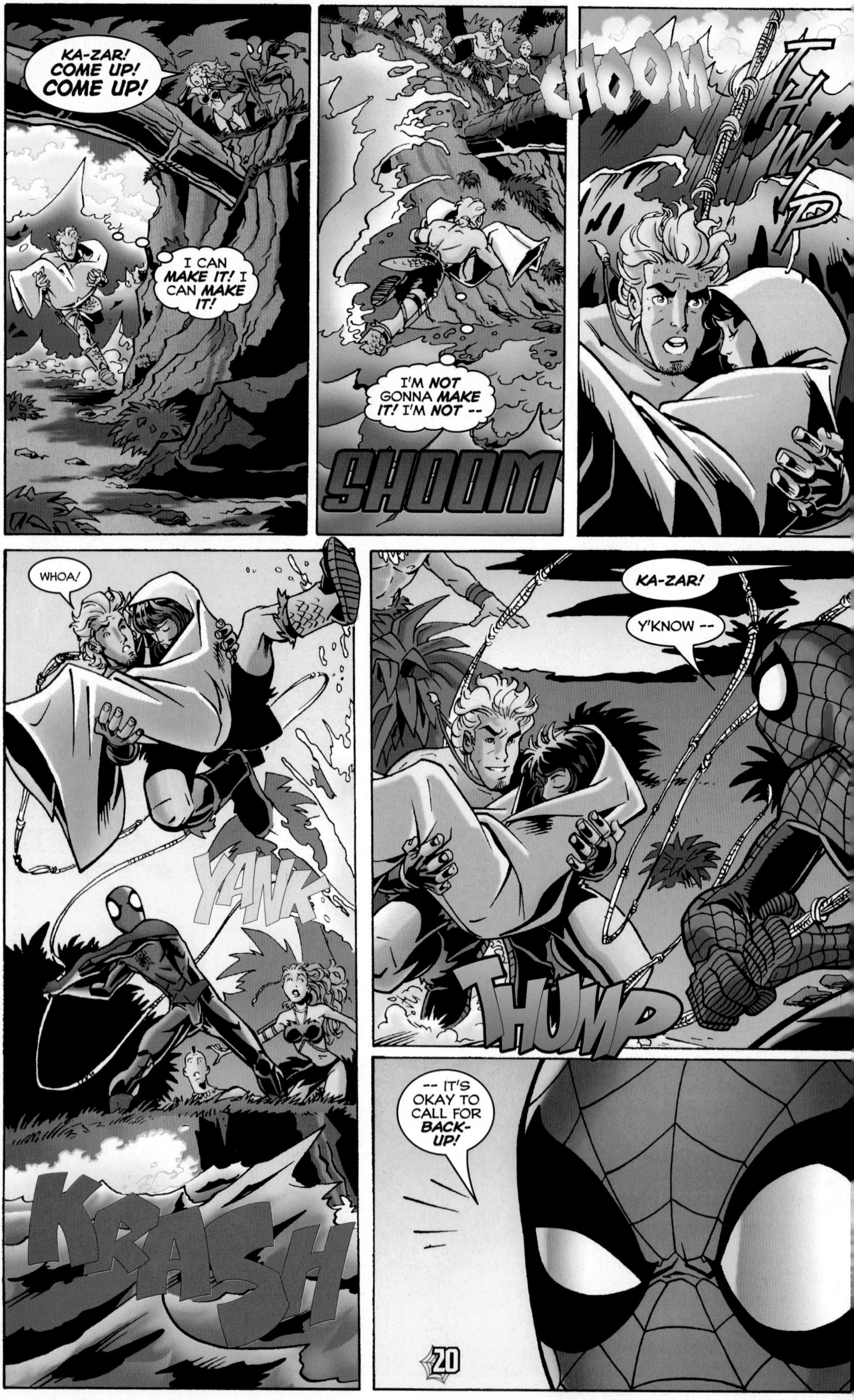

KA-ZAR! COME UP! COME UP!
I CAN MAKE IT! I CAN MAKE IT!
I'M NOT GONNA MAKE IT! I'M NOT --
SHOOM
CHOOM
THWIP
WHOA!
YANK
KRASH
KA-ZAR!
Y'KNOW --
THUMP
-- IT'S OKAY TO CALL FOR BACK-UP!

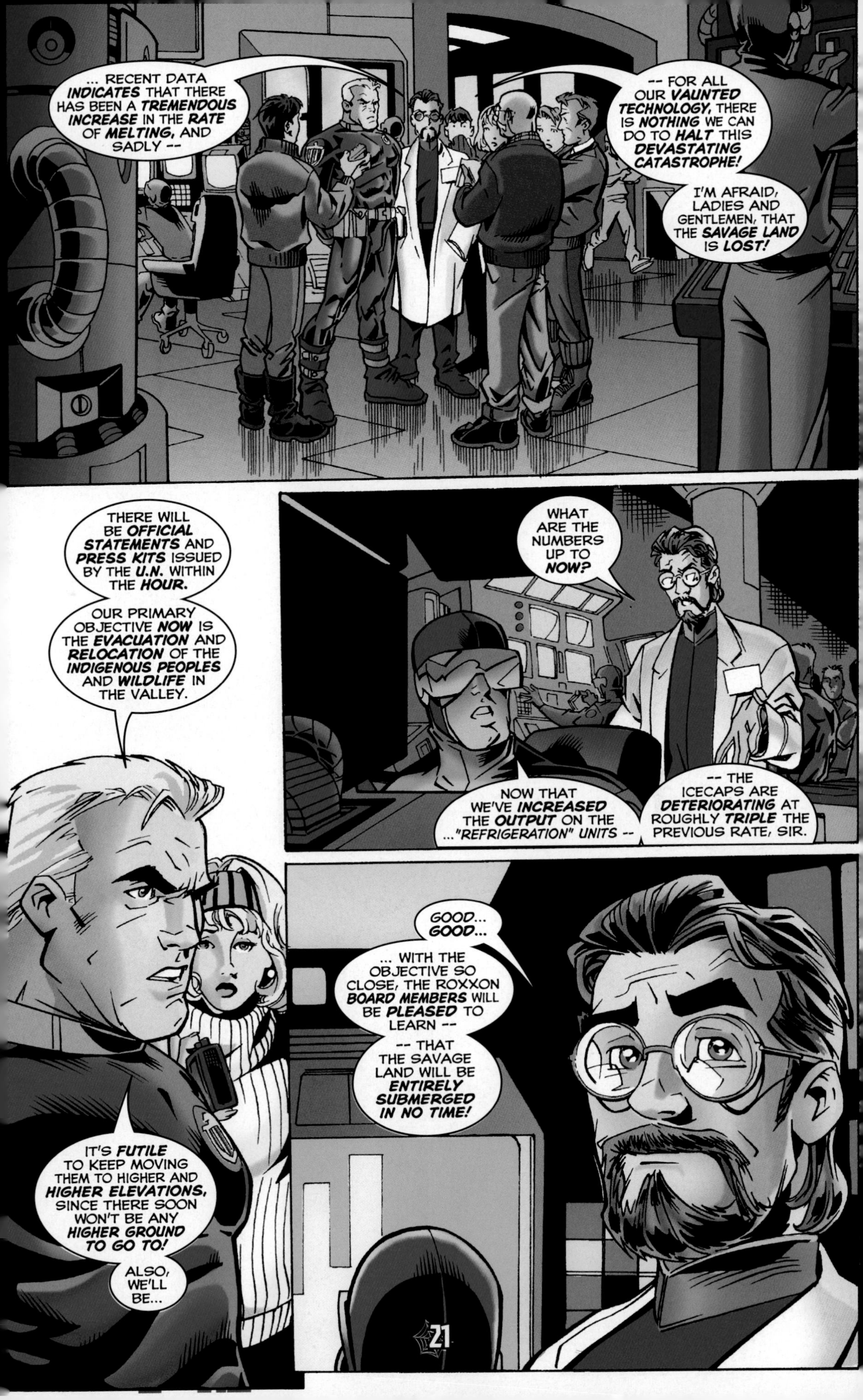

... RECENT DATA INDICATES THAT THERE HAS BEEN A TREMENDOUS INCREASE IN THE RATE OF MELTING, AND SADLY --
-- FOR ALL OUR VAUNTED TECHNOLOGY, THERE IS NOTHING WE CAN DO TO HALT THIS DEVASTATING CATASTROPHE!
I'M AFRAID, LADIES AND GENTLEMEN, THAT THE SAVAGE LAND IS LOST!
THERE WILL BE OFFICIAL STATEMENTS AND PRESS KITS ISSUED BY THE U.N. WITHIN THE HOUR.
OUR PRIMARY OBJECTIVE NOW IS THE EVACUATION AND RELOCATION OF THE INDIGENOUS PEOPLES AND WILDLIFE IN THE VALLEY.
WHAT ARE THE NUMBERS UP TO NOW?
NOW THAT WE'VE INCREASED THE OUTPUT ON THE ..."REFRIGERATION" UNITS --
-- THE ICECAPS ARE DETERIORATING AT ROUGHLY TRIPLE THE PREVIOUS RATE, SIR.
GOOD... GOOD...
... WITH THE OBJECTIVE SO CLOSE, THE ROXXON BOARD MEMBERS WILL BE PLEASED TO LEARN --
-- THAT THE SAVAGE LAND WILL BE ENTIRELY SUBMERGED IN NO TIME!
IT'S FUTILE TO KEEP MOVING THEM TO HIGHER AND HIGHER ELEVATIONS, SINCE THERE SOON WON'T BE ANY HIGHER GROUND TO GO TO!
ALSO, WE'LL BE...

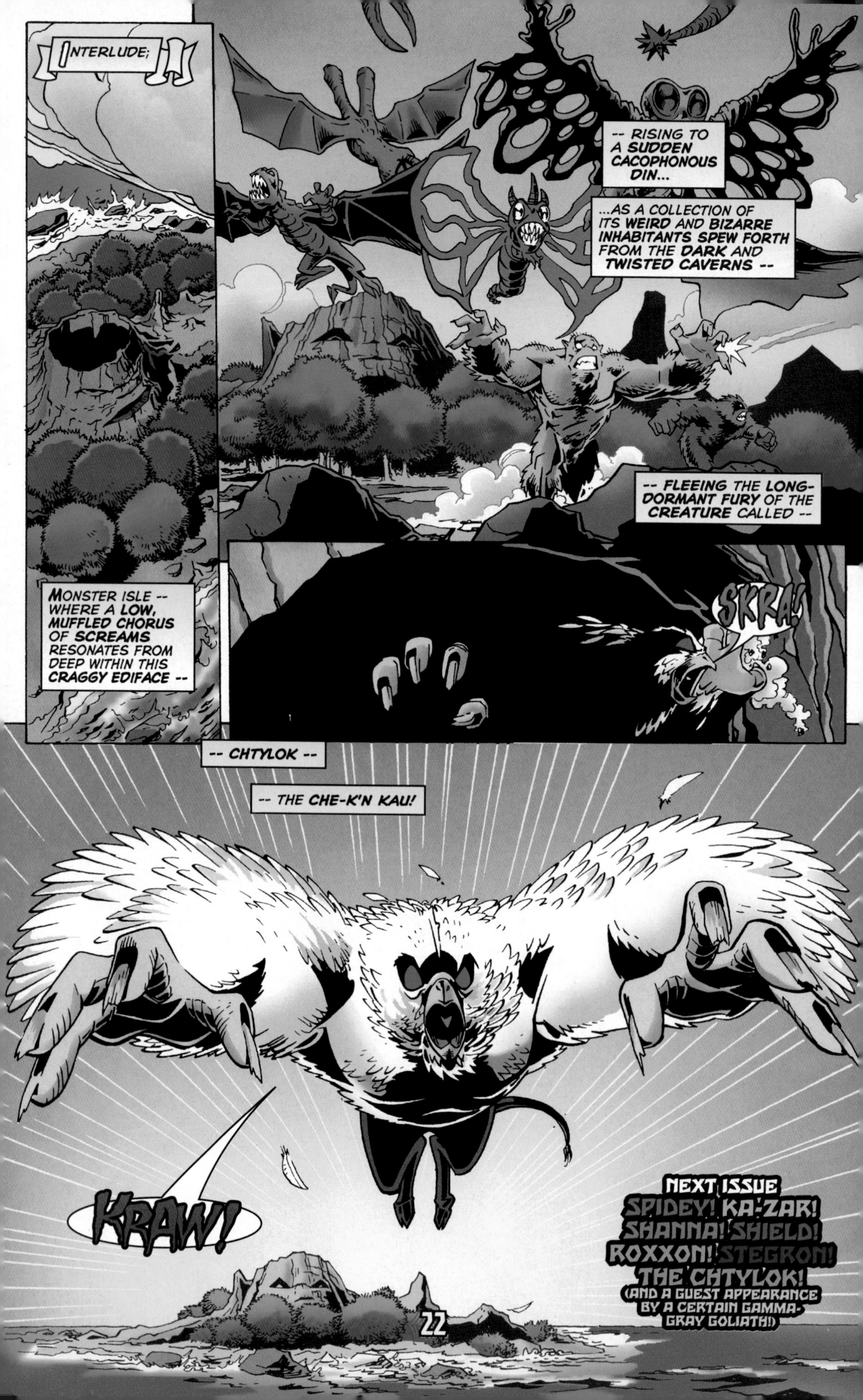
INTERLUDE;
MONSTER ISLE -- WHERE A LOW, MUFFLED CHORUS OF SCREAMS RESONATES FROM DEEP WITHIN THIS CRAGGY EDIFACE --
-- RISING TO A SUDDEN CACOPHONOUS DIN...
...AS A COLLECTION OF ITS WEIRD AND BIZARRE INHABITANTS SPEW FORTH FROM THE DARK AND TWISTED CAVERNS --
-- FLEEING THE LONG-DORMANT FURY OF THE CREATURE CALLED --
SKRA!
-- CHTYLOK --
-- THE CHE-K'N KAU!
KRAW!
NEXT ISSUE
SPIDEY! KA-ZAR! SHANNA! SHIELD! ROXXON! STEGRON! THE CHTYLOK!
(AND A GUEST APPEARANCE BY A CERTAIN GAMMA-GRAY GOLIATH!)

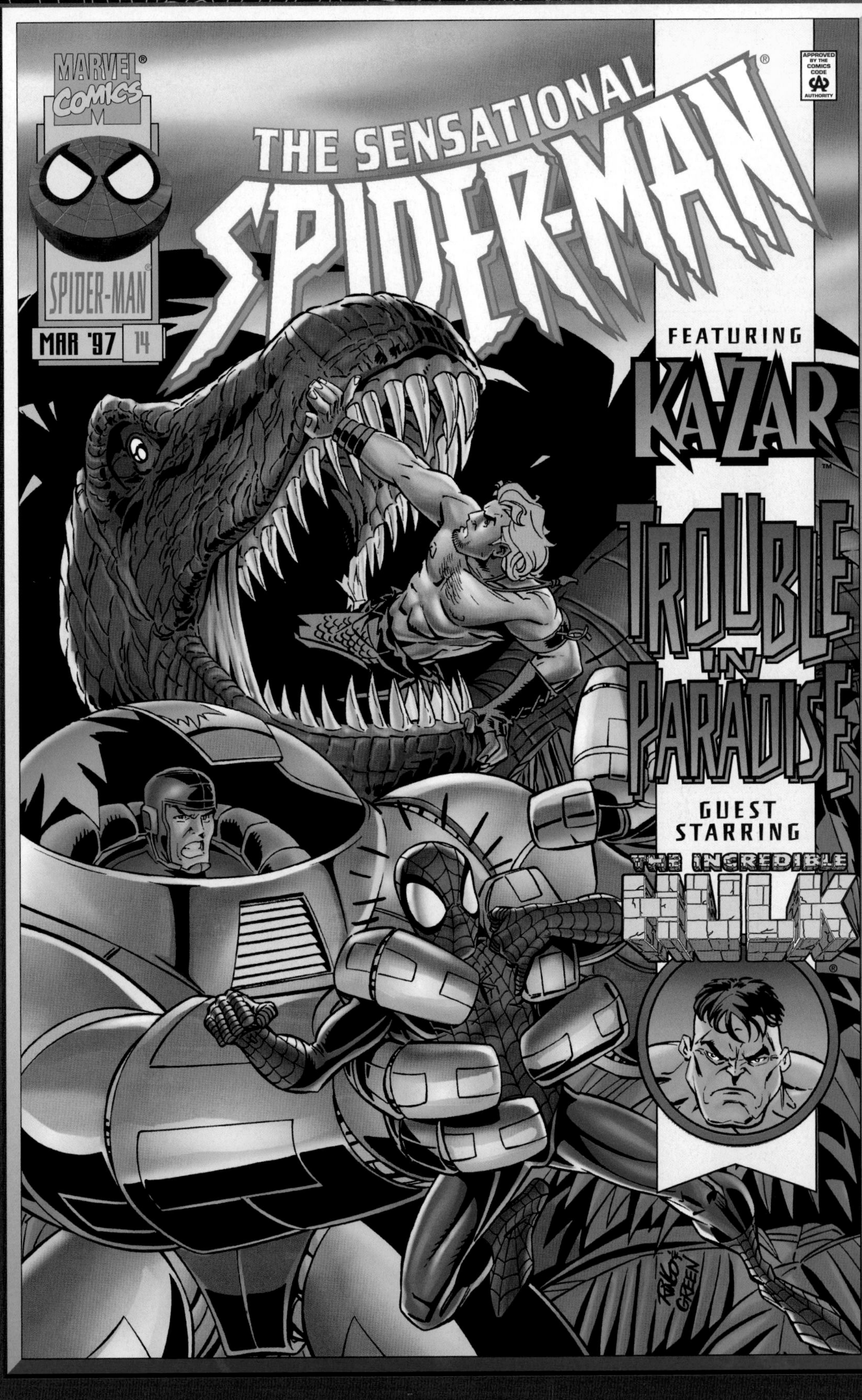
MARVEL COMICS
APPROVED BY THE COMICS CODE AUTHORITY
THE SENSATIONAL
SPIDER-MAN
SPIDER-MAN
MAR '97 14
FEATURING
KA-ZAR
TROUBLE IN PARADISE
GUEST STARRING
THE INCREDIBLE
HULK

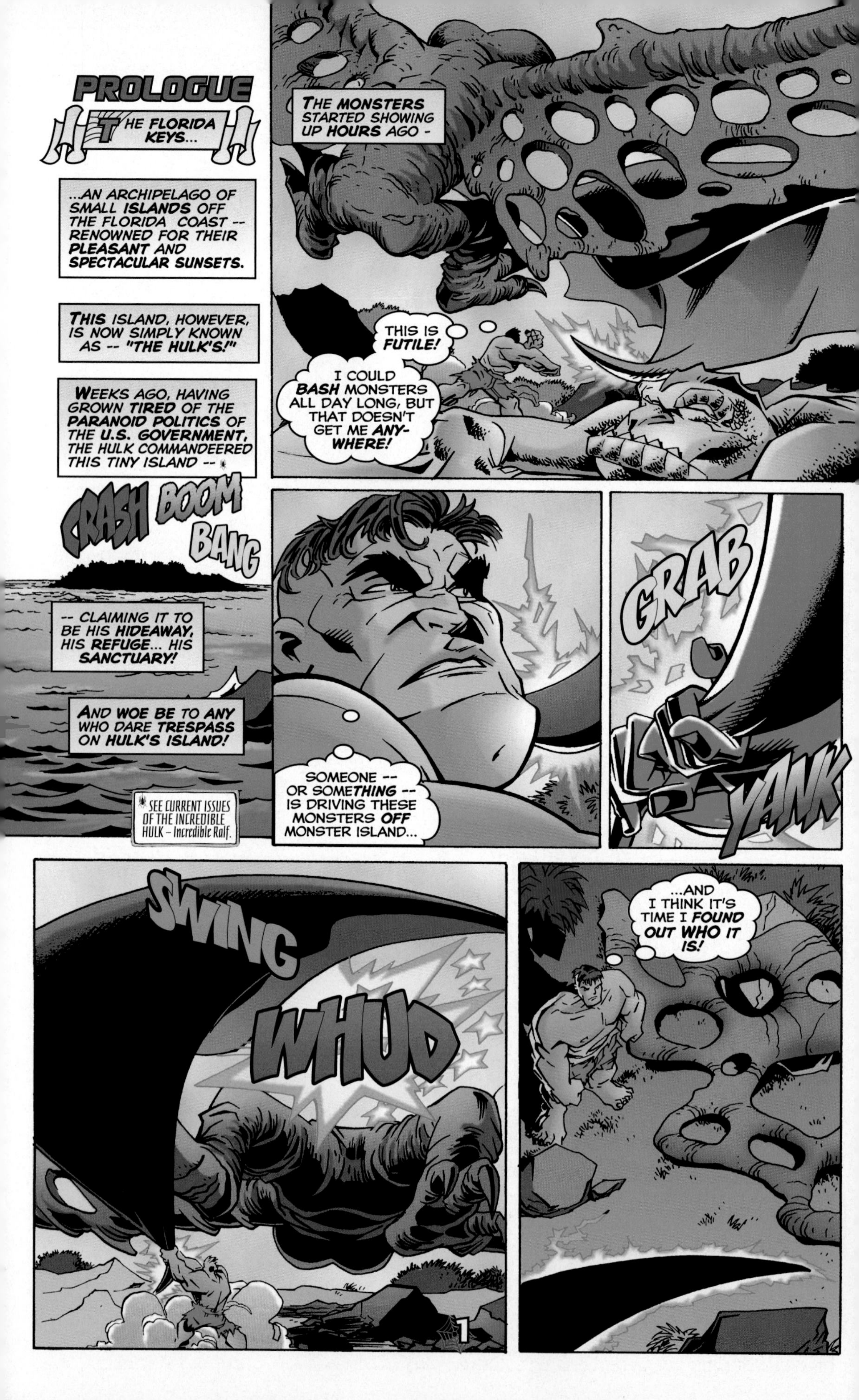
PROLOGUE
THE FLORIDA KEYS...
...AN ARCHIPELAGO OF SMALL ISLANDS OFF THE FLORIDA COAST -- RENOWNED FOR THEIR PLEASANT AND SPECTACULAR SUNSETS.
THIS ISLAND, HOWEVER, IS NOW SIMPLY KNOWN AS -- "THE HULK'S!"
WEEKS AGO, HAVING GROWN TIRED OF THE PARANOID POLITICS OF THE U.S. GOVERNMENT, THE HULK COMMANDEERED THIS TINY ISLAND --
CRASH BOOM BANG
-- CLAIMING IT TO BE HIS HIDEAWAY, HIS REFUGE... HIS SANCTUARY!
AND WOE BE TO ANY WHO DARE TRESPASS ON HULK'S ISLAND!
SEE CURRENT ISSUES OF THE INCREDIBLE HULK – Incredible Ralf.
THE MONSTERS STARTED SHOWING UP HOURS AGO -
THIS IS FUTILE!
I COULD BASH MONSTERS ALL DAY LONG, BUT THAT DOESN'T GET ME ANY-WHERE!
SOMEONE -- OR SOMETHING -- IS DRIVING THESE MONSTERS OFF MONSTER ISLAND...
GRAB
YANK
SWING
WHUD
...AND I THINK IT'S TIME I FOUND OUT WHO IT IS!

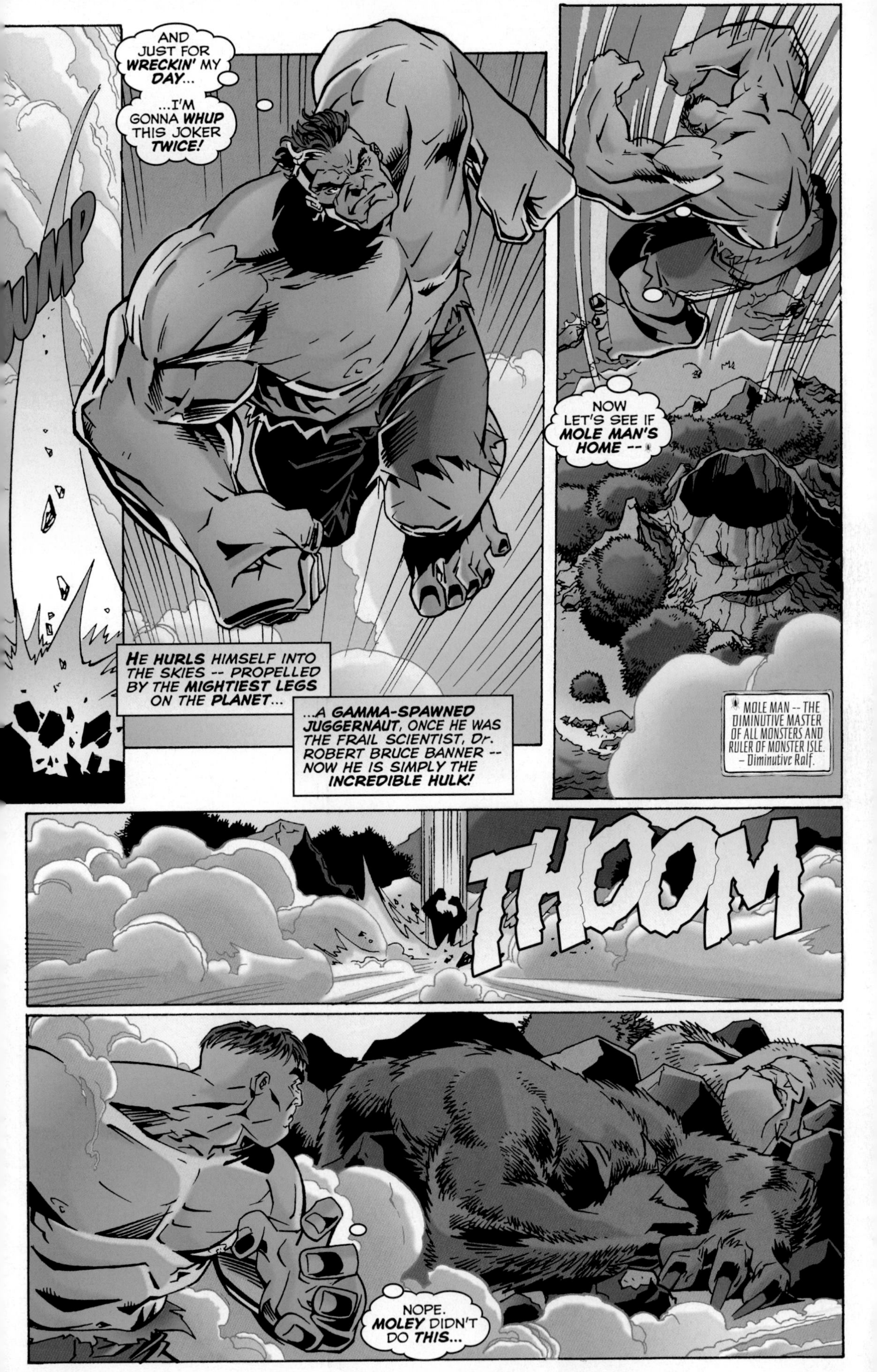
AND JUST FOR WRECKIN' MY DAY...
...I'M GONNA WHUP THIS JOKER TWICE!
HE HURLS HIMSELF INTO THE SKIES -- PROPELLED BY THE MIGHTIEST LEGS ON THE PLANET...
...A GAMMA-SPAWNED JUGGERNAUT, ONCE HE WAS THE FRAIL SCIENTIST, Dr. ROBERT BRUCE BANNER -- NOW HE IS SIMPLY THE INCREDIBLE HULK!
NOW LET'S SEE IF MOLE MAN'S HOME --
MOLE MAN -- THE DIMINUTIVE MASTER OF ALL MONSTERS AND RULER OF MONSTER ISLE. – Diminutive Ralf.
THOOM
NOPE. MOLEY DIDN'T DO THIS...

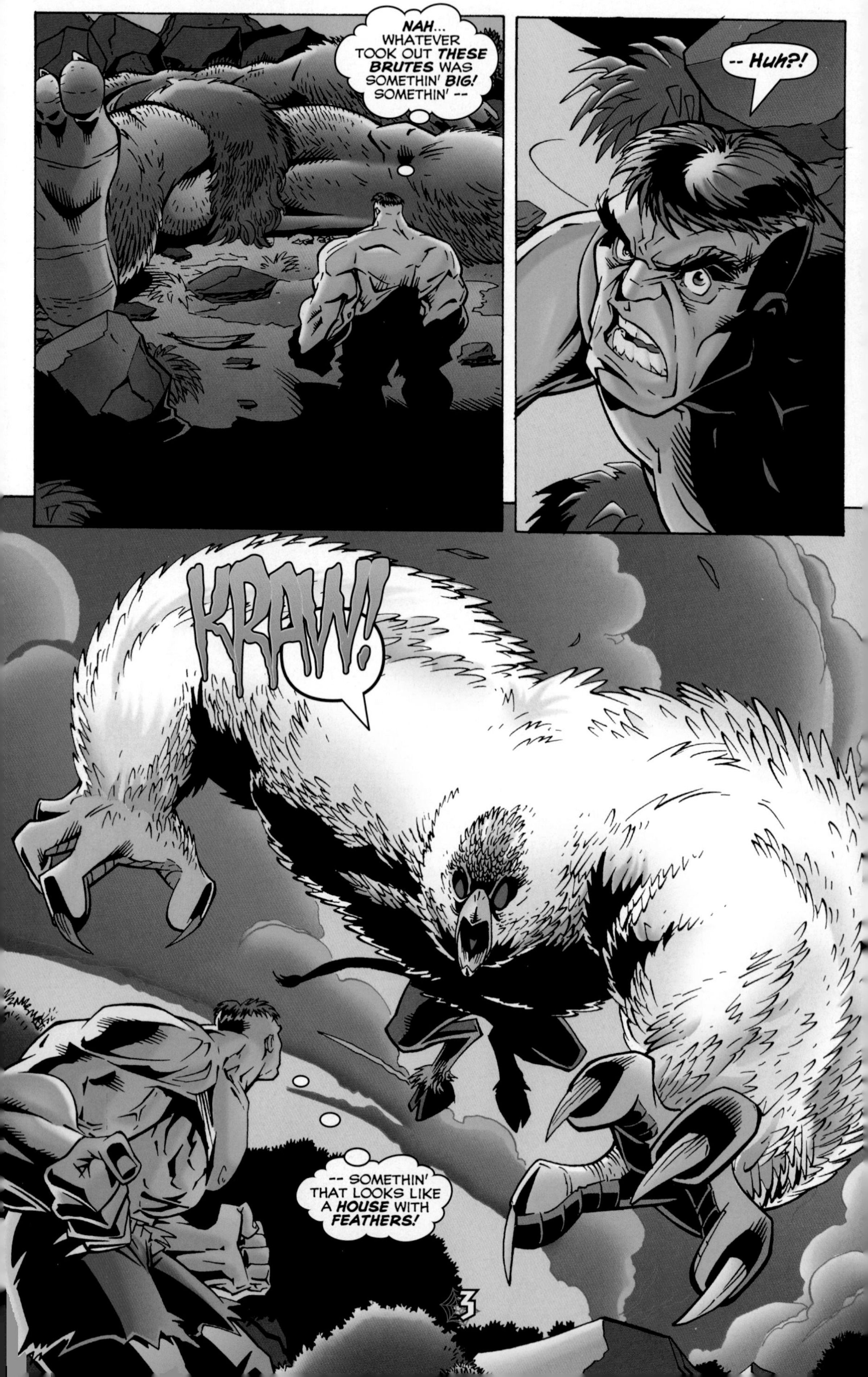
NAH... WHATEVER TOOK OUT THESE BRUTES WAS SOMETHIN' BIG! SOMETHIN' --
-- Huh?!
KRAW!
-- SOMETHIN' THAT LOOKS LIKE A HOUSE WITH FEATHERS!
3

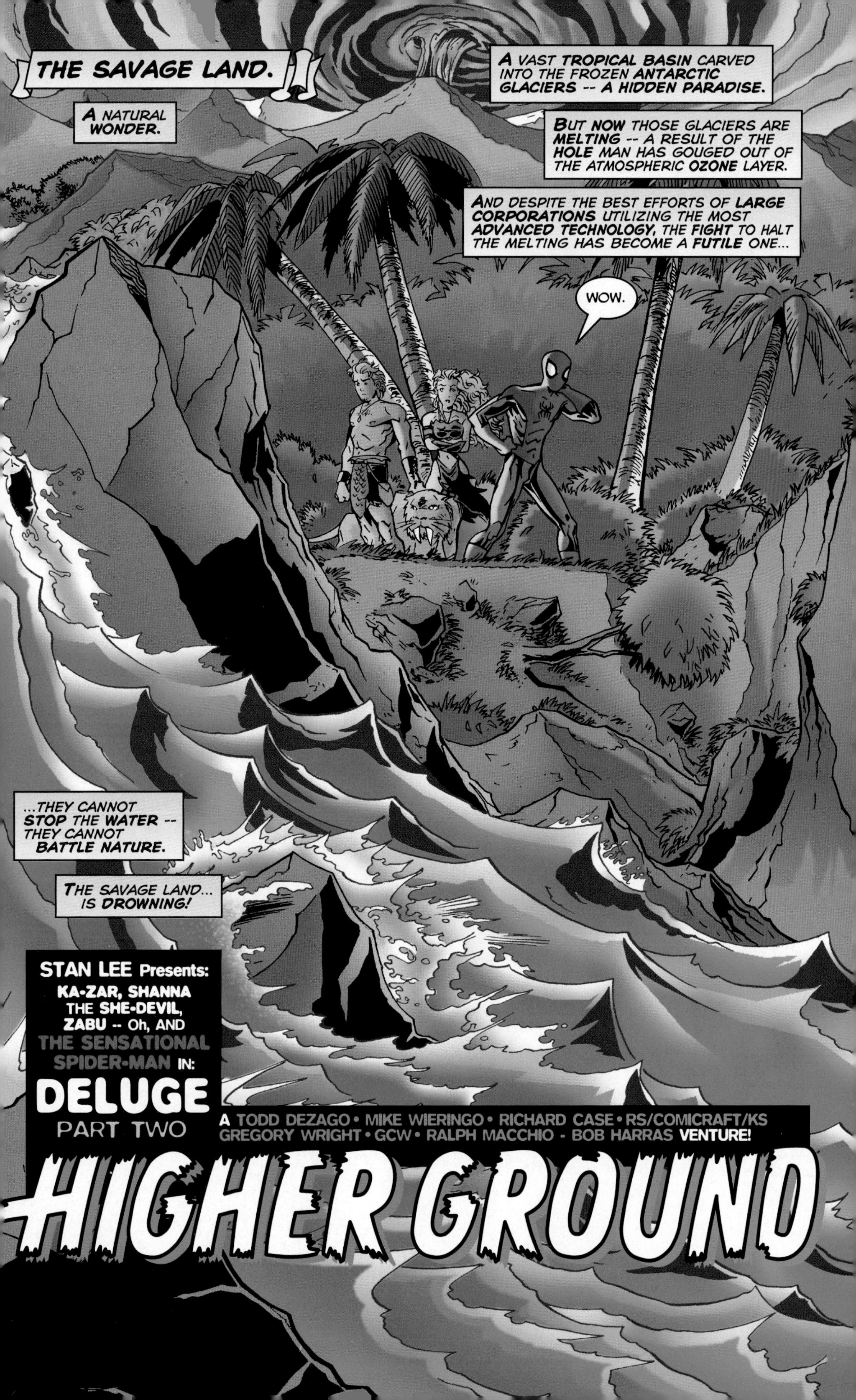
THE SAVAGE LAND.
A NATURAL WONDER.
A VAST TROPICAL BASIN CARVED INTO THE FROZEN ANTARCTIC GLACIERS -- A HIDDEN PARADISE.
BUT NOW THOSE GLACIERS ARE MELTING -- A RESULT OF THE HOLE MAN HAS GOUGED OUT OF THE ATMOSPHERIC OZONE LAYER.
AND DESPITE THE BEST EFFORTS OF LARGE CORPORATIONS UTILIZING THE MOST ADVANCED TECHNOLOGY, THE FIGHT TO HALT THE MELTING HAS BECOME A FUTILE ONE...
WOW.
...THEY CANNOT STOP THE WATER -- THEY CANNOT BATTLE NATURE.
THE SAVAGE LAND... IS DROWNING!
STAN LEE Presents: KA-ZAR, SHANNA THE SHE-DEVIL, ZABU -- Oh, AND THE SENSATIONAL SPIDER-MAN IN:
DELUGE
PART TWO
A TODD DEZAGO • MIKE WIERINGO • RICHARD CASE • RS/COMICRAFT/KS GREGORY WRIGHT • GCW • RALPH MACCHIO - BOB HARRAS VENTURE!
HIGHER GROUND

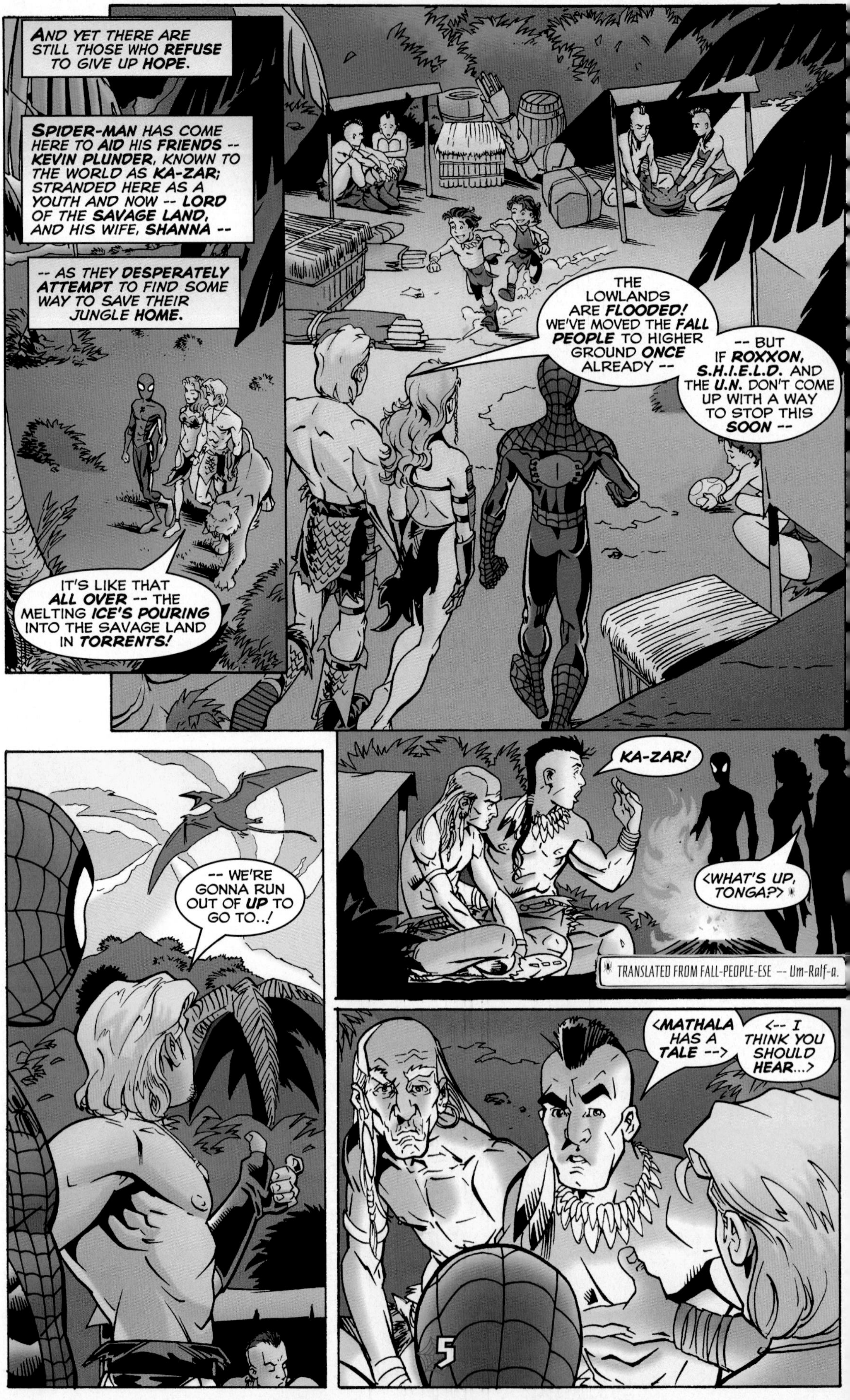
AND YET THERE ARE STILL THOSE WHO REFUSE TO GIVE UP HOPE.
SPIDER-MAN HAS COME HERE TO AID HIS FRIENDS -- KEVIN PLUNDER, KNOWN TO THE WORLD AS KA-ZAR; STRANDED HERE AS A YOUTH AND NOW -- LORD OF THE SAVAGE LAND, AND HIS WIFE, SHANNA --
-- AS THEY DESPERATELY ATTEMPT TO FIND SOME WAY TO SAVE THEIR JUNGLE HOME.
IT'S LIKE THAT ALL OVER -- THE MELTING ICE'S POURING INTO THE SAVAGE LAND IN TORRENTS!
THE LOWLANDS ARE FLOODED! WE'VE MOVED THE FALL PEOPLE TO HIGHER GROUND ONCE ALREADY --
-- BUT IF ROXXON, S.H.I.E.L.D. AND THE U.N. DON'T COME UP WITH A WAY TO STOP THIS SOON --
-- WE'RE GONNA RUN OUT OF UP TO GO TO..!
KA-ZAR!
<WHAT'S UP, TONGA?>
TRANSLATED FROM FALL-PEOPLE-ESE -- Um-Ralf-a.
<MATHALA HAS A TALE -->
<-- I THINK YOU SHOULD HEAR...>
5

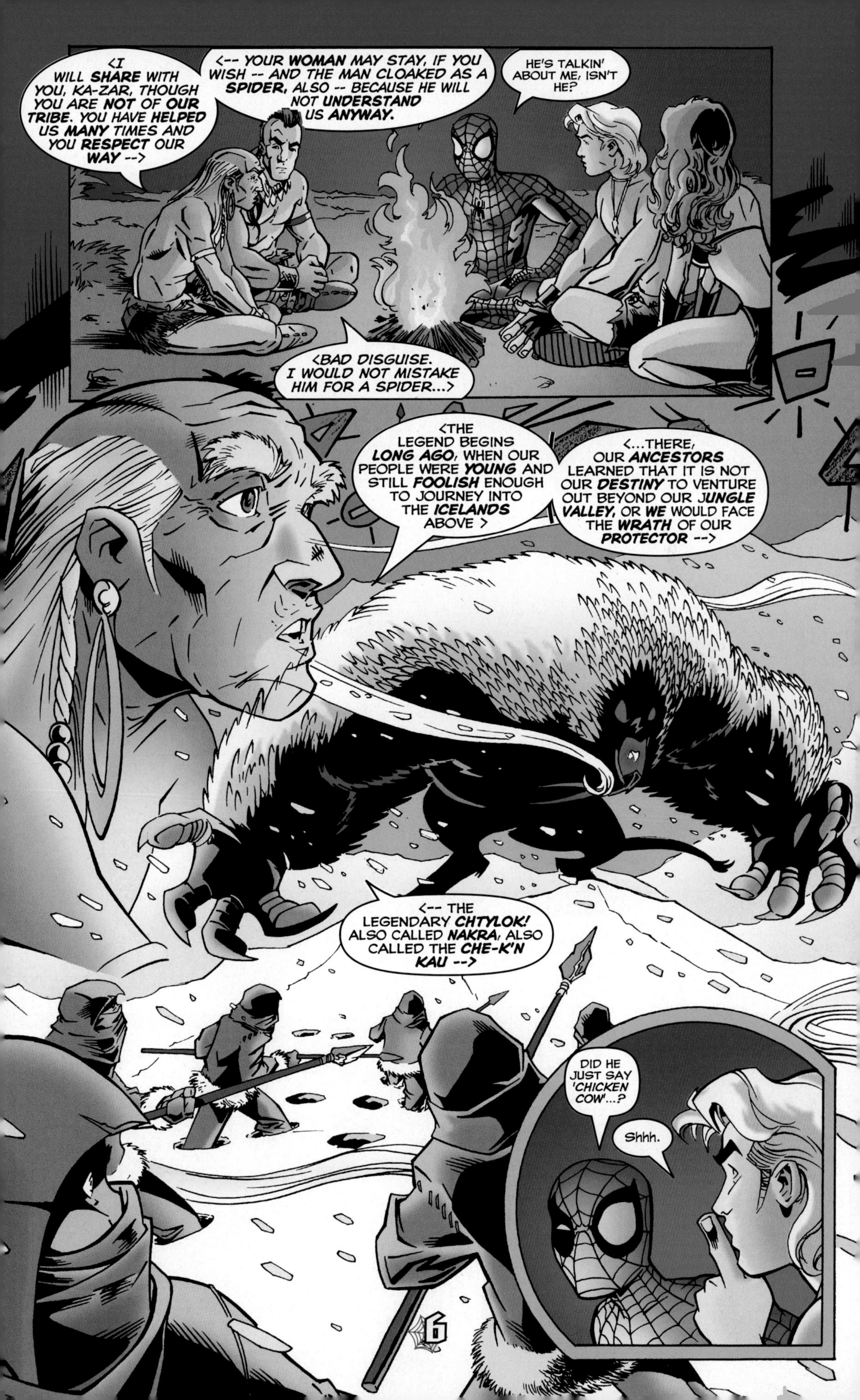
<I WILL SHARE WITH YOU, KA-ZAR, THOUGH YOU ARE NOT OF OUR TRIBE. YOU HAVE HELPED US MANY TIMES AND YOU RESPECT OUR WAY -->
<-- YOUR WOMAN MAY STAY, IF YOU WISH -- AND THE MAN CLOAKED AS A SPIDER, ALSO -- BECAUSE HE WILL NOT UNDERSTAND US ANYWAY.
HE'S TALKIN' ABOUT ME, ISN'T HE?
<BAD DISGUISE. I WOULD NOT MISTAKE HIM FOR A SPIDER...>
<THE LEGEND BEGINS LONG AGO, WHEN OUR PEOPLE WERE YOUNG AND STILL FOOLISH ENOUGH TO JOURNEY INTO THE ICELANDS ABOVE >
<...THERE, OUR ANCESTORS LEARNED THAT IT IS NOT OUR DESTINY TO VENTURE OUT BEYOND OUR JUNGLE VALLEY, OR WE WOULD FACE THE WRATH OF OUR PROTECTOR -->
<-- THE LEGENDARY CHTYLOK! ALSO CALLED NAKRA, ALSO CALLED THE CHE-K'N KAU -->
DID HE JUST SAY 'CHICKEN COW'...?
Shhh.

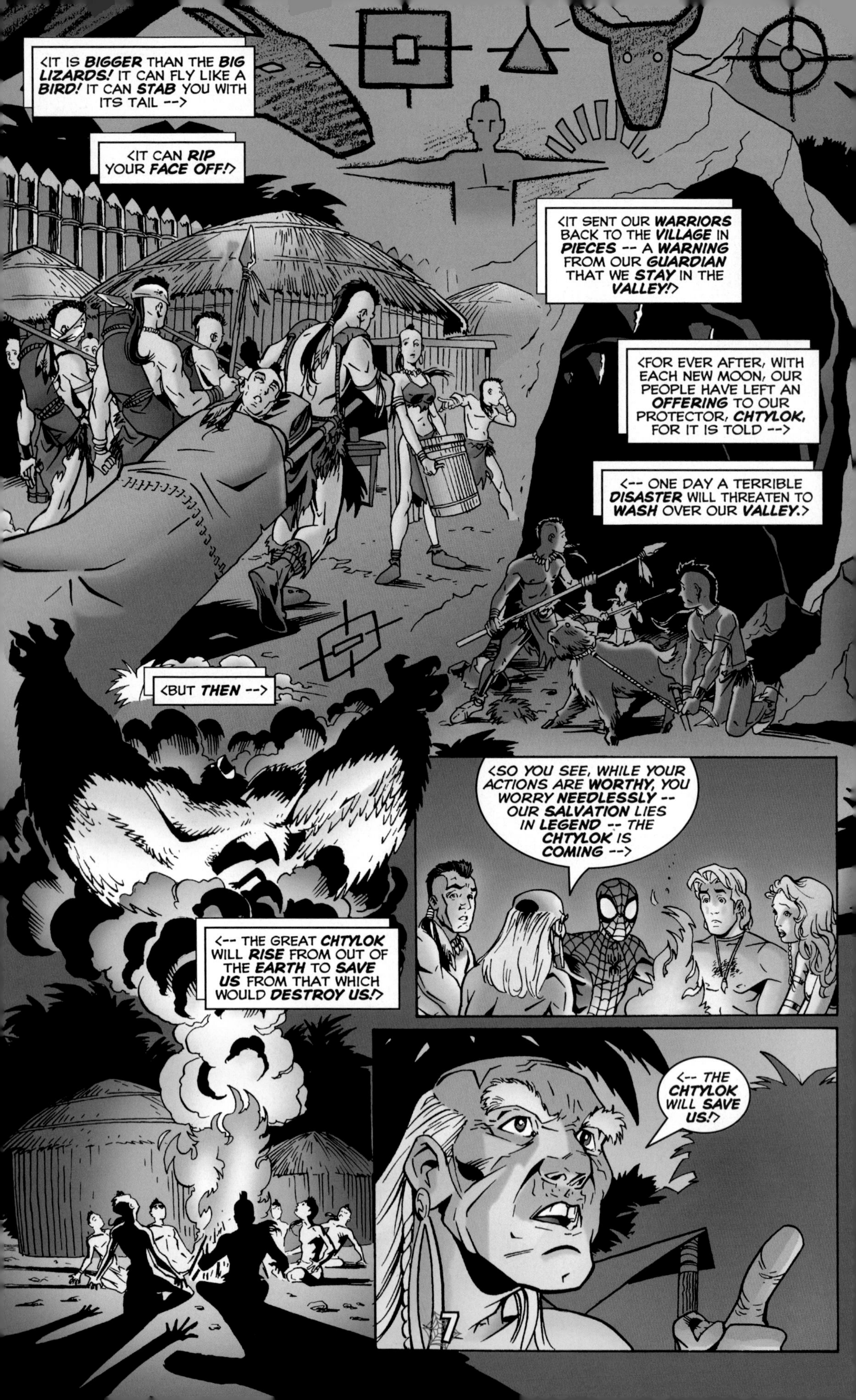

<IT IS BIGGER THAN THE BIG LIZARDS! IT CAN FLY LIKE A BIRD! IT CAN STAB YOU WITH ITS TAIL -->
<IT CAN RIP YOUR FACE OFF!>
<IT SENT OUR WARRIORS BACK TO THE VILLAGE IN PIECES -- A WARNING FROM OUR GUARDIAN THAT WE STAY IN THE VALLEY!>
<FOR EVER AFTER, WITH EACH NEW MOON, OUR PEOPLE HAVE LEFT AN OFFERING TO OUR PROTECTOR, CHTYLOK, FOR IT IS TOLD -->
<-- ONE DAY A TERRIBLE DISASTER WILL THREATEN TO WASH OVER OUR VALLEY.>
<BUT THEN -->
<-- THE GREAT CHTYLOK WILL RISE FROM OUT OF THE EARTH TO SAVE US FROM THAT WHICH WOULD DESTROY US!>
<SO YOU SEE, WHILE YOUR ACTIONS ARE WORTHY, YOU WORRY NEEDLESSLY -- OUR SALVATION LIES IN LEGEND -- THE CHTYLOK IS COMING -->
<-- THE CHTYLOK WILL SAVE US!>

SOON...

WHO'S YADA?

CRAZY WOMAN WHO LIVES ON THE OUTSKIRTS OF THE VILLAGE -- ALONE -- WITH A BUNCH OF ANIMALS...

HER HUT IS DOWN BY THE RELAY STATION.

WHAT RELAY STATION..?

<KA-ZAR! KA-ZAR -- YOU MUST COME! IT'S YADA!

<SHE IS STILL DOWN IN THE LOWLANDS -- SHE REFUSES TO LEAVE HER HOME..!>

SHOW YOU LATER.

<KA-ZAR -- NO! I DON'T WANT TO LEAVE! THIS IS MY HOME!

<THIS IS MY HOME!>

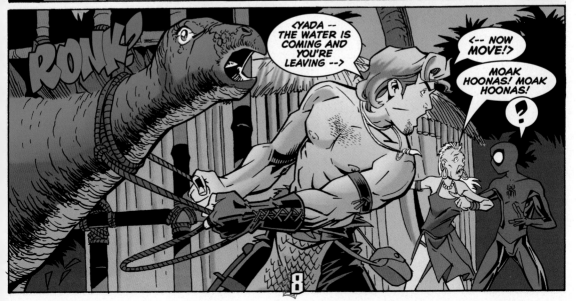

RONK

<YADA -- THE WATER IS COMING AND YOU'RE LEAVING -->

<-- NOW MOVE!>

MOAK HOONAS! MOAK HOONAS!

?

8

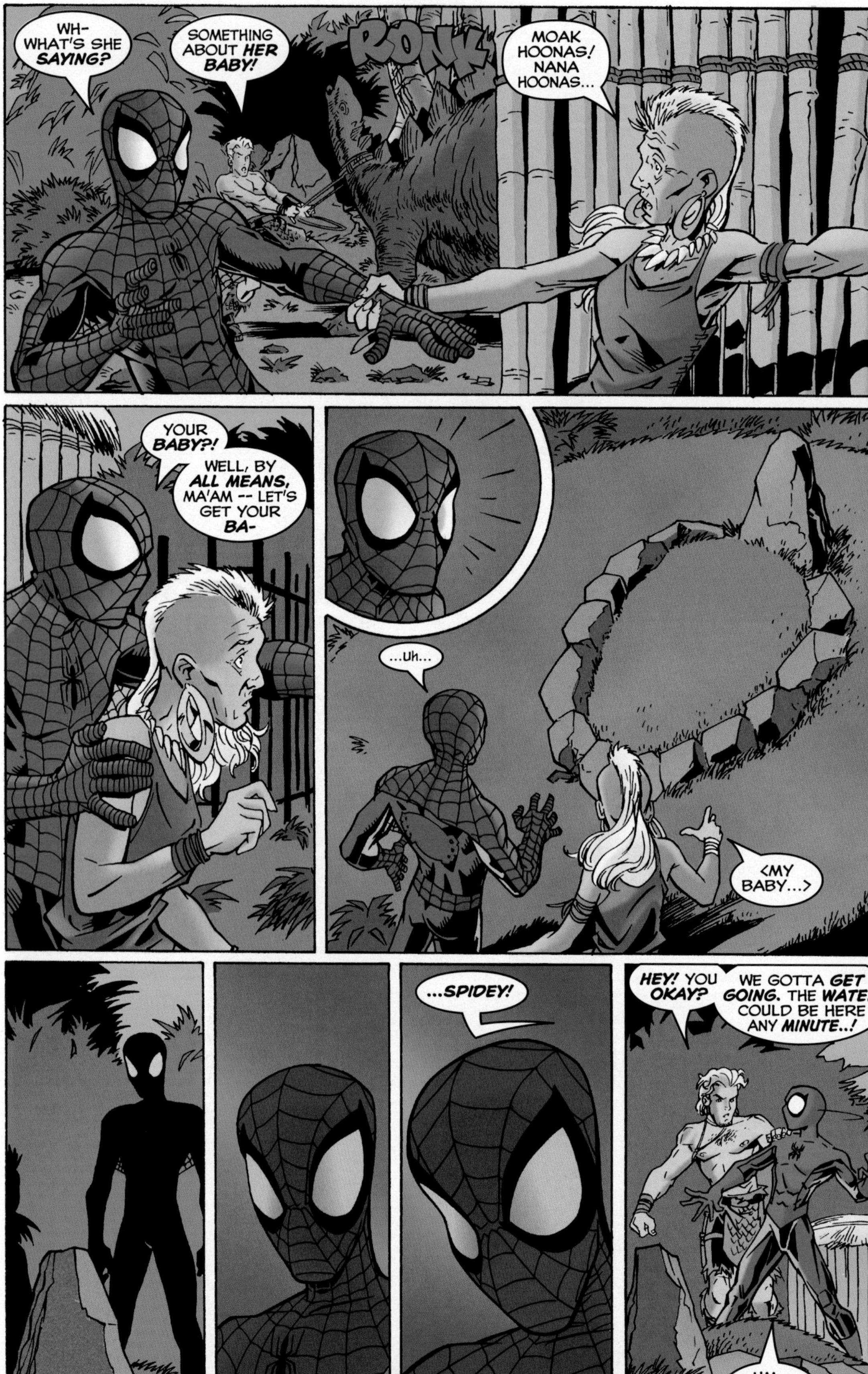
WH- WHAT'S SHE SAYING?
SOMETHING ABOUT HER BABY!
RONK
MOAK HOONAS! NANA HOONAS...
YOUR BABY?! WELL, BY ALL MEANS, MA'AM -- LET'S GET YOUR BA-
...uh...
<MY BABY...>
...SPIDEY!
HEY! YOU OKAY?
WE GOTTA GET GOING. THE WATER COULD BE HERE ANY MINUTE..!
UM... YEAH -- YEAH, LET'S GO...

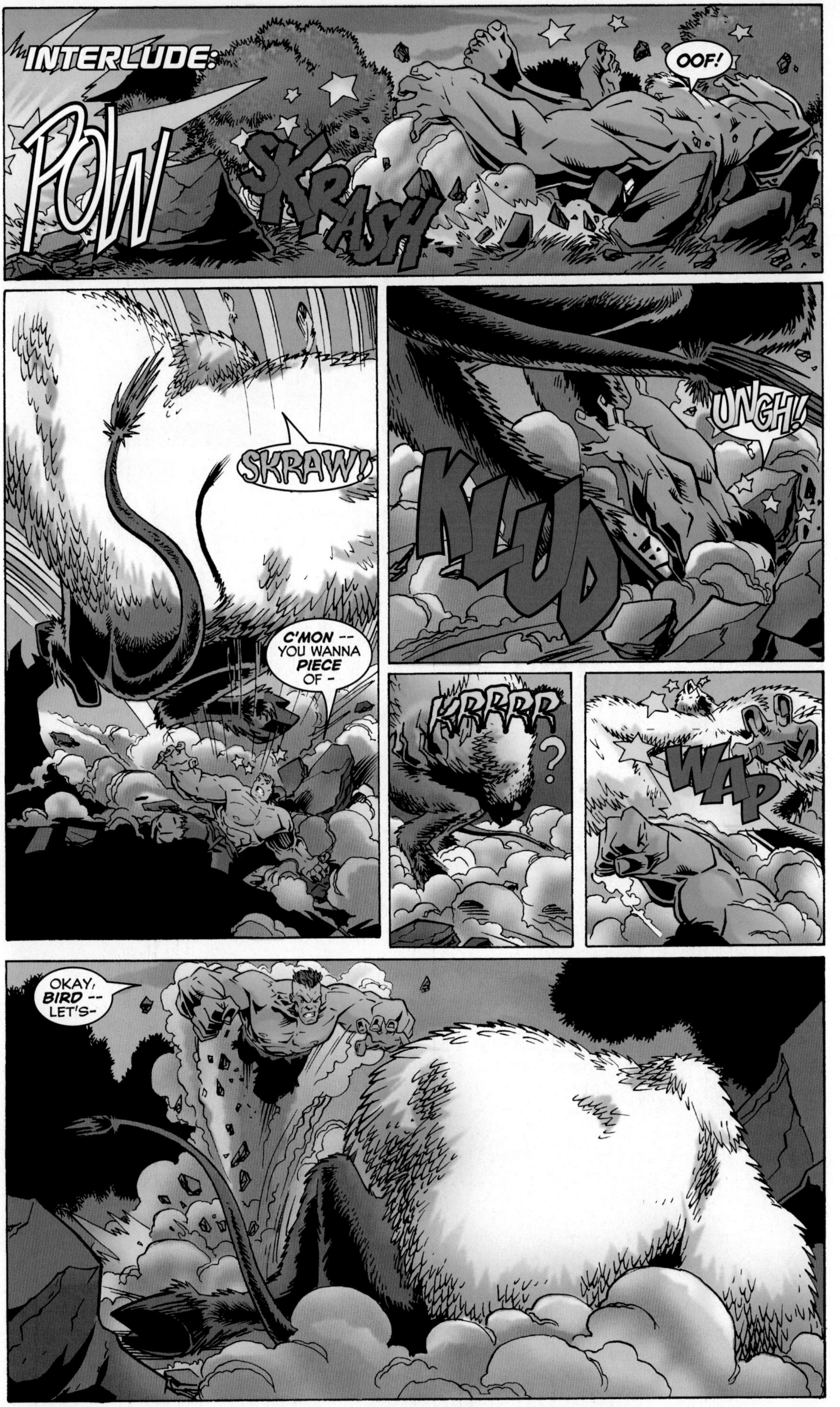
INTERLUDE:
POW
SKRASH
OOF!
SKRAW!
C'MON -- YOU WANNA PIECE OF -
KLUD
UNGH!
KRRRR
?
WAP
OKAY, BIRD -- LET'S-

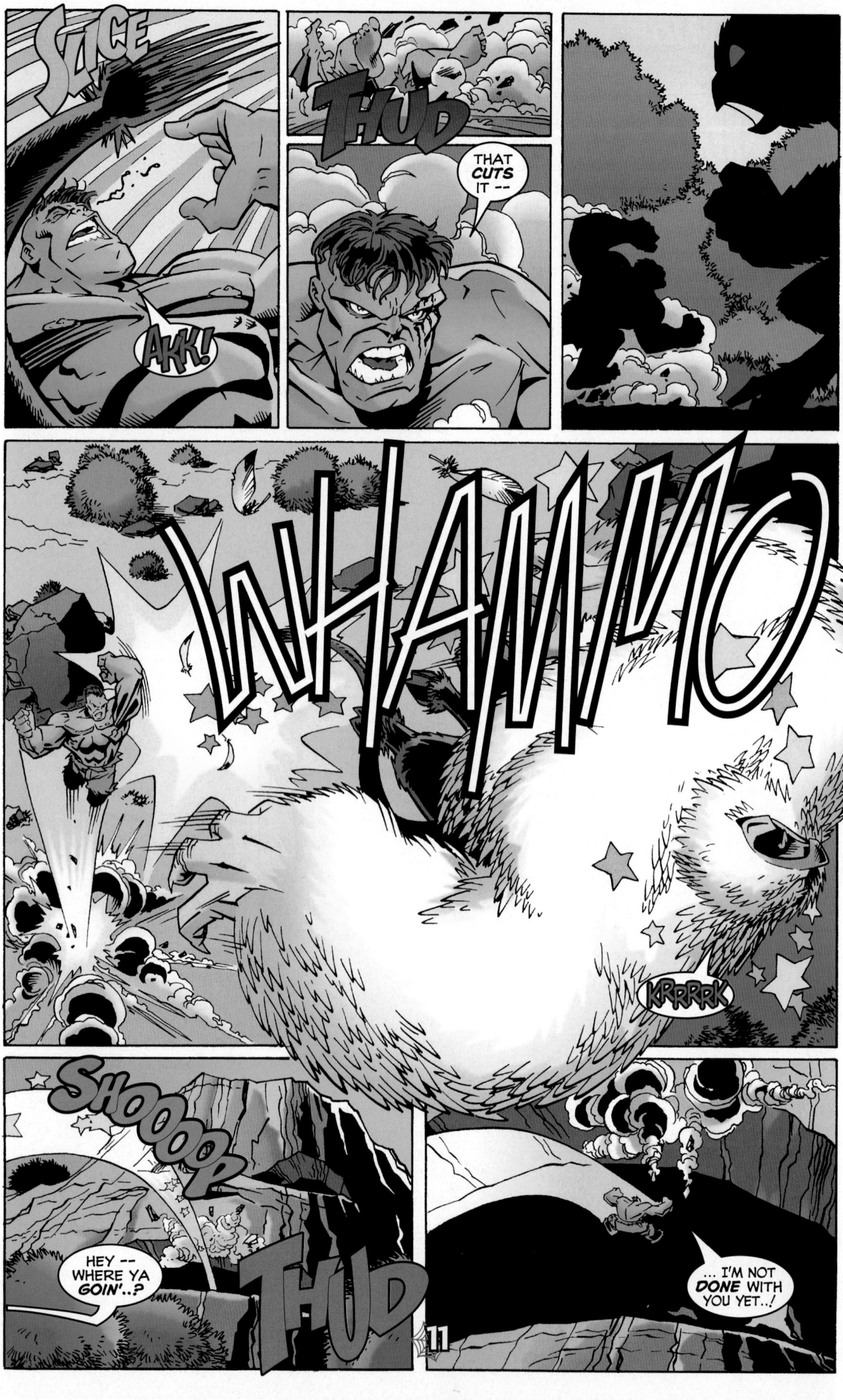
SLICE
AKK!
THUD
THAT CUTS IT --
WHAMMO
KRRRRK
SHOOOOP
HEY -- WHERE YA GOIN'..?
THUD
... I'M NOT DONE WITH YOU YET..!

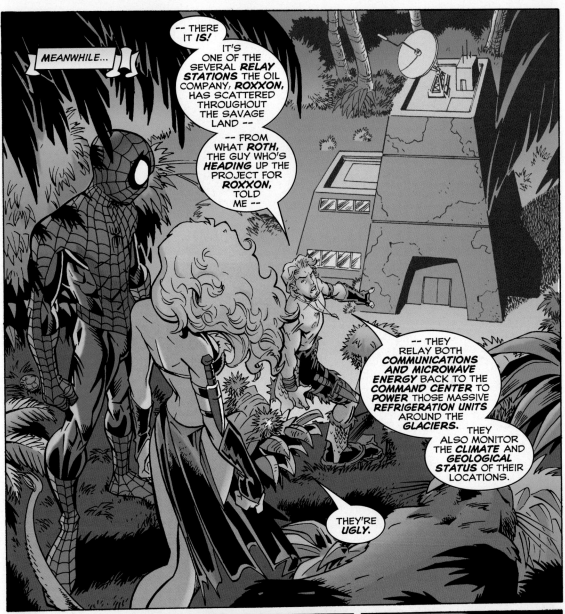

-- THERE IT **IS!** IT'S ONE OF THE SEVERAL **RELAY STATIONS** THE OIL COMPANY, **ROXXON**, HAS SCATTERED THROUGHOUT THE SAVAGE LAND --

-- FROM WHAT **ROTH**, THE GUY WHO'S **HEADING** UP THE PROJECT FOR **ROXXON**, TOLD ME --

-- THEY RELAY BOTH **COMMUNICATIONS AND MICROWAVE ENERGY** BACK TO THE **COMMAND CENTER** TO **POWER** THOSE MASSIVE **REFRIGERATION UNITS** AROUND THE **GLACIERS.** THEY ALSO MONITOR THE **CLIMATE** AND **GEOLOGICAL STATUS** OF THEIR LOCATIONS.

THEY'RE **UGLY.**

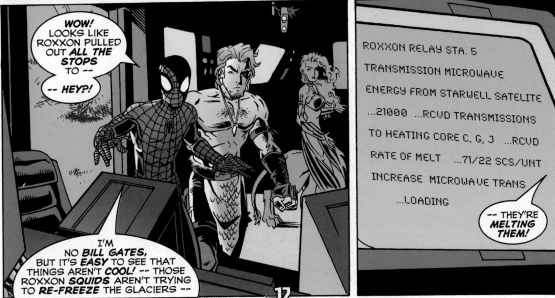

WOW! LOOKS LIKE ROXXON PULLED OUT **ALL THE STOPS** TO --

-- **HEY?!**

I'M NO **BILL GATES,** BUT IT'S **EASY** TO SEE THAT THINGS AREN'T **COOL!** -- THOSE ROXXON **SQUIDS** AREN'T TRYING TO **RE-FREEZE** THE GLACIERS --

ROXXON RELAY STA. 5

TRANSMISSION MICROWAVE

ENERGY FROM STARWELL SATELITE

...21000 ...RCVD TRANSMISSIONS

TO HEATING CORE C, G, J ...RCVD

RATE OF MELT ...71/22 SCS/UNT

INCREASE MICROWAVE TRANS

...LOADING

-- THEY'RE **MELTING THEM!**

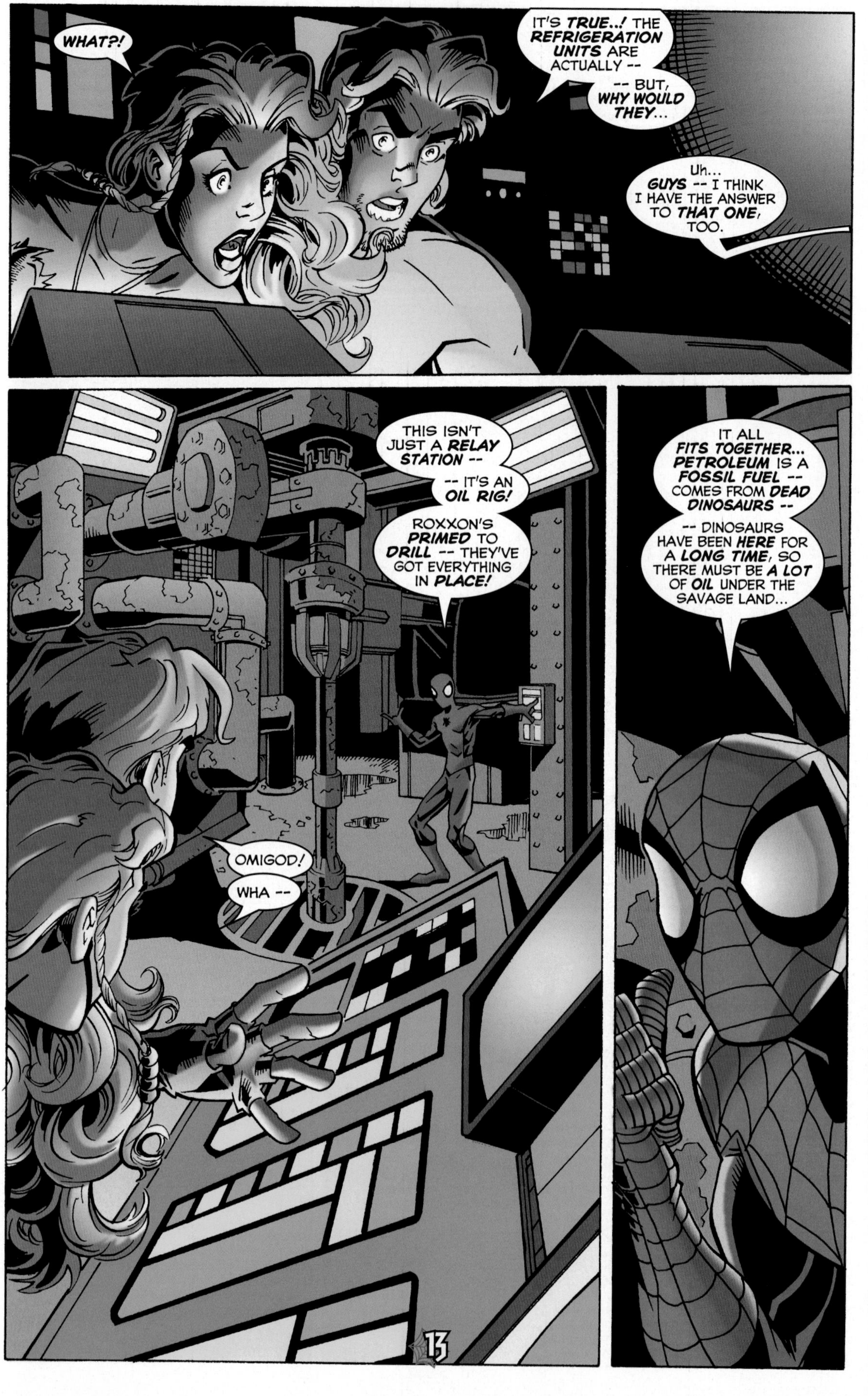
WHAT?!
IT'S TRUE..! THE REFRIGERATION UNITS ARE ACTUALLY --
-- BUT, WHY WOULD THEY...
Uh... GUYS -- I THINK I HAVE THE ANSWER TO THAT ONE, TOO.
THIS ISN'T JUST A RELAY STATION --
-- IT'S AN OIL RIG!
ROXXON'S PRIMED TO DRILL -- THEY'VE GOT EVERYTHING IN PLACE!
OMIGOD!
WHA --
IT ALL FITS TOGETHER... PETROLEUM IS A FOSSIL FUEL -- COMES FROM DEAD DINOSAURS --
-- DINOSAURS HAVE BEEN HERE FOR A LONG TIME, SO THERE MUST BE A LOT OF OIL UNDER THE SAVAGE LAND...

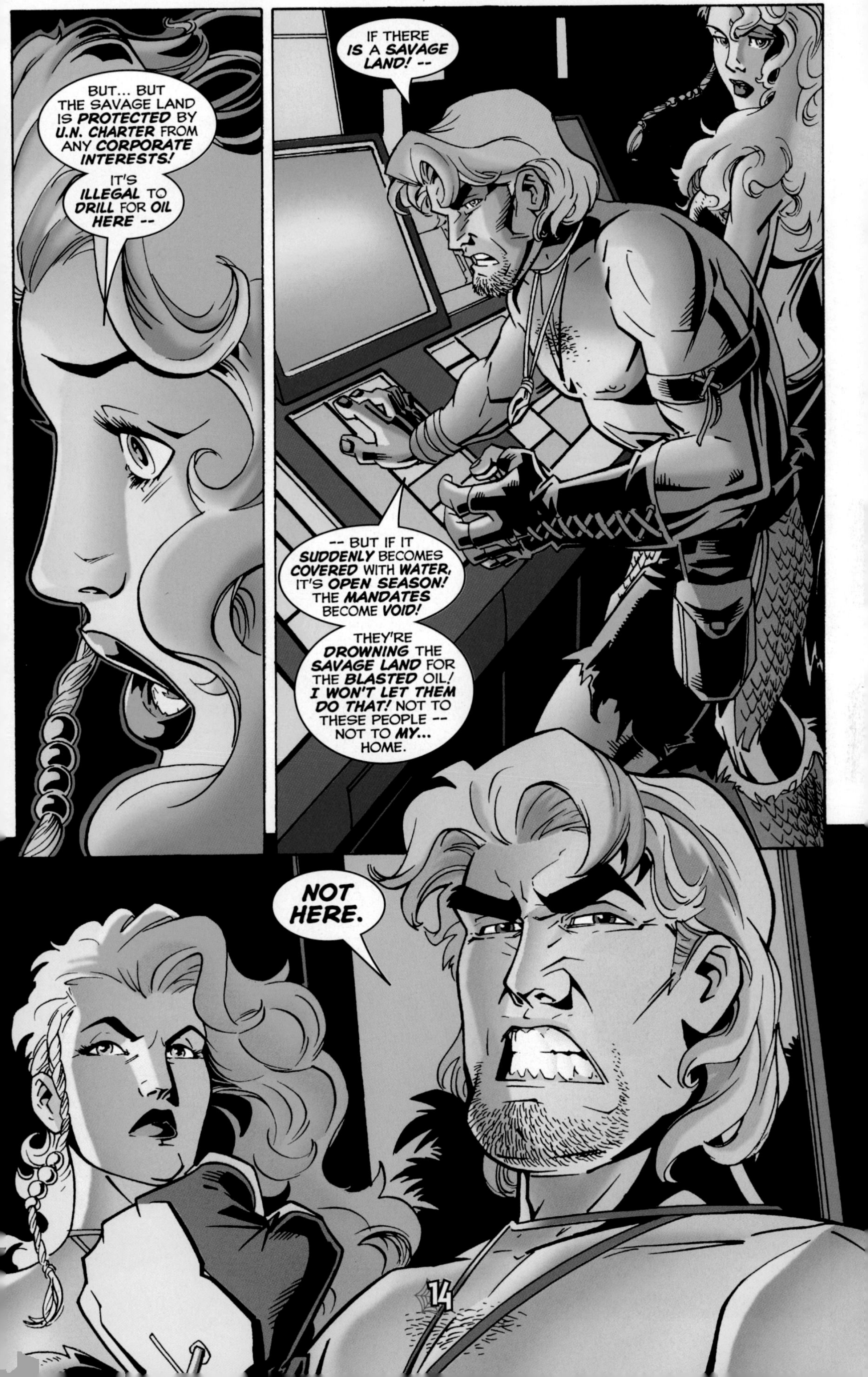

BUT... BUT THE SAVAGE LAND IS PROTECTED BY U.N. CHARTER FROM ANY CORPORATE INTERESTS!
IT'S ILLEGAL TO DRILL FOR OIL HERE --
IF THERE IS A SAVAGE LAND! --
-- BUT IF IT SUDDENLY BECOMES COVERED WITH WATER, IT'S OPEN SEASON! THE MANDATES BECOME VOID!
THEY'RE DROWNING THE SAVAGE LAND FOR THE BLASTED OIL! I WON'T LET THEM DO THAT! NOT TO THESE PEOPLE -- NOT TO MY... HOME.
NOT HERE.

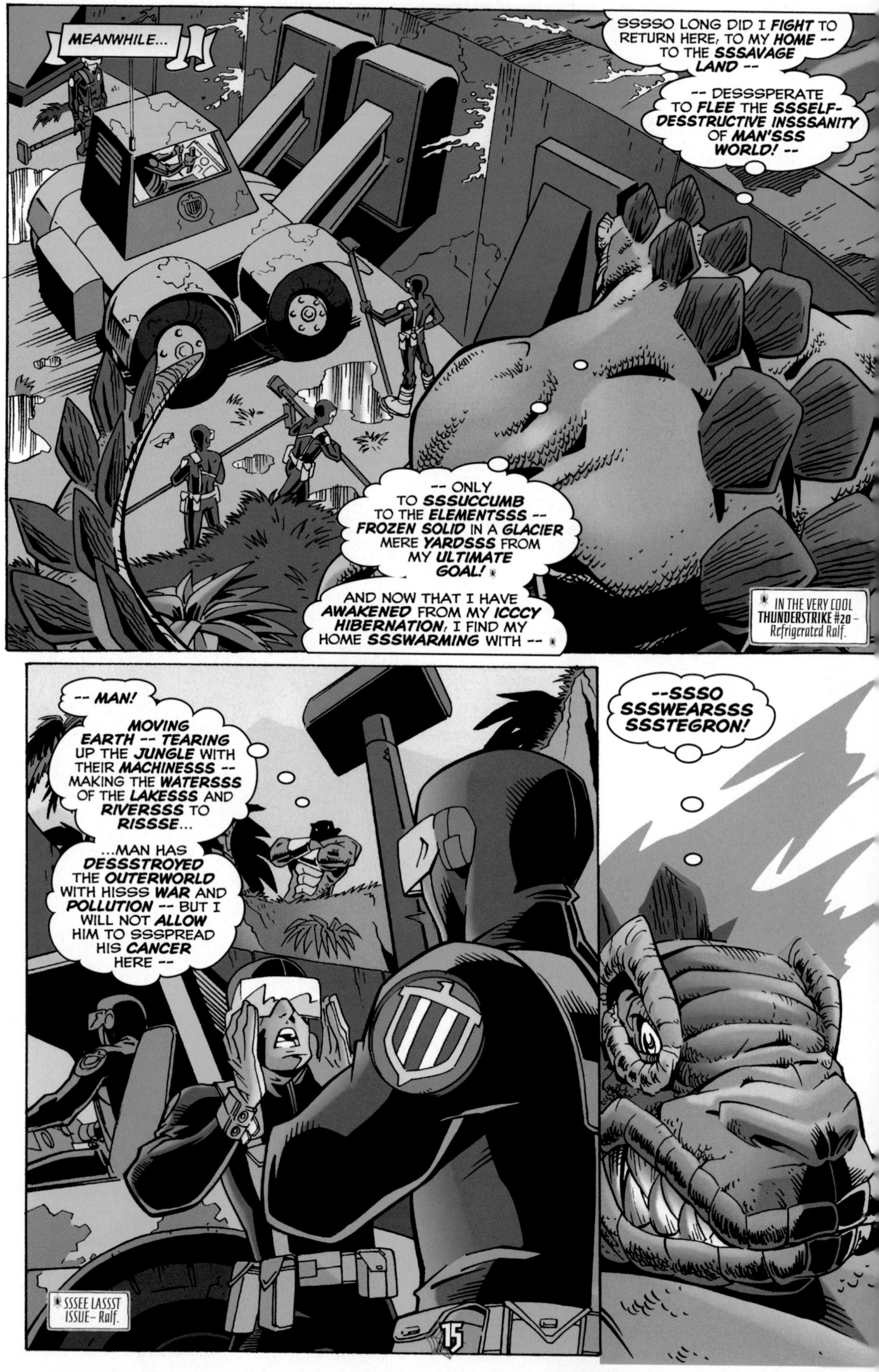

MEANWHILE...
SSSSO LONG DID I FIGHT TO RETURN HERE, TO MY HOME -- TO THE SSSAVAGE LAND --
-- DESSSPERATE TO FLEE THE SSSELF-DESSTRUCTIVE INSSSANITY OF MAN'SSS WORLD! --
-- ONLY TO SSSUCCUMB TO THE ELEMENTSSS -- FROZEN SOLID IN A GLACIER MERE YARDSSS FROM MY ULTIMATE GOAL!
AND NOW THAT I HAVE AWAKENED FROM MY ICCCY HIBERNATION, I FIND MY HOME SSSWARMING WITH --
IN THE VERY COOL THUNDERSTRIKE #20 – Refrigerated Ralf.
-- MAN!
MOVING EARTH -- TEARING UP THE JUNGLE WITH THEIR MACHINESSS -- MAKING THE WATERSSS OF THE LAKESSS AND RIVERSSS TO RISSSE...
...MAN HAS DESSSTROYED THE OUTERWORLD WITH HISSS WAR AND POLLUTION -- BUT I WILL NOT ALLOW HIM TO SSSPREAD HIS CANCER HERE --
--SSSO SSSWEARSSS SSSTEGRON!
SSSEE LASSST ISSUE– Ralf.

MILES AWAY --

-- IN THE OBSERVATION TOWER OF THE ROXXON/S.H.I.E.L.D. COMMAND CENTER --

-- WHERE PROJECT SUPERVISOR, SPECIAL AGENT CHRIS TOWNSEND, BRIEFS HIS TOP MEN ON PLANS TO EVACUATE THE SAVAGE LAND...

DR. ROTH, SIR --

...AND OF THE THREE, THE GREAT WESTERN LAKE LOOKS LIKE IT'S GONNA LET GO FIRST, SO...

-- THAT... "PROBLEM" DOWN AT RELAY STATION FIVE IS BEING DEALT WITH AS PER YOUR ORDERS.

THE STRIKE TEAM HAS BEEN DEPLOYED ALONG WITH THREE OF THE TAA UNITS.

GOOD. THAT'S VERY GOOD...

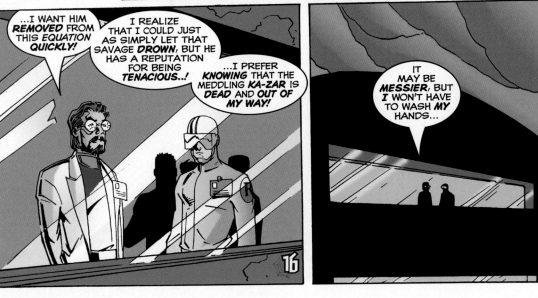

...I WANT HIM REMOVED FROM THIS EQUATION QUICKLY!

I REALIZE THAT I COULD JUST AS SIMPLY LET THAT SAVAGE DROWN, BUT HE HAS A REPUTATION FOR BEING TENACIOUS...!

...I PREFER KNOWING THAT THE MEDDLING KA-ZAR IS DEAD AND OUT OF MY WAY!

IT MAY BE MESSIER, BUT I WON'T HAVE TO WASH MY HANDS...

16

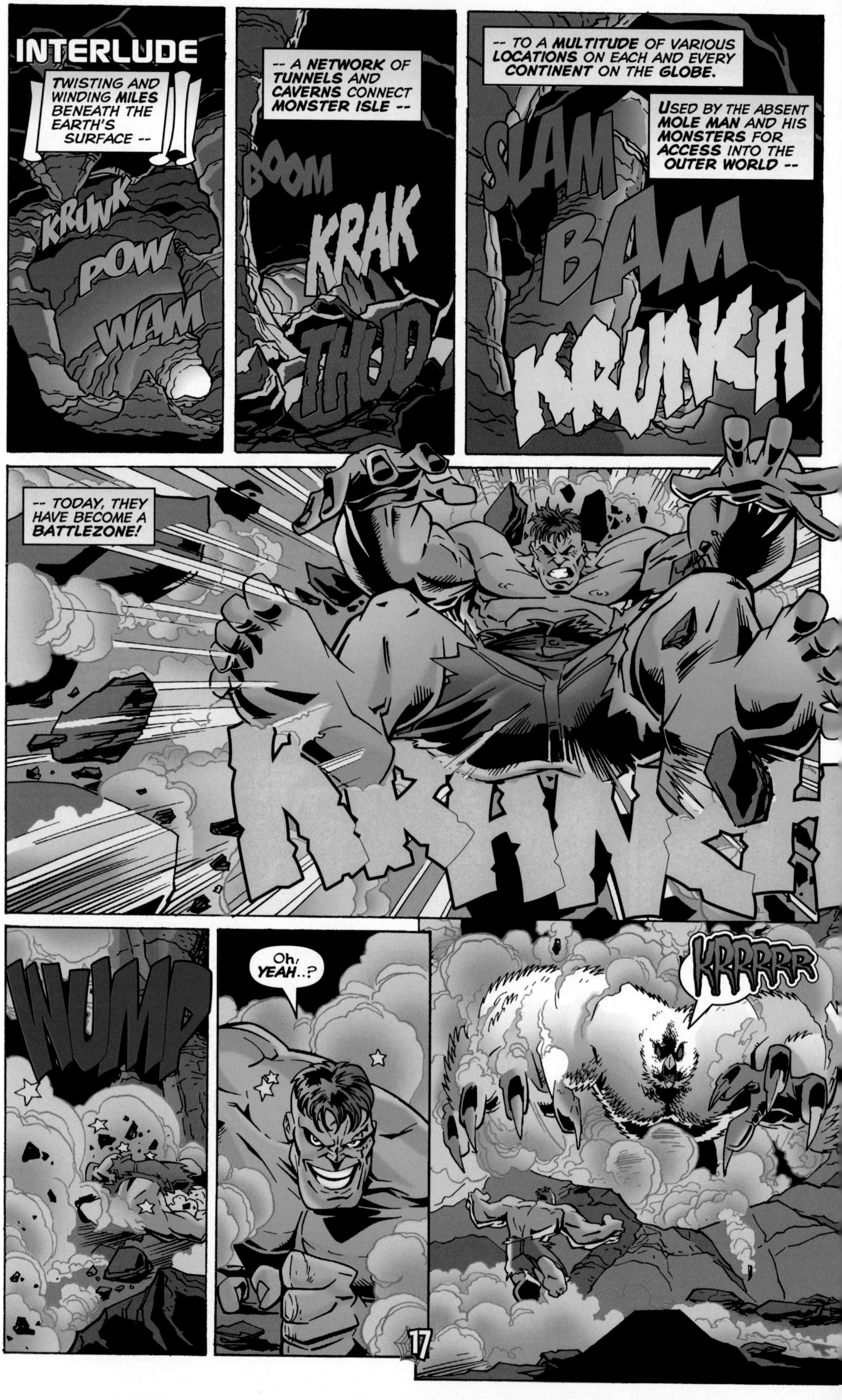
INTERLUDE
TWISTING AND WINDING MILES BENEATH THE EARTH'S SURFACE --
KRUNK
POW
WAM
-- A NETWORK OF TUNNELS AND CAVERNS CONNECT MONSTER ISLE --
BOOM
KRAK
THUD
-- TO A MULTITUDE OF VARIOUS LOCATIONS ON EACH AND EVERY CONTINENT ON THE GLOBE.
USED BY THE ABSENT MOLE MAN AND HIS MONSTERS FOR ACCESS INTO THE OUTER WORLD --
SLAM
BAM
KRUNCH
-- TODAY, THEY HAVE BECOME A BATTLEZONE!
KRANG!
WUMP
Oh, YEAH..?
KRRRRR

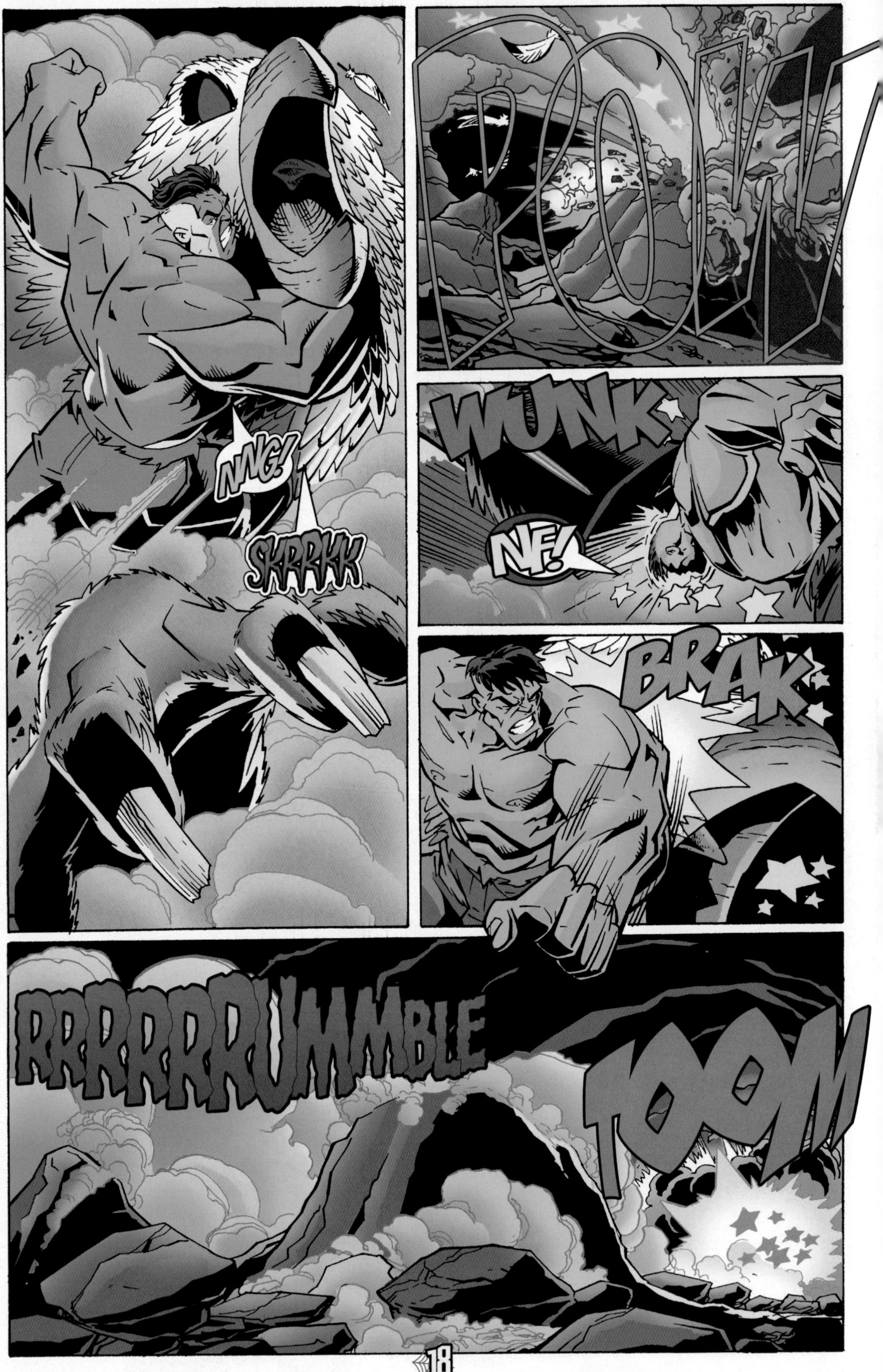
NNG!
SKRRKK
POW
WUNK
NF!
BRAK
RRRRRRUMMBLE
TOOM

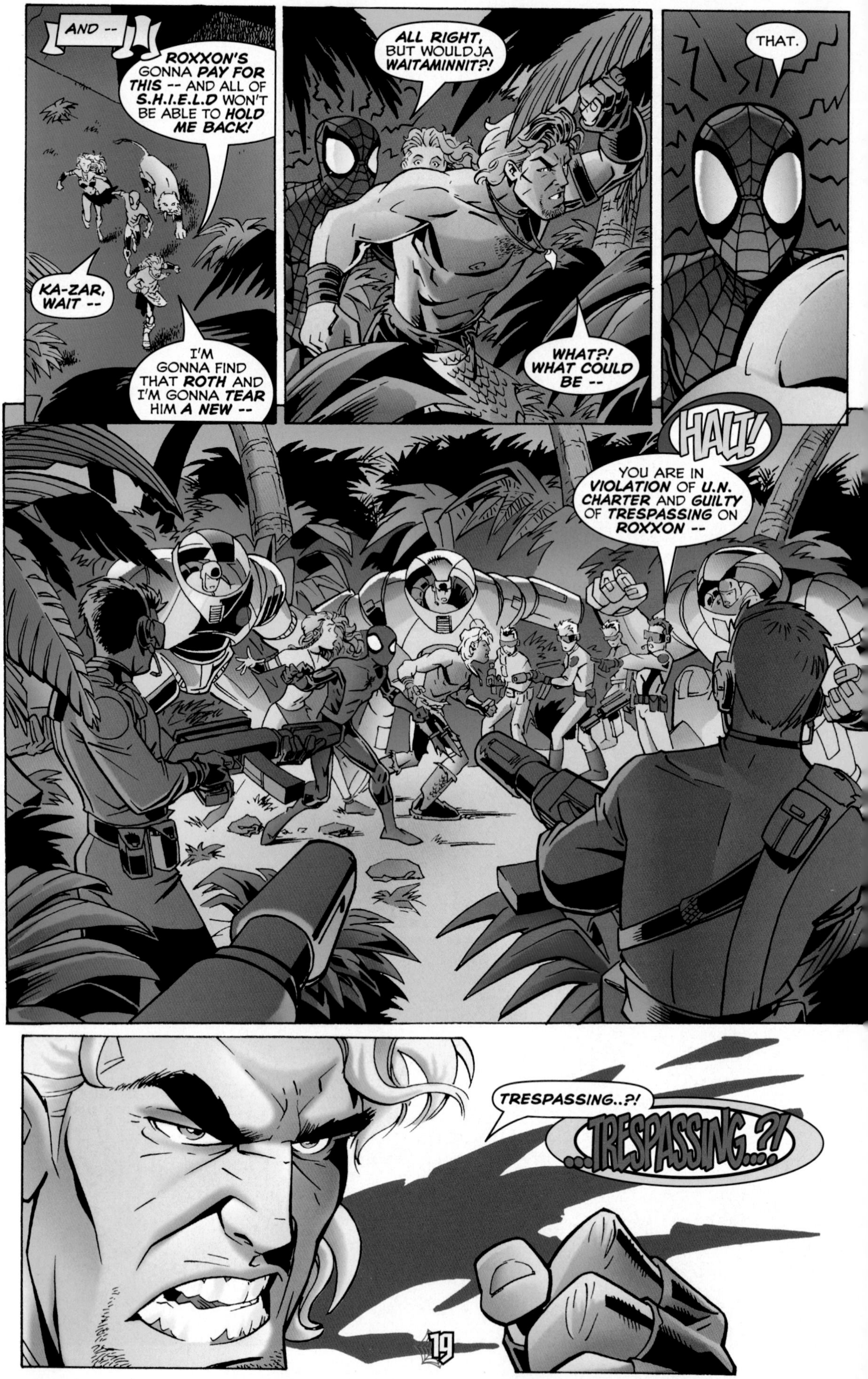
AND --
ROXXON'S GONNA PAY FOR THIS -- AND ALL OF S.H.I.E.L.D WON'T BE ABLE TO HOLD ME BACK!
KA-ZAR, WAIT --
I'M GONNA FIND THAT ROTH AND I'M GONNA TEAR HIM A NEW --
ALL RIGHT, BUT WOULDJA WAITAMINNIT?!
WHAT?! WHAT COULD BE --
THAT.
HALT!
YOU ARE IN VIOLATION OF U.N. CHARTER AND GUILTY OF TRESPASSING ON ROXXON --
TRESPASSING..?!
...TRESPASSING..?!

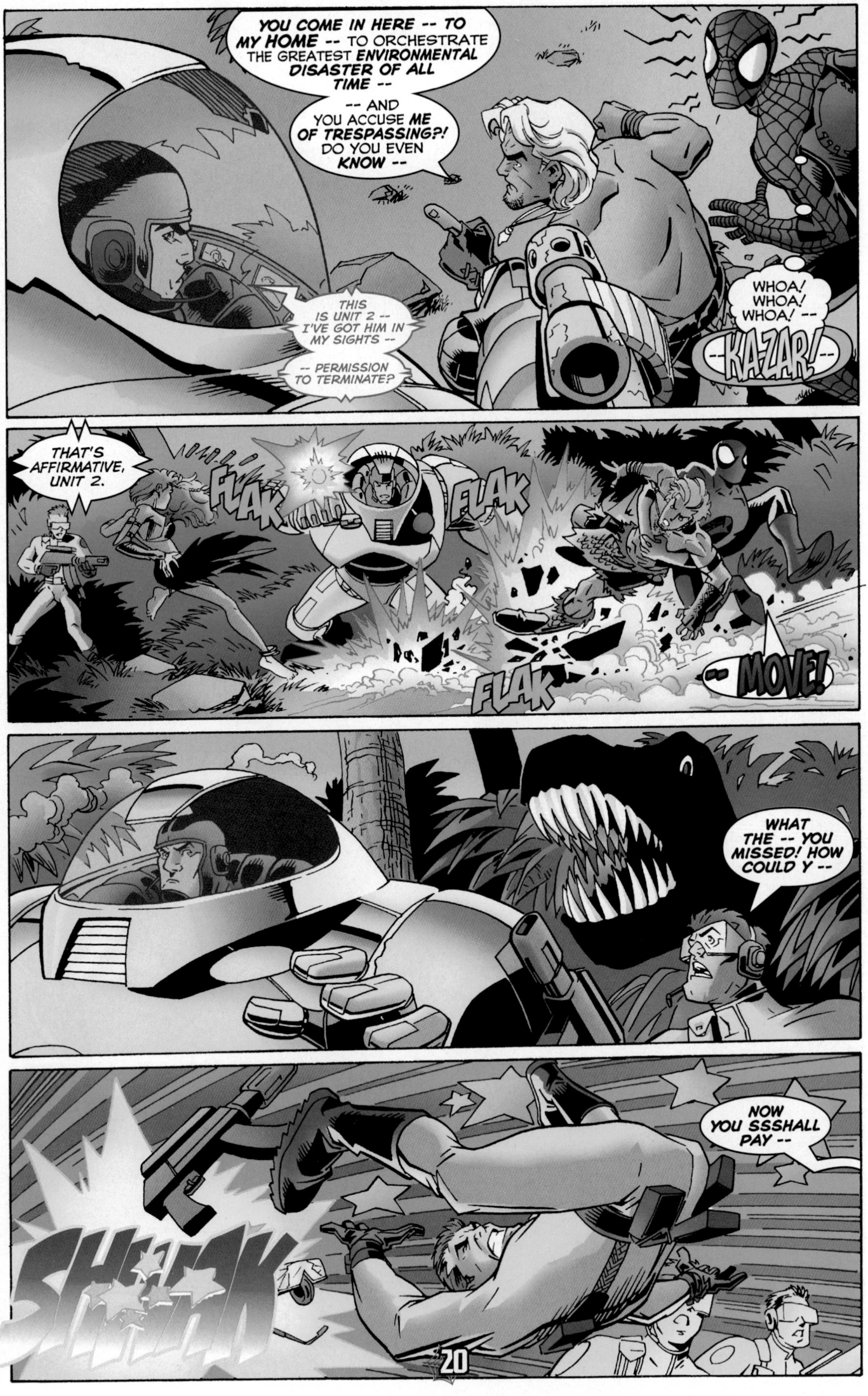

YOU COME IN HERE -- TO MY HOME -- TO ORCHESTRATE THE GREATEST ENVIRONMENTAL DISASTER OF ALL TIME --
-- AND YOU ACCUSE ME OF TRESPASSING?! DO YOU EVEN KNOW --
THIS IS UNIT 2 -- I'VE GOT HIM IN MY SIGHTS --
-- PERMISSION TO TERMINATE?
WHOA! WHOA! WHOA! --
--KAZAR!--
THAT'S AFFIRMATIVE, UNIT 2.
FLAK
FLAK
FLAK
-- MOVE!
WHAT THE -- YOU MISSED! HOW COULD Y --
NOW YOU SSSHALL PAY --
SHTAK

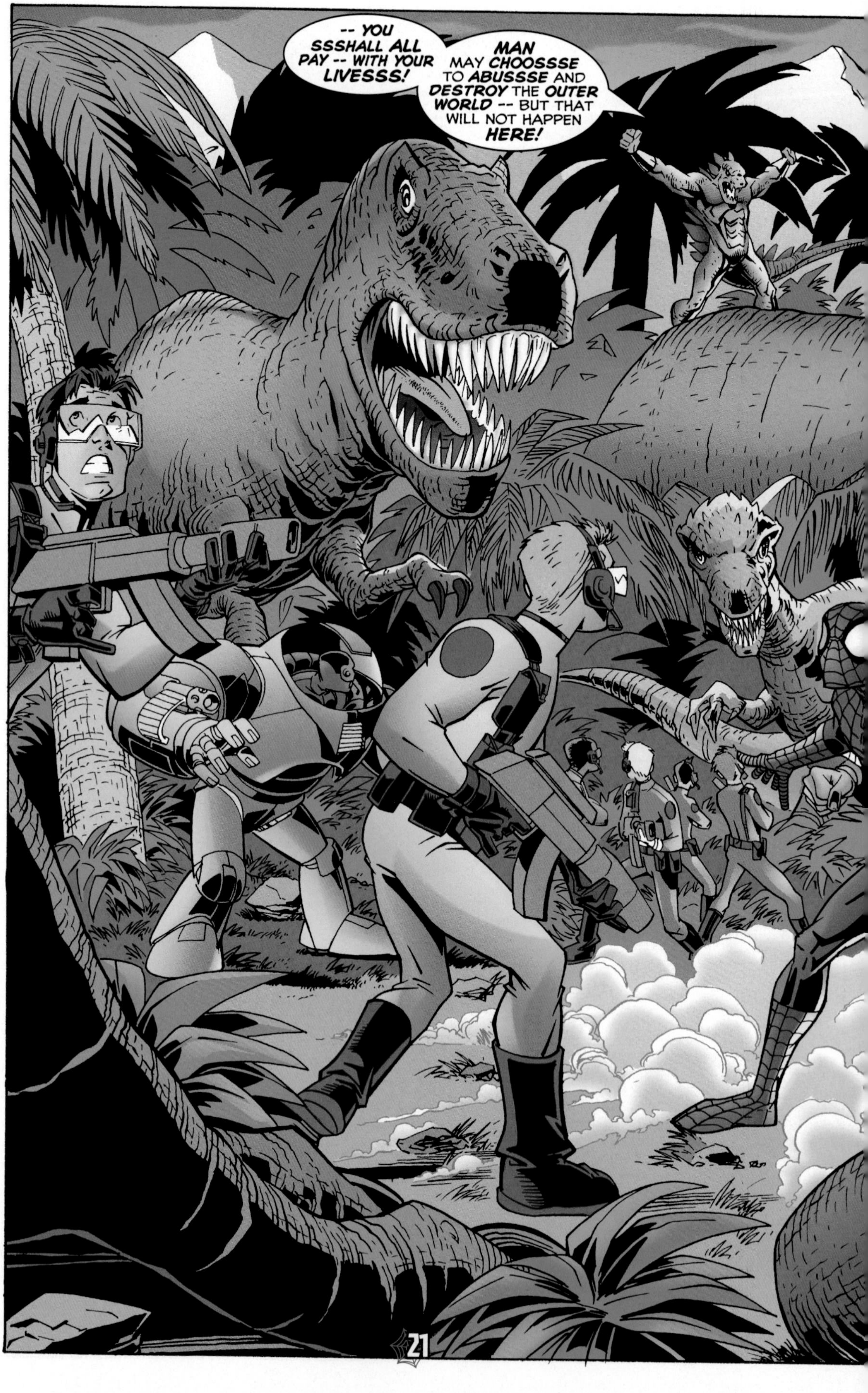
-- YOU SSSHALL ALL PAY -- WITH YOUR LIVESSS!
MAN MAY CHOOSSSE TO ABUSSSE AND DESTROY THE OUTER WORLD -- BUT THAT WILL NOT HAPPEN HERE!

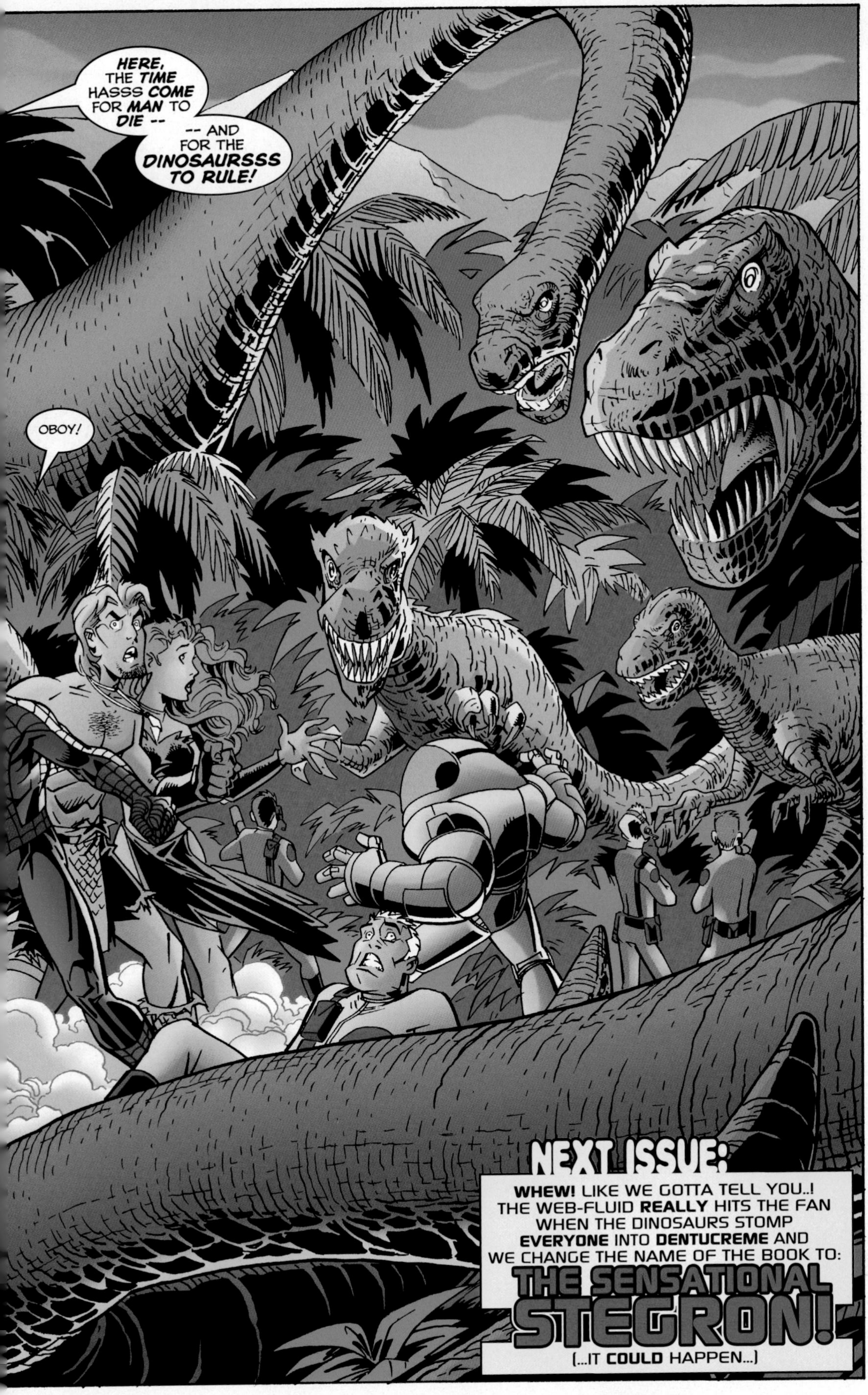

HERE, THE TIME HASSS COME FOR MAN TO DIE --
-- AND FOR THE DINOSAURSSS TO RULE!
OBOY!
NEXT ISSUE:
WHEW! LIKE WE GOTTA TELL YOU..! THE WEB-FLUID REALLY HITS THE FAN WHEN THE DINOSAURS STOMP EVERYONE INTO DENTUCREME AND WE CHANGE THE NAME OF THE BOOK TO:
THE SENSATIONAL STEGRON!
(...IT COULD HAPPEN...)

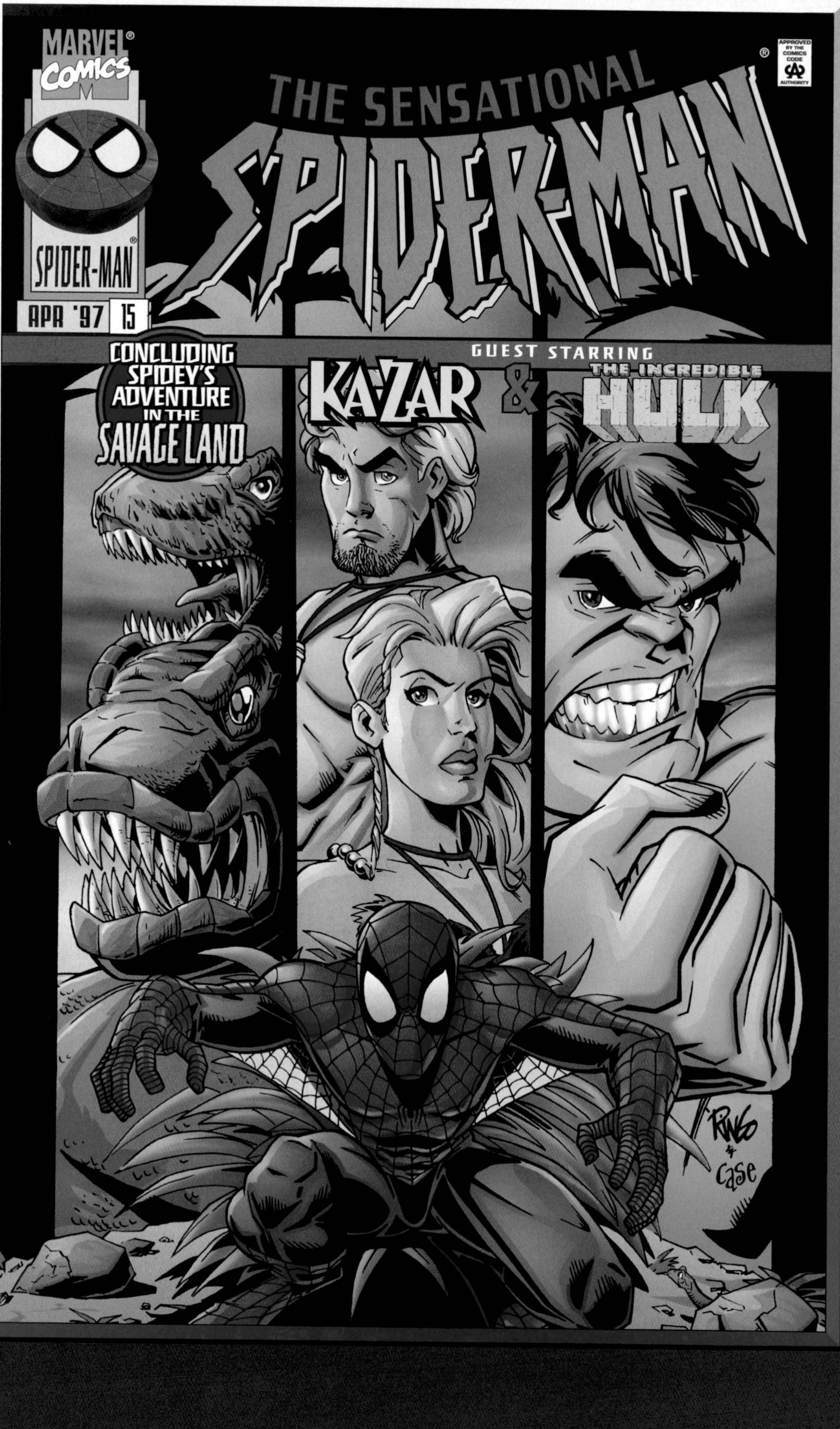
MARVEL COMICS
SPIDER-MAN
APR '97 15
APPROVED BY THE COMICS CODE AUTHORITY
THE SENSATIONAL SPIDER-MAN
CONCLUDING SPIDEY'S ADVENTURE IN THE SAVAGE LAND
GUEST STARRING
KA-ZAR
&
THE INCREDIBLE HULK
Ring & Case

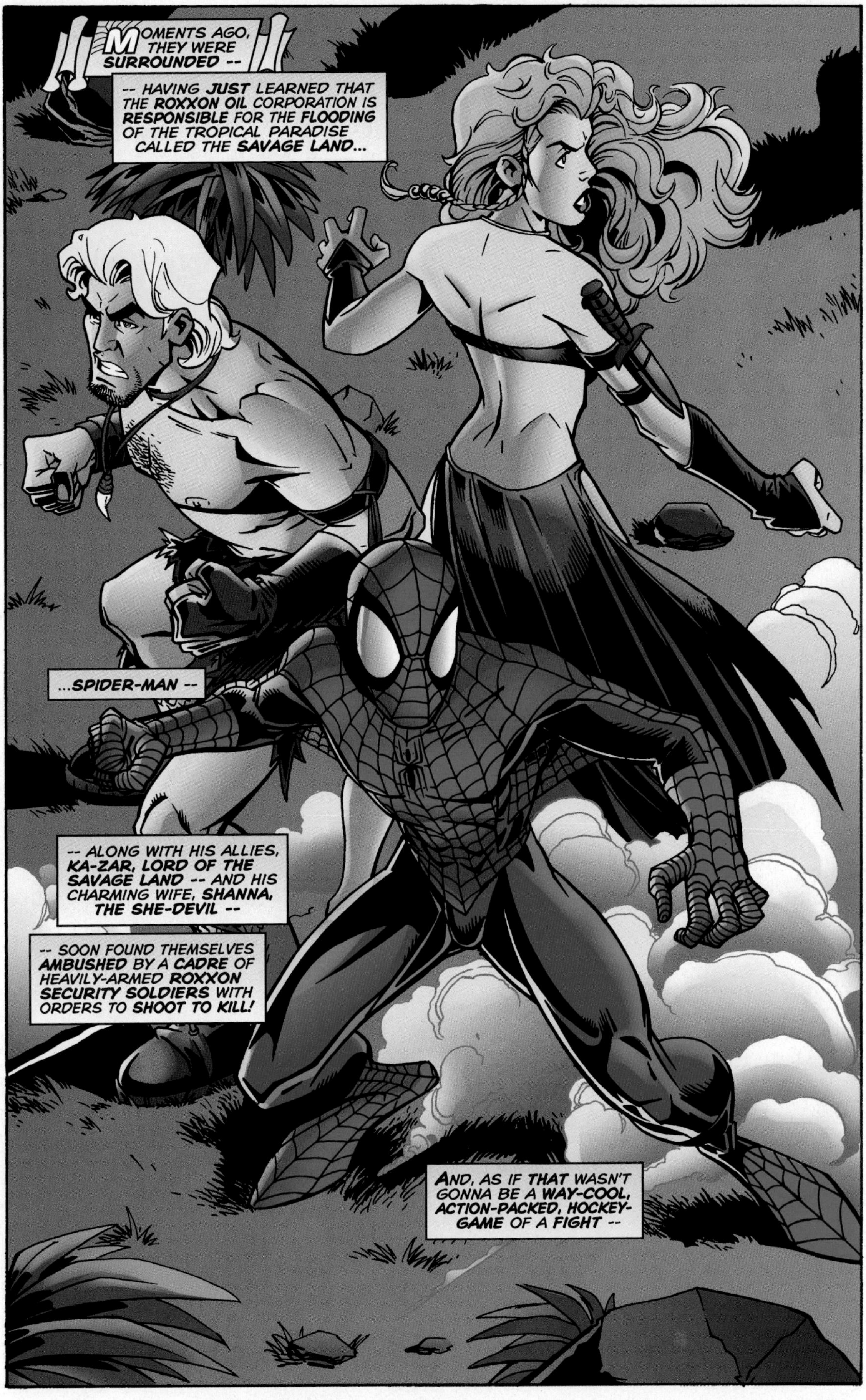
MOMENTS AGO, THEY WERE SURROUNDED --
-- HAVING JUST LEARNED THAT THE ROXXON OIL CORPORATION IS RESPONSIBLE FOR THE FLOODING OF THE TROPICAL PARADISE CALLED THE SAVAGE LAND...
...SPIDER-MAN --
-- ALONG WITH HIS ALLIES, KA-ZAR, LORD OF THE SAVAGE LAND -- AND HIS CHARMING WIFE, SHANNA, THE SHE-DEVIL --
-- SOON FOUND THEMSELVES AMBUSHED BY A CADRE OF HEAVILY-ARMED ROXXON SECURITY SOLDIERS WITH ORDERS TO SHOOT TO KILL!
AND, AS IF THAT WASN'T GONNA BE A WAY-COOL, ACTION-PACKED, HOCKEY-GAME OF A FIGHT --

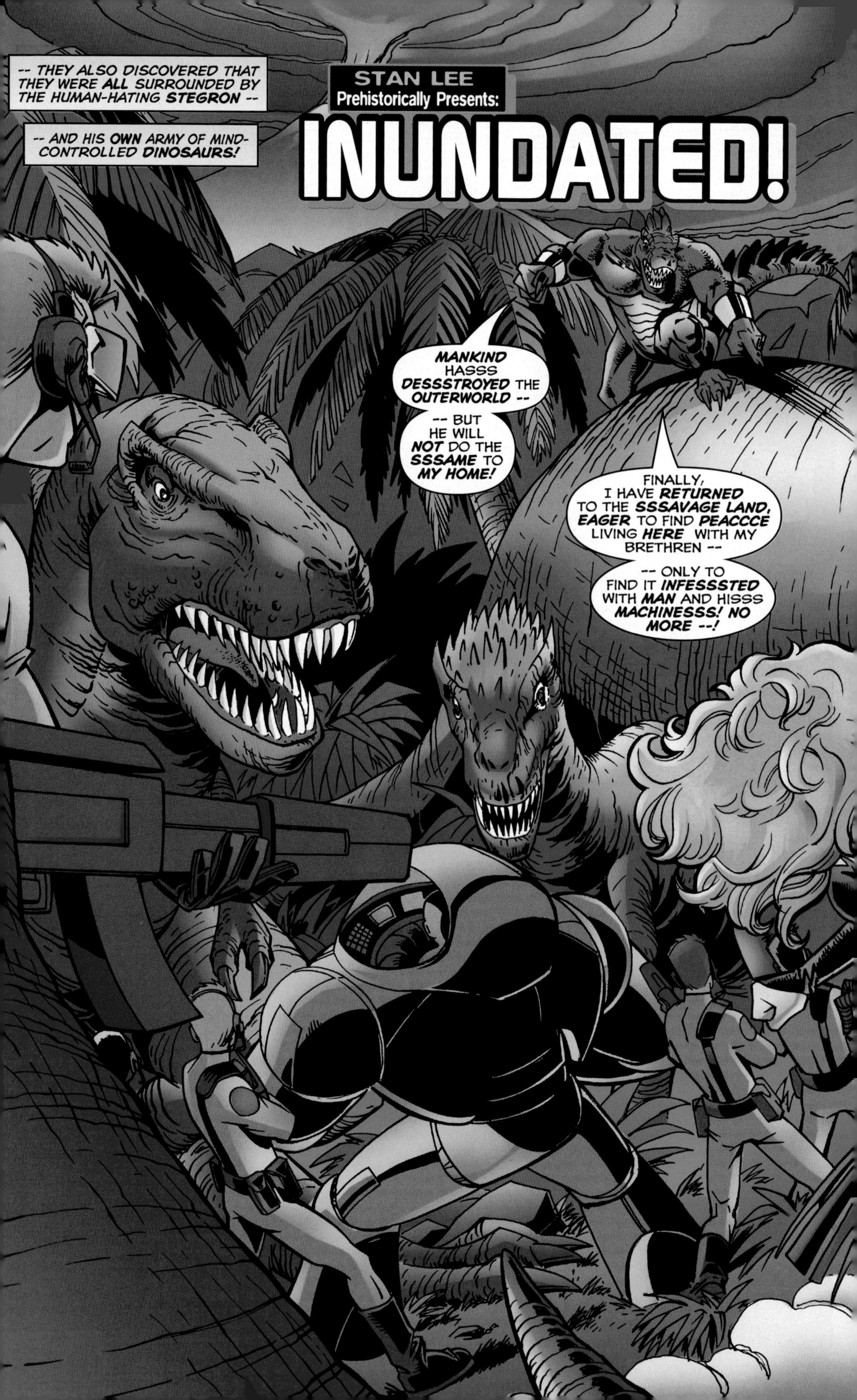
-- THEY ALSO DISCOVERED THAT THEY WERE ALL SURROUNDED BY THE HUMAN-HATING STEGRON --
-- AND HIS OWN ARMY OF MIND-CONTROLLED DINOSAURS!
STAN LEE Prehistorically Presents:
INUNDATED!
MANKIND HASSS DESSSTROYED THE OUTERWORLD --
-- BUT HE WILL NOT DO THE SSSAME TO MY HOME!
FINALLY, I HAVE RETURNED TO THE SSSAVAGE LAND, EAGER TO FIND PEACCCE LIVING HERE WITH MY BRETHREN --
-- ONLY TO FIND IT INFESSSTED WITH MAN AND HISSS MACHINESSS! NO MORE --!

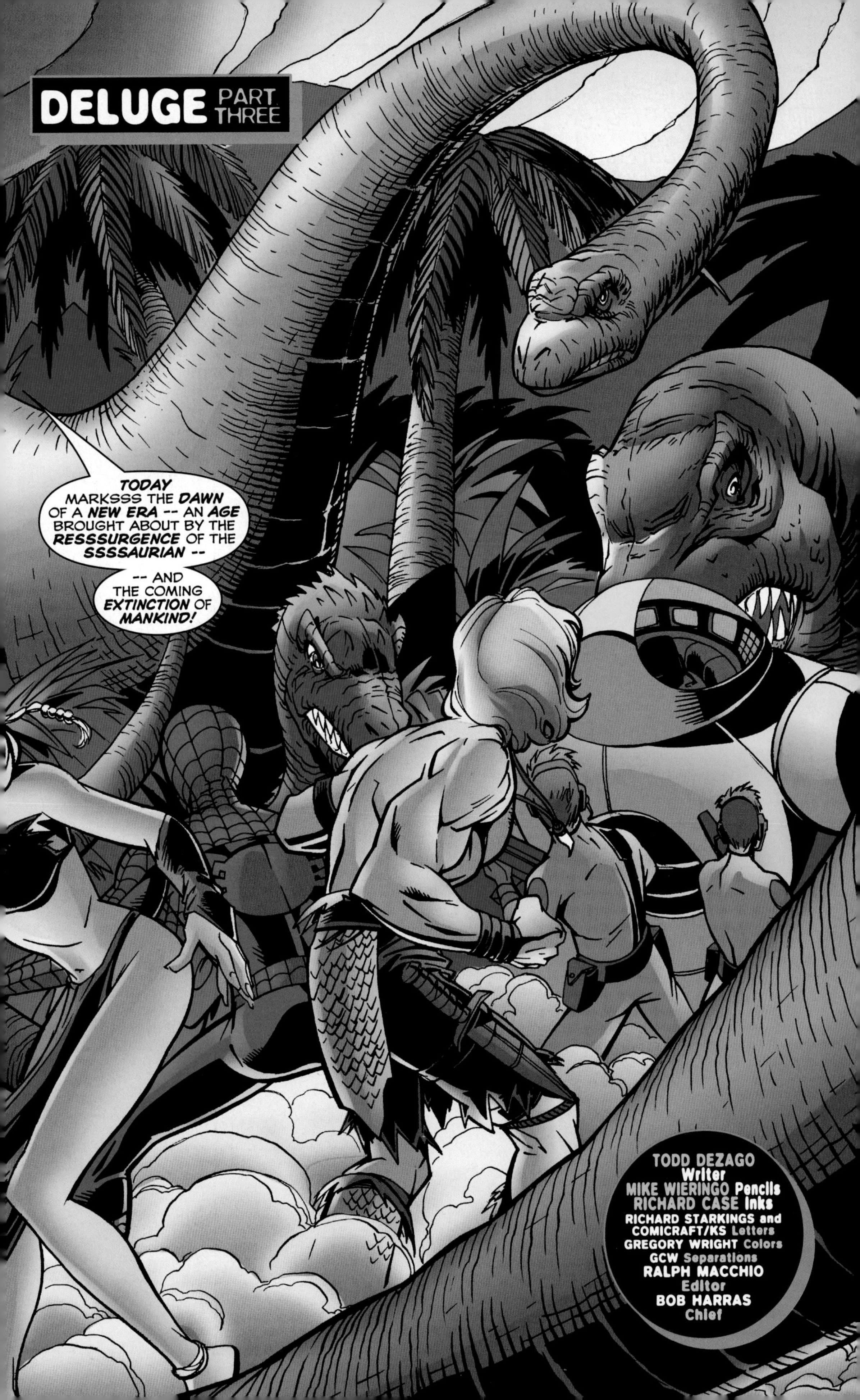
DELUGE PART THREE
TODAY MARKSSS THE DAWN OF A NEW ERA -- AN AGE BROUGHT ABOUT BY THE RESSSURGENCE OF THE SSSSAURIAN --
-- AND THE COMING EXTINCTION OF MANKIND!
TODD DEZAGO Writer
MIKE WIERINGO Pencils
RICHARD CASE Inks
RICHARD STARKINGS and COMICRAFT/KS Letters
GREGORY WRIGHT Colors
GCW Separations
RALPH MACCHIO Editor
BOB HARRAS Chief

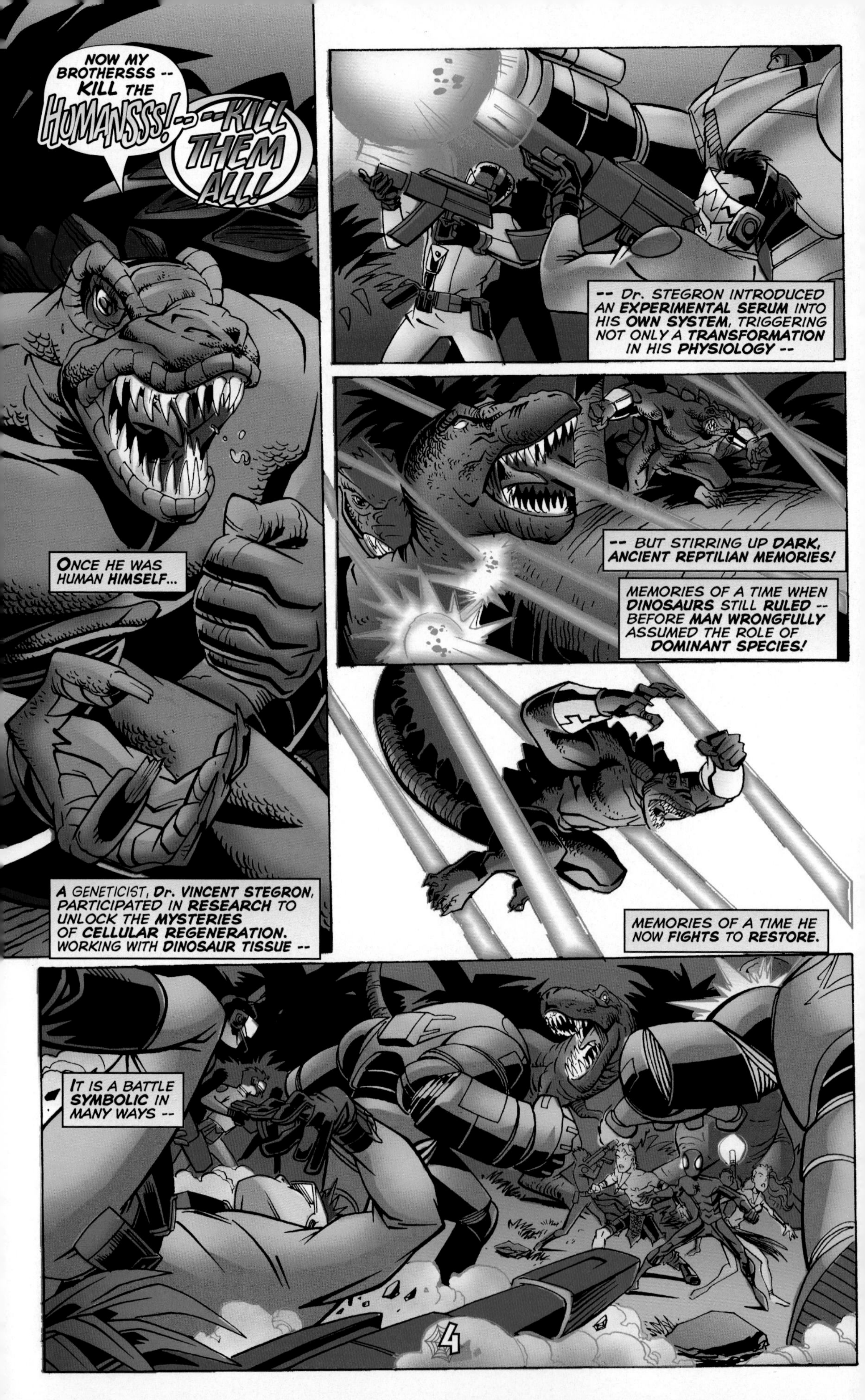

NOW MY BROTHERSSS -- KILL THE HUMANSSS! --
--KILL THEM ALL!
ONCE HE WAS HUMAN HIMSELF...
A GENETICIST, Dr. VINCENT STEGRON, PARTICIPATED IN RESEARCH TO UNLOCK THE MYSTERIES OF CELLULAR REGENERATION. WORKING WITH DINOSAUR TISSUE --
-- Dr. STEGRON INTRODUCED AN EXPERIMENTAL SERUM INTO HIS OWN SYSTEM, TRIGGERING NOT ONLY A TRANSFORMATION IN HIS PHYSIOLOGY --
-- BUT STIRRING UP DARK, ANCIENT REPTILIAN MEMORIES!
MEMORIES OF A TIME WHEN DINOSAURS STILL RULED -- BEFORE MAN WRONGFULLY ASSUMED THE ROLE OF DOMINANT SPECIES!
MEMORIES OF A TIME HE NOW FIGHTS TO RESTORE.
IT IS A BATTLE SYMBOLIC IN MANY WAYS --

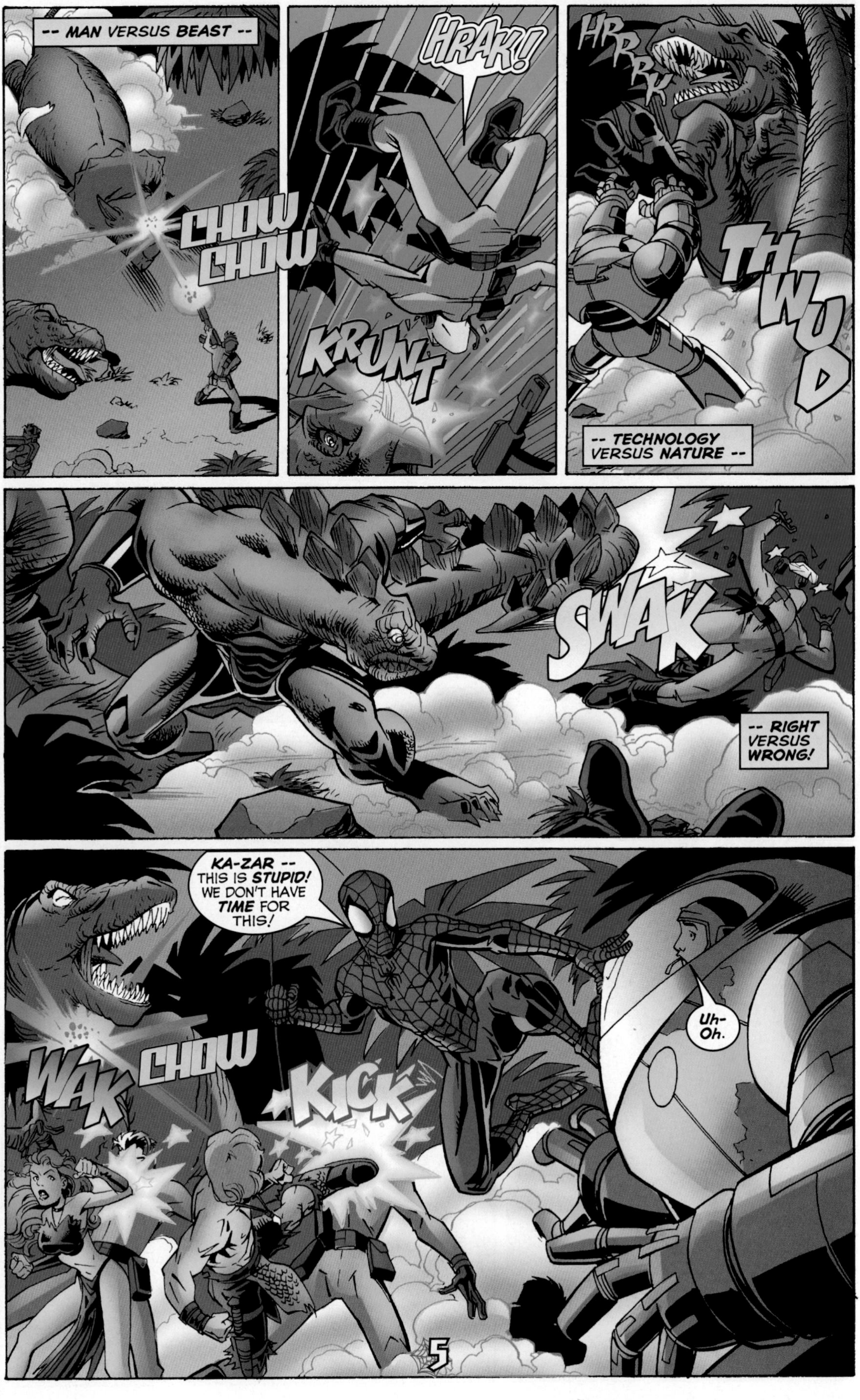
-- MAN VERSUS BEAST --
CHOW CHOW
HRAK!
KRUNT
HRRRK
THWUD
-- TECHNOLOGY VERSUS NATURE --
SWAK
-- RIGHT VERSUS WRONG!
KA-ZAR -- THIS IS STUPID! WE DON'T HAVE TIME FOR THIS!
Uh-Oh.
WAK
CHOW
KICK

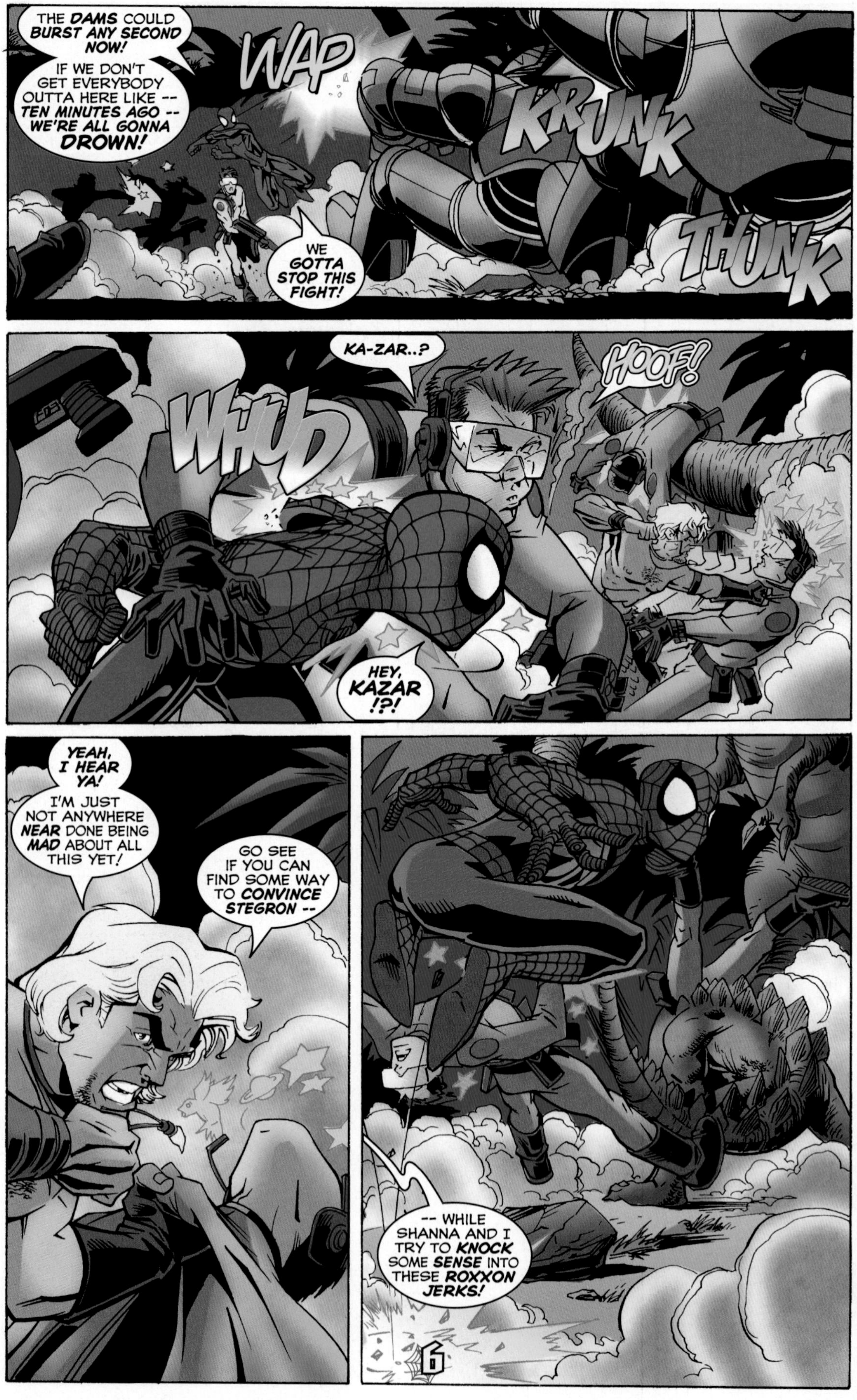
THE DAMS COULD BURST ANY SECOND NOW!
IF WE DON'T GET EVERYBODY OUTTA HERE LIKE -- TEN MINUTES AGO -- WE'RE ALL GONNA DROWN!
WAP
KRUNK
WE GOTTA STOP THIS FIGHT!
THUNK
KA-ZAR..?
WHUD
HOOF!
HEY, KAZAR !?!
YEAH, I HEAR YA!
I'M JUST NOT ANYWHERE NEAR DONE BEING MAD ABOUT ALL THIS YET!
GO SEE IF YOU CAN FIND SOME WAY TO CONVINCE STEGRON --
-- WHILE SHANNA AND I TRY TO KNOCK SOME SENSE INTO THESE ROXXON JERKS!

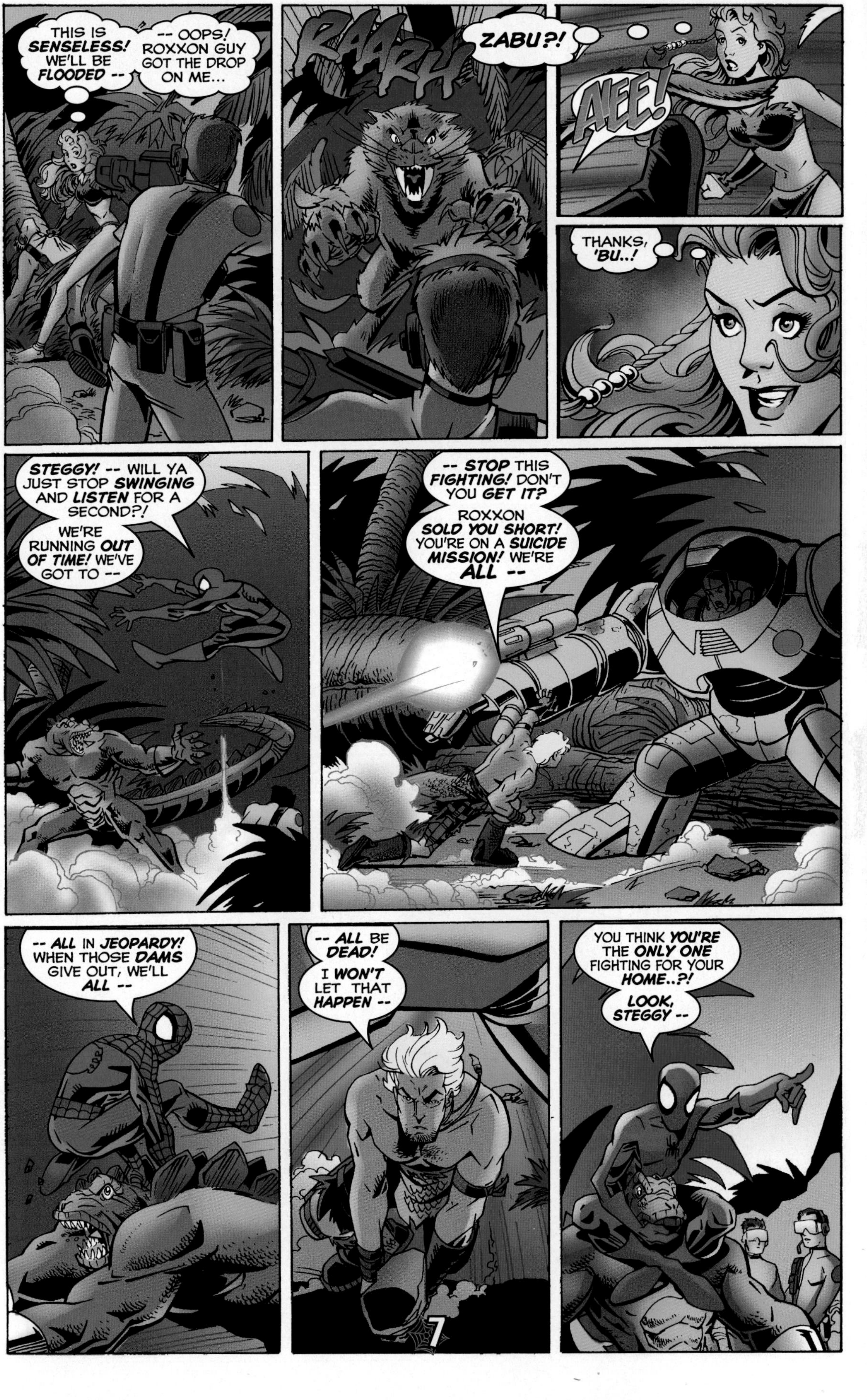
THIS IS SENSELESS! WE'LL BE FLOODED --
-- OOPS! ROXXON GUY GOT THE DROP ON ME...
RAARH
ZABU?!
AIEE!
THANKS, 'BU..!
STEGGY! -- WILL YA JUST STOP SWINGING AND LISTEN FOR A SECOND?!
WE'RE RUNNING OUT OF TIME! WE'VE GOT TO --
-- STOP THIS FIGHTING! DON'T YOU GET IT?
ROXXON SOLD YOU SHORT! YOU'RE ON A SUICIDE MISSION! WE'RE ALL --
-- ALL IN JEOPARDY! WHEN THOSE DAMS GIVE OUT, WE'LL ALL --
-- ALL BE DEAD!
I WON'T LET THAT HAPPEN --
YOU THINK YOU'RE THE ONLY ONE FIGHTING FOR YOUR HOME..?!
LOOK, STEGGY --

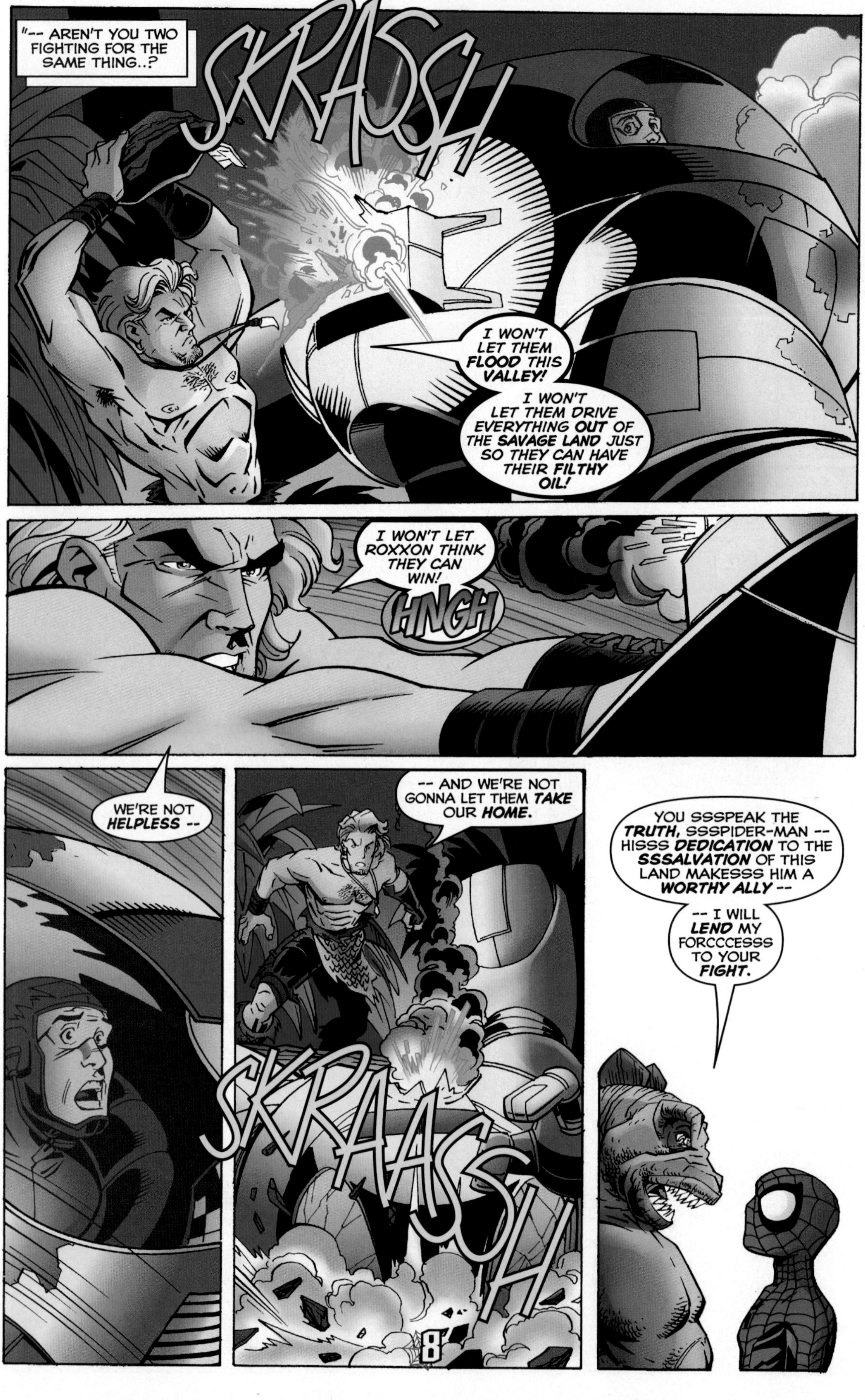
"-- AREN'T YOU TWO FIGHTING FOR THE SAME THING..?
SKRASSH
I WON'T LET THEM FLOOD THIS VALLEY!
I WON'T LET THEM DRIVE EVERYTHING OUT OF THE SAVAGE LAND JUST SO THEY CAN HAVE THEIR FILTHY OIL!
I WON'T LET ROXXON THINK THEY CAN WIN!
HNGH
WE'RE NOT HELPLESS --
-- AND WE'RE NOT GONNA LET THEM TAKE OUR HOME.
SKRAASSH
YOU SSSPEAK THE TRUTH, SSSPIDER-MAN -- HISSS DEDICATION TO THE SSSALVATION OF THIS LAND MAKESSS HIM A WORTHY ALLY --
-- I WILL LEND MY FORCCCESSS TO YOUR FIGHT.
8

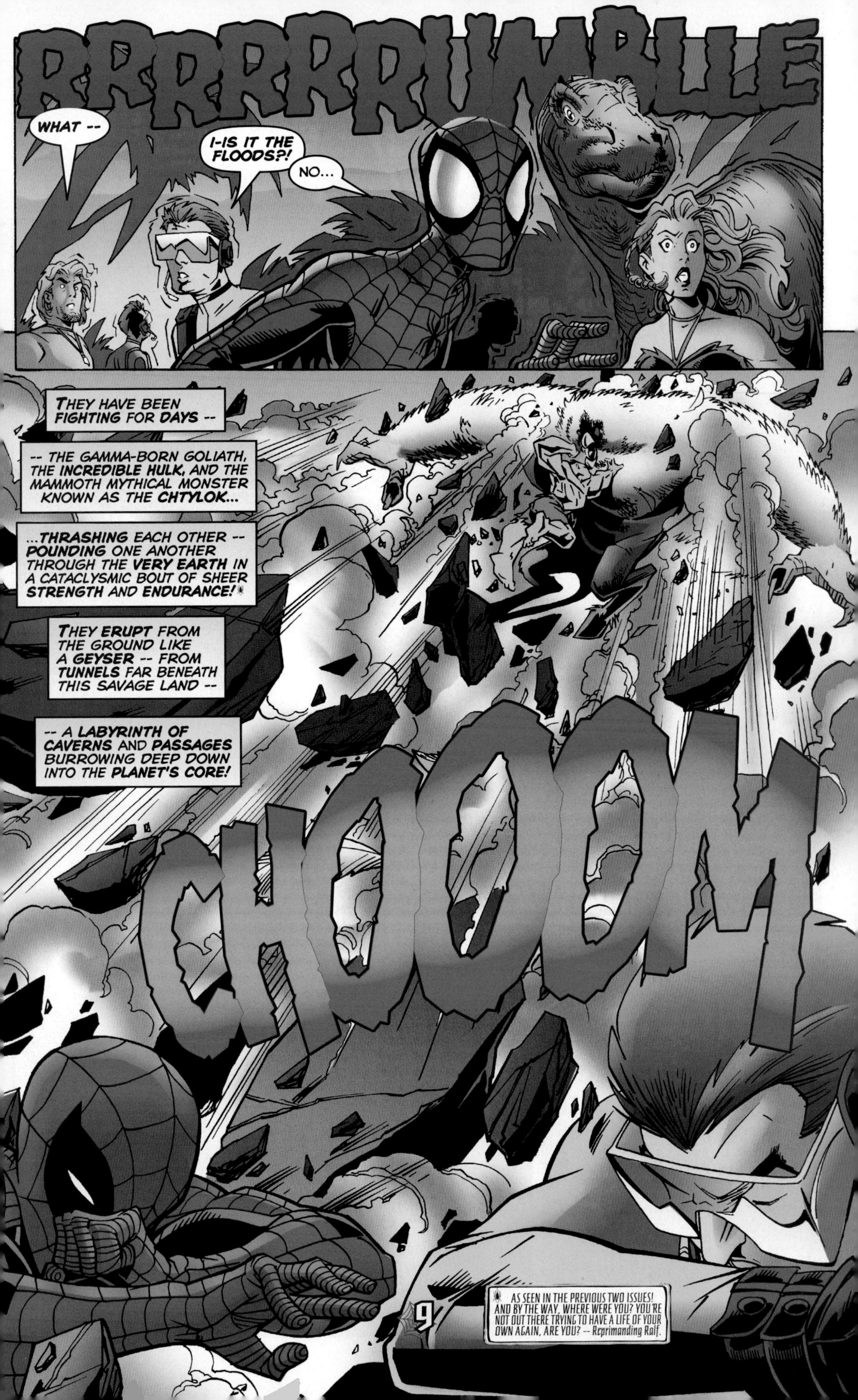
RRRRRRUMBLLE
WHAT --
I-IS IT THE FLOODS?!
NO...
THEY HAVE BEEN FIGHTING FOR DAYS --
-- THE GAMMA-BORN GOLIATH, THE INCREDIBLE HULK, AND THE MAMMOTH MYTHICAL MONSTER KNOWN AS THE CHTYLOK...
...THRASHING EACH OTHER -- POUNDING ONE ANOTHER THROUGH THE VERY EARTH IN A CATACLYSMIC BOUT OF SHEER STRENGTH AND ENDURANCE!
THEY ERUPT FROM THE GROUND LIKE A GEYSER -- FROM TUNNELS FAR BENEATH THIS SAVAGE LAND --
-- A LABYRINTH OF CAVERNS AND PASSAGES BURROWING DEEP DOWN INTO THE PLANET'S CORE!
CHOOOM
AS SEEN IN THE PREVIOUS TWO ISSUES! AND BY THE WAY, WHERE WERE YOU? YOU'RE NOT OUT THERE TRYING TO HAVE A LIFE OF YOUR OWN AGAIN, ARE YOU? -- Reprimanding Ralf.

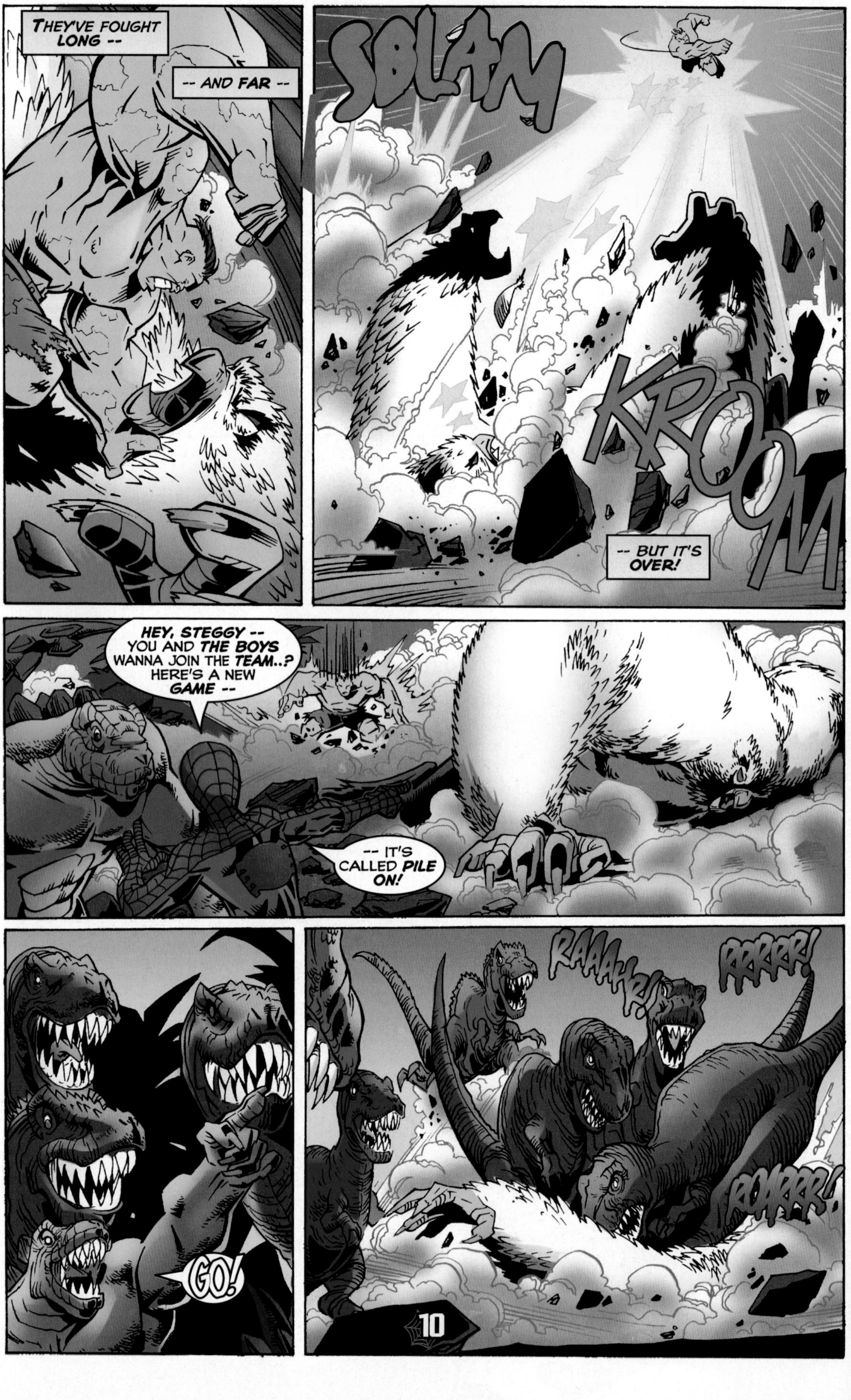
THEY'VE FOUGHT LONG --
-- AND FAR --
SBLAM
KROOM
-- BUT IT'S OVER!
HEY, STEGGY -- YOU AND THE BOYS WANNA JOIN THE TEAM..? HERE'S A NEW GAME --
-- IT'S CALLED PILE ON!
GO!
RAAAHR!
RRRRR!
ROARRR!

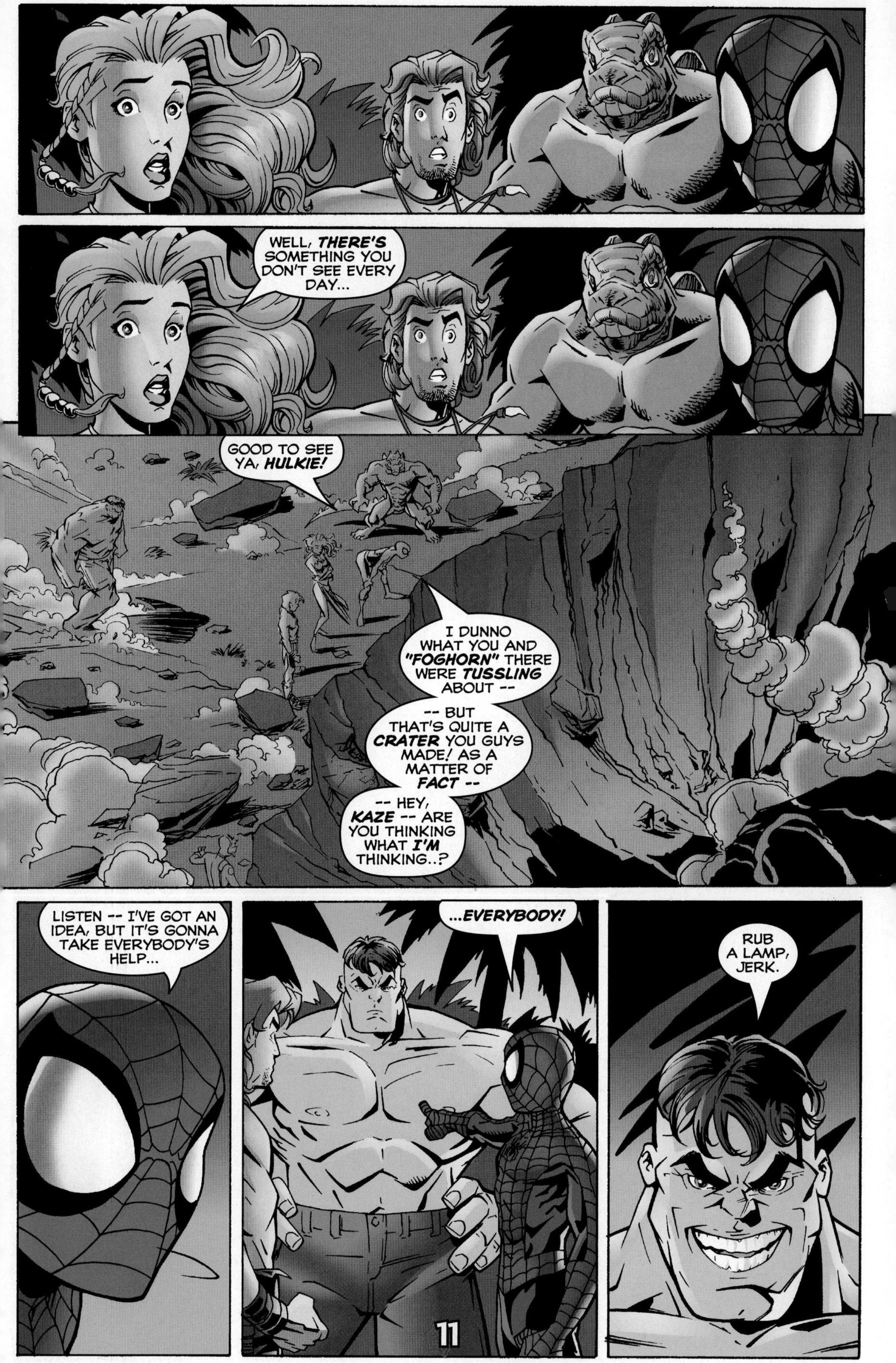
WELL, THERE'S SOMETHING YOU DON'T SEE EVERY DAY...
GOOD TO SEE YA, HULKIE!
I DUNNO WHAT YOU AND "FOGHORN" THERE WERE TUSSLING ABOUT --
-- BUT THAT'S QUITE A CRATER YOU GUYS MADE! AS A MATTER OF FACT --
-- HEY, KAZE -- ARE YOU THINKING WHAT I'M THINKING..?
LISTEN -- I'VE GOT AN IDEA, BUT IT'S GONNA TAKE EVERYBODY'S HELP...
...EVERYBODY!
RUB A LAMP, JERK.

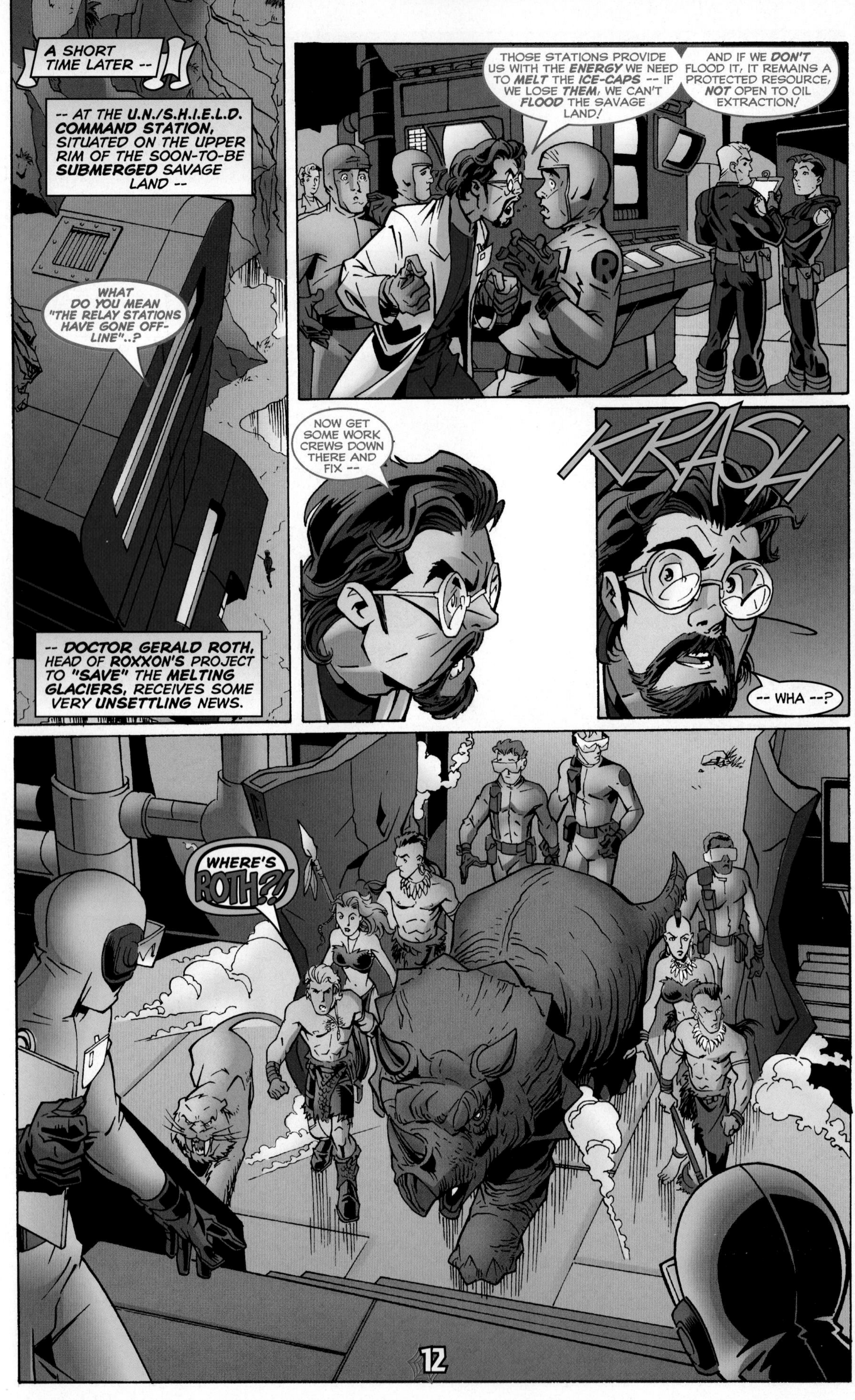
A SHORT TIME LATER --
-- AT THE U.N./S.H.I.E.L.D. COMMAND STATION, SITUATED ON THE UPPER RIM OF THE SOON-TO-BE SUBMERGED SAVAGE LAND --
WHAT DO YOU MEAN "THE RELAY STATIONS HAVE GONE OFF-LINE"..?
THOSE STATIONS PROVIDE US WITH THE ENERGY WE NEED TO MELT THE ICE-CAPS -- IF WE LOSE THEM, WE CAN'T FLOOD THE SAVAGE LAND!
AND IF WE DON'T FLOOD IT, IT REMAINS A PROTECTED RESOURCE, NOT OPEN TO OIL EXTRACTION!
-- DOCTOR GERALD ROTH, HEAD OF ROXXON'S PROJECT TO "SAVE" THE MELTING GLACIERS, RECEIVES SOME VERY UNSETTLING NEWS.
NOW GET SOME WORK CREWS DOWN THERE AND FIX --
KRASH
-- WHA --?
WHERE'S ROTH?!

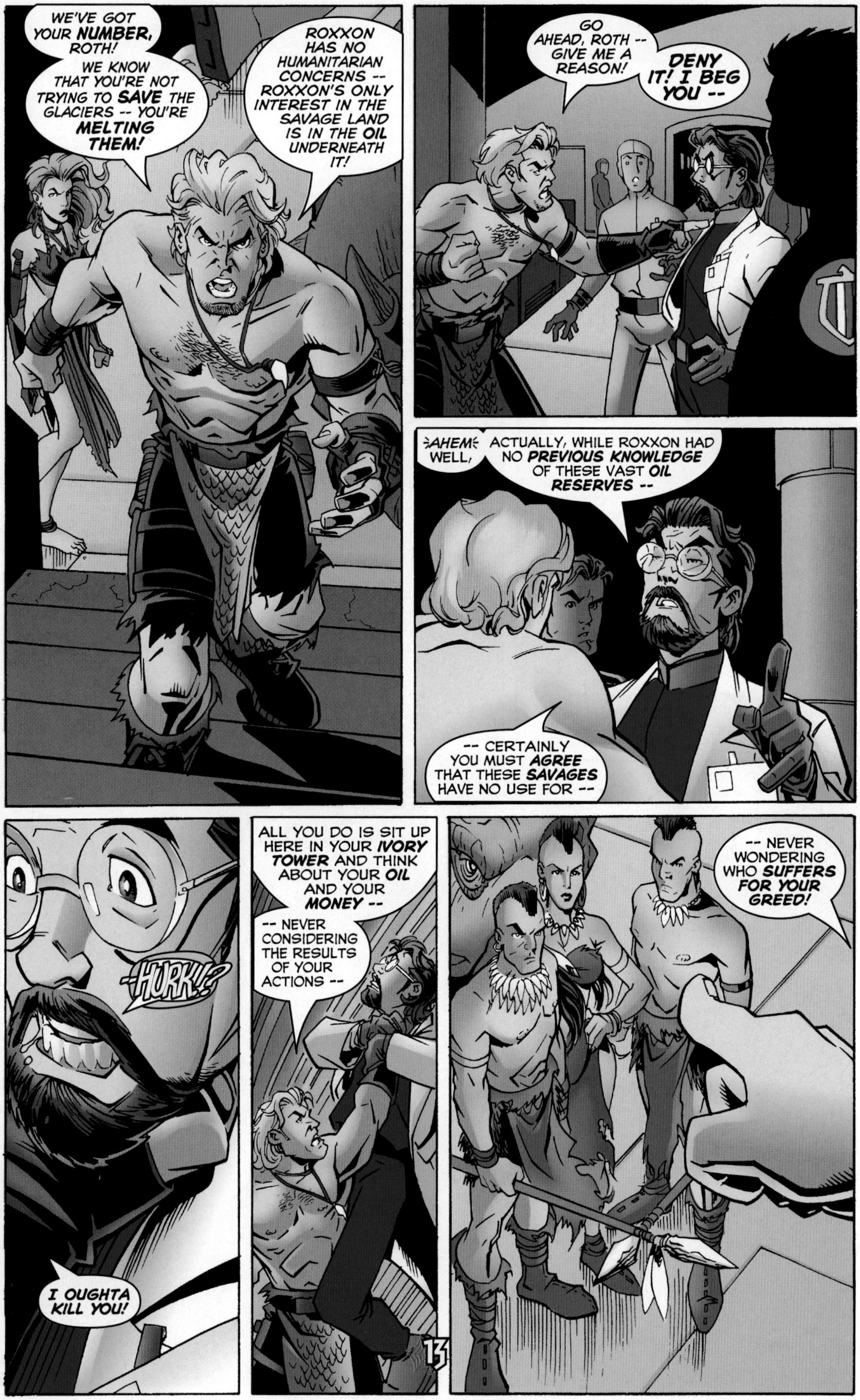
WE'VE GOT YOUR NUMBER, ROTH!
WE KNOW THAT YOU'RE NOT TRYING TO SAVE THE GLACIERS -- YOU'RE MELTING THEM!
ROXXON HAS NO HUMANITARIAN CONCERNS -- ROXXON'S ONLY INTEREST IN THE SAVAGE LAND IS IN THE OIL UNDERNEATH IT!
GO AHEAD, ROTH -- GIVE ME A REASON!
DENY IT! I BEG YOU --
AHEM WELL,
ACTUALLY, WHILE ROXXON HAD NO PREVIOUS KNOWLEDGE OF THESE VAST OIL RESERVES --
-- CERTAINLY YOU MUST AGREE THAT THESE SAVAGES HAVE NO USE FOR --
HURK!?
I OUGHTA KILL YOU!
ALL YOU DO IS SIT UP HERE IN YOUR IVORY TOWER AND THINK ABOUT YOUR OIL AND YOUR MONEY --
-- NEVER CONSIDERING THE RESULTS OF YOUR ACTIONS --
-- NEVER WONDERING WHO SUFFERS FOR YOUR GREED!
13

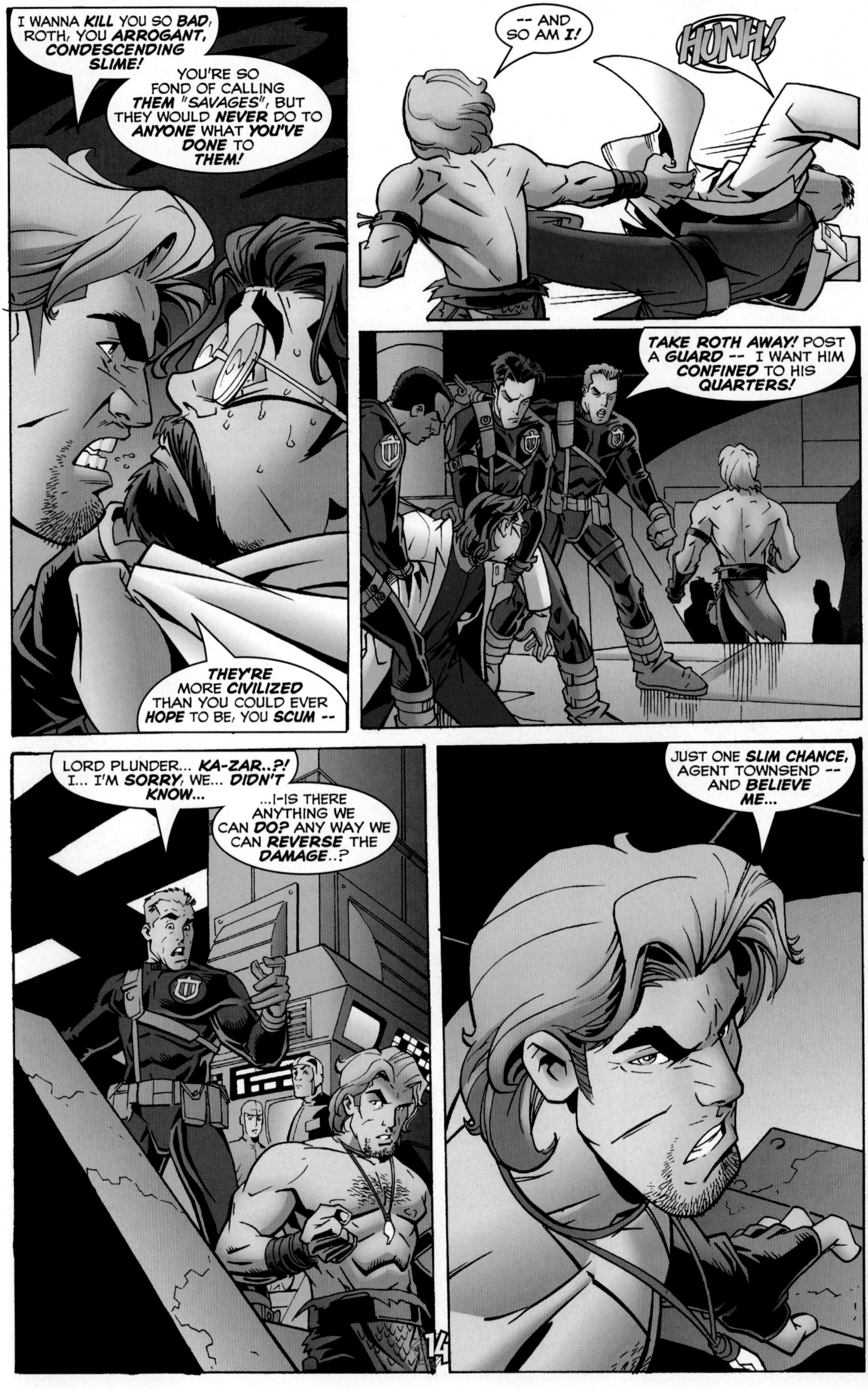

I WANNA KILL YOU SO BAD, ROTH, YOU ARROGANT, CONDESCENDING SLIME!
YOU'RE SO FOND OF CALLING THEM "SAVAGES", BUT THEY WOULD NEVER DO TO ANYONE WHAT YOU'VE DONE TO THEM!
THEY'RE MORE CIVILIZED THAN YOU COULD EVER HOPE TO BE, YOU SCUM --
-- AND SO AM I!
HUNH!
TAKE ROTH AWAY! POST A GUARD -- I WANT HIM CONFINED TO HIS QUARTERS!
LORD PLUNDER... KA-ZAR..?! I... I'M SORRY, WE... DIDN'T KNOW...
...I-IS THERE ANYTHING WE CAN DO? ANY WAY WE CAN REVERSE THE DAMAGE..?
JUST ONE SLIM CHANCE, AGENT TOWNSEND -- AND BELIEVE ME...
14

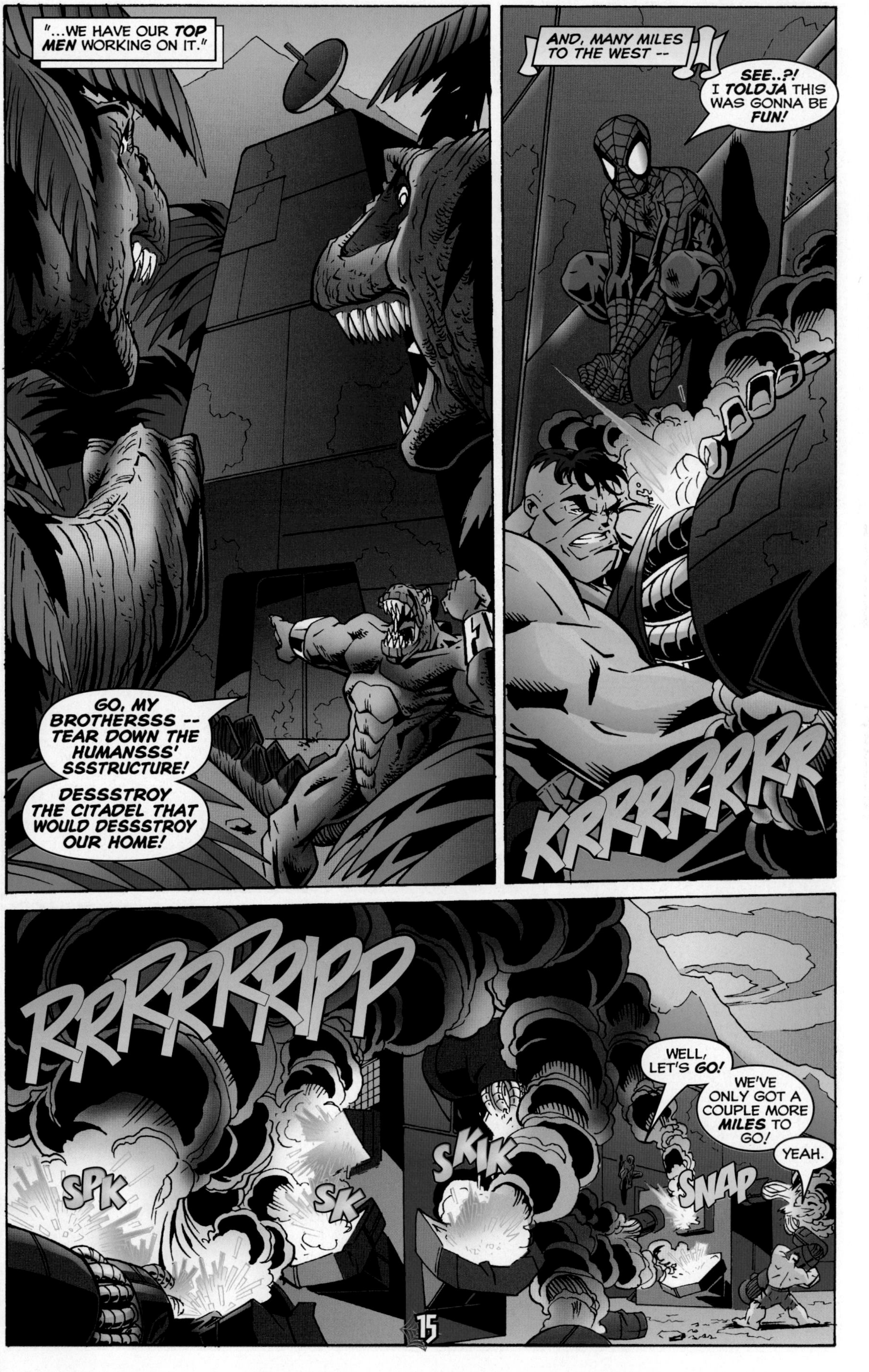
"...WE HAVE OUR TOP MEN WORKING ON IT."
GO, MY BROTHERSSS -- TEAR DOWN THE HUMANSSS' SSSTRUCTURE!
DESSSTROY THE CITADEL THAT WOULD DESSSTROY OUR HOME!
AND, MANY MILES TO THE WEST --
SEE..?! I TOLDJA THIS WAS GONNA BE FUN!
KRRRRRRRR
RRRRRRIPP
SPK
SK
SKIK
SNAP
WELL, LET'S GO!
WE'VE ONLY GOT A COUPLE MORE MILES TO GO!
YEAH.

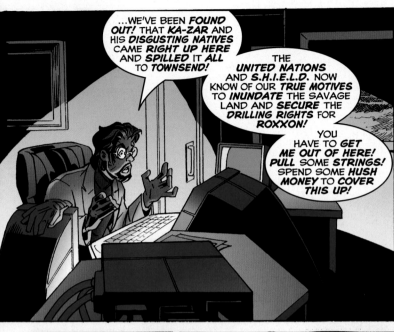

...WE'VE BEEN *FOUND OUT!* THAT *KA-ZAR* AND HIS *DISGUSTING* NATIVES CAME *RIGHT UP HERE* AND *SPILLED* IT *ALL* TO *TOWNSEND!*

THE *UNITED NATIONS* AND *S.H.I.E.L.D.* NOW KNOW OF OUR *TRUE MOTIVES* TO *INUNDATE* THE SAVAGE LAND AND *SECURE* THE *DRILLING RIGHTS* FOR *ROXXON!*

YOU HAVE TO *GET ME OUT OF HERE! PULL SOME STRINGS!* SPEND SOME *HUSH MONEY* TO COVER THIS UP!

...NO, YOU DON'T *UNDERSTAND...*

THIS WILL BE OUR *LAST* TRANSMISSION, ROTH --

-- *GOODBYE.*

THEY'VE *HUNG ME OUT TO DRY!* I'M THE *SCAPEGOAT!*

ALL THE *BLAME* WILL FALL ON *ME!*

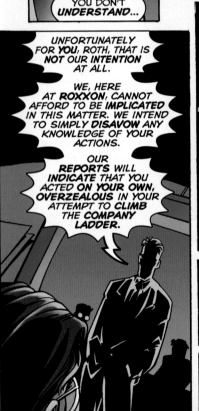

UNFORTUNATELY FOR *YOU,* ROTH, THAT IS *NOT* OUR INTENTION AT ALL.

WE, HERE AT *ROXXON,* CANNOT AFFORD TO BE *IMPLICATED* IN THIS MATTER. WE INTEND TO SIMPLY *DISAVOW* ANY KNOWLEDGE OF YOUR ACTIONS.

OUR *REPORTS* WILL INDICATE THAT YOU ACTED ON *YOUR OWN,* OVERZEALOUS IN YOUR ATTEMPT TO *CLIMB* THE *COMPANY LADDER.*

BUT... BUT...

WELL, I'M NOT GOING DOWN *ALONE!*

I CAN STILL *ACCESS* THE *EXPLOSIVES* FROM HERE --

-- AND IF I CAN *DETONATE* THEM *SIMULTANEOUSLY* -- BLOW ALL THE DAMS AT ONCE --

-- HOPEFULLY, I CAN TAKE THAT *FILTHY SAVAGE* DOWN WITH ME!

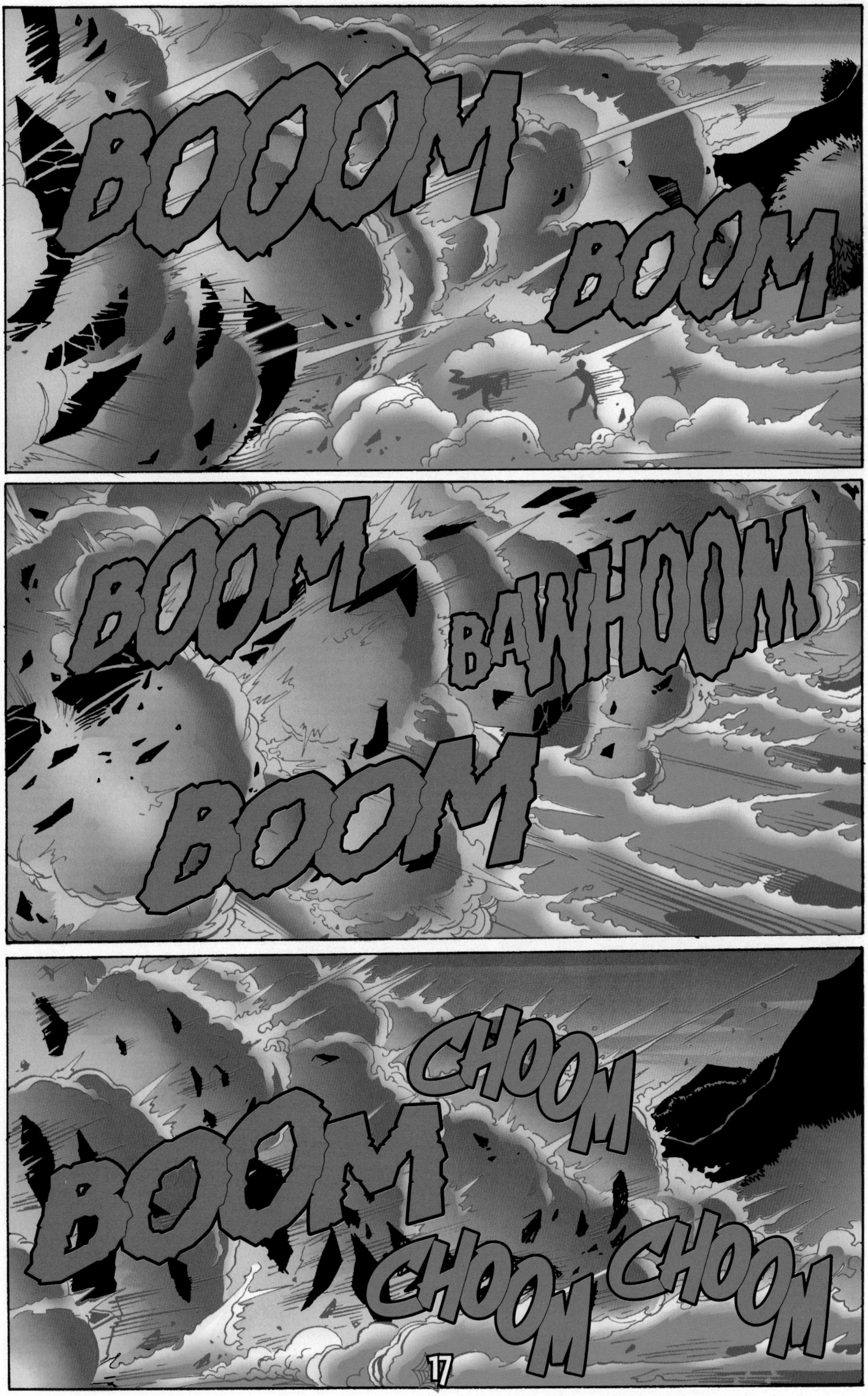
BOOOM
BOOM
BOOM
BAWHOOM
BOOM
CHOOM
BOOM
CHOOM
CHOOM

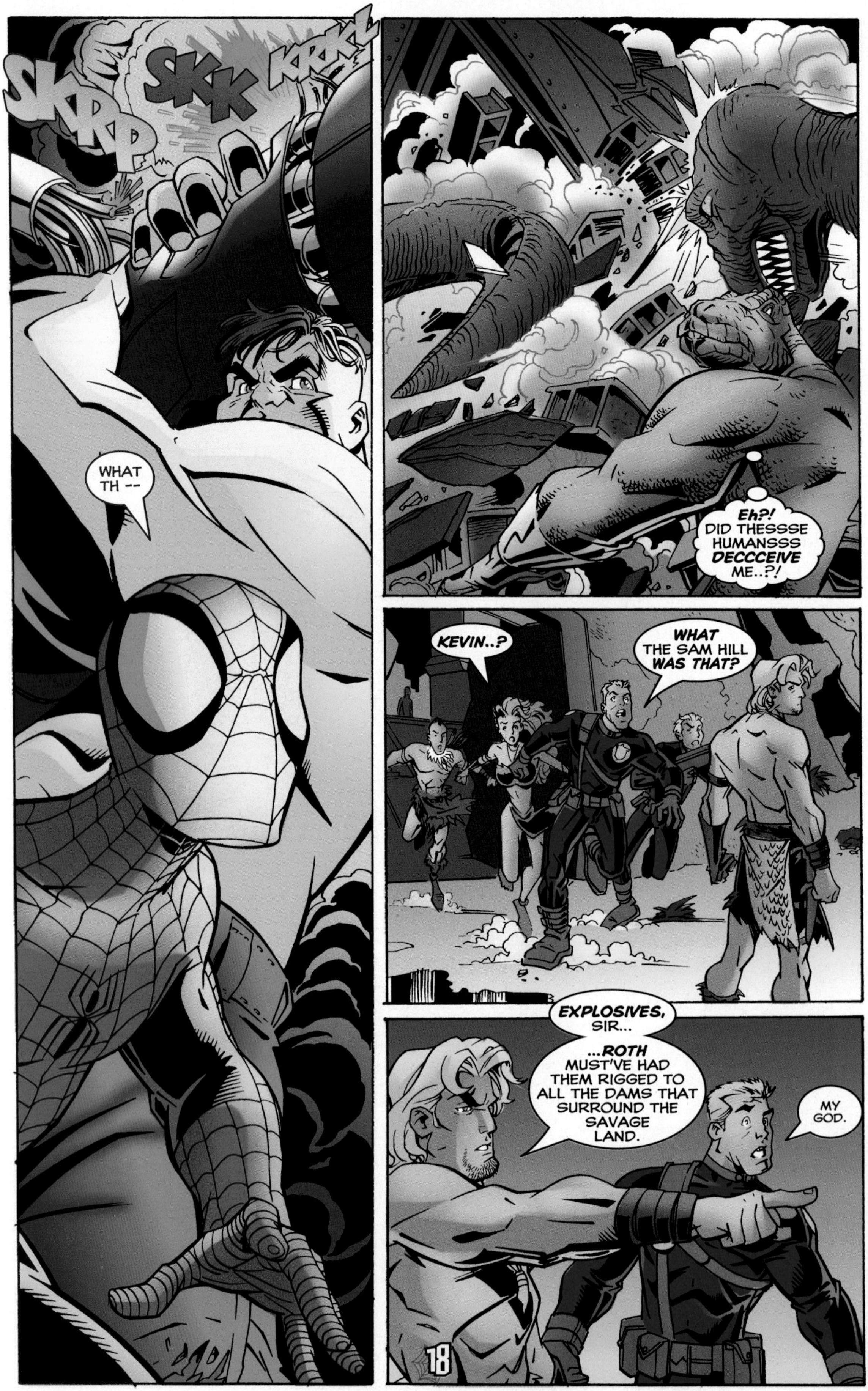
SKRP
SKK
KRKL
WHAT TH --
Eh?! DID THESSSE HUMANSSS DECCCEIVE ME..?!
KEVIN..?
WHAT THE SAM HILL WAS THAT?
EXPLOSIVES, SIR...
...ROTH MUST'VE HAD THEM RIGGED TO ALL THE DAMS THAT SURROUND THE SAVAGE LAND.
MY GOD.
18

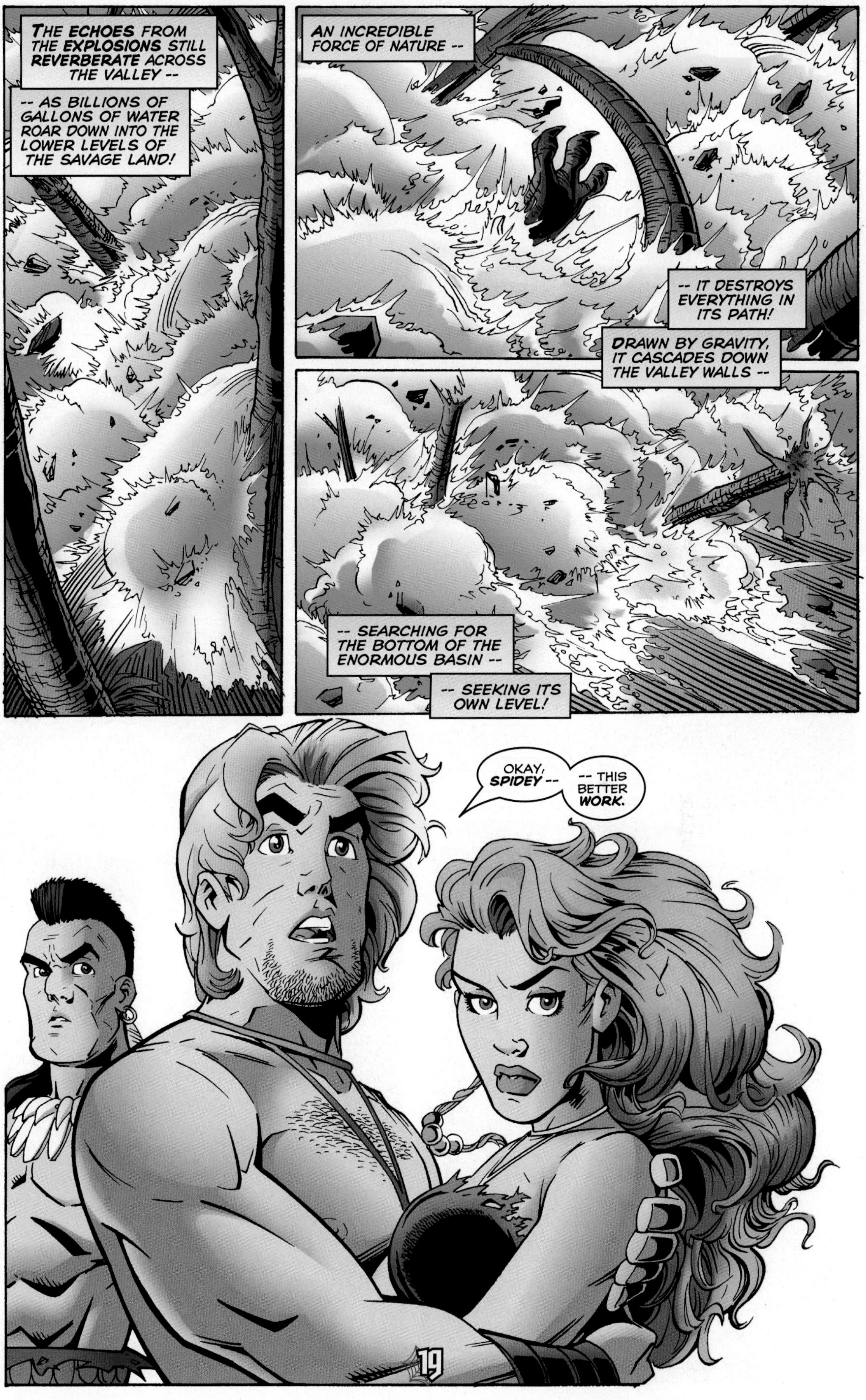
THE ECHOES FROM THE EXPLOSIONS STILL REVERBERATE ACROSS THE VALLEY --
-- AS BILLIONS OF GALLONS OF WATER ROAR DOWN INTO THE LOWER LEVELS OF THE SAVAGE LAND!
AN INCREDIBLE FORCE OF NATURE --
-- IT DESTROYS EVERYTHING IN ITS PATH!
DRAWN BY GRAVITY, IT CASCADES DOWN THE VALLEY WALLS --
-- SEARCHING FOR THE BOTTOM OF THE ENORMOUS BASIN --
-- SEEKING ITS OWN LEVEL!
OKAY, SPIDEY --
-- THIS BETTER WORK.
19

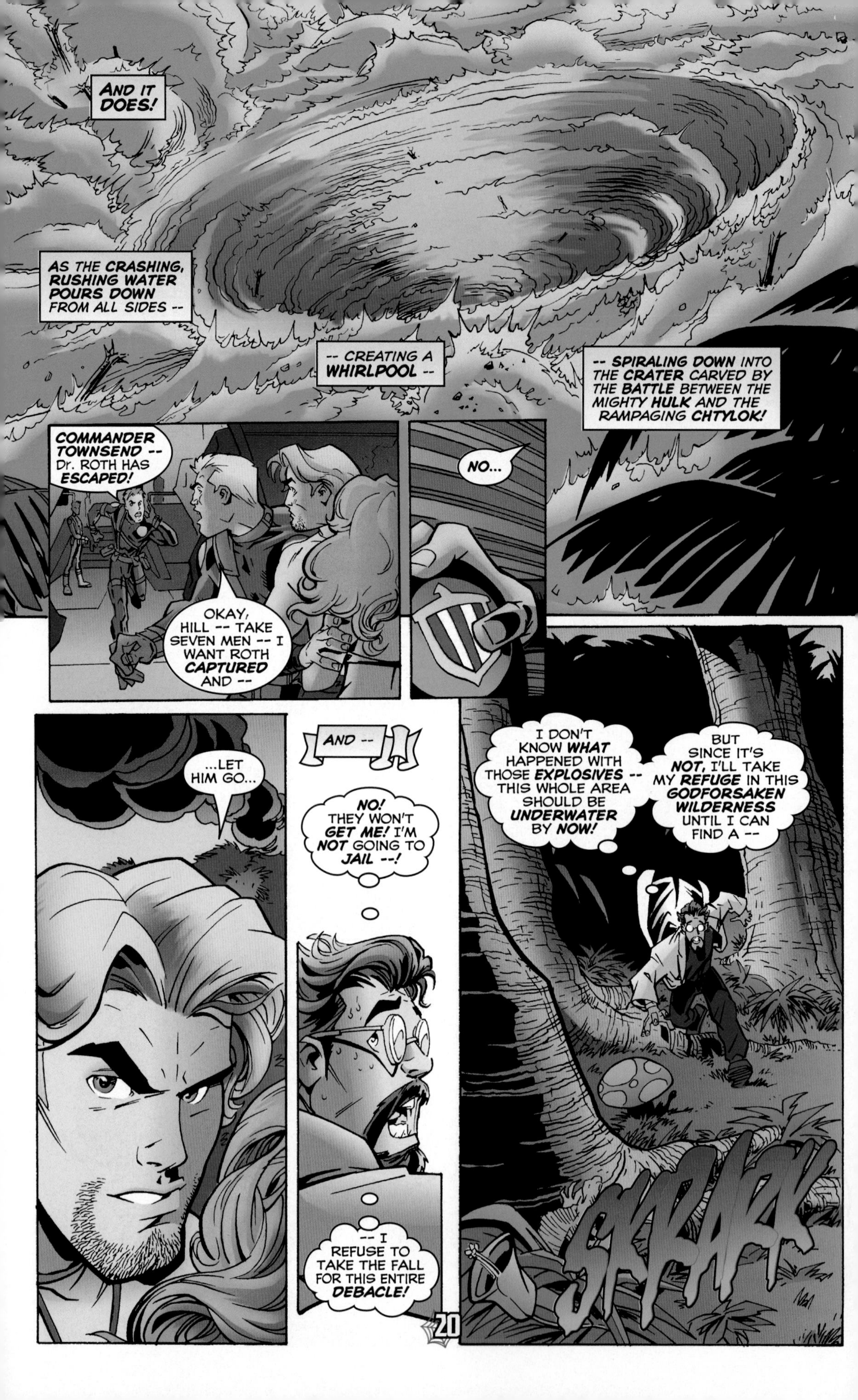

AND IT DOES!
AS THE CRASHING, RUSHING WATER POURS DOWN FROM ALL SIDES --
-- CREATING A WHIRLPOOL --
-- SPIRALING DOWN INTO THE CRATER CARVED BY THE BATTLE BETWEEN THE MIGHTY HULK AND THE RAMPAGING CHTYLOK!
COMMANDER TOWNSEND -- Dr. ROTH HAS ESCAPED!
OKAY, HILL -- TAKE SEVEN MEN -- I WANT ROTH CAPTURED AND --
NO...
...LET HIM GO...
AND --
NO! THEY WON'T GET ME! I'M NOT GOING TO JAIL --!
NO!
-- I REFUSE TO TAKE THE FALL FOR THIS ENTIRE DEBACLE!
I DON'T KNOW WHAT HAPPENED WITH THOSE EXPLOSIVES -- THIS WHOLE AREA SHOULD BE UNDERWATER BY NOW!
BUT SINCE IT'S NOT, I'LL TAKE MY REFUGE IN THIS GODFORSAKEN WILDERNESS UNTIL I CAN FIND A --
SKRAK

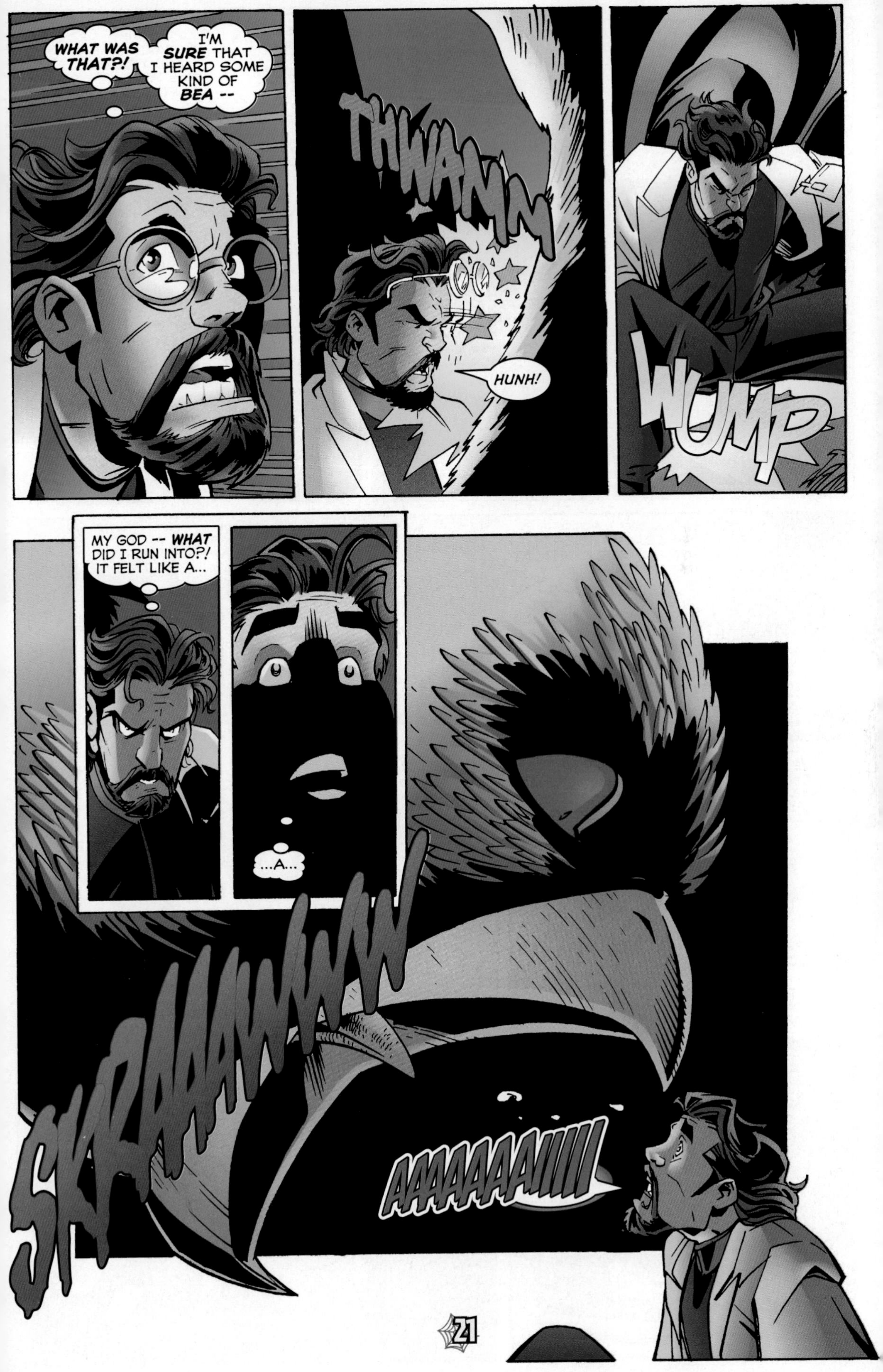
WHAT WAS THAT?!
I'M SURE THAT I HEARD SOME KIND OF BEA --
THWANNN
HUNH!
WUMP
MY GOD -- WHAT DID I RUN INTO?! IT FELT LIKE A...
...A...
SKRAAAWWW
AAAAAAIIIII

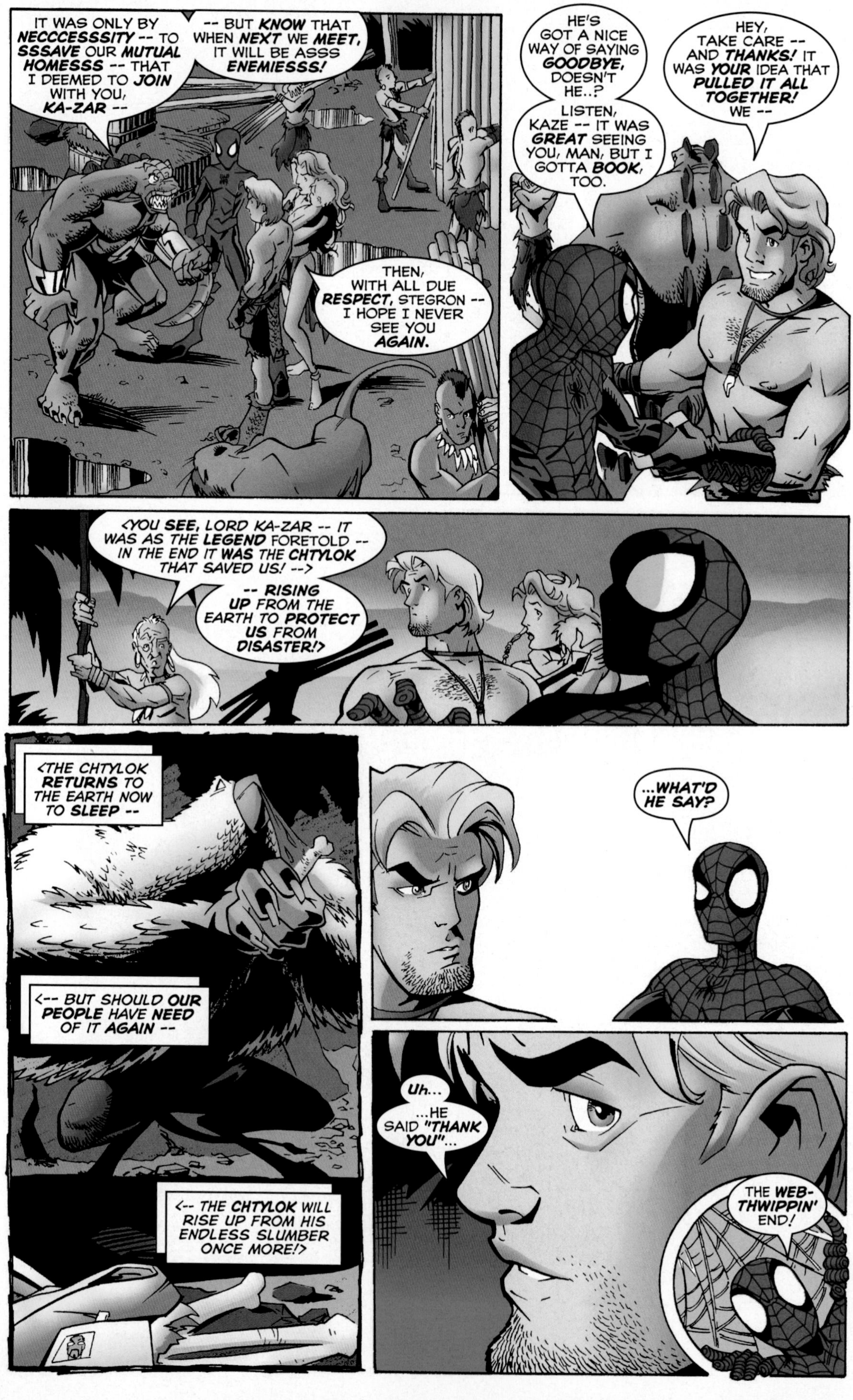
IT WAS ONLY BY NECCCESSSITY -- TO SSSAVE OUR MUTUAL HOMESSS -- THAT I DEEMED TO JOIN WITH YOU, KA-ZAR --
-- BUT KNOW THAT WHEN NEXT WE MEET, IT WILL BE ASSS ENEMIESSS!
THEN, WITH ALL DUE RESPECT, STEGRON -- I HOPE I NEVER SEE YOU AGAIN.
HE'S GOT A NICE WAY OF SAYING GOODBYE, DOESN'T HE..?
LISTEN, KAZE -- IT WAS GREAT SEEING YOU, MAN, BUT I GOTTA BOOK, TOO.
HEY, TAKE CARE -- AND THANKS! IT WAS YOUR IDEA THAT PULLED IT ALL TOGETHER! WE --
<YOU SEE, LORD KA-ZAR -- IT WAS AS THE LEGEND FORETOLD -- IN THE END IT WAS THE CHTYLOK THAT SAVED US! -->
-- RISING UP FROM THE EARTH TO PROTECT US FROM DISASTER!>
<THE CHTYLOK RETURNS TO THE EARTH NOW TO SLEEP --
<-- BUT SHOULD OUR PEOPLE HAVE NEED OF IT AGAIN --
<-- THE CHTYLOK WILL RISE UP FROM HIS ENDLESS SLUMBER ONCE MORE!>
...WHAT'D HE SAY?
Uh...
...HE SAID "THANK YOU"...
THE WEB-THWIPPIN' END!

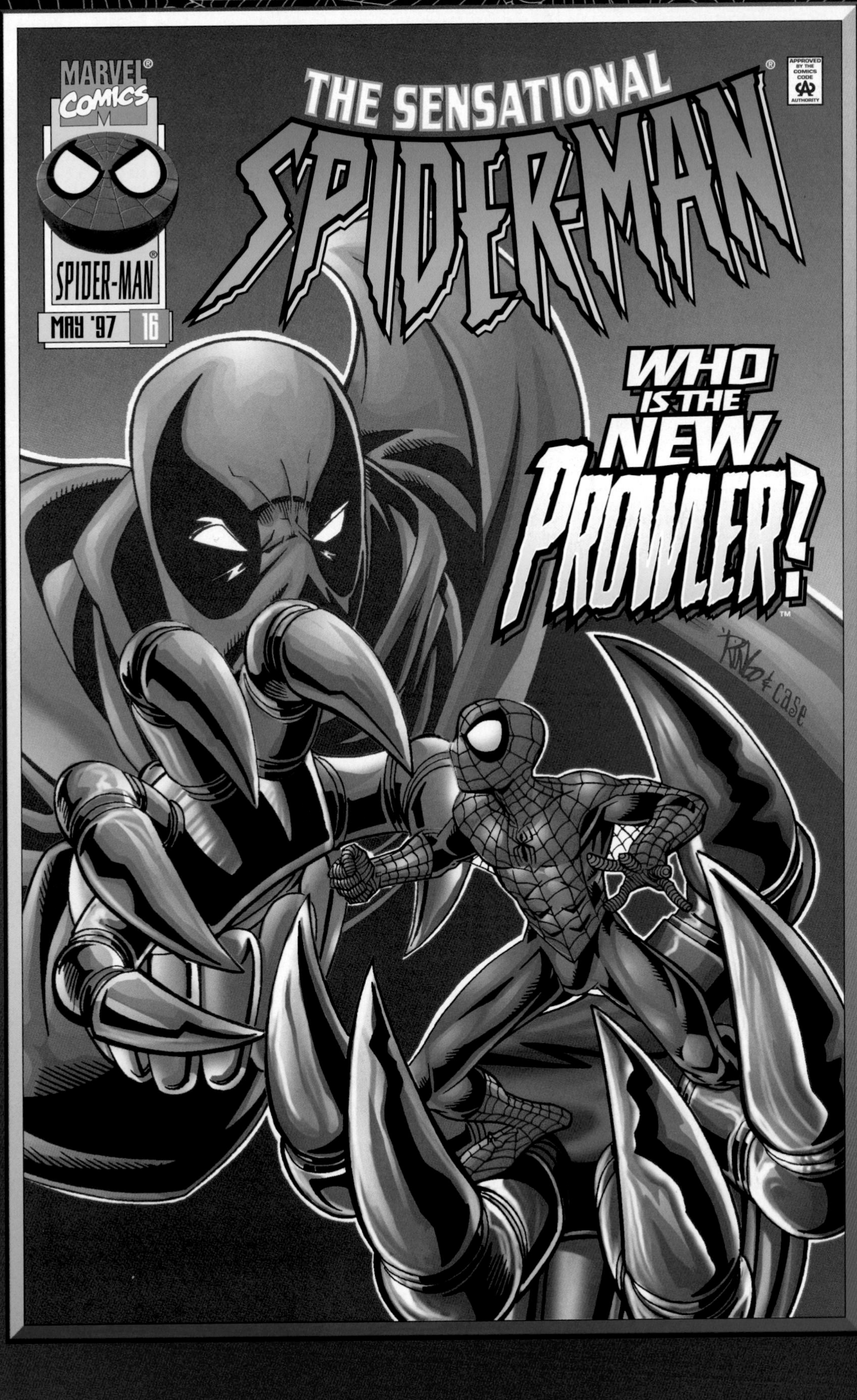
MARVEL® COMICS
THE SENSATIONAL SPIDER-MAN®
SPIDER-MAN®
MAY '97 16
APPROVED BY THE COMICS CODE AUTHORITY
WHO IS THE NEW PROWLER?™

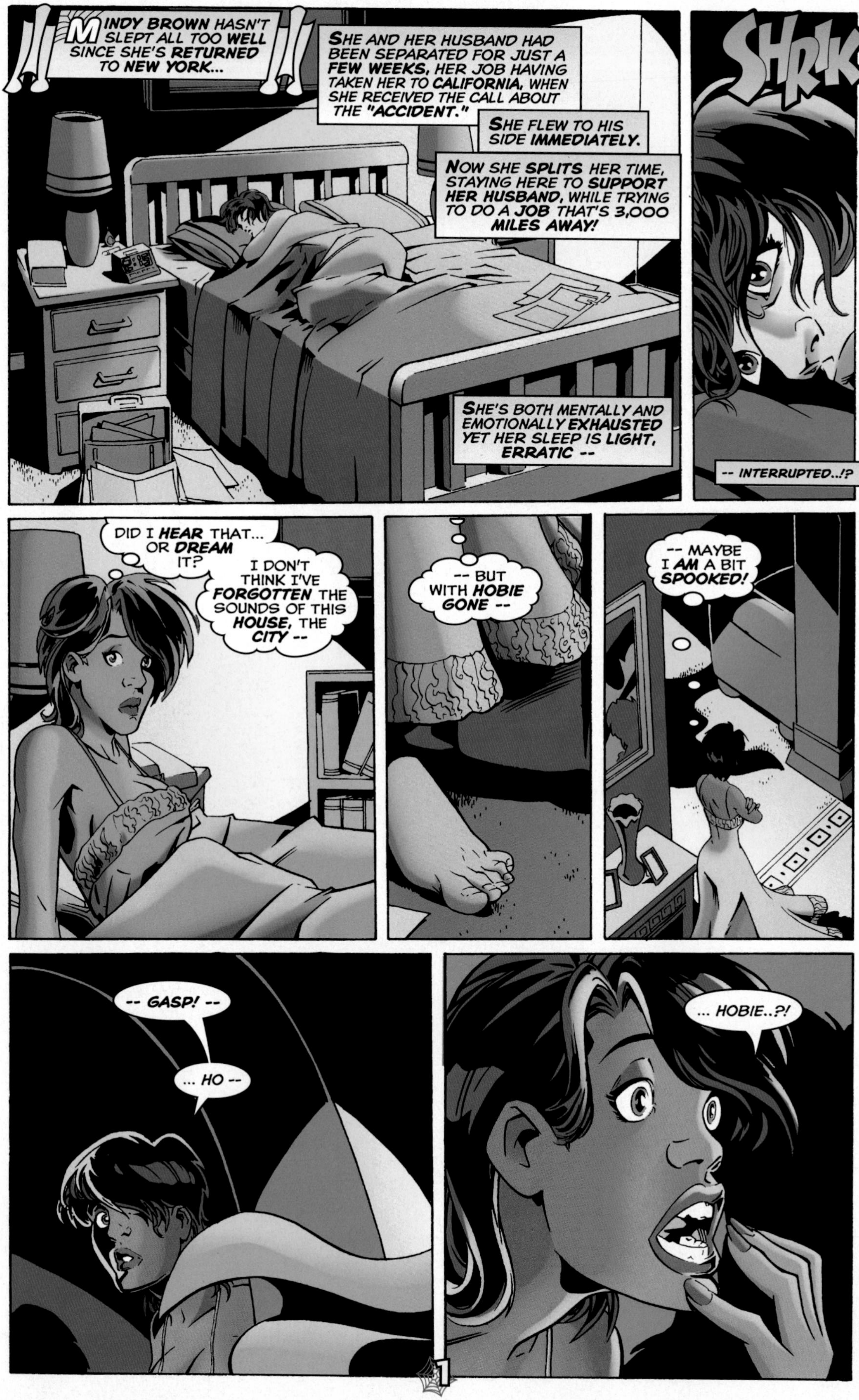
MINDY BROWN HASN'T SLEPT ALL TOO WELL SINCE SHE'S RETURNED TO NEW YORK...
SHE AND HER HUSBAND HAD BEEN SEPARATED FOR JUST A FEW WEEKS, HER JOB HAVING TAKEN HER TO CALIFORNIA, WHEN SHE RECEIVED THE CALL ABOUT THE "ACCIDENT."
SHE FLEW TO HIS SIDE IMMEDIATELY.
NOW SHE SPLITS HER TIME, STAYING HERE TO SUPPORT HER HUSBAND, WHILE TRYING TO DO A JOB THAT'S 3,000 MILES AWAY!
SHE'S BOTH MENTALLY AND EMOTIONALLY EXHAUSTED YET HER SLEEP IS LIGHT, ERRATIC --
SHRIK
-- INTERRUPTED..!?
DID I HEAR THAT... OR DREAM IT?
I DON'T THINK I'VE FORGOTTEN THE SOUNDS OF THIS HOUSE, THE CITY --
-- BUT WITH HOBIE GONE --
-- MAYBE I AM A BIT SPOOKED!
-- GASP! --
... HO --
... HOBIE..?!

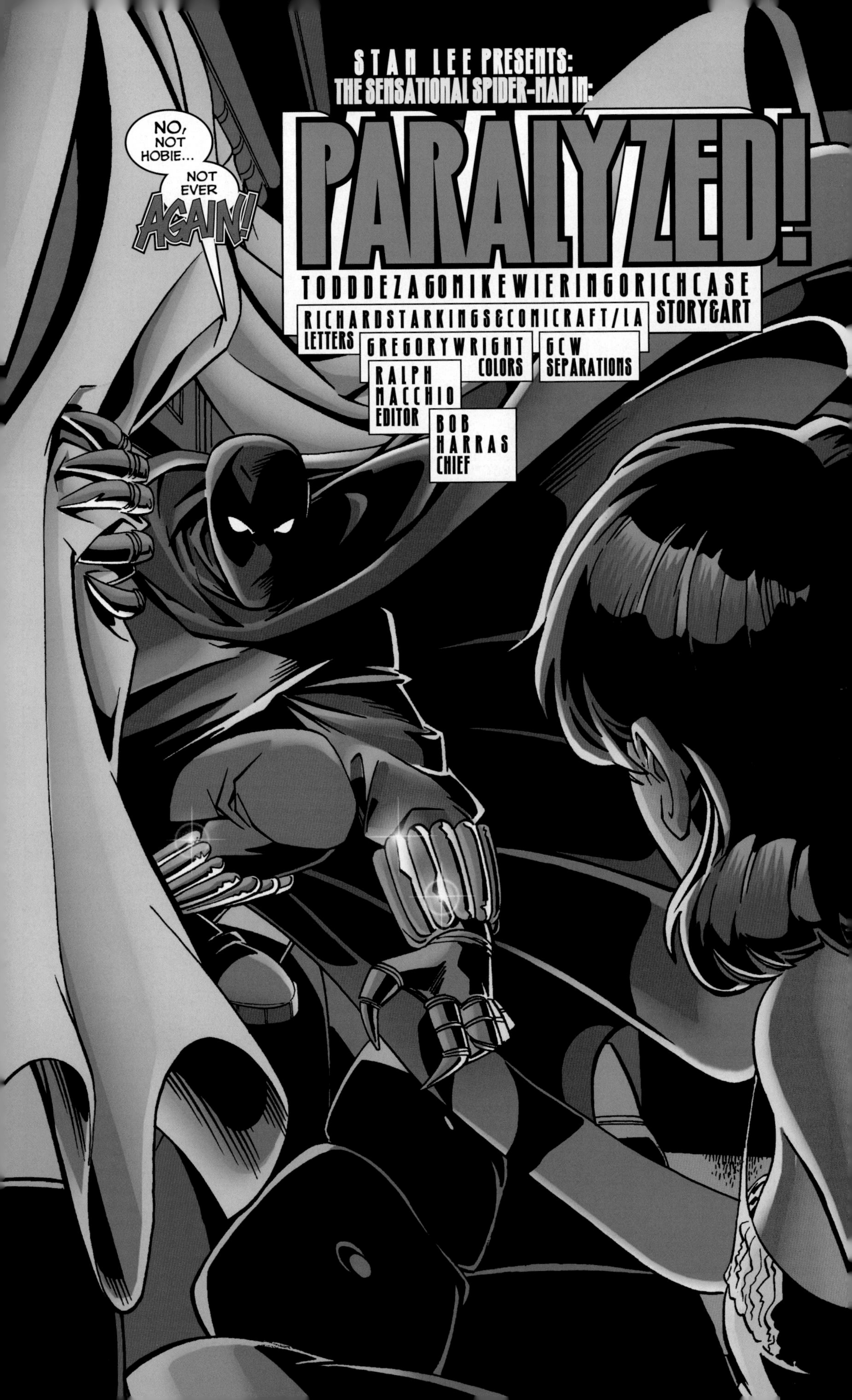
STAN LEE PRESENTS:
THE SENSATIONAL SPIDER-MAN IN:
NO, NOT HOBIE...
NOT EVER AGAIN!
PARALYZED!
TODDDEZAGOMIKEWIERINGORICHCASE STORY&ART
RICHARDSTARKINGS&COMICRAFT/LA LETTERS
GREGORYWRIGHT COLORS
GCW SEPARATIONS
RALPH MACCHIO EDITOR
BOB HARRAS CHIEF

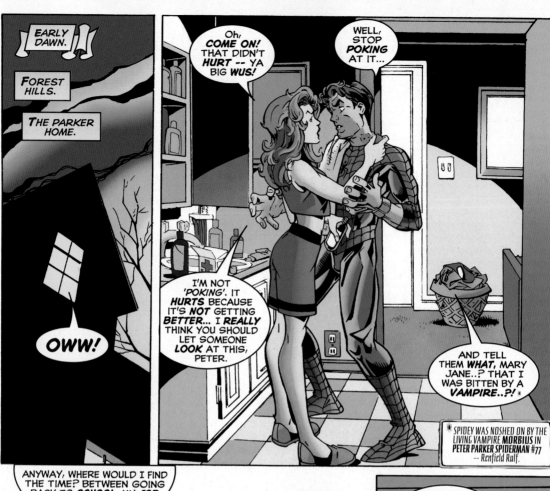

EARLY DAWN.

FOREST HILLS.

THE PARKER HOME.

OWW!

Oh, **COME ON!** THAT DIDN'T **HURT** -- YA BIG **WUS!**

WELL, STOP **POKING** AT IT...

I'M NOT 'POKING'. IT **HURTS** BECAUSE IT'S **NOT** GETTING **BETTER**... I **REALLY** THINK YOU SHOULD LET SOMEONE **LOOK** AT THIS, PETER.

AND TELL THEM **WHAT**, MARY JANE..? THAT I WAS BITTEN BY A **VAMPIRE**..?!

* SPIDEY WAS NOSHED ON BY THE LIVING VAMPIRE **MORBIUS** IN *PETER PARKER SPIDERMAN* #77 -- *Renfield Ralf.*

ANYWAY, WHERE WOULD I FIND THE TIME? BETWEEN GOING BACK TO **SCHOOL**, MY **JOB** DOWN AT THE **DAILY BUGLE** --

-- NOT TO MENTION **WACKOS** LIKE THE **CHAMELEON**, THE **ROSE**, AND **DELILAH** COMING AFTER ME WITHOUT AN **APPOINTMENT**...

* SEE CURRENT ISSUES OF **AMAZING** AND **SPECTACULAR** -- *Receptionist Ralf.*

I BARELY HAVE TIME TO **REFILL** MY **WEB-SHOOTERS!** BESIDES, IF THERE **WAS** ANYTHING TO **MORBIUS'** BITE --

-- I'M **SURE** THAT MY OWN **RADIOACTIVE BLOOD** MUST'VE **NEUTRALIZED** IT BY NOW!

Oh, **DENIAL'S** A GOOD **SIGN**... HOLD STILL --

3

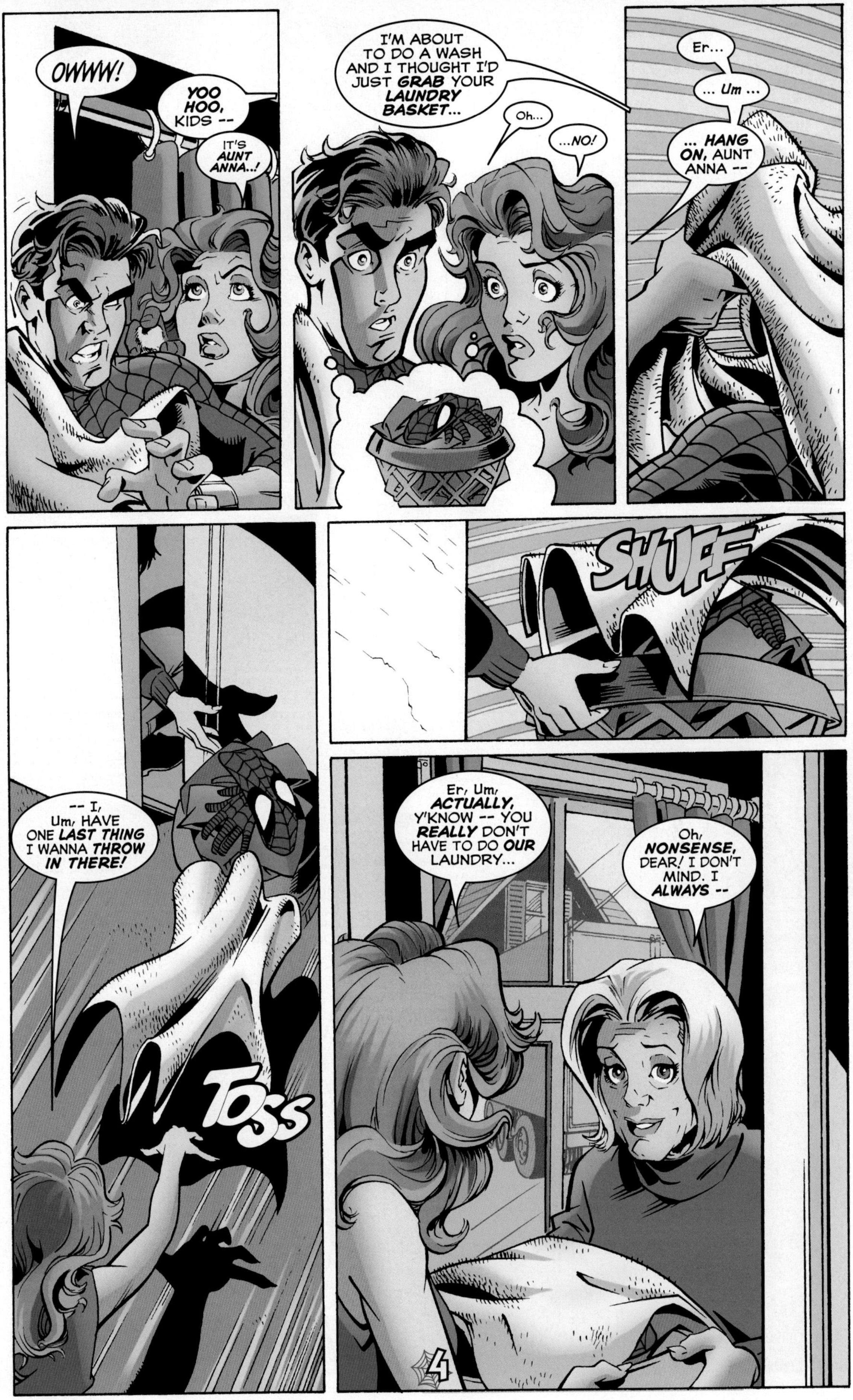
OWWW!
YOO HOO, KIDS --
IT'S AUNT ANNA..!
I'M ABOUT TO DO A WASH AND I THOUGHT I'D JUST GRAB YOUR LAUNDRY BASKET...
Oh...
...NO!
Er...
... Um ...
... HANG ON, AUNT ANNA --
SHUFF
-- I, Um, HAVE ONE LAST THING I WANNA THROW IN THERE!
TOSS
Er, Um, ACTUALLY, Y'KNOW -- YOU REALLY DON'T HAVE TO DO OUR LAUNDRY...
Oh, NONSENSE, DEAR! I DON'T MIND. I ALWAYS --
4

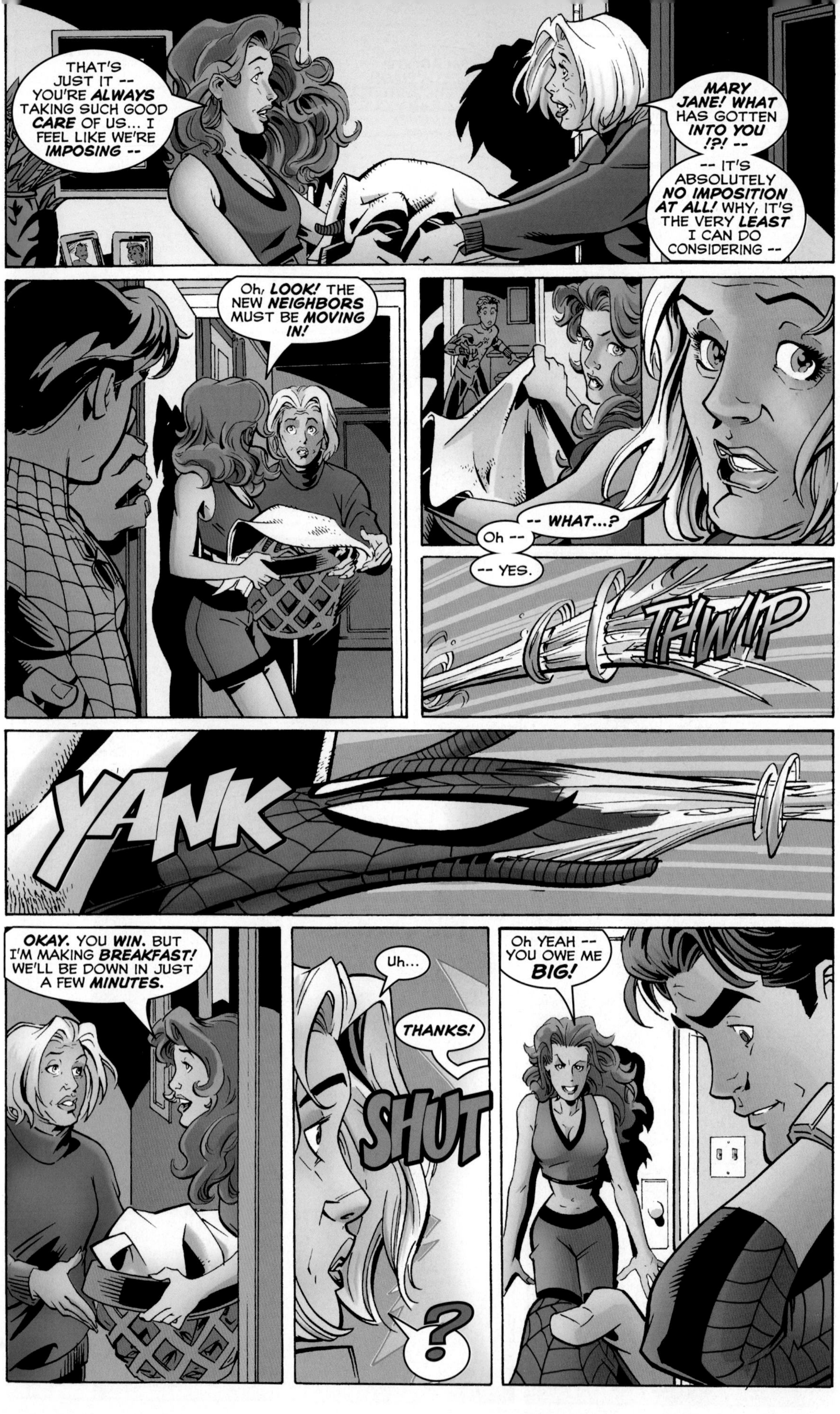
THAT'S JUST IT -- YOU'RE ALWAYS TAKING SUCH GOOD CARE OF US... I FEEL LIKE WE'RE IMPOSING --
MARY JANE! WHAT HAS GOTTEN INTO YOU !?! --
-- IT'S ABSOLUTELY NO IMPOSITION AT ALL! WHY, IT'S THE VERY LEAST I CAN DO CONSIDERING --
Oh, LOOK! THE NEW NEIGHBORS MUST BE MOVING IN!
-- WHAT...?
Oh --
-- YES.
THWIP
YANK
OKAY. YOU WIN. BUT I'M MAKING BREAKFAST! WE'LL BE DOWN IN JUST A FEW MINUTES.
Uh...
THANKS!
SHUT
?
Oh YEAH -- YOU OWE ME BIG!

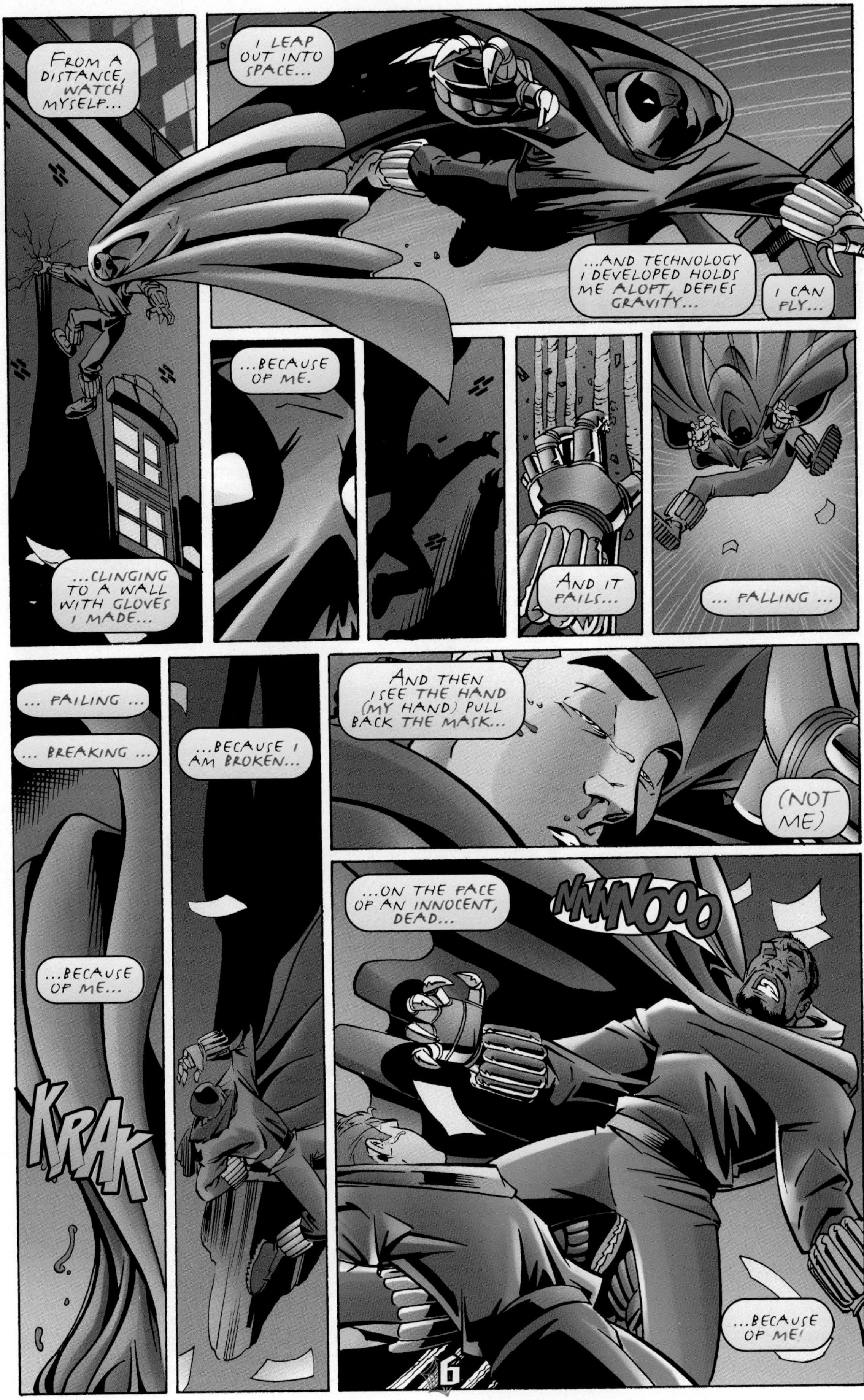
FROM A DISTANCE, WATCH MYSELF...
...CLINGING TO A WALL WITH GLOVES I MADE...
I LEAP OUT INTO SPACE...
...AND TECHNOLOGY I DEVELOPED HOLDS ME ALOFT, DEFIES GRAVITY...
I CAN FLY...
...BECAUSE OF ME.
AND IT FAILS...
... FALLING ...
... FAILING ...
... BREAKING ...
...BECAUSE OF ME...
KRAK
...BECAUSE I AM BROKEN...
AND THEN I SEE THE HAND (MY HAND) PULL BACK THE MASK...
(NOT ME)
...ON THE FACE OF AN INNOCENT, DEAD...
NNNNOOO
...BECAUSE OF ME!

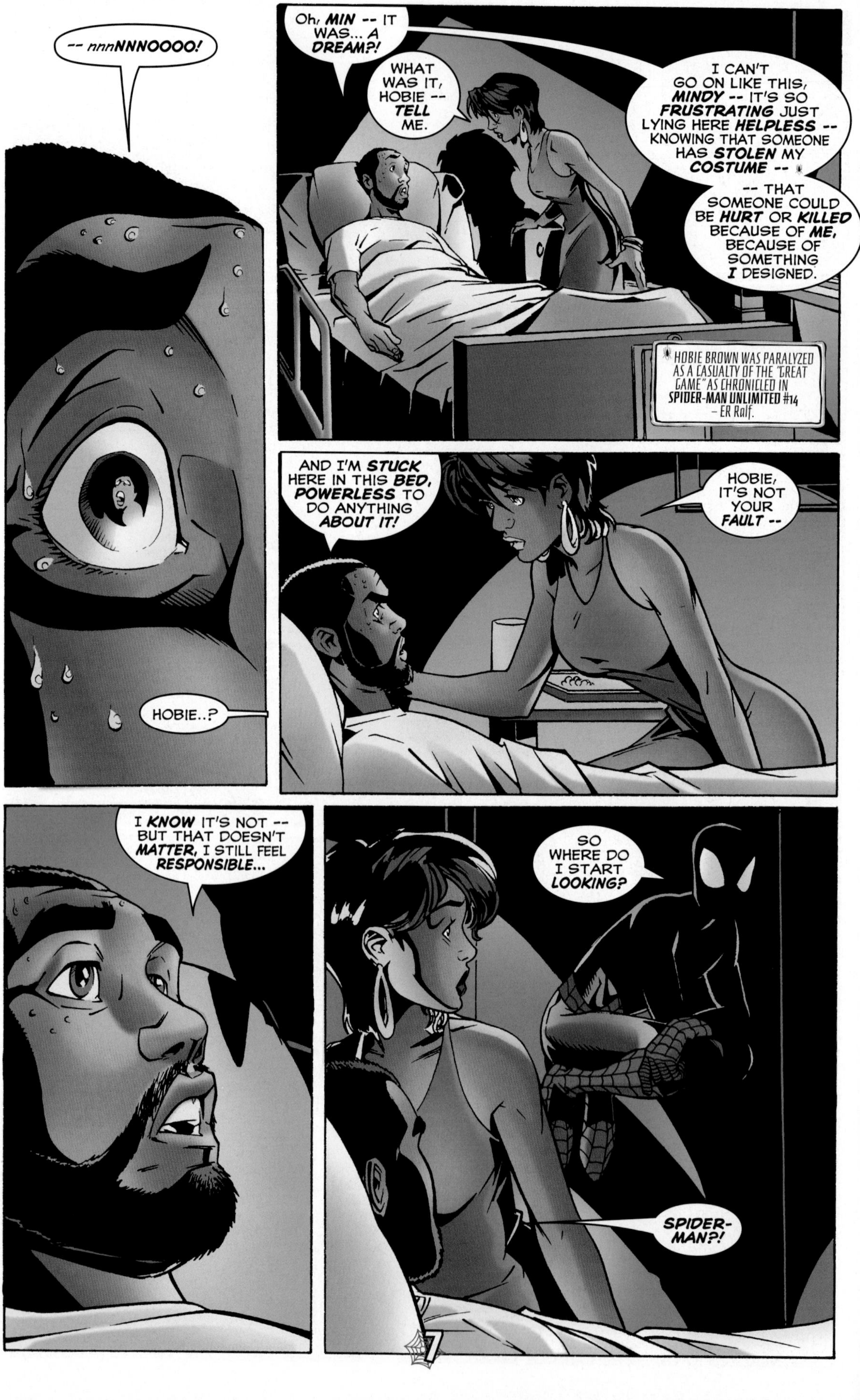
-- nnnNNNOOOO!
Oh, MIN -- IT WAS... A DREAM?!
WHAT WAS IT, HOBIE -- TELL ME.
I CAN'T GO ON LIKE THIS, MINDY -- IT'S SO FRUSTRATING JUST LYING HERE HELPLESS -- KNOWING THAT SOMEONE HAS STOLEN MY COSTUME --
-- THAT SOMEONE COULD BE HURT OR KILLED BECAUSE OF ME, BECAUSE OF SOMETHING I DESIGNED.
HOBIE BROWN WAS PARALYZED AS A CASUALTY OF THE "GREAT GAME" AS CHRONICLED IN SPIDER-MAN UNLIMITED #14 – ER Ralf.
HOBIE..?
AND I'M STUCK HERE IN THIS BED, POWERLESS TO DO ANYTHING ABOUT IT!
HOBIE, IT'S NOT YOUR FAULT --
I KNOW IT'S NOT -- BUT THAT DOESN'T MATTER, I STILL FEEL RESPONSIBLE...
SO WHERE DO I START LOOKING?
SPIDER-MAN?!
7

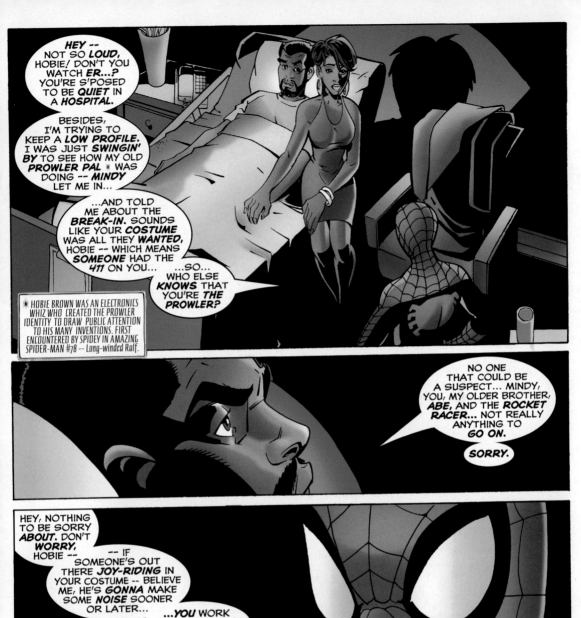

HEY -- NOT SO *LOUD*, HOBIE! DON'T YOU WATCH *ER...*? YOU'RE S'POSED TO BE *QUIET* IN A *HOSPITAL*.

BESIDES, I'M TRYING TO KEEP A *LOW PROFILE*. I WAS JUST *SWINGIN'* BY TO SEE HOW MY OLD *PROWLER PAL* ✱ WAS DOING -- MINDY LET ME IN...

...AND TOLD ME ABOUT THE *BREAK-IN.* SOUNDS LIKE YOUR *COSTUME* WAS ALL THEY *WANTED*, HOBIE -- WHICH MEANS *SOMEONE* HAD THE *411* ON YOU...

...SO... WHO ELSE *KNOWS* THAT YOU'RE *THE PROWLER*?

✱ HOBIE BROWN WAS AN ELECTRONICS WHIZ WHO CREATED THE PROWLER IDENTITY TO DRAW PUBLIC ATTENTION TO HIS MANY INVENTIONS. FIRST ENCOUNTERED BY SPIDEY IN *AMAZING SPIDER-MAN* #78 -- *Long-winded Ralf.*

NO ONE THAT COULD BE A SUSPECT... MINDY, YOU, MY OLDER BROTHER, *ABE*, AND THE *ROCKET RACER*... NOT REALLY ANYTHING TO *GO ON*.

SORRY.

HEY, NOTHING TO BE SORRY *ABOUT.* DON'T *WORRY*, HOBIE --

-- IF SOMEONE'S OUT THERE *JOY-RIDING* IN YOUR COSTUME -- BELIEVE ME, HE'S *GONNA* MAKE SOME *NOISE* SOONER OR LATER...

...*YOU* WORK ON GETTING *OUT* OF *THAT BED* --

-- AND LET ME CHASE AFTER OUR LITTLE *PROWLER WANNABE*..!

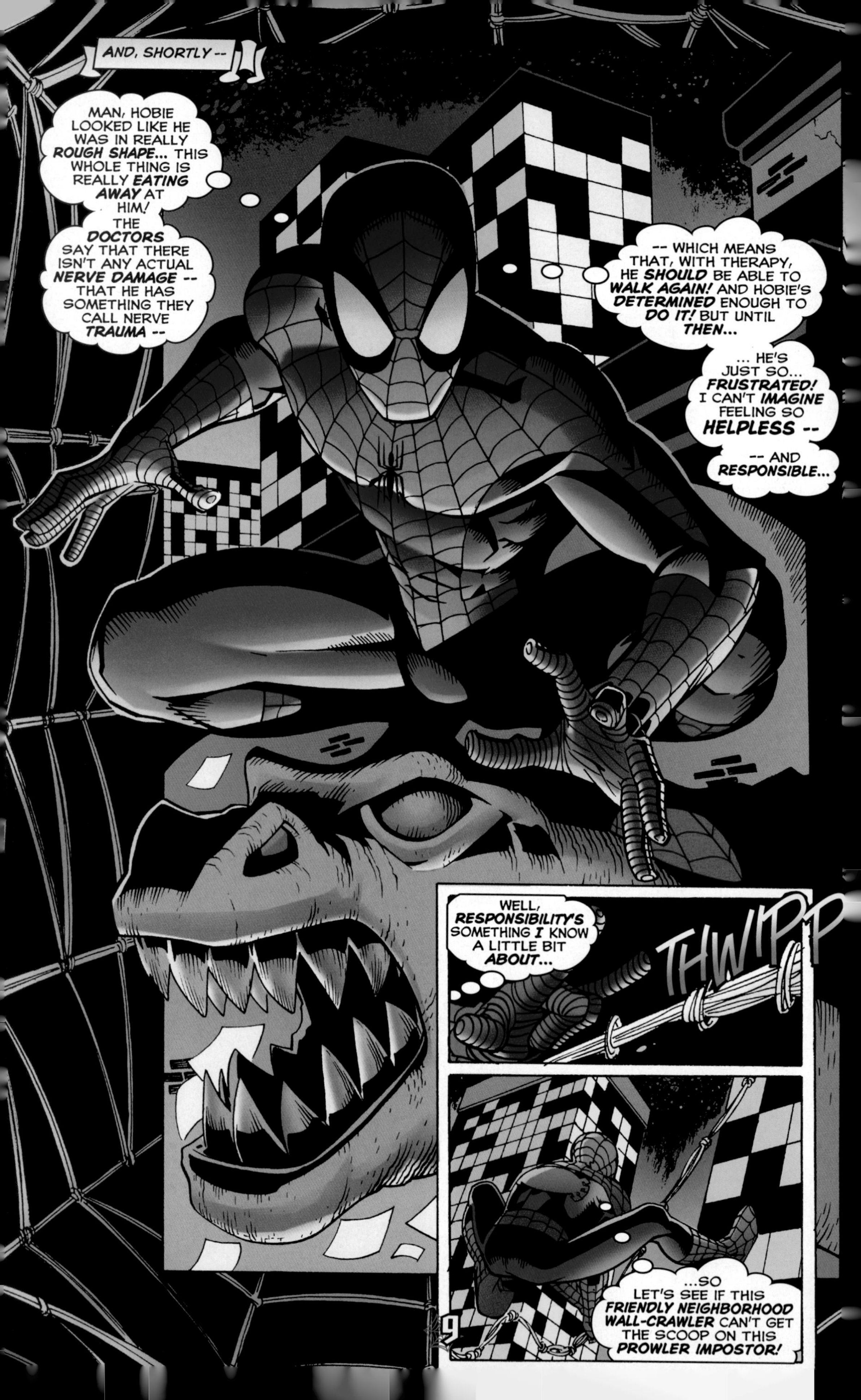
AND, SHORTLY --
MAN, HOBIE LOOKED LIKE HE WAS IN REALLY ROUGH SHAPE... THIS WHOLE THING IS REALLY EATING AWAY AT HIM!
THE DOCTORS SAY THAT THERE ISN'T ANY ACTUAL NERVE DAMAGE -- THAT HE HAS SOMETHING THEY CALL NERVE TRAUMA --
-- WHICH MEANS THAT, WITH THERAPY, HE SHOULD BE ABLE TO WALK AGAIN! AND HOBIE'S DETERMINED ENOUGH TO DO IT! BUT UNTIL THEN...
... HE'S JUST SO... FRUSTRATED! I CAN'T IMAGINE FEELING SO HELPLESS --
-- AND RESPONSIBLE...
WELL, RESPONSIBILITY'S SOMETHING I KNOW A LITTLE BIT ABOUT...
THWIPP
...SO LET'S SEE IF THIS FRIENDLY NEIGHBORHOOD WALL-CRAWLER CAN'T GET THE SCOOP ON THIS PROWLER IMPOSTOR!

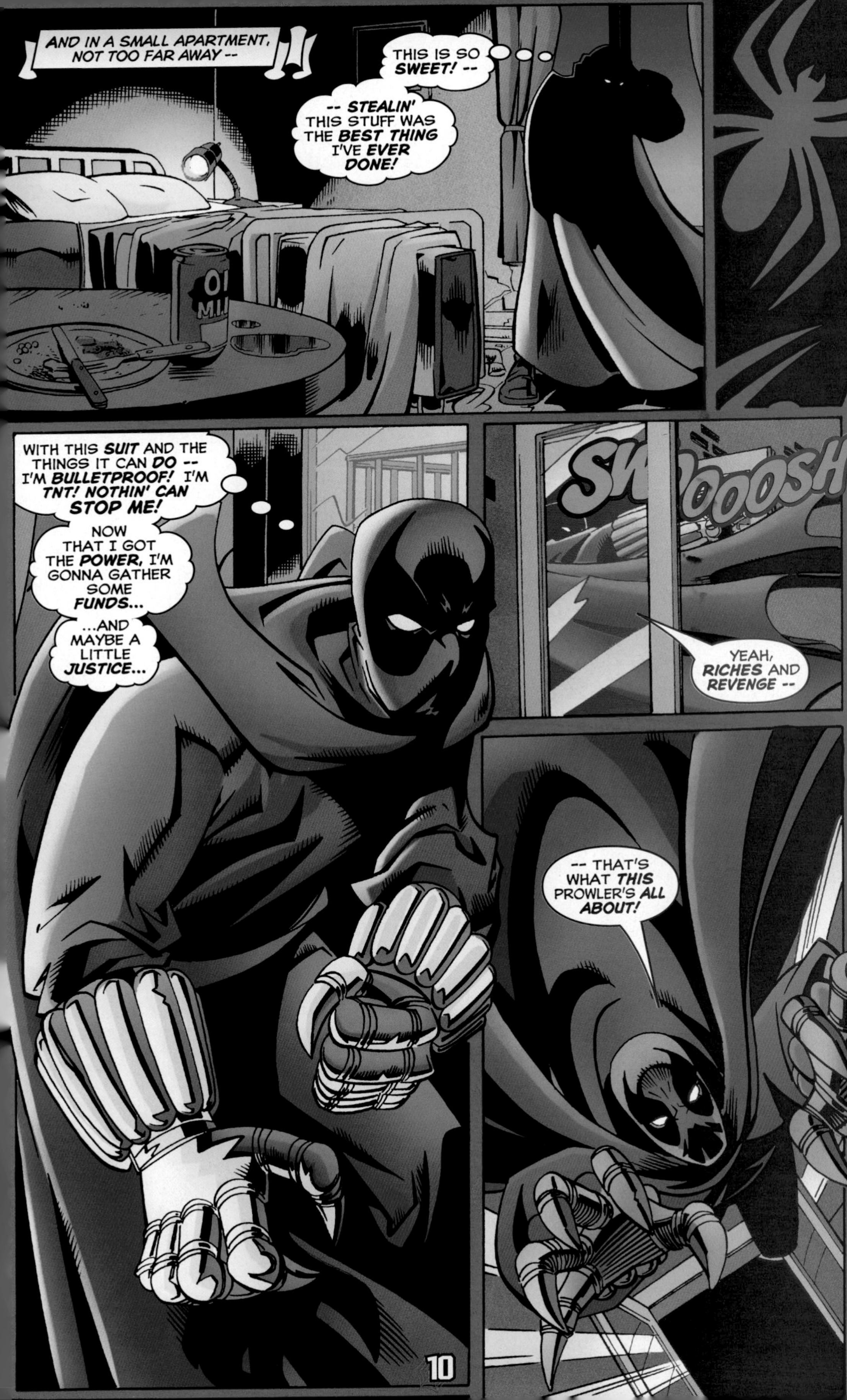
AND IN A SMALL APARTMENT, NOT TOO FAR AWAY --
THIS IS SO SWEET! --
-- STEALIN' THIS STUFF WAS THE BEST THING I'VE EVER DONE!
WITH THIS SUIT AND THE THINGS IT CAN DO -- I'M BULLETPROOF! I'M TNT! NOTHIN' CAN STOP ME!
NOW THAT I GOT THE POWER, I'M GONNA GATHER SOME FUNDS...
...AND MAYBE A LITTLE JUSTICE...
SWOOOOSH
YEAH, RICHES AND REVENGE --
-- THAT'S WHAT THIS PROWLER'S ALL ABOUT!

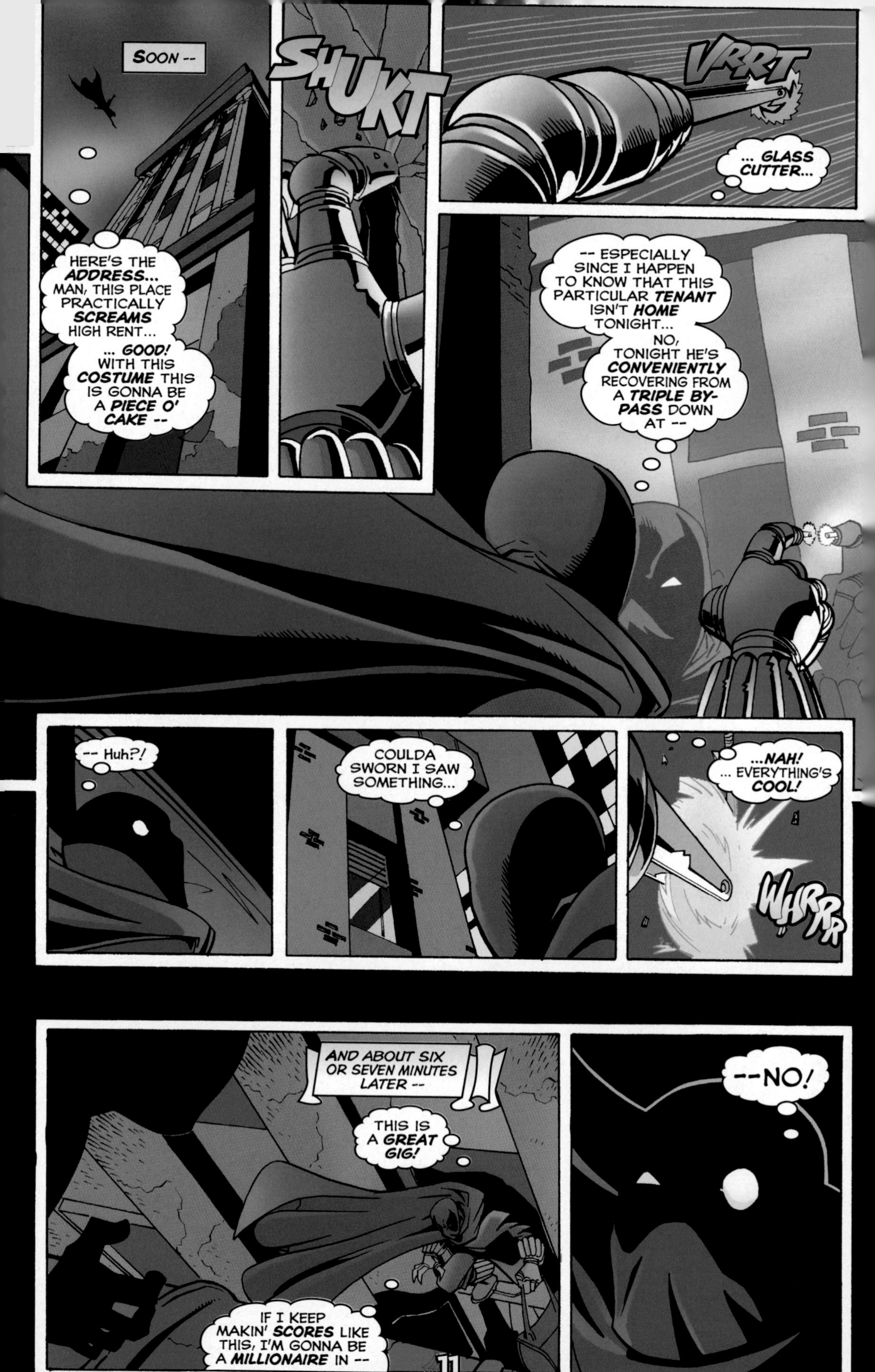
SOON --
HERE'S THE ADDRESS... MAN, THIS PLACE PRACTICALLY SCREAMS HIGH RENT...
... GOOD! WITH THIS COSTUME THIS IS GONNA BE A PIECE O' CAKE --
SHUKT
VRRT
... GLASS CUTTER...
-- ESPECIALLY SINCE I HAPPEN TO KNOW THAT THIS PARTICULAR TENANT ISN'T HOME TONIGHT...
NO, TONIGHT HE'S CONVENIENTLY RECOVERING FROM A TRIPLE BY-PASS DOWN AT --
-- Huh?!
COULDA SWORN I SAW SOMETHING...
...NAH! ... EVERYTHING'S COOL!
WHRRR
AND ABOUT SIX OR SEVEN MINUTES LATER --
THIS IS A GREAT GIG!
IF I KEEP MAKIN' SCORES LIKE THIS, I'M GONNA BE A MILLIONAIRE IN --
--NO!

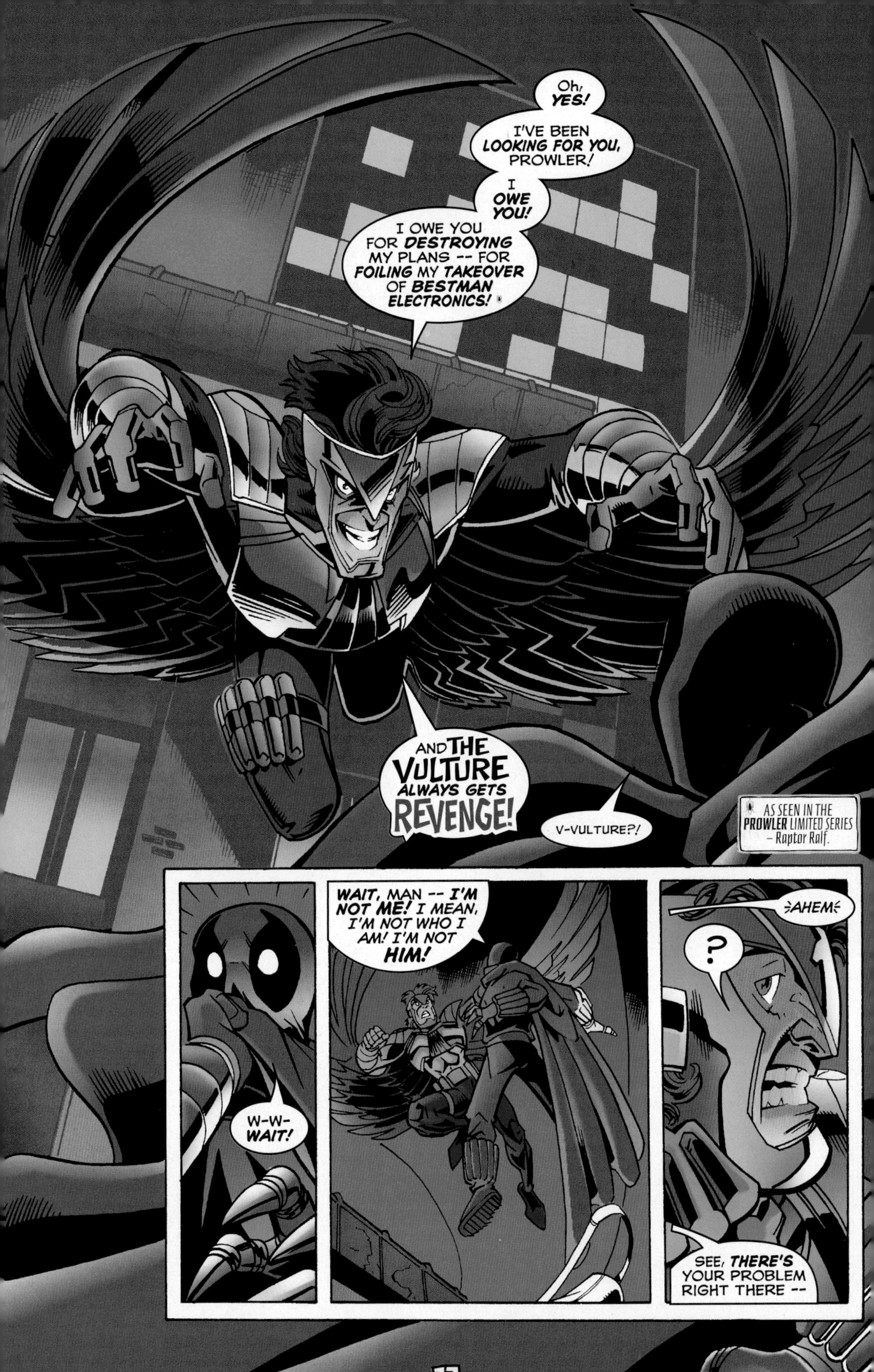

Oh, YES!
I'VE BEEN LOOKING FOR YOU, PROWLER!
I OWE YOU!
I OWE YOU FOR DESTROYING MY PLANS -- FOR FOILING MY TAKEOVER OF BESTMAN ELECTRONICS!
AND THE VULTURE ALWAYS GETS REVENGE!
V-VULTURE?!
AS SEEN IN THE PROWLER LIMITED SERIES – Raptor Ralf.
W-W-WAIT!
WAIT, MAN -- I'M NOT ME! I MEAN, I'M NOT WHO I AM! I'M NOT HIM!
AHEM
?
SEE, THERE'S YOUR PROBLEM RIGHT THERE --

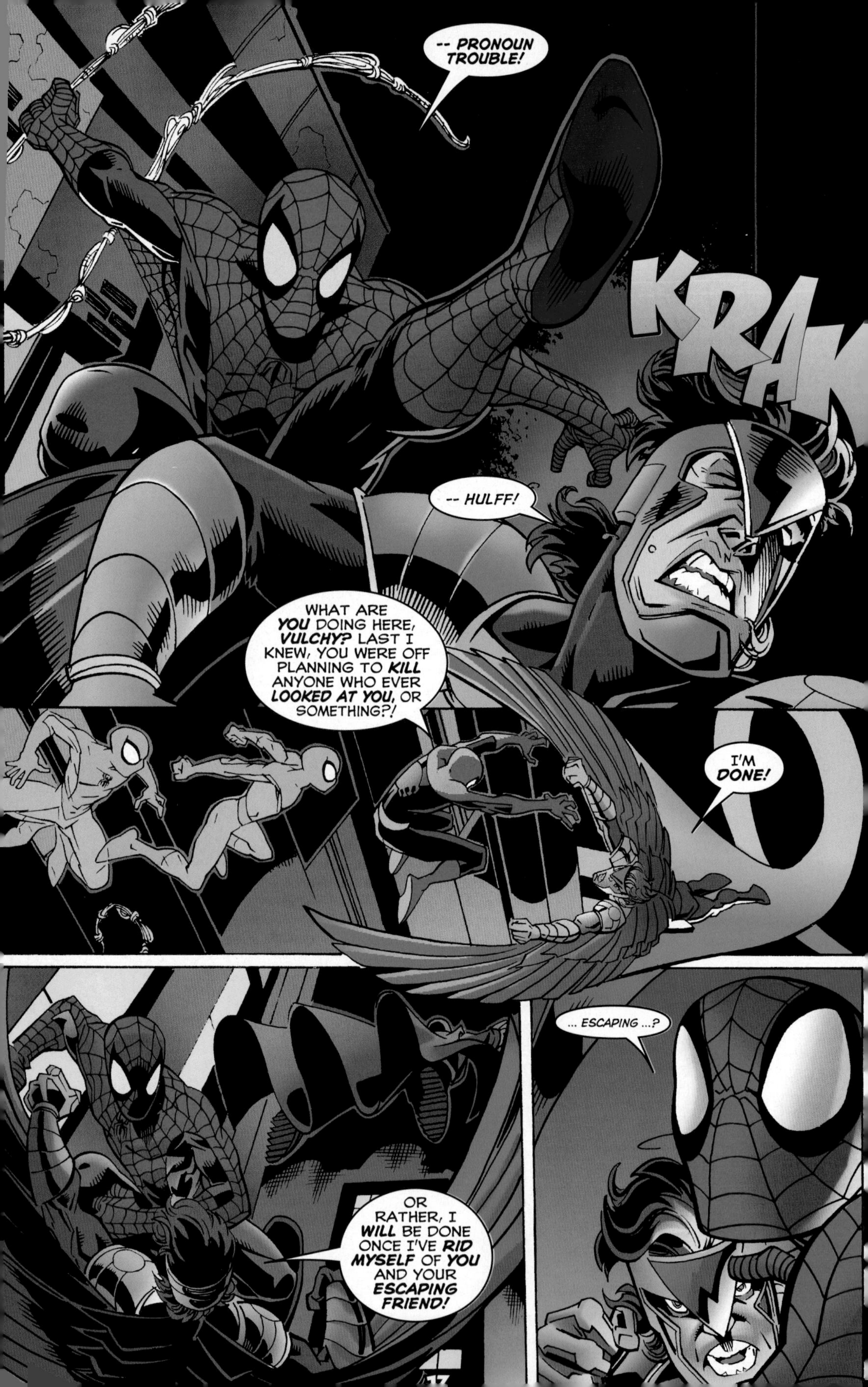
-- PRONOUN TROUBLE!
KRAK
-- HULFF!
WHAT ARE YOU DOING HERE, VULCHY? LAST I KNEW, YOU WERE OFF PLANNING TO KILL ANYONE WHO EVER LOOKED AT YOU, OR SOMETHING?!
I'M DONE!
OR RATHER, I WILL BE DONE ONCE I'VE RID MYSELF OF YOU AND YOUR ESCAPING FRIEND!
... ESCAPING ...?

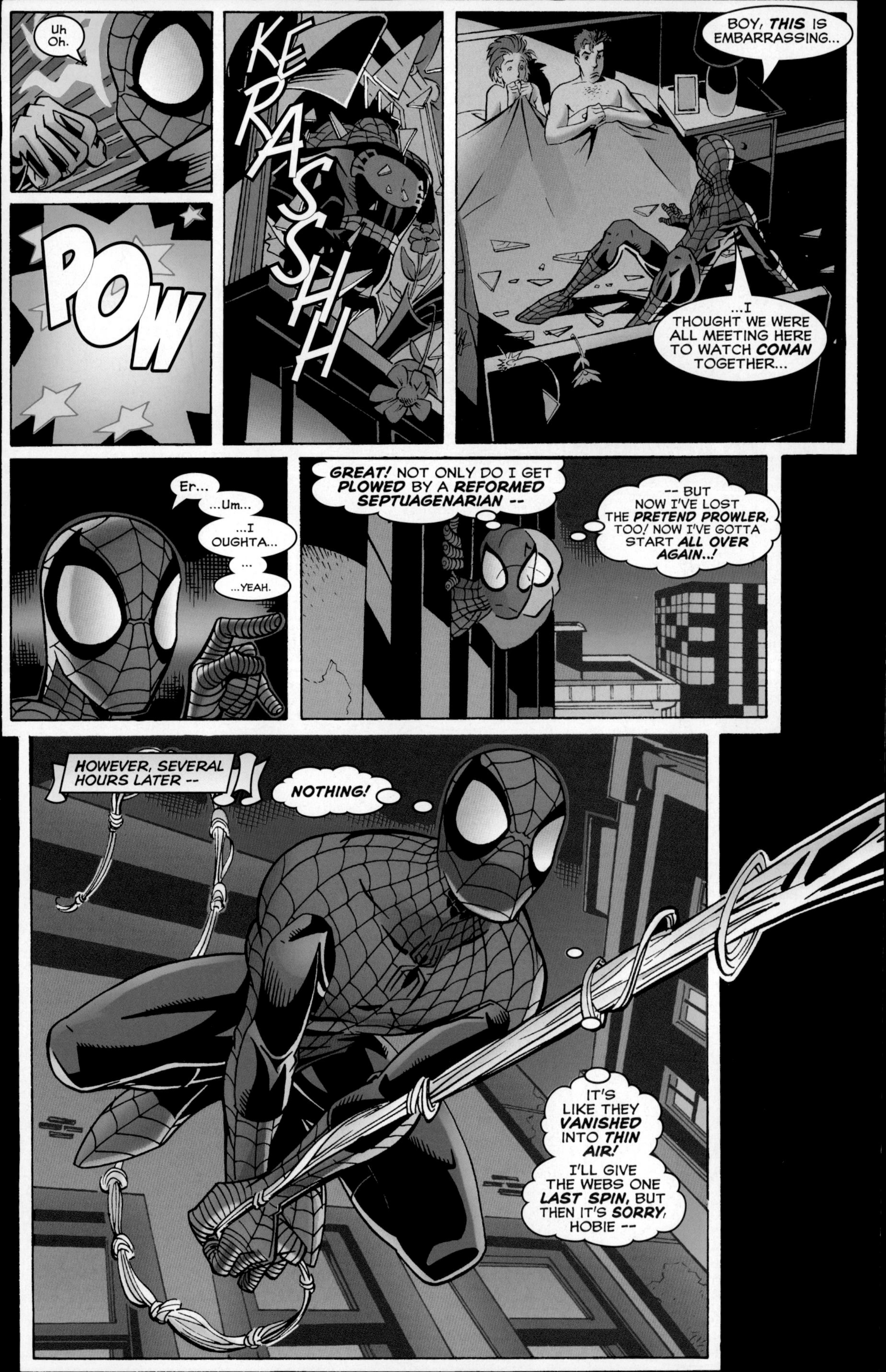
Uh Oh.
KERASHH
POW
BOY, THIS IS EMBARRASSING...
...I THOUGHT WE WERE ALL MEETING HERE TO WATCH CONAN TOGETHER...
Er...
...Um...
...I OUGHTA...
...
...YEAH.
GREAT! NOT ONLY DO I GET PLOWED BY A REFORMED SEPTUAGENARIAN --
-- BUT NOW I'VE LOST THE PRETEND PROWLER, TOO! NOW I'VE GOTTA START ALL OVER AGAIN..!
HOWEVER, SEVERAL HOURS LATER --
NOTHING!
IT'S LIKE THEY VANISHED INTO THIN AIR!
I'LL GIVE THE WEBS ONE LAST SPIN, BUT THEN IT'S SORRY, HOBIE --

"-- BUT *THIS* LITTLE SPIDER HAS TO GO TO *WORK* IN THE MORNING.!"

I WENT ALL THE WAY TO THE *SAVAGE LAND* FOR PAGE *17?!*

U N REPOR...AGE LAND OUT OF DANGER

PAGE 17?!

YOUR *POINT?*

I BROUGHT BACK *ALL THOSE* PHOTOS -- COLOR, BECAUSE YOU WERE GONNA RUN THEM IN THE SUNDAY 'MAGAZINE' --

-- NOT TO MENTION THE *STORY!* ROXXON WAS PURPOSELY *FLOODING* THE PLACE FOR THE *OIL!*

IT WAS *ENVIRONMENTAL SABOTAGE,* JONAH --

-- AND YOU RUN ONE LITTLE PHOTO ALONG- SIDE THE *U.N.'S* 'OFFICIAL' COVER-UP' STATEMENT"..?

* SEE LAST ISSUE -- J Jonah Ralf.

WHAT DO *YOU* CARE?! YOU GOT *PAID!*

BESIDES, MOST OF OUR READERS DON'T EVEN *BELIEVE* IN THE SAVAGE LAND!

THEY THINK IT'S A MYTH..! LIKE *BIGFOOT...* AND *ELVIS!*

ROXXON'S *CORRUPT,* JONAH! AND *YOU'RE* BUYING THE *WHITEWASH* IF --

PROOF! YOU'RE A GOOD *PHOTOGRAPHER,* PARKER.! BUT A LOUSY *REPORTER..!* YOU NEED *PROOF* TO RUN A STORY LIKE *THAT!*

THIS IS A *REPORTER,* PETER PARKER --BILLY WALTERS --

BILLY'S GOING TO BE A NEW *FREELANCE REPORTER* FOR THE *BUGLE,* PETER...

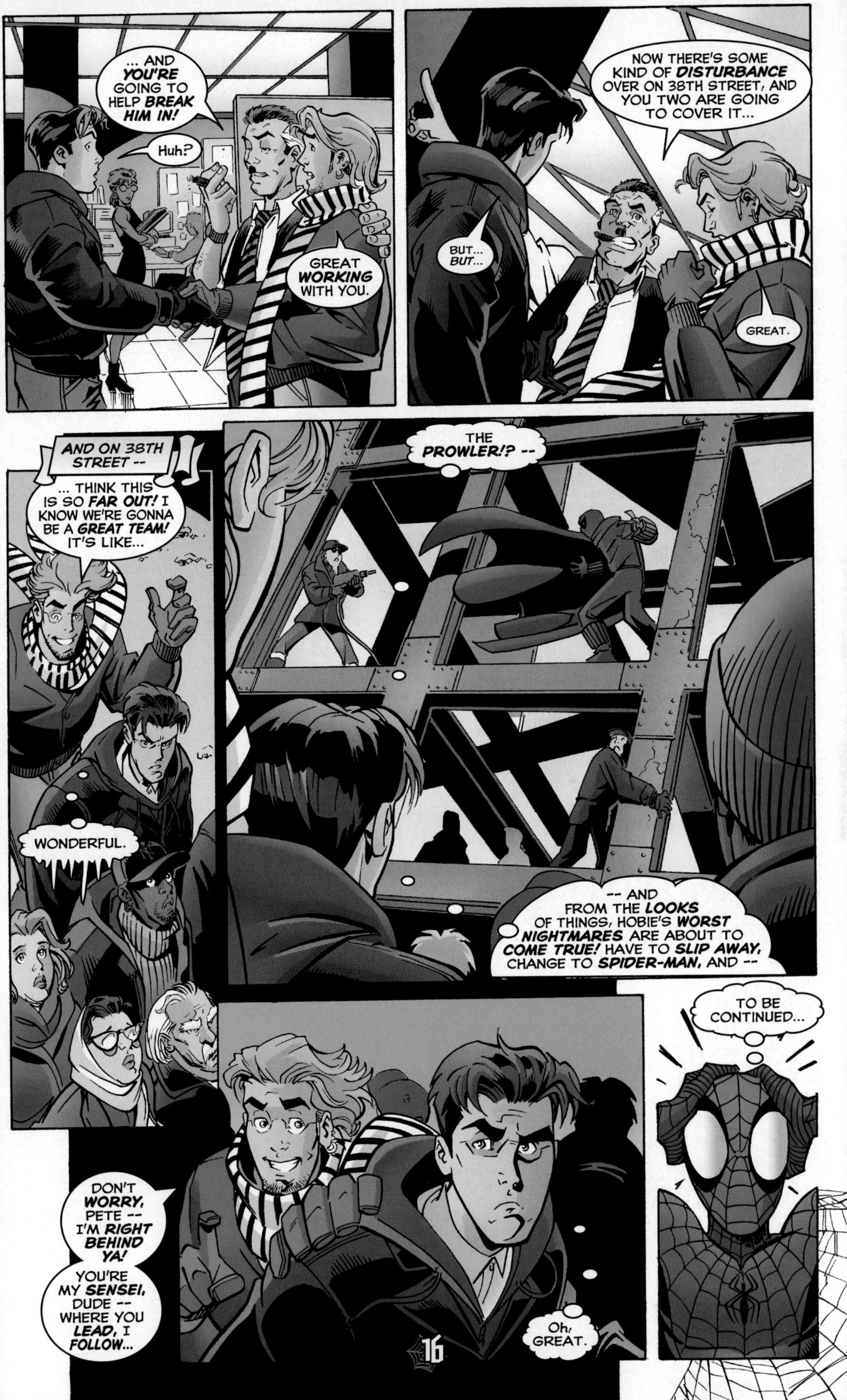
... AND YOU'RE GOING TO HELP BREAK HIM IN!
Huh?
GREAT WORKING WITH YOU.
NOW THERE'S SOME KIND OF DISTURBANCE OVER ON 38TH STREET, AND YOU TWO ARE GOING TO COVER IT...
BUT... BUT...
GREAT.
AND ON 38TH STREET --
... THINK THIS IS SO FAR OUT! I KNOW WE'RE GONNA BE A GREAT TEAM! IT'S LIKE...
WONDERFUL.
THE PROWLER!? --
-- AND FROM THE LOOKS OF THINGS, HOBIE'S WORST NIGHTMARES ARE ABOUT TO COME TRUE! HAVE TO SLIP AWAY, CHANGE TO SPIDER-MAN, AND --
DON'T WORRY, PETE -- I'M RIGHT BEHIND YA!
YOU'RE MY SENSEI, DUDE -- WHERE YOU LEAD, I FOLLOW...
Oh, GREAT.
TO BE CONTINUED...

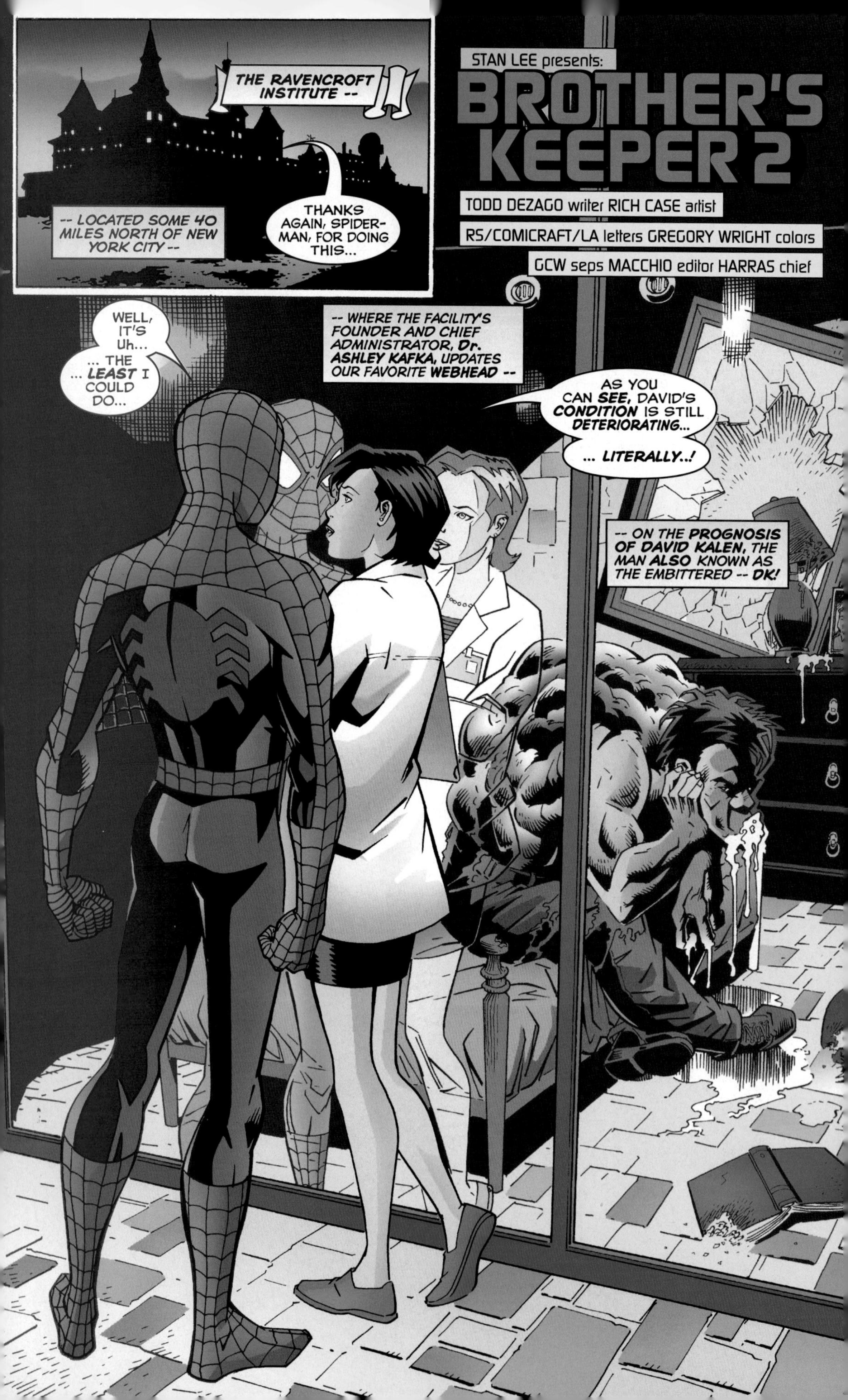
THE RAVENCROFT INSTITUTE --
-- LOCATED SOME 40 MILES NORTH OF NEW YORK CITY --
THANKS AGAIN, SPIDER-MAN, FOR DOING THIS...
STAN LEE presents:
BROTHER'S KEEPER 2
TODD DEZAGO writer RICH CASE artist
RS/COMICRAFT/LA letters GREGORY WRIGHT colors
GCW seps MACCHIO editor HARRAS chief
WELL, IT'S Uh... ... THE ... LEAST I COULD DO...
-- WHERE THE FACILITY'S FOUNDER AND CHIEF ADMINISTRATOR, Dr. ASHLEY KAFKA, UPDATES OUR FAVORITE WEBHEAD --
AS YOU CAN SEE, DAVID'S CONDITION IS STILL DETERIORATING...
... LITERALLY..!
-- ON THE PROGNOSIS OF DAVID KALEN, THE MAN ALSO KNOWN AS THE EMBITTERED -- DK!

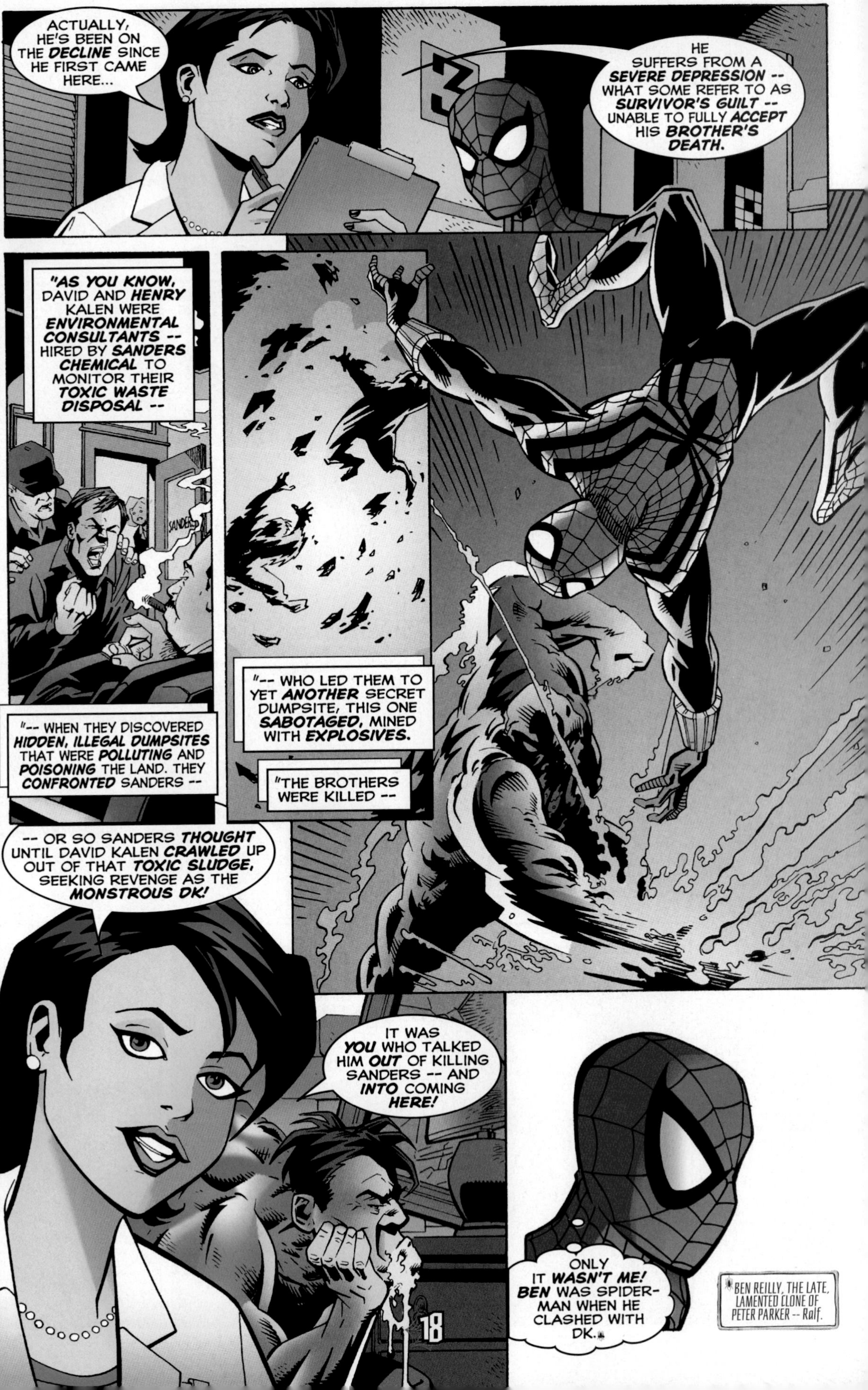
ACTUALLY, HE'S BEEN ON THE DECLINE SINCE HE FIRST CAME HERE...
HE SUFFERS FROM A SEVERE DEPRESSION -- WHAT SOME REFER TO AS SURVIVOR'S GUILT -- UNABLE TO FULLY ACCEPT HIS BROTHER'S DEATH.
"AS YOU KNOW, DAVID AND HENRY KALEN WERE ENVIRONMENTAL CONSULTANTS -- HIRED BY SANDERS CHEMICAL TO MONITOR THEIR TOXIC WASTE DISPOSAL --
"-- WHEN THEY DISCOVERED HIDDEN, ILLEGAL DUMPSITES THAT WERE POLLUTING AND POISONING THE LAND. THEY CONFRONTED SANDERS --
"-- WHO LED THEM TO YET ANOTHER SECRET DUMPSITE, THIS ONE SABOTAGED, MINED WITH EXPLOSIVES.
"THE BROTHERS WERE KILLED --
-- OR SO SANDERS THOUGHT UNTIL DAVID KALEN CRAWLED UP OUT OF THAT TOXIC SLUDGE, SEEKING REVENGE AS THE MONSTROUS DK!
IT WAS YOU WHO TALKED HIM OUT OF KILLING SANDERS -- AND INTO COMING HERE!
ONLY IT WASN'T ME! BEN WAS SPIDER-MAN WHEN HE CLASHED WITH DK.*
*BEN REILLY, THE LATE, LAMENTED CLONE OF PETER PARKER -- Ralf.

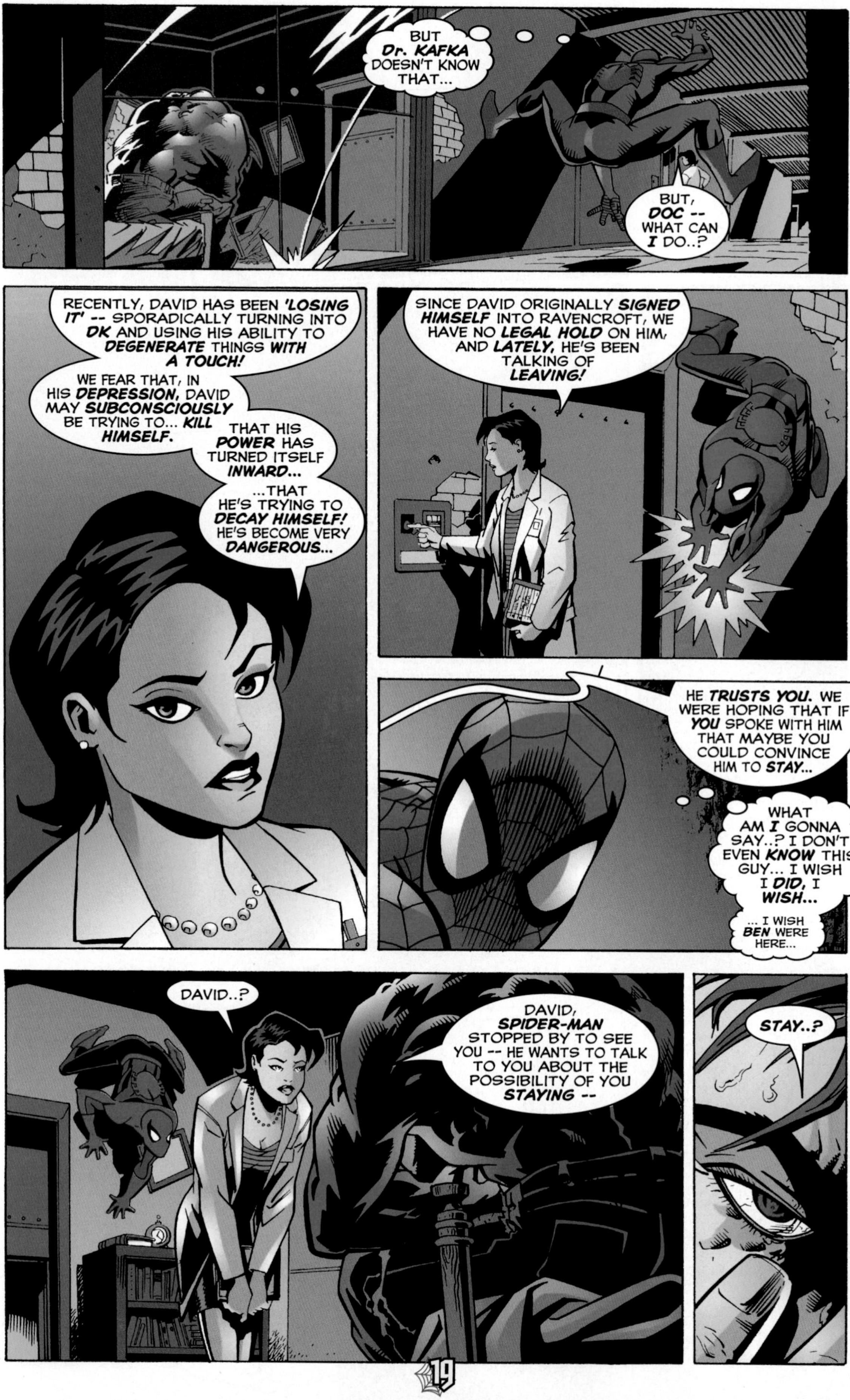

BUT Dr. KAFKA DOESN'T KNOW THAT...
BUT, DOC -- WHAT CAN I DO..?
RECENTLY, DAVID HAS BEEN 'LOSING IT' -- SPORADICALLY TURNING INTO DK AND USING HIS ABILITY TO DEGENERATE THINGS WITH A TOUCH!
WE FEAR THAT, IN HIS DEPRESSION, DAVID MAY SUBCONSCIOUSLY BE TRYING TO... KILL HIMSELF.
THAT HIS POWER HAS TURNED ITSELF INWARD...
...THAT HE'S TRYING TO DECAY HIMSELF! HE'S BECOME VERY DANGEROUS...
SINCE DAVID ORIGINALLY SIGNED HIMSELF INTO RAVENCROFT, WE HAVE NO LEGAL HOLD ON HIM, AND LATELY, HE'S BEEN TALKING OF LEAVING!
HE TRUSTS YOU. WE WERE HOPING THAT IF YOU SPOKE WITH HIM THAT MAYBE YOU COULD CONVINCE HIM TO STAY...
WHAT AM I GONNA SAY..? I DON'T EVEN KNOW THIS GUY... I WISH I DID, I WISH...
... I WISH BEN WERE HERE...
DAVID..?
DAVID, SPIDER-MAN STOPPED BY TO SEE YOU -- HE WANTS TO TALK TO YOU ABOUT THE POSSIBILITY OF YOU STAYING --
STAY..?

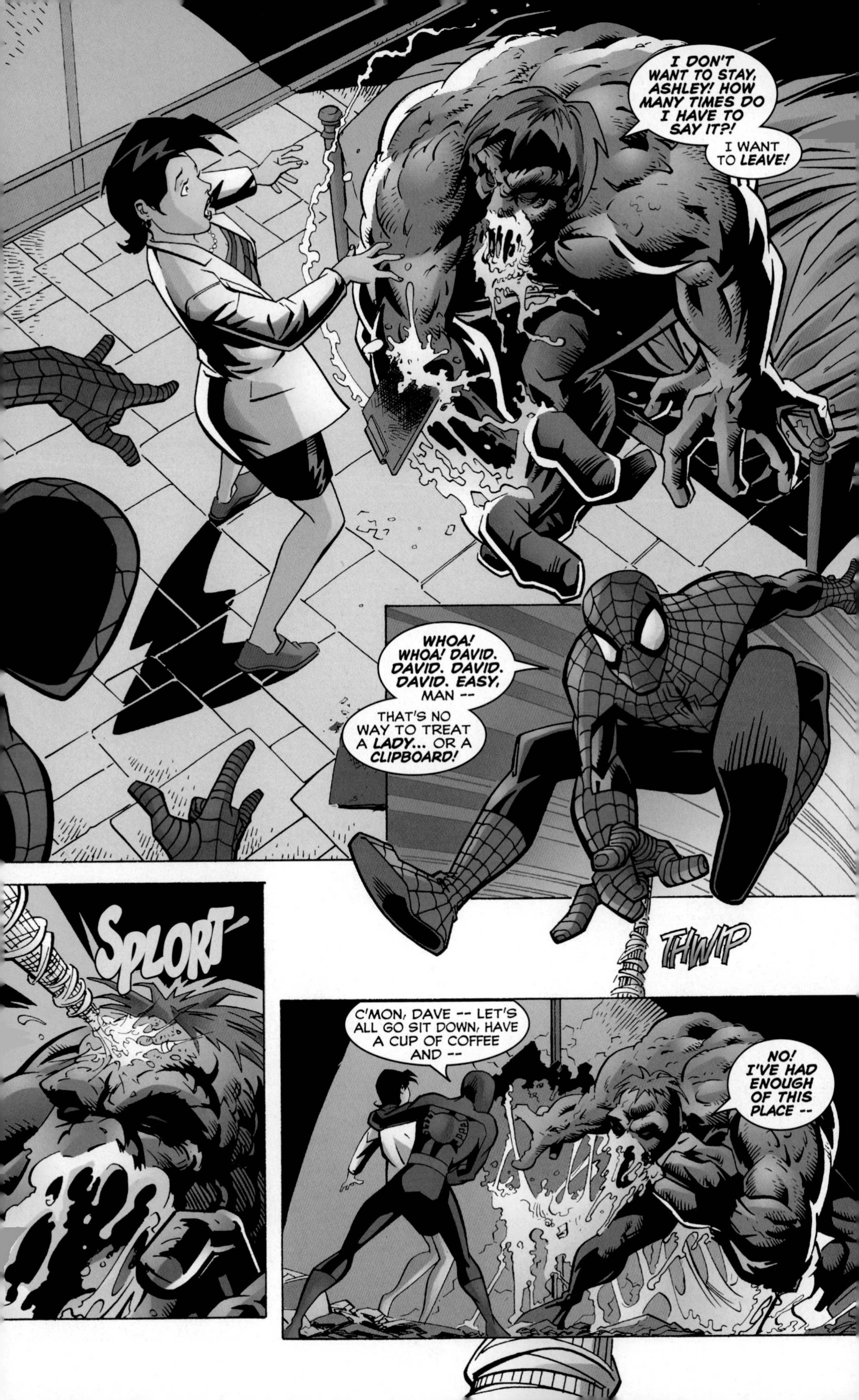
I DON'T WANT TO STAY, ASHLEY! HOW MANY TIMES DO I HAVE TO SAY IT?!
I WANT TO LEAVE!
WHOA! WHOA! DAVID. DAVID. DAVID. DAVID. EASY, MAN --
THAT'S NO WAY TO TREAT A LADY... OR A CLIPBOARD!
THWIP
SPLORT
C'MON, DAVE -- LET'S ALL GO SIT DOWN, HAVE A CUP OF COFFEE AND --
NO! I'VE HAD ENOUGH OF THIS PLACE --

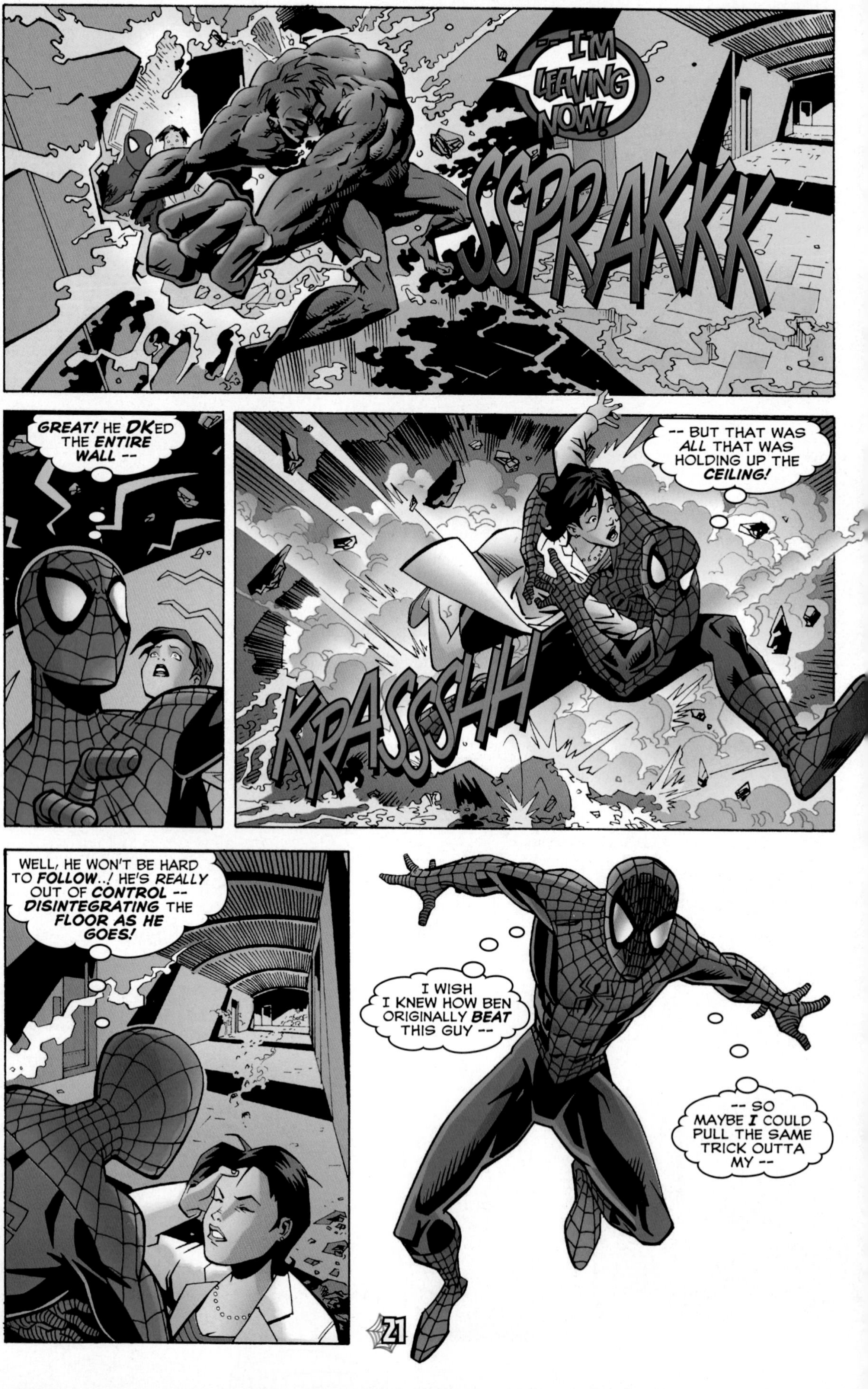
--I'M LEAVING NOW!
SSPRAKKK
GREAT! HE DKED THE ENTIRE WALL --
-- BUT THAT WAS ALL THAT WAS HOLDING UP THE CEILING!
KRASSSHH
WELL, HE WON'T BE HARD TO FOLLOW..! HE'S REALLY OUT OF CONTROL -- DISINTEGRATING THE FLOOR AS HE GOES!
I WISH I KNEW HOW BEN ORIGINALLY BEAT THIS GUY --
-- SO MAYBE I COULD PULL THE SAME TRICK OUTTA MY --

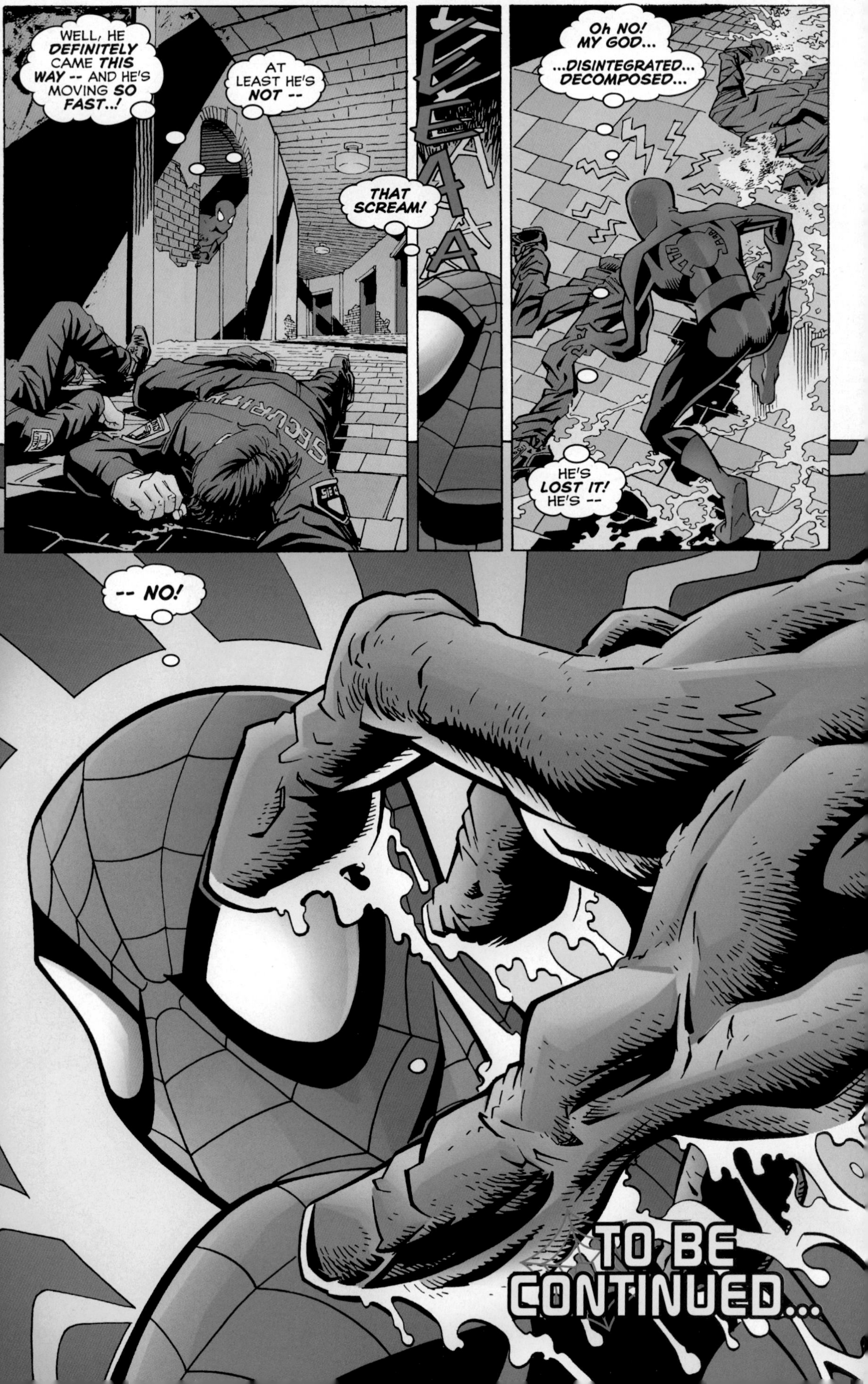
WELL, HE DEFINITELY CAME THIS WAY -- AND HE'S MOVING SO FAST..!
AT LEAST HE'S NOT --
THAT SCREAM!
Oh NO! MY GOD...
...DISINTEGRATED... DECOMPOSED...
HE'S LOST IT! HE'S --
-- NO!
TO BE CONTINUED...

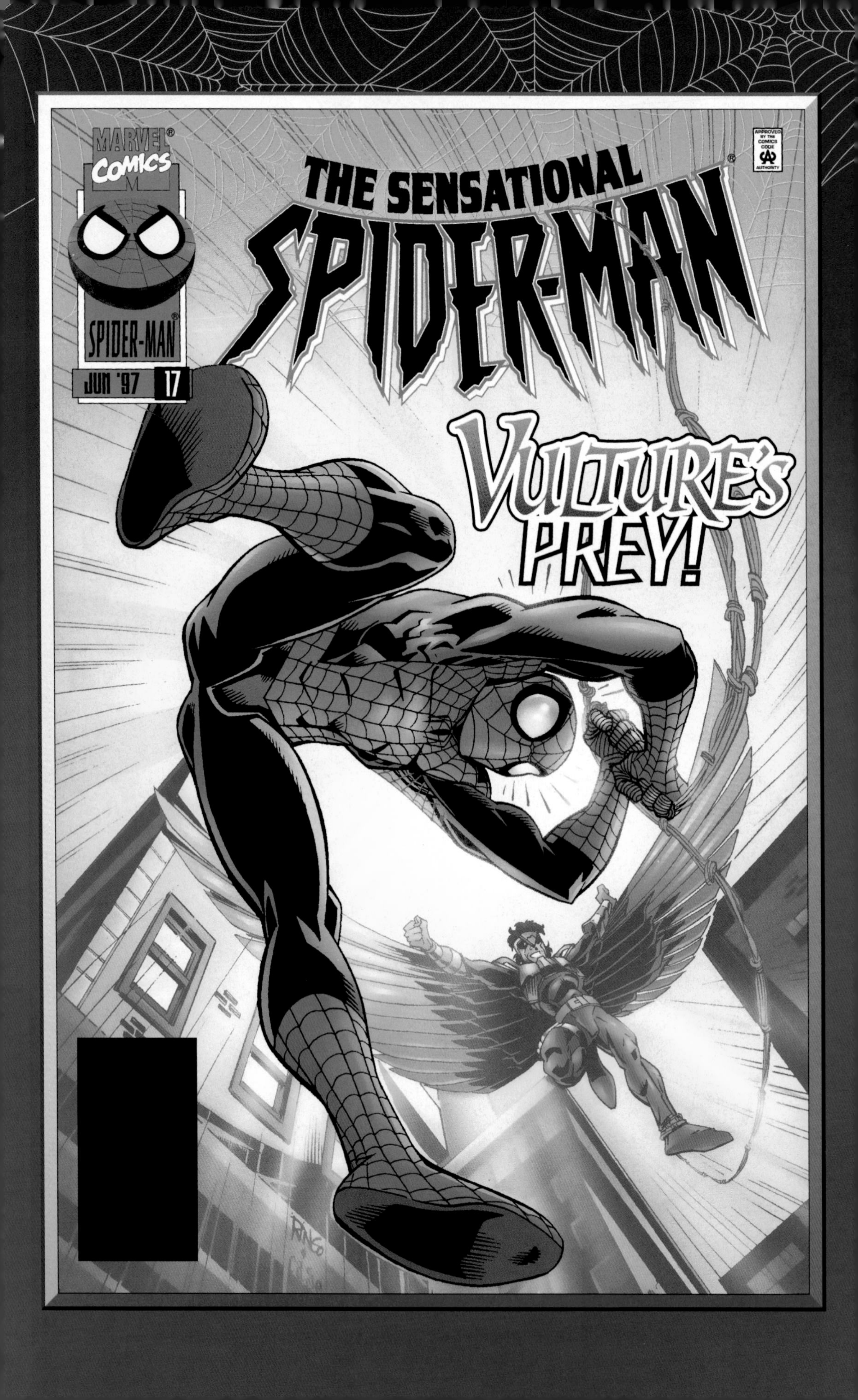
MARVEL COMICS
THE SENSATIONAL
SPIDER-MAN
SPIDER-MAN
JUN '97
17
APPROVED BY THE COMICS CODE AUTHORITY
VULTURE'S PREY!
RINGO

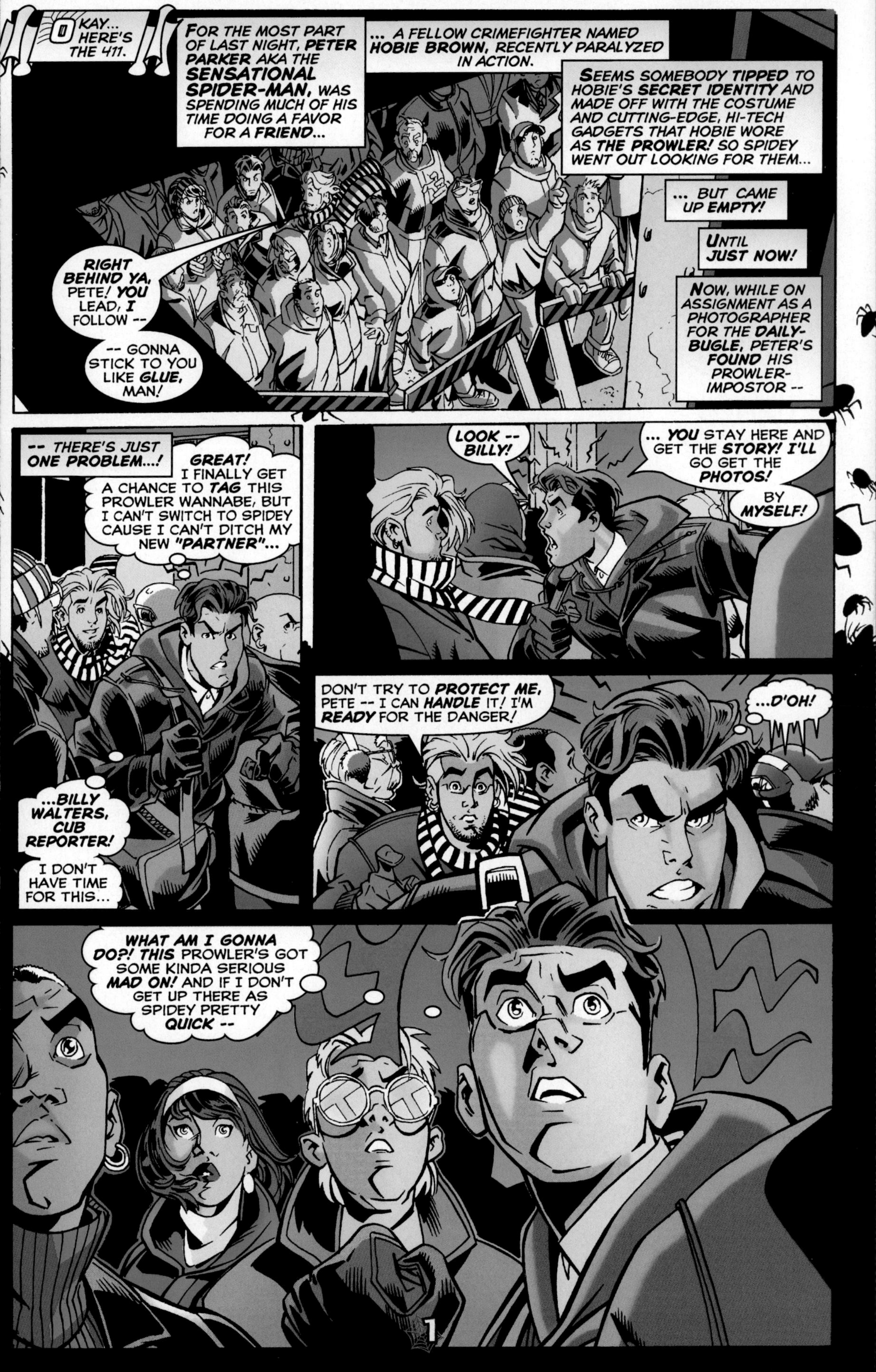
OKAY... HERE'S THE 411.
FOR THE MOST PART OF LAST NIGHT, PETER PARKER AKA THE SENSATIONAL SPIDER-MAN, WAS SPENDING MUCH OF HIS TIME DOING A FAVOR FOR A FRIEND...
... A FELLOW CRIMEFIGHTER NAMED HOBIE BROWN, RECENTLY PARALYZED IN ACTION.
SEEMS SOMEBODY TIPPED TO HOBIE'S SECRET IDENTITY AND MADE OFF WITH THE COSTUME AND CUTTING-EDGE, HI-TECH GADGETS THAT HOBIE WORE AS THE PROWLER! SO SPIDEY WENT OUT LOOKING FOR THEM...
... BUT CAME UP EMPTY!
UNTIL JUST NOW!
NOW, WHILE ON ASSIGNMENT AS A PHOTOGRAPHER FOR THE DAILY-BUGLE, PETER'S FOUND HIS PROWLER-IMPOSTOR --
RIGHT BEHIND YA, PETE! YOU LEAD, I FOLLOW --
-- GONNA STICK TO YOU LIKE GLUE, MAN!
-- THERE'S JUST ONE PROBLEM...!
GREAT! I FINALLY GET A CHANCE TO TAG THIS PROWLER WANNABE, BUT I CAN'T SWITCH TO SPIDEY CAUSE I CAN'T DITCH MY NEW "PARTNER"...
...BILLY WALTERS, CUB REPORTER!
I DON'T HAVE TIME FOR THIS...
LOOK -- BILLY!
... YOU STAY HERE AND GET THE STORY! I'LL GO GET THE PHOTOS!
BY MYSELF!
DON'T TRY TO PROTECT ME, PETE -- I CAN HANDLE IT! I'M READY FOR THE DANGER!
...D'OH!
WHAT AM I GONNA DO?! THIS PROWLER'S GOT SOME KINDA SERIOUS MAD ON! AND IF I DON'T GET UP THERE AS SPIDEY PRETTY QUICK --

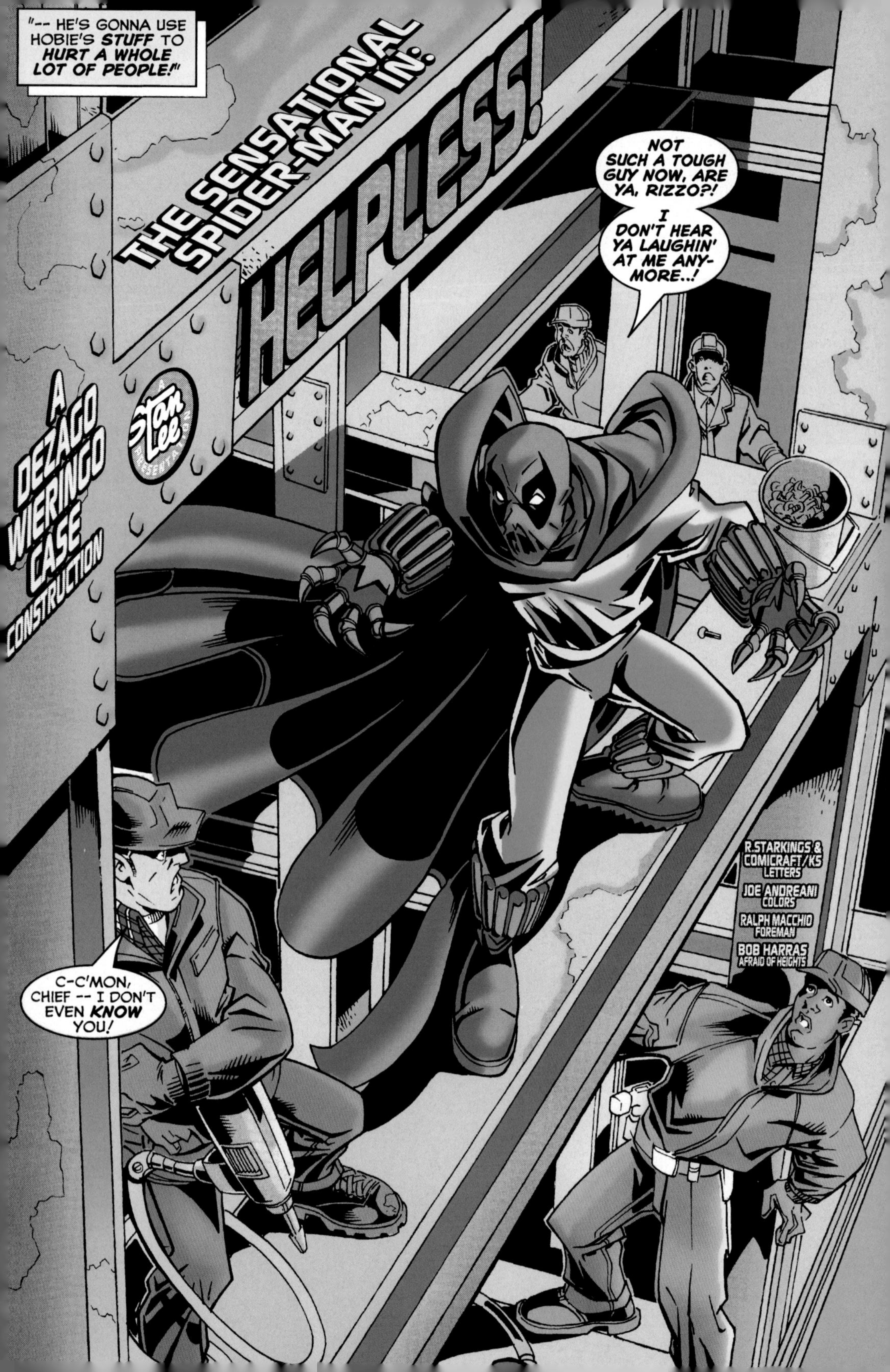
"-- HE'S GONNA USE HOBIE'S STUFF TO HURT A WHOLE LOT OF PEOPLE!"
THE SENSATIONAL SPIDER-MAN IN:
HELPLESS!
NOT SUCH A TOUGH GUY NOW, ARE YA, RIZZO?!
I DON'T HEAR YA LAUGHIN' AT ME ANY-MORE..!
A STAN LEE PRESENTATION
A DEZAGO WIERINGO CASE CONSTRUCTION
R.STARKINGS & COMICRAFT/KS LETTERS
JOE ANDREANI COLORS
RALPH MACCHIO FOREMAN
BOB HARRAS AFRAID OF HEIGHTS
C-C'MON, CHIEF -- I DON'T EVEN KNOW YOU!

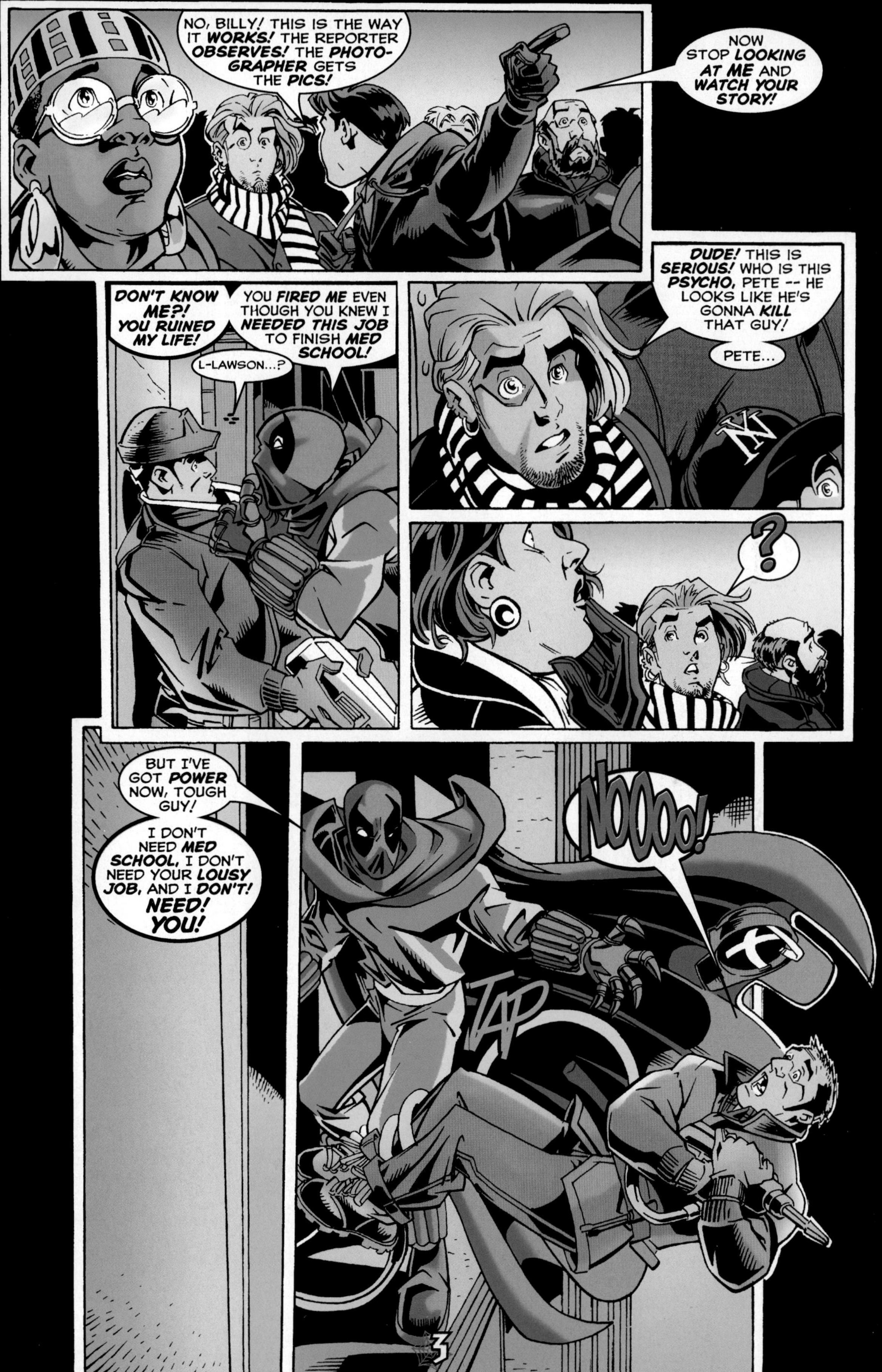
NO, BILLY! THIS IS THE WAY IT WORKS! THE REPORTER OBSERVES! THE PHOTO-GRAPHER GETS THE PICS!
NOW STOP LOOKING AT ME AND WATCH YOUR STORY!
DON'T KNOW ME?! YOU RUINED MY LIFE!
YOU FIRED ME EVEN THOUGH YOU KNEW I NEEDED THIS JOB TO FINISH MED SCHOOL!
L-LAWSON...?
DUDE! THIS IS SERIOUS! WHO IS THIS PSYCHO, PETE -- HE LOOKS LIKE HE'S GONNA KILL THAT GUY!
PETE...
?
BUT I'VE GOT POWER NOW, TOUGH GUY!
I DON'T NEED MED SCHOOL, I DON'T NEED YOUR LOUSY JOB, AND I DON'T! NEED! YOU!
NOOOo!
TAP

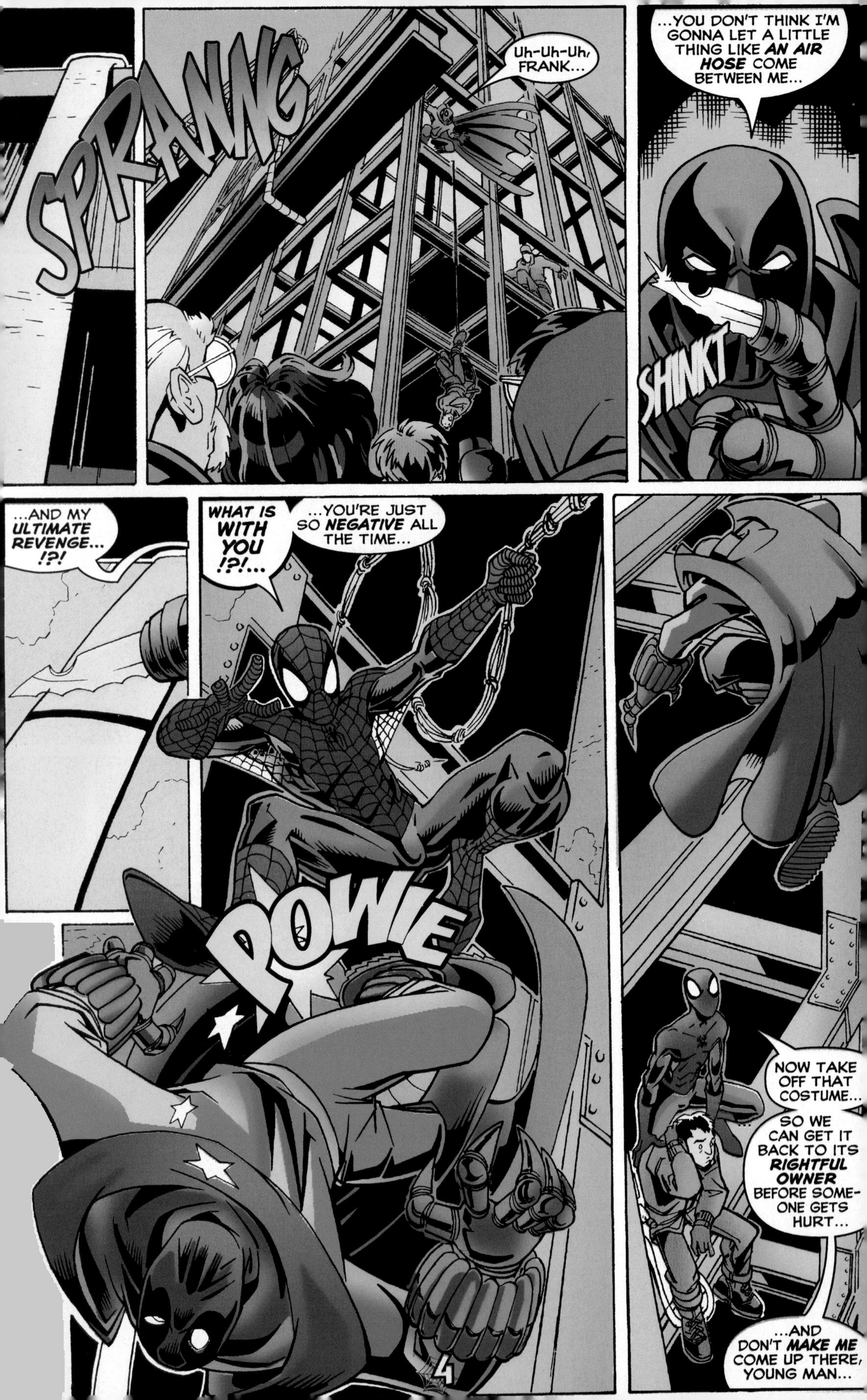
SPRANNG
Uh-Uh-Uh, FRANK...
...YOU DON'T THINK I'M GONNA LET A LITTLE THING LIKE AN AIR HOSE COME BETWEEN ME...
SHINKT
...AND MY ULTIMATE REVENGE... !?!
WHAT IS WITH YOU !?!...
...YOU'RE JUST SO NEGATIVE ALL THE TIME...
POWIE
NOW TAKE OFF THAT COSTUME...
SO WE CAN GET IT BACK TO ITS RIGHTFUL OWNER BEFORE SOME-ONE GETS HURT...
...AND DON'T MAKE ME COME UP THERE, YOUNG MAN...
4

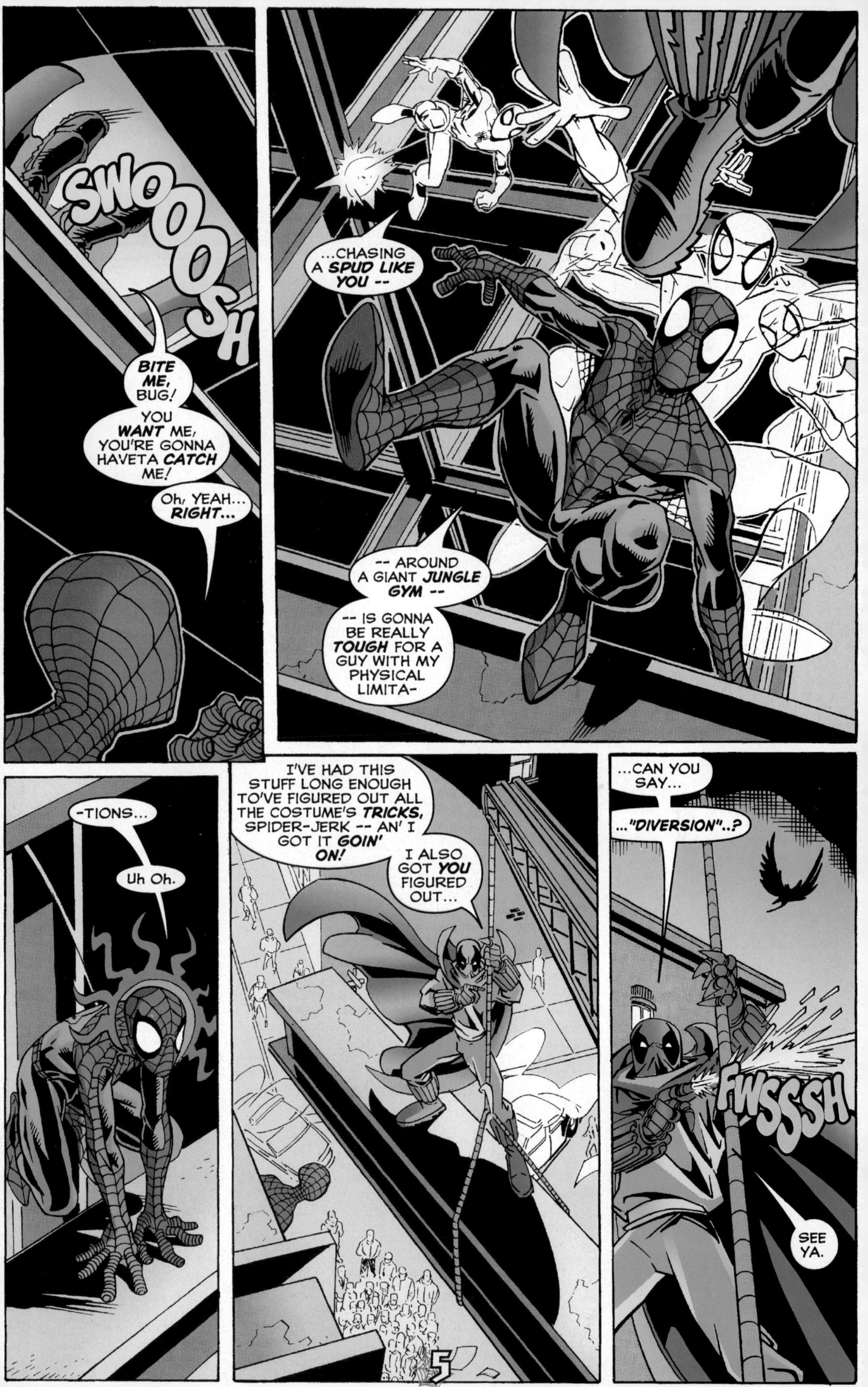
SWOOOOSH
BITE ME, BUG!
YOU WANT ME, YOU'RE GONNA HAVETA CATCH ME!
Oh, YEAH... RIGHT...
...CHASING A SPUD LIKE YOU --
-- AROUND A GIANT JUNGLE GYM --
-- IS GONNA BE REALLY TOUGH FOR A GUY WITH MY PHYSICAL LIMITA-
-TIONS...
Uh Oh.
I'VE HAD THIS STUFF LONG ENOUGH TO'VE FIGURED OUT ALL THE COSTUME'S TRICKS, SPIDER-JERK -- AN' I GOT IT GOIN' ON!
I ALSO GOT YOU FIGURED OUT...
...CAN YOU SAY...
..."DIVERSION"..?
FWSSSH
SEE YA.

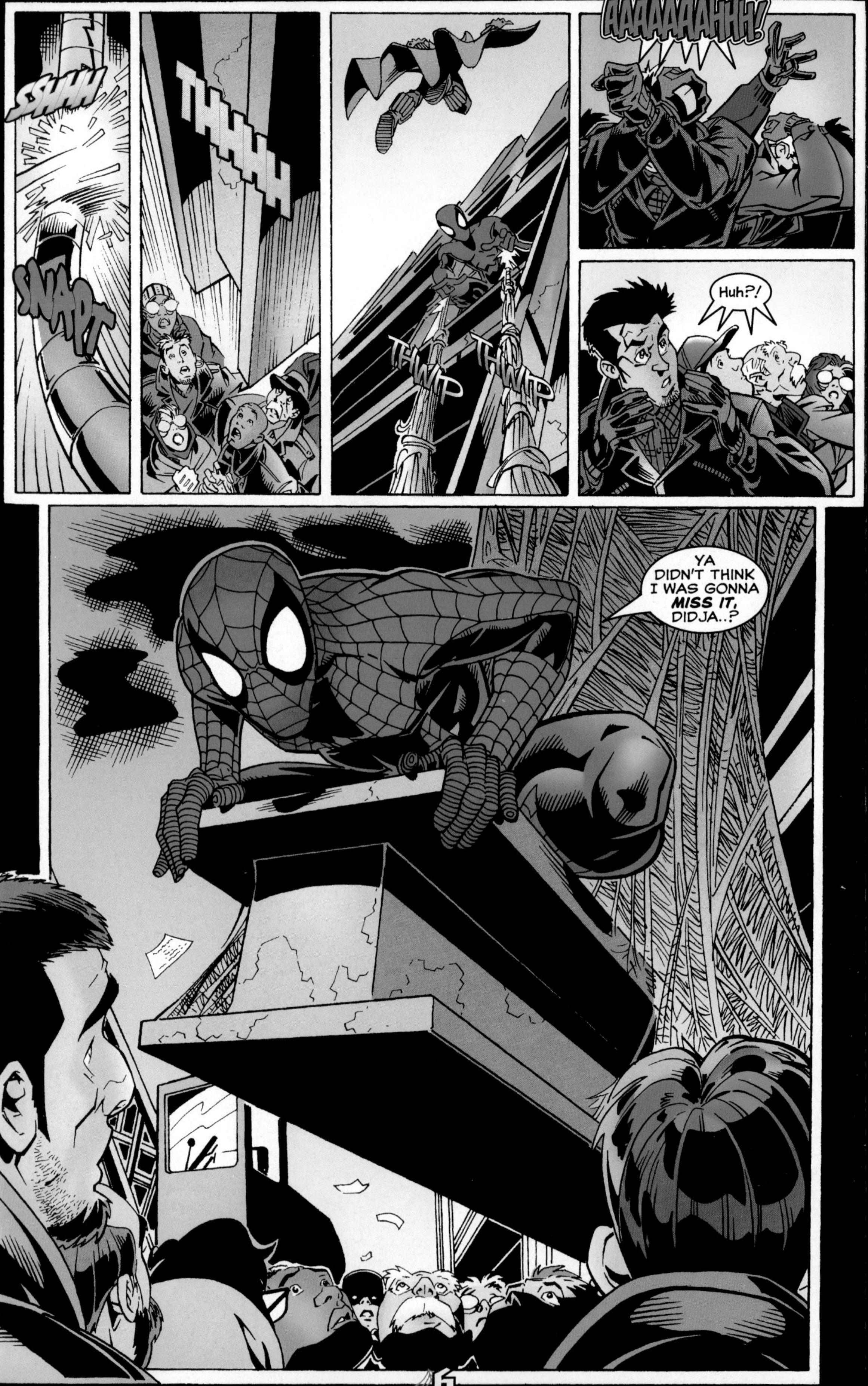
SSHH
SNAPT
THHHH
THWIP
THWIP
AAAAAAAHHH!
Huh?!
YA DIDN'T THINK I WAS GONNA **MISS IT,** DIDJA..?

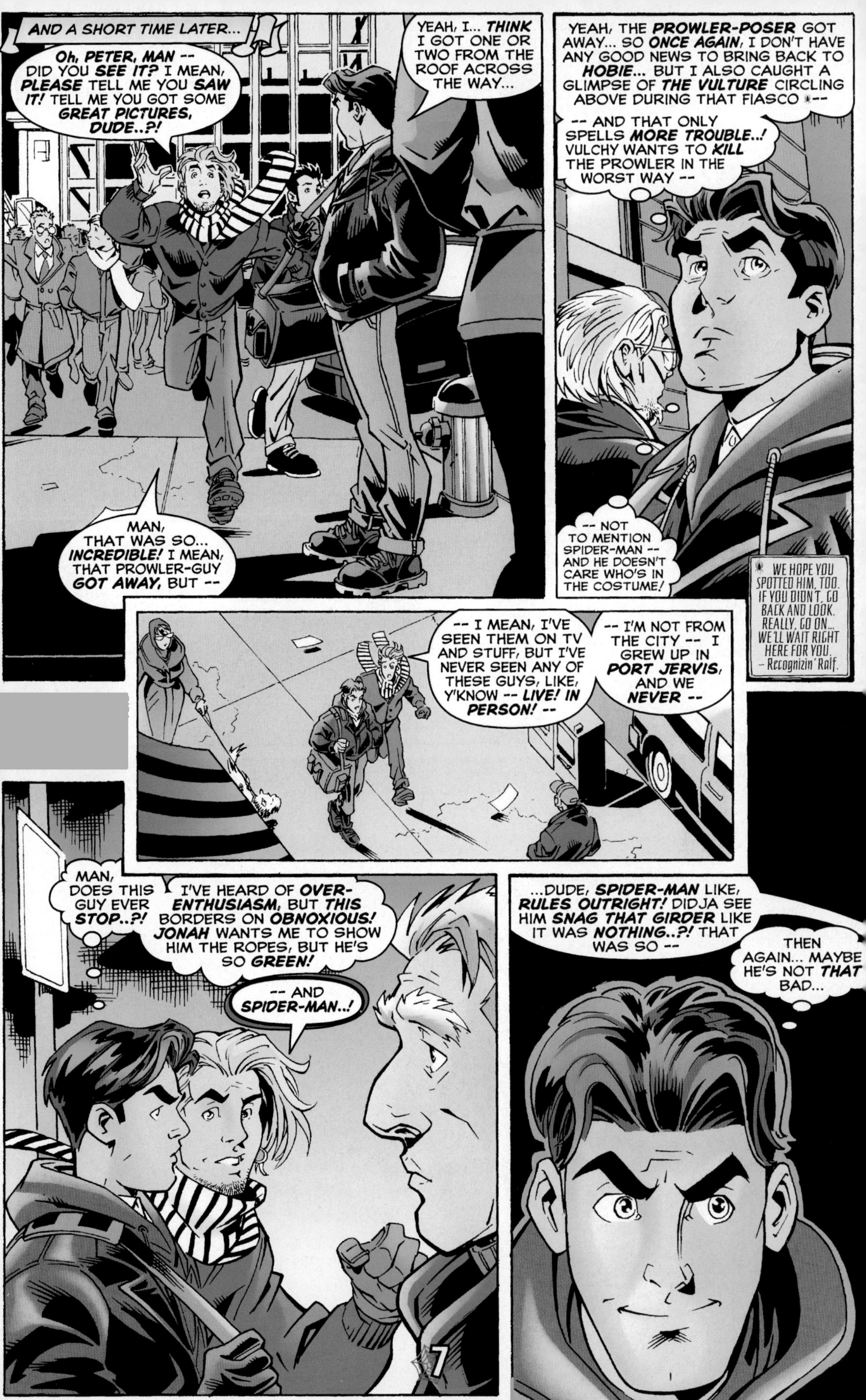
AND A SHORT TIME LATER...
Oh, PETER, MAN -- DID YOU SEE IT? I MEAN, PLEASE TELL ME YOU SAW IT! TELL ME YOU GOT SOME GREAT PICTURES, DUDE..?!
YEAH, I... THINK I GOT ONE OR TWO FROM THE ROOF ACROSS THE WAY...
MAN, THAT WAS SO... INCREDIBLE! I MEAN, THAT PROWLER-GUY GOT AWAY, BUT --
YEAH, THE PROWLER-POSER GOT AWAY... SO ONCE AGAIN, I DON'T HAVE ANY GOOD NEWS TO BRING BACK TO HOBIE... BUT I ALSO CAUGHT A GLIMPSE OF THE VULTURE CIRCLING ABOVE DURING THAT FIASCO --
-- AND THAT ONLY SPELLS MORE TROUBLE..! VULCHY WANTS TO KILL THE PROWLER IN THE WORST WAY --
-- NOT TO MENTION SPIDER-MAN -- AND HE DOESN'T CARE WHO'S IN THE COSTUME!
WE HOPE YOU SPOTTED HIM, TOO. IF YOU DIDN'T, GO BACK AND LOOK. REALLY, GO ON... WE'LL WAIT RIGHT HERE FOR YOU. – Recognizin' Ralf.
-- I MEAN, I'VE SEEN THEM ON TV AND STUFF, BUT I'VE NEVER SEEN ANY OF THESE GUYS, LIKE, Y'KNOW -- LIVE! IN PERSON! --
-- I'M NOT FROM THE CITY -- I GREW UP IN PORT JERVIS, AND WE NEVER --
MAN, DOES THIS GUY EVER STOP..?!
I'VE HEARD OF OVER-ENTHUSIASM, BUT THIS BORDERS ON OBNOXIOUS! JONAH WANTS ME TO SHOW HIM THE ROPES, BUT HE'S SO GREEN!
-- AND SPIDER-MAN..!
...DUDE, SPIDER-MAN LIKE, RULES OUTRIGHT! DIDJA SEE HIM SNAG THAT GIRDER LIKE IT WAS NOTHING..?! THAT WAS SO --
THEN AGAIN... MAYBE HE'S NOT THAT BAD...
7

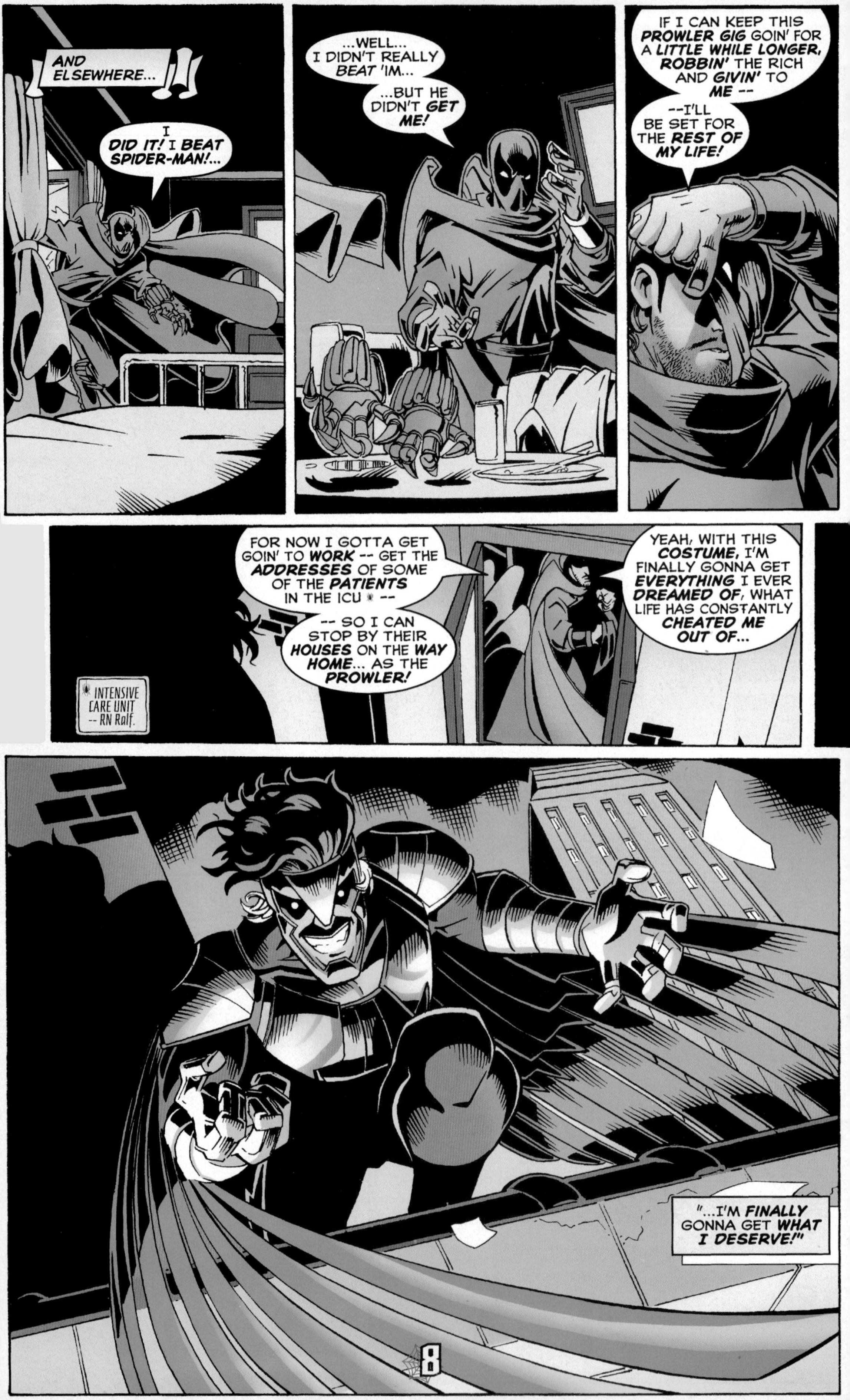
AND ELSEWHERE...
I DID IT! I BEAT SPIDER-MAN!...
...WELL... I DIDN'T REALLY BEAT 'IM...
...BUT HE DIDN'T GET ME!
IF I CAN KEEP THIS PROWLER GIG GOIN' FOR A LITTLE WHILE LONGER, ROBBIN' THE RICH AND GIVIN' TO ME --
--I'LL BE SET FOR THE REST OF MY LIFE!
FOR NOW I GOTTA GET GOIN' TO WORK -- GET THE ADDRESSES OF SOME OF THE PATIENTS IN THE ICU --
-- SO I CAN STOP BY THEIR HOUSES ON THE WAY HOME... AS THE PROWLER!
INTENSIVE CARE UNIT -- RN Ralf.
YEAH, WITH THIS COSTUME, I'M FINALLY GONNA GET EVERYTHING I EVER DREAMED OF, WHAT LIFE HAS CONSTANTLY CHEATED ME OUT OF...
"...I'M FINALLY GONNA GET WHAT I DESERVE!"
8

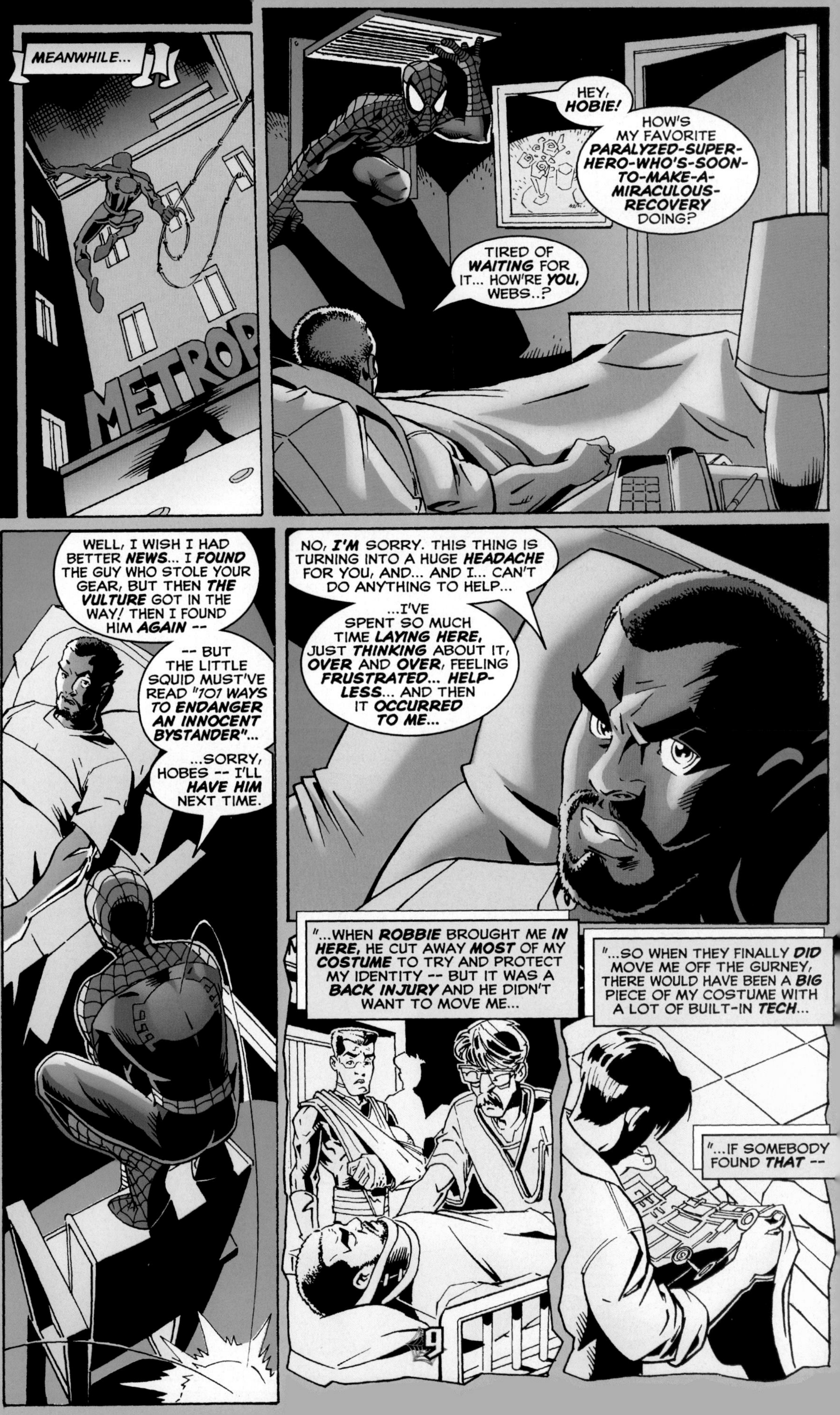
MEANWHILE...
METROP
HEY, HOBIE!
HOW'S MY FAVORITE PARALYZED-SUPER-HERO-WHO'S-SOON-TO-MAKE-A-MIRACULOUS-RECOVERY DOING?
TIRED OF WAITING FOR IT... HOW'RE YOU, WEBS..?
WELL, I WISH I HAD BETTER NEWS... I FOUND THE GUY WHO STOLE YOUR GEAR, BUT THEN THE VULTURE GOT IN THE WAY! THEN I FOUND HIM AGAIN --
-- BUT THE LITTLE SQUID MUST'VE READ "101 WAYS TO ENDANGER AN INNOCENT BYSTANDER"...
...SORRY, HOBES -- I'LL HAVE HIM NEXT TIME.
NO, I'M SORRY. THIS THING IS TURNING INTO A HUGE HEADACHE FOR YOU, AND... AND I... CAN'T DO ANYTHING TO HELP...
...I'VE SPENT SO MUCH TIME LAYING HERE, JUST THINKING ABOUT IT, OVER AND OVER, FEELING FRUSTRATED... HELP-LESS... AND THEN IT OCCURRED TO ME...
"...WHEN ROBBIE BROUGHT ME IN HERE, HE CUT AWAY MOST OF MY COSTUME TO TRY AND PROTECT MY IDENTITY -- BUT IT WAS A BACK INJURY AND HE DIDN'T WANT TO MOVE ME...
"...SO WHEN THEY FINALLY DID MOVE ME OFF THE GURNEY, THERE WOULD HAVE BEEN A BIG PIECE OF MY COSTUME WITH A LOT OF BUILT-IN TECH...
"...IF SOMEBODY FOUND THAT --

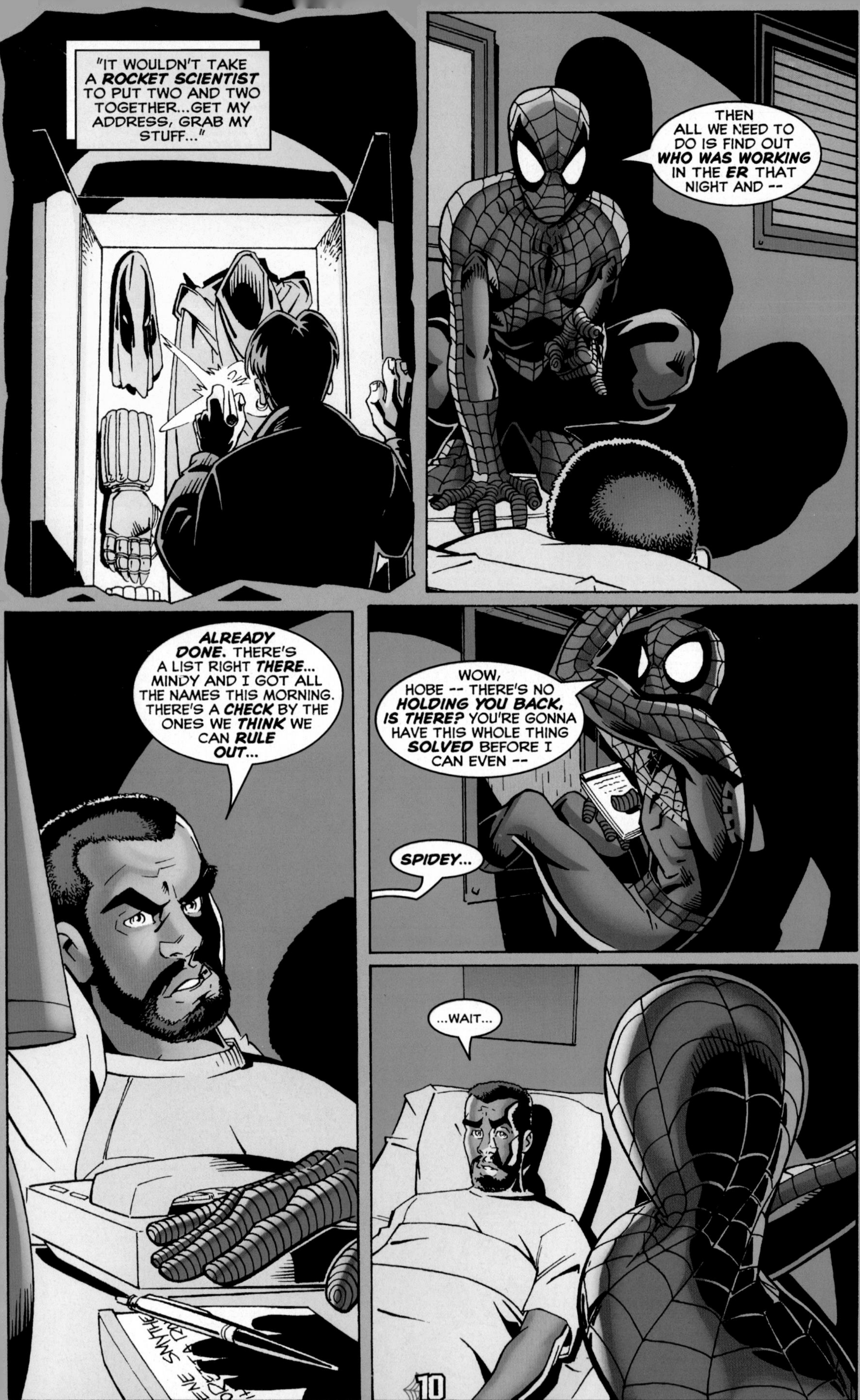
"IT WOULDN'T TAKE A ROCKET SCIENTIST TO PUT TWO AND TWO TOGETHER...GET MY ADDRESS, GRAB MY STUFF..."
THEN ALL WE NEED TO DO IS FIND OUT WHO WAS WORKING IN THE ER THAT NIGHT AND --
ALREADY DONE. THERE'S A LIST RIGHT THERE... MINDY AND I GOT ALL THE NAMES THIS MORNING. THERE'S A CHECK BY THE ONES WE THINK WE CAN RULE OUT...
WOW, HOBE -- THERE'S NO HOLDING YOU BACK, IS THERE? YOU'RE GONNA HAVE THIS WHOLE THING SOLVED BEFORE I CAN EVEN --
SPIDEY...
...WAIT...

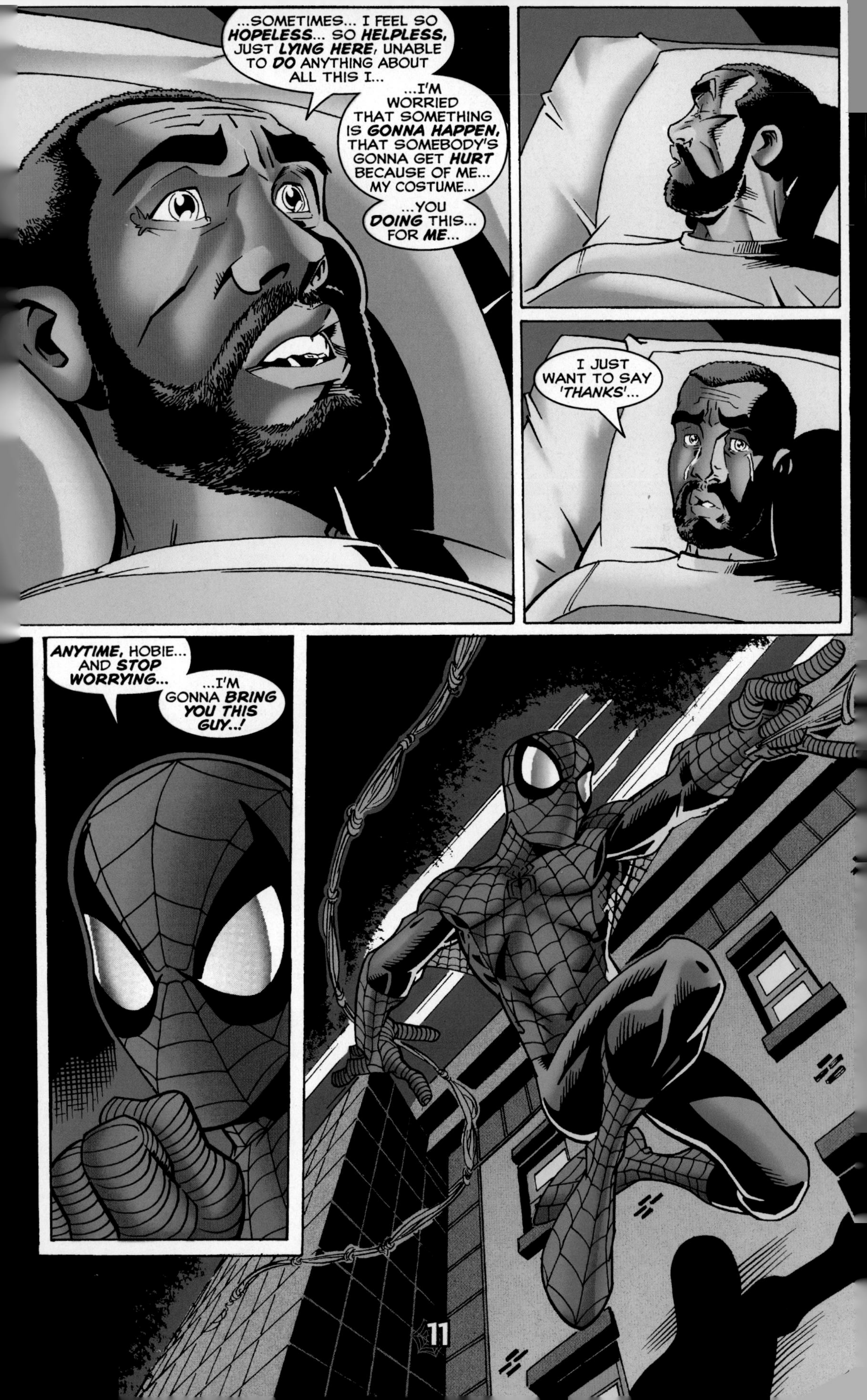
...SOMETIMES... I FEEL SO HOPELESS... SO HELPLESS, JUST LYING HERE, UNABLE TO DO ANYTHING ABOUT ALL THIS I...
...I'M WORRIED THAT SOMETHING IS GONNA HAPPEN, THAT SOMEBODY'S GONNA GET HURT BECAUSE OF ME... MY COSTUME...
...YOU DOING THIS... FOR ME...
I JUST WANT TO SAY 'THANKS'...
ANYTIME, HOBIE... AND STOP WORRYING...
...I'M GONNA BRING YOU THIS GUY..!

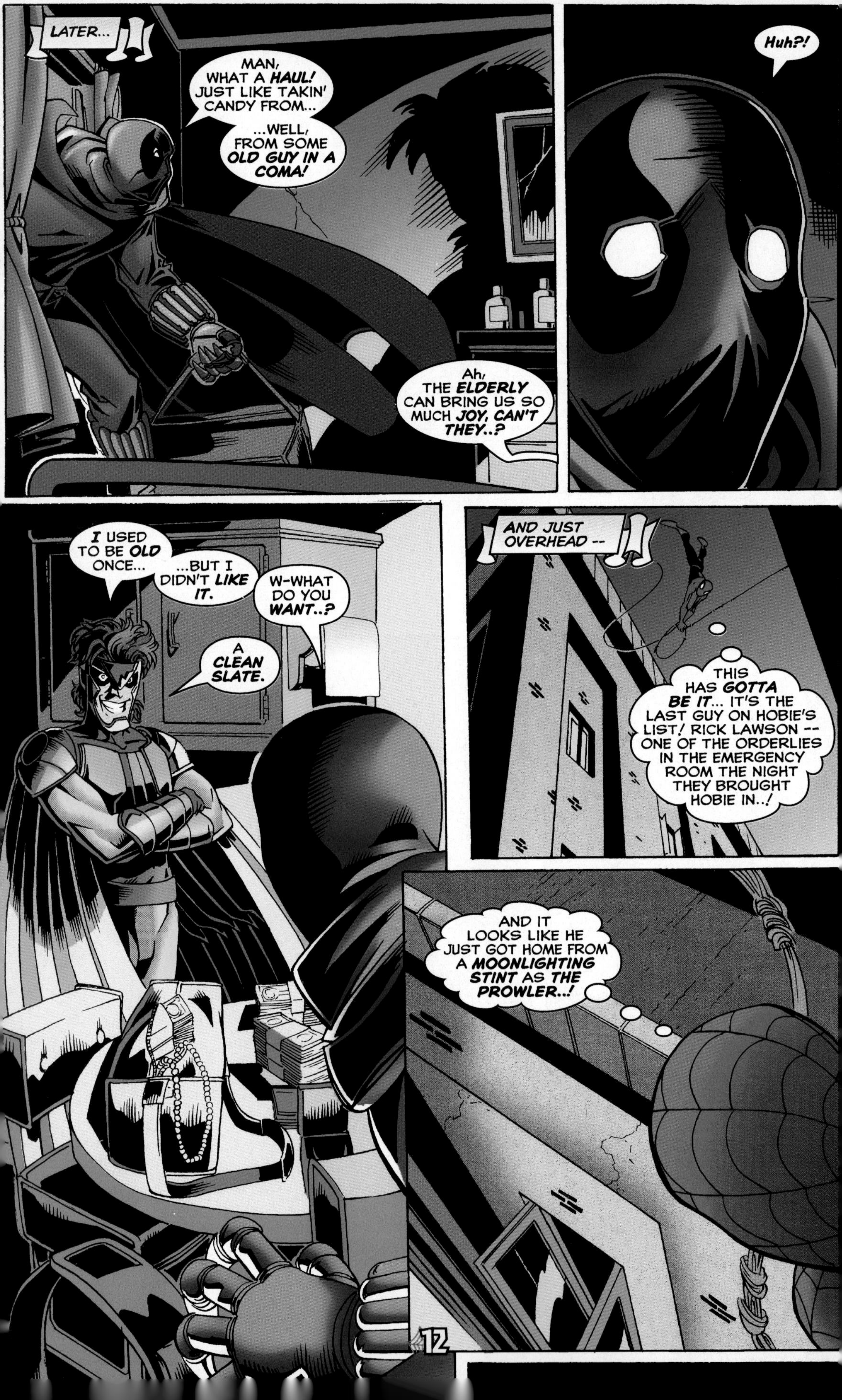
LATER...
MAN, WHAT A HAUL! JUST LIKE TAKIN' CANDY FROM...
...WELL, FROM SOME OLD GUY IN A COMA!
Huh?!
Ah, THE ELDERLY CAN BRING US SO MUCH JOY, CAN'T THEY..?
I USED TO BE OLD ONCE...
...BUT I DIDN'T LIKE IT.
W-WHAT DO YOU WANT..?
A CLEAN SLATE.
AND JUST OVERHEAD --
THIS HAS GOTTA BE IT... IT'S THE LAST GUY ON HOBIE'S LIST! RICK LAWSON -- ONE OF THE ORDERLIES IN THE EMERGENCY ROOM THE NIGHT THEY BROUGHT HOBIE IN..!
AND IT LOOKS LIKE HE JUST GOT HOME FROM A MOONLIGHTING STINT AS THE PROWLER..!
12

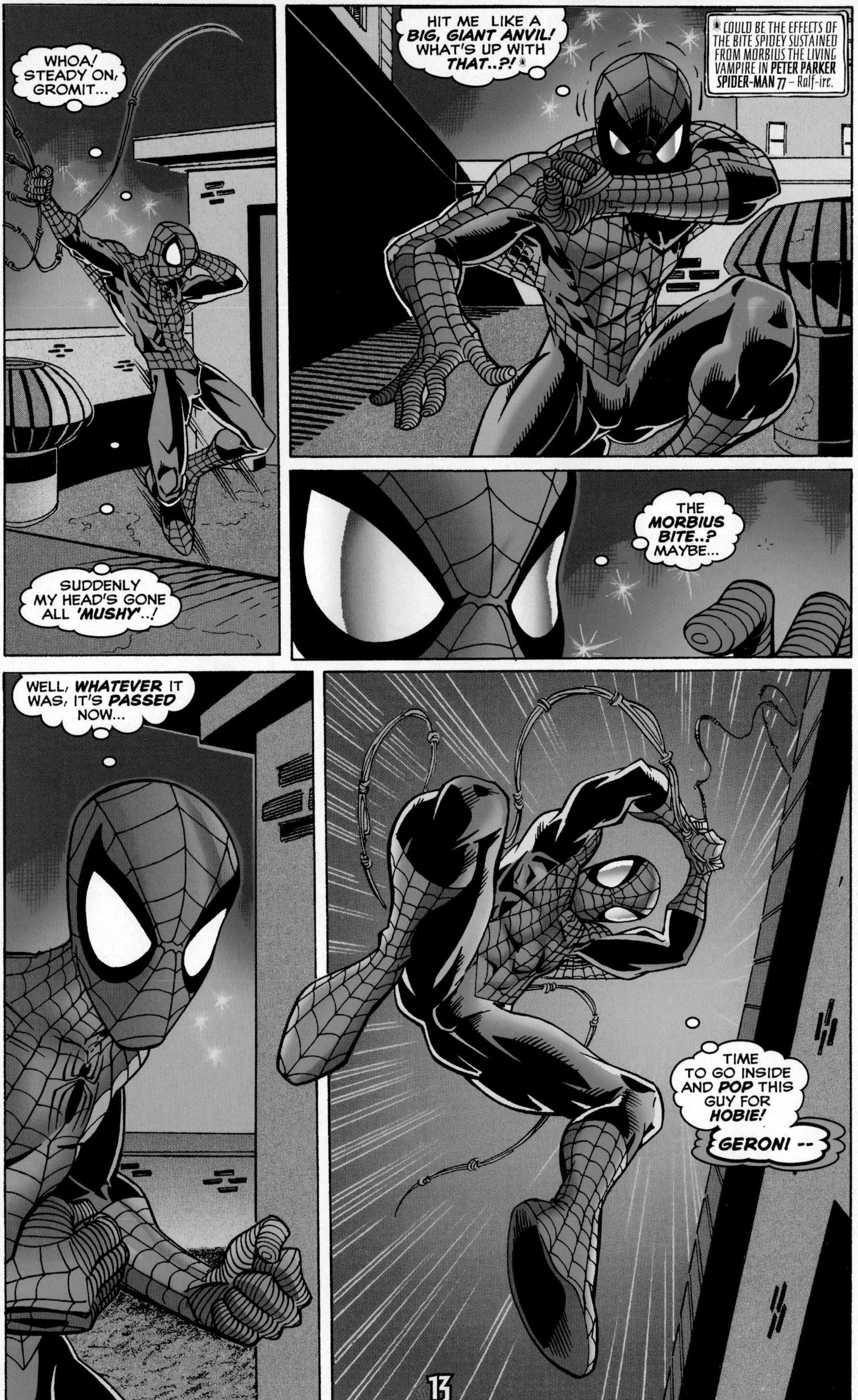
WHOA! STEADY ON, GROMIT...
SUDDENLY MY HEAD'S GONE ALL 'MUSHY'..!
HIT ME LIKE A BIG, GIANT ANVIL! WHAT'S UP WITH THAT..?!
COULD BE THE EFFECTS OF THE BITE SPIDEY SUSTAINED FROM MORBIUS THE LIVING VAMPIRE IN PETER PARKER SPIDER-MAN 77 – Ralf-ire.
THE MORBIUS BITE..? MAYBE...
WELL, WHATEVER IT WAS, IT'S PASSED NOW...
TIME TO GO INSIDE AND POP THIS GUY FOR HOBIE!
GERONI --

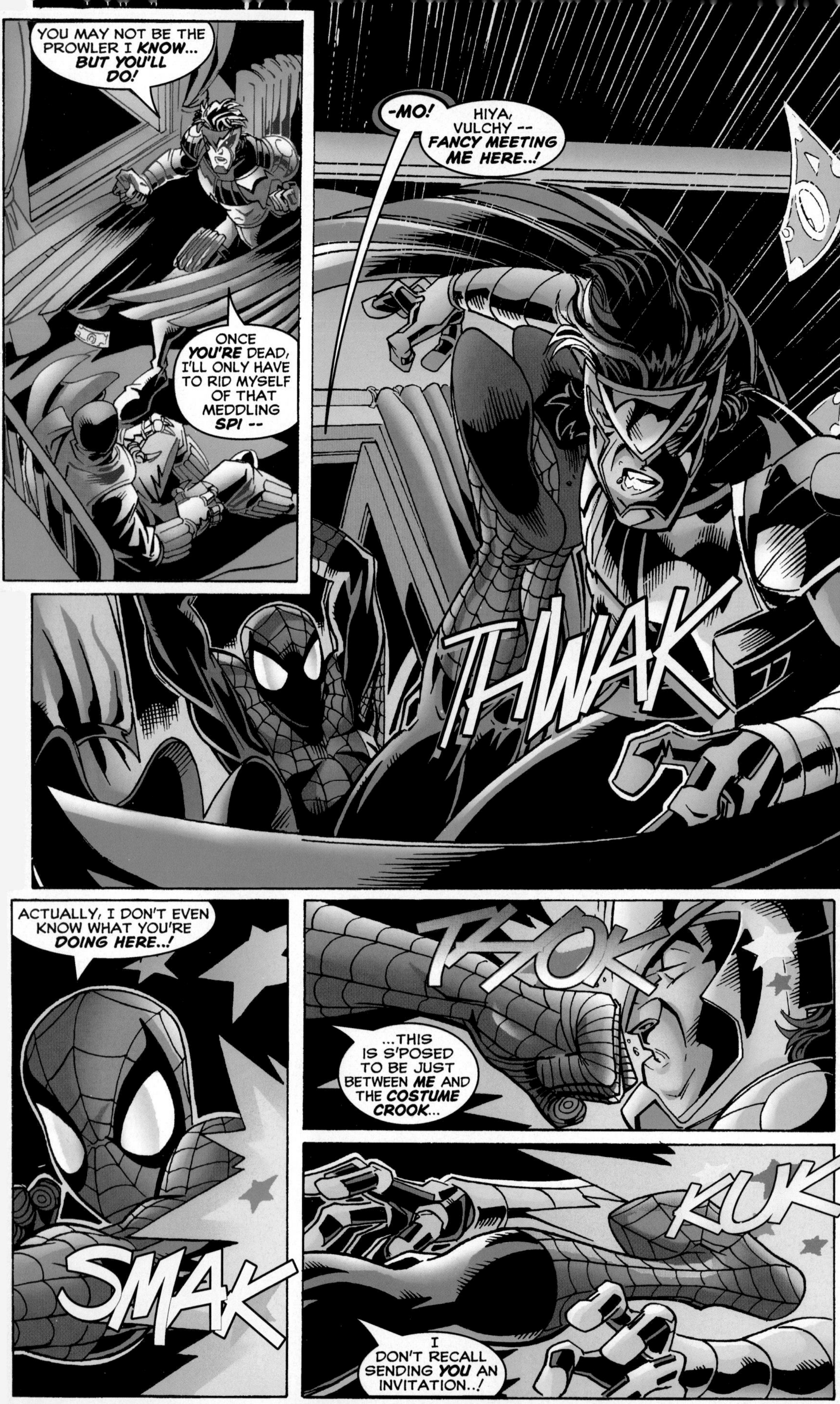
YOU MAY NOT BE THE PROWLER I KNOW... BUT YOU'LL DO!
ONCE YOU'RE DEAD, I'LL ONLY HAVE TO RID MYSELF OF THAT MEDDLING SPI --
-MO!
HIYA, VULCHY -- FANCY MEETING ME HERE..!
THWAK
ACTUALLY, I DON'T EVEN KNOW WHAT YOU'RE DOING HERE..!
SMAK
THOK
...THIS IS S'POSED TO BE JUST BETWEEN ME AND THE COSTUME CROOK...
KUK
I DON'T RECALL SENDING YOU AN INVITATION..!

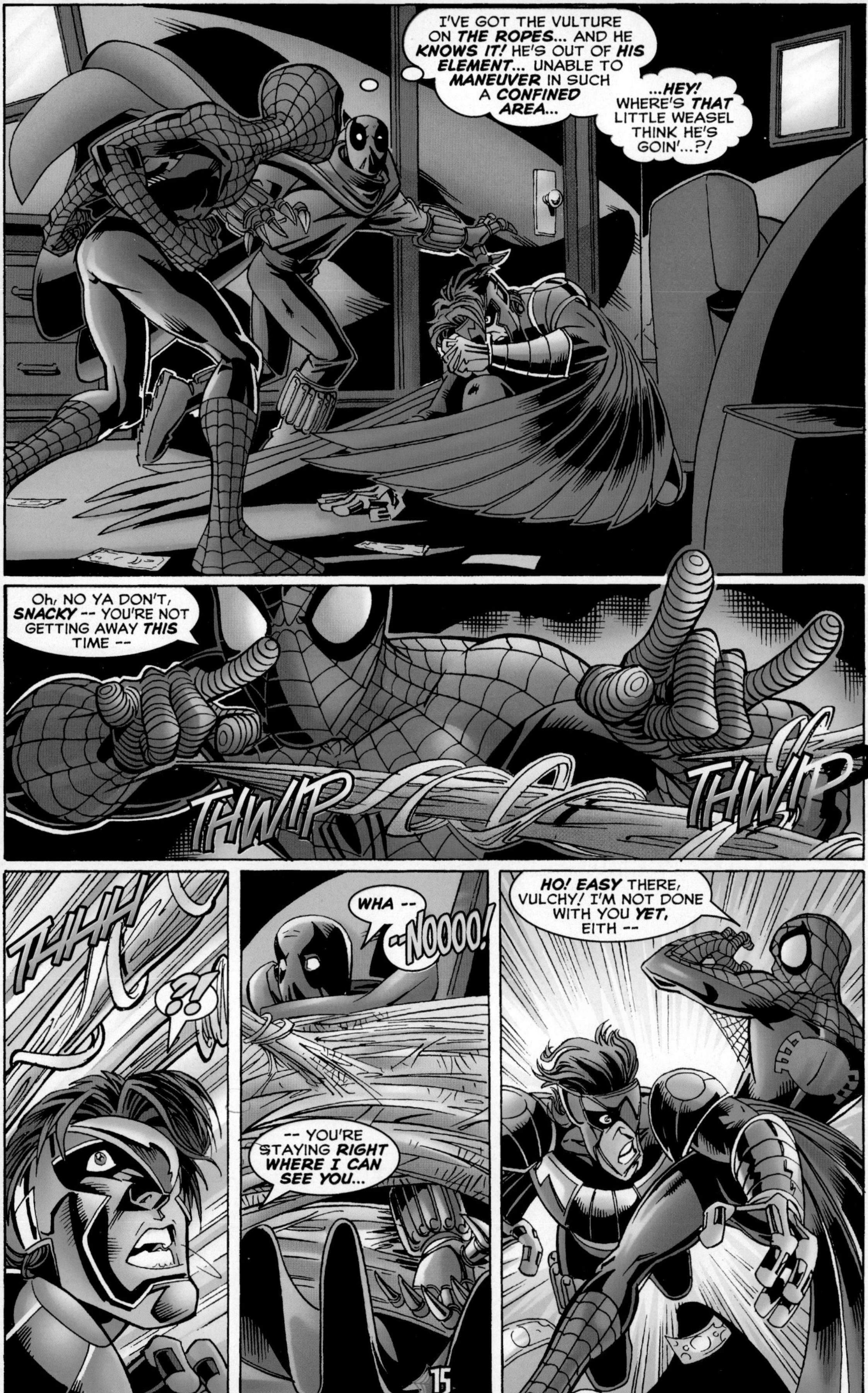
I'VE GOT THE VULTURE ON THE ROPES... AND HE KNOWS IT! HE'S OUT OF HIS ELEMENT... UNABLE TO MANEUVER IN SUCH A CONFINED AREA...
...HEY! WHERE'S THAT LITTLE WEASEL THINK HE'S GOIN'...?!
Oh, NO YA DON'T, SNACKY -- YOU'RE NOT GETTING AWAY THIS TIME --
THWIP
THWIP
THHH
?!
WHA --
--NOOOO!
-- YOU'RE STAYING RIGHT WHERE I CAN SEE YOU...
HO! EASY THERE, VULCHY! I'M NOT DONE WITH YOU YET, EITH --

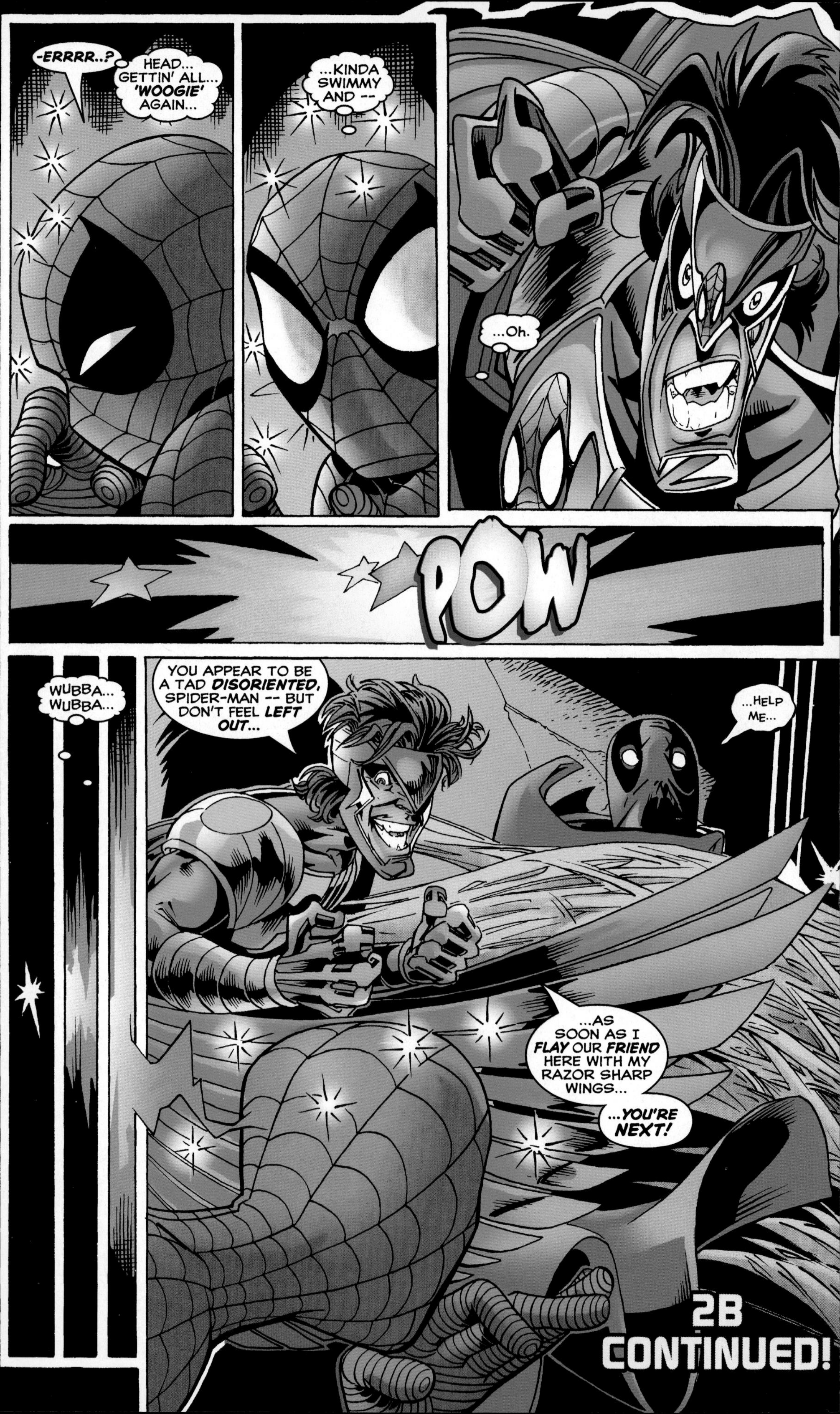
-ERRRR..?
HEAD... GETTIN' ALL... 'WOOGIE' AGAIN...
...KINDA SWIMMY AND --
...Oh.
POW
WUBBA... WUBBA...
YOU APPEAR TO BE A TAD DISORIENTED, SPIDER-MAN -- BUT DON'T FEEL LEFT OUT...
...HELP ME...
...AS SOON AS I FLAY OUR FRIEND HERE WITH MY RAZOR SHARP WINGS...
...YOU'RE NEXT!
2B CONTINUED!

BROTHER'S KEEPER, TOO

THE BIG, DRIPPY, OOZY, MAD GUY IS DK! --

-- A CREATURE CREATED WHEN **DAVID KALEN**, ALONG WITH HIS BROTHER, **HENRY**, WAS CAUGHT IN THE **HEART** OF A TERRIBLE (AND SUSPICIOUS) **TOXIC WASTE** EXPLOSION! *HENRY DIED...*

...BUT DAVID SOON FOUND THAT HE HAD ACQUIRED THE **HORRIBLE ABILITY** TO **DECAY** AND **DECOMPOSE** ANY MATERIAL WITH BUT A SINGLE TOUCH OF HIS **CORROSIVE HAND..!**

HERE AT THE **RAVENCROFT INSTITUTE**, KALEN'S SLOW DOWNWARD SPIRAL INTO THE DEPTHS OF DEPRESSION HAS FINALLY CULMINATED IN **THIS** --

A **VIOLENT** EPISODE OF [U]NCONTROLLED **RAGE**, [A]LREADY RESULTING IN [M]ANY INJURIES AND THE [G]HASTLY **DEATHS** OF TWO [S]ECURITY PERSONNEL...

...AND IT **ISN'T OVER..!**

...THE **LITTLE GUY..?**

THAT WOULD BE THE SENSATIONAL **SPIDER-MAN!**

WHOA!

STAN LEE PRESENTS

TODD DEZAGO
WRITER

RICH CASE
ARTIST

R. STARKINGS & COMICRAFT/KS
LETTERS

GREGORY WRIGHT
COLORS

RALPH MACCHIO
EDITOR

BOB HARRAS
CHIEF

HSSSSSSSS

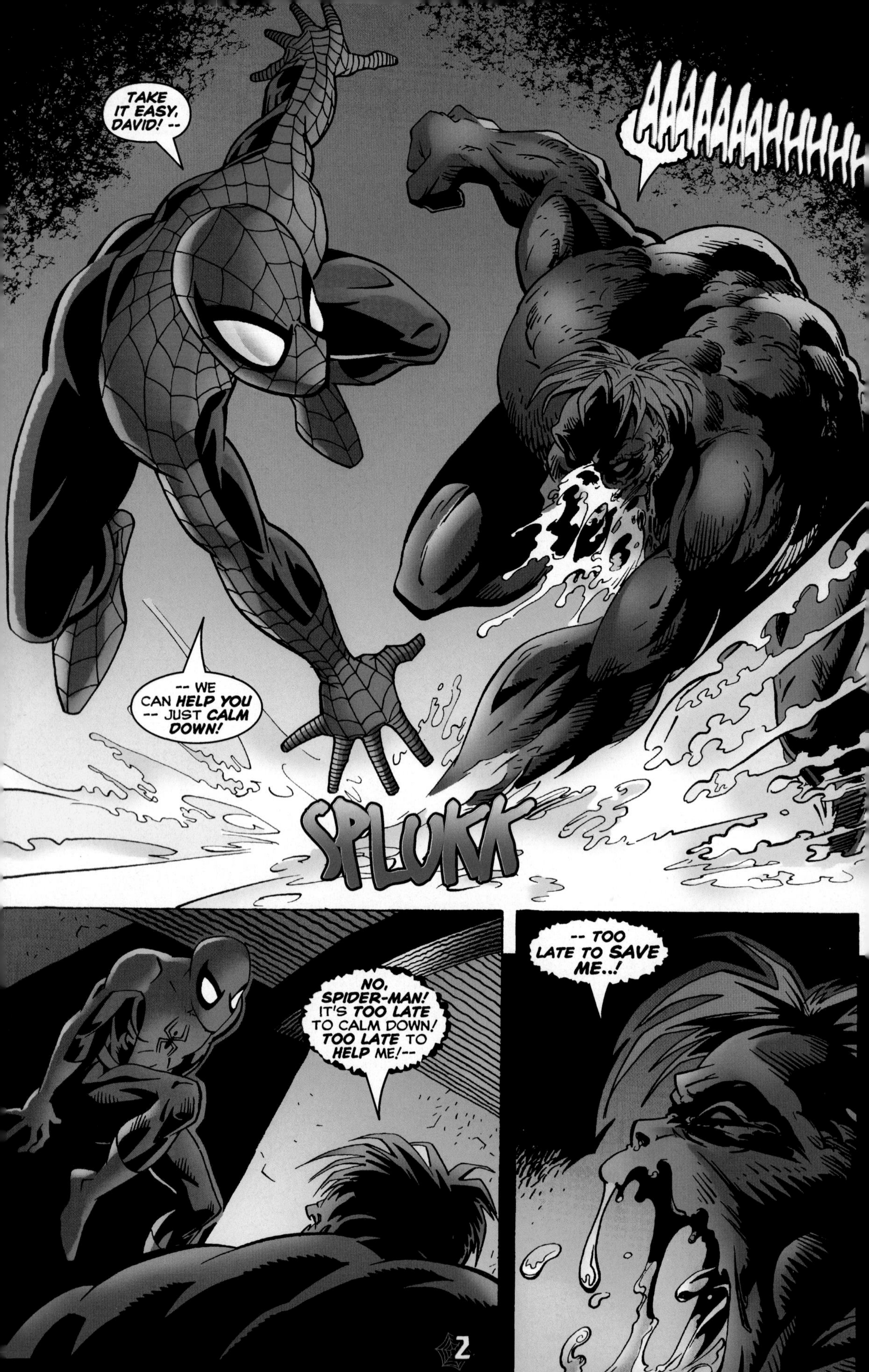
TAKE IT EASY, DAVID! --
AAAAAAAHHHHH
-- WE CAN HELP YOU -- JUST CALM DOWN!
SPLUKK
NO, SPIDER-MAN! IT'S TOO LATE TO CALM DOWN! TOO LATE TO HELP ME!--
-- TOO LATE TO SAVE ME..!

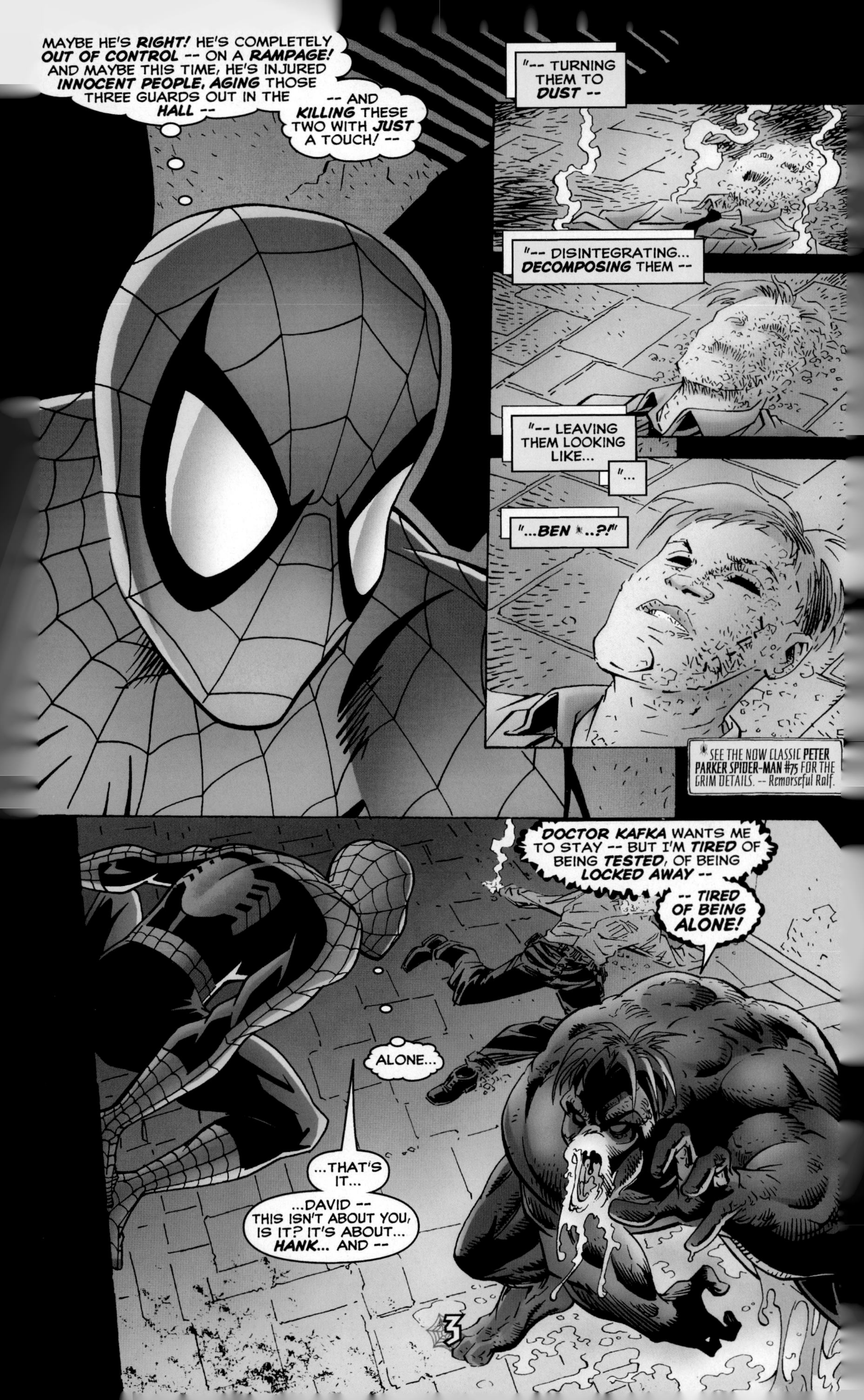

MAYBE HE'S RIGHT! HE'S COMPLETELY OUT OF CONTROL -- ON A RAMPAGE! AND MAYBE THIS TIME, HE'S INJURED INNOCENT PEOPLE, AGING THOSE THREE GUARDS OUT IN THE HALL --
-- AND KILLING THESE TWO WITH JUST A TOUCH! --
"-- TURNING THEM TO DUST --
"-- DISINTEGRATING... DECOMPOSING THEM --
"-- LEAVING THEM LOOKING LIKE...
"...
"...BEN*..?!"
*SEE THE NOW CLASSIC PETER PARKER SPIDER-MAN #75 FOR THE GRIM DETAILS. -- Remorseful Ralf.
DOCTOR KAFKA WANTS ME TO STAY -- BUT I'M TIRED OF BEING TESTED, OF BEING LOCKED AWAY --
-- TIRED OF BEING ALONE!
ALONE...
...THAT'S IT...
...DAVID -- THIS ISN'T ABOUT YOU, IS IT? IT'S ABOUT... HANK... AND --
3

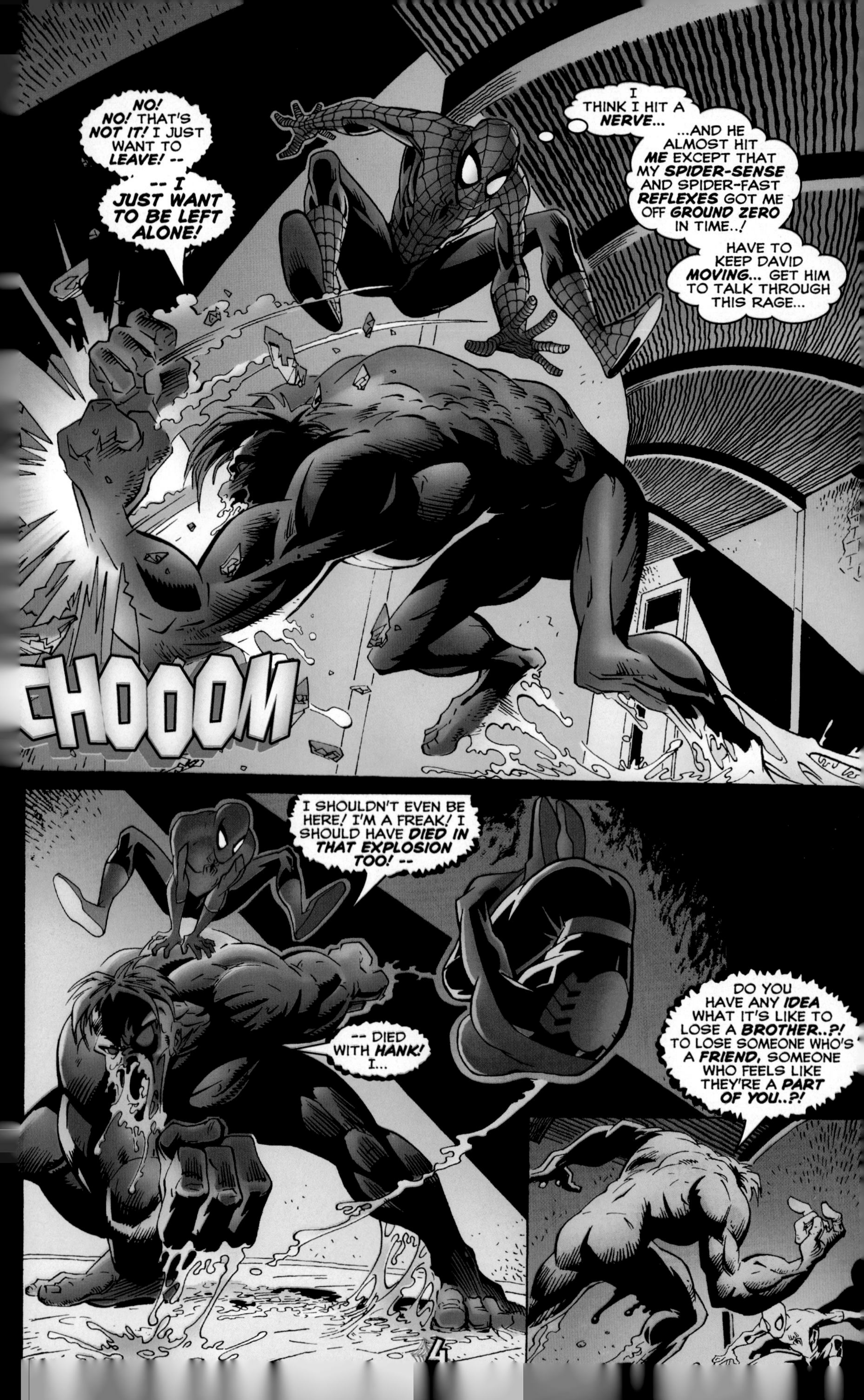

NO! NO! THAT'S NOT IT! I JUST WANT TO LEAVE! --
-- I JUST WANT TO BE LEFT ALONE!
I THINK I HIT A NERVE...
...AND HE ALMOST HIT ME EXCEPT THAT MY SPIDER-SENSE AND SPIDER-FAST REFLEXES GOT ME OFF GROUND ZERO IN TIME..!
HAVE TO KEEP DAVID MOVING... GET HIM TO TALK THROUGH THIS RAGE...
CHOOOM
I SHOULDN'T EVEN BE HERE! I'M A FREAK! I SHOULD HAVE DIED IN THAT EXPLOSION TOO! --
-- DIED WITH HANK! I...
DO YOU HAVE ANY IDEA WHAT IT'S LIKE TO LOSE A BROTHER..?! TO LOSE SOMEONE WHO'S A FRIEND, SOMEONE WHO FEELS LIKE THEY'RE A PART OF YOU..?!

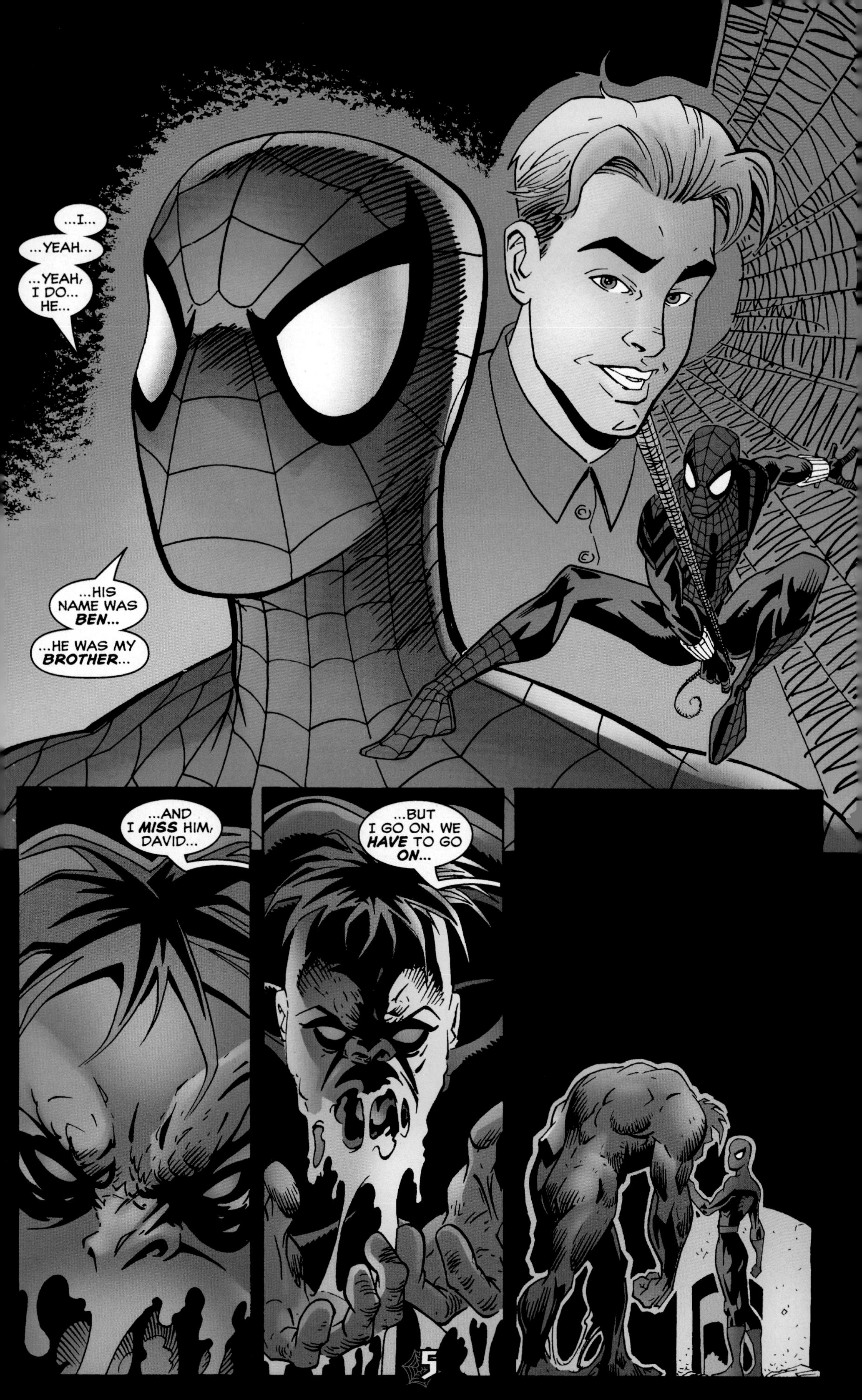

...I...
...YEAH...
...YEAH, I DO... HE...
...HIS NAME WAS BEN...
...HE WAS MY BROTHER...
...AND I MISS HIM, DAVID...
...BUT I GO ON. WE HAVE TO GO ON...

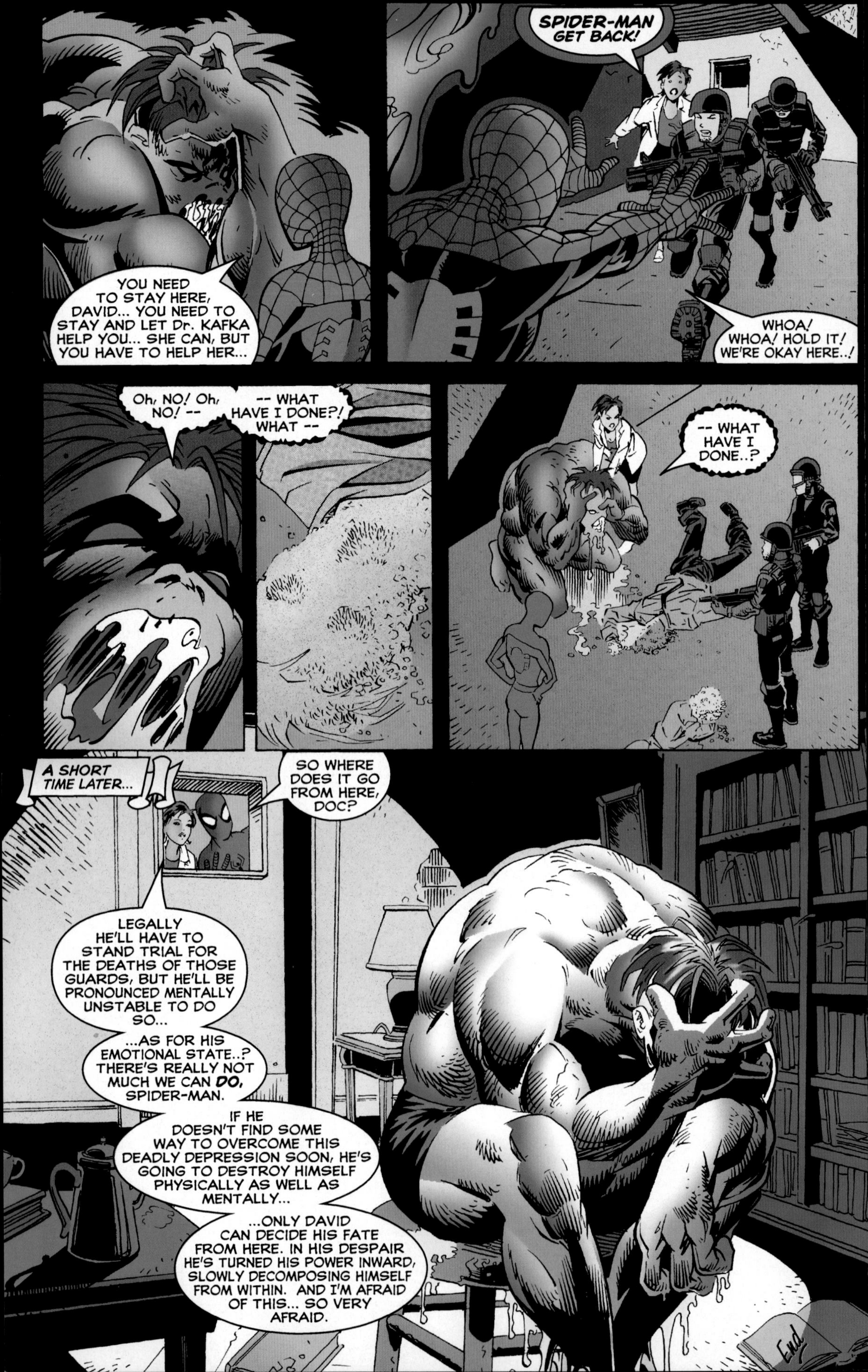
YOU NEED TO STAY HERE, DAVID... YOU NEED TO STAY AND LET Dr. KAFKA HELP YOU... SHE CAN, BUT YOU HAVE TO HELP HER...
SPIDER-MAN GET BACK!
WHOA! WHOA! HOLD IT! WE'RE OKAY HERE..!
Oh, NO! Oh, NO! --
-- WHAT HAVE I DONE?! WHAT --
-- WHAT HAVE I DONE..?
A SHORT TIME LATER...
SO WHERE DOES IT GO FROM HERE, DOC?
LEGALLY HE'LL HAVE TO STAND TRIAL FOR THE DEATHS OF THOSE GUARDS, BUT HE'LL BE PRONOUNCED MENTALLY UNSTABLE TO DO SO...
...AS FOR HIS EMOTIONAL STATE..? THERE'S REALLY NOT MUCH WE CAN DO, SPIDER-MAN.
IF HE DOESN'T FIND SOME WAY TO OVERCOME THIS DEADLY DEPRESSION SOON, HE'S GOING TO DESTROY HIMSELF PHYSICALLY AS WELL AS MENTALLY...
...ONLY DAVID CAN DECIDE HIS FATE FROM HERE. IN HIS DESPAIR HE'S TURNED HIS POWER INWARD, SLOWLY DECOMPOSING HIMSELF FROM WITHIN. AND I'M AFRAID OF THIS... SO VERY AFRAID.
End

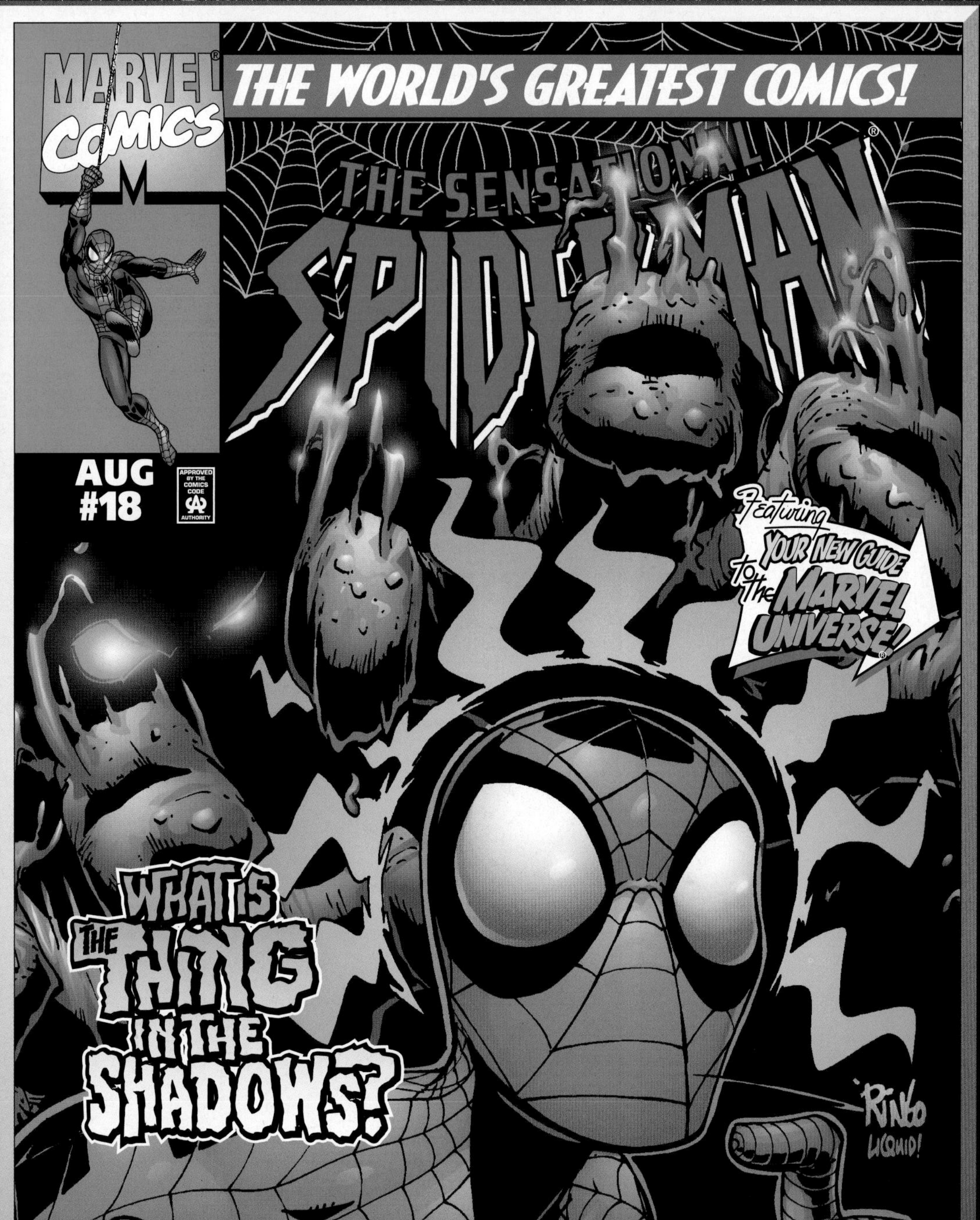
MARVEL COMICS
THE WORLD'S GREATEST COMICS!
THE SENSATIONAL
AUG #18
APPROVED BY THE COMICS CODE AUTHORITY
Featuring YOUR NEW GUIDE to the MARVEL UNIVERSE!
WHAT IS THE THING IN THE SHADOWS?
RINGO LIQUID!
DeZAGO ARMSTRONG BOYD

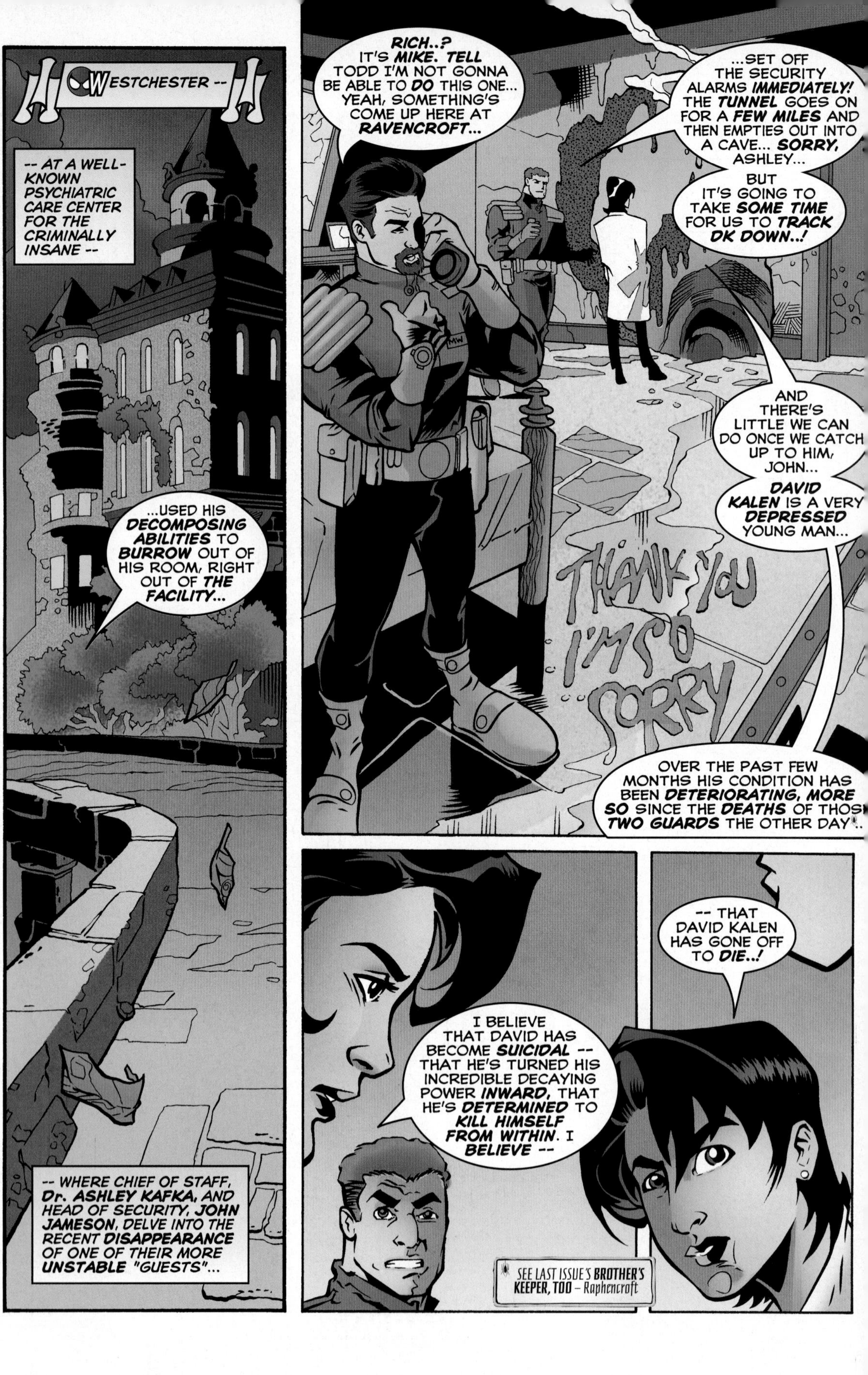
WESTCHESTER --
-- AT A WELL-KNOWN PSYCHIATRIC CARE CENTER FOR THE CRIMINALLY INSANE --
-- WHERE CHIEF OF STAFF, Dr. ASHLEY KAFKA, AND HEAD OF SECURITY, JOHN JAMESON, DELVE INTO THE RECENT DISAPPEARANCE OF ONE OF THEIR MORE UNSTABLE "GUESTS"...
...USED HIS DECOMPOSING ABILITIES TO BURROW OUT OF HIS ROOM, RIGHT OUT OF THE FACILITY...
RICH..? IT'S MIKE. TELL TODD I'M NOT GONNA BE ABLE TO DO THIS ONE... YEAH, SOMETHING'S COME UP HERE AT RAVENCROFT...
...SET OFF THE SECURITY ALARMS IMMEDIATELY! THE TUNNEL GOES ON FOR A FEW MILES AND THEN EMPTIES OUT INTO A CAVE... SORRY, ASHLEY...
BUT IT'S GOING TO TAKE SOME TIME FOR US TO TRACK DK DOWN..!
AND THERE'S LITTLE WE CAN DO ONCE WE CATCH UP TO HIM, JOHN...
DAVID KALEN IS A VERY DEPRESSED YOUNG MAN...
THANK YOU I'M SO SORRY
OVER THE PAST FEW MONTHS HIS CONDITION HAS BEEN DETERIORATING, MORE SO SINCE THE DEATHS OF THOS TWO GUARDS THE OTHER DAY*...
I BELIEVE THAT DAVID HAS BECOME SUICIDAL -- THAT HE'S TURNED HIS INCREDIBLE DECAYING POWER INWARD, THAT HE'S DETERMINED TO KILL HIMSELF FROM WITHIN. I BELIEVE --
-- THAT DAVID KALEN HAS GONE OFF TO DIE..!
* SEE LAST ISSUE'S BROTHER'S KEEPER, TOO – Raphencroft

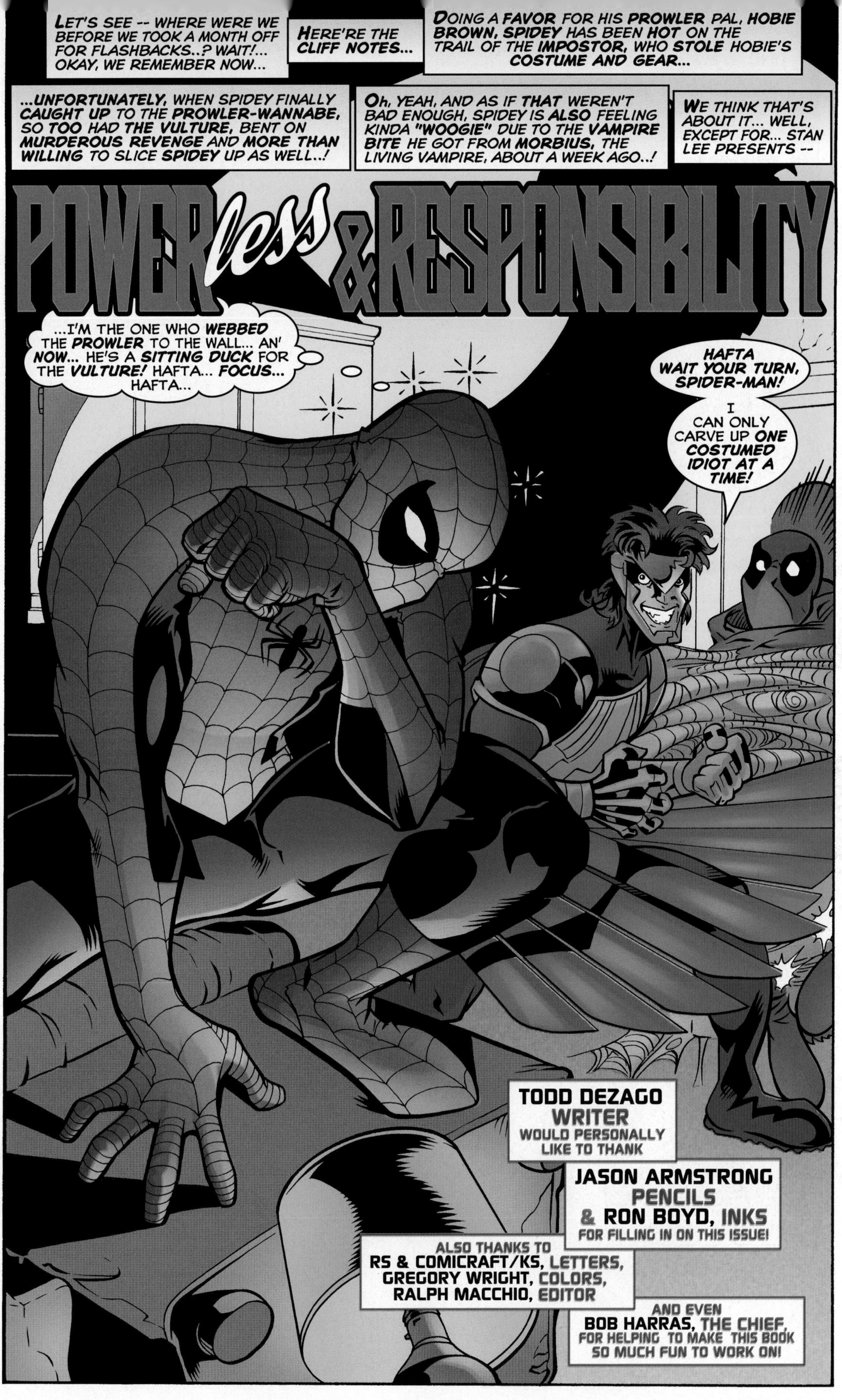
LET'S SEE -- WHERE WERE WE BEFORE WE TOOK A MONTH OFF FOR FLASHBACKS..? WAIT!... OKAY, WE REMEMBER NOW...
HERE'RE THE CLIFF NOTES...
DOING A FAVOR FOR HIS PROWLER PAL, HOBIE BROWN, SPIDEY HAS BEEN HOT ON THE TRAIL OF THE IMPOSTOR, WHO STOLE HOBIE'S COSTUME AND GEAR...
...UNFORTUNATELY, WHEN SPIDEY FINALLY CAUGHT UP TO THE PROWLER-WANNABE, SO TOO HAD THE VULTURE, BENT ON MURDEROUS REVENGE AND MORE THAN WILLING TO SLICE SPIDEY UP AS WELL..!
OH, YEAH, AND AS IF THAT WEREN'T BAD ENOUGH, SPIDEY IS ALSO FEELING KINDA "WOOGIE" DUE TO THE VAMPIRE BITE HE GOT FROM MORBIUS, THE LIVING VAMPIRE, ABOUT A WEEK AGO..!
WE THINK THAT'S ABOUT IT... WELL, EXCEPT FOR... STAN LEE PRESENTS --
POWER less & RESPONSIBILITY
...I'M THE ONE WHO WEBBED THE PROWLER TO THE WALL... AN' NOW... HE'S A SITTING DUCK FOR THE VULTURE! HAFTA... FOCUS... HAFTA...
HAFTA WAIT YOUR TURN, SPIDER-MAN!
I CAN ONLY CARVE UP ONE COSTUMED IDIOT AT A TIME!
TODD DEZAGO WRITER WOULD PERSONALLY LIKE TO THANK
JASON ARMSTRONG PENCILS & RON BOYD, INKS FOR FILLING IN ON THIS ISSUE!
ALSO THANKS TO RS & COMICRAFT/KS, LETTERS, GREGORY WRIGHT, COLORS, RALPH MACCHIO, EDITOR
AND EVEN BOB HARRAS, THE CHIEF, FOR HELPING TO MAKE THIS BOOK SO MUCH FUN TO WORK ON!

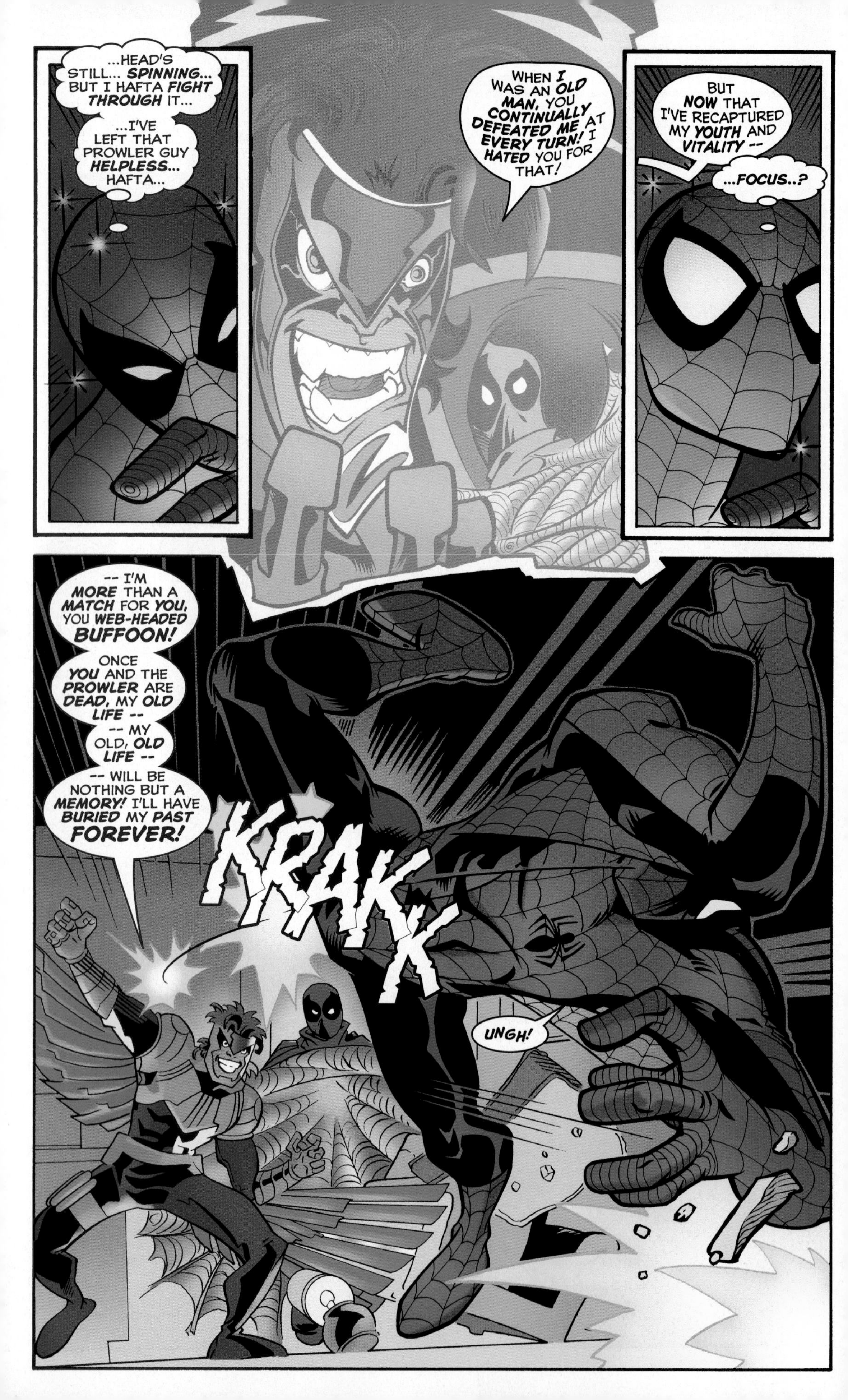

...HEAD'S STILL... SPINNING... BUT I HAFTA FIGHT THROUGH IT...
...I'VE LEFT THAT PROWLER GUY HELPLESS... HAFTA...
WHEN I WAS AN OLD MAN, YOU CONTINUALLY DEFEATED ME AT EVERY TURN! I HATED YOU FOR THAT!
BUT NOW THAT I'VE RECAPTURED MY YOUTH AND VITALITY --
...FOCUS..?
-- I'M MORE THAN A MATCH FOR YOU, YOU WEB-HEADED BUFFOON!
ONCE YOU AND THE PROWLER ARE DEAD, MY OLD LIFE --
-- MY OLD, OLD LIFE --
-- WILL BE NOTHING BUT A MEMORY! I'LL HAVE BURIED MY PAST FOREVER!
KRAKK
UNGH!

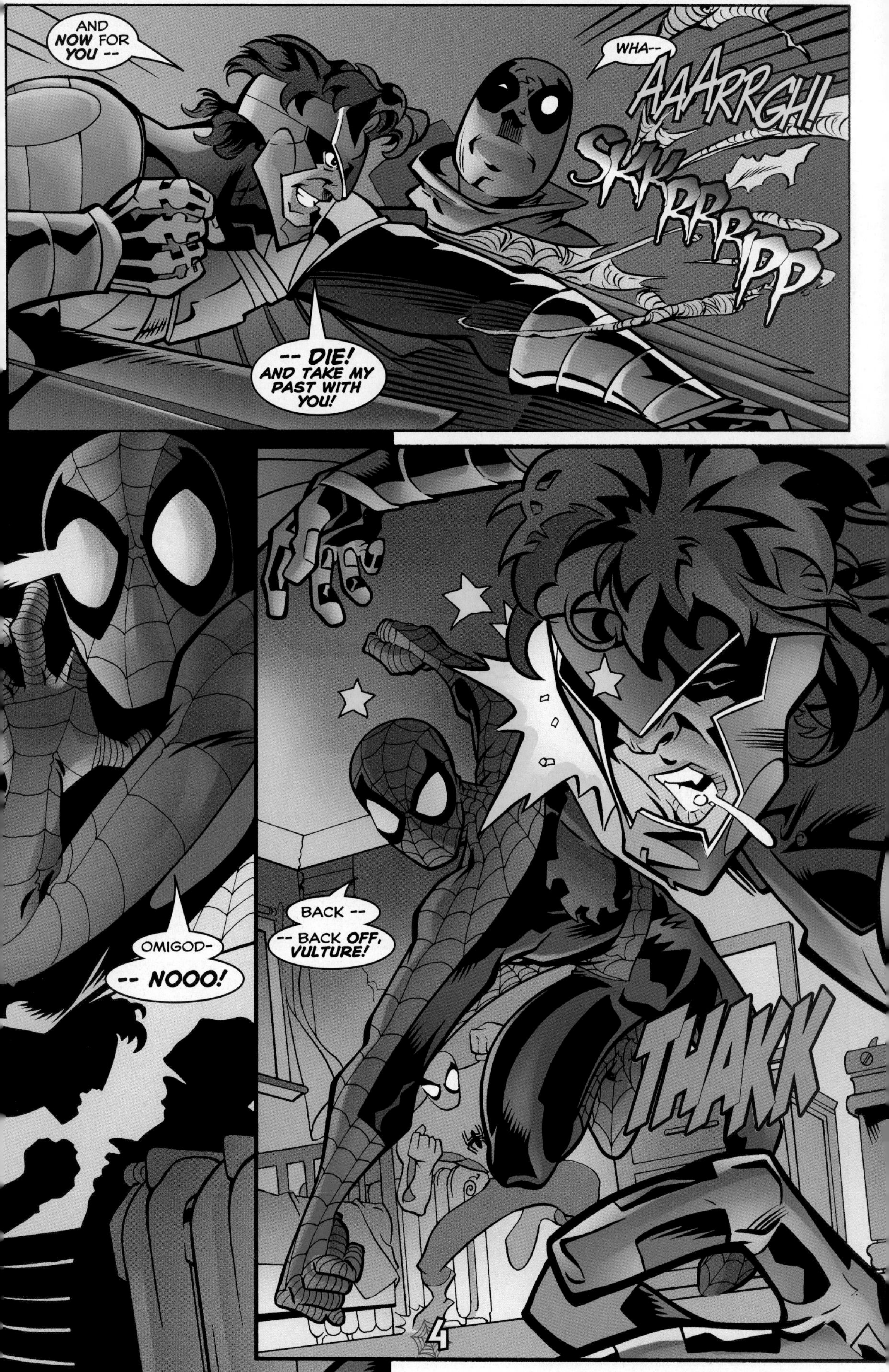
AND NOW FOR YOU --
WHA--
AAARRGH!
SKKRRRIPP
-- DIE! AND TAKE MY PAST WITH YOU!
OMIGOD-
-- NOOO!
BACK --
-- BACK OFF, VULTURE!
THAKK

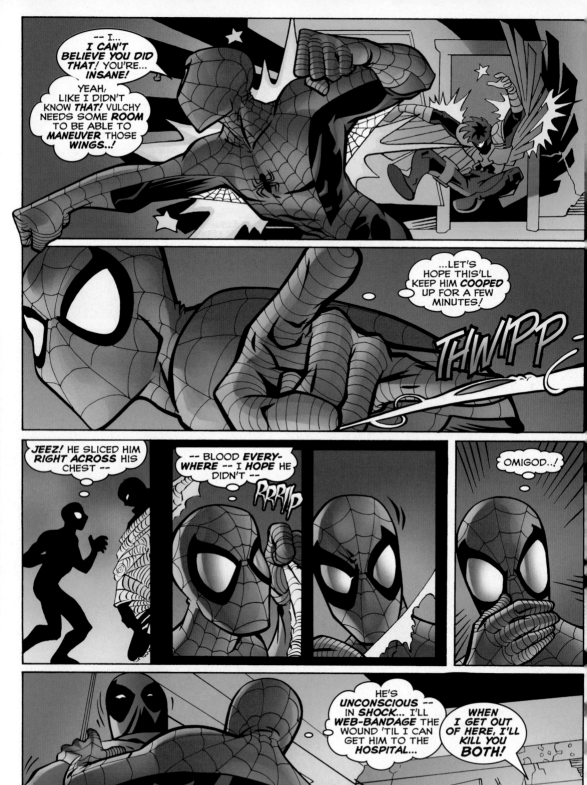

-- I... I CAN'T BELIEVE YOU DID THAT! YOU'RE... INSANE!

YEAH, LIKE I DIDN'T KNOW THAT! VULCHY NEEDS SOME ROOM TO BE ABLE TO MANEUVER THOSE WINGS..!

...LET'S HOPE THIS'LL KEEP HIM COOPED UP FOR A FEW MINUTES!

THWIPP

JEEZ! HE SLICED HIM RIGHT ACROSS HIS CHEST --

-- BLOOD EVERY-WHERE -- I HOPE HE DIDN'T --

RRRIP

OMIGOD..!

HE'S UNCONSCIOUS -- IN SHOCK... I'LL WEB-BANDAGE THE WOUND 'TIL I CAN GET HIM TO THE HOSPITAL...

WHEN I GET OUT OF HERE, I'LL KILL YOU BOTH!

SHUT UP, YOU...

...ANIMAL!

THWIP!

5

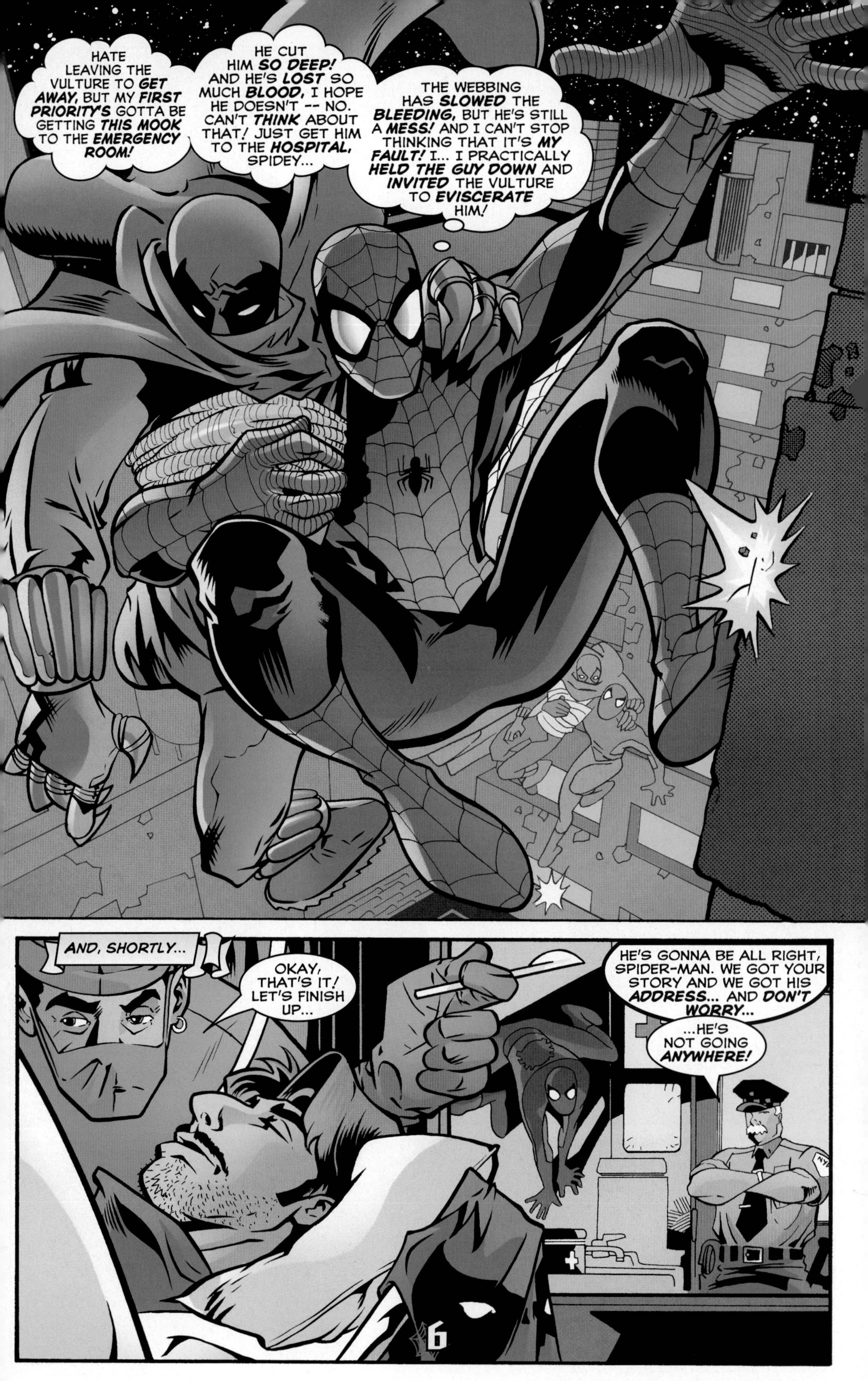
HATE LEAVING THE VULTURE TO GET AWAY, BUT MY FIRST PRIORITY'S GOTTA BE GETTING THIS MOOK TO THE EMERGENCY ROOM!
HE CUT HIM SO DEEP! AND HE'S LOST SO MUCH BLOOD, I HOPE HE DOESN'T -- NO. CAN'T THINK ABOUT THAT! JUST GET HIM TO THE HOSPITAL, SPIDEY...
THE WEBBING HAS SLOWED THE BLEEDING, BUT HE'S STILL A MESS! AND I CAN'T STOP THINKING THAT IT'S MY FAULT! I... I PRACTICALLY HELD THE GUY DOWN AND INVITED THE VULTURE TO EVISCERATE HIM!
AND, SHORTLY...
OKAY, THAT'S IT! LET'S FINISH UP...
HE'S GONNA BE ALL RIGHT, SPIDER-MAN. WE GOT YOUR STORY AND WE GOT HIS ADDRESS... AND DON'T WORRY...
...HE'S NOT GOING ANYWHERE!

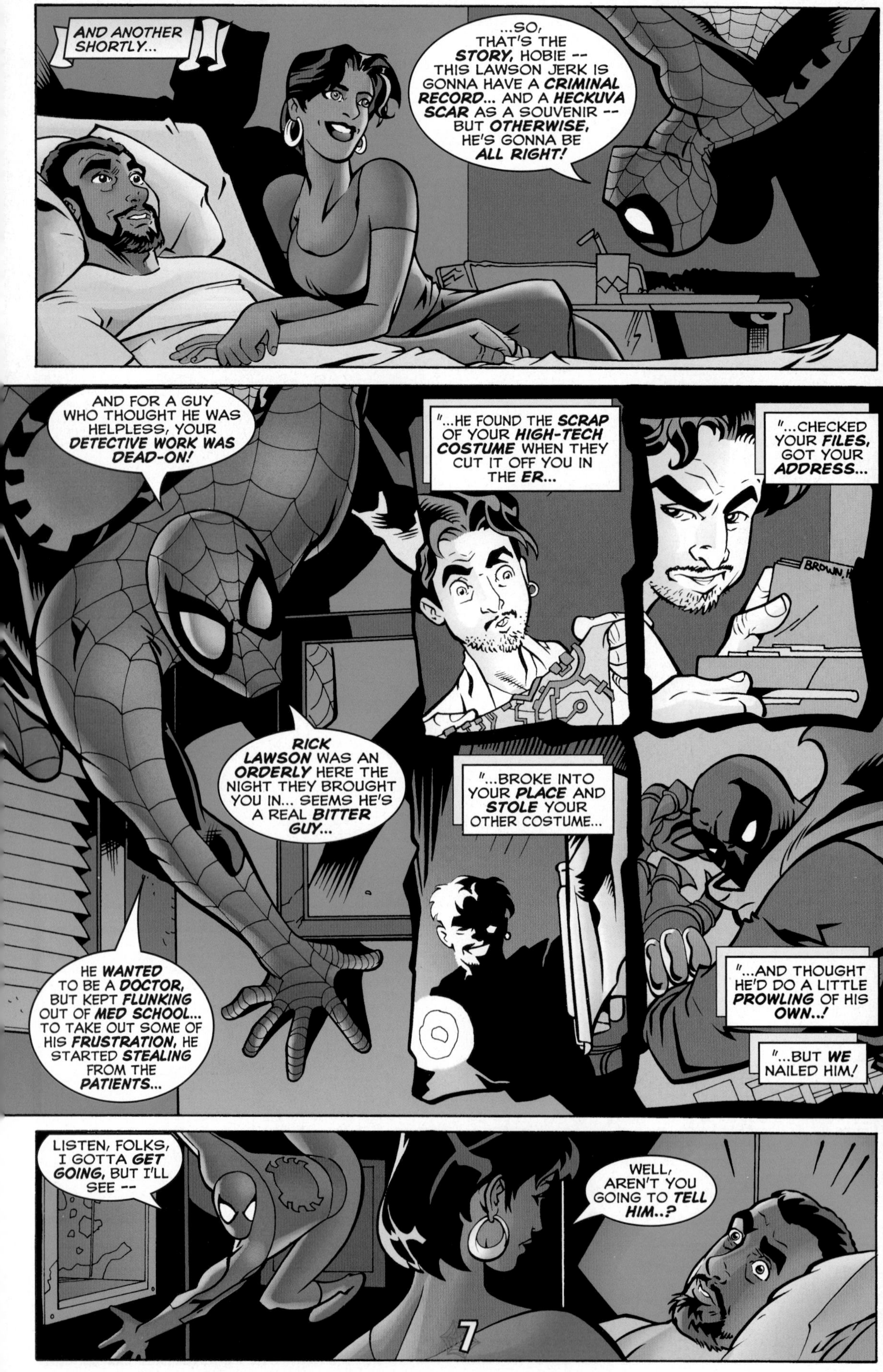
AND ANOTHER SHORTLY...
...SO, THAT'S THE STORY, HOBIE -- THIS LAWSON JERK IS GONNA HAVE A CRIMINAL RECORD... AND A HECKUVA SCAR AS A SOUVENIR -- BUT OTHERWISE, HE'S GONNA BE ALL RIGHT!
AND FOR A GUY WHO THOUGHT HE WAS HELPLESS, YOUR DETECTIVE WORK WAS DEAD-ON!
RICK LAWSON WAS AN ORDERLY HERE THE NIGHT THEY BROUGHT YOU IN... SEEMS HE'S A REAL BITTER GUY...
HE WANTED TO BE A DOCTOR, BUT KEPT FLUNKING OUT OF MED SCHOOL... TO TAKE OUT SOME OF HIS FRUSTRATION, HE STARTED STEALING FROM THE PATIENTS...
"...HE FOUND THE SCRAP OF YOUR HIGH-TECH COSTUME WHEN THEY CUT IT OFF YOU IN THE ER...
"...CHECKED YOUR FILES, GOT YOUR ADDRESS...
BROWN, H
"...BROKE INTO YOUR PLACE AND STOLE YOUR OTHER COSTUME...
"...AND THOUGHT HE'D DO A LITTLE PROWLING OF HIS OWN..!
"...BUT WE NAILED HIM!
LISTEN, FOLKS, I GOTTA GET GOING, BUT I'LL SEE --
WELL, AREN'T YOU GOING TO TELL HIM..?

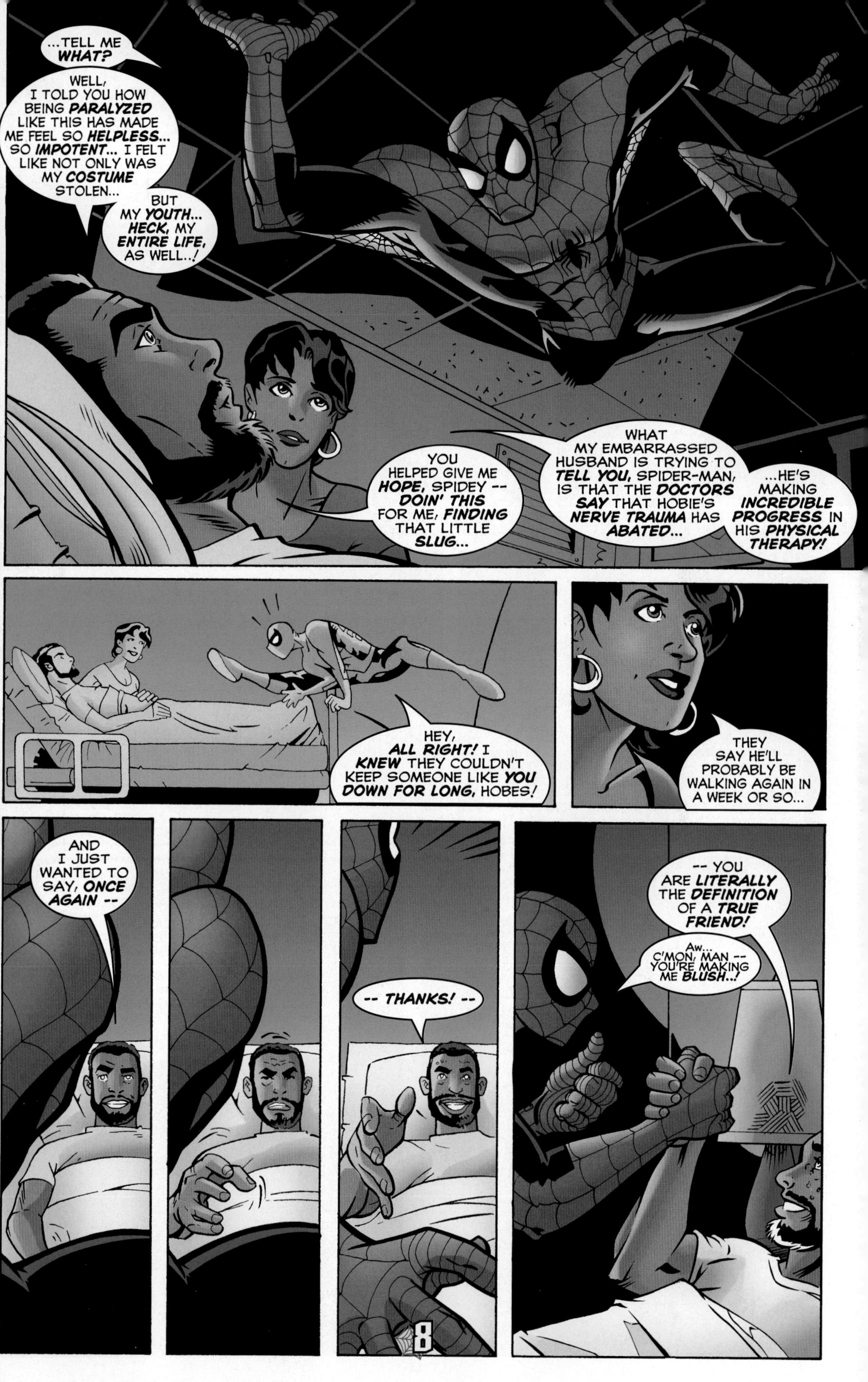
...TELL ME WHAT?
WELL, I TOLD YOU HOW BEING PARALYZED LIKE THIS HAS MADE ME FEEL SO HELPLESS... SO IMPOTENT... I FELT LIKE NOT ONLY WAS MY COSTUME STOLEN...
BUT MY YOUTH... HECK, MY ENTIRE LIFE, AS WELL..!
YOU HELPED GIVE ME HOPE, SPIDEY -- DOIN' THIS FOR ME, FINDING THAT LITTLE SLUG...
WHAT MY EMBARRASSED HUSBAND IS TRYING TO TELL YOU, SPIDER-MAN, IS THAT THE DOCTORS SAY THAT HOBIE'S NERVE TRAUMA HAS ABATED...
...HE'S MAKING INCREDIBLE PROGRESS IN HIS PHYSICAL THERAPY!
HEY, ALL RIGHT! I KNEW THEY COULDN'T KEEP SOMEONE LIKE YOU DOWN FOR LONG, HOBES!
THEY SAY HE'LL PROBABLY BE WALKING AGAIN IN A WEEK OR SO...
AND I JUST WANTED TO SAY, ONCE AGAIN --
-- THANKS! --
-- YOU ARE LITERALLY THE DEFINITION OF A TRUE FRIEND!
AW... C'MON, MAN -- YOU'RE MAKING ME BLUSH..!
8

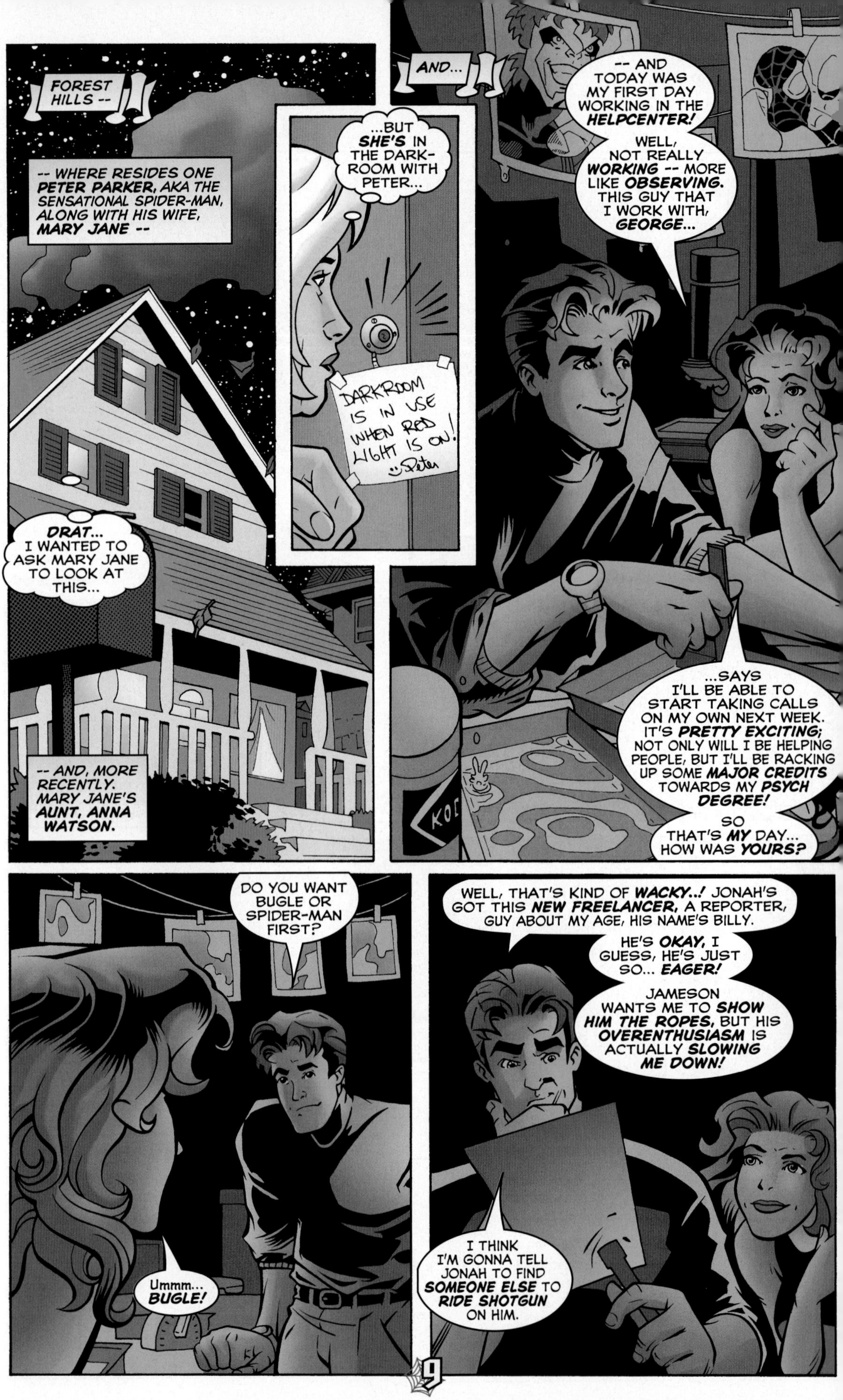
FOREST HILLS --
-- WHERE RESIDES ONE PETER PARKER, AKA THE SENSATIONAL SPIDER-MAN, ALONG WITH HIS WIFE, MARY JANE --
DRAT... I WANTED TO ASK MARY JANE TO LOOK AT THIS...
-- AND, MORE RECENTLY. MARY JANE'S AUNT, ANNA WATSON.
...BUT SHE'S IN THE DARK-ROOM WITH PETER...
DARKROOM IS IN USE WHEN RED LIGHT IS ON! Peter
AND...
-- AND TODAY WAS MY FIRST DAY WORKING IN THE HELPCENTER!
WELL, NOT REALLY WORKING -- MORE LIKE OBSERVING. THIS GUY THAT I WORK WITH, GEORGE...
...SAYS I'LL BE ABLE TO START TAKING CALLS ON MY OWN NEXT WEEK. IT'S PRETTY EXCITING; NOT ONLY WILL I BE HELPING PEOPLE, BUT I'LL BE RACKING UP SOME MAJOR CREDITS TOWARDS MY PSYCH DEGREE!
SO THAT'S MY DAY... HOW WAS YOURS?
DO YOU WANT BUGLE OR SPIDER-MAN FIRST?
Ummm... BUGLE!
WELL, THAT'S KIND OF WACKY..! JONAH'S GOT THIS NEW FREELANCER, A REPORTER, GUY ABOUT MY AGE, HIS NAME'S BILLY.
HE'S OKAY, I GUESS, HE'S JUST SO... EAGER!
JAMESON WANTS ME TO SHOW HIM THE ROPES, BUT HIS OVERENTHUSIASM IS ACTUALLY SLOWING ME DOWN!
I THINK I'M GONNA TELL JONAH TO FIND SOMEONE ELSE TO RIDE SHOTGUN ON HIM.

AS FOR *SPIDEY*...

I *FINALLY* CAUGHT UP WITH THE JERK WHO STOLE THE *PROWLER COSTUME* FROM HOBIE... BUT SO HAD *THE VULTURE*..! AND WHILE I WAS THROWING DOWN WITH *HIM* --

-- THE *PROWLER* JERK TRIED TO *SKIP OUT*, BUT I WAS SO *DETERMINED* THAT I WASN'T GONNA LET HIM *GET AWAY*, I HIT HIM WITH SOME *WEB* AND *PASTED HIM TO THE WALL!*

FOR JUST A *MOMENT*, I... THE *VULTURE* GOT THE *ADVANTAGE* AND *SLICED* THAT KID OPEN LIKE A *GRAPEFRUIT!* AND *I* PRACTICALLY *HELD THE GUY DOWN FOR HIM!* --

-- I LEFT HIM *HELPLESS*, AND I *COULDN'T DO ANYTHING ABOUT IT!* I GOT HIM TO THE *HOSPITAL*, AND HE'S GONNA BE *OKAY*, BUT --

HEY! WHAT IS IT WITH YOU ALWAYS HAVING TO FEEL *GUILTY?!* YOU DID THE *BEST YOU COULD!* THAT'S WHAT THE GOOD GUYS DO! LET IT *GO!*

NOW... ARE YOU *DONE WORKING?*

WELL, I'M DONE *PRINTING PICTURES*...

...BUT I *AIN'T DONE* WITH THE *DARKROOM*..!

ARKROOM
S IN USE
EN RED
T IS ON!
... Pete

THEY'RE STILL IN THERE... BUT I WANTED BOTH OF THEM TO *SEE* THIS...

EVER SINCE THEY MOVED IN LAST WEEK, THE NEIGHBORS HAVE BEEN SO... *QUIET*...

AND IT'S SO *STRANGE!* THE LITTLE GIRL JUST STANDS THERE IN THE BACKYARD, SOMETIMES FOR *HOURS*, JUST *STARING*...

...NEVER MAKING A *SOUND*...

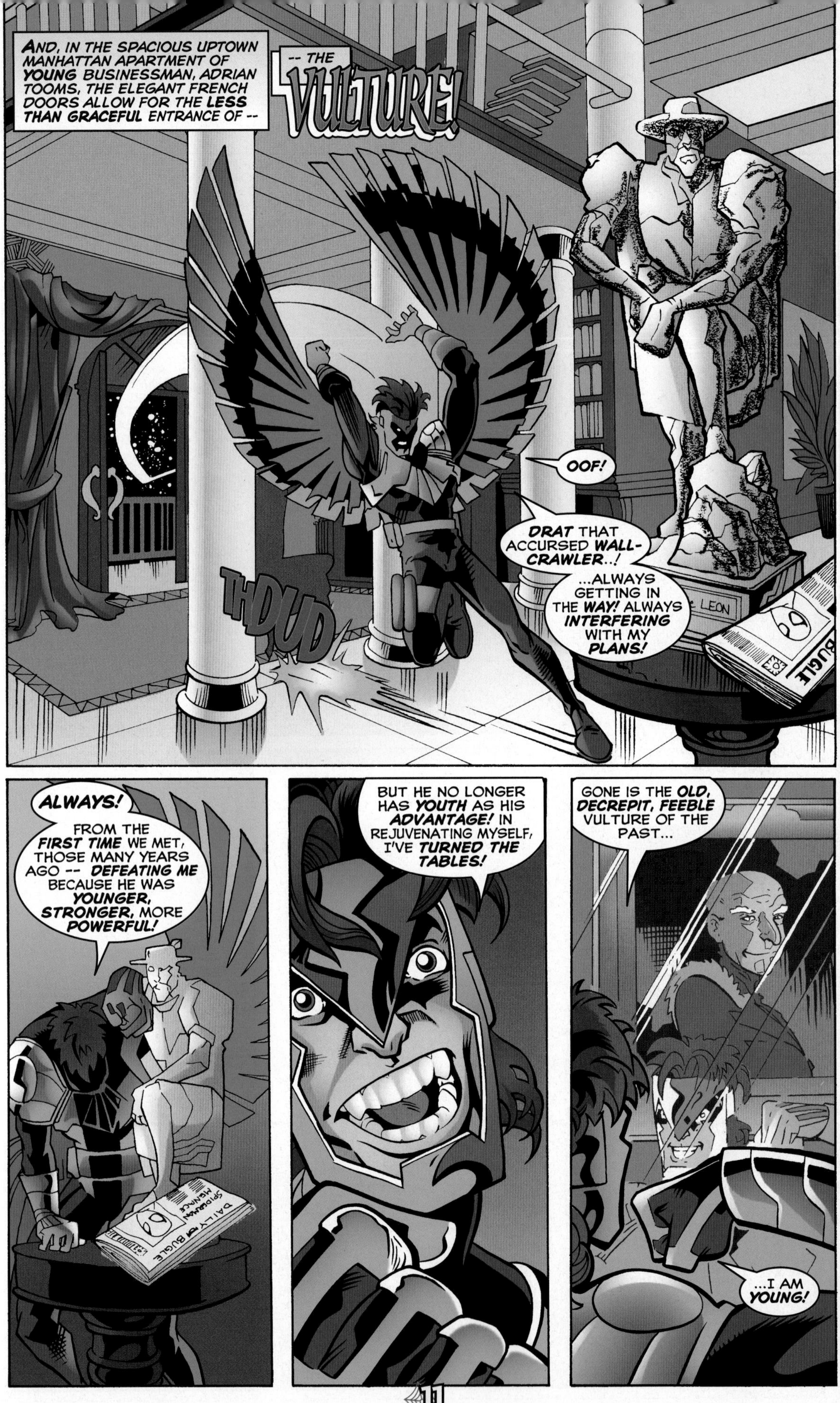
AND, IN THE SPACIOUS UPTOWN MANHATTAN APARTMENT OF YOUNG BUSINESSMAN, ADRIAN TOOMS, THE ELEGANT FRENCH DOORS ALLOW FOR THE LESS THAN GRACEFUL ENTRANCE OF --
-- THE VULTURE!
THDUD
OOF!
DRAT THAT ACCURSED WALL-CRAWLER..!
...ALWAYS GETTING IN THE WAY! ALWAYS INTERFERING WITH MY PLANS!
LEON
BUGLE
ALWAYS!
FROM THE FIRST TIME WE MET, THOSE MANY YEARS AGO -- DEFEATING ME BECAUSE HE WAS YOUNGER, STRONGER, MORE POWERFUL!
DAILY BUGLE
SPIDERMAN MENACE
BUT HE NO LONGER HAS YOUTH AS HIS ADVANTAGE! IN REJUVENATING MYSELF, I'VE TURNED THE TABLES!
GONE IS THE OLD, DECREPIT, FEEBLE VULTURE OF THE PAST...
...I AM YOUNG!

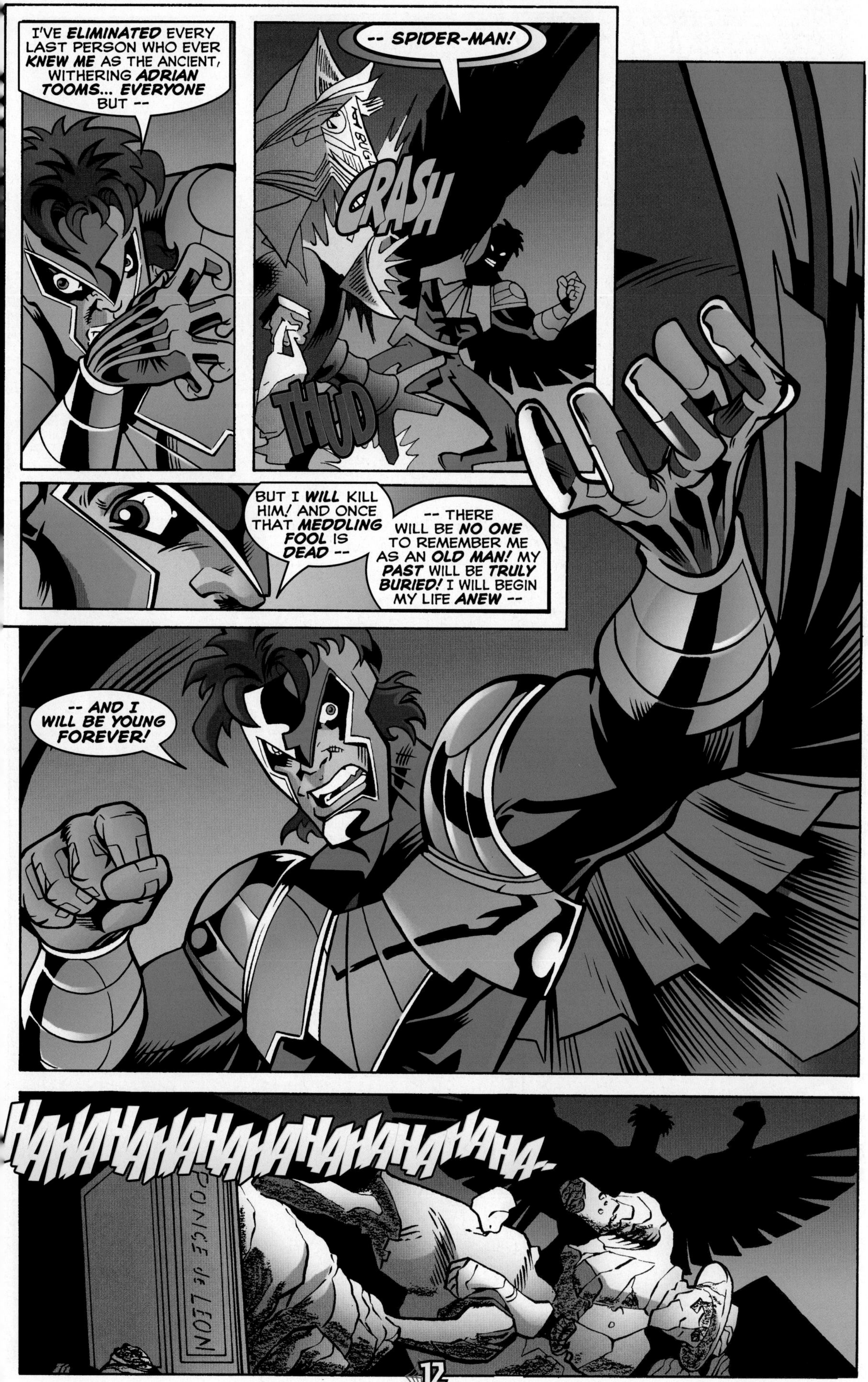
I'VE ELIMINATED EVERY LAST PERSON WHO EVER KNEW ME AS THE ANCIENT, WITHERING ADRIAN TOOMS... EVERYONE BUT --
-- SPIDER-MAN!
CRASH
THUD
BUT I WILL KILL HIM! AND ONCE THAT MEDDLING FOOL IS DEAD --
-- THERE WILL BE NO ONE TO REMEMBER ME AS AN OLD MAN! MY PAST WILL BE TRULY BURIED! I WILL BEGIN MY LIFE ANEW --
-- AND I WILL BE YOUNG FOREVER!
HAHAHAHAHAHAHAHAHAHAHAHAHAHA-
PONCE de LEON

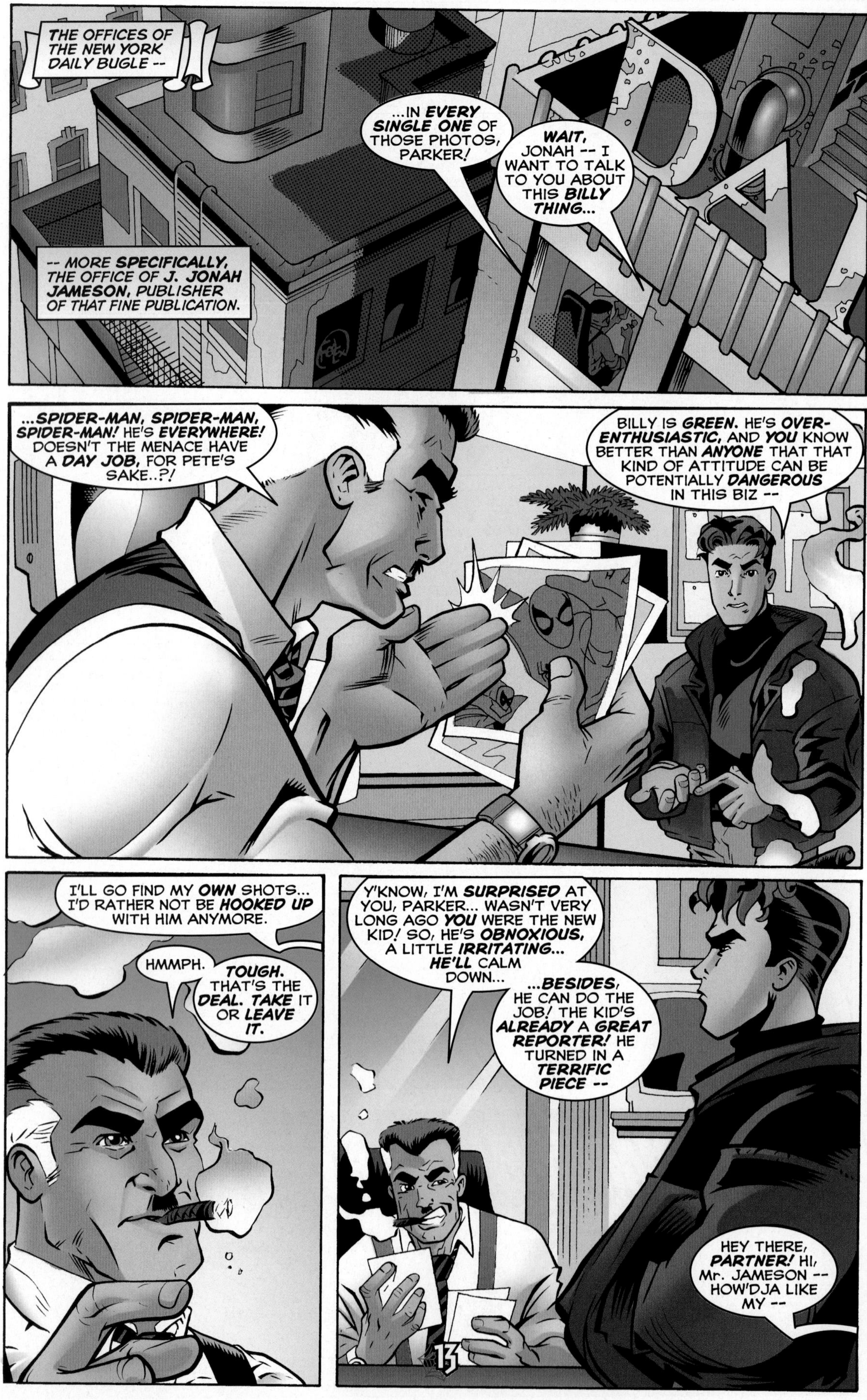
THE OFFICES OF THE NEW YORK DAILY BUGLE --
-- MORE SPECIFICALLY, THE OFFICE OF J. JONAH JAMESON, PUBLISHER OF THAT FINE PUBLICATION.
...IN EVERY SINGLE ONE OF THOSE PHOTOS, PARKER!
WAIT, JONAH -- I WANT TO TALK TO YOU ABOUT THIS BILLY THING...
...SPIDER-MAN, SPIDER-MAN, SPIDER-MAN! HE'S EVERYWHERE! DOESN'T THE MENACE HAVE A DAY JOB, FOR PETE'S SAKE..?!
BILLY IS GREEN. HE'S OVER-ENTHUSIASTIC, AND YOU KNOW BETTER THAN ANYONE THAT THAT KIND OF ATTITUDE CAN BE POTENTIALLY DANGEROUS IN THIS BIZ --
I'LL GO FIND MY OWN SHOTS... I'D RATHER NOT BE HOOKED UP WITH HIM ANYMORE.
HMMPH.
TOUGH. THAT'S THE DEAL. TAKE IT OR LEAVE IT.
Y'KNOW, I'M SURPRISED AT YOU, PARKER... WASN'T VERY LONG AGO YOU WERE THE NEW KID! SO, HE'S OBNOXIOUS, A LITTLE IRRITATING... HE'LL CALM DOWN...
...BESIDES, HE CAN DO THE JOB! THE KID'S ALREADY A GREAT REPORTER! HE TURNED IN A TERRIFIC PIECE --
HEY THERE, PARTNER! HI, Mr. JAMESON -- HOW'DJA LIKE MY --
13

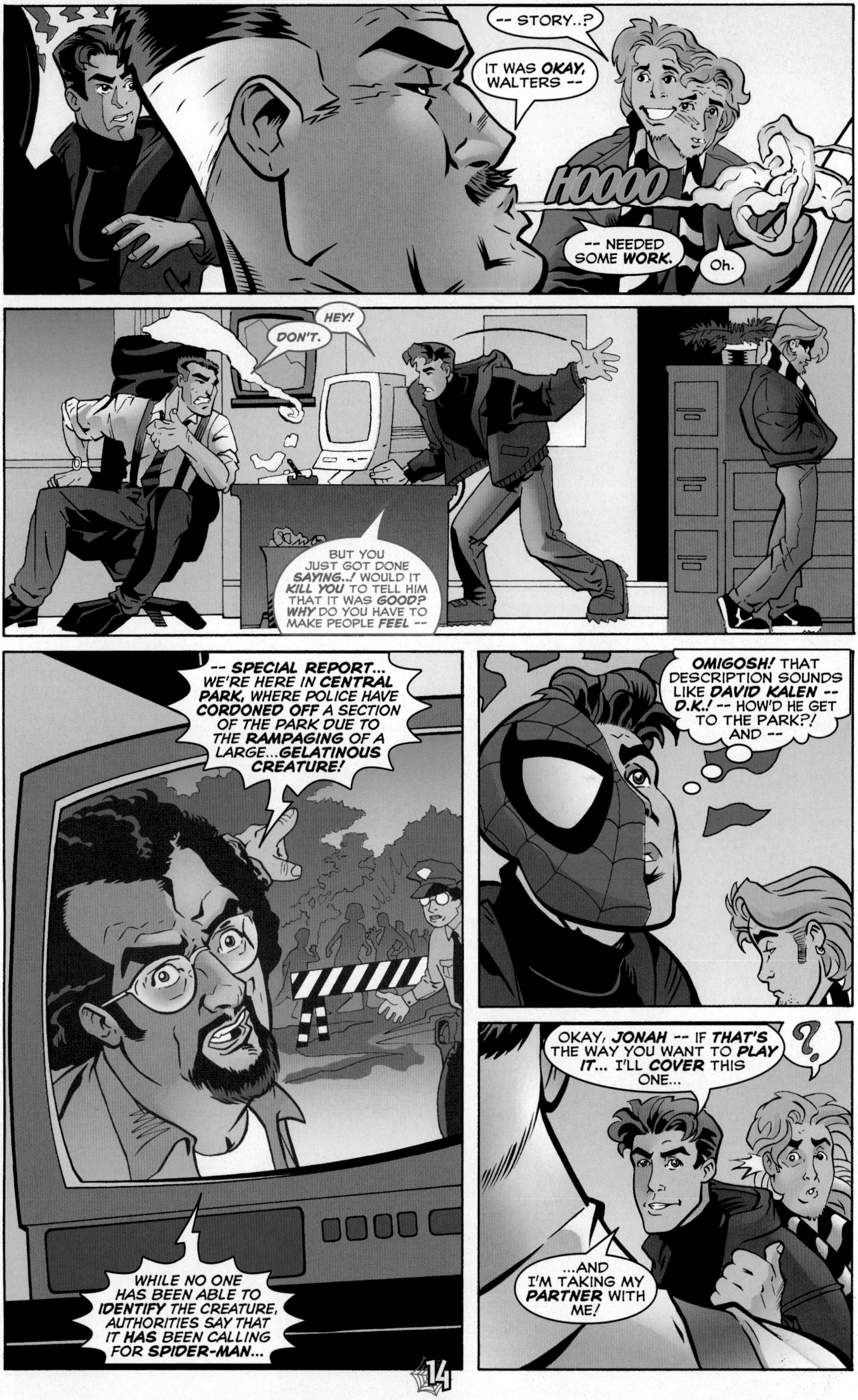
-- STORY..?
IT WAS OKAY, WALTERS --
HOOOO
-- NEEDED SOME WORK.
Oh.
DON'T.
HEY!
BUT YOU JUST GOT DONE SAYING..! WOULD IT KILL YOU TO TELL HIM THAT IT WAS GOOD? WHY DO YOU HAVE TO MAKE PEOPLE FEEL --
-- SPECIAL REPORT... WE'RE HERE IN CENTRAL PARK, WHERE POLICE HAVE CORDONED OFF A SECTION OF THE PARK DUE TO THE RAMPAGING OF A LARGE...GELATINOUS CREATURE!
WHILE NO ONE HAS BEEN ABLE TO IDENTIFY THE CREATURE, AUTHORITIES SAY THAT IT HAS BEEN CALLING FOR SPIDER-MAN...
OMIGOSH! THAT DESCRIPTION SOUNDS LIKE DAVID KALEN -- D.K.! -- HOW'D HE GET TO THE PARK?! AND --
OKAY, JONAH -- IF THAT'S THE WAY YOU WANT TO PLAY IT... I'LL COVER THIS ONE...
?
...AND I'M TAKING MY PARTNER WITH ME!

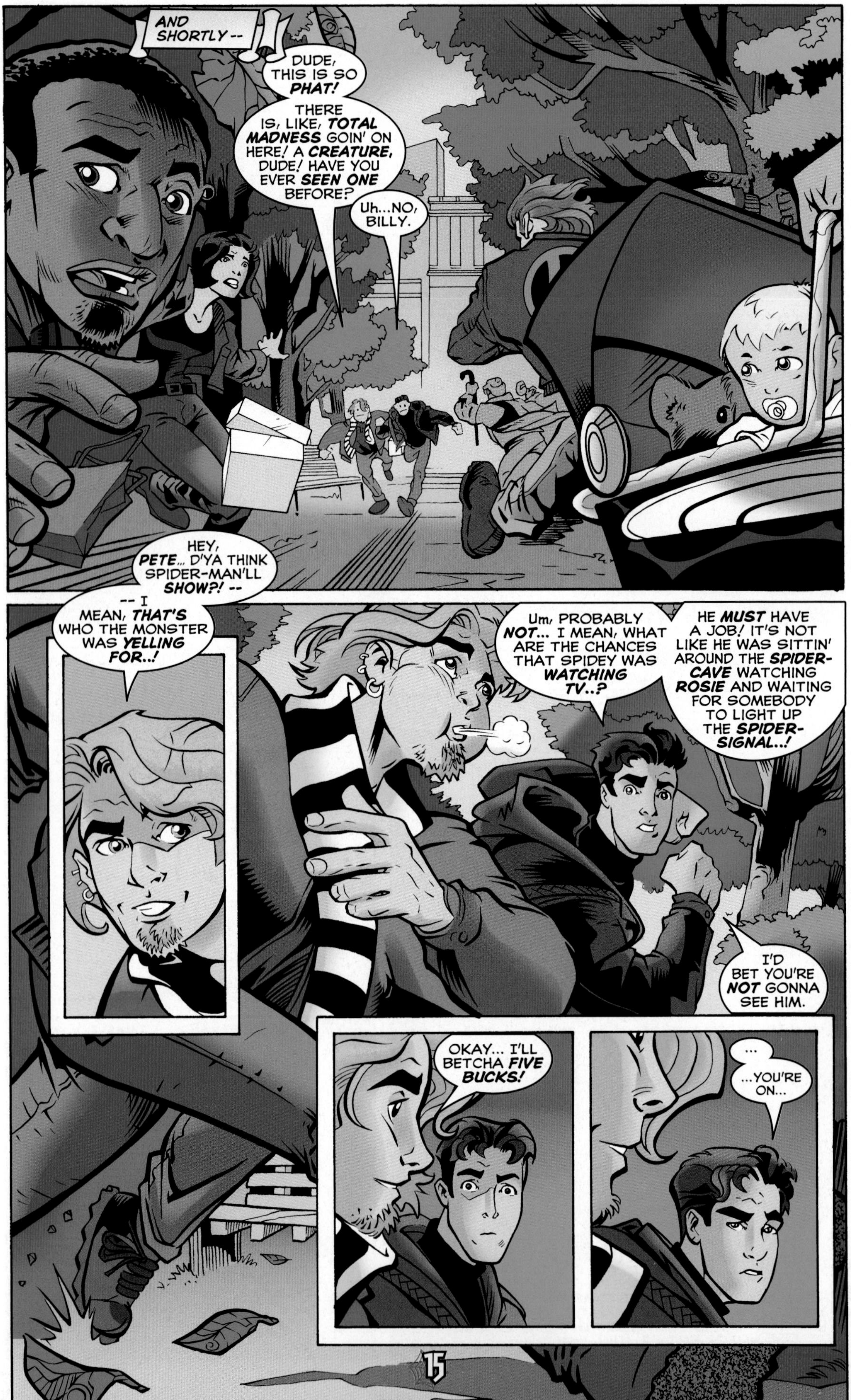

AND SHORTLY --
DUDE, THIS IS SO PHAT!
THERE IS, LIKE, TOTAL MADNESS GOIN' ON HERE! A CREATURE, DUDE! HAVE YOU EVER SEEN ONE BEFORE?
Uh...NO, BILLY.
HEY, PETE... D'YA THINK SPIDER-MAN'LL SHOW?! --
-- I MEAN, THAT'S WHO THE MONSTER WAS YELLING FOR...!
Um, PROBABLY NOT... I MEAN, WHAT ARE THE CHANCES THAT SPIDEY WAS WATCHING TV..?
HE MUST HAVE A JOB! IT'S NOT LIKE HE WAS SITTIN' AROUND THE SPIDER-CAVE WATCHING ROSIE AND WAITING FOR SOMEBODY TO LIGHT UP THE SPIDER-SIGNAL...!
I'D BET YOU'RE NOT GONNA SEE HIM.
OKAY... I'LL BETCHA FIVE BUCKS!
...
...YOU'RE ON...

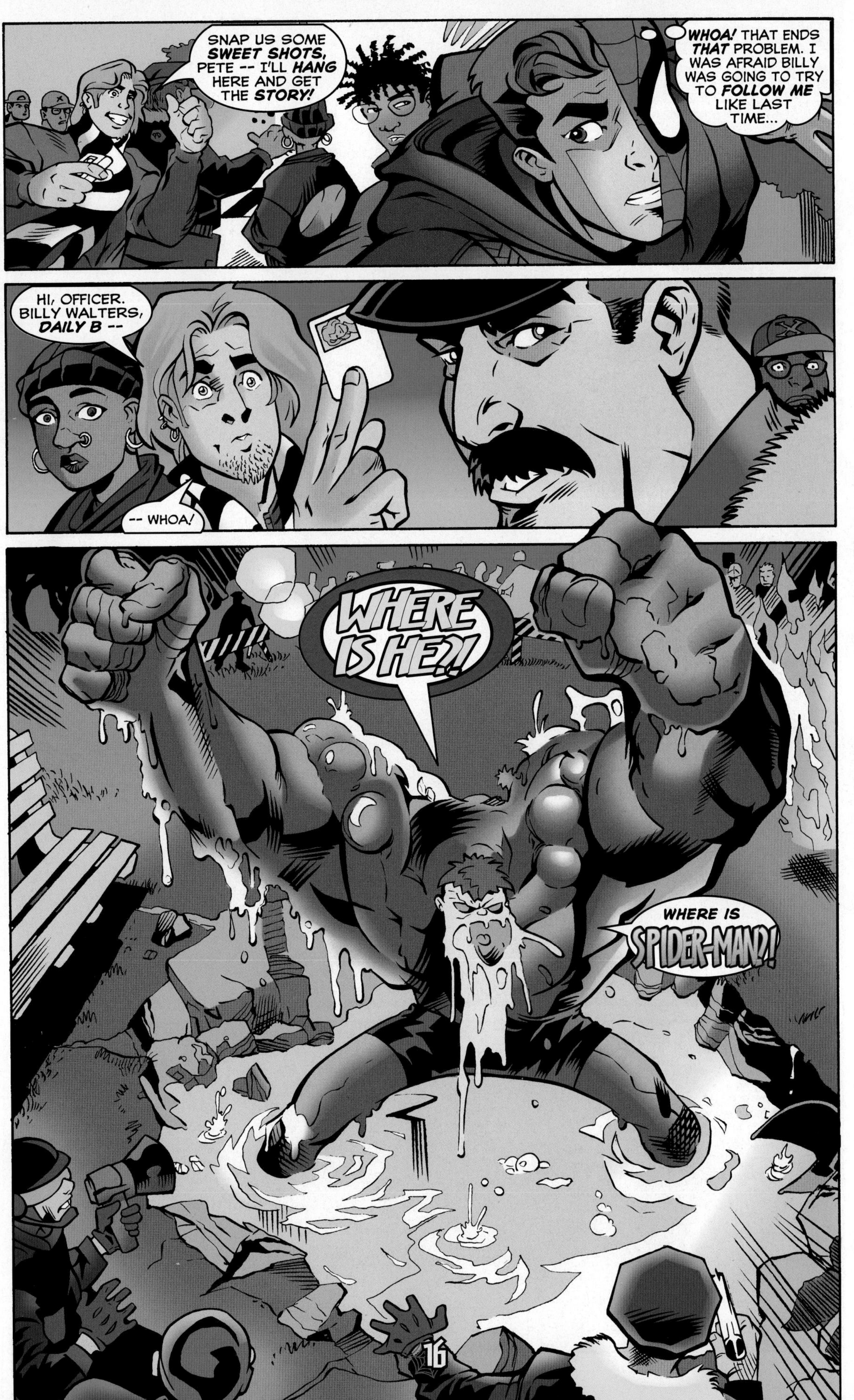
SNAP US SOME SWEET SHOTS, PETE -- I'LL HANG HERE AND GET THE STORY!
WHOA! THAT ENDS THAT PROBLEM. I WAS AFRAID BILLY WAS GOING TO TRY TO FOLLOW ME LIKE LAST TIME...
HI, OFFICER. BILLY WALTERS, DAILY B --
-- WHOA!
WHERE IS HE?!
WHERE IS SPIDER-MAN?!

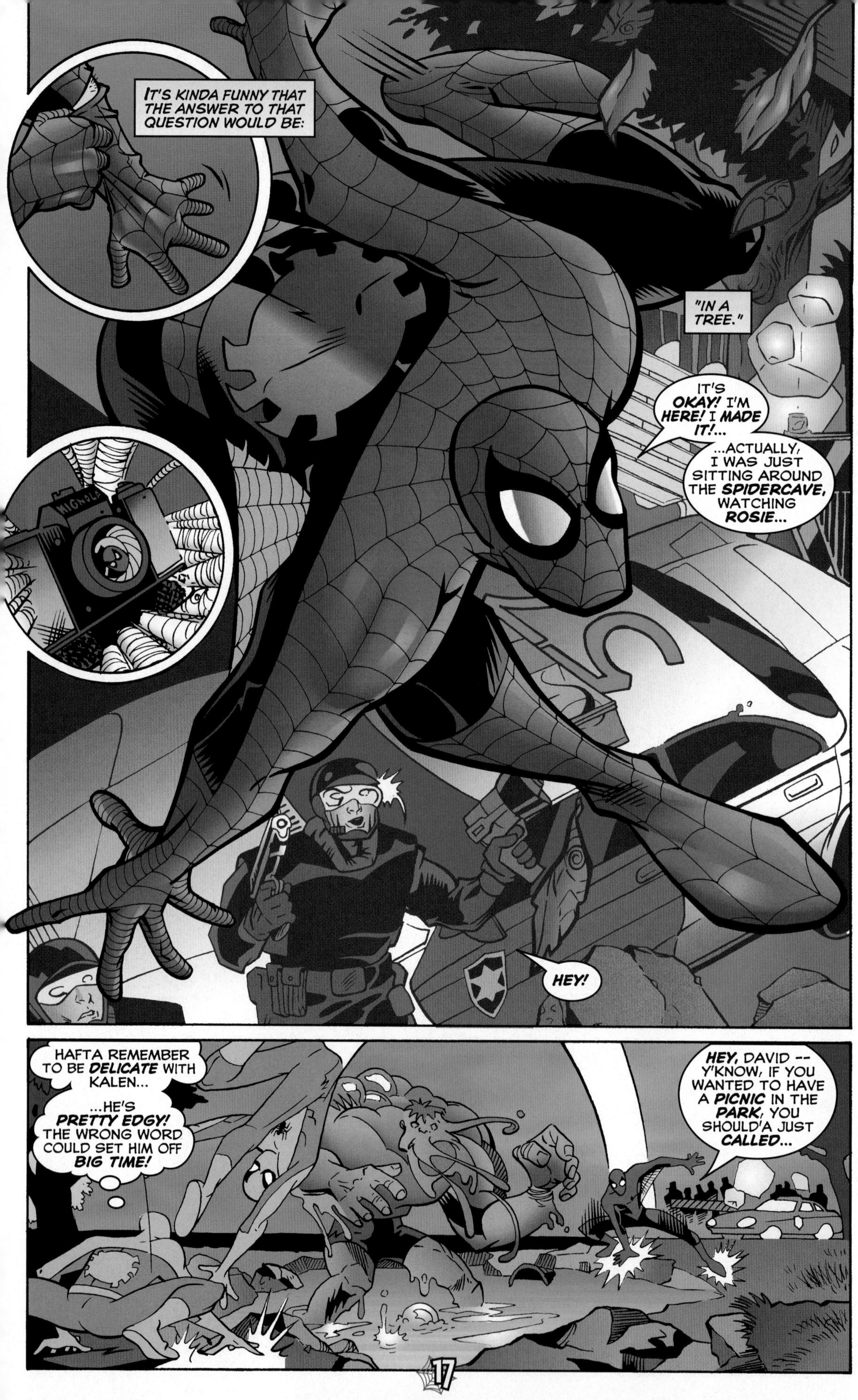
IT'S KINDA FUNNY THAT THE ANSWER TO THAT QUESTION WOULD BE:
"IN A TREE."
IT'S OKAY! I'M HERE! I MADE IT!...
...ACTUALLY, I WAS JUST SITTING AROUND THE SPIDERCAVE, WATCHING ROSIE...
HEY!
HAFTA REMEMBER TO BE DELICATE WITH KALEN...
...HE'S PRETTY EDGY! THE WRONG WORD COULD SET HIM OFF BIG TIME!
HEY, DAVID -- Y'KNOW, IF YOU WANTED TO HAVE A PICNIC IN THE PARK, YOU SHOULD'A JUST CALLED...

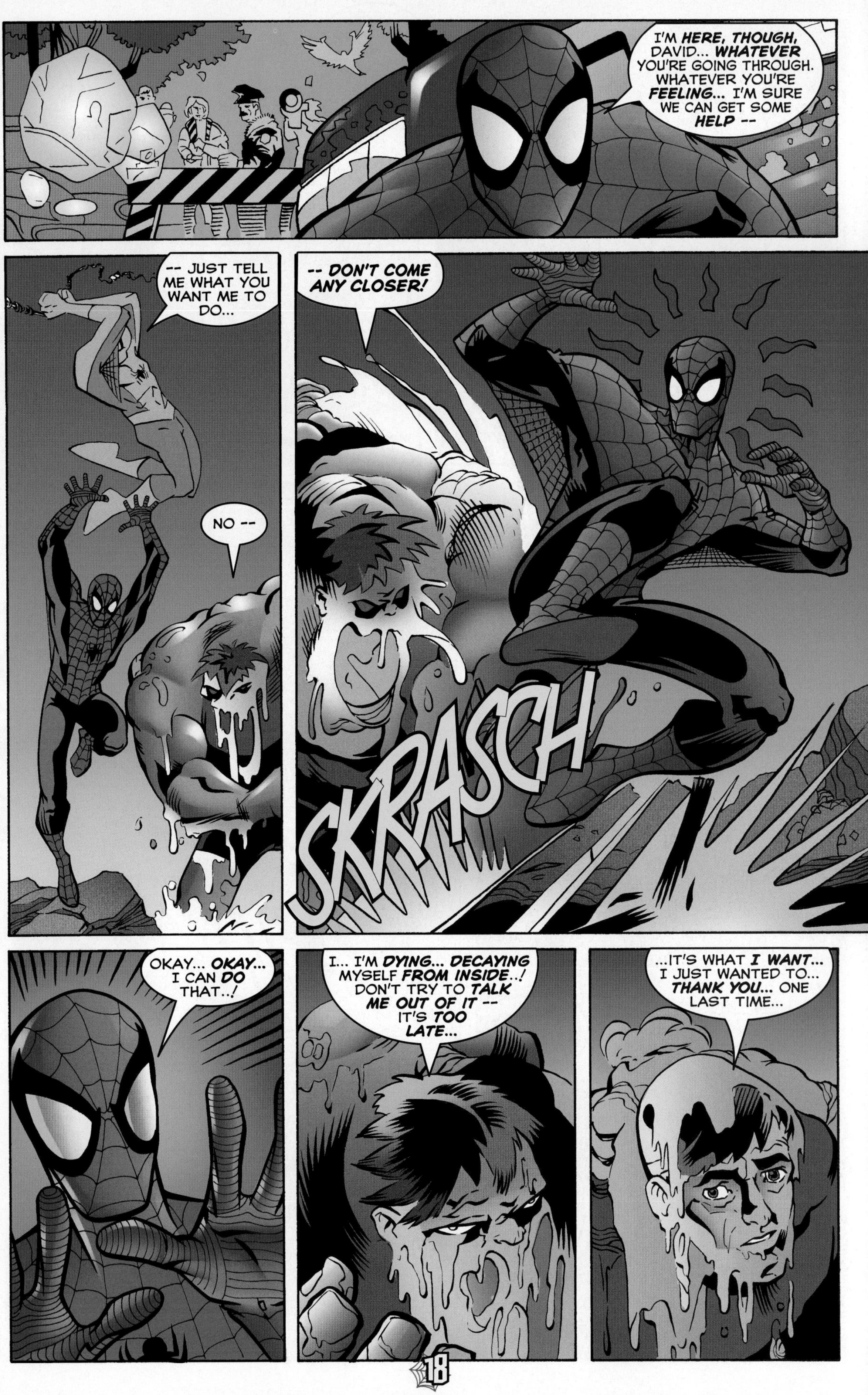
I'M HERE, THOUGH, DAVID... WHATEVER YOU'RE GOING THROUGH. WHATEVER YOU'RE FEELING... I'M SURE WE CAN GET SOME HELP --
-- JUST TELL ME WHAT YOU WANT ME TO DO...
NO --
-- DON'T COME ANY CLOSER!
SKRASCH
OKAY... OKAY... I CAN DO THAT...!
I... I'M DYING... DECAYING MYSELF FROM INSIDE...! DON'T TRY TO TALK ME OUT OF IT -- IT'S TOO LATE...
...IT'S WHAT I WANT... I JUST WANTED TO... THANK YOU... ONE LAST TIME...

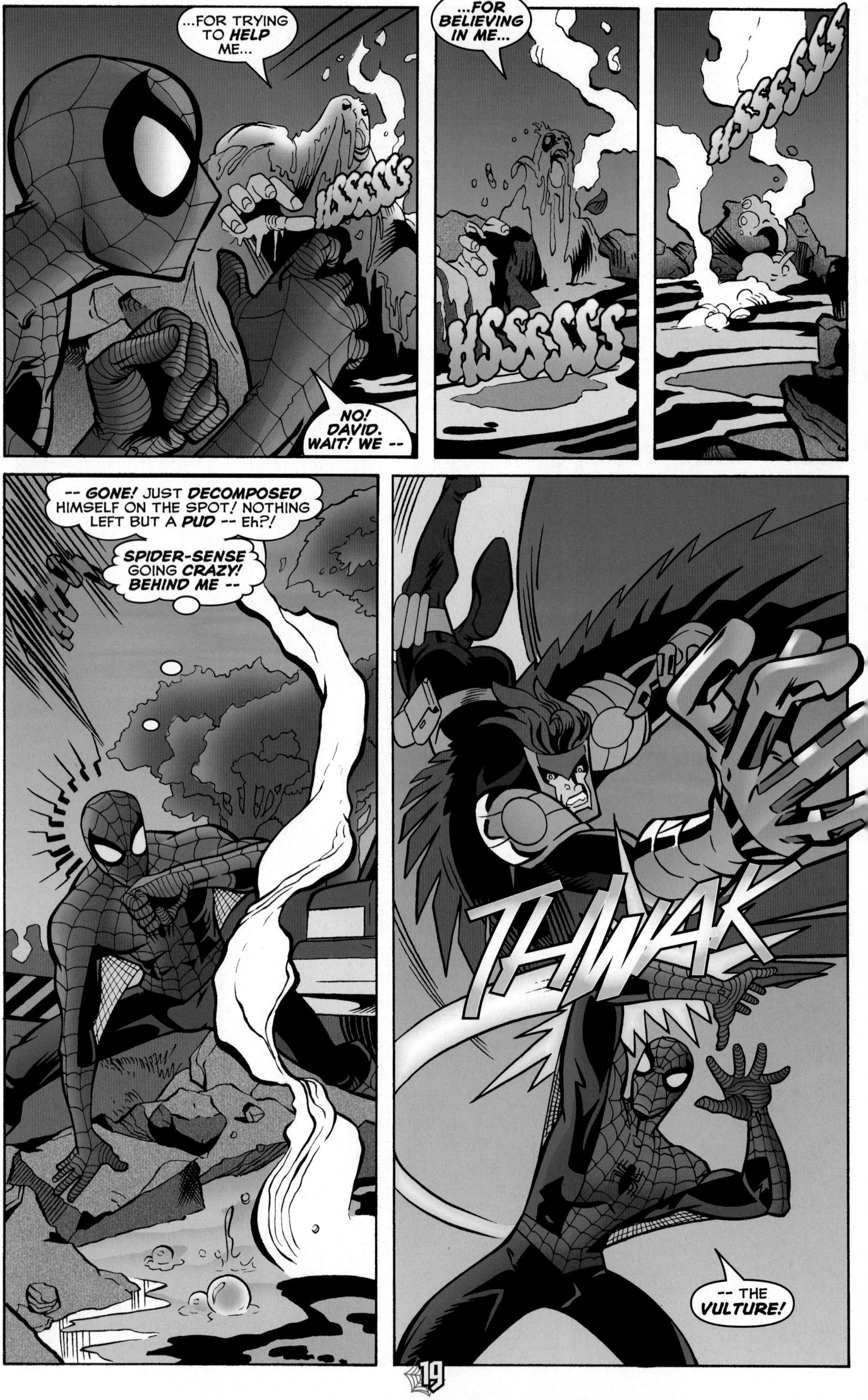
...FOR TRYING TO HELP ME...
HSSSSSS
NO! DAVID. WAIT! WE --
...FOR BELIEVING IN ME...
HSSSSSS
HSSSSSSS
-- GONE! JUST DECOMPOSED HIMSELF ON THE SPOT! NOTHING LEFT BUT A PUD -- Eh?!
SPIDER-SENSE GOING CRAZY! BEHIND ME --
THWAK
-- THE VULTURE!

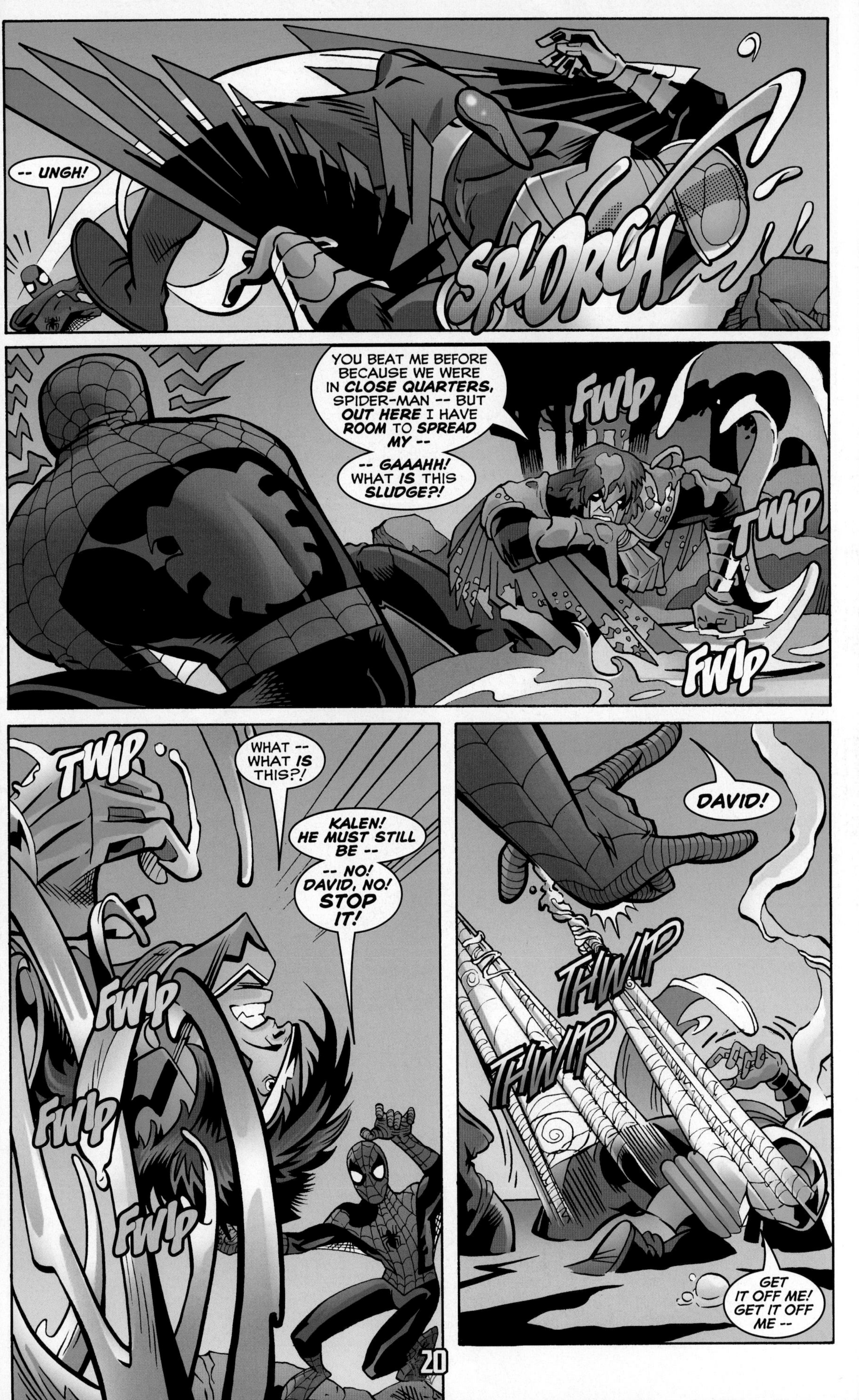

-- UNGH!
SPLORCH
YOU BEAT ME BEFORE BECAUSE WE WERE IN CLOSE QUARTERS, SPIDER-MAN -- BUT OUT HERE I HAVE ROOM TO SPREAD MY --
-- GAAAHH! WHAT IS THIS SLUDGE?!
FWIP
TWIP
FWIP
TWIP
WHAT -- WHAT IS THIS?!
KALEN! HE MUST STILL BE --
-- NO! DAVID, NO! STOP IT!
FWIP
FWIP
FWIP
DAVID!
THWIP
THWIP
GET IT OFF ME! GET IT OFF ME --

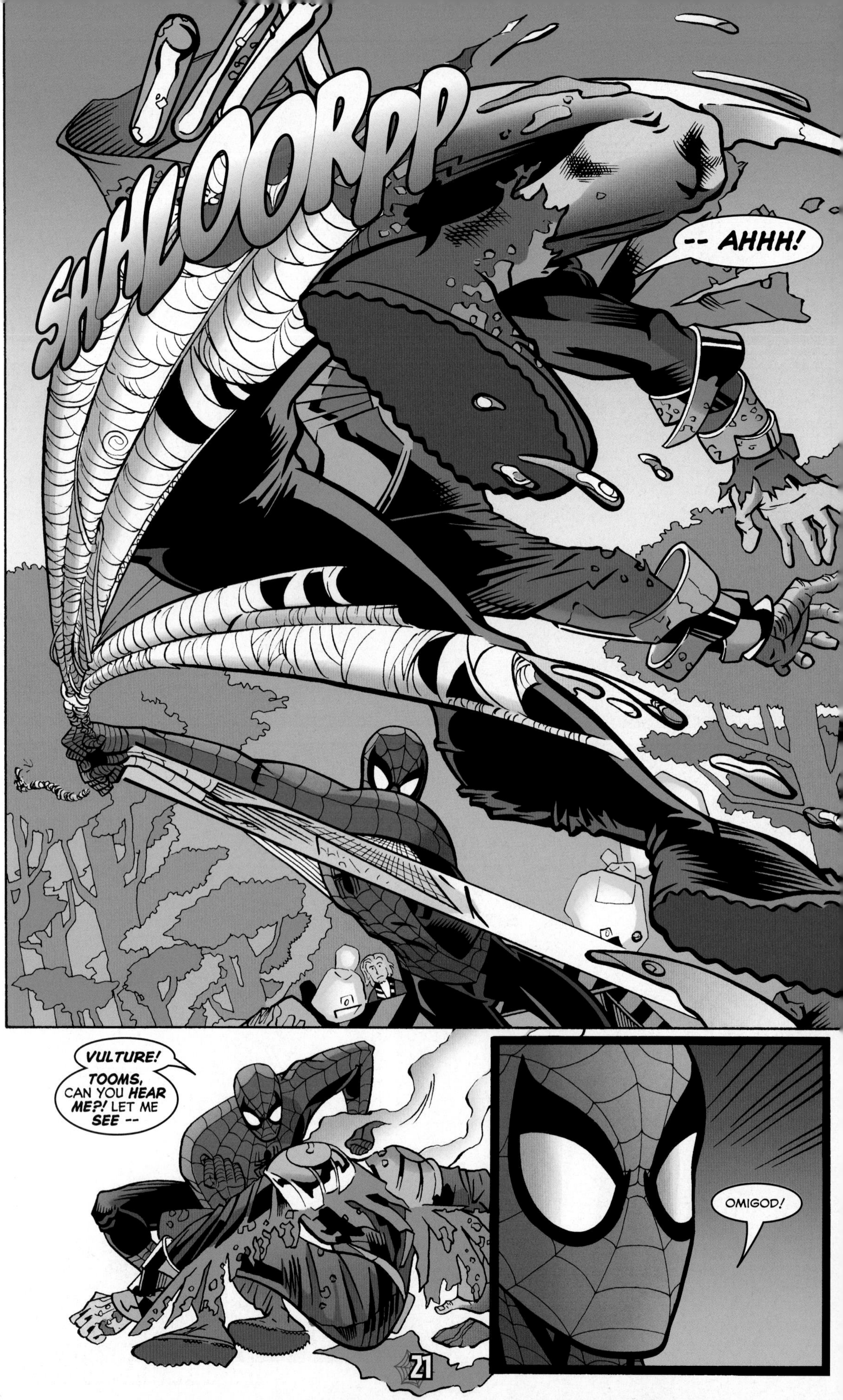
SHHLOORPP
-- AHHH!
VULTURE! TOOMS, CAN YOU HEAR ME?! LET ME SEE --
OMIGOD!

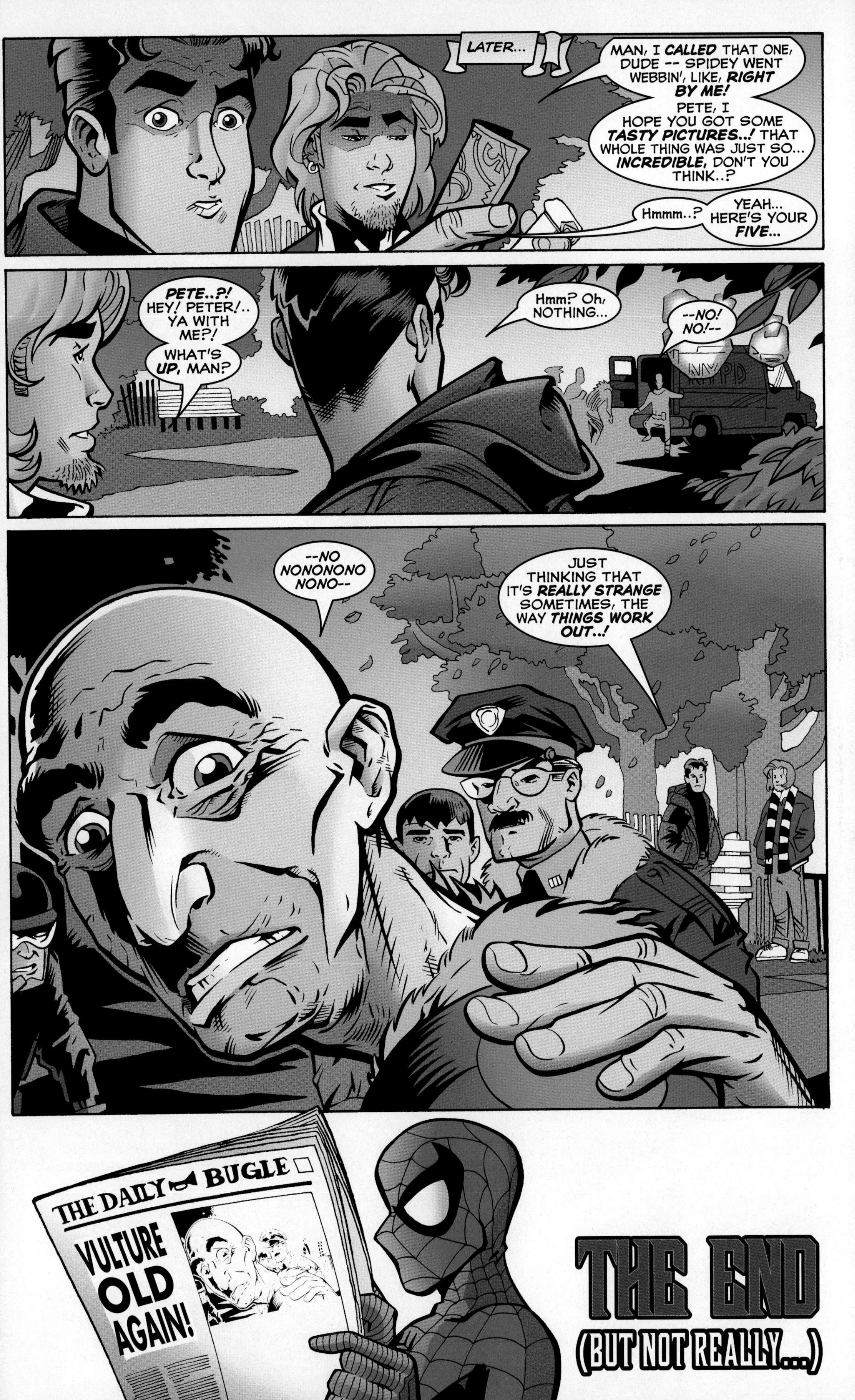
LATER...
MAN, I CALLED THAT ONE, DUDE -- SPIDEY WENT WEBBIN', LIKE, RIGHT BY ME!
PETE, I HOPE YOU GOT SOME TASTY PICTURES..! THAT WHOLE THING WAS JUST SO... INCREDIBLE, DON'T YOU THINK..?
Hmmm..?
YEAH... HERE'S YOUR FIVE...
PETE..?! HEY! PETER!.. YA WITH ME?!
WHAT'S UP, MAN?
Hmm? Oh, NOTHING...
--NO! NO!--
NYPD
--NO NONONONO NONO--
JUST THINKING THAT IT'S REALLY STRANGE SOMETIMES, THE WAY THINGS WORK OUT..!
THE DAILY BUGLE
VULTURE OLD AGAIN!
THE END
(BUT NOT REALLY...)

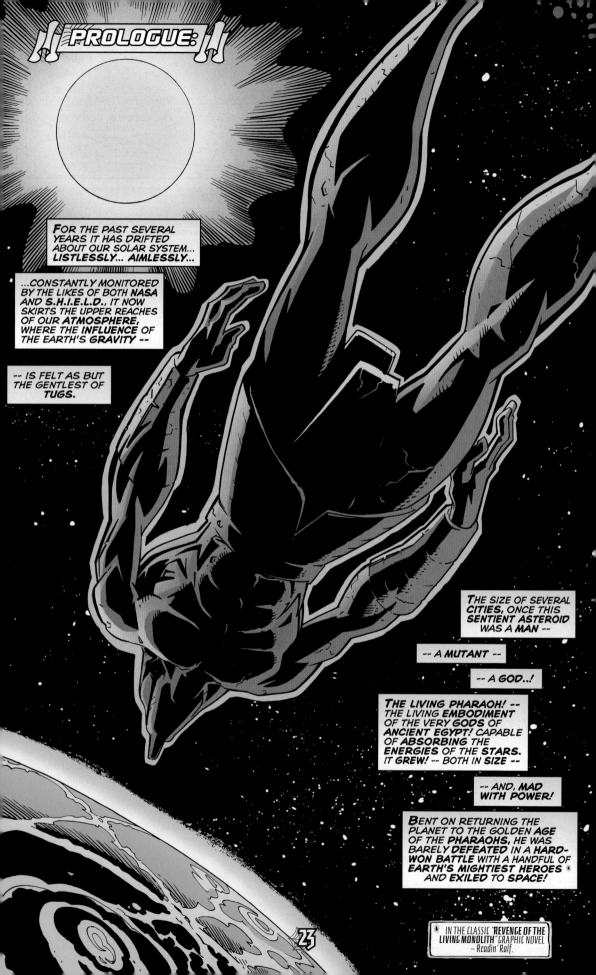

PROLOGUE:

FOR THE PAST SEVERAL YEARS IT HAS DRIFTED ABOUT OUR SOLAR SYSTEM... *LISTLESSLY... AIMLESSLY...*

...CONSTANTLY MONITORED BY THE LIKES OF BOTH *NASA* AND *S.H.I.E.L.D.*, IT NOW SKIRTS THE UPPER REACHES OF OUR *ATMOSPHERE*, WHERE THE *INFLUENCE* OF THE EARTH'S *GRAVITY* --

-- IS FELT AS BUT THE GENTLEST OF *TUGS.*

THE SIZE OF SEVERAL *CITIES*, ONCE THIS *SENTIENT ASTEROID* WAS A *MAN* --

-- A *MUTANT* --

-- A *GOD*..!

THE *LIVING PHARAOH!* -- THE LIVING *EMBODIMENT* OF THE VERY *GODS* OF *ANCIENT EGYPT!* CAPABLE OF *ABSORBING* THE *ENERGIES* OF THE STARS. IT *GREW!* -- BOTH IN *SIZE* --

-- AND, *MAD* WITH *POWER!*

BENT ON RETURNING THE PLANET TO THE GOLDEN AGE OF THE *PHARAOHS*, HE WAS BARELY *DEFEATED* IN A *HARD-WON* BATTLE WITH A HANDFUL OF EARTH'S *MIGHTIEST HEROES* AND *EXILED* TO *SPACE!*

* IN THE CLASSIC *REVENGE OF THE LIVING MONOLITH* GRAPHIC NOVEL -- Readin' Ralf.

23

IT IS BOTH ITS PRISON...

...AND FREEDOM...

...PUNISHMENT...

...AND ULTIMATE REWARD!...

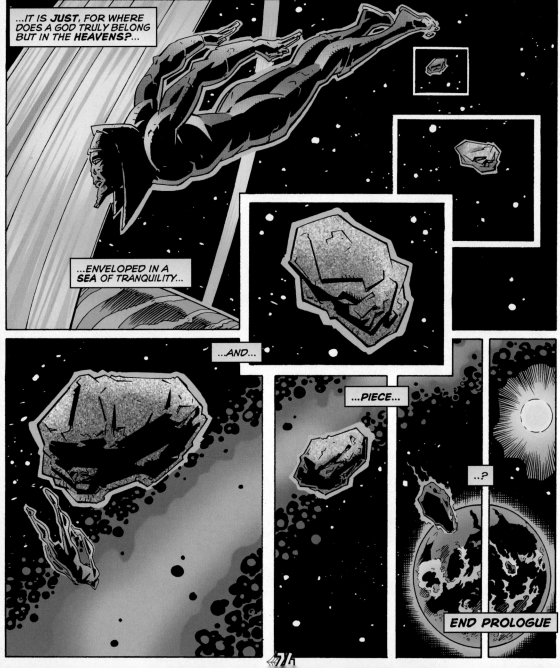

...IT IS JUST, FOR WHERE DOES A GOD TRULY BELONG BUT IN THE HEAVENS?...

...ENVELOPED IN A SEA OF TRANQUILITY...

...AND...

...PIECE...

..?

END PROLOGUE

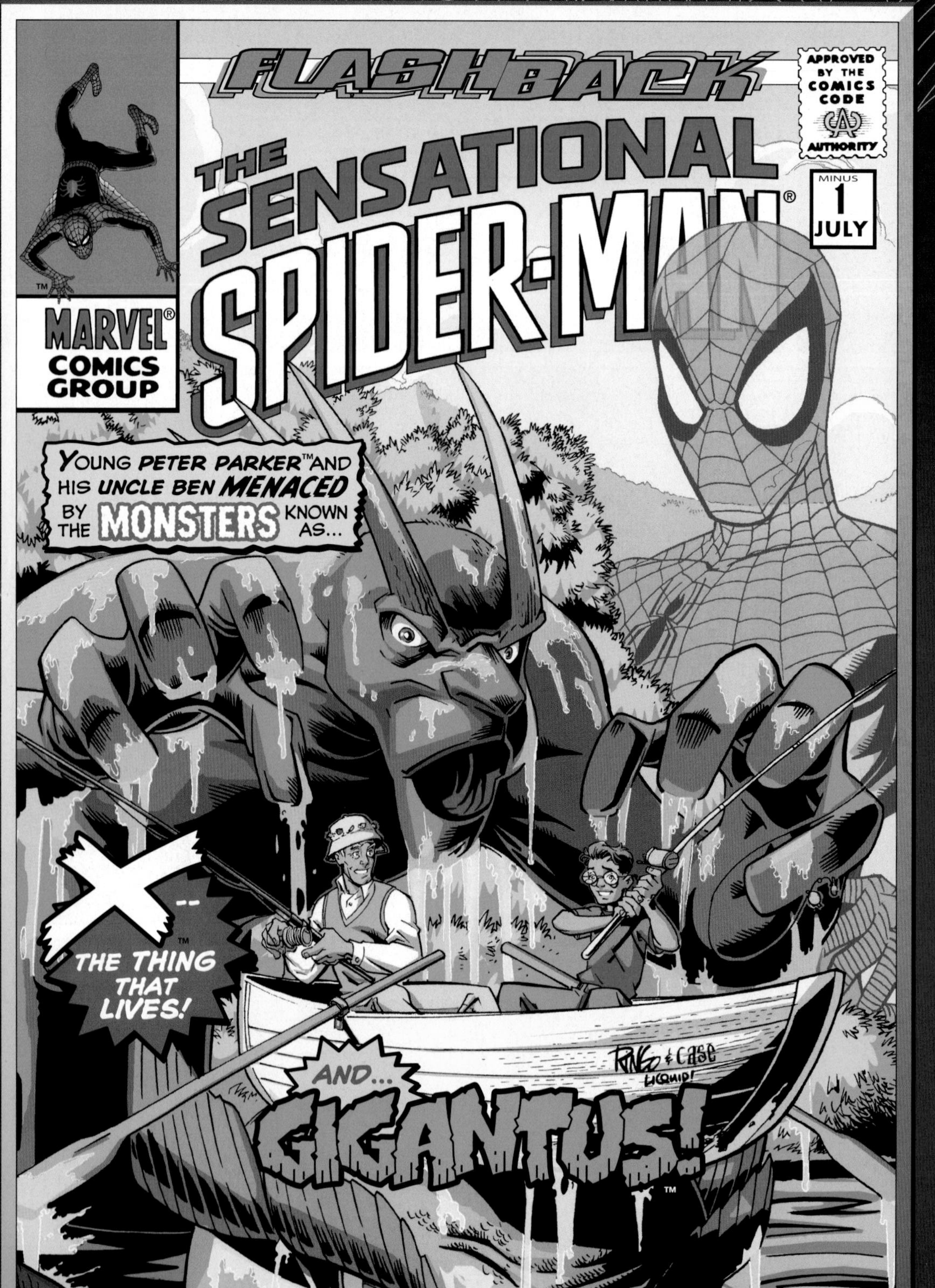
FLASHBACK
APPROVED BY THE COMICS CODE AUTHORITY
THE SENSATIONAL SPIDER-MAN®
MINUS 1 JULY
MARVEL® COMICS GROUP
YOUNG PETER PARKER™ AND HIS UNCLE BEN MENACED BY THE MONSTERS KNOWN AS...
X--™ THE THING THAT LIVES!
AND... GIGANTUS!™
RINGO & CASE LIQUID!

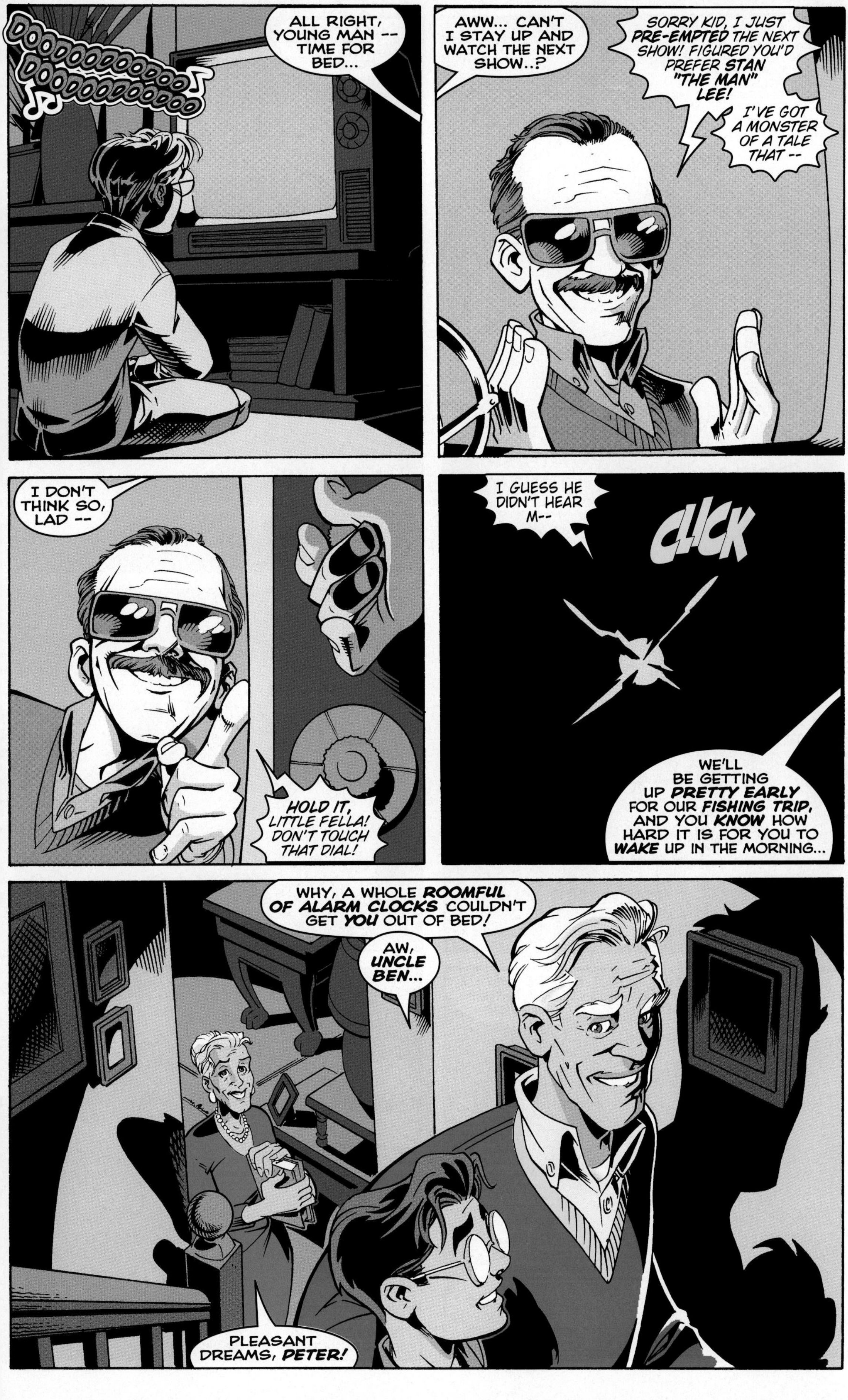

DOODOODOODOO DOODOODOODOO
ALL RIGHT, YOUNG MAN -- TIME FOR BED...
AWW... CAN'T I STAY UP AND WATCH THE NEXT SHOW..?
SORRY KID, I JUST PRE-EMPTED THE NEXT SHOW! FIGURED YOU'D PREFER STAN "THE MAN" LEE!
I'VE GOT A MONSTER OF A TALE THAT --
I DON'T THINK SO, LAD --
HOLD IT, LITTLE FELLA! DON'T TOUCH THAT DIAL!
I GUESS HE DIDN'T HEAR M--
CLICK
WE'LL BE GETTING UP PRETTY EARLY FOR OUR FISHING TRIP, AND YOU KNOW HOW HARD IT IS FOR YOU TO WAKE UP IN THE MORNING...
WHY, A WHOLE ROOMFUL OF ALARM CLOCKS COULDN'T GET YOU OUT OF BED!
AW, UNCLE BEN...
PLEASANT DREAMS, PETER!

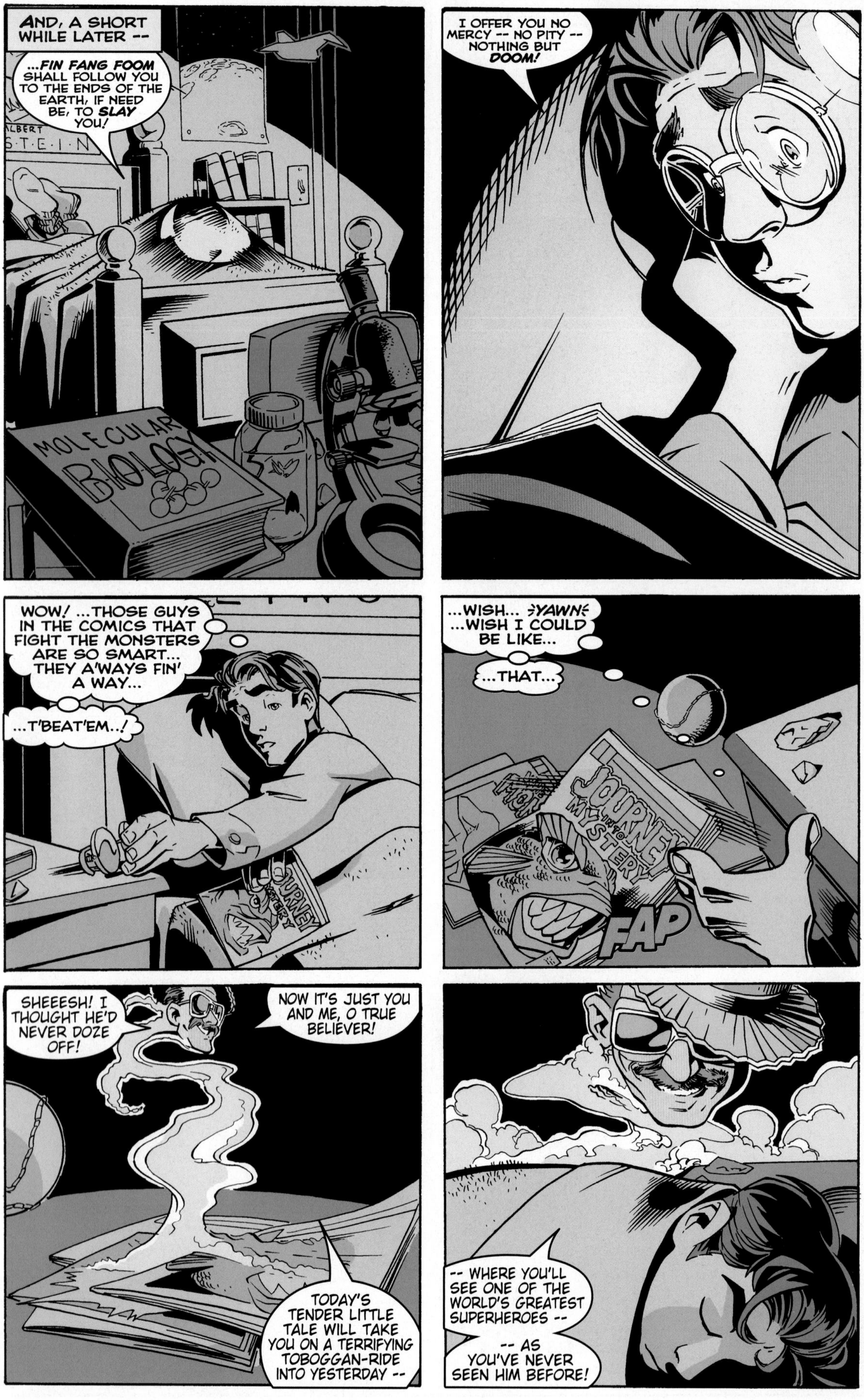
AND, A SHORT WHILE LATER --
...FIN FANG FOOM SHALL FOLLOW YOU TO THE ENDS OF THE EARTH, IF NEED BE, TO SLAY YOU!
ALBERT STEIN
MOLECULAR BIOLOGY
I OFFER YOU NO MERCY -- NO PITY -- NOTHING BUT DOOM!
WOW! ...THOSE GUYS IN THE COMICS THAT FIGHT THE MONSTERS ARE SO SMART... THEY A'WAYS FIN' A WAY...
...T'BEAT'EM..!
...WISH... *YAWN* ...WISH I COULD BE LIKE...
...THAT...
JOURNEY INTO MYSTERY
FAP
SHEEESH! I THOUGHT HE'D NEVER DOZE OFF!
NOW IT'S JUST YOU AND ME, O TRUE BELIEVER!
TODAY'S TENDER LITTLE TALE WILL TAKE YOU ON A TERRIFYING TOBOGGAN-RIDE INTO YESTERDAY --
-- WHERE YOU'LL SEE ONE OF THE WORLD'S GREATEST SUPERHEROES --
-- AS YOU'VE NEVER SEEN HIM BEFORE!

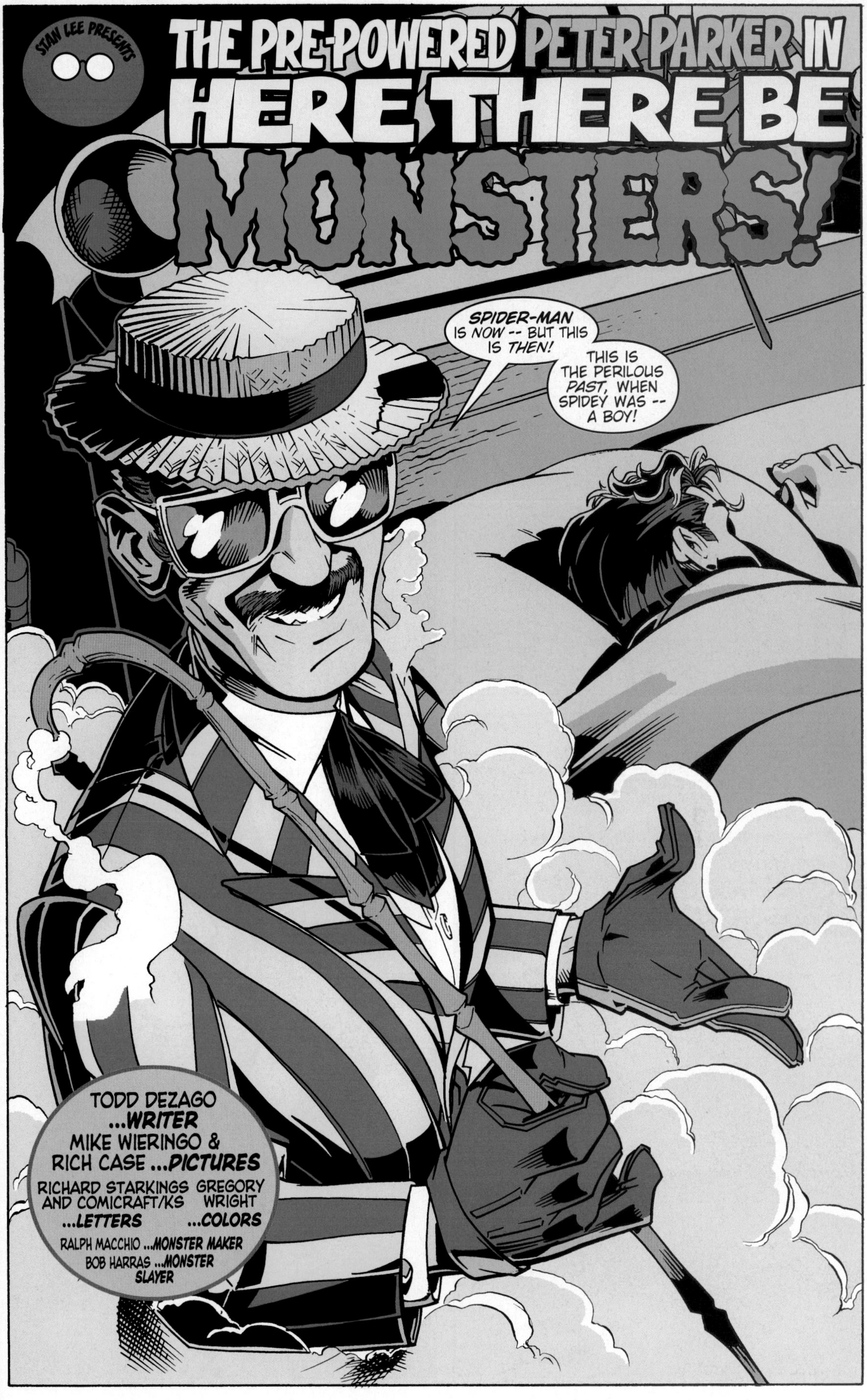
STAN LEE PRESENTS
THE PRE-POWERED PETER PARKER IN
HERE THERE BE
MONSTERS!
SPIDER-MAN IS NOW -- BUT THIS IS THEN!
THIS IS THE PERILOUS PAST, WHEN SPIDEY WAS -- A BOY!
TODD DEZAGO ...WRITER
MIKE WIERINGO & RICH CASE ...PICTURES
RICHARD STARKINGS AND COMICRAFT/KS ...LETTERS
GREGORY WRIGHT ...COLORS
RALPH MACCHIO ...MONSTER MAKER
BOB HARRAS ...MONSTER SLAYER

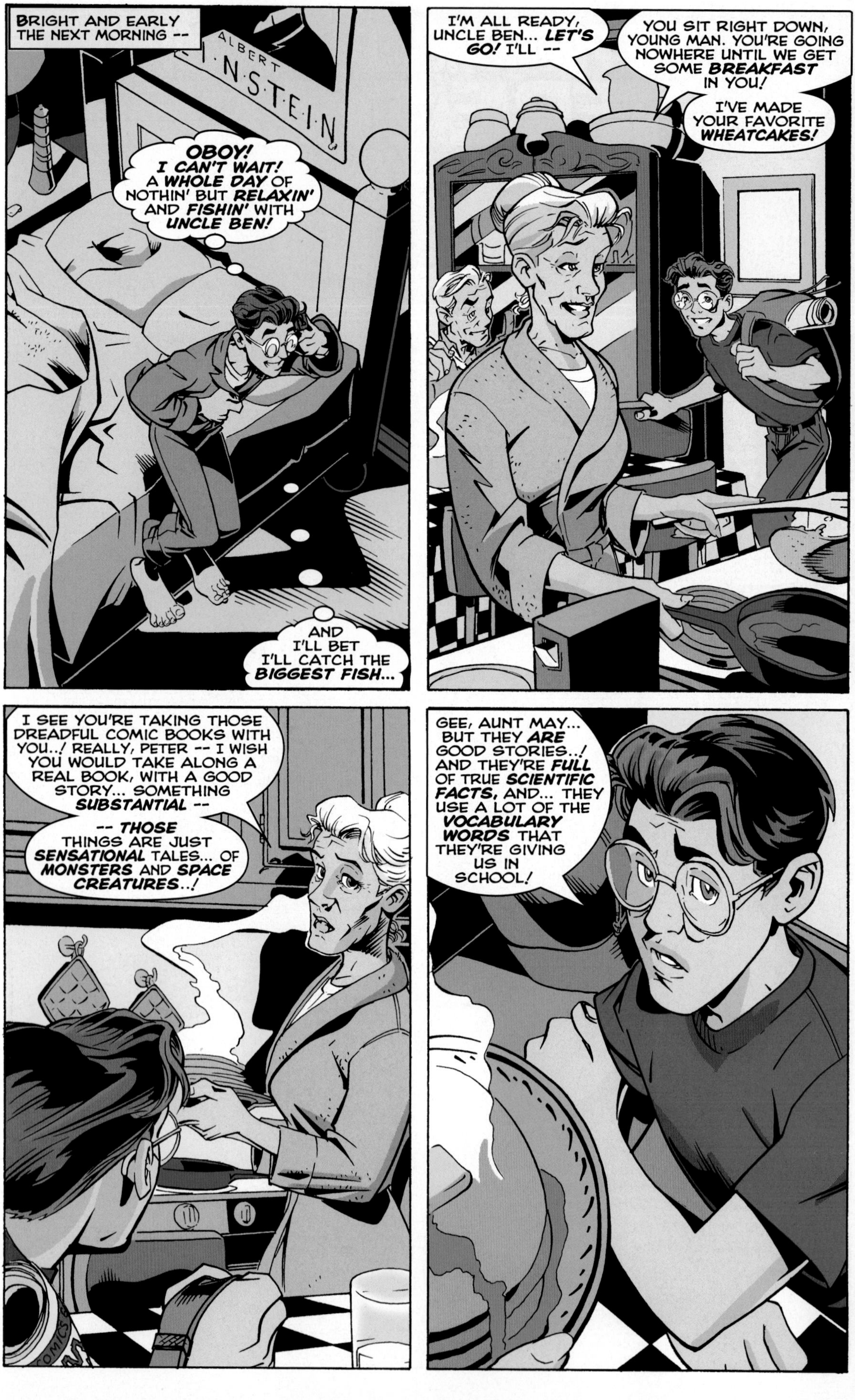
BRIGHT AND EARLY THE NEXT MORNING --
ALBERT EINSTEIN
OBOY! I CAN'T WAIT! A WHOLE DAY OF NOTHIN' BUT RELAXIN' AND FISHIN' WITH UNCLE BEN!
AND I'LL BET I'LL CATCH THE BIGGEST FISH...
I'M ALL READY, UNCLE BEN... LET'S GO! I'LL --
YOU SIT RIGHT DOWN, YOUNG MAN. YOU'RE GOING NOWHERE UNTIL WE GET SOME BREAKFAST IN YOU!
I'VE MADE YOUR FAVORITE WHEATCAKES!
I SEE YOU'RE TAKING THOSE DREADFUL COMIC BOOKS WITH YOU...! REALLY, PETER -- I WISH YOU WOULD TAKE ALONG A REAL BOOK, WITH A GOOD STORY... SOMETHING SUBSTANTIAL --
-- THOSE THINGS ARE JUST SENSATIONAL TALES... OF MONSTERS AND SPACE CREATURES...!
GEE, AUNT MAY... BUT THEY ARE GOOD STORIES...! AND THEY'RE FULL OF TRUE SCIENTIFIC FACTS, AND... THEY USE A LOT OF THE VOCABULARY WORDS THAT THEY'RE GIVING US IN SCHOOL!

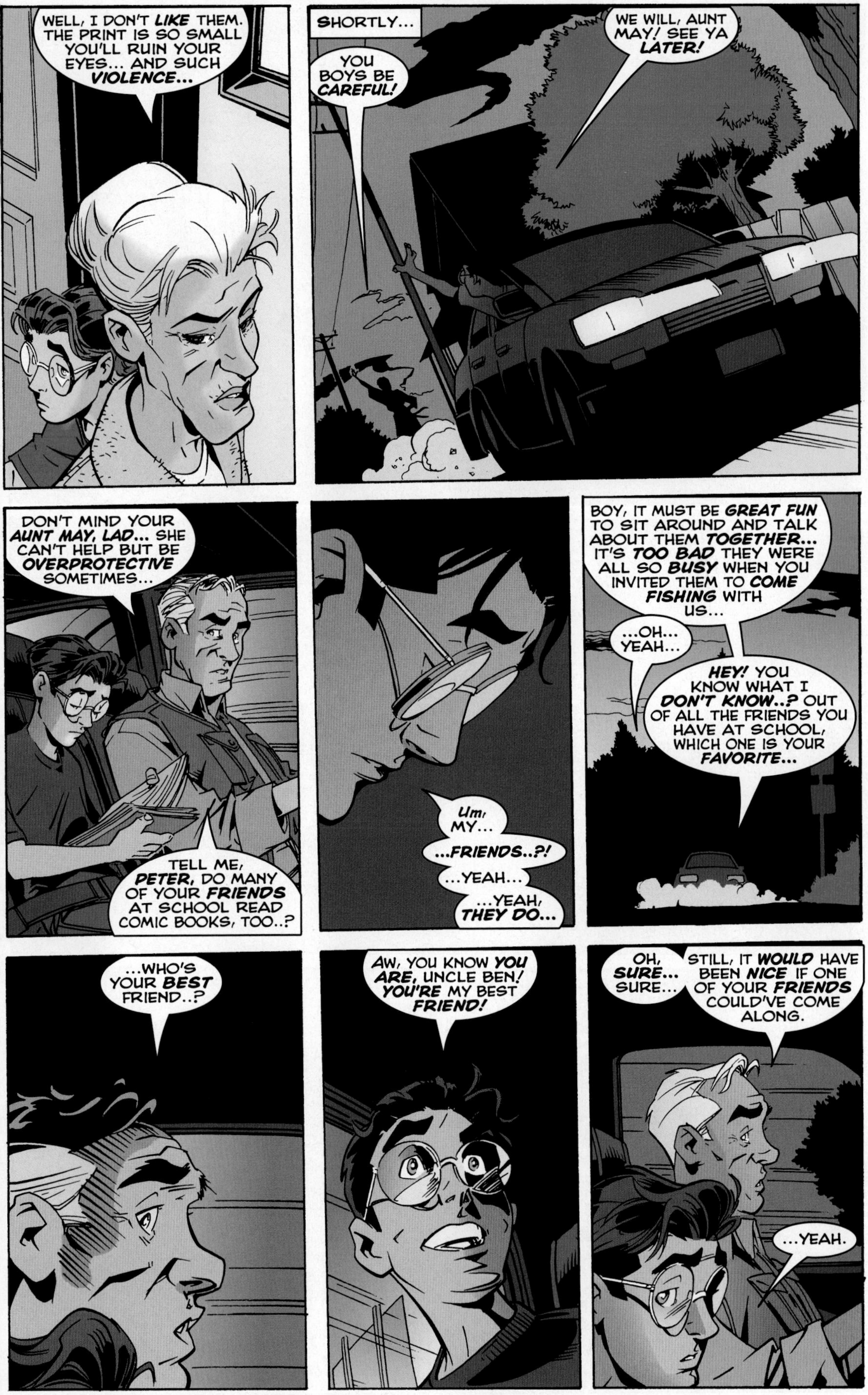

WELL, I DON'T LIKE THEM. THE PRINT IS SO SMALL YOU'LL RUIN YOUR EYES... AND SUCH VIOLENCE...
SHORTLY...
YOU BOYS BE CAREFUL!
WE WILL, AUNT MAY! SEE YA LATER!
DON'T MIND YOUR AUNT MAY, LAD... SHE CAN'T HELP BUT BE OVERPROTECTIVE SOMETIMES...
TELL ME, PETER, DO MANY OF YOUR FRIENDS AT SCHOOL READ COMIC BOOKS, TOO..?
Um, MY...
...FRIENDS..?!
...YEAH...
...YEAH, THEY DO...
BOY, IT MUST BE GREAT FUN TO SIT AROUND AND TALK ABOUT THEM TOGETHER... IT'S TOO BAD THEY WERE ALL SO BUSY WHEN YOU INVITED THEM TO COME FISHING WITH US...
...OH... YEAH...
HEY! YOU KNOW WHAT I DON'T KNOW..? OUT OF ALL THE FRIENDS YOU HAVE AT SCHOOL, WHICH ONE IS YOUR FAVORITE...
...WHO'S YOUR BEST FRIEND..?
AW, YOU KNOW YOU ARE, UNCLE BEN! YOU'RE MY BEST FRIEND!
OH, SURE... SURE...
STILL, IT WOULD HAVE BEEN NICE IF ONE OF YOUR FRIENDS COULD'VE COME ALONG.
...YEAH.

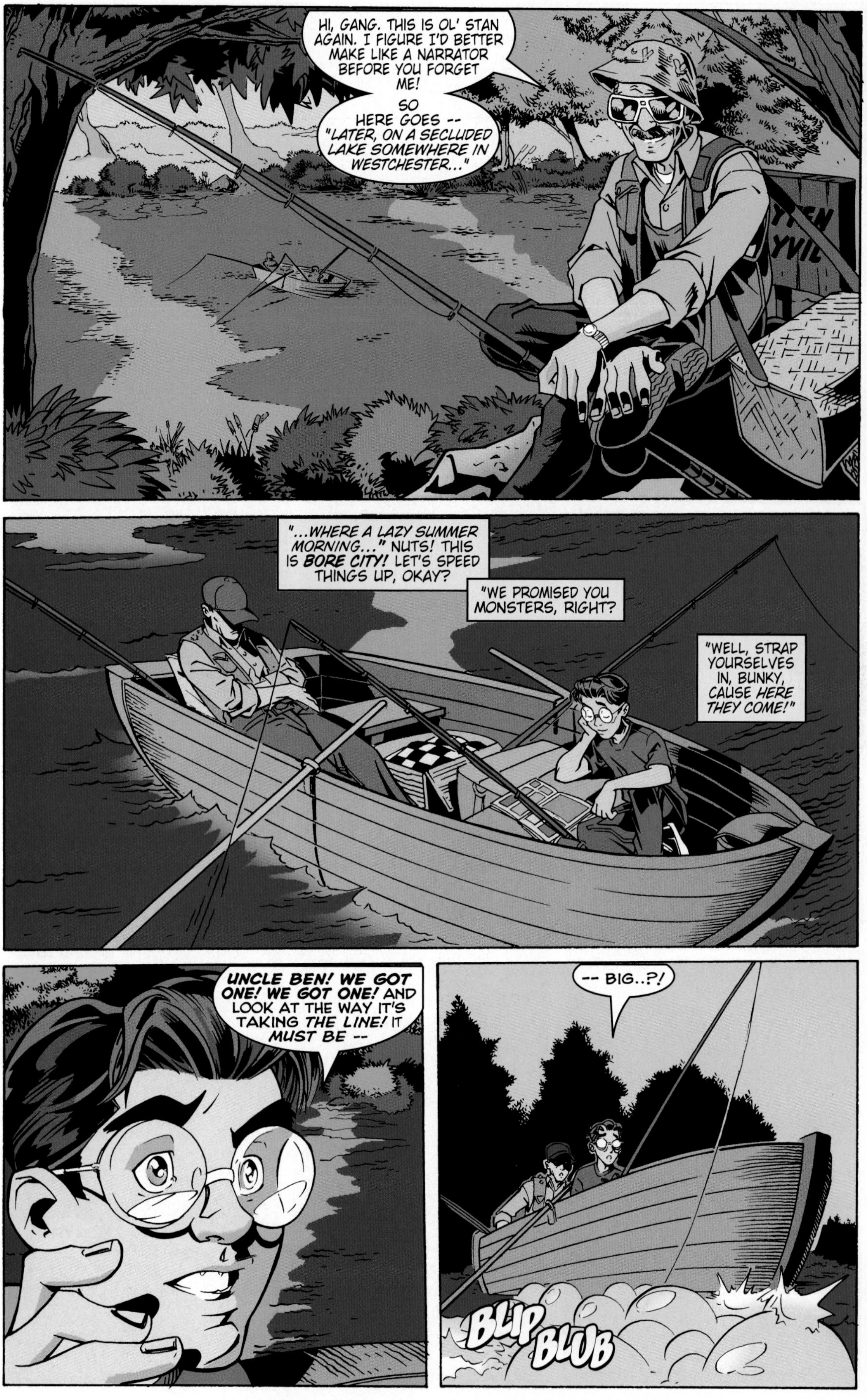
HI, GANG. THIS IS OL' STAN AGAIN. I FIGURE I'D BETTER MAKE LIKE A NARRATOR BEFORE YOU FORGET ME!
SO HERE GOES -- "LATER, ON A SECLUDED LAKE SOMEWHERE IN WESTCHESTER..."
"...WHERE A LAZY SUMMER MORNING..." NUTS! THIS IS BORE CITY! LET'S SPEED THINGS UP, OKAY?
"WE PROMISED YOU MONSTERS, RIGHT?
"WELL, STRAP YOURSELVES IN, BUNKY, CAUSE HERE THEY COME!"
UNCLE BEN! WE GOT ONE! WE GOT ONE! AND LOOK AT THE WAY IT'S TAKING THE LINE! IT MUST BE --
-- BIG..?!
BLIP
BLUB

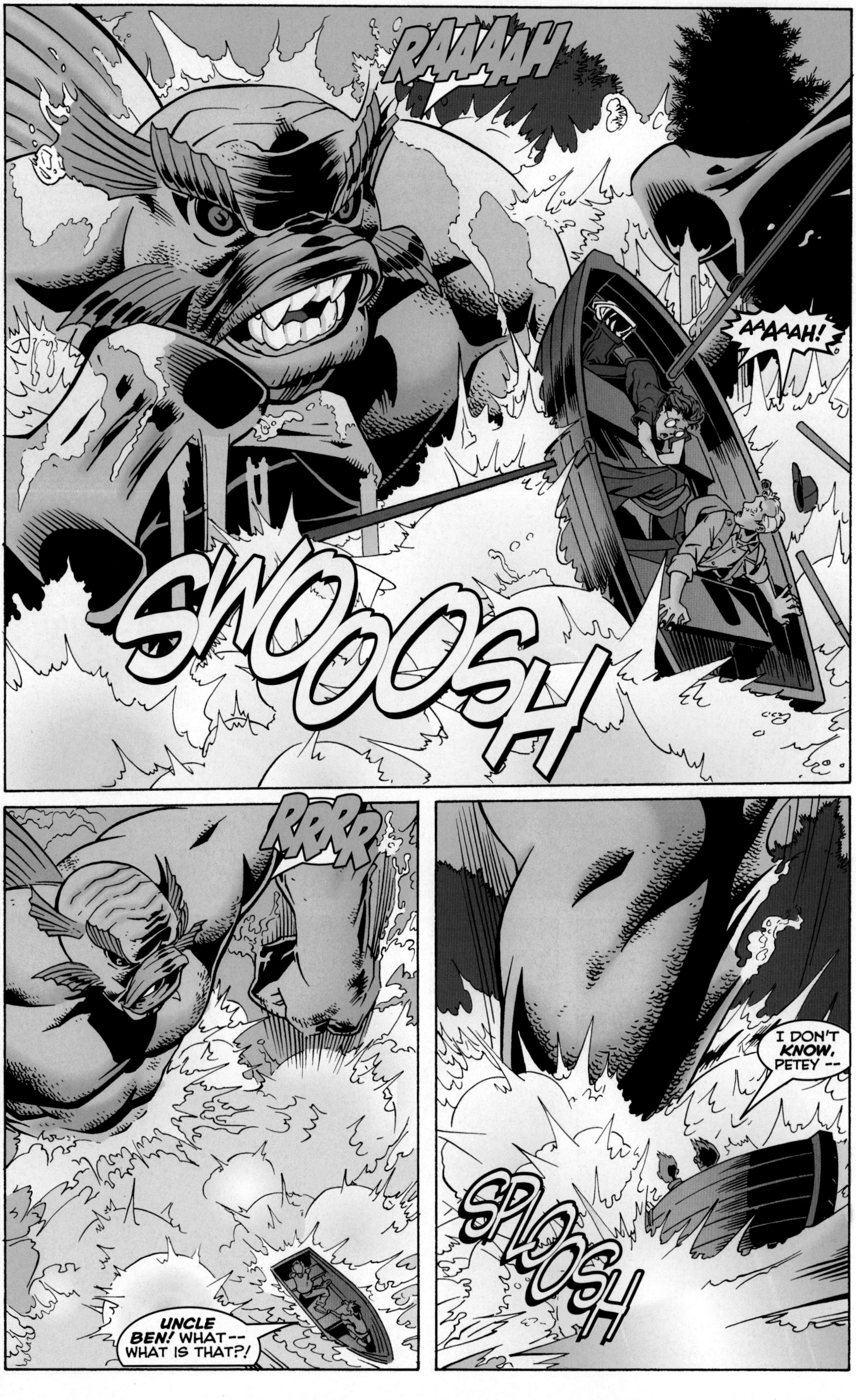
RAAAAH
AAAAAH!
SWOOOOSH
RRRR
UNCLE BEN! WHAT-- WHAT IS THAT?!
I DON'T KNOW, PETEY --
SPLOOSH

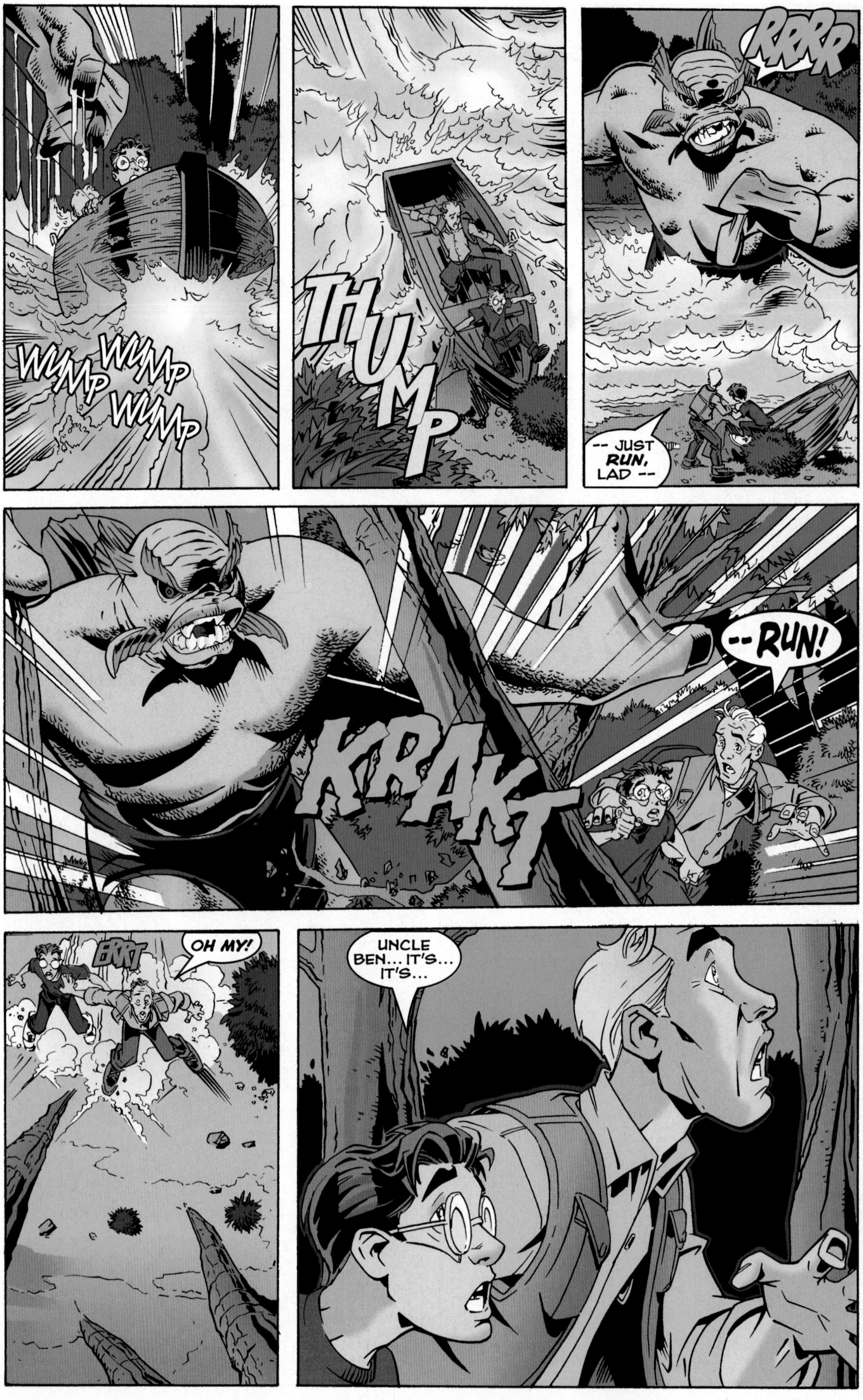
WUMP WUMP
WUMP
THUMP
RRRR
-- JUST RUN, LAD --
KRAKT
--RUN!
ERRT
OH MY!
UNCLE BEN... IT'S... IT'S...

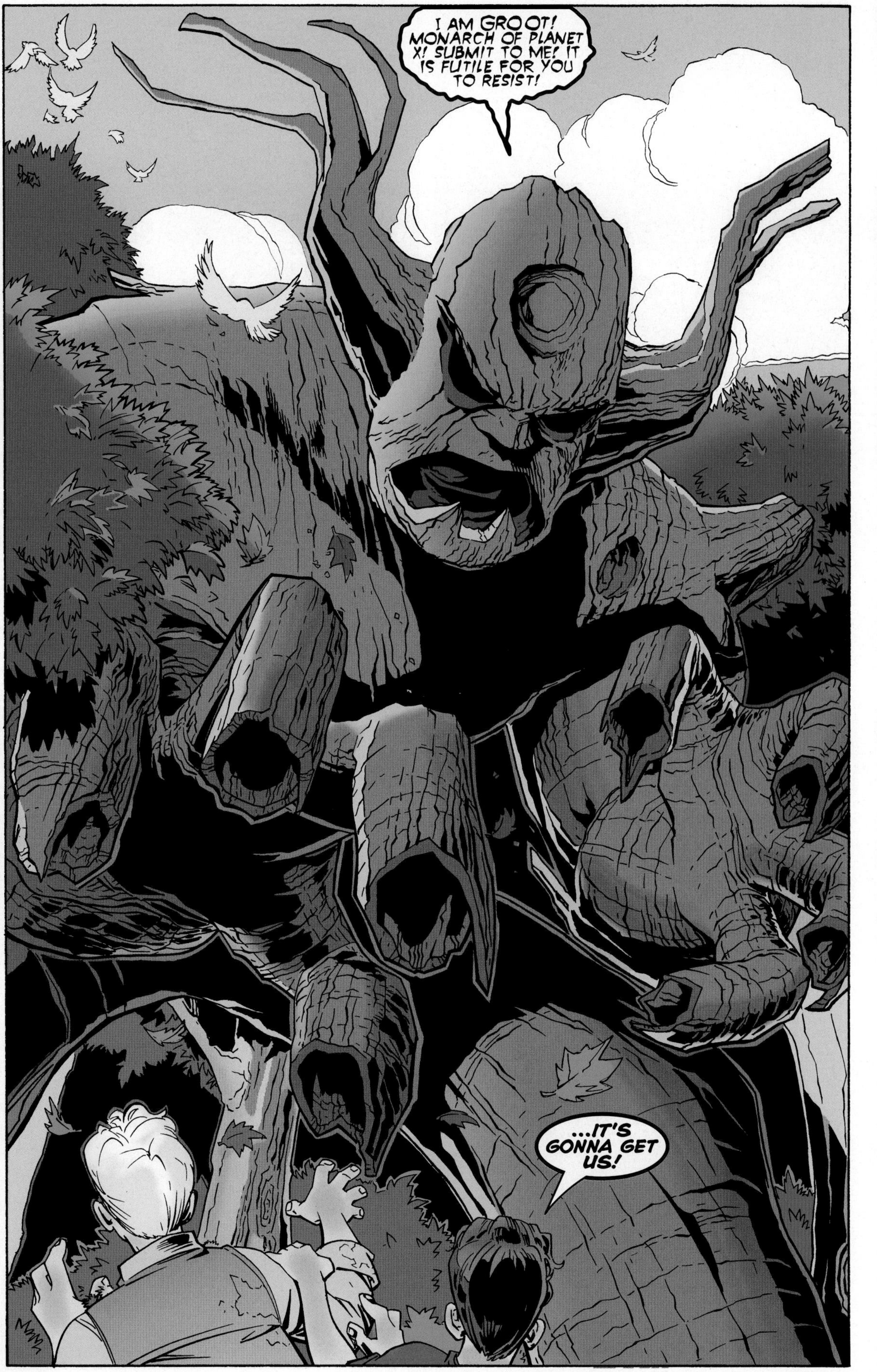
I AM GROOT! MONARCH OF PLANET X! SUBMIT TO ME! IT IS FUTILE FOR YOU TO RESIST!
...IT'S GONNA GET US!

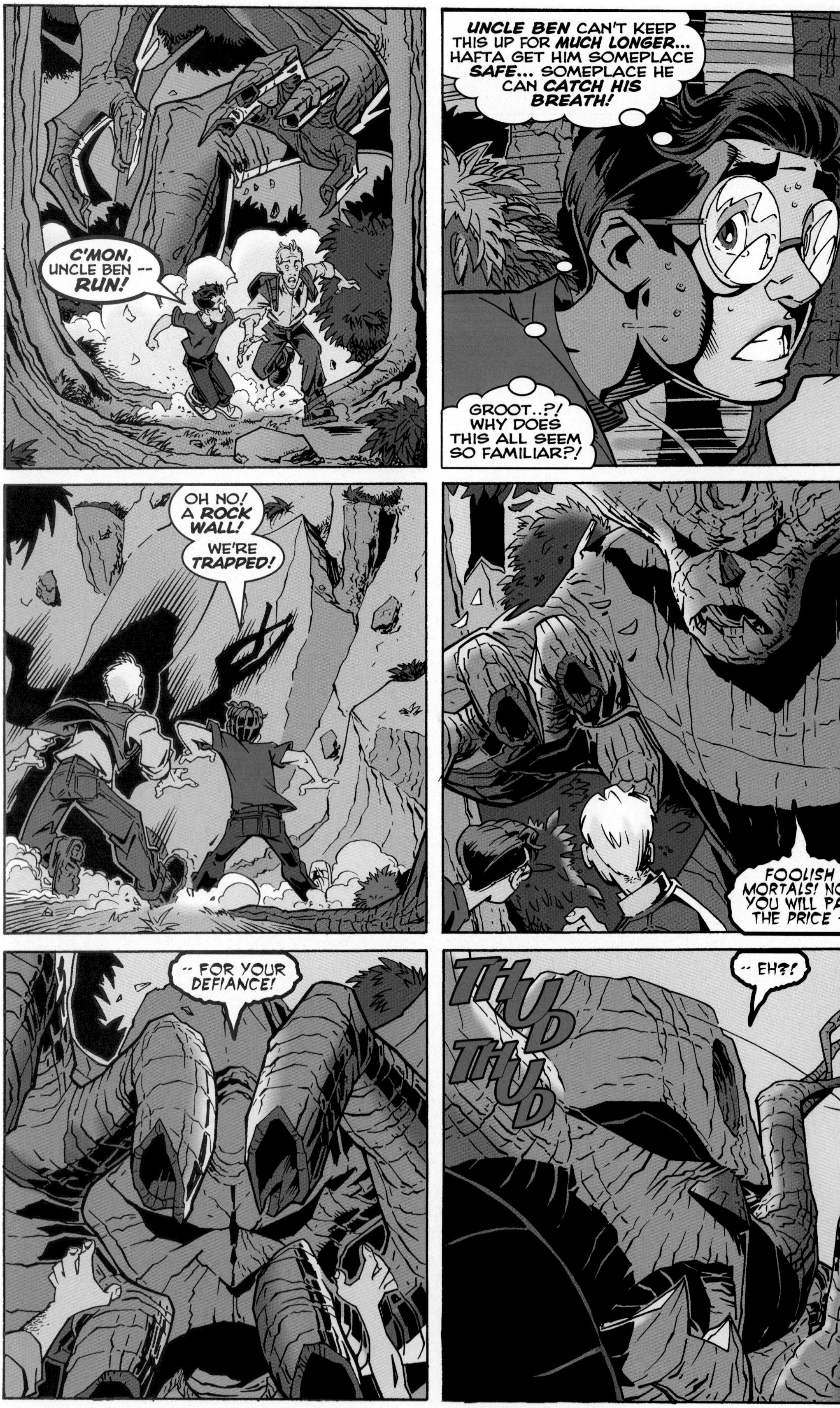
C'MON, UNCLE BEN -- RUN!
UNCLE BEN CAN'T KEEP THIS UP FOR MUCH LONGER... HAFTA GET HIM SOMEPLACE SAFE... SOMEPLACE HE CAN CATCH HIS BREATH!
GROOT..?! WHY DOES THIS ALL SEEM SO FAMILIAR?!
OH NO! A ROCK WALL!
WE'RE TRAPPED!
FOOLISH MORTALS! NOW YOU WILL PAY THE PRICE --
-- FOR YOUR DEFIANCE!
THUD
THUD
-- EH?!

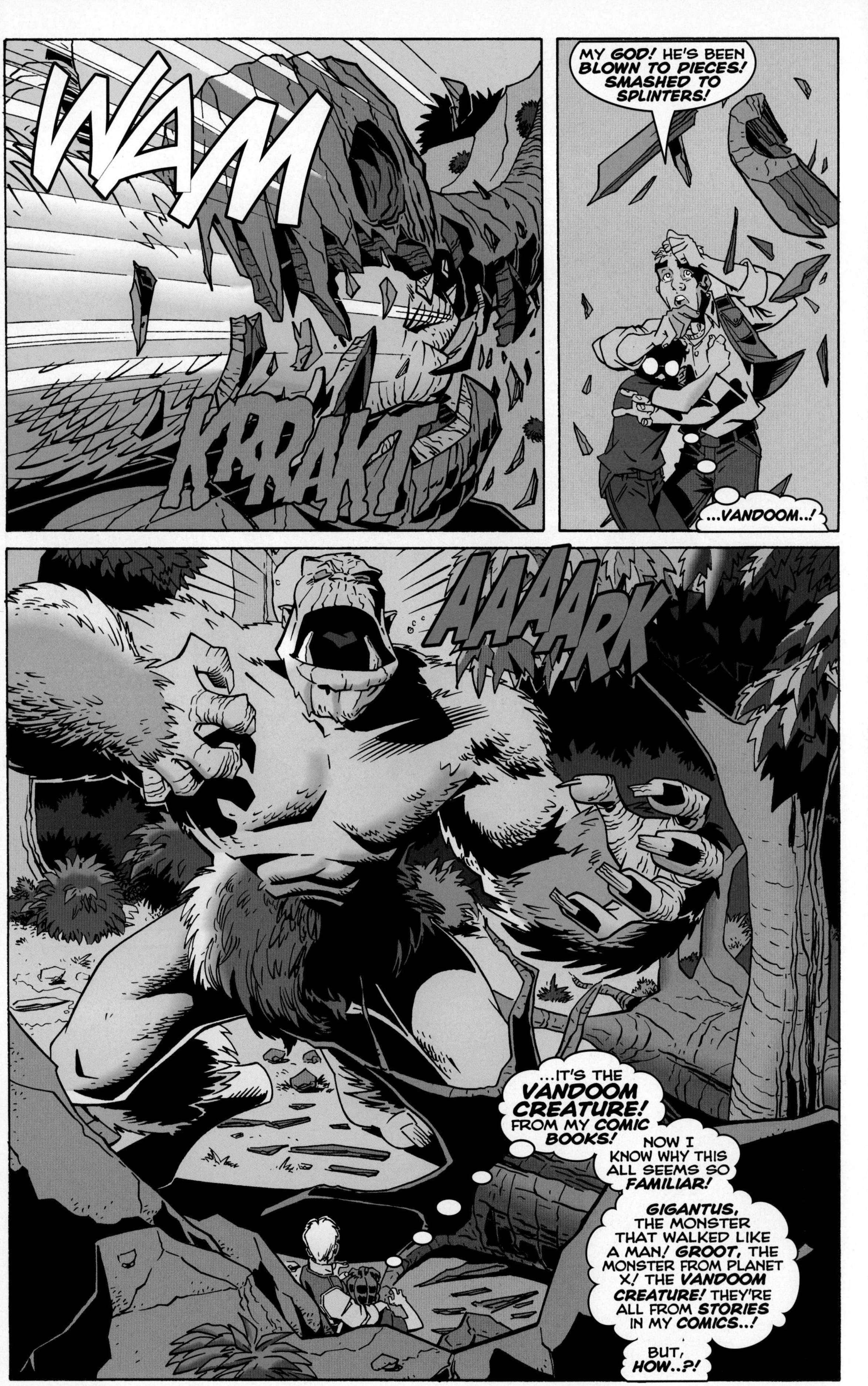
WAM
KRRAKT
MY GOD! HE'S BEEN BLOWN TO PIECES! SMASHED TO SPLINTERS!
...VANDOOM..!
AAAARK
...IT'S THE VANDOOM CREATURE! FROM MY COMIC BOOKS!
NOW I KNOW WHY THIS ALL SEEMS SO FAMILIAR!
GIGANTUS, THE MONSTER THAT WALKED LIKE A MAN! GROOT, THE MONSTER FROM PLANET X! THE VANDOOM CREATURE! THEY'RE ALL FROM STORIES IN MY COMICS..!
BUT, HOW..?!

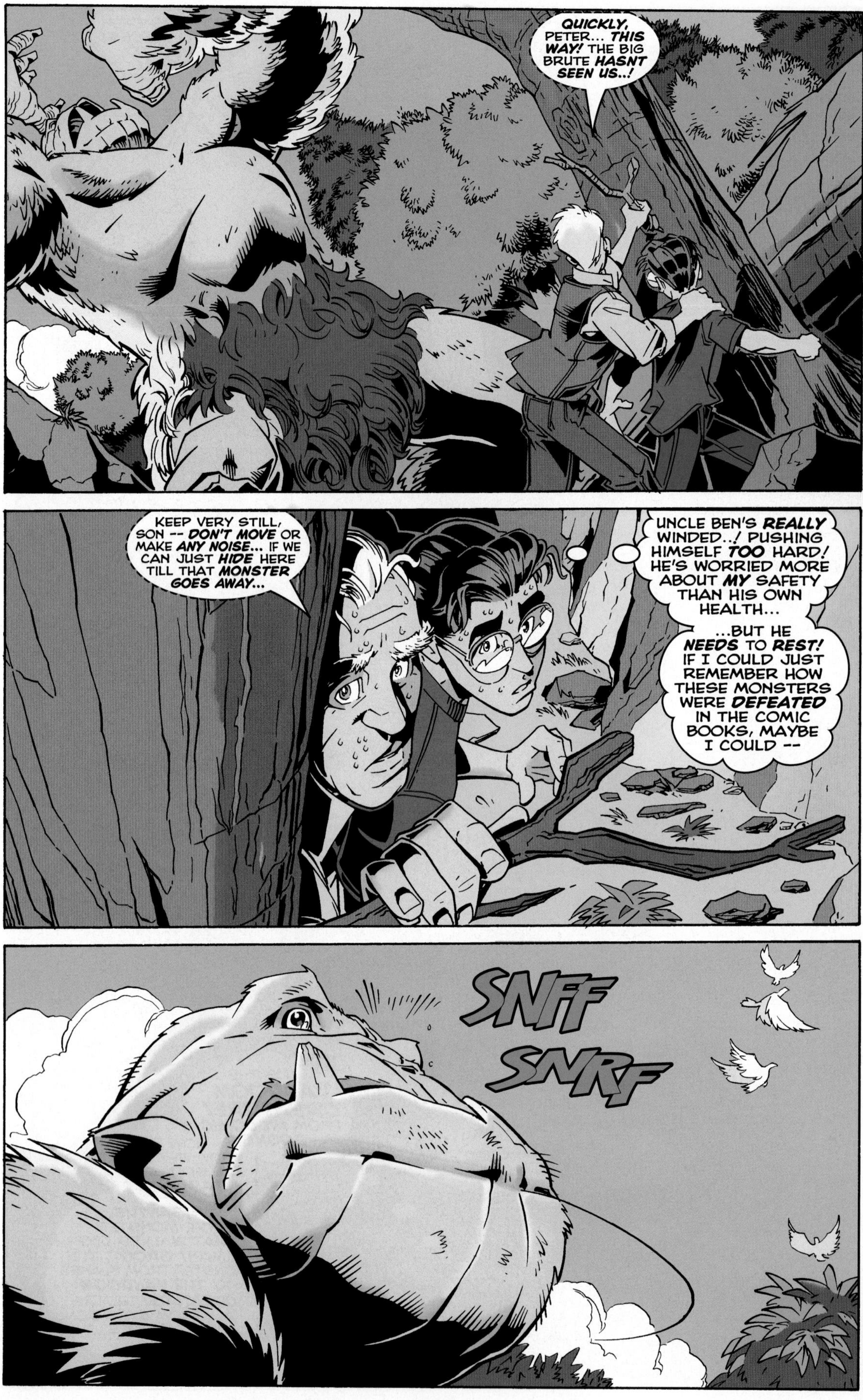
QUICKLY, PETER... THIS WAY! THE BIG BRUTE HASNT SEEN US..!
KEEP VERY STILL, SON -- DON'T MOVE OR MAKE ANY NOISE... IF WE CAN JUST HIDE HERE TILL THAT MONSTER GOES AWAY...
UNCLE BEN'S REALLY WINDED..! PUSHING HIMSELF TOO HARD! HE'S WORRIED MORE ABOUT MY SAFETY THAN HIS OWN HEALTH...
...BUT HE NEEDS TO REST! IF I COULD JUST REMEMBER HOW THESE MONSTERS WERE DEFEATED IN THE COMIC BOOKS, MAYBE I COULD --
SNFF
SNRF

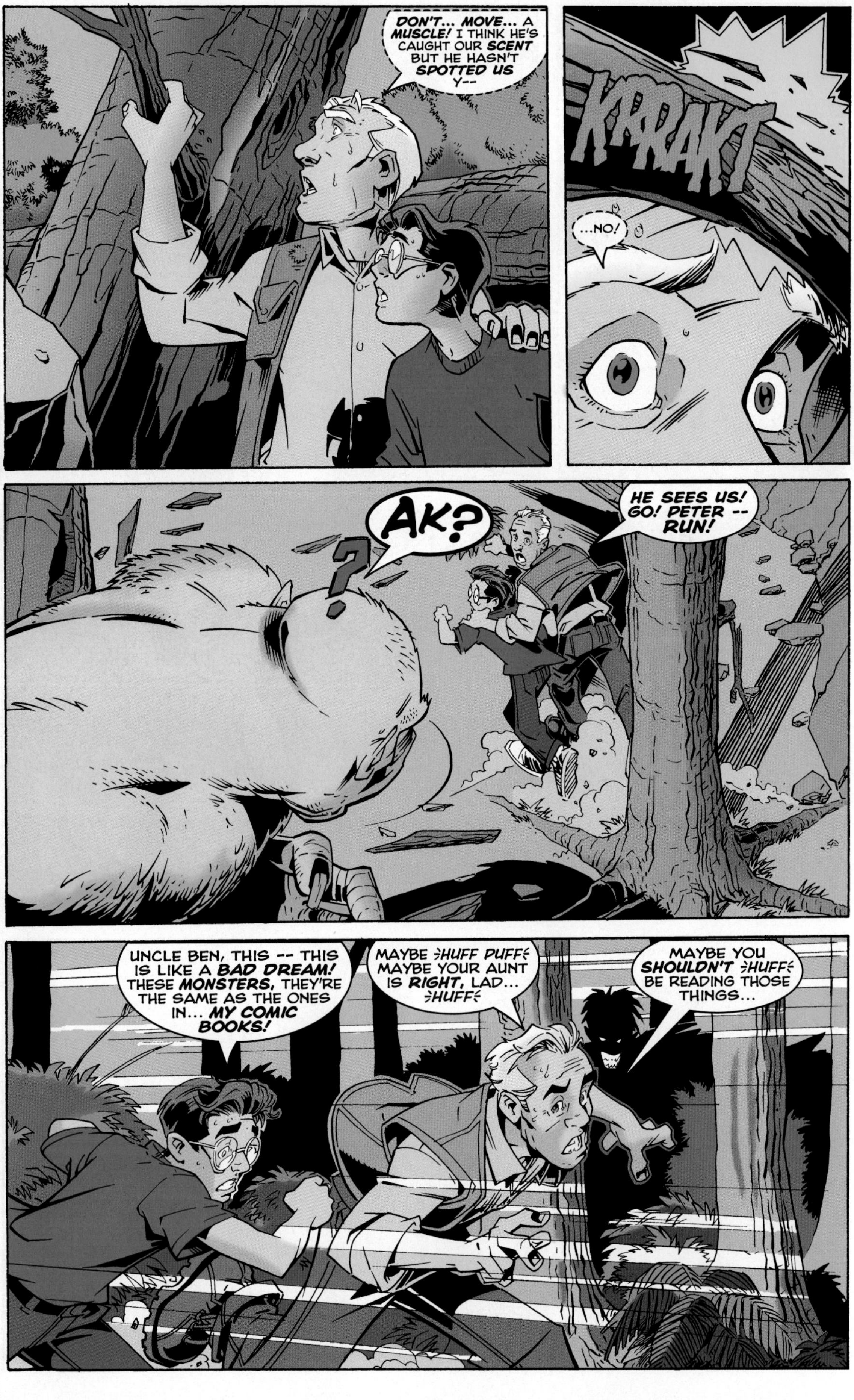
DON'T... MOVE... A MUSCLE! I THINK HE'S CAUGHT OUR SCENT BUT HE HASN'T SPOTTED US Y--
KRRAKT
...NO!
AK?
?
HE SEES US! GO! PETER -- RUN!
UNCLE BEN, THIS -- THIS IS LIKE A BAD DREAM! THESE MONSTERS, THEY'RE THE SAME AS THE ONES IN... MY COMIC BOOKS!
MAYBE *HUFF PUFF* MAYBE YOUR AUNT IS RIGHT, LAD... *HUFF*
MAYBE YOU SHOULDN'T *HUFF* BE READING THOSE THINGS...

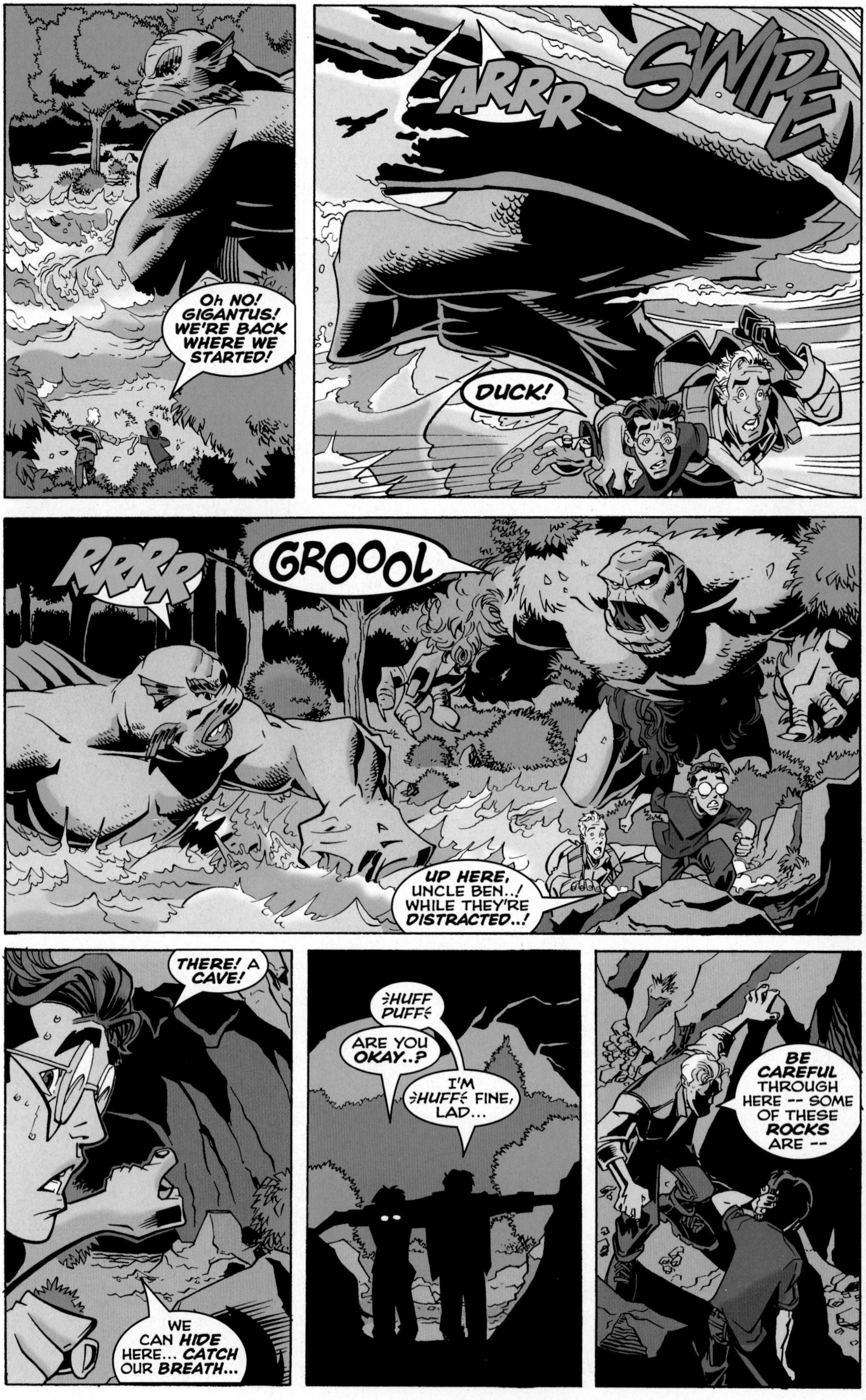
Oh NO! GIGANTUS! WE'RE BACK WHERE WE STARTED!
ARRR
SWIPE
DUCK!
RRRR
GROOOL
UP HERE, UNCLE BEN..! WHILE THEY'RE DISTRACTED..!
THERE! A CAVE!
WE CAN HIDE HERE... CATCH OUR BREATH...
HUFF PUFF
ARE YOU OKAY..?
I'M HUFF FINE, LAD...
BE CAREFUL THROUGH HERE -- SOME OF THESE ROCKS ARE --

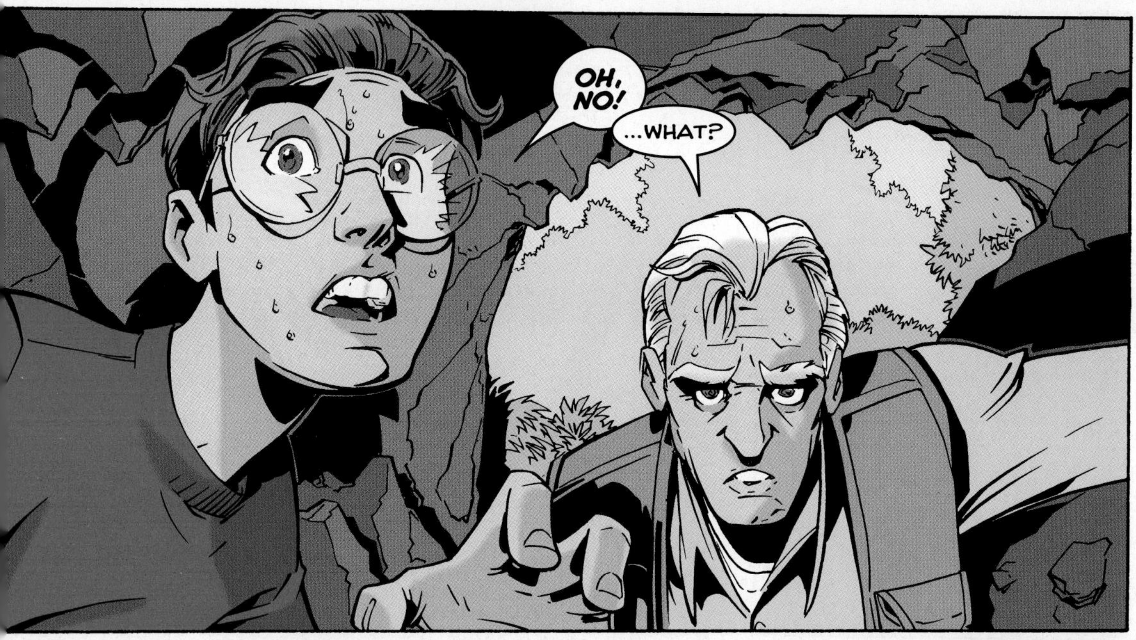
OH, NO!
...WHAT?

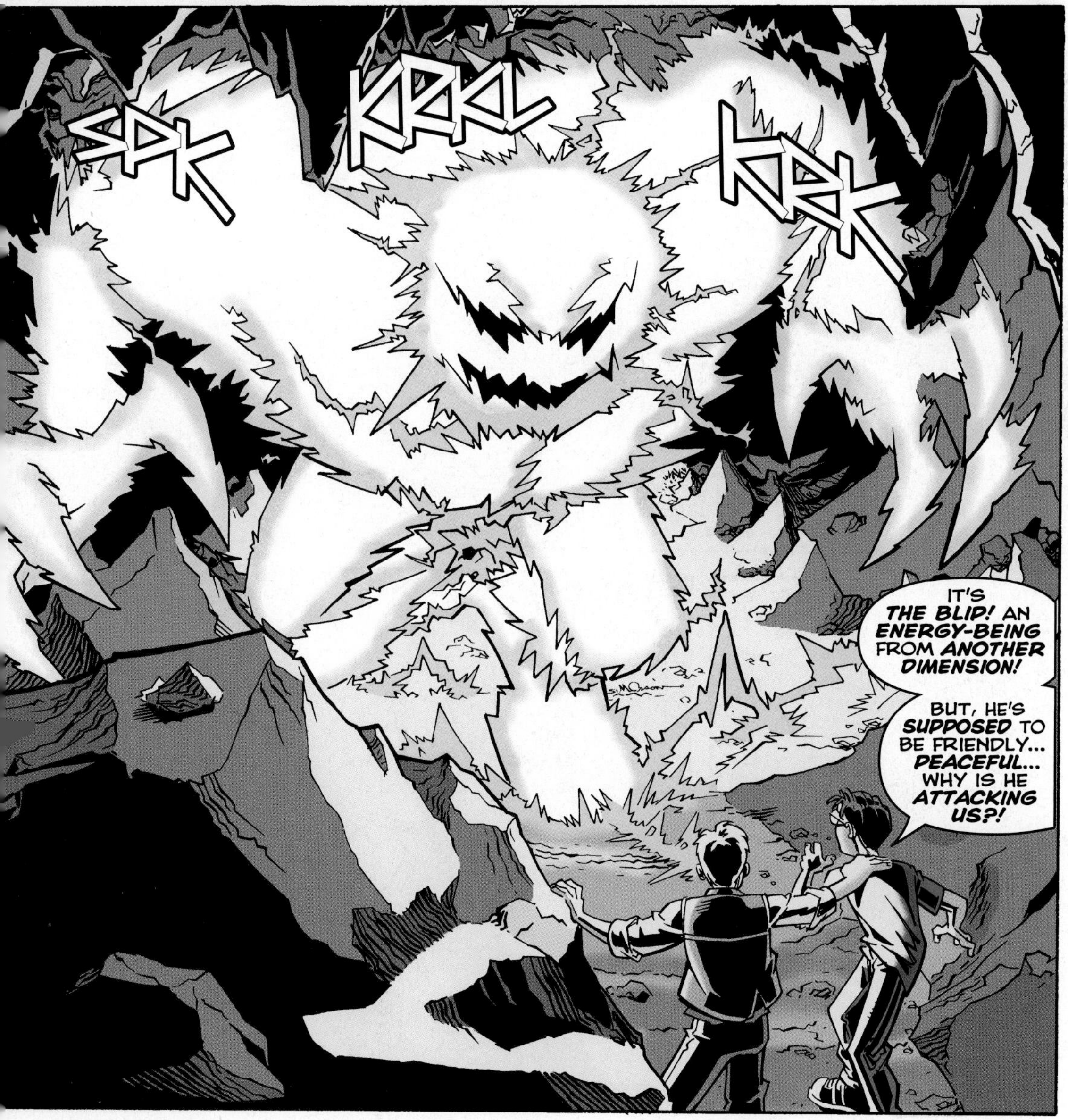
SPK
KRKL
KRK
IT'S THE BLIP! AN ENERGY-BEING FROM ANOTHER DIMENSION!
BUT, HE'S SUPPOSED TO BE FRIENDLY... PEACEFUL... WHY IS HE ATTACKING US?!

LET'S NOT *STAY* TO *FIND OUT* -- *RUN!*

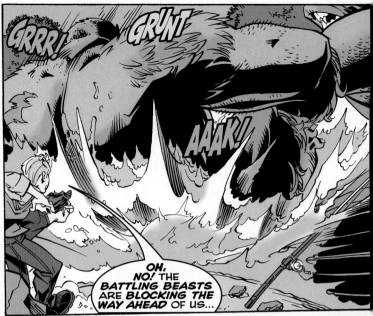

GRRR!

GRUNT

AAAK!

OH, *NO!* THE *BATTLING BEASTS* ARE *BLOCKING THE WAY AHEAD* OF US...

AND THE BLIP IS *CLOSING IN* ON US FROM *BEHIND!* WE'RE *DOOMED!*

...UNLESS...

C'MON, PETER, THINK -- *THINK!*

THAT'S IT! THE *MONEL* LINE!

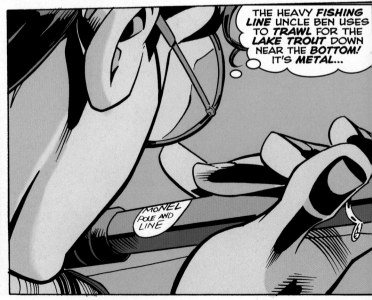

THE HEAVY *FISHING LINE* UNCLE BEN USES TO *TRAWL* FOR THE *LAKE TROUT* DOWN NEAR THE *BOTTOM!* IT'S *METAL*...

MONEL POLE AND LINE

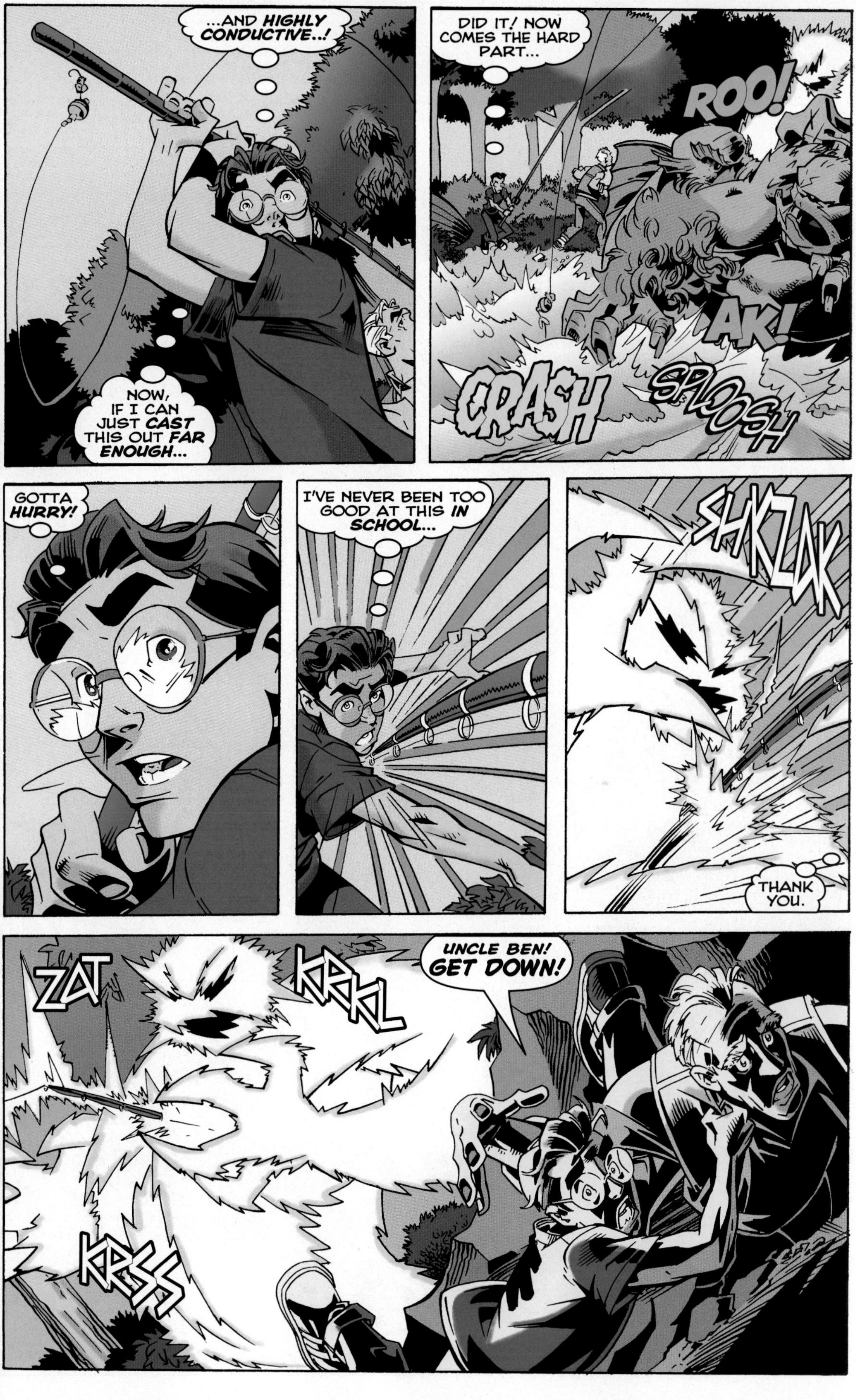

...AND HIGHLY CONDUCTIVE..!
NOW, IF I CAN JUST CAST THIS OUT FAR ENOUGH...
DID IT! NOW COMES THE HARD PART...
ROO!
AK!
CRASH
SPLOOSH
GOTTA HURRY!
I'VE NEVER BEEN TOO GOOD AT THIS IN SCHOOL...
SHKLAK
THANK YOU.
ZAT
KRKL
UNCLE BEN! GET DOWN!
KRSS

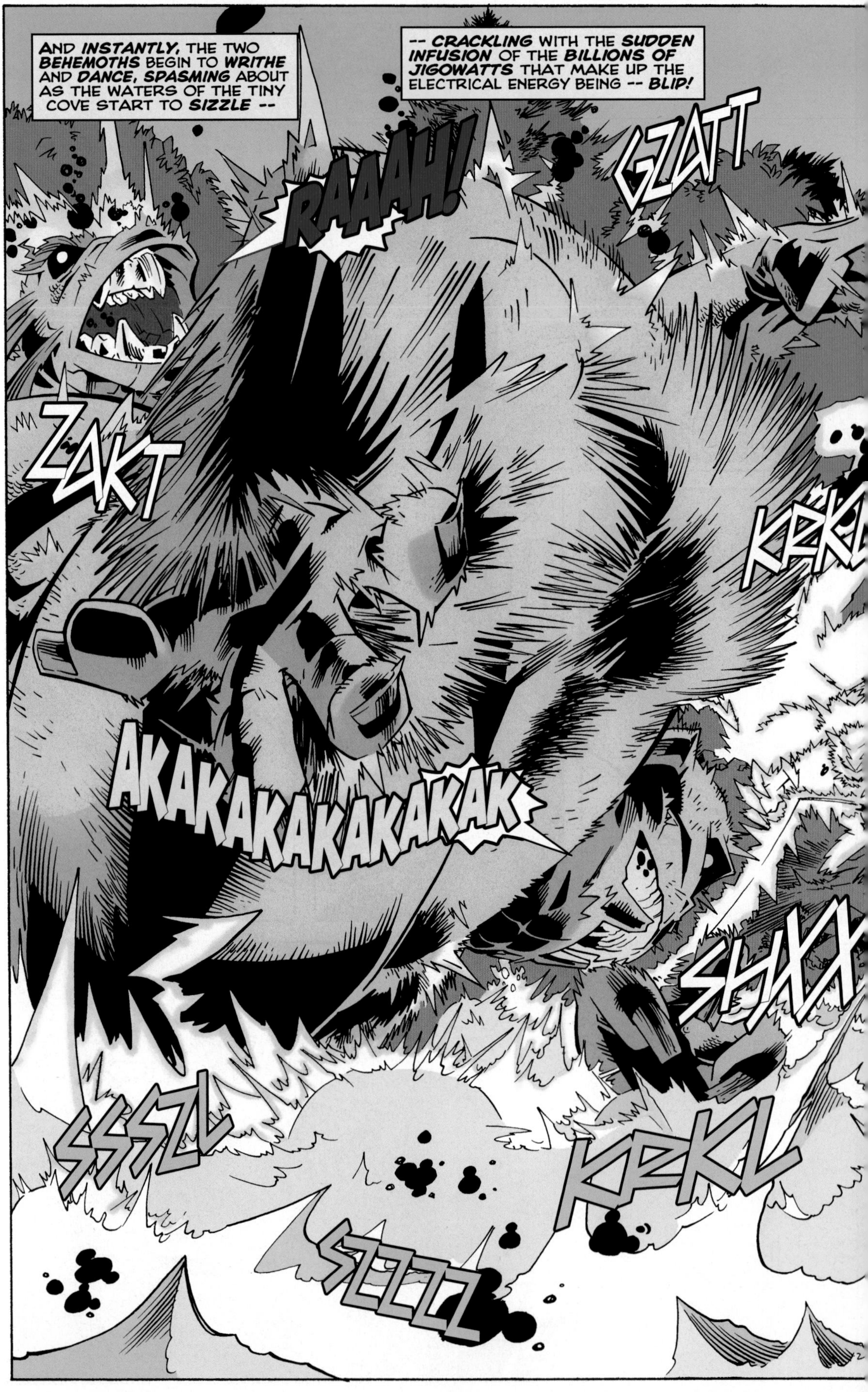
AND INSTANTLY, THE TWO BEHEMOTHS BEGIN TO WRITHE AND DANCE, SPASMING ABOUT AS THE WATERS OF THE TINY COVE START TO SIZZLE --
-- CRACKLING WITH THE SUDDEN INFUSION OF THE BILLIONS OF JIGOWATTS THAT MAKE UP THE ELECTRICAL ENERGY BEING -- BLIP!
RAAAH!
GZATT
ZAKT
AKAKAKAKAKAKAKAK
SSSZL
KRKL
SZZZZ

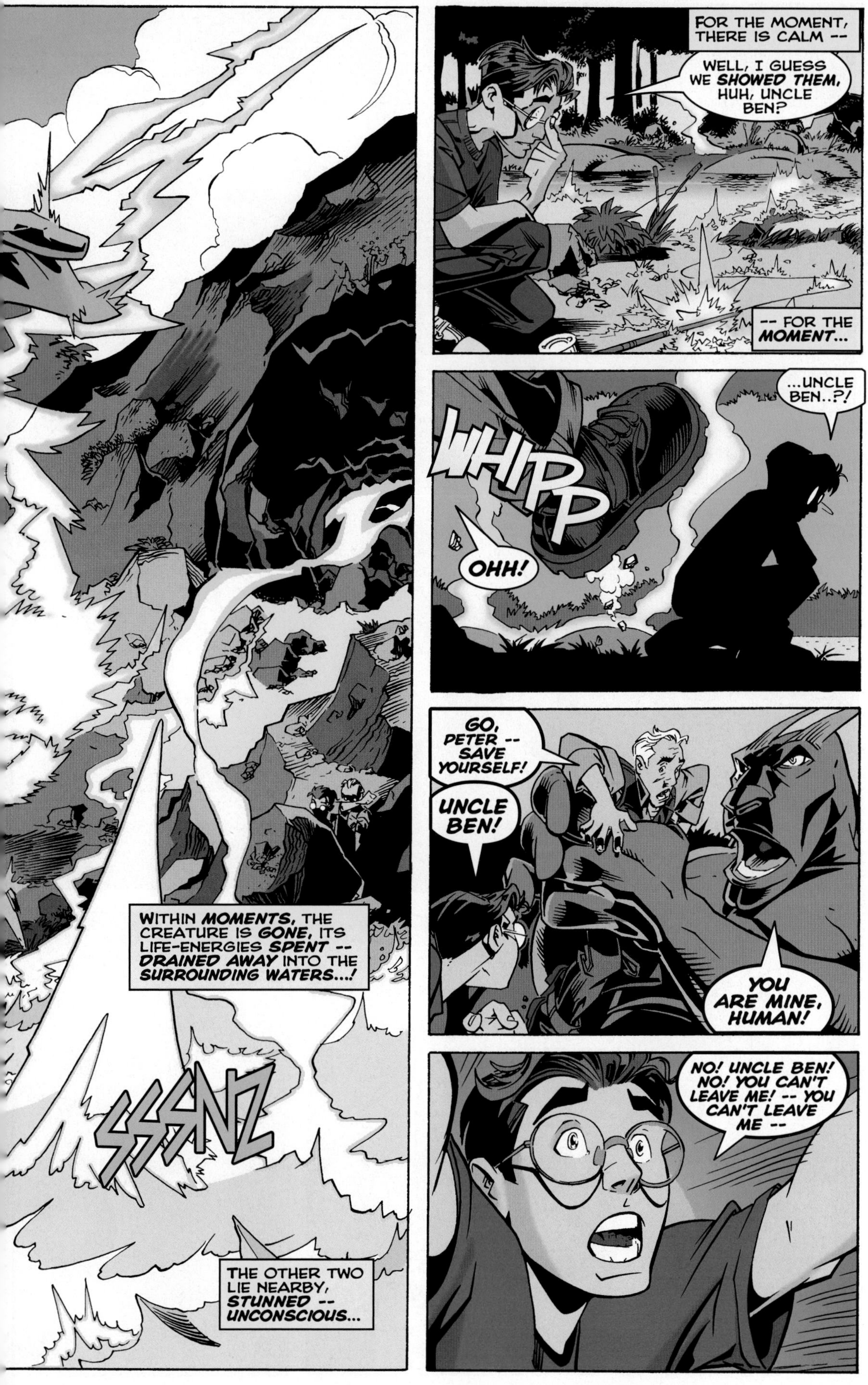
WITHIN MOMENTS, THE CREATURE IS GONE, ITS LIFE-ENERGIES SPENT -- DRAINED AWAY INTO THE SURROUNDING WATERS...!
SSSNZ
THE OTHER TWO LIE NEARBY, STUNNED -- UNCONSCIOUS...
FOR THE MOMENT, THERE IS CALM --
WELL, I GUESS WE SHOWED THEM, HUH, UNCLE BEN?
-- FOR THE MOMENT...
...UNCLE BEN..?!
WHIPP
OHH!
GO, PETER -- SAVE YOURSELF!
UNCLE BEN!
YOU ARE MINE, HUMAN!
NO! UNCLE BEN! NO! YOU CAN'T LEAVE ME! -- YOU CAN'T LEAVE ME --

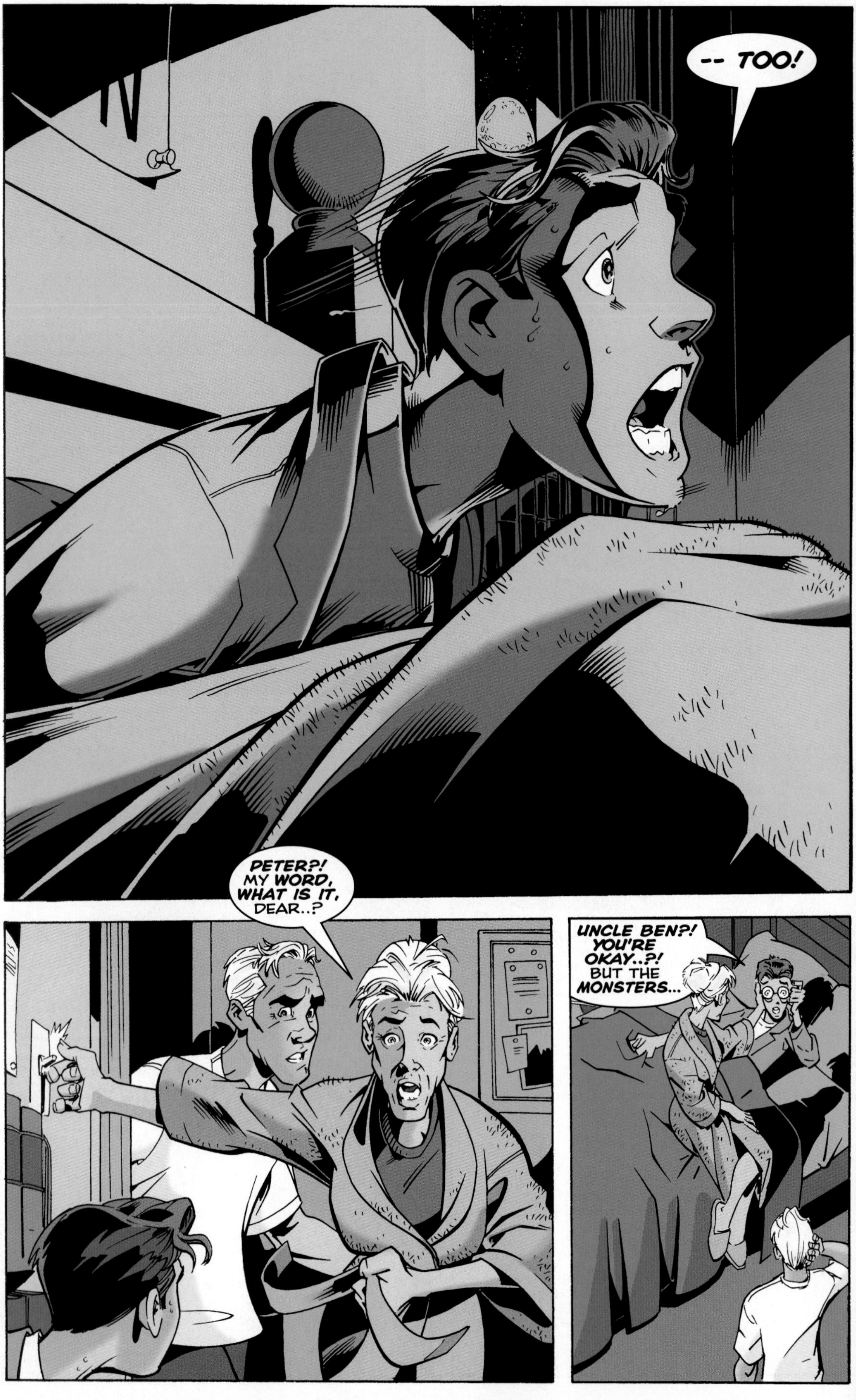
-- TOO!
PETER?! MY WORD, WHAT IS IT, DEAR..?
UNCLE BEN?! YOU'RE OKAY..?! BUT THE MONSTERS...

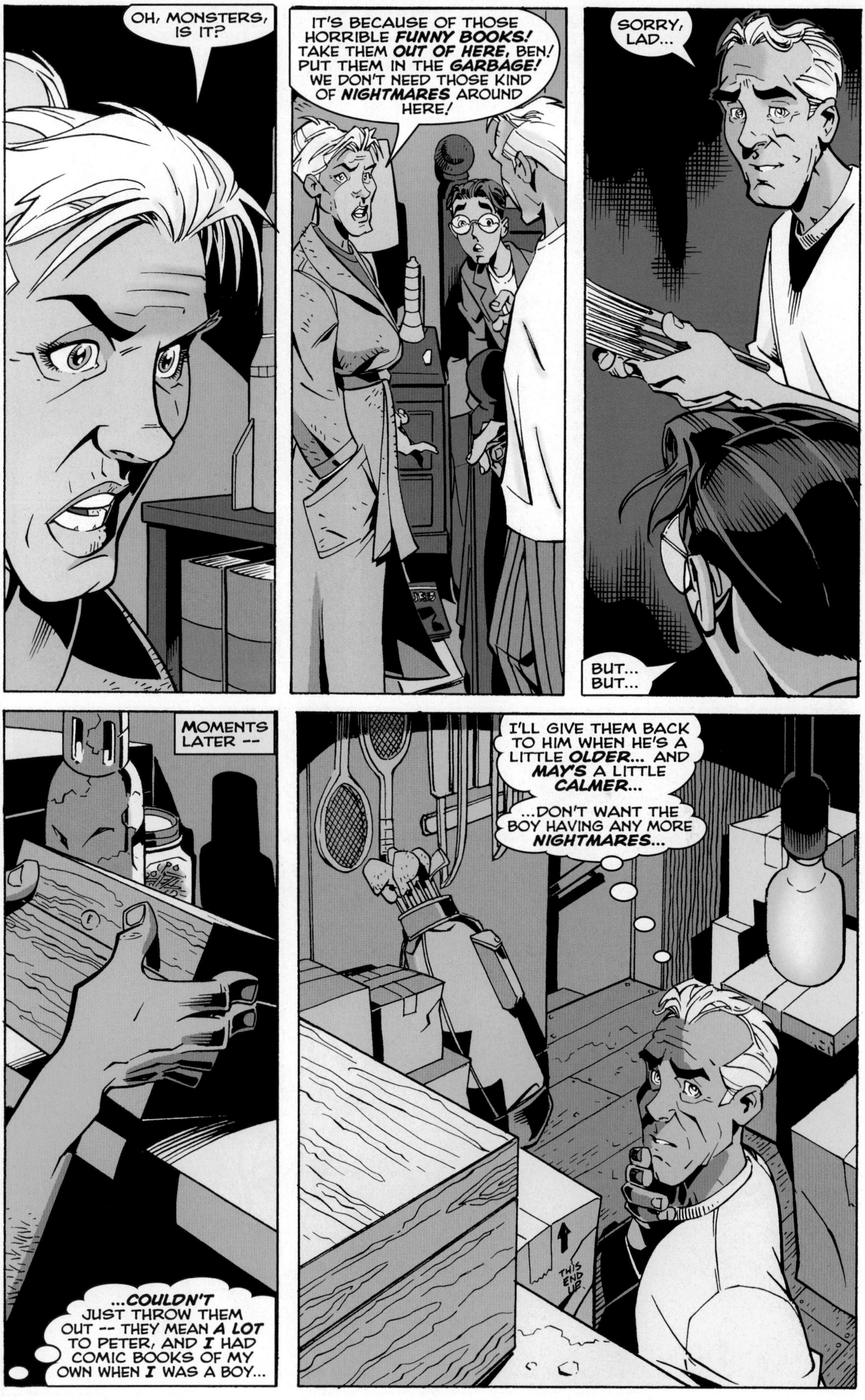
OH, MONSTERS, IS IT?
IT'S BECAUSE OF THOSE HORRIBLE FUNNY BOOKS! TAKE THEM OUT OF HERE, BEN! PUT THEM IN THE GARBAGE! WE DON'T NEED THOSE KIND OF NIGHTMARES AROUND HERE!
SORRY, LAD...
BUT... BUT...
MOMENTS LATER --
...COULDN'T JUST THROW THEM OUT -- THEY MEAN A LOT TO PETER, AND I HAD COMIC BOOKS OF MY OWN WHEN I WAS A BOY...
I'LL GIVE THEM BACK TO HIM WHEN HE'S A LITTLE OLDER... AND MAY'S A LITTLE CALMER...
...DON'T WANT THE BOY HAVING ANY MORE NIGHTMARES...
THIS END UP

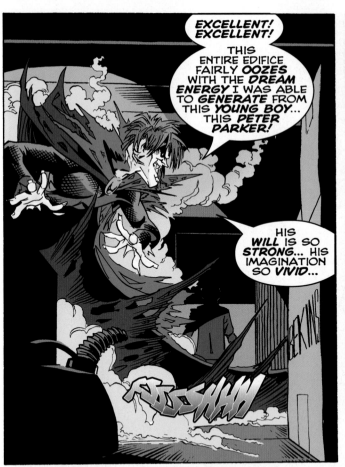

EXCELLENT! EXCELLENT! THIS ENTIRE EDIFICE FAIRLY *OOZES* WITH THE *DREAM ENERGY* I WAS ABLE TO *GENERATE* FROM THIS *YOUNG BOY...* THIS *PETER PARKER!*

HIS *WILL* IS SO *STRONG...* HIS *IMAGINATION* SO *VIVID...*

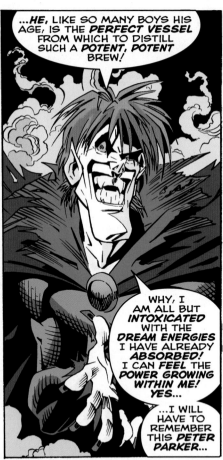

...*HE,* LIKE SO MANY BOYS HIS AGE, IS THE *PERFECT VESSEL* FROM WHICH TO DISTILL SUCH A *POTENT, POTENT* BREW!

WHY, I AM ALL BUT *INTOXICATED* WITH THE *DREAM ENERGIES* I HAVE ALREADY *ABSORBED!* I CAN *FEEL* THE *POWER* GROWING *WITHIN ME!* YES...

...I WILL HAVE TO REMEMBER THIS *PETER PARKER...*

...FOR ONLY I, *NIGHTMARE,* HAVE THE POWER TO *TWIST* AND *MANIPULATE* HIS *VERY DREAMS!* TO *DRINK* IN THE *POWER* RELEASED BY HIS *SUBCONSCIOUS ADVENTURES!* TO *PLUCK* AND *CLAW* AT HIS *INNERMOST FEA --*

OH, NIGHTY..?

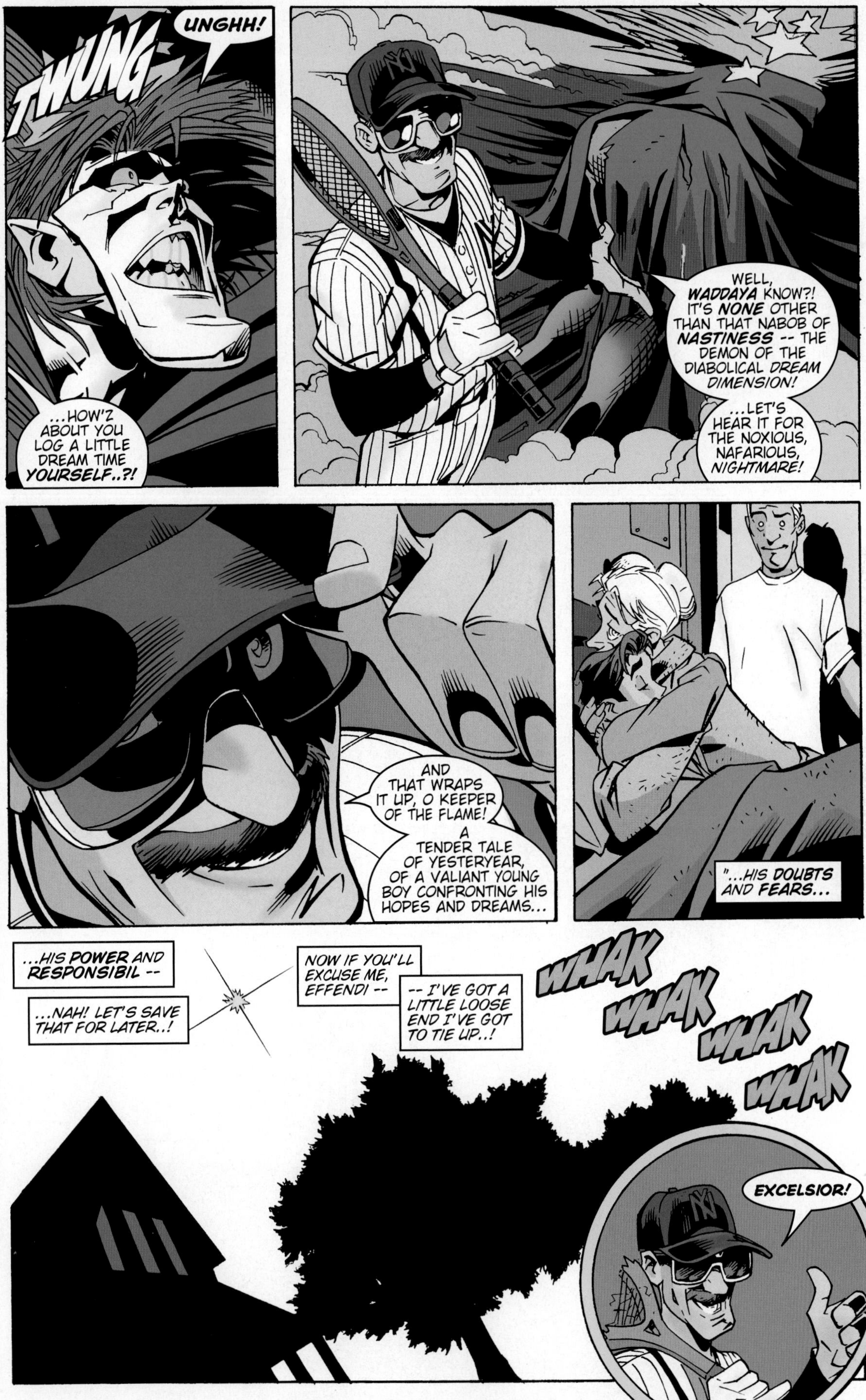
TWUNG
UNGHH!
...HOW'Z ABOUT YOU LOG A LITTLE DREAM TIME YOURSELF..?!
WELL, WADDAYA KNOW?! IT'S NONE OTHER THAN THAT NABOB OF NASTINESS -- THE DEMON OF THE DIABOLICAL DREAM DIMENSION!
...LET'S HEAR IT FOR THE NOXIOUS, NAFARIOUS, NIGHTMARE!
AND THAT WRAPS IT UP, O KEEPER OF THE FLAME!
A TENDER TALE OF YESTERYEAR, OF A VALIANT YOUNG BOY CONFRONTING HIS HOPES AND DREAMS...
"...HIS DOUBTS AND FEARS...
...HIS POWER AND RESPONSIBIL --
...NAH! LET'S SAVE THAT FOR LATER..!
NOW IF YOU'LL EXCUSE ME, EFFENDI --
-- I'VE GOT A LITTLE LOOSE END I'VE GOT TO TIE UP..!
WHAK
WHAK
WHAK
WHAK
EXCELSIOR!

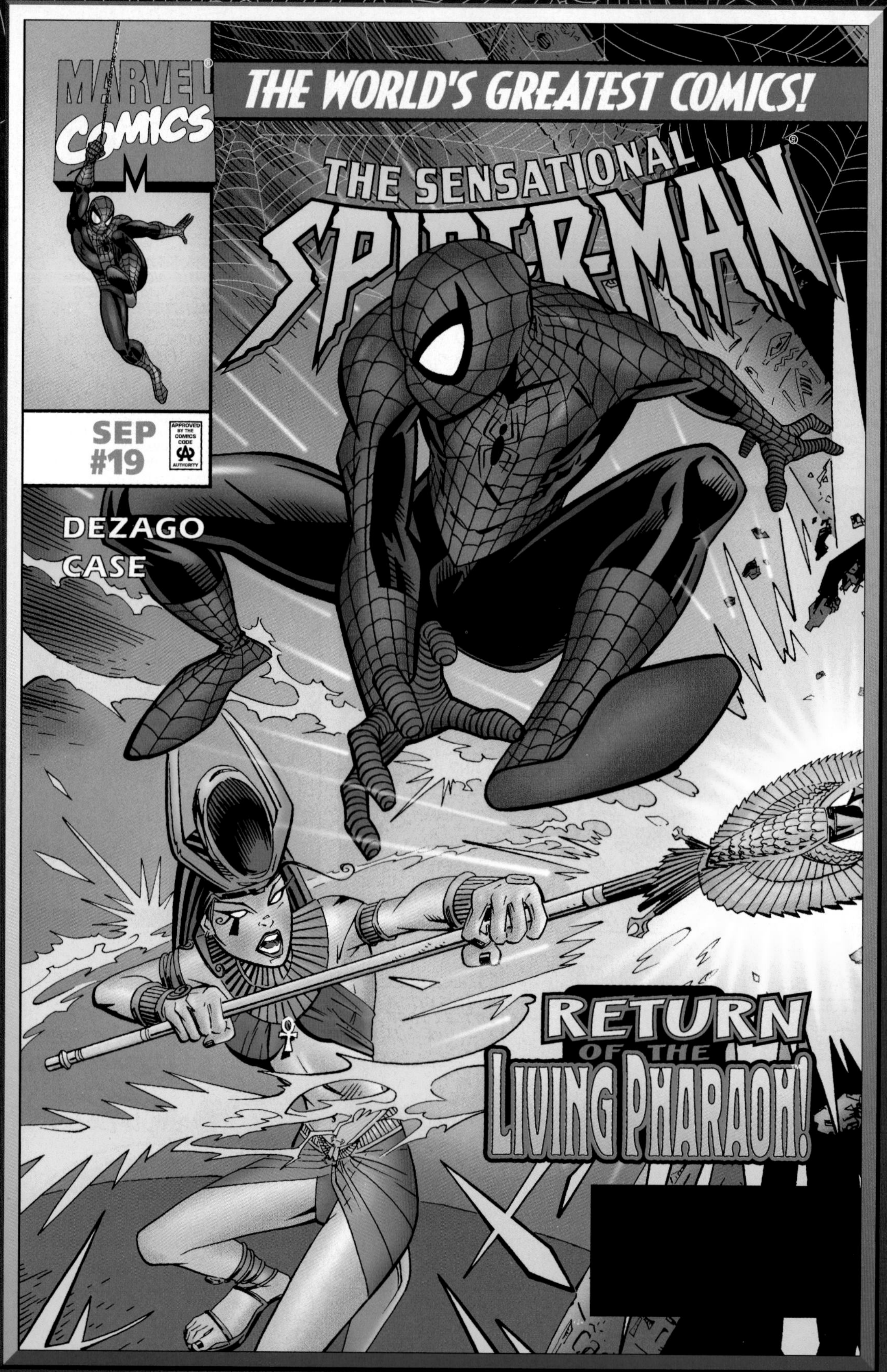
MARVEL COMICS
THE WORLD'S GREATEST COMICS!
THE SENSATIONAL
SPIDER-MAN
SEP
#19
APPROVED BY THE COMICS CODE AUTHORITY
DEZAGO
CASE
RETURN OF THE LIVING PHARAOH!

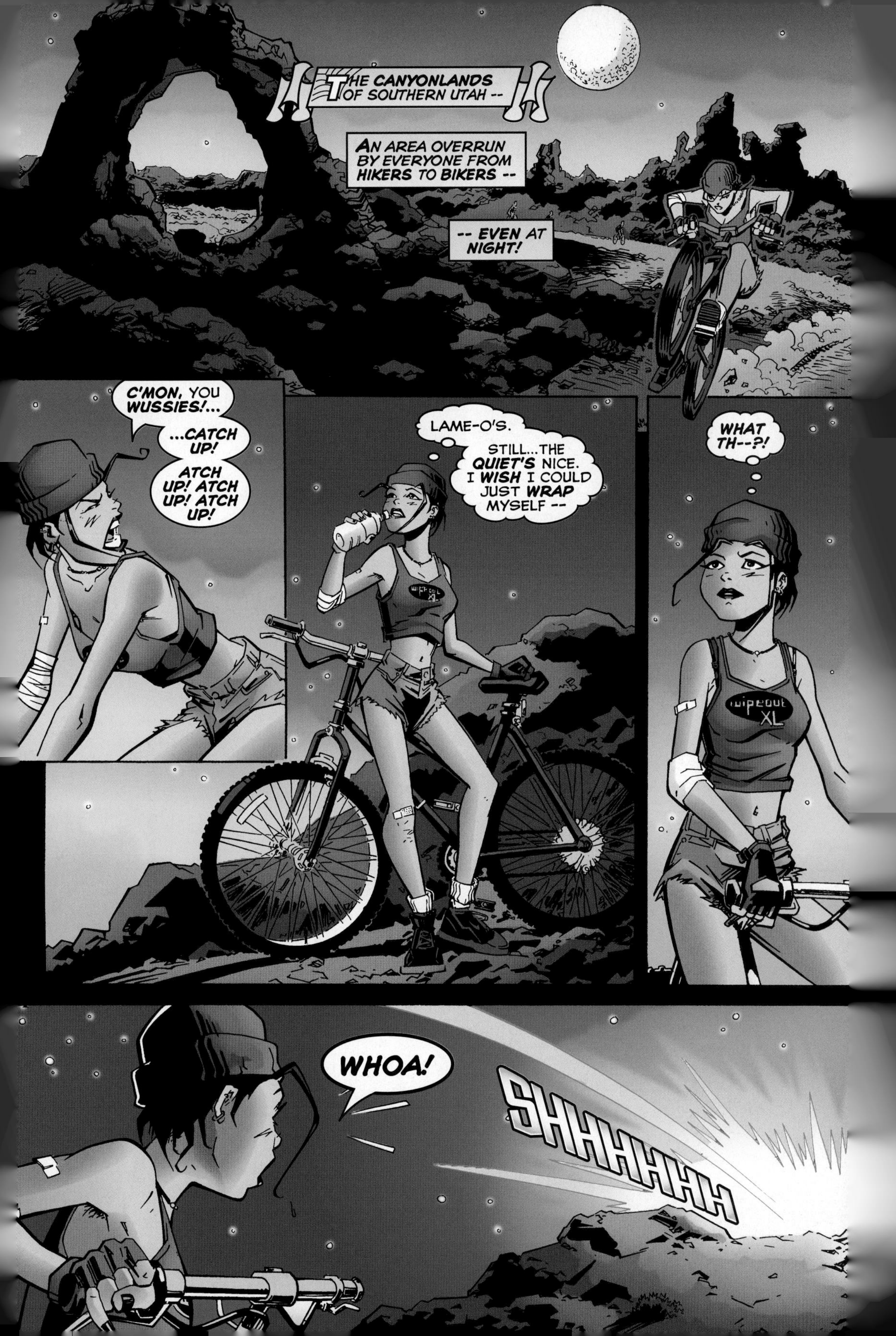
THE CANYONLANDS OF SOUTHERN UTAH --
AN AREA OVERRUN BY EVERYONE FROM HIKERS TO BIKERS --
-- EVEN AT NIGHT!
C'MON, YOU WUSSIES!...
...CATCH UP!
ATCH UP! ATCH UP! ATCH UP!
LAME-O'S.
STILL...THE QUIET'S NICE. I WISH I COULD JUST WRAP MYSELF --
WHAT TH--?!
WHOA!
SHHHHHH

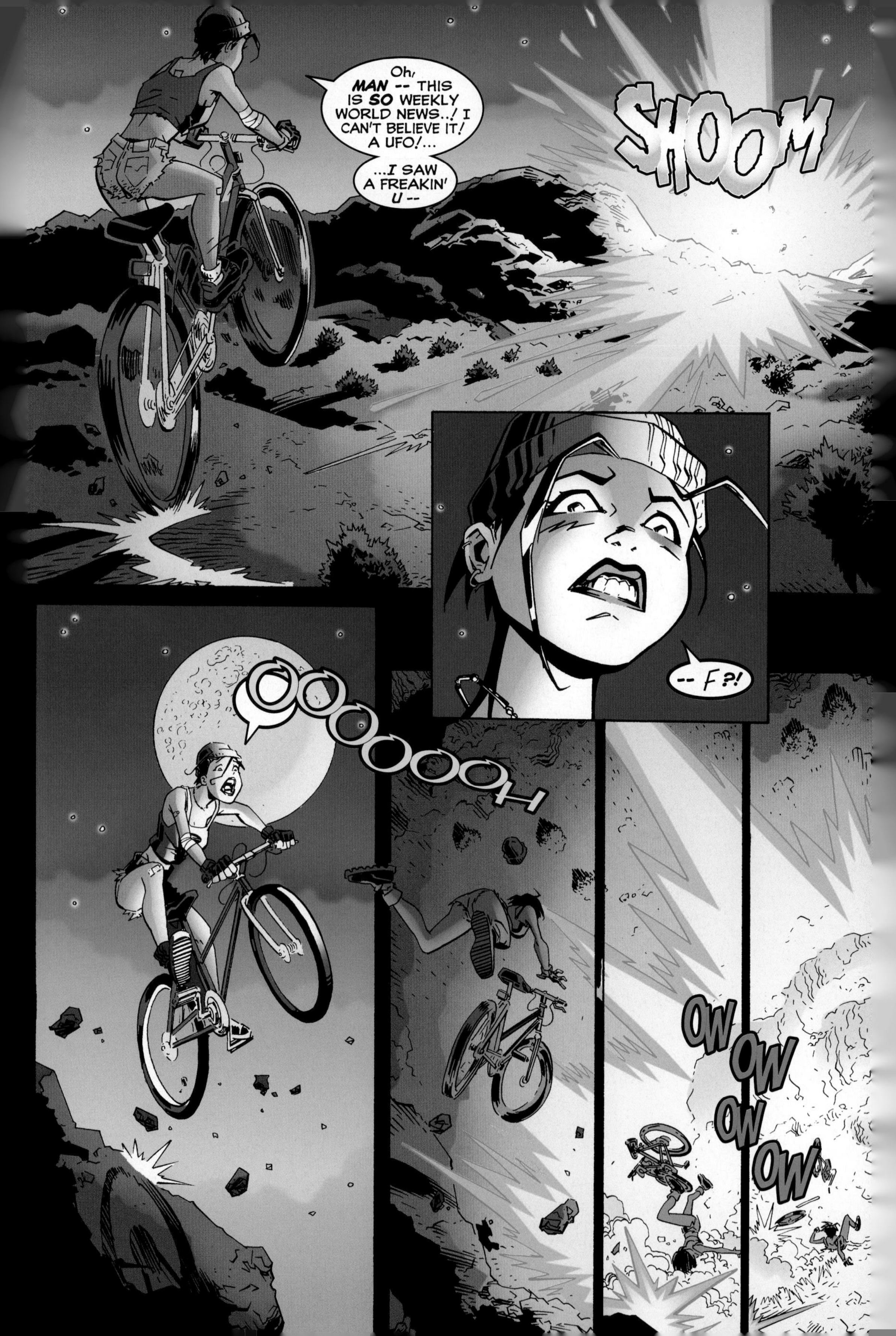

Oh, MAN -- THIS IS SO WEEKLY WORLD NEWS..! I CAN'T BELIEVE IT! A UFO!...
...I SAW A FREAKIN' U --
SHOOM
-- F?!
OOOOOOOH
OW OW OW OW

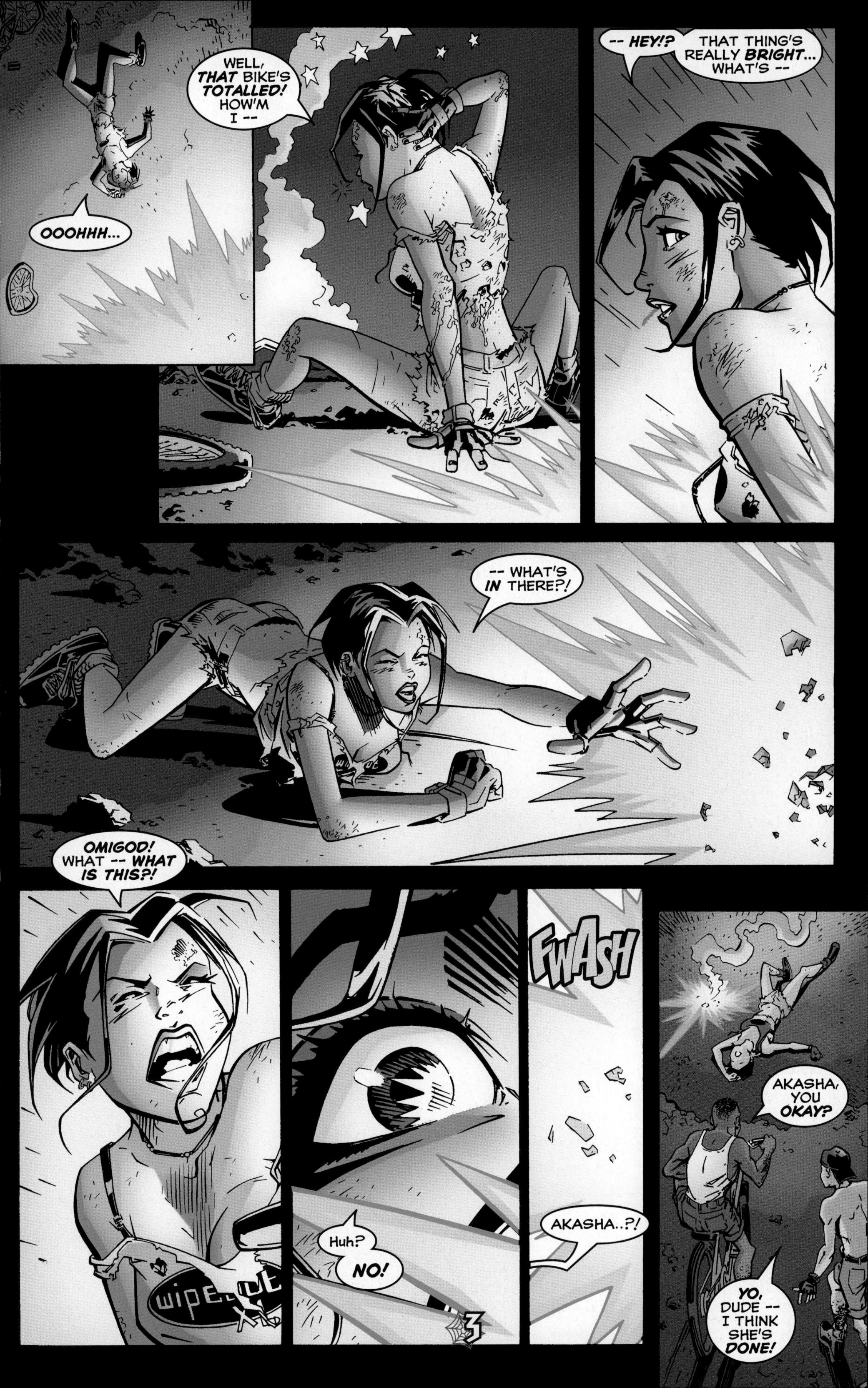

WELL, THAT BIKE'S TOTALLED! HOW'M I --
OOOHHH...
-- HEY!? THAT THING'S REALLY BRIGHT... WHAT'S --
-- WHAT'S IN THERE?!
OMIGOD! WHAT -- WHAT IS THIS?!
Huh? NO!
FWASH
AKASHA..?!
AKASHA, YOU OKAY?
YO, DUDE -- I THINK SHE'S DONE!
3

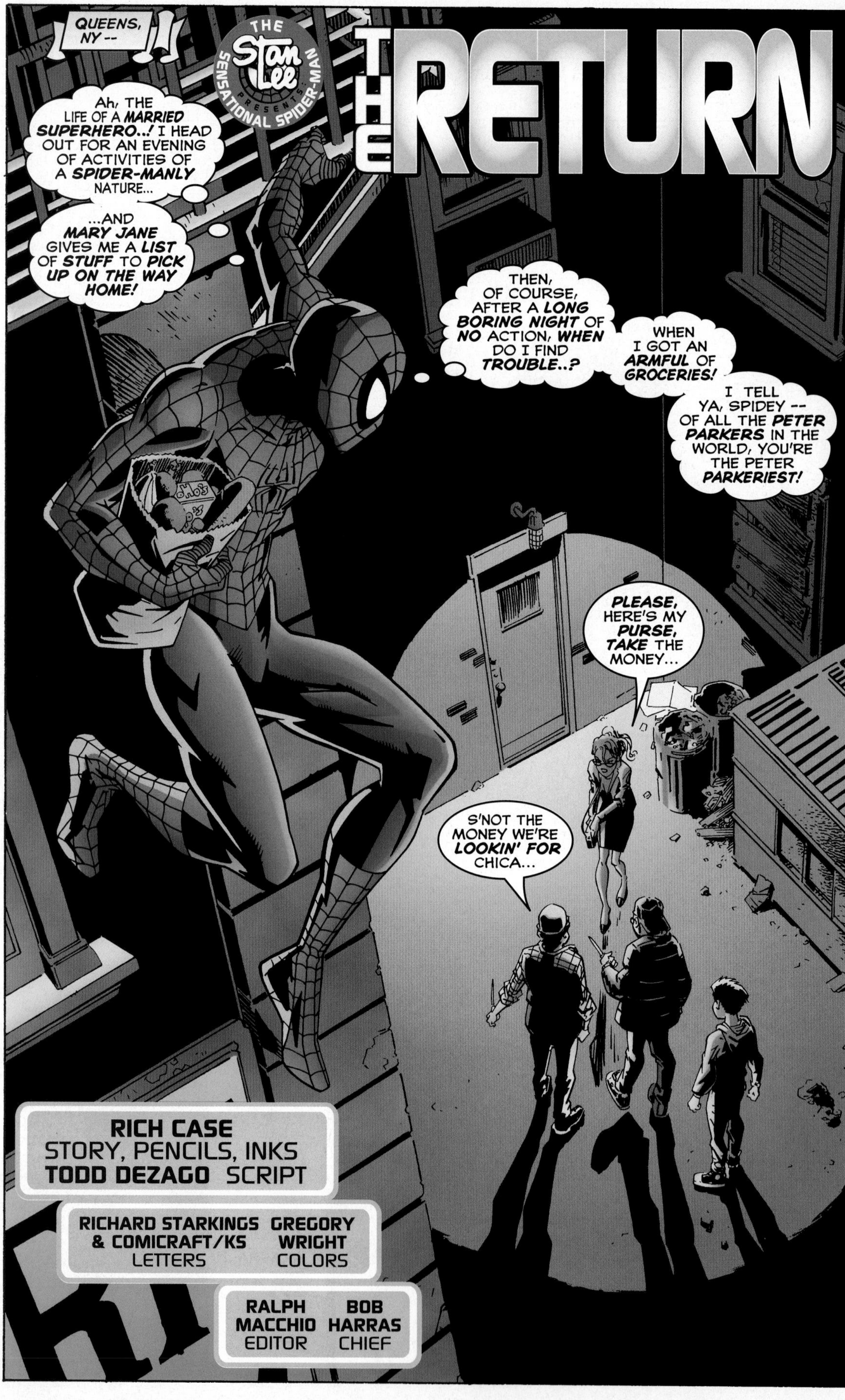

QUEENS, NY --
THE Stan Lee PRESENTS SENSATIONAL SPIDER-MAN
THE RETURN
Ah, THE LIFE OF A MARRIED SUPERHERO..! I HEAD OUT FOR AN EVENING OF ACTIVITIES OF A SPIDER-MANLY NATURE...
...AND MARY JANE GIVES ME A LIST OF STUFF TO PICK UP ON THE WAY HOME!
THEN, OF COURSE, AFTER A LONG BORING NIGHT OF NO ACTION, WHEN DO I FIND TROUBLE..?
WHEN I GOT AN ARMFUL OF GROCERIES!
I TELL YA, SPIDEY -- OF ALL THE PETER PARKERS IN THE WORLD, YOU'RE THE PETER PARKERIEST!
PLEASE, HERE'S MY PURSE, TAKE THE MONEY...
S'NOT THE MONEY WE'RE LOOKIN' FOR CHICA...
RICH CASE STORY, PENCILS, INKS
TODD DEZAGO SCRIPT
RICHARD STARKINGS & COMICRAFT/KS LETTERS
GREGORY WRIGHT COLORS
RALPH MACCHIO EDITOR
BOB HARRAS CHIEF

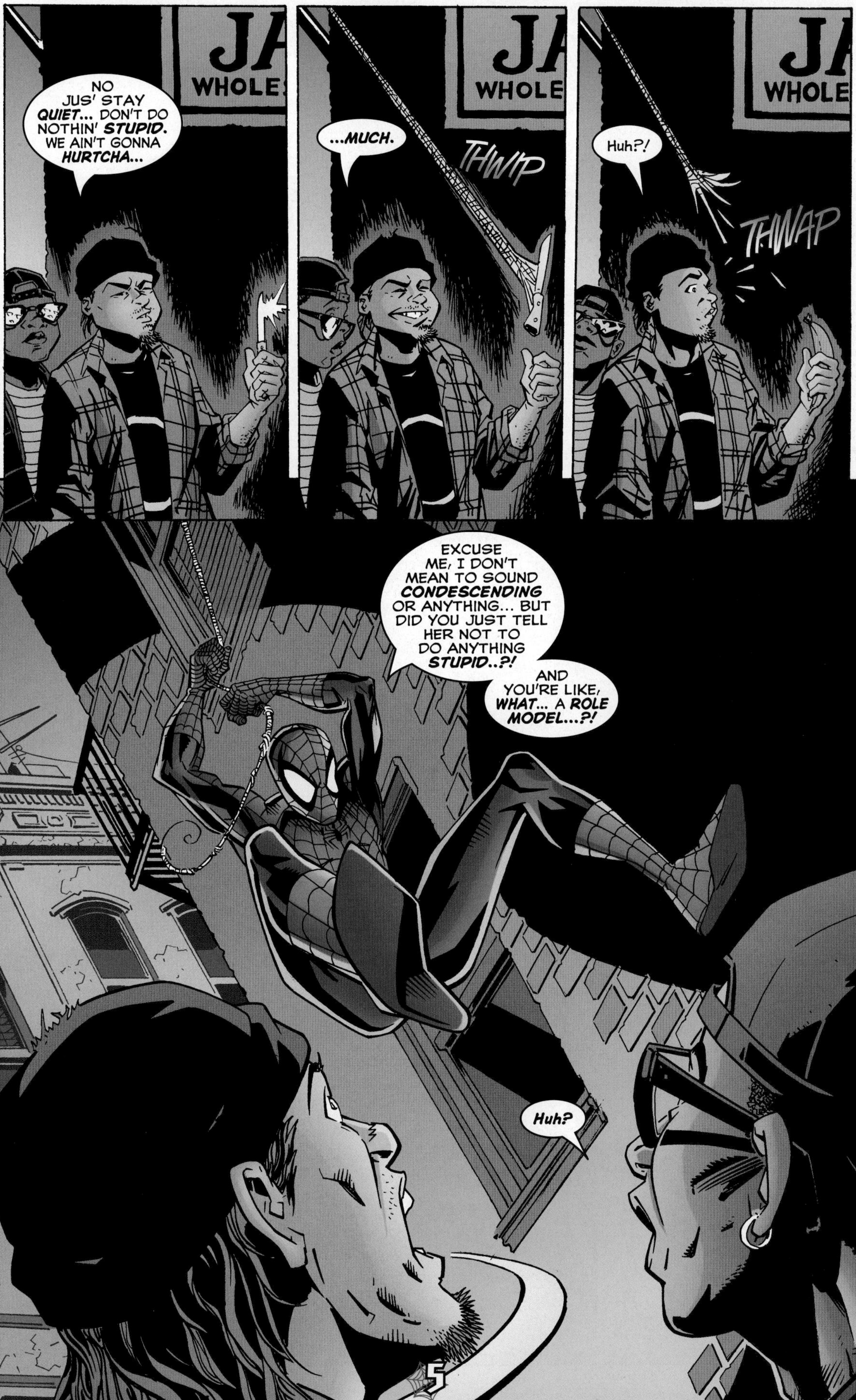
JA
WHOLES
NO JUS' STAY QUIET... DON'T DO NOTHIN' STUPID. WE AIN'T GONNA HURTCHA...
...MUCH.
THWIP
Huh?!
THWAP
EXCUSE ME, I DON'T MEAN TO SOUND CONDESCENDING OR ANYTHING... BUT DID YOU JUST TELL HER NOT TO DO ANYTHING STUPID..?!
AND YOU'RE LIKE, WHAT... A ROLE MODEL...?!
Huh?

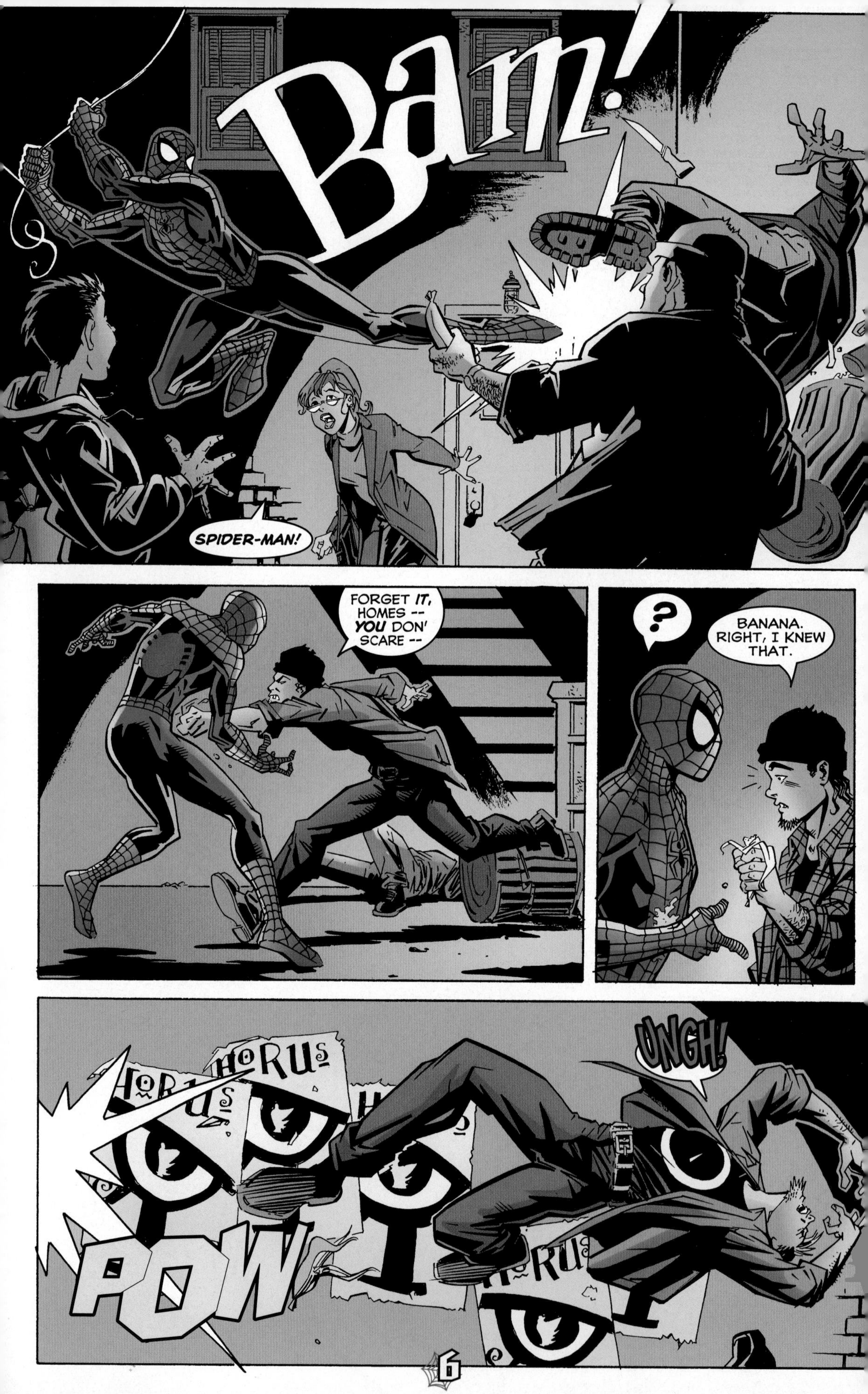
Bam!
SPIDER-MAN!
FORGET IT, HOMES -- YOU DON' SCARE --
?
BANANA. RIGHT, I KNEW THAT.
UNGH!
POW
HORUS

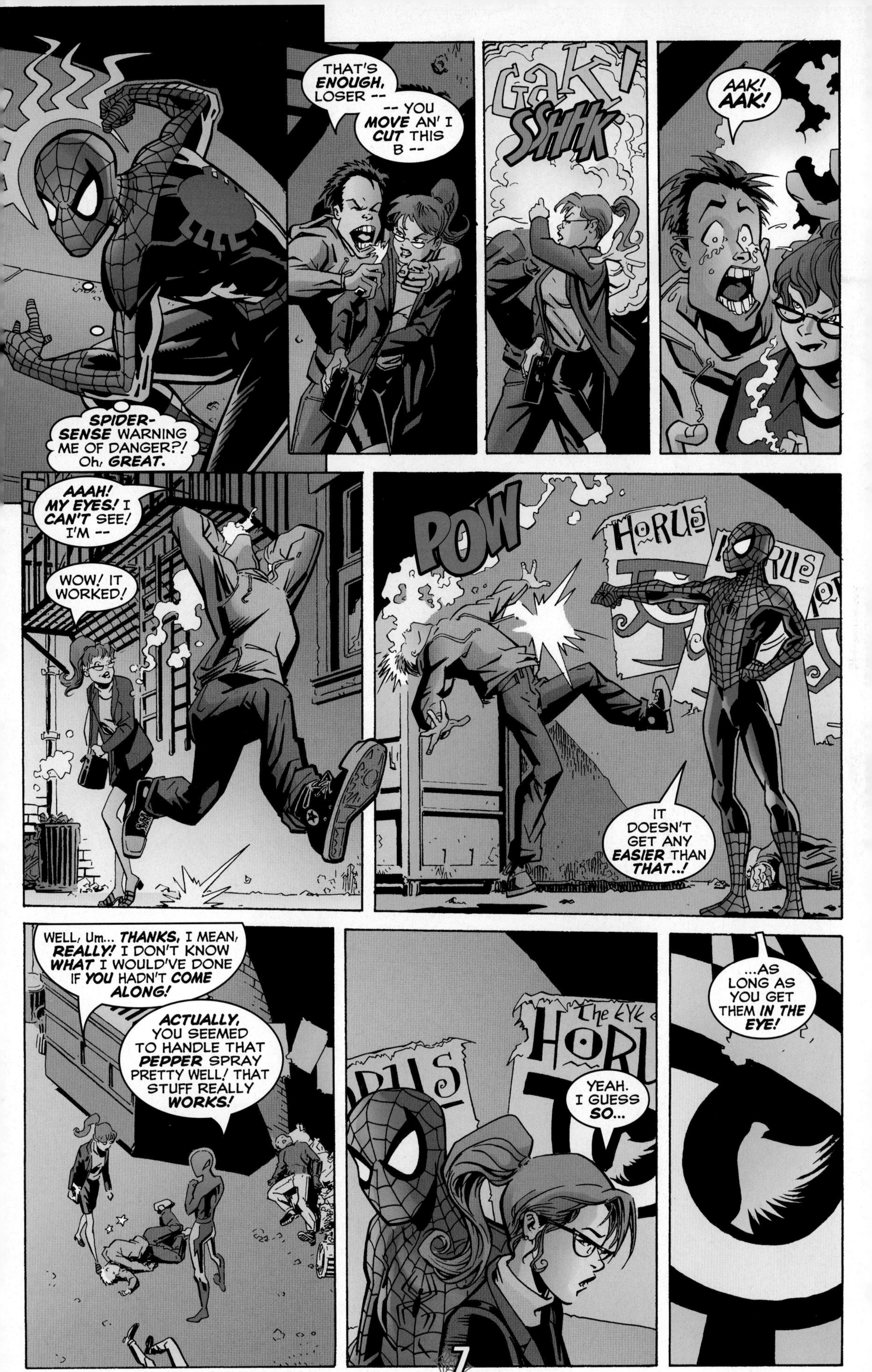
SPIDER-SENSE WARNING ME OF DANGER?! Oh, GREAT.
THAT'S ENOUGH, LOSER --
-- YOU MOVE AN' I CUT THIS B --
GAK!
SSHHK
AAK! AAK!
AAAH! MY EYES! I CAN'T SEE! I'M --
WOW! IT WORKED!
POW
HORUS
IT DOESN'T GET ANY EASIER THAN THAT..!
WELL, Um... THANKS, I MEAN, REALLY! I DON'T KNOW WHAT I WOULD'VE DONE IF YOU HADN'T COME ALONG!
ACTUALLY, YOU SEEMED TO HANDLE THAT PEPPER SPRAY PRETTY WELL! THAT STUFF REALLY WORKS!
YEAH. I GUESS SO...
...AS LONG AS YOU GET THEM IN THE EYE!

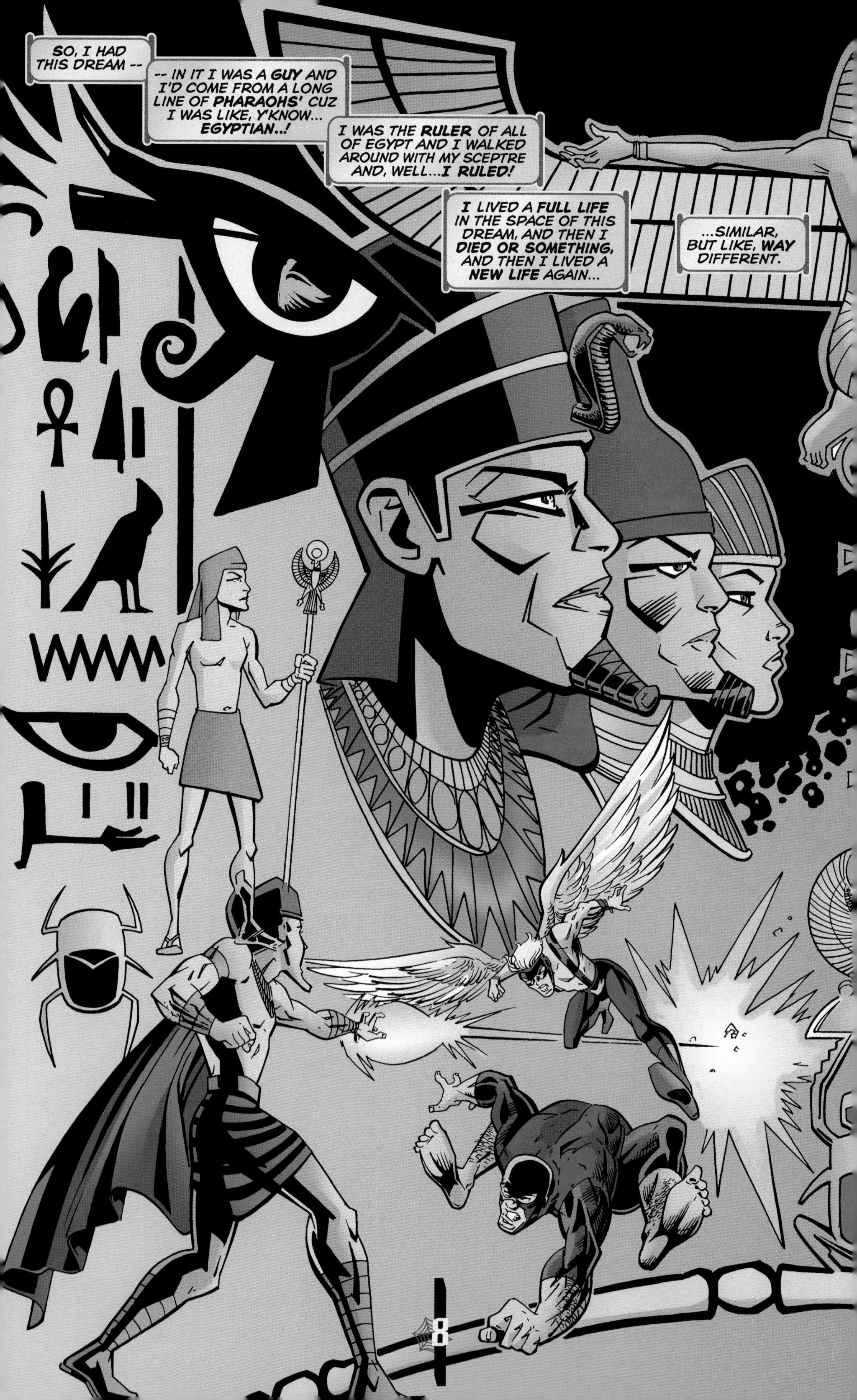

SO, I HAD THIS DREAM --
-- IN IT I WAS A **GUY** AND I'D COME FROM A LONG LINE OF **PHARAOHS'** CUZ I WAS LIKE, Y'KNOW... **EGYPTIAN**..!
I WAS THE **RULER** OF ALL OF EGYPT AND I WALKED AROUND WITH MY SCEPTRE AND, WELL...**I RULED!**
I LIVED A FULL LIFE IN THE SPACE OF THIS DREAM, AND THEN I **DIED OR SOMETHING**, AND THEN I LIVED A **NEW LIFE** AGAIN...
...SIMILAR, BUT LIKE, **WAY** DIFFERENT.

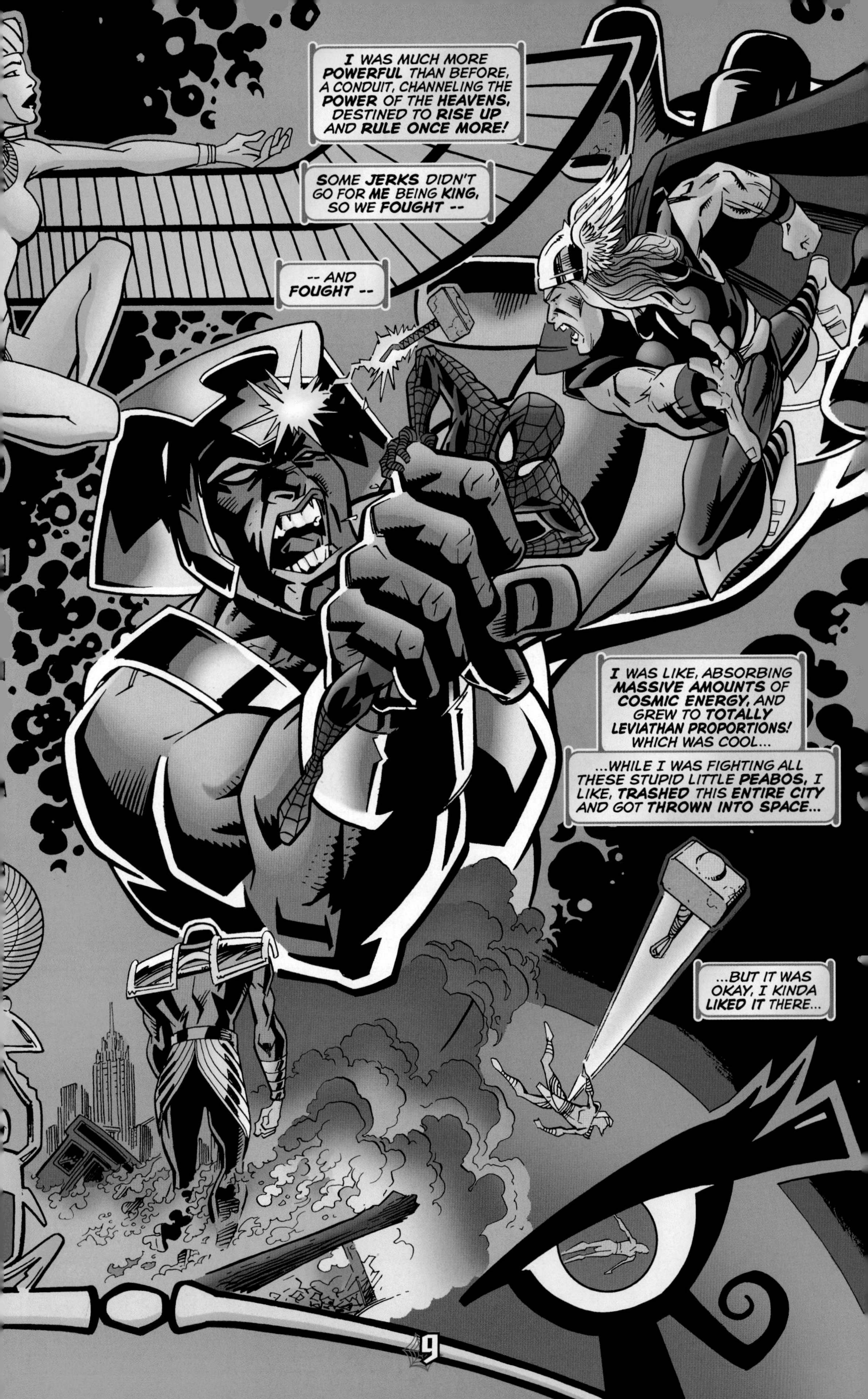
I WAS MUCH MORE POWERFUL THAN BEFORE, A CONDUIT, CHANNELING THE POWER OF THE HEAVENS, DESTINED TO RISE UP AND RULE ONCE MORE!
SOME JERKS DIDN'T GO FOR ME BEING KING, SO WE FOUGHT --
-- AND FOUGHT --
I WAS LIKE, ABSORBING MASSIVE AMOUNTS OF COSMIC ENERGY, AND GREW TO TOTALLY LEVIATHAN PROPORTIONS! WHICH WAS COOL...
...WHILE I WAS FIGHTING ALL THESE STUPID LITTLE PEABOS, I LIKE, TRASHED THIS ENTIRE CITY AND GOT THROWN INTO SPACE...
...BUT IT WAS OKAY, I KINDA LIKED IT THERE...

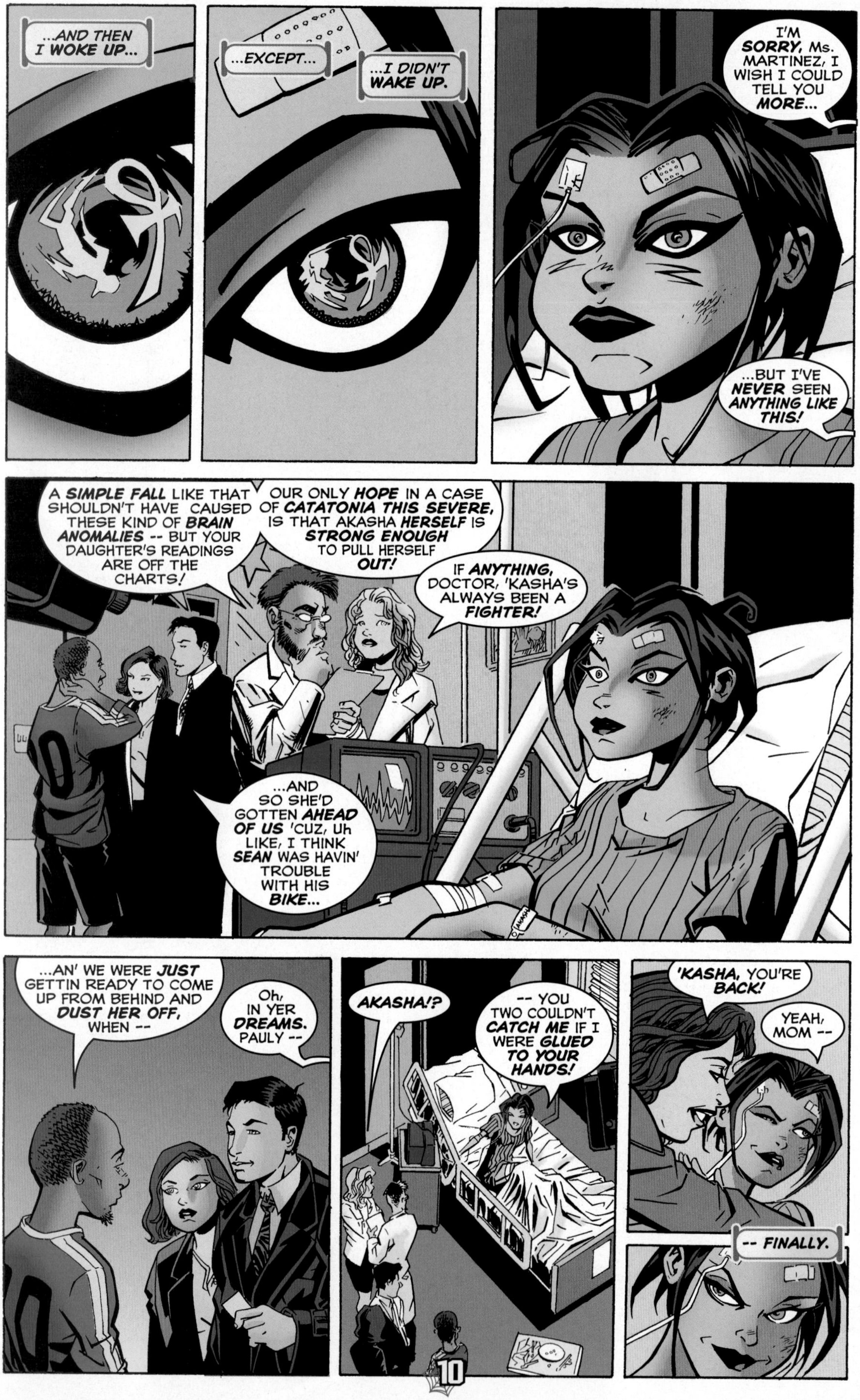
...AND THEN I WOKE UP...
...EXCEPT...
...I DIDN'T WAKE UP.
I'M SORRY, Ms. MARTINEZ, I WISH I COULD TELL YOU MORE...
...BUT I'VE NEVER SEEN ANYTHING LIKE THIS!
A SIMPLE FALL LIKE THAT SHOULDN'T HAVE CAUSED THESE KIND OF BRAIN ANOMALIES -- BUT YOUR DAUGHTER'S READINGS ARE OFF THE CHARTS!
OUR ONLY HOPE IN A CASE OF CATATONIA THIS SEVERE, IS THAT AKASHA HERSELF IS STRONG ENOUGH TO PULL HERSELF OUT!
IF ANYTHING, DOCTOR, 'KASHA'S ALWAYS BEEN A FIGHTER!
...AND SO SHE'D GOTTEN AHEAD OF US 'CUZ, Uh LIKE, I THINK SEAN WAS HAVIN' TROUBLE WITH HIS BIKE...
...AN' WE WERE JUST GETTIN READY TO COME UP FROM BEHIND AND DUST HER OFF, WHEN --
Oh, IN YER DREAMS. PAULY --
AKASHA!?
-- YOU TWO COULDN'T CATCH ME IF I WERE GLUED TO YOUR HANDS!
'KASHA, YOU'RE BACK!
YEAH, MOM --
-- FINALLY.

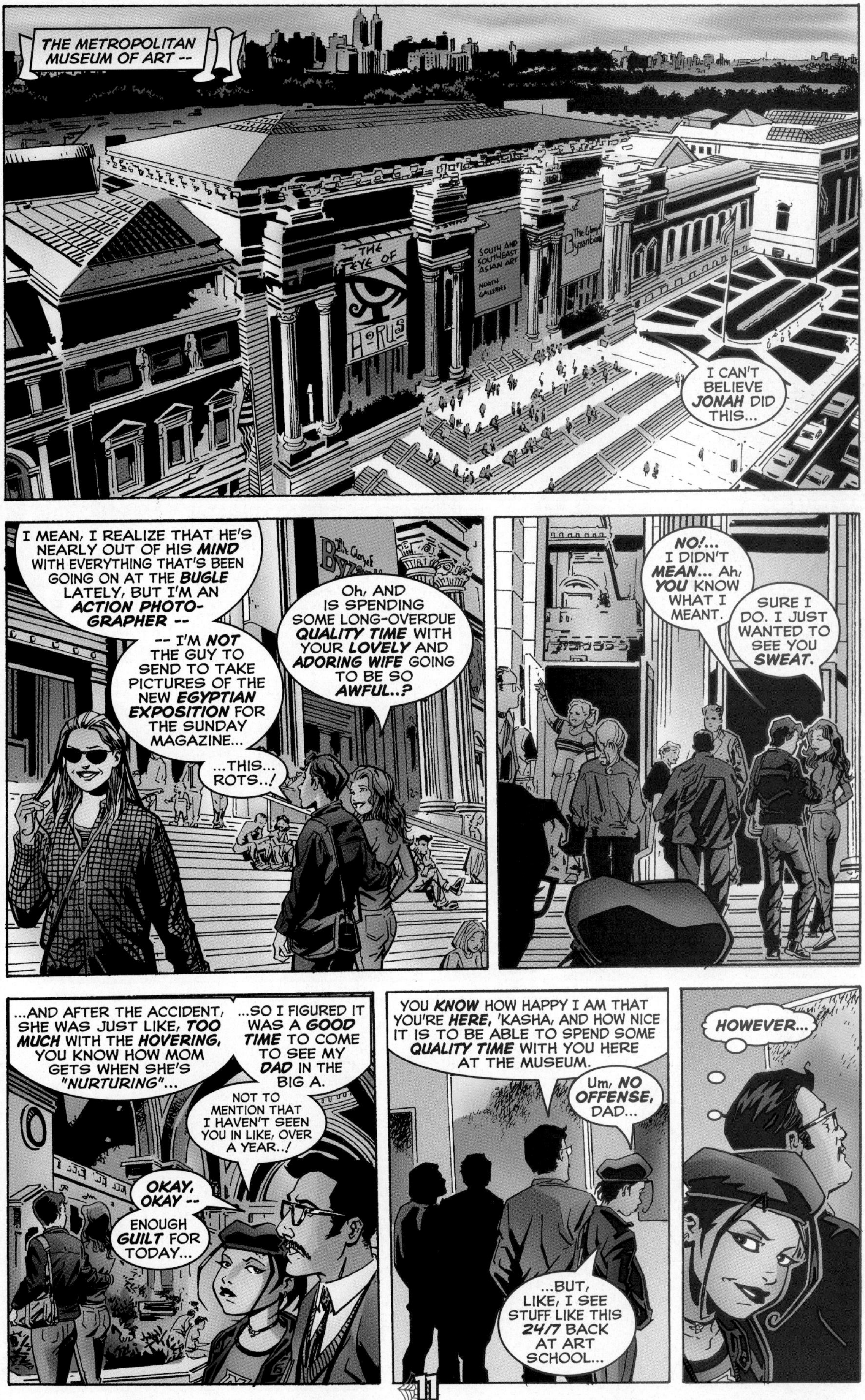
THE METROPOLITAN MUSEUM OF ART --
THE EYE OF HORUS
SOUTH AND SOUTHEAST ASIAN ART NORTH GALLERIES
The Glory of Byzantium
I CAN'T BELIEVE JONAH DID THIS...
I MEAN, I REALIZE THAT HE'S NEARLY OUT OF HIS MIND WITH EVERYTHING THAT'S BEEN GOING ON AT THE BUGLE LATELY, BUT I'M AN ACTION PHOTOGRAPHER --
-- I'M NOT THE GUY TO SEND TO TAKE PICTURES OF THE NEW EGYPTIAN EXPOSITION FOR THE SUNDAY MAGAZINE...
...THIS... ROTS...!
Oh, AND IS SPENDING SOME LONG-OVERDUE QUALITY TIME WITH YOUR LOVELY AND ADORING WIFE GOING TO BE SO AWFUL..?
NO!... I DIDN'T MEAN... Ah, YOU KNOW WHAT I MEANT.
SURE I DO. I JUST WANTED TO SEE YOU SWEAT.
...AND AFTER THE ACCIDENT, SHE WAS JUST LIKE, TOO MUCH WITH THE HOVERING, YOU KNOW HOW MOM GETS WHEN SHE'S "NURTURING"...
...SO I FIGURED IT WAS A GOOD TIME TO COME TO SEE MY DAD IN THE BIG A.
NOT TO MENTION THAT I HAVEN'T SEEN YOU IN LIKE, OVER A YEAR..!
OKAY, OKAY --
ENOUGH GUILT FOR TODAY...
YOU KNOW HOW HAPPY I AM THAT YOU'RE HERE, 'KASHA, AND HOW NICE IT IS TO BE ABLE TO SPEND SOME QUALITY TIME WITH YOU HERE AT THE MUSEUM.
Um, NO OFFENSE, DAD...
...BUT, LIKE, I SEE STUFF LIKE THIS 24/7 BACK AT ART SCHOOL...
HOWEVER...

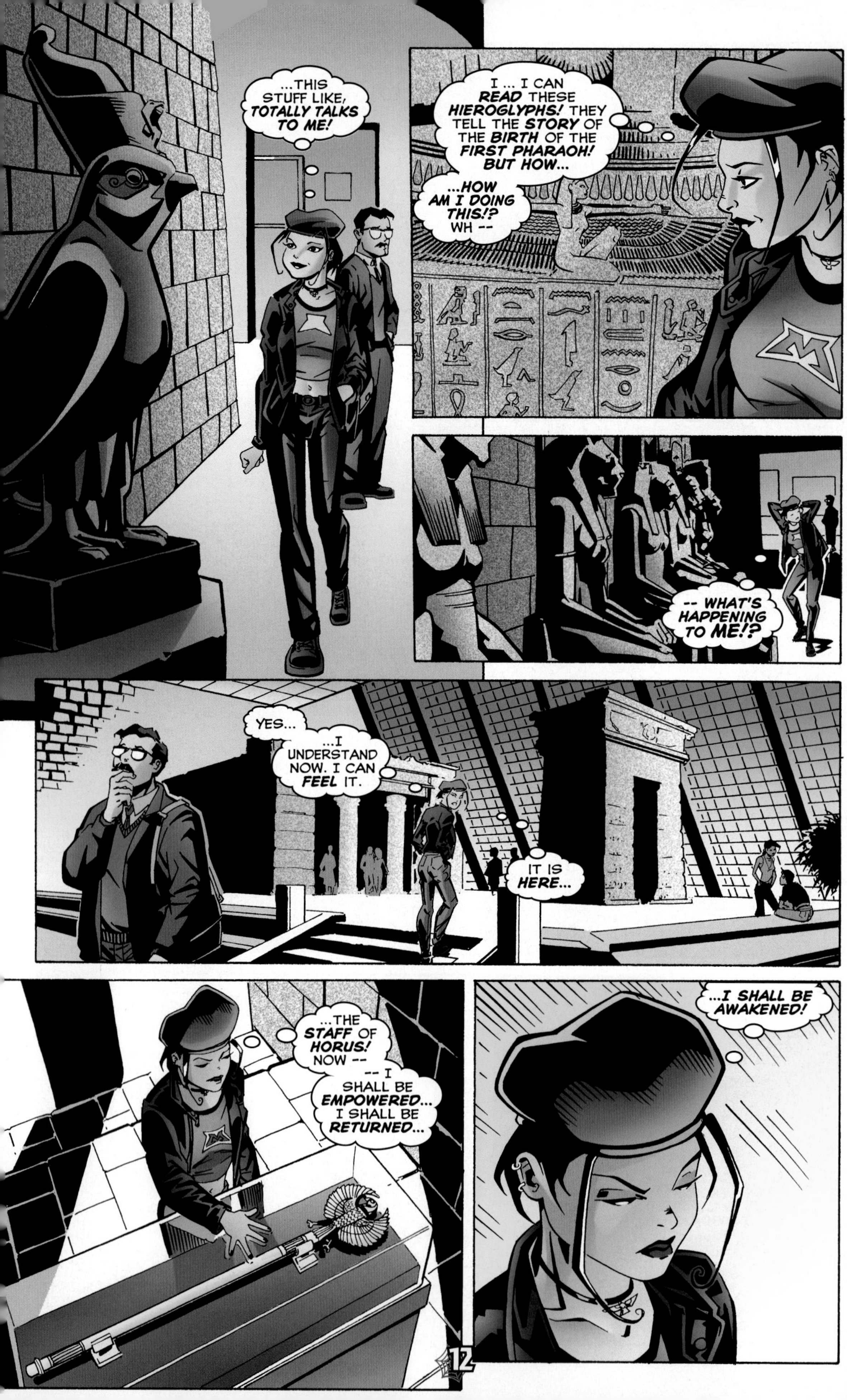
...THIS STUFF LIKE, TOTALLY TALKS TO ME!
I ... I CAN READ THESE HIEROGLYPHS! THEY TELL THE STORY OF THE BIRTH OF THE FIRST PHARAOH! BUT HOW...
...HOW AM I DOING THIS!? WH --
-- WHAT'S HAPPENING TO ME!?
YES...
...I UNDERSTAND NOW. I CAN FEEL IT.
IT IS HERE...
...THE STAFF OF HORUS! NOW --
-- I SHALL BE EMPOWERED... I SHALL BE RETURNED...
...I SHALL BE AWAKENED!
12

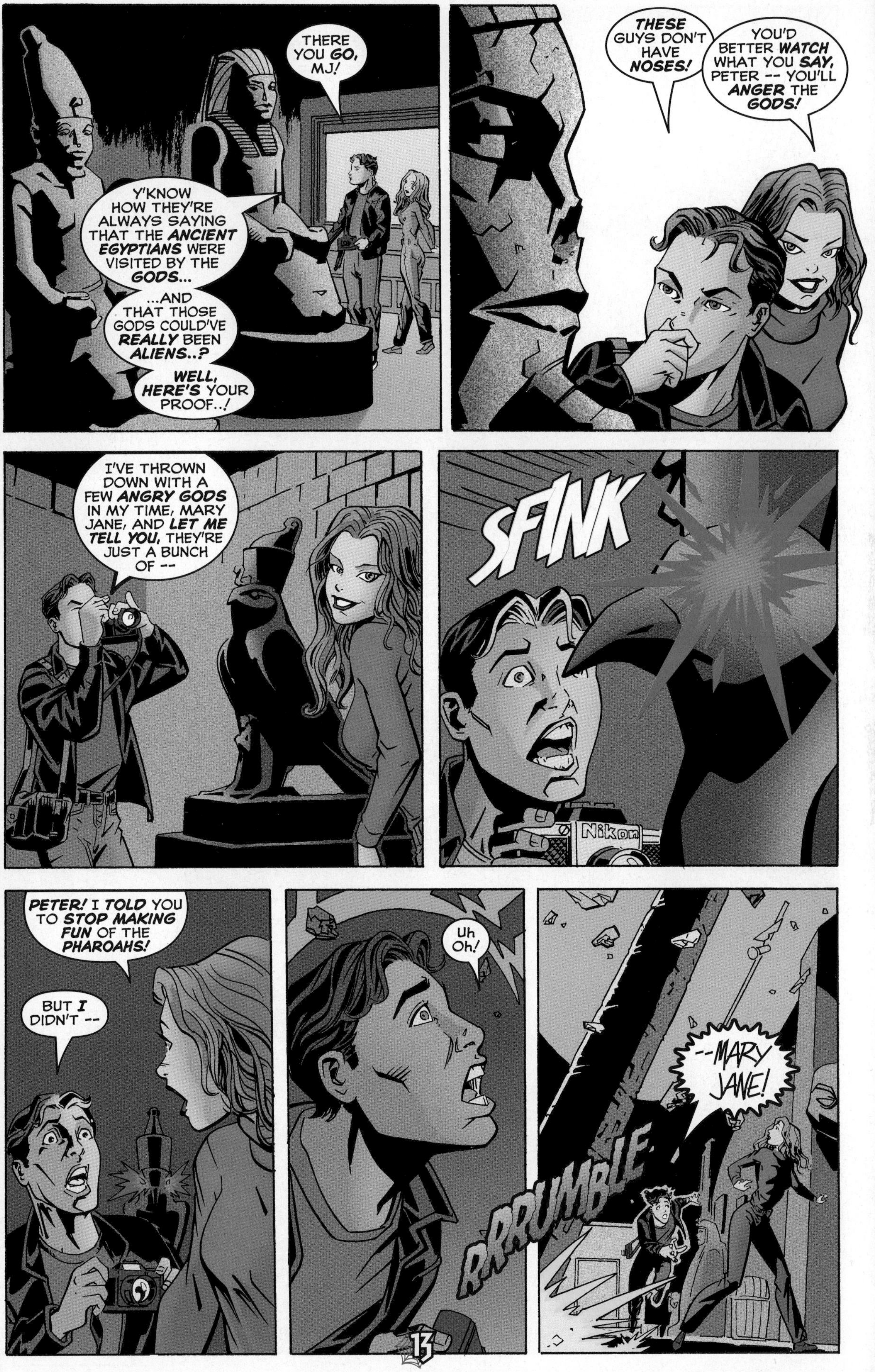
THERE YOU GO, MJ!
Y'KNOW HOW THEY'RE ALWAYS SAYING THAT THE ANCIENT EGYPTIANS WERE VISITED BY THE GODS...
...AND THAT THOSE GODS COULD'VE REALLY BEEN ALIENS..?
WELL, HERE'S YOUR PROOF..!
THESE GUYS DON'T HAVE NOSES!
YOU'D BETTER WATCH WHAT YOU SAY, PETER -- YOU'LL ANGER THE GODS!
I'VE THROWN DOWN WITH A FEW ANGRY GODS IN MY TIME, MARY JANE, AND LET ME TELL YOU, THEY'RE JUST A BUNCH OF --
SFINK
Nikon
PETER! I TOLD YOU TO STOP MAKING FUN OF THE PHAROAHS!
BUT I DIDN'T --
Uh Oh!
--MARY JANE!
R-RRUMBLE

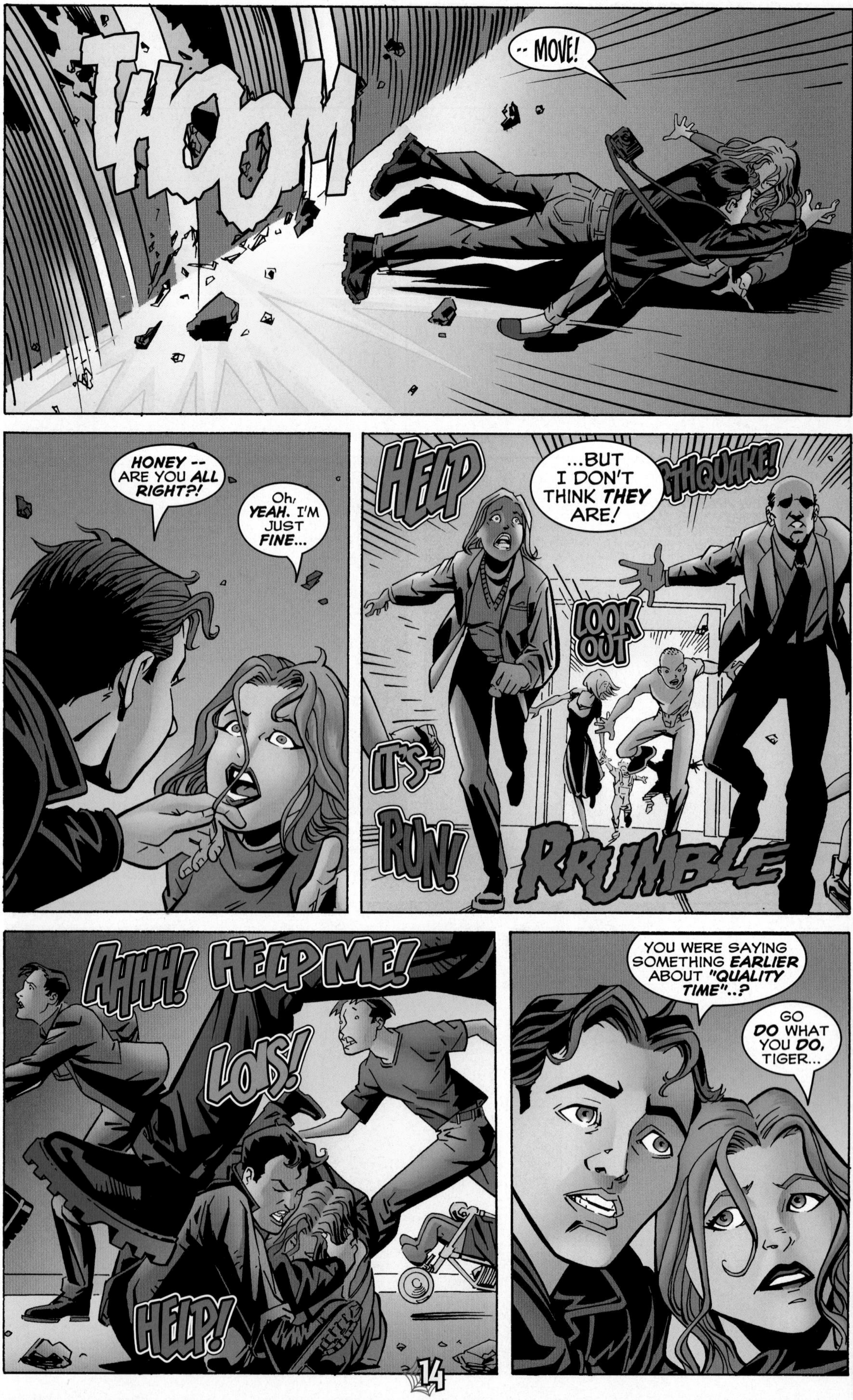
THOOM
-- MOVE!
HONEY -- ARE YOU ALL RIGHT?!
Oh, YEAH. I'M JUST FINE...
HELP
...BUT I DON'T THINK THEY ARE!
RTHQUAKE!
LOOK OUT
IT'S-
RUN!
RRUMBLE
AHHH! HELP ME!
LOIS!
HELP!
YOU WERE SAYING SOMETHING EARLIER ABOUT "QUALITY TIME"..?
GO DO WHAT YOU DO, TIGER...

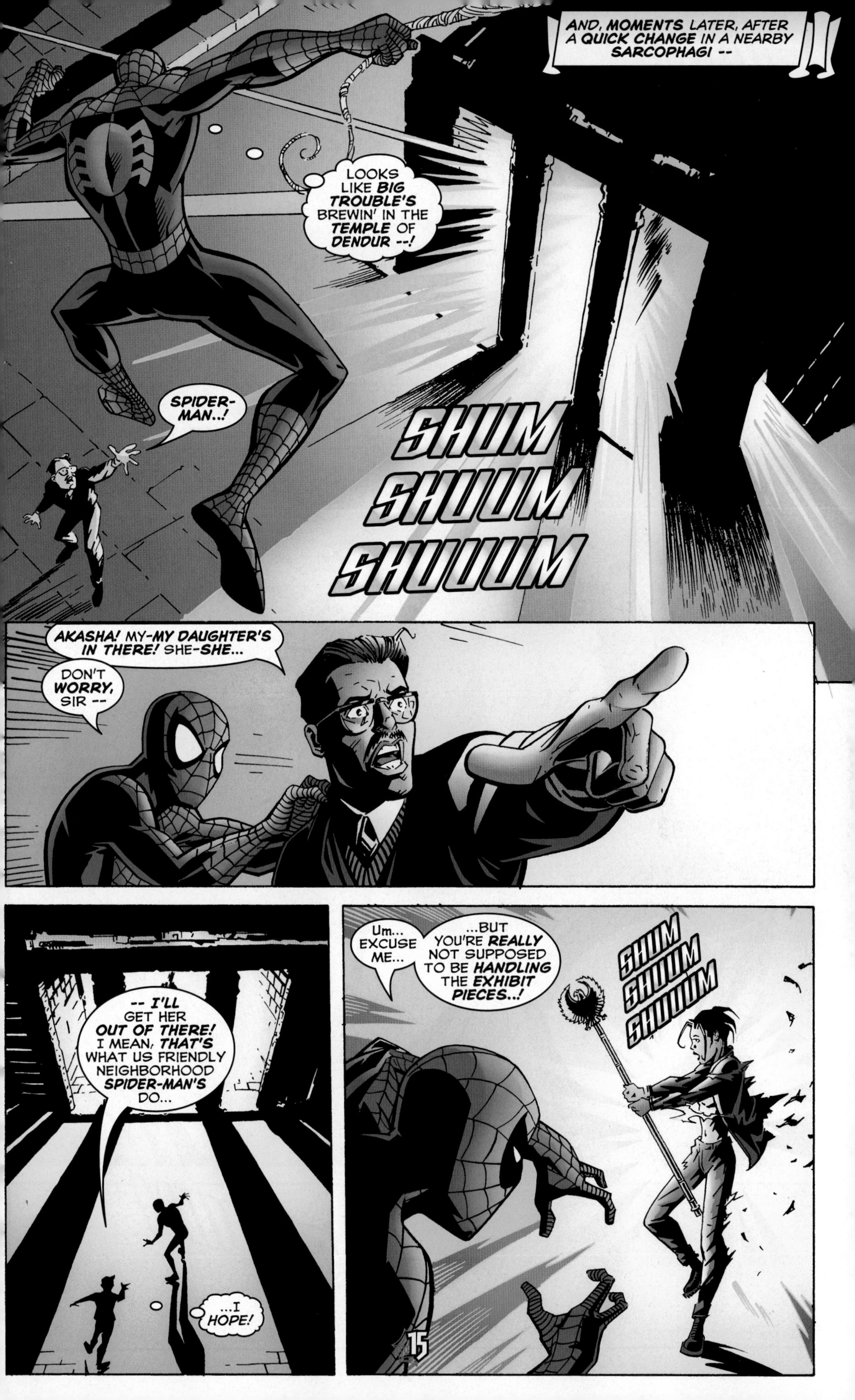
AND, MOMENTS LATER, AFTER A QUICK CHANGE IN A NEARBY SARCOPHAGI --
LOOKS LIKE BIG TROUBLE'S BREWIN' IN THE TEMPLE OF DENDUR --!
SPIDER-MAN..!
SHUM SHUUM SHUUUM
AKASHA! MY-MY DAUGHTER'S IN THERE! SHE-SHE...
DON'T WORRY, SIR --
-- I'LL GET HER OUT OF THERE! I MEAN, THAT'S WHAT US FRIENDLY NEIGHBORHOOD SPIDER-MAN'S DO...
...I HOPE!
Um... EXCUSE ME...
...BUT YOU'RE REALLY NOT SUPPOSED TO BE HANDLING THE EXHIBIT PIECES..!
SHUM SHUUM SHUUUM
15

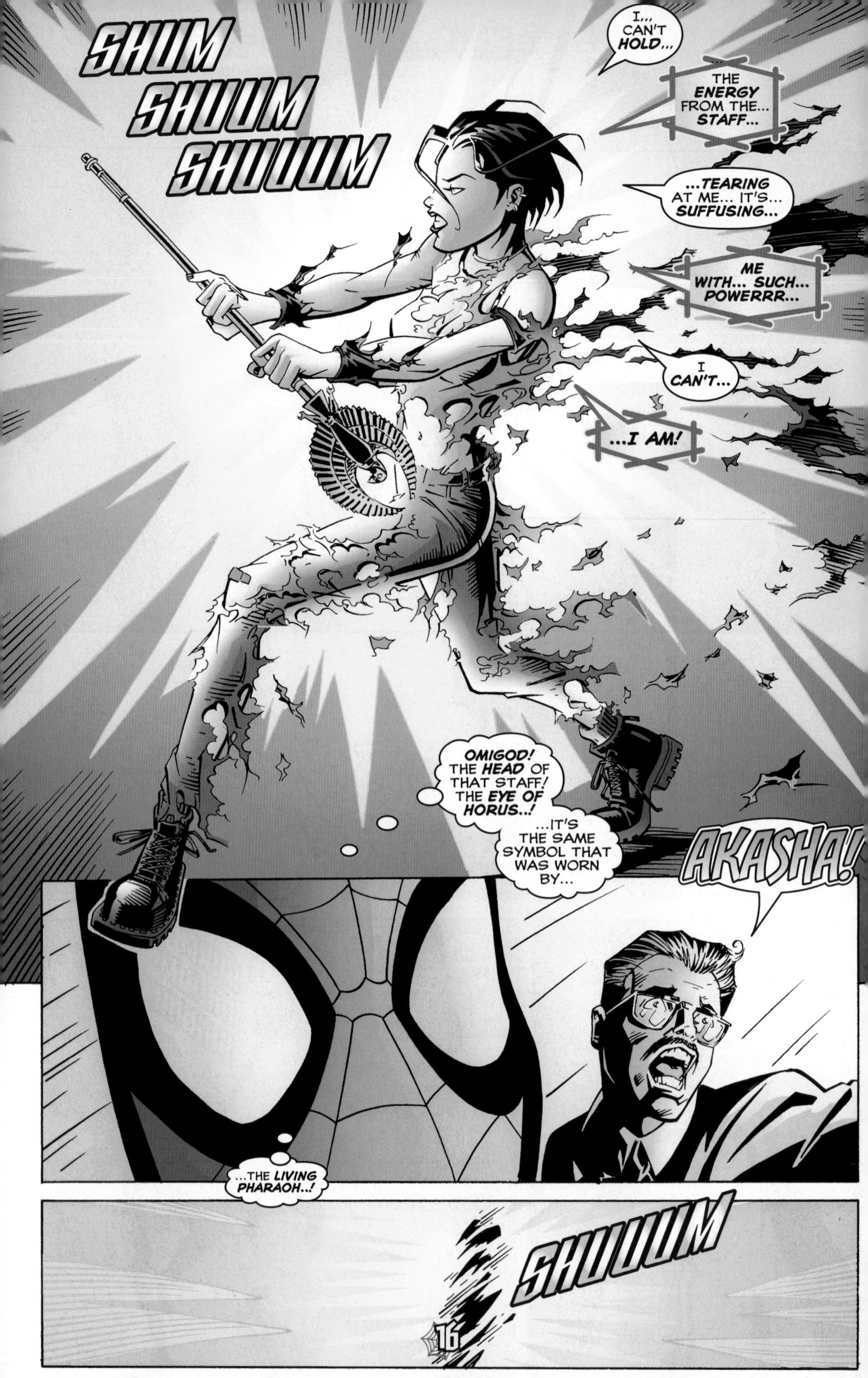
SHUM SHUUM SHUUUM
I... CAN'T HOLD...
THE ENERGY FROM THE... STAFF...
...TEARING AT ME... IT'S... SUFFUSING...
ME WITH... SUCH... POWERRR...
I CAN'T...
...I AM!
OMIGOD! THE HEAD OF THAT STAFF! THE EYE OF HORUS..!
...IT'S THE SAME SYMBOL THAT WAS WORN BY...
AKASHA!
...THE LIVING PHARAOH..!
SHUUUM

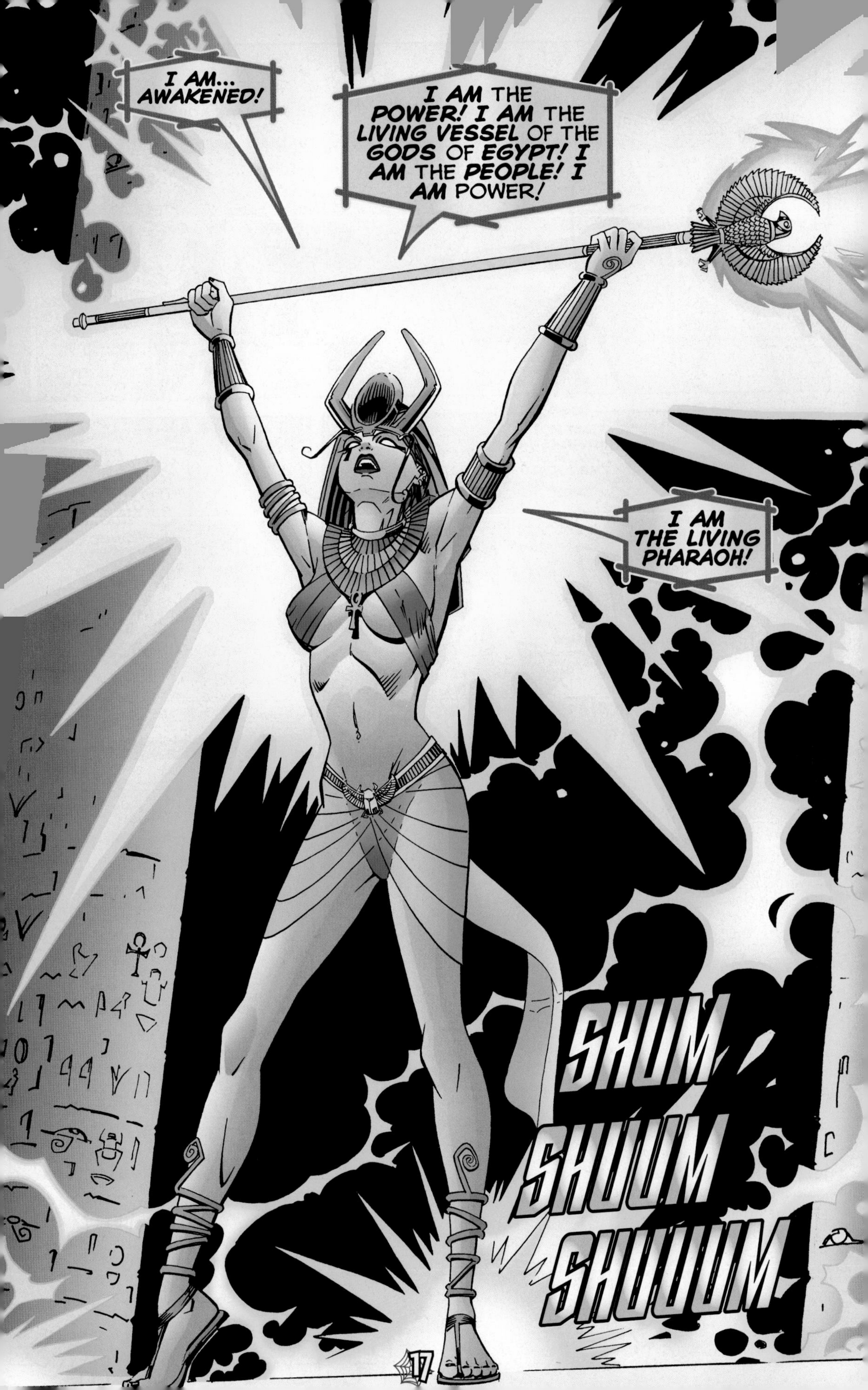
I AM... AWAKENED!
I AM THE POWER! I AM THE LIVING VESSEL OF THE GODS OF EGYPT! I AM THE PEOPLE! I AM POWER!
I AM THE LIVING PHARAOH!
SHUM SHUUM SHUUUM

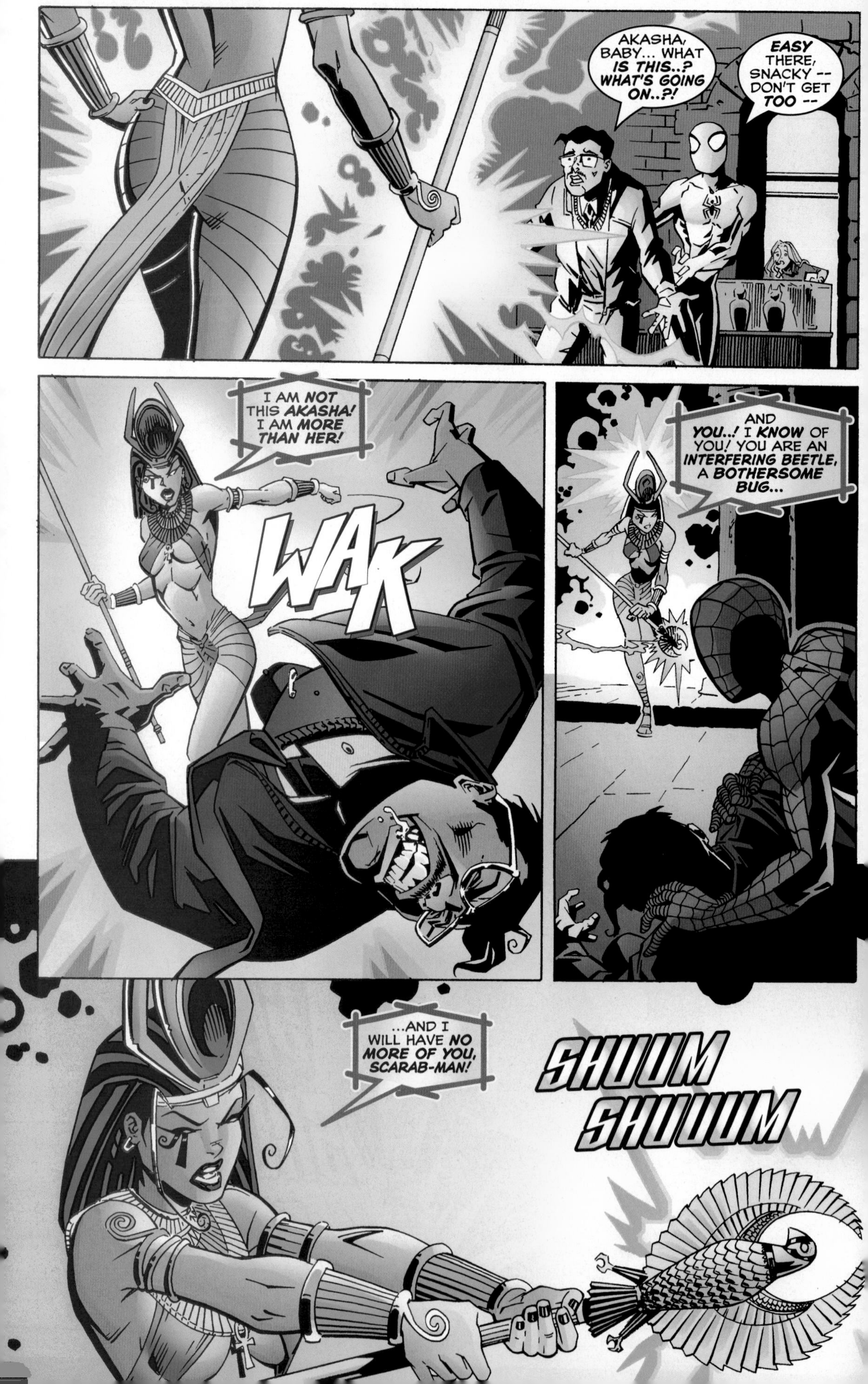

AKASHA, BABY... WHAT IS THIS..? WHAT'S GOING ON..?!
EASY THERE, SNACKY -- DON'T GET TOO --
I AM NOT THIS AKASHA! I AM MORE THAN HER!
WAK
AND YOU..! I KNOW OF YOU! YOU ARE AN INTERFERING BEETLE, A BOTHERSOME BUG...
...AND I WILL HAVE NO MORE OF YOU, SCARAB-MAN!
SHUUM
SHUUUM

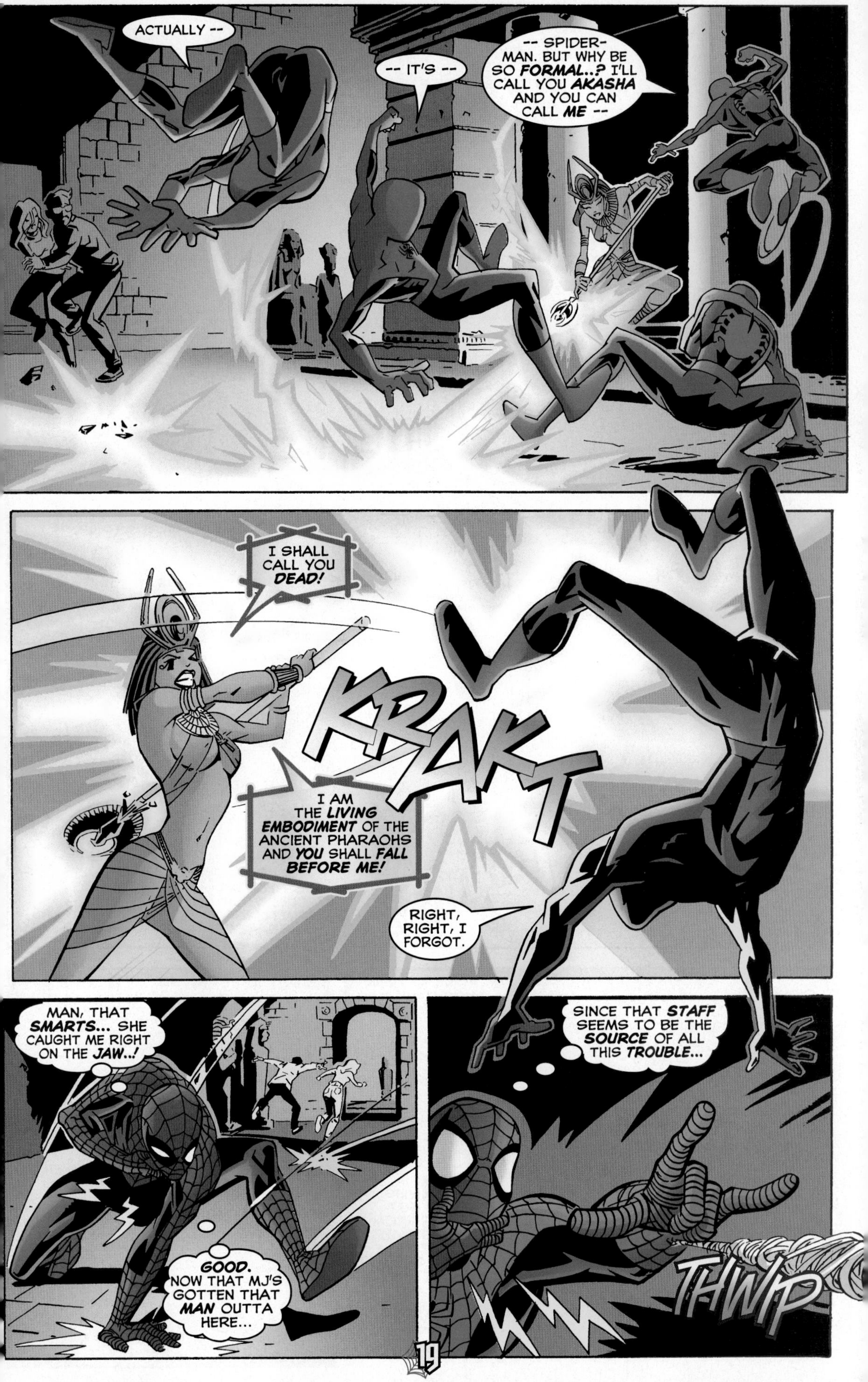

ACTUALLY --
-- IT'S --
-- SPIDER-MAN. BUT WHY BE SO FORMAL..? I'LL CALL YOU AKASHA AND YOU CAN CALL ME --
I SHALL CALL YOU DEAD!
KRAKT
I AM THE LIVING EMBODIMENT OF THE ANCIENT PHARAOHS AND YOU SHALL FALL BEFORE ME!
RIGHT, RIGHT, I FORGOT.
MAN, THAT SMARTS... SHE CAUGHT ME RIGHT ON THE JAW..!
GOOD. NOW THAT MJ'S GOTTEN THAT MAN OUTTA HERE...
SINCE THAT STAFF SEEMS TO BE THE SOURCE OF ALL THIS TROUBLE...
THWIP

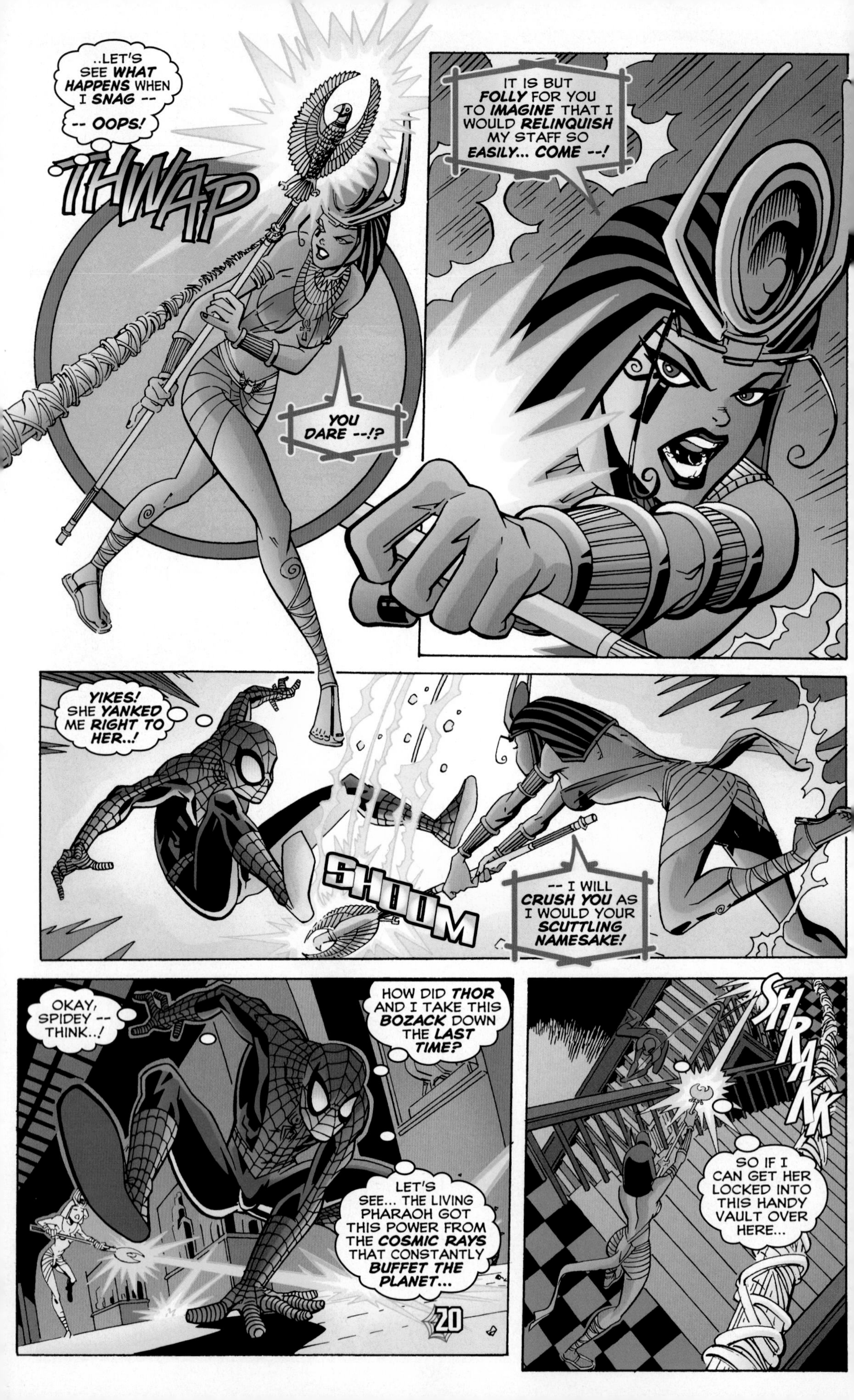

..LET'S SEE WHAT HAPPENS WHEN I SNAG --
-- OOPS!
THWAP
IT IS BUT FOLLY FOR YOU TO IMAGINE THAT I WOULD RELINQUISH MY STAFF SO EASILY... COME --!
YOU DARE --!?
YIKES! SHE YANKED ME RIGHT TO HER..!
SHOOM
-- I WILL CRUSH YOU AS I WOULD YOUR SCUTTLING NAMESAKE!
OKAY, SPIDEY -- THINK..!
HOW DID THOR AND I TAKE THIS BOZACK DOWN THE LAST TIME?
LET'S SEE... THE LIVING PHARAOH GOT THIS POWER FROM THE COSMIC RAYS THAT CONSTANTLY BUFFET THE PLANET...
SHRAKK
SO IF I CAN GET HER LOCKED INTO THIS HANDY VAULT OVER HERE...
20

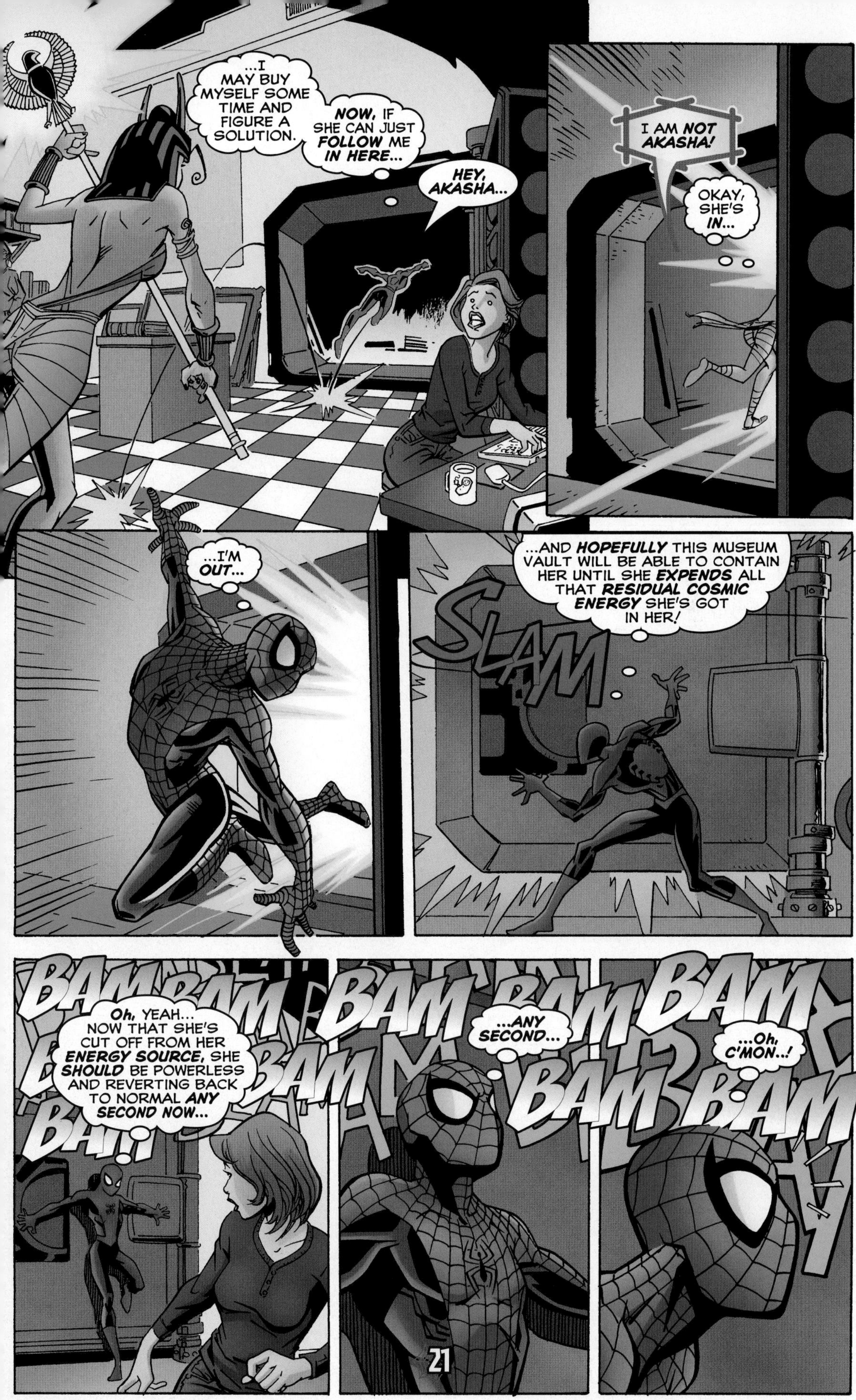
...I MAY BUY MYSELF SOME TIME AND FIGURE A SOLUTION.
NOW, IF SHE CAN JUST FOLLOW ME IN HERE...
HEY, AKASHA...
I AM NOT AKASHA!
OKAY, SHE'S IN...
...I'M OUT...
SLAM
...AND HOPEFULLY THIS MUSEUM VAULT WILL BE ABLE TO CONTAIN HER UNTIL SHE EXPENDS ALL THAT RESIDUAL COSMIC ENERGY SHE'S GOT IN HER!
BAM BAM BAM BAM
Oh, YEAH... NOW THAT SHE'S CUT OFF FROM HER ENERGY SOURCE, SHE SHOULD BE POWERLESS AND REVERTING BACK TO NORMAL ANY SECOND NOW...
BAM BAM
...ANY SECOND...
BAM BAM BAM BAM
...Oh, C'MON..!

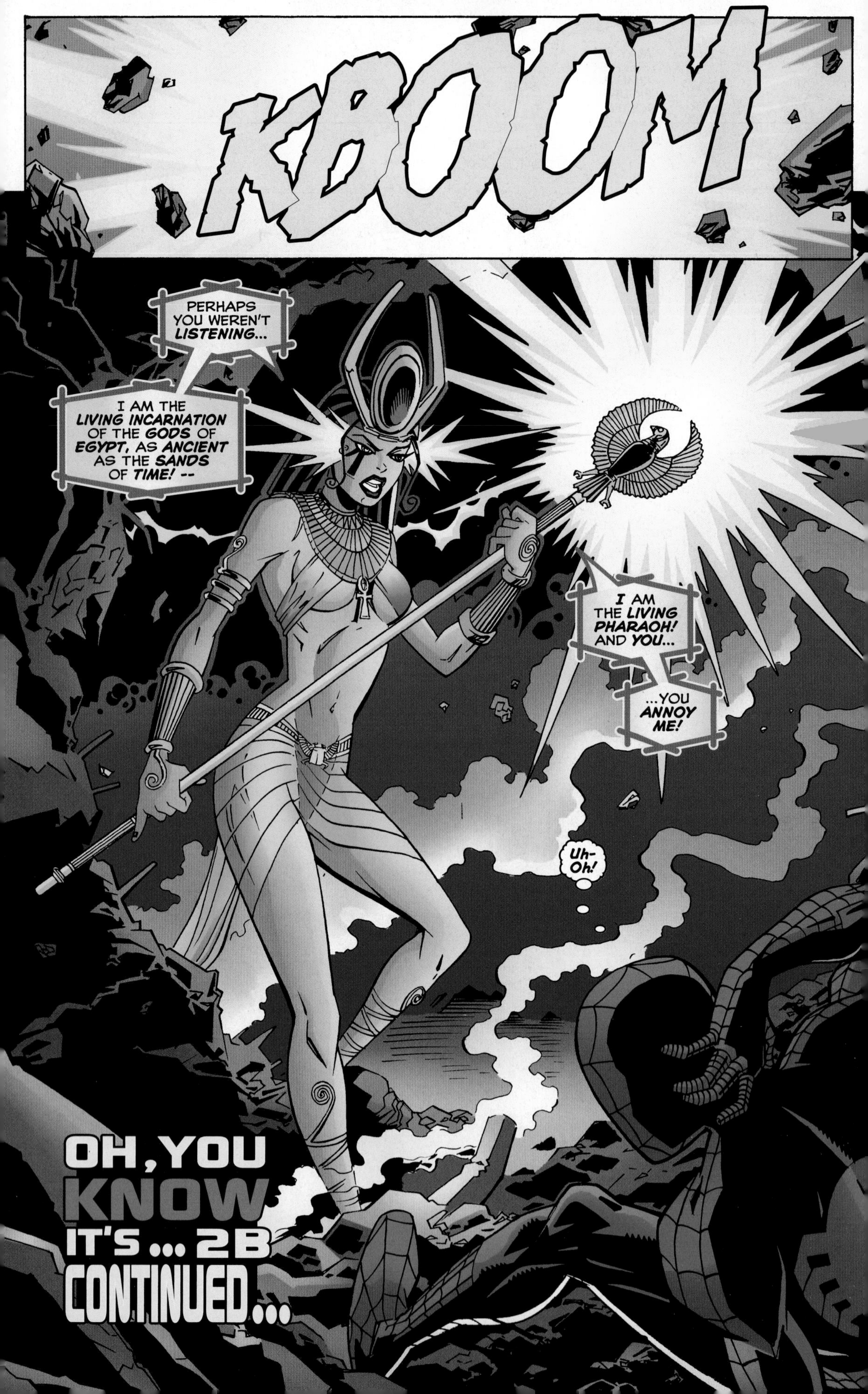
KBOOM!
PERHAPS YOU WEREN'T LISTENING...
I AM THE LIVING INCARNATION OF THE GODS OF EGYPT, AS ANCIENT AS THE SANDS OF TIME! --
I AM THE LIVING PHARAOH! AND YOU...
...YOU ANNOY ME!
Uh-Oh!
OH, YOU KNOW IT'S ... 2B CONTINUED...

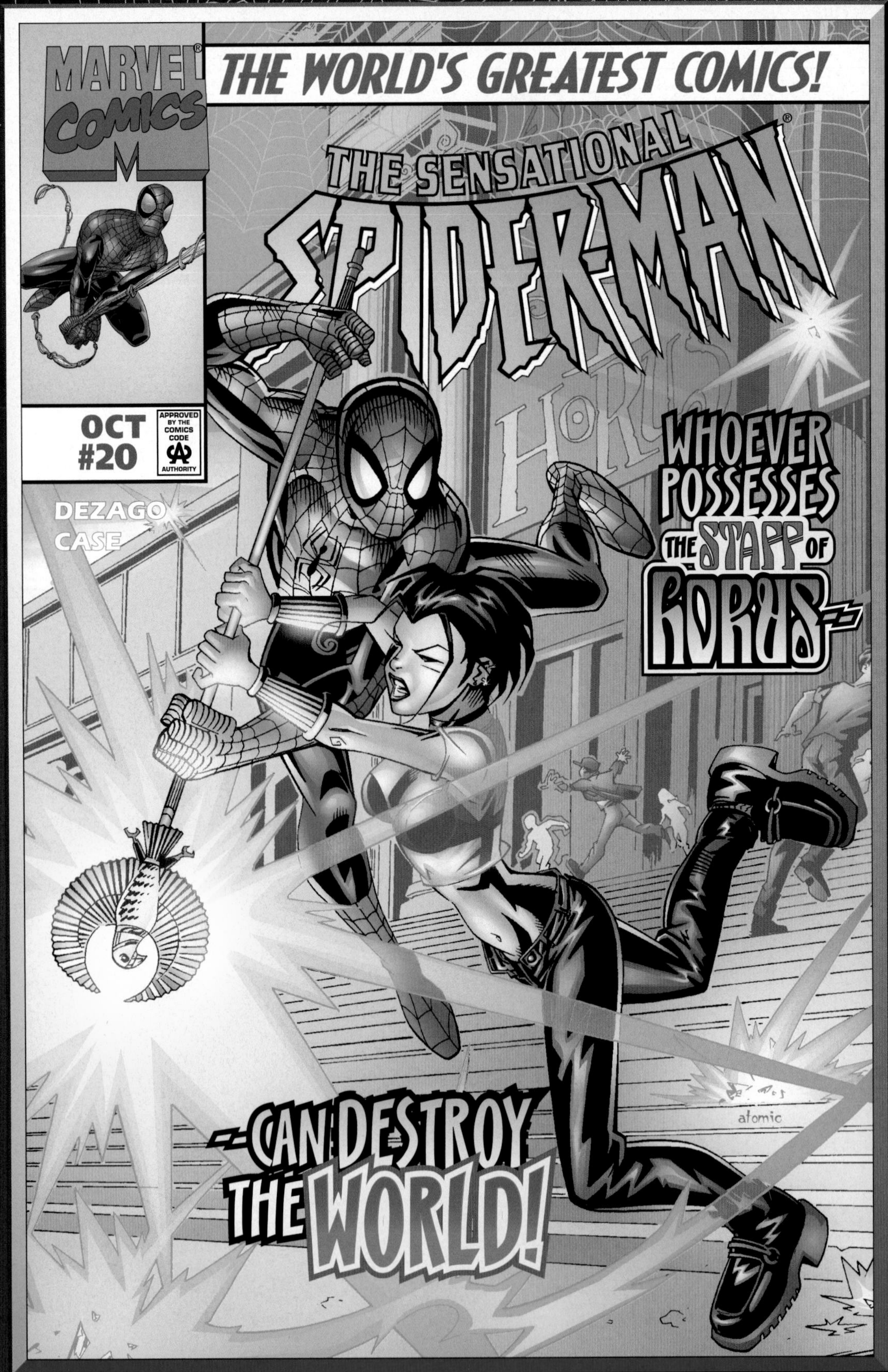
MARVEL COMICS
THE WORLD'S GREATEST COMICS!
THE SENSATIONAL SPIDER-MAN
OCT #20
APPROVED BY THE COMICS CODE AUTHORITY
DEZAGO
CASE
WHOEVER POSSESSES THE STAFF OF RORUS--
--CAN DESTROY THE WORLD!
atomic

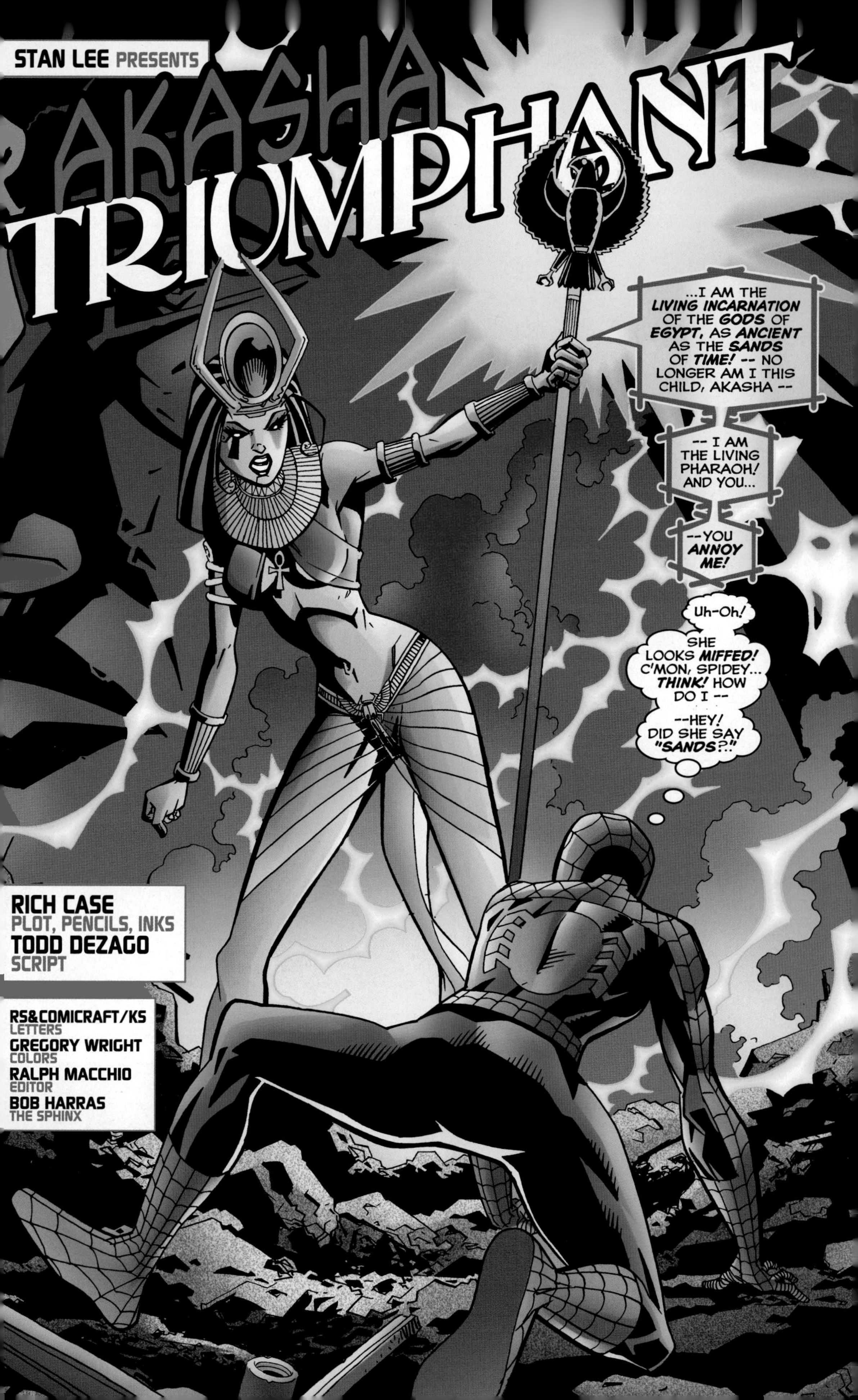
STAN LEE PRESENTS
AKASHA TRIUMPHANT
...I AM THE LIVING INCARNATION OF THE GODS OF EGYPT, AS ANCIENT AS THE SANDS OF TIME! -- NO LONGER AM I THIS CHILD, AKASHA --
-- I AM THE LIVING PHARAOH! AND YOU...
--YOU ANNOY ME!
Uh-Oh!
SHE LOOKS MIFFED! C'MON, SPIDEY... THINK! HOW DO I --
--HEY! DID SHE SAY "SANDS?!"
RICH CASE
PLOT, PENCILS, INKS
TODD DEZAGO
SCRIPT
RS&COMICRAFT/KS
LETTERS
GREGORY WRIGHT
COLORS
RALPH MACCHIO
EDITOR
BOB HARRAS
THE SPHINX

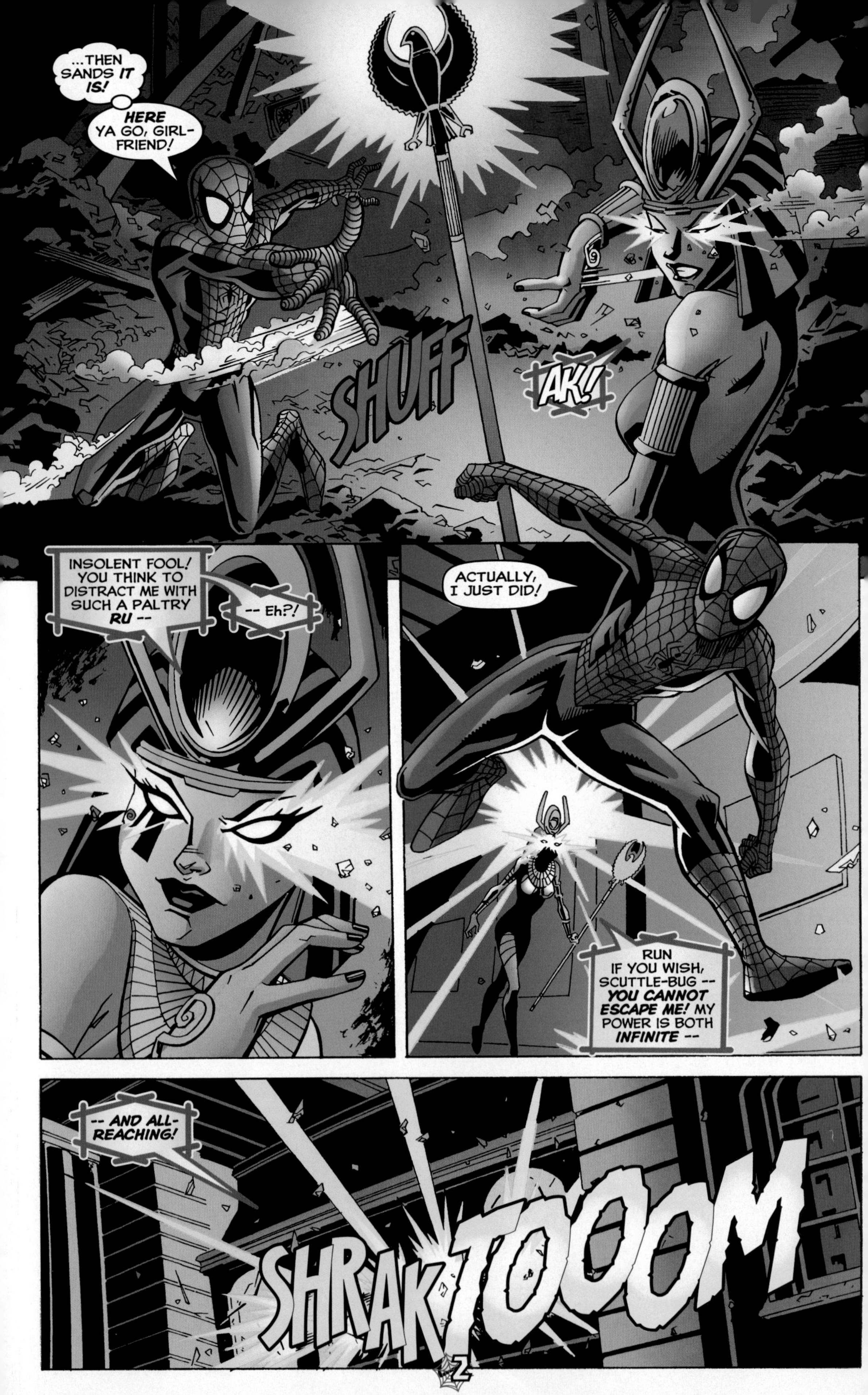

...THEN SANDS IT IS!
HERE YA GO, GIRL-FRIEND!
SHUFF
AK!
INSOLENT FOOL! YOU THINK TO DISTRACT ME WITH SUCH A PALTRY RU --
-- Eh?!
ACTUALLY, I JUST DID!
RUN IF YOU WISH, SCUTTLE-BUG -- YOU CANNOT ESCAPE ME! MY POWER IS BOTH INFINITE --
-- AND ALL-REACHING!
SHRAKTOOOM

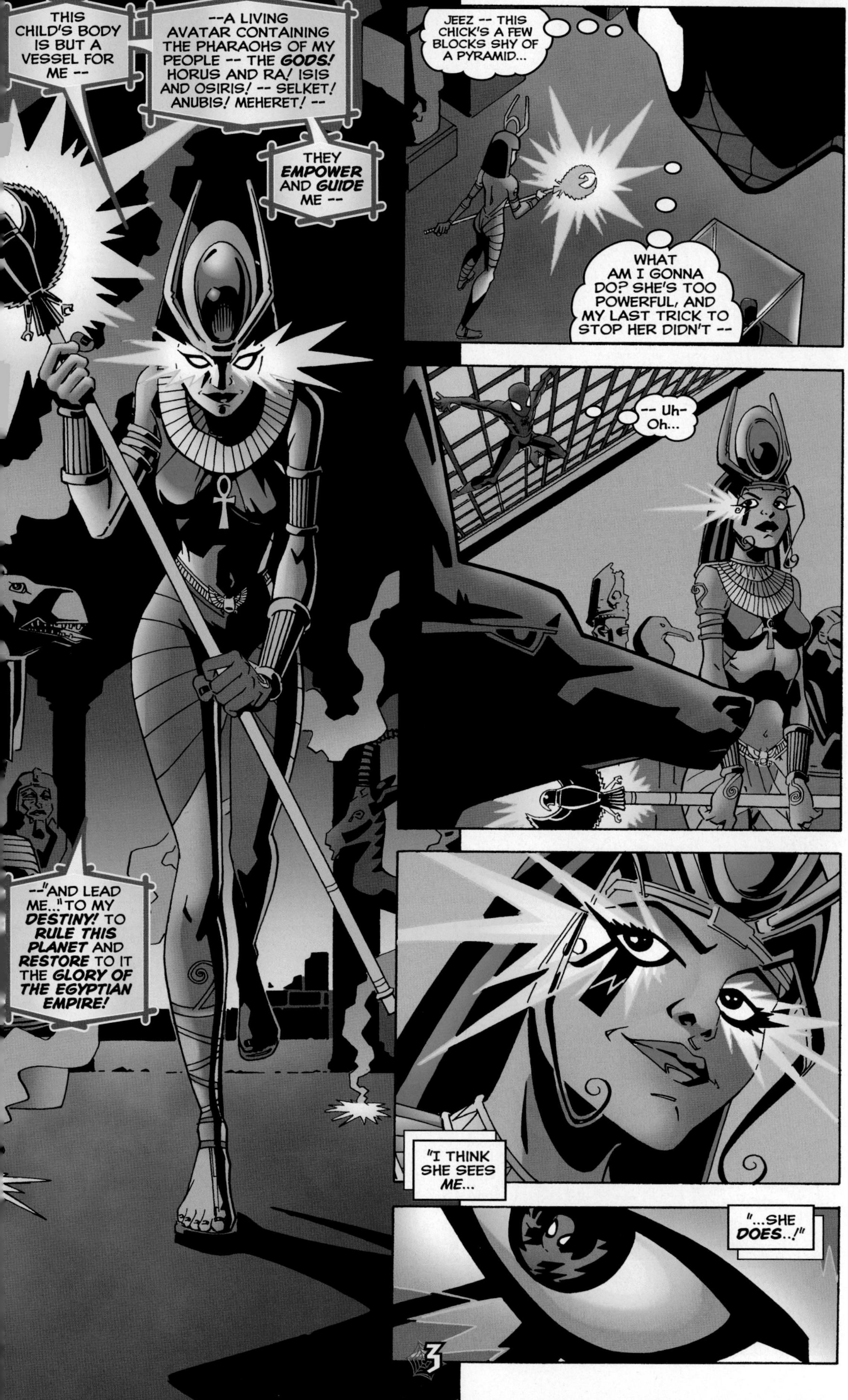
THIS CHILD'S BODY IS BUT A VESSEL FOR ME --
--A LIVING AVATAR CONTAINING THE PHARAOHS OF MY PEOPLE -- THE **GODS!** HORUS AND RA! ISIS AND OSIRIS! -- SELKET! ANUBIS! MEHERET! --
THEY **EMPOWER** AND **GUIDE** ME --
--"AND LEAD ME..." TO MY **DESTINY!** TO **RULE THIS PLANET** AND **RESTORE** TO IT THE **GLORY OF THE EGYPTIAN EMPIRE!**
JEEZ -- THIS CHICK'S A FEW BLOCKS SHY OF A PYRAMID...
WHAT AM I GONNA DO? SHE'S TOO POWERFUL, AND MY LAST TRICK TO STOP HER DIDN'T --
-- Uh-Oh...
"I THINK SHE SEES **ME**...
"...SHE **DOES**..!"

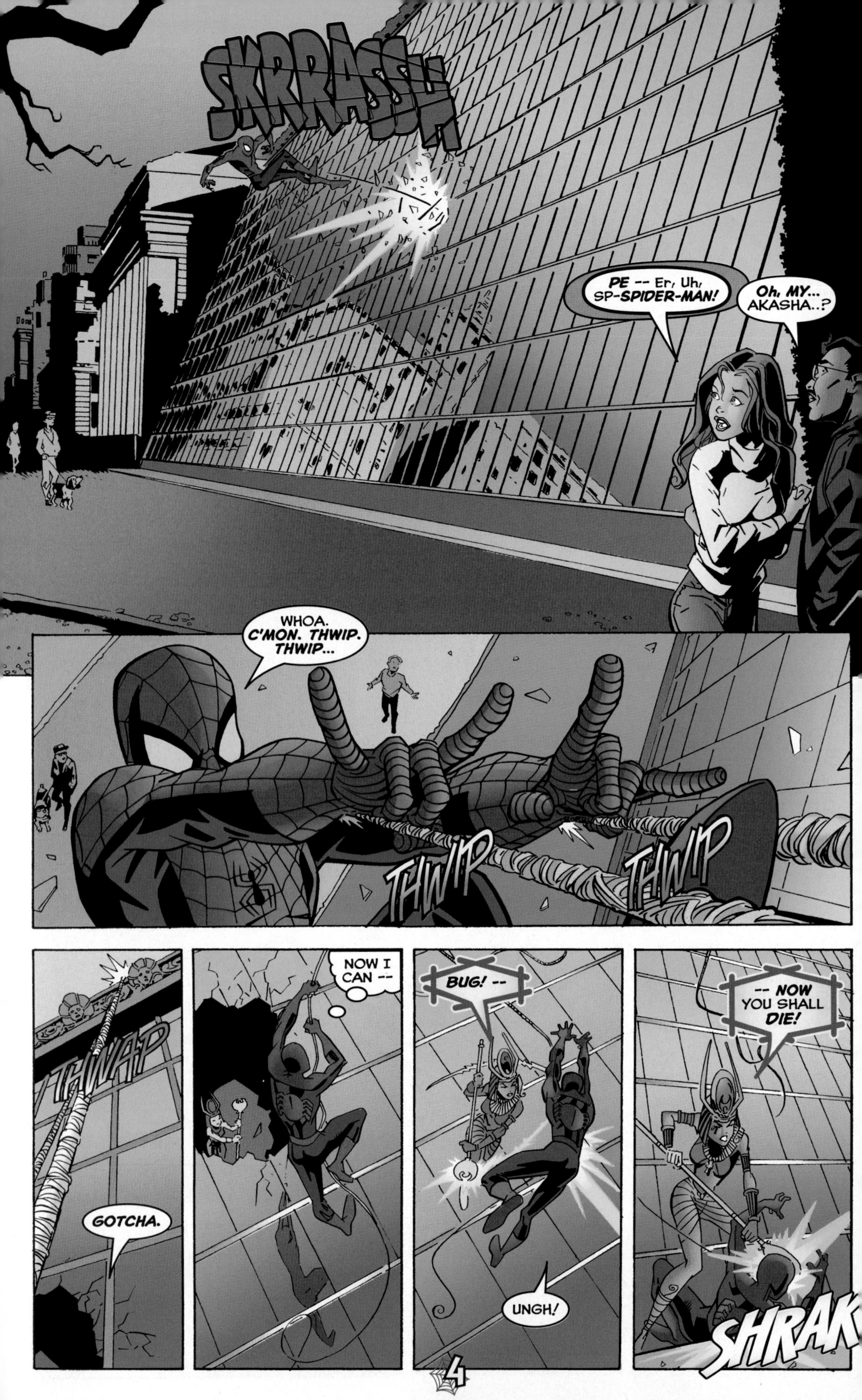
SKRRASSH
PE -- Er, Uh, SP-SPIDER-MAN!
Oh, MY... AKASHA..?
WHOA. C'MON. THWIP. THWIP...
THWIP
THWIP
THWAP
GOTCHA.
NOW I CAN --
BUG! --
UNGH!
-- NOW YOU SHALL DIE!
SHRAK

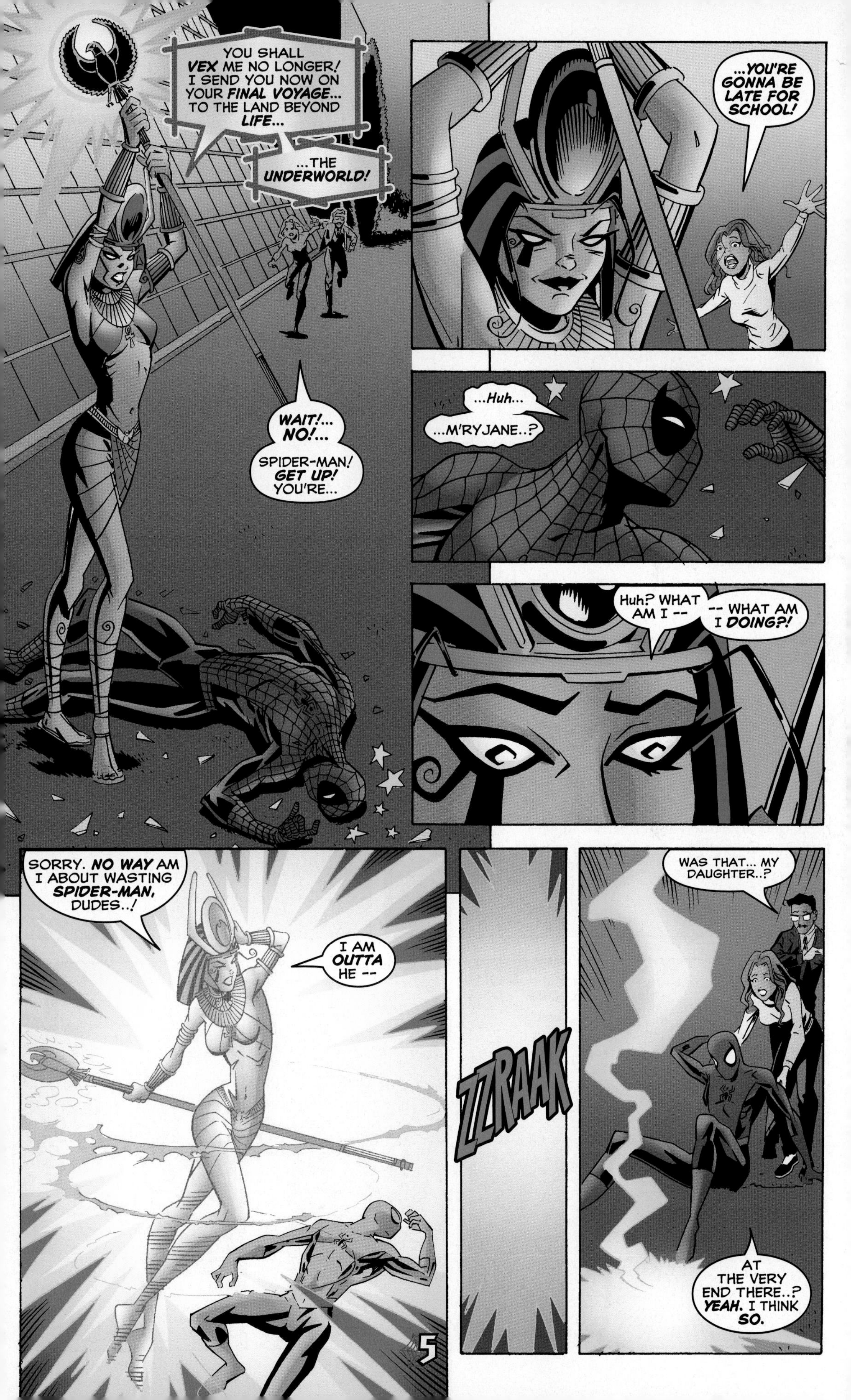

YOU SHALL VEX ME NO LONGER! I SEND YOU NOW ON YOUR FINAL VOYAGE... TO THE LAND BEYOND LIFE...
...THE UNDERWORLD!
WAIT!... NO!...
SPIDER-MAN! GET UP! YOU'RE...
...YOU'RE GONNA BE LATE FOR SCHOOL!
...Huh...
...M'RYJANE..?
Huh? WHAT AM I --
-- WHAT AM I DOING?!
SORRY. NO WAY AM I ABOUT WASTING SPIDER-MAN, DUDES..!
I AM OUTTA HE --
ZZRAAK
WAS THAT... MY DAUGHTER..?
AT THE VERY END THERE..? YEAH. I THINK SO.

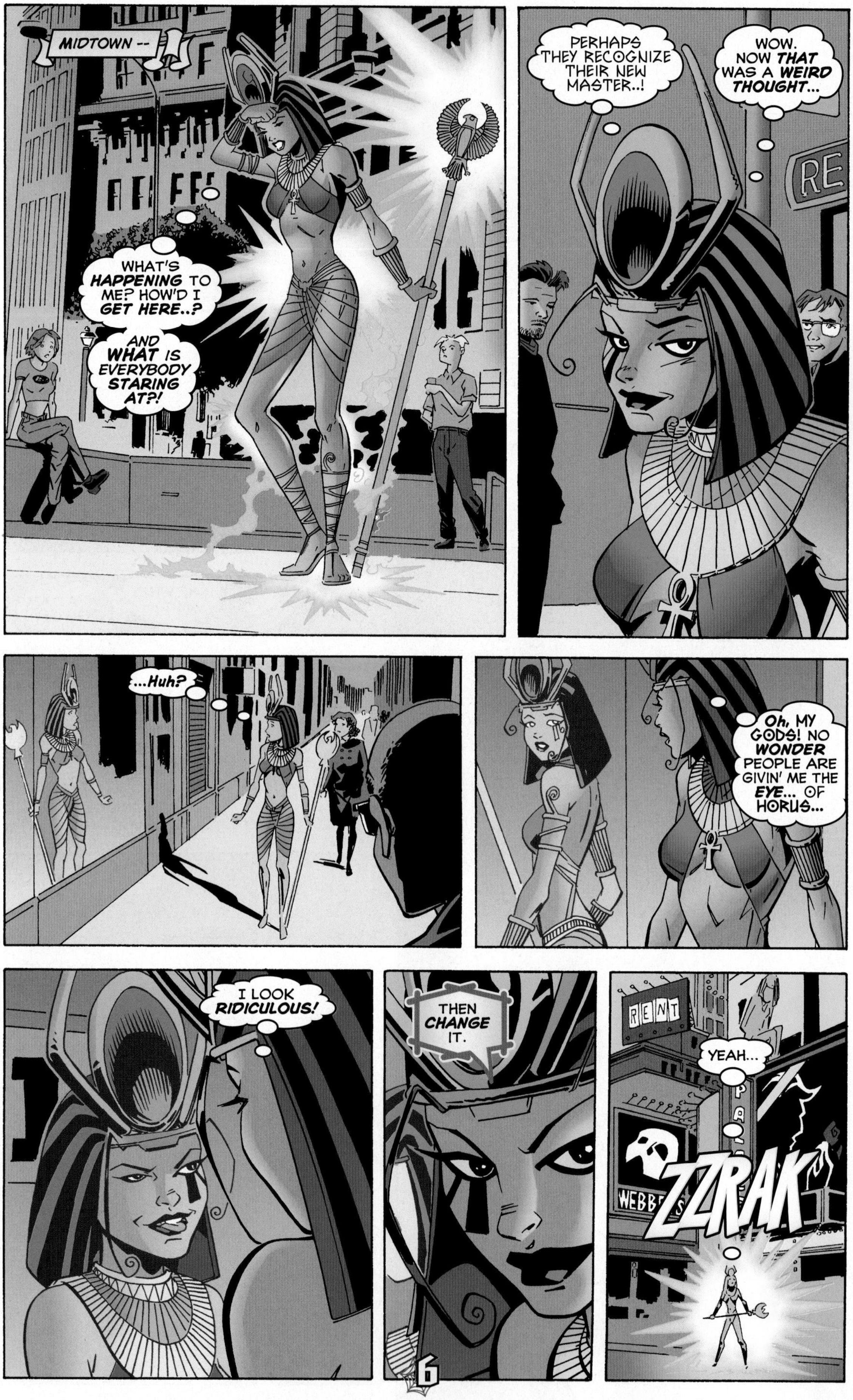
MIDTOWN --
WHAT'S HAPPENING TO ME? HOW'D I GET HERE..?
AND WHAT IS EVERYBODY STARING AT?!
PERHAPS THEY RECOGNIZE THEIR NEW MASTER..!
WOW. NOW THAT WAS A WEIRD THOUGHT...
...Huh?
Oh, MY GODS! NO WONDER PEOPLE ARE GIVIN' ME THE EYE... OF HORUS...
I LOOK RIDICULOUS!
THEN CHANGE IT.
RENT
YEAH...
WEBB
ZZRAK

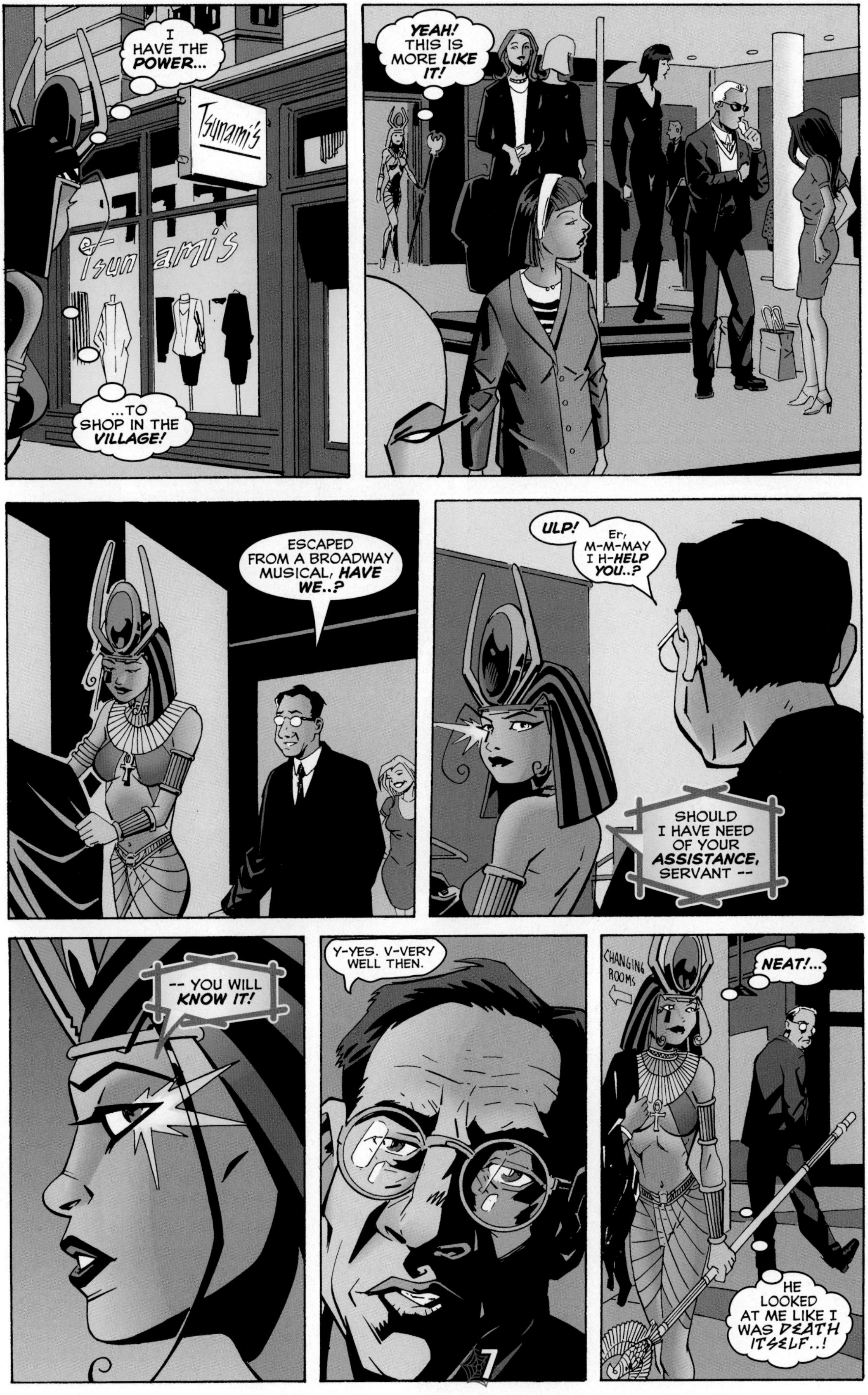
I HAVE THE POWER...
Tsunami's
Tsunami's
...TO SHOP IN THE VILLAGE!
YEAH! THIS IS MORE LIKE IT!
ESCAPED FROM A BROADWAY MUSICAL, HAVE WE..?
ULP!
Er, M-M-MAY I H-HELP YOU..?
SHOULD I HAVE NEED OF YOUR ASSISTANCE, SERVANT --
-- YOU WILL KNOW IT!
Y-YES. V-VERY WELL THEN.
CHANGING ROOMS
NEAT!...
HE LOOKED AT ME LIKE I WAS DEATH ITSELF..!

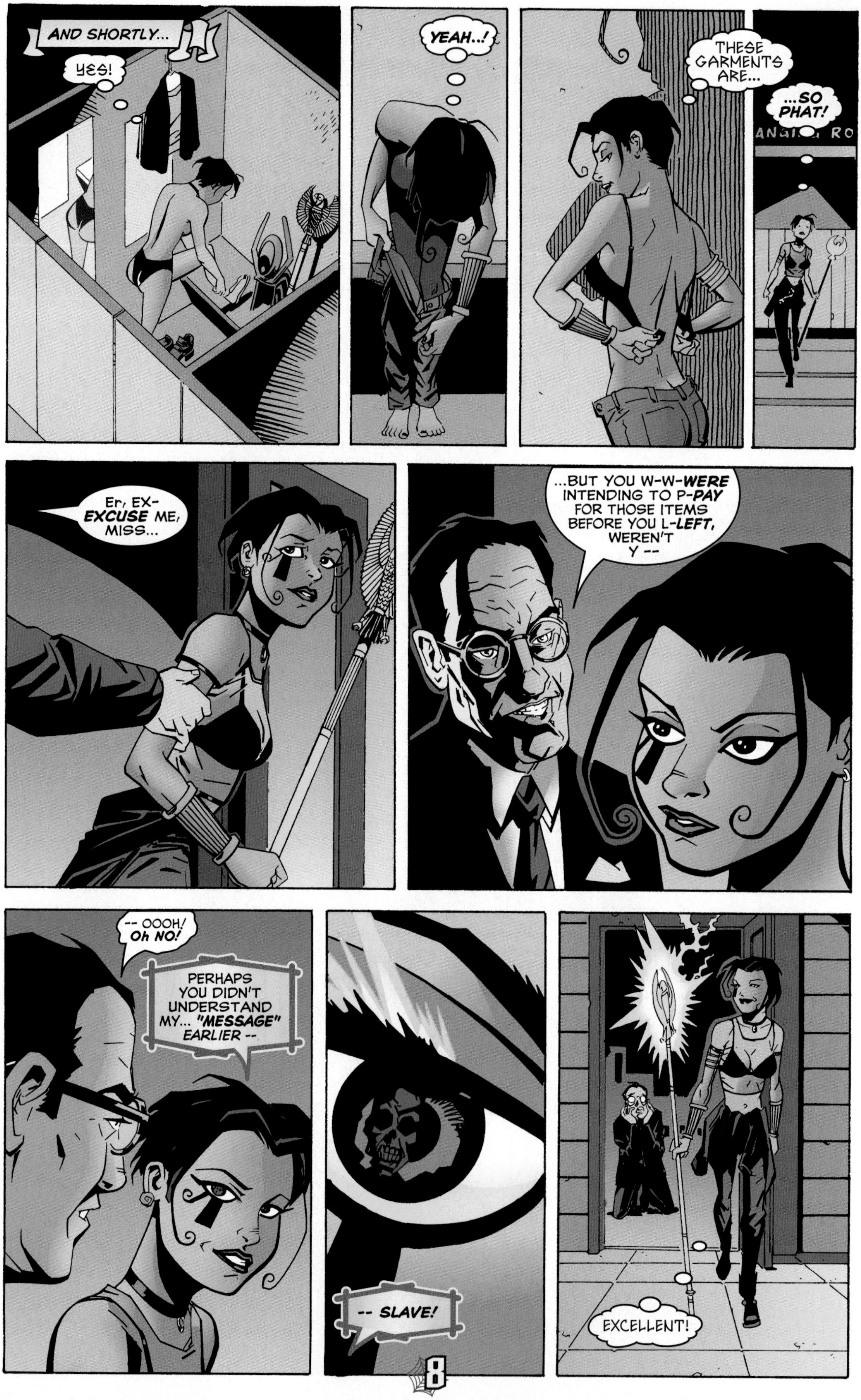
AND SHORTLY...
YES!
YEAH..!
THESE GARMENTS ARE...
...SO PHAT!
Er, EX-EXCUSE ME, MISS...
...BUT YOU W-W-WERE INTENDING TO P-PAY FOR THOSE ITEMS BEFORE YOU L-LEFT, WEREN'T Y --
-- OOOH! Oh NO!
PERHAPS YOU DIDN'T UNDERSTAND MY... "MESSAGE" EARLIER --
-- SLAVE!
EXCELLENT!

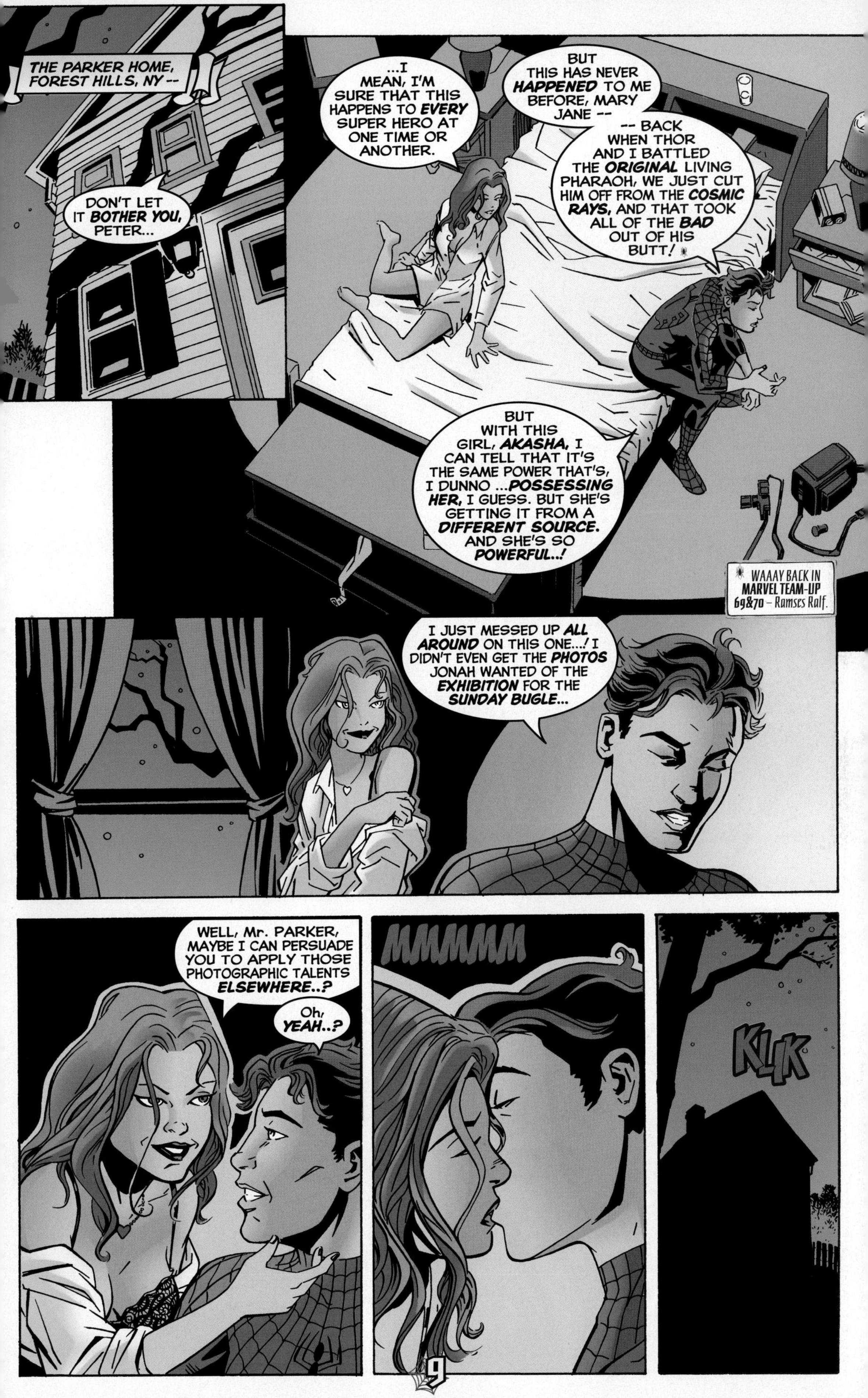
THE PARKER HOME, FOREST HILLS, NY --
DON'T LET IT BOTHER YOU, PETER...
...I MEAN, I'M SURE THAT THIS HAPPENS TO EVERY SUPER HERO AT ONE TIME OR ANOTHER.
BUT THIS HAS NEVER HAPPENED TO ME BEFORE, MARY JANE --
-- BACK WHEN THOR AND I BATTLED THE ORIGINAL LIVING PHARAOH, WE JUST CUT HIM OFF FROM THE COSMIC RAYS, AND THAT TOOK ALL OF THE BAD OUT OF HIS BUTT!
BUT WITH THIS GIRL, AKASHA, I CAN TELL THAT IT'S THE SAME POWER THAT'S, I DUNNO ...POSSESSING HER, I GUESS. BUT SHE'S GETTING IT FROM A DIFFERENT SOURCE. AND SHE'S SO POWERFUL..!
WAAAY BACK IN MARVEL TEAM-UP 69&70 – Ramses Ralf.
I JUST MESSED UP ALL AROUND ON THIS ONE...! I DIDN'T EVEN GET THE PHOTOS JONAH WANTED OF THE EXHIBITION FOR THE SUNDAY BUGLE...
WELL, Mr. PARKER, MAYBE I CAN PERSUADE YOU TO APPLY THOSE PHOTOGRAPHIC TALENTS ELSEWHERE..?
Oh, YEAH..?
MMMMMM
KLIK
9

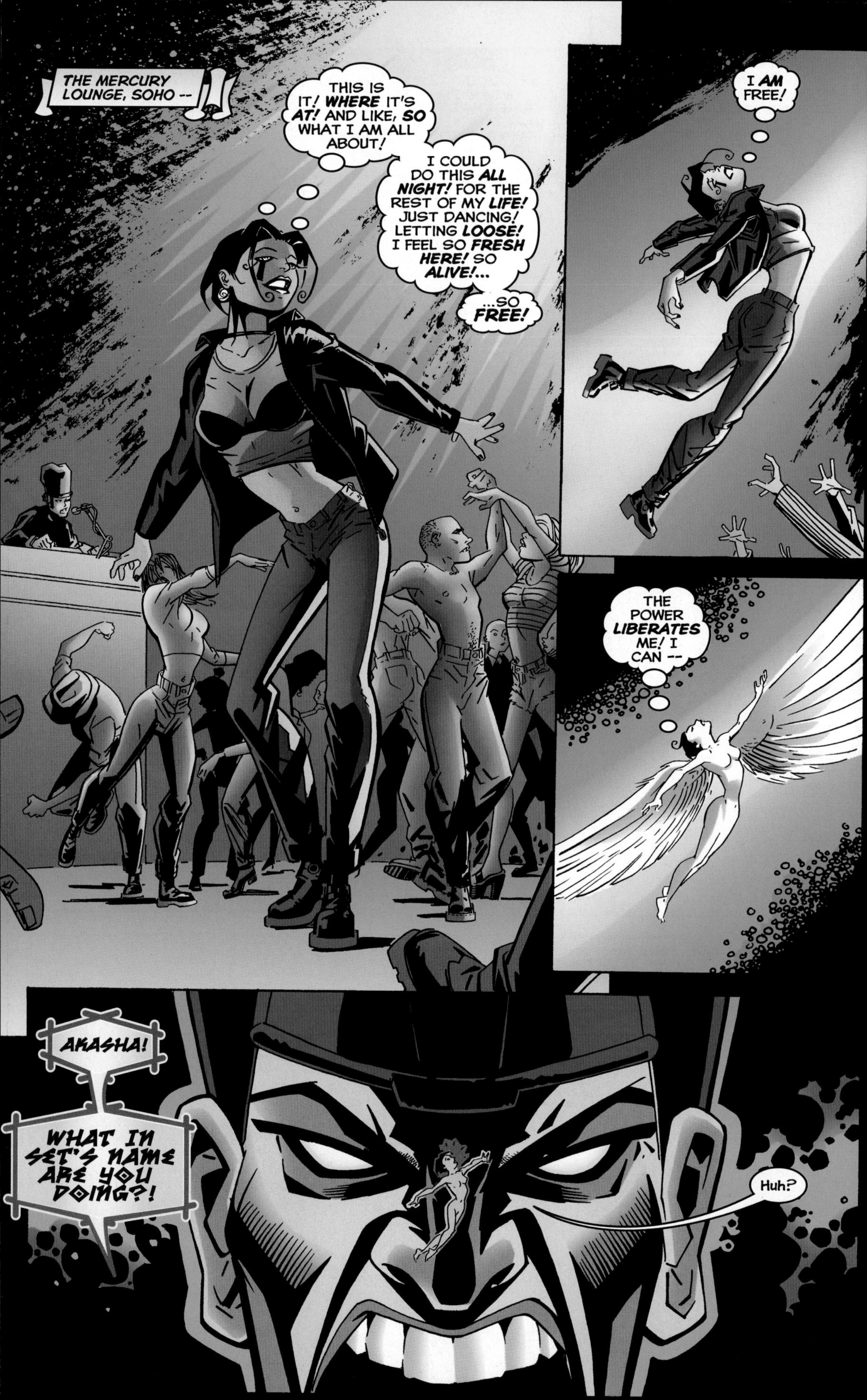
THE MERCURY LOUNGE, SOHO --
THIS IS IT! WHERE IT'S AT! AND LIKE, SO WHAT I AM ALL ABOUT!
I COULD DO THIS ALL NIGHT! FOR THE REST OF MY LIFE! JUST DANCING! LETTING LOOSE! I FEEL SO FRESH HERE! SO ALIVE!...
...SO FREE!
I AM FREE!
THE POWER LIBERATES ME! I CAN --
AKASHA!
WHAT IN SET'S NAME ARE YOU DOING?!
Huh?

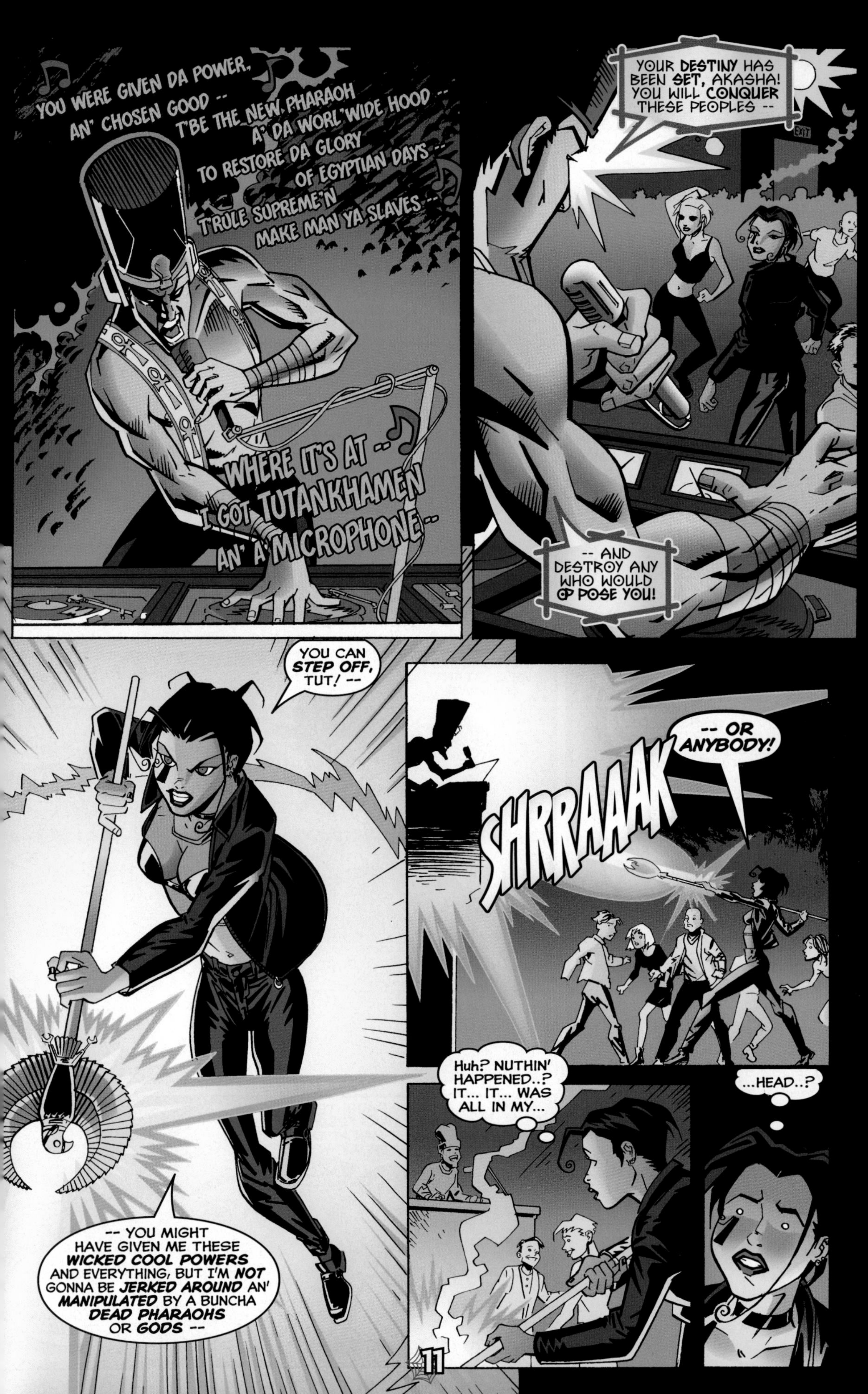

YOU WERE GIVEN DA POWER,
AN' CHOSEN GOOD --
T'BE THE NEW PHARAOH
A' DA WORL'WIDE HOOD --
TO RESTORE DA GLORY
OF EGYPTIAN DAYS --
T'RULE SUPREME'N
MAKE MAN YA SLAVES --
WHERE IT'S AT --
I GOT TUTANKHAMEN
AN' A MICROPHONE --
YOUR DESTINY HAS BEEN SET, AKASHA! YOU WILL CONQUER THESE PEOPLES --
EXIT
-- AND DESTROY ANY WHO WOULD OPPOSE YOU!
YOU CAN STEP OFF, TUT! --
-- YOU MIGHT HAVE GIVEN ME THESE WICKED COOL POWERS AND EVERYTHING, BUT I'M NOT GONNA BE JERKED AROUND AN' MANIPULATED BY A BUNCHA DEAD PHARAOHS OR GODS --
-- OR ANYBODY!
SHRRAAAK
Huh? NUTHIN' HAPPENED..? IT... IT... WAS ALL IN MY...
...HEAD..?

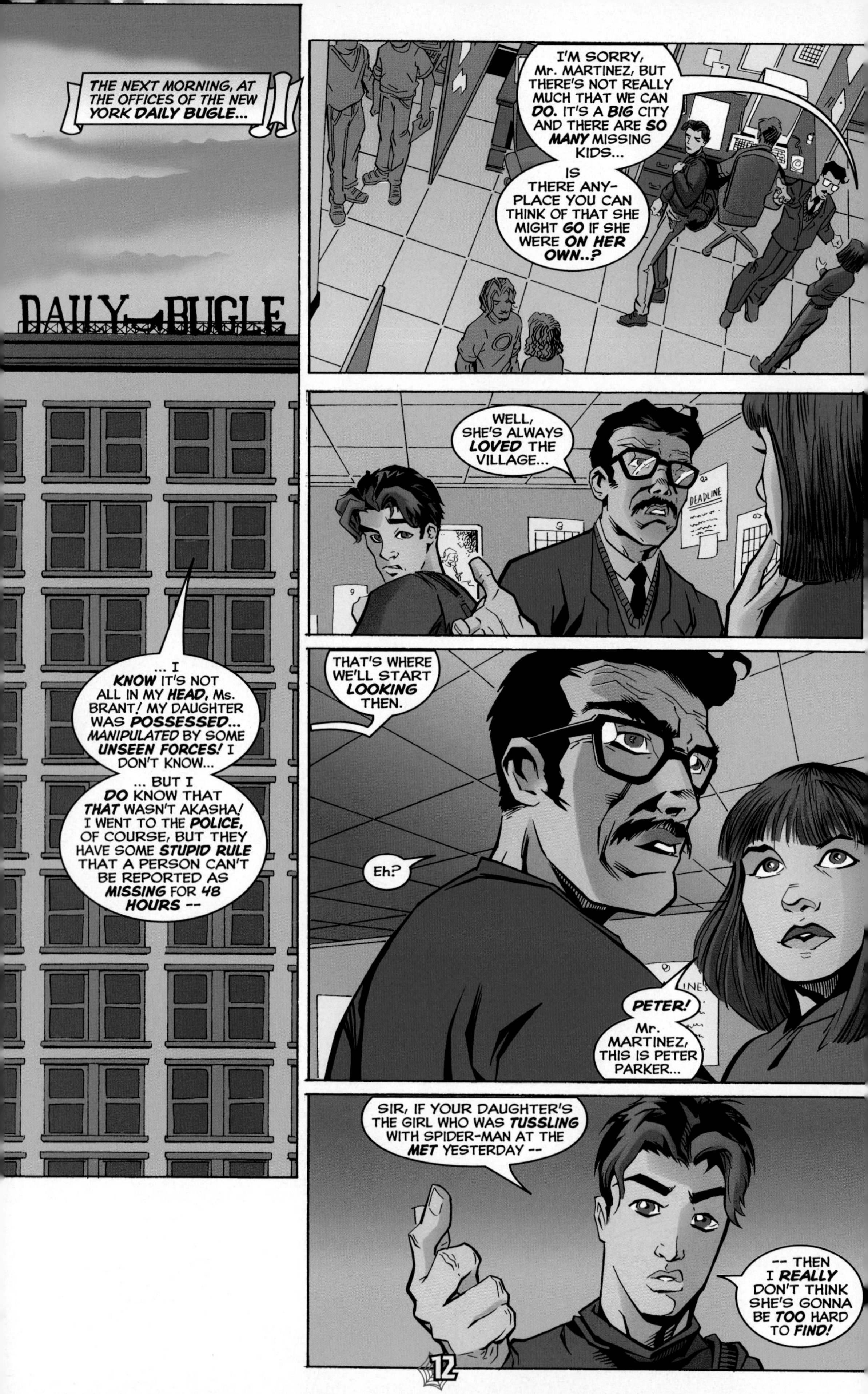
THE NEXT MORNING, AT THE OFFICES OF THE NEW YORK DAILY BUGLE...
DAILY BUGLE
... I KNOW IT'S NOT ALL IN MY HEAD, Ms. BRANT! MY DAUGHTER WAS POSSESSED... MANIPULATED BY SOME UNSEEN FORCES! I DON'T KNOW...
... BUT I DO KNOW THAT THAT WASN'T AKASHA! I WENT TO THE POLICE, OF COURSE, BUT THEY HAVE SOME STUPID RULE THAT A PERSON CAN'T BE REPORTED AS MISSING FOR 48 HOURS --
I'M SORRY, Mr. MARTINEZ, BUT THERE'S NOT REALLY MUCH THAT WE CAN DO. IT'S A BIG CITY AND THERE ARE SO MANY MISSING KIDS...
IS THERE ANY-PLACE YOU CAN THINK OF THAT SHE MIGHT GO IF SHE WERE ON HER OWN..?
WELL, SHE'S ALWAYS LOVED THE VILLAGE...
DEADLINE
THAT'S WHERE WE'LL START LOOKING THEN.
Eh?
PETER!
Mr. MARTINEZ, THIS IS PETER PARKER...
SIR, IF YOUR DAUGHTER'S THE GIRL WHO WAS TUSSLING WITH SPIDER-MAN AT THE MET YESTERDAY --
-- THEN I REALLY DON'T THINK SHE'S GONNA BE TOO HARD TO FIND!

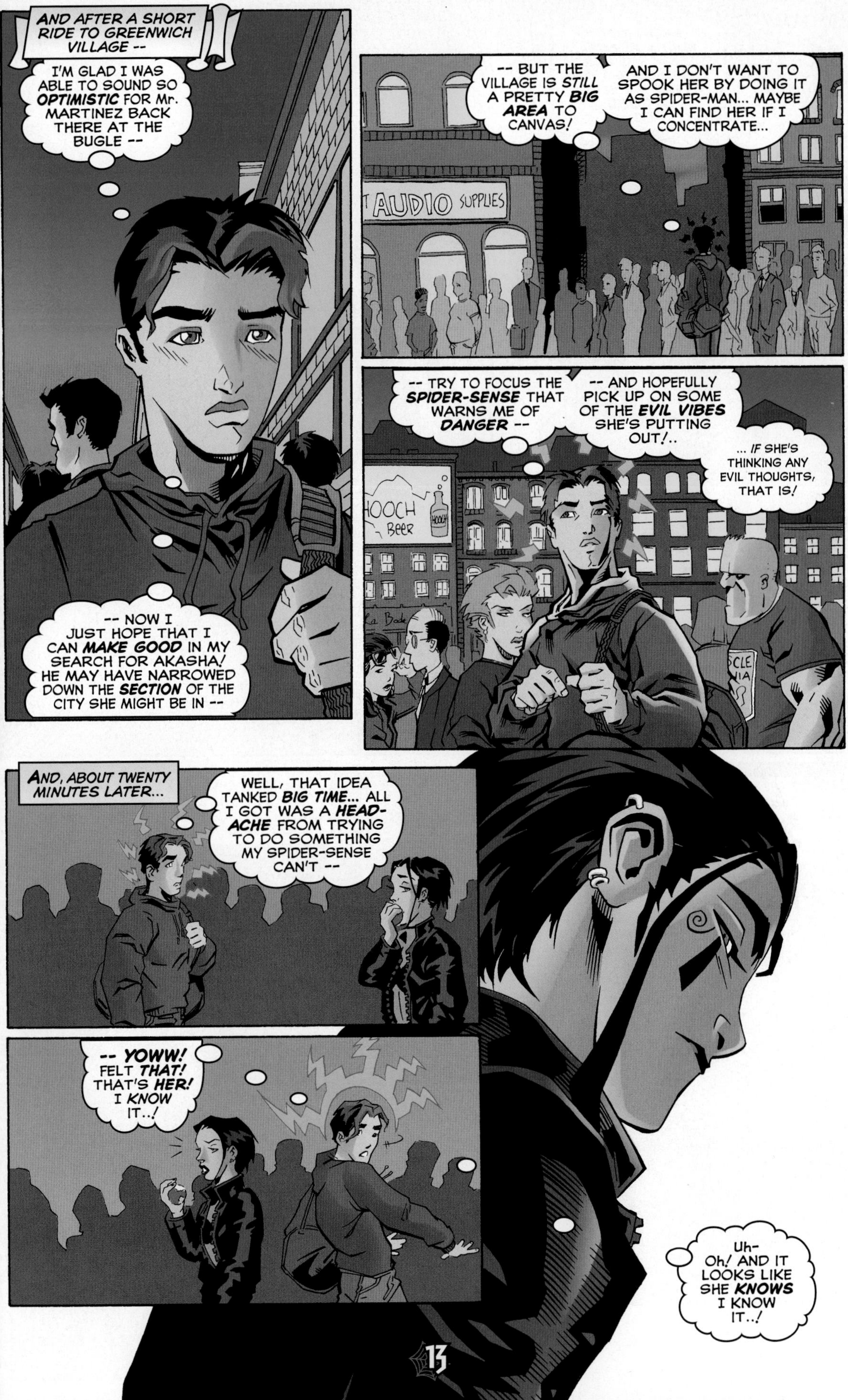

AND AFTER A SHORT RIDE TO GREENWICH VILLAGE --
I'M GLAD I WAS ABLE TO SOUND SO OPTIMISTIC FOR Mr. MARTINEZ BACK THERE AT THE BUGLE --
-- NOW I JUST HOPE THAT I CAN MAKE GOOD IN MY SEARCH FOR AKASHA! HE MAY HAVE NARROWED DOWN THE SECTION OF THE CITY SHE MIGHT BE IN --
-- BUT THE VILLAGE IS STILL A PRETTY BIG AREA TO CANVAS!
AND I DON'T WANT TO SPOOK HER BY DOING IT AS SPIDER-MAN... MAYBE I CAN FIND HER IF I CONCENTRATE...
AUDIO SUPPLIES
-- TRY TO FOCUS THE SPIDER-SENSE THAT WARNS ME OF DANGER --
-- AND HOPEFULLY PICK UP ON SOME OF THE EVIL VIBES SHE'S PUTTING OUT!..
... IF SHE'S THINKING ANY EVIL THOUGHTS, THAT IS!
HOOCH Beer
AND, ABOUT TWENTY MINUTES LATER...
WELL, THAT IDEA TANKED BIG TIME... ALL I GOT WAS A HEAD-ACHE FROM TRYING TO DO SOMETHING MY SPIDER-SENSE CAN'T --
-- YOWW! FELT THAT! THAT'S HER! I KNOW IT..!
Uh-Oh! AND IT LOOKS LIKE SHE KNOWS I KNOW IT..!

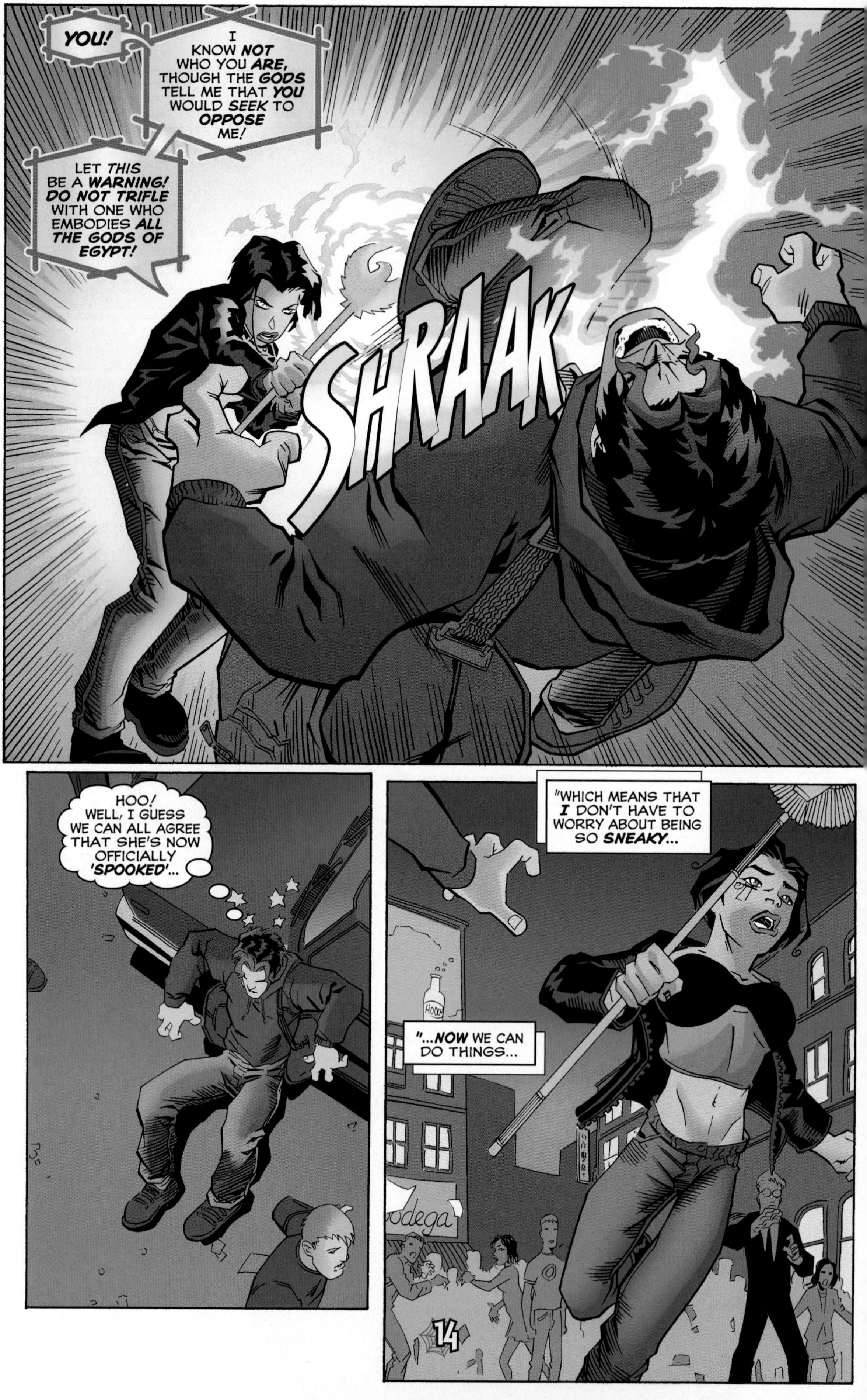
YOU!
I KNOW NOT WHO YOU ARE, THOUGH THE GODS TELL ME THAT YOU WOULD SEEK TO OPPOSE ME!
LET THIS BE A WARNING! DO NOT TRIFLE WITH ONE WHO EMBODIES ALL THE GODS OF EGYPT!
SHRAAK
HOO! WELL, I GUESS WE CAN ALL AGREE THAT SHE'S NOW OFFICIALLY 'SPOOKED'...
"WHICH MEANS THAT I DON'T HAVE TO WORRY ABOUT BEING SO SNEAKY...
"...NOW WE CAN DO THINGS...

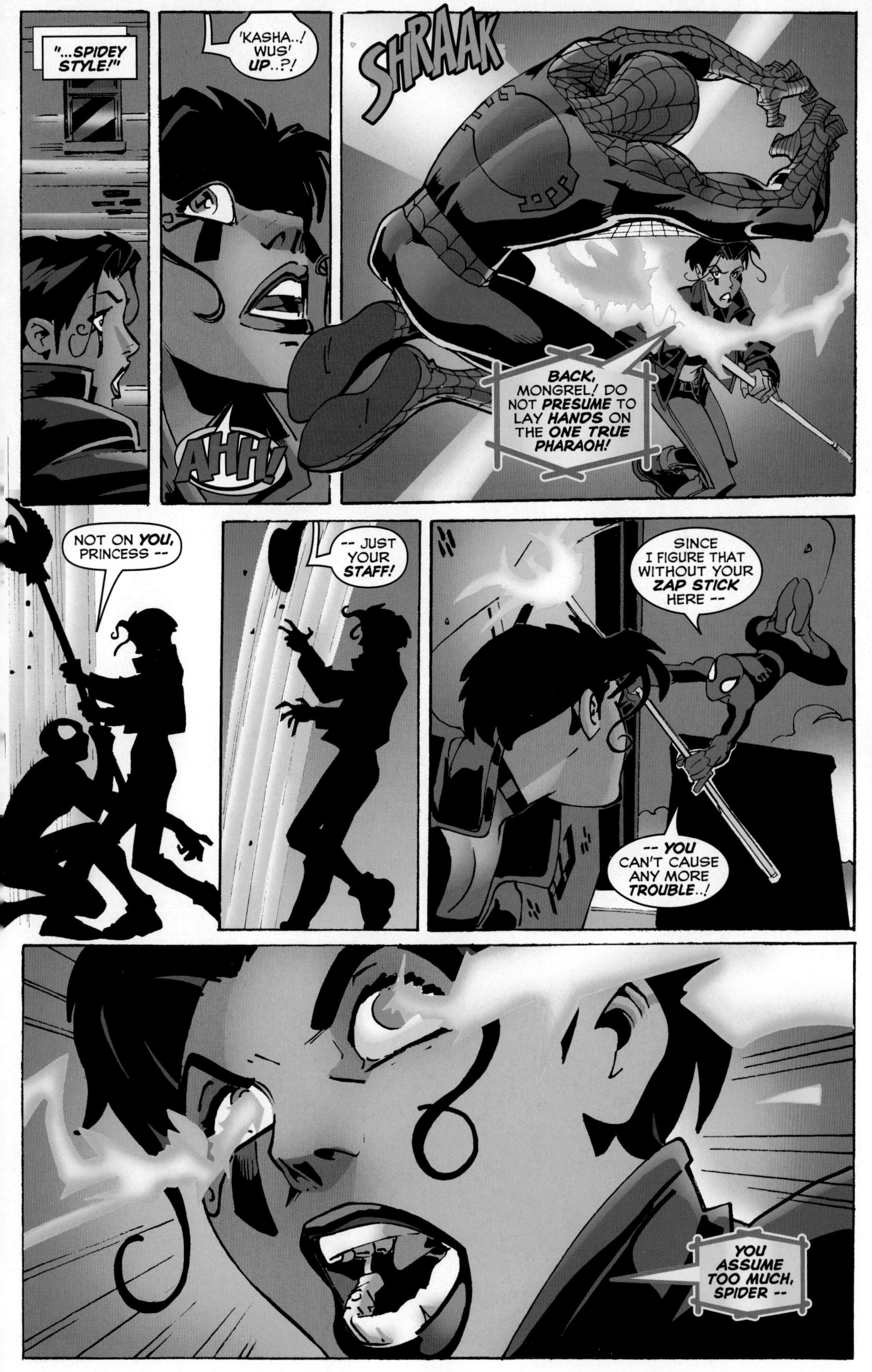
"...SPIDEY STYLE!"
'KASHA..! WUS' UP..?!
AHH!
SHRAAK
BACK, MONGREL! DO NOT PRESUME TO LAY HANDS ON THE ONE TRUE PHARAOH!
NOT ON YOU, PRINCESS --
-- JUST YOUR STAFF!
SINCE I FIGURE THAT WITHOUT YOUR ZAP STICK HERE --
-- YOU CAN'T CAUSE ANY MORE TROUBLE..!
YOU ASSUME TOO MUCH, SPIDER --

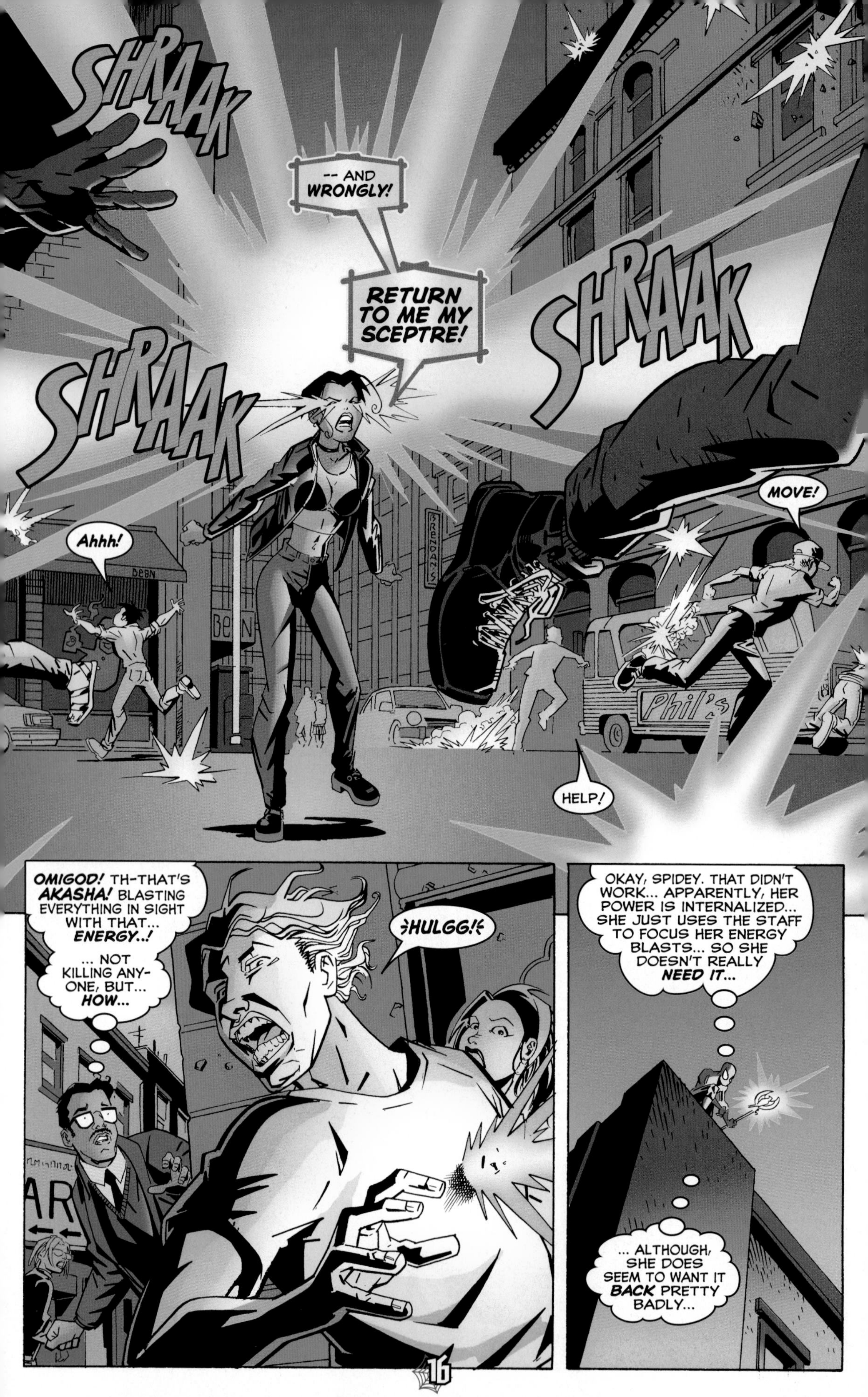
SHRAAK
-- AND WRONGLY!
RETURN TO ME MY SCEPTRE!
SHRAAK
SHRAAK
MOVE!
Ahhh!
BRENDAN'S
Phil's
HELP!
OMIGOD! TH-THAT'S AKASHA! BLASTING EVERYTHING IN SIGHT WITH THAT... ENERGY..!
... NOT KILLING ANY-ONE, BUT... HOW...
HULGG!
OKAY, SPIDEY. THAT DIDN'T WORK... APPARENTLY, HER POWER IS INTERNALIZED... SHE JUST USES THE STAFF TO FOCUS HER ENERGY BLASTS... SO SHE DOESN'T REALLY NEED IT...
... ALTHOUGH, SHE DOES SEEM TO WANT IT BACK PRETTY BADLY...

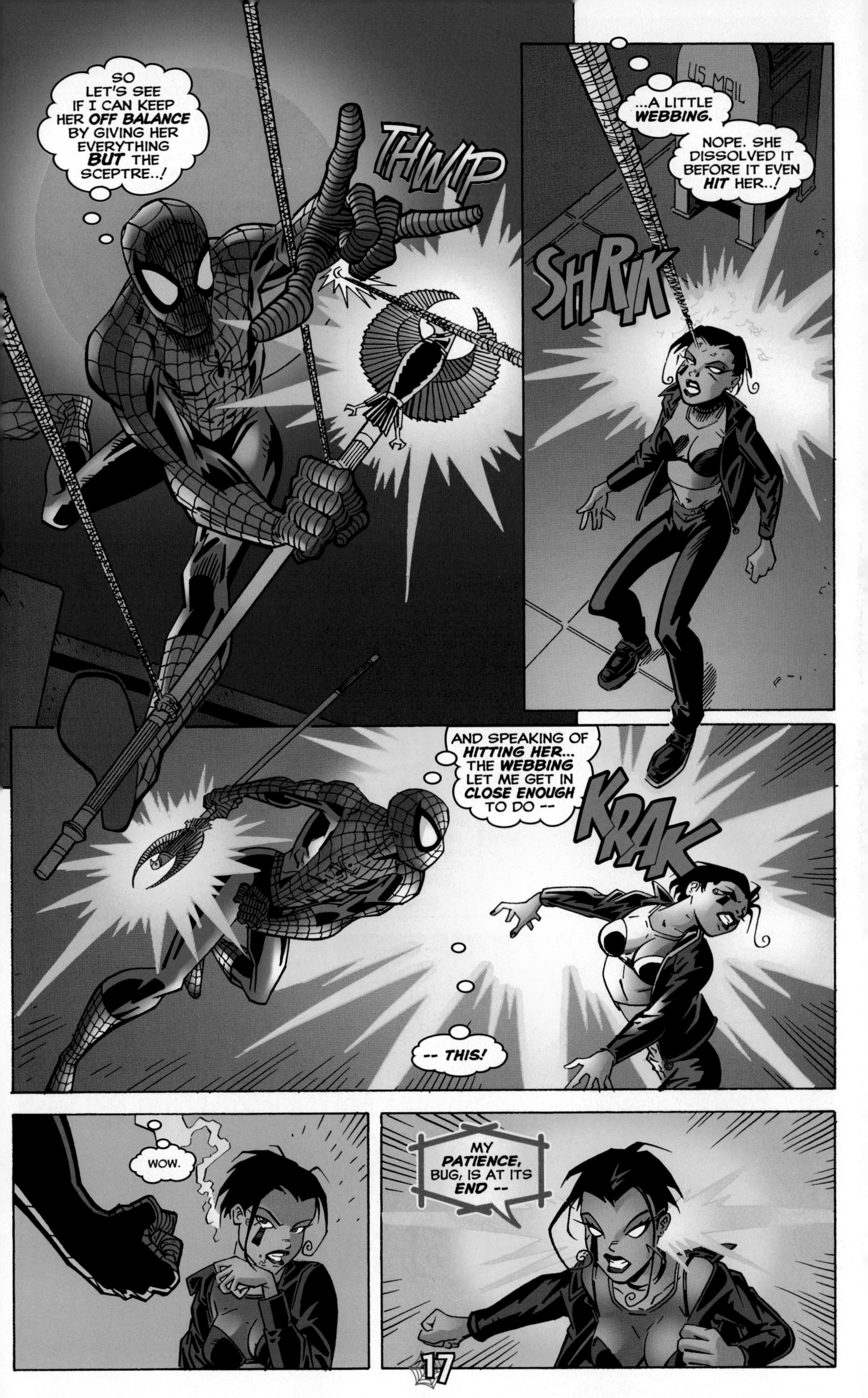

SO LET'S SEE IF I CAN KEEP HER **OFF BALANCE** BY GIVING HER EVERYTHING **BUT** THE SCEPTRE..!
THWIP
US MAIL
...A LITTLE **WEBBING.**
NOPE. SHE DISSOLVED IT BEFORE IT EVEN **HIT** HER..!
SHRIK
AND SPEAKING OF **HITTING HER...** THE **WEBBING** LET ME GET IN **CLOSE ENOUGH** TO DO --
KRAK
-- THIS!
WOW.
MY **PATIENCE,** BUG, IS AT ITS **END --**

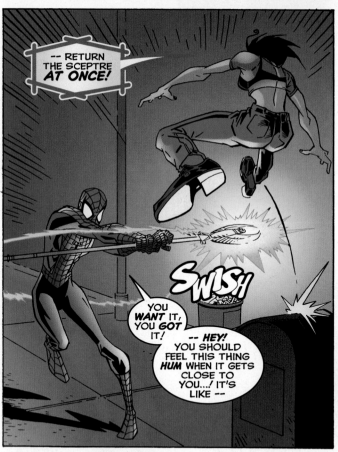

-- RETURN THE SCEPTRE *AT ONCE!*

SWISH

YOU *WANT* IT, YOU *GOT* IT!

-- HEY! YOU SHOULD FEEL THIS THING *HUM* WHEN IT GETS CLOSE TO YOU...! IT'S LIKE --

-- Oh, I *GET* IT! IT'S NOT A *WEAPON*... IT'S LIKE... A *BATTERY!* YOU USE IT TO FOCUS YOUR *ENERGY BLASTS,* BUT IT ALSO FOCUSES *POWER BACK TOWARD YOU!*

SO IF I WERE TO SOMEHOW *DESTROY* IT...

...MAYBE WE'D GET THE *REAL AKASHA* BACK..?

PRATTLING BUG! YOU DEFY *THE GODS!* THE GIRL IS *OURS!*

HER *DESTINY* HAS BEEN PRE-ORDAINED FOR *MILLENNIA!*

ERRNT! WRONG ANSWER... SORRY ABOUT YOUR *STICK!*

KRAK

NO! YOU FOOL!

SHRAK

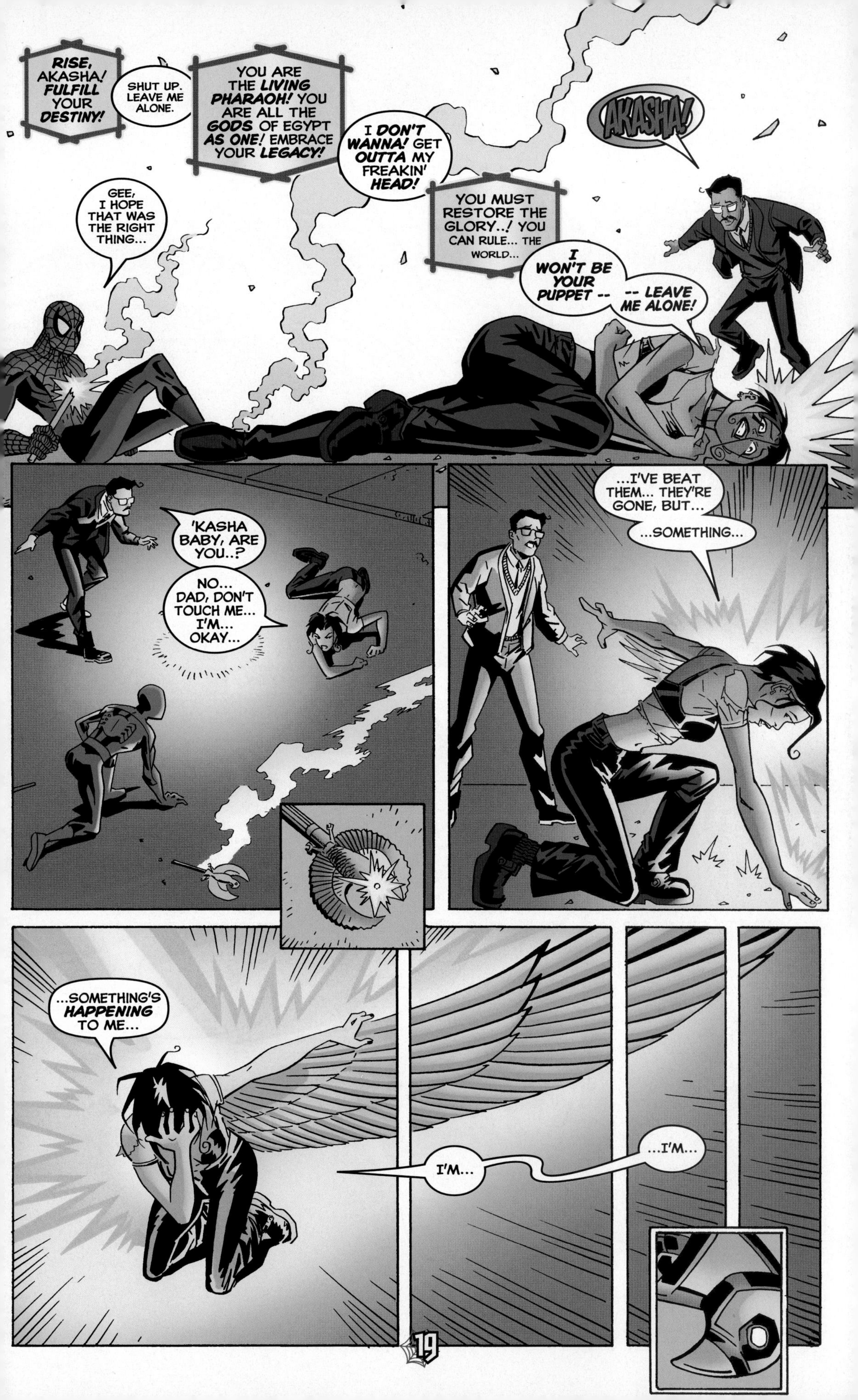
RISE, AKASHA! FULFILL YOUR DESTINY!
SHUT UP. LEAVE ME ALONE.
YOU ARE THE LIVING PHARAOH! YOU ARE ALL THE GODS OF EGYPT AS ONE! EMBRACE YOUR LEGACY!
I DON'T WANNA! GET OUTTA MY FREAKIN' HEAD!
AKASHA!
GEE, I HOPE THAT WAS THE RIGHT THING...
YOU MUST RESTORE THE GLORY..! YOU CAN RULE... THE WORLD...
I WON'T BE YOUR PUPPET --
-- LEAVE ME ALONE!
'KASHA BABY, ARE YOU..?
NO... DAD, DON'T TOUCH ME... I'M... OKAY...
...I'VE BEAT THEM... THEY'RE GONE, BUT...
...SOMETHING...
...SOMETHING'S HAPPENING TO ME...
I'M...
...I'M...
19

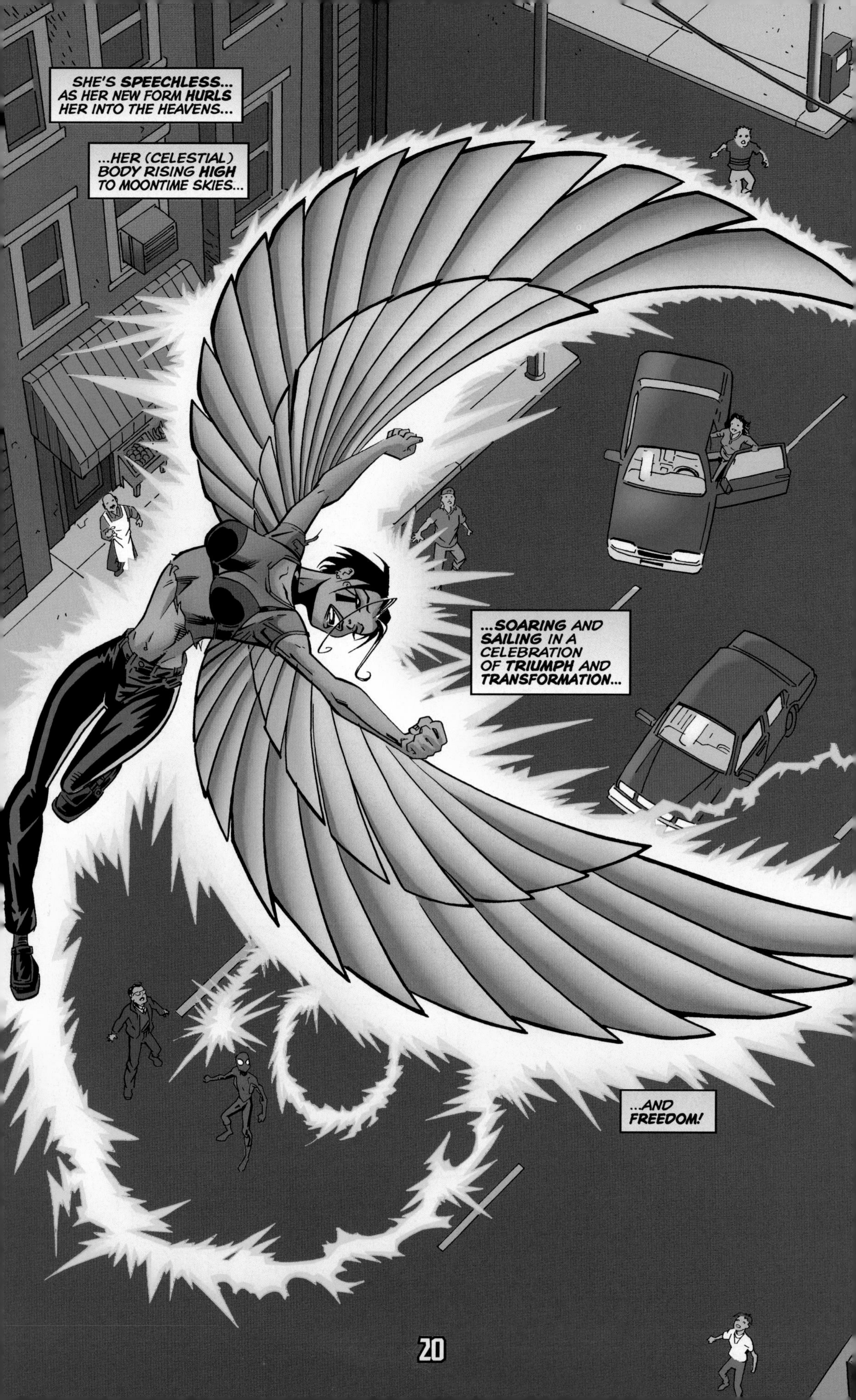
SHE'S SPEECHLESS... AS HER NEW FORM HURLS HER INTO THE HEAVENS...
...HER (CELESTIAL) BODY RISING HIGH TO MOONTIME SKIES...
...SOARING AND SAILING IN A CELEBRATION OF TRIUMPH AND TRANSFORMATION...
...AND FREEDOM!

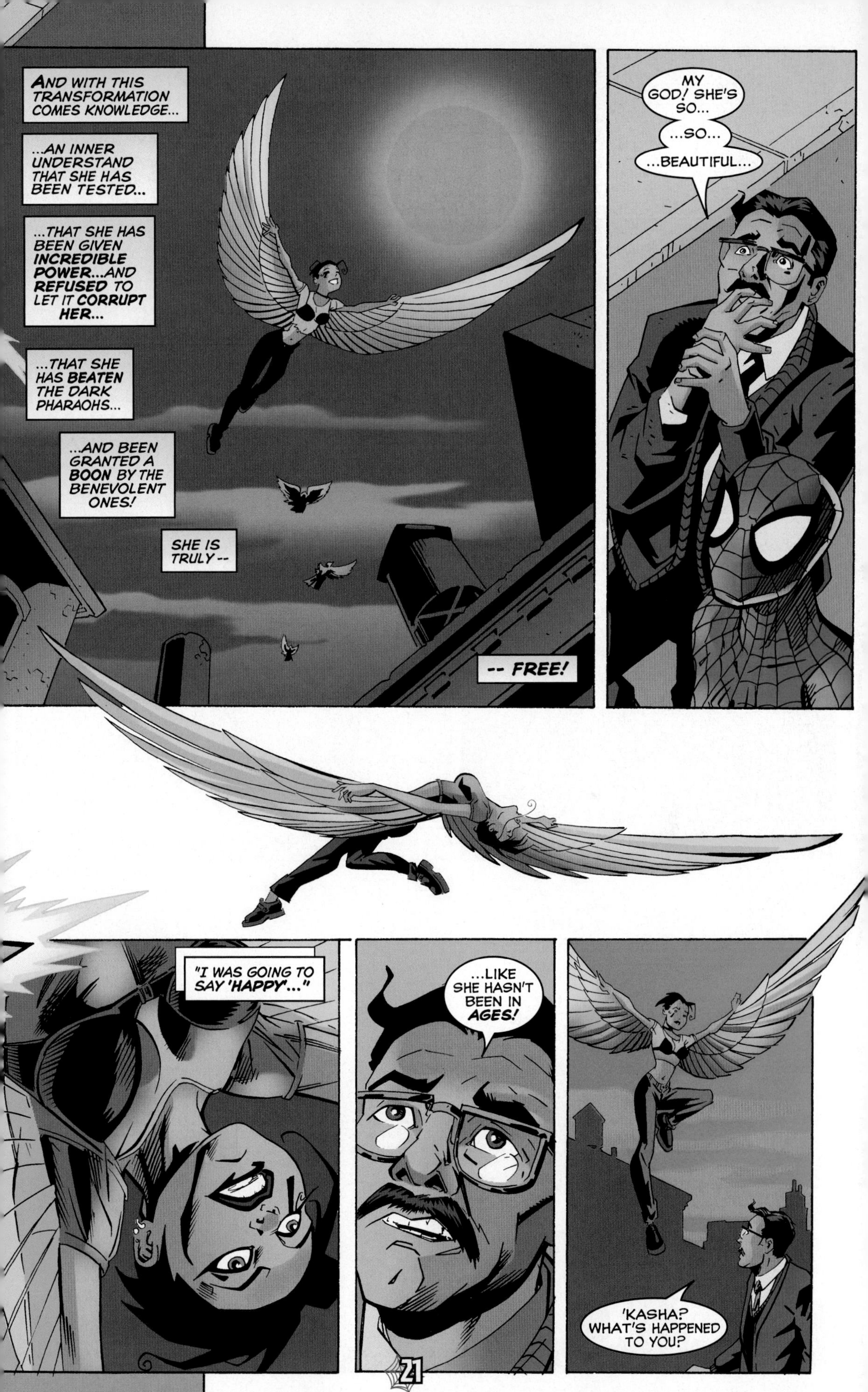
AND WITH THIS TRANSFORMATION COMES KNOWLEDGE...
...AN INNER UNDERSTAND THAT SHE HAS BEEN TESTED...
...THAT SHE HAS BEEN GIVEN INCREDIBLE POWER...AND REFUSED TO LET IT CORRUPT HER...
...THAT SHE HAS BEATEN THE DARK PHARAOHS...
...AND BEEN GRANTED A BOON BY THE BENEVOLENT ONES!
SHE IS TRULY --
-- FREE!
MY GOD! SHE'S SO...
...SO...
...BEAUTIFUL...
"I WAS GOING TO SAY 'HAPPY'..."
...LIKE SHE HASN'T BEEN IN AGES!
'KASHA? WHAT'S HAPPENED TO YOU?

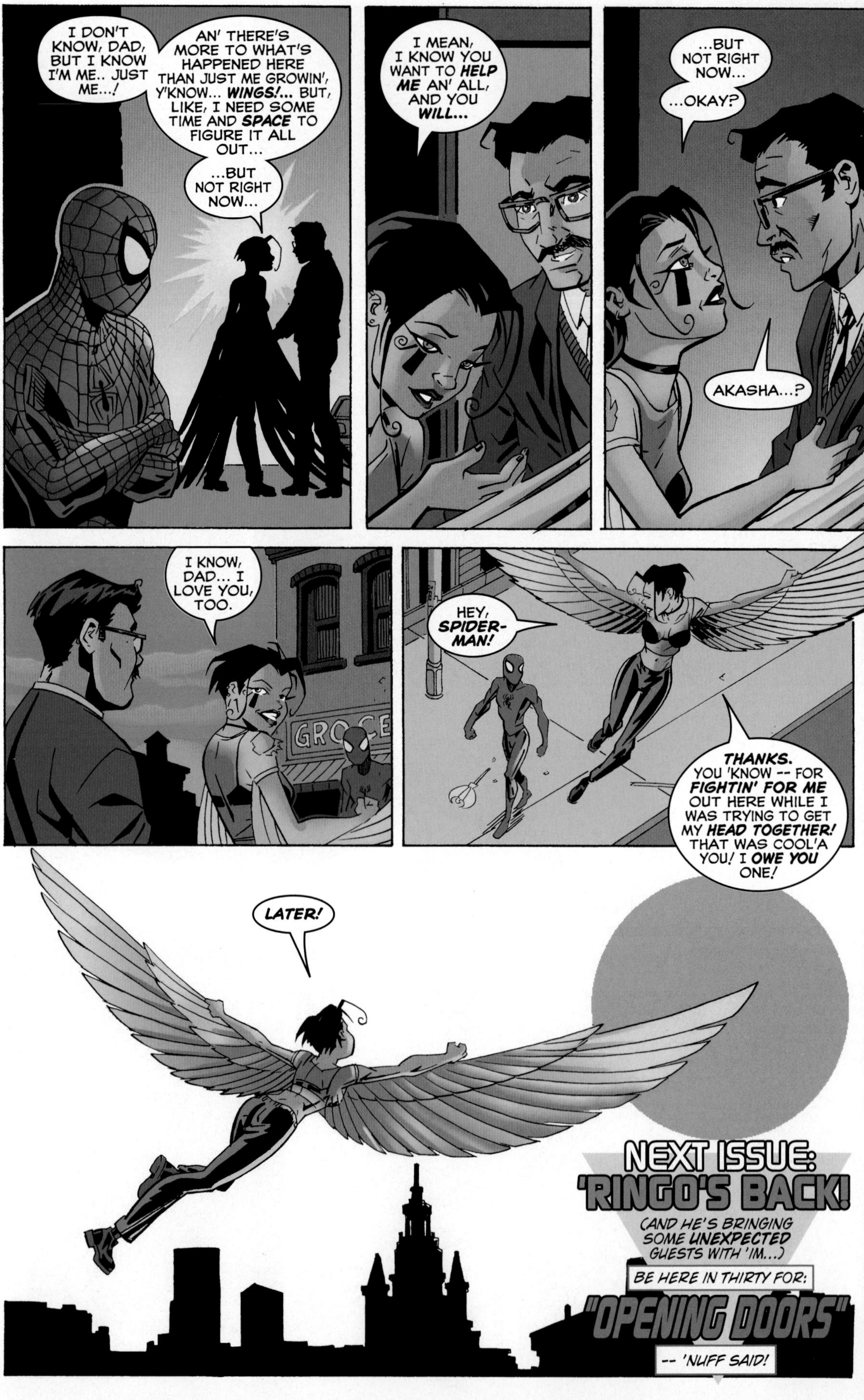

I DON'T KNOW, DAD, BUT I KNOW I'M ME.. JUST ME...!
AN' THERE'S MORE TO WHAT'S HAPPENED HERE THAN JUST ME GROWIN', Y'KNOW... WINGS!... BUT, LIKE, I NEED SOME TIME AND SPACE TO FIGURE IT ALL OUT...
...BUT NOT RIGHT NOW...
I MEAN, I KNOW YOU WANT TO HELP ME AN' ALL, AND YOU WILL...
...BUT NOT RIGHT NOW...
...OKAY?
AKASHA...?
I KNOW, DAD... I LOVE YOU, TOO.
GROCE
HEY, SPIDER-MAN!
THANKS. YOU 'KNOW -- FOR FIGHTIN' FOR ME OUT HERE WHILE I WAS TRYING TO GET MY HEAD TOGETHER! THAT WAS COOL'A YOU! I OWE YOU ONE!
LATER!
NEXT ISSUE: 'RINGO'S BACK!
(AND HE'S BRINGING SOME UNEXPECTED GUESTS WITH 'IM...)
BE HERE IN THIRTY FOR:
"OPENING DOORS"
-- 'NUFF SAID!

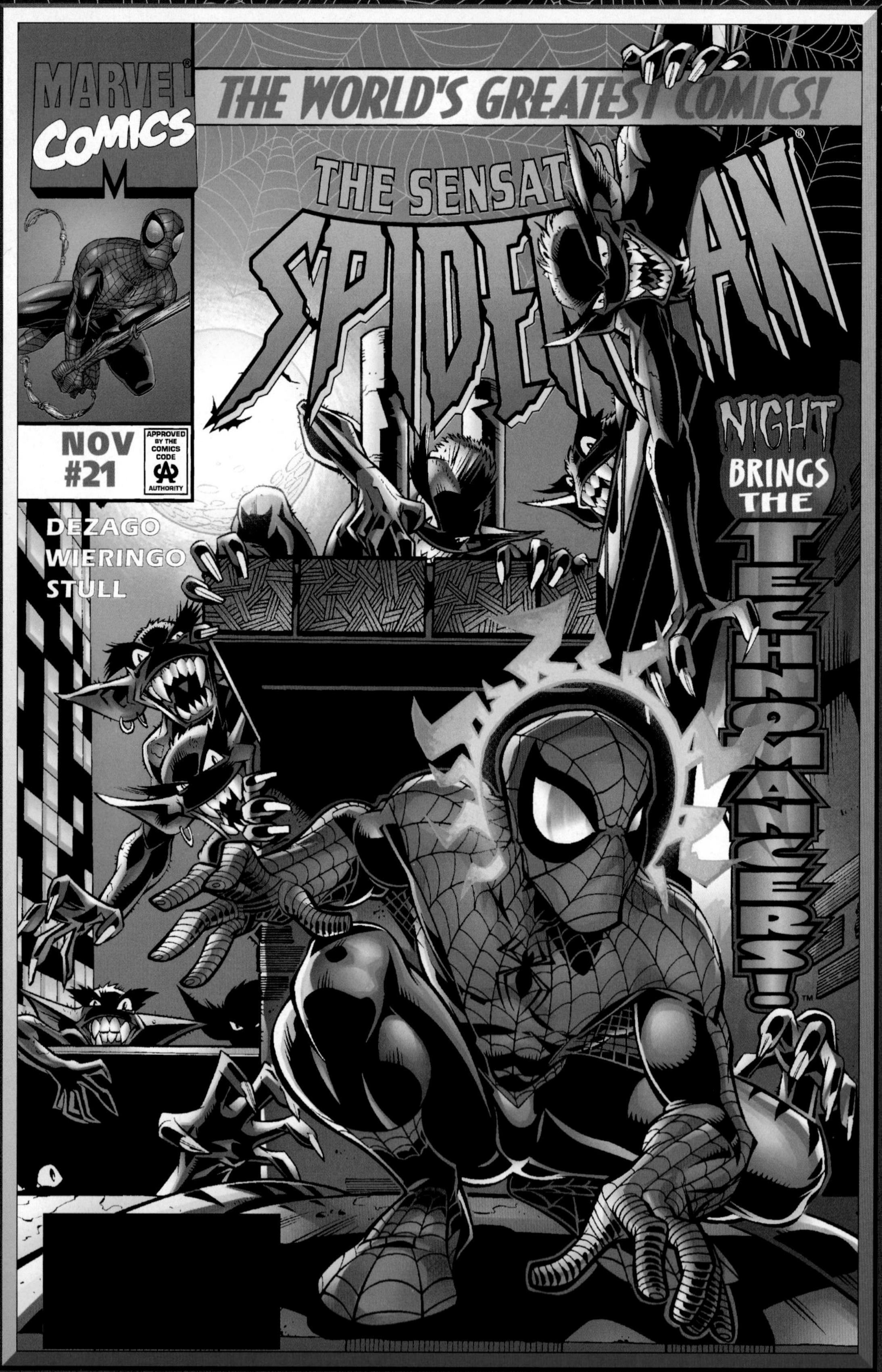
MARVEL COMICS
THE WORLD'S GREATEST COMICS!
THE SENSAT
NOV
#21
APPROVED BY THE COMICS CODE AUTHORITY
DEZAGO
WIERINGO
STULL
NIGHT BRINGS THE TECHNOMANCERS!

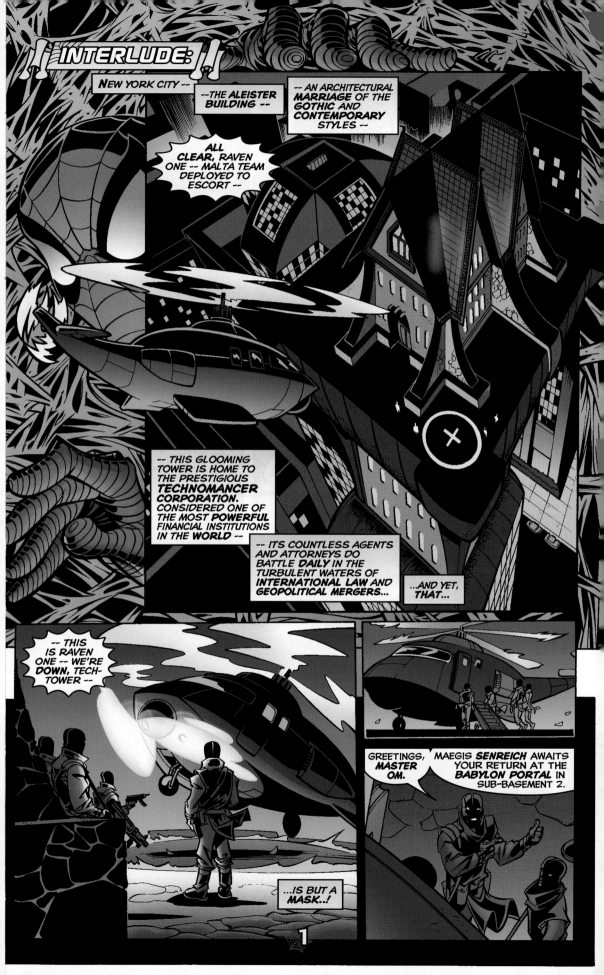

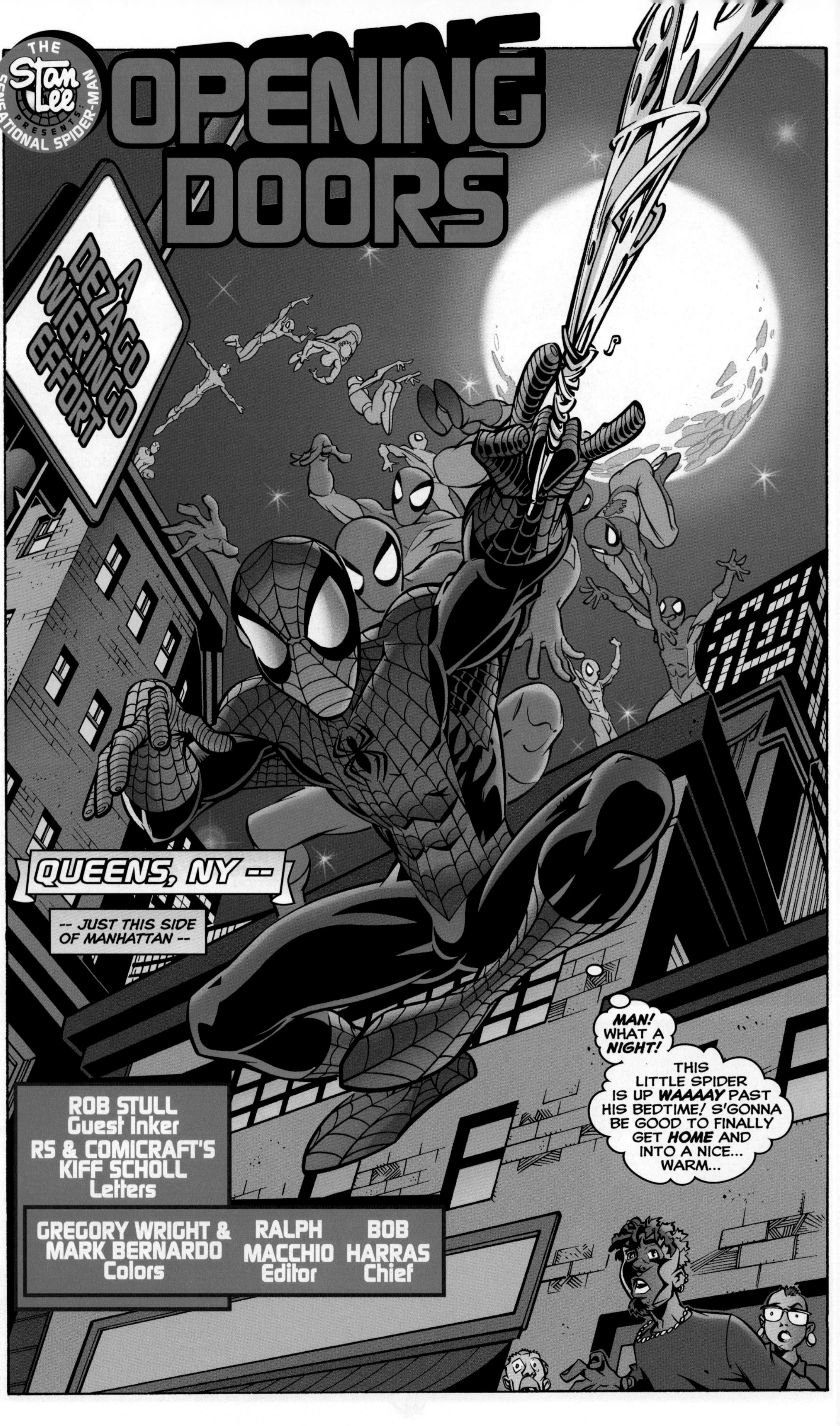

THE Stan Lee PRESENTS SENSATIONAL SPIDER-MAN
OPENING DOORS
A DEZAGO WIERINGO EFFORT
QUEENS, NY --
-- JUST THIS SIDE OF MANHATTAN --
MAN! WHAT A NIGHT!
THIS LITTLE SPIDER IS UP WAAAAY PAST HIS BEDTIME! S'GONNA BE GOOD TO FINALLY GET HOME AND INTO A NICE... WARM...
ROB STULL Guest Inker
RS & COMICRAFT'S KIFF SCHOLL Letters
GREGORY WRIGHT & MARK BERNARDO Colors
RALPH MACCHIO Editor
BOB HARRAS Chief

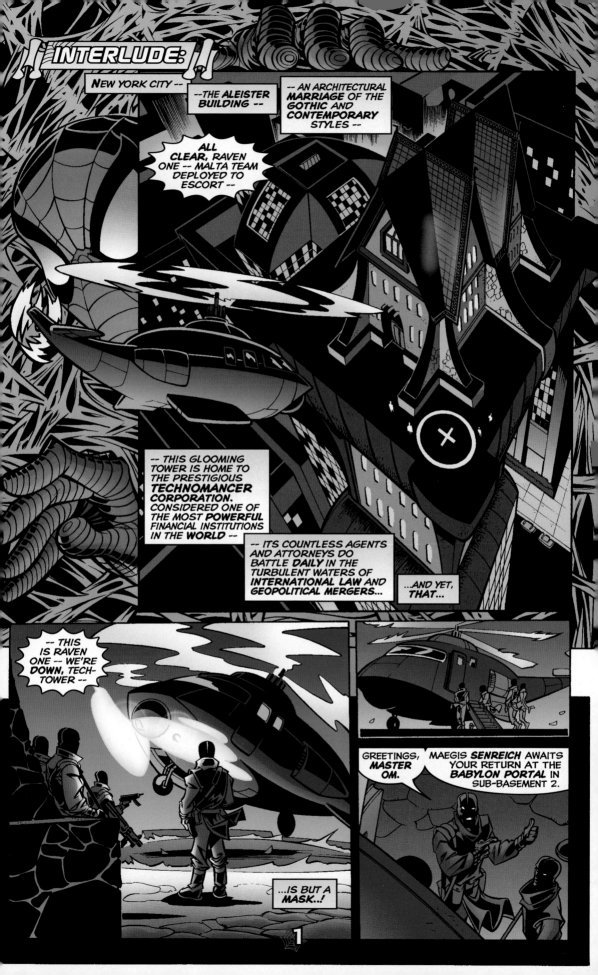

NEW YORK CITY --

--THE ALEISTER BUILDING --

-- AN ARCHITECTURAL MARRIAGE OF THE GOTHIC AND CONTEMPORARY STYLES --

ALL CLEAR, RAVEN ONE -- MALTA TEAM DEPLOYED TO ESCORT --

-- THIS GLOOMING TOWER IS HOME TO THE PRESTIGIOUS TECHNOMANCER CORPORATION. CONSIDERED ONE OF THE MOST POWERFUL FINANCIAL INSTITUTIONS IN THE WORLD --

-- ITS COUNTLESS AGENTS AND ATTORNEYS DO BATTLE DAILY IN THE TURBULENT WATERS OF INTERNATIONAL LAW AND GEOPOLITICAL MERGERS...

...AND YET, THAT...

-- THIS IS RAVEN ONE -- WE'RE DOWN, TECH-TOWER --

GREETINGS, MASTER OM.

MAEGIS SENREICH AWAITS YOUR RETURN AT THE BABYLON PORTAL IN SUB-BASEMENT 2.

...IS BUT A MASK...!

1

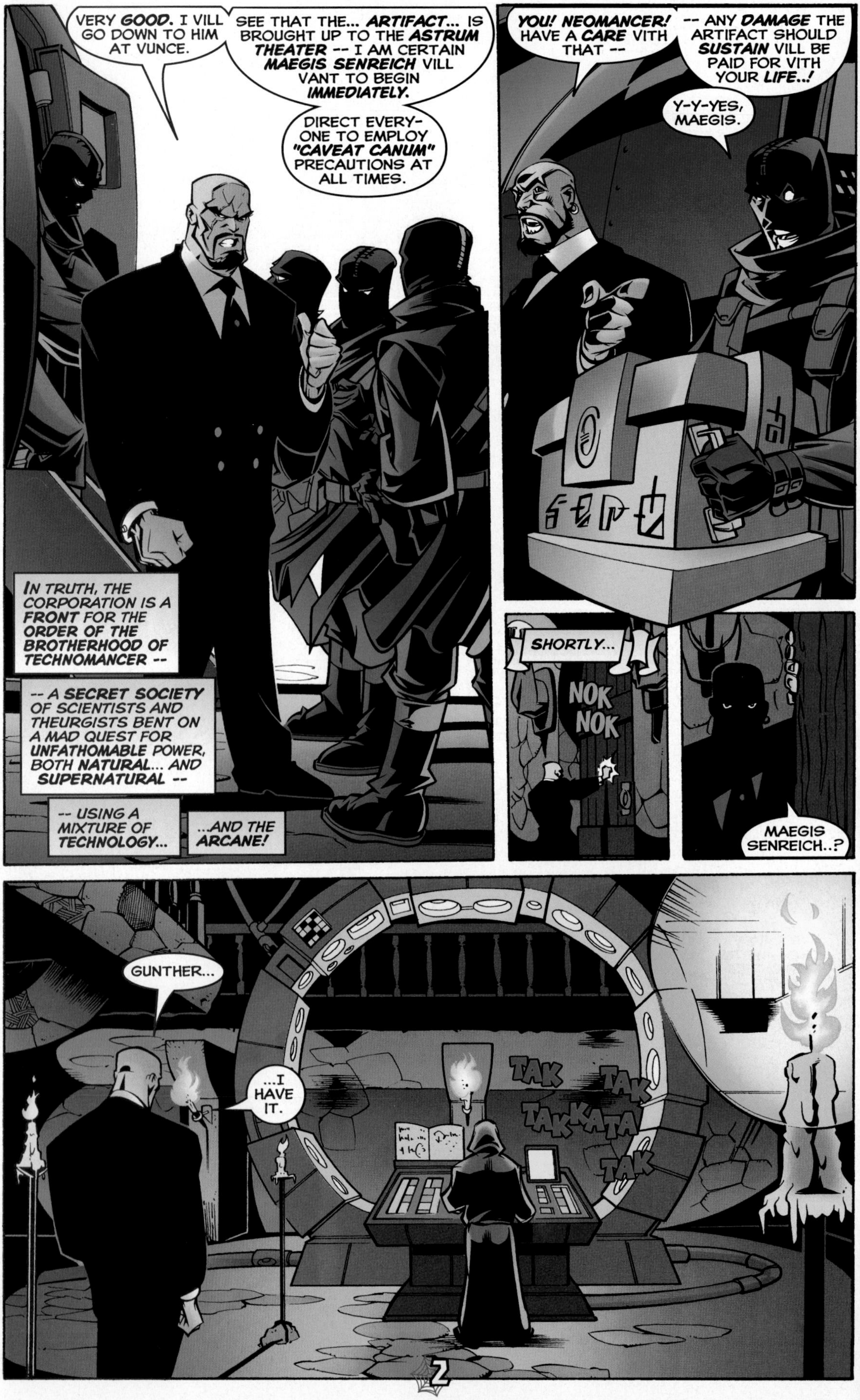

VERY GOOD. I VILL GO DOWN TO HIM AT VUNCE.
SEE THAT THE... ARTIFACT... IS BROUGHT UP TO THE ASTRUM THEATER -- I AM CERTAIN MAEGIS SENREICH VILL VANT TO BEGIN IMMEDIATELY.
DIRECT EVERYONE TO EMPLOY "CAVEAT CANUM" PRECAUTIONS AT ALL TIMES.
IN TRUTH, THE CORPORATION IS A FRONT FOR THE ORDER OF THE BROTHERHOOD OF TECHNOMANCER --
-- A SECRET SOCIETY OF SCIENTISTS AND THEURGISTS BENT ON A MAD QUEST FOR UNFATHOMABLE POWER, BOTH NATURAL... AND SUPERNATURAL --
-- USING A MIXTURE OF TECHNOLOGY...
...AND THE ARCANE!
YOU! NEOMANCER! HAVE A CARE VITH THAT --
-- ANY DAMAGE THE ARTIFACT SHOULD SUSTAIN VILL BE PAID FOR VITH YOUR LIFE..!
Y-Y-YES, MAEGIS.
SHORTLY...
NOK NOK
MAEGIS SENREICH..?
GUNTHER...
...I HAVE IT.
TAK TAK TAKKATATA TAK

IT'S... ...IT'S... HERE..?

VE ARRIVED MOMENTS AGO. IT IS BEING DELIVERED TO THE *OBSERVATORY* AS VE SPEAK.

-- THE *SPHERE* OF *SARA-KATH!*

ALREADY I HAVE IMPRESSED MY BROTHER TECHNOMANCERS BY ACHIEVING THE LEVEL OF *MAEGIS* AT SUCH AN *EARLY AGE,* BUT BY ACQUIRING THE NEAR-INFINITE ENERGIES OF THE *SARA-KATH* --

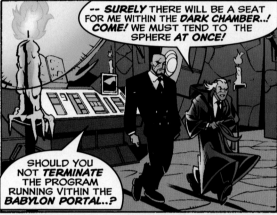

-- *SURELY* THERE WILL BE A SEAT FOR ME WITHIN THE *DARK CHAMBER..!* *COME!* WE MUST TEND TO THE SPHERE *AT ONCE!*

SHOULD YOU NOT *TERMINATE* THE PROGRAM RUNNING VITHIN THE *BABYLON PORTAL..?*

WONDERFUL! WONDERFUL! FINALLY, OM -- AFTER SO MANY YEARS OF *SEARCH* AND *STUDY* WE *HAVE IT!* ONE OF THE MOST *POWERFUL* -- AND ELUSIVE -- TALISMANS ONLY *WHISPERED ABOUT* IN THE CIRCLES OF THE SEVEN MAGIKS! --

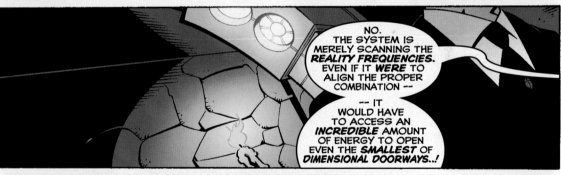

NO. THE SYSTEM IS MERELY SCANNING THE *REALITY FREQUENCIES.* EVEN IF IT *WERE* TO ALIGN THE PROPER COMBINATION --

-- IT WOULD HAVE TO ACCESS AN *INCREDIBLE* AMOUNT OF ENERGY TO OPEN EVEN THE *SMALLEST* OF *DIMENSIONAL DOORWAYS..!*

ZAT

SHRRRIKK

...IT'LL BE FINE...

...WHOA! WHOA! WHOA!

SPIDER-SENSE SAYING *"BACK OFF!"* -- SOME-BODY MUST BE WATCHING --

-- AND THE *LAST THING* WE WANT IS FOR ANYBODY TO CATCH THIS WEB-WEARY SPIDER-MAN SLIPPING IN THROUGH *PETER* AND *MARY JANE PARKER'S* BEDROOM WIND-

-- *BINGO!* THERE SHE IS! IT'S THAT NEW-LITTLE-GIRL-NEIGHBOR NEXT DOOR...

JEEZ! AUNT ANNA'S *RIGHT,* SHE IS KINDA... *SPOOKY!* JUST SITTING THERE IN THE DARK... NOT EVEN MOVING...

... *STARING...*

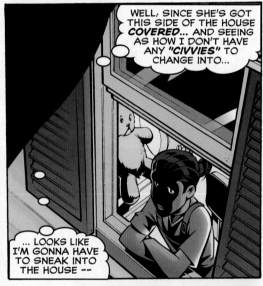

WELL, SINCE SHE'S GOT THIS SIDE OF THE HOUSE *COVERED...* AND SEEING AS HOW I DON'T HAVE ANY *"CIVVIES"* TO CHANGE INTO...

... LOOKS LIKE I'M GONNA HAVE TO SNEAK INTO THE HOUSE --

-- THROUGH THE *ATTIC!*

WOW! I HAVEN'T BEEN UP *HERE* SINCE...

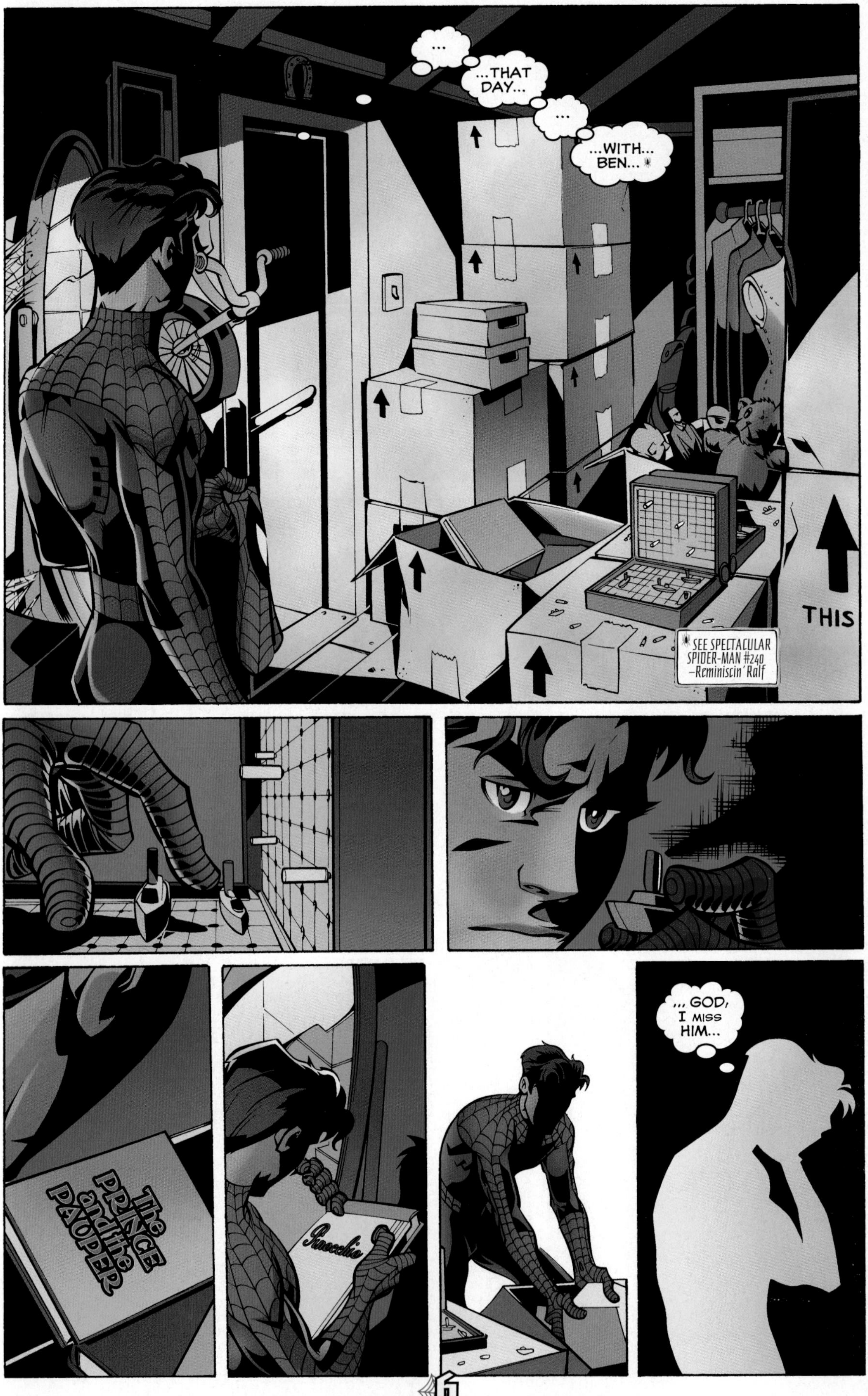
...
...THAT DAY...
...
...WITH... BEN...
THIS
SEE SPECTACULAR SPIDER-MAN #240
—Reminiscin' Ralf
The PRINCE and the PAUPER
Pinocchio
..., GOD, I MISS HIM...

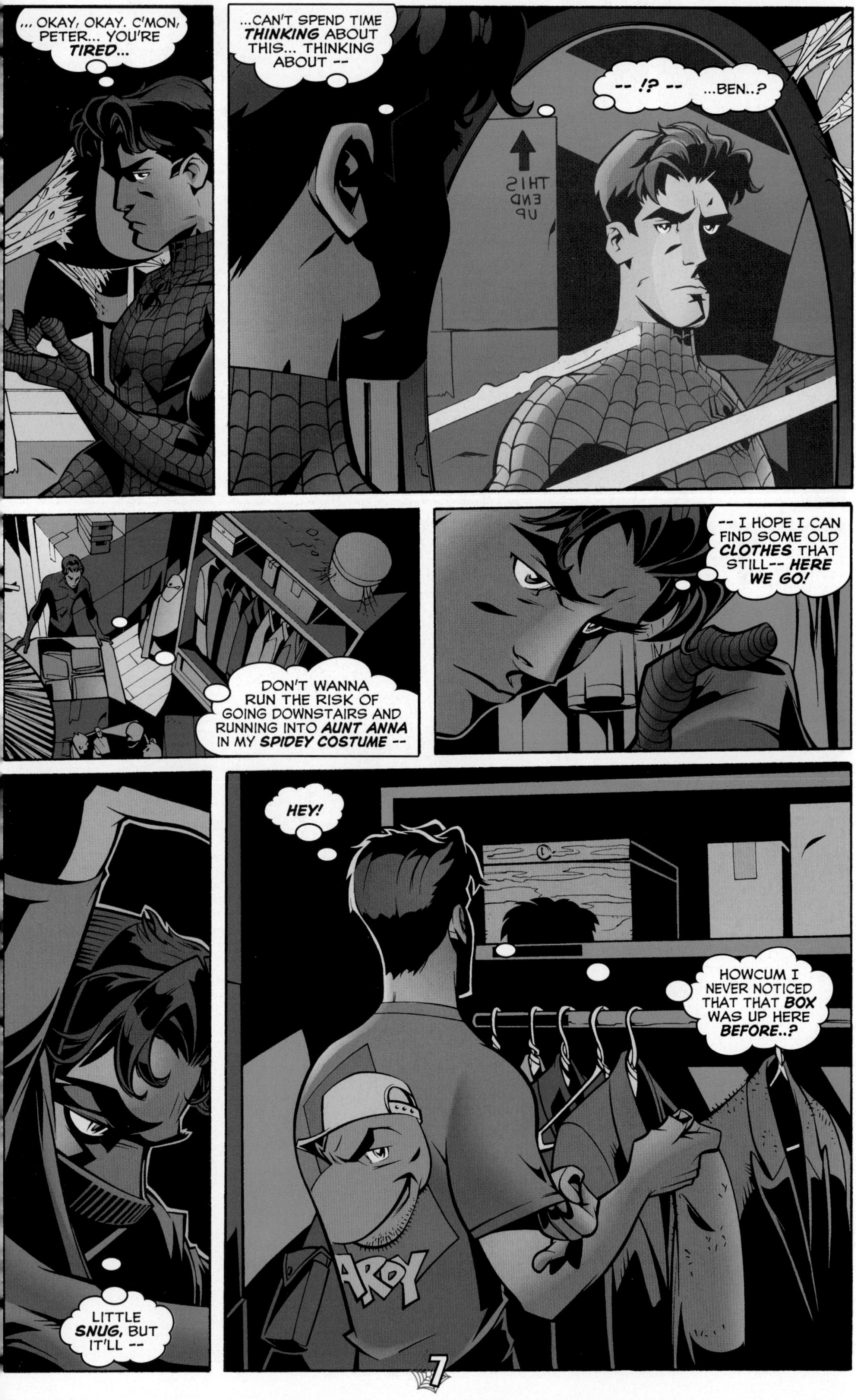
... OKAY, OKAY. C'MON, PETER... YOU'RE TIRED...
...CAN'T SPEND TIME THINKING ABOUT THIS... THINKING ABOUT --
-- !? -- ...BEN..?
THIS END UP
DON'T WANNA RUN THE RISK OF GOING DOWNSTAIRS AND RUNNING INTO AUNT ANNA IN MY SPIDEY COSTUME --
-- I HOPE I CAN FIND SOME OLD CLOTHES THAT STILL-- HERE WE GO!
LITTLE SNUG, BUT IT'LL --
HEY!
HOWCUM I NEVER NOTICED THAT THAT BOX WAS UP HERE BEFORE..?

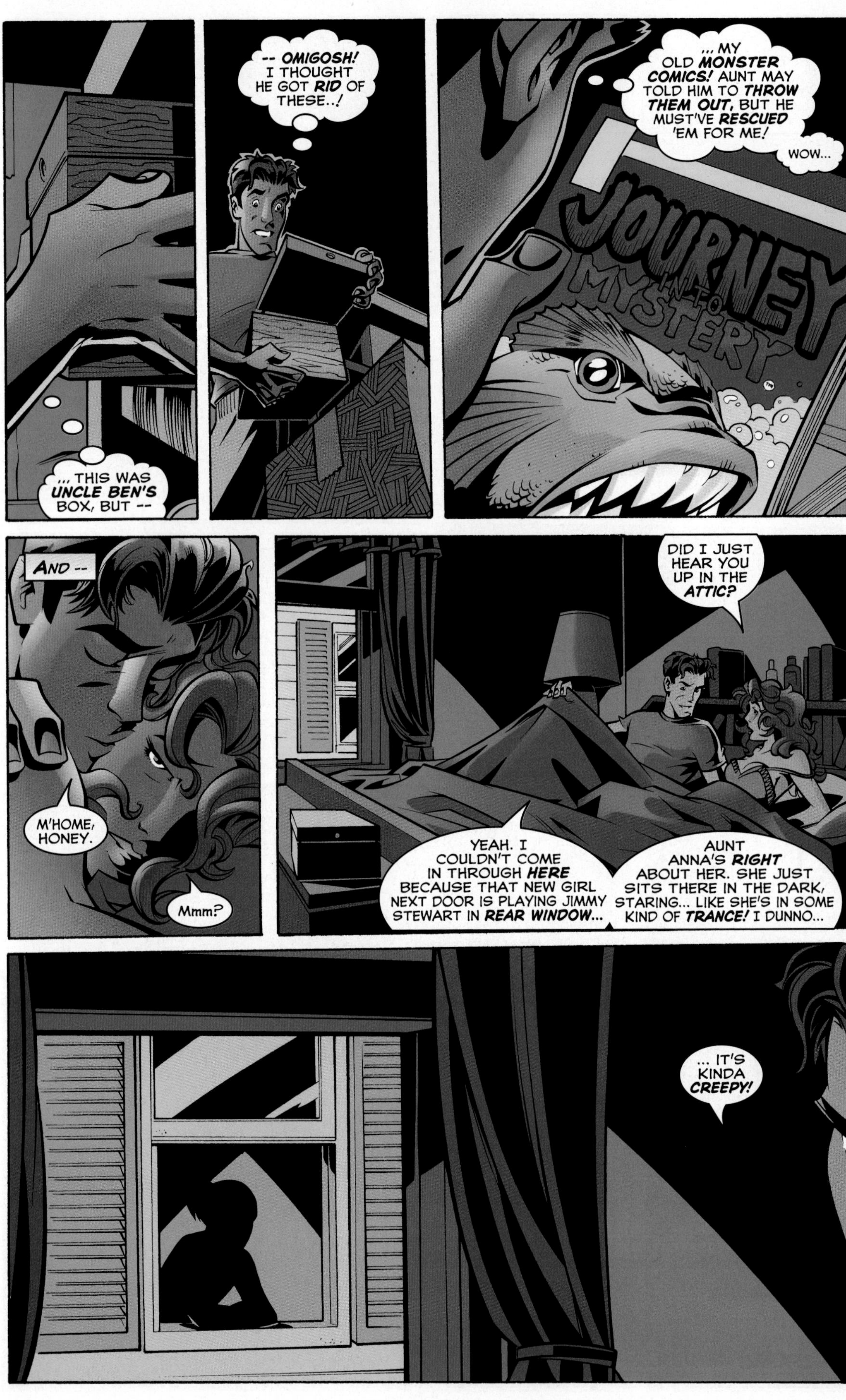

... THIS WAS UNCLE BEN'S BOX, BUT --
-- OMIGOSH! I THOUGHT HE GOT RID OF THESE..!
... MY OLD MONSTER COMICS! AUNT MAY TOLD HIM TO THROW THEM OUT, BUT HE MUST'VE RESCUED 'EM FOR ME!
WOW...
JOURNEY INTO MYSTERY
AND --
M'HOME, HONEY.
Mmm?
DID I JUST HEAR YOU UP IN THE ATTIC?
YEAH. I COULDN'T COME IN THROUGH HERE BECAUSE THAT NEW GIRL NEXT DOOR IS PLAYING JIMMY STEWART IN REAR WINDOW...
AUNT ANNA'S RIGHT ABOUT HER. SHE JUST SITS THERE IN THE DARK, STARING... LIKE SHE'S IN SOME KIND OF TRANCE! I DUNNO...
... IT'S KINDA CREEPY!

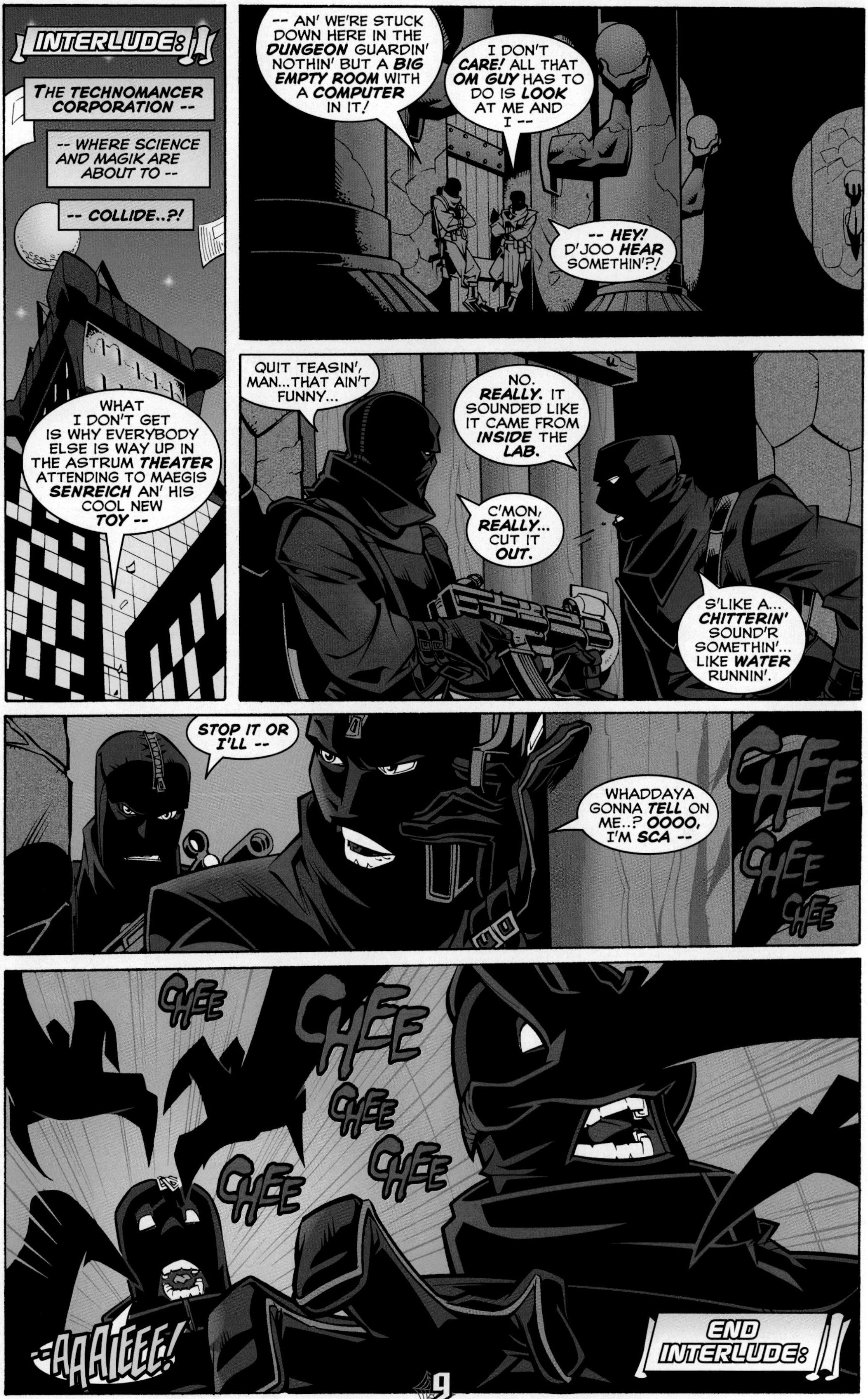
INTERLUDE:
THE TECHNOMANCER CORPORATION --
-- WHERE SCIENCE AND MAGIK ARE ABOUT TO --
-- COLLIDE..?!
WHAT I DON'T GET IS WHY EVERYBODY ELSE IS WAY UP IN THE ASTRUM THEATER ATTENDING TO MAEGIS SENREICH AN' HIS COOL NEW TOY --
-- AN' WE'RE STUCK DOWN HERE IN THE DUNGEON GUARDIN' NOTHIN' BUT A BIG EMPTY ROOM WITH A COMPUTER IN IT!
I DON'T CARE! ALL THAT OM GUY HAS TO DO IS LOOK AT ME AND I --
-- HEY! D'JOO HEAR SOMETHIN'?!
QUIT TEASIN', MAN...THAT AIN'T FUNNY...
NO. REALLY. IT SOUNDED LIKE IT CAME FROM INSIDE THE LAB.
C'MON, REALLY... CUT IT OUT.
S'LIKE A... CHITTERIN' SOUND'R SOMETHIN'... LIKE WATER RUNNIN'.
STOP IT OR I'LL --
WHADDAYA GONNA TELL ON ME..? OOOO, I'M SCA --
CHEE CHEE CHEE
CHEE CHEE CHEE CHEE CHEE
-AAAIEEE!
END INTERLUDE:

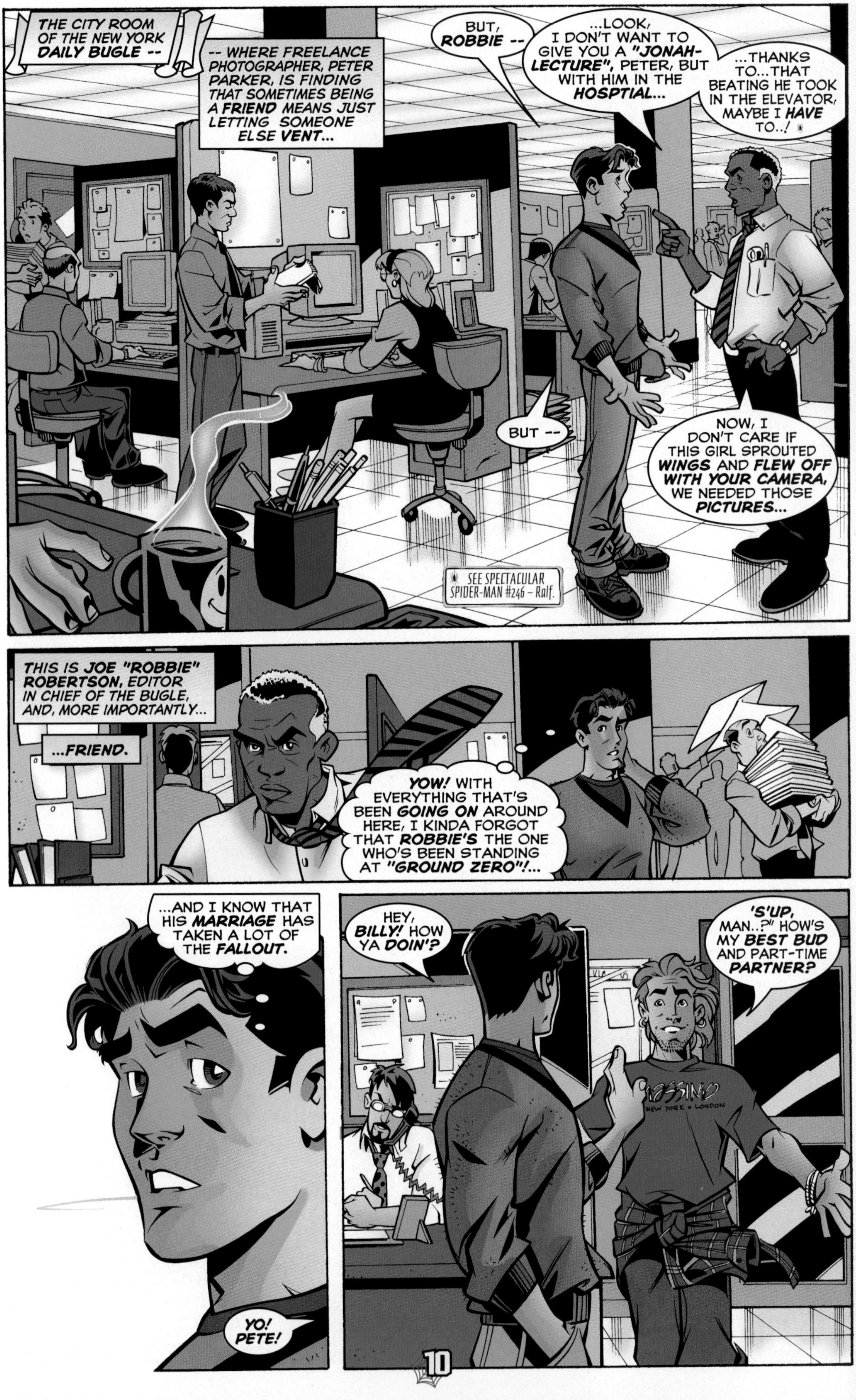

THE CITY ROOM OF THE NEW YORK DAILY BUGLE --
-- WHERE FREELANCE PHOTOGRAPHER, PETER PARKER, IS FINDING THAT SOMETIMES BEING A FRIEND MEANS JUST LETTING SOMEONE ELSE VENT...
BUT, ROBBIE --
...LOOK, I DON'T WANT TO GIVE YOU A "JONAH-LECTURE", PETER, BUT WITH HIM IN THE HOSPTIAL...
...THANKS TO...THAT BEATING HE TOOK IN THE ELEVATOR, MAYBE I HAVE TO..!
BUT --
NOW, I DON'T CARE IF THIS GIRL SPROUTED WINGS AND FLEW OFF WITH YOUR CAMERA, WE NEEDED THOSE PICTURES...
SEE SPECTACULAR SPIDER-MAN #246 – Ralf.
THIS IS JOE "ROBBIE" ROBERTSON, EDITOR IN CHIEF OF THE BUGLE, AND, MORE IMPORTANTLY...
...FRIEND.
YOW! WITH EVERYTHING THAT'S BEEN GOING ON AROUND HERE, I KINDA FORGOT THAT ROBBIE'S THE ONE WHO'S BEEN STANDING AT "GROUND ZERO"!...
...AND I KNOW THAT HIS MARRIAGE HAS TAKEN A LOT OF THE FALLOUT.
YO! PETE!
HEY, BILLY! HOW YA DOIN'?
'S'UP, MAN...?" HOW'S MY BEST BUD AND PART-TIME PARTNER?
NEW YORK • LONDON

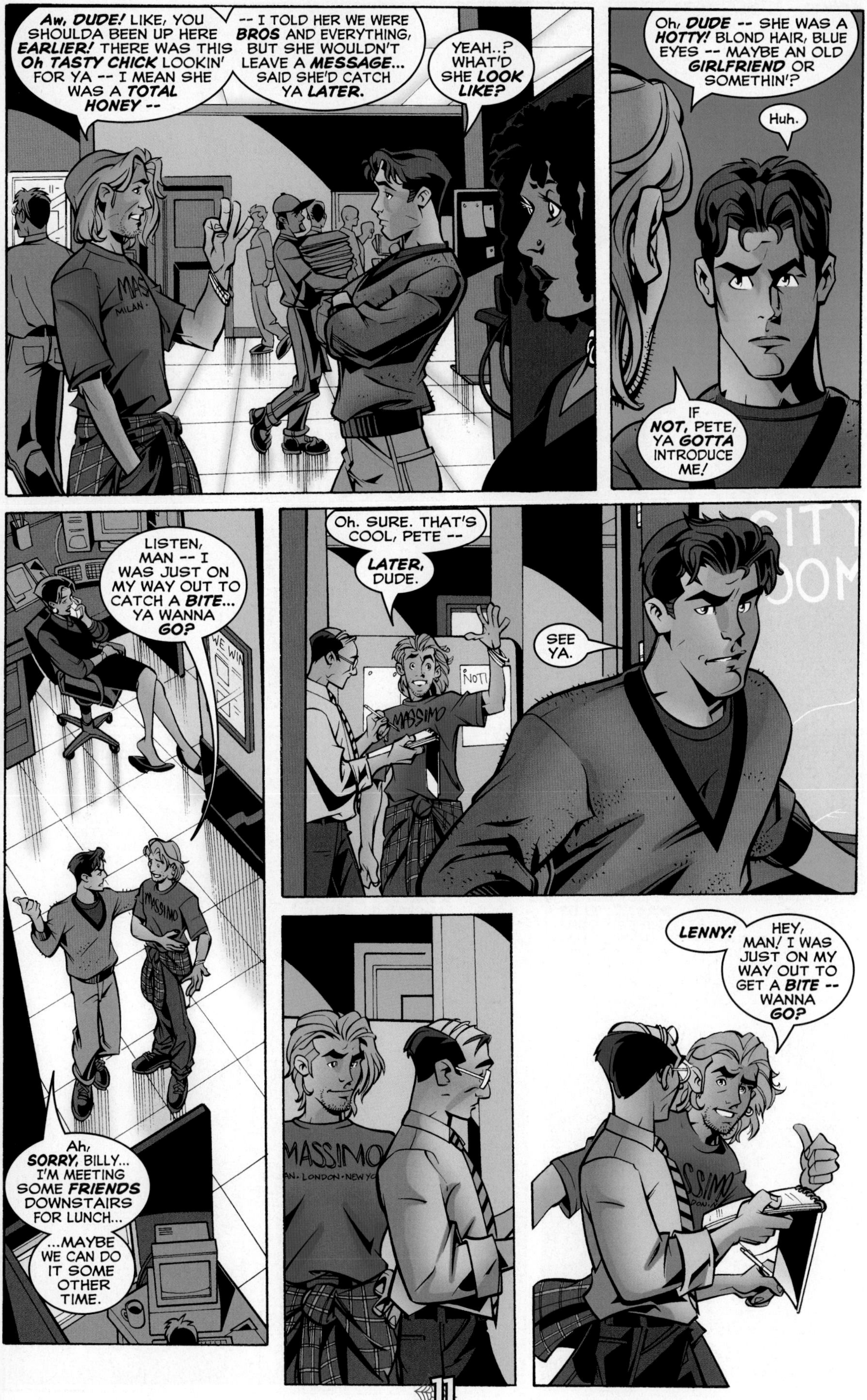
Aw, DUDE! LIKE, YOU SHOULDA BEEN UP HERE EARLIER! THERE WAS THIS Oh TASTY CHICK LOOKIN' FOR YA -- I MEAN SHE WAS A TOTAL HONEY --
-- I TOLD HER WE WERE BROS AND EVERYTHING, BUT SHE WOULDN'T LEAVE A MESSAGE... SAID SHE'D CATCH YA LATER.
YEAH..? WHAT'D SHE LOOK LIKE?
MASSIMO
MILAN
Oh, DUDE -- SHE WAS A HOTTY! BLOND HAIR, BLUE EYES -- MAYBE AN OLD GIRLFRIEND OR SOMETHIN'?
Huh.
IF NOT, PETE, YA GOTTA INTRODUCE ME!
LISTEN, MAN -- I WAS JUST ON MY WAY OUT TO CATCH A BITE... YA WANNA GO?
Ah, SORRY, BILLY... I'M MEETING SOME FRIENDS DOWNSTAIRS FOR LUNCH...
...MAYBE WE CAN DO IT SOME OTHER TIME.
Oh. SURE. THAT'S COOL, PETE --
LATER, DUDE.
SEE YA.
LENNY!
HEY, MAN! I WAS JUST ON MY WAY OUT TO GET A BITE -- WANNA GO?
MASSIMO
AN. LONDON. NEW YO

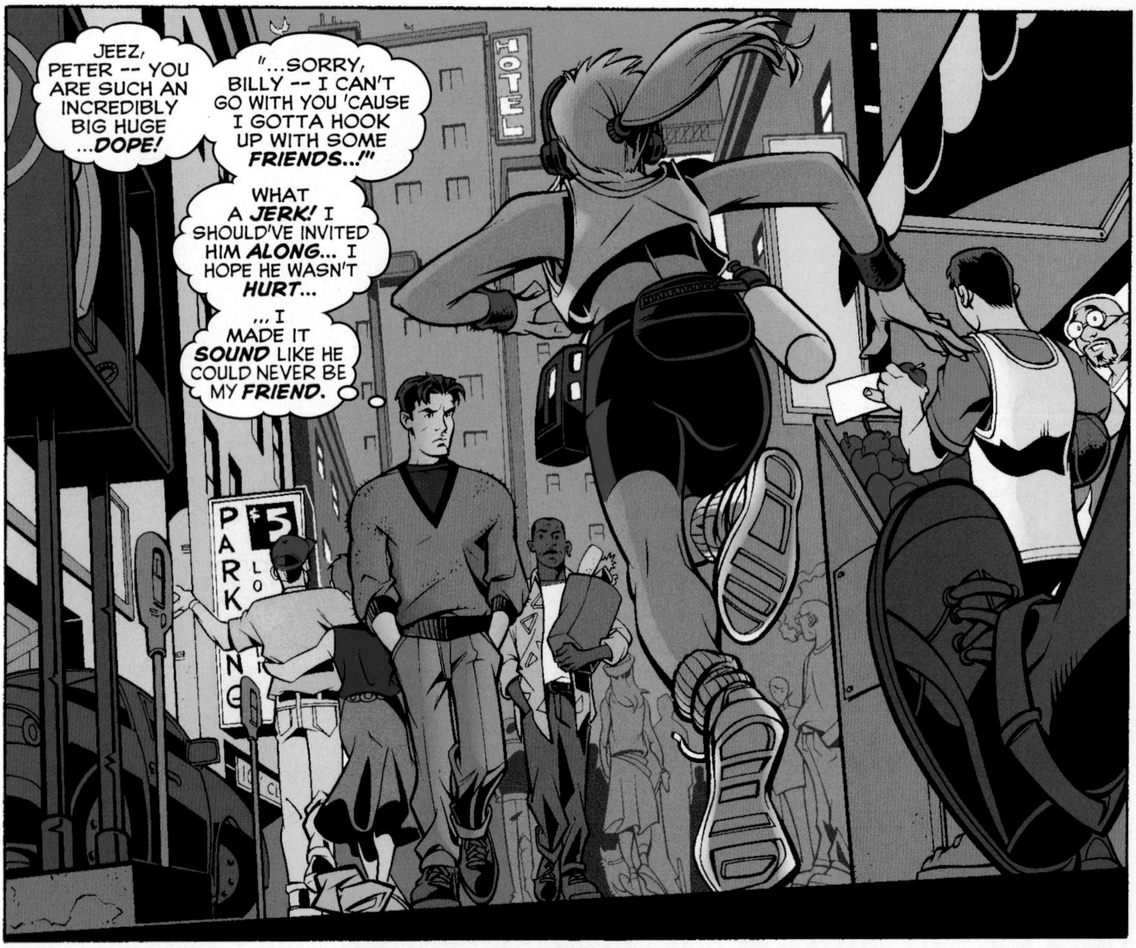
JEEZ, PETER -- YOU ARE SUCH AN INCREDIBLY BIG HUGE ...DOPE!
"...SORRY, BILLY -- I CAN'T GO WITH YOU 'CAUSE I GOTTA HOOK UP WITH SOME FRIENDS...!"
WHAT A JERK! I SHOULD'VE INVITED HIM ALONG... I HOPE HE WASN'T HURT...
...I MADE IT SOUND LIKE HE COULD NEVER BE MY FRIEND.
HOTEL
PARKING
$5

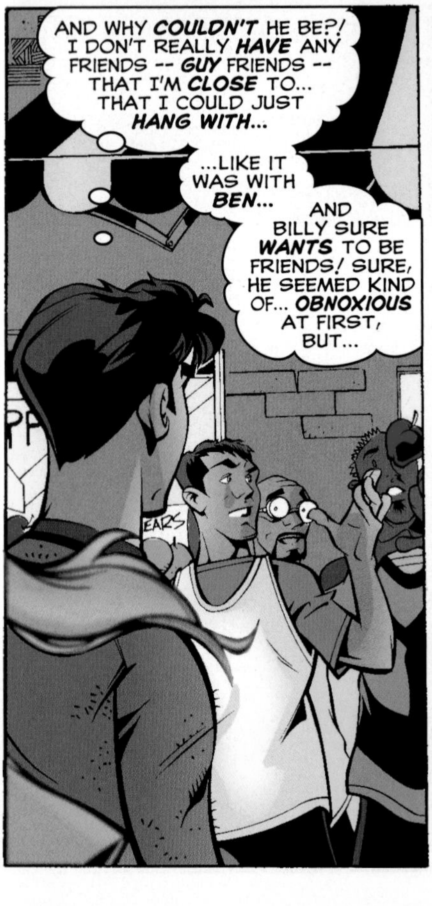
AND WHY COULDN'T HE BE?! I DON'T REALLY HAVE ANY FRIENDS -- GUY FRIENDS -- THAT I'M CLOSE TO... THAT I COULD JUST HANG WITH...
...LIKE IT WAS WITH BEN...
AND BILLY SURE WANTS TO BE FRIENDS! SURE, HE SEEMED KIND OF... OBNOXIOUS AT FIRST, BUT...

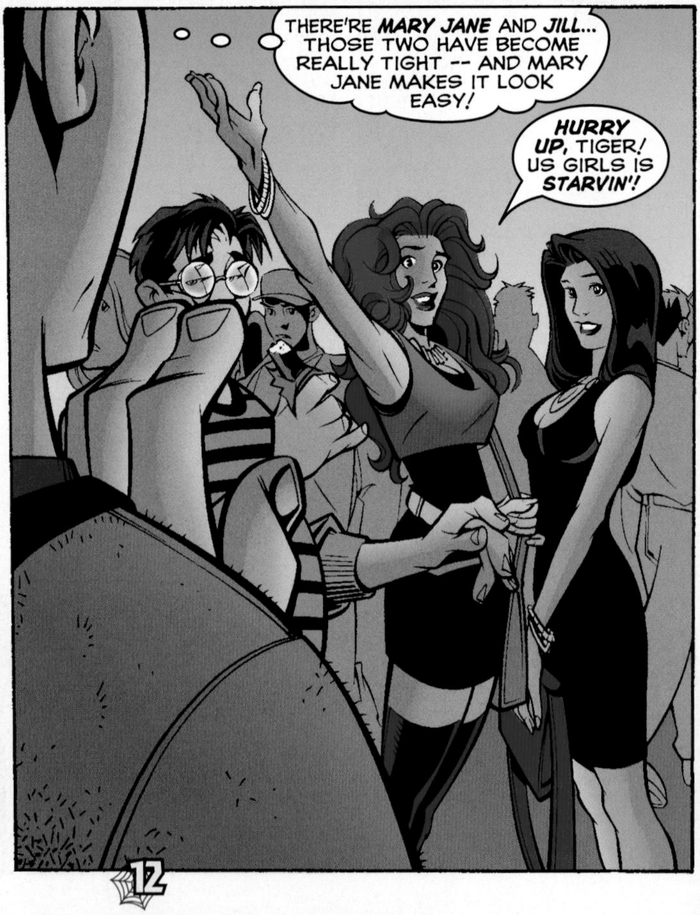
THERE'RE MARY JANE AND JILL... THOSE TWO HAVE BECOME REALLY TIGHT -- AND MARY JANE MAKES IT LOOK EASY!
HURRY UP, TIGER! US GIRLS IS STARVIN'!

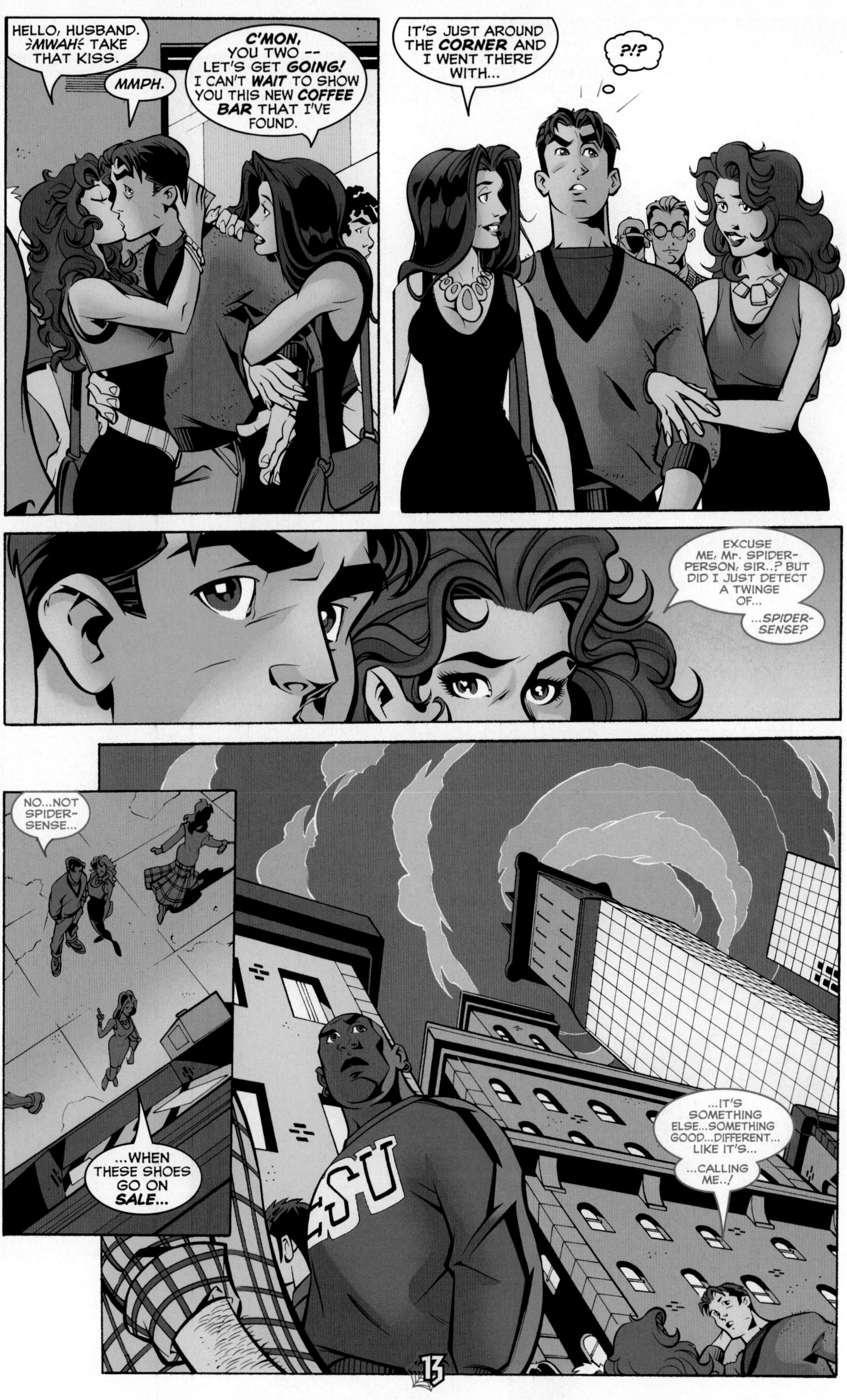
HELLO, HUSBAND. *MWAH* TAKE THAT KISS.
MMPH.
C'MON, YOU TWO -- LET'S GET GOING! I CAN'T WAIT TO SHOW YOU THIS NEW COFFEE BAR THAT I'VE FOUND.
IT'S JUST AROUND THE CORNER AND I WENT THERE WITH...
?!?
EXCUSE ME, Mr. SPIDER-PERSON, SIR..? BUT DID I JUST DETECT A TWINGE OF...
...SPIDER-SENSE?
NO...NOT SPIDER-SENSE...
...WHEN THESE SHOES GO ON SALE...
...IT'S SOMETHING ELSE...SOMETHING GOOD...DIFFERENT... LIKE IT'S...
...CALLING ME..!
ESU

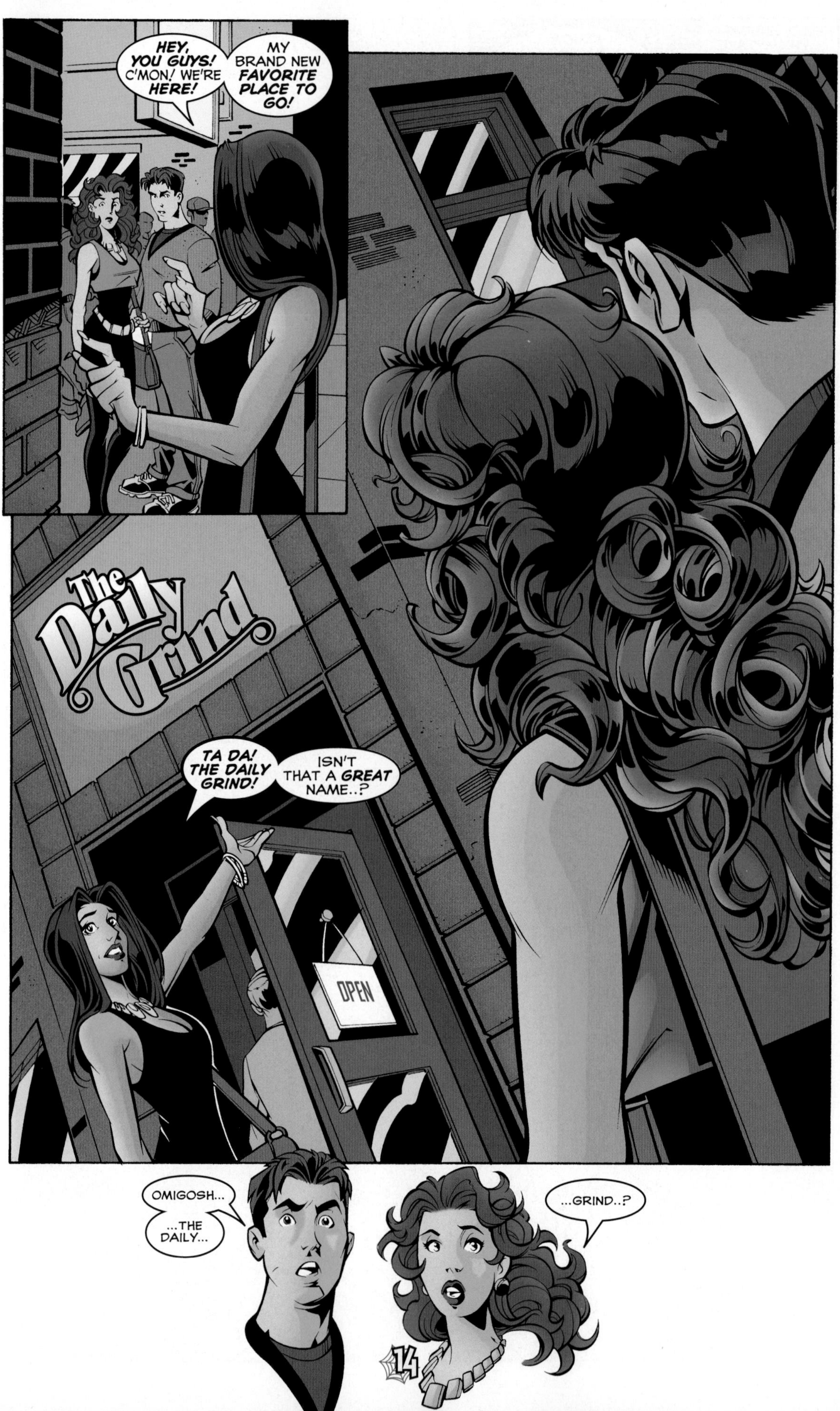
HEY, YOU GUYS! C'MON! WE'RE HERE!
MY BRAND NEW FAVORITE PLACE TO GO!
The Daily Grind
TA DA! THE DAILY GRIND!
ISN'T THAT A GREAT NAME..?
OPEN
OMIGOSH...
...THE DAILY...
...GRIND..?
14

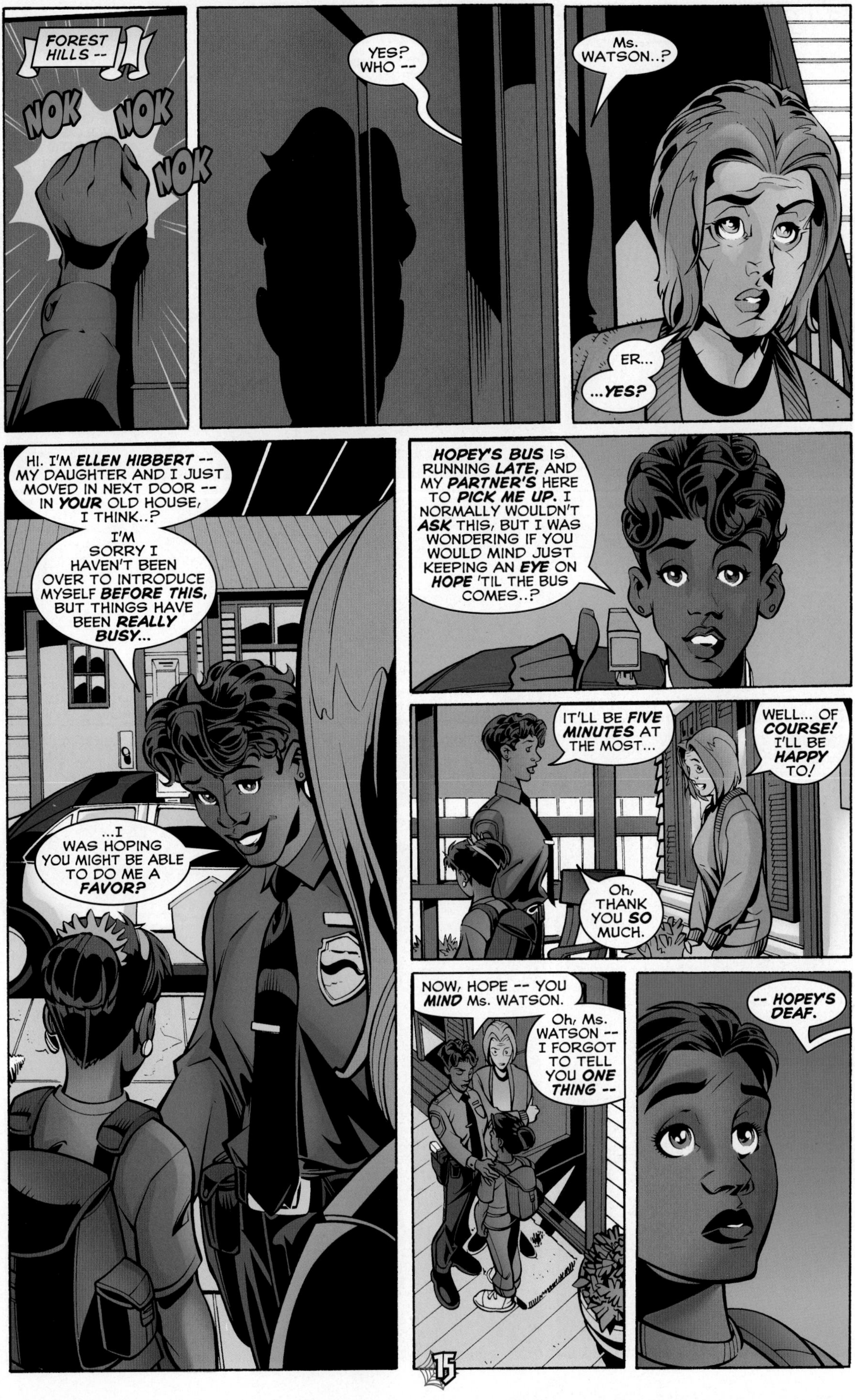
FOREST HILLS --
NOK NOK NOK
YES? WHO --
Ms. WATSON..?
ER...
...YES?
HI. I'M ELLEN HIBBERT -- MY DAUGHTER AND I JUST MOVED IN NEXT DOOR -- IN YOUR OLD HOUSE, I THINK..?
I'M SORRY I HAVEN'T BEEN OVER TO INTRODUCE MYSELF BEFORE THIS, BUT THINGS HAVE BEEN REALLY BUSY...
...I WAS HOPING YOU MIGHT BE ABLE TO DO ME A FAVOR?
HOPEY'S BUS IS RUNNING LATE, AND MY PARTNER'S HERE TO PICK ME UP. I NORMALLY WOULDN'T ASK THIS, BUT I WAS WONDERING IF YOU WOULD MIND JUST KEEPING AN EYE ON HOPE 'TIL THE BUS COMES..?
IT'LL BE FIVE MINUTES AT THE MOST...
WELL... OF COURSE! I'LL BE HAPPY TO!
Oh, THANK YOU SO MUCH.
NOW, HOPE -- YOU MIND Ms. WATSON.
Oh, Ms. WATSON -- I FORGOT TO TELL YOU ONE THING --
-- HOPEY'S DEAF.

INTERLUDE: 1

OM, IT'S...

...BEAUTIFUL! TO THINK -- WE HAVE THE LEGENDARY *'SPHERE'* OF *'SARA-KATH!* IN OUR POSSESSION --

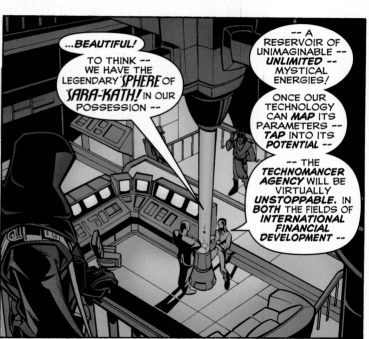

-- A RESERVOIR OF UNIMAGINABLE -- *UNLIMITED* -- MYSTICAL ENERGIES!

ONCE OUR TECHNOLOGY CAN *MAP* ITS PARAMETERS -- *TAP* INTO ITS *POTENTIAL* --

-- THE *TECHNOMANCER AGENCY* WILL BE VIRTUALLY *UNSTOPPABLE.* IN *BOTH* THE FIELDS OF *INTERNATIONAL FINANCIAL DEVELOPMENT* --

-- AND *ARCANIC* CORPORATE TAKE-OVERS!

HAAAARRGH! MAEGIS! MAEGIS SEINREICH!

WHO DARES..?!

IT'S... ...THE... ...*BABYLON PORTAL,* SIR! *AAARRGH!* IT'S... OPENED...

...AND SOMETHING...

...GOD HELP US... ...SOMETHING'S *HERE!*

CHEE

CHEEE

CHEE

CHEE

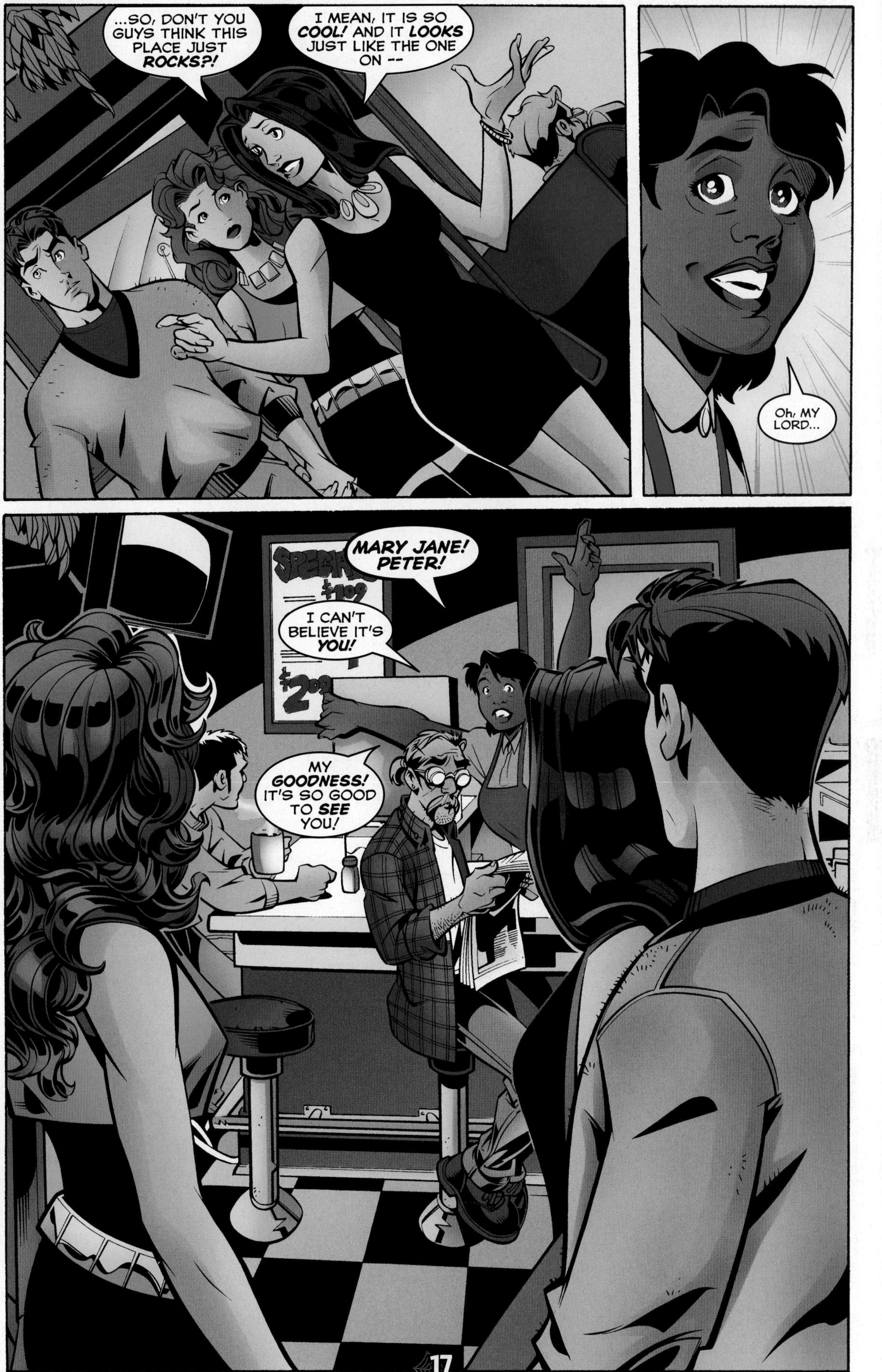
...SO, DON'T YOU GUYS THINK THIS PLACE JUST ROCKS?!
I MEAN, IT IS SO COOL! AND IT LOOKS JUST LIKE THE ONE ON --
Oh, MY LORD...
MARY JANE! PETER!
I CAN'T BELIEVE IT'S YOU!
MY GOODNESS! IT'S SO GOOD TO SEE YOU!

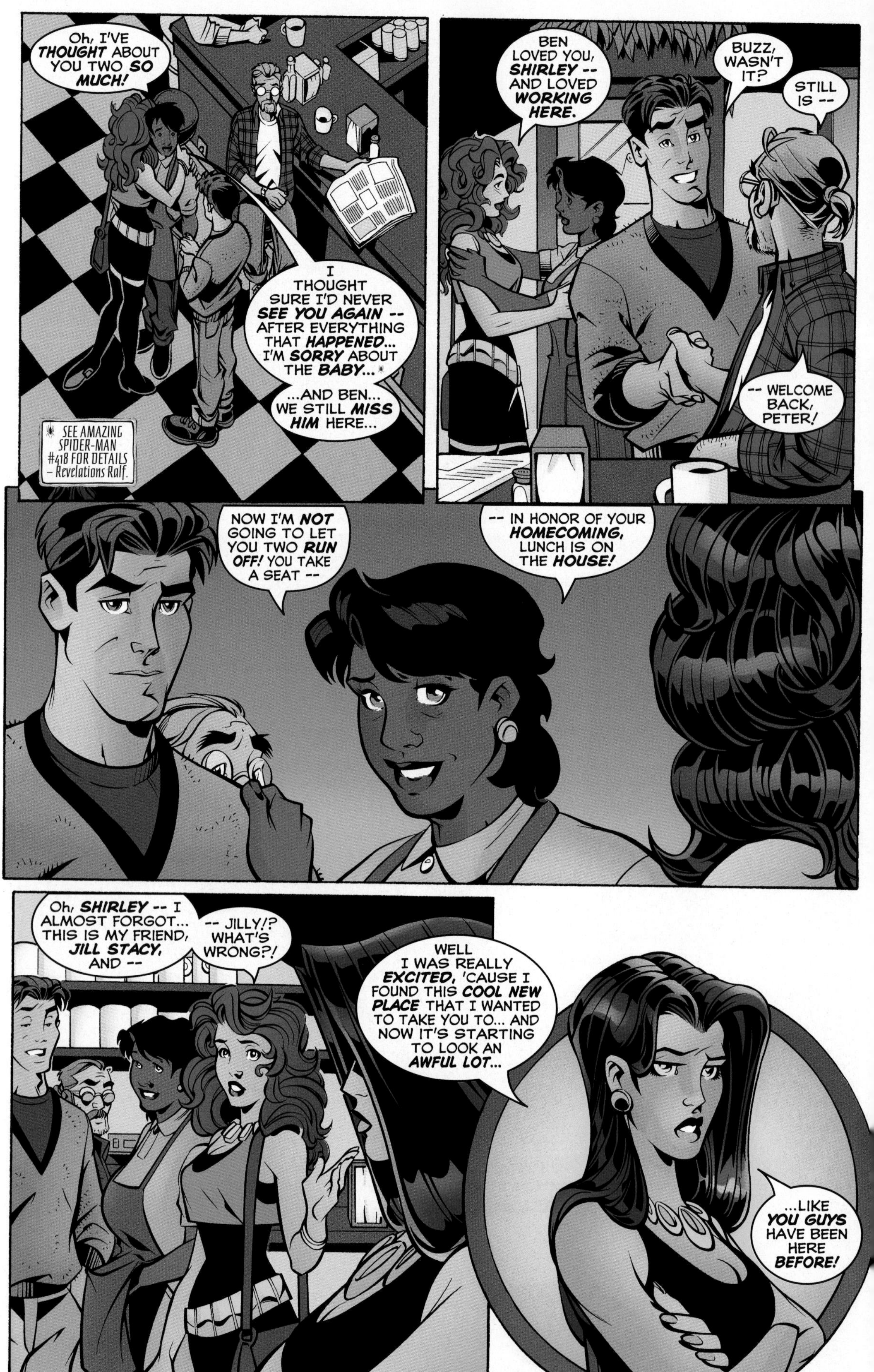
Oh, I'VE THOUGHT ABOUT YOU TWO SO MUCH!
I THOUGHT SURE I'D NEVER SEE YOU AGAIN -- AFTER EVERYTHING THAT HAPPENED... I'M SORRY ABOUT THE BABY...
...AND BEN... WE STILL MISS HIM HERE...
SEE AMAZING SPIDER-MAN #418 FOR DETAILS – Revelations Ralf.
BEN LOVED YOU, SHIRLEY -- AND LOVED WORKING HERE.
BUZZ, WASN'T IT?
STILL IS --
-- WELCOME BACK, PETER!
NOW I'M NOT GOING TO LET YOU TWO RUN OFF! YOU TAKE A SEAT --
-- IN HONOR OF YOUR HOMECOMING, LUNCH IS ON THE HOUSE!
Oh, SHIRLEY -- I ALMOST FORGOT... THIS IS MY FRIEND, JILL STACY, AND --
-- JILLY!? WHAT'S WRONG?!
WELL I WAS REALLY EXCITED, 'CAUSE I FOUND THIS COOL NEW PLACE THAT I WANTED TO TAKE YOU TO... AND NOW IT'S STARTING TO LOOK AN AWFUL LOT...
...LIKE YOU GUYS HAVE BEEN HERE BEFORE!

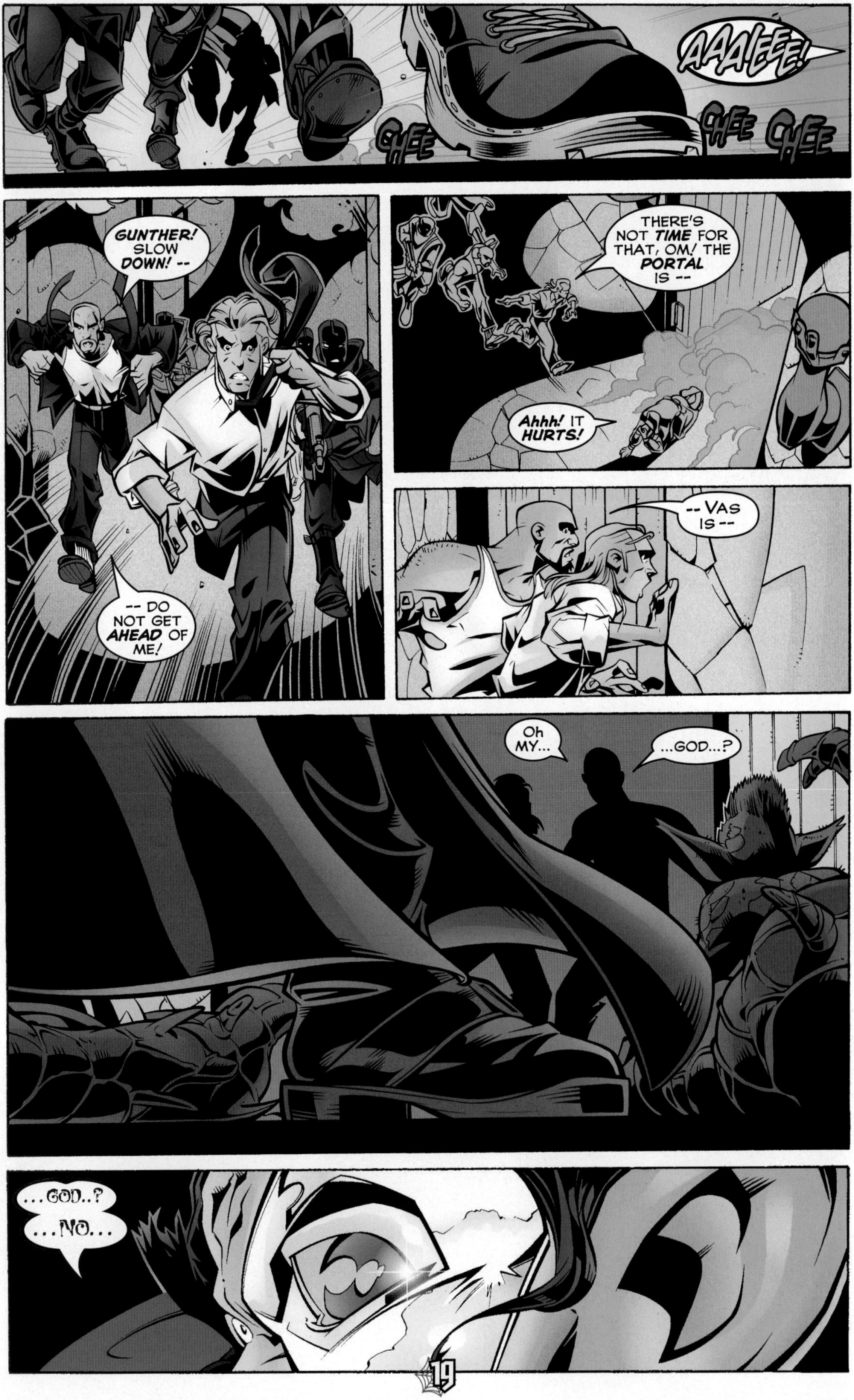
AAAIEEE!
CHEE
CHEE CHEE
GUNTHER! SLOW DOWN! --
-- DO NOT GET AHEAD OF ME!
THERE'S NOT TIME FOR THAT, OM! THE PORTAL IS --
Ahhh! IT HURTS!
-- VAS IS --
Oh MY...
...GOD...?
...GOD..?
...NO...

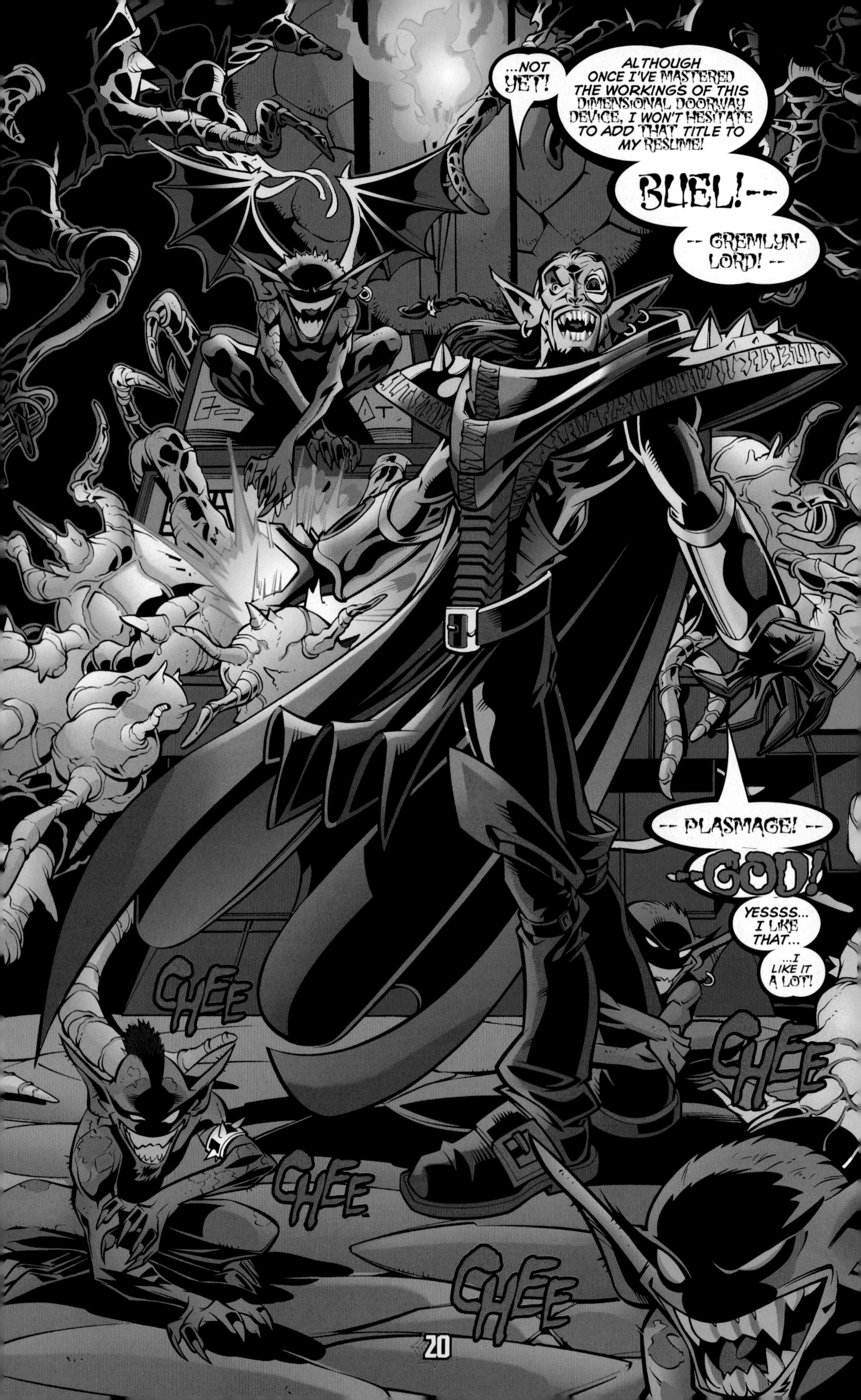
...NOT YET!
ALTHOUGH ONCE I'VE MASTERED THE WORKINGS OF THIS DIMENSIONAL DOORWAY DEVICE, I WON'T HESITATE TO ADD THAT TITLE TO MY RESUME!
BUEL!--
-- GREMLYN-LORD! --
-- PLASMAGE! --
GOD!
YESSSS... I LIKE THAT...
...I LIKE IT A LOT!
CHEE
CHEE
CHEE
CHEE

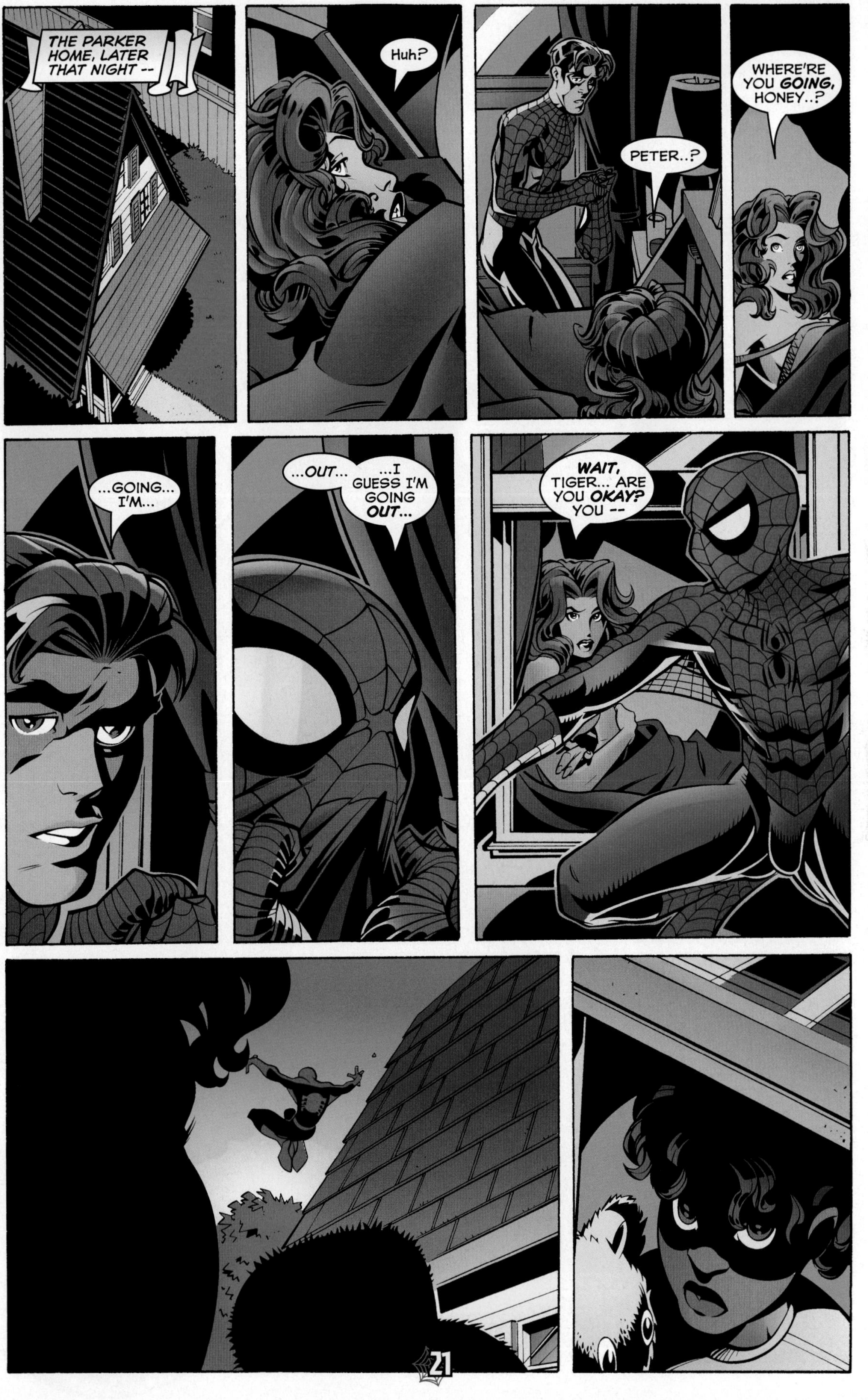
THE PARKER HOME, LATER THAT NIGHT --
Huh?
PETER...?
WHERE'RE YOU GOING, HONEY..?
...GOING... I'M...
...OUT...
...I GUESS I'M GOING OUT...
WAIT, TIGER... ARE YOU OKAY? YOU --

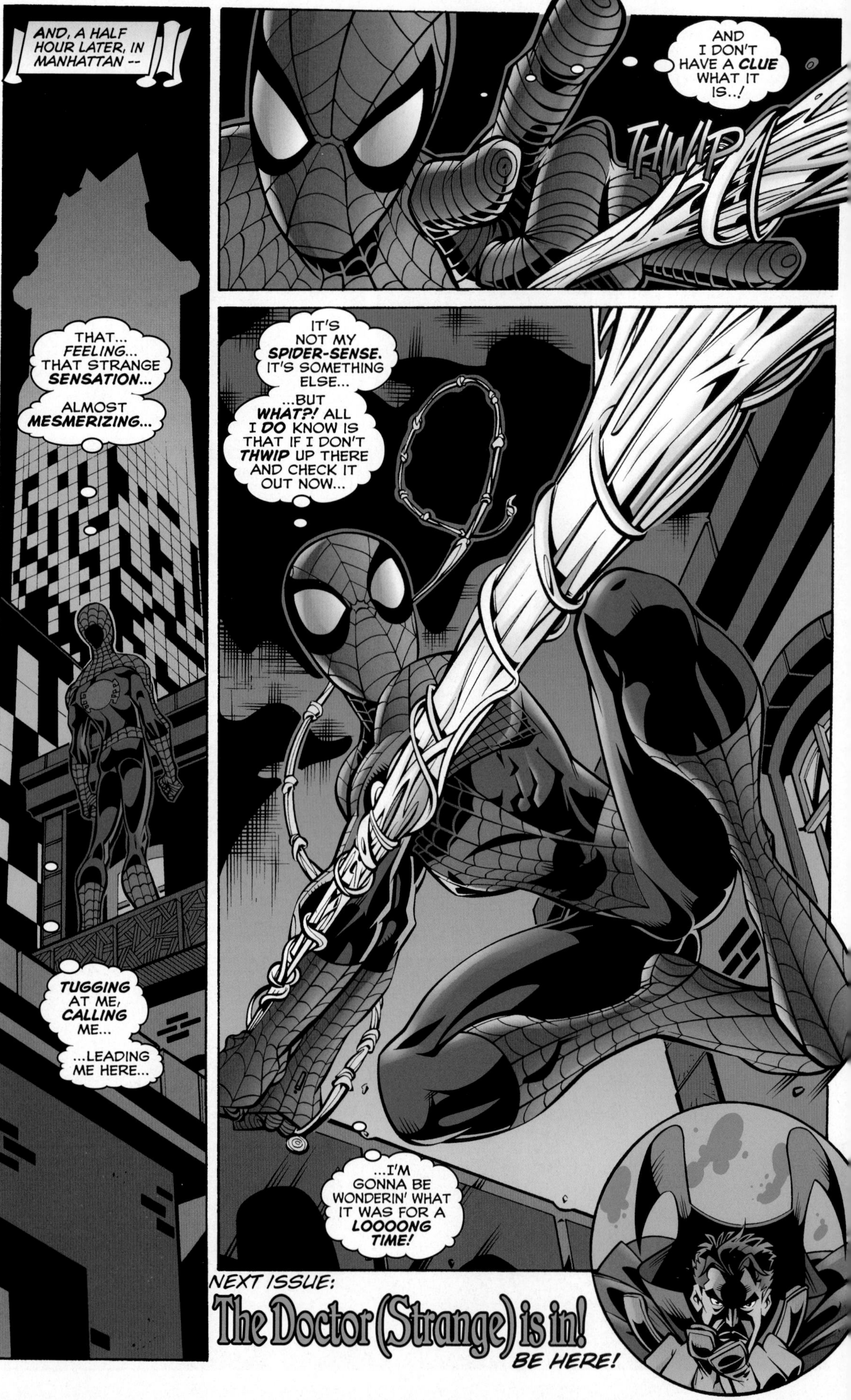

AND, A HALF HOUR LATER, IN MANHATTAN --
THAT... FEELING... THAT STRANGE SENSATION...
ALMOST MESMERIZING...
TUGGING AT ME, CALLING ME...
...LEADING ME HERE...
AND I DON'T HAVE A CLUE WHAT IT IS..!
THWIP
IT'S NOT MY SPIDER-SENSE. IT'S SOMETHING ELSE...
...BUT WHAT?! ALL I DO KNOW IS THAT IF I DON'T THWIP UP THERE AND CHECK IT OUT NOW...
...I'M GONNA BE WONDERIN' WHAT IT WAS FOR A LOOOONG TIME!
NEXT ISSUE:
The Doctor (Strange) is in!
BE HERE!

MARVEL COMICS
THE WORLD'S GREATEST COMICS!
THE SENSATIONAL SPIDER-MAN
DEC #22
APPROVED BY THE COMICS CODE AUTHORITY
SPIDEY & DOCTOR STRANGE--
--Trapped in a DARK & DISTANT DIMENSION!
ATOMIC
DEZAGO WIERINGO CASE

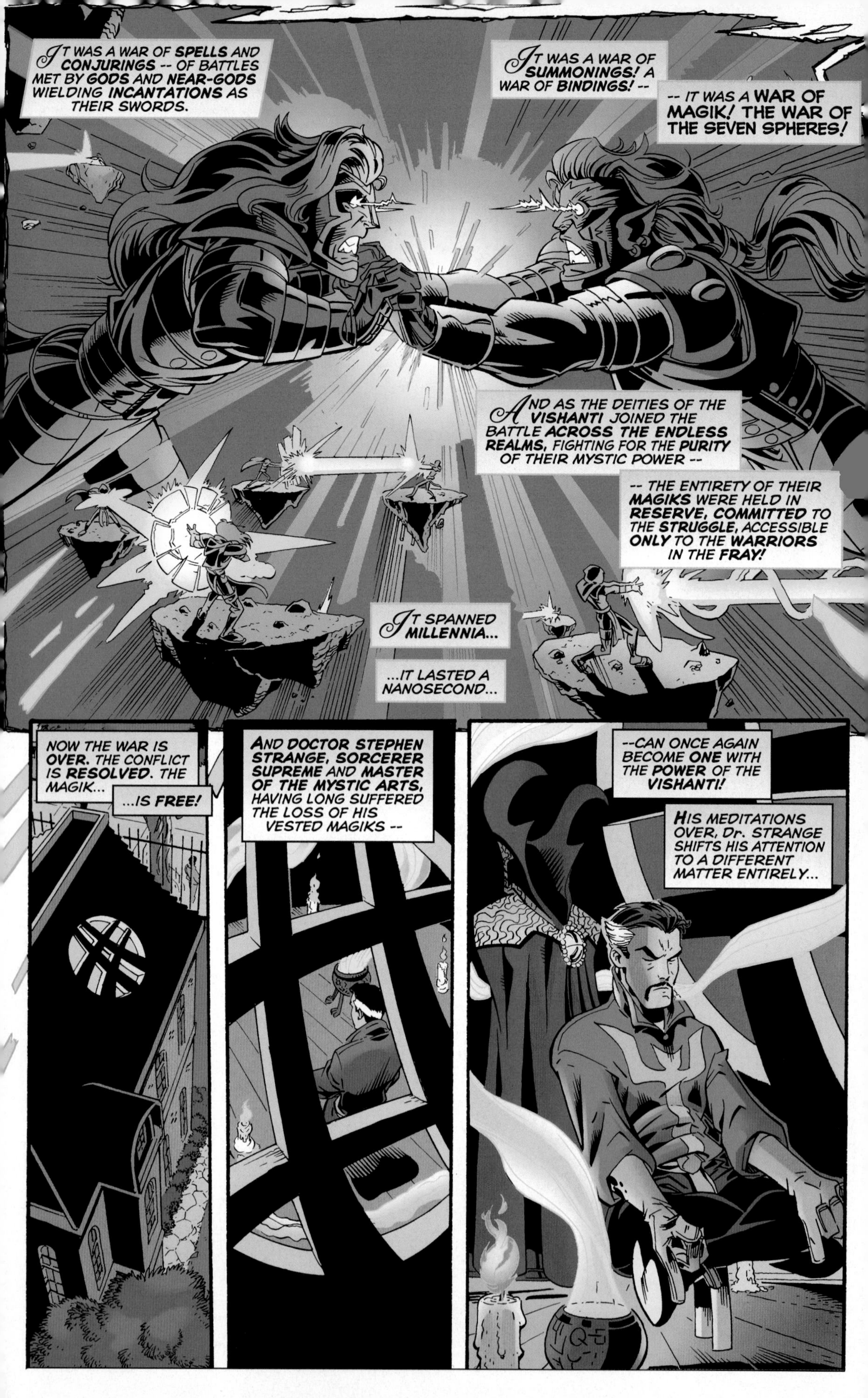
IT WAS A WAR OF SPELLS AND CONJURINGS -- OF BATTLES MET BY GODS AND NEAR-GODS WIELDING INCANTATIONS AS THEIR SWORDS.
IT WAS A WAR OF SUMMONINGS! A WAR OF BINDINGS! --
-- IT WAS A WAR OF MAGIK! THE WAR OF THE SEVEN SPHERES!
AND AS THE DEITIES OF THE VISHANTI JOINED THE BATTLE ACROSS THE ENDLESS REALMS, FIGHTING FOR THE PURITY OF THEIR MYSTIC POWER --
-- THE ENTIRETY OF THEIR MAGIKS WERE HELD IN RESERVE, COMMITTED TO THE STRUGGLE, ACCESSIBLE ONLY TO THE WARRIORS IN THE FRAY!
IT SPANNED MILLENNIA...
...IT LASTED A NANOSECOND...
NOW THE WAR IS OVER. THE CONFLICT IS RESOLVED. THE MAGIK...
...IS FREE!
AND DOCTOR STEPHEN STRANGE, SORCERER SUPREME AND MASTER OF THE MYSTIC ARTS, HAVING LONG SUFFERED THE LOSS OF HIS VESTED MAGIKS --
--CAN ONCE AGAIN BECOME ONE WITH THE POWER OF THE VISHANTI!
HIS MEDITATIONS OVER, Dr. STRANGE SHIFTS HIS ATTENTION TO A DIFFERENT MATTER ENTIRELY...

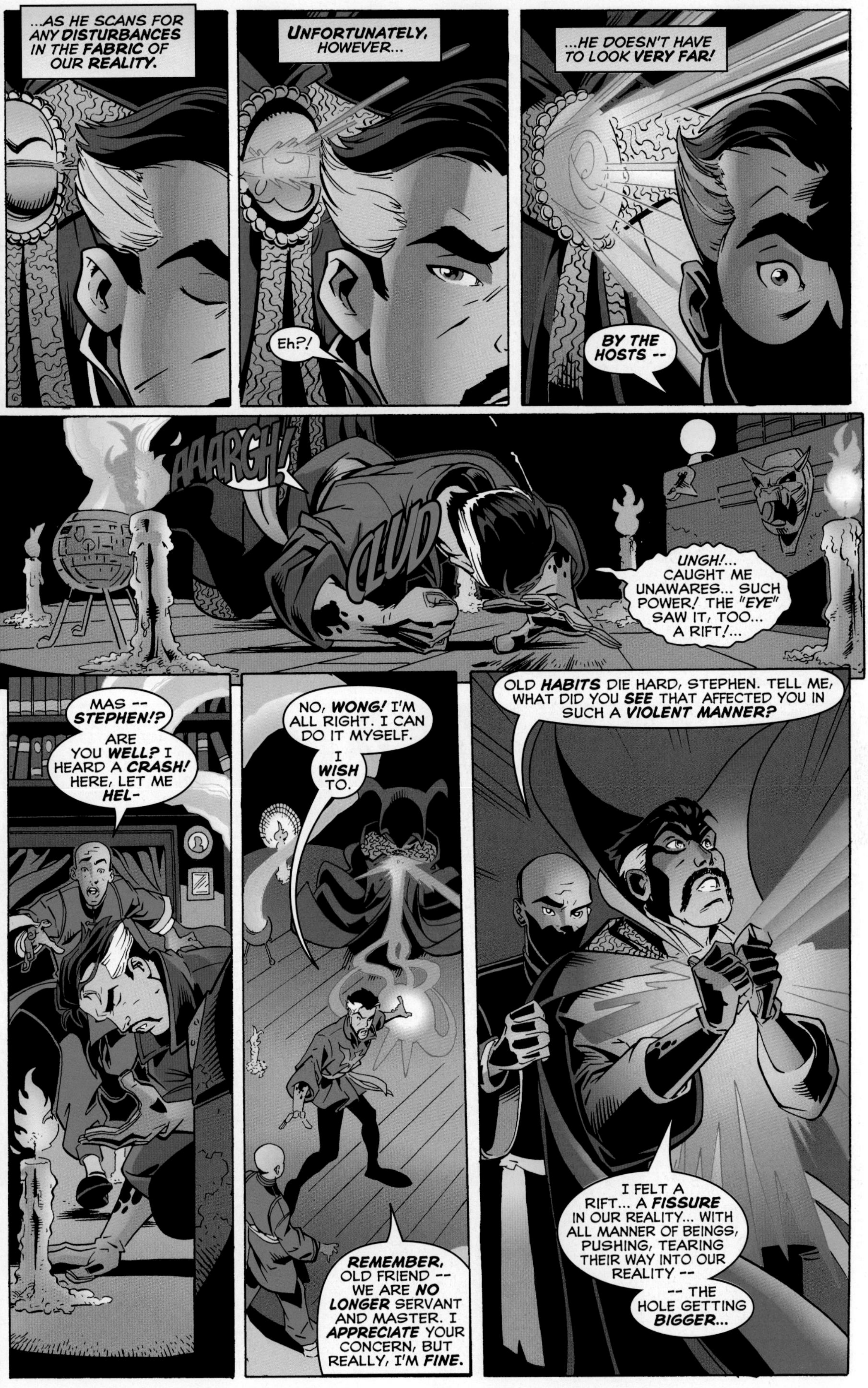
...AS HE SCANS FOR ANY DISTURBANCES IN THE FABRIC OF OUR REALITY.
UNFORTUNATELY, HOWEVER...
Eh?!
...HE DOESN'T HAVE TO LOOK VERY FAR!
BY THE HOSTS --
AAARGH!
CLUD
UNGH!... CAUGHT ME UNAWARES... SUCH POWER! THE "EYE" SAW IT, TOO... A RIFT!...
MAS -- STEPHEN!? ARE YOU WELL? I HEARD A CRASH! HERE, LET ME HEL-
NO, WONG! I'M ALL RIGHT. I CAN DO IT MYSELF.
I WISH TO.
REMEMBER, OLD FRIEND -- WE ARE NO LONGER SERVANT AND MASTER. I APPRECIATE YOUR CONCERN, BUT REALLY, I'M FINE.
OLD HABITS DIE HARD, STEPHEN. TELL ME, WHAT DID YOU SEE THAT AFFECTED YOU IN SUCH A VIOLENT MANNER?
I FELT A RIFT... A FISSURE IN OUR REALITY... WITH ALL MANNER OF BEINGS, PUSHING, TEARING THEIR WAY INTO OUR REALITY --
-- THE HOLE GETTING BIGGER...

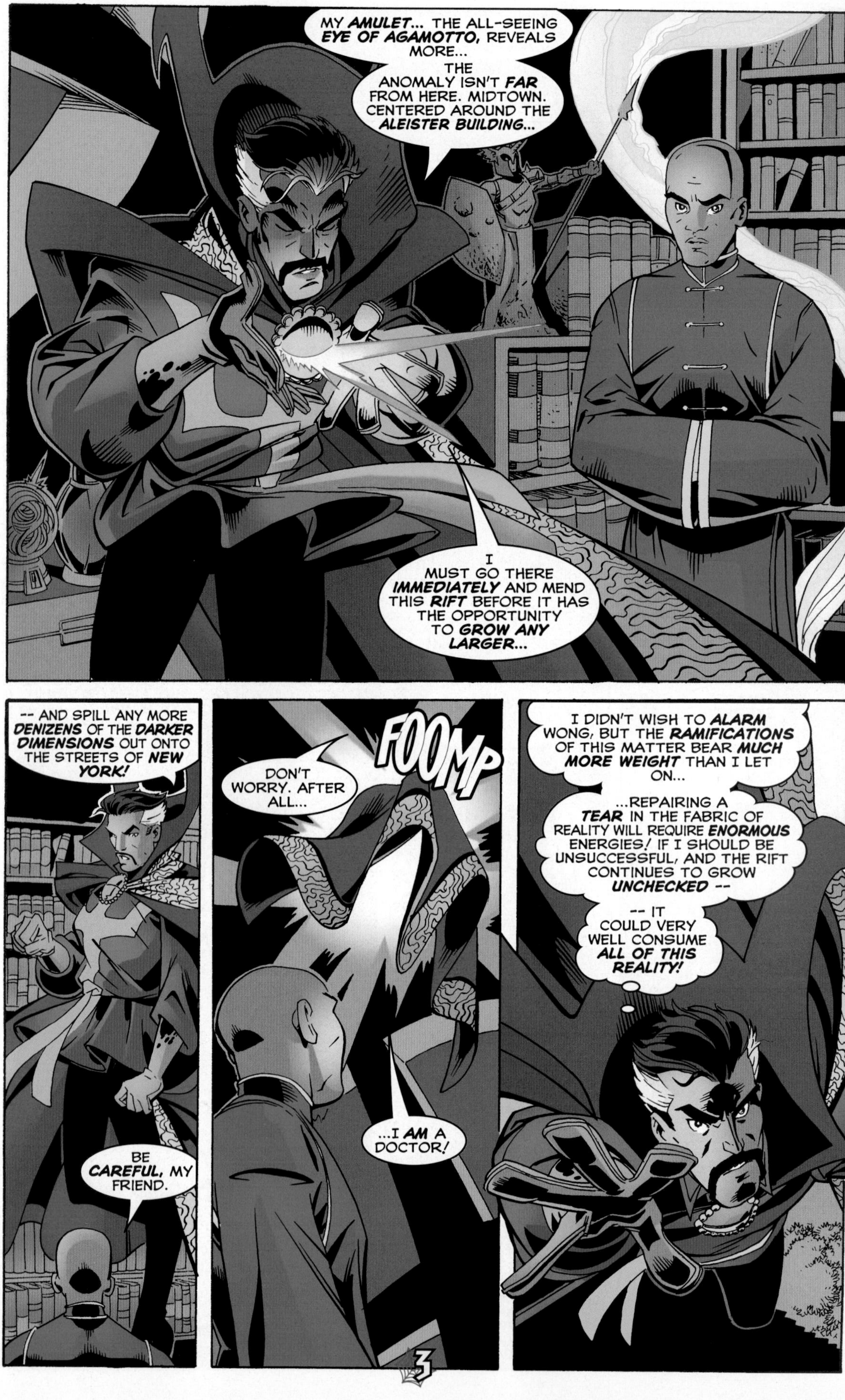
MY AMULET... THE ALL-SEEING EYE OF AGAMOTTO, REVEALS MORE...
THE ANOMALY ISN'T FAR FROM HERE. MIDTOWN. CENTERED AROUND THE ALEISTER BUILDING...
I MUST GO THERE IMMEDIATELY AND MEND THIS RIFT BEFORE IT HAS THE OPPORTUNITY TO GROW ANY LARGER...
-- AND SPILL ANY MORE DENIZENS OF THE DARKER DIMENSIONS OUT ONTO THE STREETS OF NEW YORK!
BE CAREFUL, MY FRIEND.
FOOMP
DON'T WORRY. AFTER ALL...
...I AM A DOCTOR!
I DIDN'T WISH TO ALARM WONG, BUT THE RAMIFICATIONS OF THIS MATTER BEAR MUCH MORE WEIGHT THAN I LET ON...
...REPAIRING A TEAR IN THE FABRIC OF REALITY WILL REQUIRE ENORMOUS ENERGIES! IF I SHOULD BE UNSUCCESSFUL, AND THE RIFT CONTINUES TO GROW UNCHECKED --
-- IT COULD VERY WELL CONSUME ALL OF THIS REALITY!

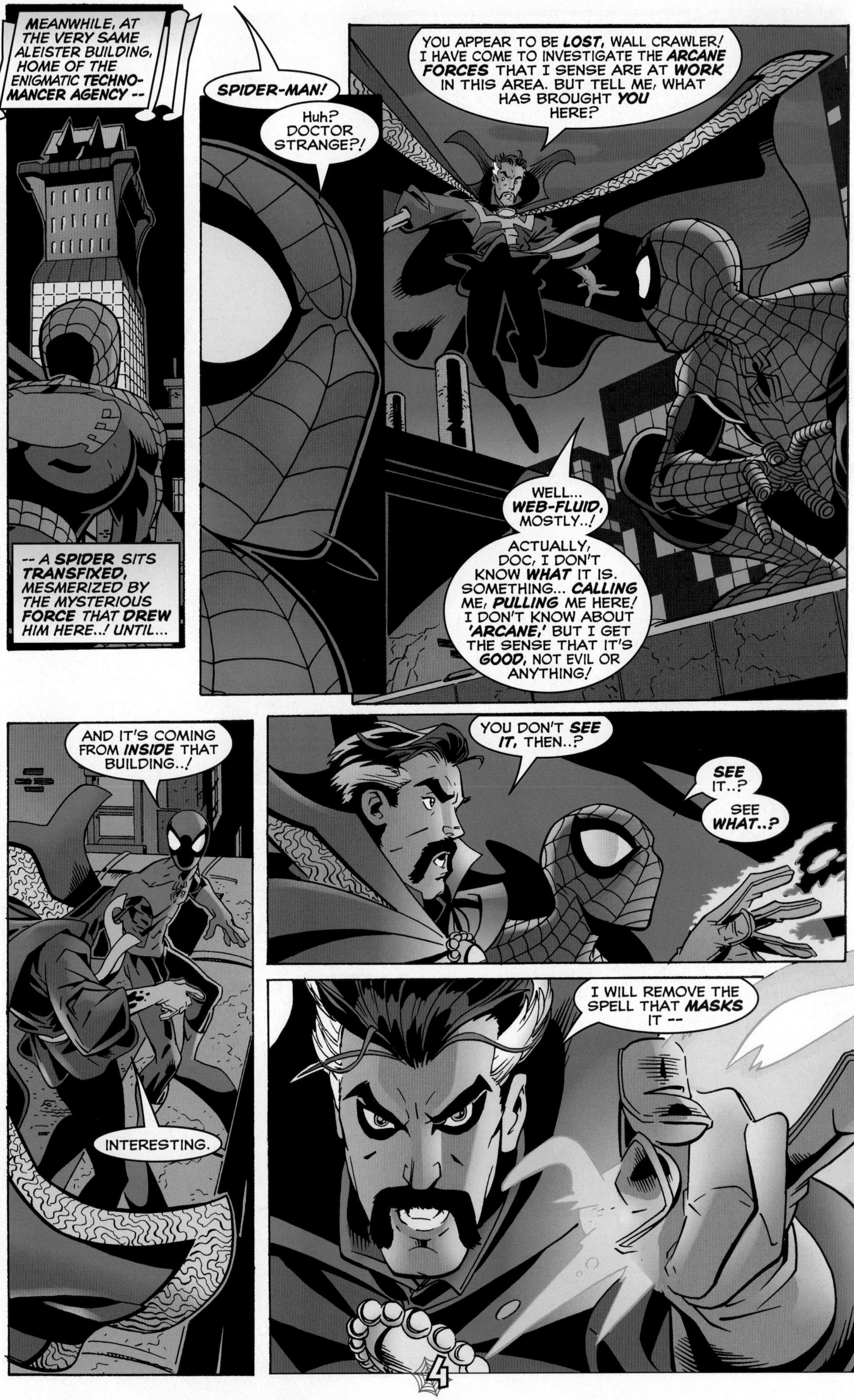

MEANWHILE, AT THE VERY SAME ALEISTER BUILDING, HOME OF THE ENIGMATIC TECHNO-MANCER AGENCY --
-- A SPIDER SITS TRANSFIXED, MESMERIZED BY THE MYSTERIOUS FORCE THAT DREW HIM HERE..! UNTIL...
SPIDER-MAN!
Huh? DOCTOR STRANGE?!
YOU APPEAR TO BE LOST, WALL CRAWLER! I HAVE COME TO INVESTIGATE THE ARCANE FORCES THAT I SENSE ARE AT WORK IN THIS AREA. BUT TELL ME, WHAT HAS BROUGHT YOU HERE?
WELL... WEB-FLUID, MOSTLY..!
ACTUALLY, DOC, I DON'T KNOW WHAT IT IS. SOMETHING... CALLING ME, PULLING ME HERE! I DON'T KNOW ABOUT 'ARCANE,' BUT I GET THE SENSE THAT IT'S GOOD, NOT EVIL OR ANYTHING!
AND IT'S COMING FROM INSIDE THAT BUILDING..!
INTERESTING.
YOU DON'T SEE IT, THEN..?
SEE IT..?
SEE WHAT..?
I WILL REMOVE THE SPELL THAT MASKS IT --

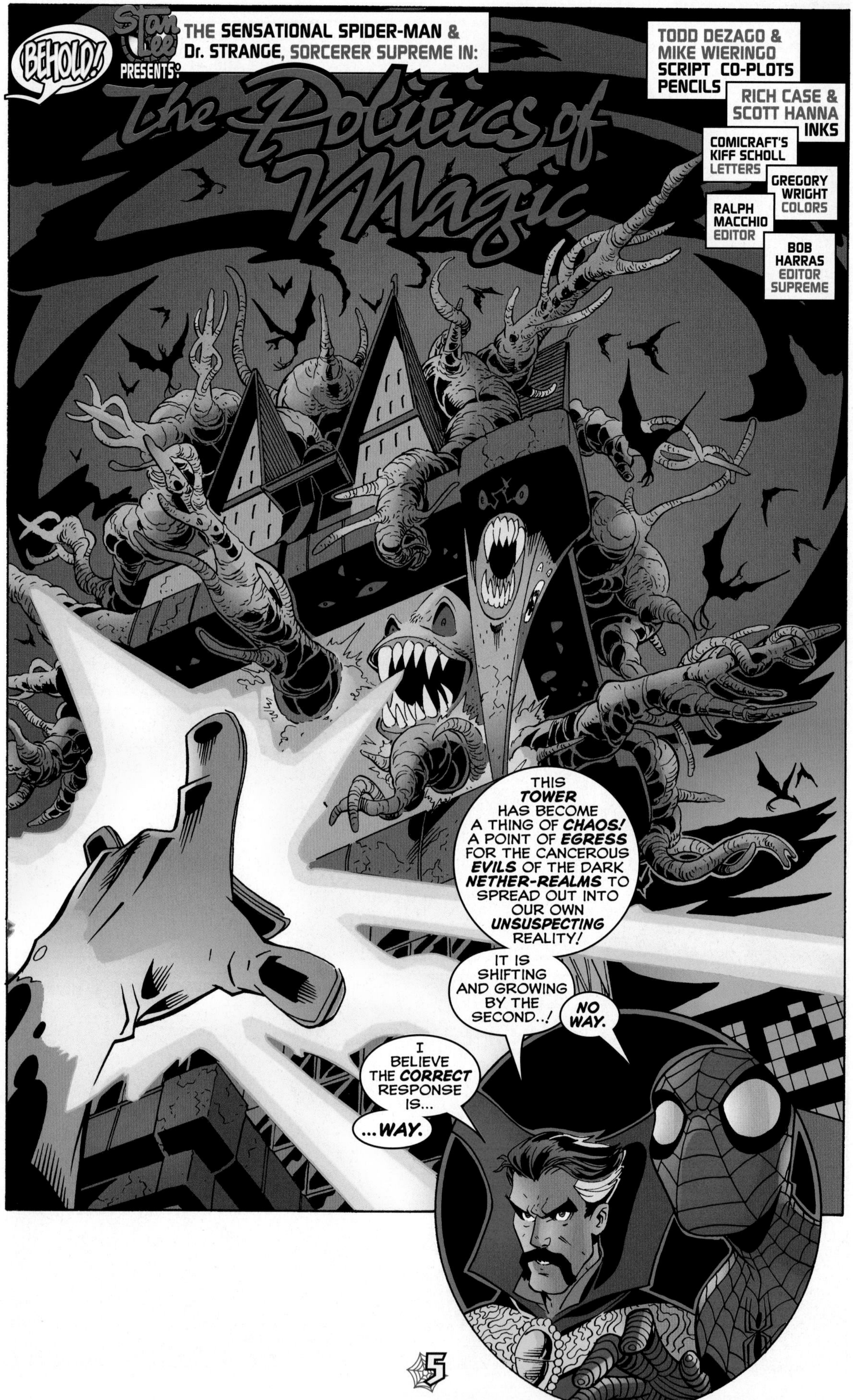
BEHOLD!
Stan Lee PRESENTS:
THE SENSATIONAL SPIDER-MAN & Dr. STRANGE, SORCERER SUPREME IN:
The Politics of Magic
TODD DEZAGO & MIKE WIERINGO SCRIPT CO-PLOTS PENCILS
RICH CASE & SCOTT HANNA INKS
COMICRAFT'S KIFF SCHOLL LETTERS
GREGORY WRIGHT COLORS
RALPH MACCHIO EDITOR
BOB HARRAS EDITOR SUPREME
THIS TOWER HAS BECOME A THING OF CHAOS! A POINT OF EGRESS FOR THE CANCEROUS EVILS OF THE DARK NETHER-REALMS TO SPREAD OUT INTO OUR OWN UNSUSPECTING REALITY!
IT IS SHIFTING AND GROWING BY THE SECOND..!
NO WAY.
I BELIEVE THE CORRECT RESPONSE IS...
...WAY.

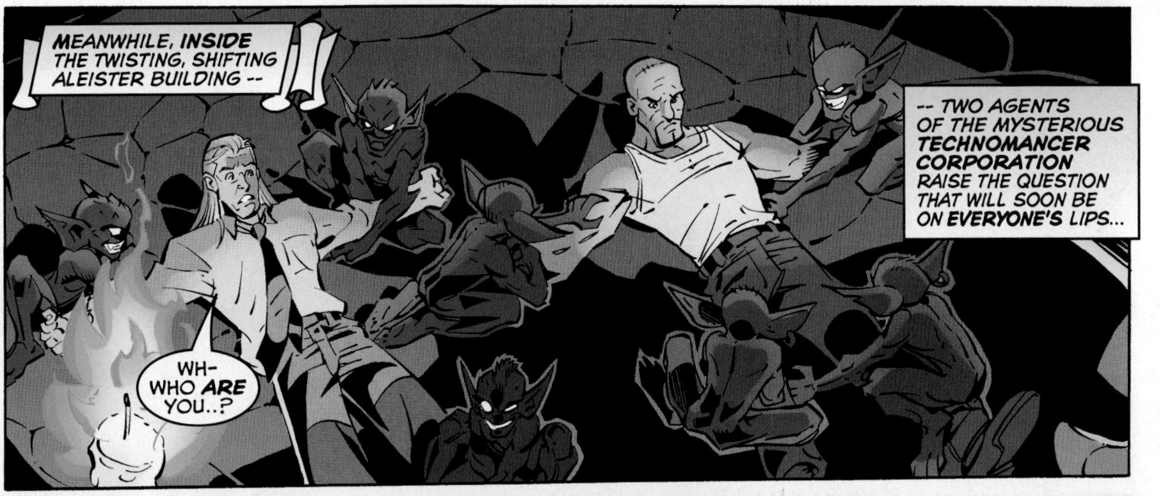
MEANWHILE, INSIDE THE TWISTING, SHIFTING ALEISTER BUILDING --
-- TWO AGENTS OF THE MYSTERIOUS TECHNOMANCER CORPORATION RAISE THE QUESTION THAT WILL SOON BE ON EVERYONE'S LIPS...
WH- WHO ARE YOU..?

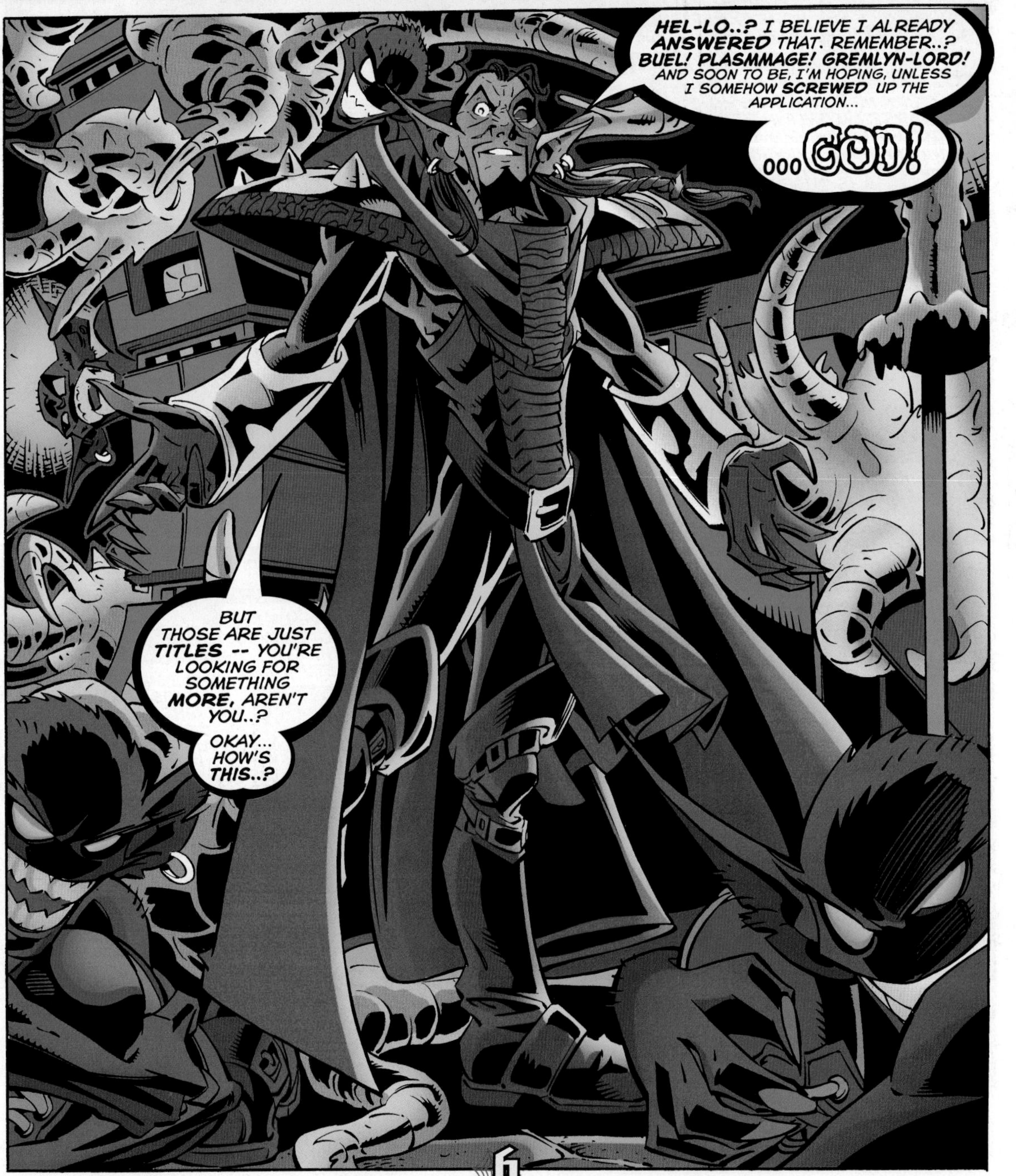
HEL-LO..? I BELIEVE I ALREADY ANSWERED THAT. REMEMBER..? BUEL! PLASMMAGE! GREMLYN-LORD! AND SOON TO BE, I'M HOPING, UNLESS I SOMEHOW SCREWED UP THE APPLICATION...
oooGOD!
BUT THOSE ARE JUST TITLES -- YOU'RE LOOKING FOR SOMETHING MORE, AREN'T YOU..?
OKAY... HOW'S THIS..?

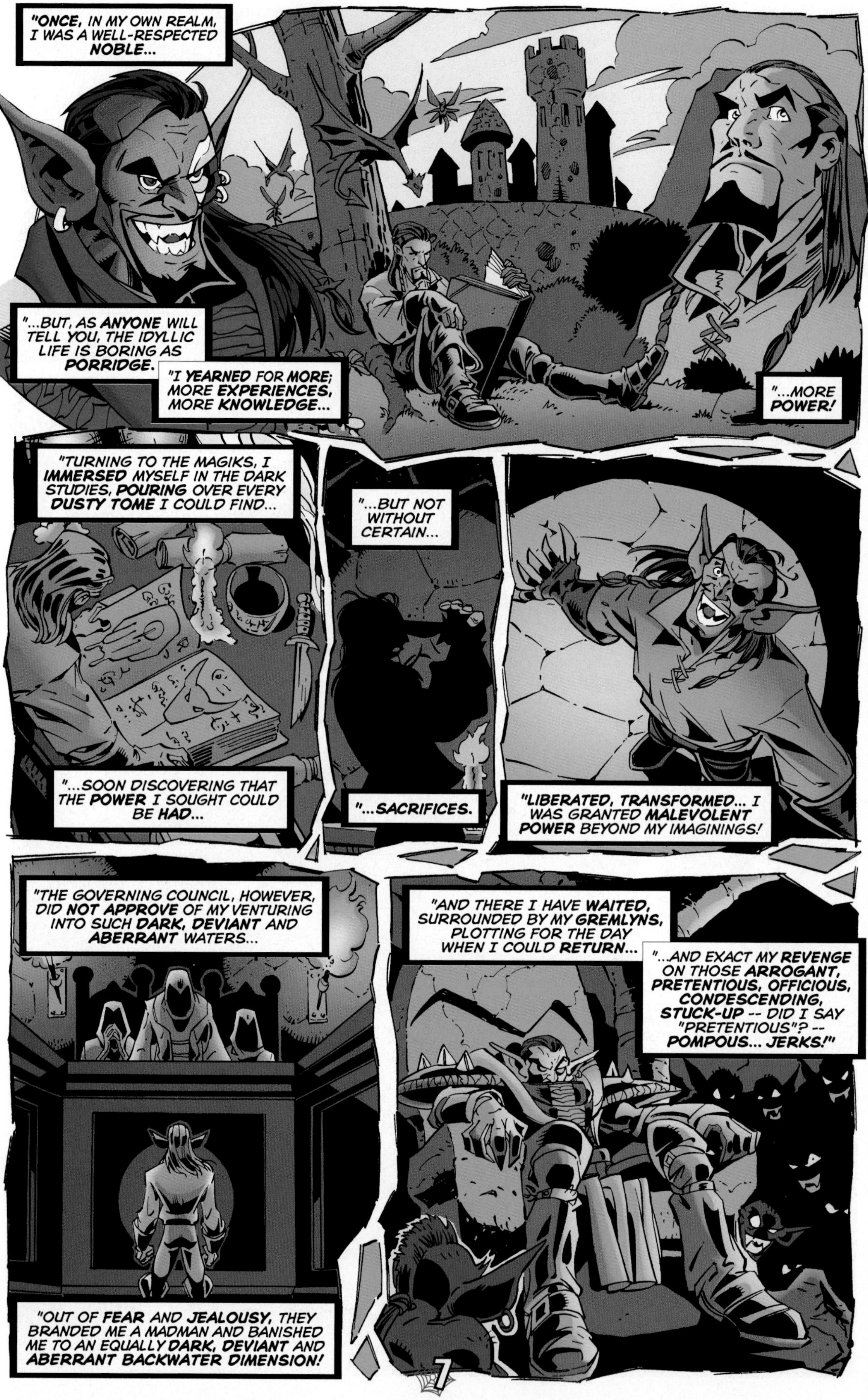
"ONCE, IN MY OWN REALM, I WAS A WELL-RESPECTED NOBLE...
"...BUT, AS ANYONE WILL TELL YOU, THE IDYLLIC LIFE IS BORING AS PORRIDGE.
"I YEARNED FOR MORE; MORE EXPERIENCES, MORE KNOWLEDGE...
"...MORE POWER!
"TURNING TO THE MAGIKS, I IMMERSED MYSELF IN THE DARK STUDIES, POURING OVER EVERY DUSTY TOME I COULD FIND...
"...SOON DISCOVERING THAT THE POWER I SOUGHT COULD BE HAD...
"...BUT NOT WITHOUT CERTAIN...
"...SACRIFICES.
"LIBERATED, TRANSFORMED... I WAS GRANTED MALEVOLENT POWER BEYOND MY IMAGININGS!
"THE GOVERNING COUNCIL, HOWEVER, DID NOT APPROVE OF MY VENTURING INTO SUCH DARK, DEVIANT AND ABERRANT WATERS...
"OUT OF FEAR AND JEALOUSY, THEY BRANDED ME A MADMAN AND BANISHED ME TO AN EQUALLY DARK, DEVIANT AND ABERRANT BACKWATER DIMENSION!
"AND THERE I HAVE WAITED, SURROUNDED BY MY GREMLYNS, PLOTTING FOR THE DAY WHEN I COULD RETURN...
"...AND EXACT MY REVENGE ON THOSE ARROGANT, PRETENTIOUS, OFFICIOUS, CONDESCENDING, STUCK-UP -- DID I SAY "PRETENTIOUS"? -- POMPOUS... JERKS!"

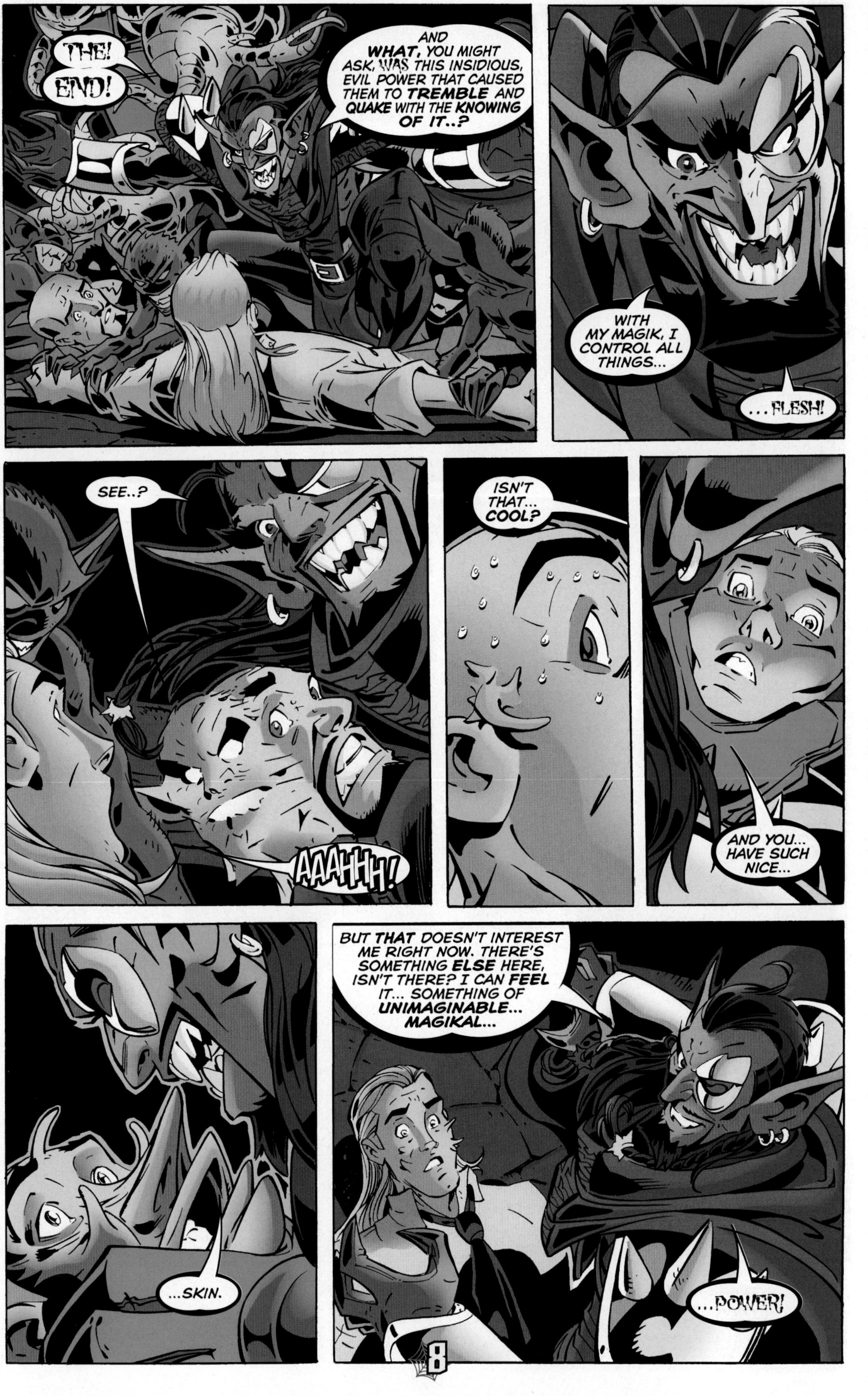
THE!
END!
AND WHAT, YOU MIGHT ASK, WAS THIS INSIDIOUS, EVIL POWER THAT CAUSED THEM TO TREMBLE AND QUAKE WITH THE KNOWING OF IT..?
WITH MY MAGIK, I CONTROL ALL THINGS...
...FLESH!
SEE..?
AAAHHH!
ISN'T THAT... COOL?
AND YOU... HAVE SUCH NICE...
...SKIN.
BUT THAT DOESN'T INTEREST ME RIGHT NOW. THERE'S SOMETHING ELSE HERE, ISN'T THERE? I CAN FEEL IT... SOMETHING OF UNIMAGINABLE... MAGIKAL...
...POWER!

THE APARTMENT OF ONE *BILLY WALTERS*, FREELANCE REPORTER FOR THE NEW YORK *DAILY BUGLE* --

NOK NOK NOK

NOK NOK NOK

DON'T GO IN THERE, SCULLY -- HE'S GOT A --

OKAY, DUDE -- I'M COMIN'! KEEP YER UNDEROOS O--

WHOA! M-M--

WALTERS... LET ME IN.

Mr. JAMESON! COME IN! SORRY ABOUT THE *MESS*, SIR. I DIDN'T -- I MEAN --

-- WHAT ARE YOU *DOING* HERE..?

LISTEN, *WALTERS* -- I DON'T KNOW WHAT YOU'VE *HEARD* ABOUT WHAT'S *GOING ON* DOWN AT THE BUGLE...

...ABOUT THE *TAKEOVER* AND *OSBORN*...

PIZZA

COLA

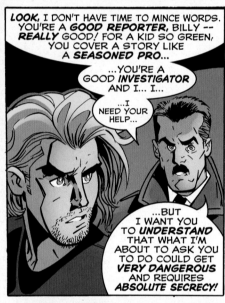

LOOK, I DON'T HAVE TIME TO MINCE WORDS. YOU'RE A *GOOD REPORTER*, BILLY -- *REALLY* GOOD! FOR A KID SO GREEN, YOU COVER A STORY LIKE A *SEASONED PRO*...

...YOU'RE A GOOD *INVESTIGATOR* AND I... I...

...I NEED YOUR HELP...

...BUT I WANT YOU TO *UNDERSTAND* THAT WHAT I'M ABOUT TO ASK YOU TO DO COULD GET *VERY DANGEROUS* AND REQUIRES *ABSOLUTE SECRECY!*

YOU --

-- YOU CAN *COUNT* ON ME, Mr. JAMESON.

I'M THERE.

GOOD... NOW HERE'S WHAT I NEED YOU TO DO...

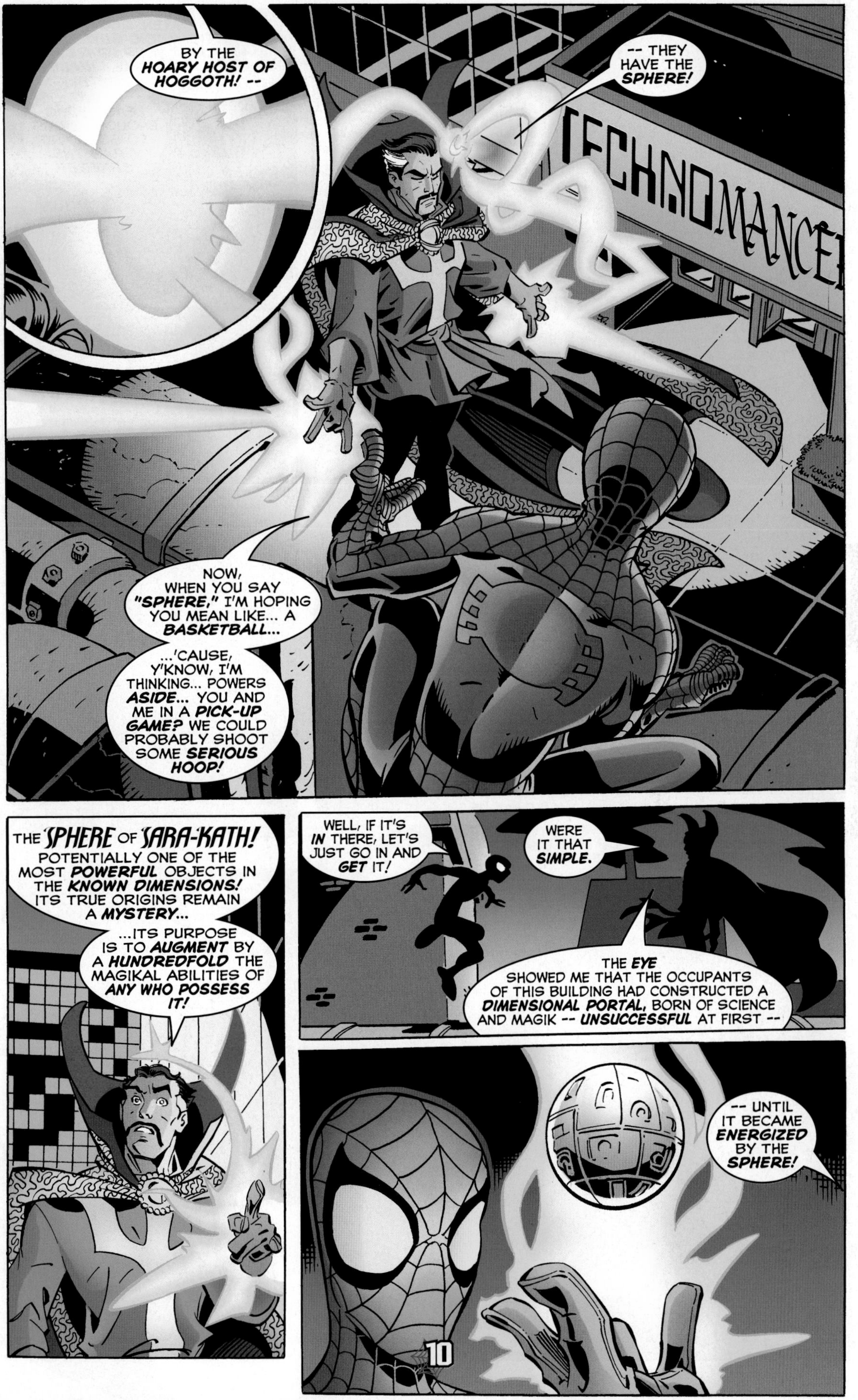
BY THE HOARY HOST OF HOGGOTH! --
-- THEY HAVE THE SPHERE!
TECHNOMANCER
NOW, WHEN YOU SAY "SPHERE," I'M HOPING YOU MEAN LIKE... A BASKETBALL...
...'CAUSE, Y'KNOW, I'M THINKING... POWERS ASIDE... YOU AND ME IN A PICK-UP GAME? WE COULD PROBABLY SHOOT SOME SERIOUS HOOP!
THE SPHERE OF SARA-KATH! POTENTIALLY ONE OF THE MOST POWERFUL OBJECTS IN THE KNOWN DIMENSIONS! ITS TRUE ORIGINS REMAIN A MYSTERY...
...ITS PURPOSE IS TO AUGMENT BY A HUNDREDFOLD THE MAGIKAL ABILITIES OF ANY WHO POSSESS IT!
WELL, IF IT'S IN THERE, LET'S JUST GO IN AND GET IT!
WERE IT THAT SIMPLE.
THE EYE SHOWED ME THAT THE OCCUPANTS OF THIS BUILDING HAD CONSTRUCTED A DIMENSIONAL PORTAL, BORN OF SCIENCE AND MAGIK -- UNSUCCESSFUL AT FIRST --
-- UNTIL IT BECAME ENERGIZED BY THE SPHERE!

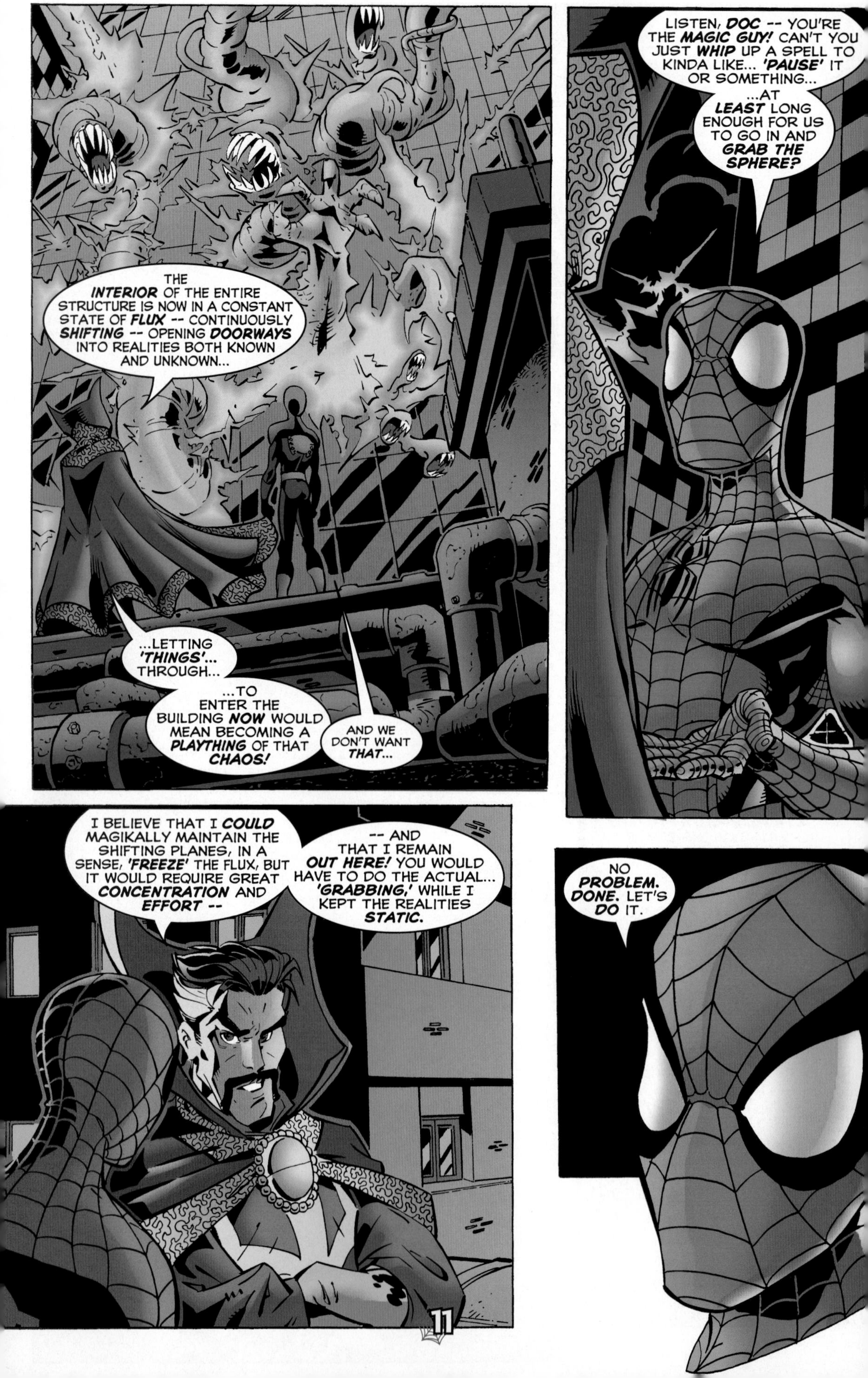
THE INTERIOR OF THE ENTIRE STRUCTURE IS NOW IN A CONSTANT STATE OF FLUX -- CONTINUOUSLY SHIFTING -- OPENING DOORWAYS INTO REALITIES BOTH KNOWN AND UNKNOWN...
...LETTING 'THINGS'... THROUGH...
...TO ENTER THE BUILDING NOW WOULD MEAN BECOMING A PLAYTHING OF THAT CHAOS!
AND WE DON'T WANT THAT...
LISTEN, DOC -- YOU'RE THE MAGIC GUY! CAN'T YOU JUST WHIP UP A SPELL TO KINDA LIKE... 'PAUSE' IT OR SOMETHING...
...AT LEAST LONG ENOUGH FOR US TO GO IN AND GRAB THE SPHERE?
I BELIEVE THAT I COULD MAGIKALLY MAINTAIN THE SHIFTING PLANES, IN A SENSE, 'FREEZE' THE FLUX, BUT IT WOULD REQUIRE GREAT CONCENTRATION AND EFFORT --
-- AND THAT I REMAIN OUT HERE! YOU WOULD HAVE TO DO THE ACTUAL... 'GRABBING,' WHILE I KEPT THE REALITIES STATIC.
NO PROBLEM. DONE. LET'S DO IT.

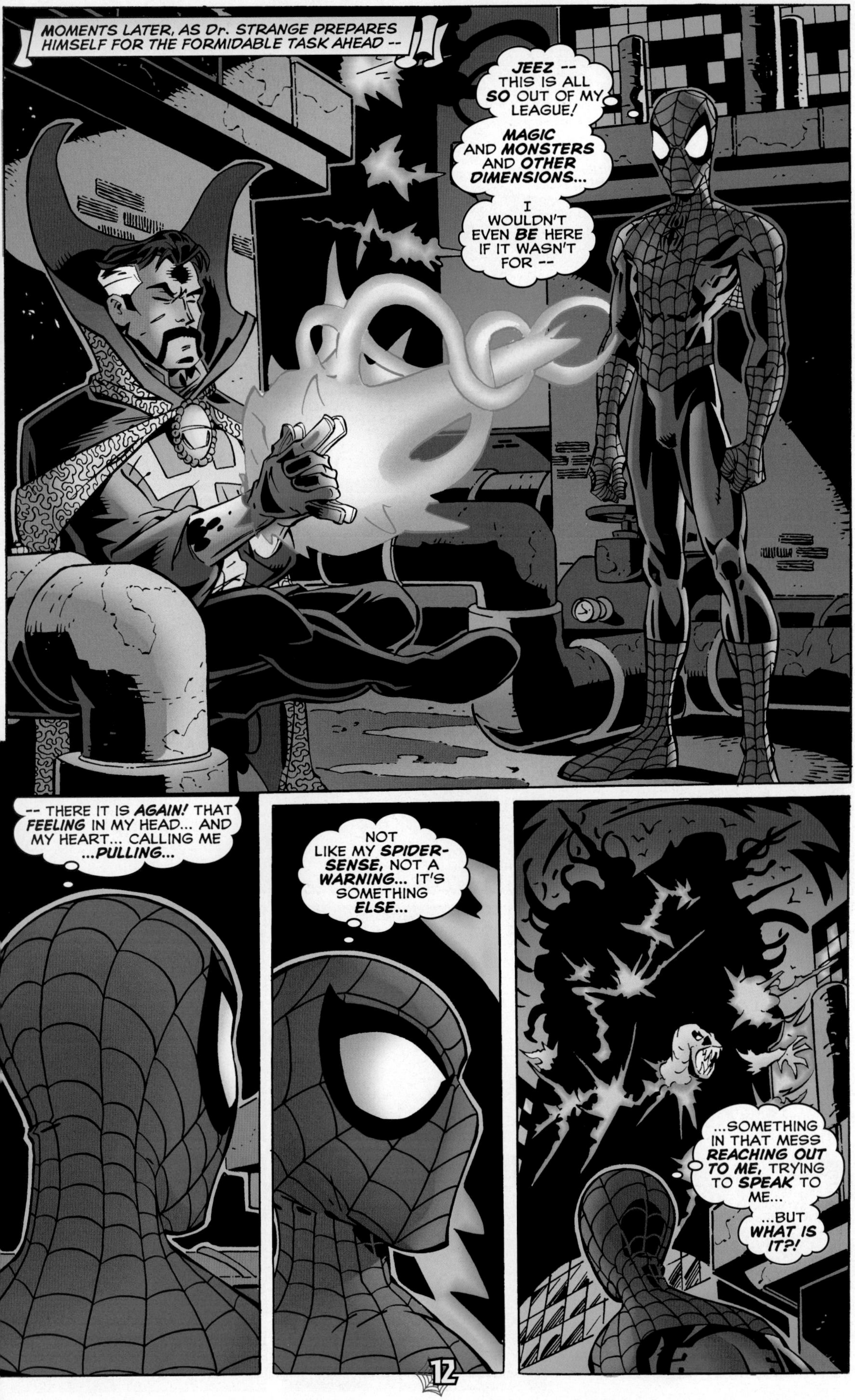
MOMENTS LATER, AS Dr. STRANGE PREPARES HIMSELF FOR THE FORMIDABLE TASK AHEAD --
JEEZ -- THIS IS ALL SO OUT OF MY LEAGUE!
MAGIC AND MONSTERS AND OTHER DIMENSIONS...
I WOULDN'T EVEN BE HERE IF IT WASN'T FOR --
-- THERE IT IS AGAIN! THAT FEELING IN MY HEAD... AND MY HEART... CALLING ME ...PULLING...
NOT LIKE MY SPIDER-SENSE, NOT A WARNING... IT'S SOMETHING ELSE...
...SOMETHING IN THAT MESS REACHING OUT TO ME, TRYING TO SPEAK TO ME...
...BUT WHAT IS IT?!

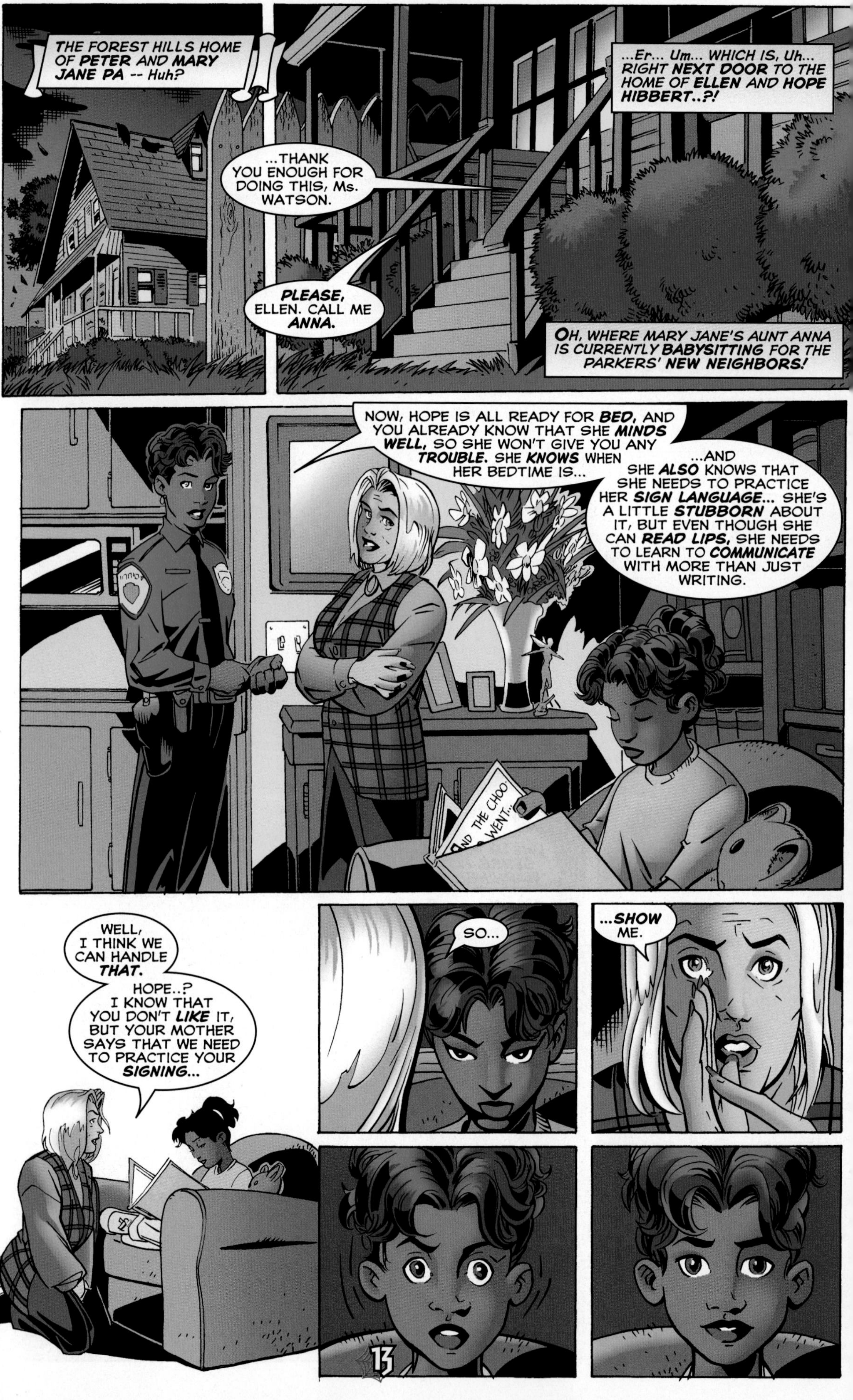
THE FOREST HILLS HOME OF PETER AND MARY JANE PA -- Huh?
...THANK YOU ENOUGH FOR DOING THIS, Ms. WATSON.
PLEASE, ELLEN. CALL ME ANNA.
...Er... Um... WHICH IS, Uh... RIGHT NEXT DOOR TO THE HOME OF ELLEN AND HOPE HIBBERT..?!
OH, WHERE MARY JANE'S AUNT ANNA IS CURRENTLY BABYSITTING FOR THE PARKERS' NEW NEIGHBORS!
NOW, HOPE IS ALL READY FOR BED, AND YOU ALREADY KNOW THAT SHE MINDS WELL, SO SHE WON'T GIVE YOU ANY TROUBLE. SHE KNOWS WHEN HER BEDTIME IS...
...AND SHE ALSO KNOWS THAT SHE NEEDS TO PRACTICE HER SIGN LANGUAGE... SHE'S A LITTLE STUBBORN ABOUT IT, BUT EVEN THOUGH SHE CAN READ LIPS, SHE NEEDS TO LEARN TO COMMUNICATE WITH MORE THAN JUST WRITING.
AND THE CHOO WENT...
WELL, I THINK WE CAN HANDLE THAT.
HOPE..? I KNOW THAT YOU DON'T LIKE IT, BUT YOUR MOTHER SAYS THAT WE NEED TO PRACTICE YOUR SIGNING...
SO...
...SHOW ME.

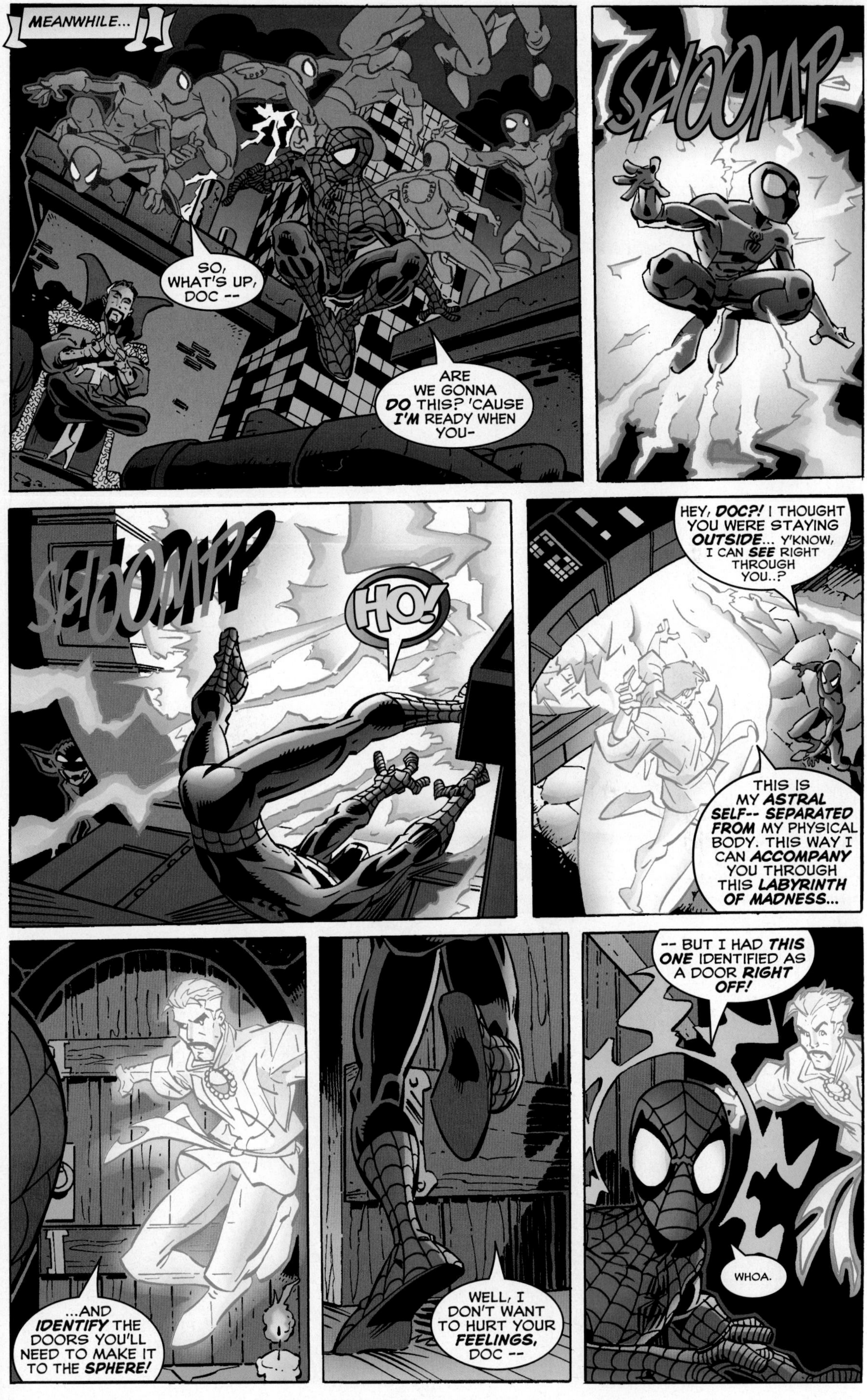

MEANWHILE...
SO, WHAT'S UP, DOC --
ARE WE GONNA DO THIS? 'CAUSE I'M READY WHEN YOU-
SHOOMP
SHOOMP
HO!
HEY, DOC?! I THOUGHT YOU WERE STAYING OUTSIDE... Y'KNOW, I CAN SEE RIGHT THROUGH YOU..?
THIS IS MY ASTRAL SELF-- SEPARATED FROM MY PHYSICAL BODY. THIS WAY I CAN ACCOMPANY YOU THROUGH THIS LABYRINTH OF MADNESS...
...AND IDENTIFY THE DOORS YOU'LL NEED TO MAKE IT TO THE SPHERE!
WELL, I DON'T WANT TO HURT YOUR FEELINGS, DOC --
-- BUT I HAD THIS ONE IDENTIFIED AS A DOOR RIGHT OFF!
WHOA.

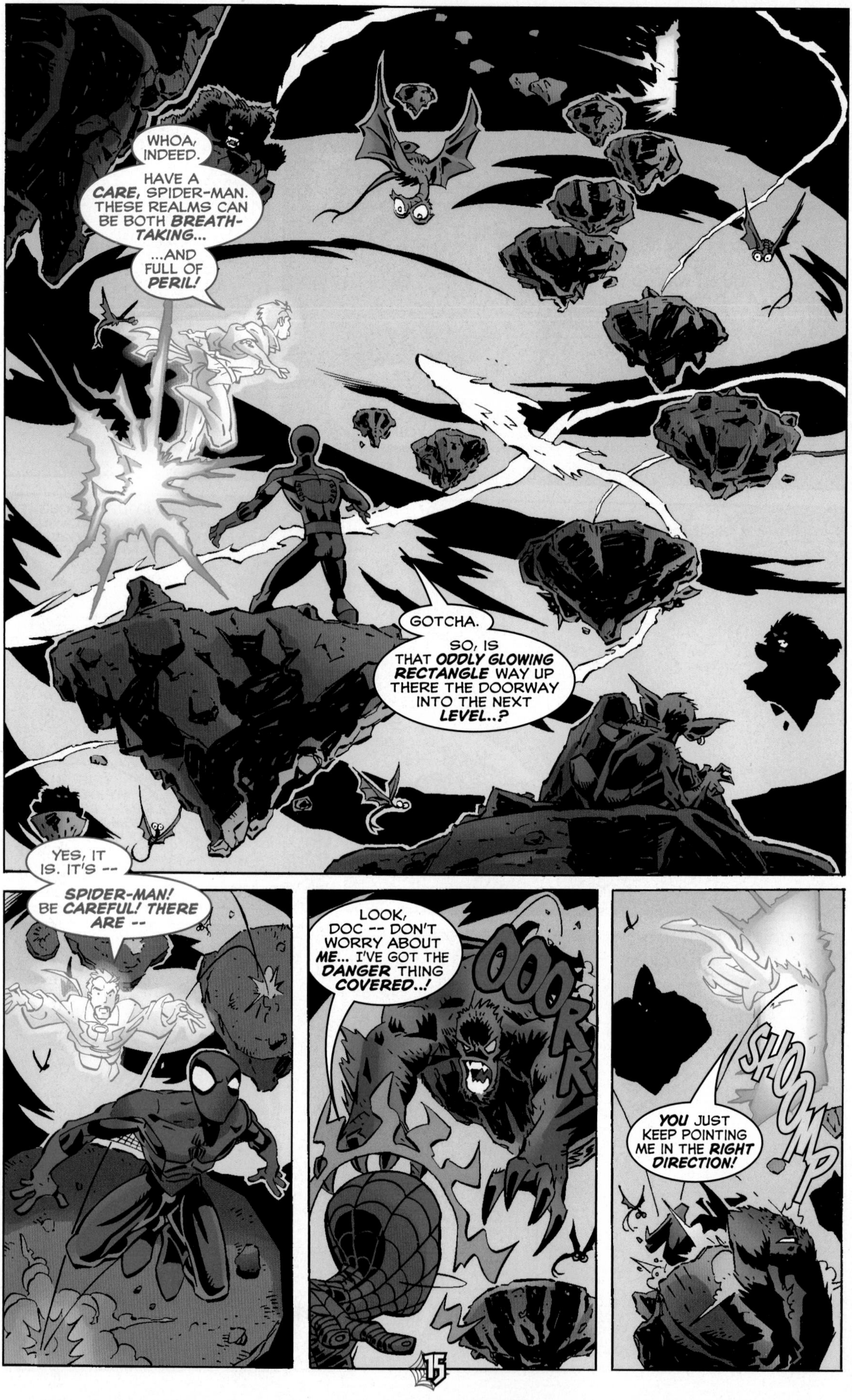
WHOA, INDEED.
HAVE A CARE, SPIDER-MAN. THESE REALMS CAN BE BOTH BREATH-TAKING...
...AND FULL OF PERIL!
GOTCHA.
SO, IS THAT ODDLY GLOWING RECTANGLE WAY UP THERE THE DOORWAY INTO THE NEXT LEVEL..?
YES, IT IS. IT'S --
SPIDER-MAN! BE CAREFUL! THERE ARE --
LOOK, DOC -- DON'T WORRY ABOUT ME... I'VE GOT THE DANGER THING COVERED..!
OOORR
SHOOMP
YOU JUST KEEP POINTING ME IN THE RIGHT DIRECTION!

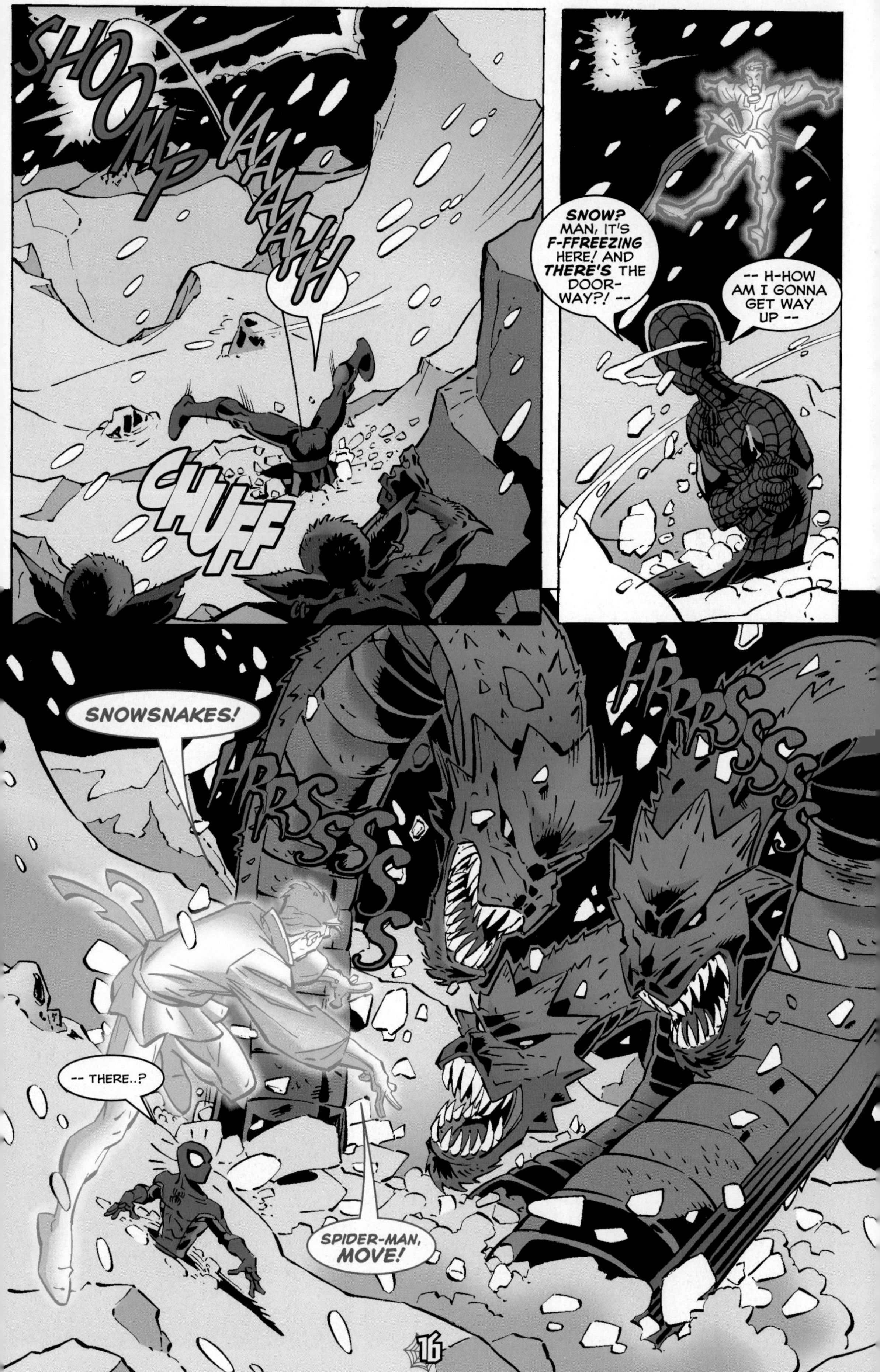
SHOOMP
YAAAAAHH
CHUFF
SNOW? MAN, IT'S F-FFREEZING HERE! AND THERE'S THE DOOR-WAY?! --
-- H-HOW AM I GONNA GET WAY UP --
SNOWSNAKES!
HRRSSSS
HRRSSSS
-- THERE..?
SPIDER-MAN, MOVE!

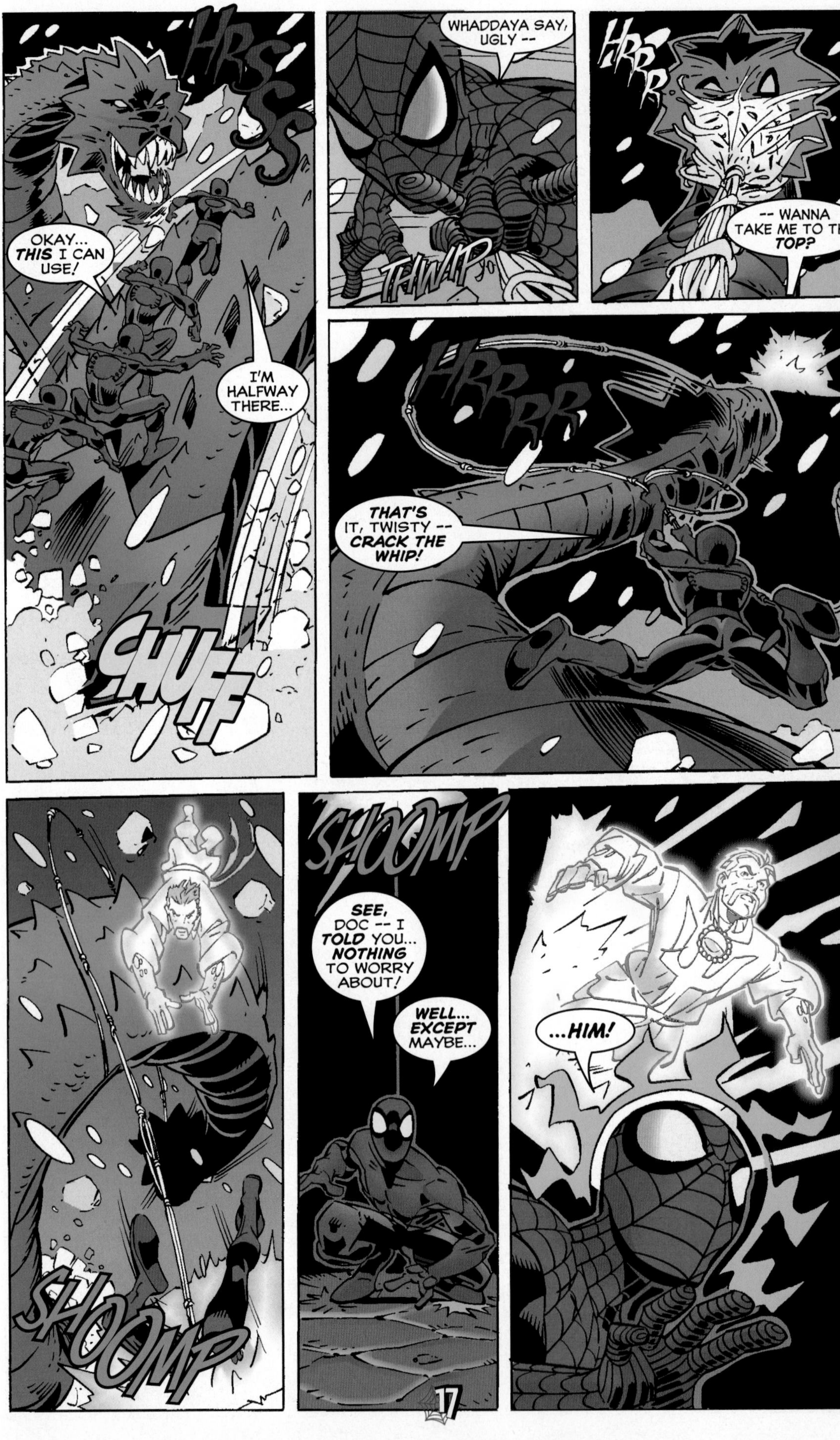

HRSSS
OKAY... THIS I CAN USE!
I'M HALFWAY THERE...
CHUFF
WHADDAYA SAY, UGLY --
THWIP
HRRR
-- WANNA TAKE ME TO THE TOP?
HRRRRR
THAT'S IT, TWISTY -- CRACK THE WHIP!
SHOOMP
SHOOMP
SEE, DOC -- I TOLD YOU... NOTHING TO WORRY ABOUT!
WELL... EXCEPT MAYBE...
...HIM!

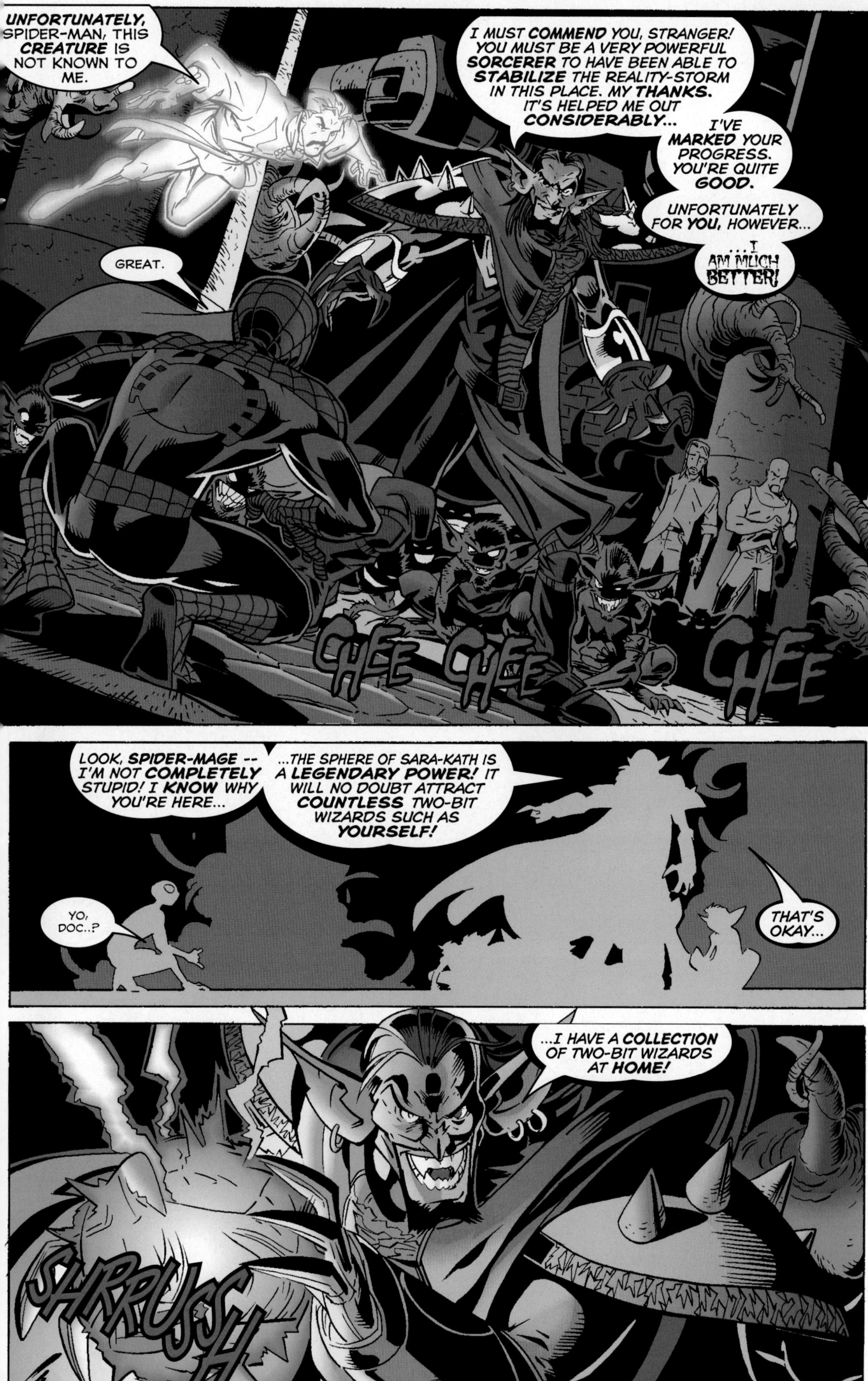

UNFORTUNATELY, SPIDER-MAN, THIS CREATURE IS NOT KNOWN TO ME.
I MUST COMMEND YOU, STRANGER! YOU MUST BE A VERY POWERFUL SORCERER TO HAVE BEEN ABLE TO STABILIZE THE REALITY-STORM IN THIS PLACE. MY THANKS. IT'S HELPED ME OUT CONSIDERABLY...
I'VE MARKED YOUR PROGRESS. YOU'RE QUITE GOOD.
UNFORTUNATELY FOR YOU, HOWEVER...
...I AM MUCH BETTER!
GREAT.
CHEE CHEE CHEE
LOOK, SPIDER-MAGE -- I'M NOT COMPLETELY STUPID! I KNOW WHY YOU'RE HERE...
...THE SPHERE OF SARA-KATH IS A LEGENDARY POWER! IT WILL NO DOUBT ATTRACT COUNTLESS TWO-BIT WIZARDS SUCH AS YOURSELF!
YO, DOC..?
THAT'S OKAY...
...I HAVE A COLLECTION OF TWO-BIT WIZARDS AT HOME!
SHRUSH

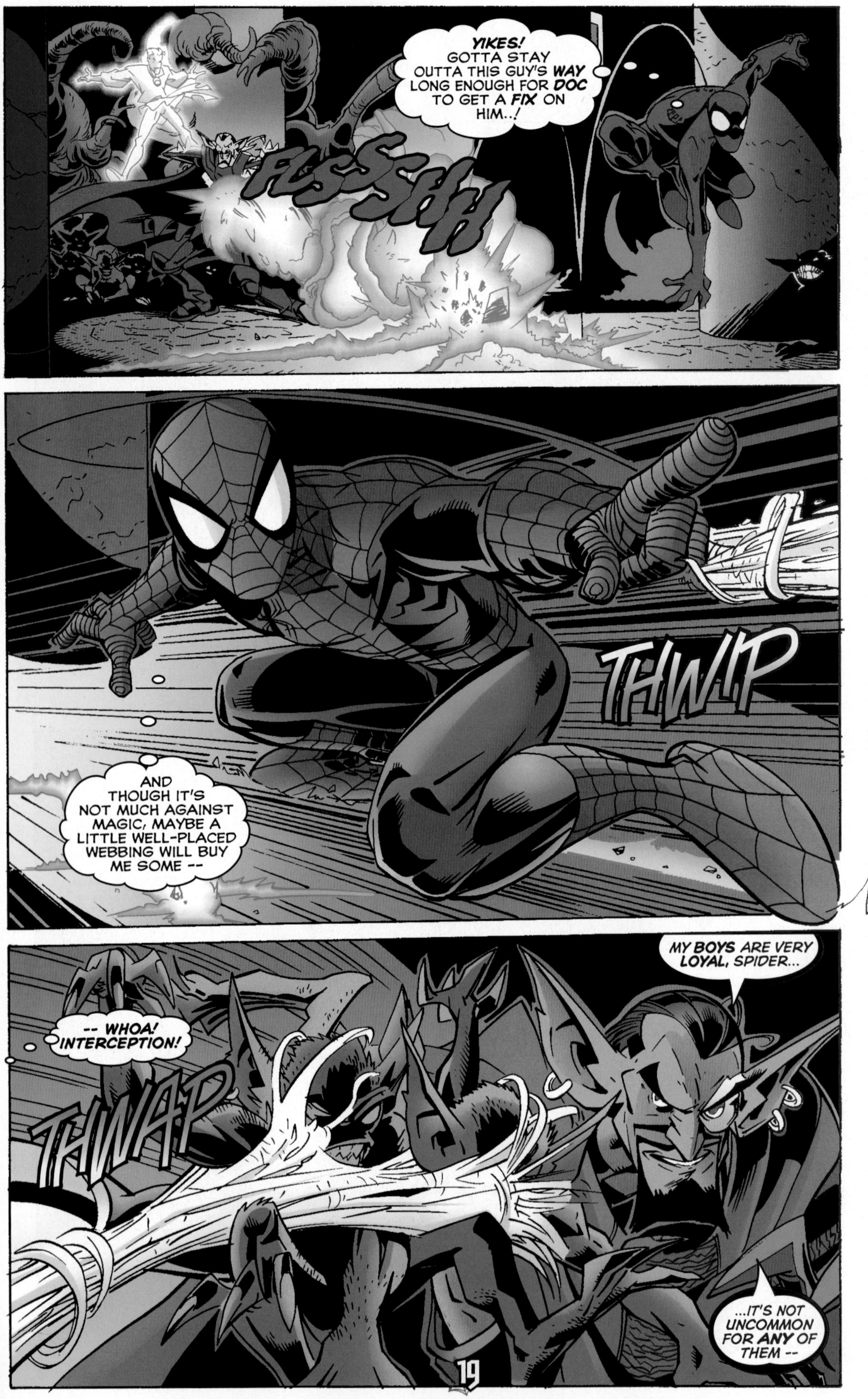

YIKES! GOTTA STAY OUTTA THIS GUY'S WAY LONG ENOUGH FOR DOC TO GET A FIX ON HIM..!
FLSSHH
AND THOUGH IT'S NOT MUCH AGAINST MAGIC, MAYBE A LITTLE WELL-PLACED WEBBING WILL BUY ME SOME --
THWIP
MY BOYS ARE VERY LOYAL, SPIDER...
-- WHOA! INTERCEPTION!
THWAP
...IT'S NOT UNCOMMON FOR ANY OF THEM --

-- TO TAKE ONE FOR THE TEAM!

CHEE CHEE

HEY, *DOC* -- I COULD USE SOME *HELP* HERE...

I'M *TRYING,* SPIDER-MAN. HIS *MAGIKS* ARE --

DOC?!... HELP?! SO YOU'RE NOT *ALONE?* YOU'RE WORKING WITH A *FAMILIAR..?!*

KSSSHH

THAT *CHANGES* THINGS!

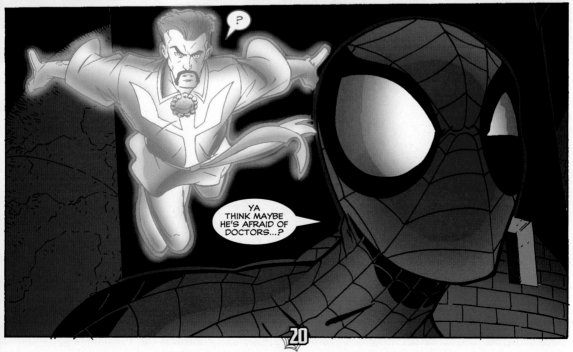

?

YA THINK MAYBE HE'S AFRAID OF *DOCTORS...?*

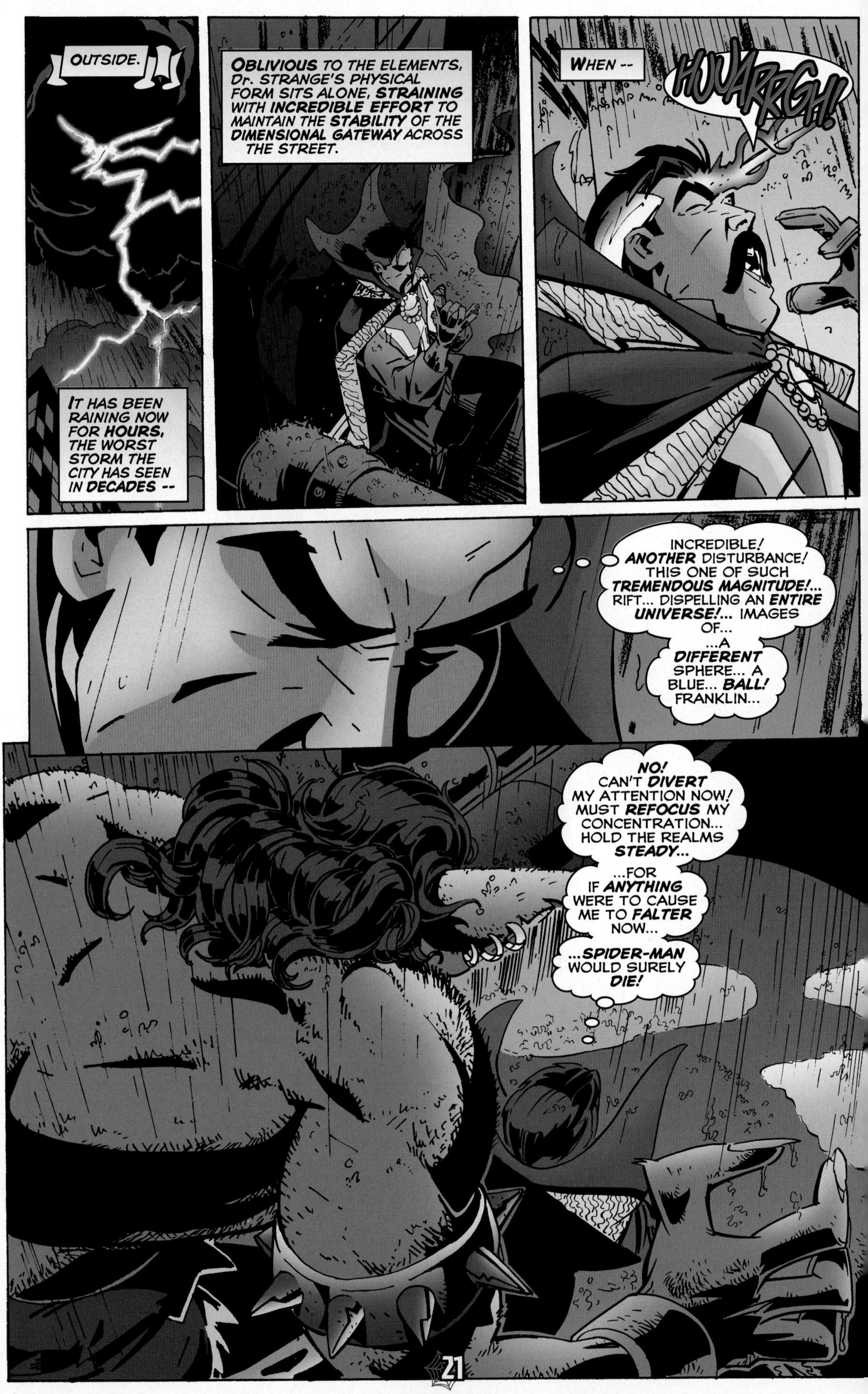
OUTSIDE.
IT HAS BEEN RAINING NOW FOR HOURS, THE WORST STORM THE CITY HAS SEEN IN DECADES --
OBLIVIOUS TO THE ELEMENTS, Dr. STRANGE'S PHYSICAL FORM SITS ALONE, STRAINING WITH INCREDIBLE EFFORT TO MAINTAIN THE STABILITY OF THE DIMENSIONAL GATEWAY ACROSS THE STREET.
WHEN --
HUUARRRGH!
INCREDIBLE! ANOTHER DISTURBANCE! THIS ONE OF SUCH TREMENDOUS MAGNITUDE!... RIFT... DISPELLING AN ENTIRE UNIVERSE!... IMAGES OF... ...A DIFFERENT SPHERE... A BLUE... BALL! FRANKLIN...
NO! CAN'T DIVERT MY ATTENTION NOW! MUST REFOCUS MY CONCENTRATION... HOLD THE REALMS STEADY...
...FOR IF ANYTHING WERE TO CAUSE ME TO FALTER NOW...
...SPIDER-MAN WOULD SURELY DIE!

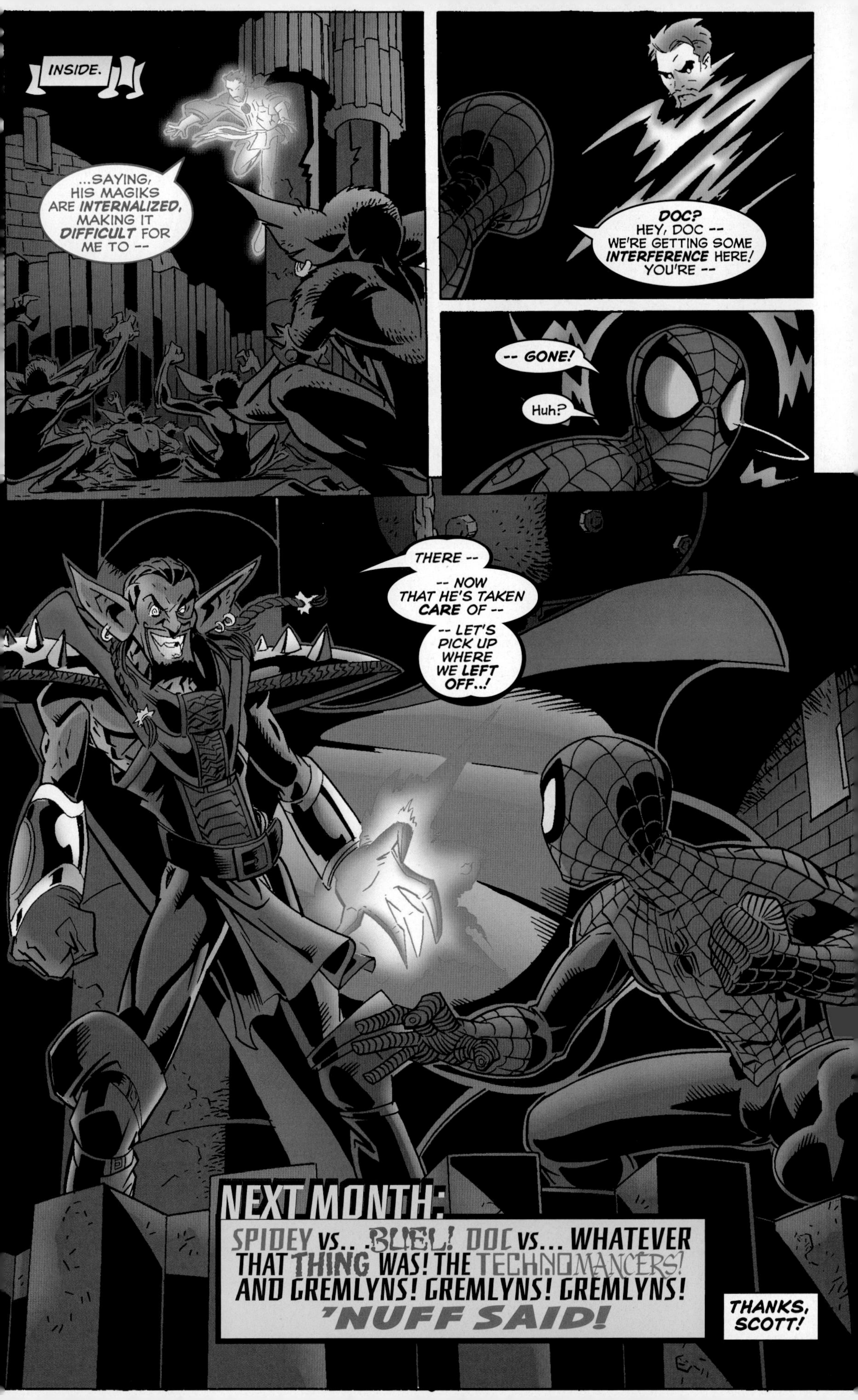
INSIDE.
...SAYING, HIS MAGIKS ARE INTERNALIZED, MAKING IT DIFFICULT FOR ME TO --
DOC? HEY, DOC -- WE'RE GETTING SOME INTERFERENCE HERE! YOU'RE --
-- GONE!
Huh?
THERE --
-- NOW THAT HE'S TAKEN CARE OF --
-- LET'S PICK UP WHERE WE LEFT OFF..!
NEXT MONTH:
SPIDEY vs.. .BUEL! DOC vs... WHATEVER THAT THING WAS! THE TECHNOMANCERS! AND GREMLYNS! GREMLYNS! GREMLYNS!
'NUFF SAID!
THANKS, SCOTT!

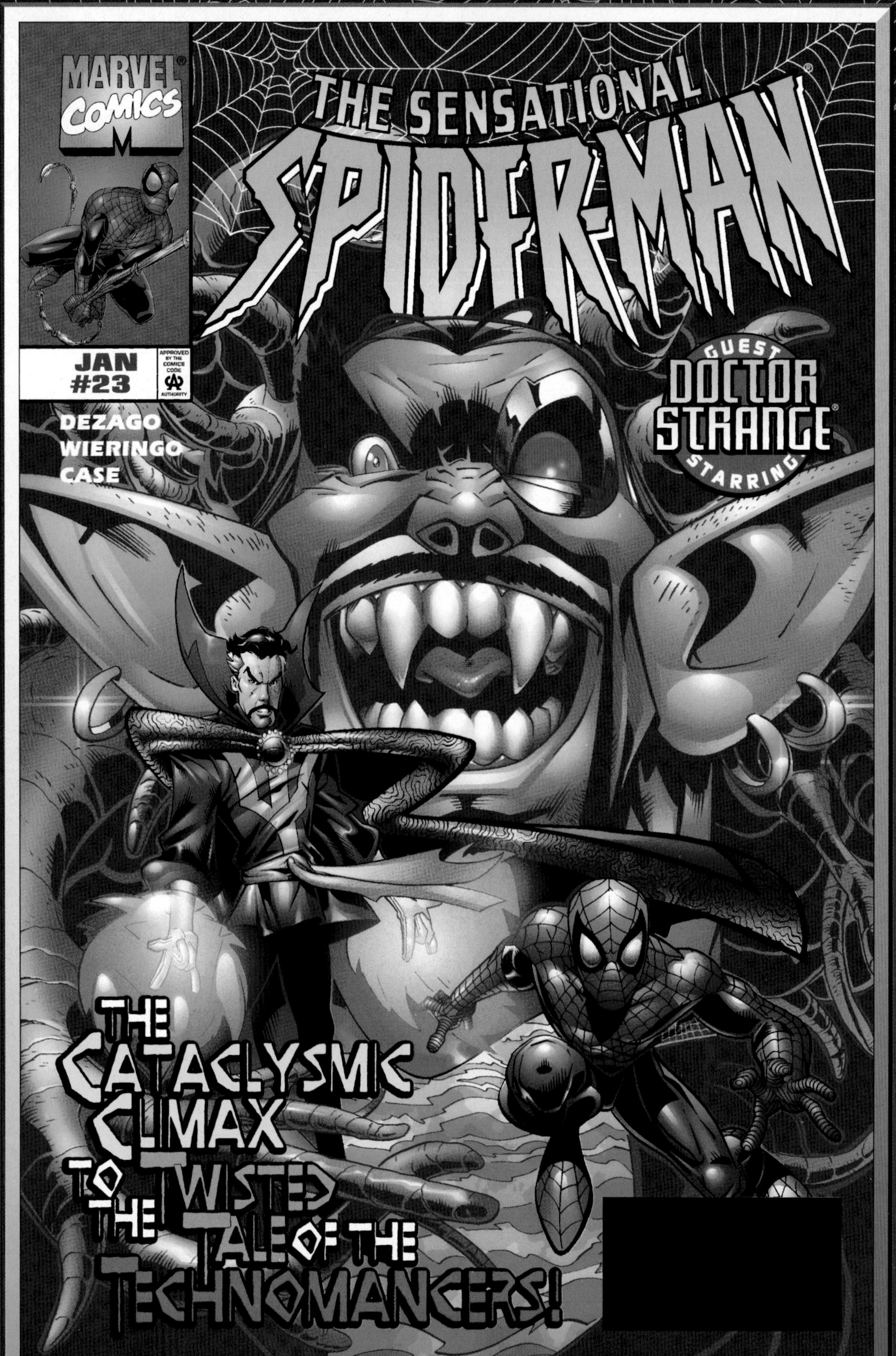
MARVEL COMICS
THE SENSATIONAL
SPIDER-MAN
JAN
#23
APPROVED BY THE COMICS CODE AUTHORITY
DEZAGO
WIERINGO
CASE
GUEST STARRING
DOCTOR STRANGE
THE CATACLYSMIC CLIMAX TO THE TWISTED TALE OF THE TECHNOMANCERS!

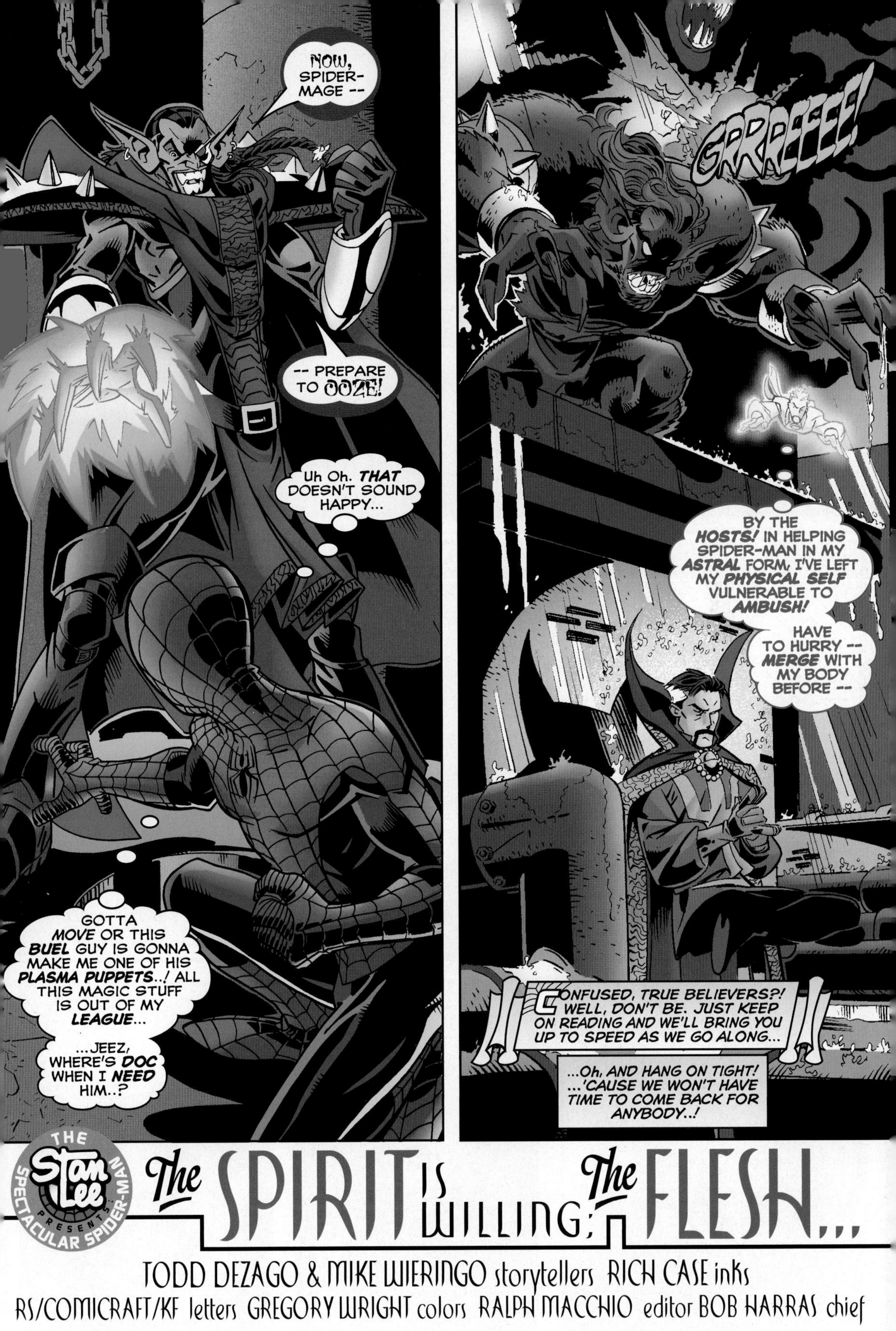
NOW, SPIDER-MAGE --
-- PREPARE TO OOZE!
Uh Oh. THAT DOESN'T SOUND HAPPY...
GOTTA MOVE OR THIS BUEL GUY IS GONNA MAKE ME ONE OF HIS PLASMA PUPPETS..! ALL THIS MAGIC STUFF IS OUT OF MY LEAGUE...
...JEEZ, WHERE'S DOC WHEN I NEED HIM..?
GRRREEEE!
BY THE HOSTS! IN HELPING SPIDER-MAN IN MY ASTRAL FORM, I'VE LEFT MY PHYSICAL SELF VULNERABLE TO AMBUSH!
HAVE TO HURRY -- MERGE WITH MY BODY BEFORE --
CONFUSED, TRUE BELIEVERS?! WELL, DON'T BE. JUST KEEP ON READING AND WE'LL BRING YOU UP TO SPEED AS WE GO ALONG...
...Oh, AND HANG ON TIGHT! ...'CAUSE WE WON'T HAVE TIME TO COME BACK FOR ANYBODY..!

THE Stan Lee PRESENTS SPECTACULAR SPIDER-MAN

The SPIRIT IS WILLING; The FLESH...

TODD DEZAGO & MIKE WIERINGO storytellers RICH CASE inks
RS/COMICRAFT/KF letters GREGORY WRIGHT colors RALPH MACCHIO editor BOB HARRAS chief

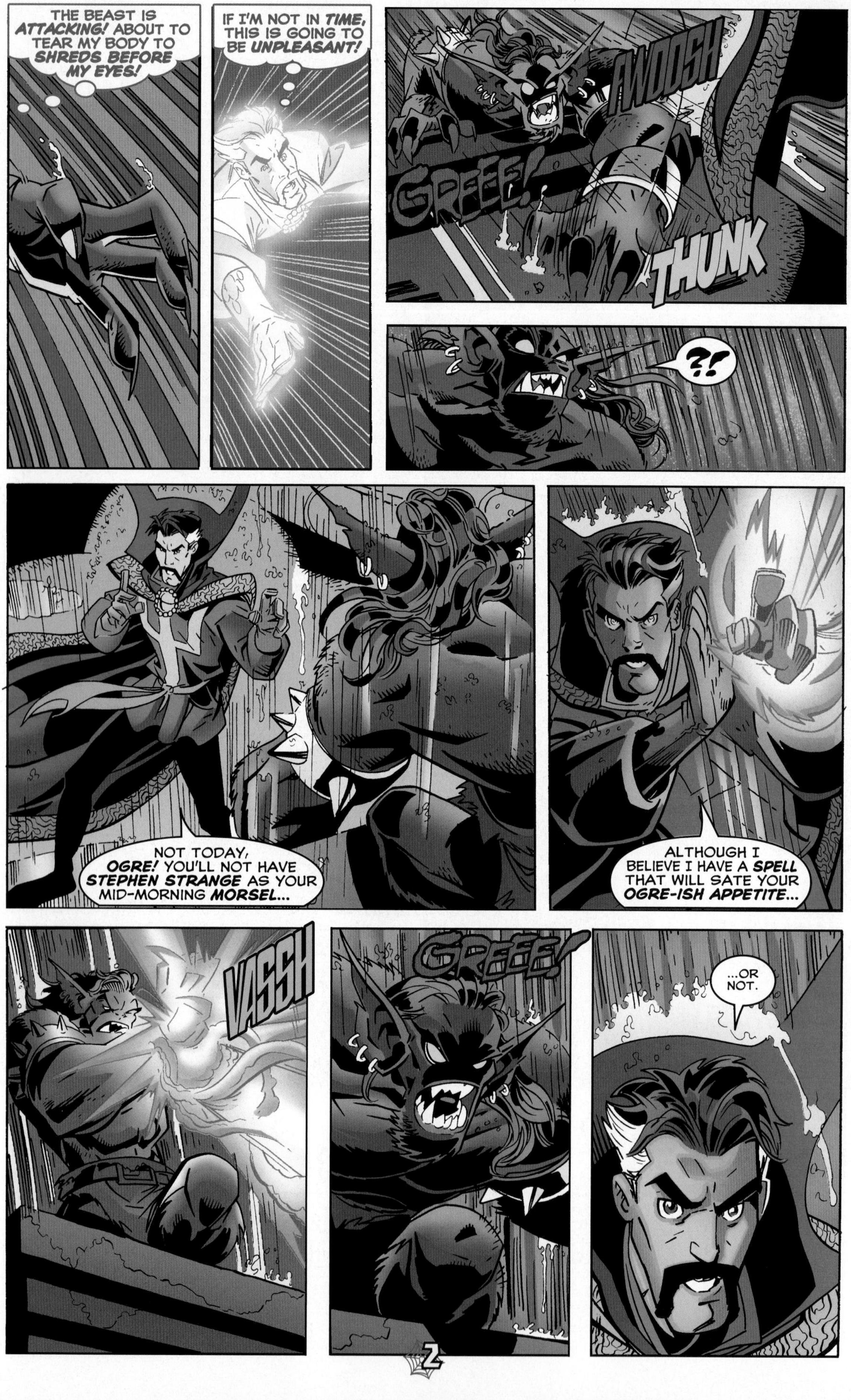
THE BEAST IS ATTACKING! ABOUT TO TEAR MY BODY TO SHREDS BEFORE MY EYES!
IF I'M NOT IN TIME, THIS IS GOING TO BE UNPLEASANT!
FWOOSH
GREEE!
THUNK
?!
NOT TODAY, OGRE! YOU'LL NOT HAVE STEPHEN STRANGE AS YOUR MID-MORNING MORSEL...
ALTHOUGH I BELIEVE I HAVE A SPELL THAT WILL SATE YOUR OGRE-ISH APPETITE...
VASSH
GREEE!
...OR NOT.

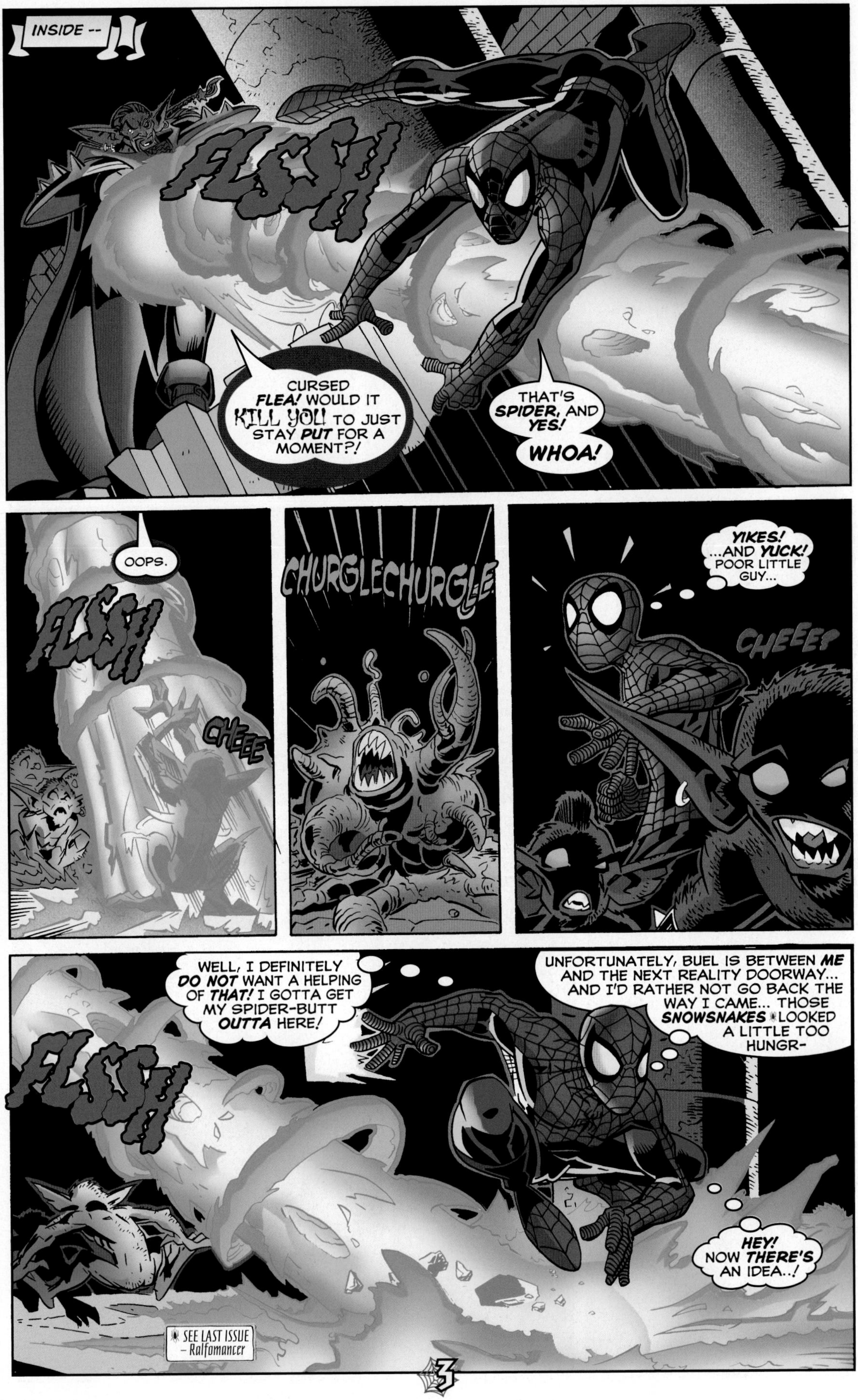
INSIDE --
FLSH!
CURSED FLEA! WOULD IT KILL YOU TO JUST STAY PUT FOR A MOMENT?!
THAT'S SPIDER, AND YES!
WHOA!
OOPS.
FLSH
CHEEE
CHURGLECHURGLE
YIKES! ...AND YUCK! POOR LITTLE GUY...
CHEEEP
WELL, I DEFINITELY DO NOT WANT A HELPING OF THAT! I GOTTA GET MY SPIDER-BUTT OUTTA HERE!
UNFORTUNATELY, BUEL IS BETWEEN ME AND THE NEXT REALITY DOORWAY... AND I'D RATHER NOT GO BACK THE WAY I CAME... THOSE SNOWSNAKES LOOKED A LITTLE TOO HUNGR-
FLSH
HEY! NOW THERE'S AN IDEA..!
SEE LAST ISSUE – Ralfomancer

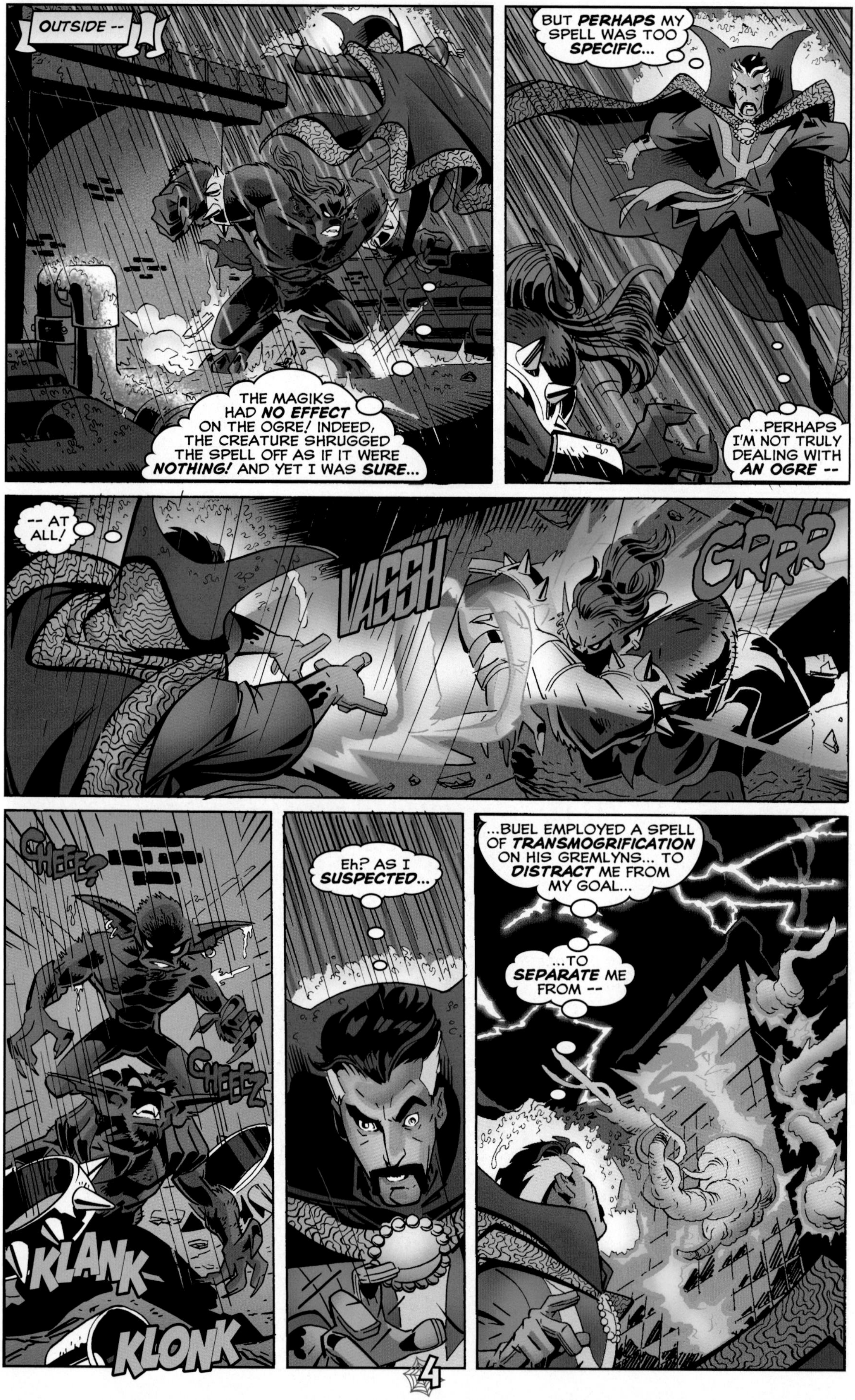
OUTSIDE --
THE MAGIKS HAD NO EFFECT ON THE OGRE! INDEED, THE CREATURE SHRUGGED THE SPELL OFF AS IF IT WERE NOTHING! AND YET I WAS SURE...
BUT PERHAPS MY SPELL WAS TOO SPECIFIC...
...PERHAPS I'M NOT TRULY DEALING WITH AN OGRE --
-- AT ALL!
VASSH
GRRR
CHEEEZ
CHEEEZ
KLANK
KLONK
Eh? AS I SUSPECTED...
...BUEL EMPLOYED A SPELL OF TRANSMOGRIFICATION ON HIS GREMLYNS... TO DISTRACT ME FROM MY GOAL...
...TO SEPARATE ME FROM --

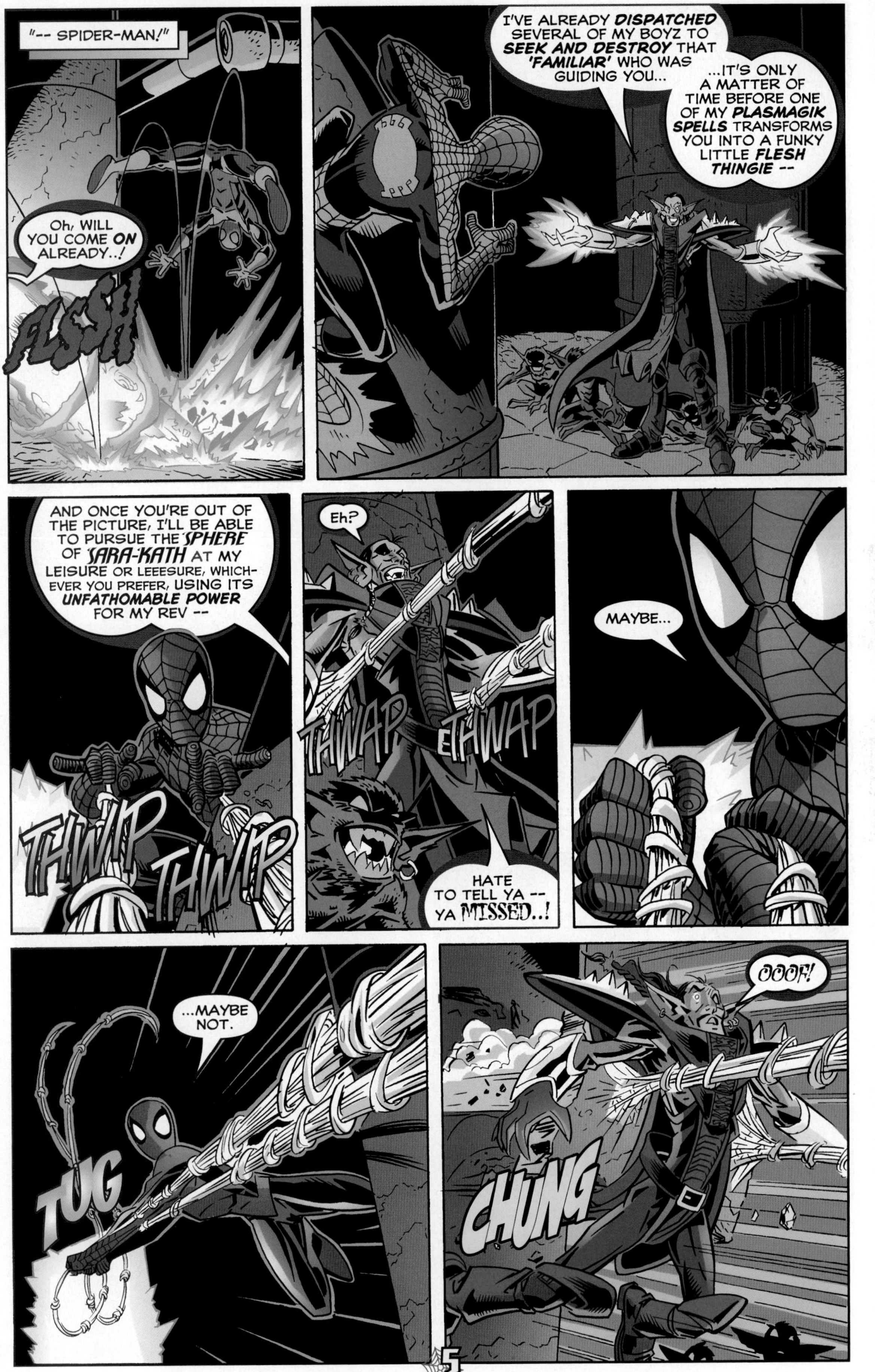
"-- SPIDER-MAN!"
Oh, WILL YOU COME ON ALREADY..!
FLSH
I'VE ALREADY DISPATCHED SEVERAL OF MY BOYZ TO SEEK AND DESTROY THAT 'FAMILIAR' WHO WAS GUIDING YOU...
...IT'S ONLY A MATTER OF TIME BEFORE ONE OF MY PLASMAGIK SPELLS TRANSFORMS YOU INTO A FUNKY LITTLE FLESH THINGIE --
AND ONCE YOU'RE OUT OF THE PICTURE, I'LL BE ABLE TO PURSUE THE SPHERE OF SARA-KATH AT MY LEISURE OR LEEESURE, WHICH-EVER YOU PREFER, USING ITS UNFATHOMABLE POWER FOR MY REV --
THWIP THWIP
Eh?
THWAP THWAP
HATE TO TELL YA -- YA MISSED..!
MAYBE...
...MAYBE NOT.
TUG
OOOF!
CHUNG

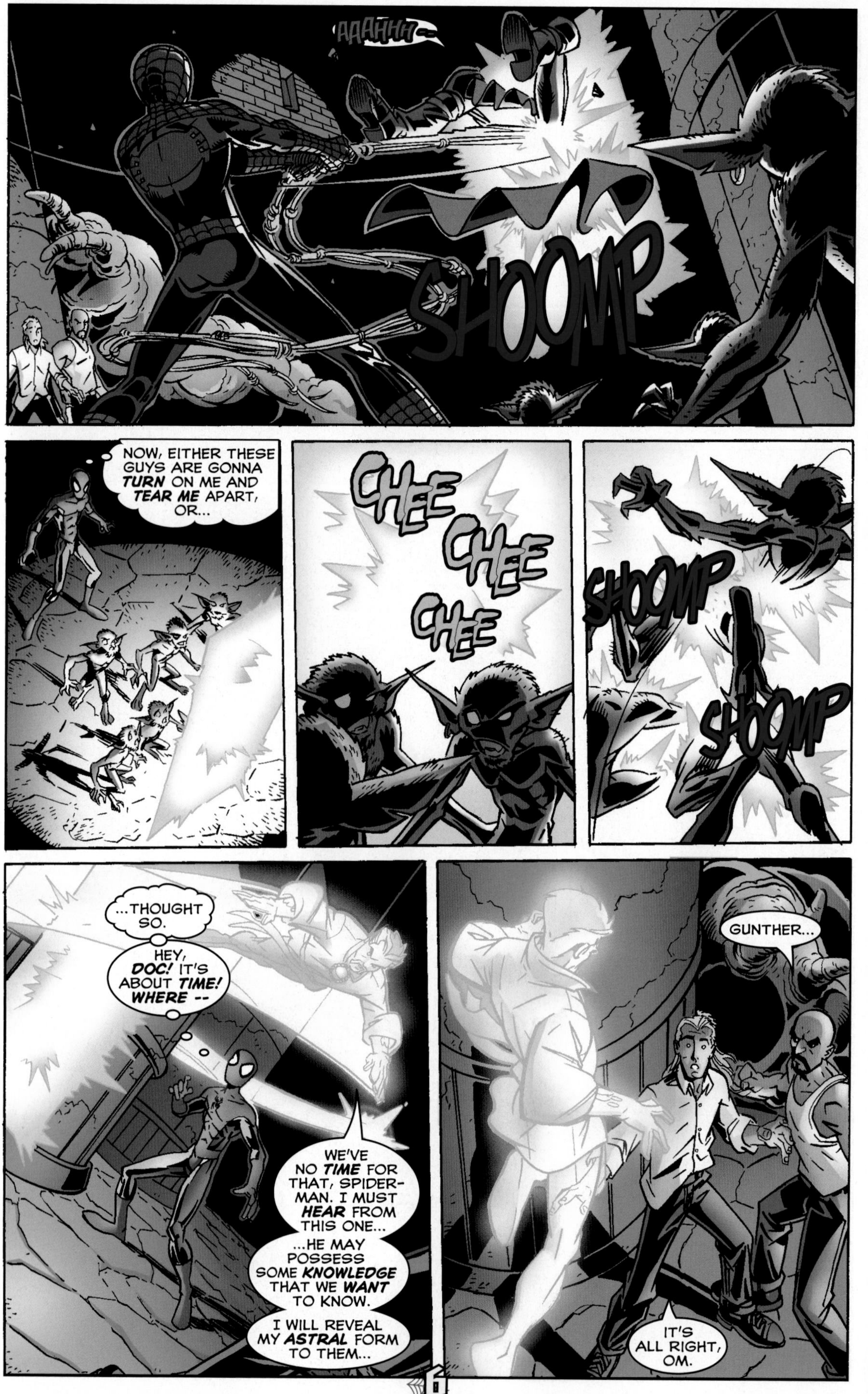
AAAHHH--
SHOOMP
NOW, EITHER THESE GUYS ARE GONNA TURN ON ME AND TEAR ME APART, OR...
CHEE CHEE CHEE
SHOOMP
SHOOMP
...THOUGHT SO.
HEY, DOC! IT'S ABOUT TIME! WHERE --
WE'VE NO TIME FOR THAT, SPIDER-MAN. I MUST HEAR FROM THIS ONE...
...HE MAY POSSESS SOME KNOWLEDGE THAT WE WANT TO KNOW.
I WILL REVEAL MY ASTRAL FORM TO THEM...
GUNTHER...
IT'S ALL RIGHT, OM.

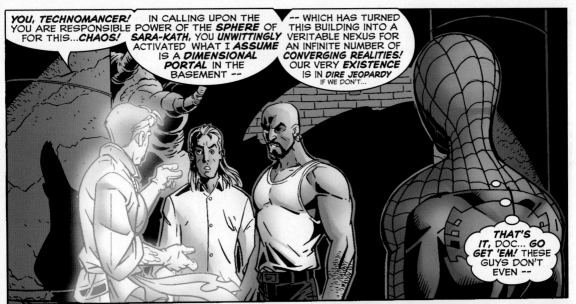

YOU, TECHNOMANCER! YOU ARE RESPONSIBLE FOR THIS...CHAOS!

IN CALLING UPON THE POWER OF THE *SPHERE* OF *SARA-KATH*, YOU *UNWITTINGLY* ACTIVATED WHAT I *ASSUME* IS A *DIMENSIONAL PORTAL* IN THE BASEMENT --

-- WHICH HAS TURNED THIS BUILDING INTO A *VERITABLE NEXUS* FOR AN INFINITE NUMBER OF *CONVERGING REALITIES!* OUR VERY *EXISTENCE* IS IN *DIRE JEOPARDY* IF WE DON'T...

THAT'S IT, DOC... *GO GET 'EM!* THESE GUYS DON'T EVEN --

Ungh! THERE IT IS *AGAIN!* BUT SO MUCH *STRONGER* THIS TIME..!

SOME... STRANGE... *FORCE...* CALLING ME...

★ LAST ISSUE
-- Relapsin' Ralf.

...ACCOUNTABLE FOR YOUR ACTIONS IN A MUCH *DIFFERENT* KIND OF COURT, AND I SUGGEST YOU PUT THAT *AWAY*, FRIEND -- AS THEY SAY, YOU DON'T BRING A *KNIFE* TO A GUN FIGHT...

...*PULLING* ME...

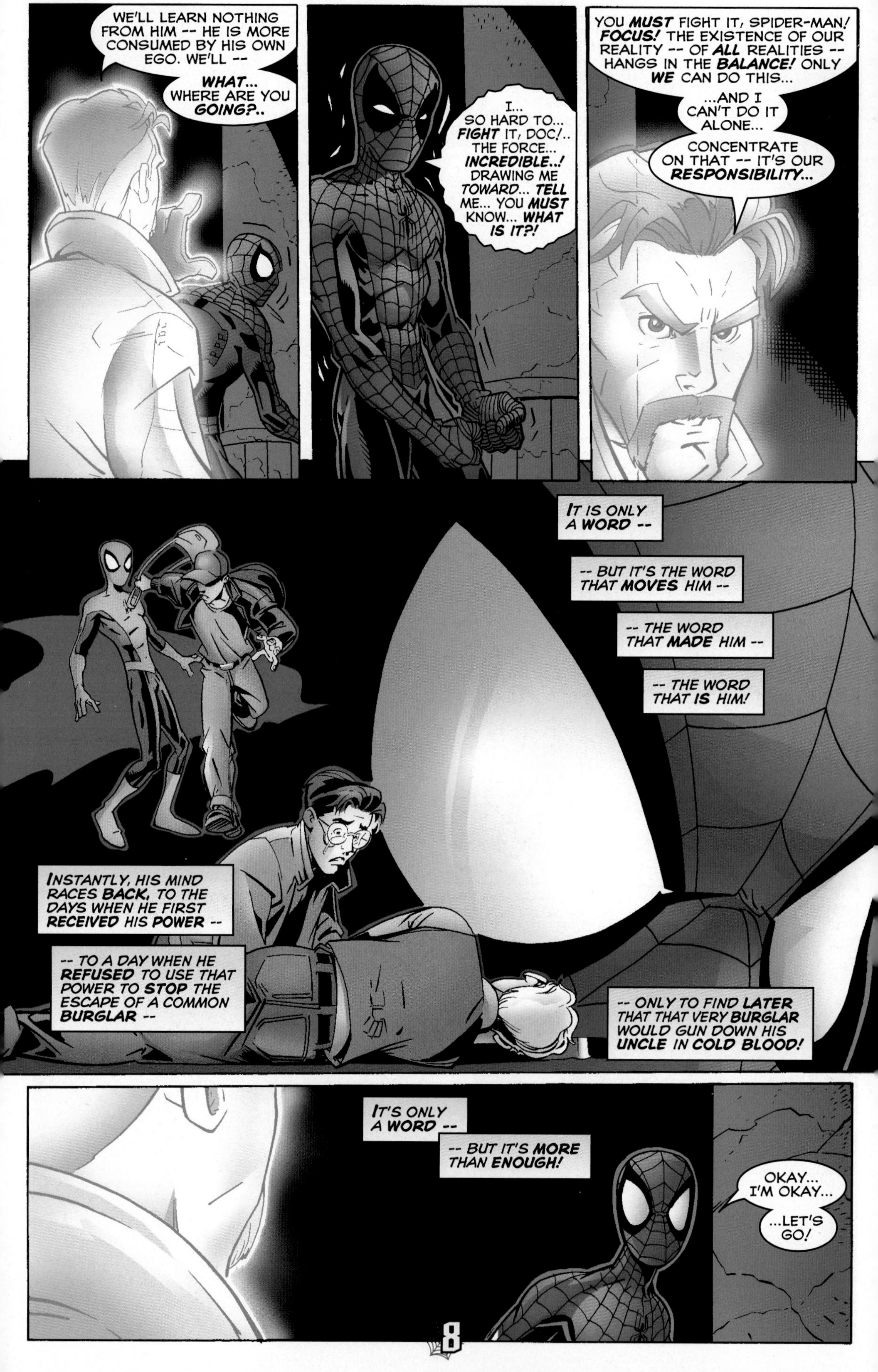
WE'LL LEARN NOTHING FROM HIM -- HE IS MORE CONSUMED BY HIS OWN EGO. WE'LL --
WHAT... WHERE ARE YOU GOING?..
I... SO HARD TO... FIGHT IT, DOC!.. THE FORCE... INCREDIBLE..! DRAWING ME TOWARD... TELL ME... YOU MUST KNOW... WHAT IS IT?!
YOU MUST FIGHT IT, SPIDER-MAN! FOCUS! THE EXISTENCE OF OUR REALITY -- OF ALL REALITIES -- HANGS IN THE BALANCE! ONLY WE CAN DO THIS...
...AND I CAN'T DO IT ALONE...
CONCENTRATE ON THAT -- IT'S OUR RESPONSIBILITY...
IT IS ONLY A WORD --
-- BUT IT'S THE WORD THAT MOVES HIM --
-- THE WORD THAT MADE HIM --
-- THE WORD THAT IS HIM!
INSTANTLY, HIS MIND RACES BACK, TO THE DAYS WHEN HE FIRST RECEIVED HIS POWER --
-- TO A DAY WHEN HE REFUSED TO USE THAT POWER TO STOP THE ESCAPE OF A COMMON BURGLAR --
-- ONLY TO FIND LATER THAT THAT VERY BURGLAR WOULD GUN DOWN HIS UNCLE IN COLD BLOOD!
IT'S ONLY A WORD --
-- BUT IT'S MORE THAN ENOUGH!
OKAY... I'M OKAY...
...LET'S GO!

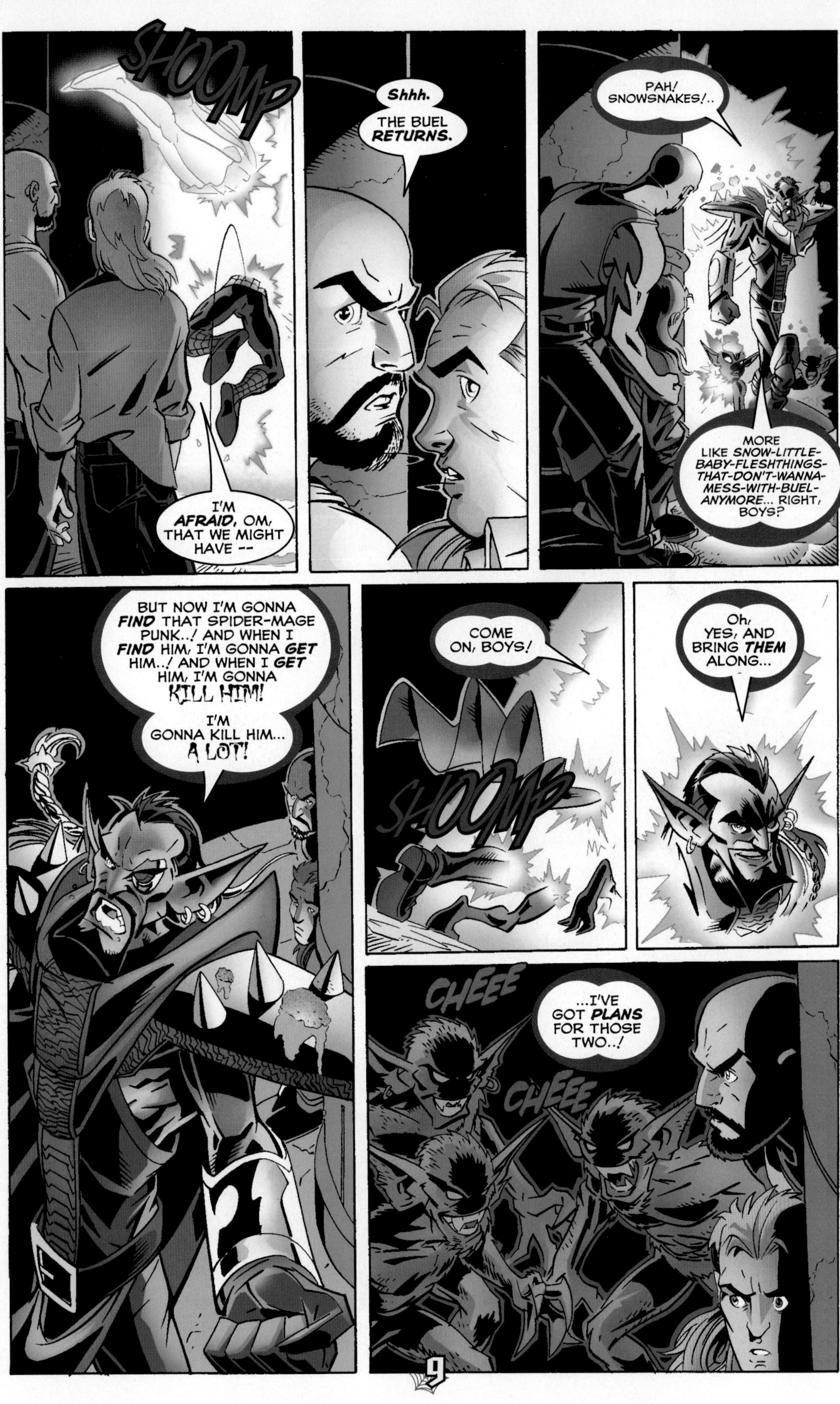
SHOOMP
I'M AFRAID, OM, THAT WE MIGHT HAVE --
Shhh. THE BUEL RETURNS.
PAH! SNOWSNAKES!..
MORE LIKE SNOW-LITTLE-BABY-FLESHTHINGS-THAT-DON'T-WANNA-MESS-WITH-BUEL-ANYMORE... RIGHT, BOYS?
BUT NOW I'M GONNA FIND THAT SPIDER-MAGE PUNK..! AND WHEN I FIND HIM, I'M GONNA GET HIM..! AND WHEN I GET HIM, I'M GONNA KILL HIM!
I'M GONNA KILL HIM... A LOT!
COME ON, BOYS!
SHOOMP
Oh, YES, AND BRING THEM ALONG...
CHEEE
CHEEE
...I'VE GOT PLANS FOR THOSE TWO..!

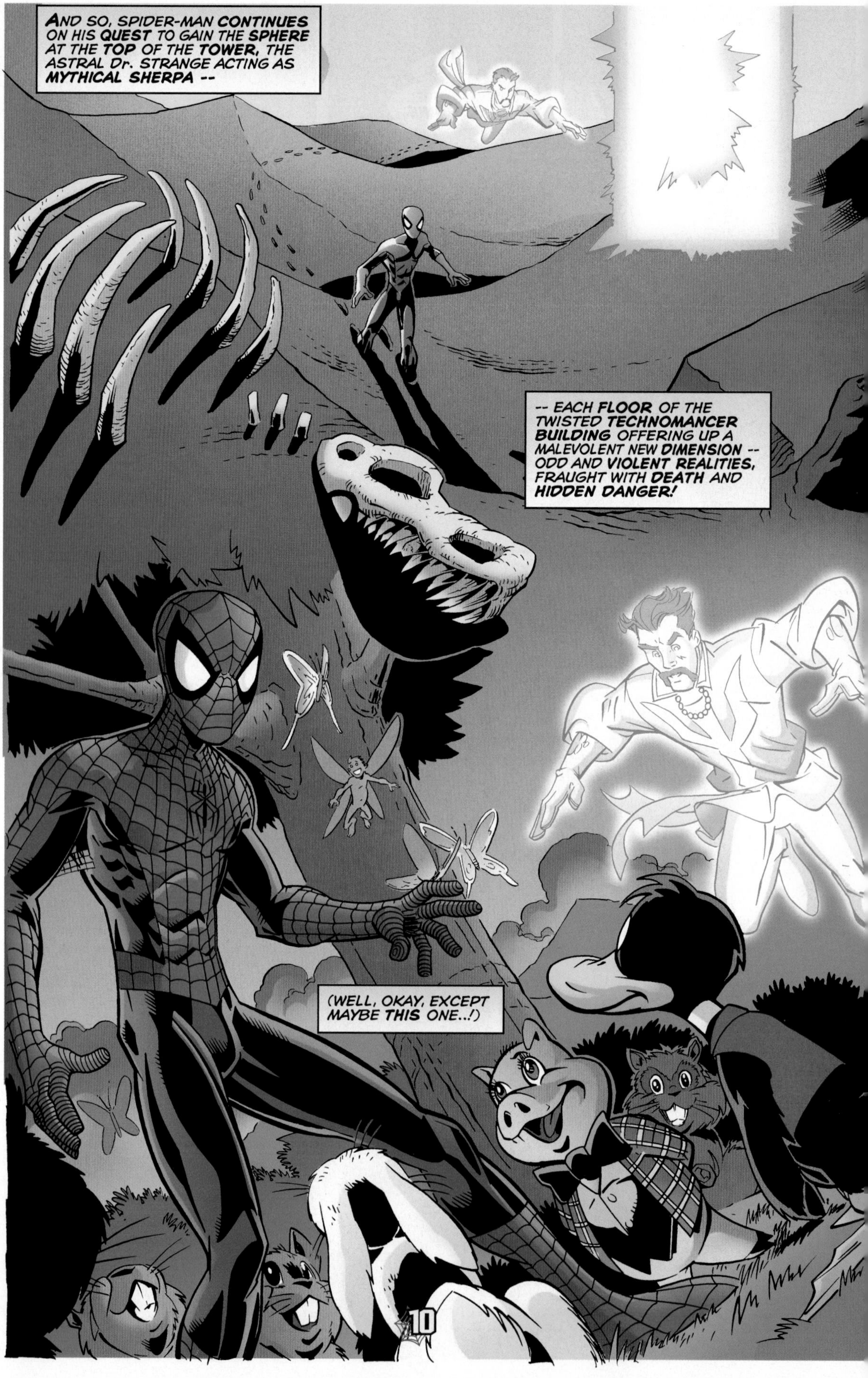
AND SO, SPIDER-MAN CONTINUES ON HIS QUEST TO GAIN THE SPHERE AT THE TOP OF THE TOWER, THE ASTRAL Dr. STRANGE ACTING AS MYTHICAL SHERPA --
-- EACH FLOOR OF THE TWISTED TECHNOMANCER BUILDING OFFERING UP A MALEVOLENT NEW DIMENSION -- ODD AND VIOLENT REALITIES, FRAUGHT WITH DEATH AND HIDDEN DANGER!
(WELL, OKAY, EXCEPT MAYBE THIS ONE..!)
10

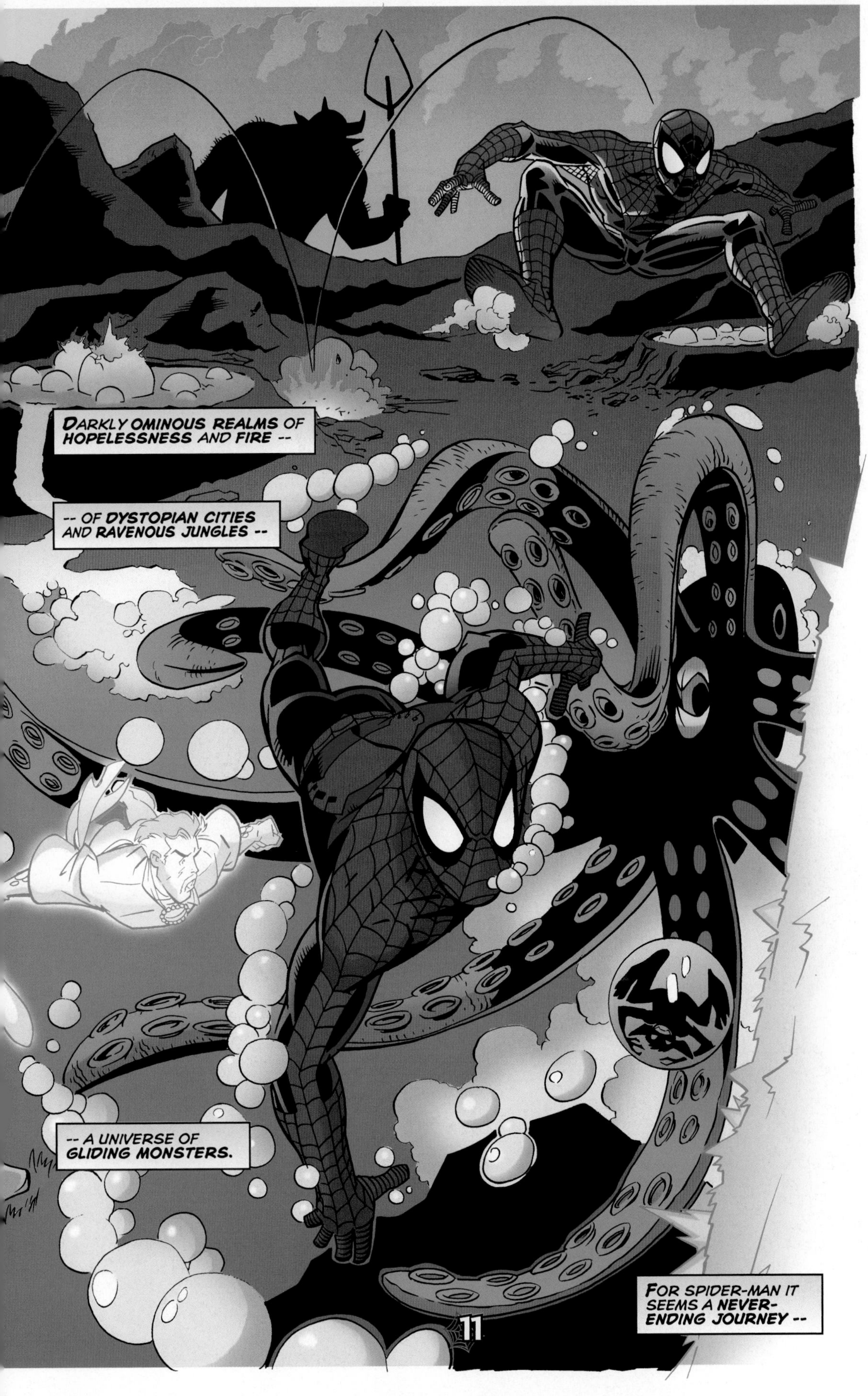

DARKLY OMINOUS REALMS OF HOPELESSNESS AND FIRE --
-- OF DYSTOPIAN CITIES AND RAVENOUS JUNGLES --
-- A UNIVERSE OF GLIDING MONSTERS.
FOR SPIDER-MAN IT SEEMS A NEVER-ENDING JOURNEY --

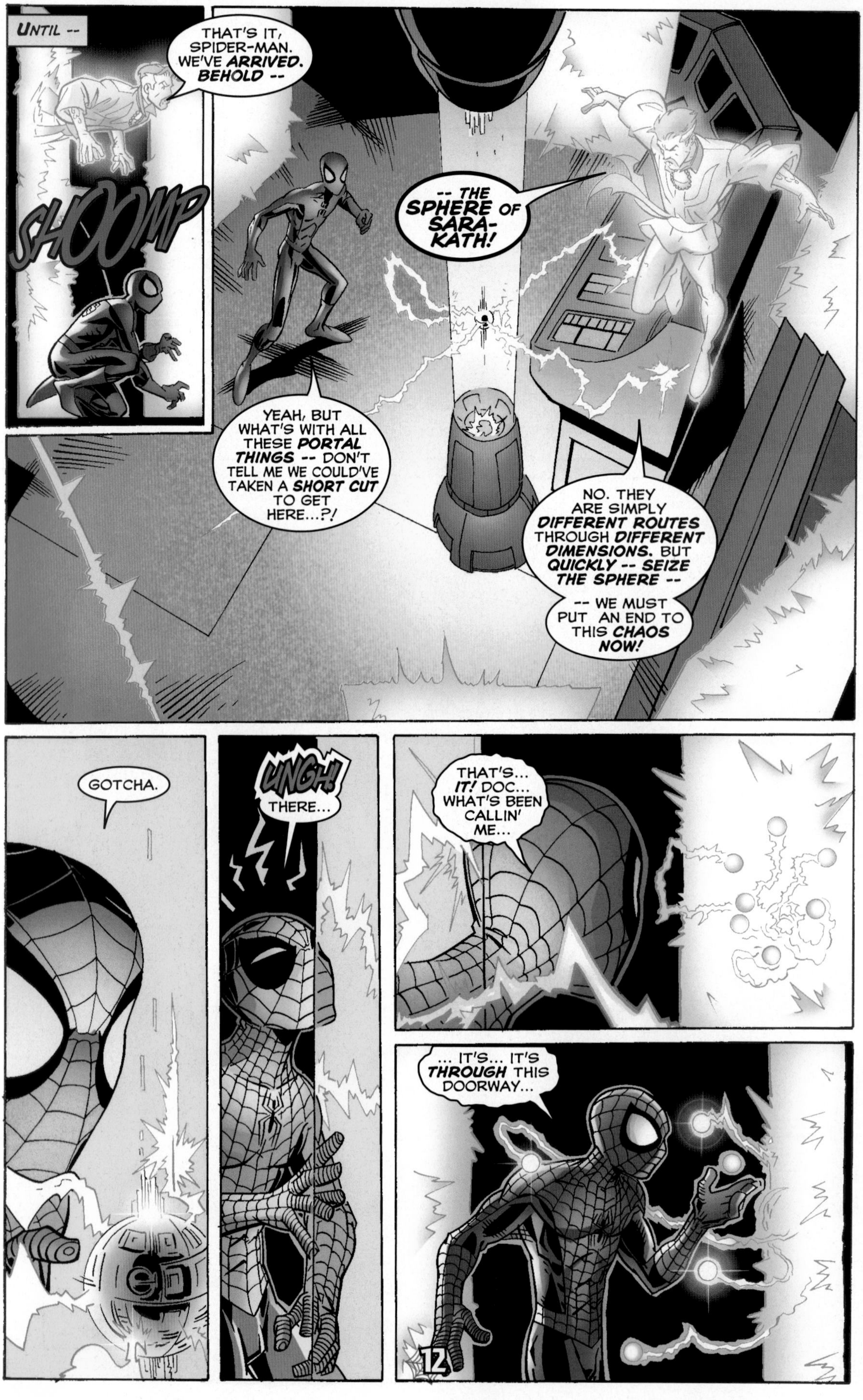
UNTIL --
THAT'S IT, SPIDER-MAN. WE'VE ARRIVED. BEHOLD --
SHOOMP
-- THE SPHERE OF SARA-KATH!
YEAH, BUT WHAT'S WITH ALL THESE PORTAL THINGS -- DON'T TELL ME WE COULD'VE TAKEN A SHORT CUT TO GET HERE...?!
NO. THEY ARE SIMPLY DIFFERENT ROUTES THROUGH DIFFERENT DIMENSIONS. BUT QUICKLY -- SEIZE THE SPHERE --
-- WE MUST PUT AN END TO THIS CHAOS NOW!
GOTCHA.
UNGH!
THERE...
THAT'S... IT! DOC... WHAT'S BEEN CALLIN' ME...
... IT'S... IT'S THROUGH THIS DOORWAY...
12

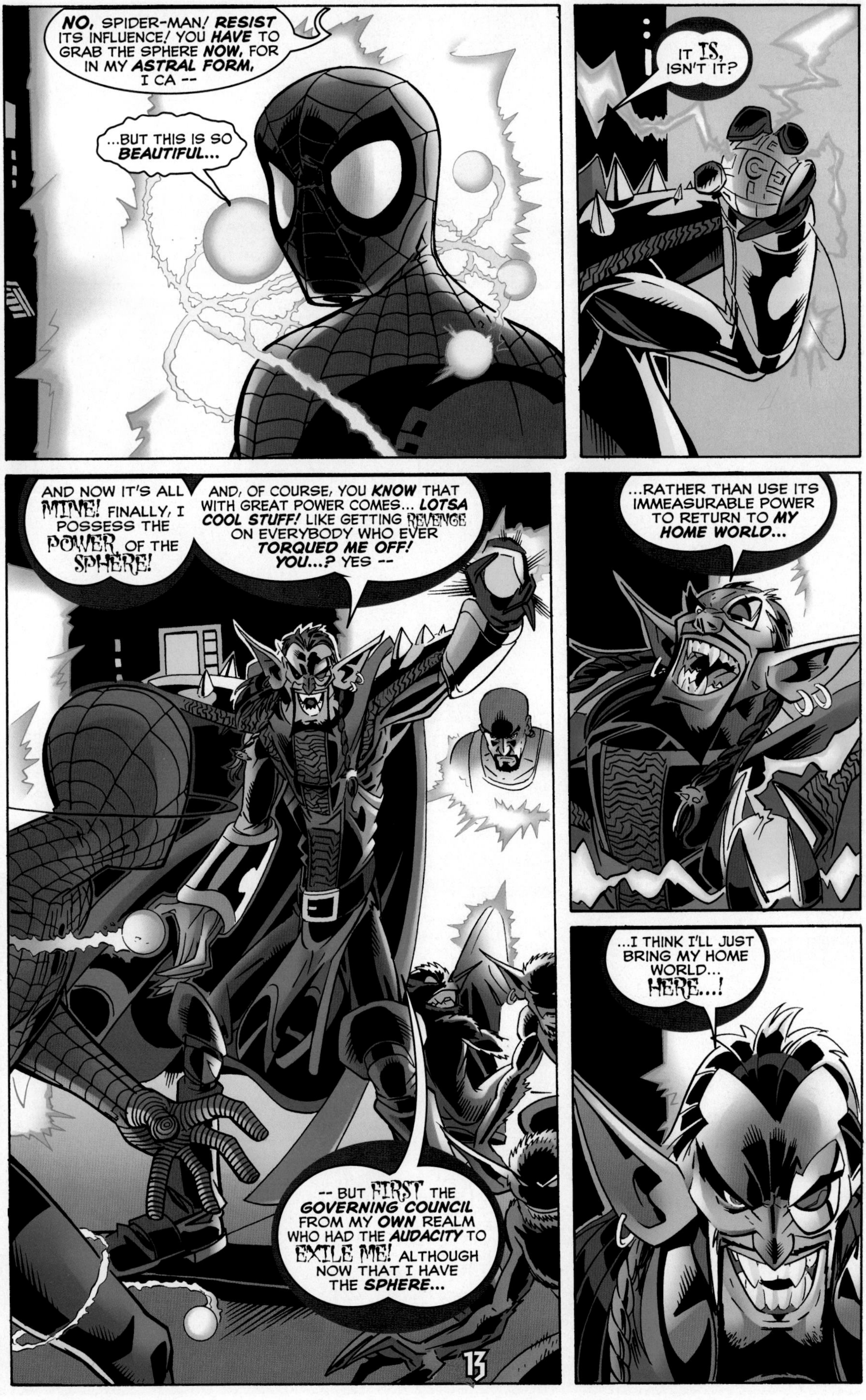
NO, SPIDER-MAN! RESIST ITS INFLUENCE! YOU HAVE TO GRAB THE SPHERE NOW, FOR IN MY ASTRAL FORM, I CA --
...BUT THIS IS SO BEAUTIFUL...
IT IS, ISN'T IT?
AND NOW IT'S ALL MINE! FINALLY, I POSSESS THE POWER OF THE SPHERE!
AND, OF COURSE, YOU KNOW THAT WITH GREAT POWER COMES... LOTSA COOL STUFF! LIKE GETTING REVENGE ON EVERYBODY WHO EVER TORQUED ME OFF! YOU...? YES --
-- BUT FIRST THE GOVERNING COUNCIL FROM MY OWN REALM WHO HAD THE AUDACITY TO EXILE ME! ALTHOUGH NOW THAT I HAVE THE SPHERE...
...RATHER THAN USE ITS IMMEASURABLE POWER TO RETURN TO MY HOME WORLD...
...I THINK I'LL JUST BRING MY HOME WORLD... HERE...!
13

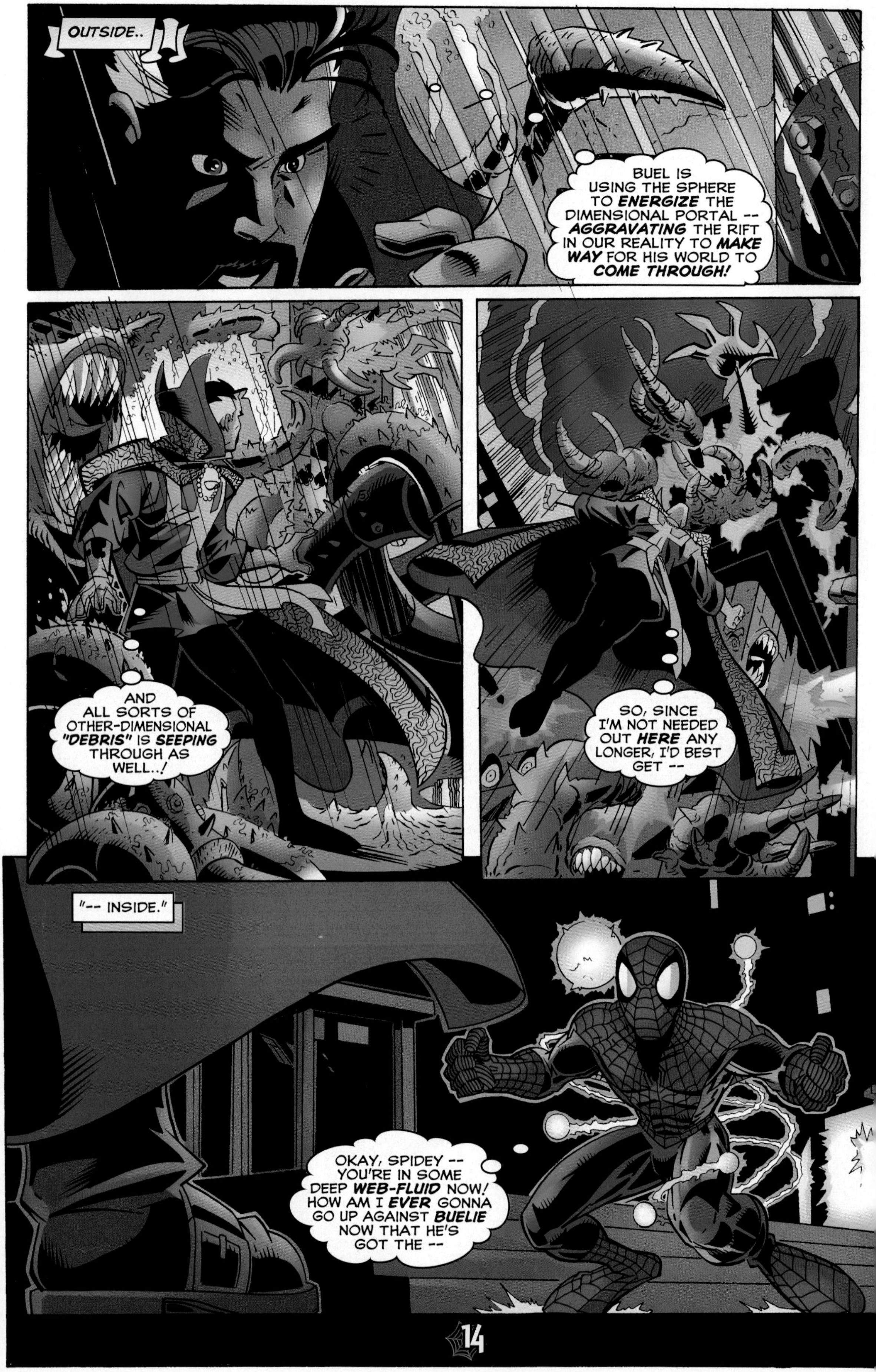
OUTSIDE..
BUEL IS USING THE SPHERE TO ENERGIZE THE DIMENSIONAL PORTAL -- AGGRAVATING THE RIFT IN OUR REALITY TO MAKE WAY FOR HIS WORLD TO COME THROUGH!
AND ALL SORTS OF OTHER-DIMENSIONAL "DEBRIS" IS SEEPING THROUGH AS WELL..!
SO, SINCE I'M NOT NEEDED OUT HERE ANY LONGER, I'D BEST GET --
"-- INSIDE."
OKAY, SPIDEY -- YOU'RE IN SOME DEEP WEB-FLUID NOW! HOW AM I EVER GONNA GO UP AGAINST BUELIE NOW THAT HE'S GOT THE --

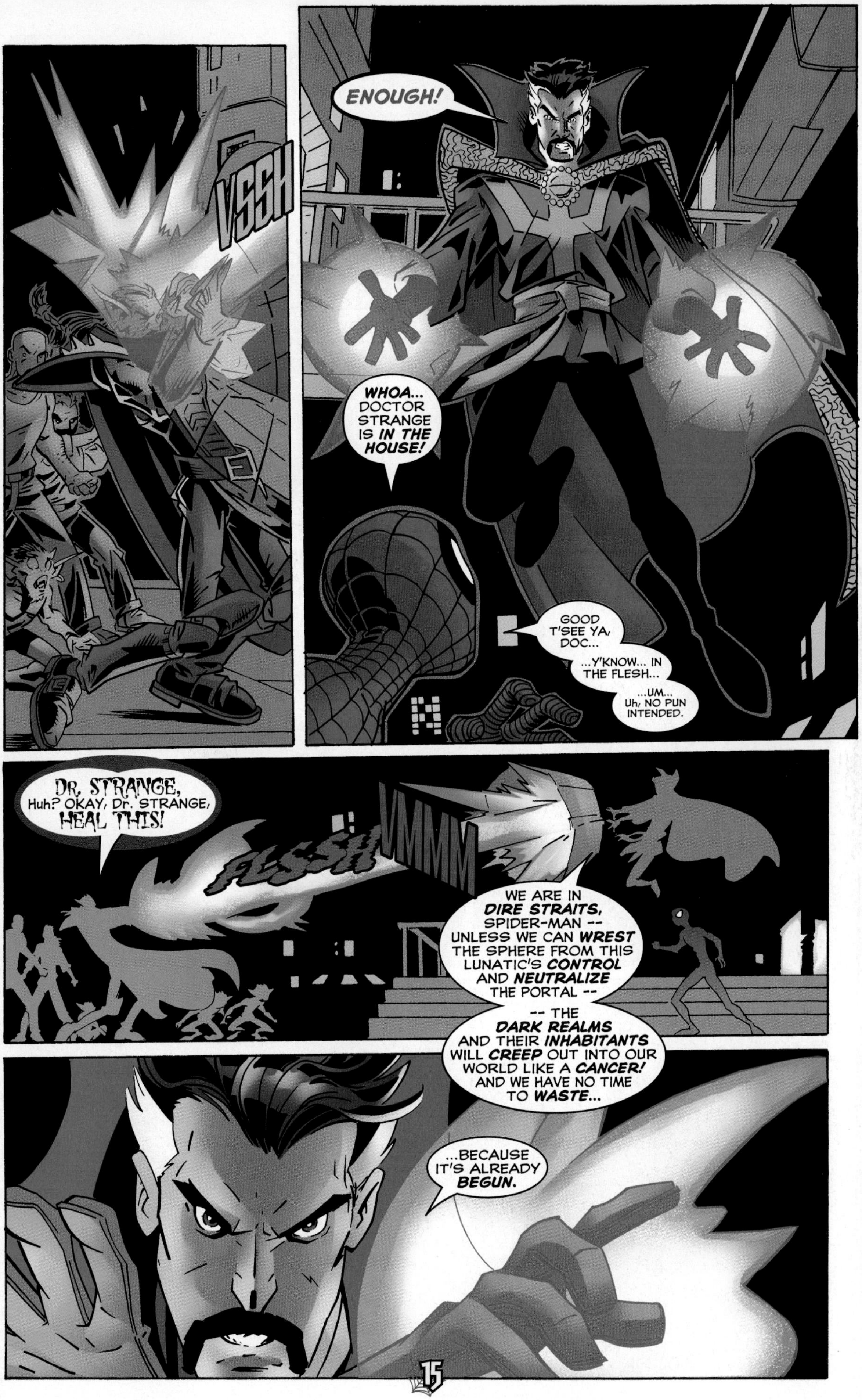
VSSH
ENOUGH!
WHOA... DOCTOR STRANGE IS IN THE HOUSE!
GOOD T'SEE YA, DOC...
...Y'KNOW... IN THE FLESH...
...UM... Uh, NO PUN INTENDED.
Dr. STRANGE, Huh? OKAY, Dr. STRANGE, HEAL THIS!
FLSSH
VMMM
WE ARE IN DIRE STRAITS, SPIDER-MAN -- UNLESS WE CAN WREST THE SPHERE FROM THIS LUNATIC'S CONTROL AND NEUTRALIZE THE PORTAL --
-- THE DARK REALMS AND THEIR INHABITANTS WILL CREEP OUT INTO OUR WORLD LIKE A CANCER! AND WE HAVE NO TIME TO WASTE...
...BECAUSE IT'S ALREADY BEGUN.

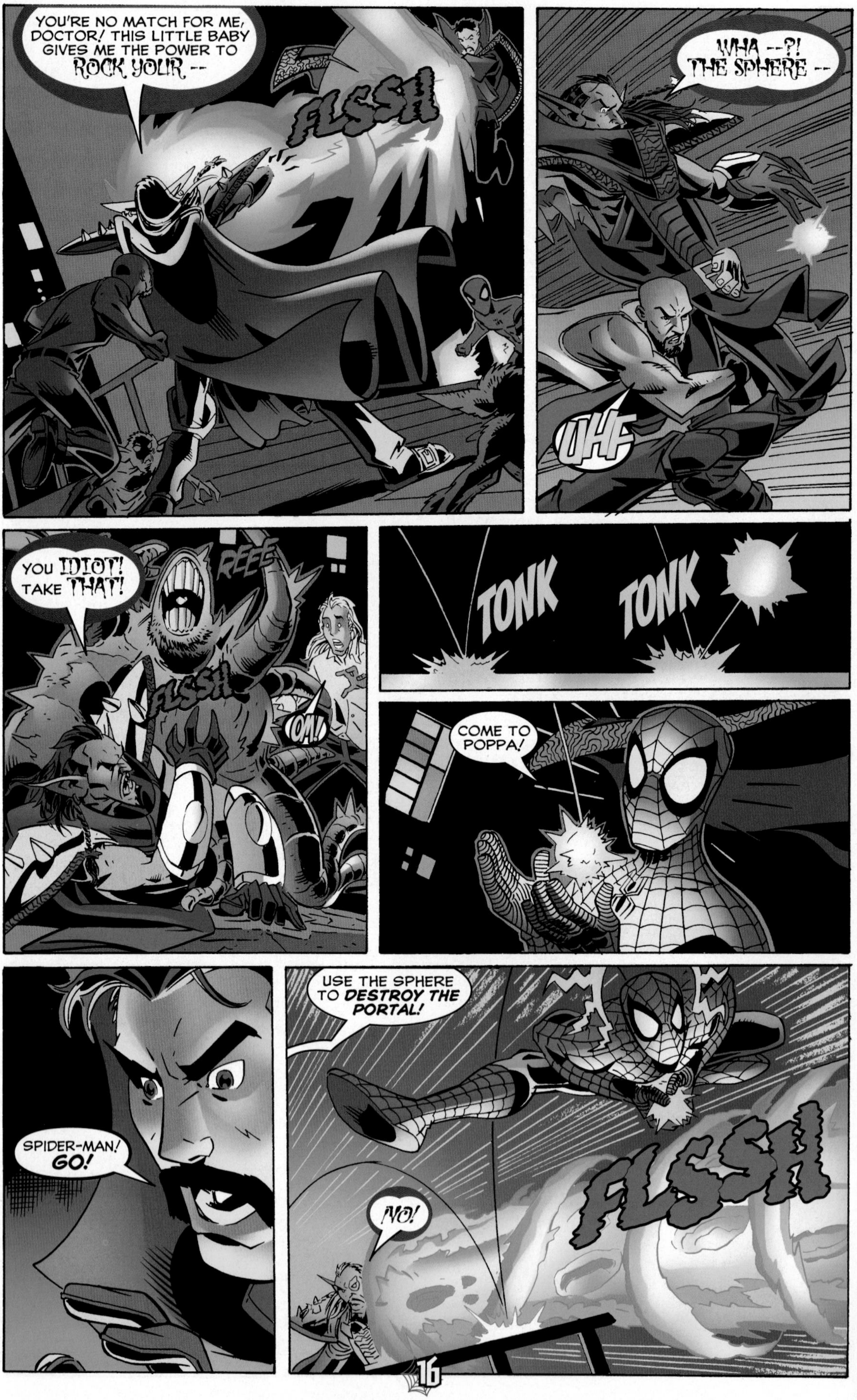
YOU'RE NO MATCH FOR ME, DOCTOR! THIS LITTLE BABY GIVES ME THE POWER TO ROCK YOUR --
FLSSH
WHA --?! THE SPHERE --
UHF
YOU IDIOT! TAKE THAT!
REEE
FLSSH
TOM!
TONK
TONK
COME TO POPPA!
SPIDER-MAN! GO!
USE THE SPHERE TO DESTROY THE PORTAL!
FLSSH
NO!

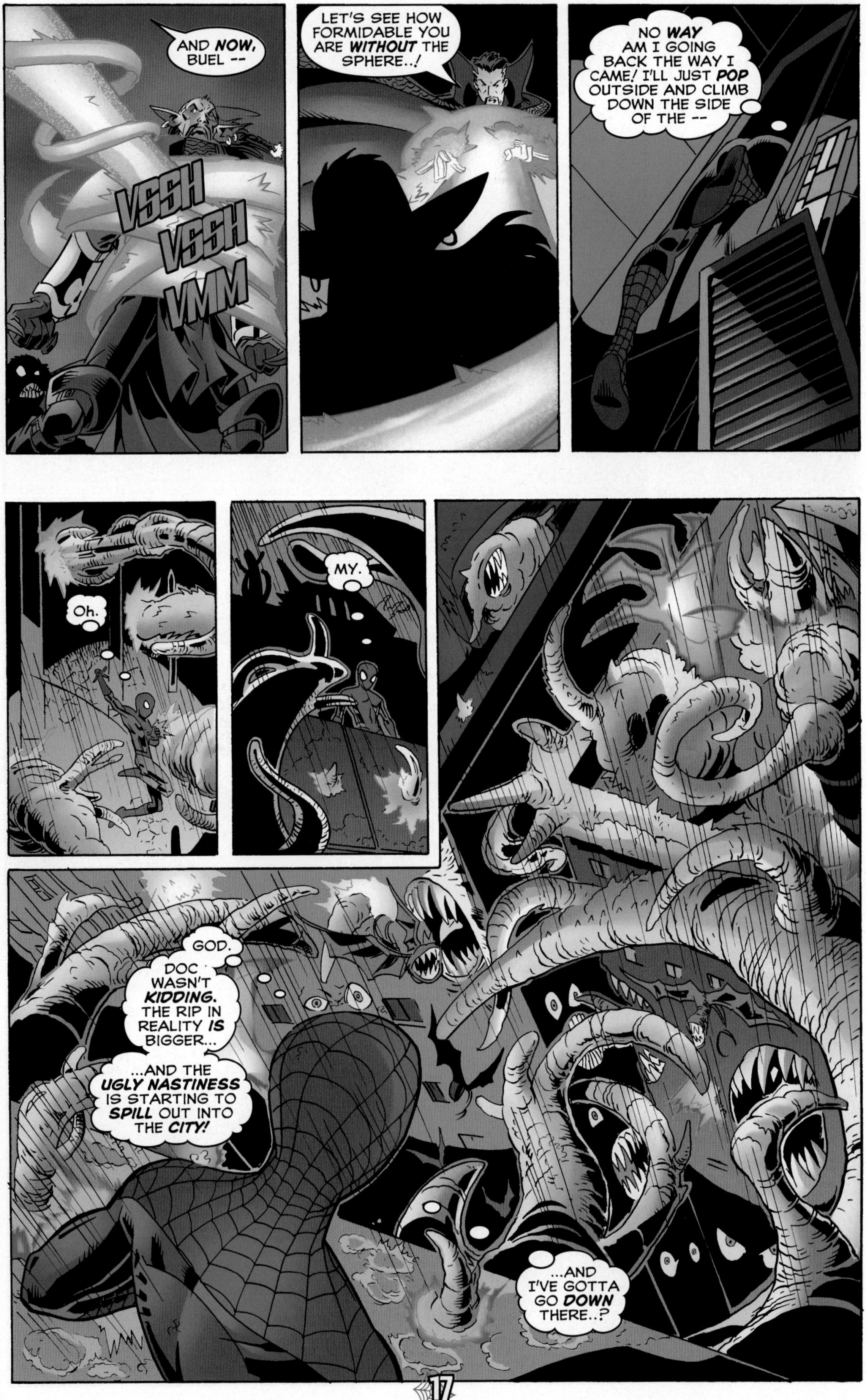
AND NOW, BUEL --
VSSH
VSSH
VMM
LET'S SEE HOW FORMIDABLE YOU ARE WITHOUT THE SPHERE..!
NO WAY AM I GOING BACK THE WAY I CAME! I'LL JUST POP OUTSIDE AND CLIMB DOWN THE SIDE OF THE --
Oh.
MY.
GOD.
DOC WASN'T KIDDING. THE RIP IN REALITY IS BIGGER...
...AND THE UGLY NASTINESS IS STARTING TO SPILL OUT INTO THE CITY!
...AND I'VE GOTTA GO DOWN THERE..?

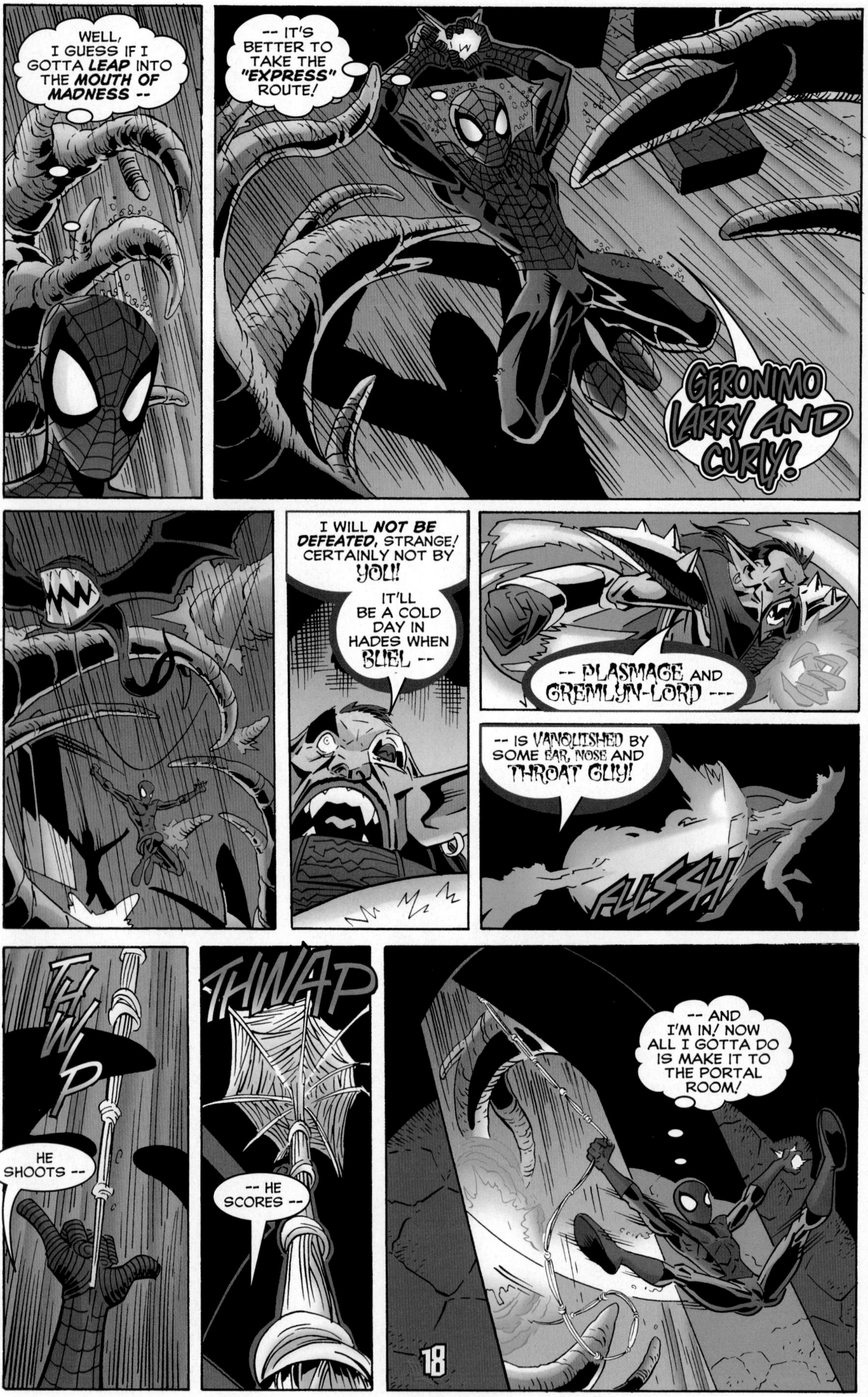
WELL, I GUESS IF I GOTTA LEAP INTO THE MOUTH OF MADNESS --
-- IT'S BETTER TO TAKE THE "EXPRESS" ROUTE!
GERONIMO LARRY AND CURLY!
I WILL NOT BE DEFEATED, STRANGE! CERTAINLY NOT BY YOU!
IT'LL BE A COLD DAY IN HADES WHEN BUEL --
-- PLASMAGE AND GREMLYN-LORD ---
-- IS VANQUISHED BY SOME EAR, NOSE AND THROAT GUY!
FUSSSH
THWIP
HE SHOOTS --
THWAP
-- HE SCORES --
-- AND I'M IN! NOW ALL I GOTTA DO IS MAKE IT TO THE PORTAL ROOM!

THE POWER OF THE SPHERE STILL *RESONATES* WITHIN ME, STRANGE --

-- SO LONG AS IT REMAINS WITHIN THE VICINITY, MY MAGIKS ARE BOLSTERED A HUNDRED-FOLD! SO GET USED TO THE NAME DR. FLESHTHING, 'CAUSE THAT'S WHAT YOU'RE GOING TO BE!

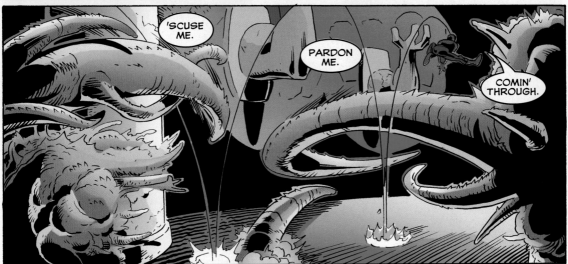

'SCUSE ME.

PARDON ME.

COMIN' THROUGH.

HOLY *COW!* THAT THING'S *GLOWING* LIKE A *MAGNESIUM* FLARE...

...*WORSE!* CAN BARELY *SEE...* AND NOW THAT I'M *HERE*, WHAT DO I DO..?

I DON'T KNOW FROM *MAGIC*, AND DOC DIDN'T HAVE TIME TO *BRIEF ME...*

...BUT I GUESS IF THIS THING IS WHAT'S *CAUSING* ALL THE TROUBLE...

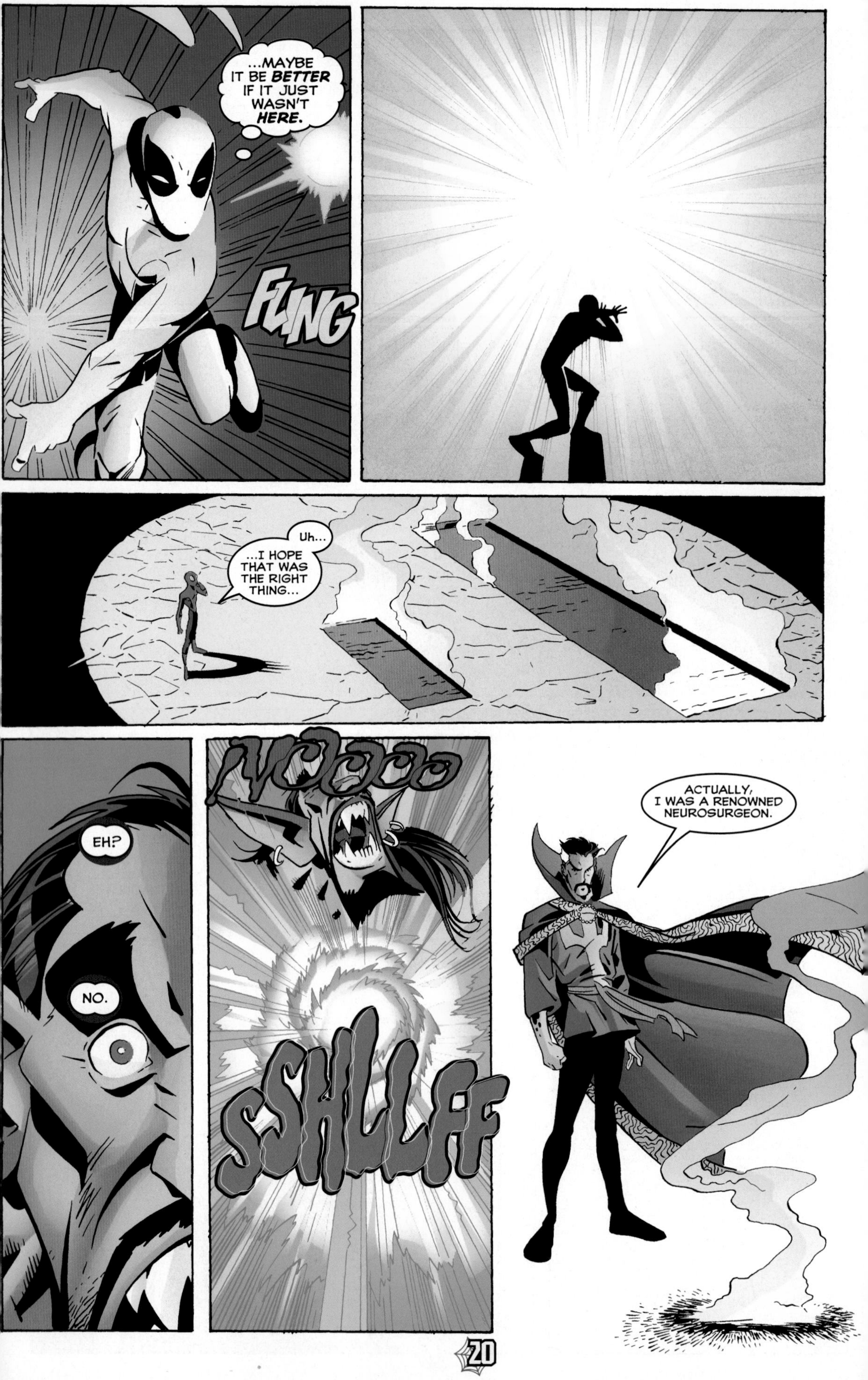

...MAYBE IT BE BETTER IF IT JUST WASN'T HERE.
FLING
Uh...
...I HOPE THAT WAS THE RIGHT THING...
EH?
NO.
NOOOOO
SSHLLFF
ACTUALLY, I WAS A RENOWNED NEUROSURGEON.

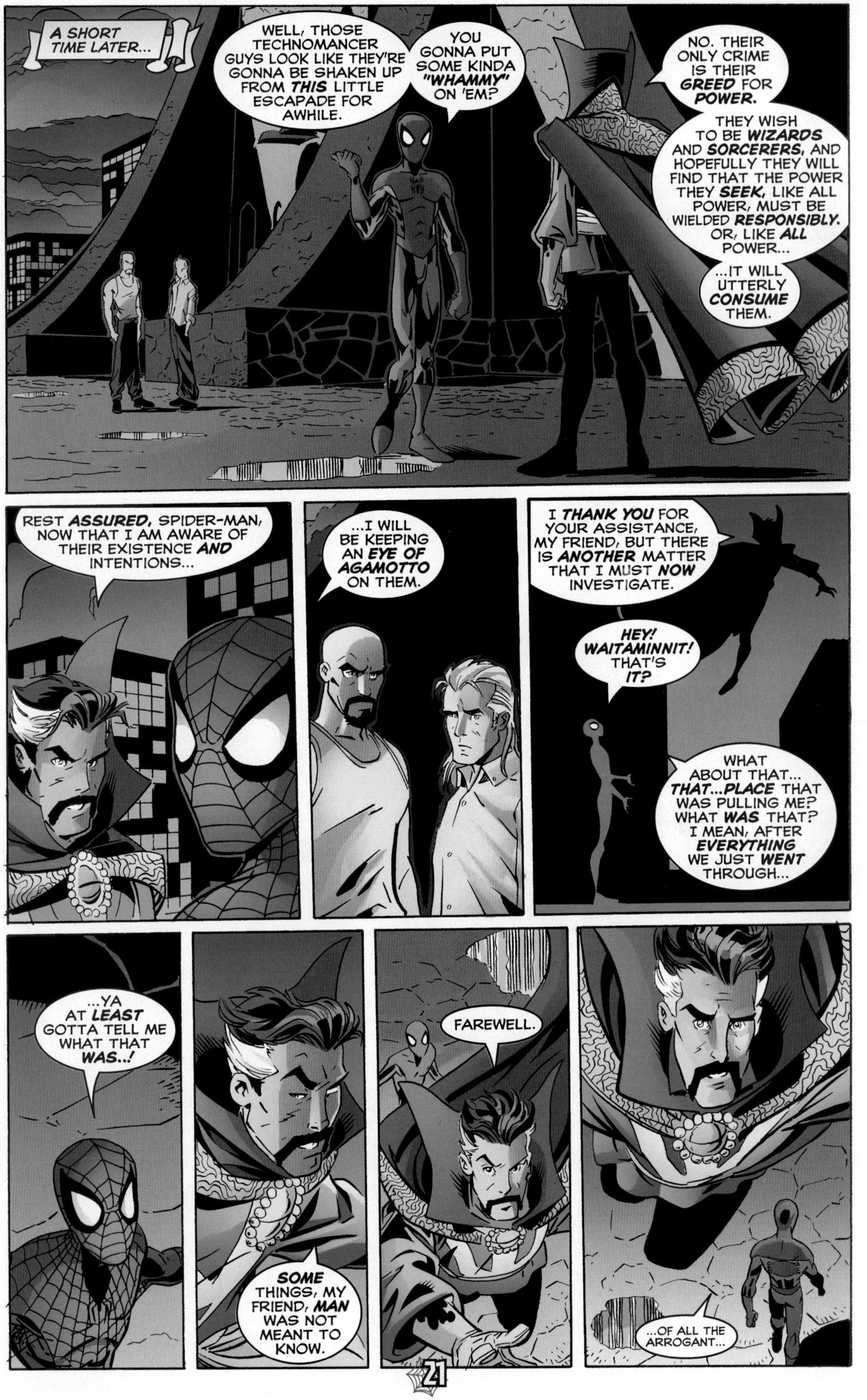
A SHORT TIME LATER...
WELL, THOSE TECHNOMANCER GUYS LOOK LIKE THEY'RE GONNA BE SHAKEN UP FROM THIS LITTLE ESCAPADE FOR AWHILE.
YOU GONNA PUT SOME KINDA "WHAMMY" ON 'EM?
NO. THEIR ONLY CRIME IS THEIR GREED FOR POWER.
THEY WISH TO BE WIZARDS AND SORCERERS, AND HOPEFULLY THEY WILL FIND THAT THE POWER THEY SEEK, LIKE ALL POWER, MUST BE WIELDED RESPONSIBLY. OR, LIKE ALL POWER...
...IT WILL UTTERLY CONSUME THEM.
REST ASSURED, SPIDER-MAN, NOW THAT I AM AWARE OF THEIR EXISTENCE AND INTENTIONS...
...I WILL BE KEEPING AN EYE OF AGAMOTTO ON THEM.
I THANK YOU FOR YOUR ASSISTANCE, MY FRIEND, BUT THERE IS ANOTHER MATTER THAT I MUST NOW INVESTIGATE.
HEY! WAITAMINNIT! THAT'S IT?
WHAT ABOUT THAT... THAT...PLACE THAT WAS PULLING ME? WHAT WAS THAT? I MEAN, AFTER EVERYTHING WE JUST WENT THROUGH...
...YA AT LEAST GOTTA TELL ME WHAT THAT WAS..!
SOME THINGS, MY FRIEND, MAN WAS NOT MEANT TO KNOW.
FAREWELL.
...OF ALL THE ARROGANT...

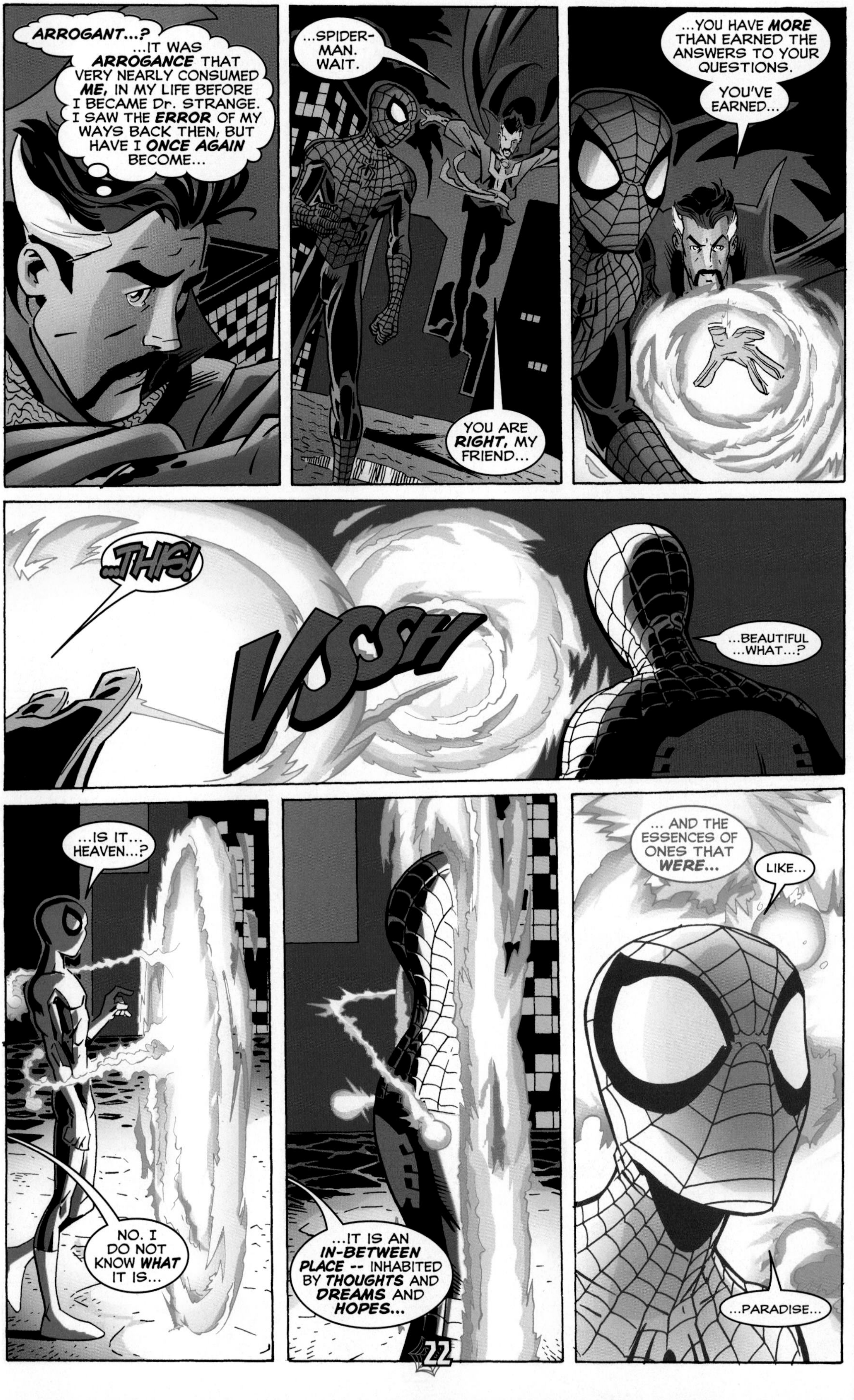
ARROGANT...? ...IT WAS ARROGANCE THAT VERY NEARLY CONSUMED ME, IN MY LIFE BEFORE I BECAME Dr. STRANGE. I SAW THE ERROR OF MY WAYS BACK THEN, BUT HAVE I ONCE AGAIN BECOME...
...SPIDER-MAN. WAIT.
YOU ARE RIGHT, MY FRIEND...
...YOU HAVE MORE THAN EARNED THE ANSWERS TO YOUR QUESTIONS.
YOU'VE EARNED...
...THIS!
VSSH
...BEAUTIFUL ...WHAT...?
...IS IT... HEAVEN...?
NO. I DO NOT KNOW WHAT IT IS...
...IT IS AN IN-BETWEEN PLACE -- INHABITED BY THOUGHTS AND DREAMS AND HOPES...
... AND THE ESSENCES OF ONES THAT WERE...
LIKE...
...PARADISE...

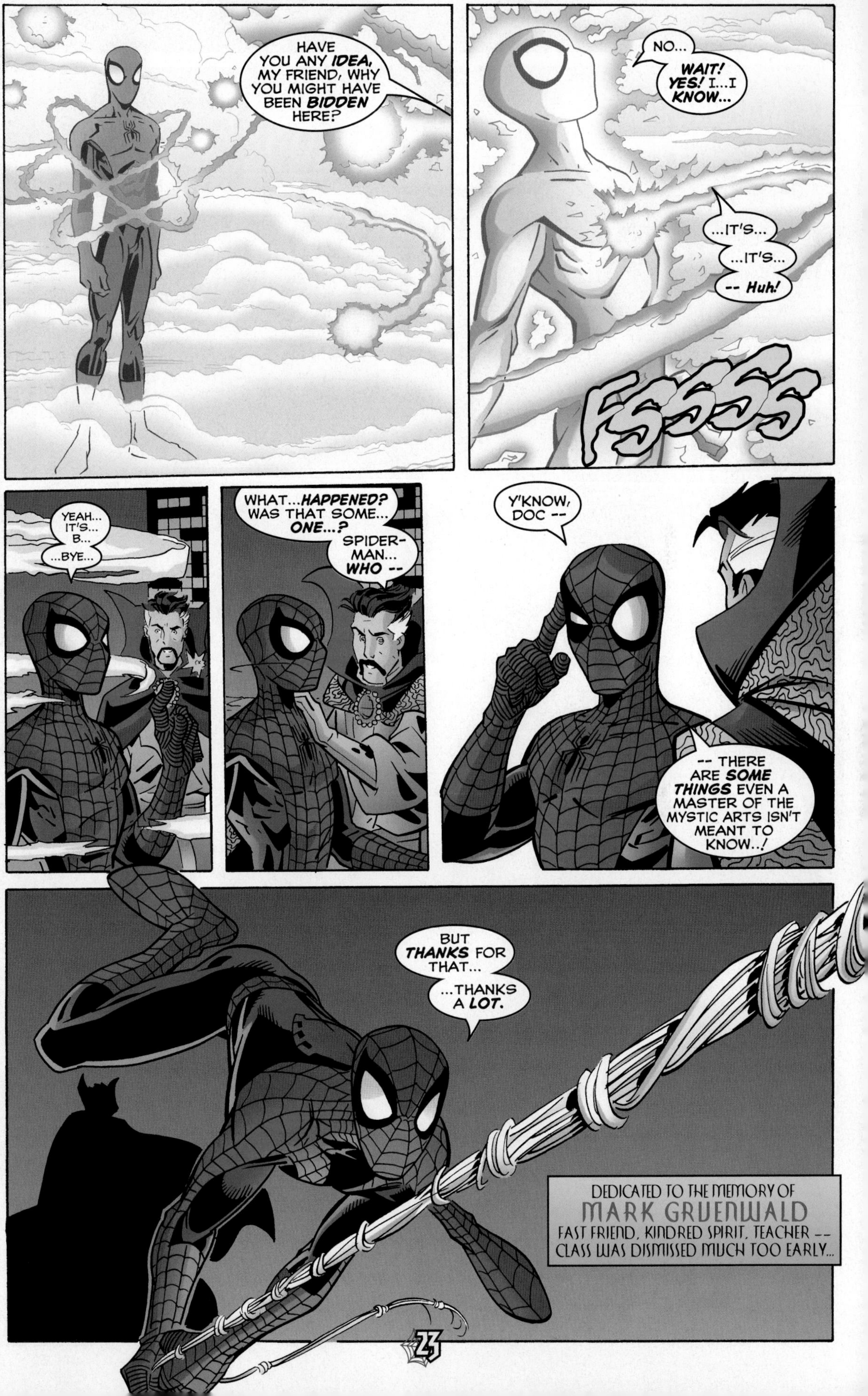

HAVE YOU ANY IDEA, MY FRIEND, WHY YOU MIGHT HAVE BEEN BIDDEN HERE?
NO...
WAIT! YES! I...I KNOW...
...IT'S...
...IT'S...
-- Huh!
FSSSS
YEAH... IT'S... B...
...BYE...
WHAT...HAPPENED? WAS THAT SOME... ONE...?
SPIDER-MAN... WHO --
Y'KNOW, DOC --
-- THERE ARE SOME THINGS EVEN A MASTER OF THE MYSTIC ARTS ISN'T MEANT TO KNOW..!
BUT THANKS FOR THAT...
...THANKS A LOT.
DEDICATED TO THE MEMORY OF
MARK GRUENWALD
FAST FRIEND, KINDRED SPIRIT, TEACHER --
CLASS WAS DISMISSED MUCH TOO EARLY...

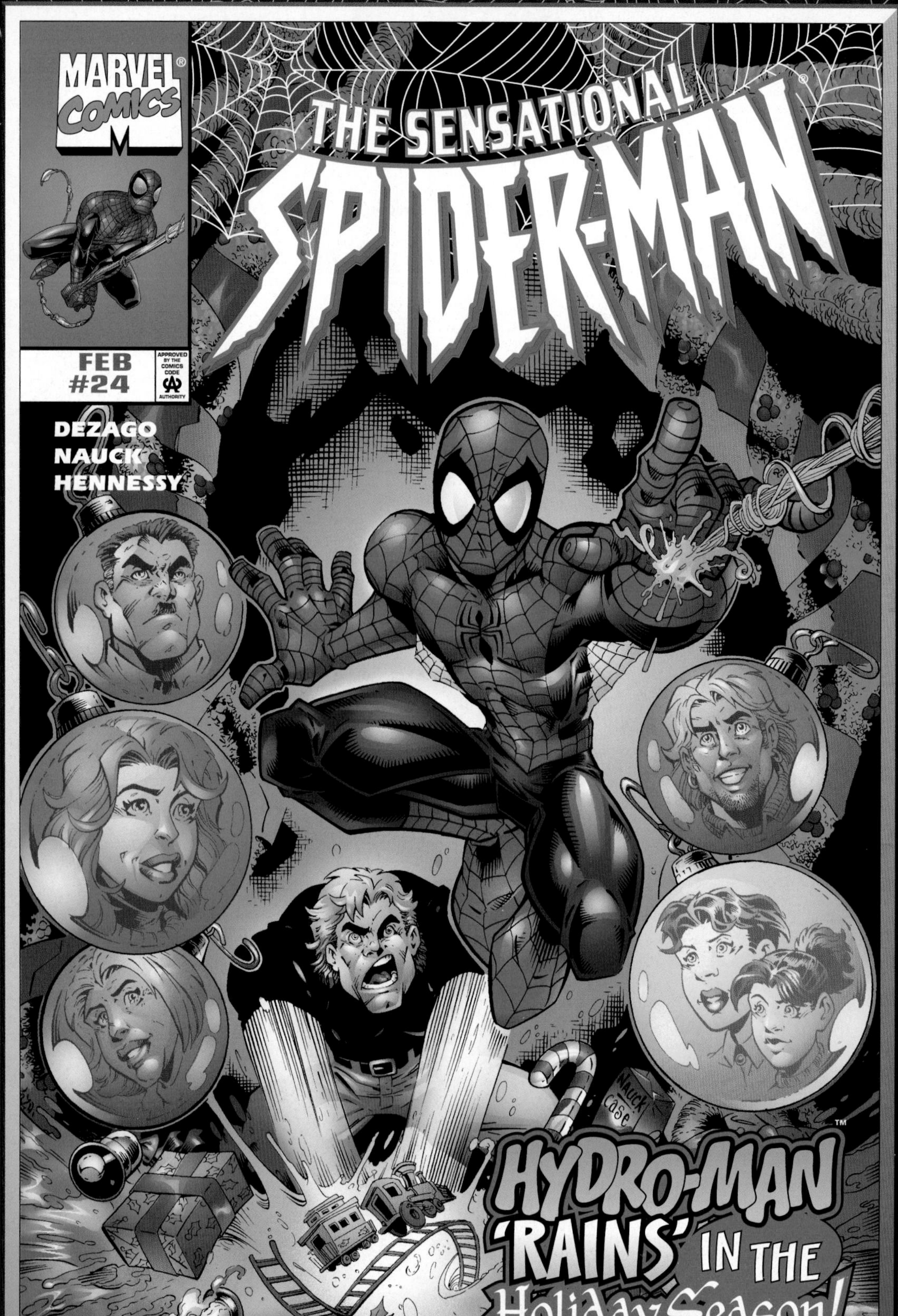

MARVEL COMICS
THE SENSATIONAL SPIDER-MAN
FEB #24
APPROVED BY THE COMICS CODE AUTHORITY
DEZAGO
NAUCK
HENNESSY
HYDRO-MAN 'RAINS' IN THE Holiday Season!

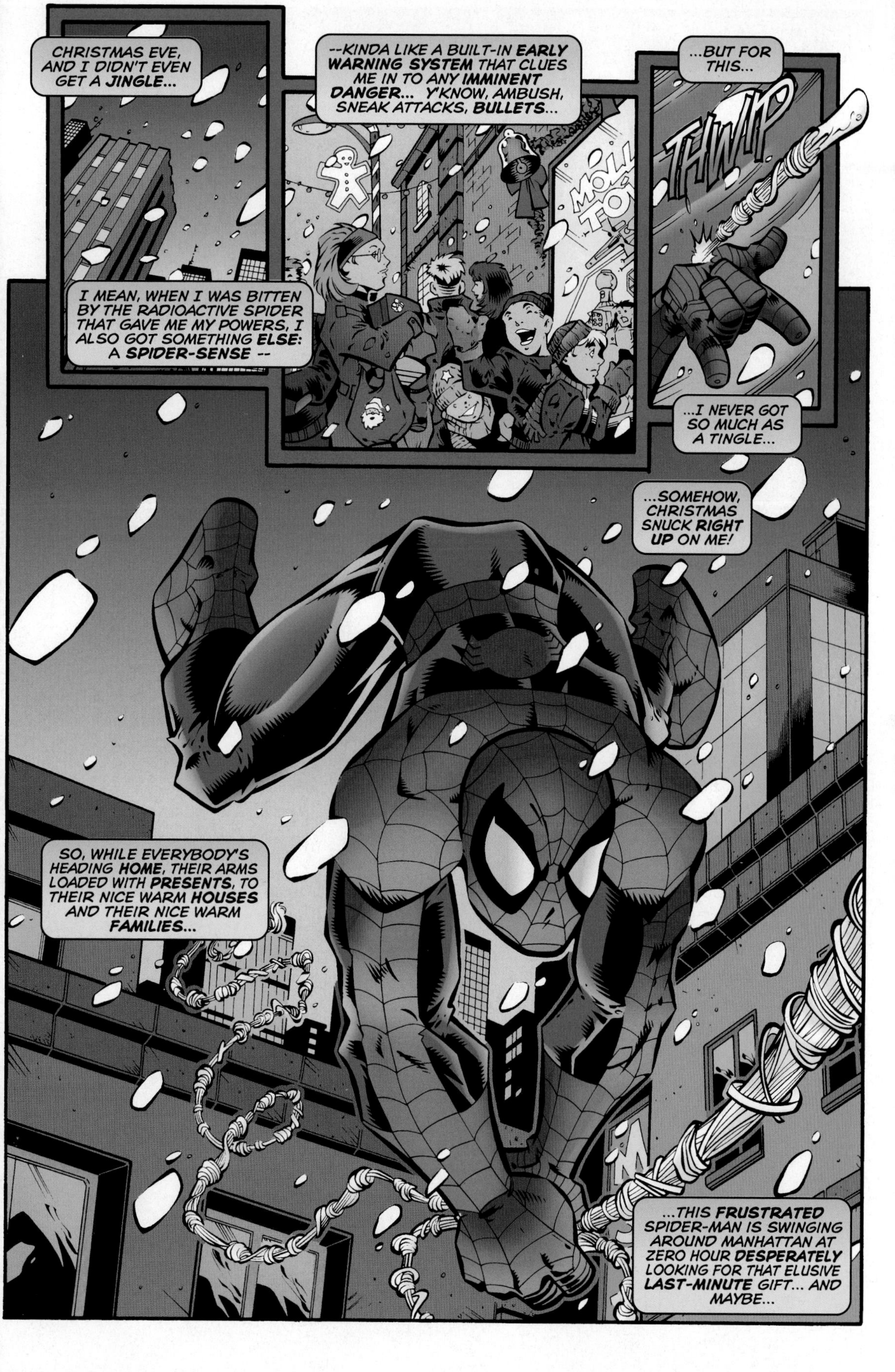
CHRISTMAS EVE, AND I DIDN'T EVEN GET A JINGLE...
I MEAN, WHEN I WAS BITTEN BY THE RADIOACTIVE SPIDER THAT GAVE ME MY POWERS, I ALSO GOT SOMETHING ELSE: A SPIDER-SENSE --
--KINDA LIKE A BUILT-IN EARLY WARNING SYSTEM THAT CLUES ME IN TO ANY IMMINENT DANGER... Y'KNOW, AMBUSH, SNEAK ATTACKS, BULLETS...
...BUT FOR THIS...
THWIP
...I NEVER GOT SO MUCH AS A TINGLE...
...SOMEHOW, CHRISTMAS SNUCK RIGHT UP ON ME!
SO, WHILE EVERYBODY'S HEADING HOME, THEIR ARMS LOADED WITH PRESENTS, TO THEIR NICE WARM HOUSES AND THEIR NICE WARM FAMILIES...
...THIS FRUSTRATED SPIDER-MAN IS SWINGING AROUND MANHATTAN AT ZERO HOUR DESPERATELY LOOKING FOR THAT ELUSIVE LAST-MINUTE GIFT... AND MAYBE...

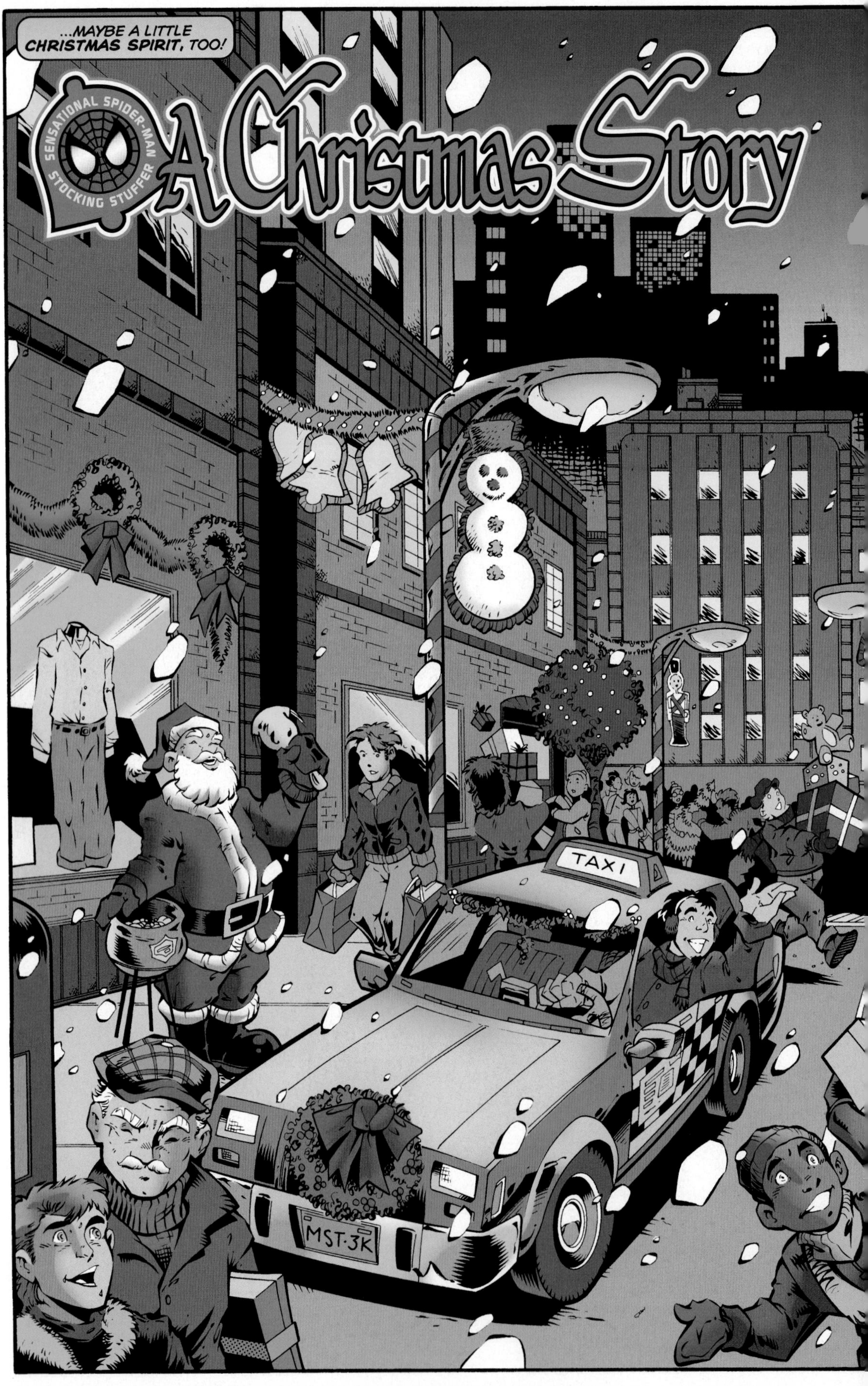
...MAYBE A LITTLE CHRISTMAS SPIRIT, TOO!
SENSATIONAL SPIDER-MAN STOCKING STUFFER
A Christmas Story
TAXI
MST-3K

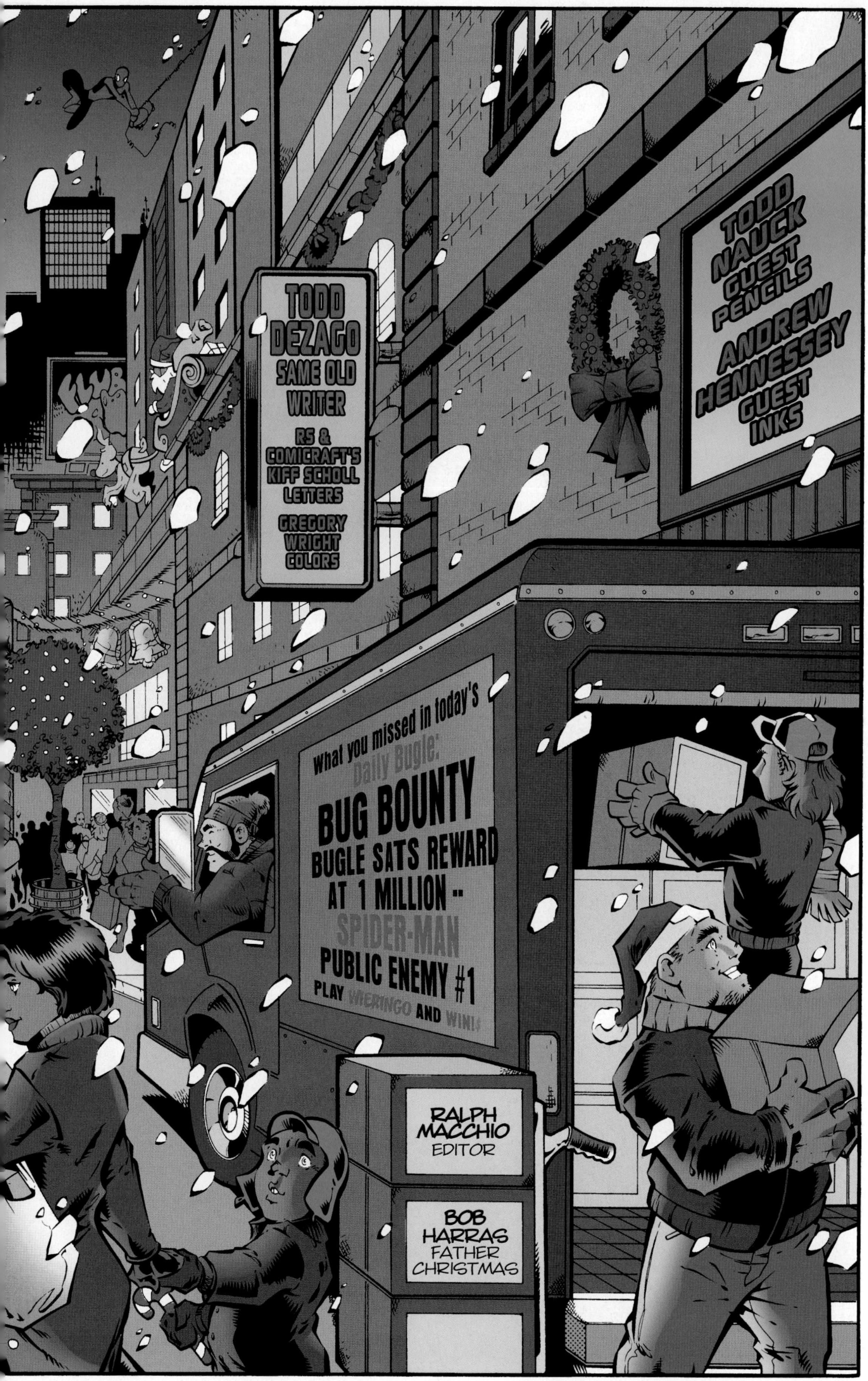
TODD DEZAGO SAME OLD WRITER
RS & COMICRAFT'S KIFF SCHOLL LETTERS
GREGORY WRIGHT COLORS
TODD NAUCK GUEST PENCILS
ANDREW HENNESSEY GUEST INKS
What you missed in today's Daily Bugle:
BUG BOUNTY
BUGLE SATS REWARD AT 1 MILLION --
SPIDER-MAN PUBLIC ENEMY #1
PLAY WIERINGO AND WIN!$
RALPH MACCHIO EDITOR
BOB HARRAS FATHER CHRISTMAS

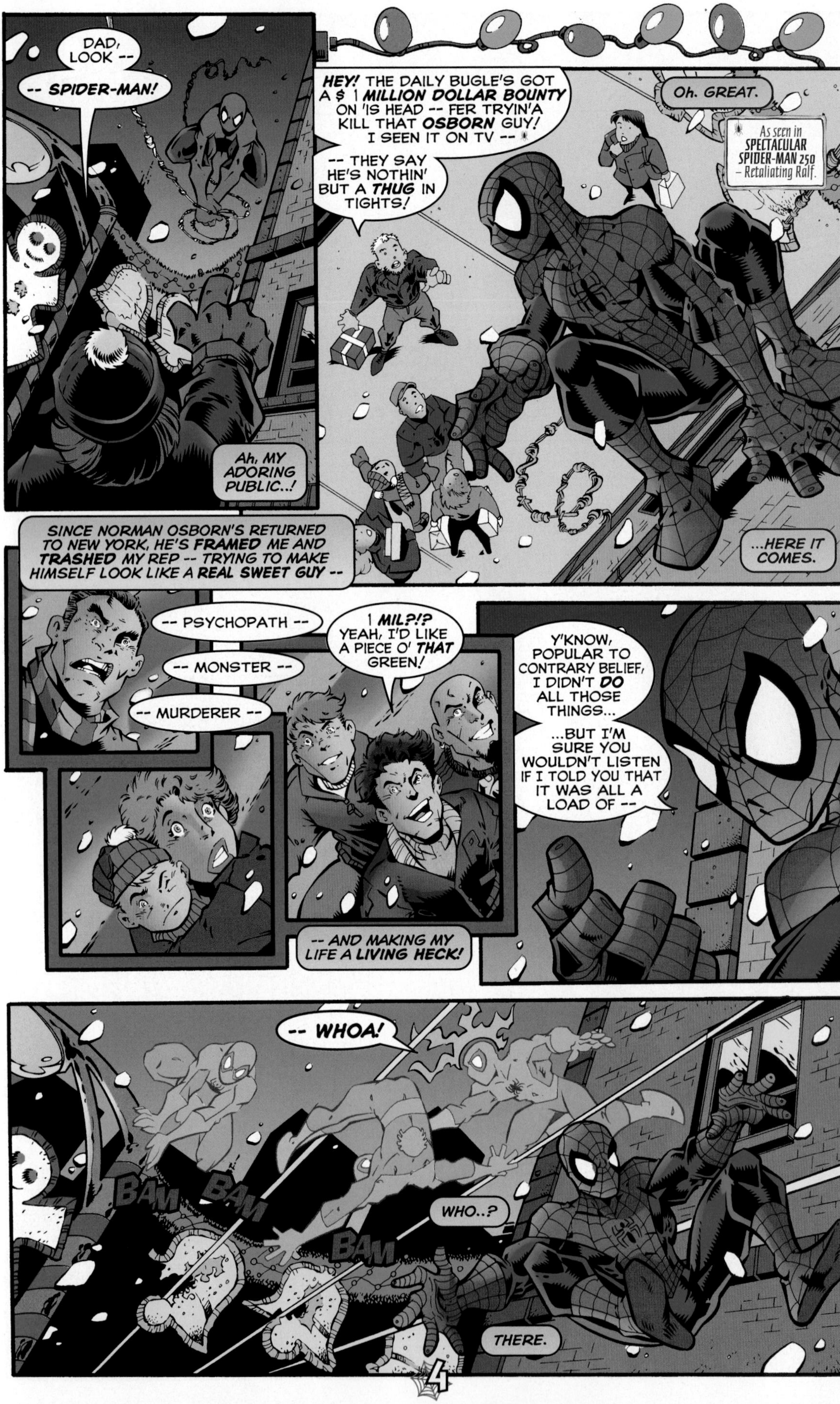

DAD, LOOK --
-- SPIDER-MAN!
Ah, MY ADORING PUBLIC..!
HEY! THE DAILY BUGLE'S GOT A $ 1 MILLION DOLLAR BOUNTY ON 'IS HEAD -- FER TRYIN'A KILL THAT OSBORN GUY! I SEEN IT ON TV --
-- THEY SAY HE'S NOTHIN' BUT A THUG IN TIGHTS!
Oh. GREAT.
As seen in SPECTACULAR SPIDER-MAN 250 – Retaliating Ralf.
...HERE IT COMES.
SINCE NORMAN OSBORN'S RETURNED TO NEW YORK, HE'S FRAMED ME AND TRASHED MY REP -- TRYING TO MAKE HIMSELF LOOK LIKE A REAL SWEET GUY --
-- PSYCHOPATH --
-- MONSTER --
-- MURDERER --
1 MIL?!? YEAH, I'D LIKE A PIECE O' THAT GREEN!
Y'KNOW, POPULAR TO CONTRARY BELIEF, I DIDN'T DO ALL THOSE THINGS...
...BUT I'M SURE YOU WOULDN'T LISTEN IF I TOLD YOU THAT IT WAS ALL A LOAD OF --
-- AND MAKING MY LIFE A LIVING HECK!
-- WHOA!
BAM
BAM
BAM
WHO..?
THERE.

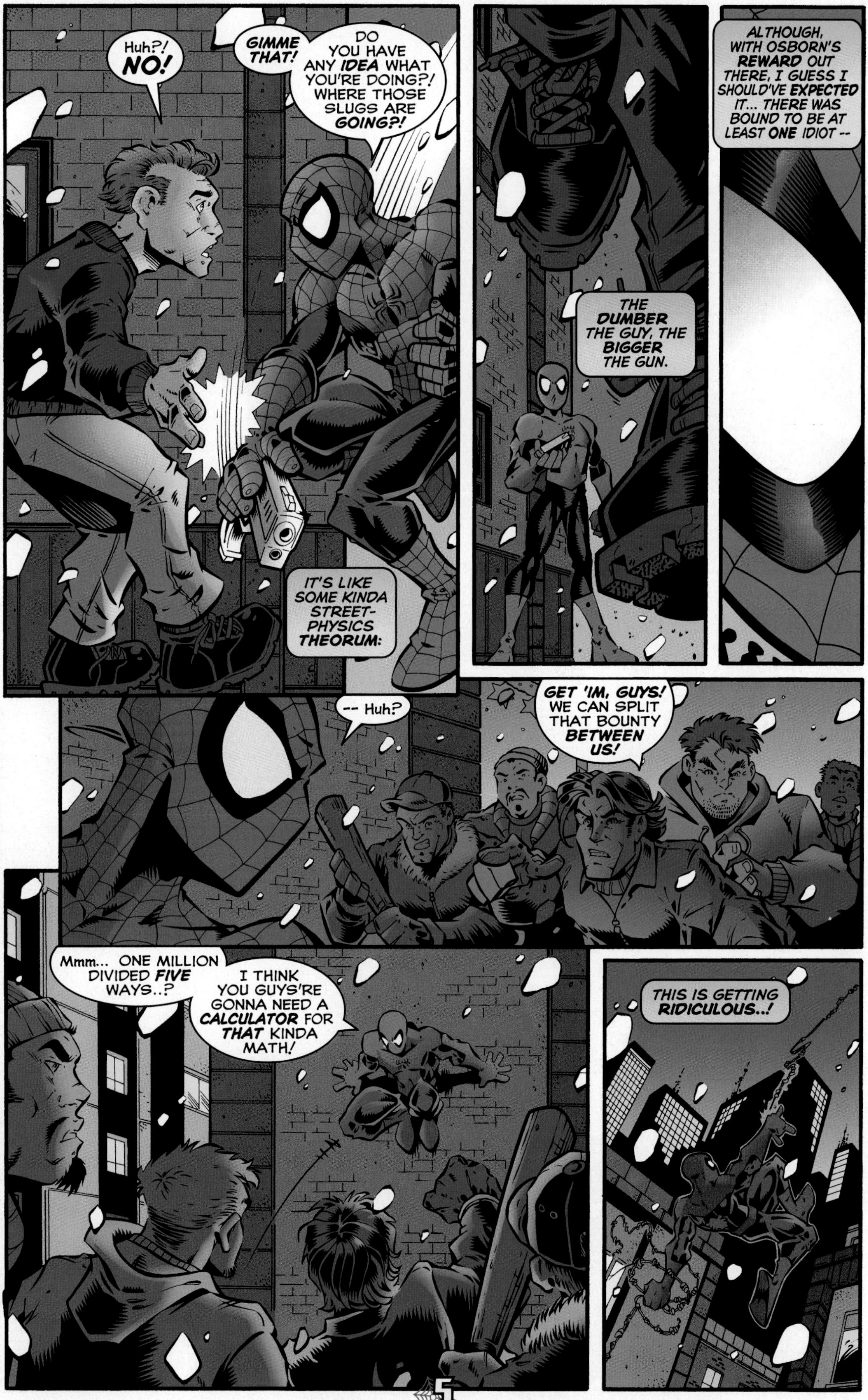

Huh?! NO!
GIMME THAT!
DO YOU HAVE ANY IDEA WHAT YOU'RE DOING?! WHERE THOSE SLUGS ARE GOING?!
IT'S LIKE SOME KINDA STREET-PHYSICS THEORUM:
THE DUMBER THE GUY, THE BIGGER THE GUN.
ALTHOUGH, WITH OSBORN'S REWARD OUT THERE, I GUESS I SHOULD'VE EXPECTED IT... THERE WAS BOUND TO BE AT LEAST ONE IDIOT --
-- Huh?
GET 'IM, GUYS! WE CAN SPLIT THAT BOUNTY BETWEEN US!
Mmm... ONE MILLION DIVIDED FIVE WAYS..?
I THINK YOU GUYS'RE GONNA NEED A CALCULATOR FOR THAT KINDA MATH!
THIS IS GETTING RIDICULOUS..!

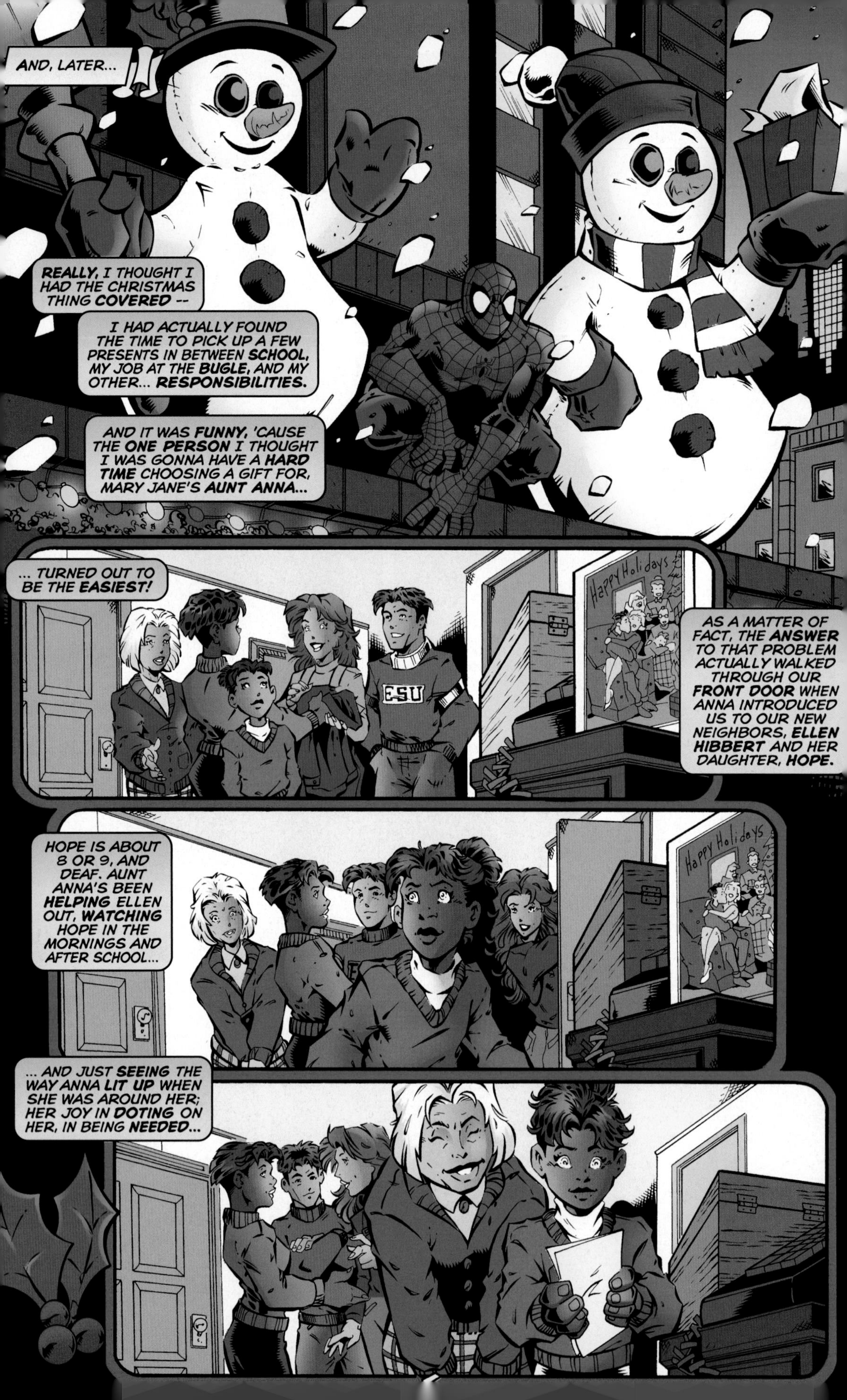
AND, LATER...
REALLY, I THOUGHT I HAD THE CHRISTMAS THING COVERED --
I HAD ACTUALLY FOUND THE TIME TO PICK UP A FEW PRESENTS IN BETWEEN SCHOOL, MY JOB AT THE BUGLE, AND MY OTHER... RESPONSIBILITIES.
AND IT WAS FUNNY, 'CAUSE THE ONE PERSON I THOUGHT I WAS GONNA HAVE A HARD TIME CHOOSING A GIFT FOR, MARY JANE'S AUNT ANNA...
... TURNED OUT TO BE THE EASIEST!
ESU
Happy Holidays
AS A MATTER OF FACT, THE ANSWER TO THAT PROBLEM ACTUALLY WALKED THROUGH OUR FRONT DOOR WHEN ANNA INTRODUCED US TO OUR NEW NEIGHBORS, ELLEN HIBBERT AND HER DAUGHTER, HOPE.
HOPE IS ABOUT 8 OR 9, AND DEAF. AUNT ANNA'S BEEN HELPING ELLEN OUT, WATCHING HOPE IN THE MORNINGS AND AFTER SCHOOL...
Happy Holidays
... AND JUST SEEING THE WAY ANNA LIT UP WHEN SHE WAS AROUND HER; HER JOY IN DOTING ON HER, IN BEING NEEDED...

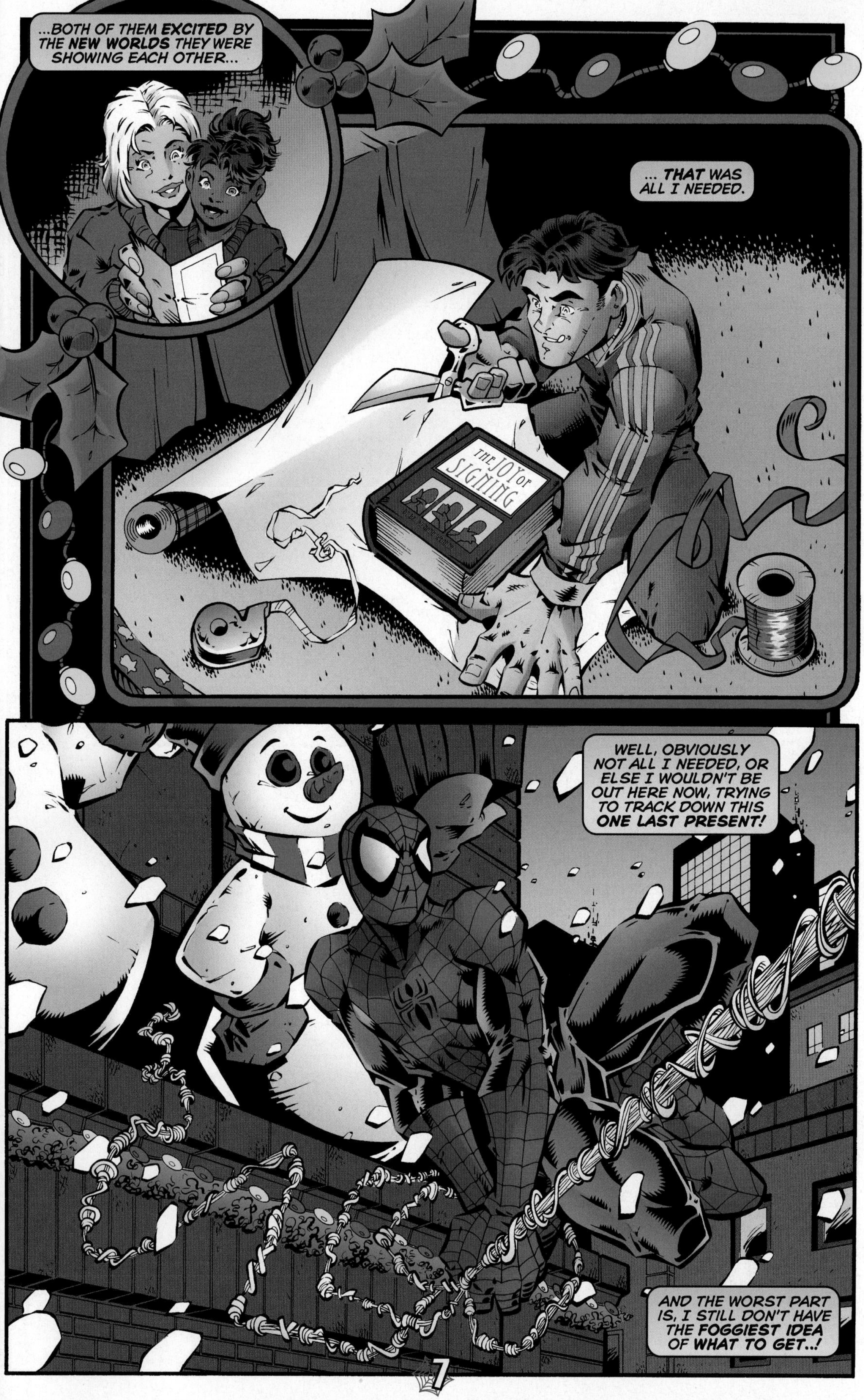
...BOTH OF THEM EXCITED BY THE NEW WORLDS THEY WERE SHOWING EACH OTHER...
... THAT WAS ALL I NEEDED.
THE JOY OF SIGNING
WELL, OBVIOUSLY NOT ALL I NEEDED, OR ELSE I WOULDN'T BE OUT HERE NOW, TRYING TO TRACK DOWN THIS ONE LAST PRESENT!
AND THE WORST PART IS, I STILL DON'T HAVE THE FOGGIEST IDEA OF WHAT TO GET..!

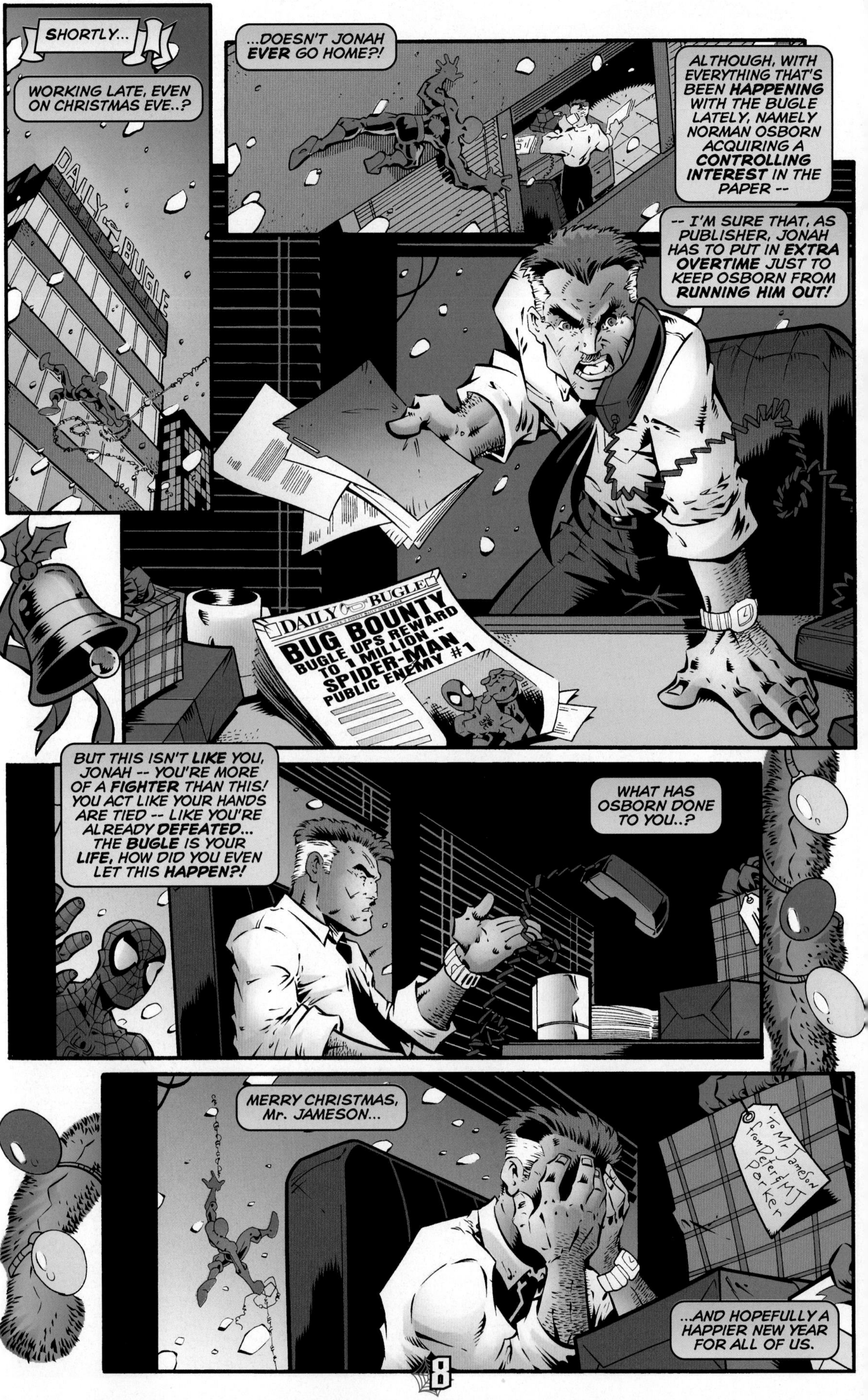
SHORTLY...
WORKING LATE, EVEN ON CHRISTMAS EVE..?
DAILY BUGLE
...DOESN'T JONAH EVER GO HOME?!
ALTHOUGH, WITH EVERYTHING THAT'S BEEN HAPPENING WITH THE BUGLE LATELY, NAMELY NORMAN OSBORN ACQUIRING A CONTROLLING INTEREST IN THE PAPER --
-- I'M SURE THAT, AS PUBLISHER, JONAH HAS TO PUT IN EXTRA OVERTIME JUST TO KEEP OSBORN FROM RUNNING HIM OUT!
DAILY BUGLE
BUG BOUNTY
BUGLE UPS REWARD TO 1 MILLION --
SPIDER-MAN PUBLIC ENEMY #1
BUT THIS ISN'T LIKE YOU, JONAH -- YOU'RE MORE OF A FIGHTER THAN THIS! YOU ACT LIKE YOUR HANDS ARE TIED -- LIKE YOU'RE ALREADY DEFEATED... THE BUGLE IS YOUR LIFE. HOW DID YOU EVEN LET THIS HAPPEN?!
WHAT HAS OSBORN DONE TO YOU..?
MERRY CHRISTMAS, Mr. JAMESON...
To Mr. Jameson from Peter & MJ Parker
...AND HOPEFULLY A HAPPIER NEW YEAR FOR ALL OF US.

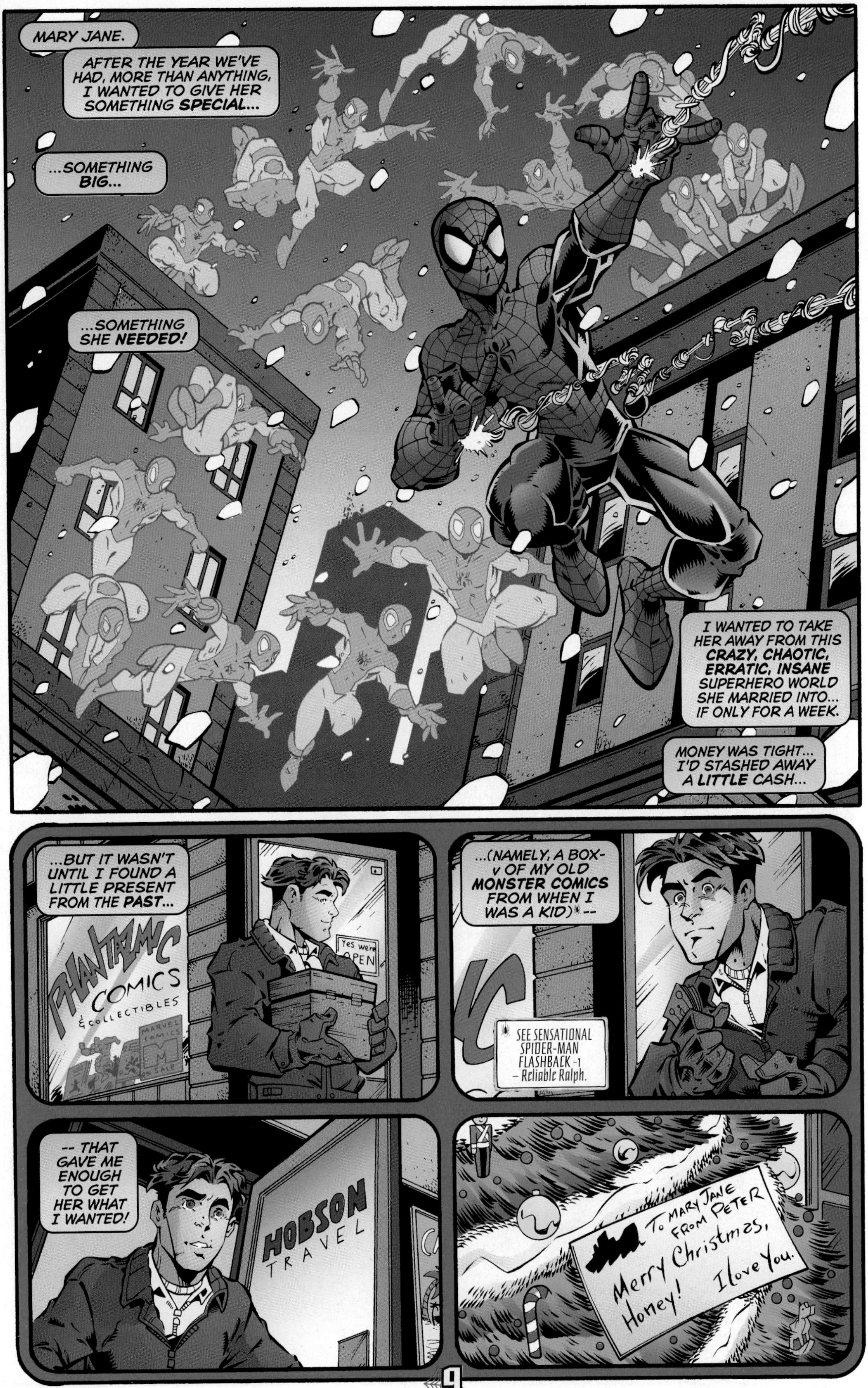
MARY JANE.
AFTER THE YEAR WE'VE HAD, MORE THAN ANYTHING, I WANTED TO GIVE HER SOMETHING SPECIAL...
...SOMETHING BIG...
...SOMETHING SHE NEEDED!
I WANTED TO TAKE HER AWAY FROM THIS CRAZY, CHAOTIC, ERRATIC, INSANE SUPERHERO WORLD SHE MARRIED INTO... IF ONLY FOR A WEEK.
MONEY WAS TIGHT... I'D STASHED AWAY A LITTLE CASH...
...BUT IT WASN'T UNTIL I FOUND A LITTLE PRESENT FROM THE PAST...
PHANTAZMIC COMICS & COLLECTIBLES
MARVEL COMICS M ON SALE
Yes we're OPEN
...(NAMELY, A BOX OF MY OLD MONSTER COMICS FROM WHEN I WAS A KID)* --
* SEE SENSATIONAL SPIDER-MAN FLASHBACK -1 – Reliable Ralph.
-- THAT GAVE ME ENOUGH TO GET HER WHAT I WANTED!
HOBSON TRAVEL
[redacted] To MARY JANE FROM PETER
Merry Christmas, Honey! I love You.

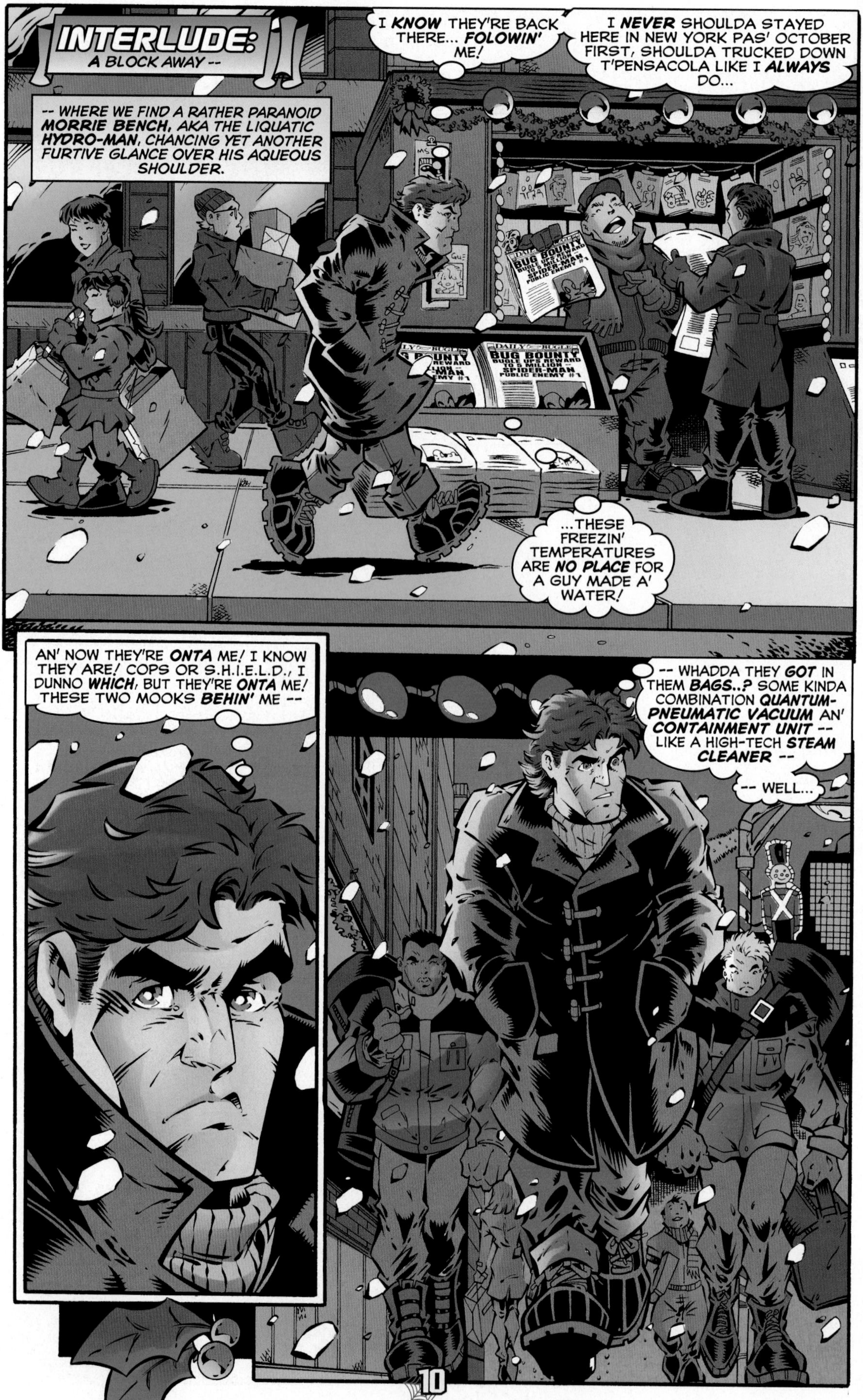
INTERLUDE: A BLOCK AWAY --
-- WHERE WE FIND A RATHER PARANOID MORRIE BENCH, AKA THE LIQUATIC HYDRO-MAN, CHANCING YET ANOTHER FURTIVE GLANCE OVER HIS AQUEOUS SHOULDER.
I KNOW THEY'RE BACK THERE... FOLOWIN' ME!
I NEVER SHOULDA STAYED HERE IN NEW YORK PAS' OCTOBER FIRST, SHOULDA TRUCKED DOWN T'PENSACOLA LIKE I ALWAYS DO...
BUG BOUNTY BUGLE UPS REWARD TO 5 MILLION -- SPIDER-MAN PUBLIC ENEMY #1
DAILY BUGLE
...THESE FREEZIN' TEMPERATURES ARE NO PLACE FOR A GUY MADE A' WATER!
AN' NOW THEY'RE ONTA ME! I KNOW THEY ARE! COPS OR S.H.I.E.L.D., I DUNNO WHICH, BUT THEY'RE ONTA ME! THESE TWO MOOKS BEHIN' ME --
-- WHADDA THEY GOT IN THEM BAGS..? SOME KINDA COMBINATION QUANTUM-PNEUMATIC VACUUM AN' CONTAINMENT UNIT -- LIKE A HIGH-TECH STEAM CLEANER --
-- WELL...

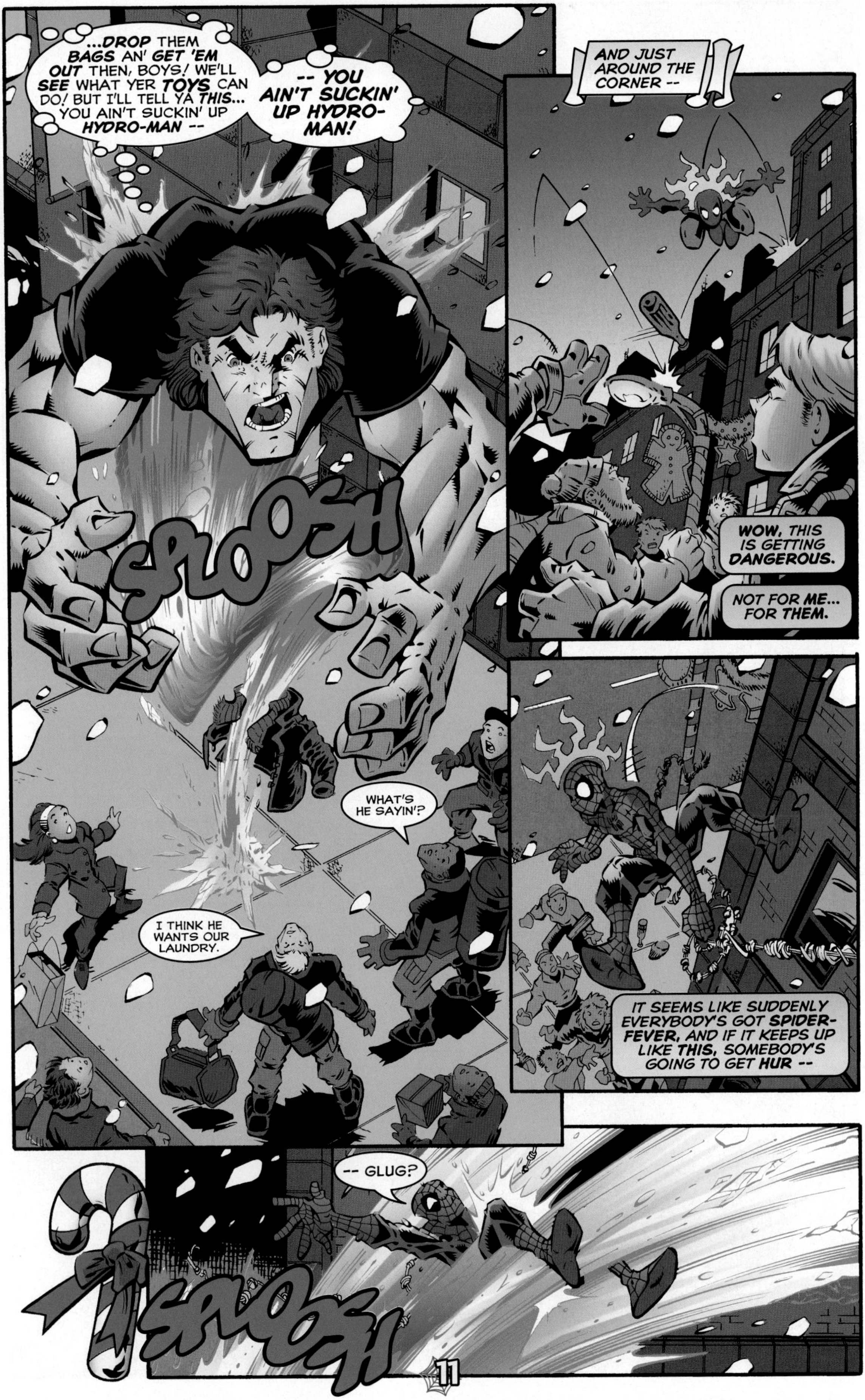

...DROP THEM BAGS AN' GET 'EM OUT THEN, BOYS! WE'LL SEE WHAT YER TOYS CAN DO! BUT I'LL TELL YA THIS... YOU AIN'T SUCKIN' UP HYDRO-MAN --
-- YOU AIN'T SUCKIN' UP HYDRO-MAN!
SPLOOSH
WHAT'S HE SAYIN'?
I THINK HE WANTS OUR LAUNDRY.
AND JUST AROUND THE CORNER --
WOW, THIS IS GETTING DANGEROUS.
NOT FOR ME... FOR THEM.
IT SEEMS LIKE SUDDENLY EVERYBODY'S GOT SPIDER-FEVER, AND IF IT KEEPS UP LIKE THIS, SOMEBODY'S GOING TO GET HUR --
-- GLUG?
SPLOOSH

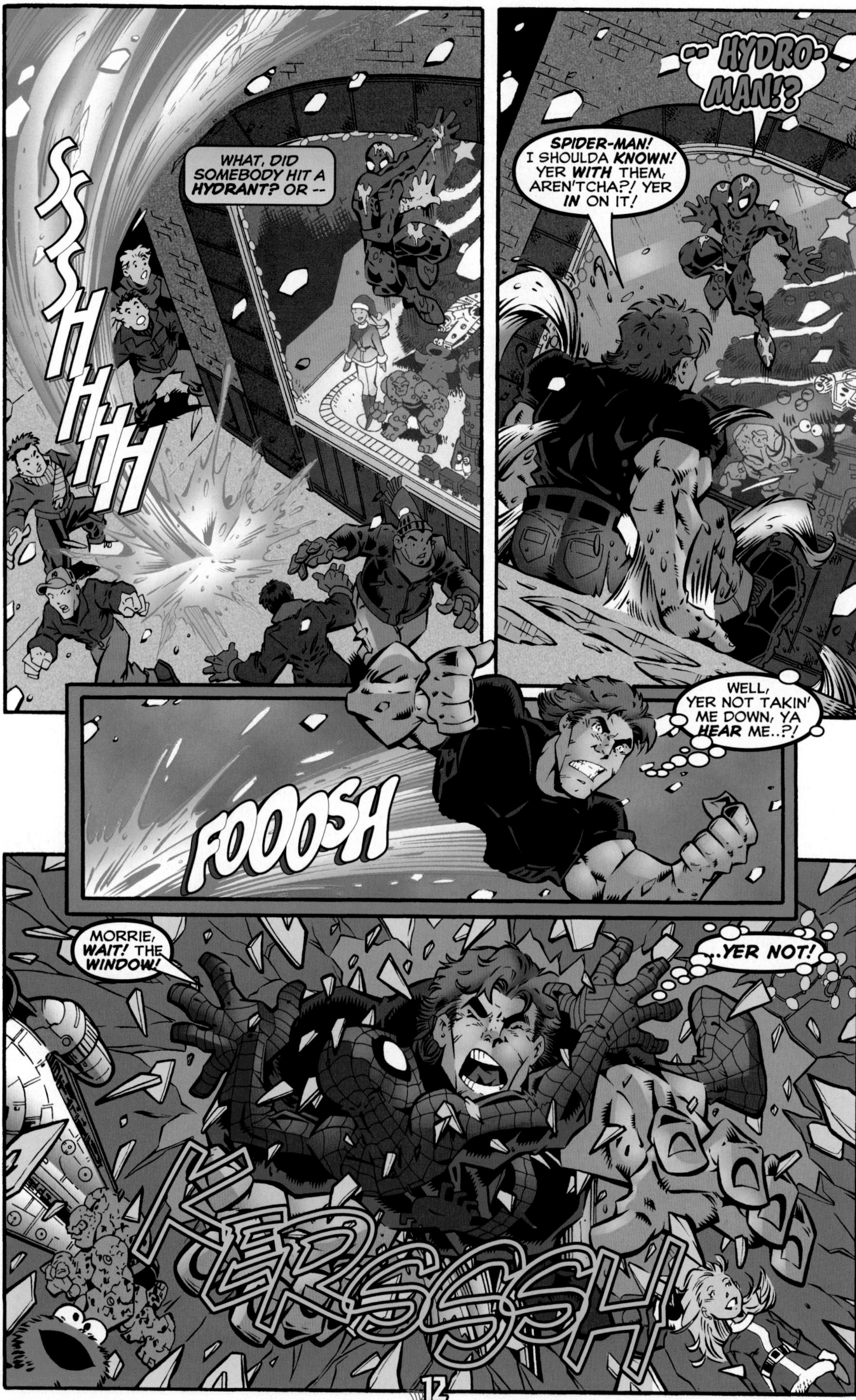
SSSHHHH
WHAT, DID SOMEBODY HIT A HYDRANT? OR --
-- HYDRO-MAN!?
SPIDER-MAN! I SHOULDA KNOWN! YER WITH THEM, AREN'TCHA?! YER IN ON IT!
FOOOSH
WELL, YER NOT TAKIN' ME DOWN, YA HEAR ME..?!
MORRIE, WAIT! THE WINDOW!
..YER NOT!
KERSSSH

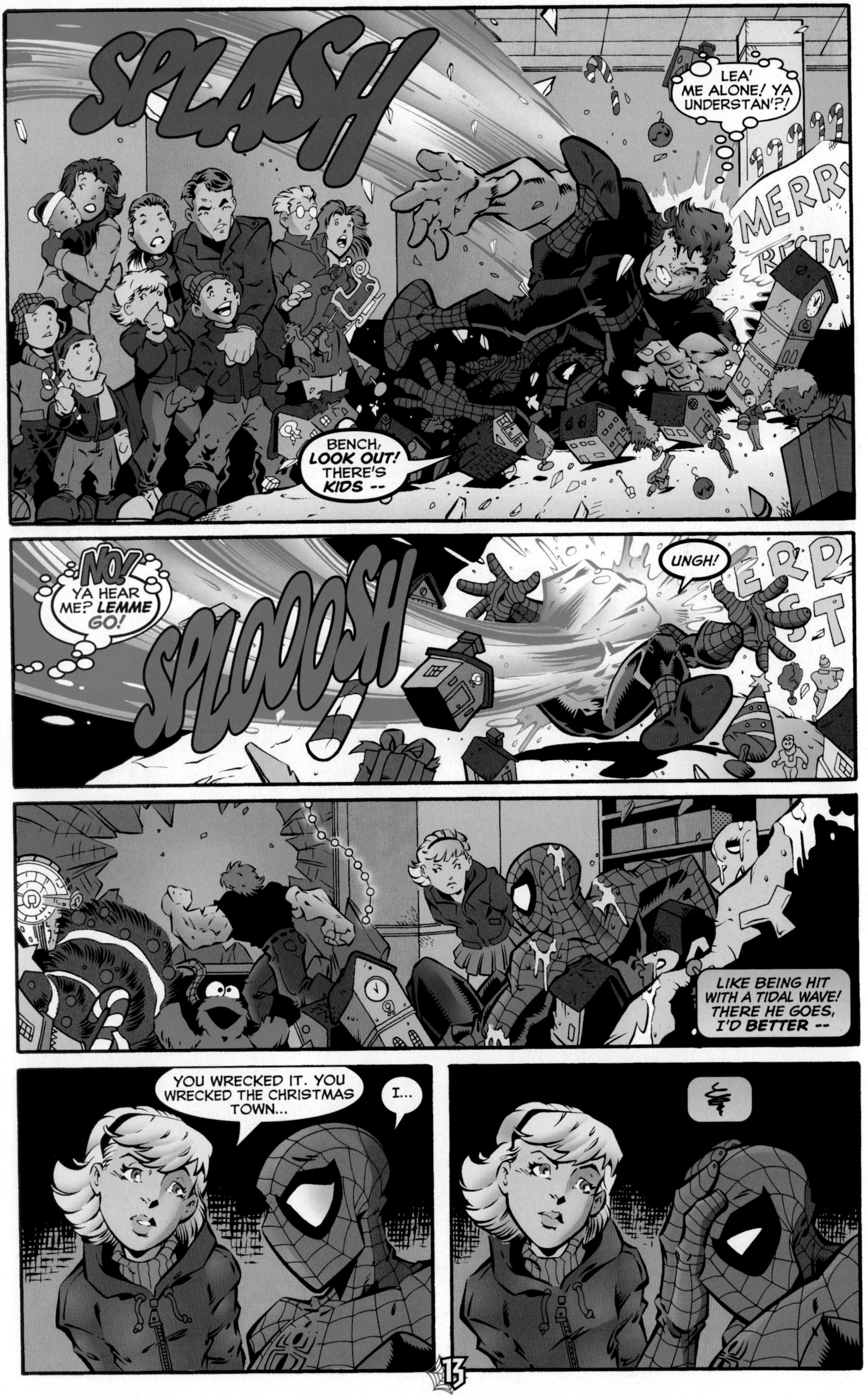
SPLASH
LEA' ME ALONE! YA UNDERSTAN'?!
BENCH, LOOK OUT! THERE'S KIDS --
NO! YA HEAR ME? LEMME GO!
SPLOOOSH
UNGH!
LIKE BEING HIT WITH A TIDAL WAVE! THERE HE GOES, I'D BETTER --
YOU WRECKED IT. YOU WRECKED THE CHRISTMAS TOWN...
I...

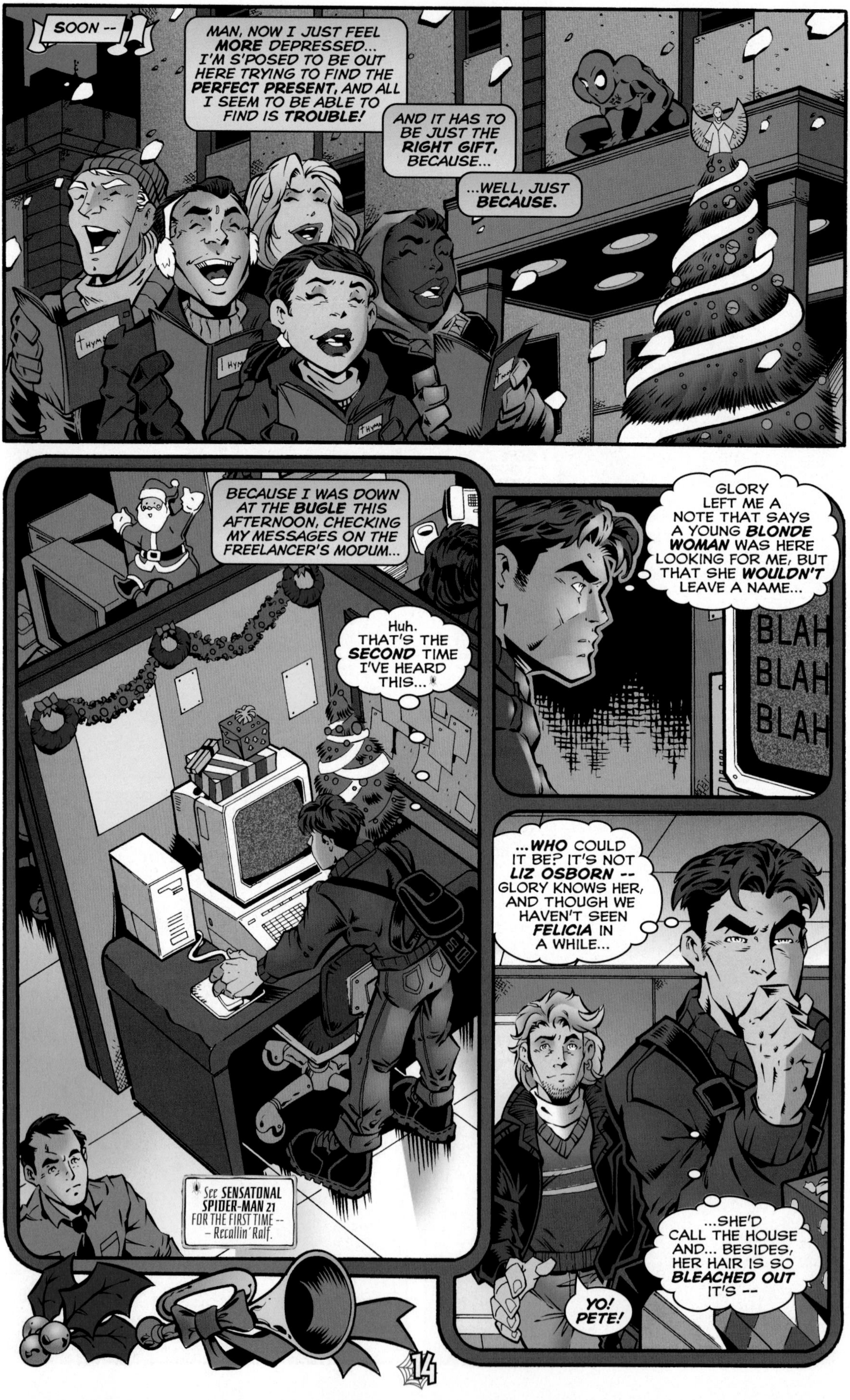
SOON --
MAN, NOW I JUST FEEL MORE DEPRESSED... I'M S'POSED TO BE OUT HERE TRYING TO FIND THE PERFECT PRESENT, AND ALL I SEEM TO BE ABLE TO FIND IS TROUBLE!
AND IT HAS TO BE JUST THE RIGHT GIFT, BECAUSE...
...WELL, JUST BECAUSE.
HYMN
BECAUSE I WAS DOWN AT THE BUGLE THIS AFTERNOON, CHECKING MY MESSAGES ON THE FREELANCER'S MODUM...
Huh. THAT'S THE SECOND TIME I'VE HEARD THIS...
See SENSATONAL SPIDER-MAN 21 FOR THE FIRST TIME -- – Recallin' Ralf.
GLORY LEFT ME A NOTE THAT SAYS A YOUNG BLONDE WOMAN WAS HERE LOOKING FOR ME, BUT THAT SHE WOULDN'T LEAVE A NAME...
BLAH BLAH BLAH
...WHO COULD IT BE? IT'S NOT LIZ OSBORN -- GLORY KNOWS HER, AND THOUGH WE HAVEN'T SEEN FELICIA IN A WHILE...
...SHE'D CALL THE HOUSE AND... BESIDES, HER HAIR IS SO BLEACHED OUT IT'S --
YO! PETE!

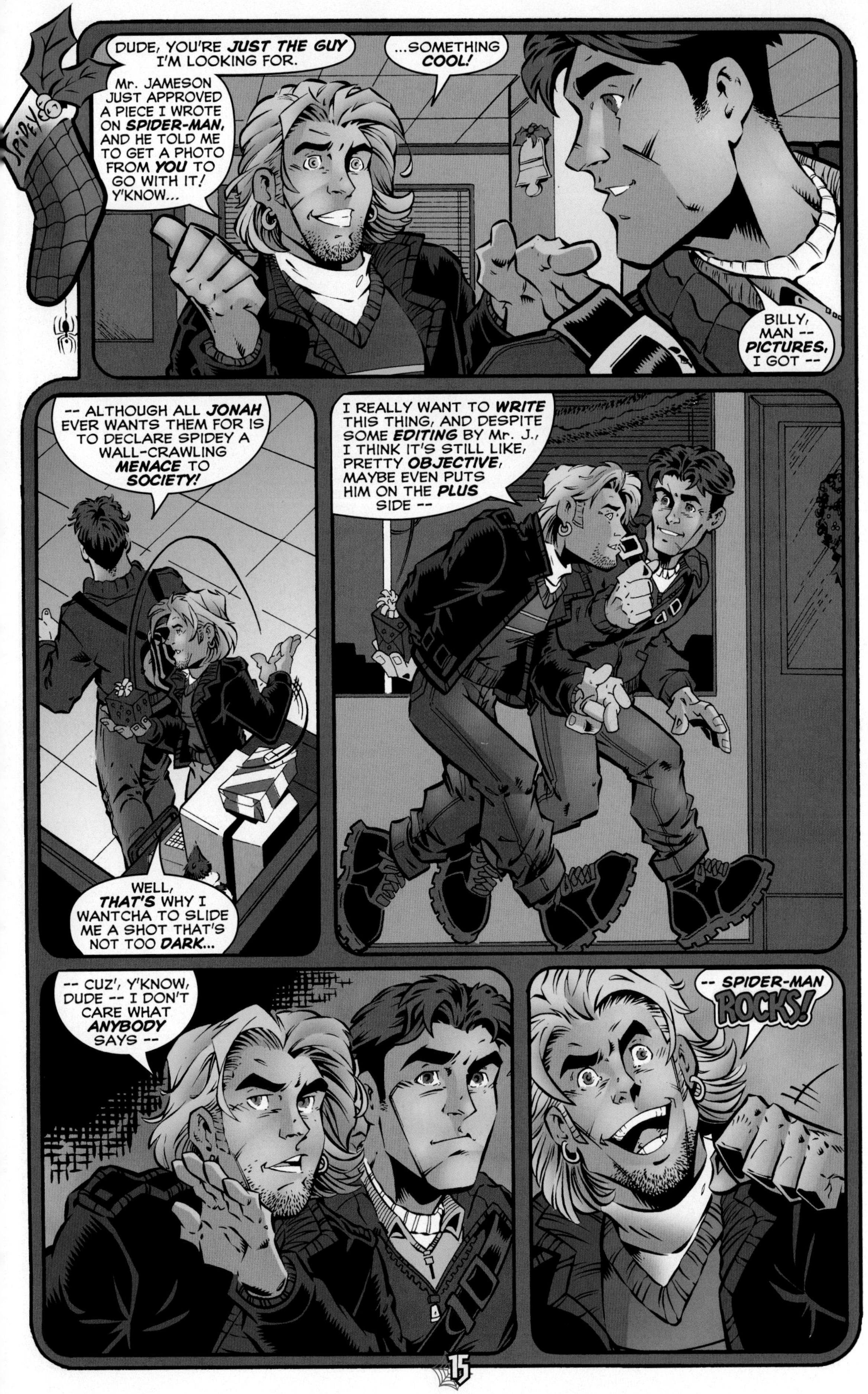
DUDE, YOU'RE JUST THE GUY I'M LOOKING FOR.
Mr. JAMESON JUST APPROVED A PIECE I WROTE ON SPIDER-MAN, AND HE TOLD ME TO GET A PHOTO FROM YOU TO GO WITH IT! Y'KNOW...
...SOMETHING COOL!
BILLY, MAN -- PICTURES, I GOT --
-- ALTHOUGH ALL JONAH EVER WANTS THEM FOR IS TO DECLARE SPIDEY A WALL-CRAWLING MENACE TO SOCIETY!
WELL, THAT'S WHY I WANTCHA TO SLIDE ME A SHOT THAT'S NOT TOO DARK...
I REALLY WANT TO WRITE THIS THING, AND DESPITE SOME EDITING BY Mr. J., I THINK IT'S STILL LIKE, PRETTY OBJECTIVE, MAYBE EVEN PUTS HIM ON THE PLUS SIDE --
-- CUZ', Y'KNOW, DUDE -- I DON'T CARE WHAT ANYBODY SAYS --
-- SPIDER-MAN ROCKS!

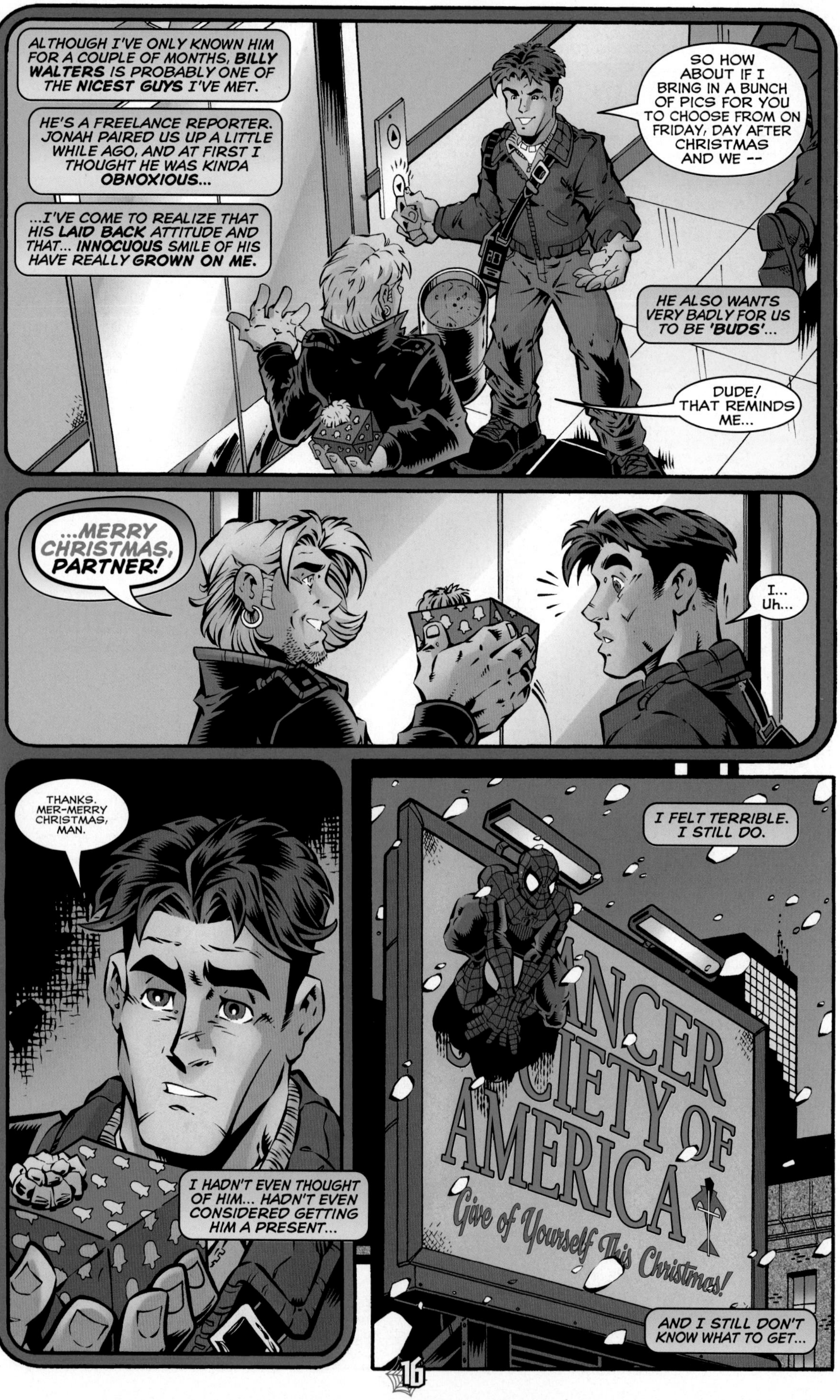
ALTHOUGH I'VE ONLY KNOWN HIM FOR A COUPLE OF MONTHS, BILLY WALTERS IS PROBABLY ONE OF THE NICEST GUYS I'VE MET.
HE'S A FREELANCE REPORTER. JONAH PAIRED US UP A LITTLE WHILE AGO, AND AT FIRST I THOUGHT HE WAS KINDA OBNOXIOUS...
...I'VE COME TO REALIZE THAT HIS LAID BACK ATTITUDE AND THAT... INNOCUOUS SMILE OF HIS HAVE REALLY GROWN ON ME.
SO HOW ABOUT IF I BRING IN A BUNCH OF PICS FOR YOU TO CHOOSE FROM ON FRIDAY, DAY AFTER CHRISTMAS AND WE --
HE ALSO WANTS VERY BADLY FOR US TO BE 'BUDS'...
DUDE! THAT REMINDS ME...
...MERRY CHRISTMAS, PARTNER!
I... Uh...
THANKS. MER-MERRY CHRISTMAS, MAN.
I HADN'T EVEN THOUGHT OF HIM... HADN'T EVEN CONSIDERED GETTING HIM A PRESENT...
I FELT TERRIBLE. I STILL DO.
ANCER CIETY OF AMERICA
Give of Yourself This Christmas!
AND I STILL DON'T KNOW WHAT TO GET...

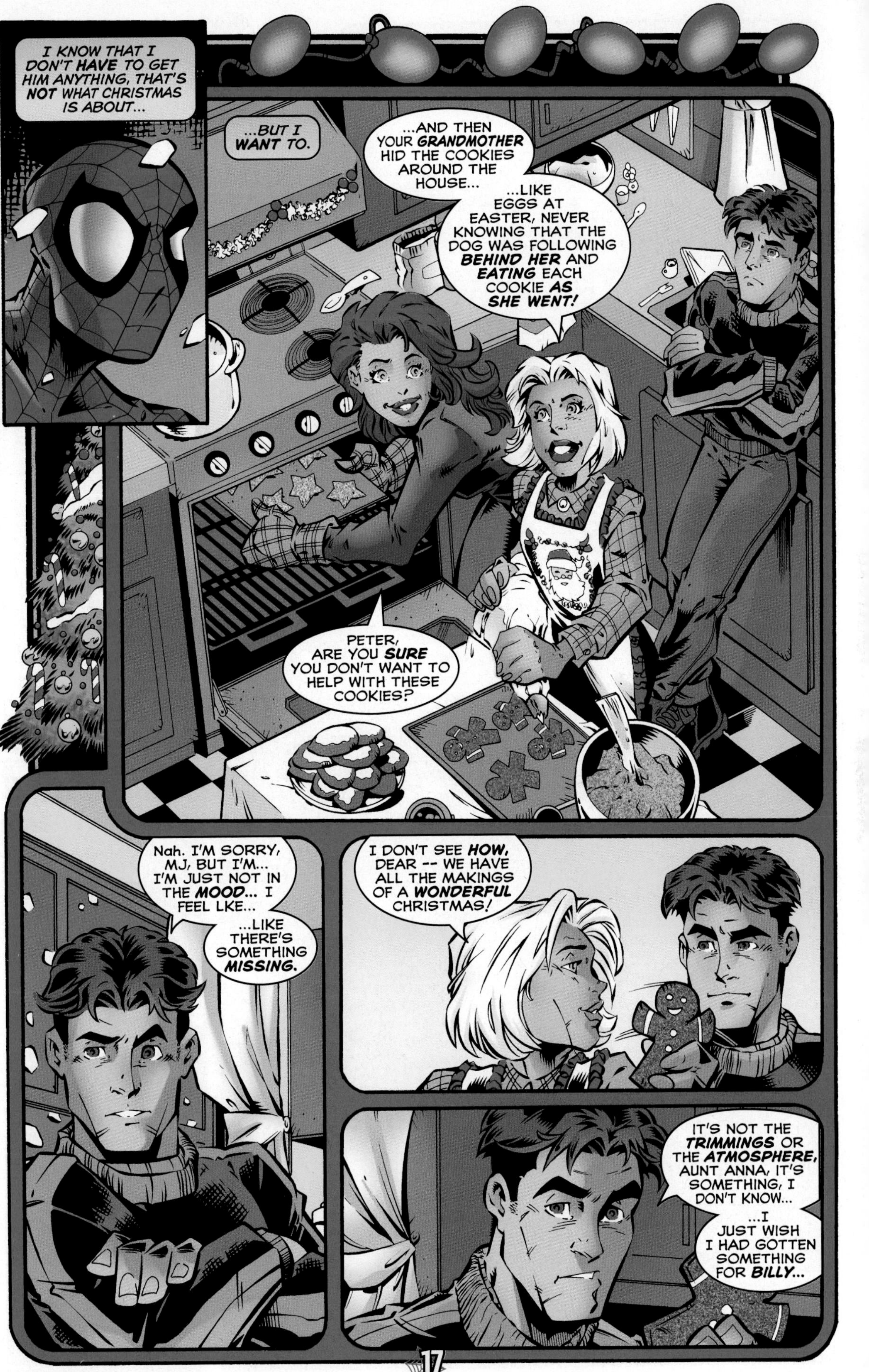
I KNOW THAT I DON'T HAVE TO GET HIM ANYTHING, THAT'S NOT WHAT CHRISTMAS IS ABOUT...
...BUT I WANT TO.
...AND THEN YOUR GRANDMOTHER HID THE COOKIES AROUND THE HOUSE...
...LIKE EGGS AT EASTER, NEVER KNOWING THAT THE DOG WAS FOLLOWING BEHIND HER AND EATING EACH COOKIE AS SHE WENT!
PETER, ARE YOU SURE YOU DON'T WANT TO HELP WITH THESE COOKIES?
Nah. I'M SORRY, MJ, BUT I'M... I'M JUST NOT IN THE MOOD... I FEEL LKE...
...LIKE THERE'S SOMETHING MISSING.
I DON'T SEE HOW, DEAR -- WE HAVE ALL THE MAKINGS OF A WONDERFUL CHRISTMAS!
IT'S NOT THE TRIMMINGS OR THE ATMOSPHERE, AUNT ANNA, IT'S SOMETHING, I DON'T KNOW...
...I JUST WISH I HAD GOTTEN SOMETHING FOR BILLY...

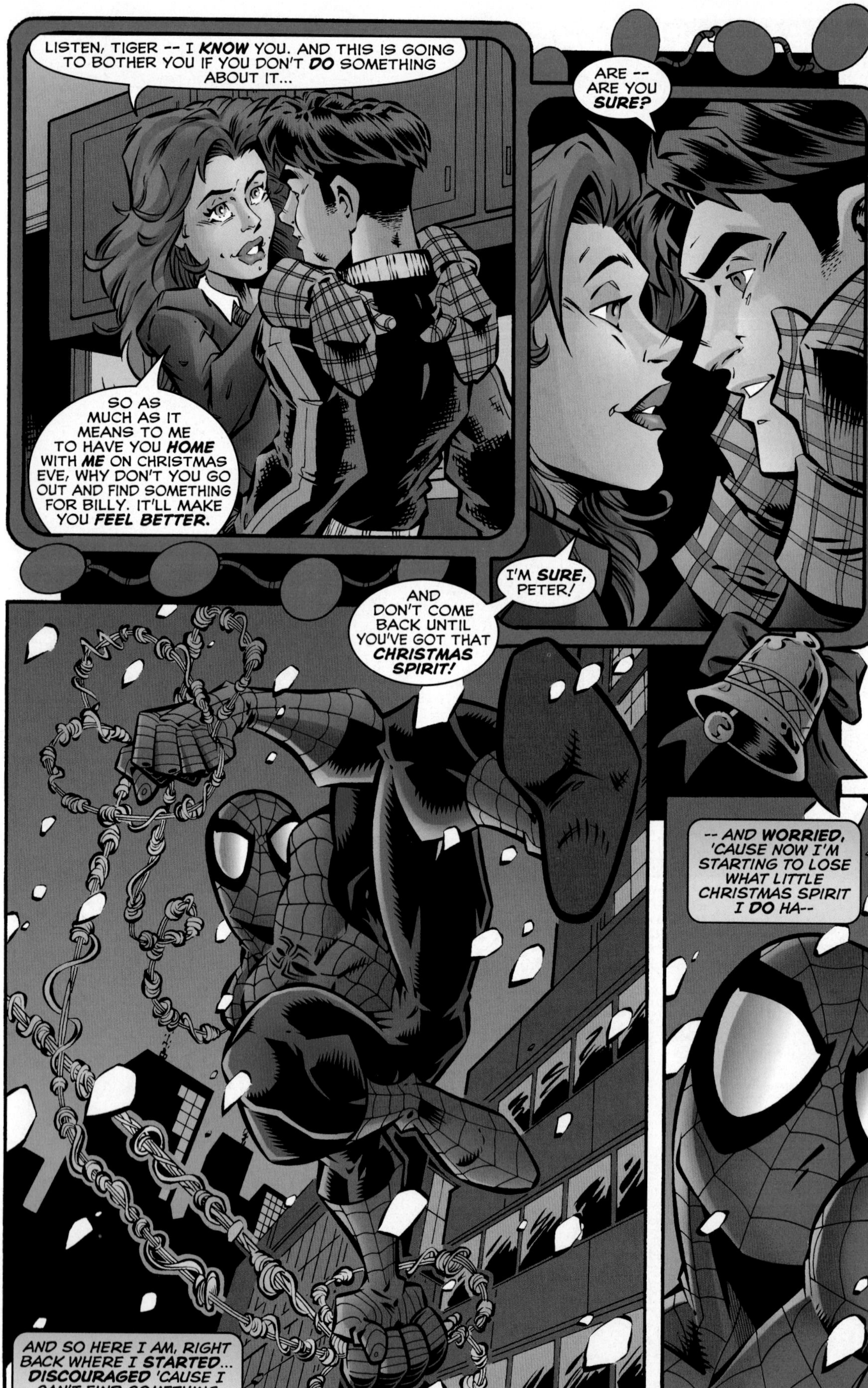
LISTEN, TIGER -- I KNOW YOU. AND THIS IS GOING TO BOTHER YOU IF YOU DON'T DO SOMETHING ABOUT IT...
SO AS MUCH AS IT MEANS TO ME TO HAVE YOU HOME WITH ME ON CHRISTMAS EVE, WHY DON'T YOU GO OUT AND FIND SOMETHING FOR BILLY. IT'LL MAKE YOU FEEL BETTER.
ARE -- ARE YOU SURE?
I'M SURE, PETER!
AND DON'T COME BACK UNTIL YOU'VE GOT THAT CHRISTMAS SPIRIT!
AND SO HERE I AM, RIGHT BACK WHERE I STARTED... DISCOURAGED 'CAUSE I CAN'T FIND SOMETHING FOR BILLY --
-- AND WORRIED, 'CAUSE NOW I'M STARTING TO LOSE WHAT LITTLE CHRISTMAS SPIRIT I DO HA--

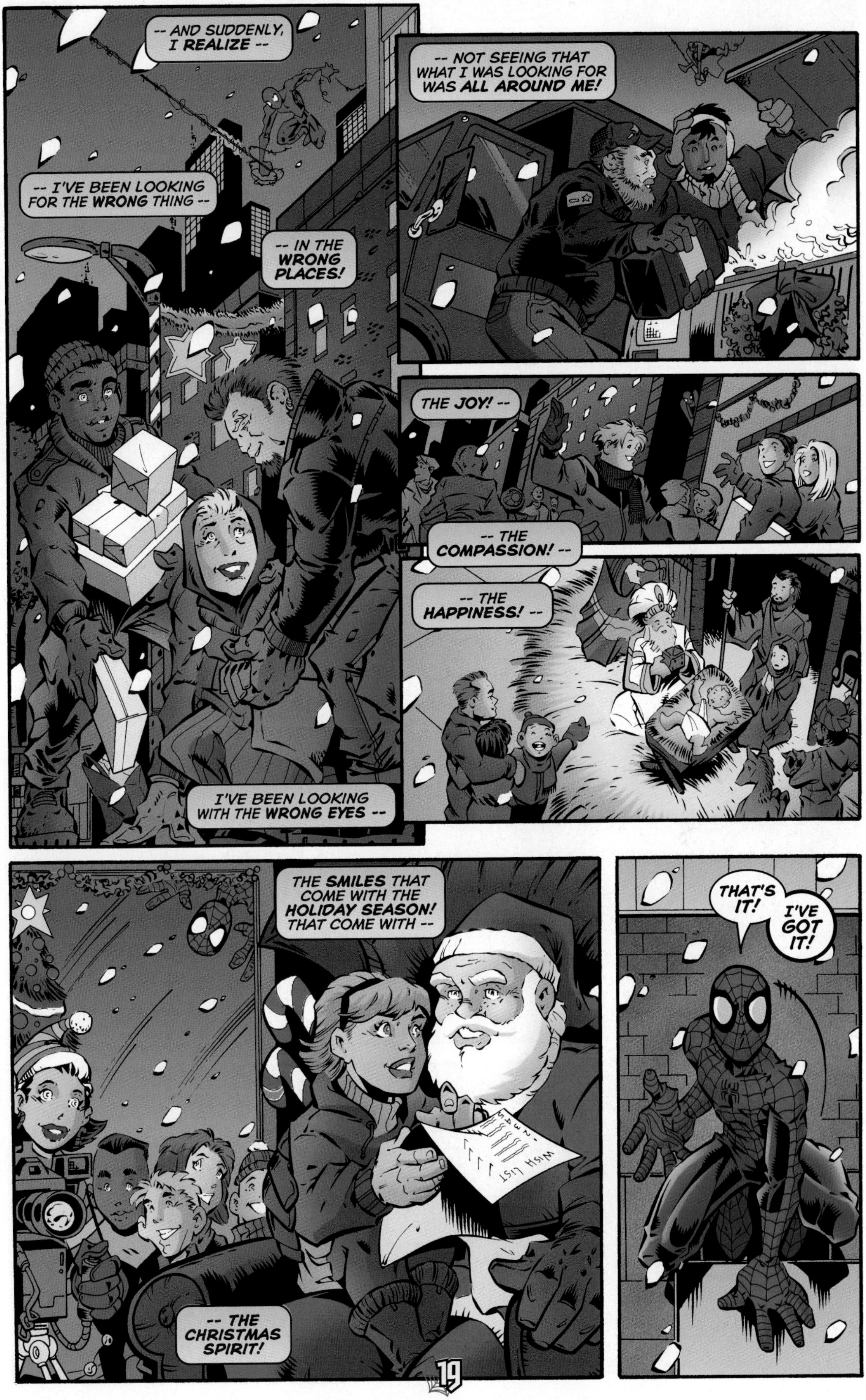
-- AND SUDDENLY, I REALIZE --
-- I'VE BEEN LOOKING FOR THE WRONG THING --
-- IN THE WRONG PLACES!
I'VE BEEN LOOKING WITH THE WRONG EYES --
-- NOT SEEING THAT WHAT I WAS LOOKING FOR WAS ALL AROUND ME!
THE JOY! --
-- THE COMPASSION! --
-- THE HAPPINESS! --
THE SMILES THAT COME WITH THE HOLIDAY SEASON! THAT COME WITH --
WISH LIST
-- THE CHRISTMAS SPIRIT!
THAT'S IT!
I'VE GOT IT!

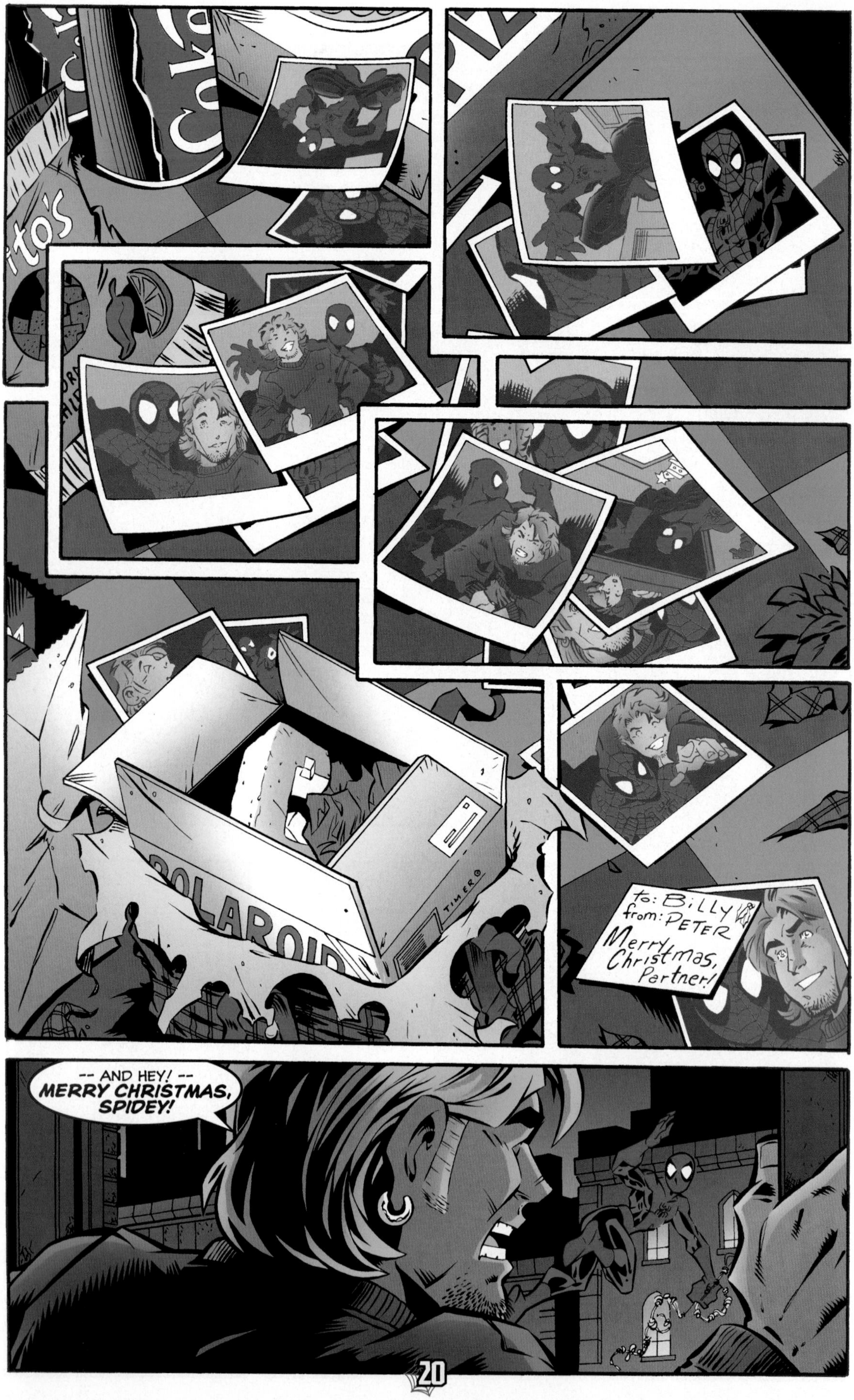
to: Billy
from: PETER
Merry Christmas, Partner!
-- AND HEY! --
MERRY CHRISTMAS, SPIDEY!

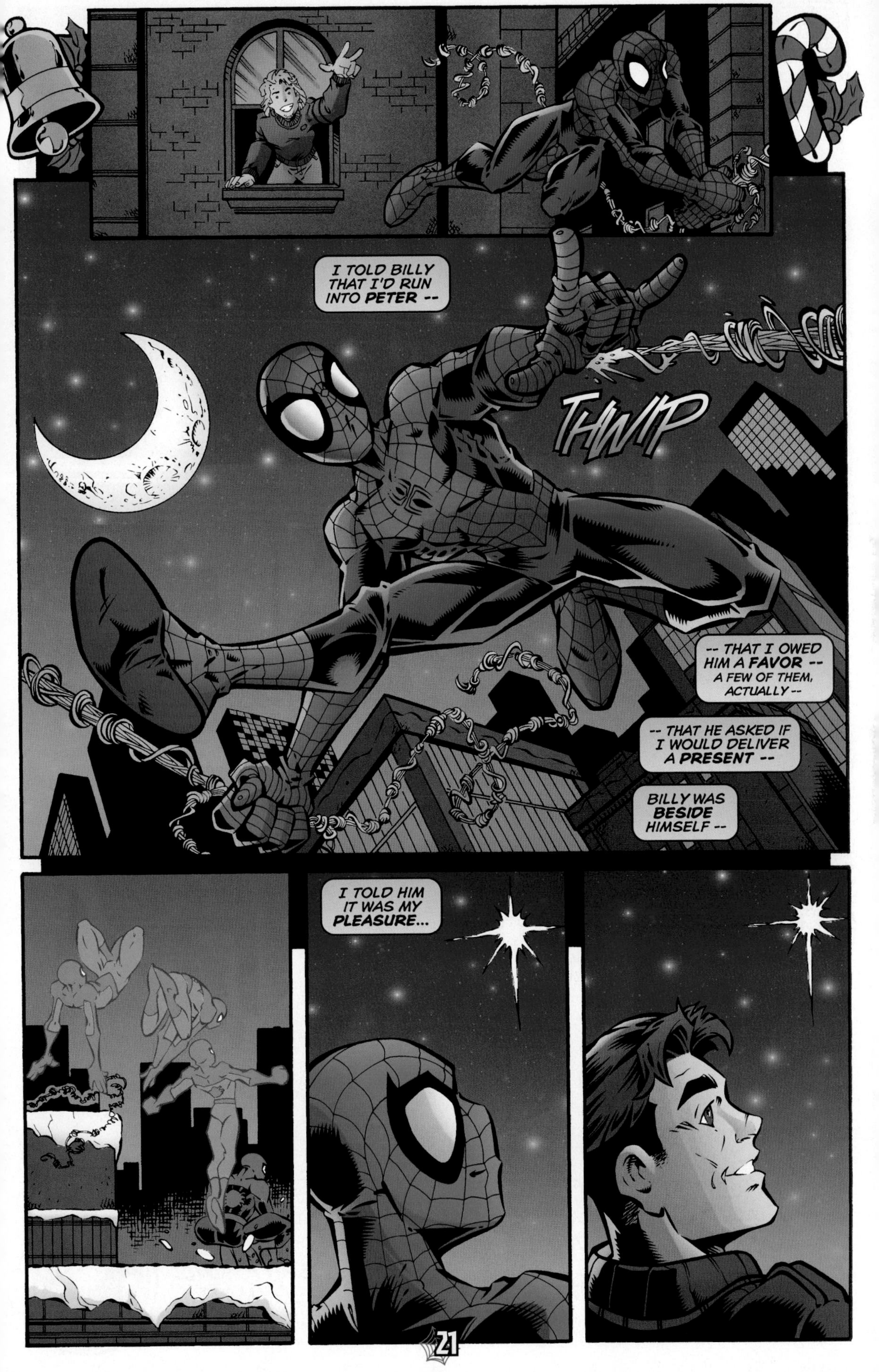
I TOLD BILLY THAT I'D RUN INTO PETER --
THWIP
-- THAT I OWED HIM A FAVOR -- A FEW OF THEM, ACTUALLY --
-- THAT HE ASKED IF I WOULD DELIVER A PRESENT --
BILLY WAS BESIDE HIMSELF --
I TOLD HIM IT WAS MY PLEASURE...

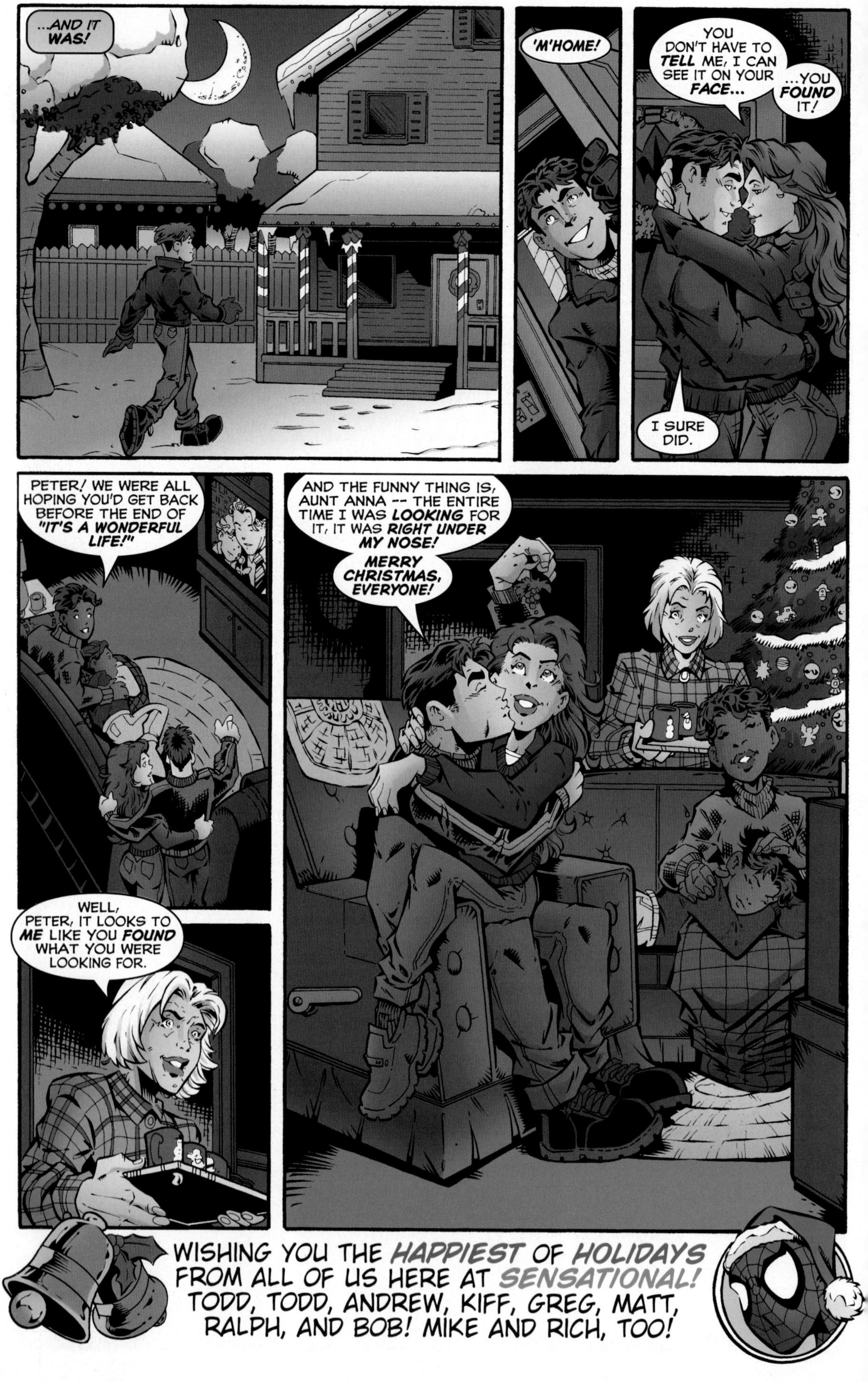
...AND IT WAS!
'M'HOME!
YOU DON'T HAVE TO TELL ME, I CAN SEE IT ON YOUR FACE...
...YOU FOUND IT!
I SURE DID.
PETER! WE WERE ALL HOPING YOU'D GET BACK BEFORE THE END OF "IT'S A WONDERFUL LIFE!"
AND THE FUNNY THING IS, AUNT ANNA -- THE ENTIRE TIME I WAS LOOKING FOR IT, IT WAS RIGHT UNDER MY NOSE!
MERRY CHRISTMAS, EVERYONE!
WELL, PETER, IT LOOKS TO ME LIKE YOU FOUND WHAT YOU WERE LOOKING FOR.
WISHING YOU THE HAPPIEST OF HOLIDAYS FROM ALL OF US HERE AT SENSATIONAL! TODD, TODD, ANDREW, KIFF, GREG, MATT, RALPH, AND BOB! MIKE AND RICH, TOO!

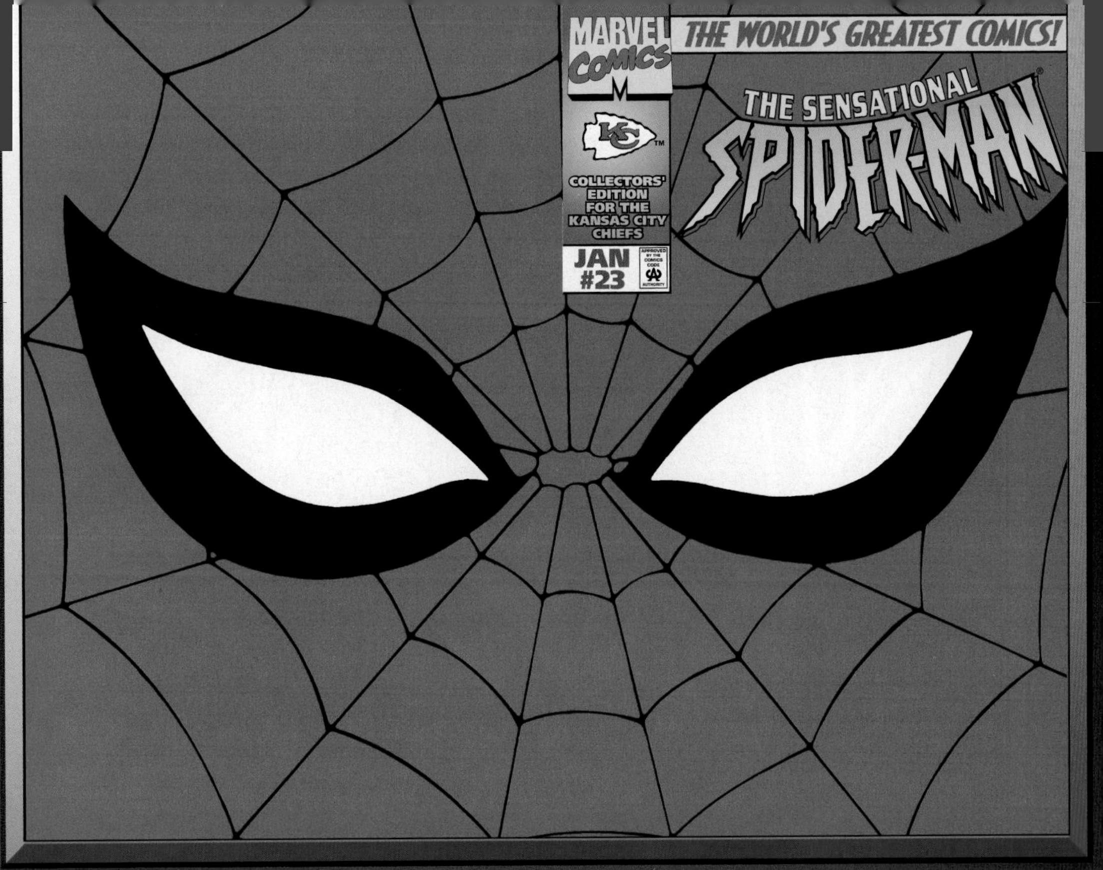
MARVEL COMICS
THE WORLD'S GREATEST COMICS!
THE SENSATIONAL
SPIDER-MAN
COLLECTORS' EDITION FOR THE KANSAS CITY CHIEFS
JAN
#23
APPROVED BY THE COMICS CODE AUTHORITY

SPIDER-MAN: THE SAVAGE LAND SAGA TPB COLLECTED *SENSATIONAL SPIDER-MAN #13-15*.
INTRODUCTION BY RALPH MACCHIO.

OCCASIONALLY, THINGS COME TOGETHER PERFECTLY. SUCH WAS THE CASE WITH OUR THREE-PART SAVAGE LAND EXTRAVAGANZA IN *SENSATIONAL SPIDER-MAN'S #13-15*. THIS WAS EXACTLY THE STORY I ENVISIONED WHEN TODD AND I FIRST DISCUSSED IT. WE KNEW THERE WERE RISKS, THOUGH. MOST SPIDEROPHILES PREFER TO SEE THEIR WEB-SPINNING WONDER DOING HIS THING AMIDST THE CONCRETE ENVIRONS OF MANHATTAN—AND THIS WAS GOING TO BE AS FAR AWAY FROM THE BIG APPLE AS YOU COULD GET. STILL, IT SEEMS READER REACTION PROVED OUR FEARS GROUNDLESS; IT WAS OVERWHELMINGLY POSITIVE. IN FACT, IT WAS SO AFFIRMATIVE, WE HAD LITTLE CHOICE BUT TO GIVE YOU HAPPY CAMPERS AN ENCORE PRESENTATION OF THOSE THREE ALREADY CLASSIC ISSUES OF *SENSATIONAL*.

AND IT WAS ALL INITIALLY POSSIBLE THANKS TO THE EXTRAORDINARY TALENTS OF MIKE WIERINGO, OUR ESTEEMED PENCILER, WHO PLANTED THE SEED WHEN HE SUGGESTED DOING A SPIDEY STORY SET DOWN UNDER; RICH CASE, OUR INCREDIBLE INKER, WHO SO BEAUTIFULLY EMBELLISHED MIKE'S SUPERB PENCILS; TODD DEZAGO, OUR WONDROUS WRITER, WHOSE SOLID PLOTTING AND CRISP DIALOGUE PULLED IT ALL TOGETHER; GREG WRIGHT, OUR CALIPH OF COLORING, WHOSE VIBRANT PALETTE MAGNIFICENTLY CAPTURED THE MANY-HUED SPLENDOR OF THE SAVAGE LAND. AND ME, I GET TO ENJOY THE FAR-OUT FANTASY A SECOND TIME—ALONG WITH ALL OF YOU. WHAT A JOB!

—RALPH MACCHIO/EDITOR

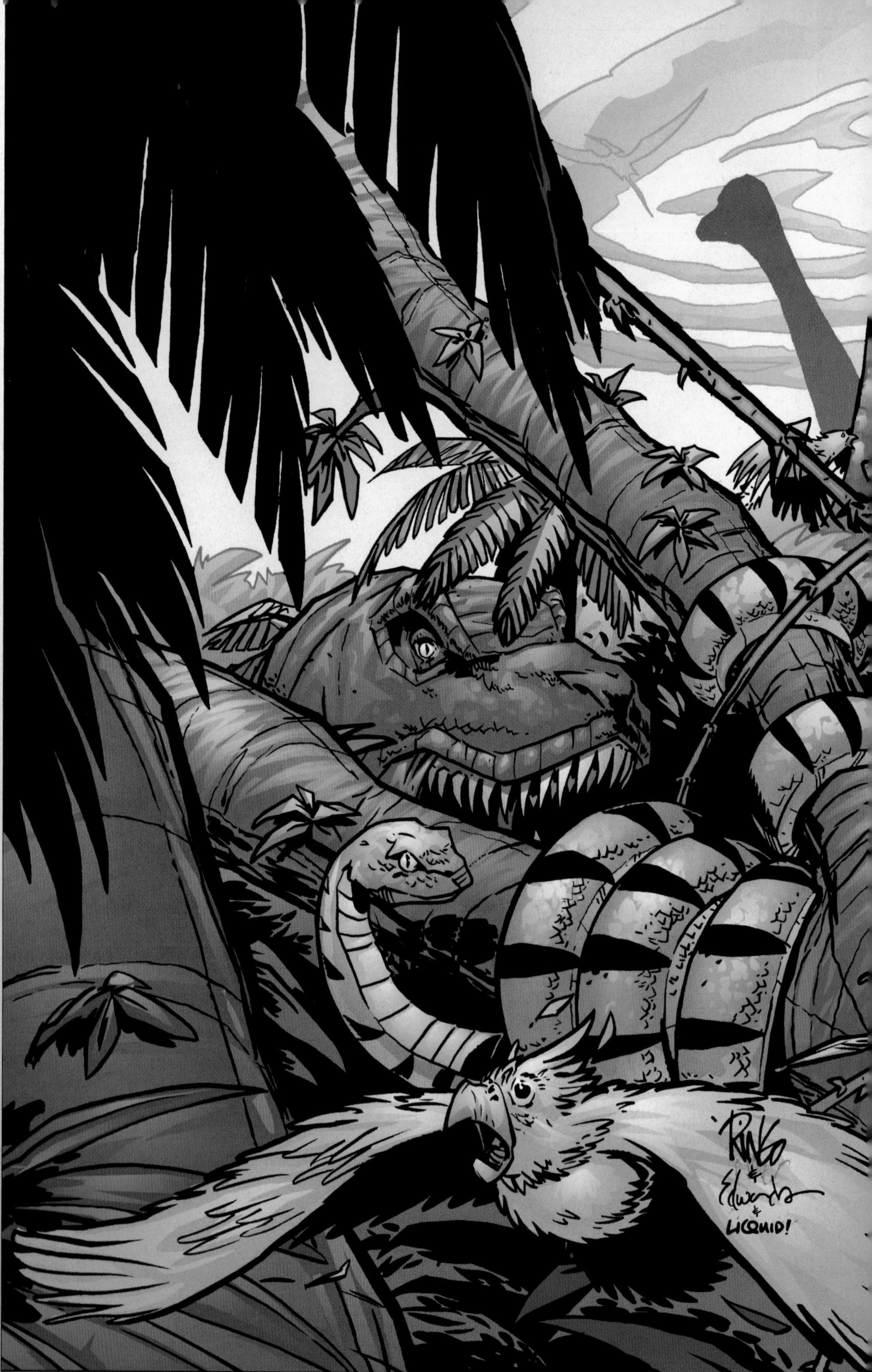
LICQUID!

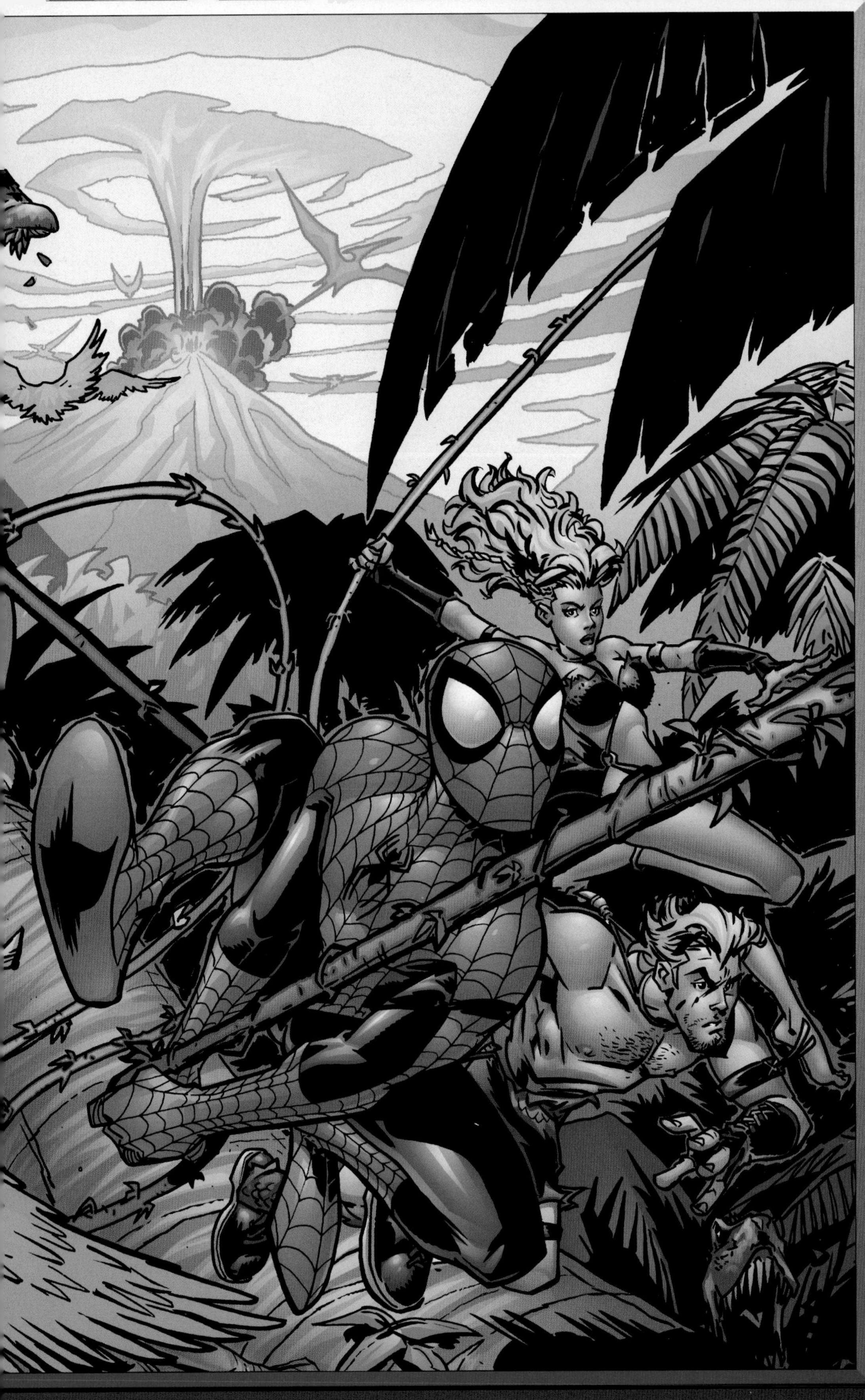

SPIDER-MAN'S GREATEST TEAM-UPS TPB COVER BY MIKE WIERINGO, GARY MARTIN & ATOMIC PAINTBRUSH

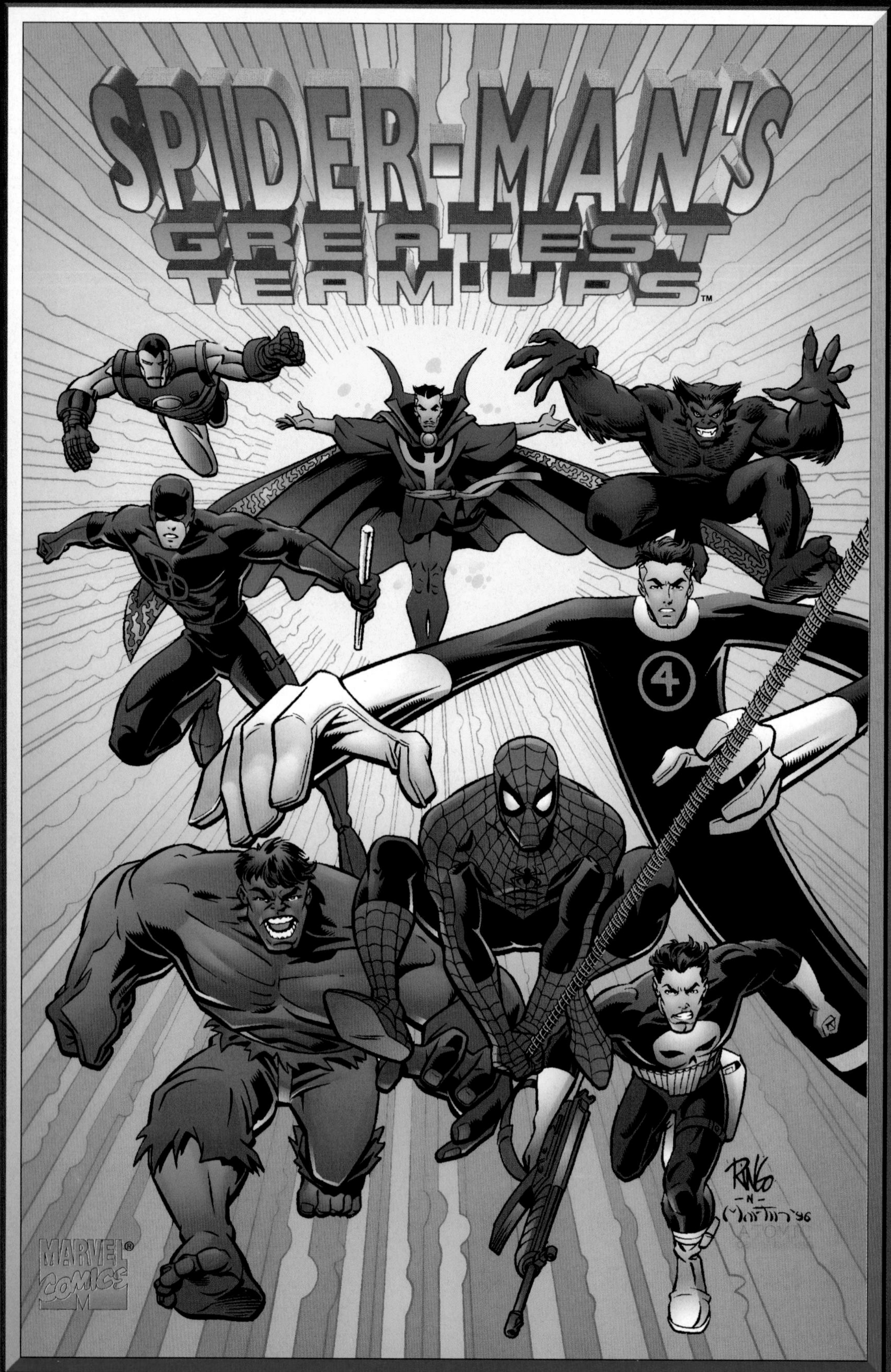
SPIDER-MAN'S
GREATEST
TEAM-UPS™
MARVEL® COMICS

MARVEL HOLIDAY SPECIAL 1996 COVER BY MIKE WIERINGO, RICH CASE & PAUL MOUNTS

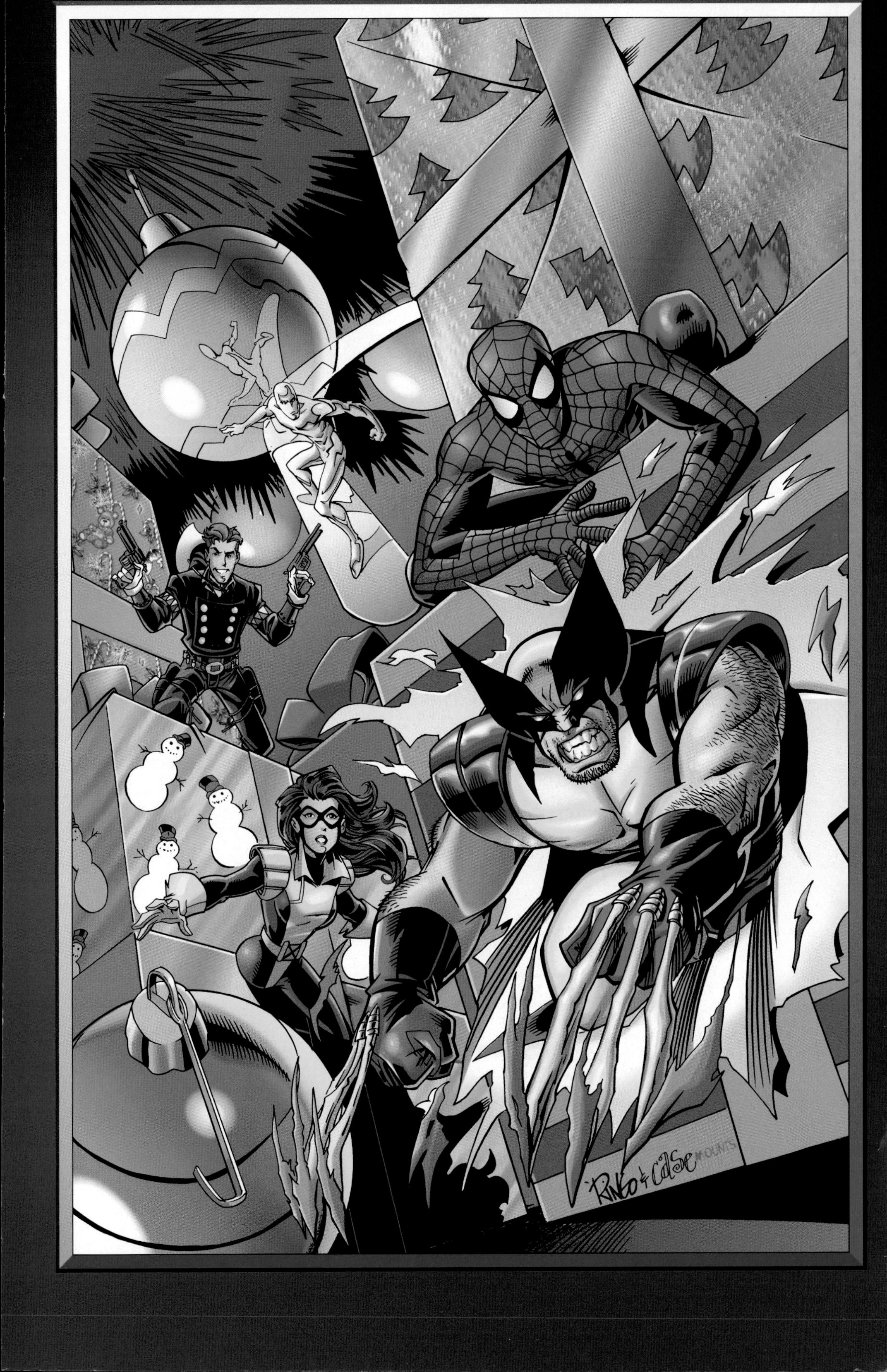

MARVEL VISION #12 COVER BY MIKE WIERINGO, RICH CASE & ATOMIC PAINTBRUSH

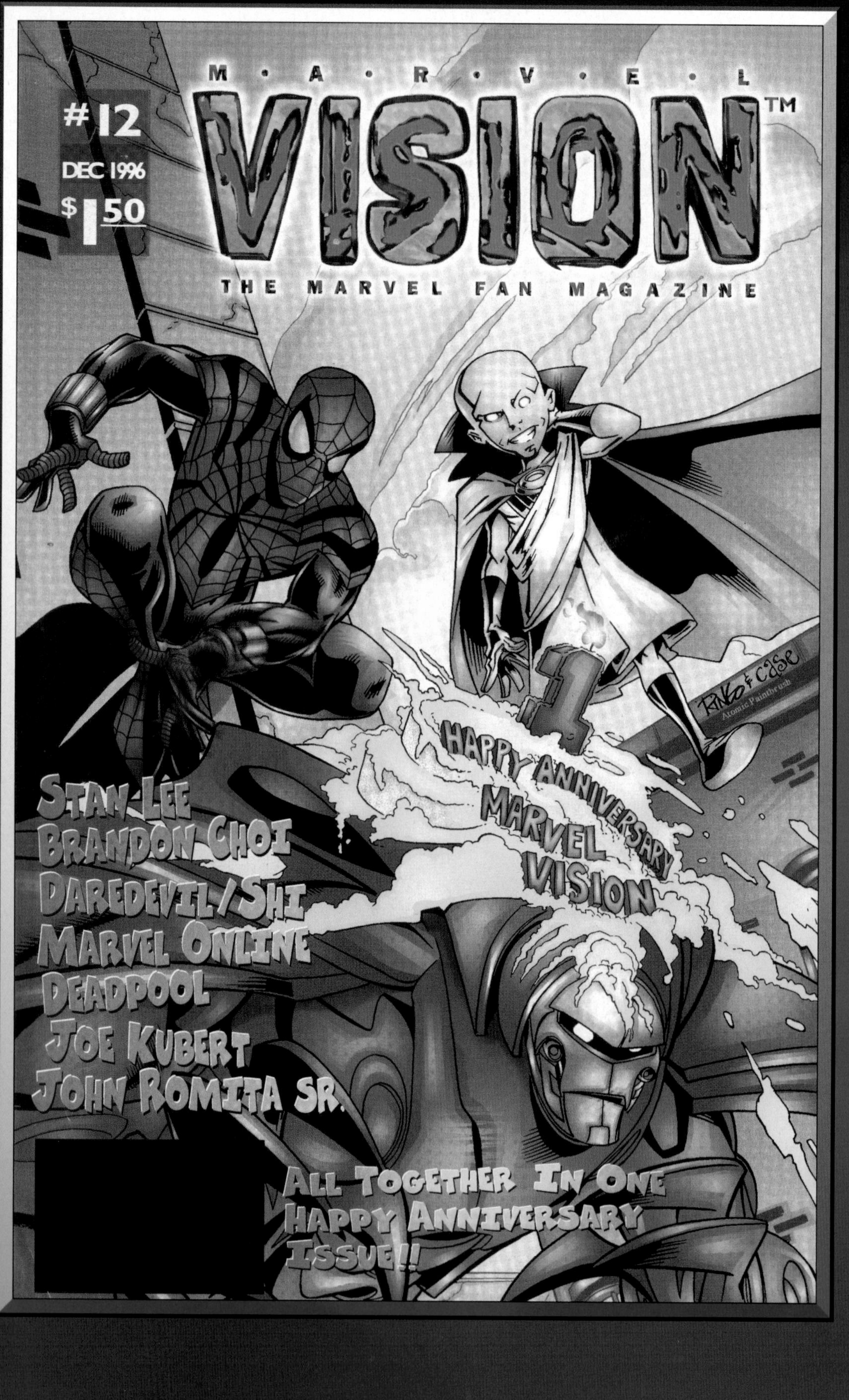

M • A • R • V • E • L
VISION™
#12
DEC 1996
$1.50
THE MARVEL FAN MAGAZINE
HAPPY ANNIVERSARY MARVEL VISION
Stan Lee
Brandon Choi
Daredevil/Shi
Marvel Online
Deadpool
Joe Kubert
John Romita Sr.
All Together In One Happy Anniversary Issue!!

WIZARD #64 COVER BY MIKE WIERINGO & TWILIGHT GRAPHICS' MICHAEL ATIYEH

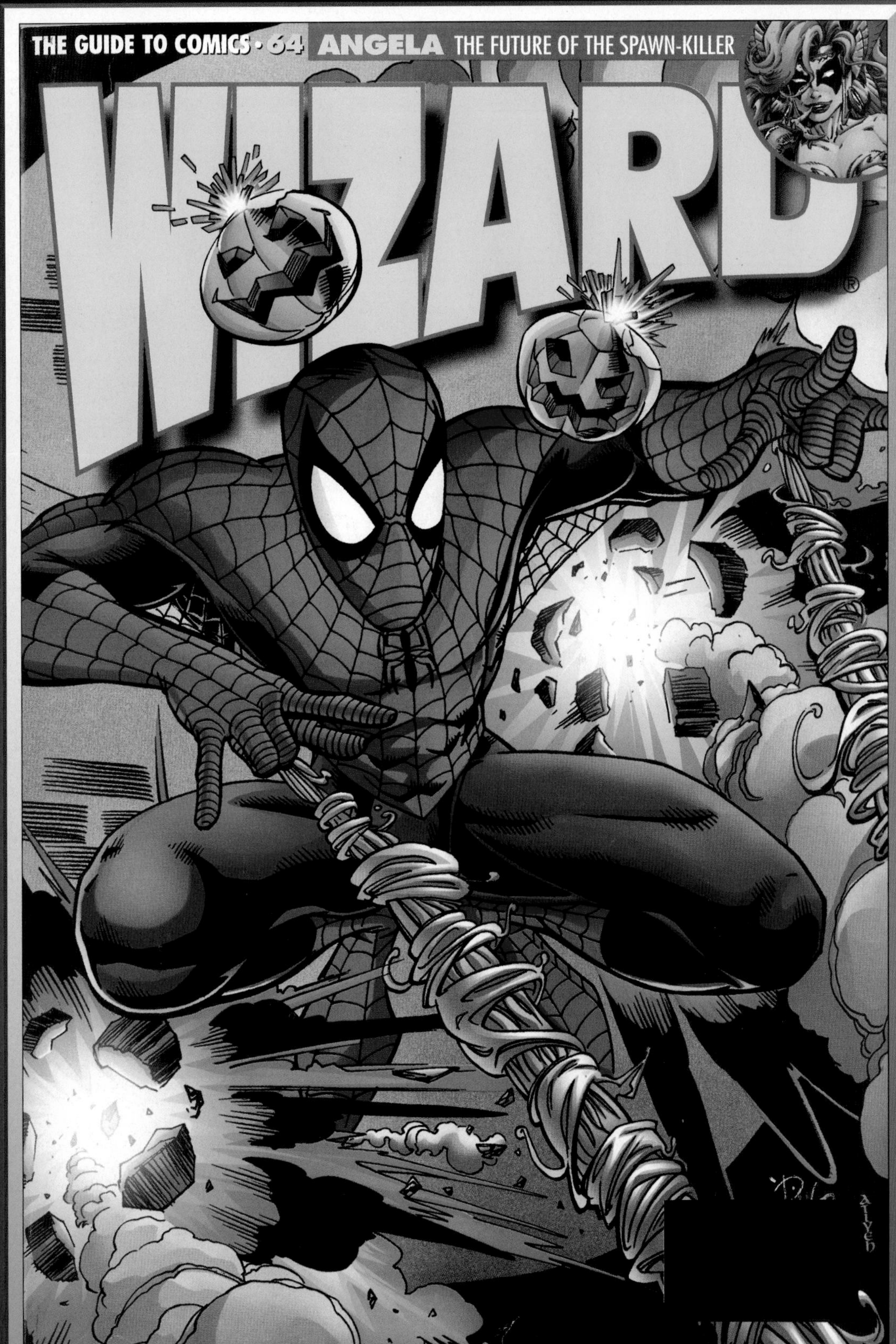
THE GUIDE TO COMICS • 64
ANGELA THE FUTURE OF THE SPAWN-KILLER
WIZARD
ATIYEH

WIZARD #72 COVER BY MIKE WIERINGO & TWILIGHT GRAPHICS' MICHAEL ATIYEH

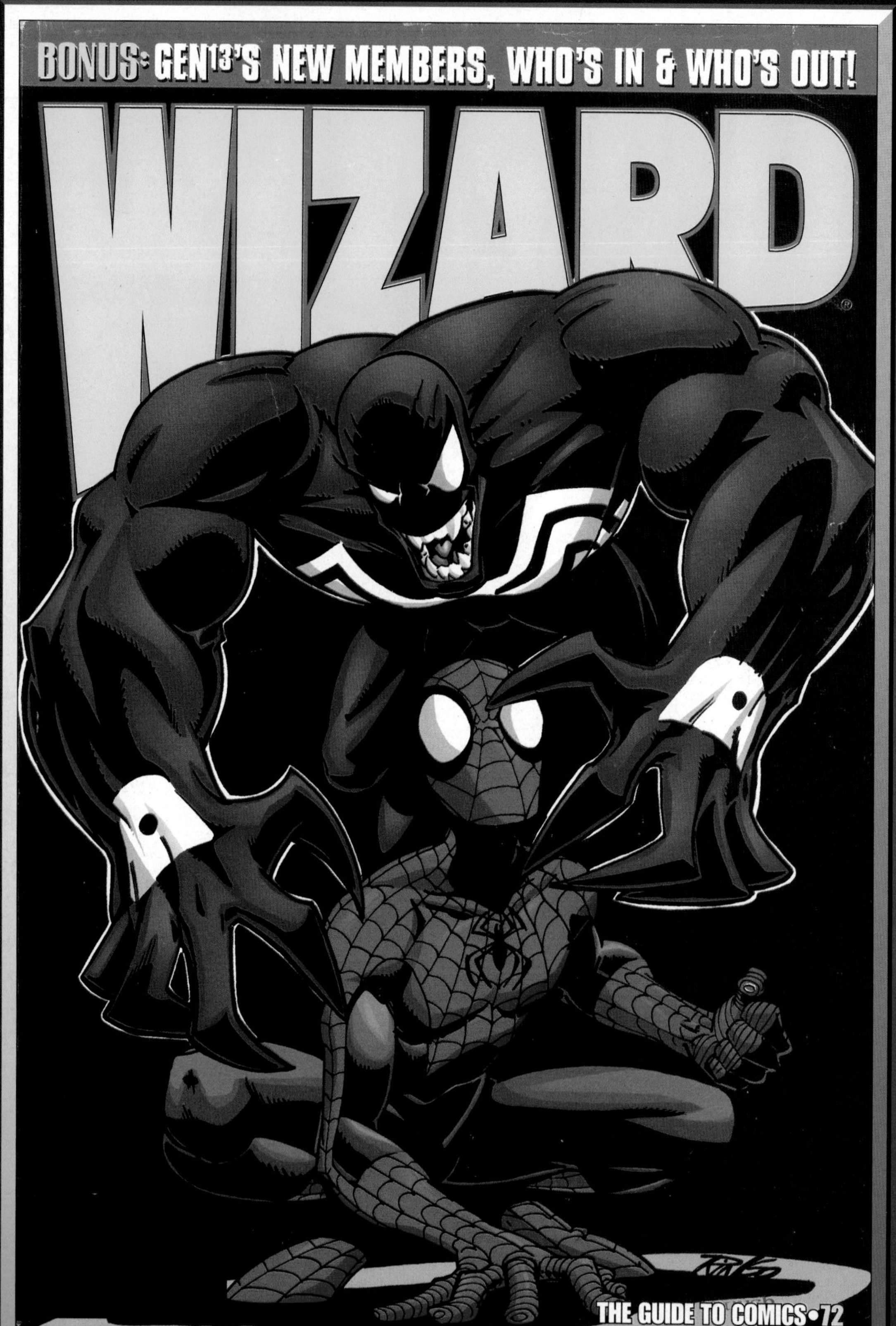

BONUS: GEN13'S NEW MEMBERS, WHO'S IN & WHO'S OUT!
WIZARD
THE GUIDE TO COMICS • 72

OVERSTREET'S FAN #22 COVER BY MIKE WIERINGO & JEFF DILLON

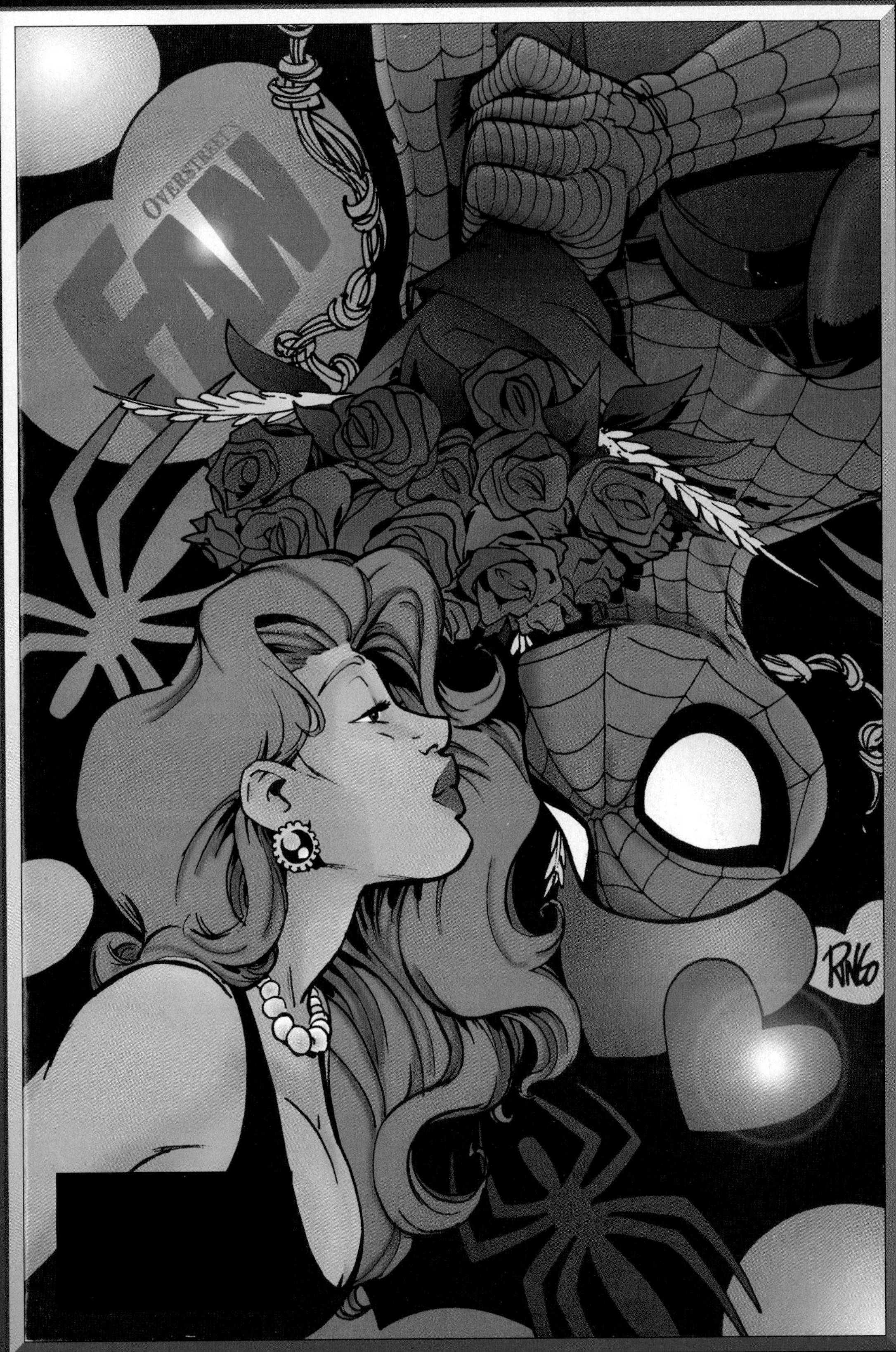
OVERSTREET'S
FAN
RINGO

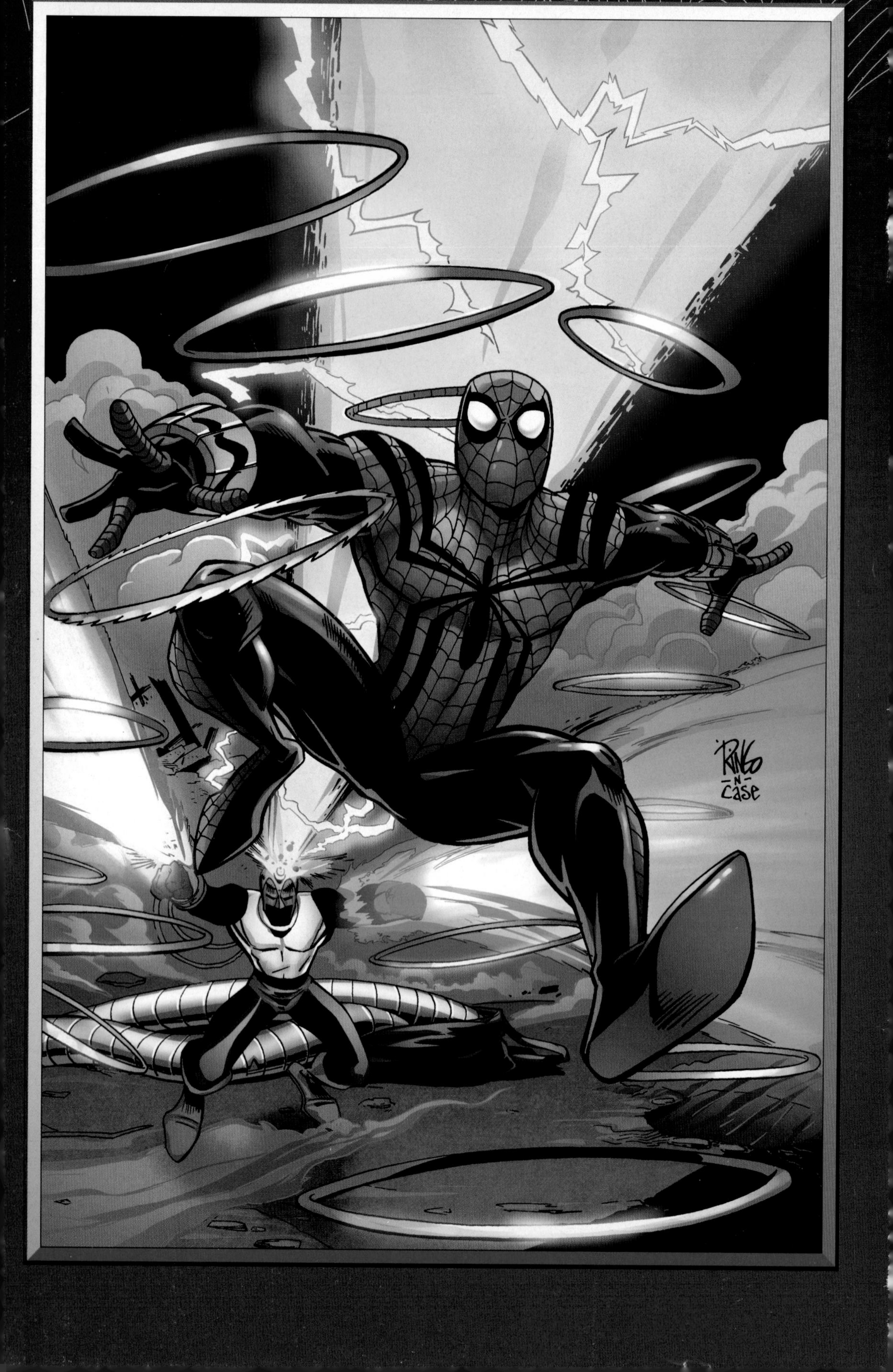
RINGO
-N-
CASE